Computer Service and Repair

4th Edition

Richard M. Roberts

Publisher

The Goodheart-Willcox Company, Inc.
Tinley Park, Illinois

www.g-w.com

Library of Congress Cataloging-in-Publication Data
Roberts, Richard M.
Computer service and repair / Richard M. Roberts. — Fourth edition.
    pages cm
    Includes index.
    ISBN 978-1-61960-795-8
    1. Microcomputers—Maintenance and repair. I. Title.
TK7887.R62 2014
004.16—dc23   2014001616

Introduction

Support for personal computers (PCs) and mobile devices has evolved into one of the largest service industries in the world. The demand for skilled technicians to maintain, support, and upgrade PCs and mobile devices is ever growing. It is a rewarding and challenging career that can take you anywhere in the world. If you enjoy tinkering with computers or have ever wondered how they work and what it takes to repair them, this course is for you. If you wish to learn computer networking, programming, administration, or any of the computer sciences, then this is the perfect place to start. A good foundation in computer technology will provide you with a base of knowledge that will make learning the other technical areas much easier.

Most computer troubleshooting is performed at the keyboard using knowledge about the computer system. You need to have a good understanding of how the components work hand-in-hand with the operating system software rather than knowing how the electronic parts (transistors, resistors, and capacitors) function. Computer repair started out as a domain dominated by electronic technicians with thousands of hours of training. It has evolved into a specialized field of PC and mobile device technicians requiring little to no electronics background at all.

The actual concepts and mechanics of computer repair are quite easy. You can show someone how to change the major components inside a PC very quickly with very few tools. For example, the mechanics of replacing a hard drive are extremely easy. Problems arise, however, if the hard drive doesn't work as expected and you start to read the technical manual specifications for help. Questions and answers are filled with unfamiliar terms such as *format, partition, active partition, sectors, block allocation units, boot sector, system files, MBR, FAT16, FAT32, exFAT, NTFS, system recovery disk, system disk, cable select, IDE,* and *SCSI.* This can prove very confusing to the novice. However, with a little effort, soon you will be speaking "techie talk" like the rest of the technicians.

Computer systems are built better than ever before. The constant problems caused by failing components encountered 30 years ago are seldom found today. Computers still do fail because of bad components, but now the majority of failures are due to software problems or they are caused by the computer users themselves. Only a small percentage of computer failures require component replacement. What is needed is someone who can diagnose the problem and determine if it is hardware related, software related, or user generated. This is the job of the computer technician. Remember that with computer repair, it is important to complete all lab activities. They are designed to give you valuable computer experiences and enhance the skills you are being taught. This will better prepare you for the CompTIA A+ exams if you choose to take them, and better prepare you for a career as a computer technician.

I wish you much success in your future.

Sincerely,
Richard M. Roberts

The Author

For the past 40 years, Richard Roberts has been designing curriculum, teaching Electricity and Electronics as well as Computer Technology, and supervising technical teachers. Mr. Roberts is an accomplished programmer and computer network technician. He has experience as the system administrator for Novell NetWare, Microsoft NT, and IBM Token Ring networking systems. He possesses a Bachelor's degree in Technical Education and a Master's degree in Administration/Supervision. He also has CompTIA A+, Network+, iNet+, and Security+ certifications and is a certified IT technician, remote desktop support technician, and depot technician.

His computer experiences started as early as 1974 when he began programming and teaching the Motorola 6800, which eventually evolved into the Motorola 68000, once the core processor of the Apple Macintosh computer system. Since then, Mr. Roberts has maintained his teaching status to both instructors and students as the technology has evolved, and he has remained at a state-of-the-art technical level through research, teaching, and applications. He is currently an adjunct instructor at South Florida State College where he teaches PC repair, A+ Certification, Network Fundamentals, Network+ Certification, and many short workshops in various Microsoft business applications. He also coauthored the textbook *Electricity and Electronics* as well as designed and programmed the accompanying interactive CD-ROM.

In addition to his current position, Mr. Roberts has taught at Erwin Technical Center and Tampa Bay Technical High School, and he has taught adults in the military service. His time is now divided between computer consulting and applications, teaching students and instructors, and writing textbooks and other ancillary instructional materials. Occasionally, he goes fishing, but not too often.

Using This Text

Each chapter begins with a number of learning objectives. These are the goals you should set to accomplish while working through the chapter. In addition to your objectives, each chapter begins with a list of these new terms, which are important for you to learn as you move through the chapter. When these words are introduced in the text, they are printed in a bold typeface.

As you read this text, you will also notice some other words or phrases that stand out. File names that you encounter will appear like notepad.exe, student.txt, or io.sys. Any data you must enter, be it by typing at the command and Run prompts or button/tabs/menus that you will click on with your mouse are set out like **dir C:** or **Start | All Programs | Accessories | System Tools**. Any Internet addresses within the text are in the traditional Web style and in blue, such as www.g-w.com. Internet addresses listed under Interesting Web Sites for More Information at the end of each chapter are in the traditional Web style, underlined, and in blue, such as www.g-w.com. Be sure to read any A+ Notes, Tech Tips, Warnings, Cautions, and Dangers that you encounter. A+ Notes contain tips that will help you study for the CompTIA A+ Certification exams. Tech Tips are useful tidbits that might come in handy in the field. Take heed when you see Warnings, Cautions, and Dangers. Warnings alert you of minor injury that may occur to yourself or to others. Cautions alert you when an act may damage your computer and incur minor injury to yourself. Losing all of your data is the most common act to be cautious of. Dangers alert you of possible serious or fatal injury to yourself or others. For example, you may encounter some dangerous voltages, especially when dealing with monitors. Most of those repairs should be left to special technicians.

Each chapter concludes with a summary of some of the key information you should take from the chapter, a large number of questions, a list of useful Web sites, and laboratory activities for you to try. Each chapter has two sets of questions. The first set of questions tests your general comprehension of the material in the chapter. The second set of questions mimics the style of the CompTIA A+ Certification exams. The questions asked here are on topics that the exams commonly probe.

Hands-on experience is the only way to become proficient in PC repair, so be sure to attempt the activities at the end of each chapter. If you can complete the activities in this text and in the accompanying laboratory manual, you should have no problem passing the A+ Certification exams. Each chapter concludes with a complete Lab Activity. Be sure to work through each of these activities. Suggested Laboratory Activities are also included. These activities are loosely structured proceedings that you can attempt on your own or if you have free time in class.

Never forget, the world of computers and mobile devices changes rapidly. Consequently, computer repair and the CompTIA A+ Certification exams must change with it. Each chapter includes a list of Web sites where you can find the latest information on the topics covered. Be sure to check the CompTIA Web site (www.comptia.org) frequently for the latest information on what subjects are being added to the exams and what subjects are being dropped. Also, check the author's Web site (www.RMRoberts.com) for text updates, interesting links, and bonus laboratory material.

Reviewers

The author and publisher would like to thank the following individuals for providing assistance and guidance in developing this textbook.

Alexander C. Bell
Career and Technical Education
  Teacher
Thomas A. Edison High School
Jamaica, NY

Stacy Byrne
Business Instructor, NBEA, NVBEA,
  NACTE, ACTE
East Career and Technical Academy
Las Vegas, NV

Matthew Champlin
Instructor, Computer Systems
Cayuga-Onondaga BOCES
Auburn, NY

James "Tommy" Davis
Department Head, Computer
  Technology Education
A. Crawford Mosley High School
Lynn Haven, FL

Beth Felts
Business, Finance, and IT Instructor
Elkin High School
Elkin, NC

Robert Hanchett
Advanced Math and Science Teacher
Westfield High School
Houston, TX

Michael High
President, Texas TSA
Texas Technology Student
  Association
Amarillo, TX

Thomas E. Hundley
Network and Cyber Security
  Instructor
Wando High School
Mt. Pleasant, SC

Michael Kalif
Engineering Technology Educator
Somerset Berkley Regional HS
Somerset, MA

Amy E. Keene
Teacher, Secondary Math
Westfield High School
Houston, TX

Rachel Newell
California TSA State Advisor
University of California, Berkeley
Berkeley, CA

Tony Newson
Instructor/Computer Installation and
  Repair Technology
Coahoma Community College
Clarksdale, MS

Stephen D. Paduhovich
Teacher, Information Technology
  Department
York County School of Technology
York, PA

R. Steven Price
President
International Technology and
  Engineering Educators Association
Reston, VA

Paul Ruiz de Velasco, M. Ed
Computer Maintenance Teacher
Lancaster High School
Lancaster, TX

Anna Marie Warren
Career and Technical Education Teacher
TSA Sponsor
Waxahachie Global High School
Waxahachie, TX

Acknowledgments

I would like to thank the following people who helped make this textbook possible by supplying information, details, photographs, artwork, and software.

Adam Forbes, Crucial Technology

Al Platt, US Postal Service

Beverly A. Summers, Fluke Corporation

Brian Burke, NVIDIA Corporation

Chris Keller, PC-Doctor, Inc.

David Goss, American Microsystems LTD

David Leong, Kingston Technology Company, Inc.

Erkki Lepre, F-Secure Corporation

Gabriel Rouchon, Swiftech Inc.

George Alfs, Intel Corporation

Heather Jardim, Kingston Technology Company, Inc.

Howard Burnside, Electronics Instructor, Retired

Jacqueline Romulo, Belkin International, Inc.

Jason Cambria, NeoWorx, Inc.

Jeremy VanWagnen, TechSmith Corporation

Jim Spare, Canesta, Inc.

Joanna Moore, IBM Corporation

John Stott, Citicorp

Kevin Franks, Winternals Software LP

Les Goldberg, D-Link Systems

Melody Chalaban, Belkin Corporation

Michelle Flippen, Tiny Software, Inc.

Ray Gorman, IBM Corporation

Sonel V. Friedman, GTCO CalComp, Inc.

Stu Sjouwerman, Sunbelt Software

Tom Way, IBM Corporation

Walter Ernie, Computer and Electronics Instructor

William Kautter, GTCO CalComp, Inc.

and special thanks to Carl Marchand and John Byrd

Trademarks

DirectX, Microsoft, MS-DOS, Outlook, Visual Basic, Windows, Windows NT, Windows Server, Windows Vista, and Windows XP are all trademarks of Microsoft Corporation.

Zip is a trademark of Iomega Corporation.

Apple, FireWire, Leopard, Mac, Macintosh, Mac OS, QuickTime, and TrueType are registered trademarks of Apple Inc.

Celeron, Celeron D, Celeron M, Enhanced Intel SpeedStep, Intel Core, Intel Core 2 Duo, Intel Core 2 Solo, Intel Core Duo, Intel Core Extreme Solo, Intel Core 2 Extreme, Intel Core 2 Extreme Quad, Core i3, Core i5, and Core i7, Intel QuickPath, Intel VT-x, Intel Atom, Intel Core Quad, Intel Core Solo, Intel Xeon, Intel386, Intel486, IntelDX2, IntelDX4, Itanium, Itanium 2, MMX, OverDrive, Pentium, Pentium 4, Pentium D, Pentium II Xeon, Pentium III Xeon, and Pentium M are registered trademarks of Intel Corporation.

AMD, AMD Athlon, AMD Duron, AMD-K6, AMD OverDrive, Athlon 64, Athlon MP, Athlon Opteron, Athlon XP, AMD Sempron, Athlon 64 X2, Athlon 64-FX, ATI, Cool 'n' Quiet HyperTransport Technology, Turbo CORE, and AMD-V are trademarks of Advanced Micro Devices, Inc.

PostScript is a trademark of Adobe Systems, Inc.

Rambus and RDRAM are trademarks of Rambus, Inc.

Other trademarks are registered by their respective owners.

CompTIA A+

How to Become CompTIA Certified

This training material can help you prepare for and pass a related CompTIA certification exam or exams. To achieve CompTIA certification, you must do the following:

1. Register for and schedule a time to take the CompTIA certification exam(s) at a convenient location.
2. Read and sign the Candidate Agreement, which will be presented at the time of the exam(s).
3. Take and pass the CompTIA certification exam(s).

For more information about CompTIA's certifications, such as their industry acceptance, benefits, or program news, please visit http://certification.comptia.org.

CompTIA is a nonprofit information technology (IT) trade association. CompTIA's certifications are designed by subject matter experts from across the IT industry. Each CompTIA certification is vendor-neutral, covers multiple technologies, and requires demonstration of skills and knowledge widely sought after by the IT industry.

To contact CompTIA with any questions or comments:
- Please call 1-866-835-8020
- or e-mail CompTIA at questions@comptia.org.

CompTIA A+ Correlation Charts

Complete mappings (correlation charts) of the CompTIA A+ objectives to the content of the *Computer Service and Repair* textbook and *Lab Manual* are located on the G-W website www.g-w.com for this textbook. On this website, you will find one correlation chart per CompTIA A+ exam:
- CompTIA A+ 220-801
- CompTIA A+ 220-802

Each correlation chart lists the exam objectives and the corresponding textbook pages and lab activities of where to find the related content.

Chapter Listing

Table of Contents

Chapter 10
Optical Storage Technology 389

Chapter 11
Printers. 419

Chapter 12
Laptops and Mobile Devices. 461

Chapter 13
Modems and Transceivers **511**

Chapter 14
Physical and Digital Security **545**

Chapter 15
PC Troubleshooting. **589**

Chapter 16
Introduction to Networking 657

Chapter 17
Network Administration 707

Introduction to a Typical PC

1

After studying this chapter, you will be able to:

- Give examples of how computers are used.
- Contrast analog and digital electronics.
- Give examples of computer data.
- Interpret binary and hexadecimal numbers *0* through *15*.
- Compare bit, byte, and word.
- Contrast serial and parallel data transfer.
- Interpret the common prefixes associated with the computer's size and speed.
- Identify external computer connections.
- Identify the major components of a typical PC.
- Explain how the major computer components interact with each other.
- Contrast electrostatic discharge, electromagnetic interference, and radio frequency interference.
- Identify common PC service tools.
- Recall common safety practices related to computer repair.

A+ Exam—Key Points

Some of the very basic questions on the A+ Certification exams deal with cable and connector identification, component handling, and safety procedures. Connector identification can be difficult for students new to PC technology, but anyone who has worked with a PC for some time will be able to answer these types of questions. As a student, you can prepare by looking at the end of the cable and noting if it uses pins or a socket. Do the same for the connection on the PC.

Key Terms

The following key terms will become important pieces of your computer vocabulary. Be sure you can define them.

A+ Certification
American Standard Code for
    Information Interchange (ASCII)
analog electronics
anti-static wrist strap
battery
binary number system
bit
byte
central processing unit (CPU)
CompTIA
computer
cooling fan
data
device bay
digital electronics
driver
electromagnetic interference (EMI)

electrostatic discharge (ESD)
expansion card
expansion card slot
external SATA
firmware
hard drive
hexadecimal number system
hot swap
integrated circuit (IC)
motherboard
parallel transfer
peripheral
power eSATA (eSATAp)
power supply
radio frequency interference (RFI)
random access memory (RAM)
serial transfer
word

This chapter introduces the basic concepts you need to understand computer hardware and software. It briefly covers many topics. These topics are expanded into complete chapters later in the textbook. This text presents the personal computer based on the IBM-compatible computer architecture, better known as the PC, and prepares you for CompTIA A+ Certification.

CompTIA is a not-for-profit, vendor-neutral organization that certifies the competency level of technicians through examinations written to test specific areas. The CompTIA organization has prepared the examinations to test individuals with approximately 12 months of PC repair, installation, and support experience. The certification awarded on successful completion of the exams is called **A+ Certification**. It is recognized throughout the industry as a certification of basic PC repair and support skills. The combination of this textbook and its accompanying Laboratory Manual and Study Guide prepares you for the certification exams. There is more information in Chapter 21—CompTIA A+ Certification Exams Preparation. You can also visit the CompTIA website for the latest certification information.

The Role of Computers

Computers are found in every aspect of our lives. There is not an industry that operates without a computer. Computers can be found in banks, Wall Street businesses, military aircraft, automobiles, televisions, communication systems, home appliances, satellites, submarines, and police stations. Computers can vary in size from the small, simple microprocessor found in a coffeepot or a clock radio to huge mainframe systems that are used in research and government agencies. **Figure 1-1** shows a microchip along with a large computer system and a typical home or business PC.

At first, the makeup of a computer can seem intimidating. However, as you progress through this text, you will see that the mechanics of a computer are quite simple. The difficulty is overcome by understanding the interaction of hardware and software, grasping different operating systems, and recognizing upgrade and compatibility issues.

If you know which part is defective, it is a relatively easy task to replace the part. The challenge is determining which part is defective

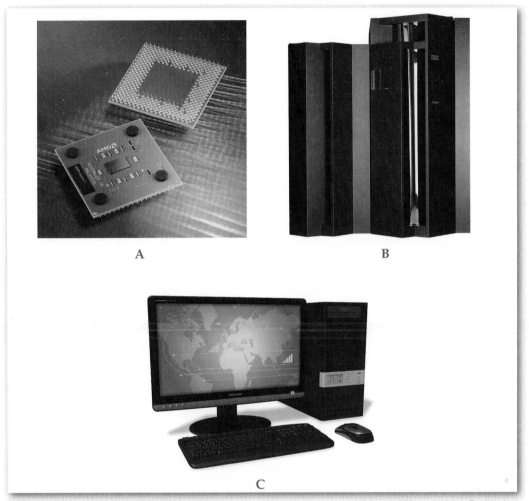

Advanced Microprocessor Devices Inc.
International Business Systems Corporation
Oleksiy Mark/Shutterstock

Figure 1-1.
Computers vary in size. A—Microchip (AMD Athlon™ XP processor). B—Large computer system for a research center. C—Typical home PC.

or determining if the problem is hardware related or software related.

The aim of this textbook is to systematically teach you the necessary skills to be successful in the world of computer technology. In this chapter, we will take a quick look at the major components of a typical PC and introduce basic computer concepts such as computer data and software. As your studies progress through the text, each part and concept will be covered in great depth, but for now it is best to have an overall view of the PC system. No component can be fully understood without realizing how it interacts with the other components in the system. This chapter covers introductory-level knowledge of the computer system before going into depth at a technician level.

Digital Electronics

All electronic components fall into one of two categories: *analog* or *digital*. **Digital electronics** is a system that is best represented by a simple switch. There can only be two conditions in the switch circuit. The switch is either on or off. No other state exists. Look at **Figure 1-2**, which shows a typical switch wired to a lamp. The switch controls power to the lamp. The lamp can be turned on or off. No other electrical condition can exist for this simple circuit. Digital electronics in computers use on and off conditions. There is either full voltage or no voltage applied to the circuit.

Analog electronics use and produce varying voltage levels. Analog electrical circuits can be

Figure 1-2.
Typical on/off switch wired to lamp.

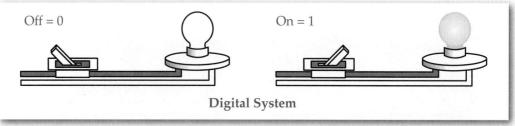

Goodheart-Willcox Publisher

represented with a dimmer switch. **Figure 1-3** shows a dimmer switch connected to a lamp. In this circuit, the intensity of the lamp varies as the dimmer switch is turned. The light from the lamp can have different intensities because the dimmer switch varies the amount of electrical energy that reaches the lamp.

A computer is constructed of some very complex digital circuits. These digital circuits are combined into modules such as circuit board cards. As a PC technician, you will usually only be responsible for replacing the module, not repairing the digital circuits. You do not need an extensive electronics background to repair a PC.

What Is a Computer?

A **computer** is an assembly of electronic modules that interact with computer programs known as *software* to create, modify, transmit, store, and display data. The computer has

rapidly evolved from a simple electronic device into a highly sophisticated piece of electronic technology.

Science fiction writers have attributed human qualities to computers such as Father in *Alien: Resurrection*. The computer can appear to be intelligent, but in reality it only processes and stores data. Processing data is limited to such things as sorting items, comparing, and locating previously stored data. In addition, computers perform mathematical calculations at amazing speeds. However, the computer cannot think. The computer can only be programmed.

This leads to another basic question: What is data? **Data** is information. This information comes in many forms. Data can be text (such as *ABC* or *123*), graphics (pictures), and sounds (music or voices). **Figure 1-4** is an illustration presenting text, sound, and a picture, followed by digital electrical voltage symbols.

Data inside the computer is represented electronically as high and low voltages. The

Figure 1-3.
Typical dimmer switch.

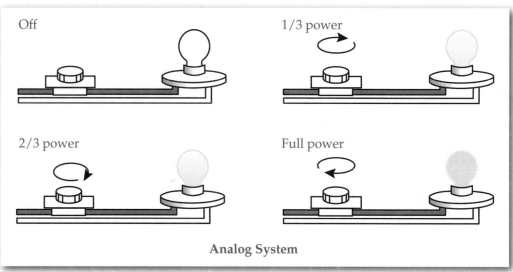

Goodheart-Willcox Publisher

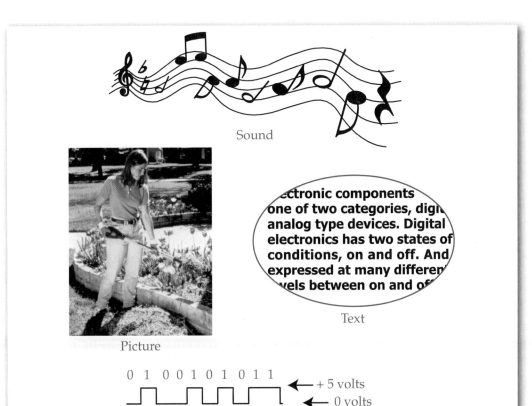

Figure 1-4.
Sound, pictures, and text are all forms of data. Each can be represented by a code consisting of ones and zeros, the binary number system.

Union Tools, Inc.
Goodheart-Willcox Publisher

voltages are pulsed through the system. These pulses of high and low voltages create what is called a *digital signal*. Many things can be done with these electrical energy pulses. Data can be displayed on a computer monitor or can be stored in memory chips or storage media such as a hard drive, flash drive, or compact disc (CD). When written to a hard drive, the electrical pulses are converted to magnetic patterns on the surface of the disk.

Data in a computer system is represented as ones and zeros. The pattern of ones and zeros is known as the *binary system*. You will be introduced to the binary system later in this chapter. Some digital patterns represent words, pictures, and sounds. Other digital patterns represent commands such as load file, find file, and save file. Remember, the computer does not contain any intelligence. It simply manipulates, stores, and displays data.

Computer Data Codes

Data can be almost anything. It can be numbers, text, pictures, and sounds. Computer data and functions are expressed in a variety of ways. They can be expressed as voltage levels, numeric systems such as binary and hexadecimal, and symbolic codes such as ASCII. Although computer data and commands can be expressed in many different forms and still have the same meaning, the form selected should be the one that is easiest to grasp for the given material. For example, it is much easier to express memory locations as hexadecimal values rather than binary values, although the memory location could be expressed in either value. The computer technician must be very familiar with each of these forms of data expression.

Binary Number Code

The **binary number system** consists of entirely ones and zeros. It is the perfect numbering system to represent digital electronic systems. Just as a digital device has only two states (on and off), the binary system uses only two numbers: *0* and *1*. Look at **Figure 1-5** to see how the binary number system is used to express different values from zero to fifteen.

Figure 1-5. The binary number system can be used to represent any integer in the decimal system. This chart shows binary numbers counting up to 15.

Binary	Decimal
0000	0
0001	1
0010	2
0011	3
0100	4
0101	5
0110	6
0111	7
1000	8
1001	9
1010	10
1011	11
1100	12
1101	13
1110	14
1111	15

Goodheart-Willcox Publisher

Binary can be compared to a switch. If the switch is closed, the lamp will be on. This state is represented by a *1*. When the switch is in the off position, the lamp is dark. This state is represented by a *0*.

This may seem like a system too simple to represent data in a computer, but let's compare it to the Morse code system. The Morse code system consists of only two tones: a short beep and a long beep. These sounds are referred to as a dot and a dash, respectively. See **Figure 1-6**. This code resembles a binary system. It has two conditions. The dots and dashes can be combined in sequences that represent the alphabet and the numerals *0* through *9*. The Morse code system has been used to transmit information all over the world.

Graphics are transmitted in a similar fashion using a facsimile (fax) machine. The light and dark areas are represented by the presence or absence of a transmitted voltage. Again, this is a form similar to digital electronics. See **Figure 1-7**, which depicts two rotating drums. One drum is a transmitter and the other is a receiver. As you can see, the two-state condition of digital electronics can be much more powerful than it first appears.

The ones and zeros of the binary system are used to represent the high and low voltage signals that travel throughout the computer system. They also represent data stored on disks or in memory chips.

Figure 1-6.
Morse code transfers letters between two antennae using combinations of two states: dots and dashes.

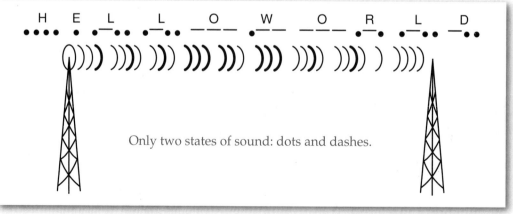

Goodheart-Willcox Publisher

Figure 1-7. Voltage highs and lows can be used to send pictures across phone lines.

Original news photograph.

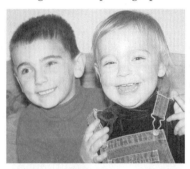

The original photo is mounted on the rotating drum. A light transmitter and receiver convert the light and dark areas of the image into matching voltage levels.

A transducer moves along the drum while it spins, converting the image into electrical signals.

Rotating drum.

Copy converted from electrical signal back to photograph.

Data is converted into electrical signals. The signals are carried across telephone lines to the destination telephoto machine where the image is recreated.

A writing stylus converts the electrical signals into an image.

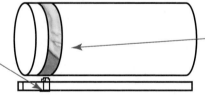

Electronic voltage levels converted to drawing.

The first facsimilie or "telephotography" machine was put into commercial use in 1924. A transparency of a photograph was placed on a spinning drum. The image was converted into electrical signals representing the light and dark areas in the photograph. The electrical signals were converted back into a photographic image at the destination.

Hexadecimal Number Code

The hexadecimal code is based on the number base 16, similar to how the binary code is based on the number base 2. The **hexadecimal number system** is a computer code system that uses 16 characters. See **Figure 1-8**.

The hexadecimal system uses numerals *0* through *9* from the decimal number system and six additional characters from the alphabet, *A* through *F*. This combination of number and letter characters forms the hexadecimal number system.

Figure 1-8. Hexadecimal numbers include the digits *0* through *9* and the letters *A* through *F*.

Hexadecimal	Decimal
0	0
1	1
2	2
3	3
4	4
5	5
6	6
7	7
8	8
9	9
A	10
B	11
C	12
D	13
E	14
F	15

Goodheart-Willcox Publisher

Binary numbers are too long and awkward to be used to express computer values such as memory locations. Thus, hexadecimal numbers are used instead. The hexadecimal code uses less space.

The hexadecimal system best matches the hardware system of most computers. As you will learn, data lines in a computer are eight, sixteen, thirty-two, or sixty-four lines wide. They use increments of eight and sixteen, which work beautifully with a hexadecimal system.

In addition, the number values you will encounter that are used to express memory sizes (such as 256, 512, and 1024) are increments of 16. As you can see, a number system based on 16 is used to best match the digital electronic system of computers.

Both the binary and hexadecimal number systems will be used to express values and illustrate computer operation many times throughout the study of computer systems.

ASCII Code

ASCII (pronounced *as-key*) stands for **American Standard Code for Information Interchange**. It was the first attempt to standardize computer character codes among the varieties of hardware and software. When a key on a computer keyboard is pressed, for example, the letter *M*, all computer systems display the letter *M* on the monitor screen. When the letter *M* is sent to the printer, the letter *M* is printed as expected. **Figure 1-9** is a listing of character codes and their ASCII code representatives.

The ASCII system was a great attempt to standardize the computer coding system, but it had limitations. The extended character set is unique to certain systems, such as IBM or equivalent machines. The extended character set must be used with a compatible software system; otherwise, unexpected characters will be generated. In addition, the standard form of ASCII does not allow for common requirements of word-processing packages such as **bold**, *italic*, underline, or variations in fonts. ASCII was meant for symbol compatibility used for basic data files. ASCII is still used today, especially when data needs to be transferred between two different software programs.

Bits, Bytes, and Words

Bit, byte, and word are basic computer units of data based on the binary number system. Short for *b*inary dig*it*, a **bit** is a single binary unit of one or zero. A **byte** is equal to eight bits. Early computers processed data in patterns of these eight-bit bytes.

A **word** is the total amount of bytes a computer can process at one time. Consequently, the length of a word can vary from computer to computer. For example, many computer systems process either 32 or 64 bits at one time. Hence, a word in those machines would consist of 32 bits (4 bytes) or 64 bits (8 bytes), respectively. Computers are often compared by the size of the word they can process.

Bit	=	0 or 1	1
Byte	=	eight bits	01011110
Word	=	1 to 8 bytes	10010010

11110000 00110011 10101010

Table of Standard ASCII Characters				(Continued)	
0	NUL	Null	64	@	
1	SOH	Start of header	65	A	
2	STX	Start of text	66	B	
3	ETX	End of text	67	C	
4	EOT	End of transmission	68	D	
5	ENQ	Enquiry	69	E	
6	ACK	Acknowledgment	70	F	
7	BEL	Bell	71	G	
8	BS	Backspace	72	H	
9	HT	Horizontal tab	73	I	
10	LF	Line feed	74	J	
11	VT	Vertical tab	75	K	
12	FF	Form feed	76	L	
13	CR	Carriage returns	77	M	
14	SO	Shift out	78	N	
15	SI	Shift in	79	O	
16	DLE	Data link escape	80	P	
17	DC1	Device control 1	81	Q	
18	DC2	Device control 2	82	R	
19	DC3	Device control 3	83	S	
20	DC4	Device control 4	84	T	
21	NAK	Negative Acknowledgment	85	U	
22	SYN	Synchronous idle	86	V	
23	ETB	End of transmit block	87	W	
24	CAN	Cancel	88	X	
25	EM	End of medium	89	Y	
26	SUB	Substitute	90	Z	
27	ESC	Escape	91	[	
28	FS	File separator	92	\	
29	GS	Group separator	93	]	
30	RS	Record separator	94	^	
31	US	Unit separator	95	_	
32	SP	Space	96	`	
33	!		97	a	
34	"		98	b	
35	#		99	c	
36	$		100	d	
37	%		101	e	
38	&		102	f	
39	'		103	g	
40	(		104	h	
41	)		105	i	
42	*		106	j	
43	+		107	k	
44	,		108	l	
45	-		109	m	
46	.		110	n	
47	/		111	o	
48	0		112	p	
49	1		113	q	
50	2		114	r	
51	3		115	s	
52	4		116	t	
53	5		117	u	
54	6		118	v	
55	7		119	w	
56	8		120	x	
57	9		121	y	
58	:		122	z	
59	;		123	{	
60	<		124			
61	=		125	}	
62	>		126	~	
63	?		127	DEL	

Figure 1-9.
ASCII code.

Goodheart-Willcox Publisher

Serial and Parallel Data Transfer

Data is transferred in one of two modes in a computer system: series or parallel. Ports on a computer are similarly classified as serial or parallel. In a **serial transfer**, data is sent through a port one bit at a time in successive order. Modems are used to communicate with other computers over telephone lines. Because of the limited capacity in a telephone line, data is transferred through modems in a serial fashion. Other examples of serial data transfer are the keyboard and mouse.

In **parallel transfer**, more than one bit is sent side by side. In parallel port transfer, data is sent eight bits at a time. In general, data is transferred at a much higher rate through a parallel port than a serial port. Data is transferred in parallel on the computer bus system between devices such as the hard drive, RAM, and the CPU. **Figure 1-10** shows a comparison between serial and parallel data transfer.

> ## A+ Note
>
> Be able to differentiate between serial and parallel data transmission.

Computer Numerical Values

Metric prefixes are commonly used to express the speed and size of computer systems and hardware. Prefixes are usually used in combination with the word bit (b) or byte (B). For example, *speed* is usually expressed in *bits*. *Storage space* is usually expressed as *bytes*. See **Figure 1-11** for a listing of commonly used metric prefixes.

There is some confusion when using metric prefixes for expressing computer sizes. This is because there are two possible values for a large expression such as a megabyte. The nominal value for megabyte using the base 10 number

Figure 1-10. Serial and parallel data transfer. Serial transfers one bit at a time. Parallel transfers multiple bits, usually multiples of 8 (1 byte), at a time.

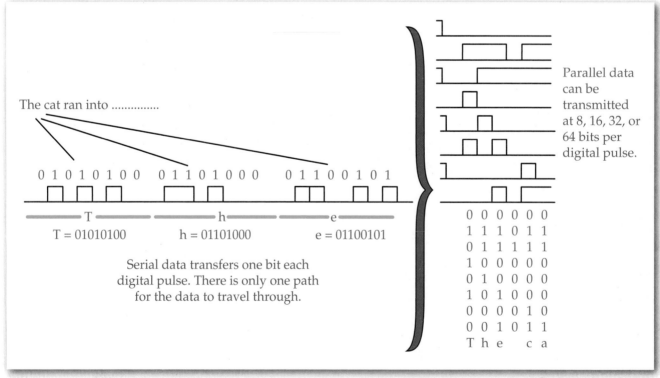

Goodheart-Willcox Publisher

Figure 1-11.
Metric prefix chart.

Metric Name	Symbol	Number Base 10	Number Base 2	Common Name	Numeric Equivalent for the Base 10 Number System
Pico	p	10^{-12}	2^{-40}	trillionth	0.000 000 000 001
Nano	n	10^{-9}	2^{-30}	billionth	0.000 000 001
Micro	μ	10^{-6}	2^{-20}	millionth	0.000 001
Milli	m	10^{-3}	2^{-10}	thousandth	0.001
Base unit		1			1
Kilo	k	10^{3}	2^{10}	thousand	1,000
Mega	M	10^{6}	2^{20}	million	1,000,000
Giga	G	10^{9}	2^{30}	billion	1,000,000,000
Tera	T	10^{12}	2^{40}	trillion	1,000,000,000,000
Peta	P	10^{15}	2^{50}	quadrillion	1,000,000,000,000,000
Exa	E	10^{18}	2^{60}	quintillion	1,000,000,000,000,000,000

Goodheart-Willcox Publisher

system is equal to 1,000,000. In computer systems, a 1-megabyte item such as memory is 1,048,576 (2^{20}) bytes (the power of 2 raised to the 20th). The large values expressed for computer systems are based on the binary number system. **Figure 1-12** compares the values of the base 10 number system and the base 2 number system.

Take a Tour Outside the Computer Case

A minimal workstation consists of a computer and input and output devices, **Figure 1-13**. The computer is a case that houses the motherboard, CPU, memory, hard drive, and other associated electronics parts and modules that make up the computer system. The typical input devices found

at a workstation are a keyboard and mouse, but there are many other devices that can be used for input. The typical output devices found at the workstation are the computer monitor, printer, and speakers.

Peripherals

The keyboard, mouse, monitor, printer, and speakers are classified as peripherals. A **peripheral** is an optional piece of equipment used to display data or to input data. The monitor displays data in the form of words and pictures. The printer displays data in a printed form on paper. The speakers convert data into sound such as music and spoken language. The mouse and keyboard are common input devices. The keyboard is used to enter alphanumeric text and

Prefix	Base 2 Number System	Base 10 Number System
Kilobyte	1,024	1,000
Megabyte	1,048,576	1,000,000
Gigabyte	1,073,741,824	1,000,000,000
Terabyte	1,099,511,627,776	1,000,000,000,000
Petabyte	1,125,899,906,842,624	1,000,000,000,000,000
Exabyte	1,152,921,504,606,846,976	1,000,000,000,000,000,000

Figure 1-12.
Base 10 and base 2 comparisons. You get more for your meg when you are using base 2 terminology.

Goodheart-Willcox Publisher

Figure 1-13. Front view of a typical PC.

Oleksiy Mark/Shutterstock.com

to issue commands through the use of special purpose keys, such as the function keys and key combinations. The mouse is used to interact with coordinates on the display. When an area on the display is selected followed by a left mouse click, a command is entered. A touch screen monitor is both an input and output device. The screen is used to display data as output and to input commands by touching the screen. These devices are covered later in the textbook.

Case Style

There are many different case styles that are used to contain and protect the electronic parts of a computer. Some of the most common case styles are referred to as desktop, tower, mini tower,

micro tower, laptop, and notebook. Case selection is usually based on individual taste.

Exterior Connections

The outside of the computer allows access to the electronic parts inside. Data can be entered into the computer system through the hard drive, optical (CD/DVD) drive, keyboard, mouse, or one of the ports in the back. See **Figure 1-14**.

The exterior connections to a computer are well worth a closer look. The connectors discussed in this section are some of the more common connectors you will find on a PC. More information is given on these connectors in the sections detailing the components with which they work.

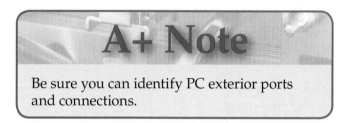

A+ Note

Be sure you can identify PC exterior ports and connections.

Mini-DIN

The mini-DIN connection is used for the mouse and keyboard, **Figure 1-15**. Be aware that this connection type may not be interchangeable on some computers as it is for the connection

Figure 1-14.
Ports accessible at the back of a typical computer.

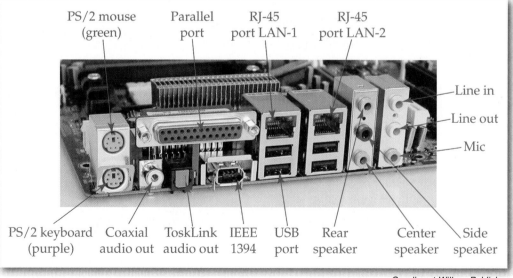

Figure 1-15. Mini-DIN connector and connection. A—Mini-DIN connector on a keyboard or mouse. B—Connection for a mini-DIN mouse or keyboard.

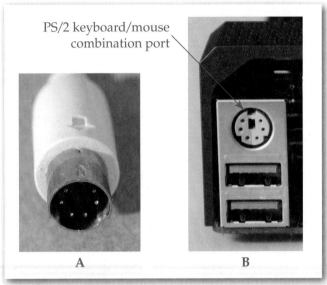

Goodheart-Willcox Publisher

in Figure 1-15. For example, on the computer in Figure 1-14, the mouse must connect to the mini-DIN connector identified for the mouse cable, and the keyboard must connect to the mini-DIN connector identified for the keyboard cable.

FireWire

The FireWire connection, also known as the IEEE-1394 connector, can connect up to 63 devices that can be hot swapped. The term **hot swap** means to plug in or unplug a device while the PC is running. FireWire was designed for Apple computers by Lucent Technologies and is proprietary. FireWire is seen more often on Apple equipment than on PC equipment. It is designed for very high-speed data transfers such as those required for video equipment. The high-speed data transfer rates make it an excellent choice to upload video images from a camera to a PC. FireWire is also used for other equipment connections such as hard drives, optical drives (CD/DVD), and printers. **Figure 1-16** shows a pair of FireWire connectors.

USB

The Universal Serial Bus (USB) is another type of connection used on PCs, **Figure 1-17**. The USB port is a multipurpose connection that allows many different devices to connect to the PC in a daisy-chain fashion or by the use of a hub. The USB design allows for connections to peripheral devices that formerly may have required opening the PC case and inserting an expansion card. With the USB port, the need to open the case to connect many of the different devices has been eliminated.

Figure 1-16. FireWire ports are high-speed connections.

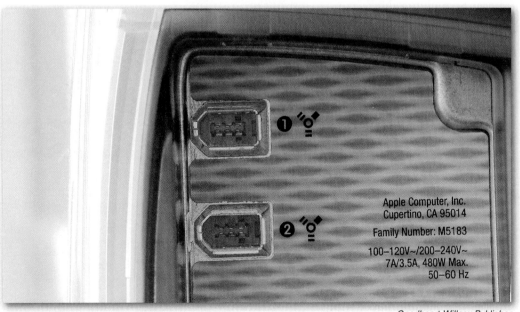

Goodheart-Willcox Publisher

Figure 1-17. USB ports.

Goodheart-Willcox Publisher

Another desirable advantage of USB is that you can connect up to 127 devices through the USB port in a daisy-chain fashion. Before USB, it was possible to run out of ports to support all of the equipment that might be needed for a special workstation. For example, a workstation used by a graphics designer might require connections to a scanner, digital camera, microphone, laser printer, color inkjet printer, poster-size plotter printer, and a digital graphics tablet for freehand drawings. USB and FireWire ports are capable of supporting numerous devices required by a single workstation. Legacy workstations could only be used to support a limited number of devices.

Device Bay

The **device bay** is a drive bay designed to accommodate the easy hot swap of devices such as hard drives, tape drives, and optical drives. The device bay is prewired for either USB or FireWire and allows devices to easily slide into or out of the PC case. A device installed into the device bay looks as though it was installed internally. By installing the device into the device bay, the problem of long cords running across and around valuable desk space can be eliminated.

RJ

There are two types of RJ connectors commonly used with a PC: RJ-11 and RJ-45. The RJ-11 is used for modem telephone connections. The RJ-45 is used for network connections. The RJ-11 uses four conductors and four pins, while the RJ-45 uses eight conductors and eight pins, see **Figure 1-18**.

DB

The DB connector looks similar in shape to the letter *D*, see **Figure 1-19**. The DB connector typically is classified as 9-, 15-, or 25-pin. The DB connector was once commonly used to connect items such as a joystick, monitor, or printer. The DB connection at the back of a sound card is sometimes referred to as a game port. When a 15-pin D shell connector is arranged with three rows of five connections, it is referred to as an *HD-15*. The HD

Figure 1-18. RJ-45 and RJ-11 connectors.

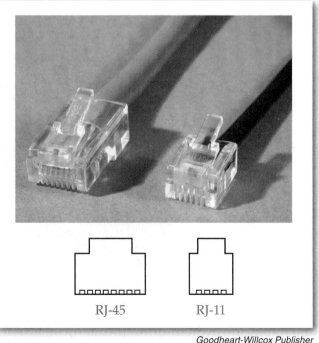

Goodheart-Willcox Publisher

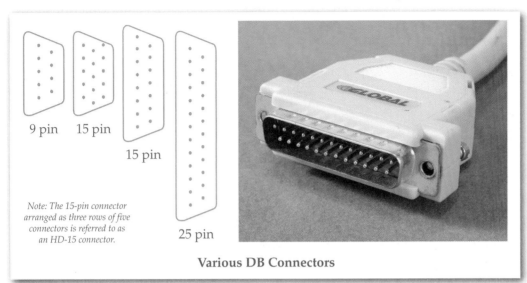

Various DB Connectors

9 pin   15 pin

15 pin

Note: The 15-pin connector arranged as three rows of five connectors is referred to as an HD-15 connector.

25 pin

Figure 1-19.
Selection of sizes of DB connectors and a typical DB connector. DB connectors are used for both serial and parallel ports.

represents *high density* and is used for monitor connections. Three-row DB-15 connectors are also referred to as DB-15HD and DE-15. Technically speaking from an electronics point of view, DE-15 is the correct term to describe a DB-15 connector designed for computer video ports.

Current computers have no DB or mini-DIN connections. USB has become the standard peripheral connection type. You may still, however, encounter DB connections on legacy PCs while doing repair work for customers.

VGA, DVI, and HDMI

Figure 1-20 shows a variety of monitor connections you may encounter on the back of a PC. Shown is a VGA, DVI, and HDMI connection. The VGA is an analog port while DVI and HDMI are digital ports. There will be much more about these connections in Chapter 8—Video and Audio Systems.

Not all computers have the same external connections. **Figure 1-21** shows the connections on a high-performance motherboard. In contrast to the external connections shown in Figure 1-20, there are no VGA, DVI, or HDMI display ports. This motherboard is designed for a video display adapter to be installed into an expansion slot.

Figure 1-20. This computer provides three different styles of video ports: VDG, DVI, and HDMI.

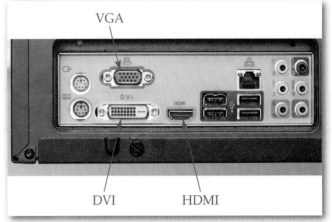

VGA

DVI   HDMI

External SATA

Another major difference in the computer in Figure 1-21 is the addition of the external SATA port and the power eSATA port. The **external SATA** port provides a data connection to an external SATA device but does not provide power to the device. The **power eSATA** port, also called *eSATAp*, provides an external SATA device with a data connection and electrical power.

There will be much more detailed information about ports and motherboards in Chapter 3—Motherboards. This chapter is intended only to

Figure 1-21.
High-performance motherboard with nonstandard connections.

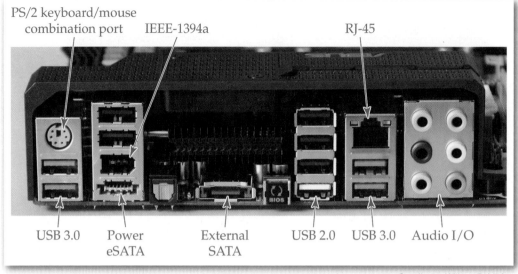

PS/2 keyboard/mouse combination port   IEEE-1394a   RJ-45

USB 3.0   Power eSATA   External SATA   USB 2.0   USB 3.0   Audio I/O

familiarize you with the exterior connections. Be sure you can visually identify each port type.

Take a Tour Inside the Computer Case

The inside of a PC is filled with a number of standard components and expansion slots that allow each computer to be customized with a tremendous variety of interesting tools, **Figure 1-22**. The equipment that follows details only the common computer components. These are devices you will find in almost every system.

CPU

In the simplest of terms, the **central processing unit (CPU)** is the brain of the computer, **Figure 1-23**. Intel® Core® i7, Intel® Pentium®, Intel® Celeron®, AMD FX 8-Core, and AMD Phenom™ identify various models of CPUs. The CPU consists of millions of microscopic electronic components called *transistors*. The transistors are electrically connected together in such a way they are able to interact with computer programs and process data.

All the other computer components depend on the actions of the CPU. The CPU controls the data in the computer. Commands are issued to the CPU via software. The CPU translates the commands into actions, such as save the data on the screen to memory, open a new file, and locate a file.

As discussed earlier, the CPU does not think or possess any human intelligence as some movies may depict. A CPU simply carries out the program codes written in the software program.

Power Supply

The **power supply** converts the 120-volt ac power from the wall outlet to dc voltage levels used by the various computer components, **Figure 1-24**. Once the 120 volts of ac power is converted to a lower dc voltage, usually 3.3, 5, or 12 volts, cables carry the electrical energy to the motherboard, hard drive, and other major components.

Hard Drive

The **hard drive** (also called the *internal drive* or *hard disk drive*) is where computer programs and data are stored, **Figure 1-25**. A hard drive is made up of several disks in a stack inside a sealed box. Computer programs and data are stored on the hard drive as magnetic patterns. Data is transmitted to and from the hard drive through a data cable attached to the hard drive on one end and to the motherboard on the opposite end. The hard drive is connected to the power supply

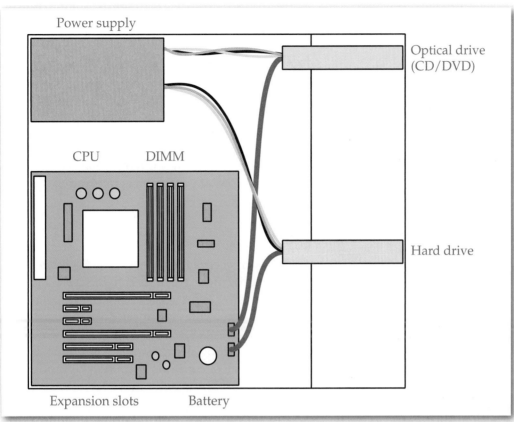

Figure 1-22.
These components are common to the PC. Depending on the style of the unit (tower, desktop, or laptop), the arrangement of the parts will vary. This sketch shows a tower PC.

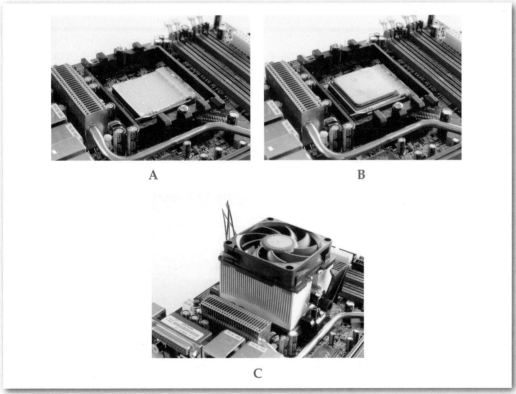

Figure 1-23.
The CPU is the brain of the computer.
A—Empty CPU socket on a motherboard.
B—CPU is inserted into the socket.
C—Heat sink is mounted on the CPU to keep it cool.

by several brightly-colored wires that supply the electrical energy needed to run the hard drive system.

Figure 1-24. The power supply converts 120 Vac input to a much lower dc output required by the computer components.

Goodheart-Willcox Publisher

Figure 1-25. Hard drives are the most common storage device used with a PC.

Goodheart-Willcox Publisher

Motherboard

The **motherboard** is usually a rectangular piece of circuit board covered with many conductors that provide electrical energy paths to the computer components and expansion slots, **Figure 1-26**. It provides a way to distribute the digital signals carrying data, control instructions, and small amounts of electrical power to the many different components mounted on the board. The electrical system of pathways is referred to as the computer bus.

RAM

Random access memory (RAM) is where computer programs are loaded to from the hard drive, **Figure 1-27**. RAM is classified as a volatile memory system. Volatile simply means that the data and programs loaded in RAM are lost when power is turned off. Increasing a computer's RAM is one of the most common computer upgrades performed. RAM is usually mounted into several parallel slots on the motherboard. The amount of RAM in a typical home PC could be 4 GB or more. Depending on the type of applications to be run, the amount of RAM required will vary.

RAM is a place where data is temporarily stored. When a computer is turned off, the RAM is emptied. When a computer is started, new information is loaded into RAM. When you draw

Figure 1-26. Almost all computer data runs through the motherboard.

Goodheart-Willcox Publisher

Figure 1-27. Three different types of RAM module. Compare the notch location at the pin edge on each module. Notice that they do not line up. That is by design so that you do not install the wrong type of memory into a motherboard.

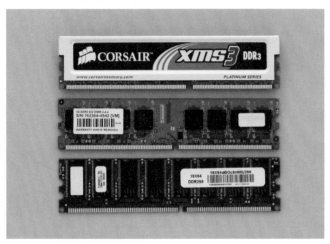

Goodheart-Willcox Publisher

a picture, the data that represents the picture is in RAM and is transferred to the screen. See **Figure 1-28**. The text on the screen is really a reflection of the data in RAM.

Firmware

Firmware is hardware-specific software required to boot the computer and support communication between the operating system and hardware devices. Firmware interprets commands of higher-level software programs, such as operating systems, and translates the commands into actions understandable by hardware devices, such as the hard drive, memory, keyboard, and mouse. **Figure 1-29** shows the relationship of firmware to hardware, application software, and the operating system.

Firmware and drivers work hand in hand. Firmware is not only found on the motherboard but is also incorporated into many computer devices such as graphic cards, hard drives, and

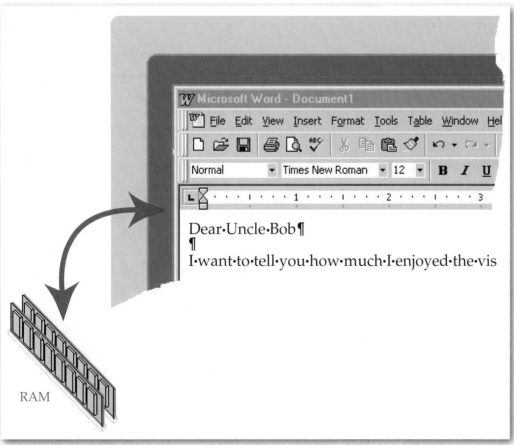

Figure 1-28. As you type data into a word-processing program, the information is stored in RAM.

Goodheart-Willcox Publisher

Figure 1-29. The relationship of firmware to hardware, application software, and the operating system.

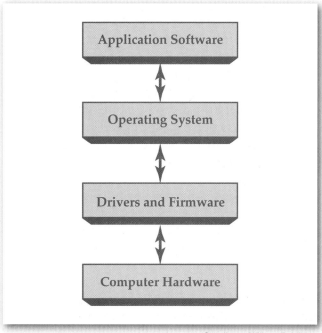

Goodheart-Willcox Publisher

SCSI drive controllers. A **driver** is a small software program written specifically for a hardware device. It allows the operating system to properly communicate with the device. For example, a printer requires a specific driver to be installed on the computer before the operating system can successfully use the printer. Without the driver, the printer will not function properly.

The terms *firmware*, *BIOS*, and *CMOS* (pronounced *c-moss*) are often interchanged, but they are really distinct concepts. *Firmware* is a combination of a special type of memory chip and software programs that support communication and compatibility. It includes the Setup utility, which is responsible for setting and storing the date and time and information about the computer hardware. *CMOS* is where the Setup utility stores information about the computer's hardware, date, and time. It is an integrated circuit. CMOS stands for complementary metal oxide semiconductor and is a type of low-power semiconductor chip technology. In the electronics field, there are many different types of devices designed from CMOS technology. In the computer field, it is understood that it refers to the location where the BIOS settings or data are stored.

Originally, firmware software was permanently etched into a ROM (read-only memory) chip. ROM firmware was permanent and could only be changed by replacing the ROM chip. Today, firmware software is stored in an EEPROM (electrically erasable programmable read-only memory) chip. An EEPROM is reprogrammable and is often referred to as flash ROM. Flash ROM can be erased electrically and reprogrammed with an updated version of a software program. It retains its data when electrical power to the computer is disconnected or turned off.

BIOS is a type of firmware. It is a small software program written in machine language. Machine language is a language that uses hexadecimal codes to write a program. It is the language that your computer understands. It is many times faster than other programming languages, but it is much more difficult to write. BIOS is typically 64 kB (kilobytes) in size and has limitations on the amount of RAM it can use. Because there is no single BIOS standard, BIOS systems are diverse. This has led to hardware compatibility problems that require BIOS upgrades. Even with these disadvantages, BIOS firmware is the most prevalent firmware in use.

EFI or UEFI is a type of firmware created to replace BIOS. EFI was introduced in the late 1990s but was not standardized until 2005. At that time it became known as UEFI. In contrast to BIOS, UEFI has a standard set of boot programs and configuration data. This allows hardware manufacturers, software companies, and operating systems to use the firmware in a consistent manner and achieve similar results without compatibility problems. It makes it much easier to develop new hardware drivers and to support hardware devices. Soon, UEFI will be the most common firmware used in computers and related hardware.

Battery

The **battery** supplies voltage to the CMOS, which contains the firmware setup data, **Figure 1-30**. Without the battery, the computer would lose the date, time, and all the important information about the hardware components when the computer power switch is turned off.

Figure 1-30. Batteries allow information such as the date and time to be saved while a PC is powered down.

Expansion Cards

Expansion cards are sometimes called *interface cards* or *host adapters*. An **expansion card** is a board that can be easily installed in a computer to enhance or expand its capabilities. An expansion card allows the computer to be custom-designed to meet the needs of different consumers, **Figure 1-31**. A certain computer may have video circuitry integrated into the motherboard or a separate video card that only allows for minimal video performance. The performance of this video system would be adequate for accounting or word-processing functions. However, it would be substandard for computer-aided drafting or

Figure 1-31. Expansion cards allow computers to do many different things. This is a PCIe video card.

game applications. To remedy this, a new video card, or video expansion card, can be added to the computer system.

Expansion cards are used for such devices as TV tuners, video cards, sound cards, and telephone modems. They can also provide additional USB ports for connecting external devices such as hard drives. Many devices that were designed as expansion cards for internal installation have been redesigned as exterior devices that connect to the computer, typically through a USB port.

Expansion Card Slots

An expansion card fits snugly into an **expansion card slot**, **Figure 1-32**. The expansion card slot, also called an *expansion slot*, allows the expansion card to connect directly to the electronic circuitry in the motherboard and to communicate directly or indirectly with other components on the motherboard or with the CPU. There are several types of expansion slots. The most common expansion slots are PCI and PCIe. Expansion cards are discussed in detail in Chapter 3—Motherboards.

Figure 1-32. A variety of expansion card slots are built into most motherboards. This motherboard has PCI and PCI Express (PCIe) expansion slots.

PCI Express (PCIe) slots   PCI slots

Cooling Fan

The **cooling fan** supplies a constant stream of air across the computer components. The typical CPU comes equipped with a fan mounted on the CPU to assist in the cooling process, as shown in Figure 1-23C. Electronic components are damaged by excessive heat.

Cables

There are several types of cables commonly used inside the PC case. These cables connect the motherboard to devices such as the hard drive and optical (CD/DVD) drive.

Figure 1-33 shows two types of cables used to connect a hard drive and optical drive to the motherboard: SATA and PATA. The acronym SATA represents Serial ATA, and the acronym PATA represents Parallel ATA. Hard drives and optical drives originally used an ATA cable which looks similar to the PATA cable in that it consists of many parallel conductors. Some of the conductors in an ATA and PATA cable are used to transfer data. Others are used to transmit control signals between the motherboard and the device.

The SATA cable uses fewer individual wires to achieve much higher data rates than PATA. The individual wires in a SATA cable are twisted together. This allows the cable to carry higher frequencies, which results in higher data rates.

The design is based on electronic engineering principles. A great deal of study is required to fully understand the principles applied to the cable design. For now, consider any cable designed with twists to be able to achieve a higher data rate than a cable designed without twists.

Electrical power for SATA and PATA devices can be transmitted through the cable conductors (wires), but many devices consume more electrical power than the cables and motherboard are designed to safely carry. When a large volume of electrical power is required for a device, a separate power cable that runs directly from the power supply is used.

eSATA cables (not shown) connect external hard drives and optical drives. eSATA technology is slightly different than SATA. The PATA, SATA, and eSATA technologies are discussed in detail in Chapter 9—Storage Devices.

How the Major Parts Work Together

The following scenario traces how a sequence of events occurs in a typical PC system. In this example, a user moves from turning on the computer through saving text data. Please note that there are many different PCs. They all have unique start-up features and program interactions.

1. When the power switch is turned to the *on* position, electrical power from the wall outlet moves through the power supply where it is converted to a much lower dc voltage (or voltages). This stepped-down power is used to run the major components of the computer system including the motherboard, hard drive, and expansion cards. The fan starts up, providing a rush of cool air across the components.

2. Next, the firmware system is activated and performs a POST. The POST (power-on self-test) checks the components in the computer such as RAM, ROM, hard drive, and keyboard to ensure they are in proper working order. Information, such as the type and model number of the firmware and the amount of memory, will flash across the computer's monitor, providing information.

Figure 1-33. SATA and PATA cables used to connect a hard drive and optical drive to the motherboard.

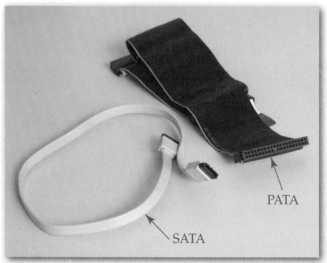

PATA

SATA

Goodheart-Willcox Publisher

3. After the firmware checks the computer components, the operating system takes control. There are many different types of operating systems, but for our example, Windows software will be used.

4. The CPU now waits for activity to be generated by the mouse, keyboard, modem, or other input device. The CPU constantly checks if a key is pressed or the mouse is moved or clicked. The CPU checks these items thousands of times per second.

5. The mouse pointer is moved to an icon, and the mouse is clicked to activate a desired program—a word-processing program in this example. The software represented by the icon is activated. It now shares control of the computer with the CPU.

6. Some typing is done, and then the save command is issued by clicking a save-the-data icon in the word-processing program. The program now attempts to save to the Documents folder. When the word-processing program saves, the operating system takes over in conjunction with the firmware. The operating system interprets the command issued from the word-processing program and translates it to a set of instructions that the firmware can interpret.

7. The firmware, in turn, translates the instructions to the storage media which is most commonly the hard drive. It activates the hard drive motor and actuator arm, moving it to the next available sector on the disk. Information about available disk space is kept in a table. The operating system and firmware work together until all data is transferred and recorded on the storage media.

8. Control is then returned to the word-processing program, so long as an error has not occurred. Possible errors are *disk full* or *unable to read disk*.

The cooperation between the word-processing program, operating system, and firmware goes unnoticed by the user.

Integrated Circuits

The term *chip* is often used in the computer industry. A chip is actually the final product of the manufacturing of an integrated circuit. An **integrated circuit (IC)** is a collection of transistors, resistors, and other electronic components reduced to an unbelievable small size. In fact, over six million transistors manufactured as an integrated circuit can fit into an area the size of a dime. Chips are commonly found on circuit boards. They are the black, square and rectangular devices.

Manufacturing an Integrated Circuit

The manufacturing process that creates an IC consists of many hundreds of steps in a process covering a period of several months. The first step in the manufacture of a chip is the design of the circuit. The circuit is drawn on a very large scale. When the design is completed and all drawings are finished, the manufacturing process is ready to begin. First, the drawings are photographed. The negative of the drawing's photograph is used as a template in the manufacturing process. See **Figure 1-34**.

An ingot of pure silicon is made and then sliced into thin wafers to serve as the base of the IC. Silicon is the same as most common beach sand, but it is extremely pure. The material cannot contain any impurities that might cause adverse effects in the manufacturing of the IC. A series of layers are produced over the surface of the silicon wafer using a process called *photolithography*.

Photolithography is described in the following sequence of events. First, a heat process vaporizes silicon dioxide. Then, various other chemicals are used to form many extremely thin layers over the surface of the wafer. After each layer is formed, a coating of a chemical called *photoresist* is laid over the entire surface of the wafer. The photoresist reacts when exposed to ultraviolet light.

The negative from the photograph of the circuit is used as a stencil. The negative is called the *photomask*. When ultraviolet light shines through the mask, it causes the photoresist to leave a pattern of soft and hard surfaces in the exact pattern of the designed circuit. The soft photoresist is then washed away leaving an etched

Figure 1-34. Manufacture of an integrated circuit. A—Circuit drawing uses a template to form circuits on silicon wafers. B—Fine layers are created in the silicon. The layers are controlled in such a way to create the millions of transistors and other electronic components used in the integrated circuit.

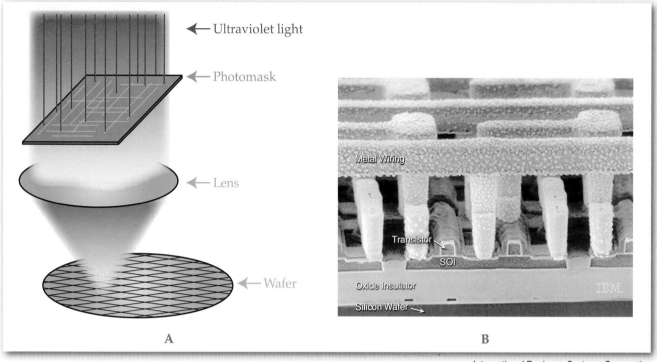

A

B

pattern of valleys and ridges on the surface of the wafer. These valleys are filled with conductive materials. The process of filling in these valleys is called *doping* or *implantation*. This process is repeated many more times until twenty or more layers are developed over the surface of the entire wafer. A single wafer consists of many integrated circuits. The wafer is cut into individual integrated circuits and then packaged.

One of the most difficult parts of packaging the integrated circuit is connecting the fine wires between the wafer circuits and the much larger pins on the outside of the package. The entire wafer and thin connection wires are encapsulated in a hard insulating material resembling black plastic.

Modern computer technology would not be possible without the techniques used in building integrated circuits. The ICs used in computers have many specialized purposes. For example, the CPU is a very large and complex IC that controls all PC activities. The computer modem, used to communicate across telephone lines, has a specialized chip that changes computer data into

a stream of various voltage levels that represent the data. It also converts the stream back into digital data at the receiving end. There are various other chips on the motherboard that have special purposes. Some assist the CPU with data flow across the motherboard. Others control devices such as the hard drive and optical drive. The RAM used in computers is nothing more than a group of ICs mounted on an insulated circuit board.

Electrostatic Discharge (ESD)

Electrostatic discharge (ESD) is best defined in the world of computer maintenance as the transfer of static electrical energy from one object to another. ESD can destroy the miniature circuits inside a computer chip. Static charges are usually created by friction. When two dissimilar materials are rubbed together, an electric charge is produced. Static buildup is always greatest when the air is dry and cool.

A common example of static electricity buildup and discharge is when you walk across a surface such as a rug and then reach out and touch a doorknob. You feel a sharp snap as the electrical charge of your body discharges to the doorknob. This is ESD.

You have learned about how ICs are manufactured and can appreciate the small scale of the circuit. An electrostatic discharge will damage the tiny circuits inside the chip. To prevent static discharge between two objects you must create a condition where both objects are at the same static voltage level or the same potential. When two objects have the same static voltage level, static discharge will not occur.

Technicians wear an **anti-static wrist strap**, also called a ground strap, when handling static-sensitive devices to avoid ESD, **Figure 1-35**. The anti-static wrist strap is designed to create an equal static voltage level between your body and the object that the strap is connected to. To prevent ESD damage to sensitive components you should connect the alligator clip to the bare metal on the computer case or power supply.

Tech Tip

There may be times when an anti-static wrist strap is not available. You can avoid ESD by touching the bare metal inside the computer case with your hand, thus becoming the same potential as the computer hardware.

Figure 1-36 shows a red mat that provides an anti-static surface for parts. The blue anti-static wrist strap goes on the wrist and is designed to bleed off any static buildup on a technician's body, allowing for the safe handling of static-sensitive devices.

Electronic parts and devices are shipped inside anti-static bags to prevent ESD, **Figure 1-37**. When removing parts from a computer, place the parts on an anti-static mat or inside an anti-static bag. You will accumulate plenty of anti-static bags while working as a computer technician. Every time you install a part, such as a hard drive or a motherboard, you will have an empty anti-static bag. Save the bag for temporarily storing static-sensitive components that you remove from a computer.

A+ Note

Be familiar with anti-static procedures, specifically the use of anti-static straps and mats and anti-static bags.

Electromagnetic Interference (EMI)

Electromagnetic interference (EMI) is interference or damage to components caused by magnets and magnetic fields. Any device that

Figure 1-35. Anti-static wrist strap.

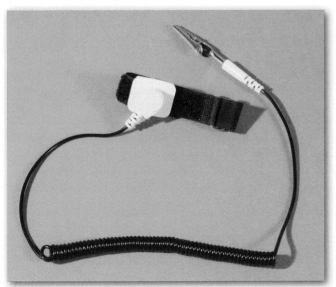

Goodheart-Willcox Publisher

Figure 1-36. Anti-static kit consisting of an anti-static wrist strap and an anti-static mat.

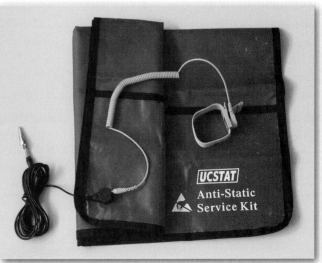

Goodheart-Willcox Publisher

Figure 1-37. Anti-static bag holding a static-sensitive device. Be sure to save anti-static bags and use them to temporarily store electronic components while making repairs.

Goodheart-Willcox Publisher

operates on magnetic principles should not come in contact or close proximity to a magnetic field. In the early days of electronics and computers, magnets were used to bulk erase data from data storage devices such as tapes and floppy disks. Bulk erasers were very powerful magnetic devices.

The most common source of magnetic field in computer repair is magnetic tools, such as screwdrivers with a magnetic tip. In the early days of computer technology, magnetic tools could destroy all data stored on a floppy disk. Floppy disks are seldom encountered today, so views have changed about the use of magnetic tools and there has been some debate. Some say the hard drive can be corrupted by magnetism, but this is not necessarily true. The case surrounding a hard drive is metallic and generally acts as a shield to protect the disks inside from a magnetic field. Some types of computer chips can be damaged by strong magnetic force, but most are designed with some form of magnetic shielding.

There are computer technicians who do use magnetic tipped tools such as screwdrivers and have never encountered a problem. However, as a general rule, you should never use magnetic tools inside a computer case.

Radio Frequency Interference (RFI)

Radio frequency interference (RFI) is interference produced by electronic devices that use radio waves. In general, radio waves are very weak and do not damage electronic components, but they can interfere with radio transmissions between electronic devices. Wireless network devices can fail or operate erratically because of radio frequencies broadcast by other devices. For example, a wireless network device can be temporarily affected by a microwave oven while the oven is running. Some common devices that generate RFI are baby monitors, cell phones, cordless phones, wireless network components, and microwave ovens.

Tool Kit

Computer repair requires a minimum number of tools, **Figure 1-38**. A standard tool kit can vary from a small pouch to a more elaborate tool case.

A variety of flat tip, Phillips, and star drivers are needed. Canned compressed air, a chip puller, anti-static wrist strap, multimeter, extra screws, and a Torx driver set are also helpful tools. Additionally, some type of extraction tool for retrieving dropped screws and other parts is definitely needed.

Figure 1-38. Standard small tool kit. This kit contains the basics. More elaborate kits are available.

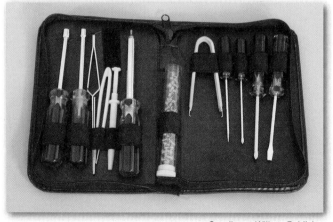

Goodheart-Willcox Publisher

You will find that a software tool kit is just as important as a hardware tool kit. You will probably depend more on your skills using software than hardware to troubleshoot, diagnose, and repair PCs. As you progress through the textbook, there will be many suggestions about software to add to your tool kit. There will also be many references to third-party suppliers and shareware available for your use.

Many software tools can be found as shareware. Shareware is software that is freely distributed, usually by downloading from the Internet. Shareware is not always free for your unlimited use. It is usually intended for use on a trial basis only. The distributor expects the subscriber to purchase the software at a later date.

Safety

Safety is the responsibility of all personnel in the classroom and laboratory areas. This includes students and instructors. A general understanding of common safety practices is a must to help avoid classroom, laboratory, and on-the-job injuries. Safety is best practiced as a habit, not as a written test. You must develop safety habits to avoid possible injury. This section covers safety as related to the computer repair environment. Detailed safety information is provided later in this textbook as it relates to specific topics. For example, computer power supply, CRT displays, and grounding will be covered later after you are more familiar with the technologies.

Physical Safety

One of the most common physical dangers in the classroom or work environment is cables, such as power cords and network cables, lying across the floor. Cables cause a tripping hazard, which can result in injury. Avoid running cables across pathways. When cables must be laid across a floor, the pathway should be blocked to prevent pedestrian traffic. When the pathway cannot be blocked, simply tape the cable to the floor with duct tape. You can also use a cable floor runner or cord protector designed specifically for running cables across a floor, **Figure 1-39**.

When working with computers, there is a real possibility of burns caused by electronic components. Common high-temperature

Figure 1-39. Cables floor runner covering network cables. The runner protects the cables and prevents a tripping hazard.

Goodheart-Willcox Publisher

components are the CPU and some associate motherboard chips. The high-frequency electrical power passing through these components generates the high temperature. Avoid touching electronic components while the computer is energized or soon after the computer has been turned off. Laser printers also have high-temperature parts capable of causing skin surface burns.

Loose clothing and inappropriate footwear (flip flops, sandals) should not be worn in the computer repair environment. Technicians often lift and move computers and battery backup power supplies, both of which can be quite heavy. Dropping a computer or backup power supply on an unprotected foot can cause severe injury. Loose clothing can snag on a computer case or computer parts, causing the computer or parts to fall to the floor. This can possibly damage the items or cause injury. Many insurance companies refuse to cover employees who willfully disobey safety practices specifically stated in the insurance company policy.

One of the most common work-related injuries is the back injury caused by lifting heavy objects. Most physical injuries can be avoided when safety standards are followed. A comprehensive source of safety information for all occupations is regulated by the Occupational Safety and Health Administration (OSHA). OSHA is part of the Department of Labor. It enforces safety standards as well as trains, educates, and provides assistance to employers and employees. Because there are a great many work-related back injuries, OSHA has developed a formula to determine the maximum weight a person can lift without causing physical injury. The formula includes factors such as the height of the object being lifted, the distance it is moved, and how many times the movement is repeated within a given period. Most employers restrict their employees to a maximum lift of 50 pounds. When the weight of an object exceeds 50 pounds, you should wait for assistance from coworkers or special equipment designed for lifting and hauling heavy objects. **Figure 1-40** shows a typical cart used to transport heavy equipment.

OSHA also provides standards for such areas as ladders, electrical cords, grounding, working surfaces, adequate lighting, and computer workstation-related injuries. As a student and as a computer technician, chances are you spend a lot of time at a computer workstation. Check out the OSHA website to learn how to avoid computer workstation-related injuries. You may be surprised at some bad habits you have developed over the years.

Electrical Safety

Students who first enter a computer course typically do not have an electronics background that would enable them to understand fully the electrical hazards in a computer laboratory environment. As you progress through this course, you will gain more knowledge about potentially hazardous practices and devices. At this point, the best practice to follow concerning electrical safety is the following: *Do not attempt to open, inspect, or repair any electronic device that you have not been trained on by your instructor or if you have not received your instructor's permission.*

Figure 1-40. Computers are moved using a cart which helps protect the technician from injury.

Goodheart-Willcox Publisher

In general, before opening the case to begin work, disconnect the electrical power from the computer. The recommended practice is to unplug the ac power cord from the computer's power supply. The reason is many motherboards and power supplies maintain a small electrical current to some critical parts when the computer is turned off. After the powering off a computer with the on/off switch, you can actually see small lights known as LEDs lit on the motherboard.

Removing jewelry before working inside a computer case is also recommended. Jewelry can snag on electronic components, damaging the component. If the component was accidentally energized, the jewelry could make an excellent electrical path, causing electric shock.

Fire Safety

The possibility of fire is always a threat in a computer laboratory as well as on the job or in your home. You should have a basic understanding of fire extinguisher types and how to use them in the event of a fire. Pay particular attention to the information related to electrical fires. Always follow your teacher's instructions concerning fire safety procedures and fire safety in the classroom and lab.

Fire extinguishers are divided into five classes and assigned letters to represent the classification, **Figure 1-41**.

The following table lists the classes and a description of each.

Class	Description
Class A	Ordinary materials such as paper, wood, cardboard, most plastics, and similar materials.
Class B	Flammable liquids such as gasoline, kerosene, oil, and common combustible solvents.
Class C	Energized electrical equipment, appliances, fuse boxes, electrical power tools, wiring, and other electrical devices.
Class D	Combustible metals such as magnesium, sodium, potassium, and titanium.
Class K	Kitchen fires caused by cooking grease and oils.

Some fire extinguishers are designated with a combination of letters, which means they are suitable for each classification indicated by letter. For example, a fire extinguisher with the letters *A*, *B*, and *C* would be suitable for a Class A, B, or C fire.

Obviously, a computer lab should be equipped with a Class C fire extinguisher or one that is designated with a combination of letters, as long as the letter *C* is clearly marked.

Water extinguishers are only appropriate for Class A fires and should never be used on a Class B, C, D, or K fire. Class A uses water or a liquid that reacts violently with Class B, C, D, and K fires and could cause the fire to spread rather than extinguish.

Figure 1-41. Always know the location of the nearest fire extinguisher and how to properly use one.

Pin
Handles
Gauge

Goodheart-Willcox Publisher

A+ Note

The CompTIA A+ exams often have at least one question related to fire safety.

The handy acronym PASS is used to remember the proper procedure for using a fire extinguisher. This acronym was developed to match the recommended procedures by the National Fire Protection Agency (NFPA) for fire extinguisher use. While standing approximately six to eight feet from the fire, follow the procedure as outlined.

P = Pull the pin.
A = Aim at the base of the fire.
S = Squeeze the handles together slowly to discharge the fire extinguisher.
S = Sweep the nozzle from side to side, moving carefully toward the fire while keeping the discharge aimed at the base of the fire.

Be sure you know the location of all fire extinguishers in your classroom and lab area. Also, know the fire exit procedure and the designated area where the class will regroup.

Chemical Safety

As a computer technician, you will come in contact with hazardous materials to some extent, for example, toner used in the laser printers. A Material Safety Data Sheet (MSDS) is required by federal law for such hazardous materials. An MSDS provides information such as proper handling, storage, and disposal of the material. It also contains information about health effects or harmful effects from breathing and contact with the skin or eyes. Material Safety Data Sheets are meant to be used by emergency response personnel, such as firefighters and emergency medical technicians, and workers who commonly come in contact with the chemicals.

Electronic devices often contain material considered harmful to the environment. The Environmental Protection Agency (EPA) provides information about how to properly dispose of and recycle electronic equipment. Cities, counties, and states often have regulations that exceed the federal government concerning the disposal of computer and electronic equipment. Always check the local regulations on proper disposal. The EPA website has a link to the current state regulations.

An electronic device that causes the most concern is the CRT. The CRT is a legacy-style computer or television monitor. It contains sufficient quantities of lead to warrant it as hazardous material. Local authorities typically require CRTs to be recycled and do not allow the CRT to be handled as normal garbage. It is usually required that the CRT be recycled or disposed of by a local agency for a small fee. Not many states have regulations about how to properly dispose of CRTs, and there is no one universal regulation.

Other potentially hazardous computer-related materials are LCD monitors, batteries, and printer toner. The hazards for these devices are discussed in detail later in the textbook.

Chapter Summary

- Computers are used in every aspect of daily life and in all industries.
- An analog system uses varying voltage levels, whereas a digital system uses only two voltage levels.
- Data can be text, graphics, and sounds.
- The binary system consists of only two numbers: *0* and *1*; whereas, the hexadecimal system has sixteen characters: *0–9* and *A–F*.
- A *bit* consists of a single *0* or *1*, a *byte* consists of eight bits, and a *word* is the total amount of bytes a computer can process at one time.
- Serial data transfer sends one bit at a time in successive order, whereas parallel data transfer sends more than one bit at the same time.
- Computer speed is usually expressed in bits, whereas storage space is usually expressed in bytes.
- Some common external connections on a typical PC are video (VGA, DVI, HDMI), PS/2, USB, FireWire, RJ-45, and audio.
- Some common internal components in a typical PC are CPU, cooling fan, motherboard, RAM, power supply, hard drive, expansion cards, and cables.
- When a command in a software program is initiated, the operating system interprets the command and translates it into a set of instructions that the firmware can interpret, and then control is returned to the software program.

- ESD is a static charge of electricity that can damage integrated circuits; EMI is interference or damage to components caused by magnets and magnetic fields; and RFI is interference produced by electronic devices that use radio waves.
- Typical tools used in computer repair are flat tip screwdriver, Phillips screwdriver, star drivers, compressed air, anti-static wrist strap, multimeter, extraction tool, and extra screws.
- Some common safety practices related to computer repair are to disconnect electrical power from the computer before beginning repair and to avoid touching electronic components while the computer is energized or soon after the computer has been turned off.

Review Questions

Answer the following questions on a separate sheet of paper. Please do not write in this book.

1. Give three examples of how computers are used in industry.
2. Describe the difference between a digital and an analog electronic device.
3. Which of the following items acts like an analog system, and which is most like a digital system?
   a. automobile gas pedal
   b. streetlight
   c. drawbridge
   d. car horn
   e. wind speed
   f. slide trombone
   g. drum
   h. flashlight
4. Data can be _____.
   a. text
   b. sound
   c. pictures
   d. All the answers are correct.
5. The binary number system consists of the decimal numbers _____ and _____.
6. List the characters for the hexadecimal number system from zero to fifteen.

   0 = _____   1 = _____   2 = _____   3 = _____   4 = _____   5 = _____   6 = _____
   7 = _____   8 = _____   9 = _____   10 = _____   11 = _____   12 = _____
   13 = _____   14 = _____   15 = _____

7. Complete the following statement about the basic computer units of data. There are eight _____ in one _____.
8. What letter symbol represents bit?
9. What letter symbol represents byte?
10. How many bytes are in a 32-bit word?
11. Describe the difference between serial data transfer and parallel data transfer.

12. What are the two numeric values for 1 megabyte?
    a. Base 10 _____ = 1M
    b. Base 2 or binary _____ = 1M

13. What are the two numeric values for 1 kilobyte?
    a. Base 10 _____ = 1k
    b. Base 2 or binary _____ = 1k

14. What are the two numeric values for 1 gigabyte?
    a. Base 10 _____ = 1G
    b. Base 2 or binary _____ = 1G

15. Name two port types a keyboard or mouse can connect to.

16. The _____ connection is used to connect to the network.

17. Name three types of video connectors.

18. What components are found in a typical computer workstation?

19. RAM provides (temporary, permanent) _____ storage of data.

20. What is the purpose of the battery mounted on the motherboard?

21. Explain the difference between the CMOS chip and firmware.

22. What are the two types of firmware used today?

23. Why are expansion slots provided on a computer motherboard?

24. What happens during the POST?

25. What happens when the save command is initiated in a software program?

26. Describe the differences between ESD, EMI, and RFI.

27. Which of the following can be harmful to integrated circuits?
    a. EMI and RFI
    b. ESD and EMI
    c. RFI and ESD
    d. Only ESD

28. What are some common tools used by a computer technician?

29. Which type of fire extinguisher is used for electrical fires?

30. What does the fire protection acronym PASS represent?

31. What government organization is responsible for safety education and enforcement in the work area?

32. What is the maximum amount of weight employers allow employees to lift?

Sample A+ Exam Questions

Answer the following questions on a separate sheet of paper. Please do not write in this book.

1. An analog display monitor typically uses which type of cable connector?
   a. DB-9
   b. DB-15
   c. 9-pin serial
   d. 25-pin parallel

2. A hard drive uses which type of cable connector?
   a. flat ribbon cable
   b. DB-15
   c. RJ-45
   d. PS/2

3. A telephone modem typically uses which type of connector to connect to the telephone line?
   a. RJ-45
   b. DB-9
   c. RJ-11
   d. PS/2

4. The maximum number of devices that can be connected to an IEEE-1394 connector is _____.
   a. 7
   b. 24
   c. 63
   d. 127

5. The maximum number of devices that can be connected using a USB connector is _____.
   a. 7
   b. 24
   c. 63
   d. 127

6. Firmware is associated with which of the following items?
   a. RAM
   b. BIOS
   c. DVD
   d. Speaker amplifier system

7. Which two are the most commonly encountered slot types? (Select two.)
   a. ISA
   b. PCI
   c. EISA
   d. PCIe

8. The acronym CMOS represents which of the following answers?
   a. Complementary mechanical operating system
   b. Complementary metal oxide semiconductor
   c. Complementary media operating system
   d. Complementary metallic opposition semiconductor

9. Which is the accepted method for a technician to manage ESD?
   a. Always use insulated hand tools.
   b. Place the PC on a rubber mat before disassembly.
   c. Disconnect the ground before servicing a PC.
   d. Always wear an anti-static wrist strap before touching PC components.
10. Which type of fire extinguisher is used on electrical fires?
    a. Class A
    b. Class B
    c. Class C
    d. Class A and Class B

Suggested Laboratory Activities

Do not attempt any suggested laboratory activities without your instructor's permission. Certain activities can render the PC operating system inoperable.

1. Remove the case from three different PCs and compare the hardware. The PCs may differ by age or manufacturer. Take note of similarities as well as differences. Identify all the major components.

2. Select a major brand of PC and use the Internet to access the website of the manufacturer. Look for technical reference material to help you identify the component locations on the motherboard and on the outside of the case.

Operating Systems

After studying this chapter, you will be able to:

- Explain the basic model of an operating system.
- Recall the common characteristics of all operating systems.
- Compare Windows features.
- Carry out a Windows operating system installation.
- Explain the Windows boot sequence.
- Give examples of common portable devices and tasks.
- Give examples of cloud computing resources and services.
- Summarize the guidelines for selecting software and drivers for 32-bit and 64-bit systems.

A+ Exam—Key Points

You must know the system requirements for Windows XP and later operating systems and be familiar with the features of each operating system.

You should also know the basic text-based commands such as **cmd**, **dir**, **rd**, **md**, **del**, **fdisk**, **format**, **copy**, **xcopy**, **diskpart**, **sfc**, **attrib**, **defrag**, **edit**, and **ckdsk**. Many of these commands are covered in more detail in later chapters of this textbook. Even with an excellent knowledge of the Microsoft Windows operating system, the lack of sufficient knowledge of text-based commands can result in failure on the CompTIA A+ Certification exams.

In addition, be sure you can define multitasking, both preemptive and cooperative. You should know how to navigate a directory structure from Windows Explorer and from the command line interface and how to create and manage files and directories.

Key Terms

The following key terms will become important pieces of your computer vocabulary. Be sure you can define them.

app	graphical user interface (GUI)
application software	internal commands
boot sequence	kernel
bootstrap program	multiple-boot system
bug	multitasking
cloud computing	multithreading
cold boot	operating system (OS)
command interpreter	pathname
command line interface (CLI)	power-on self-test (POST)
command prompt	preemptive multitasking
configuration file	registry
cooperative multitasking	root directory
directory	software driver
dual-boot system	software patch
executable file	subdirectory
external commands	thin client
file	Tile
file extension	virtual machine
file system	virtualization
file table	warm boot

This chapter introduces you to the Microsoft Windows XP, Windows Vista, Windows 7, and Windows 8 operating systems. Understanding the operating system is essential for troubleshooting a PC. To gain in-depth knowledge of an operating system, the operating system and its various options must be put to use. It is imperative that you supplement textbook studies through hands-on practice with current Windows operating systems. The Laboratory Manual for this textbook will give you the necessary skills and first-hand knowledge required to pass the A+ Certification exams and to become a proficient PC technician.

What Is an Operating System?

An **operating system (OS)** is software that provides a computer user with a file system structure and with a means of communicating with the computer hardware. The operating system communicates with disk storage units, monitors, printers, memory, and other computer components. It is also the job of the operating system to make sure programs running on the computer do not interfere with each other. Before operating systems were commonplace, users had to write code for all of the common tasks. If you wanted to save data, you had to write the code that told your computer to do so.

Operating system software has evolved over the years. Think of the evolution of computer software and hardware as a group of inventors constantly building a better mousetrap. What is a leading-edge operating system one day may not be the next day. In fact, it will likely become obsolete only a few years later. It is the constant evolution of the computer that makes it so confusing. Each operating system has its individual strengths and weaknesses.

The core of any operating system is referred to as the **kernel**. Just as plants bud and grow from a single seed or kernel, so does the operating system software. The core program is enhanced by other software applications that refine the computer system. Associated with the core can be programs that provide for user interface style, security, and specialized file systems.

Operating systems allow application software to communicate with the BIOS. The BIOS translates the application software requests into instructions the hardware can understand. Examine **Figure 2-1**.

As you can see, users give instructions to the computer system via application software such as word-processing, graphics, and gaming. The user can also give instructions directly to the operating system. The operating system communicates with the BIOS, which then communicates with the computer hardware and peripherals.

Operating System Characteristics

The way an operating system handles activities, such as storing data, interfacing with the user, and presenting information on the screen, can be referred to as operating system characteristics. Most operating systems appear similar when judged by their screen display. However, there are many differences in the way they handle activities, especially data storage.

Multitasking

Multitasking is the ability of an operating system to support two or more programs running at the same time. When multitasking, it seems to the user that both programs are running simultaneously. However, in reality, they are not. The computer simply switches control between the programs, giving the illusion they are running at the same time.

An example of multitasking is using the printer while at the same time using e-mail, surfing the Internet, or running another computer application. The computer runs the software in between sending packets of data to the printer.

Most operating systems support multitasking, but the hardware may not. Systems designed with minimal hardware, such as tablets and smartphones, do not support multitasking very well. If you attempt to perform more than one task, the system will either not allow you to run an additional program or the system will run sluggishly because of the shared resources (CPU, RAM, and chipset). The two major classifications of multitasking are preemptive and cooperative.

Preemptive multitasking, sometimes referred to as *time slicing*, is the process which allows multiple programs to share control of the operating system. For example, two or more programs can share the CPU for processing information. No single program can totally take charge of the computer system. All programs running in the preemptive mode of multitasking share RAM. If two programs attempt to use the same area of RAM at the same time, the computer will lock up. Windows 95, Windows Me, Windows XP, Windows Vista, Windows NT, Windows 2000, OS/2, and MAC OS X use preemptive multitasking.

Cooperative Multitasking

With **cooperative multitasking**, one program dominates the operating system but will allow another program to run while it is idle. This type of multitasking is common to MAC OS 9 and earlier and to Windows 3.x.

Figure 2-1. Typical relationship of computer hardware and software components.

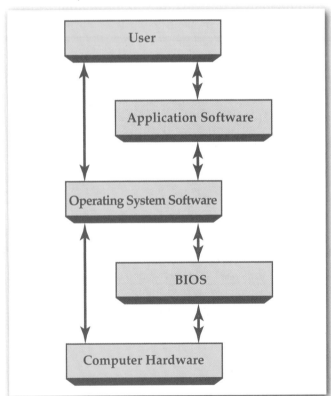

Multithreading

You may have heard the term *thread* or *threads* used when referring to computer processing. These terms refer to passing small portions of a computer program through the core of the processor. Data and parts of a program can be shared between two or more CPUs or between the two cores of a single CPU. This is called **multithreading** instead of *multitasking*.

32-Bit and 64-Bit

Operating systems, hardware devices, and software applications are identified using the terms *32-bit* and *64-bit*. The terms *32-bit* and *64-bit* are used to describe the amount of data that can be stored or processed. For example, how much data can be processed at once by the CPU or how much total memory the operating system can access.

The maximum amount of memory a 32-bit Windows operating system can access is 4 GB. Even if the computer contains more than 4 GB of RAM, only 4 GB will be accessible by the 32-bit operating system. A 64-bit Windows 7 operating system recognizes a maximum of 8 GB or 128 GB of memory depending on the operating system edition.

Upgrading from one operating system to another operating system or edition can be affected by the number of bits it was written for. For example, you can only directly upgrade a 32-bit operating system to another operating 32-bit system or a 64-bit operating system to another 64-bit operating system. Upgrading directly from a 32-bit operating system to a 64-bit operating system would delete all data files (documents, photos, music, etc.) stored on the computer. You would have to back up all files, perform the upgrade from 32-bit to 64-bit, and then reinstall the data files and software applications.

User Interface

There are two dominant user interfaces used to issue commands on a computer system: command line interface and graphical user interface. Graphical user interface is referred to as GUI (pronounced *gooey*). The command line interface is commonly referred to by Microsoft as the *command prompt*.

Command Line Interface

The **command line interface (CLI)** allows commands for the computer to be issued by typing in text at a command prompt. **Figure 2-2** shows a command line interface.

Some common commands are **dir**, **cd**, and **copy**. These commands call up a directory, change directories, and copy a file or disk, respectively. See **Figure 2-3** for a table of some common commands. There are many more commands than the few listed, but these are some of the most commonly used.

DOS was the major operating system used by PCs in the 1980s. However, DOS was difficult to use. Users had to memorize many different commands to become proficient with the operating system.

Today, text-based commands are still used, especially when troubleshooting. Text-based commands are particularly important when a PC fails to complete its startup process and take the user to the GUI. Troubleshooting tools such

Figure 2-2.
Command line interface.

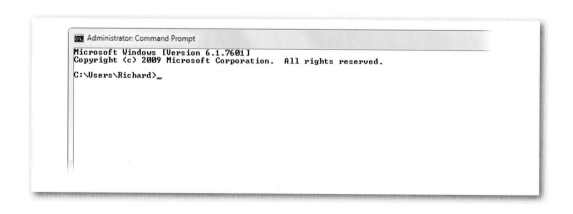

```
Administrator: Command Prompt
Microsoft Windows [Version 6.1.7601]
Copyright (c) 2009 Microsoft Corporation.  All rights reserved.

C:\Users\Richard>_
```

Command	Example	Description
cd	c:\>cd\games	Changes from the current location in a directory to another directory.
chkdsk	c:\>chkdsk c:	Checks a disk for errors and displays the results.
copy	c:\>copy d:memo.txt c:	Copies data from one location to another.
del	c:\>del memo.txt	Deletes a file.
dir	c:\>dir	Displays a list of files, directories, and subdirectories.
exit	c:\>exit	Exits the command prompt window and returns to the Windows desktop.
format	c:\>format a:	Prepares a disk for first-time use.
md	c:\>md c:\games	Creates, or makes, a directory.
rd	c:\>rd c:\games	Deletes, or removes, a directory.
xcopy	c:\>xcopy c:\games d:	Copies multiple files and directories.

Figure 2-3.
Table of commonly used Windows text-based commands.

Goodheart-Willcox Publisher

as Recovery Console, used in Windows 2000 and Windows XP, can only be run using text-based commands. It is important that the technician be able to use the command prompt.

Modern Windows systems do not use DOS but rather a DOS emulator. The DOS emulator has the look and feel of a real DOS prompt and functions similarly. Many of the restrictions or limitations of DOS are not found in the emulator program. For example, many of the restricted characters not allowed in DOS file names can be used.

Windows XP also uses DOS-like commands in the Recovery Console utility. The Recovery Console utility allows a computer technician to communicate with the Windows XP operating system after a system GUI failure. When a computer system fails during the startup process, there is no GUI. The only means of communicating with the computer system is by using a non-graphical user interface such as the Recovery Console. Many of the commands used in Recovery Console look and work exactly like the DOS commands and DOS emulator commands. **Figure 2-4** lists the most commonly used Recovery Console commands.

Windows Vista replaced the Recovery Console with a utility called the Recovery Environment. Both provide access to a command prompt. However, Windows Vista Recovery Environment

provides a menu of tools to repair a system as well as an option to access the command prompt. The menu options are **Startup Repair**, **System Restore**, **CompletePC Restore**, **Windows Memory Diagnostic Tool**, and **Command Prompt**.

There are also newer text-based commands that complement today's more sophisticated operating systems. There will be much more about command line support in Chapter 15—PC Troubleshooting and in the Laboratory Manual.

A+ Note

Text-based commands are still very much a part of the A+ Certification exams. To pass the exams, you must be familiar with each command's function.

Graphical User Interface

A **graphical user interface (GUI)** allows the user to perform functions by selecting on-screen icons rather than by issuing text-based commands. Although DOS and DOS-like systems controlled over 80% of the market during the 1980s, the user-friendly graphical user interface (GUI) of Macintosh gained popularity. Creating GUIs for the PC in the form of Windows 3.1 and

Recovery Console Command	Function
attrib	View or set the attributes of a file or directory.
cd	View or change the current directory.
chkdsk	Check and display the status of a hard drive.
copy	Copy a file.
del	Delete a file.
dir	Display the files and subdirectories of the current working directory.
disable	Disable a service or a driver.
diskpart	Partition a hard drive.
enable	Enable a service or a driver.
exit	Exit Recovery Console.
fixmbr	Repair the master boot record.
format	Format a hard drive or floppy disk.
help	Display a list of Recovery Console commands.
md	Create a directory.
ren	Rename a file.
rd	Delete a directory.

Goodheart-Willcox Publisher

Windows NT helped Microsoft retain control of the operating system market.

In most operating systems that are used today, the GUI displays the file system consisting of folders, icons, and names. One great advantage of using the GUI is that the entire file structure is easily displayed and interpreted. **Figure 2-5** shows a typical GUI display of a file system organization. A typical GUI is seen in **Figure 2-6**. Although this is a Windows XP desktop, all Windows GUIs are very similar. On the desktop are a number of program icons.

File System Structure

There are many different file systems, but they all have common characteristics. Programs and files are stored on computers in much the same way regardless of the operating system used. The basic structure is made of directories, subdirectories, and files. A **file** is a program or a collection of data that forms a single unit. A **directory** and **subdirectory** are groupings of files. The distinction between a directory and subdirectory is in how they relate to each other.

This will become apparent shortly. Examine **Figure 2-7**. This is a typical directory and file structure. It shows the relationship of the root directory, directories, subdirectories, and files.

The **root directory** is at the top of the directory structure. In this case, C:\ appears at the top. Thus, the root directory is C: (the hard drive). Next, there are two directories stemming from the root directory: Games and School. *Directory* and *subdirectory* are relative terms. Looking at the example again, you will see that English is a subdirectory to School. Both English and School are directories, but the placement in the structure determines if it is a subdirectory. Directories and subdirectories can contain files. Under the directory Games, you can see several game files such as Hearts and Solitaire.

A **pathname** is used to identify the location of a specific file. Look at **Figure 2-8**. The pathname for the file is Computer → Local Disk(C:) → Users → Richa_000 → My Pictures. The "Computer" in the directory structure identifies the local user computer or workstation. C:\ is the root directory, Users is the first directory, and Richa_000 is a subdirectory of Users. My Pictures is the final

Figure 2-5. Directory structure displayed by a GUI.

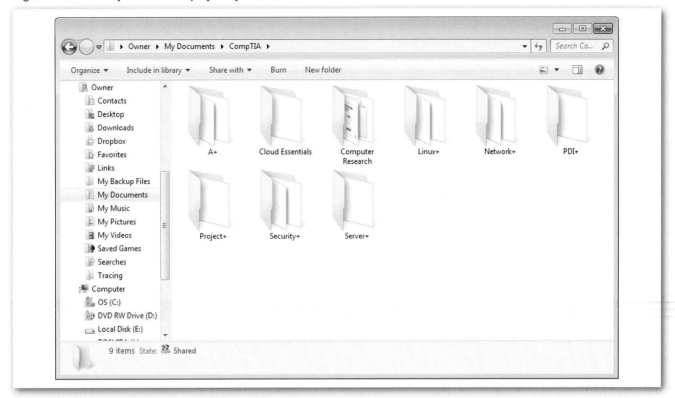

Figure 2-6.
Typical opening GUI for Windows. While the mechanics behind the interface can be very different between the various versions of Windows, the appearance of the GUI has remained fairly constant.

Figure 2-7. Typical directory and file structure.

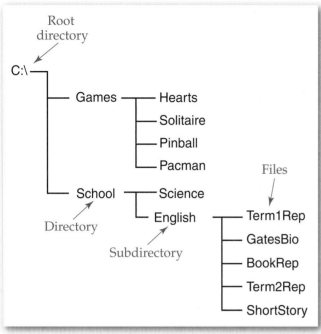

Goodheart-Willcox Publisher

subdirectory folder in the path. This subdirectory reveals a collection of folders, which are subdirectories, and a collection of picture files.

Most of the Windows operating system files are located by default in the Windows folder on the C: partition or drive. The pathname for this location is C:\Windows. In reality, this folder can be located on any partition. In Microsoft technical literature, the exact location of the Windows folder is indicated as %systemroot% rather than C:\Windows. The %systemroot% variable is used in the path to represent the location of the Windows folder.

File Systems

No introduction to operating systems would be complete without mentioning file systems. A **file system** refers to the method of organizing files on a storage device. It is used by the operating system to keep track of all files on the disk. The

Figure 2-8. Pathnames indicate locations for files on a specific computer or even across a network system.

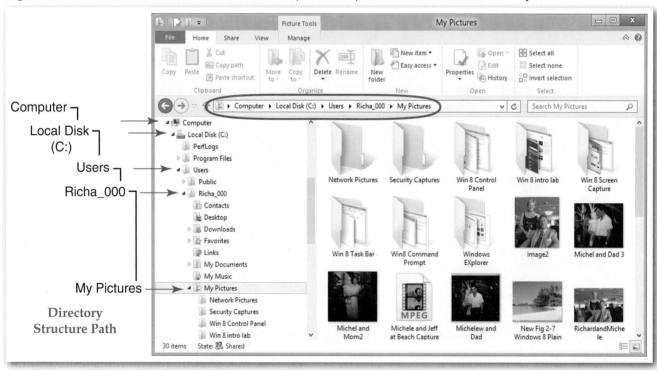

file system maintains a **file table** of all areas on the disk, and it tracks which areas are used and which are not. File systems are covered in greater depth in Chapter 9—Storage Devices.

The file systems with which you should be familiar are FAT12, FAT16, FAT32, and NTFS. The default file system used by Windows operating systems since Windows XP is NTFS. The FAT16 and FAT32 file systems are still available for use in formatting partitions under the control of Windows XP and Windows Vista. FAT is still an option for Windows 7 and Windows 8 when formatting flash drives. As you study operating systems more in-depth, you will see the need for other types of file systems.

> # A+ Note
>
> You need to be familiar with all available file systems in preparation for the A+ Certification exams.

Configuration Files

When a computer system is configured, the type of hardware and software the system has planned for use is recorded in a **configuration file**. Configuration files contain information such as the amount of memory and the type of video adapter present in the system. Configuration information is stored in the config.sys file of DOS systems. The config.sys file is still used in newer operating systems, but it is included only to support legacy software applications.

Early Windows systems stored configuration information in the win.ini and system.ini files. Software applications also stored configuration setting in .ini files. These configuration files are replaced by the Windows registry settings for the Windows 95 and later operating systems. Many computer systems still contain .ini files to maintain a downward compatibility with some software programs.

The registry is found in Windows 95 and later operating systems. The **registry** is essentially a database that stores configuration information. The major sections of the registry are listed as follows.

- **HKEY_CLASSES_ROOT**: Object linking and embedding (OLE) information and how files are associated with each other.
- **HKEY_CURRENT_USERS**: Information for the current user of this workstation.
- **HKEY_LOCAL_MACHINE**: Information specific to the local computer.
- **HKEY_USERS**: Information for each user of this workstation.
- **HKEY_CURRENT_CONFIG**: Display and printer settings.

The registry is accessed by entering **regedit** in the **Run** dialog box found in the **Start** menu or by entering **regedit** at the command prompt. **Figure 2-9** shows the Windows XP Registry Editor.

> **Tech Tip**
>
> Changes in the registry can completely disable your computer operating system. Do *not* experiment with registry settings unless under supervision of your instructor.

There are two main registry files: system.dat and user.dat. The system.dat file contains information about the computer settings. The user.dat file contains information about individuals who use the computer. Registry files can be copied to disk, installed on another computer, backed up, and modified. The registry is repaired through the System Restore utility. Rarely does a technician need to access the registry files directly. When a technician does access the registry files, it is usually as part of repair steps outlined by Microsoft on its TechNet website. Direct modification of the registry should be a last resort effort.

Microsoft Windows Operating System

The most widely used operating system is Microsoft Windows. You will encounter Windows XP, Windows Vista, Windows 7, or Windows 8 on most computers. This section references all of the mentioned Windows operating system versions. Differences between operating systems are pointed out when appropriate.

Figure 2-9.
Windows XP Registry Editor.

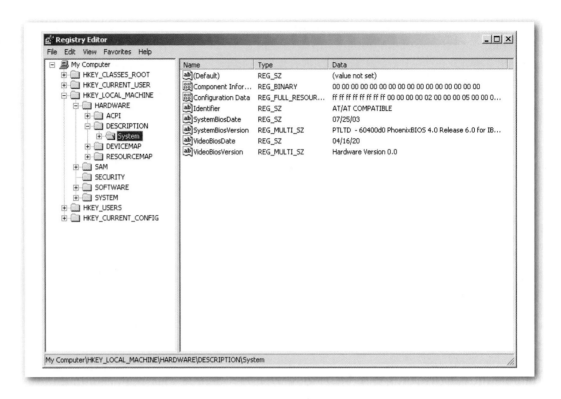

Windows Vista was released to the public in January 2007. It was not well received by users, mainly because of the added security features. The previous edition, Windows XP, was criticized for being too lax on security. Many people in the technical areas felt that Windows XP was too vulnerable to malicious software, such as viruses and worms. Windows Vista, therefore, was designed with enhanced security to make it less vulnerable to such attacks. As a result, the user was constantly prompted for approval at an administrator level whenever critical changes were about to be made to the system configuration. The constant prompting for permission proved to be annoying to the average user. There were also issues with older software and drivers not working properly with Windows Vista. Public reception of this operating system was so bad, many computer suppliers offered to replace Windows Vista with Windows XP at no extra cost.

In October 2009, Microsoft released the Windows 7 operating system. The public was hesitant to accept Windows 7, but soon Windows 7 became a well-respected operating system. Windows 7 did have some software and driver issues, but that is typical with any new version of an operating system. Because the release dates of

Windows Vista and Windows 7 were close, the two operating systems share the same or similar features. There are some differences. These differences will be pointed out as we cover the major features of the Windows operating system.

Windows Directory Structure

The Microsoft approach to software is like constantly trying to improve a mousetrap. They keep reinventing existing features. Nowhere is there a better example of this process than comparing the directory structure of the various Windows operating system versions. As new approaches to old problems are solved and new technologies are introduced, changes are reflected in the directory structure.

A directory structure consists of files, folders, documents, and items such as hard drive partitions, CD/DVD drives, and network locations. To make a quick comparison of the Windows XP, Windows Vista, Windows 7, and Windows 8 directory structures, look at **Figure 2-10**.

The Windows XP directory is simple in comparison to Windows Vista, which introduced the concept of a Public folder to make sharing easier for users. The Windows 7 directory structure is even more complex than previous versions. Windows 7 introduced Libraries and HomeGroup into the directory structure. The HomeGroup is an improved sharing feature, and Libraries allows easier access to files and folders located in multiple locations. Changes in the directory structure is one of the biggest reasons people have trouble locating their files after upgrading to a new operating system or buying a computer with a newer version of an operating system.

Windows File Names

Originally, file names had to conform to the DOS standards. DOS required that file names be no longer than eight characters followed by a period and three additional characters. The three additional characters are called the **file extension**. In modern operating systems, the file extension is not necessary but does help identify the file type. The table in **Figure 2-11** lists common file extensions and the type of program they are related to.

The file name structure allows for file names of up to 255 characters and is referred to by many references as *long file names*. Long file names allow for the content of the file to be described in some detail. This provides relief from brief, cryptic, eight-character file names. For example, a file could be saved as Term1 Science Paper The Factors Affecting Ocean Tides.

Figure 2-10. Windows directory structure comparison.

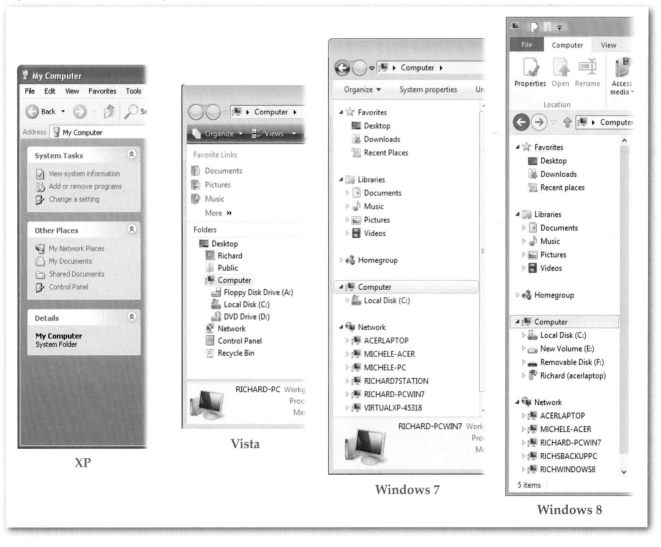

Figure 2-11. Common file extensions.

File Extension	Description
.avi	Audio video file.
.bmp	Bitmap graphics file.
.com	Executable file.
.doc	Document file.
.exe	Executable file. A program that runs when the file name is entered at the command prompt.
.ini	File containing configuration data.
.jpg	Picture file.
.log	File listing actions that have occurred or containing a brief record or collection of data.
.mpg	Video file.
.tmp	Temporary file. Typically associated with Internet downloads and software installations.
.txt	Text file.
.wav	Wave audio file.
.wmv	Windows media video file.
.wps	Microsoft Windows word-processor document.

Goodheart-Willcox Publisher

There are certain characters or symbols that cannot be used in the file name. The characters that are not allowed in the long file name system are the following:

| *   >   <   ?   :   \   /   "

These characters have a special meaning to the operating system and will produce errors or unwanted results when used. As you can see in **Figure 2-12**, Windows 8 displays an error message when the user attempts to use a restricted character in the folder file name. Restricted characters also provide backward compatibility to legacy operating systems.

Windows Desktop

The Windows desktop has maintained a similar user interface from Windows XP to Windows 7. **Figure 2-13** shows a comparison of the Windows **Start** menu for Windows XP, Windows Vista, and Windows 7. The **Start** menu is located at the bottom-left corner of the desktop. Notice the similarities. From this menu, programs are launched, folders such as Documents and Pictures are accessed, and commands such as **Shut Down** are initiated.

Windows 8 does not support the **Start** menu feature. The default screen is Start, **Figure 2-14**. Start contains a set of objects called *Tiles*. Tiles are similar to icons used on earlier Windows operating system desktops. A **Tile** represents a shortcut to a Windows 8 program applications referred to as an *app*. Tiles can easily be added or removed from Start. The new design was made for devices with touch screens, such as the tablet and smartphone. However, you can still use a mouse to navigate.

An alternate desktop that resembles the traditional Windows desktop can be used instead of Start, **Figure 2-15**. It looks similar to the desktop of earlier Windows operating systems except that it does not have a **Start** menu icon. A taskbar is displayed across the bottom of the desktop and the familiar icons displayed. You can create desktop shortcuts or pin programs to the taskbar for quick access to commonly used software applications.

Cmd.exe

Cmd.exe is a compact program that allows the user to interact with the computer using commands entered at the command prompt.

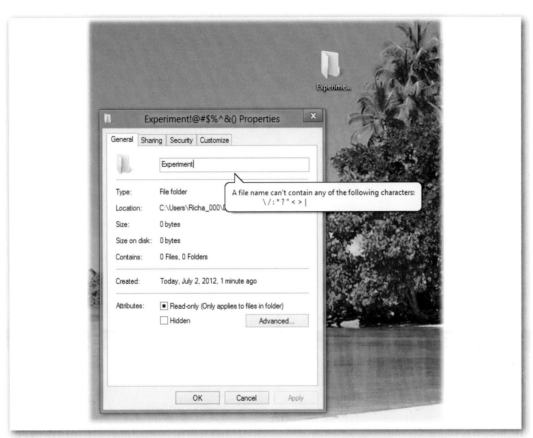

Figure 2-12. An error message displays when a user enters a file name with a restricted character.

The earlier version of cmd.exe was command.com. The command.com program is considered legacy by modern operating systems. Another name for command.com and cmd.exe is **command interpreter**. The command interpreter contains a set of programs that are activated by text entered at the command prompt. These commands are known as **internal commands** because the required software to run them resides inside command.com and cmd.exe. Following are examples of several common internal commands.

Command	System Response
copy	Copies a file or group of files from one location to another location.
date	Displays the date.
del	Deletes a file.
dir	Displays a list of files, directories, and subdirectories.
rename	Changes the name of a file.
time	Displays the time.
ver	Displays the software version running on the computer.

The command interpreter also uses several **external commands**. These are individual, executable files found in addition to the internal commands. The external commands can be viewed in the Windows directory structure, usually under C:/Windows/System32 for 32-bit systems and C:/Windows/sysWOW64 for 64-bit systems. The external commands in modern operating systems are identified as an "Application" but use the .exe file extension. Following are several examples of common external commands.

Command	System Response
chkdsk	Checks the condition of a disk and displays a report.
edit	Starts a text editor program similar to a word processor.
format	Prepares a disk for storing data.
print	Prints a text file to a printer.

Microsoft refers to the program that produces the command line as the **command prompt**. The

Figure 2-13.
Comparison of
Windows **Start** menus.

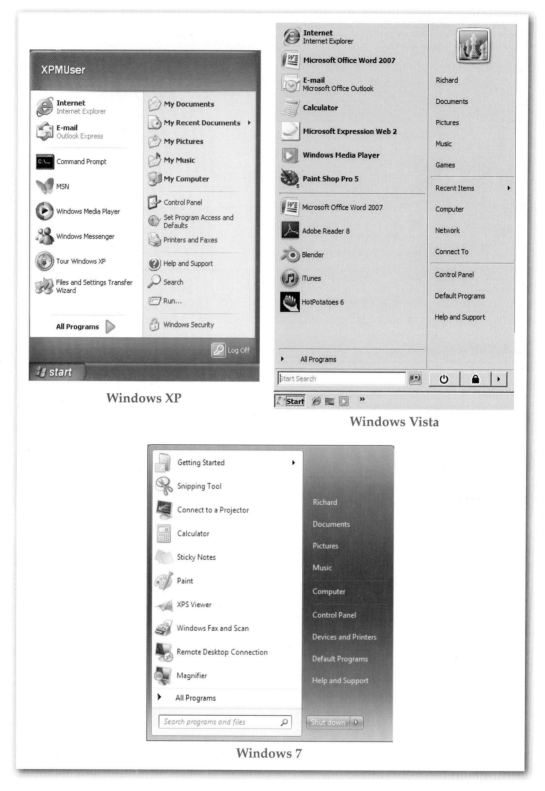

Windows XP

Windows Vista

Windows 7

Figure 2-14.
Windows 8 Start.

Figure 2-15.
Windows 8 alternative desktop.

command.com produces an MS-DOS command prompt, whereas cmd.exe produces a 32-bit console application. Both command.com and cmd.exe are executable files. An **executable file** has an .exe or .com file extension. Executable files are complete software programs that run when the file name is entered at the command prompt. Similar results occur when a program is selected from the **Start** menu or when clicking a desktop shortcut that represents a program.

Command.com can be run in Windows Vista, Windows 7, and Windows 8 when required for legacy programs. It is run as a DOS interpreter inside a Windows NT virtual machine. The Windows NT virtual machine is not a physical machine. A virtual machine or computer only exists in the computer's memory but appears to the user as a real machine or computer. This command interpreter contains many of the same DOS internal and external commands, plus additional commands.

Windows Features

The most important Windows features are introduced in this section. Not all of the features are available to all versions of Windows. You can use the table **Figure 2-16** to quickly identify which version of Windows has the feature integrated into the operating system. Features unique to Windows 8 are covered in the following section.

For a more detailed list of Windows operating system features, check the Microsoft website. You can conduct an Internet search using the key terms "Microsoft Windows feature comparison." Be sure to add the operating version or versions in the search key terms.

A+ Note

The A+ Certification requires knowledge of a variety of Windows operating systems and features. Always check the CompTIA website for a list of operating systems that are covered on the exams.

Windows Aero

Windows Aero is an enhanced user interface. It is much more sophisticated than the user interfaces of operating systems previous to Windows Vista. It is designed to have a glass-like appearance with various degrees of transparency, **Figure 2-17**. The Windows Aero feature is one of the main reasons a greater amount of RAM and a quality 3-D graphics card or motherboard is required. Windows Aero is also one of the main reasons for the slow performance of Windows Vista when compared to Windows XP loaded on a similar PC.

BitLocker Drive Encryption

BitLocker Drive Encryption is an encryption feature. Encryption is the process of rendering the contents of a file unreadable by people other than those who are allowed to read it. It differs from earlier versions of file encryption in that it encrypts the entire volume, including the system files required for startup and logon, rather than just data files. BitLocker ensures that data remains encrypted even when the operating system is not running. For example, if someone removes a hard drive and then attempts to access the data from another computer using a different operating system or software utility, BitLocker prevents the data from being accessed because the data remains encrypted.

BitLocker is transparent to the user after it is activated. It is designed to be used with a computer that has a Trusted Platform Module (TPM) or firmware that can read a USB flash drive. The TPM is a microchip designed to work with the BitLocker software. The TPM ensures that encryption is intact throughout the boot sequence of the computer. If the TPM is missing or has changed, the user is required to supply a password to access the encrypted data. If BitLocker is configured on a system that does not have a TPM, a startup key is required when it is first configured. A typical startup key is a software program loaded on a USB flash drive. The software program contains the encryption key used to access the encrypted drive.

Figure 2-16. Comparison table of common Windows features.

Windows Feature	Windows XP	Windows Vista	Windows 7	Windows 8
BitLocker Drive Encryption	No	Yes	Yes	Yes
BitLocker To Go	No	No	Yes	Yes
Gadgets	No	Yes	Yes	No
Libraries	No	No	Yes	Yes
Microsoft User Account	No	No	No	Yes
Network Discovery	No	Yes	Yes	Yes
Picture Password	No	No	No	Yes
Recovery Refresh and Reset	No	No	No	Yes
Sync Your Settings	No	No	No	Yes
Tablet PC Settings	Yes	Yes	Yes	Yes
Windows Aero	No	Yes	Yes	Yes
Windows Media Center	No	Yes	Yes	No
Windows Meeting Space	No	Yes	No	No
Windows Mobility Center	No	Yes	Yes	Yes
Windows Ready Boost	No	Yes	Yes	Yes
Windows Shadow Copy and Previous Versions	No	Yes	Yes	Yes
Windows To Go	No	No	No	Yes
XP Mode	No	No	Yes	No

Note: Some features may only be available in specific Windows editions. Also, Window Media Center is available as an add-on for some editions of Windows 8.

Goodheart-Willcox Publisher

Windows Media Center

Windows Media Center is a collection of media manipulation utilities or tools. With Windows Media Center, you can edit digital movies; modify or adjust digital photos; and record, copy, and create DVDs. If your PC has a television tuner card installed, you can also watch live television. Windows Media Center is only available in Windows Vista Home Premium and Windows Vista Ultimate. Windows Media Center continues to be available in all Windows 7 versions and is available as an add-on feature for Windows 8.

Windows Mobility Center

Windows Mobility Center provides a central location for accessing the most commonly used features for laptops, such as presentation configurations for a projector and energy conservation configurations. It also automatically configures common network connections, such as for the home, office, or work location.

The Windows Hot Start feature allows a laptop to instantly start a selected program with the touch of a single button. There is no need to wait long periods of time while the program is located, opened, and loaded into memory. It will start an application directly out of sleep mode or hibernation and even when the computer has been turned off. The feature was designed specifically for mobile PCs.

Windows Meeting Space

Windows Meeting Space is designed for collaborating over a network. The meeting can vary from two to nine persons using personal computers connected by cables or wireless devices. The users can share documents, PowerPoint presentations, audio, video images, and anything else they might share at a typical

Figure 2-17.
The Windows Vista
Aero feature provides
an adjustable
transparency for
Windows dialog boxes.

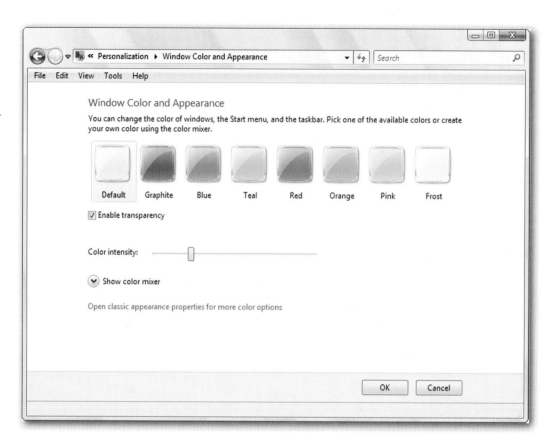

Network Discovery

Network Discovery was introduced with
Windows Vista and continues to be supported by
Windows 7 and Windows 8. It makes setting up
and configuring a network easy as it automatically
detects and configures a network and sets up
a share and Internet connection. It also allows
files to be shared much easier in a peer-to-
peer network, while still providing security
from the Internet. The main exception arises if
there is a router or gateway being used that is
not compatible with the automatic networking
features.

Figure 2-18 shows the Network and Sharing
Center. Notice the **Network discovery** option in
the **Sharing and Discovery** section of the dialog
box. This option lets you enable and disable the
Network Discovery feature.

meeting. Windows Meeting Space is also referred
to as People Near Me. Windows 7 continues to
support People Near Me, but with the introduction
of Windows 8, collaboration activities are designed
more as a cloud activity.

**Windows Shadow Copy and Previous
Versions**

The Windows Shadow Copy feature
automatically makes a copy of files that have
changed and have been saved. This feature allows
a user to open an earlier version of a file using
the Previous Versions feature. To restore a file
using the Previous Versions feature, open the
Properties dialog box of the folder that held that
file or of the current version of that file. Click the
Previous Versions tab. Previous versions of the
file will be listed. Select the desired file and then
click **Restore**. Notice that in **Figure 2-19** there are
four earlier versions of the document titled *CSR
Chapter 2 Revision 2012* that can be restored.

Windows Shadow Copy was first introduced
in Windows Server 2003. It is only available in
Windows Vista Business, Enterprise, and Ultimate
editions and in Windows 7 and Windows 8.

Windows Ready Boost

Many software programs require a great
deal of RAM to operate efficiently. Otherwise,
the program responds slowly or may not

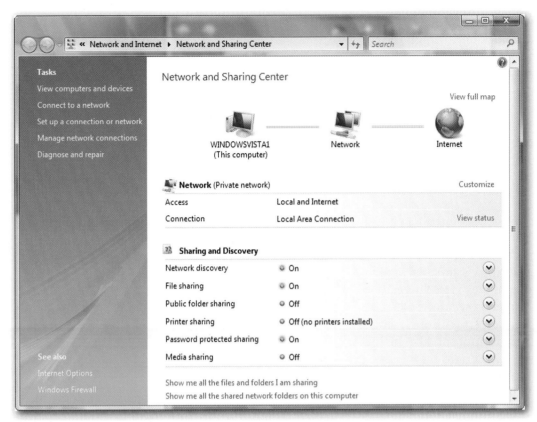

Figure 2-18.
When the **Network discovery** option is enabled, Windows can automatically detect and conFigure a network.

work at all, or the system will seem to freeze up. Operating systems typically use the hard drive to temporarily store limited amounts of program information when RAM is full. For example, a computer with 1 GB of RAM may use 500 kB of memory, referred to as a *page file*, to temporarily store information. This keeps the program working reasonably well when the RAM is full. However, compared to RAM, the hard drive is notoriously slow when accessing and manipulating data.

Windows Ready Boost allows a flash drive to temporarily store this information. Data on a flash drive can be accessed and manipulated much faster than data on a hard drive. Windows Ready Boost is a great improvement to overall performance when a computer system is overworked. It is also an excellent feature for legacy laptops, which typically have much less memory than desktop computers.

Windows Defender

Windows Defender works directly with Internet Explorer 7 or later to protect the

Figure 2-19. The Previous Versions feature allows a user to go back and open an earlier version of a file, called shadow copies.

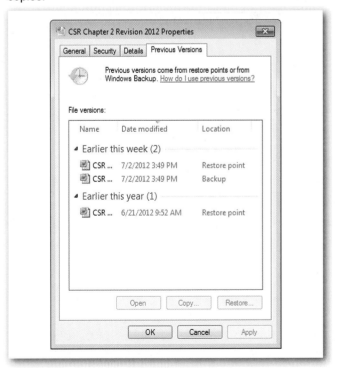

computer from spyware. It scans files as they are downloaded to the computer through the Internet browser. Windows Defender identifies what appears to be spyware, but allows the user to decide what action to take. The possible actions are ignore, allow, quarantine, and always allow. Quarantine isolates and stores the suspected spyware file, allowing the user to install it at a later date if it is found not to be spyware.

Tablet PC Settings

Tablet PC Settings were first introduced in Windows XP Service Pack 2 (SP2) and continue through newer versions of Windows. The newest enhancement to tablet settings is touch screen support. This enhancement was introduced in Windows Vista. Touch screens are designed for users to simply touch the screen with their finger or a pen (stylus). Keyboard input can also be touch generated by displaying a keyboard on the screen and simply touching the desired keys.

Tablet settings allow the user to adjust the pen and tablet features related to the display area. The tablet settings are designed for tablet computers which use a pointing device or a desktop PC that is attached to a tablet-style input device. **Figure 2-20** shows the **Tablet PC Settings** dialog boxes. As you can see, the settings provide selections to conFigure the pen and touch display,

calibrate pen input, and customize the Tablet PC Input Panel. There is also a calibration feature to convert handwriting into fonts associated with typing from a keyboard. After handwriting calibration is configured, handwriting can be converted to a typed document. Tablet devices commonly have their own configuration software application and may not use the Microsoft Windows version.

Offline Files

The Offline Files feature was first introduced with Windows 2000 and further enhanced in later operating systems. This feature synchronizes file content that is stored on a network server with a copy on the computer. The file on the computer can be used whenever the network is not available. Cloud storage offers the same ability as Offline Files.

Gadgets

Windows Vista introduced a desktop feature called *gadgets*. It was continued for Windows 7, but not for Windows 8. This feature resides by default on the right side of the desktop, **Figure 2-21**. Gadgets are mini software programs that provide services, such as an online dictionary, a notepad, a clock, a calendar, a weather report, and a CPU

Figure 2-20. Table PC Settings configuration options. A—**Display** tab options. B—**Other** tab options.

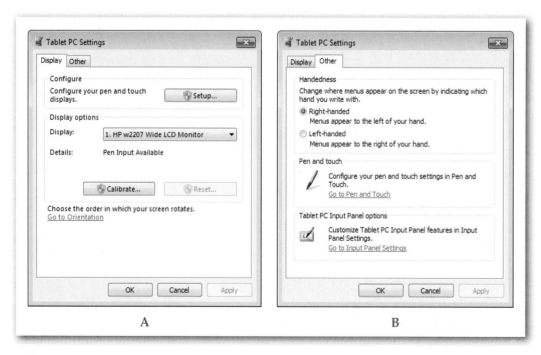

A

B

Figure 2-21.
Windows Vista
Business Edition
desktop. Note the
gadgets on the right
side of the desktop.

monitor. Microsoft discontinued support for gadgets in 2012 because of security problems, and it no longer provides gadgets as a download from the Microsoft website.

XP Mode

Introduced in Windows 7 is XP Mode. XP Mode is not installed by default during the operating system installation. It is installed from a free download from the Microsoft website. The download is actually two separate downloads. The first is Windows Virtual PC. When it is downloaded, the software is installed and a virtual machine automatically configured. The second is XP Mode, a full version of Windows XP. This software is installed on the virtual machine.

After XP Mode is installed and configured, you can install software programs and applications that run under the Windows XP operating system onto the virtual machine. This is not a dual-boot system but rather Windows XP is running simultaneously as Windows 7 is running. Dual-boot systems and virtual machines are covered later in this chapter.

The screen capture in **Figure 2-22** shows Windows 7 running Microsoft Word while Windows XP Mode is running. The Windows XP

My Documents folder is opened. Files can be copied between the Windows XP Mode program and the Windows 7 programs. XP Mode allows you to successfully run a software program designed for the Windows XP environment. XP Mode is only available in Windows 7 Professional, Ultimate, and Enterprise editions.

Libraries

Libraries are new in Windows 7 and differ from the My Documents and Documents folders in Windows XP and Windows Vista. A library is a virtual container of user content, such as documents, music, and pictures. It is a virtual container because the content included in a library can be located on the local computer, remote locations such as network shares, and on exterior storage devices. Libraries serve as a pointer to content. The idea is to have one central virtual storage location for the user.

There are four default folders in a library: Documents, Music, Pictures, and Videos. See **Figure 2-23**. Libraries are not the only way folders can be organized on a Windows 7 computer. The Public folders, which were first introduced in Windows Vista, can also be used.

Figure 2-22.
XP Mode allows the Windows XP operating system and applications to run in a virtual machine.

Figure 2-23.
Windows 7 libraries serve as a virtual container for files located on the local computer, remote locations, and on exterior storage devices. The default library folders are Documents, Pictures, Music, and Videos.

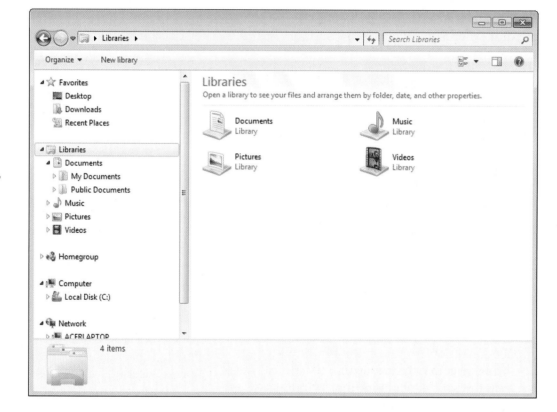

BitLocker To Go

BitLocker To Go was first introduced in Windows 7. It is an enhanced version of the BitLocker application that allows encryption of USB storage devices. As the name implies, you can encrypt files on a USB drive, remove the drive, and take it to another computer. Microsoft provides the

BitLocker To Go Reader as a free download. This program can be installed on a Windows Vista or Windows XP computer. It allows the user to read the contents of the encrypted flash drive. BitLocker To Go is automatically added to the USB flash drive or storage media by default.

Windows 8 Specific Features

Windows 8 has many of the same features found in Windows Vista and Windows 7. The most significant differences are the Windows 8 user interface, which was discussed earlier, the logon option called Microsoft logon, and the incorporation of cloud access by default.

Microsoft User Account

There are two general user account types associated with Windows 8. They are the *local user account* and the *Microsoft account*. The Microsoft account is a combination of your e-mail address, such as Student1481@comcast.net, and a password. The local user account name is simply a user name such as *Student1481* and a password. The e-mail address used for the Microsoft account does not need to be a Microsoft email account. Any e-mail account you own can be used. For example, you could use your Gmail account or the account provided by your Internet service provider.

The Microsoft account is configured during the operating system installation or when a user account is created. When you log on to the computer using your Microsoft account, you automatically connect to the Internet. If configured, you will also automatically connect to your e-mail account, Facebook, Twitter, LinkedIn, and to an assortment of other accounts. When you log on using the local user account, you do not automatically connect to the Internet.

Windows To Go

Windows To Go is a feature specific to the Windows 8 Enterprise edition. It allows a Windows 8 Enterprise operating system and desired files and folders to run from a USB storage device, such as a flash drive or external hard drive. The idea is to allow technicians in the corporate or enterprise environment to plug their USB storage

device into any computer and boot to their own personal computer configuration.

Sync Your Settings

File synchronization is not new to Windows, but the **Sync your settings** option in Windows 8 is redesigned with many additional features. The screen capture in **Figure 2-24** shows the **Sync your settings** options. Notice the list of items that can be synchronized between all your Windows 8 devices, such as other Windows 8 PCs and tablets. This is a great improvement over earlier versions of synchronization because it requires little effort or technical skills on the user's part. To sync your settings requires a user to log on to the computer with the Microsoft account so that the settings will be saved on any of the Microsoft cloud services. This means that when you use a device that automatically connects to cloud services using your Microsoft account, your personal settings will match on each device.

Picture Password

Windows 8 introduces two authentication methods for logging on to a Windows 8 device. The new authentication methods were designed to more easily accommodate touch screen devices such as tablets and phones. A user can authenticate using either a PIN number or a picture. The PIN is a four-digit number created by the user. When using the picture authentication method, you first select a picture. Then you draw directly on the touch screen creating a combination of circles, straight lines, and taps locations. The size, direction, and location of your gestures become your picture password. You can still log on to your PC using a standard password.

Recovery Refresh and Reset

The System Recovery feature has been changed from previous versions of Windows by introducing two new wizards: Refresh and Reset. The recovery wizards are designed to automatically repair your Windows 8 system with limited user interaction. Look at the screen capture in **Figure 2-25**.

When the Refresh wizard is run, the operating system is reinstalled and personal files,

Figure 2-24.
Windows 8 **Sync your settings** options list the items that can be synchronized between personal Windows 8 devices.

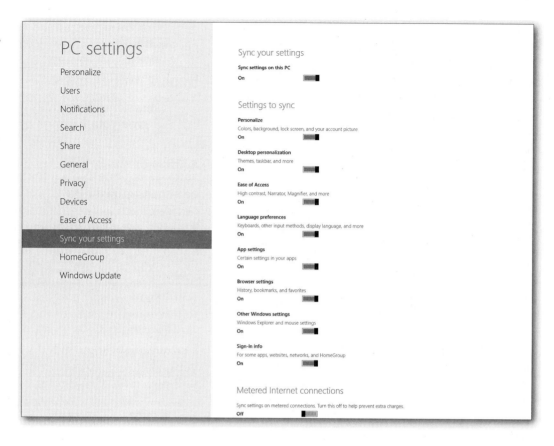

Figure 2-25.
Windows 8 Recovery options.

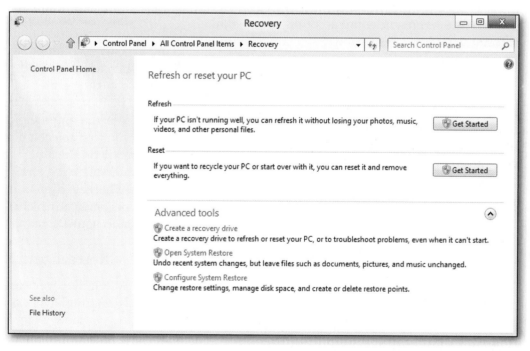

settings, and apps that come with Windows 8 or from the Microsoft Application Store are retained. Any apps from other vendors will not be reinstalled. A list of these apps will be created so you can reinstall them, either from the vendors or from a backup copy.

When the Reset wizard is run, the operating system is reinstalled and all personal files, settings, apps, and user configurations are lost. Only the standard apps that come with the operating system are reinstalled. The advanced options located under **Advanced tools** in the **Recovery** dialog box allow you to create a recovery drive, open a system restore point, or conFigure a system restore point. These three features were available in previous versions of the operating system.

Microsoft Windows Installation

When installing Windows, you can perform an *upgrade* or a clean install. An upgrade means that you can install Windows on an existing operating system and retain files, settings, and applications. A *clean install* means that the previous operating system is completely replaced and you will lose all files, settings, and applications. Windows 7 and Windows 8 use the term *custom* to refer to a clean install. Before performing a clean install or custom installation, you must back up all data. After the installation process, the data can be restored to the system.

Sometimes, upgrading from a previous version of a Windows operating system to a newer version requires a clean install. For example, to upgrade from Windows XP to Windows 7, you would need to do a custom install, which would wipe out all data on the hard drive and perform a clean installation of Windows 7. Be aware that hardware, software applications, and drivers used for the previous operating system may not be supported in a newer version of Windows. So, before performing an upgrade or clean install, run the Windows Upgrade Advisor to ensure compatibility.

A+ Note

The CompTIA A+ exams often ask questions requiring you to match which operating system edition can be upgraded to another. For example, to which edition of Windows 7 can Windows Vista Business be upgraded? Be sure you can answer these types of questions.

It is recommended that in most cases, you do a clean install after partitioning and reformatting the hard drive. This will eliminate any file fragments and most registry corruption from the previous operating system version. Before you perform a clean install, be sure you have all hardware device drivers available and a copy of all previously installed applications. Back up all files and be sure to turn off any antivirus programs.

Tech Tip

Always back up of the entire computer system before performing an upgrade or a custom install. Anything might go wrong. Without a complete backup, you may not be able to rescue the system files or data files.

Windows Vista Editions and Requirements

The editions of Windows Vista you will most likely encounter are Home Basic, Home Premium, Business, and Ultimate. The requirements in the following table will give you a good idea of the hardware needed for a Windows Vista Premium Ready PC and Windows Vista Capable PC. The terms *premium* and *capable* are another way of saying *recommended* and *minimum hardware*. Windows Vista Premium Ready PC hardware requirements support advanced features, such as Windows Aero. A Windows Vista Capable PC will run Windows Vista, but without the special Aero effects. Some software capabilities will be limited also.

Hardware	Windows Vista Capable	Windows Vista Premium
CPU	800 MHz	1 GHz
RAM	512 MB	1 GB
Hard drive size	20 GB	40 GB
Hard drive free space	15 GB	15 GB
Installation media	CD/DVD	DVD
Graphics card	DirectX 9, SVGA 800 × 600	DirectX 9, 128 MB RAM
Optical drive	CD drive	DVD drive

Windows 7 Editions and Requirements

The editions of Windows 7 you will most likely encounter are Home Premium, Professional, and Ultimate. There are additional editions such as Starter, Enterprise, and those with the letter *N* affixed to the edition name. The Starter edition is limited to emerging countries and not sold as a retail copy in the United States. Only an original equipment manufacturer (OEM) may purchase the Starter edition and install it on certain minimal systems, such as tablets. The Enterprise edition is not available for retail purchase and can only be sold through the volume licensing program. Volume licensing is when multiple copies of the operating system are sold to a large consumer, such as a corporation, government, or educational institution. It allows multiple copies of the same operating system to be installed using the same activation key and is based on the number of users or workstations in the organization. The Professional and Ultimate editions are also available through volume licensing, but not to the general public or OEMs. When you see the letter *N* affixed to the name of the version it means the operating system does not include Windows Media Player or Movie Maker. The following table lists the Windows 7 system requirements.

Hardware	32-bit	64-bit
CPU	1 GHz	1 GHz
RAM	1 GB	2GB
Hard drive space	16 GB	20 GB
Graphics support	DirectX 9 and Windows Display Driver Model (WDDM) 1.0	
DVD drive	Required for installation or upgrade using a retail version of the operating system.	

Not all versions of an operating system are upgradeable. For some editions, you must back up all important files and then install the new operating system. During the installation process, all existing files are destroyed because the new operating system deletes existing files and replaces the old operating system. When performing an upgrade, the new operating system preserves existing user files such as documents, pictures, and movies. Even the old operating system is typically saved in a folder identified as "OldWindows." Saving the old operating system will usually allow the installation of a new operating system to be reversed if something goes wrong. It is best to back up all important files before installing a new operating system, even before performing an upgrade. Things can go wrong, and valuable files can be lost. The table in **Figure 2-26** identifies the Windows Vista editions that can be upgraded to a particular Windows 7 edition.

A+ Note

For the A+ Certification exams, be sure to know the difference between hardware recommendations for 32-bit, 64-bit, and tablet versions.

Windows 8 Editions and Requirements

Windows 8 is available in just four editions: Windows 8, Windows 8 Pro, Windows 8 Enterprise, and Windows 8 RT. Some Windows 8 editions are designed especially for portable devices, such as tablets and phones. Other editions are designed for devices with more resources such as a powerful CPU and lots of memory.

Windows 8 will run on 32-bit or 64-bit systems and on an ARM device. ARM devices are also referred to as advanced RISC machines. They are typically portable devices with limited computer resources and are designed for very little power consumption so that the battery lasts as long as possible. ARM is used in devices such as smartphones, tablets, iPads, and some gaming devices. Some tablets use processors other than ARM, such as the Intel Atom.

Legacy devices that do not support a minimum screen resolution of 1024×768 will not properly display apps designed for Windows 8. Windows 8 has a feature first released in Windows 7 called Snap. The Snap feature allows

Windows Vista Edition	Windows 7 Home Premium	Windows 7 Professional	Windows 7 Ultimate
Windows Vista Home Basic	Yes	No	Yes
Windows Vista Home Premium	Yes	No	Yes
Windows Vista Business	No	Yes	Yes
Windows Vista Ultimate	No	No	Yes

Figure 2-26.
Use this table to determine if a particular edition of Windows Vista can be upgraded to Windows 7.

Goodheart-Willcox Publisher

two applications to be displayed side by side on the screen at the same time. It requires a minimum screen resolution of 1366 × 768.

The following table lists the Windows 8 system requirements. To learn more about any particular operating system, visit the Microsoft website or conduct a search using the key terms "Microsoft features" followed by the name of the edition such as "Windows 8."

Hardware	32-bit	64-bit
CPU	1 GHz	1 GHz
RAM	1 GB	2 GB
Hard drive space	16 GB	20 GB
Screen resolution, for Start interface	1024 × 768	1024 × 768
Screen resolution, for Snap feature	1366 × 768	1366 × 768
Graphics support	DirectX 9 or higher	DirectX 9 or higher

The table in **Figure 2-27** identifies if a particular Windows 7 edition can be upgraded to a particular Windows 8 edition. While you can upgrade to Windows 8 and Windows Pro from any previous Windows 7 edition, you may not retain all your system settings. Also, you cannot upgrade a 32-bit operating system to a 64-bit operating system and retain Windows settings, personal files, or applications. The Microsoft TechNet website lists detailed information on upgrading to Windows 8 and retaining system settings and data. You can find this information by entering "TechNet Windows 8 upgrade path" in the search box of your Internet browser.

Before installing or performing an upgrade to Windows 8, Microsoft recommends you verify that the processor can support the following CPU features: PAE, NX, and SSE2. All modern processors have these features. If SSE2 is not supported, some drivers and software applications may not perform as intended. If a computer was purchased after 2006, it should have no problem running Windows 8. You can run the Windows 8 Upgrade Advisor to determine if the computer can support Windows 8 features. The Upgrade Advisor will check program and hardware compatibility and advise of any expected problems.

Physical Address Extension (PAE)

Operating systems that are 32-bit can only access 4 GB of RAM, but a processor that has the Physical Address Extension (PAE) feature can access more than 4 GB. This feature allows Windows 8 to be installed on a 32-bit system and to access more than 4 GB of RAM.

Windows 7 Edition	Windows 8	Windows 8 Pro	Windows 8 Enterprise
Windows 7 Home Premium	Yes	Yes	No
Windows 7 Professional	Yes	Yes	Yes
Windows 7 Ultimate	Yes	Yes	Yes

Figure 2-27.
Use this table to determine if a particular edition of Windows 7 can be upgraded to Windows 8.

Goodheart-Willcox Publisher

Never eXecute (NX)

Never eXecute (NX) is a coding feature that allows a processor to separate memory into sections and to prevent software other than the designated operating system to execute. NX is a security feature that helps prevent malicious software from attacking the operating system.

SSE2

Streaming SIMD Extensions 2 (SSE2) is a collection of over 70 different processor instructions and has been included in processor design for many years. SIMD stands for Single Instruction Multiple Data. SSE has been expanded over the years. The latest version is SSE4, but only SSE2 is required for Windows 8. The SEE instruction set and SIMD allow multiple data to be processed at the same time. This feature can best be described as required to support parallel processing and multi-core processing.

Windows Easy Transfer

Windows 7 provides the Windows Easy Transfer tool to assist you during a custom install, **Figure 2-28**. You can use it to transfer user accounts, files, and settings to a USB storage drive, similar to performing a backup. Then, after performing a custom install, use Windows Easy Transfer tool to reinstall the files and settings to the new operating system. You can also use this tool to transfer user accounts, files, and settings from an old computer to a new computer.

Some of the types of files you can transfer are documents, music, pictures, e-mail settings, contacts, messages, program settings, user accounts, desktop backgrounds, network connections, screen savers, **Start** menu options, taskbar options, network printers and drives, and Internet and web browser settings.

Not everything on an old computer system is transferable. For example, most application software will not work after being transferred. You will need to reinstall the software using the original disc. Also, when updating an operating system, especially when going from a 32-bit to a 64-bit system, you will most likely need new hardware drivers and new versions of antivirus software. The Windows Easy Transfer tool can generate a report identifying most problem areas that might be encountered.

Windows Anytime Upgrade

The Windows Anytime Upgrade allows a user to upgrade to a Windows edition that has more features than the Windows edition being used. A link to this utility is located on the **Start** menu.

Figure 2-28.
Windows 7 Easy Transfer tool allows you to transfer user accounts, files, and settings.

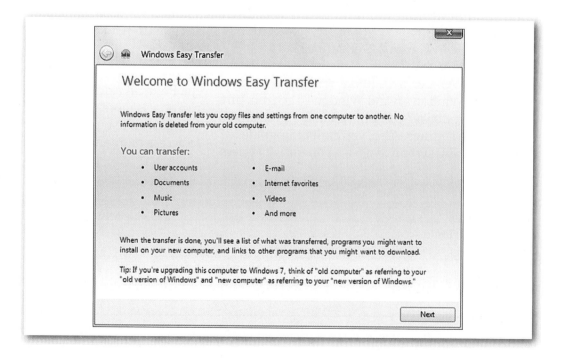

When selected, a dialog box similar to the one in **Figure 2-29** is displayed.

The process uses the Internet to obtain an upgrade key. During the upgrade, application software, files, and settings are preserved. This is handy when a user discovers a feature is needed. Windows Anytime Upgrade is available in most Windows operating systems, but the ability to upgrade is phased out when a newer operating system becomes available. For example, the Windows Vista version of Windows Anytime Upgrade was disabled after the release of Windows 7 to encourage users to purchase the newer operating system.

Windows PE

Windows Pre-installation Environment (Windows PE) is a minimal 32-bit Windows operating system that prepares a disk storage system before the complete operating system is installed. In addition, Windows PE supports CD, DVD, and USB flash drives, all of which may be required for the complete operating system installation. Windows PE supports the Remote Installation Services (RIS), which allows an operating system to be installed from across a network. Windows PE is part of the Windows installation program when performing a complete installation from a Windows DVD. The latest version at the time of this writing is Windows PE 3.0 and is based on the Windows 7 operating system.

In addition to preparing a computer for operating system installation, Windows PE can be used to recover a failed computer or for troubleshooting purposes. Windows PE is part of the Windows Automated Installation Kit (WAIK). The WAIK is a set of installation tools available for free download from the Microsoft Support website. The tools allow a computer technician to create disc images, deploy operating systems automatically to computers that have no operating systems, manage existing systems by automatically installing new device drivers, and create a Windows Pre-installation Environment on disc or flash memory device.

Microsoft Windows Boot Sequences

A **boot sequence** is the step-by-step process of bringing a computer to an operational state. This involves a combination of hardware and software control to initialize hardware and load

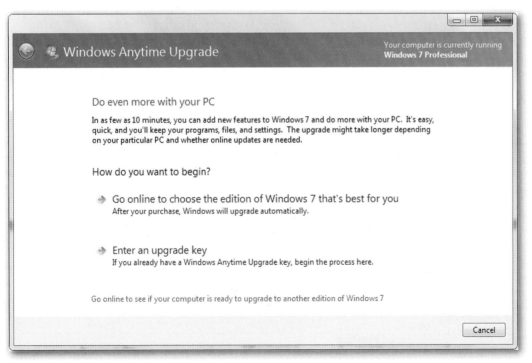

Figure 2-29. Windows Anytime Upgrade allows a user to upgrade from one Windows edition to another that has more features.

operating system files. This section serves as an introduction to the boot sequences of Windows XP, Windows Vista, Windows 7, and Windows 8. An in-depth understanding of boot sequences is essential to troubleshooting startup problems. Therefore, a more detailed description is presented in Chapter 15—PC Troubleshooting.

A+ Note

The A+ Certification exams usually stress knowledge of the boot sequence. Exercises in the accompanying Laboratory Manual will help you to better understand the boot process.

Warm and Cold Booting

A computer cannot begin the boot sequence if it is not initiated. When the boot sequence is initiated, it is called *booting the computer*. There are two styles of booting a computer: cold boot and warm boot. A **cold boot**, also called a *hard boot*, means that the electrical power switch is used to turn on the computer. A **warm boot**, or *soft boot*, is used to restart a computer that is already running. A warm boot can be initiated by a software program as part of a typical installation, such as installing a game. Another common style of initiating a warm boot is by pressing the [Ctrl], [Alt], and [Delete] keys simultaneously or clicking the **Restart** command located in the **Start** menu, **Figure 2-30**.

Figure 2-30. A warm boot can be performed by clicking the **Restart** command on the **Start** menu or pressing the [Ctrl], [Alt], and [Delete] keys simultaneously.

POST

As you can see in **Figure 2-31**, all operating systems start out with a power-on self-test. The **power-on self-test (POST)** is a simple diagnostic program that is initiated when electrical power is applied to the computer system. It is common to all operating systems, even to MAC OS X and all versions of Linux. The POST does a quick system check to determine if all major hardware components, such as the CPU, RAM, keyboard, mouse, video system, and storage devices, are in proper working order. The devices checked may vary slightly from computer to computer depending on the firmware.

The test it performs is not as sophisticated as diagnostic software, but it will check for major problems. When the POST is finished, it usually makes one "beep" sound to let you know that the POST is complete and everything is in working order. If an error is detected during the POST, an error code is usually displayed on the screen and a series of beeps are heard that match the code. The codes and beep pattern vary according to the different BIOS or UEFI chip manufacturers. A list of error codes and beep codes can be obtained from the website of the manufacturer.

BIOS

In a BIOS-based system, the POST is initiated by the bootstrap program in the firmware. The **bootstrap program** is a short program that runs the POST; searches for the Master Boot Record

Figure 2-31. Comparison of Windows operating system boot sequences.

Windows 2000 and XP	Windows Vista, 7, and 8
POST	POST
Initial startup phase	Initial startup phase
Boot loader phase	Windows Boot Manager phase
Detect and conFigure hardware phase	Windows Boot Loader phase
Kernel loading phase	Kernel loading phase
Logon phase	Logon phase

Goodheart-Willcox Publisher

(MBR), which is typically located on the first section of the hard drive; loads into memory some basic files; and then turns the boot operation over to the operating system. The word *bootstrap* comes from the expression "to pull oneself up by one's bootstraps."

UEFI

The boot sequence is slightly different for a computer equipped with UEFI, or EFI. The Unified Extensible Firmware Interface (UEFI) is a modern approach to the BIOS system and an enhancement to the boot process. When a device equipped with UEFI completes POST, control is turned over to a built-in boot manager program rather than the MBR, which contains the bootstrap program. The UEFI firmware uses an improved hard drive technology known as GUID partition table. There will be more about UEFI and GUID later in this textbook when you have a better understanding of data storage and system files.

Some computers have an UEFI boot manager and an MBR to ensure backward compatibility. UEFI is backward compatible with devices and software that require BIOS firmware. The UEFI firmware directly supports BIOS features using a compatibility support module (CSM), which is programmed into the UEFI. The CSM emulates the BIOS features. For example, when a computer system that has BIOS firmware is upgraded to a new operating system that uses UEFI firmware and supports the GUID partition table, the UEFI technology will use CSM to support a BIOS MBR partition. This way, backward compatibility is maintained.

Windows operating systems began support for EFI and UEFI with the release of Windows Vista. Windows operating systems must be 64-bit versions to use UEFI.

Windows 8 was designed with a secure boot-sequence to prevent malware and unauthorized changes to the operating system. By default, Windows 8 installs the boot-sequence for the use of UEFI firmware. Windows 8 does have the ability to run on computers designed with BIOS, but some of the security features will not be installed because BIOS cannot implement these features. UEFI firmware protects the computer before the start of the Windows 8 operating system. The UEFI system allows the anti-malware program to begin before the operating system starts. The early start of anti-malware software helps to prevent attacks on the computer before operating system is loaded. Also, Windows 8 only allows the installation of Microsoft preapproved software applications. The purpose of this is to prevent malware applications from altering or damaging the system configuration. There will be much more about UEFI protection later in Chapter 14—Physical and Digital Security.

> **Tech Tip**
>
> Because the term *BIOS* is so ingrained in computer technician jargon, it will still be used for many years to represent the correct term *firmware* and *UEFI*. Although not technically correct, this is the way technical language commonly evolves. You will often encounter terms that are not always correct when reading resource materials and talking to other technicians.

Windows NT-Based Boot Sequence

Windows NT was the first Microsoft operating system to be fully developed so that it is independent of the restrictions of DOS. It is a completely redesigned operating system with a new kernel. Windows 2000 and Windows XP are typically identified as Windows NT-based operating systems because they are built on the Windows NT kernel.

The Windows NT boot sequence is described as a series of phases rather than a series of files executed one after another. These phases are listed in the first column of the table in Figure 2-31. Some files are loaded into memory during the boot process and are used to provide information to the file that is presently in control of the boot operation. You might say that the boot operation is no longer a series of files taking over one by one, but rather several files working together to complete the boot operation. **Figure 2-32** provides a description of the Windows NT-based boot process files. The following details the Windows NT boot sequence.

1. BIOS performs the POST.
2. BIOS locates the MBR and loads it into memory.

Figure 2-32.
Windows NT-based
(Windows 2000
and Windows XP)
boot sequence and
configuration files.

Windows NT-Based Boot Sequence File	Description
boot.ini	File used to identify the default operating system and other operating systems if more than one is present. The boot.ini file has been replaced by the Boot Configuration Data (BCD) file in Windows Vista.
bootcfg.exe	Used in dual-boot and multiple-boot systems to allow the user to select which operating system to boot.
hal.dll	Provides information and supports communication between software applications and hardware devices. Software applications are not allowed to directly communicate with hardware. Loads at the same stage as the kernel, and then works directly with the kernel.
ntbootdd.sys	The driver used to communicate with hardware devices that do not communicate directly with BIOS, such as SCSI drives and some ATA drives.
ntdetect.com	File responsible for identifying hardware information for ntldr. Ntdetect.com has been merged into the Windows Vista kernel.
ntldr	File responsible for loading the operating system. Ntldr has been replaced by the Windows Boot Manager in Windows Vista.
ntoskrnl.exe	The core of the operating system, referred to as the kernel.
winlogon.exe	The file that controls the system logon by the user.

Goodheart-Willcox Publisher

3. The MBR loads the operating system loader, ntldr.
4. Ntldr reads the boot.ini file.
5. If the boot.ini file contains a reference to a SCSII disk drive system, the ntbootdd.sys file is loaded.
6. Ntldr calls the ntdetect.com program.
7. The ntdetect.com program detects system hardware information and passes the information to ntldr.
8. Ntldr passes the hardware information and control over to ntoskrnl.exe.
9. The ntoskrnl.exe program loads the device drivers and hal.dll, and then initializes the computer settings using the values stored in the system registry.
10. Winlogon.exe loads, allowing the user to begin the logon process.
11. The user successfully logs on to the computer.

Windows Vista and Later Boot Sequence

Starting with Windows Vista, Microsoft made several changes to the boot sequence. First, Windows Vista and later operating systems can boot from the BIOS or UEFI. This section focuses only on the BIOS-based boot sequence.

Look again at the table in Figure 2-31. The second column lists the major phases of the Windows Vista, Windows 7, and Windows 8 boot sequence. Notice that after the POST, Windows progresses through the initial startup phase in similar fashion as the Windows NT-based operating systems. However, the next phase for Windows Vista, Windows 7, and Windows 8 is the Windows Boot Manager phase.

In this phase, the Windows Boot Manager (bootmgr) reads a registry-type file called the Boot Configuration Data (BCD) file. This file stores boot configuration information, such as the names of the operating systems to list in a boot menu, the amount of time the boot menu should be displayed while waiting for user input, and the default operating system to load if no user input is entered.

The Windows Boot Manager (bootmgr) replaces bootcfg.exe used by Windows NT-based operating systems. The Windows Boot Manager will not display a selection of operating systems if there is only one operating system on the computer. If there are two or more operating systems, the Windows Boot Manager appears for approximately 30 seconds to allow the user to select which operating system to boot. If no selection is made, the default operating system is started.

When the Windows Boot Manager phase completes, the Windows Boot Loader (winload.exe) phase begins. First, the kernel (ntoskrnl.exe) is loaded into memory but not executed. The hal.dll file and registry data are also loaded into memory. The Windows Boot Loader phase ends by executing the kernel. The kernel loading phase begins.

In this phase, the kernel starts the Session Manager (smss.exe), which creates the system environment. Up until now, the operating system has been in a text-based mode; however, with smss.exe loaded, the operating system switches to graphics mode by loading the GUI. It is at this point that the familiar progress bar appears at the bottom of the screen.

The kernel interacts with hal.dll and the registry information in memory to load hardware drivers and other files necessary to complete the boot operation. The last phase in the boot sequence is the logon phase, which is initiated by the loading of the Logon Manager (winlogon.exe). After a successful user logon, the desktop appears, and the user can start using the various software applications.

Certain files are automatically loaded into RAM after a successful user logon. These files are generally referred to as startup programs, and will start quickly after they are selected from the **Start** menu or from a shortcut icon because they are already loaded into RAM. If a program is not a startup program, it will need to be loaded to RAM before it starts, thus causing a short delay in program response when selected. **Figure 2-33** provides a description of the files for this boot

Windows Vista, 7, and 8 Boot Sequence File	Description
BCD	The Boot Configuration Data file, which is a registry file containing information such as the names of the operating systems to list in a boot menu.
BCDEdit.exe	Used to edit the Boot Configuration Data file. Replaces bootcfg.exe in Windows NT-based operating systems.
winload.exe	The Windows Boot Loader file, which loads ntoskrnl.exe and hal.dll into memory and scans the registry for device drivers to load. It then passes control to the ntoskrnl.exe.
bootmgr	The Windows Boot Manager file, which reads the BCD file and displays the boot menu.
hal.dll	Provides information and supports communication between software applications and hardware devices. Software applications are not allowed to directly communicate with hardware. Loads at the same stage as the kernel and then works directly with the kernel.
ntoskrnl.exe	The core of the operating system referred to as the kernel.
smss.exe	The Session Manager file, which creates the user session environment and the graphical user interface.
winlogon.exe	The Logon Manager file, which controls system logon by the user.

Figure 2-33. Windows Vista, Windows 7, and Windows 8 boot sequence and configuration files.

process. The following details the Windows Vista, Windows 7, Windows 8 boot sequence:

1. BIOS performs the POST.
2. BIOS locates the MBR and loads it into memory.
3. BIOS locates and loads the Windows Boot Manager (bootmgr).
4. Windows Boot Manager reads the BCD file and displays the boot menu.
5. Windows Boot Manager starts the Windows Boot Loader (winload.exe) when Windows Vista, Windows 7, or Windows 8 is selected or if started automatically.
6. The Windows Boot Manager loads ntoskrnl.exe and hal.dll into memory and scans the registry for device drivers to load. It then passes control to the kernel.
7. The kernel loads the device drivers and hal.dll and initializes the computer settings using the values stored in the system registry.
8. The kernel starts the Session Manager (smss.exe), which creates the system environment.
9. The operating system switches to graphics mode and the winlogon.exe file is loaded, thus starting the Logon Manager (winlogon.exe).
10. The Logon Manager allows the user to begin the logon process.

A+ Note

When answering questions related to the Windows Vista, Windows 7, and Windows 8 boot sequence, remember these operating systems use the Windows Boot Loader file, winload.exe, not ntldr.

Dual-Boot and Multiple-Boot Systems

When two operating systems are installed on a single computer, it is referred to as a **dual-boot system**. For example, Windows Vista and Windows 7 can both be installed on the same computer, resulting in a dual-boot configuration. The Windows 7 Windows Boot Manager allows

the user to select which operating system to start. If no selection is made, the Windows 7 operating system will start by default.

You could also conFigure a **multiple-boot system**, which contains more than two operating systems. For example, you could have Windows 2000, Windows XP, Windows Vista, and Windows 7 installed on the same computer. You could also add a non-Microsoft operating system, such as Linux.

Tech Tip

At the time of this writing, you cannot create a dual-boot or multiple-boot system with Windows 8. It is only possible by installing a virtual software program on an existing operating system and then installing Windows 8 into the virtual partition.

Virtual Machine

When a computer is configured as a dual-boot or multiple-boot system, you can only run one operating system at a time. However, a virtual machine can be created using a special software application that allows more than one operating system to be executed at the same time. A computer that runs two operating systems at the same time is referred to as a **virtual machine** or *virtual PC*. The Microsoft application for creating a virtual machine is called *Windows Virtual PC*. There is also a third-party vender that markets virtual machine software called *VMware*.

When two operating systems are running at the same time, they must share the CPU and the RAM. Sharing the CPU and RAM negatively impacts computer performance when compared to a dual-boot or multiple-boot system.

Common Mobile Device Operating Systems

In general, mobile operating systems are designed for portable devices with limited hardware resources, such as cell phones, tablets, and some gaming hardware. Although some mobile operating systems do appear on larger devices, such as laptops and tablets, they are typically designed with limited CPU and memory support. For example, they will not support extensive graphics associated with games or sophisticated graphic design programs, such as some web design software or computer-aided drafting and engineering software. In general, the mobile operating system is designed to provide the widest assortment of popular user applications on limited hardware with a minimal amount of software required to perform a task. Common portable device tasks are Internet access and collaboration activities, such as instant messaging, texting, Facebook, Twitter, taking photos, and sharing music and photos. As mobile device operating systems and mobile devices evolve, it will soon be difficult to discern between what is considered a mobile device and what is not.

Cloud Computing

Cloud computing is accessing a shared pool of resources and specialized services over the Internet. Examples of shared resources and services are storage, application software, instant messaging, e-mail, and database support. The term *cloud* is synonymous with the Internet symbol used in network drawings, **Figure 2-34**. The cloud symbol represents the Internet location of a service. The cloud computing concept is not as new as you might think. It has actually been around for many years, even before the term *cloud* was used. If you have ever used Hotmail, Facebook, or an online photo sharing or online gaming program, then you have used a cloud-based system.

Cloud services have expanded rapidly in recent years because of mobile devices, such as smartphones and tablets. These two types of mobile devices do not have sufficient memory, storage space, or powerful CPUs, which is why the demand for cloud services has increased. The cloud provides storage services and the ability to use large software applications, which cannot possibly be installed on the portable device. For example, a mobile user can access the complete Microsoft Office suite via the Internet using a portable device. The success of mobile devices depends greatly on cloud computing.

Typically, users install the entire software application on their computer. After installation, they have complete access and control over the use and configuration of the software application. Users can also store files on their computer as related to the software application. In a cloud computing setting, the user would install a small software application, or **app**, which allows the user to access the larger software application on the cloud service. The software appears to the user as though it is installed entirely on the PC or portable device, when in reality the software application is installed on the cloud server. In this scenario, the user's computer is referred to as a **thin client**. A thin client depends on the cloud-based software application to do most of the work. The user has the option to store the document on the cloud location or on the computer. When software applications are provided through cloud services, it is often referred to as **virtualization**.

Cloud services can be provided free of charge or for a cost. When free of charge, fewer services and less storage space are provided as compared to pay services. There are many cloud service providers such as Google, Apple, Microsoft, Amazon, VMware, IBM, and other private companies.

The real strength of cloud computing is resource pooling and sharing of resources. Computer resources such as documents, pictures, videos, and other types of files can be easily shared with members of the cloud service. In addition to sharing resources, the cloud service provider typically makes available software applications appropriate for the type of cloud

Figure 2-34. The Internet is represented as a cloud on network drawings.

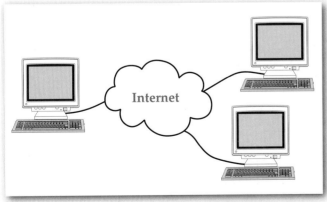

Internet

membership. For example, word-processing, database, e-mail, and digital photo software applications may be provided as a service. The cloud member does not need to install the software application on the mobile device but instead is able to connect to the host cloud as a thin client. The advantage of the software application being installed on the cloud service server means that the software application will be available no matter which device the user decides to use. Users can run the software application from their desktop, tablet, or cell phone. Another advantage is the cloud service provider is responsible for updating the software application, making backup files, and providing the necessary technical support.

Microsoft offers several versions of cloud services at this time, such as Windows Live, Microsoft Office 365, Windows Azure, and Windows Intune. Some of these services are free,

but most are not. The fees vary in range based on the desired services and number of users. For example, the cost of the service can be based on the number of users determined by the number of unique e-mail accounts. Microsoft Windows Live is a cloud service provided for free for common PC users, **Figure 2-35**.

Common Operating System Terminology

There is a tremendous amount of operating system terminology that is common to all operating systems. A few terms are required to be mastered early, such as application software, software driver, and software patch. There will be many more terms introduced throughout the textbook and your instruction. Be sure to master these three for now.

Figure 2-35. Screen shot of the Microsoft Windows Live website. Windows Live offers free cloud-based services.

Application Software

Application software, also referred to as *end-user software,* is designed for a specific purpose, such as creating databases or spreadsheets, word processing, producing graphics, or just for entertainment. It is not an operating system.

Typical application software rely on the operating system to communicate with PC hardware such as the hard drive or CD-ROM drive. When a word-processing program issues a save command, the command is interpreted by the operating system, which in turn passes it through the CPU and on to the hardware. While most 32-bit software applications will run on a 64-bit computer system, some will not. Antivirus programs are a classic example of a software application that must match the system type: 32-bit or 64-bit.

Software Driver

A **software driver** is a small package of programs that allow proper communication between the computer and the peripheral device. Common devices that require drivers are printers, modems, monitors, and storage devices. Software drivers act as translators, converting common commands issued from the CPU to the device in use.

PC and software systems are constantly evolving, but not necessarily in the same time frame. For example, you may install a printer that is much newer than the software installed on a computer. The computer may not have the software programs necessary to communicate correctly with the printer. A typical scenario is when a new printer is installed on a PC and the self-test runs perfectly. However, when a file you have created on the PC is sent to the printer, it prints out a garbled set of meaningless symbols or an endless stream of blank pages. This is a classic case of incorrect driver software.

Software drivers are typically classified as 32-bit and 64-bit and are not interchangeable. You must match the driver to the type of operating system. Microsoft operating systems require 64-bit driver software to be digitally signed. A digitally-signed driver contains a security code which identifies and verifies the developer

of the software driver. Because the driver is verified, Microsoft recognizes it as a driver from a legitimate software vendor and that does not contain malware.

Windows operating systems incorporate options to allow you to run legacy software applications and legacy drivers. The screen capture in **Figure 2-36** shows the options for configuring a program to run as if it was installed on a previous version of Windows. In this example, the Battlefield 3 game is configured to run as if it was installed on a Windows XP (Service Pack 3) edition of the Windows operating system. Microsoft provides a compatibility troubleshooter called Program Compatibility, which automatically detects possible compatibility problems associated with various programs, **Figure 2-37.**

Software Patch

A **software patch** is a fix for operating systems and application software that have already been released. It also contains security updates when the operating system or software has been compromised. Although operating

Figure 2-36. Windows operating systems provide compatibility options for configuring legacy software applications.

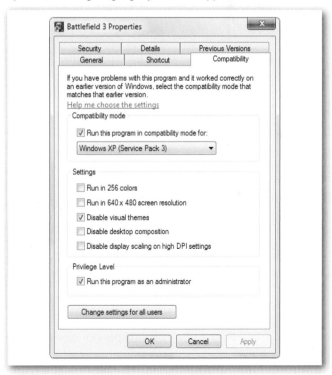

Figure 2-37. The Program Compatibility tool detects possible compatibility problems associated with legacy software applications.

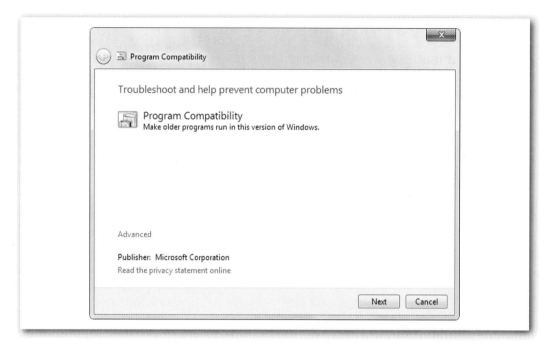

systems and software go through countless hours of testing, many have errors in programming. This type of error is referred to as a **bug**. Patches for software programs can assist in correcting bugs and are readily available for download off the Internet. Periodically, a large collection of patches are released at once and referred to as a *service pack*.

Chapter Summary

- Operating systems provide a file system structure and a means of communicating with the computer hardware.
- All operating systems have a user interface, a file system structure, a file table, configuration files, and the ability to multitask.
- The most significant differences between Windows 8 and earlier Windows operating systems are its user interface, user account settings, and the incorporation of cloud access.
- Carrying out a Windows installation calls for knowledge of an operating system's hardware requirements and determining whether an upgrade or clean install should be performed.
- Windows Vista, Windows 7, and Windows 8 share a common boot sequence: POST, initial startup phase, Windows Boot Manager phase, Windows Boot Loader phase, kernel loading phase, and logon phase.
- Common portable devices are cell phones, tablets, and some gaming hardware; common portable device tasks are Internet access and collaboration activities.
- Examples of cloud computing shared resources and services are storage, application software, instant messaging, e-mail, and database support.

- Most 32-bit software applications will run on a 64-bit computer system, some will not; 32-bit and 64-bit drivers will only run on the system they were designed for.

Review Questions

Answer the following questions on a separate sheet of paper. Please do not write in this book.

1. An operating system does what? Select all that apply.
   a. Manages file storage
   b. Provides communication between the user and the computer system
   c. Provides software to communicate with the BIOS
   d. Provides communication between the user and the hard drive

2. What is a kernel?

3. Which type of multitasking allows data and parts of a program to be shared between two or more CPUs.
   a. Cooperative multitasking
   b. Multithreading
   c. Preemptive multitasking
   d. Time slicing

4. What are two main advantages of 64-bit systems over 32-bit systems?

5. What is the maximum amount of memory supported by 32-bit operating systems?

6. What are the two dominant user interfaces used to issue commands on a computer?

7. Where is the root directory located?

8. What are pathnames used for?

9. The purpose of file table is to _____.
   a. keep track of the number of times the PC starts
   b. record the amount of memory used
   c. record file locations on disk
   d. supply power to the screen display

10. List five symbols that are *not* allowed in the Windows long file name system.

11. Which file names are invalid using the Windows long file name format? (Indicate why each is not acceptable.)
    a. myreport
    b. MYREPORT#12
    c. mymemo*for*jim
    d. MYMEMO/TO/JIM
    e. my+memo+to+jim
    f. mymemo:jim
    g. MEMO1999~CA$H
    h. memo1999?
    i. MEMOJune2001=

12. What is the name of the Windows feature that supplements the system RAM using a USB flash drive?

13. What is the purpose of Windows Defender?

14. Which operating system introduced Windows XP Mode?

15. Which Windows version introduced Libraries and HomeGroup into the directory structure?
    a. Windows XP
    b. Windows Vista
    c. Windows 7
    d. Windows 8

16. What is a library in a Windows directory structure?

17. What new user account type was introduced in Windows 8?

18. What is the name of the feature that allows a Windows 8 Enterprise operating system and desired files and folders to run from a USB storage device such as a flash drive or external hard drive?

19. What needs to be done to preserve user data before performing a custom install?

20. What is the recommended amount of RAM for a 32-bit and 64-bit Windows 7 installation?

21. What tool does Windows 7 provide to transfer user accounts, files, and settings to a USB storage drive before performing a custom install?

22. A warm boot may be initiated by pressing which three keys simultaneously?

23. Which part of the boot sequence is common to all operating systems?

24. What is the name of the Windows Vista and later file that loads the kernel?
    a. bootmgr
    b. ntldr
    c. boot.ini
    d. ntoskrnl.exe

25. What is the name of the Windows XP file that detects system hardware components?
    a. ntdetect.com
    b. ntldr
    c. boot.ini
    d. ntoskrnl.exe

26. Which Windows Vista and later file is referred to as the kernel?

27. Which phase in the Windows Vista and later boot sequence replaced the boot loader phase of Windows XP?

28. Which phase of the Windows Vista or later boot sequence allows a user to select the operating system to load when two operating systems are installed on the same computer?

29. During which phase of the Windows Vista or later boot sequence does it change from the text mode to the graphic mode?

30. Give at least two examples of portable devices.

31. Give at least three examples of common portable device tasks.

32. Give two examples of cloud computing resources.

33. Give three examples of cloud computing services.

34. Can a 32-bit software application run on a 64-bit operating system?

35. Can a 32-bit driver be installed on a 64-bit operating system?

36. Can a 64-bit drive be installed on a 32-bit operating system?

Sample A+ Exam Questions

Answer the following questions on a separate sheet of paper. Please do not write in this book.

1. What is the recommended RAM for a 32-bit Windows 7 installation?
   a. 500 MB
   b. 1 GB
   c. 1.5 GB
   d. 2 GB

2. The operating feature that allows two programs to appear to be running simultaneously is called _____.
   a. multiprocessing
   b. multitasking
   c. program coordination
   d. kernel sharing

3. The registry is accessed by entering which command at the command prompt?
   a. cmd
   b. help
   c. regedit
   d. registry32

4. What is the maximum amount of RAM supported by 32-bit Windows 7 system?
   a. 1 GB
   b. 2 GB
   c. 4 GB
   d. 8 GB

5. Which device would contain the POST program?
   a. Hard drive
   b. RAM
   c. USB flash drive
   d. BIOS chip

6. Which of the following are no longer required by Windows Vista or later? Select two.
   a. ntdetect
   b. ntoskrnl
   c. boot.ini
   d. POST

7. Which command entered in the **Search** box will produce the command prompt in Windows 7?
   a. prompt
   b. msdos.sys
   c. cmd
   d. doscom.com

8. Which program is executed first during the boot process?
   a. ntldr
   b. POST
   c. bootcfg
   d. ntdetect

9. Which Microsoft security feature is used to encrypt an entire hard disk drive?
   a. Sync
   b. BitLocker
   c. VPN
   d. XP Mode

10. Which of the following allows more than one operating system to be executed at the same time? Select two.
    a. dual-boot
    b. multiple-boot
    c. XP Mode
    d. virtual machine

Suggested Laboratory Activities

Do not attempt any suggested lab activities without your instructor's permission. Certain lab activities could render the PC operating system inoperable.

1. Access the command prompt and explore some text-based commands. To access the command prompt in Windows Vista or Windows 7, type **cmd** into the **Search** box located on the **Start** menu. In Windows 8, use the **Command Prompt** app located on the **App** screen or enter **cmd** into the **Search** box. Try the following commands: **help**, **ver**, **mem**, **dir**, **dir/?**, **time**, **date**, and **cls**.

Tech Tip   Do not attempt to use the **format** command. It can damage stored data if the command is recognized.

2. Experiment with long file names. Try the special symbols and see what effect they have when attempting to save a file.

3. Do an Internet search to find more information about Windows text-based commands.

4. Visit the Microsoft website and search for a list of operating system features for each current operating system edition.

Motherboards  3

After studying this chapter, you will be able to:

- Recall motherboard bus systems and their function.
- Identify common motherboard form factors.
- Explain motherboard bus architecture.
- Identify expansion card slot architectures.
- Use Device Manager and System Information to identify system resources.
- Carry out a software driver installation.
- Carry out a BIOS upgrade.
- Use the Setup utility to view system settings.
- Identify major parts of a motherboard.
- Check a motherboard for pinched cables, loose connections, oxidation, and high-voltage damage.

A+ Exam—Key Points

This chapter covers many of the objectives on the CompTIA A+ exam. Be sure you can access the Setup utility for several different computer systems and understand the terminology associated with the settings. Motherboard technical manuals are available on the Internet and provide detailed Setup utility information. Be sure to look at several manuals thoroughly. Typical questions on the exam will address upgrading the firmware and changing the Setup utility configuration and its password.

There will be questions related to motherboard expansion architecture, such as the data rate of PCI, PCIe, USB, SATA, eSATA, and IEEE-1394. There may also be questions to test basic knowledge of form factors.

Key Terms

The following key terms will become important pieces of your computer vocabulary. Be sure you can define them.

Accelerated Graphics Port (AGP)
address bus
backplane
bus
chipset
control bus
data bus
direct memory access (DMA)
expansion card slots
Flash BIOS
form factor
I/O bus
I/O port address

IEEE-1394
internal bus
local bus
memory address range
memory bus
north bridge
Peripheral Components
     Interconnect (PCI)
Plug and Play (PnP)
power bus
south bridge
Universal Serial Bus (USB)

The *motherboard* is considered the most important element of a computer's design. All major components connect to and transmit data across the motherboard. The motherboard is the communications center for input and output devices such as the memory, CPU, keyboard, mouse, monitor, and network connection. The motherboard also provides the connection points required by the fans, speaker, on/off switch, LED indicator lights, and CMOS battery.

The motherboard provides a means for expanding and customizing the system by inserting expansion boards into slots, which support a direct connection to the bus architecture. Various special purpose chips control communication between the different buses and devices mounted on the motherboard. The motherboard is also referred to as the *system board*, *main board*, and *planar board*.

Motherboard Construction

The motherboard provides a physical surface on which to mount electronic components such as resistors, capacitors, chips, slots, and sockets. The motherboard is a combination of insulating material and electronic circuit paths constructed of thin conductors. See **Figure 3-1**. The motherboard is constructed mainly from electrical insulation material. Insulation material does not conduct electrical energy. The electrical circuits

that run across the surface of the motherboard are called *traces*. Traces provide the paths between all the different components mounted on the motherboard. This confines the flow of electrical energy to the path created by the traces. The electrical circuit paths provide a means of sending and receiving data between the components connected to the motherboard.

The insulated motherboard does not allow the electrical energy to come in contact with the case. An electrical short circuit would be created if electrical energy were allowed to flow to the metal PC case. A short circuit would also be created if electrical energy could flow directly between the traces on the motherboard.

The thin conductors also provide electrical energy to low-power devices. High-power consumption devices, such as the disk drives, are provided power directly from the power supply through much thicker conductors. Many of the thin conductors on the motherboard are grouped together to make up what is referred to as a bus. A **bus** is a collection of conductors that works together for a specific purpose.

There are many bus types, such as data bus, control bus, memory bus, internal bus, I/O bus, address bus, and power bus. The **data bus** is used to move data between components. The data is moved between components in groups of 8, 16, 32, or 64 bits. The amount of data that can be moved at one time is referred to as the bus width.

Figure 3-1. Close-up of motherboard circuit paths.

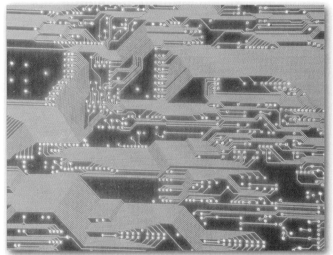

Goodheart-Willcox Publisher

Signals are transmitted across the **control bus** to activate devices such as hard drives and modems. The **memory bus** connects the processor directly to the memory, and the **I/O bus**, also called an *expansion bus*, connects the processor to the expansion slots. The **internal bus** is part of the integrated circuit inside the CPU unit. The **local bus**, or *system bus*, connects directly to the CPU and provides communications to high-speed devices mounted closely to the CPU. The **address bus** connects the CPU with the main memory module. It identifies memory locations where data is to be stored or retrieved. Lastly, the **power bus** is used to send electrical power to low-consumption devices such as speakers, lights, and switches. High-consumption devices, such as disk drives, connect directly to the power supply using larger conductors. As you can see, there are many different bus types and classifications. The name usually implies the purpose of the bus.

A bus may also be a collection of bus types. For example, the local bus consists of power, data, control, and memory bus lines. Therefore, it consists of the power bus, data bus, control bus, and memory bus. For this reason, the local bus may be referred to by other names such as the *system bus* or *memory bus*. Intel has coined the local bus as the *front side bus (FSB)*. This term is used quite often when specifying motherboard bus speeds. It is also often used to describe any motherboard bus that connects directly to the

CPU. The term *backside bus* is used to describe an internal bus inside the CPU.

Form Factors

The **form factor** is the physical shape or outline of a motherboard and the location of the mounting holes. Sometimes the form factor is called the *footprint*. A motherboard form factor must be considered when upgrading a PC. The form factor determines if the motherboard will fit the PC case style you intend to use, **Figure 3-2**. Another device that conforms to a form factor is the power supply. The power supply must match the form factor of the case and motherboard. The form factors that have been developed over the years are the XT, AT, ATX, mini-ITX, LPX, NLX, BTX, and backplane. ATX is the most common form factor used for full-size computers.

XT, AT, and Baby AT

The original PC by IBM used an XT form factor for its motherboard. This was in 1983 and was the first standardized form factor for motherboards. The XT used an 8-bit data bus system. The next standard size was the AT (Advanced Technology) form factor. It was slightly larger than the XT and provided a 16-bit data bus.

As chip technology advanced, it became possible to reduce the size of the motherboard to the original size and shape of the XT. This next motherboard was called the *Baby AT*. Even though it was the same size as the XT board, there would have been a lot of confusion caused by naming it XT. There would have been two different boards, one 8-bit and the other 16-bit, that were the same size. This is the reason for calling the 16-bit board the Baby AT. See **Figure 3-3**.

ATX

The Baby AT remained popular until 1996 when the ATX, a new style of motherboard, gained popularity. The ATX is incompatible with most other motherboard form factors.

ATX form factor has three common sizes: ATX, microATX, and flexATX. The flexATX is sometimes referred to as miniATX. The three standard sizes are 12.0″ × 9.6″ (ATX), 9.6″ × 9.6″ (microATX), and

Figure 3-2.
This case can house a variety of motherboard form factors. The legend at the bottom of the case (enlarged in the exploded view) includes capital letters to identify the mount points for specific form factors. The letter A represents ATX mount points, M represents MicroATX mount points, and B represents BTX mount points.

Goodheart-Willcox Publisher

Figure 3-3.
Comparison of Baby AT and full-size AT form factors.

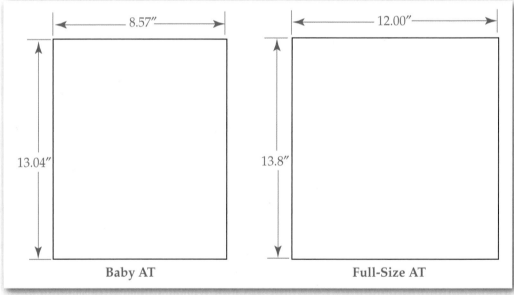

Goodheart-Willcox Publisher

7.5″ × 9.6″ (flexATX), **Figure 3-4**. The overall size of the ATX motherboard is reduced by decreasing the total number of adapter slots for each ATX form factor.

The ATX board looks similar to a Baby AT board that has been turned 90° inside the computer case. The ATX requires a new shape of power supply so that both the motherboard and power supply will fit inside the same case. The most welcomed feature of this form factor is the ATX power supply connector mounted on the motherboard. The ATX power supply connector is designed to prevent the power supply from being plugged into the motherboard with the

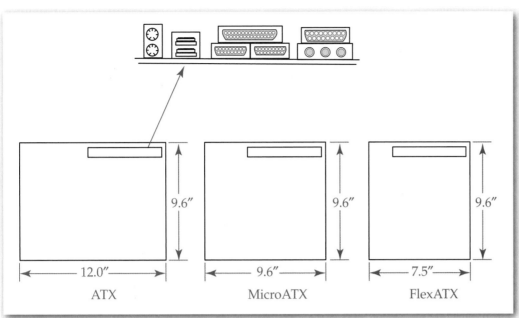

Figure 3-4.
ATX form factors and
back view.

ATX   MicroATX   FlexATX

polarity reversed. This would result in a blown motherboard.

We will take a closer look at power supply connectors in Chapter 5—Power Supplies. For quick identification, an ATX form factor motherboard uses a 20-pin power supply connector, and an AT form factor motherboard uses a 12-pin connector. A newer style of the ATX form factor, called ATX12V, uses a 24-pin connector.

Mini-ITX

The mini-ITX, which was developed by Via Technologies, is a smaller version of the microATX. It provides for a compact system using the same standard components (CPU, RAM, I/O ports, etc.) as the ATX, microATX, and flexATX. **Figure 3-5** shows the size relationship of the ATX, microATX and mini-ITX form factors.

The mini-ITX form factor is used for small desktop computers. There are even smaller ITX form factors used for mobile devices with the sizes 4.7″ × 4.7″ (nano-ITX), 3.94″ × 2.83″ (pico-ITX), and 2.36″ × 2.36″ (mobile-ITX). Many proprietary small form factors (SFF) exist and are used for a wide variety of mobile devices.

LPX

The LPX form factor was designed for a low-profile desktop computer or a slim tower. This motherboard does not have expansion slots like a typical motherboard. Instead, it has a single expansion slot usually mounted in the middle of the motherboard. This expansion slot hosts a bus riser card. See **Figure 3-6**.

Expansion cards are plugged into the bus riser card at right angles so that they are parallel to the motherboard. This is what allows for a low-profile computer case.

The LPX is not considered a true standard and cannot be easily upgraded. Rather, it is a proprietary style. The bus riser card is not always located in the same spot. This variation can be a problem when changing or upgrading the motherboard. Obtaining a motherboard from the same manufacturer is usually required to get the correct layout. This style of motherboard is popular in low-priced computer systems.

NLX

Another form factor, the NLX, uses the same principle as the bus riser card design. However, rather than placing the bus riser card in the middle of the motherboard, it is located at the end

Figure 3-5.
Size comparison of the ATX, microATX, flexATX, and mini-ITX form factors.

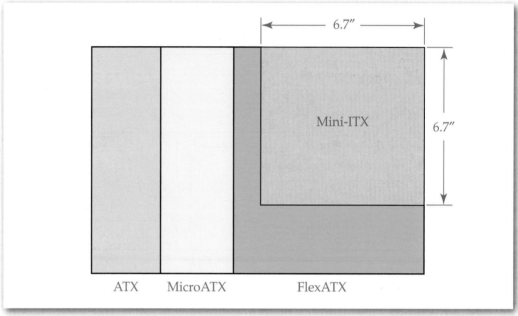

Goodheart-Willcox Publisher

Figure 3-6.
LPX form factor and back view.

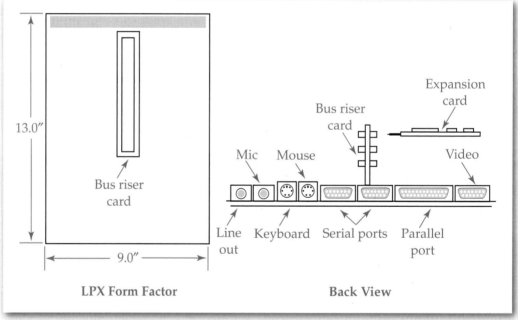

Goodheart-Willcox Publisher

of the board. In fact, the edge of the motherboard plugs into the riser card. See **Figure 3-7** and **Figure 3-8**.

The major advantage of the NLX board over the LPX is that the NLX is standardized in the industry. This means you can replace or upgrade any NLX board with any other NLX board. The NLX was popular among leading PC manufacturers such as Gateway, Hewlett-Packard, IBM, NEC, and Micron. The board width is a standard 9.0″ while the length can vary from 10.0″ to 13.6″. Even though the length may vary, it is still considered a standard. The ATX and NLX continue to be the most popular design used by computer manufacturers. They should stay standard for some time.

BTX

Balanced Technology Extended (BTX) is designed for improved system cooling and acoustics. Many PC components, such as CPUs,

Figure 3-7. NLX form factor. Notice the edge connector on the left side of the motherboard. The motherboard fits into the riser expansion card.

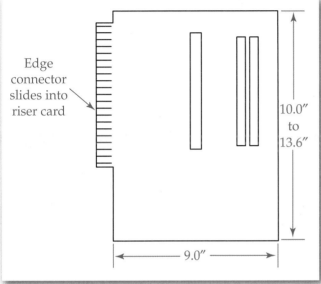

Edge connector slides into riser card

10.0"
to
13.6"

9.0"

Goodheart-Willcox Publisher

chipsets, and graphic cards, operate at a much higher frequency than their predecessors. Therefore, PCs require a superior cooling system. The BTX form factor allows for a direct stream of air across the CPU and other heat-generating components. Another key part of the design is the ability to reduce the noise level of PC cooling system fans.

The BTX design is not compatible with the ATX design, but the BTX can use a typical ATX power supply and any standard device that is not form factor dependent, such as CD/DVD drives, hard drives, CPUs, and expansion cards.

The BTX motherboard has four form factor sizes: 10.5" × 12.8" (BTX), 10.5" × 10.4" (microBTX), 10.5" × 8.8" (nanoBTX), and 10.5" × 8.0" (picoBTX), **Figure 3-9**. The width of the BTX form factor is reduced by reducing the number of expansion slots. The full BTX has up to seven expansion slots, the microBTX has four expansion slots, the nanoBTX has two expansion slots, and the picoBTX has only one expansion slot.

Computer cases today are designed with many openings and several fans to allow as much air to pass through the case as possible. BTX is now obsolete as a case form factor design.

Figure 3-8. NLX motherboard.

Intel Corp.

Figure 3-9.
BTX form factors. Notice that the length is retained and the width is shorted by reducing the number of available expansion slots.

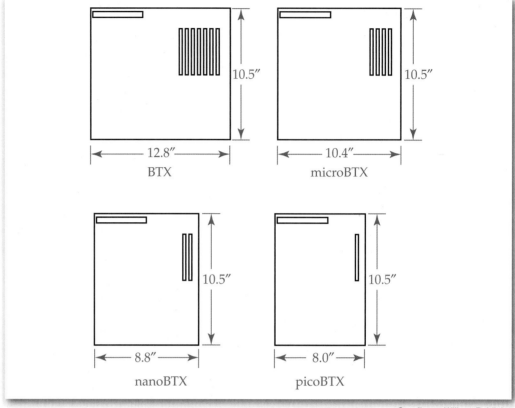

BTX

microBTX

nanoBTX

picoBTX

Goodheart-Willcox Publisher

Backplane

A backplane is not a true form factor design, but it must be considered with a discussion on form factors and motherboards. A **backplane** is a circuit board with an abundance of slots along the length of the board, **Figure 3-10**. Expansion cards slide into the expansion slots. Even the CPU can insert into an expansion slot on the backplane. The main idea of the design is to ensure easy upgrades of any and all components. This style is very popular in heavy industry. The backplane is considered proprietary.

There are two main classifications of backplane boards: active and passive. In a *passive* design, all typical motherboard circuits and chips are located on the expansion cards and not on the backplane. An *active* backplane design contains the usual circuitry found on any typical motherboard with the exception of the main processor. The processor is usually installed into an expansion slot to allow for an easy upgrade as more advanced processors come on the market. To learn more about form factors, visit the FormFactors.org website.

Figure 3-10. Typical backplane design is simply a series of slots across the motherboard.

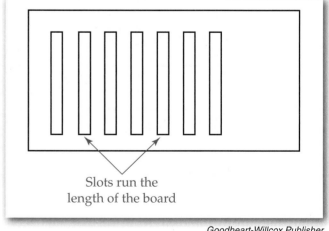

Slots run the length of the board

Goodheart-Willcox Publisher

Motherboard Bus System Architecture

The original PC had a simple bus architecture. One bus connected all major components to the RAM and CPU. The CPU transmitted data to and from components on the motherboard at the same speed. See **Figure 3-11**. The original bus architecture consisted of one bus. The speed of the bus matched the processor speed.

As the PC evolved, the CPU processing speed increased and soon surpassed the speed capabilities of the bus structure. At high frequencies, a bus system can transmit electromagnetic energy just like a radio transmitter. The bus inside the CPU is very short. In fact, it is microscopic. This allows data to move at high speeds without generating electromagnetic interference. The bus outside the CPU is a great deal longer, and interference is a significant problem. This is the main reason for limited data transmission speed on a bus system.

The electrical occurrence of *inductive reactance* limits the speed of electrical energy flow through a conductor. Inductive reactance has a choking effect on the flow of electrical energy. The amount of choking effect is directly related to the speed of data transmission (frequency) and the length of the conductor (bus wire length). The choking effect increases in direct proportion with the speed of data transmission and the length of the data path.

A PC motherboard is designed with many different bus speeds. For example, it may have PCIe, USB, SATA, and eSATA ports and buses of different bandwidths (data rates) connecting to the CPU and RAM. Because of the different bandwidths, there must be a way of joining the different systems together and making them compatible with each other. This is the main function of a chipset. A **chipset** connects the motherboard buses and ports that run at different speeds. It supports the flow of data and control signals of different bus technologies to and from the CPU, RAM, hard drive, and video system.

Originally, chipsets consisted of two discreet chips referred to as the north bridge and south bridge. The north bridge was placed near the CPU, and the south bridge was placed farther away. The **south bridge** was previously used to connect slower devices, such as keyboard, mouse, printer, hard drive and USB ports. The **north bridge** was used to connect high-speed devices to the CPU, such as RAM and PCI slots. Today, motherboards have only one chipset, but the terminology still lingers. The single chipset is often referred to as the *south bridge*. Technically, it is simply a chipset.

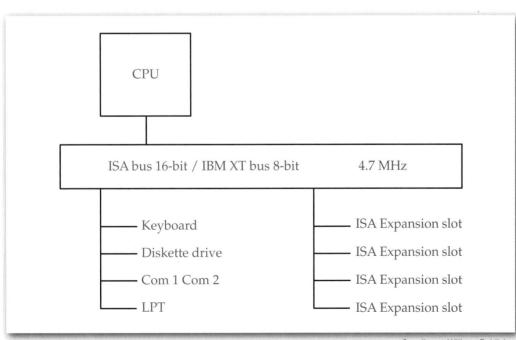

Figure 3-11. PC using a single bus to communicate and transfer data to all components inside and outside the computer. All components run at the same speed as the CPU.

Goodheart-Willcox Publisher

The high-speed devices that originally connected to the north bridge, such as RAM and the PCIe slots designed for video, connect directly to the CPU.

Intel phased out the north bridge and south bridge and replaced it with a bus they refer to as the Intel QuickPath Interconnect (QPI). **Figure 3-12** illustrates a generic layout of a modern Intel chipset. The devices that demand high-speed connections are the PCI Express (PCIe) 3.0 slots used for video cards and DDR3 RAM. These devices connect directly to the CPU. The Intel chipset connects slower devices to the CPU, such as WiMAX/WiFi, Serial ATA (SATA), USB 2.0 and 3.0, audio, network, and BIOS. There can also be digital display bus connecting to the chipset used when there is no high-performance video card installed in the high-performance PCIe slot(s).

AMD invented and developed the HyperTransport Technology to improve the performance of the front side bus (FSB), north bridge, and south bridge. The HyperTransport Technology allows devices to connect directly to each other using bidirectional communications and to negotiate data transfer speed. It does not use a north bridge chip or an FSB. It connects directly to the south bridge, additional CPUs, and other devices. See **Figure 3-13**.

HyperTransport Technology only works with processors that support the technology. For example, AMD processors work with the HyperTransport bus system, but Intel processors do not. HyperTransport Technology is maintained by a consortium of computer-related industries, such as AMD, NVIDIA, Apple Computer, Cisco Systems, and Sun Microsystems. To learn more about the HyperTransport Technology and the organization, visit the HyperTransport Technology Consortium website.

Tech Tip
The terms *north bridge* and *south bridge* are still used by many technicians when describing motherboard features, even though it is technically incorrect.

Without chipsets, the CPU would be required to handle all computer data operations through its own core. This would greatly reduce the efficiency of the CPU. For example, if every byte of data representing a picture transferred from the hard drive to the RAM had to pass through the CPU, the computer would run slowly.

There are also chipsets designed to handle additional functions such as enabling

Figure 3-12.
The Intel chipset in this bus architecture provides communication between buses of different speeds.

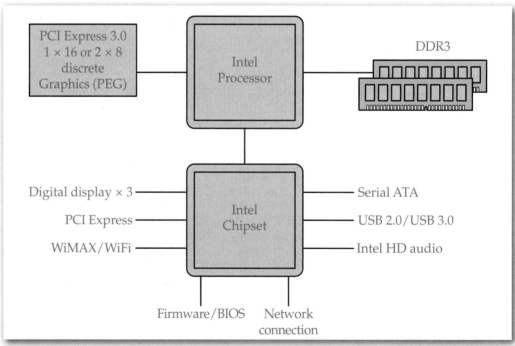

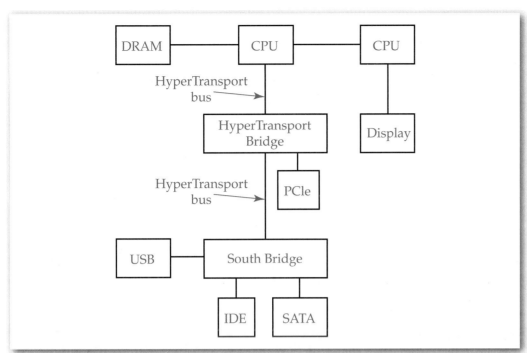

Figure 3-13.
Example of AMD
HyperTransport™
Technology. Be
aware that the exact
design will vary by
manufacturer.

Goodheart-Willcox Publisher

motherboard expansion slots to work with RAM and other computer components with minimal CPU intervention.

Chipset specifications vary a great deal. Some of ways they vary are in what they can support, such as maximum amount of memory, type of memory, number and type of USB and SATA ports, type of video (DVI, VGA, HDMI), type of audio, type of firmware support (EUFI, BIOS, or both), and type of processor. As technology evolves, chipsets also evolve to support the newer technologies. For example, when a newer version of SATA or USB technology is released, a newer chipset will also be released to support that specific technology. Some major chipset manufacturers are Intel, SIS, and VIA.

Chipsets are an integral part of the motherboard and not field replacement units. You cannot change the chipset. Instead, you must replace the entire motherboard.

Expansion Card Slots

Expansion card slots provide a quick and easy method of connecting devices directly into the motherboard bus system. They are designed to hold inserted cards called *adapters*, *expansion cards*, *interface cards*, and *daughter boards*. This allows the technician to modify the existing computer system for additional hardware, such as network cards, which allow communications with a network, and television and radio adapter cards, which allow tuning a favorite radio station or watching television programs on the PC.

The most common expansion slot encountered is the PCI Express. USB and IEEE-1394 are not physically designed as a traditional slot. However, they are a type of hardware expansion architecture and are therefore covered in this section.

A+ Note

You may encounter information about legacy expansion card slots such as ISA, EISA, MCA, and VESA. You do not need to study these particular expansion card slots for the CompTIA A+ Certification.

PCI

Peripheral Components Interconnect (PCI) was introduced in the early 1990s and was the best choice for general purpose expansion cards, **Figure 3-14**. PCI has a 32-bit data width that transfers data at a rate of 132 MBps. The original PCI adapter had a frequency of 33 MHz which was later increased to 66 MHz with the PCI 2.0 standard.

PCI incorporates a chipset with a buffer, which is used for a temporary data storage area. The buffer makes it possible to communicate with a slow motherboard bus by providing a place to store data until the bus becomes available.

PCI dominated the motherboard adapter design for over ten years. However, demands for even greater data transfer rates spurred faster versions of PCI.

PCI-X

PCI Extended (PCI-X) was designed as a replacement for PCI. It has a 64-bit data width and is capable of operating at a higher frequency (speed) than PCI. It is fully downward compatible with PCI. You can install a PCI or PCI-X in the same expansion slot because they use the same pin assignments and same voltages. The only real difference is the higher frequency capability of PCI-X, which causes high data transfer rates. For example, the standard frequency of PCI-X 1.0 is 133 MHz. PCI-X 2.0 introduced the double data rate (DDR), which operates at 266 MHz, and the quad data rate (QDR), which operates at 533 MHz. These speeds are high enough to support data transfers to gigabit Ethernet network cards as the following table shows.

Bus Type	Speed	Capacity
PCI-X 1.0	133 MHz	8.5 Gbps
PCI-X 2.0 (DDR)	266 MHz	17 Gbps
PCI-X 3.0 (QDR)	533 MHz	34 Gbps

PCI-X was not widely accepted in desktop models of computers. Rather, it was limited to network servers and high-end desktop models. PCI-X was quickly replaced by the PCI Express standard.

PCI Express

PCI Express has two common acronyms: PCIe and PCI-E. It is often confused with PCI-X. PCI Express was introduced in 2004 as an expansion card technology designed to replace earlier versions of adapters such as PCI, PCI-X, and AGP. See **Figure 3-15**.

While the original PCI adapter is based on parallel data transfer, PCIe uses serial data transfer. Ordinarily, data transferred in parallel moves much more data than a serial connection. But, when it comes to electronics, you must understand electronic principles to see the advantage of serial data transfer over parallel.

At lower frequencies, parallel data transfer is better than serial, but at high speeds, serial data transfer is better than parallel. As the speed of computers has increased over the years, serial has become the preferred method of data transfer. This is because at high frequencies there are

Figure 3-14.
The edge connector of a 32-bit PCI expansion card. PCI cards are not compatible with other types of expansion slots.

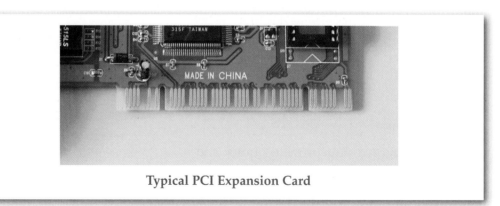

Typical PCI Expansion Card

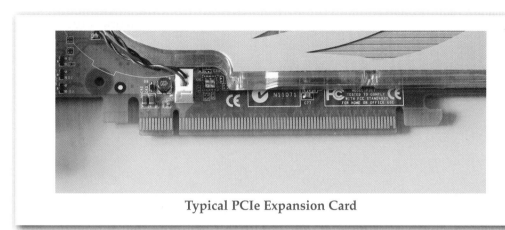

Typical PCIe Expansion Card

Figure 3-15.
Edge connector of a PCIe expansion card. PCIe uses serial data transfer and is designed to replace earlier versions of adapters such as PCI, PCI-X, and AGP.

Goodheart-Willcox Publisher

electrical limitations imposed by the parallel data bus design. Basically, there are two main circuit construction principles that must be followed to achieve high data rates:

- All circuit conductors need to be the same length.
- All conductors need to be bundled together, or in close proximity, to reduce the effects of inductive reactance.

The simple PCIe design meets both design principles and results in higher data rates. All PCIe conductors are the same length and are in close proximity.

Conductor Length

When conductors have the same length, data transferred across the bus system arrive at their destination at the same time. Parallel bus design involves right angle turns, which cause the length of the outside conductor to be many times longer than the inside conductor, **Figure 3-16**. Notice how the outside conductor length in Figure 13-16A is drastically longer in comparison to the inside conductor. This means that if data were sent in parallel over the conductors, the data would arrive at the ends of the conductors at different times. However, when conductors are run in pairs, as shown in Figure 3-16B, the overall length is more closely matched and a higher data rate can be achieved.

Conductor Proximity

Inductive reactance is an electronics term that basically describes a resistance to the flow of electrons through a conductor. All conductors have a degree of inductive reactance when functioning as an electrical path. Inductive reactance reduces the ability of the conductor to achieve high data rates. When the conductors are bundled together, inductive reactance is reduced to a minimum or nearly canceled, thus allowing for higher data rates than a flat ribbon data cable.

Since PCIe uses a pair of conductors in close proximity to each other, most of the effect of inductive reactance is canceled. This same principle of conductor pairs is used for IEEE-1394, USB, and SATA cables. These cables have all but replaced original flat ribbon data cable designs. **Figure 3-17** compares the design of PCIe ×1 conductors to traditional parallel conductors.

PCIe is designed from serial links referred to as *lanes*. The simplest PCIe identified as PCIe ×1 consists of a single lane. A single lane consists of two pairs of conductors, or four conductors total. One conductor of each pair is used to send data, and the other conductor of each pair is used to receive data. PCIe is bidirectional, which means it can send and receive data at the same time. A collection of lanes is referred to as a *link*.

The number of lanes used for PCIe is represented by the symbol "×" followed by a number. The symbol "×" represents the word "by."

Figure 3-16.
PCIe conductor pairs in a 64-conductor path. Notice the difference in total length of the outside conductors compared to the inside conductors. The PCIe conductor pairs closely match conductor lengths and are thus able to achieve a higher data rate.

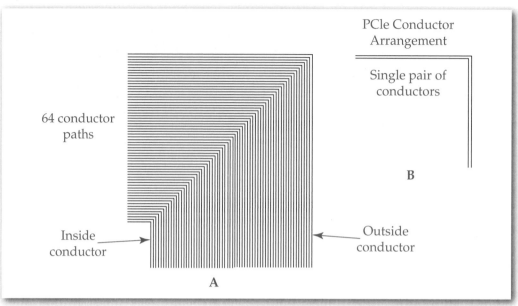

Figure 3-17.
Comparison of PCIe and parallel conductors. A—A PCIe lane consists of two pairs of conductors. Each pair forms a single communication pair. The pairs cancel most of the effect of inductive reactance, thus allowing a high data rate. B—Parallel conductors carry data in the same direction and do not cancel the effect of inductive reactance. This results in lower overall data rates when compared to PCIe.

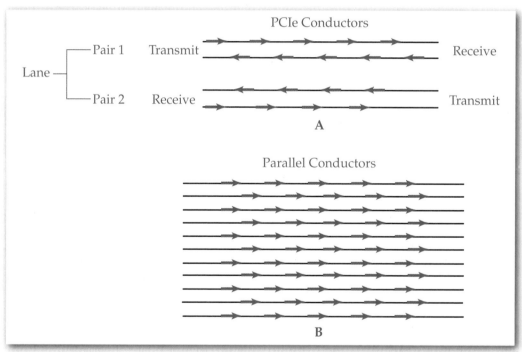

For example, PCIe ×16 means "PCIe by 16" and represents a PCIe adapter with 16 lanes, or pairs of conductors. There is a PCIe ×32 specification, but it has not been applied to desktop motherboard designs at the time of this writing.

PCIe Specifications

The original PCIe specification, PCIe 1.1, typically runs at 2.5 GHz and transfers data at a rate of 250 Mbps per lane. In January of 2007, the PCI Express 2.0 specification was released with an increase that doubled the throughput of data. The PCIe 2.0 specification raised the bandwidth from

2.5 GHz to 5.0 GHz and raised the data rate from 250 Mbps to 500 Mbps. The PCIe 3.0 standard raised the data rate to 1 Gbps. The following table compares these specifications as well as other specifications you may encounter.

Bus Type	PCIe 1.1	PCIe 2.0	PCIe 3.0
Raw Data Rate GT/s	2.5 GT/s	5 GT/s	8 GT/s
Interconnect Bandwidth	2 Gbps	4 Gbps	8 Gbps
Bandwidth per Lane per Direction	250 Mb/s	500 MB/s	1 Gb/s
Total Bandwidth for ×16 Link	8 Gb/s	16 Gb/s	32 Gb/s

Note: PCIe 4.0 is scheduled for 2014–2015 release and is proposed at this time by the PCI Special Interest Group (PCI-SIG). PCIe 4.0 is expected to double the PCIe 3.0 rates.

The second row in the table provides the raw data rate expressed in GT/s or gigatransfers per second. This rate is in gigabits per second and is the total amount of bits transferred across the data bus, including control and timing signals, which is commonly referred to as overhead. For example, to move 2 gigabits of image data across the PCI 1.1 bus, an additional 0.5 Gb (500 Mb) of data is required to control the flow of the 2 Gb image.

The next row, labeled Interconnect Bandwidth, lists the expected data rate between two devices connected with the PCIe bus. It is the expected data rate after the overhead has been accounted for. The row labeled Bandwidth per Lane is as stated: the data rate per lane. The final row, labeled Total Bandwidth for ×16 Link, is the total amount of data rate when using all 16 lanes to transfer data.

Parallel circuits are most often expressed in bytes (B) and serial is expressed in bits (b). This can add to the confusion when comparing the various bus technologies. The bus data width must also be considered. Early PCI and PCI-X used

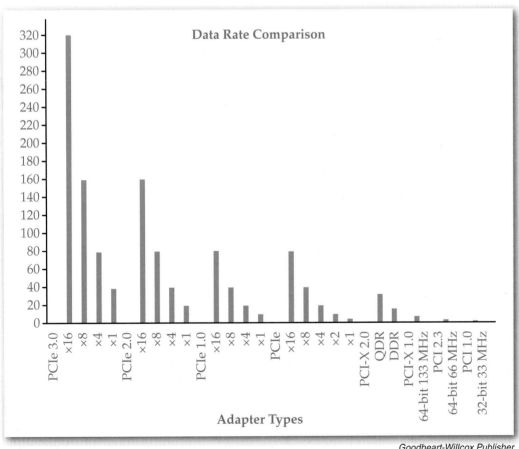

Figure 3-18.
PCI, PCI-X, and PCIe data rate comparison.

32-bit and 64-bit data bus widths. The bus width for PCIe is two, based on two pairs of conductors per lane. The chart in **Figure 3-18** compares the data speed of PCI, PCI-X, and PCIe standards. Notice that there is a tremendous performance difference between PCIe and earlier adapter technologies such as PCI.

A+ Note

The CompTIA A+ Certification exams may contain several questions based on expansion card speeds. You should memorize the total bandwidth values of PCIe 1.1, PCIe 2.0, and PCIe 3.0. After 2015, the CompTIA A+ exams will most likely include PCIe 4.0 when the finalized standard has been released. Always check the CompTIA website for the latest A+ exam objectives.

The PCIe standard maintains physical and electrical backward compatibility. This means you can install a PCIe 1.1 or PCIe 2.0 device into a PCIe 3.0 slot or install a PCIe 3.0 or PCIe 2.0 device into a PCIe 1.1 slot. The problem is when you mix two versions of PCIe slot and hardware devices, the result will be the device will operate at the lowest bandwidth of the two. In other words, if you install a PCIe 2.0 device with a bandwidth of 500 MB/s into a PCIe 1.1 expansion slot with a bandwidth of 250 MB/s, the result will be that the 500 MB/s device will only operate at 250 MB/s.

PCIe expansion cards are somewhat compatible. For example, a PCIe ×1 can be inserted into a PCIe ×4 slot and will perform without a problem. However, you cannot insert a PCIe ×4 into a PCIe ×1 slot because it is physically impossible. A variety of PCIe and PCI expansion slots on a motherboard are shown in **Figure 3-19**. PCIe provides better video performance than AGP and can be used for more devices than video cards. AGP is used only for video cards. To learn the latest up-to-date information about PCIe, visit the PCI-SIG (PCI Special Interest Group) website.

Figure 3-19.
This motherboard has a variety of PCIe expansion slots. Notice how they compare with one another and with the standard PCI expansion slots.

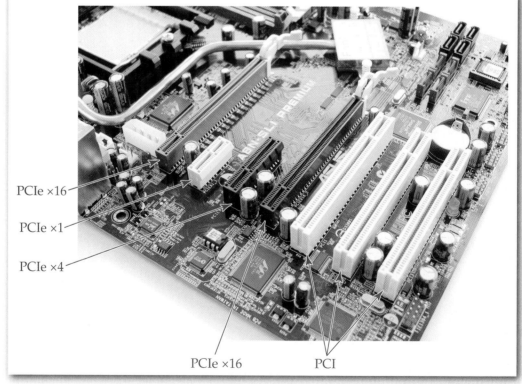

PCIe ×16

PCIe ×1

PCIe ×4

PCIe ×16   PCI

Goodheart-Willcox Publisher

MiniPCI and MiniPCIe

MiniPCI and mini PCIe are smaller versions of the full-size PCI and PCIe expansion cards. They are designed for laptops, notebooks, and similar portable devices. The design is typically used for wireless network cards. **Figure 3-20** shows a miniPCIe card next to a standard-size PCIe expansion card.

USB

The **Universal Serial Bus (USB)** system was designed to replace the existing variety of ports and expansion slots, such as serial and parallel ports and any expansion slot type, with the exception of high data-rate video expansion slots. USB is designed as a port rather than a traditional slot. The USB port connects to many different types of input and output peripherals and can support up to 127 devices. It is accessed by plugging a USB device or cable with attached device into the bus at a port opening in the case. Devices are simply daisy-chained when using USB cables. There is no need to open the computer case. **Figure 3-21** shows variety of USB 1.1 and 2.0 cable end connectors.

USB is designed for Plug and Play support. Devices connected to the port are automatically

Figure 3-20. Comparison of a miniPCIe expansion card to a standard-size PCIe expansion card.

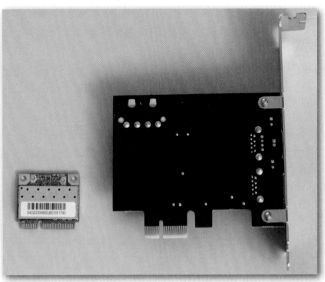

Goodheart-Willcox Publisher

detected, and communication between the computer system and the device begins. USB technologies conserve the use of IRQ assignments because each port only requires one IRQ, no matter how many devices are connected to it. For example, when two or more devices are connected to a USB port, they automatically share the same IRQ address without creating a conflict. Each

Figure 3-21. Three most commonly encountered USB 1.1 and USB 2.0 connectors used with desktop PCs.

Goodheart-Willcox Publisher

device that connects to the USB port is assigned an address for identification purposes. The devices take turns communicating through the USB port. Data is moved along the data lines as packets of information. This is similar to the way networks communicate.

For USB to work properly, an operating system and a recently developed chipset, such as Intel's 440LX, must be used. For example, when a newer USB standard is released, existing motherboard chipsets do not automatically support the new standard, even when the operating system does by using a software patch. The chipset and motherboard may not be designed for the improvements.

The following table lists the names associated with each USB standard and its data rate. The USB names, Low-Speed, Full-Speed, Hi-Speed, and SuperSpeed, were designated by the USB Implementers Forum (USB-IF). The USB-IF is responsible for developing the USB specifications.

Name	USB Standard	Data Rate
Low-Speed	1.0	1.5 Mbps
Full-Speed	1.1	12 Mbps
Hi-Speed	2.0	480 Mbps
SuperSpeed	3.0	5 Gbps

Note: The USB Implementers Forum (ISB-IF) refers to high-speed USB as "Hi-Speed" USB.

USB 3.0, also known as SuperSpeed USB, made many improvements over the USB 2.0 standard. The USB 3.0 standard provides much higher data transfer rates, raising the previous 2.0 standard from 480 Mbps to 5 Gbps—providing approximately 10 times more bandwidth. USB 3.0 also increased the output electrical power to 900 mA (milliamps) from the previous 500 mA associated with USB 2.0 standard. The 3.0 standard specifies that data can be transferred in both directions at the same time. This is technically referred to as full-duplex. USB 2.0 is limited to half-duplex transmissions, which means data can only be transferred in one direction at a time. For example, two devices connected by USB 2.0 must take turns when communicating.

Another improvement of USB 3.0 is less power consumption. USB 3.0 devices use less

power because the port is not constantly "poled" like it is with previous USB versions to see if a device is attached. The other major power-saving factor is the transfer speed. While USB 3.0 requires approximately twice as much power while performing data transfers, it transfers 10 times as much data. This is a net result of 1/5 total power consumed when transferring the same amount of data as USB 2.0. The last power-saving factor is data transfer overhead. USB 3.0 sends larger packets than USB 2.0, thus requiring less packet overhead (control signals). Therefore, no poling, faster data transfer, and less data transfer overhead result in less power consumption. This is good for devices that use batteries, such as cell phones and tablets.

USB Cables and Connectors

A USB 2.0 and earlier cable consists of four wires or conductors—two data lines (D+ and D–), a voltage bus (Vbus), and a ground (GND). See **Figure 3-22**. The combination of the Vbus and GND carry power to each device connected to the USB port. Since the actual amount of electrical power carried on the electrical power lines is low, devices requiring additional power use their own electrical power supply.

USB carries commands and data on the two twisted data lines. The twist in the data pair reduces the amount of inductive reactance and helps achieve the high data rates. This technique is also incorporated in some other computer high data-rate cables like SATA and network cables.

USB 3.0 increased the number of conductors (wires) and connection pins to achieve high bandwidth. **Figure 3-23** compares the USB 2.0

Figure 3-22. USB cable design.

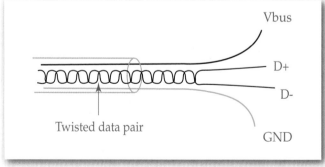

Goodheart-Willcox Publisher

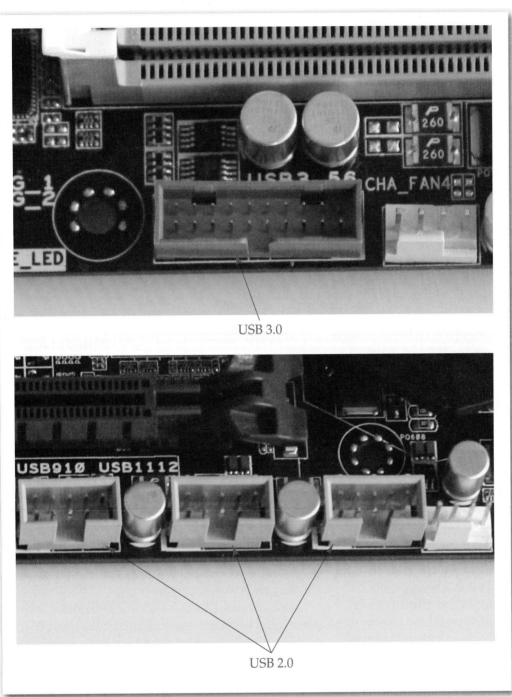

Figure 3-23.
USB 3.0 and USB 2.0
motherboard
connection
comparison. The
USB 3.0 connection
provides additional
pins to achieve higher
bandwidth than
USB 2.0.

USB 3.0

USB 2.0

Goodheart-Willcox Publisher

motherboard connections with the USB 3.0 connections. Notice the increased pin count for USB 3.0 compared to USB 2.0. The tables in **Figure 2-24** list and describe the pinouts for USB 2.0 and earlier and USB 3.0. Notice that USB 3.0 has an additional two pairs of data transmission wires labeled TX–, TX+, RX–, and RX+. The two pairs of additional data lines are in addition to the single pair of USB 2.0 data lines labeled D– and D+. The additional USB 3.0 data lines are why USB 3.0 has a higher data rate than USB 2.0. Also notice how the first four pins of the USB 3.0 pinout perfectly match the USB 2.0 and earlier pinouts.

USB 2.0 cable length is 5 meters. USB 3.0 has no specified length, but is generally 3 meters

Figure 3-24. USB connector pinouts for USB 2.0 and earlier and USB 3.0.

USB 1.0, 1.1, and 2.0		
Pin Number	Identification	Purpose
1	Vbus	Electrical 5 volts
2	D–	Data
3	D+	Data
4	GND	Electrical ground
USB 3.0		
Pin Number	Identification	Purpose
1	Vbus	Electrical 5 volts
2	D–	USB 2.0 data
3	D+	USB 2.0 data
4	GND	Electrical ground for power
5	RX–	USB 3.0 signal receive
6	RX+	USB 3.0 signal receive
7	GND	Electrical ground for signals
8	TX–	USB 3.0 signal transmit
9	TX+	USB 3.0 signal transmit
10	GND	Connection shield ground

Goodheart-Willcox Publisher

Figure 3-25. USB connector types. (Not to scale.)

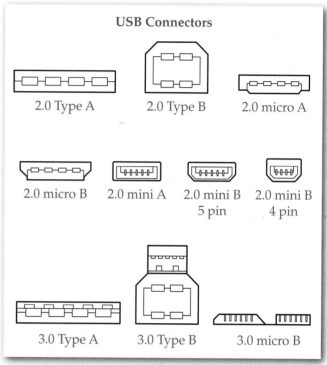

Goodheart-Willcox Publisher

long. There are two general variations of USB connectors: Type A and Type B. The Type A USB connectors and ports are found on almost every full-size desktop computer. Type B USB connectors and ports are found mostly on printers, scanners, and external storage devices. The micro and mini styles are found typically on portable devices, such as cell phones, music players, cameras, tablets, GPS, and palmtops.

Figure 3-25 shows the general shape and number of connection pins for each USB 2.0 and USB 3.0 connector, Type A and Type B. Not included is USB 1.0, which is obsolete but has the same physical shape as USB 2.0. There are also several proprietary connector shapes not included that are similar to the micro and mini connector shapes.

The USB Type A for 2.0 and 3.0 are physically the same shape. The difference between the two is that USB 2.0 has four pins and the USB 3.0 has nine pins. The USB 2.0 mini Type B comes in two varieties: five pin and four pin. Even though they share the same name, they are physically different. Other similar USB connectors exist that are proprietary. They are typically found on mobile devices such as cell phones.

When both USB 2.0 and USB 3.0 ports are available on a computer, the USB 3.0 port is typically identified with a blue connector, **Figure 3-26.** The USB 3.0 standard does not specify that the color blue be used, but blue has been widely accepted and will most likely become a "de facto" standard. Also, most computers use some type of port shield with markings, indicating the location of the USB 3.0 and USB 2.0 ports. Because the two ports are physically compatible, they need to be properly identified. If a person attaches a USB 3.0 device to a USB 2.0 port, the device would not achieve the expected bandwidth. The same problem could occur if the user attached a USB 3.0 device to a USB 3.0 port but used a cable designed for USB 2.0 or older.

Tech Tip

You must use high-speed USB 3.0 cables when connecting to USB 3.0 ports to achieve the 5 Gbps bandwidth. If you use a USB 2.0 cable with a USB 3.0 port, you will only achieve the USB 2.0 standard bandwidth, or 480 Mbps.

Upgrading to USB 3.0

To upgrade a computer from 2.0 to 3.0 is easy. An expansion card like the one shown in **Figure 3-27** can be installed into a PCIe slot to provide additional USB 3.0 ports. Notice that the disc provides the necessary software drivers. Windows XP, Windows Vista, and Windows 7 do not directly support USB 3.0 devices, which means you must install new drivers. After the

Figure 3-26.
USB 2.0 and USB 3.0 ports on the back of a computer.

Goodheart-Willcox Publisher

Figure 3-27.
An expansion card can be installed into a PCIe slot to provide additional USB 3.0 ports on an existing system.

Goodheart-Willcox Publisher

drivers are installed, the USB 3.0 ports can be used. Without the proper drivers, the USB 3.0 data speeds cannot be achieved. The USB port would behave like USB 2.0 port, or not at all. Windows XP and Windows Vista do not have a service pack that provides drivers for USB 3.0. Also, Windows 7 may or may not provide a service pack or hot fix for USB 3.0. Windows 8 supports USB 3.0, so the provided drivers would not have to be installed.

Notice the white connector on the expansion card in Figure 3-27. This is a typical Molex power connector. USB 3.0 is designed to provide up to 900 mA of current to USB 3.0 devices. This is almost one full ampere of electrical current. The PCIe bus is not designed to supply this amount of current. That is why a separate power connection is provided to the expansion card.

To upgrade to USB 3.0, you can also install exterior ports using an adapter similar to the one in **Figure 3-28**. The adapter is installed into an empty slot in the back of the PC case, and the cables are plugged into the appropriate port on the motherboard. There are also adapters made to fit into the front of the PC case.

External SATA

SATA technology was originally limited to internal PC connections used for hard drives and DVD drives. External SATA (eSATA) allows devices to be connected outside the PC case.

Figure 3-28.
This adapter provides extra USB 3.0 ports to a computer.

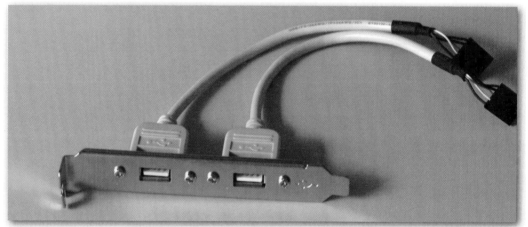

Goodheart-Willcox Publisher

Figure 3-29.
SATA and eSATA cable end connectors.

SATA   eSATA

Goodheart-Willcox Publisher

Figure 3-29 shows SATA and eSATA cables. These cables and ports are often confused with USB cables and ports. Upon a closer examination you will notice that SATA and eSATA both have physical differences when compared to USB Type A ports and connectors. Figure 3-26 also shows an example of an eSATA port. There will be much more about SATA in Chapter 9—Storage Devices.

IEEE-1394

Specification **IEEE-1394** was first introduced by Apple Computer systems and called by the trade name *FireWire*, **Figure 3-30**. Other manufacturers call their similar systems names such as *i.link* and *Lynx*. There are two IEEE-1394 standards: IEEE-1394a and IEEE-1394b. The IEEE-1394a standard provides a high rate of data transfer at 400 Mbps. IEEE-1394b is twice as fast at 800 Mbps. FireWire is needed for devices such as video cameras, which require a high data rate. A single IEEE-1394 port can serve up to 63 external devices in daisy-chain fashion.

With the introduction of USB and IEEE-1394, manufacturers have been reducing the number of slots available on the motherboard. The use of USB and IEEE-1394 has eliminated the need for expansion slots and parallel and serial ports. USB and IEEE-1394 can be used to connect any device that presently uses motherboard adapter slot technology.

IEEE-1394 is becoming less common to find on a PC. When a computer requires an IEEE-1394 port, you can easily add one by installing an IEEE-1394 adapter card into an available PCIe slot on the motherboard.

AGP

The **Accelerated Graphics Port (AGP)** was designed exclusively for the video card, **Figure 3-31**, especially for 3-D graphic support. There is usually only one slot of this type on any motherboard. The slot is designed to fit as close as possible to the CPU and RAM to allow for high data transfer rates. The bandwidth for transferring data to and from the AGP can be significantly faster than PCI. AGP supports 32-bit data transfers at speeds ranging from 266 MBps for AGP 1.0 to 2,133 MBps for AGP 2.0, as shown in the following table.

Standard	Speed	Data Rate
AGP 1.0	1×	266 MBps
AGP 1.0	2×	533 MBps
AGP 2.0	4×	1,066 MBps
AGP 3.0	8×	2,133 MBps

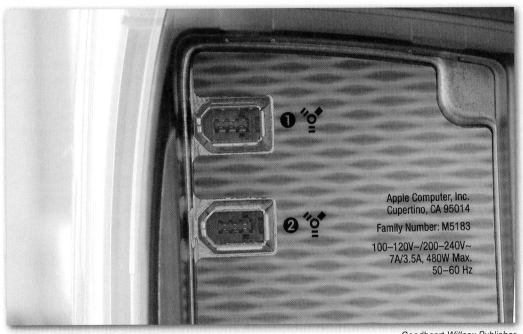

Figure 3-30. IEEE-1394 (FireWire) ports.

Figure 3-31.
The edge connector of a 32-bit AGP expansion card.

Goodheart-Willcox Publisher

AGP offered excellent support for graphics programs until the introduction of PCIe. The most powerful feature of AGP is DIME (Direct Memory Execute). DIME is the direct access to main memory used strictly to support video. This means the video card can use large portions of RAM rather than only the memory modules located on the video card.

AGP is almost obsolete at the time of this writing and most video cards are PCIe. You may still need to replace an AGP video card when repairing a legacy PC. There will be much more about AGP, PCI, and PCIe as applied to video cards later in the textbook. For now, be able to identify these technologies and explain what they are used for most commonly.

AMR, ACR, and CNR

There are many devices that are commonly used in a standard desktop computer. By combining the functions of several separate technologies into a single unit, a more economical device can be produced. Manufacturers can combine the functions of audio, USB, modem, DSL, network connection (Ethernet), wireless access technologies, and more. Three special motherboard slot specifications that meet this need are Audio/Modem Riser (AMR), Advanced Communications Riser (ACR), and Communications and Networking Riser (CNR). The combined technologies are incorporated into one riser board, which is inserted into a slot on the motherboard. See **Figure 3-32**.

CNR is a royalty-free standard developed by Intel Corporation. ACR is an organization that developed the ACR standard and is supported by 3COM, AMD, Lucent Technologies, VIA

Technologies, Motorola, Texas Instruments, ACER, PCTEL, and others.

The AMR technology was released first and was closely followed by CNR. CNR is the more popular choice by computer hardware manufacturers because it is royalty free and uses the same space as the PCI slot. With CNR sharing a PCI slot on the motherboard, the manufacturer does not need to make a major design change in the motherboard structure and circuitry the way they would for an AMR slot. AMR was later replaced by ACR. ACR is backward compatible with AMR.

The Intel CNR board supports on a single card up to four different devices out of a possible seven types of devices. The slot location is typically located at the edge of the motherboard, far away from components that produce interference. The riser cards incorporate audio devices. Audio can be corrupted by stray electromagnetic interference generated by other high-speed components.

Riser board technology is favorable for development of low-cost motherboard manufacturing, but there are two problems. First, if one or more of the devices incorporated into the riser board goes bad, the entire board will need to be replaced at a higher cost than if replacing a single item such as a modem card. Second, the cost of a replacement board is higher because you need to go through the original manufacturer.

System Resources

System resources must be assigned and made available for devices such as printers, modems, hard drives, DVD drives, and sound cards. The major system resources to consider are the I/O port address, memory addresses, IRQ, and

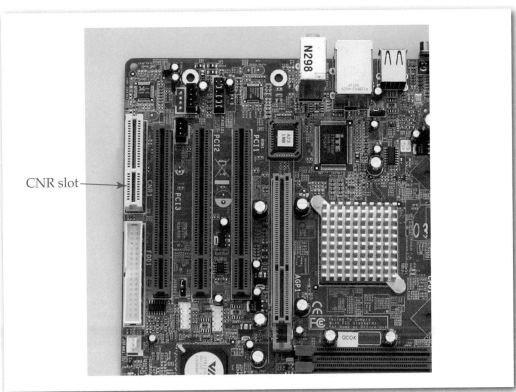

Figure 3-32.
Notice that the CNR slot is located at the edge of the motherboard.

DMA settings. Typically, system resources are automatically assigned by the operating system and device drivers. The PC technician rarely has to manually conFigure a hardware device but must be prepared to reconFigure the device if needed.

Device Manager

System resource assignments can be viewed in Windows Device Manager. To see the system resources assigned to a Windows 7 or Windows Vista computer, right-click **Computer** on the **Start** menu. The right-click brings up a shortcut menu. Click **Properties**. The **System** dialog box will display, **Figure 3-33**. Select the **Device Manager** option. You should see a screen similar to the one in **Figure 3-34**.

On a Windows XP computer, right-click the **My Computer** icon located on the desktop. The right-click brings up a shortcut menu. Click **Properties**. The **System Properties** dialog box will display. Select the **Hardware** tab, and then click the **Device Manager** button.

You can also access Device Manager by typing "Device Manager" in the **Search** box located on the **Start** menu. The **Search** box is a common way to access Device Manager in Windows 8.

Device Manager presents you with a list of hardware devices installed in the computer system. The general hardware items listed can be expanded to show individual hardware devices identified by name.

> ## A+ Note
> Be sure you know the various ways to access Device Manager and what modifications can be made to hardware devices from Device Manager.

To access the **Properties** dialog box for a specific hardware device, you can either right-click the device and select **Properties** from the shortcut menu or select **Properties** from the **Action** menu listed at the top of Device Manager. The

Figure 3-33.
The **System** dialog box.

Figure 3-34.
Device Manager is used to view hardware devices in the computer system and to conFigure or modify device resources and hardware drivers.

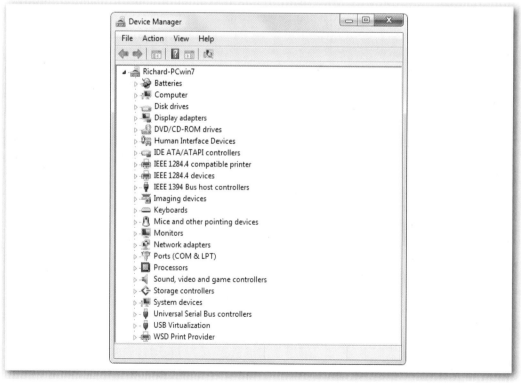

Properties dialog box displays information about the hardware configuration and resources. There are options to make changes to the hardware device driver. **Figure 3-35** shows the information revealed by each of the four tabs associated with the **Properties** dialog box of an AMD Radeon HD 6800 series video card. Notice that you can view driver details as well as update the driver, disable the hardware device, uninstall a driver, and roll back a driver to an earlier version if a driver has been installed previously. The **Resources** tab reveals the system resources assigned to the hardware device. Windows 8 added the **Event** tab, **Figure 3-36**. The **Event** tab reveals information

about changes that have occurred to the hardware device over time.

System Information

System resources can also be viewed from the System Information program, **Figure 3-37**. This program is accessed by running msinfo32.exe. To run this file, you can enter **msinfo32** or **System Information** in the **Search** box and then select the appropriate result.

The left pane lists the categories of information that can be viewed. When a category or subcategory is selected, the related information

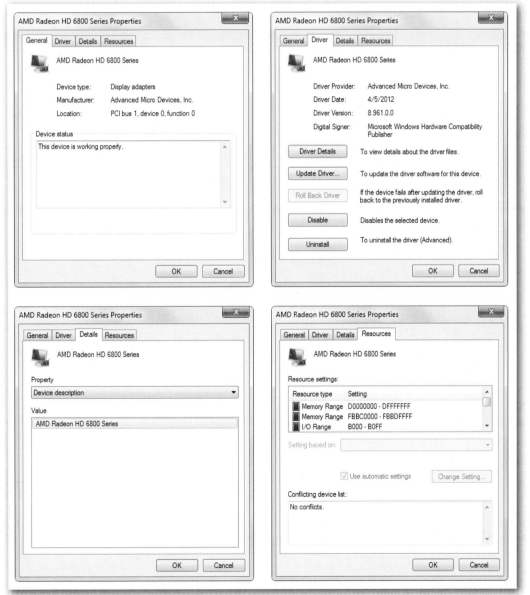

Figure 3-35.
Screen captures of the four tabs associated with the **Properties** dialog box of an AMD Radeon HD 6800 series video card.

Figure 3-36. Windows 8 adds an **Events** tab to the **Properties** dialog box for a hardware device.

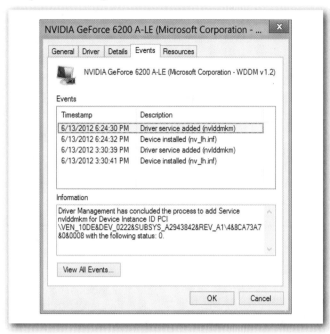

is displayed in the right pane. When **System Summary** is selected, information, such as the operating system name and version, system (computer) name, user name, processor type, and BIOS version is displayed. The system resources are located in the subcategories under the **Hardware Resources** category. These subcategories are **Conflict/Sharing**, **DMA**, **Forced Hardware**, **I/O**, **IRQs**, and **Memory**. Click the plus (+) sign next to **Hardware Resources** to see the subcategories. In **Figure 3-38**, the **IRQs** subcategory is selected and information about the assigned IRQs are shown in the right pane. You can see which IRQs are assigned to which device. This is a handy way to view the hardware resource assignments. There are menu options to save the system information into a text file format or to print the summary.

Figure 3-37. System Information program.

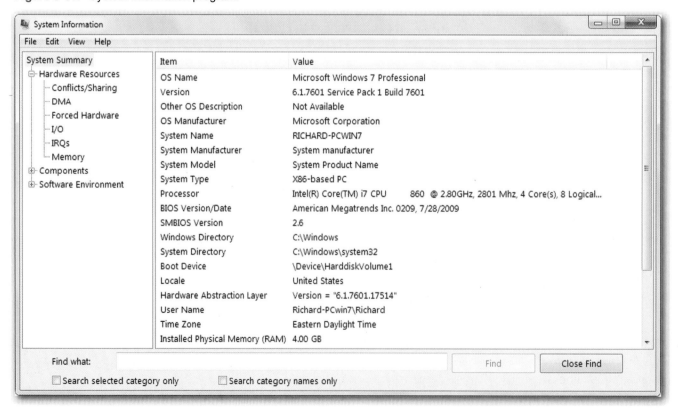

Figure 3-38. System resources can be viewed in System Information.

Resource	Device	Status
IRQ 0	System timer	OK
IRQ 3	Intel(R) 5 Series/3400 Series Chipset Family SMB...	OK
IRQ 4	Communications Port (COM1)	OK
IRQ 8	System CMOS/real time clock	OK
IRQ 13	Numeric data processor	OK
IRQ 14	ATA Channel 0	OK
IRQ 15	ATA Channel 1	OK
IRQ 16	Intel(R) 5 Series/3400 Series Chipset Family USB...	OK
IRQ 16	Intel(R) processor PCI Express Root Port 1 - D138	OK
IRQ 16	Intel(R) 5 Series/3400 Series Chipset Family PCI ...	OK
IRQ 17	High Definition Audio Controller	OK
IRQ 17	Intel(R) 5 Series/3400 Series Chipset Family PCI ...	OK
IRQ 17	Intel(R) 5 Series/3400 Series Chipset Family PCI ...	OK
IRQ 18	Intel(R) 5 Series/3400 Series Chipset Family PCI ...	OK
IRQ 18	VIA 1394 OHCI Compliant Host Controller	OK
IRQ 18	JMicron JMB36X Controller	OK
IRQ 19	Intel(R) 5 Series/3400 Series Chipset Family PCI ...	OK
IRQ 19	Realtek PCI GBE Family Controller	OK
IRQ 21	Intel(R) 5 Series/3400 Series Chipset Family 2 p...	OK

I/O Port and Memory Address Range

Each device has a unique memory address range. Components such as DVD drives, hard drives, and monitors require part of the computer system's memory to be used for temporary data storage. A **memory address range** is an assigned section of memory used as a temporary storage area for data before it is transferred. An **I/O port address** is assigned to a device for identification. A device must be identified for communication purposes. Both the I/O port and the memory address are expressed as a range and in hexadecimal notation such as 03B0–03BB. Some devices have an I/O port address and a name.

A memory address is often mistaken for an I/O port address because a memory address also uses hexadecimal numbers for their assignments. Look at the resources assigned to a video card in **Figure 3-39**. The memory address range is the area used to store large amounts of video information, and the I/O port is used to control communication between the video card and the CPU. For example,

Figure 3-39. Resources assigned to a video graphics card.

if a command is issued on the bus for I/O port address number B000–B0FF, then the device that is assigned port number B000–B0FF accepts the command. If a large amount of video information is sent to the video card, the information is temporarily stored in the memory location range of FBBC0000–FBBDFFFF. Video cards require a large amount (range) of memory. Not all hardware devices have an assigned memory range, but most do have an assigned I/O port address range.

IRQ Settings

Devices connected to a computer motherboard need the attention of the CPU. The only way to share the attention of the CPU is through an orderly system of IRQ settings. *IRQ* is an acronym for interrupt request. An IRQ literally interrupts the processes taking place in the CPU to give attention to some device such as a keyboard. In addition to hardware interrupts are software interrupts. Software interrupts are programmed into the software and call for the CPU's attention. Hardware interrupts are physically wired to the computer bus.

Figure 3-40 shows a listing of typical hardware IRQ assignments. Early PC designs used only eight IRQs numbered 0 through 7. Today, 16 IRQ settings are used, numbered 0 through 15. Many of the IRQ settings are standard, such as the system timer, keyboard, COM1, LPT, primary IDE, and secondary IDE. Also, computer systems are not limited to 16 hardware IRQ assignments. An unlimited number of IRQ assignments can be assigned through software. When an IRQ assignment is created using software, it is a logical or virtual assignment. The virtual assignments allow for flexibility and solve system conflicts much more easily. Look again at Figure 3-38 to see IRQ assignments higher than IRQ 16.

> **Tech Tip**
> When the IRQ design evolved from 8 to 16 IRQs, IRQ 2 was cascaded with IRQ 9. This means that IRQ 2 should never be assigned to any device because IRQ 2 communicates with IRQ 9.

IRQs are also assigned priorities. A lower number for an IRQ means a higher priority. Look at the system timer in Figure 3-40. It is assigned to IRQ 0. This gives it the highest priority, as it

Figure 3-40.
Table of IRQ settings cascading from IRQ 2 to IRQ 9. Notice that this is a typical set of IRQ assignments. They will not match all computers. Many IRQs will have more than one device assigned to them, especially controller chips.

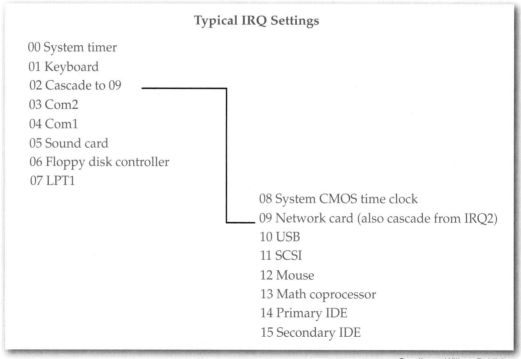

Typical IRQ Settings

00 System timer
01 Keyboard
02 Cascade to 09
03 Com2
04 Com1
05 Sound card
06 Floppy disk controller
07 LPT1

08 System CMOS time clock
09 Network card (also cascade from IRQ2)
10 USB
11 SCSI
12 Mouse
13 Math coprocessor
14 Primary IDE
15 Secondary IDE

should be. The system timer is responsible for the timing of all devices, including the CPU.

Another important aspect of IRQ assignments are IRQ conflicts that arise when two or more devices assigned the same IRQ setting try to access the CPU at the same time. When this happens, the conflicting request for attention can cause some strange occurrences. Usually only one of the two devices will have access to the CPU, leaving the other the appearance of being dead.

Two IRQ assignments can be shared if the devices are not going to be used at the same time. An example of two such devices would be a scanner and a camera. A digital camera can share an IRQ assignment with a scanner because it is highly unlikely both would be used at the same time. However, if the mouse and a floppy drive were assigned the same IRQ setting, a problem would arise. If the mouse was identified first by the CPU, then the floppy drive would appear disabled. If the floppy drive was identified first by the CPU, the mouse would appear to be disabled. Today, many chipsets are identified by IRQs and are shared with other chipsets and devices. Plug and Play (PnP) technology remedies most of the assignment problems. This technology is covered later in this chapter.

Examine **Figure 3-41**. Here you see an interrupt request assignment viewed through the **Properties** dialog box for a system device. This dialog box is often used to verify or change IRQ settings. To view these settings for a device, in Device Manager, double-click the device you are interested in. You can also right-click the device and select **Properties**.

DMA Channels

In the early days of computers, the CPU was designed to control all devices and their functions. For example, when data was moved from the hard drive to the RAM memory, each bit would have to be transferred to the CPU, and then the CPU would transfer the bit to the memory location. **Direct memory access (DMA),** is a combination of hardware and software that allows the hard drive to transfer all the data directly to memory without involving the CPU. Waiting for the CPU to take action caused a bottleneck for the transfer of data in the computer system. If the data did not need the CPU's attention, a device that has DMA could transfer the data directly into memory via the DMA controller.

The DMA controller is a chip that connects certain devices directly to memory, bypassing the CPU. Each DMA controller has four channels. There is one device connected per channel. A motherboard with a DMA controller has a total of eight channels available for devices. **Figure 3-42**

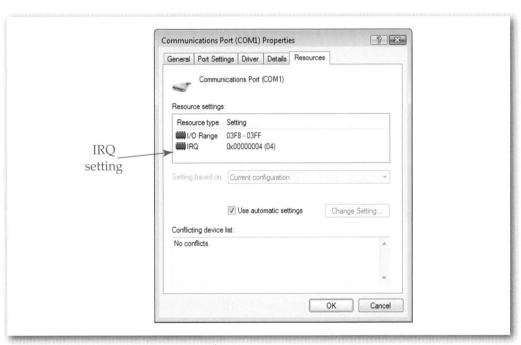

Figure 3-41. Through the **Properties** dialog box of a system device, you can view specific device properties. This can show you the IRQ being used by the device.

Figure 3-42.
The **Properties** dialog
box for a system device
will also show you
DMA assignments for
devices.

DMA
setting

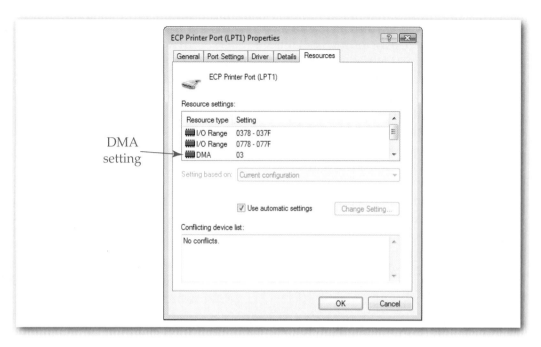

shows the DMA assignment for a printer port (LPT1) on a PC. DMA settings, like IRQ and I/O settings, can be viewed through the **Properties** dialog box for a system device.

DMA technology was used mainly for PATA hard drives, legacy printers, and floppy drives. Today, DMA assigned to a device is seldom encountered. Chipsets eliminate the need for DMA assignments. The DMA controller still exists on modern computers to ensure backward compatibility with legacy devices. You can still see DMA assignment for floppy drives, some types of PATA hard drives, and legacy type printers using RS232 type connections.

Bus Mastering

Bus mastering was another method of control that allowed data to be transferred directly between two devices without the intervention of the CPU. Control of the bus is usually taken while the CPU is busy with a task that does not require the use of the bus system.

Even though bus mastering and DMA sound similar, they are different. The main difference between bus mastering and DMA is the intent of the device. Bus mastering takes control of the bus system to which it is attached, while DMA is used to access the memory system. DMA is designed to allow devices to communicate directly to and

from the memory (RAM) without the intervention of the CPU. Bus mastering technology allows devices to carry out specific tasks such as communicating with each other without direct intervention of the CPU. It allows devices to carry out their individual tasks without using the CPU for each and every bit transfer. While the CPU is busy with other tasks such as calculations, the bus master controller controls the communication between two devices on the bus system.

Both DMA and bus mastering were designed to speed up the common operations involving data flow. To use either technology, the device as well as the BIOS, the operating system software, and the motherboard chipset must be designed to support the technology. The function of Bus mastering and DMA has been incorporated into modern motherboard chipsets.

Plug and Play

Plug and Play (PnP) is the automatic assignment of system resources such as DMA channels, interrupts, memory, and port assignments. As the name implies, with Plug and Play you simply plug in a device, for example a network card, and the system software automatically assigns the system resources. There is no need to manually conFigure the system resources. For Plug and Play to work, the BIOS, the hardware being installed, and the operating system must all support Plug and Play technology.

Before Plug and Play, expansion cards required the installer to set jumpers or dip switches into specific configurations to identify such things as the card's IRQ setting and port address.

Plug and Play works well most of the time, but not for every case. There are times when you must intervene. For example, you may encounter some difficulty when installing a device that incorporates newer technology than when the operating system was developed.

Installing Software Drivers

Many hardware device manufacturers recommend that you install the software drivers before installing the device. By installing the drivers first, the operating system can find the correct drivers. If the device is installed before the correct driver is installed, the operating system may choose a generic driver or incorrectly identify the device. When this happens, the device may not function properly. Software drivers, also called device drivers, are typically on the accompanying CD/DVD. If the hardware driver did not come with the device, you can typically download it from the manufacturer's website.

Device Manager has a **Roll Back Driver** option, which can be used to replace the current driver with an earlier version. There is also an **Update Driver** option, which as the name implies, automatically searches for a newer version of the driver. One problem that is often encountered is when a new hardware device is installed, the operating system may incorrectly identify the device and either install the incorrect updated driver or not install an updated driver at all. As stated earlier, these problems can be solved by using the information at the manufacturer's website.

Motherboard chipsets also require software drivers. A common mistake made by novices when building a computer system or replacing the motherboard is to not install the motherboard drivers. When this occurs, the computer system may fail to correctly support hardware devices connected to the motherboard. Motherboard drivers are located on a setup CD/DVD that

typically accompanies the motherboard. The drivers for the motherboard are not the same as the firmware software in the BIOS or UEFI. Also, the setup CD/DVD typically contains other commercial software, such as trial versions of antivirus software.

> **Tech Tip**
>
> Motherboard drivers are located at the motherboard manufacturer's website or through the vendor of the computer system, such as ASUS or Intel.

When installing the motherboard drivers using the setup CD/DVD, it is important to read all the information provided on the disc and to perform a custom install rather than a default install. The default install will typically install all software that comes on the disc, which includes trial versions of commercial products such as web browser software, security suites, and computer utilities. When a custom install is selected, you can choose exactly which products you wish to install. If you install a security suite from the motherboard disc and then install another security suite or antivirus program, computer performance will be greatly decreased. Multiple security system software on the same computer is not a good practice. There will be more about this issue later in the textbook.

Upgrading the BIOS

Upgrading the BIOS is fairly common when upgrading hardware systems on older computers. In addition, upgrading the BIOS is not just for hardware concerns. Certain software programs can require an upgraded version of the BIOS. For example, when Plug and Play was introduced to consumers, problems arose when trying to use the new Plug and Play technology. The appropriate operating system may have been available and a Plug and Play device installed, however, the system could not detect or support the device until the BIOS was upgraded.

To upgrade the BIOS program on early computer motherboards, the BIOS chip had to be replaced or an ultraviolet light had to be used to erase the program stored on the BIOS chip in order to reprogram it. The first programs were electrically etched into the microscopic circuitry inside the BIOS chip. The style of chip was referred to as programmable read-only memory (PROM). These chips were programmed once by the manufacturer and could not be reprogrammed. They simply had to be replaced.

Another variation of the BIOS chip called the erasable programmable read-only memory (EPROM) was developed. This chip had a transparent window usually covered by a foil patch. The foil patch was a sticker with the BIOS manufacturer name and part identification on it. When the label was removed, a window exposing the circuitry inside the chip was revealed. If an ultraviolet light was shined through the exposed window, the program in the chip would be erased. This process allowed the chip to be reprogrammed. These past techniques are no longer used.

Modern PCs use flash BIOS. **Flash BIOS** is an electrically erasable programmable read-only memory (EEPROM) module, which can be erased electrically and then reprogrammed. Flash BIOS is easily reprogrammed using software available through the motherboard manufacturer's website and an updated BIOS program file.

> **Tech Tip**
> Upgrading the BIOS can render the PC inoperable. Visit the manufacturer's website first and read all information pertaining to upgrading the BIOS. Follow the manufacturer's instructions for upgrading your particular BIOS.

The following are general instructions for upgrading flash BIOS. Be sure to always follow the manufacturer's instructions for upgrading a specific BIOS.

1. Download the BIOS upgrade program and the updated BIOS program file from the motherboard manufacturer's website.
2. Copy the BIOS upgrade program and the updated BIOS program file onto a USB flash drive.
3. Boot the PC with the USB flash drive inserted into a USB port.
4. Run the BIOS upgrade program.
5. When the BIOS upgrade program asks for the name of the BIOS program file, enter the exact name of the BIOS program file.
6. If the BIOS upgrade program asks you if you want to back up the contents of the BIOS, answer "yes." Having a backup of the BIOS is vital if you need to return the BIOS to its original state. The BIOS upgrade program will then back up the original contents of the BIOS, erase the contents from the BIOS, and write the new BIOS program file to the BIOS.
7. When the procedure has successfully completed, reboot your PC and enter the Setup utility. Do not be alarmed if you do not see the new BIOS date and information in the Setup utility screen.
8. Enter the Setup utility and set it to its default settings.
9. Save the changes and reboot the computer.
10. When the computer is rebooting, enter the Setup utility again. You will now see the date of the new BIOS program.
11. Enter the correct settings for your system.
12. Save the changes and reboot the computer.

> **Tech Tip**
> Details vary somewhat for different motherboards and BIOS upgrade procedures. For detailed steps on upgrading a particular BIOS, consult the manufacturer's website.

On most current motherboards, the BIOS can be automatically upgraded through the Windows operating system. For example, the Intel Express BIOS Update utility can be downloaded via the Internet and saved as an executable file (.exe) in the default Downloads folder. To start the upgrade process, you simply double-click the executable file. The familiar InstallShield Wizard followed by the typical license agreement will display. When you click **Finish**, the computer will automatically reboot and start the upgrade process. The status of the upgrade process will appear on the screen in text format. The computer will restart once again when the BIOS upgrade process is complete.

The USB BIOS Flashback button found on the back of some ASUS motherboards, **Figure 3-43**, also allows a PC technician to update the system

USB Flashback button / White USB 2.0 port

Figure 3-43.
The USB BIOS Flashback button and white USB 2.0 port on the back of this ASUS motherboard allows a PC technician to update the system BIOS.

Goodheart-Willcox Publisher

BIOS. The technician must first download the newest version of firmware to a USB flash drive and then insert the drive into the white USB 2.0 port beside the USB BIOS Flashback button. Next, the technician presses the button. The firmware is automatically upgraded.

Setup Utility

To store a computer's date and time and information about its hardware in CMOS, the Setup utility is used. The Setup utility allows you to do the following:

- Identify the type of hard drive and other storage systems installed.
- Identify the type of chipset installed.
- Set up a password for accessing the Setup utility.
- Select power management features.
- ConFigure the boot order of the hard drive, CD/DVD drive, USB flash drive, and solid-state drive (SSD).

The Setup utility is activated by a special set of keyboard strokes during the boot up period. The instructions for accessing the Setup utility are often displayed on the screen. When they are not displayed, accessing a computer's Setup utility can be difficult. There are many different ways to access the Setup utility. Examine **Figure 3-44**. These key combinations could prove helpful for the troublesome computer. Keep in mind that what works for a particular brand one day

Figure 3-44. Possible key combinations for accessing the Setup utility.

BIOS Manufacturer	Key(s) to Press
AMI	[Del] or [Esc] key during POST
Award, Phoenix	[Ctrl] + [Alt] + [Esc] or [Ctrl] + [Alt] + [S] or [F2] during POST
Computer Manufacturer	
Dell	[Ctrl] + [Alt] + [Enter]
Compact	[F2] or [F10] or [Ctrl] + [Alt] + [F2]
DTK	[Esc]
IBM PS/2	[Ctrl] + [Alt] + [Del] followed by [Ctrl] + [Alt] + [Ins]
Gateway 2000	[F1]
Sony PC	[F3] while booting followed by [F1] at Sony logo
NEC	[F1] when cursor flashes on screen

Goodheart-Willcox Publisher

may not work in the future. Another way to find the right key combination is to check the manufacturer's website. You may have to open the computer case and look at the brand and model number on the BIOS chip.

Figure 3-45 shows a typical Setup utility screen. Not all Setup utility screens look the same, but they are similar in appearance and in function. The most obvious difference between traditional BIOS and UEFI Setup utilities is the appearance. UEFI firmware has a true high-resolution GUI and

Figure 3-45. Screen displays for Setup utility and exit screen.

```
System Time:              [14:45:47]
System Date               [06/09/2000]

Language                  English
Diskette A:               [1.44 MB, 31/2]
Diskette B:               [Not Installed]
>IDE Adapter 0 Master     [C:2.2 GB]
>IDE Adapter 0 Slave      [None]
>IDE Adapter 1 Master     [None]
>IDE Adapter 1 Slave      [None]
Video Systems             [EGA/VGA]
>Memory and Cache
>Boot Options
>Keyboard Features
```

```
Save Changes & Exit
Discard Changes & Exit
Get Default Values
Load Previous Values
Save Changes
```

Typical exit screen leaving
the Setup utility routine

Above is a typical first screen display
of Setup utility program.

Goodheart-Willcox Publisher

allows for the use of a mouse or similar pointing device. The traditional BIOS Setup utility is a text-based interface that only allows keyboard input. The traditional BIOS Setup utility may use low-resolution graphic images to display during the boot process, but the images are low resolution. The text-based interface at times appears to be graphic, but on closer examination, you can see that the graphics, such as lines, boxes, and shading, are really made from ASCII characters. UEFI firmware uses graphics consisting of drawn lines and shapes.

The usual default setting for the boot sequence is the hard drive followed by the CD/DVD drive, also referred to as an optical drive. You may also see an option for a floppy drive. Older computer systems may present the floppy drive as a choice whether the drive is installed or not. Modern computer systems will present a floppy drive as a choice only if it is physically installed and detected. Sometimes, computers are set to boot from the hard drive first as a time-saving measure or for security reasons.

Another interesting feature is password protection for the Setup utility. By password protecting the Setup program, unauthorized personnel cannot change the settings either intentionally or accidentally. Curious PC users often inadvertently change the system settings.

Sometimes people forget their password. If this happens, the CMOS will have to be erased. This will allow a new password to be programmed into CMOS. Some motherboards are equipped with a jumper for erasing the data in CMOS. Moving the jumper to the "clear CMOS" position erases all CMOS data, even the password. Moving the jumper back to its original location will allow the settings to be reentered.

Tech Tip   The exact process and terminology of clearing the CMOS data can vary between motherboard manufacturers.

Identifying Motherboard Components

There are many different motherboard manufacturers. The process of identifying the jumper and connection locations, chips, and other major components can be very confusing. Motherboard manufacturers include a drawing of the motherboard in the motherboard user's guide. The drawing represents the approximate locations of all common connection points on the motherboard, such as the USB ports, power, fan power ports, CPU socket, PCI slots, and PCIe slots. The parts in the drawing are numbered and the numbers are correlated to their related component name and listed in a table. A motherboard user guide comes with a motherboard when purchased or it can be downloaded from the manufacturer's website.

Figure 3-46 shows a photo of the motherboard with the components labeled. Motherboard components can be easily identified by their relative position and outline on each motherboard. A close-up of the pin locations for the front panel connection is shown in **Figure 3-47**. The front panel connection is used to provide a connection point for the power switch, system reset switch, power-on LED, hard drive activity LED, and simple speaker, which is used to sound out diagnostic beeps. You can also see a close-up of a typical fan connection and USB 2.0 port connection.

Some motherboards provide a front panel connector kit to make it easier when connecting front panel cables to the motherboard, **Figure 3-48**. You simply use the kit to make connections between the cables in the front of the PC and the front panel pins located on the motherboard. The

Figure 3-46. ASUS Sabertooth X79 motherboard with components labeled.

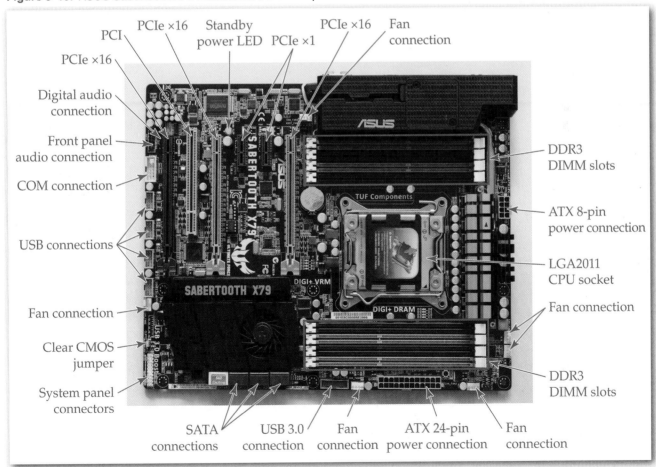

Figure 3-47.
Front panel cable connections. Notice the jumper to clear the data from CMOS.

USB 2.0   Fan   CMOS clear   Front panel

Goodheart-Willcox Publisher

Figure 3-48.
Front and back side of a motherboard front panel connector kit. This kit provides an easy way to make connections between the motherboard and cables running to the front of the PC.

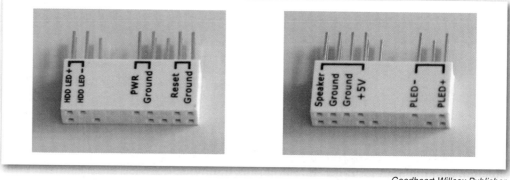

Goodheart-Willcox Publisher

connector kit adapter slips over the connection pins (sometimes referred to as the *header*) on the motherboard. As you can see, the connection pins are clearly marked. This makes it much easier than trying to read the connection pin locations on the motherboard. Notice that the electrical polarity plus (+) and minus (–) is indicated on the connector. Electrical devices such as LED lights must connect with the correct polarity or they will not work properly.

Troubleshooting Motherboards

The motherboard is one of the most expensive parts to replace, and problems with it are some of the most difficult to diagnose. Understanding all the peripheral devices that are associated with the PC is required to effectively diagnose a defective motherboard. Many times, the process of diagnosing a problem requires third-party diagnostic software or hardware.

The difficulty in diagnosing a motherboard fault is that all major components use the motherboard circuitry. For example, a technician is troubleshooting a modem problem. The technician first examines the modem and all of its connections. After all methods of diagnosing the modem have been exhausted, the motherboard chipset or circuitry could be at fault. The motherboard must be changed in order to be absolutely sure.

Substitution can be expensive when trying to determine if the CPU or motherboard is at fault. Both are expensive parts. Before replacing the motherboard, always start with a simple inspection of some common failure points. Many times electronic equipment failures are nothing more than loose connections. All the jumpers and connections on and to the motherboard should be checked. A detailed drawing of the component layout (from the manufacturer's website) will help locate all possible connections and jumpers. Many times, the simple act of reconnecting jumpers and connections will remedy the problem.

Sometimes a computer can be repaired simply by removing and reinstalling the CPU. The connection pins can become oxidized and stop the flow of electrical energy. Removing and reinserting often clears a sufficient amount of the thin coating of oxidation to clear the fault.

Obvious signs of lightning or high voltage surge damage should be sought. A small burnt area on the motherboard bus at the connection to a component is a sure sign. The back side of the motherboard should also be inspected for damage.

Figure 3-49 shows damage caused by a loose connection to the motherboard power connector. The computer would shut down randomly after a few minutes to as long as a few days. The damage to the connection is not apparent until the connector is removed from the motherboard.

At times, a fault disappears when the cover is removed from the PC. This is often a sign of a pinched cable or a loose connection. Wires and cables can become trapped between the case and metal framework during assembly. The cable may not be completely damaged at the time it becomes caught, but over time, the framework pinches through the cable.

Many motherboard manufacturers provide tools at their website to assist you with diagnosing possible motherboard problems. Always check the motherboard manufacturer's website for information and procedures when diagnosing problems. As you progress through your studies, your knowledge base will grow and so will your troubleshooting skills.

Figure 3-49. A loose power connector can damage the power supply connector and the motherboard connection.

Goodheart-Willcox Publisher

Chapter Summary

- Some common motherboard buses are the data bus, control bus, memory bus, I/O bus, internal bus, local bus, address bus, and power bus.

- The most common motherboard form factors are microATX and ATX.

- A motherboard chipset connects slower devices, such as WiMAX/WiFi, Serial ATA (SATA), USB, and audio to the CPU, whereas high-speed devices, such as video and memory, connect directly to a CPU.

- There are several types of motherboard slots available, such as AGP, PCI, and PCIe.

- Device Manager and System Information can be used to view system resources.

- Manufacturer's typically recommend that software drivers for a device be installed before installing the device.

- BIOS upgrade procedures vary somewhat for different motherboards; therefore, you should always consult the manufacturer's website for detailed steps on upgrading a particular BIOS.

- A Setup utility is used to view and modify system settings and can be accessed by a special set of keyboard strokes during the boot up period.

- Motherboard manufacturers include a drawing of the motherboard in a user's guide, which can be used to identify the major parts of a motherboard.

- When troubleshooting a motherboard, look for pinched cables, loose connections, oxidation, and high-voltage damage.

Review Questions

Answer the following questions on a separate sheet of paper. Please do not write in this book.

1. Define the following bus types.
   a. Memory
   b. Address
   c. Data
   d. Power
   e. Local
   f. Expansion
   g. Internal
   h. Control

2. A bus can consist of two or more other types of buses. True or False?

3. Form factor describes the _____ of the motherboard.
   a. bus type
   b. shape
   c. voltage level
   d. chipset

4. What is the major difference between an NLX and an LPX form factor?

5. What form factor was specifically designed for airflow across heat-generating components?

6. What does the acronym BTX represent?

7. Arrange the following form factors from largest to smallest.
   a. MicroATX
   b. Mini-ITX
   c. FlexATX

8. On a motherboard, devices that demand high-speed connections connect to the _____, whereas slower devices connect to the _____.

9. What is the data width of PCI?

10. What does the acronym PCI-X represent?

11. What is the data width of PCI-X?

12. What does the acronym PCIe represent?

13. How many conductors are in a single PCIe lane?

14. What is the total number of conductors for a PCIe ×1 lane?

15. As a PC technician, where would you most likely encounter a miniPCIe card?

16. What is the maximum data rate of USB 1.1?

17. What is the maximum data rate of USB 2.0?

18. What is the maximum data rate of USB 3.0?

19. What is the maximum length of USB 2.0 cable according to the standard?

20. Which USB versions are backward compatible with USB 3.0?

21. What speed will result from connecting a USB 2.0 device into a USB 3.0 port?

22. What is the maximum number of devices that can be attached to an IEEE-1394 port?

23. Which has the highest data rate: USB or IEEE-1394?

24. What are the advantages to incorporating the CNR or ACR riser system into a motherboard design?

25. What are the four major system resources used by computer devices?

26. List how to access **Device Manager** for a Windows Vista or Windows 7 PC. Start with *Right-click* **Computer**.

27. Explain the purpose of Device Manager.

28. What executable file is used to access System Information?

29. Explain how to access System Information.

30. Which IRQ has the highest priority?
   a. 3
   b. 5
   c. 2
   d. 15

31. What three things are necessary for Plug and Play to work?

32. When do manufacturers typically recommend installing software drivers for a new device?

33. When upgrading a Flash BIOS, what two items should be downloaded from the motherboard manufacturer's website?

34. What is the general procedure for upgrading a BIOS through the Windows operating system?

35. How is a computer's Setup utility accessed?

36. What can be done to protect the Setup utility from accidental changes?

37. What can a PC technician use to aid in component identification on a motherboard?

38. When troubleshooting a motherboard, what are some things a PC technician should check?

Sample A+ Exam Questions

Answer the following questions on a separate sheet of paper. Please do not write in this book.

1. Which is the smallest motherboard form factor?
   a. AT
   b. Mini-ATX
   c. Flex-ATX
   d. Mini-ITX

2. Which technology supports the fastest transfer speeds?
   a. PCI
   b. USB 3.0
   c. PCIe
   d. IEEE-1394b

3. Which slot design is exclusively used for video cards?
   a. PCI
   b. AGP
   c. USB
   d. IEEE-1394

4. IRQ settings can be accessed and modified in Windows through the _____.
   a. Device Manager
   b. System Resource icon in Control Panel
   c. IRQ icon in Control Panel
   d. System Resources dialog box

5. Which program will display information about all the system resource assignments at once?
   a. Internet Explorer
   b. Device Manager
   c. System Information
   d. Event Viewer

6. What is the UEFI standard concerned with?
   a. Software drivers
   b. Motherboard ports
   c. System firmware
   d. System video

7. Where does the computer store information about the type of hard drive installed?
   a. At sector 2 of the hard drive
   b. In the CMOS
   c. In the system ROM chip
   d. In the system RAM chip

8. What is required for Plug and Play technology to work correctly? Select all that apply.
   a. Plug and Play BIOS
   b. An operating system that supports Plug and Play
   c. Device Manager must support Plug and Play
   d. The hardware device being installed must be equipped to support Plug and Play

9. What is the name of the executable file that produces the System Information window?
   a. msinfo32.exe
   b. 32.exe
   c. system32.exe
   d. information32.exe

10. Which of the following items controls the speed of data flow across different bus architectures on a motherboard?
   a. BIOS
   b. Motherboard chipsets
   c. DMA channels
   d. IEEE-1394

Suggested Laboratory Activities

Do not attempt any suggested laboratory activities without your instructor's permission. Certain activities can render the PC operating system inoperable.

1. Completely remove a motherboard. Make a drawing and label all connections to the motherboard to assist you during reinstallation.

2. Access the website of the motherboard's manufacturer. Look for a drawing on the site that identifies all of the major parts of the motherboard. Identify the type of chipset and firmware (BIOS or UEFI) that it uses. List the various features associated with the motherboard chipset.

3. Access the Setup utility on your assigned PC. Write down all the settings you find in the Setup utility, such as the hard drive, floppy disk drive, and CD/DVD drive configurations. Look for a **Help** option. It will usually be displayed on the screen as you move the cursor into each setting's input field. Locate the security password system in the BIOS.

4. Open Device Manager and study the way the system resources are displayed and assigned. Identify the IRQ, memory, and DMA assignments for various devices. Record your findings and use them as a study guide.

5. Open System Information and examine the information displayed, such as memory, DMA, and I/O assignments. Look at the various information that can be displayed and explore the options available in the **Tools** menu.

6. Conduct an Internet search for Intel desktop beep codes. Use the terms "Intel desktop beep codes" in your search. Access the website in the result that has Intel.com in its name. Examine the information provided about the beep codes for Intel desktops.

7. Visit the Bios Central website and view beep and post codes for various BIOS manufacturers.

Central Processing Unit (CPU)

4

After studying this chapter, you will be able to:

- Recall the purpose of an instruction set.
- Explain the basic operation of a CPU.
- Recall the technologies used to enhance CPU operation.
- Use processor descriptive terminology to explain, identify, and compare CPUs.
- Identify the three top CPU manufacturers.
- Compare Intel and AMD CPUs.
- Explain the construction and operation of multi-core processors.
- Use Task Manager to set processor affinity.
- Identify sockets associated with the CPU.
- Evaluate a computer system's performance.
- Evaluate whether to upgrade a CPU.
- Carry out a CPU installation.
- Carry out a cooling system installation.

A+ Exam—Key Points

The CompTIA A+ exams ask basic questions about the CPU, CPU sockets, CPU terminology, and CPU cooling. Be prepared to answer questions such as the following:

- How is CPU performance measured?
- Which CPU fits which socket?
- What effect does overclocking have on a CPU?
- What is the difference between 32-bit and 64-bit processing?
- What is the purpose of thermal compound?
- What purpose does processor throttling serve?

Key Terms

The following key terms will become important pieces of your computer vocabulary. Be sure you can define them.

arithmetic logic unit (ALU)
assembly language
bus unit
cache
compiler
complex instruction set computer (CISC)
control unit
decode unit
Dual Independent Bus (DIB)
dynamic execution
floating point unit (FPU)
front side bus (FSB)
instruction set
instructions
Integrated Memory Controller (IMC)

L1 cache
L2 cache
MMX processor
multiple branch prediction
overclocking
processor affinity
processor throttling
reduced instruction set computer (RISC)
register unit
register
simultaneous threading
superscalar execution
System Management Mode (SMM)
thread
zero insertion force (ZIF) socket

CPU stands for *central processing unit*, and it does exactly what its name implies. It is *central* in that all other components are dependent on the CPU, **Figure 4-1**. It is a *processor* in that it processes data. It is a *unit* in that it is very much a self-contained device that is modular in design. The CPU is replaced as an entire unit.

Instructions and Data

The CPU has been given the status of the computer's brain. It has evolved over the years from a simple chip composed of only 27,000 transistors in early 1978 to a highly sophisticated integrated chip composed of over 2.5 billion

Figure 4-1.
The CPU and its relationship with other components.

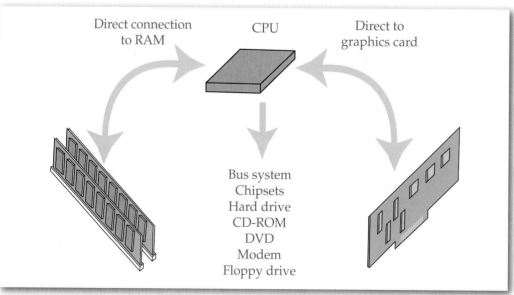

Direct connection to RAM   CPU   Direct to graphics card

Bus system
Chipsets
Hard drive
CD-ROM
DVD
Modem
Floppy drive

transistors. The CPU follows commands called **instructions** and then processes data. The data is normally stored in RAM or introduced into the system by some device such as a keyboard, mouse, microphone, hard drive, or optical drive.

Every processor runs from a set of basic commands called the **instruction set**. The instruction set is the lowest language level used to program a computer. The instruction set is written in **assembly language**. Assembly is one step above machine language. When code is written in a high-level language such as BASIC or C++, it must be compiled before it can run the computer as a stand-alone program or executive program. A **compiler** is a program that translates the higher-level language into machine language based on the CPU's instruction set. The instruction set contains commands such as add; subtract; compare; add one to; subtract one from; get the next one, two, or four bytes from; and put the next one, two, or four bytes at.

The CPU has several registers. A **register** is a small pocket of memory used to temporarily store data that is being processed by the CPU. For example, when adding two numbers together, one number is stored in register A and the other number is stored in register B. The add command adds the contents of register A to the contents of register B and places the result in register C. Next, the contents can be moved from register C to a RAM address.

Assembly language programs are translated into machine code. The assembly program is written as a series of commands and bytes of data to be acted on byte by byte. Writing code in assembly is painstakingly difficult. It takes an extremely long time to write even a simple program. However, it produces the fastest execution possible. Assembly language translated into machine code is used when speed or compact size is a necessity. The kernel code of operating systems and BIOS programs are usually written to some degree in assembly. Most other common programs are written for computers using a higher-level language that is then translated from the higher-level language to machine-like code. However, using a higher-level language and then compiling the code results in a larger, slower program.

Machine-level programs are lengthy but appear transparent to the user because of the sheer speed at which the instructions are carried out by the computer. Programming in machine language is an entire science, but only needs to be briefly explained to give you the necessary insight on how a CPU functions with data.

CPU Operation

A CPU is in a state of constant operation. When not processing commands to process data, the CPU is:

- Refreshing memory.
- Checking for communication from other devices through the system of hardwired IRQs and software IRQs.
- Monitoring system power.
- Performing any other programmed duties.

Look at **Figure 4-2** to see how a CPU performs the simple operation of addition. This series demonstrates how the registers are used to manipulate data. To add the numerical value of two numbers, three registers are used. The value 3 is placed in register A. The value 4 is placed in register B. Then the contents of the two registers are added together and stored in register C. While this action seems simple, there are many other activities going on at the same time that are controlled by the CPU. For example, the CPU is refreshing the RAM, checking IRQ status (checking for keyboard input, mouse input, and other such input), and displaying the contents of the registers on the monitor.

CPU Parts

The following is a simplified discussion of CPU operation, but it should give you some idea of how the major parts work together to perform operations on data. A **bus unit** is a network of circuitry that connects all the other major components together, accepts data, and sends data through the input and output bus sections. There is an instruction cache and a data cache. The term **cache** (pronounced *cash*) means a small temporary memory storage area. Cache is used to separate and store incoming data and instructions.

Figure 4-2. Illustrated in this series are the steps that a CPU takes to add two numbers together.

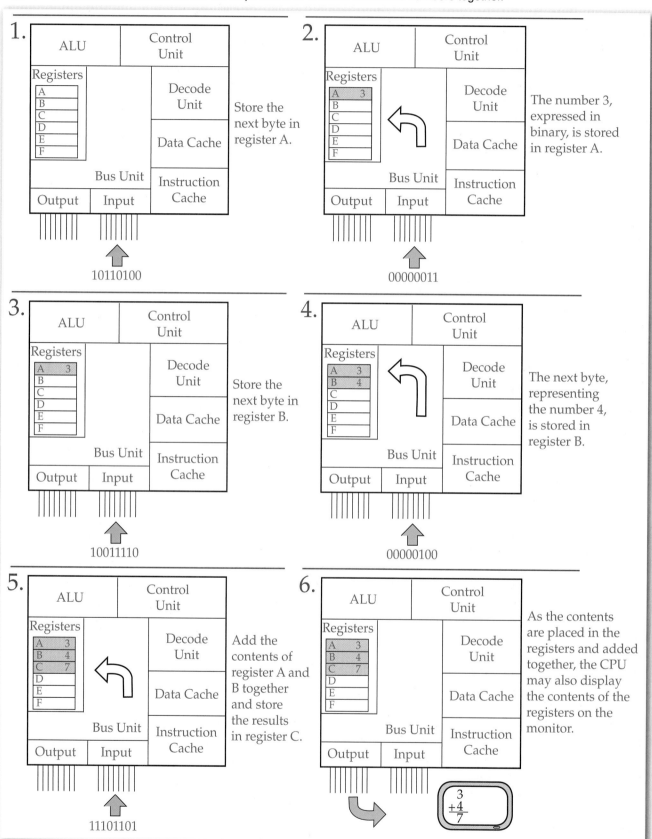

1. Store the next byte in register A.

10110100

2. The number 3, expressed in binary, is stored in register A.

00000011

3. Store the next byte in register B.

10011110

4. The next byte, representing the number 4, is stored in register B.

00000100

5. Add the contents of register A and B together and store the results in register C.

11101101

6. As the contents are placed in the registers and added together, the CPU may also display the contents of the registers on the monitor.

3
+4
7

Goodheart-Willcox Publisher

A **decode unit** does what the name implies. It decodes instructions sent to the CPU. Under the direction of a control unit, it not only decodes the series of instructions and data but also sends the data on to other areas in an understandable format.

The **control unit** controls the overall operation of the CPU. It takes instructions from the decode unit and directs command instructions to the arithmetic logic unit and data to be manipulated to the register area. The **arithmetic logic unit (ALU)** performs mathematical functions on data stored in the register area. It also performs data manipulations such as comparing two pieces of data stored in the registry unit. It can do comparisons such as "equal to," "greater than," and "less than."

The **register unit** is composed of many separate storage units smaller than cache. Each register has a unique identity. In our model, each is labeled with a letter of the alphabet. The main difference between register storage and cache is that registers contain a single data element. A single data element is a number or a letter. The data and instruction cache can hold multiple pieces of data and commands. The ALU performs manipulations on the data stored in registers, such as adding or subtracting the contents of register A to or from the contents of register B. The ALU can also do comparisons on the contents of A or B, such as determining which is larger.

Manipulating a list of words in alphabetical order is an example of a comparison of the contents of two or more registers. Each letter is given a numeric value, processed through the CPU in pairs, and then stored in either cache or RAM in the appropriate order. The series of comparisons can consist of over a thousand repetitions. The CPU operates at such a high speed that the process appears very brief. This is the great value of the computer. A computer can perform repetitive tasks such as sorting the addresses of 2,000,000 names for a phone book in a few minutes. Performed manually, the same operation would take weeks or even months to perform. Animation on the screen of the display unit has also been made possible because of the great speed of the control unit, the ALU, and the registers. See **Figure 4-3**.

Figure 4-3. A list of words are entered into the CPU and stored in cache. The control unit sends pairs of words to the registry broken down by letter and then compares each pair until all possible combinations are exhausted.

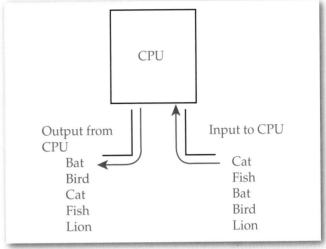

Goodheart-Willcox Publisher

CPU Power

Not all business conducted with a PC requires the use of a powerful CPU. A simple word-processing package will work with most any CPU. However, extreme software gaming, CAD/CAM (computer-aided drafting/computer-aided manufacturing), scientific simulations and research, and large corporate financial record calculations require powerful CPUs. CPU power can be taken even further. Many sophisticated operations, such as weather prediction and medical research, have requirements well beyond a PC and must use a mainframe or a super computer.

Imagine a CAD drawing of a shopping center or mall that can be manipulated on the display unit. People can walk through the virtual mall and look at the simulation as though they were actually in the mall itself. They can see the entire layout through a shopper's perspective. Or, imagine many popular game scenarios as you navigate through a maze of hallways. Animation, especially those involving three-dimensional images, is CPU intensive.

One form of animation technology requires the redrawing of every line in the image for each display change. See **Figure 4-4**. Before redrawing each line, a calculation has to be made based on the X, Y, and Z coordinates of each end of the line. The distance and angle of the new location is used as part of the algorithm. An algorithm is similar to a recipe. You simply insert the X, Y, and Z coordinates of the existing position of each line end and then input the new X, Y, and Z coordinates.

Figure 4-4.
These three illustrations show the concept behind animation technology using X, Y, and Z coordinates.

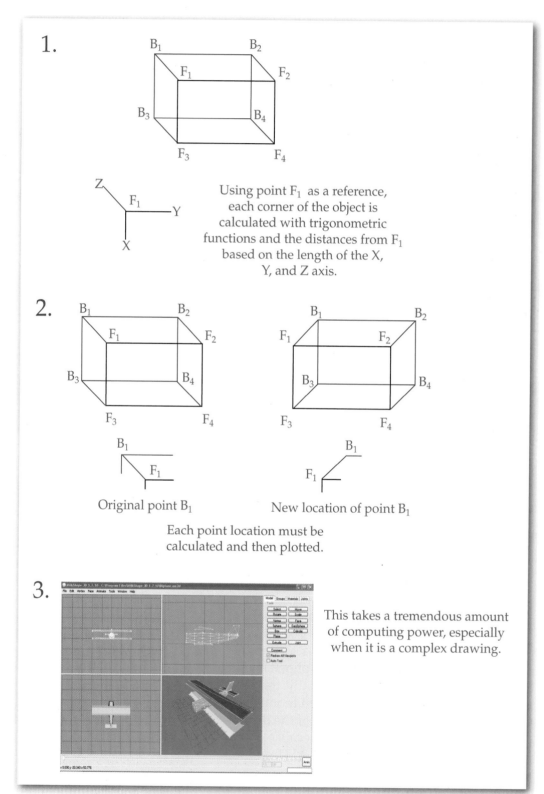

1. Using point F_1 as a reference, each corner of the object is calculated with trigonometric functions and the distances from F_1 based on the length of the X, Y, and Z axis.

2. Original point B_1 New location of point B_1

Each point location must be calculated and then plotted.

3. This takes a tremendous amount of computing power, especially when it is a complex drawing.

Rather than inputting the exact coordinates manually, they can be "implied" by the use of a mouse, keyboard, or game control device. To give a realistic feeling, an illustration containing hundreds or even thousands of lines must be computed in a fraction of a second and then displayed on the screen. This type of operation requires a high-speed CPU with many advanced data processing techniques.

Remember that the CPU receives a constant stream of alternating commands and data. Early CPUs required all data to be transferred through the CPU. For example, if a memo was being typed, the CPU would act on each letter in the memo. Now, modern systems allow for bus mastering and direct memory access. These additions allow repetitive actions that do not require manipulation of data to simply be passed on to memory, the screen, the printer, or data storage areas such as the hard drive.

Each step of the processor requires a clock beat. The clock sends a repetitive signal to all parts of the computer system to keep data transmissions in step with the other parts. The transmission of data throughout the PC is a combination of series and parallel transmissions and many different devices operating at different speeds. For example, the keyboard is a serial device. Keyboard data must be converted to parallel data and then be transmitted in step with the other parts of the computer.

CPU Speed

The CPU has been progressively made to operate faster and more efficiently. The modifications to data processing methods are given special names to describe their actions. Modifications to the CPU include RISC, superscalar technology, dynamic execution, and additional cache. In the next section, we will take a closer look at processor speed and these special modifications to the CPU.

Comparison of CPUs is usually based on speed and bus width. The speed is how fast the CPU can process data and commands. The bus width is how many bits can be passed simultaneously on parallel circuits, for example 8, 16, 32, and 64 bits simultaneously.

The CPU moves data and carries out commands as a series of binary numbers. The CPU or processor speed is measured in hertz (Hz), or cycles per second (frequency). With CPUs, this means the number of digital pulses in one second. A digital signal is a fluctuation of electrical energy. In digital electronics, a complete cycle is one complete sequence of the digital signal shape. Look at **Figure 4-5** to see a complete cycle of the digital signal illustrated.

The term *frequency* is used to express the number of cycles in one second. Thus, if there are 25 complete digital cycles in one second, the frequency is 25 hertz (25 Hz). A CPU that runs at 1 MHz carries out instructions and data

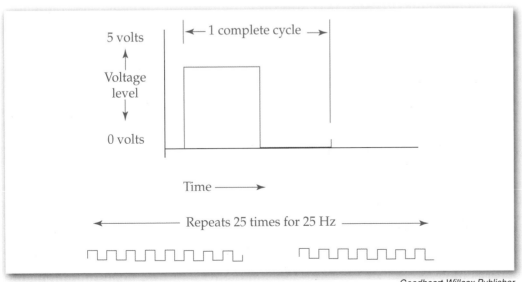

Figure 4-5. Complete cycle of a digital signal. A 5-volt digital signal rises and falls to a 5-volt level. The number of times it repeats the pattern in one second is the frequency of the signal. A 25-Hz signal repeats 25 times in one second.

Goodheart-Willcox Publisher

movement at one million digital pulses per second. Bus width and speed combine to express amount of data transfer. See **Figure 4-6** for a drawing explaining the speed of a CPU.

As computer systems shifted from text-based command operating systems to Graphical User Interface (GUI), speed became an extremely important factor. For example, the intense graphics of Windows requires a faster computer system. Graphics functions demand a lot of processor attention.

Keep in mind that the speed of processing data is not entirely dependent on the speed of the electronics. The instruction set used to process data as well as special methods such as pipeline burst, RISC, and cache technique also influence the speed of processing data.

Enhancing CPU Operation

Processors are continually getting faster and more powerful. Each new generation of CPU can operate on shorter clock cycles. However, a CPU's abilities can be enhanced in a number of ways in addition to simply producing chips that operate at a faster rate. These improvements include changes to the local bus, the addition of cache, the addition of a math coprocessor, and the way a processor executes instructions.

A+ Note

Be able to identify which features most influence a processor's ability to process data quickly.

Local Bus

The local bus is connected directly to the CPU. It is always the highest speed bus in the entire computer system. The local bus is the bus system connecting certain components directly to the CPU. RAM and video card slots are examples of components connected directly to the CPU to better enhance performance. The local bus is also referred to as the *system bus* or the *front side bus*. A lot of the terminology used is dependent on the manufacturer of the product or even the generation of the technology. At one time, Intel used the term **front side bus (FSB)** when referring to the local bus of Pentium processors.

The shorter the distance between two devices, the higher the data transfer rate can be. It is not the length the data has to travel, but rather the effect of inductive reactance that causes a choking effect on the electrical impulses. As the length of the data path increases, so does the choking

Figure 4-6.
The rate of data transfer is based on the width and speed of the bus system.

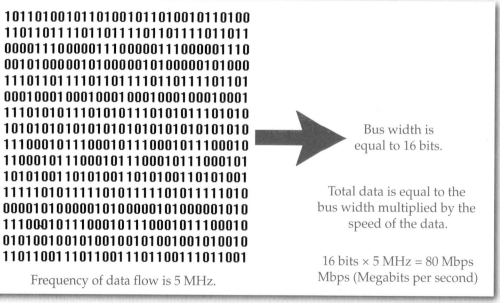

Frequency of data flow is 5 MHz.

Bus width is equal to 16 bits.

Total data is equal to the bus width multiplied by the speed of the data.

16 bits × 5 MHz = 80 Mbps
Mbps (Megabits per second)

effect. The only practical way to decrease this choking effect as the length of the path increases is to lower the data flow rate. Thus, the inductive reactance slows down the speed that a processor can run.

Today, AMD uses HyperTransport Technology and Intel uses QuickPath Interconnect (QPI) to connect the processor core directly to RAM, thus eliminating the need for the front side bus.

Cache

The processor bus speed is the highest data transfer speed in the entire computer system. To enhance the speed of data processing, a special block of RAM was developed and manufactured as an integral part of the processor. This feature began with the 486 processor. This special memory unit is called *cache*.

The cache in the CPU is called the **L1 cache**. L1 cache is designed to run at the same speed as the CPU. It is the most costly memory to produce when compared on a per byte basis. As design engineers must create a CPU and computer system that will work at a high speed while staying within a reasonable cost that the customer can afford, L1 cache is smaller on less expensive processors.

L1 cache enables the CPU to quickly process data. Data can be stored temporarily in the L1 cache rather than in a RAM module. The bus speed to L1 cache is many times faster than the bus speed from the CPU to the RAM. By storing data in L1 cache, the movement of data being manipulated by the CPU is greatly increased.

L2 cache is separate from the processor but mounted as close as possible to the processor to keep the transfer rates high. The **L2 cache** is used to increase the speed of data transmission to and from the processor to other parts of the motherboard.

L1 and L2 cache also differ in one other significant way. L1 cache is made from static RAM technology. L2 cache uses dynamic RAM technology, which is slower than the L1 cache. The terms *static memory* and *dynamic memory* will become clearer when you complete Chapter 6—Memory. **Figure 4-7** shows the layout of a legacy cache system.

Figure 4-7. Starting with the 486 processor, L1 cache was incorporated into the CPU and L2 cache was mounted on the motherboard in close proximity to the CPU.

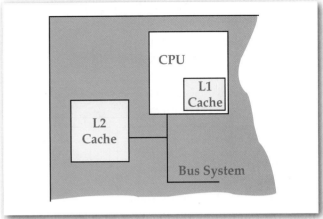

Goodheart-Willcox Publisher

The Pentium III incorporates both L1 and L2 cache into the CPU die. The L1 cache is divided into a data cache and an instruction cache. The L2 cache performs at a much higher rate of data transfer than previous L2 caches since it is built into the processing unit.

The Intel Core 2 Duo and Quad processors have just an L1 and L2 cache incorporated into the CPU die. The L3 cache is located on the motherboard close to the CPU. Today, CPU architecture incorporates L1, L2, and L3 cache in the CPU unit. See **Figure 4-8**, which shows the architecture of an Intel Core i7 CPU.

Notice that each core has two L1 caches: one for data and the other for instructions. Each core has its own L2 cache, and all cores share a common L3 cache. Every core supports two threads, which is equal to two logical processors. The CPU has a DDR3 controller that connects directly to three channels of DDR memory mounted on the motherboard. There are two Intel QuickPath Interconnect (QPI) controllers incorporated into the CPU. An Intel QPI controller connects to a high-speed I/O controller mounted directly on the motherboard in close proximity to the CPU. The combination of the QPI controller and high-speed I/O controller has replaced the front side bus.

The latest processors have an Integrated Memory Controller (IMC) and Integrated Graphics Processing Unit (GPU) incorporated into the

Figure 4-8. Intel Core i7 architecture.

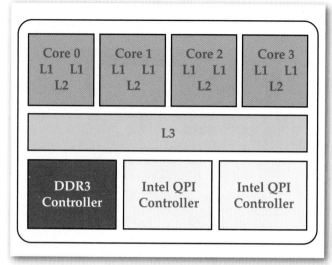

Goodheart-Willcox Publisher

processor die. Originally, the IMC was a separate chip mounted on the motherboard. The IMC and processor communicated across a bus on the motherboard. By incorporating the IMC into the processor, access to RAM is improved.

Floating Point Unit

The **floating point unit (FPU)** is a set of circuits incorporated into the processor that is used for mathematic computation. Originally, computer systems had a special chip on the motherboard called the *math coprocessor* that served as the mathematical computation unit. Incorporating the mathematical computation unit into the processor produces more computation speed when compared to a separate chip on the motherboard.

Multiple Branch Prediction

Multiple branch prediction is a technique that guesses what data element will be needed next rather than waiting for the next command to be issued. It is especially accurate in repetitive tasks and can significantly speed up CPU operations. Multiple branch prediction has proven to be over 90% accurate.

Superscalar Technology

The 486 and all processors before it could only process one instruction at a time. Beginning with the Pentium, processing multiple instructions at the same time was possible. The act of processing more than one instruction at the same time is called **superscalar execution**.

CPUs are designed with two pipelines. Pipelines are parallel paths on which data travels to the CPU sections. This parallel path concept is what makes the CPU capable of performing two data manipulation functions at the same time. Two data words can be processed during the same clock tick. Again, the speed of the processor is improved far beyond the limits of the clock. Superscalar technology is dependent not only on a new physical design of the processor, but also on an additional set of instructional commands to operate the twin pipelines while still maintaining backward compatibility with previous processors. All modern processors use superscalar technology.

Dynamic Execution

The term **dynamic execution** was coined by Intel to describe the enhanced superscalar and multiple branch prediction features associated with the Pentium II processor. Dynamic execution is a combination of new physical features and additional instruction set commands manufactured into the processor. It is also a technique that looks ahead at instructions coming to the processor. If an instruction can be carried out faster than the instruction preceding it, it is moved ahead of its current position and then executed.

Integrated Memory Controller

The memory controller for early processors was a chip mounted on the motherboard close to the CPU and RAM. It controlled data flow between the processor and RAM over the front side bus. Current processors integrate the memory controller into the processor. When the memory controller is part of the processor, it is referred to as the **Integrated Memory Controller (IMC)**. A short motherboard bus makes a connection from the processor directly to the motherboard RAM. By incorporating the memory controller into the processor and providing a direct connection to system RAM, the performance of the computer system is greatly enhanced.

Integrated Graphics Processing

Earlier motherboards had a chip called the Graphics Processing Unit (GPU), which supported graphics and processed images. Today, Intel and AMD processors integrate the GPU. Intel refers to this integrated unit as the Graphics Processing Unit (GPU). AMD refers to a processor with an integrated GPU as the Accelerated Processing Unit (APU). The integrated graphics processing feature is not available for all new processor models, but most feature it.

Integrating the GPU into the processor enhances the ability of the computer system to produce video and 3-D images. Processing images and 3-D information between separate devices across the motherboard is not as efficient as when the individual parts are incorporated into the same die. Higher frequencies can be used, thus processing the video data more quickly. High-speed processing of video data is a requirement for streaming live video, DVD movies, high-definition live television, and similar video. While this is a good way to process video, it is not as good as using a separate graphics card mounted in a motherboard slot. An integrated graphics unit is not nearly as powerful as a separate graphics card.

Dual Independent Bus

Dual Independent Bus (DIB) is a bus architecture introduced with the Pentium Pro and Pentium II. As the name implies, there are two separate or independent bus systems incorporated into the processor chip. One bus connects to the main memory and the other connects with the L2 cache. Both buses can be used simultaneously rather than singly to increase program execution speed. Today, DIB has been replaced by Intel QuickPath Interconnect and AMD HyperTransport Technology.

Simultaneous Threading

In software programming, a **thread** is part of a software program that can be executed independently of the entire program. When two or more threads are executed at the same time, it is called **simultaneous threading**. Intel coined the term *Hyper-Threading* to describe in their advertisements the simultaneous threading technology. Hardware and software companies often coin new terminology to describe computer technology in their advertisement campaigns. Sometimes the technology is new, but often only the marketing term is new.

Intel Hyper-Threading Technology was introduced many years ago and is still a vital part of the Intel processor design. The Intel Core series of multi-core CPUs uses two threads per core, resulting in twice the processing power for the number of cores. For example, a quad-core processor in which each core has the capability of supporting two threads has the logical processing power of eight processors. The processing power of the quad core is doubled as a direct result of simultaneous threading.

In **Figure 4-9**, Windows Task Manager shows the performance of an Intel Core i7 processor, which has four cores. Notice that there are eight graphs displayed, not just four. Each of the four processor cores supports two threads. This results in a total of eight logical processors, and hence, eight performance graphs.

Overclocking

Processors have design specifications which indicate the maximum frequency that should be applied to that particular processor. Applying a higher frequency than specified results in excessive heat, which can damage a processor. Processors can withstand short periods of time under excessive heat conditions without damage, but this condition should be watched closely.

Applying higher frequencies to a processor than the design specification is referred to as **overclocking**. Higher frequencies applied to a processor results in overall enhanced performance. In other words, the processor can accomplish more tasks in a shorter time. The amount of tasks performed by a processor is

Figure 4-9. Windows Task Manager displaying the performance of an Intel Core i7 processor, which has four cores. Notice that there is a graph for each processor thread.

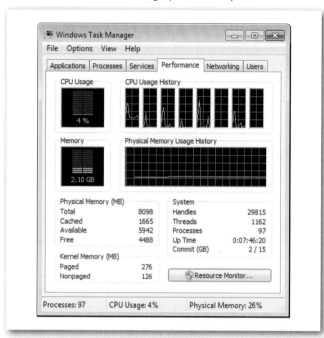

directly related to the applied frequency. The applied frequency to a processor can be controlled by software or by BIOS configuration.

An example of overclocking of the Intel processor is Intel Turbo Boost Technology. This technology increases processor performance by increasing the applied frequency for short periods of time while monitoring the processor core temperature and electrical power consumption. Excessive temperature and excessive electrical power consumption can damage a processor. Processors are manufactured in part by using a heat process. Because the processor is created in part by heat during manufacturing, excessively high heat can damage a processor. AMD has a similar technology called Turbo CORE.

Excessive electrical power consumption damages a processor much in the same way any electrical device is damaged by excessive electrical current. Electrical devices are protected by fuses. The fuse blows when a predetermined electrical current value is reached. Processors have no fuses or equivalent circuitry. The only practical solution is monitoring the amount of electrical current flowing through to the processor. When a predetermined current value is reached,

overclocking is halted by returning the applied frequency to its specified value.

Intel provides a software utility free for download called Intel Extreme Tuning Utility that allows the user to overclock the CPU, system clock, and RAM. It also monitors the CPU temperature, frequency, voltage, and fan speeds. AMD has a similar software utility called AMD OverDrive which performs the same functions as the Intel overclocking software.

The practice of overclocking is not supported by the manufacturing industry and voids the warranty status of the processor. When a processor runs at a higher speed (frequency) than it is designed for, excessive heat develops that may damage the chip. The CPU may freeze and come to a complete stop with or without a fatal error message. This is because fatal error messages are issued by normally working processors that have a software or hardware problem.

Even though Intel provides a *Performance Tuning Guide* about how to overclock the system and provides the software application to perform the overclocking, it also provides a disclaimer in the guide, **Figure 4-10**. Intel warns that altering the frequency or voltage levels of a system processor and memory can cause failure or damage and it does not warranty the operation of the Intel processor beyond its specification. The same disclaimer applies to other manufacturers' memory modules.

A user might attempt to overclock the CPU and cause the system to fail or lock up during post. You can usually correct this problem by resetting the BIOS to its default settings. To reset the BIOS, consult the manufacturer's motherboard manual. Resetting the BIOS is typically performed by using the jumper located near the CMOS battery. A second method is the Back-to-BIOS button located on some motherboards. You simply press the button to reboot the system and enter the Setup utility.

A third method of resetting the BIOS is the watchdog timer embedded into the motherboard circuitry. The watchdog senses a boot system failure and then automatically opens the Setup utility, allowing the technician to make changes. The availability of each method is determined by the motherboard chipset and BIOS.

Figure 4-10. Overclocking warning in an *Intel Performance Tuning Guide*.

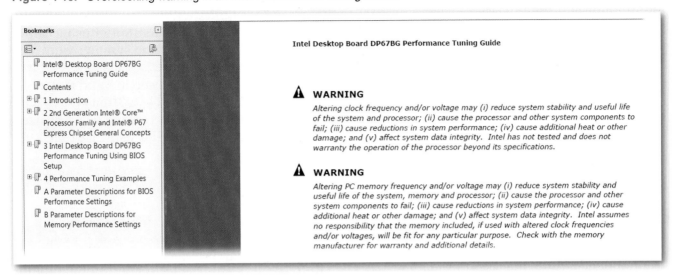

A+ Note

To prepare for the CompTIA A+ exams, you should be able to explain the concepts of virtualization, cache, Hyper-Threading, and integrated GPU as related to the processor.

Processor Descriptive Features

Processor descriptive features are a collection of terms used to explain, identify, and compare processing units. Some of the terms covered are RISC, CISC, and virtualizaton.

RISC

Reduced instruction set computer (RISC) is a type of CPU architecture that is designed with a fewer number of transistors and commands. This architecture produces a CPU that is both inexpensive and fast. The trade-off is that the system software has to carry modifications to allow for fewer CPU instructions. This puts greater responsibility on the software.

RISC processors are found in devices such as the iPOD, iPAD, Android tablet, smartphone, game controller, printer, netbook, digital camera, and digital video camera. They are also used for applications such as electronic engine controls, televisions, airplane electronic controls, and robots.

Some of the most common RISC processors are produced and designed by ARM (Cortex) and Intel (Atom). While RISC processors are commonly found in small portable devices, they are also used in server hardware, which is often assumed to be more powerful than desktop computer systems.

Ironically, as RISC processors become more powerful and more complicated, the difference between RISC and traditional processors is becoming more difficult to determine and classify. RISC processors have always had a limited set of programming instructions as compared to a CISC. However, an old CISC CPU would be about equal to today's RISC processor. For example, the RISC processor in a smartphone is more powerful than a 486 CPU.

CISC

Complex instruction set computer (CISC) is, as the name implies, a CPU with a complex instruction set. The CPU die is designed to accept many machine language commands that manipulate or process complex mathematical formulas.

An increased number of transistors are required to produce a CISC-based CPU. The added complexity causes an increase in clock cycles to carry out an expanded and more complex set of programming instructions. This type of system is best used by complex programming techniques.

MMX

In 1997, the **MMX processor** was introduced. The MMX processor was based on a standard processor with the addition of 57 commands that enhanced its abilities to support graphics technology. Many of the commands replaced functions normally carried out by the sound and video card. This allowed for faster processing of video and sound data. The L1 cache was made larger to assist in speeding up the processing of video frames.

The meaning behind letters *MMX* is debatable. Some claim it stands for Multi-Media eXtensions. Others claim it stands for Matrix Math eXtensions. Intel, the company that developed MMX technology, claims that MMX was not meant to be an acronym at all. The term *MMX* is still used today as a processor feature for many Intel processors.

32-Bit and 64-Bit Technology

CPUs and other computer devices as well as software are often referred to as 32-bit and 64-bit. What is being described is the amount of data that can be processed in parallel during one cycle or clock beat. This is also referred to as the data width. The 64-bit technology provides data paths twice as wide as 32-bit technology. This means that large volumes of data can be transferred much quicker with a 64-bit processor than with a 32-bit processor. The 64-bit technology is superior to 32-bit technology when large amounts of program storage are required.

The 64-bit technology provides access to vast amounts of memory for programs that require it, such as CAD/CAM, digital image creation and manipulation, in-depth financial analysis, computer games with rich graphic content, or any application requiring a great deal of memory and processor throughput.

For a computer system to take full advantage of 64-bit technology, four things are required in addition to a 64-bit processor:

- BIOS that supports a 64-bit processor.
- 64-bit operating system.
- 64-bit device drivers.
- Software applications written for 64-bit.

Take note that for data to transfer using 64-bit technology the 64-bit operating system requires 64-bit device drivers, otherwise data will be transferred as 32-bit. Also, keep in mind that a software program designed as a 32-bit system will not show any significant increase in performance when running on a 64-bit CPU using a 64-bit operating system.

Virtualization

Virtualization makes a single physical processor appear as multiple processors to the computer software system and the user. It allows for a single computer to run multiple operating systems, multiple software applications, and multiple users simultaneously. Virtualization for multiple users is typically applied to network server systems rather than to desktop systems.

Both Intel and AMD processors support virtualization and have trademark names for their virtualization technologies: Intel Virtualization (VT-x) and AMD Virtualization (AMD-V).

XP Mode in Windows 7 is an example of virtualization. After the Windows 7 operating system is installed, a full version of Windows XP can be installed on the same computer. Then, both Windows 7 and Windows XP can be run at the same time.

System Management Mode

System Management Mode (SMM) was first developed for laptop computers to save electrical energy when using a battery. SMM was introduced in the 486SL processor and became a standard for all Pentium processors and later.

The power management is controlled by software, usually the Setup utility. Power management puts the CPU and the computer system into a state of rest or sleep and can also shut down the computer.

Cool 'n' Quiet

The Cool 'n' Quiet feature from AMD adjusts the processor speed and power consumption automatically based on the temperature and processing demands of a running program. Fan speed is also automatically adjusted. Intel has a similar technology called Intel Precision Cooling technology.

Controlling processor frequency is referred to as **processor throttling**. Processor throttling is used to conserve portable computer battery life. The frequency of the CPU is directly proportional to the demand of the software application(s) running on the system. If no software application is running, the frequency of the processor is automatically lowered to conserve battery life and produce less heat. Power Now is the AMD mobile computer version of Cool 'n' Quiet. There will be more about this feature in Chapter 12—Portable Devices.

Enhanced Intel SpeedStep Technology

Intel originally developed Enhanced Intel SpeedStep® Technology for its line of portable computers. This technology is designed to change the applied system voltage and CPU frequency under certain conditions. For example, when a laptop is connected to an AC source, the CPU frequency is 2.6 GHz and the applied system voltage is 1.3 volts. The overall power consumed is 30 watts. When the same laptop is run on battery power, the CPU frequency is reduced to 1.2 GHz and the applied system voltage is reduced to 1.2 volts. The overall power consumed is 20.8 watts, a reduction of almost 10 watts. To take advantage of this technology, the computer's operating system, BIOS, and chipset must support it. Enhanced Intel SpeedStep Technology is already incorporated into Windows XP and later operating systems. It can be accessed on a portable computer under the **Power Options** icon in Control Panel.

Figure 4-11 shows the Windows 7 **Advanced settings** tab in the **Power Options** dialog box. This dialog box allows the user to select specific devices and control device performance as related to power consumption. The **Processor power management** item has been expanded. Notice the options for controlling the processor's state of operation. The maximum processor state has been set to 100%. There is even an option for controlling the processor cooling device. These features are standard on all Microsoft operating systems.

CPU Voltages

CPU operating voltage has decreased over the years. The reason for decreasing the operating voltage levels is to reduce the amount of heat generated by the CPU when processing data.

Motherboards are designed in different ways to achieve different CPU voltage levels. Some boards are equipped with a set of jumpers located beside the CPU. Various voltage levels can be achieved by moving the jumper position. This is a very common method on third-party motherboards. Another method is the use of a voltage regulator. A voltage regulator is installed on the motherboard beside the CPU. The voltage regulator is easy to spot. It is usually equipped with its own small heat sink for cooling purposes. Some overclocking software can manipulate the voltage level of the processor.

Starting with the Pentium, applied voltage from the motherboard was reduced from 5 volts to 3.3 volts. Today, processor core voltage can be less than 1 volt. Lowering a processor's core voltage results in less wattage, and thus, less heat.

Processor Size

The physical size of processors has not changed significantly over the years, but the electronics inside the chip have become more compact over the years. There are many more transistors packed into the processor chips. The density of transistor circuits in a CPU is expressed in nanometers. A nanometer is one billionth of a meter. This measurement is applied to processors by expressing half the distance between two distinct electronic surfaces inside a processor, for example, one half the distance between two circuit paths inside a CPU. The first generation of Intel Core processors is 45-nm, and the third generation is 22-nm.

Moore's Law

In 1965, Gordon Moore, cofounder of Intel, predicted that computers would double in calculating power approximately every 12 months. So far, he has been pretty close to correct. The amount of time has slightly lengthened to about 18 months.

Figure 4-11.
Windows 7 laptop
Power Options dialog
box.

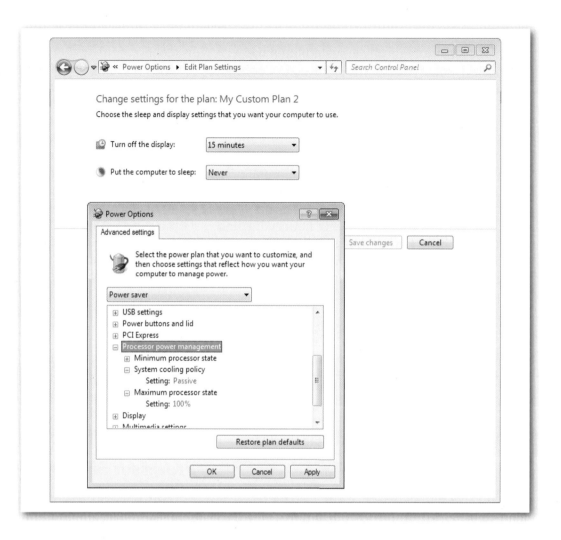

Computers have evolved technically at a rate unsurpassed by any other technology in history. Other technologies have evolved at a snail's pace when compared to the computer. The continuing rapid development of the computer is difficult to predict, but most experts agree that this present rate will continue for some time.

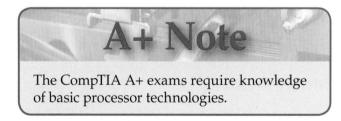

A+ Note

The CompTIA A+ exams require knowledge of basic processor technologies.

Processor Manufacturers

While there are a large number of past and present CPUs to choose from, three companies have produced most of these chips. These three competitors are Intel, AMD, and VIA Technologies.

Intel

Intel is the dominant force in the manufacturing of CPUs for PCs. Intel has been at the top in sales since introducing the 8086 processor to the market in the 1970s. Sales of Intel's 8088 chip were great enough to propel Intel into the Fortune 500.

Intel has continued to dominate the computer processor manufacturing market through the years. Today, Intel controls the vast majority of computer chip manufacturing. Intel not only manufactures CPUs but also chipsets, motherboards, wireless devices, and networking devices.

AMD

Advanced Micro Devices (AMD) has long been Intel's biggest competitor. Originally, AMD manufactured math coprocessors, but when the math coprocessor began to be integrated into the CPU, AMD began manufacturing its own CPU. AMD began its series with the 486 and designed its processor to be compatible with the Intel series. Both Intel and AMD manufacture excellent CPUs.

VIA Technologies

VIA Technologies is not nearly as big as Intel or AMD, but they do produce a lot of computer-related devices as well as their own processor. They specialize in low power-consumption embedded computers and peripherals. They market miniature form factor motherboards with embedded processors from Intel, AMD, and their own processor. VIA Technologies also manufactures specialized power supplies, automobile PCs, and storage devices, such as solid-state hard drives and compact flash drives.

Processor Evolution

Processors have evolved over the years, and as they do, manufacturers reinvent the way processors work. Each generation of processors has its own unique technologies that make the processor run more powerfully than its predecessor. Manufacturers continue to develop processors with more and more transistors and other electronic components. In this section, we will take a brief look at some of the most significant processors used in computing. Major emphasis is on the very latest processors.

Intel Pentium

The first Intel Pentium processor was introduced by Intel in 1993. The Pentium is used today, but it is not the same as the Pentium introduced over 12 years ago. The Pentium uses the front side bus and many of what are considered legacy technologies. The Pentium and the Celeron are often used in mobile applications such as laptops and netbooks.

Intel Pentium Xeon

The Intel Pentium Xeon processor was introduced in 1998 and is referred to as simply Xeon (pronounced *zee-on*). It was designed for

high-end applications such as network servers and for communication between multiple CPUs installed on the same server. Xeon processors differ from desktop processors in the available types of features. While Xeon has many of the same features that are incorporated into other Intel processors, such as Hyper-Threading, they are not designed for video streaming 3-D and such. Xeon processors are not designed for entertainment but rather to work together as a large collection of processors sharing tasks. For example, blade servers are specialized equipment that contain multiple motherboards with two or more processors on each board, **Figure 4-12**. The term *blade server* is used to describe the individual modules. The individual blade server modules are installed in an enclosure like the one in **Figure 4-13**. Blade server modules are thin in design when compared to a desktop model.

The entire blade server system is used to provide web services, cloud storage, network services, and similar applications. The individual blade server modules are typically made "hot swappable," which means they can be replaced without shutting down the the system.

Intel Celeron

The Intel Celeron was introduced in 1999. It is a budget-minded processor designed for general-purpose applications. The limited size of the Celeron L1 and L2 cache counters the high speed of the processor, resulting in less overall performance when compared to other Intel processors. Motherboards designed for the Intel Celeron and Pentium processors use front side bus (FSB) technology.

AMD Athlon 64

The AMD Athlon 64, introduced in 2002, is an extremely powerful desktop CPU. As the name implies, it uses 32-bit and 64-bit processing technology. L1 and L2 cache are integrated into the CPU, and an L3 cache is mounted on the motherboard. The Athlon 64 is designed to mount in a 940-pin socket. Normally, an increased number of pins would increase the overall dimensions of the CPU socket. The Athlon 64 CPU, however, uses the Socket 940 micro PGA. The micro PGA

Figure 4-12.
This blade server has two sockets used to mount two separate Xeon processors.

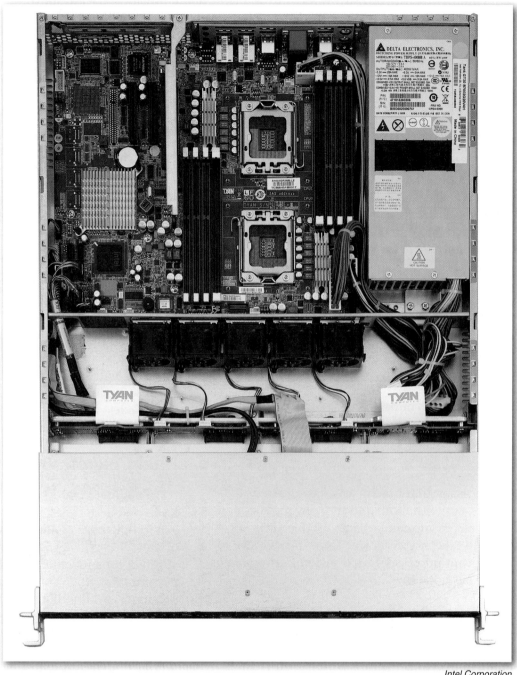

reduces the socket pin grid array area, reducing the overall size of the CPU socket, even with an increase in the number of pins.

AMD Opteron

The AMD Opteron, introduced in 2003, is a high-end processor designed and developed for network servers. The Opteron eliminated the 4 GB memory address barrier associated with earlier processors. The 4 GB memory access limitation is a trait of the 32-bit design, but the Opteron uses a 64-bit memory address design, allowing for greater memory capacity. Total possible accessible memory is 256 TB, but that number is impractical for now. The typical core processor speeds range from 800 MHz to 2.6 GHz, but the processor can produce a throughput of 19 GB or more by using

Figure 4-13.
Eight blade servers installed in an enclosure. The motherboard in each blade server has 2 Xeon processors. The blade servers work together as a single server with a total of 16 processors.

Intel Corporation

multiple paths to process data. The 64 kB L1 cache and the 1024 kB (1 MB) L2 cache are both integrated into the CPU chip. The Opteron mounts into a Socket 940 micro PGA.

AMD Sempron

AMD Sempron, introduced in 2004, is the successor to the AMD Duron processor and is designed for use in low-cost computer systems like the Intel Celeron. The Sempron requires a socket 754 on the motherboard. The interesting thing about the Sempron is that it comes in two very different styles—front side bus with a north bridge chipset and HyperTransport. You must be sure of which Sempron you are going to install or replace.

For CPUs that use HyperTransport, speed is represented by megatransfers per second (MT/s), not frequency (Hz). AMD claims 2000 MT/s is equal to 4 GBps in each direction of the bus.

The transfer speed can also be measured as gigatransfers (GT/s), but AMD has chosen to represent the transfer speed in MT/s. To a casual reader with no real computer expertise, 2000 MT/s looks much more impressive than 2 GT/s.

AMD Athlon 64 X2

The AMD Athlon 64 X2, introduced in 2005, is a dual-core processor that incorporates a new technique of accessing frequently used data. The Athlon 64 X2 cores are capable of higher data throughput than the single-core Athlon 64. The Athlon 64 X2 is intended to be used in all computer systems except in high-end or high-performance models.

AMD Athlon 64 FX

In 2006, AMD introduced the Athlon 64 FX and a new socket design called *AM2*. Although, the Athlon 64 FX processor is physically and electrically compatible with the socket 939 and socket 940. This means that the Athlon 64 FX can be used to upgrade an older computer that uses the previous version CPU mounted in a socket 939 or socket 940. The AM2 socket, however, is not compatible with previous versions of AMD processors that fit into the socket 939 and socket 940. The Athlon 64 FX is comparable to the Intel Core 2 Extreme. Both are intended for use in high-end or high-performance computer systems, which require intense processing performance.

Intel Core Solo

The first Intel Core processor, referred to as Intel Core Solo, was introduced in the summer of 2006. The Intel Core Solo is a single core processor designed for laptop and other portable computer systems. Intel changed the physical and electrical design of its processor to meet the demands for less power consumption and high data throughput. Low power consumption was a desirable feature for marketing laptop and portable devices. High data throughput is the most common design characteristic of CPU evolution and is expected in all new models. The Core Solo core design is also used by the Intel dual-core and quad-core CPUs.

Intel Core Duo

The Intel Core Duo was also introduced in the summer of 2006. It was the first dual-core processor designed by Intel and at first, was intended for the laptop market. At this point in computer development, laptops were becoming more popular than desktops. To take advantage of this growth market, Intel revised the CPU design to better capture a large market share of laptop computer sales. This was done by developing the Intel Core Duo processor. The dual-core design provided greater processing power with reduced electrical power to decrease heat.

Intel Core 2 Duo

The Intel Core 2 Duo, introduced in 2006, has two processor cores mounted inside one CPU chip. The Core 2 Duo differs from the AMD dual-core

processors in two main design issues. First, the Intel Core 2 Duo uses a front side bus, which connects the CPU to the RAM and north bridge chipset through one common bus. The AMD dual-core processors use the HyperTransport bus system. Second, the Intel Core 2 Duo varies the amount of L2 cache used by each core based on program demand. The AMD design does not share the L2 cache.

Intel Core 2 Extreme

The Intel Core 2 Extreme, introduced in 2007, is comparable to the AMD Athlon 64 FX processor. The Core 2 Extreme has the highest dual-core processor throughput and the largest L2 cache (8 MB at the time of this writing). It is designed for use in intense computing such as gaming, computer-aided drafting, three-dimensional rendering, and scientific formula processing. The Core 2 Extreme is also referred to as Core 2 X, where the X represents *extreme*.

Intel Core 2 Extreme Quad

The Intel Core 2 Extreme Quad, introduced in 2007, is also referred to as Core 2 Quad and Core 2 Q. It is the first quad-core processor design. The Core 2 Extreme Quad houses four independent processor cores on the same CPU die. It uses the same core as the Core 2 Extreme processor. The main idea is to double the capabilities of the Core 2 Extreme processor by doubling the core on a single chip. To take advantage of quad-core processing, a software application must be designed for this type of processing. Otherwise, there will not be a significant increase in software application performance.

Intel Core i3, i5, and i7

For improved video and entertainment, Intel rapidly developed a series of processors called the Intel Core processor family. It started with the introduction of the first generation Intel Core i3 processor in January 2010 and soon followed with the second and third generations of the Intel Core processors known as Core i3, Core i5, and Core i7. There are over thirty different processors included in the Intel Core family of processors, spanning three generations from January 2010 to October 2012.

This first release of the Core i3, Core i5, and Core i7 processors are known now as the first generation of Core processors. In addition to processor improvements such as cache size, number of cores, and high processor frequencies, the Core series of processors made major improvements in graphics for entertainment. The emphasis in recent years has been to improve the quality of streaming videos for high-definition television, improve 3-D graphics support, and allow for video editing without the need for a high-performance video card. The video improvements are incorporated into the processor design.

2nd Generation Intel Core i3, i5, and i7

The second generation of Intel Core processors were introduced in January 2011. These processors are built using 32-nanometer architecture. It was the first generation of Intel Core processors to put the processor, memory controller, and graphics unit on the same die. While incorporating the graphics processor on the same die as the CPU does improve graphics performance, the improvement is limited to graphics such as streaming video, television, and movies. For the very best video and 3-D performance, a separate video card with its own processor is required.

Intel advertises the second generation Core processors to have a 60% improvement in performance over the previous generation. These processors have up to six processors on one die, each processor supporting two threads. This is equal to 12 logical processors. Intel Turbo Boost Technology 2.0 was also introduced with this generation, which is an enhanced version of the original Turbo Boost Technology.

There are over 30 different processors in the second generation. The processors vary by specifications such as maximum core frequency, technologies supported, and amount of internal cache.

3rd Generation Intel Core i3, i5, and i7

The third generation of Intel Core processors was released in the summer of 2012. This generation is built using 22-nanometer

architecture. It can support more RAM than previous generations and has faster processing abilities. The third generation continues to enhance video and improve 3-D graphics. See **Figure 4-14** to compare the features of the 3rd Generation Intel Core i3/i5/i7 processors.

The table in **Figure 4-15** provides a snapshot of the overall specifications of the 3rd Generation Intel Core processors for comparison. The specifications are constantly changing and may be higher than those recorded at the time of this writing.

Figure 4-14. Feature comparison of 3rd Generation Intel Core processors.

Features	i3	i5	i7
Number of cores/threads	2/4	4/8	4/8
Turbo Boost 2.0 Technology	No	Yes	Yes
Hyper-Threading Technology	Yes	No	Yes
Smart Cache w/shared L3	3 MB	6 MB	8 MB
Performance Tuning enabled	No	Yes	Yes
Recommended chipset	H61	H77	Z77

Goodheart-Willcox Publisher

Intel Core i3

The Intel Core i3 is designed for minimal computing power and is not intended for high-performance applications. The Core i3 will perform word-processing functions, e-mail services, and web-browsing applications. This processor is ideal for a computer that uses cloud services, which provide the processing power needed for more intense software applications. Compared to the Core i5 and i7, the Core i3 has the smallest L3 cache size. Also, Turbo Boost 2.0 Technology and Performance Tuning are not available for the Intel Core i3.

Intel Core i5

The Intel Core i5 processor is designed as an intermediate processor with performance between

Figure 4-15.
Comparison of Intel Core processor cores, threads, speed, and cache.

Processor	Cores	Threads	Clock Speed	Cache
Core i7 Extreme	4–6	8–12	2 GHz–2.9 GHz	8 MB–15 MB
Core i7	2–6	4–12	1.2 GHz–2.8 GHz	4 MB–8 MB
Core i5	2	4	1.2 GHz–2.8 GHz	3 MB–6 MB
Core i3	2	4	1.2 GHz–2.66 GHz	3 MB

Note: These specifications are constantly changing and may not reflect the latest changes.

Goodheart-Willcox Publisher

the Core i3 and i7. The Core i5 does not support Intel Hyper-Threading Technology but does have many of the other processor features such as performance tuning. The addition of Performance Tuning enhances overall system performance for gaming, video editing, and computation but not to the level expected from a Core i7 processor. The L3 cache of Core i5 is bigger than that of the Core i3 but smaller than that of the Core i7. This means that processor performance is better than the Core i3 but less than the Core i7. This processor is perfect for users looking for an average computer system with limited multimedia-editing capabilities.

Intel Core i7 and i7 Extreme

The Intel Core i7 processor comes in two versions: Intel Core i7 and Intel Core i7 Extreme. Both processors have the most processor cores and threads as compared to Core i3 and i5. Both versions of Core i7 have the most desirable features for high performance such as Intel Turbo Boost 2.0 Technology, Intel Hyper-Threading Technology, Performance Tuning, and the largest L3 cache.

The main difference between the Core i7 and Core i7 Extreme edition is the Extreme edition provides better graphics performance than the Core i7. The Intel Core i7 Extreme processor is the best Intel processor designed for high-performance software applications, such as gaming with intense 3-D graphics. This processor supports up to 32 GB of DDR3 memory. The Core i7 has additional cache and is capable of higher clock speeds when compared to the Core i7.

Intel Atom

The Intel Atom is a specialized processor designed for low power consumption and low heat production. It is available in 32-bit and 64-bit and in single-core and dual-core. The Atom is limited to applications requiring minimal processor performance. It is used in netbooks, tablets, smartphones, and similar devices. The Atom is soldered to the motherboard, which makes replacement difficult. The motherboard would need to be replaced if the processor was defective.

AMD FX

The AMD FX is the best performance AMD processor so far. It is a multi-core processor available in 4-core, 6-core, and 8-core. The AMD FX is used in applications which demand high-performance processing, such as for 3-D graphics. It is designed for overclocking using the software utility AMD Overdrive and AMD Catalyst. The AMD FX was the first multi-core processor with eight cores beating Intel in the processor development race.

AMD A-Series

The AMD A-Series consist of a collection of processors identified as A4, A6, A8, and A10. The A-Series is similar to the Intel Core i3/i5/i7 processors in that they are designed with an integrated GPU. The AMD A-Series refers to the integrated graphics unit as Accelerated Processing Unit (APU). To compare AMD with similar Intel processors, see **Figure 4-16**.

Expectations	Intel	AMD
High-end performance, such as intense graphics, audio, and video processing.	Core i7, Core i7 Extreme	Athlon 64 X2, Phenom, Phenom II, FX, A-Series
Average performance, such as multimedia editing and processing by the average user.	Core i5	Sempron, Athlon II
Low performance, such as an introductory-level PC not designed for intense graphics and multimedia processing.	Pentium, Celeron, Core 2 Duo, Core i3	Sempron

Figure 4-16.
Comparison of Intel and AMD processors.

Goodheart-Willcox Publisher

Multi-Core Processors

A multi-core processor is two or more processor cores constructed on the same die. Increased data throughput is achieved mainly by using a dual core. Both Intel and AMD manufacture multi-core processors.

Figure 4-17 compares the internal architecture of an AMD Athlon 64 processor and an AMD Athlon 64 FX processor. The AMD Athlon 64 processor in Figure 4-17A contains a single core and two L1 caches. One L1 cache is used to temporarily store processing instructions and commands, and the other L1 cache is used to temporary store data being processed. The two L1 caches make the processing of data twice as fast as processors that contain a single L1 cache. L1 cache is typically smaller and faster than L2 cache. The AMD Athlon 64 uses an L1 cache of 64 kB while L2 cache is typically 1 MB or more. The DDR memory controller connects directly with RAM. The HyperTransport link connects to other devices and buses across the motherboard.

As you can see in Figure 4-17B, the AMD Athlon 64 FX processor consists of two complete AMD Athlon 64 processors on the same die. Each processor has its own set of L1 caches, and each has its own L2 cache. The two processors share the DDR memory controller and the HyperTransport link.

The Intel Core Duo has two L1 caches per core, just like the AMD Athlon 64 FX processor, **Figure 4-18**. The big difference between the AMD and Intel multi-core processors is the L2 cache design. The AMD Athlon 64 FX processor has an L2 cache for each core; the Intel Core Duo has one L2 cache, which is shared by each core. The

reason Intel decided to share the L2 cache is so the amount of L2 cache used by each core is directly proportional to the processing demand of each core. For example, if only one core is used, then that one core will use the entire L2 cache. If one core is running at 25% and the other at 75%, the L2 cache will also be split at 25% and 75%. This means that the entire L2 cache is used at all times. In the AMD design, the L2 cache can only be used by the corresponding processor core.

Another significant difference between the Intel Core Duo and the AMD Athlon 64 FX is the AMD multi-core design makes use of HyperTransport Technology and does not use a north bridge chip. The data throughput using the HyperTransport Technology is used to connect directly to the south bridge, additional CPUs, or other devices. The AMD multi-core processor also connects directly to the RAM and does not have a front side bus as the first Intel multi-core designs did. The FSB design of Intel multi-core system requires that the RAM share the FSB with the north bridge. See **Figure 4-19**.

AMD and Intel both introduced newer multi-core technologies that are designed with the individual core processors communicating directly with each other and directly to memory. In earlier versions of processor and motherboard architecture, the processor had to communicate with memory through chipsets mounted on the motherboard. Also, early versions of multi-core processors communicated with each other through the processor L3 cache rather than directly. The AMD version is called Direct Connect Architecture and the Intel version is called QuickPath Technology.

Figure 4-17. The internal architecture of a single-core and dual-core AMD Athlon processor. A—AMD Athlon 64 (single-core) processor. B—AMD Athlon 64 FX (dual-core) processor.

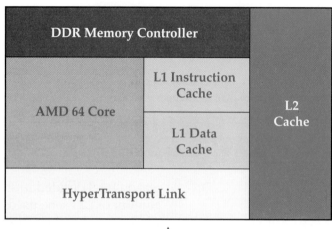

Goodheart-Willcox Publisher

AMD and Intel have been competing for many years. Whenever one of the organizations develops a new technology, the other soon develops its own version of a very similar technology. AMD Direct Connect Architecture and Intel QuickPath Technology are a great example of this competition. The technologies are very similar but never an exact duplicate which would result in patent infringement.

Processor Affinity

Processor affinity is the ability to select the number of CPU cores to apply to a software application. To take advantage of multi-core

Figure 4-18. Intel Core Duo internal architecture. Notice it has one L2 cache, which is shared by each core.

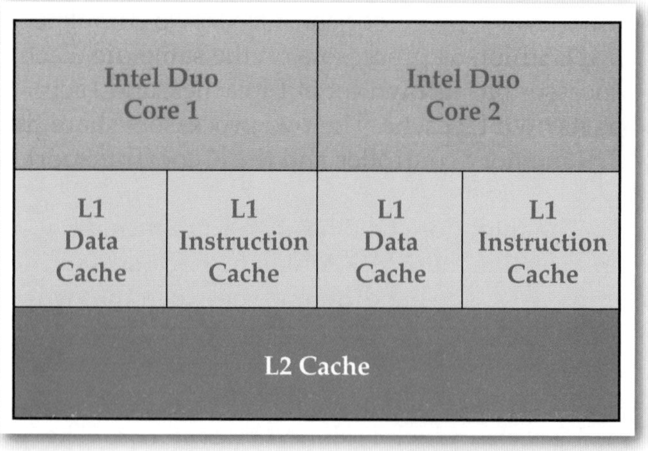

Goodheart-Willcox Publisher

Figure 4-19. An AMD multi-core processor and an Intel multi-core processor interface differently with motherboard devices, chipsets, and other CPUs. A—AMD multi-core processor connects directly to the south bridge chip, RAM, and other devices. B—Intel Core Duo connects directly to the front side bus.

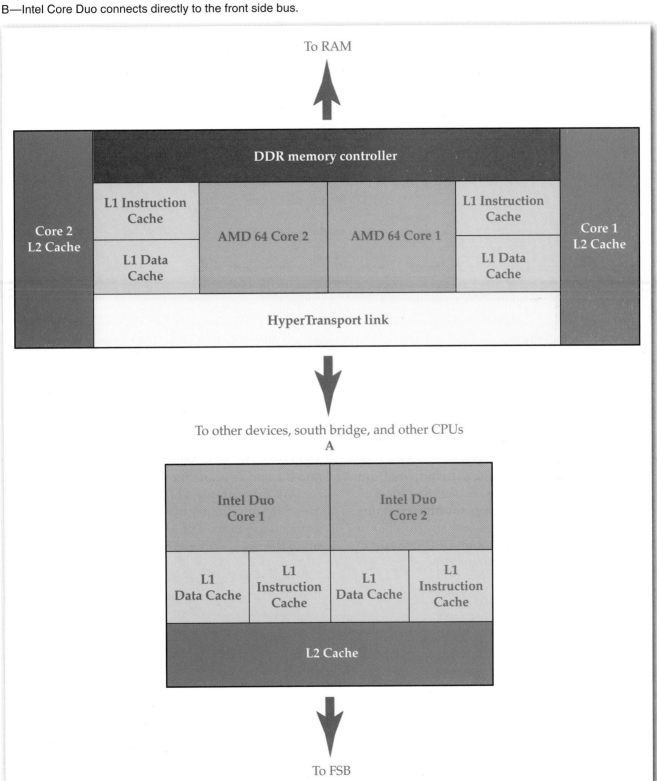

Figure 4-20.
To disable the use of multiple CPUs for a program that is not designed to work with multiple CPUs, access **Task Manager** and right-click the program. Select **Set Affinity** from the shortcut menu. The **Processor Affinity** dialog box will display.

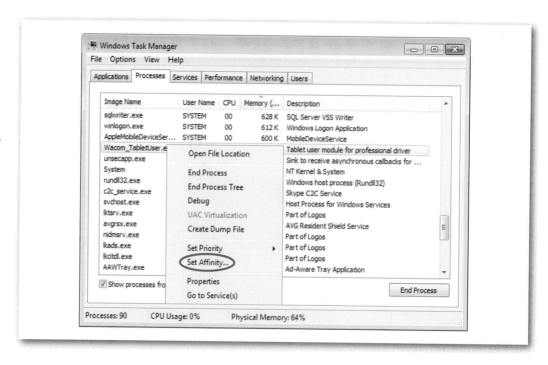

processors, the operating system and the software application must be designed to operate in the multi-core environment. If a software program or application is not designed to work with a multi-core processor, the software could lock up. It may be necessary to disable the multiple cores so that the software application can run properly. To disable one of the cores, you simply open the Task Manager, right-click the software program, and select **Set Affinity** from the shortcut menu. See **Figure 4-20**. In the **Processor Affinity** dialog box, **Figure 4-21**, simply deselect any number of processors from CPU 0 through CPU 7 to run the software application on a single processor.

Processor Sockets

Processor sockets vary according to the number of electrical connections and the pattern of the connections that are made between the processor and the socket. Common Intel CPU sockets are LGA 775, LGA115, LGA 1156, LGA 1366, and LGA 2011. Some common AMD CPU sockets are 940, AM2, AM2+, AM3, AM3+, F, FM1, and FM2. See **Figure 4-22** to match Intel and AMD sockets and processors. The most important thing to remember about processor sockets is you cannot install an Intel processor into a socket designed for an AMD processor, and you cannot

install an AMD processor into a socket designed for an Intel processor.

The terms **Land Grid Array (LGA)** and **Pin Grid Array (PGA)** are used to identify the physical and electrical connections made between the socket and the processor. Current Intel sockets use LGA, and current AMD sockets use PGA and LGA. The acronym LGA is incorporated into the socket name for many Intel processor sockets, for example, LGA 2011. Land Grid Array uses a design or an array of "lands" as electrical connection points. The term *land* refers to the small flat area used as an electrical connection

Figure 4-21. Processor Affinity dialog box.

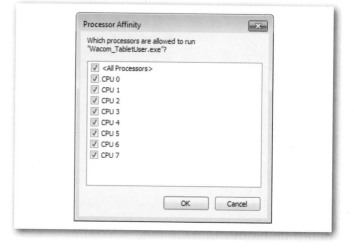

Intel Socket	Intel Processor	AMD Socket	AMD Processor
LGA 775	Pentium, Celeron, Xeon, Core 2 Duo, Core 2 Quad	940	Opteron, Athlon 64 FX
LGA 115	Pentium, Celeron, Xeon, Core i3/i5/i7	AM2	Athlon 64, Athlon 64 X2, AMD 64 FX
LGA 1156	Pentium, Celeron, Xeon, Core i3/i5/i7	AM2+	Phenom, Phenon II, Athlon 64, Athlon 64 X2
LGA 1366	Xeon, Core i7	AM3, AM3+, F	Opteron, Sempron, Phenon II, Athlon II, FX, Liano
LGA 2011	Xeon, Core i7	FM1, FM2	A4, A6, A8, A10, E2

Figure 4-22. Intel and AMD processors and sockets.

Note: The table contains only a partial list of sockets and processors. Check the manufacturer's website for the latest information about sockets and processors.

Goodheart-Willcox Publisher

point on the back of the processor. Pin Grid Array uses an array of pins for the electrical connections.

The original processor sockets were designed for the technician to press the processor into the socket. This required many pounds of force. The processor had an array of long pins on the back which were forced into the socket. If the processor pins were misaligned with the processor socket, the force of the insertion would bend some of the pins. When the pins were straightened back out they would sometimes break off, resulting in a processor that could not be repaired. To alleviate the use of severe force, the **zero insertion force (ZIF) socket** was designed. ZIF sockets have a lever to assist in the installation of the CPU. This type of socket requires practically no force at all to insert the CPU into the socket while the lever arm is raised. Once the CPU is inserted into the socket, the lever is lowered, which in turn causes each pin to fit tightly into the socket. The ZIF socket literally clamps each pin into place.

Intel identifies its processor sockets with numbers. For example, an Intel LGA 2011 socket has 2,011 locations or connection points. In contrast a LGA 775 socket has 775 connection points. This means the socket and the motherboard is only compatible with a specific set of processors. AMD identifies its processor sockets with numbers and letters. AMD is moving away from number identification and is now using more letters.

AMD features two sockets: socket 939 and socket 940. They appear almost identical except for the one pin difference. The one pin difference is very significant. The socket 939 does not require registered RAM. Socket 940 does. Registered RAM is typically used for servers and mission-critical computers. Most desktop PCs do not require registered type RAM. Therefore, you will find that most AMD desktop PCs use a socket 939.

The AMD AM2 socket closely resembles the 939 and 940 sockets, but it is not compatible electrically or physically with CPUs designed for 939 and 940 sockets. The reason for the change is the HyperTransport interface on an AM2 socket processor. AMD CPUs that use the HyperTransport technology are no longer compatible with motherboards which use a north bridge chip in the chipset. The AMD Athlon 64 FX will physically fit into a 939, 940, and AM2 socket, but it can only take advantage of the larger L2 cache design when installed in an AM2 socket.

The AM2 socket also supports direct data transfers to DDR2 RAM. The 939 and 940 sockets do not. DDR2 RAM is a high-performance RAM that is covered in detail in Chapter 6—Memory. The original name of the AM2 socket was simply M2 but later was changed because it was confused with the M2 socket introduced by Cyrix.

Processor Performance

Because the Intel and AMD physical designs are so different, they cannot be evaluated by the specific features. Both companies claim superior performance based on their CPU designs. The only way to fairly evaluate CPU performance is when it is running software applications.

The true performance of a CPU can only be measured by evaluating the performance of two different computer systems using similar hardware. However, it is nearly impossible to exactly match the two systems because of the motherboard chipset and bus system. Rather than try to evaluate a specific CPU, you are better off evaluating a complete computer system and how the same software application performs on each computer system. A CPU analyzer can also be used to evaluate a processor's performance. A free CPU analyzer, called CPU-Z, can be downloaded from CPUID. It will identify the CPU, size of the L1 and L2 cache, socket type, core speed, bus speed, and more.

The CPU-Z utility shown in **Figure 4-23** has identified four cores for the processor and additional related information. This is an excellent tool for obtaining processor specifications as well as motherboard and memory specifications without opening the computer case and looking for part numbers. Intel and AMD also provide similar software utilities to inspect the processor. **Figure 4-24** shows the Intel Processor Identification Utility.

Figure 4-23. The CPU-Z utility available from CPUID can be used to identify the CPU, size of L1 and L2 cache, socket type, core speed, bus speed, and more.

Tech Tip

A software utility that identifies the processor, motherboard, and memory specifications is a valuable asset to a PC technician's tool kit.

Questions to Ask Before Upgrading a CPU

The process of upgrading the CPU can range from easy to nearly impossible. The degree of likelihood for a logical upgrade is based on several computer system conditions. Questions you should first answer include the following:

- What are you trying to achieve by upgrading the CPU?
- Is the upgrade processor compatible physically with the motherboard?
- Will the chipset and BIOS support the upgraded processor?
- Does the motherboard bus speed and chipset, rather than the CPU speed, limit the increase in speed you desire?
- Does the motherboard chipset support the desired features of the new CPU, such as a new 3-D technology?

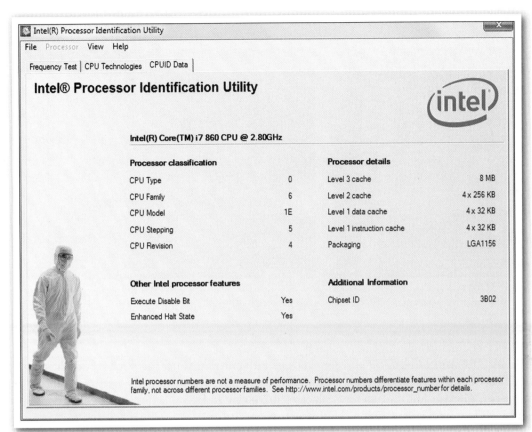

Figure 4-24.
The Intel Processor Identification Utility identifies data about the installed processor, such as the processor name, processor model number, cache sizes, and socket type.

You may wish to upgrade from a low-end processor such as an Intel Celeron or Intel Core i3 to a Core i7, but the higher performance expected may not be encountered. The motherboard chipset is most likely matched to the processor. Simply replacing the existing processor with a much better one may not achieve your desired purpose.

Transferring data to and from the hard drive or a scanner is mostly an issue involving the motherboard bus speed and port speeds and not the speed of the CPU. If an increase in the speed of downloading information from the Internet is the challenge, a new processor is not likely to increase the download speed. Download speed is more dependent on the cabling system between the downloading site and the computer and the modem speed. If typing is the main function performed at the computer, upgrading the CPU will have little to no effect on the user's typing speed.

As you can see, upgrading a processor may not meet your desires. If you crunch a lot of data or play games that contain intensive graphics and sound, you may very well improve the performance of the computer system by upgrading the CPU. Often, it is more practical to replace the CPU and the motherboard to achieve the desired results.

Installing a Processor

Installing or replacing a processor is not a difficult task. If it is your first time installing a particular processor, you need to do your research before beginning, especially when matching the correct cooling device to the processor. Processor installation has always been a fairly easy task, but cooling device installation has been known to be much more difficult. The information presented in this section is to serve as a general guide for installing a processor and cooling device. You should always consult the manufacturer's website before performing a complete processor installation or replacement.

A CPU socket is designed as a mechanical assembly with a mounting plate and lever(s) which secure the processor in the socket.

Figure 4-25. Comparison of a one-lever and two-lever processor socket.

LGA 2011

LGA 775

Figure 4-25 shows the LGA 2011 and LGA 775 sockets for comparison. The LGA 775 has a single lever called a load plate lever. The LGA 2011 has two socket levers, the active lever and hinge lever. These levers are designed to place equal physical pressure on both ends of the loading plate, ensuring that the processor is firmly mounted in place. Having an additional lever helps secure the processor in place when a heavy cooling unit is mounted on the socket.

The LGA 2011 socket has been designed to accommodate heavy processor cooling devices. The socket is made of a heavy-duty metal frame, which is securely fastened to the motherboard. The metal frame has four threaded mounting studs used to secure the cooling device. The cooling device can be a simple lightweight heat sink and fan combination, a heat sink and heat tube combination, or a radiator and liquid cooler pump combination. The lightweight heat sink and fan combination is used for the average processor. The heat sink and tube combination and radiator and liquid cooler pump combination are used for high-performance processors and for those used in overclocking applications.

The major parts of an LGA 2011 socket are identified in **Figure 4-26**. The entire socket assembly is fabricated on a metal frame, which is mounted to the motherboard. The motherboard typically has a plate on its reverse side. The plate

is in direct alignment with the socket mounting plate, **Figure 4-27**. Motherboards without a back plate require one to be installed with certain types of cooling devices.

When a motherboard is removed from the shipping box, the socket will come with a cover over the socket held in place by the load plate. The cover is designed to keep foreign objects such as dust out of the socket and protect the electrical connections from accidental physical damage. The levers must be released to remove the cover from under the loading plate.

The two levers on the LGA 2011 have a specific sequence for opening and closing. To open the socket load plate, the hinge lever must be released first followed by the active lever. When closing the load plate, the operational sequence is reversed. The active lever is closed first, and then the hinge lever is closed. The hinge lever is designed to keep the active lever from being opened first, **Figure 4-28**. After both the hinge lever and the active lever are released, the load plate can be tilted back and the cover removed, thus exposing the processor socket.

After the processor socket is exposed, the processor can be installed. There is only one way to correctly install the processor. It must be aligned with the socket. If you look closely at the processor in **Figure 4-29**, you will see an orientation mark in the top corner. This mark

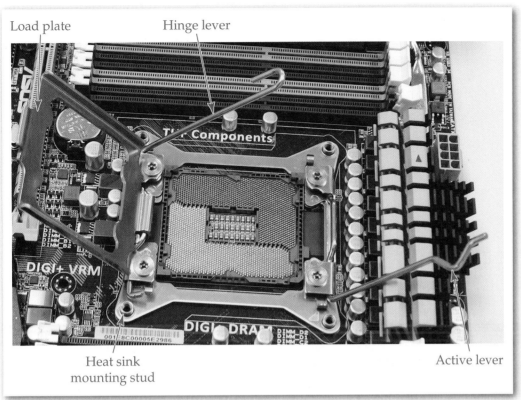

Load plate   Hinge lever

Heat sink
mounting stud

Active lever

Goodheart-Willcox Publisher

Figure 4-26.
LGA 2011 major socket parts.

Figure 4-27. The socket back plate is required to prevent damage to the motherboard when mounting cooling devices.

Back plate

Goodheart-Willcox Publisher

is used to assist with proper orientation. Some processors use a dot. Some use a triangle or some other mark. You can also visually compare the pin pattern on the socket and processor to determine

the correct orientation or use the notches provided along the edge of the processor that align with the notches along the edge of the socket. There is no need to force the processor into the socket. Simply drop it into place, gently.

After the processor is installed, close the active lever and then the hinge lever to snuggly close the loading plate over the processor and secure it into the socket. Now the processor is ready for the cooling system.

Cooling the Processor

As the CPU evolved to higher data speeds, the heat generated by the processor circuits also increased. Electrical circuits generate heat in proportion to the speed of data flow. Electronic integrated circuits start to break down at approximately 160°F (71°C). There are three main choices of cooling the processor:

- Simple heat sink and fan assembly.
- Heat pipe cooling system.
- Liquid cooling system.

Figure 4-28.
The LGA 2011 is equipped with a hinge lever locking mechanism.

Hinge lever must be released first

Hinge lever prevents active lever from opening

Figure 4-29.
Processor and socket orientation.

Notches

Notches

Triangles used for orientation

A simple heat sink and fan assembly is most commonly used. Heat sinks are attached to the CPU by heat conductive paste, also called *thermal compound*. The paste ensures a good fit between the surface of the processor and heat sink. Without the paste, the heat sink could warp slightly, resulting in poor physical contact between the surfaces. The CPU could heat up to a dangerous level.

A heat pipe cooling system is more expensive than a simple heat sink and fan and is generally much heavier. A liquid cooling system is the most expensive. Both the heat pipe and the liquid cooling systems are commonly used in overclocking applications. The heat pipe and liquid cooling types reduce the heat from the processor much more efficiently than a simple heat sink and fan assembly.

The difficulty of installing a cooling system ranges from simple to complicated, depending on the type of system you choose to install. Also, some of the assembly kits can contain many parts, and the instructions are not always as clear. Experience is a great help when installing cooling kits. The cooling kit manufacturer typically provides detailed instructions at their website. There are also several YouTube videos designed to show how to install a cooling system for a particular type of CPU and motherboard combination.

A+ Note

When preparing for the A+ Certification exams, remember that overclocking, even when using a liquid cooling device, generally voids the processor warranty.

Heat Sink and Fan Assembly

For general purpose computer systems, you will most likely use a heat sink and fan assembly. The simple fan and heat sink assembly is the least expensive of the three cooling systems. The fan assembly screws into place on a LGA 2011 socket. Another type of fan assembly used with a different physical socket does not use threaded screws. It uses plastic legs that are pushed through the physical connections points. See **Figure 4-30**.

After the heat sink and fan assembly is physically installed over the processor, you must connect the fan wiring to the motherboard. A typical motherboard has several fan connections. One is usually designated as the CPU fan connection, **Figure 4-31**. The CPU fan connection can be monitored by the BIOS. The BIOS will warn the user when the fan is running too slowly

Figure 4-30. Installing a fan and heat sink assembly. A—The fan assembly is screwed into the mounting studs of the LGA 2011 socket assembly. B—This fan assembly uses plastic mounting legs that are inserted and twisted into the mounting holes of the processor socket assembly.

A

B

Figure 4-31. Four-pin CPU fan connection.

Goodheart-Willcox Publisher

or when the CPU is generating excessive heat. The motherboard manual usually contains all information needed for proper installation of a simple fan and heat sink.

When a motherboard manual is not available, you can check the motherboard manufacturer's website or processor manufacturer's website to correctly match the cooling device to the processor and motherboard socket. The website or manual will contain detailed instructions for the correct installation of the processor and the cooling system. An illustrated manual usually accompanies a non-standard cooling device. Again, you can consult the manufacturer's website for detailed instructions on how to install the cooling device. YouTube commonly has videos explaining the installation procedure. These are provided by other technicians or by the manufacturer.

Heat Pipe Cooling System

A heat pipe is constructed of a collection of hollow tubes that run from the processor heat sink through a series of cooling fins used to dissipate heat. The tubes contain a cooling liquid that absorbs the heat generated by the processor. The liquid absorbs heat and evaporates into a gas form.

This process is referred to as evaporation. The gas then rises through the tubes to the cooling fins or radiator. The gas then condenses as the heat is released through the cooling fins and turns back into a liquid. This process is called condensation. The liquid returns to the processor end of the tube using gravity or capillary action. The heat pipe system repeats the cooling cycle continuously. Generally, no pump is used to return the liquid. The cooling liquid is circulated using only the principles of evaporation, condensation, and gravity or capillary action. See **Figure 4-32**.

Capillary action refers to the physics principle when liquid travels through or is drawn through a narrow passage or through a thin surface material or slot. As an example of capillary action, think of how a paper towel or cloth absorbs liquid into the material when only a corner touches the liquid. This same principle is used in the heat tube circulation system. The heat tube has an absorbent material lining which channels the condensation to the heat source using the capillary action. Gravity is not always best because the heat pipe can be mounted in a position that does not support gravity flow to the bottom of the heat pipe. For example, when a heat tube is mounted on a motherboard inside a tower case, the heat tube is mounted on its side. The capillary principle will return the liquid to the heat source.

Liquid Cooling System

A liquid cooling system is by far the most expensive of the three choices of cooling systems. The pump and a heat sink are mounted directly on the processor. The heat generated by the processor is absorbed by the heat sink and transferred to the liquid. The liquid is circulated by a small pump that is mounted on the processor heat sink. The liquid is circulated to the radiator where the heat is released. A fan is mounted on the radiator to assist with the removal of the heat. See **Figure 4-33**.

The cooling system can be monitored by the BIOS. When the temperature and the fan speed are monitored, the computer system will automatically shut down if a predetermined temperature is reached or if the cooling system

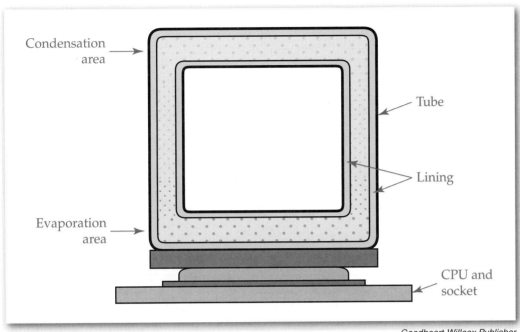

Condensation area

Tube

Lining

Evaporation area

CPU and socket

Figure 4-32.
The CPU heats the liquid in the heat tube. The liquid turns to vapor. The cooling action of the cooling fins returns the vapor to a liquid. The liquid returns to the evaporation area, and the process begins again.

Goodheart-Willcox Publisher

Figure 4-33. A liquid cooling system consists of a pump and a radiator. The pump circulates the liquid, and the radiator releases the heat generated by the processor.

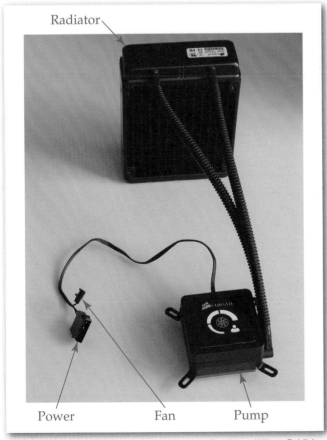

Radiator

Power   Fan   Pump

Goodheart-Willcox Publisher

fails, such as the fan goes below a preset RPM. To monitor the cooling system, a three- or four-wire fan connection is required. To simply power a cooling fan, only a two-wire fan connection is required.

Look again at Figure 4-33. Notice that the liquid cooling pump uses two different electrical connections. One is a typical fan connection, which provides monitoring information. The other is a Molex-type power connection, which provides electrical power to the pump. The pump requires more electrical power than a fan. This is why the Molex connector is required.

Cooling devices may come with a wide variety of hardware accessories that are used for a variety of different sockets. An Intel processor socket and an AMD processor socket usually require different mounting accessories. Be sure to read all instructions carefully before attempting to install the cooling devices. **Figure 4-34** shows the final stage of installing a liquid cooling device. The radiator has been mounted to the rear case fan and the liquid cooling pump is screwed down over the processor.

After installing the liquid cooling unit, the computer can be booted. If a problem occurs, the computer BIOS will automatically stop the boot process. **Figure 4-35** shows the ASUS UEFI BIOS monitoring the computer system. The system was halted because of a cooling fan problem detected.

The information for the fan at fault is displayed in red. The BIOS has detected that the CPU cooling fan RPM is too low and has stopped the boot process. A high-performance CPU can rapidly generate excessive heat and lock up during the boot process. After the problem is corrected, the computer can be safely booted. There is also an option which will allow you to ignore the problem. Not all computers have this type of monitoring. The availability of the monitoring program depends on the motherboard BIOS system.

Figure 4-34. Installing a liquid cooling system.

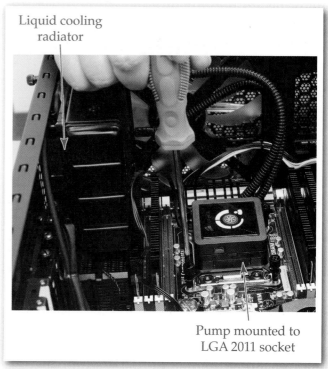

Liquid cooling radiator

Pump mounted to LGA 2011 socket

Goodheart-Willcox Publisher

Figure 4-35. Cooling error displayed by the UEFI BIOS Utility.

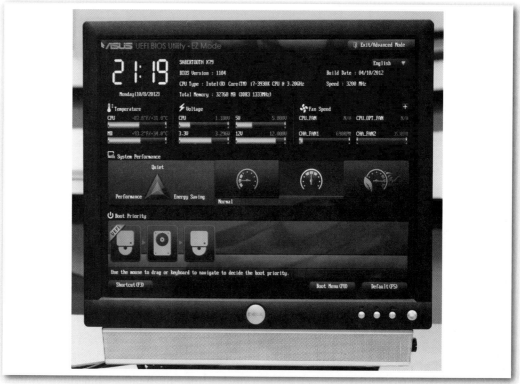

Goodheart-Willcox Publisher

Chapter Summary

- An instruction set is the lowest language level used to program a computer and is written in assembly language.
- A CPU processes commands and data, refreshes memory, checks for communication from system devices, monitors the system power, and performs other programmed duties.
- Some of the technologies used to enhance CPU operation are local bus, cache, floating point unit, multiple branch prediction, and overclocking.
- Some of the terminology used to describe a processor is RISC, CISC, 32-bit and 64-bit, and processor virtualization.
- The three leading CPU manufacturers are Intel, AMD, and VIA Technologies.
- The AMD A-Series of processors, identified as A4, A6, A8, and A10, are similar to the Intel Core i3/i5/i7 processors in that they are designed with an integrated GPU.
- The individual cores in AMD and Intel multi-core processors communicate directly with each other and directly with memory.
- Windows Task Manager can be used to select the processor(s) to run an application program.
- Common Intel CPU sockets are LGA 775, LGA 115. LGA 1156, LGA 1366, and LGA 2011; and some common AMD CPU sockets are 940, AM2, AM2+, AM3, AM3+, F, FM1, and FM2.
- The performance of a CPU can be measured by evaluating the performance of two different computer systems using similar hardware.
- Before upgrading a CPU, a series of questions should be asked relating to what is to be achieved by the upgrade and whether the new CPU will be compatible with the motherboard.
- To align a processor with a socket, the markings on the top of the processor or the pin pattern on the processor and socket can be used.
- Three choices of cooling the processor are a simple heat sink and fan assembly, heat pipe cooling system, and liquid cooling system.

Review Questions

Answer the following questions on a separate sheet of paper. Please do not write in this book.

1. What is an instruction set?
2. What is the unit of measure for CPU or processor speed?
3. What is the purpose of a decode unit?
4. What is the purpose of a control unit?
5. What is a register unit and what is it used for?
6. What AMD technology is comparable to Intel QuickPath Technology?

7. What is cache?
8. What is superscalar execution?
9. When did superscalar technology begin?
10. What do GPU and APU stand for?
11. What is a Dual Independent Bus, and when was it introduced?
12. What is Intel's term for simultaneous threading?
13. What does overclocking mean?
14. What is the difference between a RISC and CISC processor?
15. What four things are required of a computer system to take full advantage of 64-bit processing?
16. What is processor virtualization?
17. What is System Management Mode?
18. What is Enhanced Intel SpeedStep® Technology?
19. State Moore's law.
20. Name the three top CPU manufacturers.
21. Which Intel processor is designed exclusively for server applications?
22. Does the AMD Sempron use an FSB or a HyperTransport bus system?
23. Which AMD processor is considered comparable to the Intel Celeron processor?
24. Which Intel processor would have the best performance: Core i3 or Core i7?
25. Which AMD processor was designed as the first 8-core processor?
26. Which Intel processors are considered comparable to the AMD FX processor?
27. AMD multi-core processors use _____ Technology to connect directly to the south bridge, additional CPUs, or other devices.
28. What is processor affinity?
29. What Windows program can be used to set the processor affinity?
30. Can you replace an AMD processor with an Intel processor?
31. What is the main difference between the AMD 940 and 939 sockets?
32. What socket is used for an AMD Athlon 64 processor?
33. Can you install an Intel Core i5 into an LGA 1156 socket?
34. Can you install an Intel Core i7 into an AMD2+ socket?
35. What is the only way to fairly evaluate a CPU performance?
36. List at least three questions to ask to determine if a CPU upgrade is desirable or possible.
37. What can be used to properly align a CPU before inserting it into a socket?
38. What are the three major types of processor cooling system?
39. Which type of cooling system is the most expensive?
40. Which cooling system is most common?

Sample A+ Exam Questions

Answer the following questions on a separate sheet of paper. Please do not write in this book.

1. Which of the following are true statements concerning the L1 cache? Select all that apply.
   a. It is generally incorporated into the CPU.
   b. It generally transfers data faster than external cache.
   c. It is usually much larger in storage size than motherboard RAM.
   d. It is a form of temporary memory storage.

2. A CPU register is best described as what?
   a. Cache memory used to store hardware information
   b. Temporary memory storage unit
   c. CPU clock signal generator
   d. Trademark associated with the brand of CPU

3. What does the acronym GPU represent?
   a. Graded Processor Unit
   b. Graphics Processor Unit
   c. Grounded Physical Unit
   d. Graphics Production Utility

4. What is the relationship between CPU frequency, temperature, and performance?
   a. Raising the applied processor frequency results in faster processor performance and increased processor heat.
   b. Raising the applied processor frequency results in faster processor performance and makes the fan run faster, which results in lower overall processor temperature.
   c. Raising the applied processor frequency results in slower processor performance and lower processor heat.
   d. Raising the applied processor frequency results in no change in processor performance and no change in processor temperature.

5. Which processor is commonly used in tablet PCs?
   a. Intel Core i7
   b. AMD A8
   c. Intel Atom
   d. Intel Pentium Xeon

6. When upgrading a CPU, which three items should be given consideration? Select three.
   a. BIOS version
   b. CPU socket/slot type
   c. Size of the RAM
   d. Motherboard chipset

7. Which CPU cooling method is most commonly used for Intel processors?
   a. Heat sink and fan assembly
   b. Passive heat pipe
   c. Heat pipe and fan assembly
   d. Liquid cooling and fan assembly

8. Which processor is compatible with an AM2+ socket?
   a. Core i7
   b. Pentium
   c. Celeron
   d. Athlon 64

9. Which factors directly affect the speed of data manipulation by the CPU? Select two.
   a. Clock frequency
   b. Bus width
   c. Voltage level
   d. System temperature

10. When replacing or upgrading the CPU, you should always do what?
    a. Leave the fan assembly off and run the system for a while to be sure the new CPU is operating correctly.
    b. Move the jumpers on the motherboard to test for the highest overclocking speed that the CPU can safely handle.
    c. Check the manufacturer's website for the latest upgrade or replacement information.
    d. Replace the BIOS as a matter of routine practice.

Suggested Laboratory Activities

Do not attempt any suggested laboratory activities without your instructor's permission. Certain activities can render the PC operating system inoperable.

1. Go to the AMD website and access the instructions for installing and replacing an AMD processor.

2. Go to the Intel website and access the instructions for installing and replacing an Intel Core i7 processor.

3. Select a PC in the lab, visit the manufacturer's website, and locate step-by-step procedures for replacing the CPU.

4. Go on the Internet and download a shareware utility to measure CPU performance.

5. Visit the Intel and AMD websites and research the latest CPU technologies.

6. Download and install a copy of the CPU-Z analyzer from CPUID.

7. Open Task Manager and view the **Processor Affinity** dialog box for a multi-core processor.

8. Go to the AMD website and locate the *AMD Builders Guide*. Survey the material, including how to install the various types of AMD processors.

Power Supplies

After studying this chapter, you will be able to:

- Explain the terms *voltage*, *current*, *resistance*, and *power* in relation to electrical energy.
- Use a digital multimeter to check a fuse, cable, switch, and power outlet.
- Identify possible commercial power problems.
- Identify the signs of a bad power supply.
- Explain the operation of UPS systems and power strips.
- Use the appropriate guidelines when handling and disposing of a battery.
- Use Windows Power Options to control PC power consumption.

A+ Exam—Key Points

Expect some basic questions about meters and reading the resistance values of wires and fuses. There may also be questions related to power supplies, such as wattage, connector identification, and voltage levels as well as items related to UPS systems, battery disposal, and power management.

Key Terms

The following key terms will become important pieces of your computer vocabulary. Be sure you can define them.

four-pin peripheral power connector
Advanced Configuration and Power
     Interface (ACPI)
alternating current (ac)
amperes (A)
backfeed
blackout
brownout
continuity
current
dedicated circuit
direct current (dc)
floppy drive power connector
fuse

metal oxide varistor (MOV)
ohm
power
power good signal
rails
resistance
standby power connection
surge
uninterruptible power supply (UPS)
voltage
volt-amperes (VA)
volts (V)
watts (W)

This chapter introduces you to the basic concepts of electrical energy. It will not turn you into an electronics technician. Rather, it will familiarize you with the terminology and basic electrical concepts needed to ensure success as a computer technician and success on the A+ Certification exams.

You will learn how to use a multimeter to test voltage and resistance and to test the standard features of computer power supplies. The basis of this chapter is the discussion and illustration of the PC power supply unit. The power supply is easy to understand and simple to replace, but improperly installing a power supply can damage the motherboard. This would be a very expensive mistake.

What Is Electrical Energy?

Electrical energy is best defined as the flow of electrons. Most people only know that electricity can be supplied from a wall outlet or from a battery. This is fine for what you need to achieve as a computer technician. In fact, these two power sources will likely be the only areas of concern you will have when working with PCs.

The flow of electrons is described by terms that express electrical values such as *voltage*, *current*, *resistance*, and *power*. Each term will be explained individually and in relation to each other. The terminology may seem confusing at first, but it is fairly simple. Familiarity with these terms is essential for A+ Certification.

AC and DC

Direct current (dc) electrical energy flows in one direction, from negative to positive. A dc power source has two terminals: positive and negative. The positive terminal is indicated by the color red and a plus (+) sign. The negative terminal is indicated by the color black and a minus (−) sign. See the left side of **Figure 5-1**. DC electrical energy flows steadily from negative to positive.

Alternating current (ac) has no negative or positive markings because it is in a state of constant change or alternating polarities. The current in an ac circuit flows in one direction and then in the opposite direction. Examine the right side of Figure 5-1. The completed sequence of flow, first in one direction and then in the other, is called a *cycle*. Current flows in one direction during the first half cycle and then flows in the opposite direction the next half. **Figure 5-2** illustrates a complete ac cycle.

This pattern is repeated as long as power is applied to the circuit. The frequency of how often the cycle is repeated is expressed in hertz (Hz) and is based on a time period of one second. Standard

Figure 5-1.
Illustrations of ac and dc flow.

Alternating Current

First half cycle

Second half cycle

Direct Current

— → → → → → +

Goodheart-Willcox Publisher

Figure 5-2. An ac voltage is commonly drawn as a graph with the voltage level plotted along the vertical axis and the time plotted along the horizontal axis.

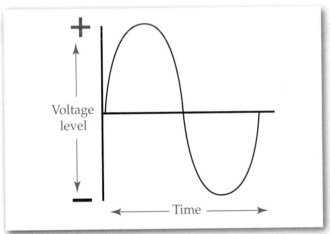

Voltage level

Time

Goodheart-Willcox Publisher

household electrical energy is 60 Hz. This means that the direction of the current changes at a rate of 60 times per second, or 60 Hz. See **Figure 5-3**.

Voltage and Current

Voltage and current are two measurements of electrical power that are tested by technicians when diagnosing problems related to the PC. These measurements are usually taken with a universal multimeter. The multimeter and its operation are covered later in this chapter.

Voltage and current are directly related to each other. **Voltage**, measured in **volts (V)**, is the amount of electrical pressure present in a circuit or power source. **Current**, measured in **amperes (A)**, is the amount of electron flow. Do

not mistake the ampere measurement of electrical energy as speed. It is the measure of volume of electrical energy flowing through the system.

Electrical energy can be compared to water in a pipe. Water flow is measured in gallons per minute (GPM) as well as pounds per square inch (PSI). GPM is the rate of flow or volume of water while PSI is the amount of pressure used to produce the flow. Electrical energy is similar. The voltage of the electrical source produces the force for moving electrical energy through the wires and devices. The amount of electrical energy, or current, moved depends on the amount of voltage applied and the amount of resistance in the path.

Resistance

Resistance is the opposition to the flow of electrical energy. The unit of resistance is the **ohm** and is expressed with the letter R or the symbol omega (Ω).

Electrical components that manipulate the voltage and current levels in a circuit have measurable resistance values that can be expressed in ohms. Computer technicians very seldom, if ever, are required to take accurate resistance readings. The resistance readings taken by PC technicians are usually to check for electrical continuity. **Continuity** is the ability of a device or component to allow an unobstructed flow of electrical energy. Examine **Figure 5-4**.

In the illustration, there are two electrical wires. These wires are referred to as conductors when using electrical terminology. A complete conductor, one that has no breaks, will have a resistance reading of zero. There is no significant

Figure 5-3. A complete ac cycle and a series of ac cycles. The cycle pattern represents the rise and fall of a voltage level. This pattern repeats 60 times in one second (60 Hz) for standard household electrical energy.

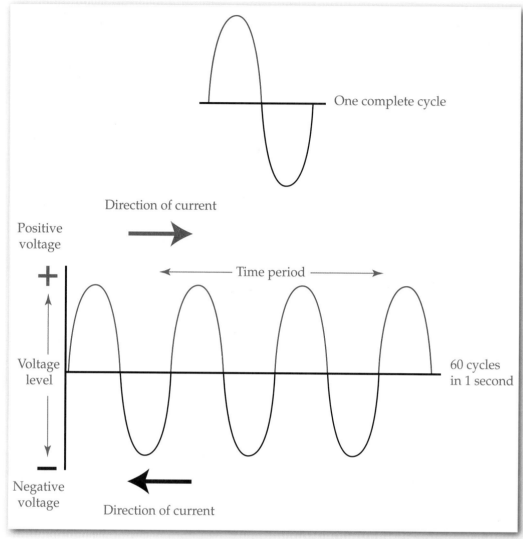

One complete cycle

Direction of current

Positive voltage

Time period

Voltage level

60 cycles in 1 second

Negative voltage

Direction of current

Goodheart-Willcox Publisher

Figure 5-4. Drawing of two wires: one complete and the other open. A complete circuit has (almost) no resistance. An open circuit (like a broken wire) has a very high or infinite resistance.

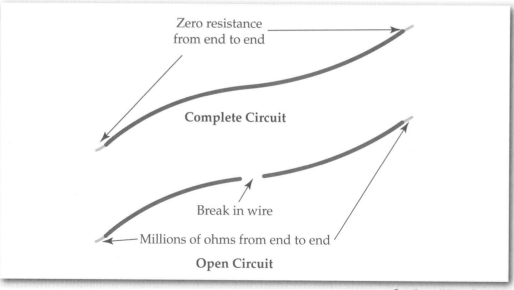

Zero resistance from end to end

Complete Circuit

Break in wire

Millions of ohms from end to end

Open Circuit

Goodheart-Willcox Publisher

resistance to be measured. When a conductor has a break in its path, referred to as an open, there is an immeasurable amount of resistance. This extreme condition of high resistance is referred to as infinity. As the term *infinity* implies, the reading is so high it is beyond the capability of the multimeter to read it. It is imperative that you learn these two readings, what they mean, and the conditions that cause them. This is the key to using the ohmmeter function to troubleshoot certain PC items. Checking the resistance values of fuses, cables, and switches is covered later in this chapter.

Power

The amount of electrical energy provided or used by equipment is **power**, and it is measured in **watts (W)**. Wattage is the product of voltage and current. In other words, to determine the amount of power expressed in watts that a dc circuit is using, the electrical pressure measured in volts is multiplied by the electrical current measured in amps.

$$\text{watts} = \text{volts} \times \text{amps}$$

A computer drawing 3 amps when connected to a 120-volt source would consume approximately 360 watts of electrical energy. Notice that the term *approximately* is used here. When calculating wattage values associated with ac power, there are other electrical factors, such as induction, to be taken into account. The power value of an ac circuit is expressed in **volt-amperes (VA)**, an alternative scale for measuring electrical power.

A power supply's output capacity is rated in watts and in VA. Watts and VA are not the same expression. Wattage is considered the "true" power rating of a device. It is measured with a very expensive wattmeter or calculated with a more exact formula. VA is considered the "apparent" power. It is called the apparent power because the voltage and ampere values derived from a multimeter are not true values. These values are distorted from electrical factors in the circuit, such as induction. See **Figure 5-5**. Total

Figure 5-5. The total wattage rating can be quite a bit different than the calculated wattage rating based on the formula volts × amps. It is not unusual for the calculated wattage using volts and amps to be larger than the wattage totals.

Each Monitor = 140 Watts	140 W	+	140 W	+	140 W	+	140 W	+		560 Watts
Each CPU = 180 Watts	180 W	+	180 W	+	180 W	+	180 W	+		720 Watts
One Printer = 300 Watts									300 W	300 Watts
										1580 Watts Total

Each Monitor = 1.6 Amps	1.6 Amps	+	1.6 Amps	+	1.6 Amps	+	1.6 Amps	+		6.4 Amps
Each CPU = 2.0 Amps	2.0 Amps	+	2.0 Amps	+	2.0 Amps	+	2.0 Amps	+		8.0 Amps
One Printer = 3.5 Amps									3.5 Amps	3.5 Amps
										17.9 Amps Total

Printer

Volts × Amps = VA
120 volts × 17.9 Amps = 2148 VA

Volt-amperes (VA) equal 2148 while Watts equal 1580.

Always use the equipment wattage rating when sizing power supplies. Do not calculate wattage based on volts and amps. The result will be volt-amperes (VA), not true Watts.

load is calculated from a group of computers and a printer, which are rated by amperes, and wattage. Notice that the calculated power rating derived from the formula V × A is higher than the total power rating derived from adding the individual watt values. The power rating derived from adding the individual watt values is the true power rating. This is a very brief explanation of a very complicated topic. The electronic theory involved for a complete understanding of electronic system loads is beyond the scope of this text. If you have a real desire to know more about electronics, an introductory level course in basic dc and ac circuits is recommended.

When sizing the load capacity of a computer configuration, there are two choices. All the watt values can be added together to arrive at the total load in watts, or all the ampere loads can be added together and then compared to the amperage rating of the power supply.

Wattage measurements are used in two primary ways: power consumption and power supplied. The amount of power consumed by devices such as monitors or hard drives is expressed in watts. When wattage is written on a device that uses or consumes electrical power, the watts label is used to express the amount of power used or consumed by that device. When *watts* is used as a label on a device that supplies electrical energy, such as a generator or power supply, it represents the amount of power that can be provided safely from that unit. Power supplies and generators can actually supply more power than they are rated for. However, when excess amounts of power are taken from a power supply, excessive heating occurs. This can permanently damage the power supply.

When changing power supplies, a power supply with equal or greater wattage marked on the label must be used. A power supply with less wattage capability may work for a while, but it will surely burn up after a period of time.

To determine how much equipment can be connected to a power strip, the wattage ratings of each piece of equipment should be added together. A typical power strip should not connect to a total of over 1600 watts of equipment. Also, *never* daisy-chain (string in series) power strips, **Figure 5-6**. When daisy-chained, the first strip carries the total load of both strips.

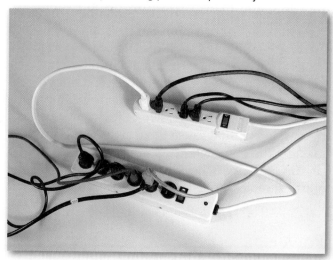

Figure 5-6. Daisy-chaining power strips is very unwise.

Goodheart-Willcox Publisher

Another consideration when using extension cords is wire size. A cord with less than number 16-gauge wire should not be used. Wire smaller than 16 gauge can pose a fire hazard. Wire gauge is used to indicate the size of wire and how much current it can safely handle without excessive heat. Remember, the larger the number, the smaller the wire. **Figure 5-7** shows a wire size chart with current ratings.

Clean Electrical Power

Clean power is a term that means the commercial electrical supply is steady at the correct voltage level and does not contain voltage spikes. Clean power can be difficult to obtain without additional equipment added to the supply

Figure 5-7. Wire size chart with current ratings. Note that this chart reflects the current-carrying capacities of typical conductors. It does not take into consideration the type of insulation or the application, which can change the current rating for the listed conductors.

Wire Size	Ampere Rating
12	20
14	15
16	7
18	5

Goodheart-Willcox Publisher

system. High-voltage power line switching, lightning, cars hitting electric poles, or routine line maintenance can cause voltage spikes. When a spike occurs, an abnormally high level of voltage is sent through the electrical system. See **Figure 5-8** for an illustration of line spike in relation to normal ac voltage pattern.

Figure 5-8. A voltage line spike can be caused by many things (motors, switches, lightning). The increased voltage in the spike damages electronic components by exceeding the voltage limitation of the component.

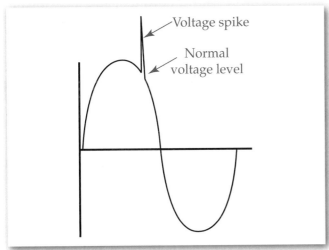

Goodheart-Willcox Publisher

Line voltage spikes can be reduced or eliminated by the use of line conditioning equipment. A common method of ensuring a constant supply of clean power is the use of an uninterruptible power supply (UPS). The UPS system will be discussed later in this chapter.

Using a Digital Multimeter

A digital multimeter is used to measure current, resistance, and voltage values. As the name implies, the meter is constructed from digital circuits, and it is used in place of multiple meters. The multimeter replaces the use of individual volt, ohm, and amp meters. It is an all-in-one type of meter. See **Figure 5-9**, which shows a typical digital multimeter with major parts labeled.

Probes and Test Leads

The meter is equipped with two test leads with probes at the end of each. The probes are used for touching test points. One test lead is black and the other is red. This color combination is universal. The black lead is for the negative side of a reading. It plugs into the meter at the jack that is marked in black, has a negative sign, or both. The

Figure 5-9.
A typical auto-range meter is very simple in design. You simply select the function you wish (volts or resistance) and then touch the parts with the probe tips.

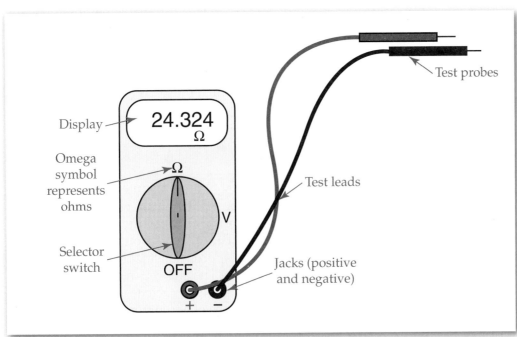

Goodheart-Willcox Publisher

jack may also be marked with the word "COM," as it is on the meter in **Figure 5-10**. The red lead plugs into the jack with the red marking or the plus sign for voltage and resistance readings. For current readings, there is usually a different position in which to plug the red lead.

As a PC technician, you typically never need to take a current reading. Current readings are much more complicated and require knowledge of electronic components to correctly connect the meter. Voltage readings and occasionally resistance readings are required.

Never touch the probes with your fingertips when taking readings, even when the voltage is low. Forming safe habits is essential. If you touch the bare tip of the probe during routine checks of low voltage where there is not sufficient voltage to harm you, you may create a bad habit. This can lead to touching the tips when reading dangerously high voltages. Low voltages (below 50 volts) will not normally harm you, and you normally do not feel any electrical sensation. Touching a 120-volt ac line is an entirely different story. You will definitely feel the sensation of electrical energy. It is possible to incur a permanent injury or even death. Safety is a habit. Develop safe habits when reading low voltages

and you will automatically use the same habits when reading a much higher voltage.

Range Selector

The range selector is used to choose the appropriate value to be read: voltage, current, or resistance. The dial indicator should be placed in the lowest range that is greater than the value to be read. For example, a meter with voltage ranges of 5, 50, and 500 should be set to 50 to take an expected 12-volt reading. If it is placed higher than the next highest value, an accurate reading will not be obtained. The reading will be a rounded-off value, rather than an accurate reading. If you go below the desired level, you will probably not get a reading at all. In fact, a warning will appear in the display area of most good meters.

Some meters are equipped with an auto-range feature. This feature automatically selects the correct range for the reading you are taking. This type of meter is recommended for anyone not familiar with basic electronics.

Display Area

The display area is where the measured value is shown, such as voltage, current, or resistance. For example, when reading voltage, the display will give a numeric value of the voltage and possibly indicate if it is ac or dc. It may also indicate if you are out of the correct range selection value. The value is expressed with a decimal point when appropriate and is coordinated with the range selector setting and the jacks into which the leads are plugged.

Figure 5-10. Meters come with multiple jacks for the test probes. Be sure to place the test probes in the proper jacks.

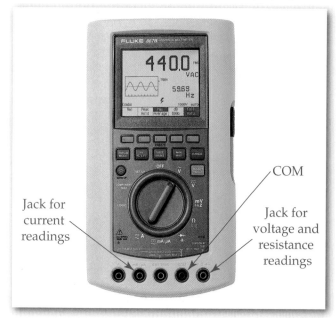

Jack for current readings

COM

Jack for voltage and resistance readings

Fluke Corp.

A+ Note

You will most likely encounter a scenario-type question asking you to choose the most appropriate test instrument for an application. For example, you may be asked to select the appropriate tool for testing wall outlet voltage. The answers may include multimeter, crimper, cable tester, tone probe, or similar types of equipment.

Procedures for Reading Voltage

Before taking any readings, you should have some idea of the level of voltage you expect to read. For example, a common wall outlet is 120 volts ac. A power supply unit might be 12, 5, or 3.3 volts dc depending on the exact power supply connection.

> **Danger !** Never wear an anti-static strap or ground strap while taking meter readings. The strap makes you an excellent conductor of electricity, which can result in fatal injury.

To read ac or dc voltages:
1. Insert the meter leads into the appropriate jacks on the meter. The red lead is inserted into the jack marked with the letter "V" or plus (+) symbol. (Generally, you will never use the jacks marked with "A" or "mA" as they are used for current readings.) The input voltage jack is usually red.
2. Insert the black lead into the jack marked "COM" or the minus (–) symbol. The common (COM) jack is usually black.
3. Turn the selector switch to voltage AC. On some meters this can require the use of two separate switches. One switch selects ac or dc voltage and the other switch selects the voltage range. If you do not have an auto-range meter, set the range selector to the next highest voltage level over what you expect to read.
4. Touch the test locations with the probes. Keep your fingers away from the tips of the probes.
5. Read the display and record the voltage. It should be within 10% of the expected voltage level.

Procedures for Reading Resistance

To read resistance:
1. Insert the meter leads into the appropriate jacks on the meter. The red lead is inserted into the jack marked with the letter "V" or plus (+) symbol.

2. Insert the black lead into the jack marked with "COM" or the minus (–) symbol. The common (COM) jack is usually black.
3. Be absolutely sure the power is OFF before attempting to read resistance.
4. Set the selector switch to the highest value of resistance.
5. Touch the test probes together to see if the meter is working properly. The reading should be zero. If not, the battery inside the unit could be weak. The ohmmeter portion of a multimeter depends on battery power to take a resistance reading.
6. Touch the probes to the part (fuse or cable) to be tested.
7. When checking resistance of a fuse or a cable, you should read either zero resistance or infinity. A good fuse will cause a reading of zero resistance as will a good cable. A bad fuse will cause a reading of infinity as will a cable that is not complete from end to end.

> **Caution !** Electrical voltage can damage a meter if the meter is set to read resistance.

Checking Fuses, Cables, and Switches

When checking fuses, cables, and switches there are only two resistance values that are typically displayed on a digital meter: zero ohms and infinity. A typical low-ampere fuse found in electronic equipment is simple in construction. The **fuse** is a cylinder shape of glass or ceramic with a metal cap on each end. Inside the cylinder is the fuse link. The fuse link is a thin metal wire that burns and splits into two parts at a predetermined ampere value.

The easiest way to tell if the fuse is good (or not) is to remove it from the fuse holder and take a resistance reading across the fuse, **Figure 5-11**. Since the fuse is made of a thin metal wire, it will have very low resistance. When tested with the ohmmeter, the meter will indicate zero resistance.

Figure 5-11. A blown fuse will have a resistance reading too high to be displayed, even in the megaohm range. A good fuse will display zero resistance.

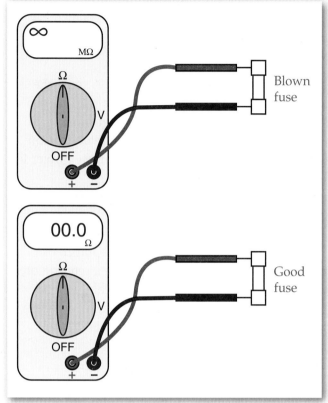

Goodheart-Willcox Publisher

If the fuse is burned open, it will have a resistance value too high to read. You would be trying to read through the air or space inside the tube. This reading is known as *infinity*. This means the resistance reading is beyond the capabilities of the meter range.

A+ Note

Remember that a fuse must be removed from the circuit before taking a resistance reading.

The same principle applies to a cable and switches. Before reading a switch or cable with an ohmmeter, they must be removed from the PC. A cable should read zero resistance from one end to the other. A cable with a broken wire will read infinity. See **Figure 5-12** for an illustration of a cable with a meter attached, showing both a good reading and a bad cable reading.

Testing switches is very similar to testing fuses. An open switch will show an infinite resistance. A closed switch should show zero ohms of resistance, **Figure 5-13**. As with testing a fuse, **make sure the switch is removed from the PC**.

A switch can be difficult to remove from the circuit and the type of switch present must be identified. Some switches are capacitor-type switches. These switches cannot be adequately diagnosed with an ohmmeter. Capacitor switches are usually very small in comparison to the physical size of mechanical switches. If a switch is suspected as the problem, it may be best to simply replace the switch with a known good switch rather than attempt to diagnose it with a meter.

Resistance values can fool an untrained electronics technician. There is a situation when a resistance reading taken on a circuit component such as a switch will give false information. An open switch can, in fact, have what appears as a resistance value other than infinity. The meter may be reading through the electronic components mounted in the system and indicate a value anywhere between zero and infinity.

Look at the drawing in **Figure 5-14**. In the illustration, the ohmmeter is reading through the circuit components even after the switch is opened. This is referred to as **backfeed** and is a very common condition. To avoid backfeed situations, the component to be read should be removed from the circuit whenever possible. This is not always practical. At times, it is more appropriate to take voltage readings to indicate the condition of fuses, breakers, and switches.

Checking Power Outlets

Checking a power outlet is a very common task. See **Figure 5-15**. The meter probes are simply inserted into a wall outlet to check for electrical power. There is no polarity when reading ac voltage sources, so the polarity markings on the meter need not be observed.

| Warning ! | Never touch the tips of the meter leads when taking readings. |

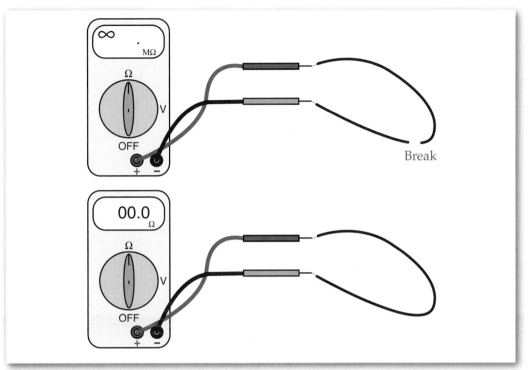

Figure 5-12.
A good conductor will read zero resistance. A conductor with a break (or open) will read infinity, the highest possible resistance reading.

Goodheart-Willcox Publisher

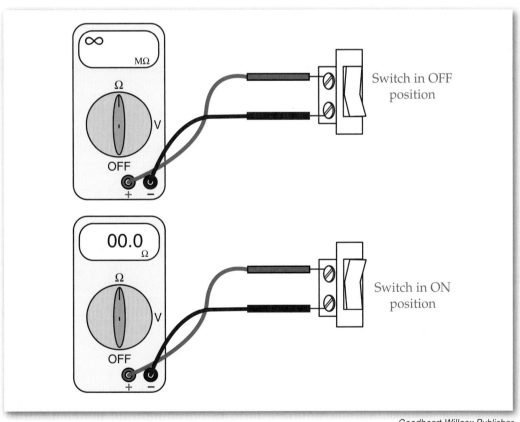

Figure 5-13.
A closed switch has zero resistance while an open switch has infinite resistance.

Goodheart-Willcox Publisher

Figure 5-14.
Reading resistance across an open switch can give you a false reading. The ohmmeter reads the resistance through the rest of the circuit instead of the resistance across the open switch.

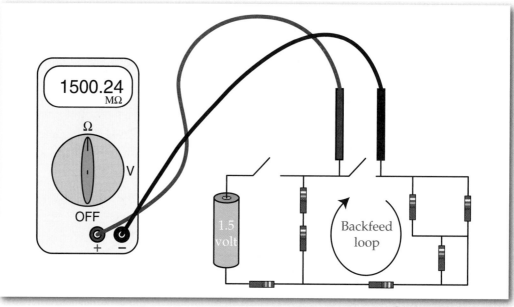

Goodheart-Willcox Publisher

Figure 5-15. Meter connected to a wall outlet. Polarity need not be observed. Be careful when making this test. Keep your fingers away from the exposed probe tips.

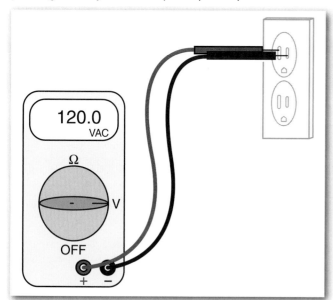

Goodheart-Willcox Publisher

A good voltage reading is considered to be plus or minus 10% of the 120-volt rating. In actuality, the voltage can drop or rise considerably more before affecting a PC.

Two other important considerations when taking voltage readings are the weather and the time of day. Low voltage is common on extremely hot or cold days when electrical heat or air conditioning control building temperature. Heating and air conditioning call for a large demand on the electrical system inside a building. The highest demand for electrical power is usually between the hours of 4:00 p.m. and 6:00 p.m. During this period, most households are actively using power because of those coming home from school or work. The demand for heating or cooling increases and often combines with the power needed for the preparation of the evening meal. During the same period, many businesses are still operating. This is the time that most brownouts occur.

Tech Tip

When checking for low voltage, it is best to have the air conditioning or heating system operating at maximum, so you can see the system under maximum strain. This is especially important when checking an intermittent problem and a low-voltage condition is suspected.

Branch Circuits

Many computer problems can be generated by the electrical system inside a home or small business. The electrical power in a home setting and in some businesses originates from an electrical panel. Electrical equipment running anywhere in those environments can cause a power problem for the computer system.

For example, the operation of a vacuum cleaner or a power tool can generate voltage spikes that can disrupt the computer process. The computer can be damaged, develop a glitch, or simply lock up. It is imperative that a surge protector be installed at the computer location. See **Figure 5-16** for a drawing of a typical home distribution system.

Branch circuit is the technical name for the wiring from an electrical panel to the final outlet on that circuit. A typical commercial installation uses two electrical distribution panels: one panel for lighting and the other panel for distributing power to equipment. **Figure 5-17** is an illustration showing side-by-side panels. One panel is for lighting and the other is for power.

Computers are located in every type of business location from small travel agency offices to heavy manufacturing companies. It is important to know the type of equipment the company operates from and the electrical distribution panel that serves the computer stations. The type of electrical distribution and the equipment connected to that electrical system is of major concern to reliable computer operation. An office located in a large industrial building can be misleading to a technician. While the immediate environment may look like a typical office setting, the same electrical circuits in the office can be serving heavy printing press equipment directly behind the office wall. A surge protector power strip may not be adequate in this type of location. A more reliable device is a quality uninterruptible power supply (UPS) system. UPS systems are covered later in this chapter.

Dedicated Circuit

A **dedicated circuit** is an electrical power distribution system that is designed to serve *only* computer equipment. It is wired separately from other electrical circuits. A typical installation uses an isolation transformer to separate the computer electrical power from other power circuits. An isolation transformer converts electrical energy to magnetic energy and then back to electrical energy. The transformer helps to buffer the circuit against voltage spikes generated inside and outside the building.

Figure 5-16. Typical home power distribution.

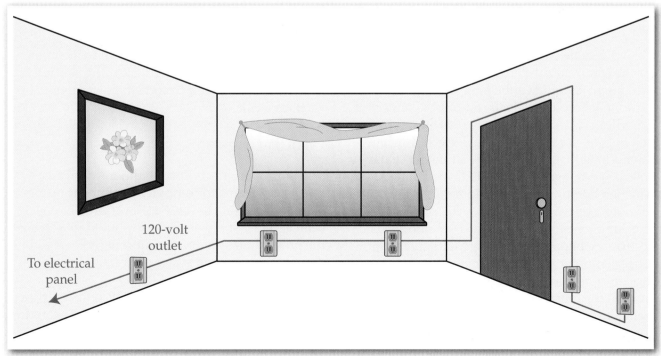

Figure 5-17.
Heavy machinery should have its own electrical panel. It should not be on the same panel as computer equipment.

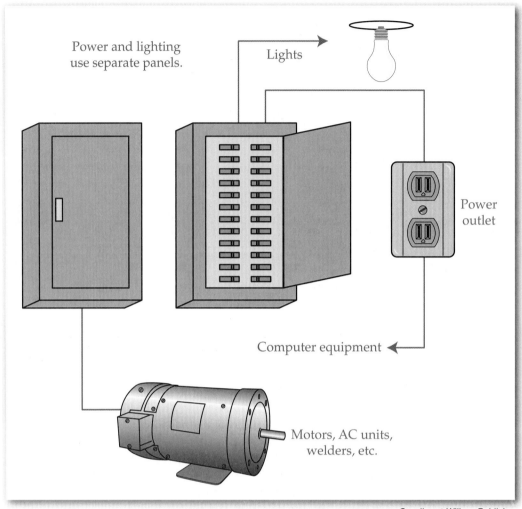

Power and lighting use separate panels.

Lights

Power outlet

Computer equipment

Motors, AC units, welders, etc.

Goodheart-Willcox Publisher

A separate electrical panel is used strictly for the computers in the building. No additional equipment should ever be plugged into the dedicated circuit outlets. If computers connected to dedicated circuits suddenly develop problems that appear to be power related, the technician should look for some type of equipment that may have been plugged into the dedicated outlets. Any non-computer type equipment that is found should be removed.

An interesting, and all too common, occurrence happens to network equipment and office computer systems that are left constantly in the "on" position. When office workers return to work in the morning, they find their computers locked up or crashed. After rebooting, everything appears fine again. However, a few days later, or even the next day, the computer system is down again. This problem is usually solved when it is discovered that the overnight cleaning service is using the dedicated circuits to power their vacuum cleaners.

Grounding

Improper grounding conditions can cause serious problems to computer equipment. After all other attempts to solve a power problem have been exhausted, the technician should investigate the grounding system. An improperly-installed or damaged grounding system can cause problems that appear as voltage problems.

To check out the grounding system, a certified electrician or power company technician should make the inspection. Specialized equipment is used to perform grounding tests. It is expensive and special training is needed to use it. This is one time when the computer tech must call another specialist.

The PC Power Supply

The power supply is responsible for converting standard 120-volt ac power from the wall outlet to dc voltage levels appropriate for the electronics systems of the computer. Typical dc voltage levels are +12, +5, +3.3, –12, and –5. These voltages are provided to the motherboard, which, in turn, distributes these voltage levels to motherboard components and expansion slots. The expansion slots provide the voltage levels required by adapter card electronic parts. Voltages are also distributed to peripherals inside the computer, such as the hard drive and DVD drive.

Power supplies have form factors just as motherboards do. The power supply must fit into the case and also allow room for the motherboard. Some of the standard form factors are named after the motherboard form factors, such as AT, Baby AT, LPX, ATX, ATX12V and NLX. In addition, they can be broken down further to tower or desktop models. You should be aware of a variety of nonstandard power supplies that are proprietary. The color coding on the wiring for these types of power supplies are not truly standard. You must be careful. As a matter of fact, any implied standardization should not be taken for granted. Always check with the manufacturer's specifications for definitive information about color and voltages.

Tech Tip

When upgrading a computer, always consider the effect on the power supply. For example, many high-performance video cards consume large amounts of electrical power. Video card manufacturers will recommend a minimum power supply size for a given video card.

Main Power Connectors

To assist in making the proper voltage level connections, power plugs have a special shape that matches the voltage level required by the motherboard or peripheral. **Figure 5-18** illustrates two styles of motherboard main power connections: ATX and ATX12V. Notice that both connectors have a PWR_OK connection. This refers to the power good signal. This signal is transmitted from the power supply to the motherboard and on to the CPU. The **power good signal** is used during POST to verify the power supply is working properly.

The +5VSB (standby) connection provides voltage even when the power switch is set to off. The computer is said to "wake up" on an event. The exception is when the AC plug is physically unplugged from the wall outlet or the power supply. The **standby power connection**, also called *soft power*, provides power to the keyboard when the computer system is in sleep mode. Power is reduced to the entire system, but some power must remain to reactivate or wake the system. This is the purpose of the standby power connection. The power on and the standby power connections are also used jointly by Windows operating systems to turn the computer off using software commands rather than a physical switch. For example, the +5VSB connection can provide electrical power to a network card so that the computer can be activated when a network event occurs. The BIOS/UEFI Setup utility is used to configure the computer to "wake up on LAN," which means network activity can wake or start the computer system. This is a common feature of all modern computer systems.

The ATX and ATX12V form factors also have 3.3-volt power connectors. The addition of 3.3 volts at the power connection has eliminated the need for a voltage regulator located at the CPU. The regulator was used to convert the 5 volts from the power supply to the lower voltage required by the new CPU units. ATX is one of the most popular power supply form factors on the market.

The ATX12V power supply is a redesign of the ATX power supply. Changes to the design were made to accommodate new power requirements such as that for PCIe devices and power-hungry video cards. The ATX motherboard main power connection has 20 pins. The newer ATX12V motherboard main power connection has 24 pins. Look closely at Figure 5-18 and you can see that the main difference between the 20-pin and

Figure 5-18. ATX and ATX12V main power connections.

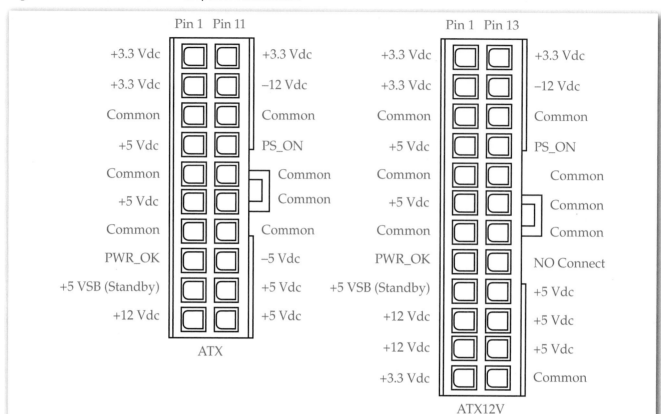

24-pin connection is the bottom four pins. These four additional pins on the ATX12V are used to supply additional electrical power required by the more modern motherboards.

Most ATX motherboard designs will accept an ATX12V connector. The ATX12V standard is backward compatible with older motherboards. This is useful when purchasing an ATX12V power supply to replace a defective ATX power supply. Conversion kits are available to change a 20-pin connector into a 24-pin connector and also the opposite, change a 24-pin to a 20-pin connector. Many motherboards have no problem with a pin conversion kit. The conversion kit is simply two connections, one 24-pin and one 20-pin joined by wires. If you study the pin assignments carefully in Figure 5-18, you will see that the first set of 20 pins of an ATX power supply connector closely match the first 20-pins of the 24-pin ATX12V power supply.

Figure 5-19 and **Figure 5-20** show the ATX and ATX12V power connectors respectively. The plastic of these plugs are molded so that the connector can connect to the motherboard in only one way. This prevents an improper connection that will destroy the motherboard. Do keep in mind that nothing along these lines is truly impossible. If sufficient force is applied, it can be plugged in backward. The connector should attach easily. If it does not, do not force it.

Other Power Connectors

There is a wide assortment of power connectors besides the main motherboard power connectors that can be used with a computer power system. **Figure 5-21** shows three of the more common ones you will encounter. The +12-volt power connector, Figure 5-21A, is also referred to as a 2 × 2, 12-volt connector. The designation

Figure 5-19. ATX motherboard power connector.

Goodheart-Willcox Publisher

Figure 5-20. ATX12V main motherboard power connector. Most motherboards designed to work with a 20-pin ATX power supply will work with a 24-pin ATX12V power supply.

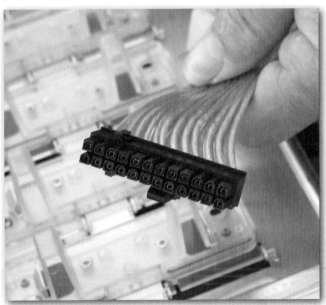

Goodheart-Willcox Publisher

Figure 5-21. Assorted power connectors.

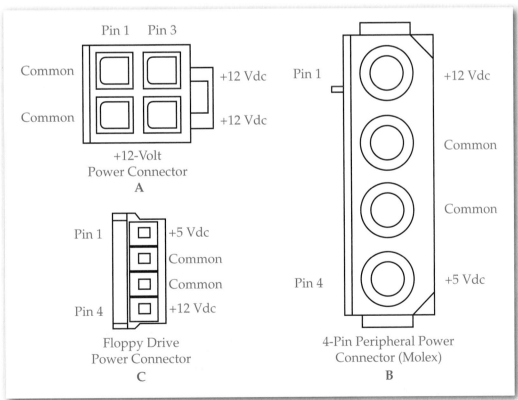

Pin 1   Pin 3

Common

Common

+12 Vdc

+12 Vdc

+12-Volt
Power Connector
A

Pin 1   +5 Vdc

Common

Common

Pin 4   +12 Vdc

Floppy Drive
Power Connector
C

Pin 1   +12 Vdc

Common

Common

Pin 4   +5 Vdc

4-Pin Peripheral Power
Connector (Molex)
B

Goodheart-Willcox Publisher

2×2 represents the pin configuration as two pins in two rows. The 2×2 designation is a way to differentiate it from the 4-pin peripheral power connector, Figure 5-21B. The 4-pin peripheral power connector would be designated as 1×4. Power supply main motherboard connectors are referred to in the same fashion. For example, a 20-pin ATX connector is referred to as a 2×10 connector, while the 24-pin ATX12V connector is referred to as a 2×12 connector.

The 2×2, 12-volt power connector in Figure 5-21A is used to supply 12 volts to newer high-performance CPUs. There are also 2×4, 12-volt power connectors on many power supplies. **Figure 5-22** shows a power splitter cable with a 2×4 and 2×2, 12-volt connector. The voltage applied to the processor was raised from 5 Vdc to 12 Vdc. Therefore, the ATX12V power supply uses a 4-pin or more power connector attached directly to the motherboard near the processor rather than through the main motherboard power connector. **Figure 5-23** shows an auxiliary power connector.

Tech Tip

Always check your motherboard manual or support documentation to determine the location of and type of power connections to use.

Figure 5-22. Two-by-four (2×4) and two-by-two (2×2), 12-volt power connectors.

Goodheart-Willcox Publisher

Figure 5-23. Auxiliary power connector.

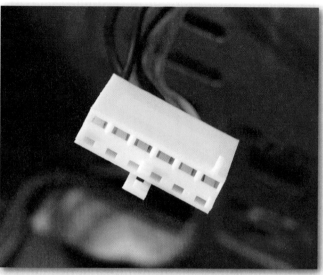

Goodheart-Willcox Publisher

The ATX style could only carry voltage and higher current to the CPU through the very thin conductors on the motherboard referred to as *traces*. Traces are very limited in the amount of current that they can carry. Power connections made directly to locations on the motherboard as well as directly to devices overcome the current limitations of motherboard traces. The power connection near the CPU is critical on motherboards with high-performance processors. Without the direct connection, the computer will not boot.

The **four-pin peripheral power connector**, Figure 5-21B, is also called a *Molex connector*. It is used to connect to ATA hard drives, CD-ROM drives, and DVD drives. These devices typically use the +12-volt level from the connector. The **floppy drive power connector**, Figure 5-21C, is also called a *mini connector*. It is used for 3 1/2" floppy drives. **Figure 5-24** shows a picture of the four-pin peripheral power connector, and **Figure 5-25** shows the mini connector.

Tech Tip

The term *Molex* is commonly used and universally accepted to identify the 4-pin peripheral power connection, although this is incorrect. Molex is the name of the company that designed and markets this type of connection.

Figure 5-24. Four-pin peripheral power connector, also called a *Molex connector*. This connector is typically used to power ATA hard drives, CD-ROM drives, and DVD drives.

Goodheart-Willcox Publisher

Figure 5-26. A power supply connector labeled with PCI-E is intended for use with a PCIe video card.

Goodheart-Willcox Publisher

Figure 5-25. Mini connector. This connector is used to power 3 1/2″ floppy drives.

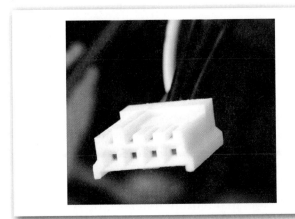

Goodheart-Willcox Publisher

There are also power connectors designed to connect directly from the power supply to a PCIe card. For example, video cards with high-performance processors require a separate power supply connected directly to the card. Graphic cards can consume a wide range of power, from just a few watts to over 500 watts. Typically, a 2 × 3 or 2 × 4 power connector is required to provide ample power directly to the video card. Some power supply manufacturers identify which power connector is designed especially for use with a video graphics card. Look at the connector in **Figure 5-26**. It shows the letters "PCI-E" on the side of a 2 × 3 connector, identifying it for use with a PCI Express graphics card.

Serial ATA (SATA) hard drives use a SATA power connector, **Figure 5-27**, which has 14 pins at three different voltage levels. Adapter wiring kits are available so that you can connect a SATA hard disk drive to a power supply that does not have a SATA power connector.

Input and Output Voltage Levels

Input voltage levels are specified by the Form Factors Organization. This organization makes a set of recommended nonbinding specifications that are used as a guideline for power supply manufacturers, as shown in the following table.

Input	Minimum VAC	Nominal VAC	Maximum VAC
115 Vac	90	115	135
230 Vac	180	230	265
Frequency (Hz)	47	50/60	63

Computers are used worldwide, and as a result, they are typically designed with two voltage levels available either through use of a switch or by automatic electrical sensing and switching circuitry. Most countries in the world use 50-Hz electrical power rated at 230 volts. Some use 115 volts at 50 Hz. The United States is one of the few countries that use a 115-volt and 230-volt,

Figure 5-27. SATA power connector and pinouts.

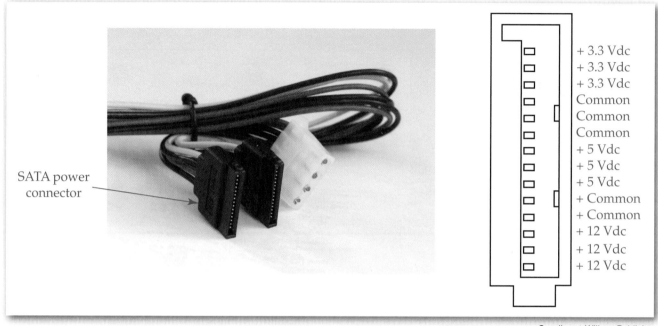

+ 3.3 Vdc
+ 3.3 Vdc
+ 3.3 Vdc
Common
Common
Common
+ 5 Vdc
+ 5 Vdc
+ 5 Vdc
+ Common
+ Common
+ 12 Vdc
+ 12 Vdc
+ 12 Vdc

SATA power connector

Goodheart-Willcox Publisher

60-Hz electrical system. While a computer will run on 230 volts at 50 Hz, the 120-volt, 60 Hz standard electrical plug will not fit physically into the 230-volt, 50-Hz wall outlet. A special adapter must be used to make the computer power supply physically compatible. Always check the foreign country that the client or customer is going to, so you can best advise them as to the electrical requirements.

To learn more about specific countries throughout the world, visit the Europlugs website. This site has a comprehensive list of countries and their standard electrical power systems, voltage, frequency, and power plug and socket types.

The DC output levels of an ATX12V power supply are +12, –12, +5, and +3.3 volts. The following table lists the tolerance levels for these voltages. Thus, a connection that is designated to output +12 volts may actually output +11.40 volts to +12.60 volts.

Output Vdc	Range	Minimum	Maximum
+12	± 5%	+11.40	+12.60
+5	± 5%	+ 4.75	+ 5.25
+3.3	± 5%	+ 3.14	+ 3.47
–12	± 10%	–10.80	–13.20

All power supplies use a transformer that converts the voltage levels identified in the table. These voltage levels are distributed by **rails**, which is the electrical term used to describe the conductor paths inside the metal power supply case. It was introduced with the ATX12V power supply. There is one rail for each voltage level. Each rail supplies the electrical voltage level to all connectors that require that specific voltage. In other words, every connector that requires +5 volts will connect to the same +5 rail inside the power supply.

Some power supplies use a dual rail for a specific voltage. For example, a power supply designed to provide large amounts of wattage will have dual +12-volt rails, each supplying 18 to 20 amperes. When you look at a set of manufacturer specifications for a specific power supply, the voltages available will be stated by rail.

Power Supply Label

The typical information found on a power supply label includes the output voltages and the power in watts the unit can deliver. See **Figure 5-28**. Notice that the power supply label indicates a +5VSB entry. The acronym VSB

Goodheart-Willcox Publisher

Figure 5-28. The label on the power supply provides information such as the total amount of power measured in watts that the power supply can safely deliver.

represents "Volts Standby." The +5VSB is the electrical power present when the power supply is plugged in but not turned on. It is used to keep the computer in standby mode. For example, it allows the computer to "wake up" when a signal is sent to the network card from the network. The VSB is also used to keep devices powered at a minimum level during sleep mode.

Troubleshooting the Power Supply

In general, there are no serviceable parts inside the power supply. It is considered a field replacement unit. Although it is possible to repair a power supply, it is not cost-effective. The cost of most power supplies does not come near the cost of having an electronic technician repair the unit. See **Figure 5-29** for a picture of the inside of a power supply. A power supply is usually sealed to make it difficult to open.

Power supply failure is quite frequent when compared to the failure of other computer components. Although some of the indicators can be caused by other system components, it is most likely that the power supply has caused the occurrence. The following are the common signs of a defective power supply:

- **Inoperable cooling fans:** Cooling fans that are not running are a fairly consistent sign that the power supply has failed. (Cooling fans receive their power directly from the power supply.)
- **No indicator lights:** No lights or lit LEDs is a good sign that the power supply has failed.
- **Smoke:** Smoke coming from the power supply is an indicator of electronic component or circuit board damage. Electronic components usually burn up from an overload condition. This almost always results in excessive heat, which generates the smoke.
- **Burnt smell:** The distinctive smell of a burnt electrical device in proximity of a failed computer is an indication that the power supply is defective. The smell can linger for hours after a system failure.
- **Circuit breaker tripping:** If a circuit breaker is tripped, it is most likely caused by the power supply unit in the computer. With the exception of the monitor, no other component will generate a condition to trip the breaker. To verify that the problem is with the power supply, unplug the monitor to isolate the computer power supply.
- **Automatic rebooting:** If the computer reboots automatically while on standby or during normal operation, it is a good indication of a bad power supply. The power level dropping and rising is a common occurrence as the

Figure 5-29.
Inside a power supply.
Power supplies are
field replacement units.

power supply breaks down. This fluctuating voltage level causes the computer system to reboot for no apparent reason.

- **Electric shock:** Any electric shock received from the computer case is a sign of a bad power supply or one that is breaking down. *Always use extreme caution when troubleshooting a suspected power supply unit. Remember that 120-volt ac power can be deadly.*

- **Excessive heat:** This troubleshooting diagnosis is made through experience. Even a normally functioning power supply will produce a certain amount of heat. Heat is a normal by-product of electrical equipment. However, excessive heat is a sure sign that complete failure of an electronic component is imminent. The excessive heat in combination with the other signs can leave little doubt that the power supply is failing. If the power supply is too hot to touch, it has excessive heat. Electronic components usually start to break down at 160°F (71°C).

Electronic technicians can repair power supplies, but it is usually not cost-effective. The time taken to diagnose the power supply, locate the component, and replace the defective component is simply cost-prohibitive. It's much quicker and more economical to replace rather than repair. Power supplies are low-cost components. The cost of labor and availability of replacement parts are the major factors that determine when a unit is repaired or replaced.

Figure 5-30 shows a typical ATX power checker with the cover removed to better expose the LED indicators. The LEDs light up to indicate the presence of +12, –5, +5, –12, and +3.3 voltage levels corresponding to the ATX main motherboard connection. This is the preferred method of checking power. Also, notice that the two large white rectangular areas at the top corners of the device are resistors. The resistors are used to simulate an actual electrical load. To measure a true voltage output level, some electrical load must be used. Many times a false good reading is indicated on a voltage power supply output when there is no electrical load.

Figure 5-30. ATX power checker.

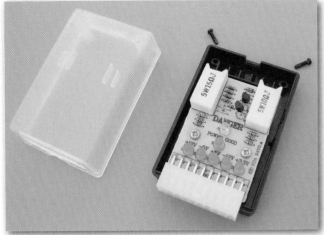

Goodheart-Willcox Publisher

This is one of the short comings of using a digital voltmeter to check the power supply output voltage.

Replacing a Power Supply

Replacing a power supply is an easy task. You must make sure the replacement is an acceptable form factor to match the case and motherboard. You must also make sure there is an adequate watt capacity provided by the replacement unit. *The watts capacity should either match or exceed the unit being replaced.*

Steps for power supply replacement:

1. Be absolutely sure the power is off. (Do *not* use an anti-static wrist strap for this operation.)
2. Sketch all the connections between the old power supply unit and the other computer components. (This will save you a great deal of time later.)
3. Remove the power connections carefully. Try not to disturb other cable connections on the motherboard or other devices. Also, remove the power cord attached to the power supply.
4. Remove retaining/mounting screws from the case that secure the power supply in place.
5. Place the new power supply into the case and secure the retaining/mounting screws.
6. Reconnect the power connections to the motherboard and devices using your sketch as a map.

7. Place any extra connections from the power supply in a neat bundle. Keep the loose connectors away from the motherboard. A loose connector could easily slip over a motherboard bare jumper causing destruction during power on. It can also catch in the fan blades, thus stopping the fan and causing the CPU to overheat.
8. Take one last look around at the connections. Verify that they are all secure, and then power on the computer before replacing the case cover. The cover should be left off until you are satisfied the PC is working properly. Any error messages at this time could be generated by a loose or improper connection during installation.
9. If everything is fine, replace the case cover and power on the PC once more. When replacing the case cover, be careful not to pinch any of the cables between the case frame and cover.

Surge Protection Devices

An electrical surge, brownout, or blackout can happen at any time. A **surge** is when a higher voltage than desired is present in the electrical system. A **brownout** is when low voltage is present. In a **blackout** condition, there is no voltage present. A momentary blackout can happen at any time and go completely unnoticed by the human eye. All that is required is the absence of one electrical cycle of power, or less, to cause a computer crash or lockup. **Figure 5-31** shows a series of cycles with one flatlined. Below it is a series of digital signals with a large group of flat digital pulses in relation to the one cycle.

Surge protection devices are designed to protect computer and other electronic devices against harmful surges of electrical energy. Two of the most common methods of providing protection are the use of power strips and UPS systems. UPS systems also protect against brownouts and blackouts.

Figure 5-31.
Series of cycles with a few cycles flatlined. Below it is a series of digital signals with a large group of flat digital pulses. A few lost cycles can eliminate many digital pulses.

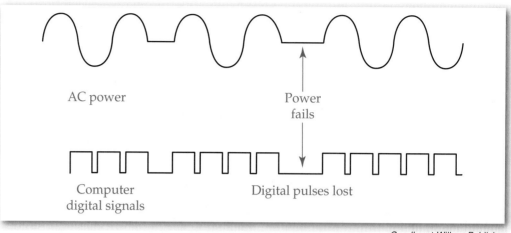

AC power

Power fails

Computer digital signals

Digital pulses lost

UPS Systems

An **uninterruptible power supply (UPS)** is designed to ensure a constant supply of quality electrical power to the computer system. *Quality power* means a power supply that eliminates surges, low voltage, and complete power outage conditions. **Figure 5-32** illustrates a typical UPS system showing outlets, surge protection, batteries, and charger. **Figure 5-33** shows two typical UPS systems.

A UPS system monitors the power input to the computer while maintaining a fully-charged battery. The AC/DC inverter is used to convert some of the 120 Vac from the outlet to 12 Vdc used to keep the batteries fully charged. When commercial power fails, the inverter changes the 12 Vdc from the battery back into 120 Vac. The 120 Vac is then used to maintain power to the computer until the PC can be properly shut down, preventing the loss of data. Without the UPS system, the PC would crash when the power failed, and all data in RAM would be lost.

Low-voltage situations and brownouts are common occurrences in electrical distribution systems. Some low-voltage occurrences last only a few milliseconds and go completely unnoticed by the users. Even low voltage levels of a few milliseconds can cause a computer to crash. Remember that the digital traffic in a computer is traveling at megahertz speeds. Many commands can be issued in a few milliseconds or thousands of bits of data can be sent. All of it could be lost during the momentary voltage loss.

Many computer system lockups are caused by momentary low-voltage conditions. This condition can be prevented by using a UPS. A power strip does not provide protection against blackout or brownout conditions.

Power Strips

Not all power strips protect against power surges. Some are designed as a strip of convenient outlets to plug equipment into. Power strips that are designed for power surge protection have a **metal oxide varistor (MOV)** connected across the internal electrical line.

The MOV does not normally conduct electricity until a certain voltage level is reached. Then the MOV acts much like a direct short, providing an alternate path for current. This diverts the current from the path through the electronic equipment plugged into the strip.

Power strips offer some degree of protection against power surges. While there is no true protection against extreme power surges, such as those generated by a direct hit from a bolt of lightning, the surge protector does protect against lower forms of power surge. A power surge can occur naturally many times a day in high-voltage power distribution systems. Most of them go unnoticed, but there are some that are quite severe. Surges are produced in the normal course of events such as in the opening and closing of electrical switch gear. Electrical distribution systems are normally rerouted while performing routine or emergency maintenance.

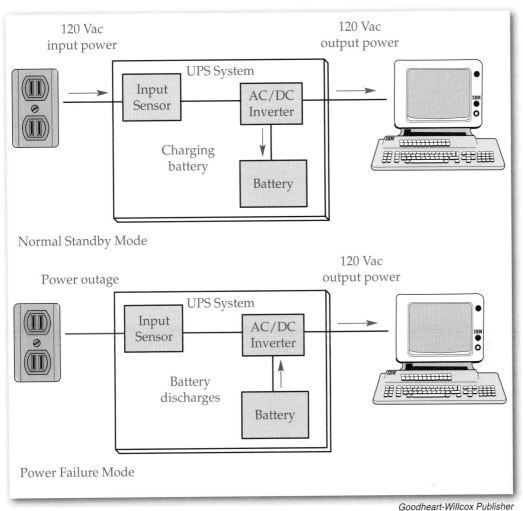

120 Vac
input power

120 Vac
output power

UPS System

Input
Sensor

AC/DC
Inverter

Charging
battery

Battery

Normal Standby Mode

Power outage

120 Vac
output power

UPS System

Input
Sensor

AC/DC
Inverter

Battery
discharges

Battery

Power Failure Mode

Goodheart-Willcox Publisher

Figure 5-32.
A typical UPS monitors the 120 Vac input. When power is normal, the battery is kept fully charged and ac power is supplied to the computer. When the 120 Vac input fails, the battery discharges through the inverter to create 120 Vac for the computer.

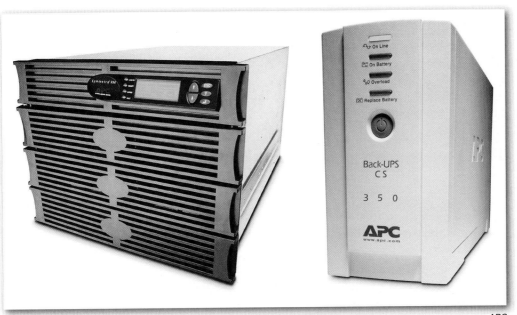

APC

Figure 5-33.
Uninterruptible power supply systems protect PCs and servers from power loss and power surges. All critical PC systems should be protected by a UPS unit.

Other sources of voltage surges are caused by running brush-type motors, such as those found in vacuum cleaners, drills, saws, and most any type of power tool or appliance. These types of surges show up as line spikes.

These surges can produce very large spikes in the electrical system many times greater than the normal voltage and can damage sensitive electronic equipment. Many electronic components have maximum operating voltages. When a voltage surge exceeds this value, the component is damaged.

Batteries

Computers keep a variety of information stored in their CMOS. In this way, when your computer is turned on, it knows the settings describing the hard drive and floppy drive as well as items like the time and date. The information cannot be stored in ROM and must match the hardware installed in the computer. It is saved to the CMOS chip and maintained by a battery so that it remains intact even when the computer power is disconnected or turned off. Thus, a battery is used to power the CMOS chip when the main power supply to the computer is shut down. See **Figure 5-34**.

Batteries are constructed in a simple manner. When two dissimilar metals are placed in contact with a chemical solution, called an electrolyte, a voltage is produced. **Figure 5-35** illustrates the principles behind a battery. It shows two metal plates and an electrolyte with a lightbulb as the load.

The most common types of batteries used for motherboards are alkaline, nickel metal hydride, nickel cadmium (also called NiCad), and lithium. All are rechargeable batteries. The charge on a lithium battery lasts longer than the other three types of battery. This is why lithium is the preferred choice, especially for laptop computers.

A sure sign of failure of the CMOS battery is the PC's failure to correctly keep the date and time. Battery failure can also cause the system to fail to recognize the hard drive and other devices that store information in CMOS. A typical PC battery should last five to seven years, but they have been known to fail sooner. You can reset and save the information with the Setup utility and use the computer as normal until the battery is replaced.

The batteries used for a UPS system are usually lead-acid or a gel-type. These batteries can provide power for a substantial period of time. The biggest advantage of gel-type is the lack of regular maintenance required as compared to lead-acid. Newer lead-acid batteries should also be maintenance free. Both types should be periodically inspected for corrosion on the battery terminals.

Figure 5-34. Typical motherboard battery.

Goodheart-Willcox Publisher

Figure 5-35. Illustration of battery principles. Two metal plates in an electrolyte solution produce energy to power a light.

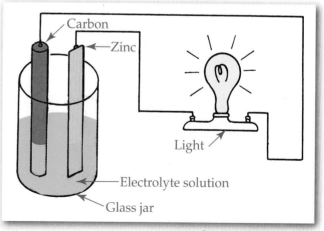

Goodheart-Willcox Publisher

Battery Disposal

Batteries must be disposed of in the manner outlined by the Environmental Protection Agency (EPA). Most manufacturers will readily accept the old battery in return for the purchase of a new one. They have the proper means of disposal at hand that the typical technician does not. You simply do not throw an old battery into the trash, especially large UPS batteries. More information on battery recycling can be found on the EPA website. Also, be aware that local jurisdictions, such as counties and cities, may have their own set of regulations on battery disposal.

A Material Safety Data Sheet (MSDS) is required for batteries that contain hazardous materials such as lead, zinc, magnesium chloride, mercury, and cobalt. Manufacturers must supply an MSDS when requested. The MSDS contains information about how to safely handle the product, what to do if a person is contaminated by the product, and how to dispose of the product properly. A complete list of Material Safety Data Sheets for the most common batteries are available at the BatteriesPlus website.

Battery Safety

Some battery manufacturers print information about safety and proper disposal on their labels.

The APC battery in **Figure 5-36** lists the following safety warnings:

- **Do not charge in gas tight container.** The gases could accumulate and then a spark would cause an explosion.
- **Do not short battery terminals.** Short-circuited battery terminals cause excessive current flow. This can cause severe flash burns and possible explosion.
- **Do not incinerate.** Incineration can cause battery cells to expand and explode. Also, burning some types of batteries causes toxic materials to be released into the atmosphere.
- **Flush with water at once if contaminated with electrolyte (acid).** The acid in this type of battery can cause skin irritation. When splashed or rubbed into the eye area, it can cause blindness.

Power Management Standards

Power management is a critical issue when it comes to power consumption of desktops, laptops, and servers. Controlling power consumption on laptops is critical for battery life before charging is required. Controlling power consumption for desktops and servers can result in significant electrical energy costs,

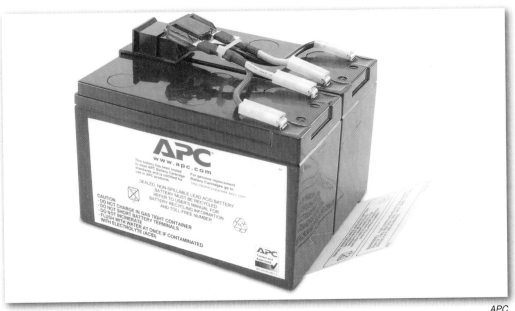

Figure 5-36.
A UPS battery with safety and proper disposal information printed on the side.

APC

especially in an environment of several hundred or even thousands of computers. Turning off computer displays and putting the computer into hibernation can save thousands of dollars in energy costs. The savings are not just directly related to electrical energy consumed by the computer system, but also to electrical energy consumed by air conditioning. Computers and displays generate a lot of heat, especially CRT displays.

Advanced Configuration and Power Interface (ACPI) is an open industry power management standard for desktops, laptops, and servers. ACPI allows the operating system to control the power management features. The original implementation of computer power management is Advanced Power Management (APM). APM was designed for the BIOS to control power management features of the computer system. APM was configured in the BIOS Setup utility and determined the amount of time before the display screen and hard disk drive would be turned off. It was later replaced by ACPI.

ACPI is enabled in the BIOS/UEFI Setup utility but not controlled or configured by it. It is configured through the operating system. The operating system then determines when to implement the energy saving features.

Windows Vista, Windows 7, and Windows 8 provide three general options for power savings: **Balanced**, **Power saver**, and **High performance**. **Figure 5-37** shows these options in Windows 8. To the right of each option, you can see the relationship of energy savings to computer performance. For example, the **Power saver** option would be the best choice for the maximum life of a laptop battery charge. There will be much more about power saving and laptops later in Chapter 12—Portable Devices.

The **Power Options** dialog box is accessed through **Control Panel | Performance and Maintenance** in Windows XP, through **Control Panel | System and Maintenance** in Windows Vista, and through **Control Panel | System and Security** in Windows 7 and Windows 8.

Figure 5-37.
Windows 8 **Power Options** dialog box.

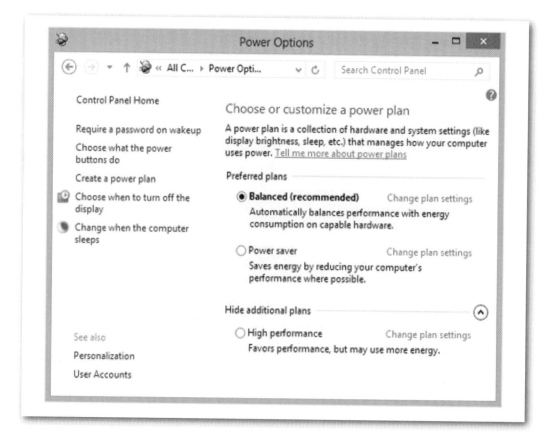

If your folders are set up to use the Classic view in Windows XP and Windows Vista, the **Power Options** dialog box is accessed through **Control Panel | Power Options**. There is no **Classic View** option in Windows 7 and Windows 8. To produce the same effect as Classic view, select either the **Small icons** viewing option or **Large icons** viewing option in Control Panel.

Windows uses dynamic processor throttling to control the processor when in certain processor management modes. The Windows operating system can automatically throttle CPU performance to conserve electrical energy. The following table lists the various modes.

Mode	Description
None	Run at highest performance possible.
Constant	Always run at lowest possible performance to conserve maximum energy.
Adaptive	Performance based on demand.
Degrade	Always run at lowest performance state. Used mainly for laptops to conserve maximum amount of energy.

A+ Note

You will most likely see a question concerning power options for desktop and laptop computers. Be sure you can identify which power options are available for all current Windows operating systems.

Chapter Summary

- Voltage is the pressure that pushes electrons through a circuit; current is the amount of electron flow; resistance is the opposition to current; and power is calculated by multiplying voltage (volts) with current (amperes).

- A good fuse or cable produces a zero resistance reading, and an open fuse or cable produces an infinity reading.

- Electrical equipment running on the same circuit as a computer can cause a power problem for the computer system.

- The signs that a power supply is bad are inoperable cooling fans, no indicator lights, smoke, burnt smell, circuit breaker tripping, automatic rebooting, electric shock, and excessive heat.

- A UPS system provides protection against power surges, low voltage, and temporary power outages; a surge protector power strip provides protection against power surges.

- Information on battery recycling can be found on the Environmental Protection Agency's website and Material Safety Data Sheets.

- The Windows **Power Options** dialog box located in **Control Panel** can be used to control PC power consumption.

Review Questions

Answer the following questions on a separate sheet of paper. Please do not write in this book.

1. Define *electrical energy*.
2. Water pressure, expressed in PSI, is similar to what value in electronics?
3. What value in electrical energy is similar to gallons per minute in water?
4. Opposition to electron flow is expressed in _____.
5. Wattage and VA are exactly the same. True or False?
6. The wattage rating on a power supply unit is an indication of how much _____.
   a. electrical energy can be safely supplied to the PC's devices
   b. electrical energy the power supply will consume
   c. current the power supply unit will draw from the PC's devices
   d. voltage the power supply unit needs to operate the PC
7. What resistance value will a good fuse indicate on a digital multimeter?
8. A blown fuse should indicate how much resistance on an ohmmeter?
9. A good cable should read how much resistance from one end to the other end?
10. When checking voltage at a wall outlet, plus or minus _____% of the 120-volt rating is considered a good voltage reading.
11. When troubleshooting computer electrical damage, glitches, and lockups in a commercial location, what should you know about the distribution system?
12. What is a dedicated circuit?
13. What are the typical dc voltage levels from a PC power supply unit?
14. What is the difference between an ATX and an ATX12V motherboard main power connection?
15. What is the typical electrical voltage supply in European countries?
16. What should you warn a computer customer about when they plan a trip to Europe and they want to take their laptop along with them?
17. What is the minimum input voltage level of a standard ATX12V power supply used in the United States?
18. List eight signs that a power supply is bad.
19. What is the difference between an electrical surge and a brownout?
20. A UPS unit delivers a constant level of power to a PC during _____. Select all that apply.
    a. electrical surges
    b. low voltage
    c. power outage conditions
    d. brownouts
21. Explain the operation of the AC/DC inverter in a UPS unit.

22. All power strips provide surge protection. True or False?
23. What is a metal oxide varistor used for?
24. What government agency outlines the proper disposal of batteries?
25. What is the difference between APM and APCI?
26. What are the three main power conservation settings available in Windows Vista, Windows 7, and Windows 8 systems?
27. What is the path to access the **Power Options** dialog box in Windows 7 and Windows 8? Start with Control Panel.

A+

Sample A+ Exam Questions

Answer the following questions on a separate sheet of paper. Please do not write in this book.

1. Select the best definition of a PC power supply.
   a. A power supply converts 120 Vac power into 3.3, 5, and 12 Vdc levels that are used by the motherboard and various components.
   b. A power supply converts 120 Vdc power into 3.3, 5, and 12 Vdc levels that are used by the motherboard and various components.
   c. A power supply converts 120 Vac power into 5, 12, and 18 Vdc levels that is used by the motherboard and various components.
   d. A power supply converts 120 Vdc power into 5, 12, and 18 Vdc levels that is used by the motherboard and various components.

2. Which unit below is used to express electrical pressure?
   a. Ampere
   b. Volt
   c. Watt
   d. Ohm

3. Which electrical characteristics does a digital multimeter measure? Select all that apply.
   a. Voltage
   b. Resistance
   c. Amperes
   d. Wire size

4. Which item ensures a steady and clean supply of electrical energy during power outages?
   a. VOM
   b. DMM
   c. UPS
   d. APC

5. Electrical power is usually expressed by which letter?
   a. V
   b. A
   c. W
   d. R

6. What is the maximum electrical load that may be connected to a typical 120-Vac power strip supplying computer equipment?
   a. 1000 W
   b. 1600 W
   c. 2000 W
   d. 2400 W

7. Which of the following is the closest to the resistance reading of a blown fuse?
   a. 0 Ω
   b. 120 volts
   c. 10 MΩ
   d. Infinity

8. Which is a typical procedure when a power supply is suspected to be bad?
    a. Open the power supply unit and replace the fuse.
    b. Check the output voltage levels of the wall outlet.
    c. Run **msinfo32** from **Run** in the **Start** menu to diagnose the power output.
    d. Put on an anti-static wrist strap and then open the power supply box to replace the fuse.
9. Which system is controlled by the operating system to conserve electrical energy?
    a. ACPI
    b. APM
    c. DDR
    d. DMA
10. Which dc voltage levels are associated with a typical ATX power supply?
    a. 3.3, 5, 12
    b. 5, 12, 18
    c. 3.3, 5, 12, 18
    d. 12, 18, 24

Suggested Laboratory Activities

Do not attempt any suggested laboratory activities without your instructor's permission. Certain activities can render the PC operating system inoperable.

1. Remove a power supply from a typical PC and then reinstall it.
2. Practice taking resistance readings of various conductors.
3. Gather several small batteries of different voltages. Practice taking dc voltage readings.
4. Take voltage readings of the 120-Vac outlets in your classroom. See what the actual voltage levels are. Take readings throughout the day to see if the voltage levels change.
5. Take voltage readings from the output of a typical PC power supply. Make note of the voltage type (whether ac or dc) and the voltage levels.
6. Take resistance readings of a fuse known to be good and then of a fuse known to be blown. Compare the results.
7. Go to a multimeter manufacturer's website, such as Fluke Corporation, and download a user's manual for one of their digital multimeters. Read about the meter's jacks and dial settings.

Memory 6

After studying this chapter, you will be able to:

- Evaluate the type and amount of memory needed for an upgrade.
- Identify physical memory packages.
- Recall various memory types and their characteristics.
- Use proper procedures to install memory.
- Apply knowledge of RAM characteristics when adding or replacing RAM modules.
- Explain the construction of flash memory devices.
- Identify memory map areas and functions.
- Explain the benefits and operation of virtual memory and Windows ReadyBoost.
- Recognize typical memory problems.

A+ Exam—Key Points

For the CompTIA A+ exams, you should be familiar with compatibility issues between the various types of DDR memory. You should also master the terminology and acronyms presented in this chapter.

Key Terms

The following key terms will become important pieces of your computer vocabulary. Be sure you can define them.

buffer
Column Address Select (CAS)
dual-channel mode
dual in-line memory module (DIMM)
dual in-line package (DIP)
dynamic RAM
electrically erasable programmable read-only memory (EEPROM)
erasable programmable read-only memory (EPROM)
error correction code (ECC)
even parity checking
fake parity
flash memory
flash ROM
flex mode
heap
heat spreader
MicroDIMM
nanosecond (ns)
odd parity checking
page file

parity
programmable read-only memory (PROM)
protected mode
quad-channel mode
random access memory
read-only memory (ROM)
real mode
registered memory
Row Address Selection (RAS)
safe mode
serial presence detect (SPD)
single-channel mode
single in-line memory module (SIMM)
single in-line package (SIP)
small outline DIMM (SO-DIMM)
small outline RIMM (SO-RIMM)
solid-state disk (SSD)
static RAM
triple-channel mode
virtual memory

The memory in a computer is one of the most difficult components to explain and understand. It is imperative that you carefully examine the illustrations provided in this chapter while studying the concept of memory. You may also need your instructor's help to completely grasp this difficult concept. While memory is, without question, one of the easiest upgrades that can be made to a PC, understanding system memory and its evolution is very complex and confusing.

This chapter covers memory types, memory terminology, memory diagnostics, and memory management used by the various Microsoft operating systems. It will also help you understand the complexity of PC memory and develop troubleshooting strategies. A large part of the A+ Certification exams is dedicated to questions regarding memory terminology. The terminology associated with memory can be confusing, but with a little concentration and effort, you will master the subject of PC memory.

Questions to Ask Before Upgrading Memory

Before you begin your study of memory types, let's look at the issues you must consider when upgrading memory. There are a number of items of which you must be aware. Novices simply plug memory modules into motherboards and expect the amount of memory and performance to increase. This will not always be the result. Improperly identified memory modules and improper installation can decrease PC performance and possibly damage the motherboard.

The questions that need to be answered before upgrading memory involve the following:

- **Compatibility:** With which type of memory is the motherboard compatible?
- **Quantity:** What is the total amount of RAM desired? Are you adding to existing RAM or replacing it?

- **Parity or non-parity:** Does the existing memory have parity checking? Does the existing system support parity checking?
- **Speed:** Will the existing chipset support the speed (frequency) of the memory module?
- **Memory specifics:** Must the memory be installed in pairs? Must the size and latency match when installed in pairs? Are there any other specifics that must be adhered to?

These questions should all be answered before attempting a memory upgrade on a PC. Deciding on these issues will save time and money. The rest of this chapter assists with answering these questions. It also covers important concepts that will aid in your understanding of technical manuals and memory issues.

Tech Tip

Windows 32-bit systems will only access 4 GB of memory. Adding more memory will serve no useful purpose. To utilize more than 4 GB, you must install a Windows 64-bit operating system.

Physical Memory Packages

PC memory chips are packaged in several different physical styles. Some of these are SIP, DIP, SIMM, and DIMM. Physical size of the memory package is important when assessing an upgrade or a replacement.

SIP

A **single in-line package (SIP)** is a memory chip that has a single row of connections that run along the length of a chip, **Figure 6-1**. SIPs are sometimes referred to as SIPPs, single in-line pin packages, because the row of connections along the modules are pins. This type of module is not often used today because it has a high physical profile and the pins are easily bent.

DIP

A **dual in-line package (DIP)** is a chip that has two rows of connections, one row per side of the chip, **Figure 6-2**. This style is commonly used for cache memory or for memory that must be mounted permanently on a circuit board. Memory of this type is found on older model motherboards. It is mounted in rows near the CPU.

SIMM

A **single in-line memory module (SIMM)** is a memory module containing a row of DIP memory chips mounted on a circuit board. The circuit board has flat contacts that run along both sides of the bottom edge. This type of connection is called an *edge connector*. The circuit board is then inserted into a SIMM memory slot on the motherboard. The SIMM is designed so that, when plugged into the memory socket, each side of the edge connector is the same circuit. This eliminates easily damaged pins. SIMMs come in 30-pin and 72-pin packages.

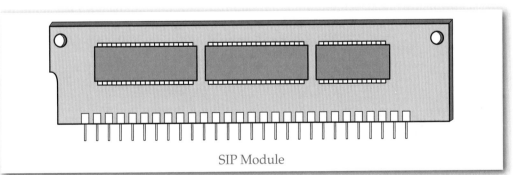

SIP Module

Figure 6-1.
Early PC memory modules were SIPs.

Figure 6-2. Another early form of PC memory was the DIP.

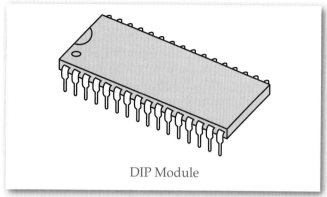

DIP Module

Goodheart-Willcox Publisher

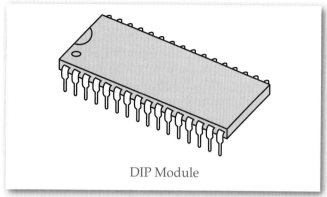

Tech Tip

Flat edge contacts are also referred to as pins.

DIMM

A **dual in-line memory module (DIMM)** is a memory module constructed much like a SIMM. The major difference is that the edge connectors located directly across the circuit board from each other do not connect electrically. They are not the same electrical connection as they are on the SIMM board. The DIMM design allows for more electrical connections per inch than the SIMM design, **Figure 6-3**. DIMMs come in 168-pin, 184-pin, and 240-pin packages.

SO-DIMM and SO-RIMM

Small outline DIMM (SO-DIMM) and **small outline RIMM (SO-RIMM)** are small outline packages of regular DIMM and RIMM modules. They are used especially for laptop applications where space is compact. The small outline package is designed to fit easily into the small confines of a laptop computer.

Figure 6-3. The various packages of memory can be easily identified by size. Shown are two SIMMs and a 168-pin DIMM.

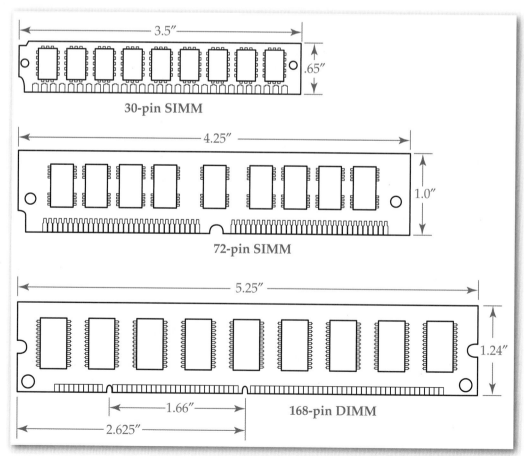

3.5″

.65″

30-pin SIMM

4.25″

1.0″

72-pin SIMM

5.25″

1.24″

1.66″

168-pin DIMM

2.625″

Goodheart-Willcox Publisher

MicroDIMM

MicroDIMM is a more compact version of the standard SO-DIMM package. KINGMAX Semiconductor coined the term "MicroDIMM" to distinguish it from the already existing SO-DIMM package and to emphasize its smaller size. Other memory manufacturers such as Kingston use SO-DIMM as the name of the smaller module. Either way, the module is quickly identified because of the overall smaller dimensions and pin count. The MicroDIMM has a 172-pin count while the standard SO-DIMM has a 200-pin count, **Figure 6-4**. The MicroDIMM memory module is used in many notebook and laptop computers, but not in desktops.

ROM and RAM Memory

Computer systems contain both read-only memory (ROM) and random access memory (RAM) memory. **Read-only memory (ROM)** is designed to store the program information in a permanent fashion, while **random access memory (RAM)** is designed to temporarily store data or programs. Content in RAM can be erased and reloaded again and again. All programming and data in RAM is lost when power is removed from the chip. ROM retains data and programs after power is removed.

To help you understand the difference between RAM and ROM, think of a typical "whiteboard" found in classrooms or in corporate boardrooms. The whiteboard requires the use of a nonpermanent marker. If information is written

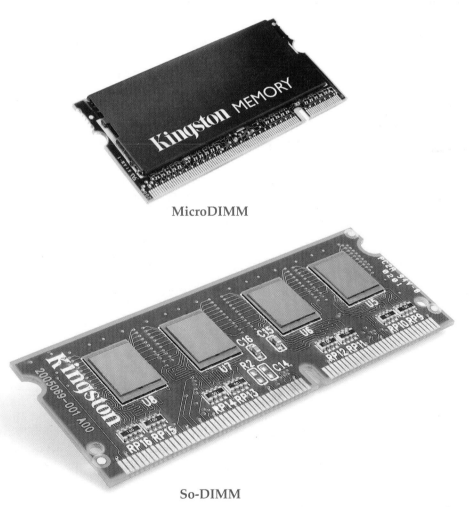

Figure 6-4.
MicroDIMM is a compact version of the standard SO-DIMM. Some manufacturers also call the MicroDIMM a SO-DIMM.

MicroDIMM

So-DIMM

on a whiteboard using a permanent marker, the information will remain on the board forever, similar to the information written in a ROM memory chip. If an erasable marker is used on the whiteboard, the information can be wiped clean from the board, allowing new and different information to be written on the board. This is similar to RAM.

The terms *volatile* and *nonvolatile* are often used to describe computer memory. RAM is considered volatile memory. Like RAM, a volatile memory chip loses its data when power is removed from the computer. ROM chips are nonvolatile. Nonvolatile memory chips retain their information when the power is removed from the computer.

Types of ROM

There has been a good deal of innovation involving ROM memory. Not all ROM chips have programs that are permanently embedded. Many variations of ROM chips can actually be reprogrammed with different data or programs. They are still classified as ROM chips because, in normal applications, they retain their information even after power is removed from the computer.

PROM

The original ROM chips were manufactured with a program etched into the chip. The technically correct term for this type of ROM chip is *mask ROM*. The manufacturer uses a mask to create the circuitry. This circuitry represents the program when the chip is manufactured. Recall the discussion from Chapter 1—Introduction to a Typical PC about the chip manufacturing process. The programs in these chips cannot be altered.

Programmable read-only memory (PROM) is similar to mask ROM. It is used extensively in computer program development. Blank ROM chips are purchased and then programmed using a device called a PROM burner. A PROM burner is connected to a PC. A program or data is written on the PC and then transferred to the burner where it electrically burns the program into the blank PROM chip. The PROM chip then retains the program indefinitely, but it cannot be reprogrammed.

EPROM

Erasable programmable read-only memory (EPROM) was an advancement of the PROM. These chips can be programmed, erased, and then reprogrammed. The EPROM has a small clear window that exposes the miniature circuitry inside the chip. The chip is erased by shining an ultraviolet light through the window. This returns the EPROM to its original blank state.

EEPROM

Electrically erasable programmable read-only memory (EEPROM) eliminated the need for using an ultraviolet light to erase the memory chip. It uses a higher electrical charge to erase the chip than the original charge used to program it. The EEPROM was designed to be erased one bit at a time. In this way, part of a program could be erased rather then the entire program at one time.

Flash ROM

Flash ROM behaves in a similar manner to RAM. It is possible to replace the memory contents of flash ROM. It is similar to EEPROM, but it uses a much higher voltage to erase the chip and also erases the entire block of memory at one time.

It is important to note that EEPROM and flash ROM can only be reprogrammed a limited number of times. At some point, the chip will become damaged by the application of the higher than normal voltage used in the erase operation.

Types of RAM

Random access memory is a matrix of individual storage areas where information can be stored as bits. The name *random access* means that the CPU can access any bit anywhere in the memory. The CPU does not have to go through the memory in sequential fashion. Early computer systems did not have the advantage of RAM chips or disk drive systems. They used ROM chips and stored data on magnetic tape. The data on the tape was stored sequentially, bit by bit, along the entire length of tape. To access any information on the tape, the tape would have to play back bit by bit until the desired information could be retrieved.

Dynamic RAM vs. Static RAM

There are two basic forms of RAM. One type, dynamic RAM, uses capacitors to store the information. The second type, static RAM, uses devices called flip-flops.

Dynamic RAM (referred to as DRAM and pronounced *dee-ram*) is a type of integrated circuit that uses capacitors to assist in storing data in the transistors. Capacitors are capable of storing electrical charges. The presence or absence of the electrical charge in the capacitor represents the binary data being stored. Because of their microscopic size, the capacitors in the integrated circuit lose their charge over a short period of time. To retain the charge, the capacitors must be constantly refreshed (recharged) with electrical energy. Dynamic RAM is used in the CPU because it is very small and is low cost when compared to static RAM.

Static RAM (referred to as SRAM and pronounced *es-ram*) is an integrated circuit technology based on digital flip-flop components. The flip-flop does not use a capacitor to hold the data condition as dynamic RAM does. It transmits data faster than dynamic RAM because it does not have to be constantly refreshed. To take advantage of the faster data transfer speed, most PC cache systems use static RAM as opposed to dynamic RAM. However, SRAM is approximately four times larger than DRAM, and it is considerably more expensive. Consequently, a computer's RAM will be some variant of DRAM.

DRAM

The basic *dynamic RAM (DRAM)* is the typical memory chip installed in older PCs, **Figure 6-5**. When someone says a computer has 2 GB of RAM, they are generally saying that the computer has DRAM. DRAM memory chips must be refreshed periodically to retain the information stored on them.

EDO DRAM

Extended Data Output DRAM (EDO DRAM) is faster than conventional DRAM. Conventional DRAM accesses only one block of memory at a time and then passes the data completely on to the next component before it transfers in new data.

Figure 6-5. Basic DRAM found in older PCs.

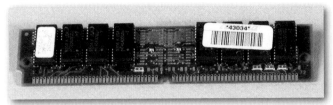

Goodheart-Willcox Publisher

EDO DRAM is designed to access and transfer in new data before the previous data stored on the chip is transferred out. This technique greatly improves the transfer rate of memory.

BEDO DRAM

Burst Extended Data Output DRAM (BEDO DRAM) is an improved version of EDO DRAM. It can transfer data in groups or "bursts" of four memory addresses at one time. BEDO DRAM cannot keep up with a motherboard bus that runs faster than 66 MHz. Consequently, there are few current applications for this type of memory.

SDRAM

Synchronous dynamic RAM (SDRAM) is much faster than conventional DRAM, **Figure 6-6**. SDRAM can transfer data at speeds exceeding 100 MHz. The SDRAM synchronizes the transfer of data with the CPU chip. Synchronizing data transfer timing increases data transfer rates. This is because the chip does not have to wait for the next tick of the CPU clock system to begin transferring data. SDRAM can be found on video cards because of its high-speed transfer rate.

DDR1

Double Data Rate-SDRAM or simply *DDR1* was designed to replace SDRAM. DDR1 was originally referred to as DDR-SDRAM or simply DDR. When DDR2 was introduced, DDR became referred to as DDR1. Names of components constantly change as newer technologies are introduced, especially when the newer technology is based on a previous one.

The principle applied in DDR is exactly as the name indicates. DDR doubles the rate at which data is transferred by using both the rising and falling edges of a typical digital pulse. Earlier

Figure 6-6.
The original SDRAM had exposed memory chips. Today, SDRAM used in high-performance memory applications have heat spreaders to dissipate heat created by high frequencies.

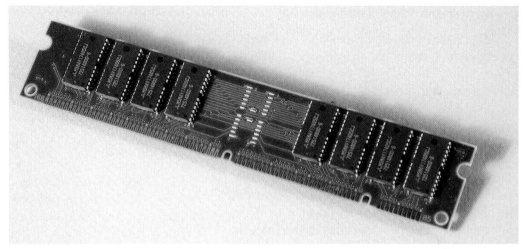

memory technology, such as SDRAM, transferred data after one complete digital pulse. DDR transfers data twice as fast by transferring data on both the rising and falling edges of the digital pulse. Examine **Figure 6-7**. As you can see, DDR can transfer twice the data as SDRAM.

DDR2

DDR2 is the next generation of memory developed after DDR. It has a greater data transfer rate (bandwidth) than DDR1. This is achieved by increasing its operational frequency to match the front side bus (FSB) frequencies and by doubling

Figure 6-7.
Comparison of SDRAM and DDR data transfers. A—SDRAM transfers data on a complete digital signal pulse. B—DDR transfers data on the rising edge and falling edge of a digital signal pulse, thus transferring twice as much data as SDRAM.

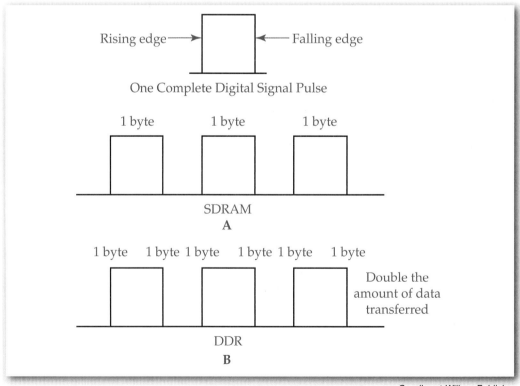

the prefetch buffer data rate. The memory prefetch buffer data rate is discussed in detail later in this chapter.

DDR2 is a 240-pin DIMM design that operates at 1.8 volts. The lower voltage counters the heat effect caused by high-frequency data transfer. DDR1 operates at 2.5 volts and is a 184-pin DIMM design. DDR2 uses a different motherboard socket than DDR1 and is not compatible with motherboards designed for DDR1. The DDR2 DIMM key will not align with DDR DIMM key. Forcing a DDR2 into a DDR1 socket will damage the socket, and the memory will be exposed to a high voltage level.

DDR3

DDR3 was introduced in the summer of 2007 and is the natural successor to DDR2, **Figure 6-8**. DDR3 increased the prefetch buffer size to 8 bits and increased the operating frequency, resulting in higher data transfer rates than DDR2. In addition, the voltage level was lowered to 1.5 volts to counter the heating effects of the high frequency. By now, you can see the trend of memory is to increase the prefetch buffer size, increase the operating frequency, and lower the operational voltage level to counter the effects of heat.

In 2009, the Joint Electron Devices Engineering Council (JEDEC), an organization that develops and distributes specifications for memory modules, modified the DDR3 standard to lower the voltage levels to 1.35 volts and 1.25 volts. A DDR3 1.35-volt module is identified as DDR3L. A DDR3 1.25-volt module is identified as DDR3U. The "L" represents "low voltage," and the "U" represents "ultra low voltage."

By lowering the operational voltages, the amount of current is also lowered and so is the amount of wattage the memory module consumes. Lower wattage means less heat. When applied to portable devices such as laptops, it means a slightly longer battery life between charges. When used in server applications, it means greatly reduced heat and less electricity to be consumed. Think of a large server facility such as at Google. The total number of memory modules for all the servers collectively would be in the thousands. Not only is there a direct savings in energy costs due to less wattage consumed by the servers, there is also direct energy savings for cooling and air conditioning because less heat is generated.

The computer system firmware detects the presence of the memory module and then automatically configures the voltage level so that is compatible with the memory module.

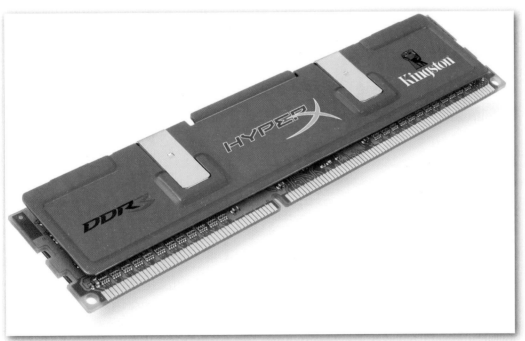

Figure 6-8.
Kingston DDR3 DIMM.

Kingston Technology

The DDR3 is designed with 240 pins like the DDR2, but the notch is in a different position to prevent insertion into a DDR2 socket. DDR3 is both electrically and physically incompatible with other versions of DDR RAM. See the location of the notch placed along the bottom edge of the memory modules in **Figure 6-9**. The notch is used to match the proper memory module to the proper socket. Insertion of the wrong memory module into the wrong socket will damage the socket.

In addition to high frequency capabilities and a lower applied voltage level, the DDR3 has a memory reset feature. This feature allows the memory to be cleared by a software reset action. Other memory types do not have this feature, and thus their memory state is uncertain after a system

Figure 6-9.
DDR DIMM comparison.

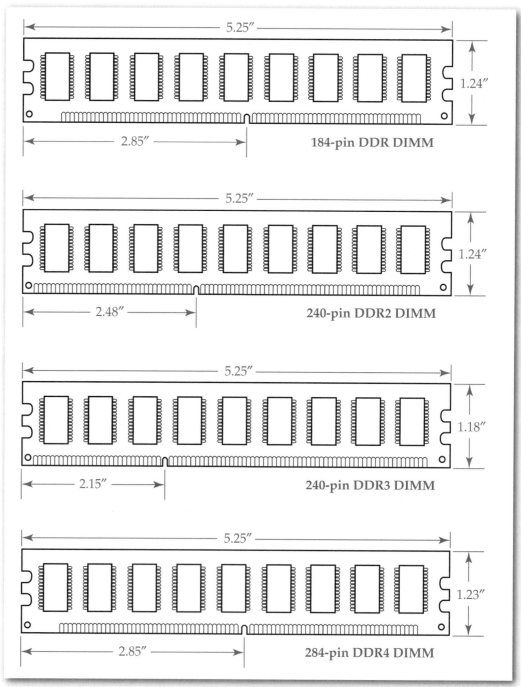

reboot. The memory reset feature ensures that the memory will be clean or empty after a system reboot. This feature causes a more stable memory system.

DDR4

The JEDEC standard for DDR4 was released in late 2012. DDR4 has an operating voltage of 1.2 volts and is designed with 284 pins. The SO-DIMM DDR4 has 256 pins. DDR4 has a greater bandwidth than DDR3. The lowest bandwidth rate of DDR4 overlaps the DDR3 bandwidth rate and continues to increase. DDR4 is not expected to enter the PC market until approximately 2014. The standard will continue to evolve over the next few years. Check the JEDEC website or RMRoberts website for the latest DDR4 memory standards.

Figure 6-10 lists the memory module PC classification, memory chip classification, and memory module bandwidth of various SDRAM and DDR memory modules. The memory chip classification correlates to the memory chip frequency design. For example, a DDR2-400 is designed to operate at 400 MHz. The memory module PC classification correlates to the memory module frequency times 8. For example, a DDR2-400 would be identified as a PC2-3200. The 3200 is equal to 8 times 400 MHz.

The memory module bandwidth is the theoretical amount of data that can be transferred, even though it is expressed as an exact value such as 12.8 GB. The table is based on theoretical throughputs and does not take into account the memory controller, BIOS, or chipset. For a motherboard designed with dual-channel architecture, the memory module bandwidth is theoretically doubled, for triple-channel it is tripled, and for quad-channel it is quadrupled. The theoretical speed is just a value used to compare the various RAM types and classifications. Actual speed will be much lower than the theoretical speed.

Memory Module PC Classification	Memory Chip Classification	Memory Module Bandwidth
PC100	SDRAM	800 MB
PC133	SDRAM	1.10 GB
PC1600	DDR	1.60 GB
PC2100	DDR	2.10 GB
PC2700	DDR	2.70 GB
PC2-3200	DDR2-400	3.20 GB
PC2-4200	DDR2-533	4.20 GB
PC2-5300	DDR2-667	5.30 GB
PC2-6400	DDR2-800	6.40 GB
PC2-8500	DDR2-1066	8.50 GB
PC3-6400	DDR3-800	6.40 GB
PC3-8500	DDR3-1066	8.53 GB
PC3-10600	DDR3-1333	10.67 GB
PC3-12800	DDR3-1600	12.80 GB
PC3-14900	DDR3-1866	14.9 GB
PC3-17000	DDR3-2133	17 GB
PC4-XXXX	DDR4-2133–DDR4-4266	17 GB–34 GB

Note: The PC4 stats are the expected data rates.

Figure 6-10. Memory chip and memory module classifications. The memory module PC classification correlates to the memory module frequency times 8.

Tech Tip   DDR1, DDR2, DDR3, and DDR4 are not interchangeable because they are not physically or electrically compatible.

GDDR

Graphic DDR (GDDR) is RAM used exclusively for video cards. GDDR is incorporated into the video card and does not fit into slots as motherboard RAM does. Even though video cards use the same individual memory chips that are found on motherboard RAM, the electronic specifications are different than motherboard RAM. GDDR is designed to transfer data to and from the video processor directly at much higher frequencies than motherboard RAM. Because the Video RAM runs at higher frequencies, it generates more heat than motherboard RAM. Fans are incorporated into high-performance video cards that use high-performance RAM. The fans are standard for cooling the video card RAM. Video RAM generations are sequential just like DDR, for example GDDR3, GDDR4, and GDDR5.

RDRAM

Rambus DRAM (RDRAM), developed by Rambus, Inc., is a proprietary memory system. See **Figure 6-11**. RDRAM uses a DDR (double data rate) technique to double the speed of the data transfer. Data transfer rates as high as 800 MHz can be accomplished using RDRAM and a motherboard and CPU that support a 400-MHz front side bus. Intel originally incorporated Rambus RDRAM into its line of motherboards but has since discontinued it.

RIMM is the trade name for Direct Rambus memory module. It is longer than a 168-pin DIMM, and it reaches speeds of 800 MHz. It also uses a package capable of dissipating the heat generated by the high-speed data transfer rate. The package is an aluminum sheath, called a **heat spreader**. The heat spreader covers the chips and acts as a heat sink.

RIMM must be installed in pairs to function. However, one RIMM module may contain more than enough memory for a user. In that case, to achieve the effect of two RIMM modules when using only one RIMM module, a continuity RIMM (C-RIMM) must be installed in the second slot, **Figure 6-12**. The C-RIMM does not contain any memory chips. It simply acts as an electrical connection allowing data to pass through as if there were an additional RIMM installed. When C-RIMM is used in conjunction with a RIMM, the exact slot sequence should be checked against the manufacturer's specifications.

Tech Tip   Memory chip technology is rapidly changing. There has been at least one new memory type developed every year for the last five years.

Cache

Cache is a temporary storage location for data. The data remains in cache until the bus system is ready to transfer it to another component. Cache can be found throughout the computer system. For example, the CPU has cache (small pocket of RAM). Hard drives, modems, and video cards have cache, too. A hard drive uses cache (RAM

Figure 6-11.
RDRAM has data transfer rates of up to 800 MHz.

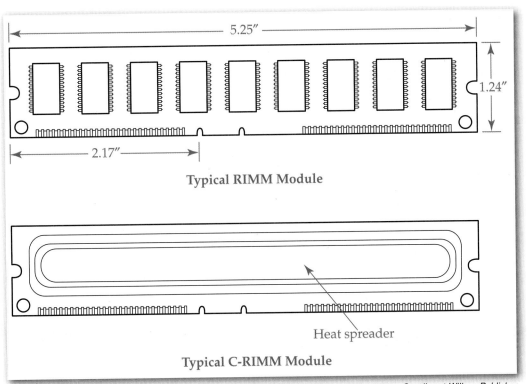

Figure 6-12. Sketch of RIMM and C-RIMM. In the diagram, the RIMM is shown with the heat spreader removed, exposing the individual memory chips.

Typical RIMM Module

5.25″

1.24″

2.17″

Typical C-RIMM Module

Heat spreader

Goodheart-Willcox Publisher

chip) to temporarily store data during a disc read/write operation. A typical modem uses cache to store data while waiting to transfer data into the computer bus system. Anywhere data transfer is taking place, you can be sure there is a cache system designed in the circuit board.

The size of cache directly affects the rate of data transfer. The larger the cache, the more data can be transferred. This results in a higher data rate, which is interpreted as high data speeds. Speed of data is based on how much data can be transferred in a given time period. Discussion of L1, L2 and L3 cache can be found in Chapter 4—CPU.

SPD

Serial presence detect (SPD) is a technology that identifies the type of RAM installed on a computer. It involves the presence of an extra chip on the memory module, which contains technical information about the module. The information provided by SPD is used by the BIOS to automatically configure the BIOS RAM settings to match the installed RAM. You can still change the RAM settings manually with the Setup utility, but this is not advised.

Increasing the RAM access clock speed is commonly performed by PC enthusiasts who wish to increase the performance of their computer. This group of enthusiasts is referred to as "overclockers." They not only overclock the RAM performance, but also the CPU. When you manually override the automatic SPD detection and configuration with the Setup utility, you run the risk of overheating the memory chips and causing a system failure or lockup. After failing to tweak the speed of the RAM, the computer BIOS must be reset, thus allowing the SPD to automatically reconfigure the BIOS RAM configuration correctly.

A+ Note

There is sure to be several questions that require you to compare and contrast different types of memory modules. For example, you will be asked to select the correct type of memory based on the characteristics described in the question

Installing RAM Modules

Adding memory is one of the easiest upgrades you can make to a computer. You simply insert the module and the computer's BIOS recognizes the new memory when you start your computer. However, the memory and the slots on the motherboard can be damaged if you are not careful, so there are a few important facts to keep in mind when installing memory.

> **Caution !**
>
> Do *not* force the memory module into the socket. Doing so may damage the memory module or socket. The memory module should fit snuggly, and you should experience only a little physical resistance when inserting the module.

Memory modules are extremely sensitive to static discharge. Always wear an anti-static or grounding wrist strap when handling memory chips. Do not touch the edge of the module where the electrical circuit connections are located. Touching the exposed electrical connections could cause ESD damage. In **Figure 6-13** the technician is holding the memory module by the heat spreader.

Figure 6-13. Do not touch the memory module electrical connections running along the bottom of the memory module. Align the notch on the bottom of the memory module with the key in the memory slot.

Goodheart-Willcox Publisher

Each memory type has a notch that is used to properly orientate the memory module with the memory slot and to ensure the correct type of memory is used to match the motherboard system, **Figure 6-14**. The slot has a corresponding key that fits into the notch.

After properly aligning the memory notch with the slot key, press the module firmly into the slot using your thumbs similar to that in **Figure 6-15**. When the memory is firmly seated in the slot, the clips at each end of the slot will clamp onto the module, thus holding it securely in place.

To achieve better performance, install DIMMs in sets as prescribed by the technology. For example, to achieve dual-channel capability, the modules must be installed in pairs. The following section covers various DIMM installation arrangements.

> ## A+ Note
>
> The CompTIA A+ exams often ask a question about the proper way to insert a DIMM as related to angle.

DIMM Physical Arrangements

Motherboards are capable of many different DIMM physical arrangements. The five DIMM arrangements you should be familiar with are the following:

- Single-channel mode.
- Dual-channel mode.
- Triple-channel mode.
- Quad-channel mode.
- Flex mode.

To determine the correct arrangement for a specific motherboard, you need to consult the motherboard manual or consult the motherboard manufacturer's website or computer manufacturer's website. Also, memory manufacturers provide online resources for matching memory to motherboards or computers.

Figure 6-14.
Each type of DDR memory module has a different notch location. A—Comparison of DDR, DDR2, and DDR3. B—DDR, DDR2, and DDR3 modules stacked one on top of the other to show the different notch locations.

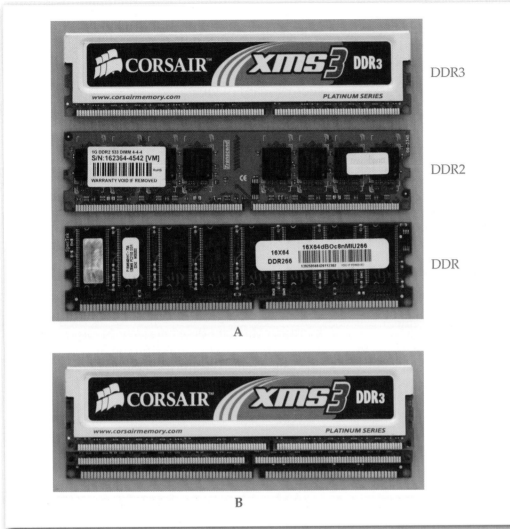

DDR3

DDR2

DDR

A

B

Goodheart-Willcox Publisher

Figure 6-15. Press the memory module down into the slot until the clips at each end close, locking down the memory module.

Goodheart-Willcox Publisher

Caution ! The drawings in this section are made solely as an aid for explanation of the way the various channel modes are configured. Do *not* use these drawings as a practical example to be copied. You must consult the motherboard manual or the manufacturer's website for the correct physical configuration.

Single-Channel Mode

Single-channel mode, also referred to as *asymmetric mode,* is when a single DIMM is installed, or multiple DIMMS of different memory capacity are installed in the motherboard memory slots. **Figure 6-16** shows an example of single-channel mode with one DIMM. **Figure 6-17** shows an example of single-channel mode with DIMMs of different values. In this example, the different value DIMMs may have a total memory capacity of 6 GB or less depending on the motherboard and if the DIMM has been installed in the correct sequence as specified by the motherboard manufacturer. If the DIMM arrangement is incorrect, the computer may fail to boot or all of the memory may not be detected.

When different memory modules have different speed specifications, the memory performance will be based on the slowest speed. For example, when installing a 400-MHz memory module with a 533-MHz memory module, the performance will be based on 400 MHz. Also, most motherboards require that memory modules be placed in a specific order of arrangement. Random arrangement will most likely generate an error message and the computer may not boot properly.

Dual-Channel Mode

Dual-channel mode, also known as *interleaved mode*, is when the DIMMs are arranged as a pair and in a specific way according to the motherboard manual.

Dual-channel DDR memory takes advantage of dual-channel technology developed by Intel in 2003. The RAM bus system, also known as the front side bus (FSB), consisted of a single bus system. The Intel Corporation redesigned the motherboard to provide two memory busses between the RAM and the north bridge chipset, **Figure 6-18**. In this design, north bridge chipset contains the memory controller, which controls the flow of data between the RAM and CPU. (Today, computers incorporate the memory controller into the CPU chip and the north bridge is eliminated.) Dual-channel technology greatly increases the data flow between the processor and the RAM. It does not actually double the data rate to the CPU, but the data rate is increased significantly.

Figure 6-16.
Single-channel mode with one DIMM.

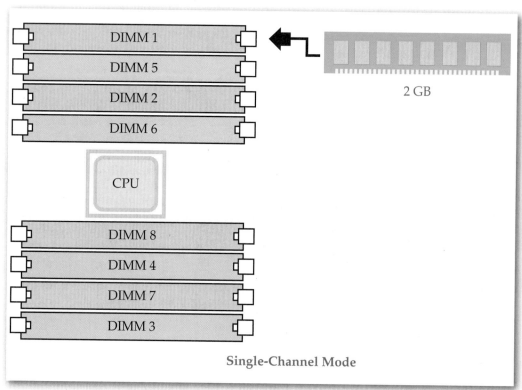

Single-Channel Mode

Goodheart-Willcox Publisher

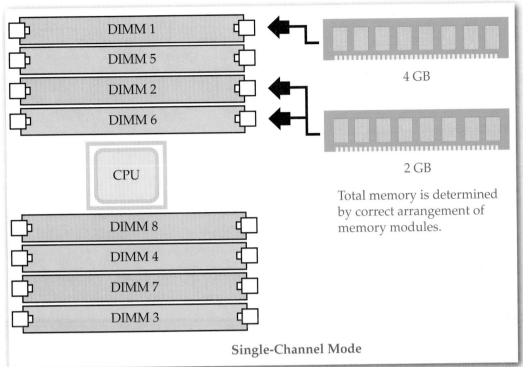

Goodheart-Willcox Publisher

Figure 6-17.
Single-channel mode with DIMMs of different values.

Figure 6-18. The Intel dual-channel DDR memory motherboard architecture significantly increases the data throughput from the RAM to the north bridge.

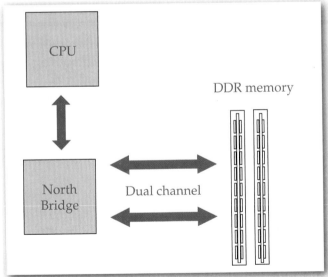

Goodheart-Willcox Publisher

To implement dual-channel mode, you must install DRAM as a pair. The pair does not necessarily need to match, but it is highly recommended that they match for best performance. When the pair does not match, the module with the least amount of memory will be matched by the other module. For example, a 2-GB memory module and a 4-GB memory module paired in a dual-channel arrangement will result in the same effect as two 2 GB modules. Also, be aware that the worst latency will apply to both modules as a pair.

When installing pairs of memory in dual-channel mode, the size, speed, and latency should be matched; otherwise, unexpected and intermitted problems could occur. Latency is covered later in this chapter.

Triple-Channel Mode

Triple-channel mode is interleaved in the same way as dual-channel mode. The difference is triple-channel mode uses three channels to support memory access.

To configure a triple-channel mode of operation, three identical memory modules are inserted into the three identified memory slots, **Figure 6-19**. If only two memory modules are installed, the mode of operation will be dual-channel, not triple-channel. If a single memory

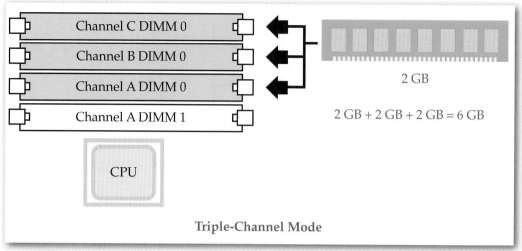

Figure 6-19.
Triple-channel mode.
For this mode, three
DIMMS of the same
value are installed.

2 GB

2 GB + 2 GB + 2 GB = 6 GB

Channel C DIMM 0

Channel B DIMM 0

Channel A DIMM 0

Channel A DIMM 1

CPU

Triple-Channel Mode

module is installed, the mode of operation will be single-channel.

When configured for triple-channel mode, the memory size is equal to adding the three separate memory capacities together. For example, three 2-GB memory modules would equal 6 GB of total memory. The speed is greatly increased, but not actually tripled.

Quad-Channel Mode

As the name implies, **quad-channel mode** supports four identical memory modules into the designated quad-channel slots. Again, the speed is greatly increased, but is not four times faster. **Figure 6-20** shows two different quad-channel mode arrangements. In Figure 6-20A, four 2-GB DIMMs are arranged in quad-channel mode for a total of 8 GB. In Figure 6-20B, eight 2-GB DIMMs are arranged in quad-channel mode for a total of 16 GB of RAM.

The quad-channel motherboard can also be configured for the triple-channel, dual-channel, and single-channel mode of operation. Quad-channel is not yet common in PC systems, except for in some high-performance systems such as network servers. These systems often contain large amounts of memory to better perform while being accessed by multiple clients.

Figure 6-21 shows the quad-channel locations identified on an ASUS Sabertooth X79 motherboard. The DIMM channel identifications are printed on the motherboard beside the DIMM

sockets. The DIMM sockets are identified as DIMM_D2, DIMM_D1, DIMM_C2, and DIMM_C1. This means the channels are identified as channel "C" and channel "D." Each channel consists of two DIMM sockets identified as "1" and "2." For example, DIMM_C1 identifies DIMM channel C, slot 1. The top set of DIMM slot identification markings are obscured by the chipset fan housing. You would need to use the motherboard manual to correctly identify the other four DIMM slots as DIMM_A1, DIMM_A2, DIMM_B1, and DIMM_B2.

Memory slots pairs are also identified with color. For the ASUS Sabertooth X79 motherboard, the pairs are identified with the colors brown and tan. This particular motherboard is designed to hold eight memory modules in quad-channel configuration. The maximum amount of memory for this motherboard is 64 GB.

Flex Mode

The DIMM memory modules can also be arranged in **flex mode**, which is a hybrid arrangement. See **Figure 6-22**. Notice the 2-GB and 4-GB DIMM arranged in a dual-channel configuration. In this arrangement, the total memory capacity is the total amount of RAM installed, or for this example, 6 GB. The memory is arranged in both dual-channel mode and single-channel mode. The dual-channel configuration consists of the single 2-GB memory module and the first 2-GB of the 4-GB module. The remaining 2 GB of the 4-GB module operates in single-

Figure 6-20. Quad-channel mode. A—Four 2-GB DIMMs are used for a total of 8 GB of RAM. B—Eight 2-GB DIMMs are used for a total of 16 GB of RAM.

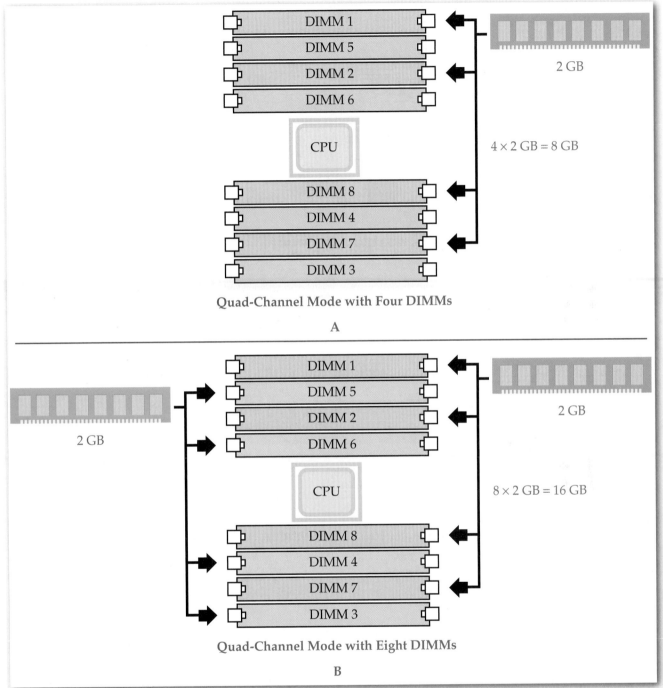

Quad-Channel Mode with Four DIMMs

A

Quad-Channel Mode with Eight DIMMs

B

channel mode. In other words, this example is operating in dual-channel and single-channel mode at the same time.

To further explain how the speed is increased by the various modes of operation, look at the following memory bandwidth relationship table. Notice that the bandwidth for single-channel operation is 64 bits wide. This means that there are 64 separate paths to and from the memory controller and the processor. As the channel

Figure 6-21.
Quad-channel memory location identification. The identification labels are in close proximity to the DIMM slots, and the slots are color-coded to help identify the different channel pairs.

Quad-channel DIMM slot identification
DIMM_D2
DIMM_D1
DIMM_C2
DIMM_C1

Goodheart-Willcox Publisher

Figure 6-22.
Flex mode DIMM configuration. The 2-GB module and the 2 GB of the 4-GB module operate in dual-channel mode. The remaining 2 GB from the 4-GB module operates in single channel mode.

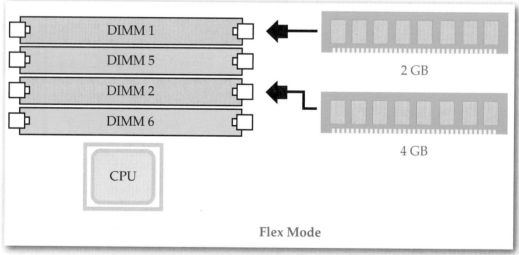

Goodheart-Willcox Publisher

number is increased so is the number of paths. For example, when dual-channel mode is configured, the number of paths is doubled from 64 to 128. In triple-channel mode, the bandwidth is tripled, and in quad-channel mode, the bandwidth is quadrupled.

Channels	Bandwidth in Bits
Single	64
Double	128
Triple	192
Quad	256

The speed of data transfer is not actually doubled, tripled, or quadrupled. The speed expressed in terms of doubled, tripled, or quadrupled is theoretical. In actual application, factors such as computer hardware and software reduce the speed from the theoretical speed to actual speed. For example, data is not transferred continuously with every beat of the processor frequency. The processor does not strictly communicate with the DIMM. It communicates with all the devices in the computer system. Data transferred to and from the processor and memory is held in cache for an undetermined amount of time. The data waiting in cache reduces the theoretical transfer rate of the memory read or write operation.

> **Tech Tip**
>
> You will see memory kits advertised such as "2 GB (1 GB × 2)." This means it contains two identical 1-GB memory modules.

Memory Overclocking

Just as some processors can be overclocked to increase performance, so can some types of memory. Some memory modules have two speed ratings: standard and maximum. The standard memory frequency is the speed at which the memory is designed to be used. The maximum speed is the maximum speed the memory has been tested for in actual applications. The maximum speed typically requires additional cooling just as overclocked processors require additional cooling. Cooling devices are available, such as fans that attach to the memory modules and eliminate excessive heat. When memory is normally installed in a computer system, it is automatically detected and configured for the standard speed. To maximize the memory, you would need to manually configure the memory speed.

Matching RAM Characteristics

When adding or replacing RAM modules, it is important that certain characteristics of the modules are matched. The two most important characteristics of RAM chips are the speed and the integrity of the chips. In addition to speed and integrity, you need to understand the terms used to describe memory performance such as *latency*, *buffered chips*, and *registered memory*. You should be familiar with these terms not only as a technician but also to be prepared for the CompTIA A+ Certification exam.

Memory Chip Speed

The speed of the CPU is measured in megahertz (MHz) or gigahertz (GHz). Memory chip speed is measured in nanoseconds. A **nanosecond (ns)** is a unit of time equal to one billionth of a second.

When adding more memory to a PC, it is best to match the speed of the existing memory chips. If faster memory chips are added to an existing slower memory chip bank, the faster chips will run at the same speed as the existing chips. The chips will run, so if you have them, they can be used successfully. However, because they will run at a slower speed, they are not cost-effective. While faster RAM will slow down to run on a computer with a slower bus speed, RAM modules with a speed slower than that of the motherboard bus will not run.

Another consideration is the maximum speed that the motherboard system bus can support as well as the chipsets. You must check the PC, chipset, and BIOS documentation before attempting to upgrade RAM. This is especially true if the PC you are attempting to upgrade is several years old.

Latency

To understand latency, you must first understand how computers locate and transfer data stored in memory locations. The RAM can be thought of as a matrix of storage bins, each bin containing a bit of information in a binary format. Each location corresponds to a specific column and row identification. Look at **Figure 6-23**.

Reading or writing to a memory location takes time. The time required to complete a memory read or write operation is measured in clock signals. A clock signal is when the voltage level switches between high and low. There are two main measurements and several minor measurements of read-write access: RAS and CAS.

Figure 6-23.
Each memory location in the matrix is described by a column and a row hexadecimal number, such as 08A2h 3B5Fh.

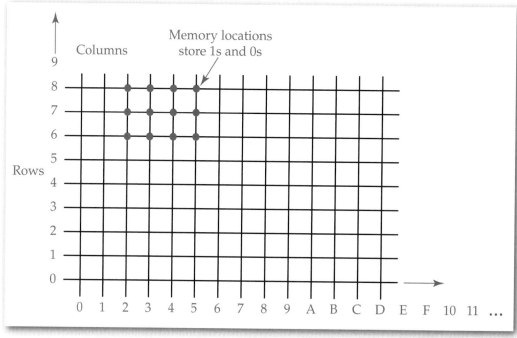

Goodheart-Willcox Publisher

Row Address Selection (RAS) is a term that describes the time it takes to start a memory read or to write the row location in the memory matrix. RAS is the first step of a memory access operation. This is followed by CAS.

Column Address Select (CAS) is a term that describes the time it takes to access the exact column location in the memory matrix after RAS. There is a minimum amount of time the CAS must remain active to complete the read operation. For example, a CAS 3 means that three clock signals will occur before the CAS can complete the read of the memory location.

CAS is considered by most experts as the most important number when expressing latency. You will find that in most cases, CAS is the primary way latency is measured. In other words, when a publication such as a computer parts catalog or technical article appears and it states that the latency is 5, they are generally basing the latency measure on the CAS.

Other latency measures are used when memory latency is expressed as a series of numbers. For example, it may be expressed as 3-3-3-5. These numbers represent tCL, tRCD, tRP, and tRAS respectively. The following table describes each term.

Term	Description
tCL	This is equal to CAS or Column Access Strobe.
tRCD	The amount of delay between the RAS and CAS.
tRP	How long it takes to precharge the RAS.
tRAS	The delay to precharge the RAS.

Now you can see why most articles simply use the CAS value. These other latency terms require a more in-depth understanding of digital electronics; otherwise, they are very cryptic to the average reader.

In general, the lower the number used to describe the latency, the better the performance. There is an exception to this rule. You must compare latency between similar DDR technologies for a fair comparison. As frequencies rise, memory latency rises. For example, DDR has latencies in the range of 1.5 to 3, DDR2 has latency range from 2 to 5, and DDR3 has latency from 7 to 11. While DDR3 has the largest latency number compared to DDR or DDR2, it provides much better system performance. If you double the memory frequency, you will of course double the latency.

Buffered Chips

The term *buffer*, in relationship to a PC, can be likened to a temporary waiting or holding area. A **buffer** is used to temporarily store data before transferring it to a device. Data can be temporarily stored for a few microseconds before continuing its journey. Remember that there are several different bus systems on the computer motherboard, and all of them are running at different speeds. In addition, many of the devices attached to the computer have speeds much slower than memory chips. For this reason, fast memory requires buffering when exchanging data with other components in the PC.

The buffer area can be provided in the motherboard chipset or as an additional chip on the memory module. DIMM memory modules have definitive notch patterns that match the memory module slots on the motherboard.

This design prevents improper installation of a buffered DIMM into a motherboard that already contains memory buffer chips. See **Figure 6-24** to view a drawing of notch locations on a DIMM and how they vary.

DDR Prefetch Memory Buffer

Memory chips can operate at extremely high frequencies inside the memory chip structure. The frequencies of the logic transistors inside the chip operate at a much higher frequency than the outside connections, such as the FSB or the HyperTransport bus. The transferring data is stored in a buffer located on the chip. At the proper time, it is transferred to the motherboard bus. The entire operation is referred to as the memory prefetch.

The term *prefetch* is followed by the lowercase letter n and a number that represents the number of data bits. For example, DDR1 has a prefetch 2n, which means it can store 2 bits of data in each prefetch buffer. DDR2 uses a prefetch 4n, or 4-bit buffer, thus doubling the amount of data transferred from the buffer as compared to DDR1. DDR3 uses a prefetch 8n, double the size of the prefetch used in DDR2. Look at the following table and compare the prefetch buffer, voltage level,

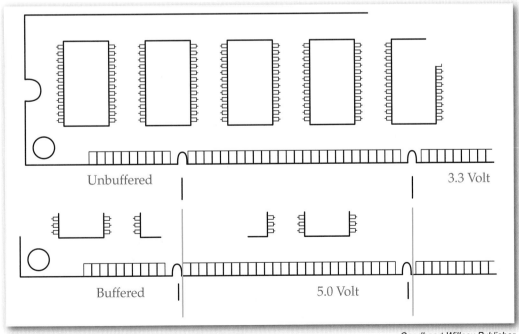

Figure 6-24. Buffering and voltage can be identified by the position of the notch at the bottom of the DIMM. This is how manufacturers ensure the correct type of DIMM is installed on the motherboard when replacing or upgrading memory modules.

Unbuffered — 3.3 Volt

Buffered — 5.0 Volt

and FSB data rates of DDR1, DDR2, DDR3, and DDR4. Increasing the size of the prefetch buffer and the memory bus operational frequency allows each generation of DDR to increase the overall throughput.

	Prefetch Buffer	Voltage Level	Data Rates (in MHz)
DDR1	2-bits	2.5 V	200, 266, 333, 400
DDR2	4-bits	1.8 V	400, 533, 677, 800
DDR3	8-bits	1.5 V	800, 1066, 1330, 1600
DDR4	8-bits	1.2 V	1600, 2133, 2400, 2667

Note: Prefetch buffer size for DDR4 could increase to 16-bits in later standard revisions. Also, the data rates could change.

Registered Memory

Registered memory is a memory module that incorporates a registry chip to drive and synchronize the memory without depending on the motherboard. Typical motherboards incorporate a chipset with functions to drive and synchronize the memory unit with the motherboard bus system. Registered memory is sometimes referred to as buffered memory because it works in a similar fashion as *buffered memory*. Some computer systems incorporate a memory register or buffer on the motherboard. The important thing to remember is that registered and nonregistered memory modules cannot be mixed. Registered memory is not typically found on standard PCs. It is found more commonly on high-end PCs and network servers.

Memory Data Integrity

Data can become corrupted while waiting in memory. Some causes of data corruption are electrical voltage leaking from the memory module, electrical interference, power surges, and electrostatic discharges. Even cosmic rays can corrupt data. Think for a moment about a 16-MB SIMM memory module. It is composed of 128 million memory cells, so there is always a possibility of corrupted data being transmitted. Corrupt data that is processed through the RAM can result in mathematical computation errors as well as program run errors that can cause a computer system to lock up. There are two common methods for checking the integrity of data transferred in and out of memory: parity and error correction code.

Parity

As you have learned, all data transmitted through a PC system consists of ones and zeros together in groups of eight. These groups of eight are known as bytes. **Parity** is simply the counting of either odd or even bits of the bytes transmitted.

To understand the role of parity, we must first look at how memory is constructed. A memory chip consists of millions of tiny cells that store data. Each cell can contain either a zero or one. The ones and zeros represent the state of electrical charge in the cell. Typically, a 5-volt electrical charge represents a one and no electrical charge represents a zero. The cells are grouped together in sets of eight cells (one byte).

When memory chips and data transfer techniques were first developed, they were not as reliable as they are today. Out of the millions of cells designed in the memory module, a few of the individual cells might be flawed. These flawed cells tend to lose their electrical charge. Cells that lose their charge are said to *leak*. If a single cell changes its charge state from 5 volts to 0 volts while it is stored, then the data it represents also changes. For example, the stored binary number 00001010 represents the decimal number *10*. If one cell loses its charge, the binary format of the data could look like 00000010. It now represents the decimal number *2*. The data stored as a byte has changed its value from the decimal *10* to the decimal *2*. Data stored in a changing byte is not limited to data that represents numbers. The stored byte could represent letters, sound, part of an illustration, or even a program command.

Data can also change while being transferred from one module to another. Remember that data is processed through a PC. It could be loaded from a disk to the memory (RAM) and then moved to the CPU to be manipulated and then routed simultaneously to the screen and to RAM. While the data is transferred around the PC system, any of the bits that form a complete byte could be changed by outside electrical interference or by a slightly defective part such as a circuit board trace that is starting to fail.

To check that data received by RAM and transferred to other parts is still valid, parity was developed. Instead of just the usual eight bits being stored to represent one byte, an additional bit was added to make a total of nine bits. The ninth bit is referred to as the *parity bit*. The parity bit reflects the number of ones and zeros contained in the data byte.

For example, assume the number of ones being transmitted to or from the memory is counted. Every time the number of bits counted is *odd*, a parity bit of one is sent to indicate the number of bits is odd. This is an example of **odd parity checking**. The system could also be designed to do **even parity checking** by transmitting an extra bit each time there was an even number of bits in the byte of data being transmitted. See **Figure 6-25**. Parity checking is not simply limited to memory; it is also used for transmitting data across telephone and network lines.

The only problem with a parity check using this method is it assumes that only one bit will change. If two bits change, the parity will not change and the error will go undetected.

Figure 6-25. For odd parity checking, a parity bit of one is generated whenever the number of ones in a byte is odd. In even parity checking, a parity bit of one is generated whenever the number of ones in a byte is even.

Odd Parity Checking

Data bit value is odd	Parity bit is added
1 0 0 0 1 0 1 0	1
Data bit value is even	No parity bit is added
1 0 1 0 1 1 1 1	0

Even Parity Checking

Data bit value is odd	No parity bit is added
1 0 0 0 1 0 1 0	0
Data bit value is even	Parity bit is added
1 0 1 0 1 1 1 1	1

Goodheart-Willcox Publisher

Today, memory chips and circuit board designs are very dependable. Relatively few errors are generated by individual memory cells or motherboard parts. Many PCs use memory modules that do not check parity, or they use what is described as fake parity. With **fake parity**, the parity bit is set to a constant value, say, for instance, a one. This is done by electronic circuit design. Since the parity bit is always set to one regardless of the true number of ones contained in the byte, parity will always match when data is transferred. In other words, a true parity check is never performed. The fake parity bit always confirms the data as good. Some PC systems require parity checking memory modules. On these systems, fake parity memory modules can be used.

The term *fake parity* can also refer to the manufacture of memory chips that are advertised as containing parity but in reality are fake. Memory designed with actual parity checking costs more than memory that is not designed with actual parity checking. Manufacturing fake parity memory in place of true parity checking memory brings additional profit.

SIMM modules usually contain eight chips to store memory and a ninth chip to check parity. The only way to be certain if a memory module uses fake parity checking or not is to check the part number. All information needed about the chip is usually listed on the company website.

Error Correction Code

Another form of checking the integrity of data is error correction code. **Error correction code (ECC)** not only checks for errors but also corrects most errors. Parity checking simply generates an error code, which is displayed on the screen and then stops the program. Error correction code requires an additional chip designed especially for this type of error checking and correcting. ECC cannot correct all errors, only the usual corrupt single bit. If multiple bits are corrupt, the ECC chip cannot correct the data. ECC is not often found in desktop PCs. It is usually only found in high-end computers such as servers.

Single-Sided and Double-Sided

According to Intel, double-sided memory modules contain two rows of SDRAM and single-sided memory modules contain one row of SDRAM. The memory modules are identified as "SS" for single-sided and "DS" for double-sided. The memory designation is unique to Intel motherboards.

Crucial refers to single-sided and double-sided as ranked modules. A memory module that has chips on both sides of the printed circuit board is double-ranked, and a memory module that has chips only on one side is single-ranked.

Most Intel motherboards work with either single-sided or double-sided memory modules. You must consult the motherboard manual or manufacturer's website to verify what type of memory module is compatible with a particular motherboard.

> **Tech Tip**
>
> Always check the motherboard documentation for the memory type that is compatible with the motherboard and motherboard chipset.

Flash Memory Devices

Flash memory is a solid-state, reusable data storage device that can retain data even when the electrical power is disconnected. It is derived from EEPROM technology and takes advantage of the EEPROM's ability to be programmed and reprogrammed. However, unlike the original EEPROM, flash memory only stores data, not computer programs. Like the EEPROM, flash memory does not require a power source to retain data. Since it does not require a power source, the size and weight is reduced significantly.

Flash memory devices are often referred to as "hot swappable" devices. The term *hot swap* means that the device can be plugged into or unplugged from a computer system while the computer is running.

Some typical devices that use flash memory technology are miniature data drives, personal digital assistants (PDAs), global positioning systems (GPS), digital cameras, cellular phones, pagers, electronic instruments, MP3 players, and personal computer systems. Flash memory in this chapter is limited directly to computer memory and storage applications.

USB Flash Drives

A typical flash drive is constructed from EEPROM chips. Data is "flashed" to the EEPROM chip similar to the way BIOS chips are flashed. There are many different names used for the EEPROM memory devices such as pen drives, jump drives, micro drives, thumb drives, micro vaults, stick drives, and more. In this textbook, the term *USB flash drive* is used. USB flash drives are reusable storage systems that connect to the computer system via a USB port, **Figure 6-26**. The electrical power for energizing the USB flash drive is delivered by the USB port. There is no need for an external power supply. After data is transferred to the USB flash drive, the drive can be removed from the system and will retain the data for a long time. The data on the USB flash drive can be transferred to another computer or to a similar device. The USB flash drive can have additional data added to it or it can be completely erased similar to most other storage media.

At the time of this writing, USB flash drives range from a modest 128 MB to over 128 GB. A 16-GB USB flash drive has the same storage capacity as approximately twenty-four standard 650 CD-RW discs or approximately four

Figure 6-26. USB flash drive.

Goodheart-Willcox Publisher

4.7-GB DVDs. This is an incredible amount of data for such a compact device. USB flash drives will compete with traditional hard drives soon and have already replaced compact discs for many storage applications. The main advantage of the USB flash drive is it has no moving parts to wear out or misalign. The entire system is designed from integrated chip technology.

When connected to a computer system through the USB port, the USB flash drive is recognized as a removable hard drive. Look at **Figure 6-27**. The USB flash drive is listed beneath **Devices with Removable Storage** and is identified as **Lexar Media (F:)**.

A USB flash drive is automatically detected and configured when inserted into the computer system's USB port. As a precaution, the USB flash drive should be deactivated before removing it from the port. This is especially true while data is being transferred to or from the USB flash drive. **Figure 6-28** shows a Windows XP **Safely Remove Hardware** dialog box.

The **Safely Remove Hardware** dialog box identifies the USB flash drive as a USB Mass Storage Device. The user simply clicks the **Stop** button and then proceeds to unplug the USB flash drive from the port. Many users simply unplug the USB flash drive, unaware of the possible damage that could occur to the drive.

A+ Note

You may be asked to identify types of boot media that can contain an operating system and be used to boot a PC. Remember that a flash drive, CD, or DVD can be used as a bootable media.

Flash Memory Cards

Flash memory cards hold text data, image data, and sound data. Flash memory technology has been incorporated into many digital systems, such as cameras, music players, notebook computers, cell phones, electronic test equipment, MP3 players, cam recorders, and personal digital assistants. Some flash memory cards are especially

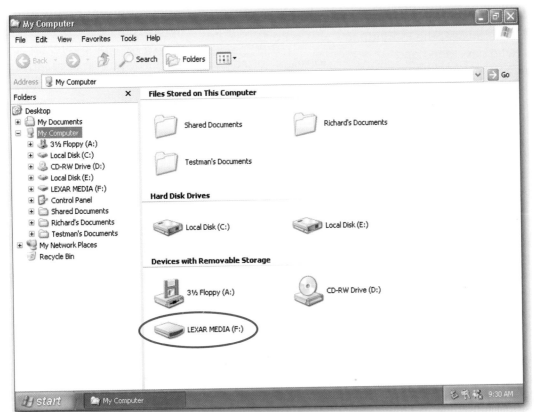

Figure 6-27. Removable storage devices such as the USB flash drive are automatically detected when inserted into the computer system's USB port and are listed in **My Computer** (or **Computer**) beneath **Devices with Removable Storage**.

Figure 6-28. The USB flash drive, as with any other removable computer device, should first be stopped with the Safely Remove Hardware program.

Figure 6-29. The Belkin 8-in-1 Media Reader/Writer reads a variety of flash memory card types.

Belkin Corporation

designed for security systems. They contain user passwords required to log on to the computer system, and they support data encryption.

Flash memory cards go by many different names such as SmartMedia, CompactFlash, MultiMediaCard, Memory Stick, and Secure Digital. The names vary because of the individual competing companies who developed and marketed the flash memory cards. Although they are all designed on the same principles of flash memory technology, they differ in their overall physical design, electrical characteristics, and software system requirements for reading and writing to the media. Because they have different attributes, you have to either match the card type to a particular reader or use one of the readers that support multiple card formats.

One such card reader is the Belkin 8-in-1 Media Reader/Writer, **Figure 6-29**, which reads and writes to eight different types of flash memory cards. The reader connects to any standard PC through the USB port.

Solid-State Disks

Solid-state disk (SSD) is a storage system designed with no moving parts and that consists entirely of DRAM chips. The SSD is also referred to as a RAM drive. The SSD is very advantageous to laptop designs because it requires less electrical power, is much lighter than mechanical drives, boots faster, and does not generate noise the way mechanical drives do. It is also not as easily damaged as mechanical drives when dropped nor does it experience mechanical shock.

SSDs are designed mainly for laptops and other forms of portable equipment. As the cost to produce SSD drives drops, they will become common on desktop models of computers. There will be more about SSD in Chapter 12—Portable Devices.

Memory Map Structure and Development

Memory map structure is a description of the way memory is allocated in the PC. Because of the issue of backward compatibility in the PC industry, the development of the memory structure has become complex and confusing. The desire for the latest computer system to be compatible with ancient 8-bit system technology has created the evolution of a difficult memory structure. There have been many different software attempts to overcome these structural limitations.

The terminology of memory structure dates back to the original PC and the oldest DOS operating system. The early PC could only access 1 MB of memory (1,024,000 bytes). The restrictions of 1 MB of memory are DOS and Windows 3.x restrictions. They do not apply to Windows 95 or later operating systems. Windows 95 and later follow the DOS memory pattern *only* when dealing with legacy cards or 16-bit software programs. Windows NT and later are not affected at all by DOS memory structure. These operating systems handle individual memory areas as one big block, referred to as the **heap**. The memory is then portioned out as needed. The only exception is during the POST when using a BIOS type of firmware. The BIOS limits access of memory to the first 1 MB of RAM. Let's look at how the memory system structure was designed and labeled.

Conventional Memory

The memory structure is illustrated in **Figure 6-30**. This illustration shows the layout of conventional, upper, high, and extended memory.

The original PC was limited to 1 MB (1024 kB) of random access memory. This first memory was originally divided in half (512 kB each). After the

original PC was on the market for a short time, the memory system was redesigned into parts that were no longer equal. The bottom part was given 640 kB and was called *conventional memory*. The top part was given 384 kB and was called *upper memory*, or *reserved memory*. This division of the first 1 MB of memory into two unequal parts, conventional (640 kB) and reserved (384 kB), became the industry standard.

Conventional memory was where application programs were loaded. The reserve memory was reserved for use by the video system, expansion cards, and the BIOS. The reserved memory is dedicated (or reserved) for hardware drivers and cannot be used by application programs. For many years, conventional memory (640 kB) was referred to as the *memory barrier*. Early computer programmers were required to write programs that could fit into the 640 kB space of conventional memory.

The term *conventional memory* is still in use. However, the 32-bit operating systems of newer models easily work around the 640 kB barrier. Programs, as well as drivers, can be loaded into memory well beyond the first 1 MB.

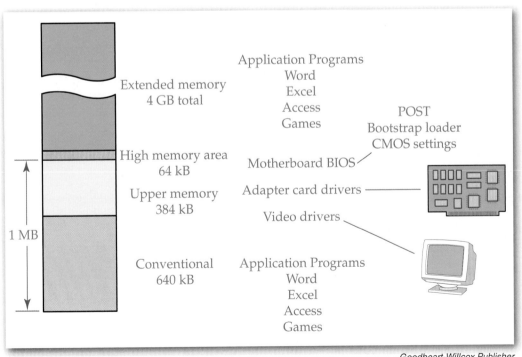

Figure 6-30.
To the right of the memory map are examples of what you might find loaded into each of these portions of memory.

Goodheart-Willcox Publisher

Examine **Figure 6-31**. This illustration diagrams the relation of the various areas in RAM and how they developed.

Upper Memory Area (Reserved Memory)

The upper memory area (UMA), or reserved memory, is the 384 kB of memory remaining after the first 640 kB of conventional memory. The term *reserved* means that only the PC system software drivers used to run and interface with the system hardware components can be loaded into this area. The reserved memory cannot be used for application software such as word processor programs, gaming, or other software.

The upper memory is divided into sections that are determined by their function. The first

Figure 6-31. The use of RAM has evolved over the years.

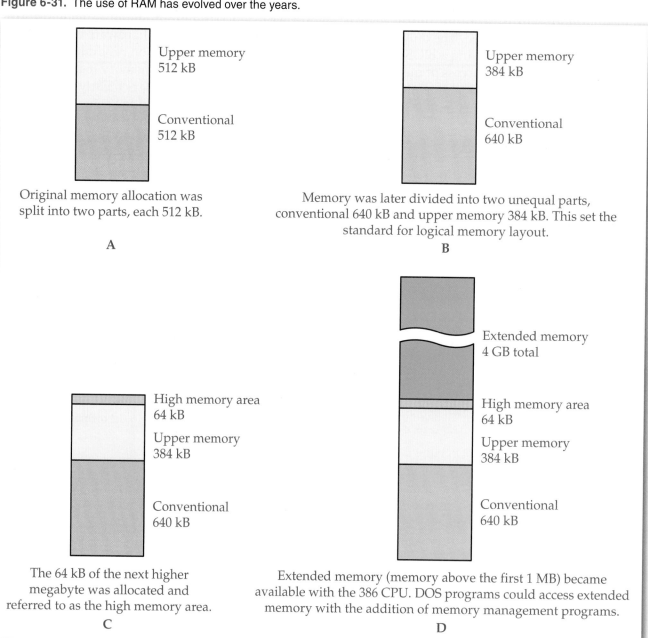

Upper memory
512 kB

Conventional
512 kB

Original memory allocation was split into two parts, each 512 kB.

A

Upper memory
384 kB

Conventional
640 kB

Memory was later divided into two unequal parts, conventional 640 kB and upper memory 384 kB. This set the standard for logical memory layout.

B

High memory area
64 kB

Upper memory
384 kB

Conventional
640 kB

The 64 kB of the next higher megabyte was allocated and referred to as the high memory area.

C

Extended memory
4 GB total

High memory area
64 kB

Upper memory
384 kB

Conventional
640 kB

Extended memory (memory above the first 1 MB) became available with the 386 CPU. DOS programs could access extended memory with the addition of memory management programs.

D

part of the UMA (128 kB) is used for the video system. The information about the computer monitor is stored in this area. The next part of the UMA (128 kB) is used for adapter boards mounted in slots on the motherboard. Examples of these adapter boards are boards for the modem or network cards. VGA adapter cards sometimes utilize the first 32 kB of this area of memory. The last part of the UMA (128 kB) is used for the motherboard BIOS, CMOS settings, POST program, and bootstrap program.

Many types of device drivers are also loaded into the UMA. A section of UMA can also be occupied by a memory manager program, which permits certain programs to use memory beyond the 1 MB barrier. Again, modern operating systems have no problem accessing RAM beyond the first 1 MB. This was a restriction of earlier operating systems.

High Memory Area

It is easy to confuse a high memory area with upper memory. The *high memory area (HMA)* is the first 64 kB of the extended memory area. (Actually, it is 16 bytes short of a full 64 kB.)

This area was first discovered as a design flaw in the memory access data lines, but it soon became the standard method to gain more conventional memory space. Conventional memory not only holds application programs but also basic DOS files, such as the kernel, needed to operate the PC. The DOS kernel file is approximately 45 kB in size. Transferring a DOS kernel to the high memory area releases 45 kB of conventional memory space for use by application programs. To use the HMA, the line DOS=HIGH is added to the config.sys file.

In DOS 5.0 and later versions, the DOS=HIGH command loads the DOS program kernel into the high memory area. The high memory area can also be used to store a software driver instead of the DOS kernel, but note that only one program can be stored in the high memory area.

Expanded Memory

Expanded memory was an early method to move past the 1 MB memory barrier. *Expanded memory standard (EMS)* was designed to increase the amount of memory available for applications. An expanded memory adapter board loaded with memory chips was inserted into a motherboard expansion slot. Unlike RAM, the expanded memory adapter board was not accessed directly by the CPU, but rather by a software-driver program, which was loaded into reserved memory. The software-driver program transferred data to and from the memory adapter board to the 64 kB EMS window established in upper memory. See **Figure 6-32** for a memory map illustrating the 64 kB EMS window and expanded memory available on the expanded memory adapter board.

The memory adapter board could contain a maximum data content of 32 MB. Data was transferred through the EMS window in 16 kB segments, or pages, to and from the memory on the adapter board.

EMS is obsolete, and the memory boards are no longer manufactured. The transfer rate of data with EMS is extremely slow because it is limited to the speed of the motherboard bus slot. EMS was designed for the ISA bus slot, which is very slow when compared to the data transfer rates of SIMM or DIMM. SIMM and DIMM connect via the system bus, directly to the CPU. The concept of EMS was readily accepted when memory space was needed and the 1 MB barrier was a problem.

Extended Memory

The *extended memory system (XMS)* includes all of the PC's memory beyond the first 1 MB when the CPU is running in real mode. As operating systems evolved over time, the CPU was designed to access more memory than the early predecessors. Today, a 32-bit operating system can access 4 GB of RAM. A 64-bit operating system can access theoretically 16 TB (terabytes) of RAM. The 64-bit upper memory access limit is not realistic at this time. No computer system

Figure 6-32.
Expanded memory is provided by a memory adapter board inserted into a motherboard expansion slot. A small EMS window is set up in the upper memory area and transfers data to and from the expanded memory in increments of 4 kB to 16 kB pages of data totaling 64 kB.

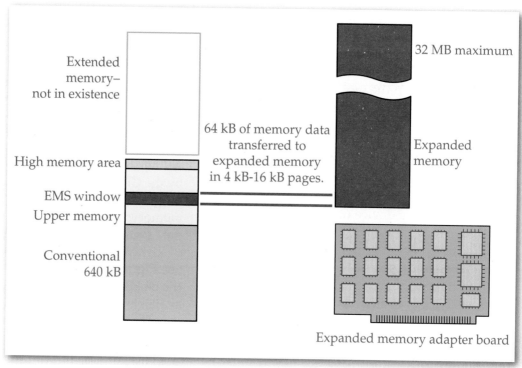

Goodheart-Willcox Publisher

hardware is designed to allow for 16 TB of memory. A more realistic maximum RAM value of 8 GB to 128 GB can be expected for desktops.

Real Mode, Protected Mode, and Safe Mode

The terms *real mode* and *protected mode* are used by programmers to describe the boundaries of memory as related to programming code and structure of memory. **Real mode** is designed on the DOS system of memory access. When operating in real mode, only the first 1 MB of RAM can be accessed. **Protected mode** includes all of real mode plus extended memory. Multitasking can only occur in protected mode or when more than the first 1 MB is accessed by the system. The limitations of protected mode also depend on the firmware installed. The BIOS typically follows the DOS guidelines and limits the access to the first 1 MB or RAM. UEFI can exceed the 1-MB limit during the POST.

The term **safe mode** is used by technicians to describe starting the computer in protected mode. Safe mode is accessed by pressing the [F8] key during the startup or boot operation for all Windows operating system versions. Computers systems boot very fast now and it is almost impossible to press the [F8] key at the exact time between the finish of the POST and the loading of the operating system. The best way to enter safe mode is to repeatedly press [F8] during the boot operation, starting during the post and continuing until the menu options or **Advanced Boot Options** menu (in Windows Vista and Windows 7) appears.

Putting Windows 8 into safe mode can be a great deal more complicated and difficult. The combination of the Windows 8 operating system and more modern computers has greatly increased the boot speed. There is an extremely short period of time between the POST and the loading of the operating system. Thus, it can be difficult to access safe mode. To access Windows 8 safe mode, press and hold the [Shift] key while quickly tapping the [F8] key. You also have an option to hold down the [Shift] key while rebooting the computer.

Windows 8 is designed to detect errors during the boot process and then present a screen with an option to go into safe mode when an error is automatically detected. There is also an option to automatically start the computer in safe mode. This will be covered in detail in Chapter 15— PC Troubleshooting.

Starting Windows in safe mode is a very common troubleshooting technique. Safe mode only loads minimal drivers and limits the memory access to the first 1 MB of RAM, thus eliminating any problems caused by 32-bit or 64-bit drivers and software applications. If the computer starts in safe mode, then it is a good indication that the problem is software related rather than a hardware problem. Many troubleshooting features are available while in safe mode.

Virtual Memory

Virtual memory is memory that supplements physical memory known as RAM. Virtual memory is located on the hard drive and is referred to as a **page file** or *swap file*. The virtual memory is divided into units called *pages*. RAM is used to hold data content as well as the software application. If data or sections of an application program are not accessed for a period of time, then the data or application section is transferred to virtual memory as a page of information. The transfer to the page file is called *paging* or *swapping*. When needed, the data is transferred back to RAM from the hard drive page file.

Figure 6-33 shows the virtual memory configuration page in Windows 7. It is accessed through **Control Panel | System and Security | System | Advanced system settings**. The **Advanced** tab of the **System Properties** dialog box will display. Under the **Performance** section, click **Settings**. The **Performance Options** dialog box will display. Click the **Advanced** tab to see the virtual memory configuration. A similar configuration feature is available in all Windows operating systems.

One sign that the computer is running out of RAM and using the page file is when there is a lot of hard drive activity. The use of virtual memory causes an overall drop in software performance. You need to install more RAM if virtual memory is being used.

A new feature for virtual memory first introduced in Windows Vista is ReadyBoost. Windows ReadyBoost allows removable storage devices, such as USB flash drives, to supplement the memory installed on the computer system. The flash drive must be able to support a sufficient

Figure 6-33. Windows 7 path for accessing the virtual memory (paging file) settings. Accessing the paging file settings is similar in Windows Vista and Windows 8.

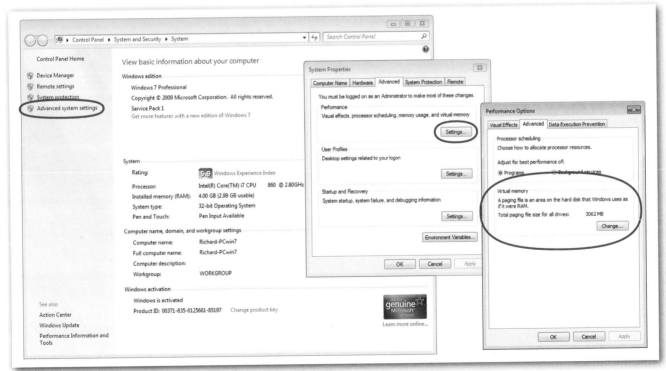

size and speed; otherwise, this feature will not be available.

ReadyBoost will not work with all types of USB flash drives. You should only use USB 2.0 or later. However, the device may still fail to work properly. When the removable storage device is attached to the PC, the operating system will automatically detect it and display a menu option for ReadyBoost like that shown in **Figure 6-34**. The option **Speed up my system using Windows ReadyBoost** is located at the bottom of the **AutoPlay** dialog box. If the removable flash drive is compatible with the ReadyBoost feature, a dialog box like that in **Figure 6-35** will appear after choosing the **Speed up my system using Windows ReadyBoost** option. You can select to use or not use the removable device. The device in the example is limited to only 350 MB, so it would not provide sufficient space to supplement the 2 GB of RAM already installed on the PC. You could delete files from the removable device to free up space, which would allow more space to be usable by ReadyBoost.

Microsoft recommends the space on the removable drive be one to three times the amount of installed physical RAM. For example, if the

system has 512 MB of RAM, the recommended maximum amount of USB flash memory is 1.5 GB. ReadyBoost will perform faster than the page file system that uses space on the hard disk drive. The USB flash drive has a faster read and write rate than the hard drive.

Troubleshooting Memory

Memory problems can be quite difficult to diagnose, especially intermittent problems. Fortunately, Microsoft has provided a memory diagnostic tool as part of the operating system. In this section, you will learn about the Windows Memory Diagnostics tool and the effects of oxidation and excessive heat on memory.

Windows Memory Diagnostics Tool

The Windows Memory Diagnostics Tool was introduced in Windows Vista. To access this tool in Windows Vista or Windows 7, enter **mdsched** in the **Search** box on the **Start** menu or

Figure 6-34. The **Speed up my system using Windows ReadyBoost** option appears in the **AutoPlay** dialog box when a removable storage device is attached to the PC.

Figure 6-35. In the **ReadyBoost** dialog box, you can select to use or not use the removable device. Also, the USB flash drive can be configured to help with startup by augmenting the system RAM using the free space provided on the flash drive.

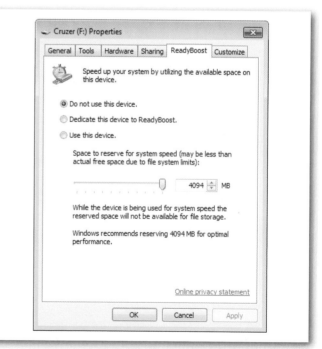

at the command prompt. You must be the system administrator or equal to run it. For Windows 8, enter **mdsched** at the command prompt or in the **Search** box for Apps accessed through **Charms Bar | Search**.

You will be prompted to have Windows automatically restart the computer to begin the memory diagnostics or to start the diagnostics the next time the computer reboots, **Figure 6-36**. When the Memory Diagnostics Tool does run, it will look similar to that in **Figure 6-37**.

Figure 6-36. When the **Windows Memory Diagnostic** window appears, you can select to restart the computer now and begin diagnostics or check for problems the next time you start the computer.

Figure 6-37. Windows Memory Diagnostics Tool.

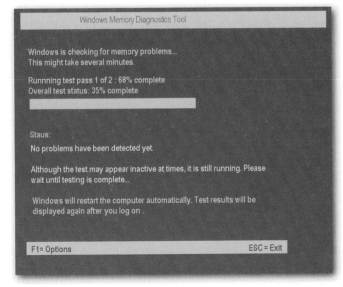

For a quick check of how much memory is installed in a Windows Vista or Windows 7 PC, right-click **Computer** and then select **Properties** from the shortcut menu. You will see a dialog box similar to that in **Figure 6-38**.

You might use the command prompt to display what appears as the total amount of memory for the computer system, but the result would be inaccurate. **Figure 6-39** shows a screen capture of Windows Vista after the **mem** command has been issued at the command prompt. This is very similar in Windows 7 and Windows 8. Look at the amount of conventional memory, largest executive program size, total contiguous extended memory, and total extended memory available. Notice that only 1 MB of memory is indicated. This is incorrect for this particular computer. The **mem** command is a DOS-based memory command and cannot detect memory above 1 MB. The command failed to identify the total amount of physical memory installed in this computer. The total physical memory for this system is 2 GB. Using the **mem** command is not recommended for determining the total amount of memory installed.

Gold vs. Tin Edge Connectors

There are two types of edge connector finishes used on memory modules: gold and tin. The memory module (SIMM or DIMM) edge connector should match the connector finish inside the expansion slot. When two different types of metal are in contact with each other, a condition occurs that causes increased oxidation. When first installed, the memory will not show any signs of a problem. It should work perfectly. But as time goes by, oxidation develops. The PC starts to generate error codes, such as parity errors, more frequently. The amount of use and the conditions of the environment determines how long the oxidation process will take. Once it reaches a point that the electrical connection between the memory edge connector and the slot connector has totally degenerated, errors will constantly occur.

Some oxidation can be removed by simply removing and reinserting the memory module. This action alone may correct the error. However, the condition can be so bad, it renders the

Figure 6-38.
You can quickly check the amount of installed RAM by accessing the **System** window.

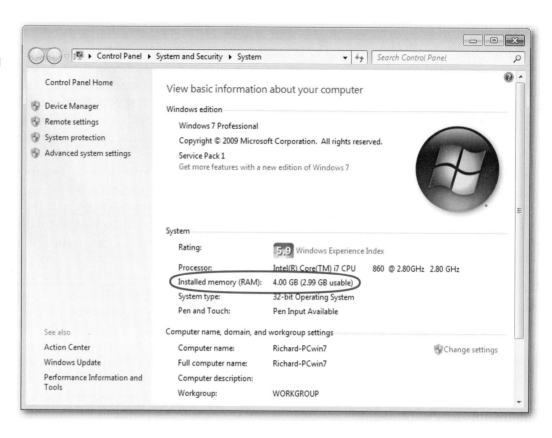

Figure 6-39.
The **mem** command only gives information for the first 1 MB of memory.

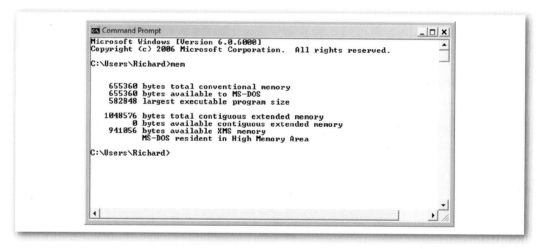

motherboard slot useless. Always match the type of metals used.

Memory and Heat

Heat will destroy a chip or cause temporary chaos in a computer. A common symptom of excessive heat causing memory problems is when a PC works fine for a short period of time (20 minutes) and then locks up. At the time the PC locks up, a sufficient level of heat has been generated to cause a circuit problem inside one of the memory chips. This causes the PC to fail. Fans should be checked, filters cleaned, and dirt and dust removed to prevent heat buildup.

High-performance memory modules generate a lot of heat. The amount of heat generated is directly related to the operational frequency of the memory module. The higher the frequency, the higher the temperature generated. One cooling method is using a heat spreader. Another cooling method is to add a fan that is especially designed for cooling memory modules. Cooling fans for memory are used in many overclocking systems.

A+ Note

There is typically at least one question on the CompTIA A+ exam requiring you to identify which memory module matches a particular pin count.

Chapter Summary

- Before upgrading RAM, questions related to compatibility, quantity, parity, speed, and other memory specifics should be answered.
- Memory chips are packaged in several different physical styles such as SIP, DIP, SIMM, DIMM, SO-DIMM, SO-RIMM, and MicroDIMM.
- ROM retains data after the power is removed, and RAM loses data after power is removed.
- To install memory, hold the module by the heat spreader, properly orientate the module in the slot, and firmly press the module into place.
- Typical memory characteristics to consider when adding or replacing RAM modules relate to chip speed and integrity.
- Flash memory is derived from EEPROM technology.
- The four logical areas of RAM are conventional, upper, high memory, and extended memory.
- Virtual memory is located on the hard drive and is used to supplement available RAM; Windows ReadyBoost allows a USB flash drive to supplement RAM.
- Oxidation on memory module contacts can generate error codes; excessive heat can cause a PC to lock up.

Review Questions

Answer the following questions on a separate sheet of paper. Please do not write in this book.

1. What questions should be asked before installing or replacing memory?
2. What is the difference between SIMM and DIMM?
3. What is the difference between SO-DIMM and MicroDIMM?
4. What is the maximum data rate for a PC-3200 memory module used in a motherboard with an FSB of 200 MHz?
5. What is the PC2 classification of a DDR2-800 memory module?
6. What is the bandwidth of a PC2-6400 memory module?

7. Why can you not replace a DDR2-800 with a DDR3-1600 memory module to achieve better overall PC performance?

8. List the number of pins for each DDR type.
   a. DDR
   b. DDR2
   c. DDR3
   d. DDR4

9. Briefly describe dual-channel DDR memory technology.

10. What is the purpose of memory SPD?

11. How should memory modules be handled?

12. What is the purpose of the notch on a DDR memory module?

13. List the five DIMM physical arrangements.

14. What will happen when only two matching DIMMs are installed into a system designed to operate in triple-channel mode?

15. A technician installs one 4-GB and one 2-GB memory module into a dual-channel mode system. How much memory will operate in interleaved mode, and how much memory will operate in asymmetric mode?

16. RAM chip speed is measured in _____.

17. What will happen to latency when you double a memory module frequency?

18. What does "prefetch 2n" mean in regards to a DDR memory module?

19. What is flash memory?

20. What is flash memory derived from?

21. What is a solid-state disk made of?

22. What is the maximum amount of RAM that the original PC's processor could access?

23. What are the four logical areas of RAM?

24. Draw the logical memory layout of RAM for DOS and label each part and indicate the size in kB.

25. What is the maximum amount of memory accessible by a 32-bit operating system?

26. What is the maximum theoretical limit for RAM access when using a 64-bit operating system?

27. What is virtual memory?

28. What is Windows ReadyBoost?

29. How can oxidation on memory contacts affect computer operation?

30. How can excessive heat affect computer memory?

Sample A+ Exam Questions

Answer the following questions on a separate sheet of paper. Please do not write in this book.

1. During the system boot, the following error message is displayed: "Parity check failure!" What particular system component would the message be referring to?
   a. RAM
   b. ROM
   c. HDD
   d. USB

2. In the Windows 7 operating system, how would you display the amount of RAM installed on a PC?
   a. Select the **Start** menu, right-click **Computer**, and select **Properties** from the shortcut menu.
   b. Select the **Start** menu, right-click **Computer**, and then select **System Status** from the shortcut menu.
   c. Open **Control Panel** and double-click the **RAM** icon.
   d. Open **Control Panel** and double-click the **System Memory** icon.

3. Which command will evoke a memory diagnostic routine for Windows 7?
   a. **mdsched**
   b. **sysconfig**
   c. **msinfo32**
   d. **memprob**

4. Which memory module is compatible with DDR3?
   a. DDR2
   b DDR1
   c. DDR4
   d. No other memory module is compatible with DDR3.

5. Which type of memory must constantly be refreshed to retain the stored data?
   a. SRAM
   b. PROM
   c. DRAM
   d. CRIMM

6. What affect will adding more RAM have on a desktop PC?
   a. Improve the Internet connection speed
   b. Improve overall computer performance
   c. Increase HDD storage capacity
   d. Reduce the overall POST time

7. How can you access the **Advanced Boot Options** menu when using the Windows 7 operating system?
   a. Hold down [F1] during the POST.
   b. Press [F8] immediately after the POST.
   c. Press [Ctrl] [Alt] [Delete] at the same time.
   d. You cannot access safe mode when using a Windows 7 operating system.

8. A memory chip's speed is measured in which standard unit?
   a. Megahertz
   b. Gigahertz
   c. Nanoseconds
   d. Cycles per second

9. Which memory module is designed with DDR2 memory chips?
   a. PC2100
   b. PC2700
   c. PC2-6400
   d. PC3-12800

10. Which items listed below should be practiced to ensure correct installation of additional memory? Select all that apply.
    a. Use an anti-static wrist strap.
    b. Put the PC into real mode to prevent accessing the upper memory area until after the installation is complete.
    c. Turn off all electrical power to the system.
    d. Disconnect all peripheral components until after complete memory installation has been verified by system setup.

Suggested Laboratory Activities

Do not attempt any suggested laboratory activities without your instructor's permission. Certain activities can render the PC operating system inoperable.

1. Run **msinfo32** and reveal the properties of the memory.

2. Remove the RAM chips from a lab PC and observe the boot operation. Observe all proper ESD precautions. Does the system boot? If it does, what part of the system startup sequence does not rely on RAM? Also, observe any error messages that are displayed.

3. Add additional memory to a lab PC.

4. Identify any markings on the lab PC (such as the manufacturer, serial number, and model number) and then try to obtain a definitive identification from the Internet websites.

5. Go to the Kingston website and view its support section. Watch the available videos that show how to install RAM.

6. Visit the Intel website and look up the specifications of several Intel motherboards. Find out what is the maximum RAM supported by the motherboard. Be sure to include motherboards for servers and desktops.

7. Run the **mem** command from the command prompt and view the information concerning conventional, XMS, extended, and HMA memory.

8. Start the computer and use the [F8] key to access the **Advanced Boot Options** menu. View the options available, such as **Safe Mode**.

Input Devices

7

- Recall the purpose of the Human Interface Device standard for USB devices.
- Explain how a keyboard scan code is generated and interpreted.
- Explain how an optical mouse operates.
- Explain how a bar code reader, scanner, and digital camera operate.
- Recall the characteristics of the major touch screen technologies.
- Recall the characteristics of Bluetooth, Wi-Fi, WUSB, and UWB.
- Use Device Manager, Devices and Printers, and the Ease of Access Center to manage computer input devices.

A+ Exam—Key Points

Basic input devices are always a source of questions on the A+ Certification exams. Some of the devices are touch screen, microphone, KVM switch, webcam, and scanner. Always check the CompTIA website for the latest list of input devices that you may encounter.

Key Terms

The following key terms will become important pieces of your computer vocabulary. Be sure you can define them.

bar code reader	optical character recognition (OCR)
Bluetooth standard	optical mouse
carpal tunnel syndrome	protocol
charged-coupled device (CCD)	scanner
digital camera	stylus
digitizer pad	synchronous
game pad	touch screen display
Human Interface Device (HID) standard	trackball
	Ultra-Wideband (UWB) standard
input device	USB standard
Keyboard-Video-Mouse (KVM) switch	Wi-Fi standard
light pen	Wireless USB (WUSB) standard

An **input device** is any piece of equipment used to communicate with the PC system and provide the PC with data. The keyboard is one of the most common and useful input devices, but there is a broad spectrum of input devices for computers. Some devices, such as the mouse, find widespread use in a variety of different computer applications. Other input devices, like bar code scanners, have more specific uses.

While specific plugs and jacks are common to certain input devices, you may encounter a keyboard, mouse, or other device that installs in some unique way. Some devices have standard connections on the back of the motherboard. The keyboard and mouse usually attach this way. Most input devices, however, connect to the PC through the USB port. Other devices require a card to be inserted into a motherboard expansion slot.

USB Implementers Forum

The USB Implementers Forum (USB-IF) consists of industry people with a common interest in creating a standard guideline for the development of drivers for USB input and output devices. This forum designates hardware devices into groups and refers to the groups as classifications. Each classification has a set of standards to follow for software programming. With a system of standards, companies can develop and distribute software templates of code for their device, thus ensuring the device will work correctly with different operating systems and other devices. For example, all keyboards are designed to interpret keyboard key strokes

and then convert them to digital signals that are transmitted to the PC for interpretation by the operating system and then the software application, such as Microsoft Word.

The USB-IF provides example software driver programs as a guide to follow when writing drivers for each device. Manufacturers are free to add additional features to the driver program if they so desire. The USB-IF is responsible for the development of the USB standard and Human Interface Device (HID) standard.

USB Standard

Most input and many output devices are based on the **USB standard**. This standard, developed by the USB Implementations Forum, describes how different classifications of devices should communicate with a PC. Common device classifications are keyboards, mice, joysticks, bar code readers, magnetic card readers, game pads, printers, and digital cameras.

The USB standard supports bidirectional communication, which means that data can flow to and from the PC and USB device, **Figure 7-1**. For example, a digital camera can transmit digital photos to a software application on the computer. In turn, the computer software application can delete the data located on the digital camera. Another example of bidirectional communication is an Internet connection provided through a modem with a USB port. The USB port supports data flow in both directions, to and from the Internet.

The USB standard is not limited to USB wired devices. The standard also has a prevision for USB

Figure 7-1.
The USB standard allows for bi-directional communication between a USB device and PC.

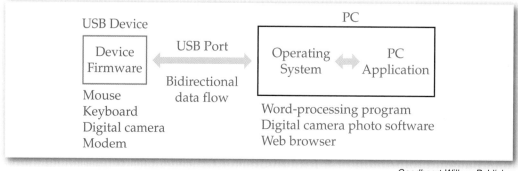

Goodheart-Willcox Publisher

wireless devices, which is a combination of USB, Bluetooth, and Wi-Fi standards. Wireless USB is covered later in this chapter. You can also visit the USB Implementers Forum website to learn more about the USB wireless device standard.

HID Standard

The USB Implementers Forum also developed the **Human Interface Device (HID) standard**. HID is a classification of USB devices. It is also a set of standards written for hardware device drivers to ensure compatibility between hardware devices and computers. It describes the programming for Human Input Devices, identifies variable names, and provides a uniform set of coding standards so that HID software drivers are the same for all input devices except for the features unique to a particular input device.

Before the HID specification, each company who produced a USB input device had to write the code for the driver from scratch. Now, they can simply download the example code, modify it for unique device features, and leave the required code that ensures compatibility with all PCs and operating systems.

Keyboard

The standard keyboard is a common serial input device. It changes keystrokes into computer data. The typical keyboard has a small microprocessor installed as a keyboard controller, **Figure 7-2**. The keyboard controller is not as powerful as the processor inside a PC. Rather, it is a limited processor used for small device applications such as telephones, automobiles, and appliances. The keyboard controller is contained on a circuit board that connects to the keyboard circuit traces and to the USB cable port.

Several types of switches are used under the keys in keyboards. See **Figure 7-3**. The most common types are the following:

- Mechanical.
- Membrane.
- Rubber Dome.
- Capacitor.

The mechanical switch, Figure 7-3A, is constructed from a set of typical electrical contacts that are normally open (separated). When the key is pressed, the contacts close.

A membrane switch, Figure 7-3B, is constructed differently than the typical contact switch. A piece of foam with foil on one side is

Figure 7-2. Inside a keyboard. A—Keyboard controller connected between the circuitry for the keys and the USB port wiring. B—The controller converts the electrical signals generated from keyboard scan codes to numbers represented by digital signals.

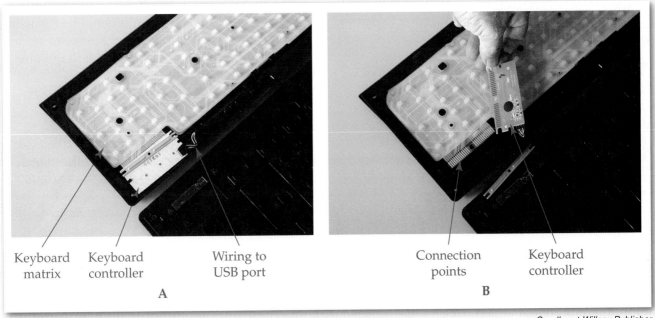

Keyboard matrix   Keyboard controller   Wiring to USB port

A

Connection points   Keyboard controller

B

Figure 7-3. The mechanics of the four most common types of keyboard switches.

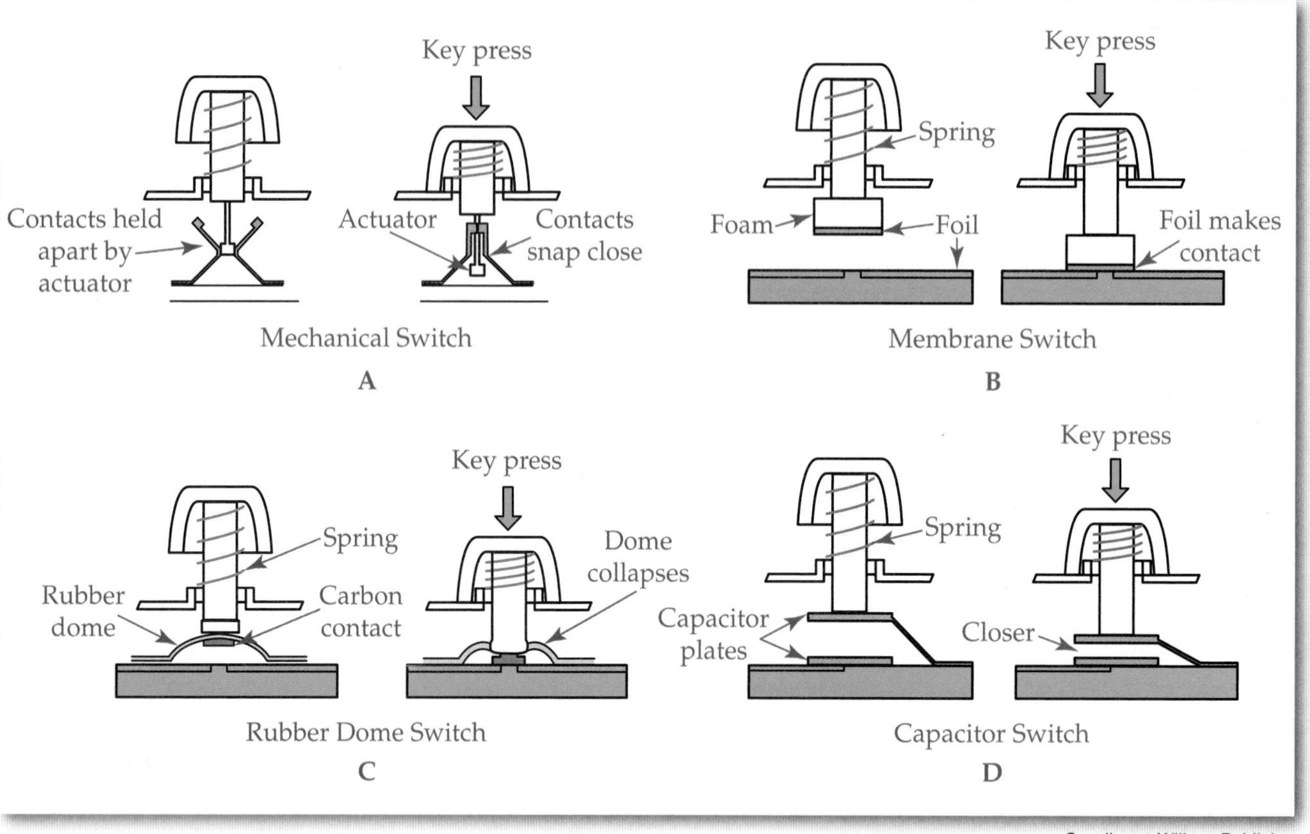

Goodheart-Willcox Publisher

attached to the switch actuator. A circuit board is used as the base of the switch. The circuit board has a pair of contact points on the surface of the board. When the key is pressed, a conductive piece of foil located on the foam completes the circuit across the circuit board contact points.

Another type of keyboard switch is the rubber dome, Figure 7-3C. The rubber dome is constructed, as the name implies, with a small rubber dome under the actuator. When the key is pressed, the rubber dome folds down. This causes a small carbon contact to complete the circuit on the circuit board. The rubber dome switch is less likely to allow dirt particles to accumulate between the carbon contact and the circuit board contact area. This keeps the switch working reliably.

The last type of switch is the capacitor switch, Figure 7-3D. The capacitor switch derives its name from the fact that it operates on the principle of an electronic capacitor. A capacitor is simply two plates of conductive material in close proximity to each other. The distance between the two capacitor plates directly affects the strength and electrical characteristics of the capacitor. When the key is pressed on the capacitor switch, the plates move closer together, but they never touch. The capacitor switch is the most reliable type of keyboard switch available. Dirt particles or corrosion will not affect the switch. The other three types of switches are susceptible to corrosion, which causes an open circuit and a failure to complete the electrical circuit.

When comparing types of switches, the first obvious difference is the tactile feel of the switch. While the difference in the "feel" of the various switches may not be important to a PC technician, it may be the most important characteristic to a professional typist. Most PC users have a keyboard preference even if they do not realize the reason for the difference. Because of this, you may be required to install an older keyboard when replacing an old PC with a newer one.

The keyboard in **Figure 7-4** has two layers of printed circuits on clear plastic. The two printed circuit boards have a pattern or matrix of circular points. When the rubber dome is pressed by the keys, the circular points on the circuit boards come close to each other, increasing the capacitance and in turn identifying the key(s) being pressed. The process of key identification is referred to as "generating a scan code." The scan code is interpreted by the keyboard controller and then translated into a digital code which is sent to the computer via the USB port, **Figure 7-5**.

Keyboard Scan Codes

The keyboard is a matrix of electrical connections. Each junction in the matrix is a key location. Each position on the matrix has an assigned number. When a key is pressed, the electrical signal (digital binary) is sent to the keyboard controller as a scan code. The scan code is interpreted by the system BIOS and the application software and is turned into an ASCII character. The scan code represents the position of

Figure 7-4. Keyboards typically have two layers of printed circuits on plastic.

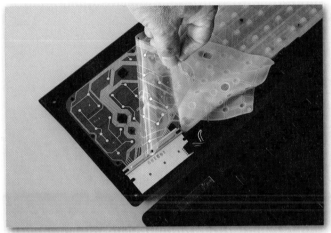

Goodheart-Willcox Publisher

Figure 7-5. A typical keyboard and how it works.

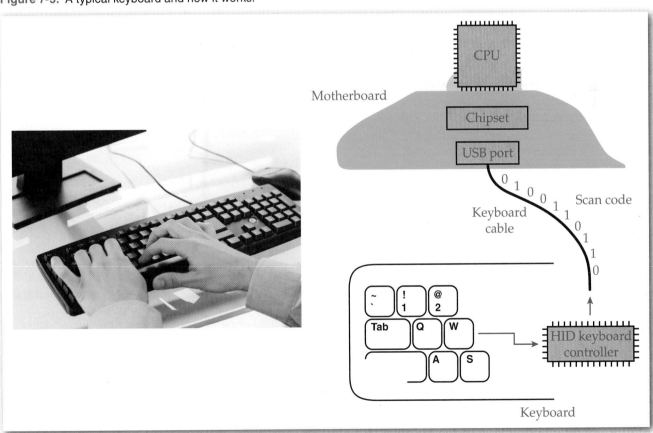

wavebreakmedia/Shutterstock.com
Goodheart-Willcox Publisher

the pressed key. Another scan code is generated when the same key is released.

The scan code is not the ASCII code nor is it the printed letter, number, or symbol on the physical key. The scan code is used to identify the exact symbol to be displayed on the screen or to be printed on the printer. Keyboards can have multiple sets of scan codes. Programmers use the scan codes to convert the action of a certain key being pressed into an action by the computer. Usually, the action is converting the code to an ASCII character, but not always. The scan codes are what allow multiple languages to be assigned to a particular computer. The scan code from the key is converted into the letter symbol of the language for which the system has been set up.

Look at **Figure 7-6** for a listing of scan codes for several keys. Note that the key press and release codes are expressed in hexadecimal values.

Keyboard Connectors

Most computers use USB ports for keyboard connections. A keyboard can connect to a USB port by wire or wirelessly. PS/2 connections still exist on many computers, but this type of port is rapidly becoming obsolete. An example of a PS/2 connector is shown in **Figure 7-7**.

Notice that for the PS/2 connection, data is sent through only one of the five pins. The keyboard is a serial device. The data sent to the motherboard is sequential. After the data reaches the motherboard, it is converted into parallel form, usually two bytes. A clock signal is also transmitted through the keyboard connector wiring. The keyboard data transfer is **synchronous**, which means that the data is transferred based on the same timing as the computer's clock signal.

Many people will purchase a computer that has no PS/2 port and still want to use their original PS/2 mouse and/or keyboard. A USB PS/2 adapter can be used to connect a PS/2 device to a USB connection or a USB device to a PS/2 connection.

There are two different types of USB PS/2 adapters. One type is referred to as a *converter* or *signal converter*. It is used to connect a USB mouse or keyboard to a PS/2 port on the computer, **Figure 7-8**. This type of adapter has electronics

Figure 7-6. Hexadecimal scan codes for the pressing and releasing of selected keys.

Key	Key Press Code	Key Release Code
A	1E	9E
B	30	B0
Esc	01	81
F2	3C	BC
Home	E047	E0C7
Delete	E053	E0D3
Page Down	E051	E0D1
Spacebar	39	B9
4 $	05	85

Goodheart-Willcox Publisher

built into it, which translates the USB signal into a serial signal understood by the PS/2 port.

The other type of adapter is passive. It is used to connect a PS/2 device to a USB port. This type of adapter has no electronics embedded inside it, thus the term *passive*. The keyboard or mouse, if designed to do so, automatically detects the type of port being used and converts the signals accordingly to ensure compatibility.

Some passive USB PS/2 adapters are designed as a replacement for a product that originally shipped with a USB to PS/2 converter. The mouse or keyboard was designed to automatically detect the type of port, USB or PS/2, and then send the appropriate signal. If the device was packaged with USB PS/2 passive adapter, any passive adapter will work with it. If the device did not ship with a passive adapter, it most likely will not work correctly. A USB PS/2 converter adapter will be required.

Tech Tip   If a customer complains that their new USB keyboard does not work with their old computer, they most likely are using the wrong type of USB adapter.

Ergonomic Keyboards

Ergonomic keyboards are keyboards shaped for comfort and to help prevent injury. Many

Figure 7-7. A PS/2 connector, diagram, and pinout. The PS/2 connector is still encountered, but it is considered a legacy port and may not appear as a connection on modern computers.

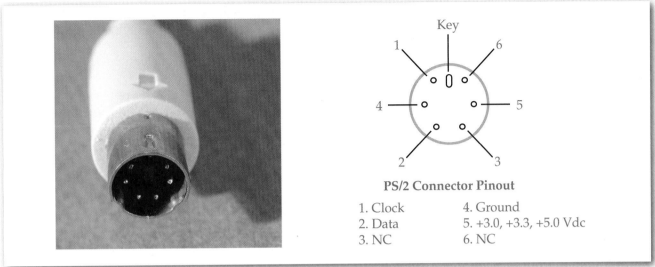

Key

PS/2 Connector Pinout
1. Clock   4. Ground
2. Data   5. +3.0, +3.3, +5.0 Vdc
3. NC   6. NC

Goodheart-Willcox Publisher

Figure 7-8. Adapters are available for connecting PS/2 devices to USB ports and vice versa. This adapter connects a USB mouse or keyboard to a PS/2 port.

Goodheart-Willcox Publisher

people suffer from **carpal tunnel syndrome**, an inflammation of the tendons in the hands and wrist. It is caused by repeating the same movement over and over without proper rest or support. An example of this type of repetitive movement, and a common cause of carpal tunnel syndrome, is inputting data at a keyboard day after day.

Figure 7-9. Logitech Wave-design comfort keyboard.

Logitech

It is believed that by shaping a keyboard so that the hands and fingers contact the keyboard in a more natural alignment, carpal tunnel syndrome can be prevented. A variety of different designs for keyboards have been developed. One design is shown in **Figure 7-9.**

Virtual Keyboard

Canesta has developed a virtual keyboard that works with PCs, personal digital assistants (PDAs), smartphones, and any application where an input device might be required. The Canesta system consists of three main components: light sensor module, infrared light source, and pattern projector, **Figure 7-10**.

The infrared light source and pattern projector work together to create an image of a keyboard. The keyboard image can be projected onto any surface. The light of the keyboard image is reflected off the surface to a set of light sensors. The user simply types on the image just as though it was a real keyboard. The user's finger motions interrupt the light pattern representing the keyboard. The light sensors detect interruptions in the reflected light. The light sensor module converts the interruptions into digital signals that represent the keys touched by the user. See **Figure 7-11**.

Troubleshooting Keyboards

In general, it is not cost-effective to repair damaged keyboards. It is usually less expensive to simply replace the keyboard. However, preventive maintenance can be used to extend the life of a keyboard.

Preventive Maintenance

Most of the problems with keyboards are associated with dirt in and around the keys. As you have seen, the keyboard keys can easily be disabled by dirt or corrosion. A keyboard should be cleaned on a regular basis. A small vacuum cleaner or a can of dry compressed air can be used to clean the keyboard.

When using vacuum cleaners, remember that they generate a lot of electrical noise and static. Electrical noise consists of high voltage spikes. If the vacuum is plugged into the same outlet as the computer being cleaned, be sure the computer is off. Do not equate a computer being off as a computer in a suspended state. When in doubt, unplug the computer. Also, remember that computers other than the one being cleaned might be connected to the same circuit. A battery-operated vacuum is the safest, but be sure it contains sufficient power. Be careful of static electricity. Static electricity is a common and hazardous by-product produced by the plastic parts on a vacuum cleaner. Be sure to follow all anti-static procedures to prevent damage to equipment.

Most computer users understand the hazards of keeping liquids (coffee or soda) near the computer equipment. If a liquid is spilled on the keyboard, the keyboard should be flushed with distilled water as soon as possible. Residue from soda or any other liquid containing sugar

Figure 7-10.
The virtual keyboard by Canesta is constructed from three main devices: light sensor module, infrared light source, and pattern projector.

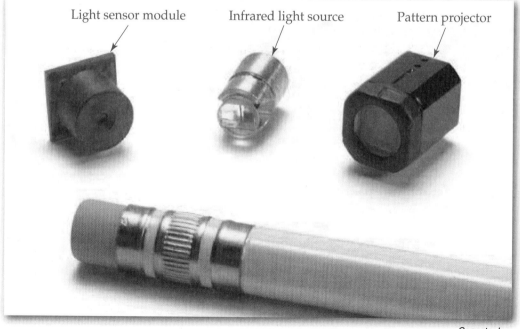

Light sensor module   Infrared light source   Pattern projector

Canesta, Inc.

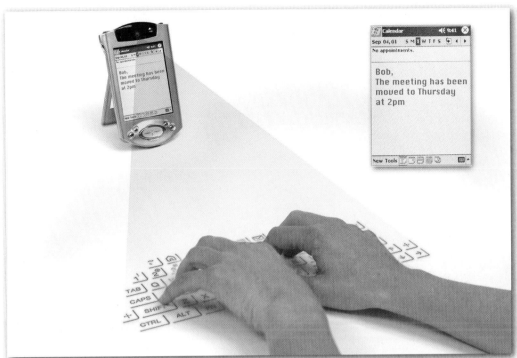

Figure 7-11.
The user's finger movements interrupt the light pattern representing the keyboard. The light sensor module detects the interruptions and converts them into digital signals that represent the keys touched by the user.

Canesta, Inc.

will leave a sticky film when dry. This film will quickly collect dirt and dust and the keys will begin to stick. Certain drinks contain materials that are very corrosive to electrical parts. Distilled water does not contain any minerals that will cause corrosion. Flush the keyboard liberally with distilled water.

Keys on the keyboard can be easily removed using a chip puller. A paper clip can also be bent to hook under the individual keys. Care should be used when attempting to remove the spacebar. The typical spacebar can be very difficult to reconnect to the keyboard after removal.

Warning ! Be careful when disassembling a keyboard. Many styles of keyboards are assembled at the factory in ways that make them nearly impossible to reassemble.

Adjusting Keyboard Properties

Certain keyboard properties can be adjusted for preference in the **Keyboard Properties** dialog box. Keyboard Properties for Windows XP is

located at **Control Panel | Printers and Other Hardware | Keyboard**. For Windows Vista, it is located at **Control Panel | Hardware and Sound | Keyboard**. In Windows 8, it can be accessed through **Control Panel | All Control Panel Items | Keyboard**. To access it in Windows 7 through **Control Panel**, you must be in **Small icon** or **Large icon** view, not the default **Category** view.

A+ Note

Many times a question will appear on a CompTIA A+ exam asking for the correct path to an option or dialog box. Be sure to learn the paths for Windows XP, Windows Vista, Windows 7, and Windows 8.

All Windows operating systems use a very similar **Keyboard Properties** dialog box. You can easily change the repeat delay and the repeat rate as well as the cursor blink rate, **Figure 7-12**. Under the **Speed** tab, you will find the **Repeat delay** and **Repeat rate** adjustments, which control the actions of a pressed key. These adjustments control the length of a pause after pressing a key and the time

Figure 7-12. Windows 7 **Keyboard Properties** dialog box. It is accessible through **Control Panel** and **Small icon** or **Large icon** view.

Figure 7-13. Keyboards and languages are changed through the **Region and Language** dialog box.

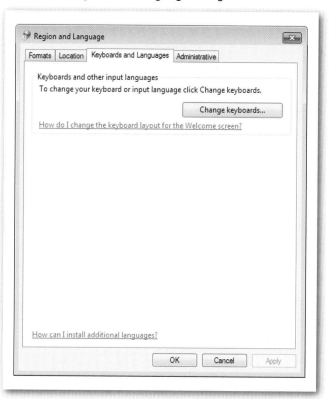

required to hold a key in place before it repeats a character. A typical application of this timing method is when a user holds the spacebar down to continuously move the cursor across the screen. The number of times per second a character can be typed is usually expressed as characters per second (CPS). The **Cursor blink rate** adjustment modifies how fast the cursor blinks on and off. It does not affect your typing in any way.

The computer can also be configured to allow a different language to be displayed on the screen. The computer is an international electronic device marketed worldwide. This window allows you to add and change the language entered by the keyboard. There are keyboards for all major languages in the world. Language is configured in the **Region and Language** dialog box, **Figure 7-13**.

In Windows Vista and Windows 7, you can access the **Region and Language** dialog box through **Control Panel | Clock, Language, and Region | Region and Language**. In Windows 8, it is accessed through **Control Panel** in similar fashion as Windows Vista and Windows 7. The only difference is Windows 8 uses two distinct property windows: one for language and one for region. In Windows XP, you can access the

language options through **Control Panel | Date, Time, Language, and Regional Options | Regional and Language Options**. Changing the physical keyboard layout in Windows XP to match the language is not as easy as it is in Windows Vista and later and requires several additional steps.

Optical Mouse

An **optical mouse** traces movement by transmitting a light beam to a surface, such as a desk, **Figure 7-14**. The light beam is reflected from the surface to a built-in receiver in the mouse. The receiver contains a CMOS digital camera, which captures the image of the surface that is directly under the mouse. The images are taken in rapid succession and compared to one another to determine the direction of motion. The optical mouse may take thousands of images per second. A microprocessor inside the mouse compares the images and translates them into relative direction of movement and speed. There are no mechanical moving parts as found in a ball mouse.

Figure 7-14. Optical mouse. A—Typical optical wireless mouse. B—Beneath the optical mouse is a light source and receiver.

Light source and receiver

A

B

Two light sources commonly used with optical mice are LED and laser. A laser can produce more precise movement increments than an LED. The LED depends on a light-shaping optical lens to produce a fine beam of light. A laser has a natural fine line of light and requires no special light-shaping lens.

Mouse quality is measured and compared by frames per second (FPS) and dots per inch (DPI). The term *frames per second* as related to an optical mouse means how often the mouse sensor reads the surface and transmits the data collected. *Dots per inch* is the degree of accuracy that a mouse can produce when sliding across a surface. The higher the number represented by DPI and FPS, the better the quality of the mouse system.

It is not unusual for a laser light mouse to produce increments of 1600 DPI and transfer 6000 FPS or more. This is quite an improvement over earlier versions of ball mice movement of less than 100 DPI and 100 FPS.

Tech Tip

Some modern office furniture designs incorporate a clear plastic or glass writing surface. You should avoid using an optical mouse on a transparent surface or material.

The mouse is available in three interface styles:
- Motherboard PS/2.
- USB.
- Wireless.

Most mice connect through a USB port. A wireless mouse also uses a USB port. A wireless receiver is inserted into the port. The receiver receives wireless signals from the mouse and converts them into a signal to be sent over the USB bus to the processor. While PS/2 mice do exist, they are rapidly becoming obsolete.

When the mouse connector is built into the motherboard using a PS/2 port connection, the IRQ setting assigned is typically IRQ 12. When using a USB port, the IRQ assignment is shared with all other USB devices using that port.

Troubleshooting the Optical Mouse

As with keyboards, it is not cost-effective to spend any large amount of time fixing a malfunctioning mouse. You simply replace the mouse and do not attempt to make electrical repairs. Since there are no mechanical parts, there is never an issue of worn parts. If an optical mouse begins to jump or behave erratically, the source of trouble is usually a buildup of dust and foreign particles on the light source or light receiver surfaces. The suspect area should be cleaned with a lint-free cloth. No special chemical cleaners are required. When a wireless mouse stops working completely, it is usually a sign that the batteries are weak and require replacement, **Figure 7-15**.

Adjusting Mouse Properties

As with keyboards, certain properties of the mouse can be adjusted for preference. The **Mouse Properties** dialog box is used to make adjustments to the mouse. See **Figure 7-16**. This dialog box can be accessed in Windows XP and Windows Vista, through **Control Panel | Printers and Other Hardware | Mouse**. In Windows 7 and Windows 8, it is accessed through **Control Panel | Hardware and Sound | Mouse**.

Once the properties window for the mouse is open, adjustments to functionality, such as speed of pointer travel across the screen and the speed used to double-click can be adjusted. The type of mouse used can be selected. One special change allows you to reverse the features (such as dragging) associated with the right and left buttons. Adjustments for purely aesthetic reasons can be performed here as well. For example, the length of the trailing mouse tail can be adjusted. The style, color, and size of the pointer can also be changed, **Figure 7-17**.

Figure 7-16. **Mouse Properties** dialog box in Windows 7. The appearance of this box will vary depending on the mouse installed.

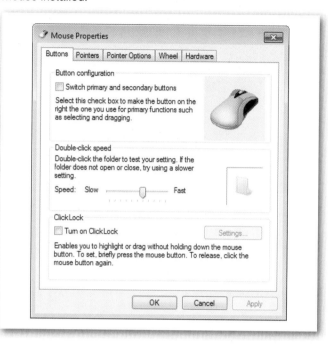

Figure 7-17. The **Mouse Properties** dialog box allows you to adjust the mouse for purely aesthetic reasons in addition to functional reasons.

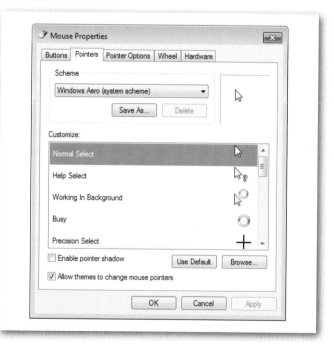

Figure 7-15. Wireless mouse and battery.

Goodheart-Willcox Publisher

Other Input Devices

There are many other types of input devices used with computers. In this section, we will limit the instruction to the most commonly encountered input devices and to those that might be presented on a typical A+ Certification exam.

Trackball

A **trackball** is a mouse with a ball embedded in the top of it, **Figure 7-18**. The ball is used to position the curser on the screen display. The advantage of a trackball as compared to a traditional mouse is the trackball remains stationary. You do not need to move the trackball device, only the ball. The disadvantage of a trackball is the ball may need periodic cleaning.

Game Pad

The term **game pad** applies to any device used as an input for a game application. This includes joysticks, steering wheels, or specialty items such as the Logitech G13 Advanced Gameboard in **Figure 7-19**.

The Logitech G13 Advanced Gameboard is a hybrid gaming keypad designed for comfort as a game input device for a MAC or PC. It is physically designed as an ergonomic device for many hours of constant use. What all game pads

Figure 7-18. A trackball is equipped with a ball embedded into the top of the device. The ball is spun using the fingertips, which results in cursor movement.

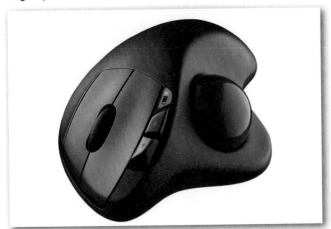

Logitech

Figure 7-19. The Logitech G13 Advanced Gameboard is a PC game input device.

Logitech

have in common is their ability to allow keys to be programmed to perform specific tasks such as run, jump, shoot, pick up, and throw. This particular device has 25 programmable keys and a programmable analog stick. The LCD panel displays game statistics, system information, and player messages.

To hook up a game pad, the device drivers must be installed. The drivers are provided on the CD or DVD that comes with the game pad or are available for download from the manufacturer's website. Without proper drivers, the game pad will most likely fail to operate as intended. It is not uncommon for a game pad to be automatically configured by the operating system but without the latest drivers. In this case, some features may not work correctly.

Digitizer Pad

Digitizer pads are input devices for graphic software applications such as Adobe Photoshop, AutoCAD, or most any paint or drawing program. The **digitizer pad** is a virtual drawing surface that allows the user to create or modify drawings or modify photos, **Figure 7-20**. The pen used with the digitizer is also referred to as a **stylus**. It is used as a virtual pencil, paintbrush, or ink pen. When you draw on the digitizer pad using the stylus, a line or brushstroke appears on the screen in a similar fashion as when using a pencil or paintbrush with art medium.

Figure 7-20.
A digitizer pad is used as an input device for graphics software applications.

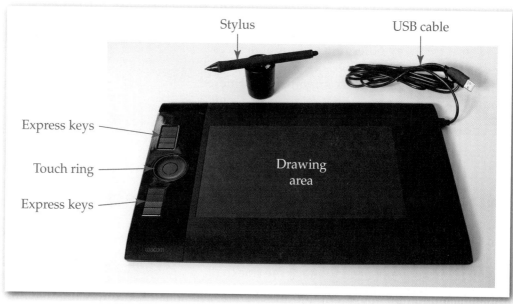

Figure 7-21 shows a close-up of the left side of the digitizer pad in Figure 7-20. It contains express keys and a touch ring. The express keys are programmable function keys. The exact function of the keys and touch ring depend on the software application used with the digitizer pad. For example, some of the functions of the express keys can produce special menus, control drawing precision, and pan and/or scroll the image. The touch ring is typically used for zooming in or out of an image, modifying line thickness, rotating the drawing, and cycling through drawing layers. The toggle button in the center of the touch ring is used to select assigned functions.

A group of four LEDs along the edge of the touch ring are used to indicate the activation of specific functions associated with the touch ring and toggle button. In Figure 7-21, only one LED is lit.

Problems associated with a digitizer pad are similar to any other input device. The manufacturer provides the latest software drivers and user manual, explaining the use and configuration of the digitizer pad.

Bar Code Readers

A **bar code reader** simply converts bar code images into data. The operation of a bar code scanner is simple, **Figure 7-22**. It is designed with a light source transmitter and a light source

Figure 7-21.
Controls are located on the left side of the digitizer pad and provide common key functions and more.

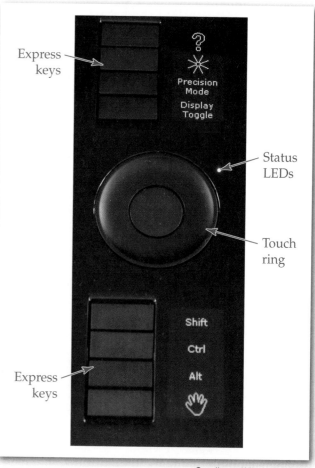

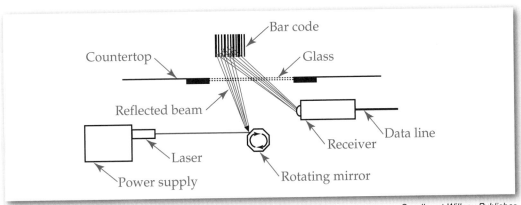

Goodheart-Willcox Publisher

Figure 7-22.
Shown are the workings of a bar code reader that can be found at the checkout counter of many stores. Using these fixed readers, bar codes dragged across the glass can be read.

receiver. The light source transmitter projects a light beam across the bar code. The bar code is made up of dark lines of varying width and spacing. The widths of the dark lines combine with the white spaces to form a code that represents ASCII letters and numbers. Look at **Figure 7-23**, which shows a typical bar code.

The light from the source is reflected by the white spaces and absorbed by the dark lines. The receiver converts the reflected light into electrical pulses representing the data contained in the bar code. The electrical pulses are then passed along as ASCII data to the PC through either a wireless or a wired connection. The PC has software driver programs that use the ASCII data for application programs that manage inventory or drive a cash register program.

Figure 7-23.
A typical bar code. Note the variation in the thickness of the black lines of the code.

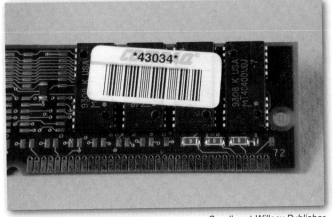

Goodheart-Willcox Publisher

Scanners and Digital Cameras

A **scanner** is a tool that takes in an optical image and digitizes it, **Figure 7-24**. Scanners can be used to read text into a computer or to create a digital version of an image. To read text into a format that can be used with word-processing software, a scanner uses optical character recognition software. This **optical character recognition (OCR)** software determines which letters, numbers, and symbols match with images taken by the scanner. The output is a fairly accurate text version of a printed document. A **digital camera** takes pictures like a regular camera, but it captures and stores images as digital data instead of on photographic film. See **Figure 7-25**. Scanners and digital cameras rely on either the charged-coupled device (CCD) or CMOS technology to capture digital images.

CCD

Think of a **charged-coupled device (CCD)** as a series of light-activated capacitors contained in a single chip. These capacitors convert light into electrical energy. When light strikes the CCD, a voltage is produced in direct proportion to the intensity of the light.

The voltage produced is analog, which means the voltage level is a variable signal. To be used by a computer system, the voltage must be converted to a digital signal, a sequence of discrete voltages. A special chip called an *analog-to-digital converter (ADC)* receives the analog electrical charge from the CCD and converts it to a series of digital signals that represent the light intensity of the

Figure 7-24. A scanner changes reflected light into digital signals.

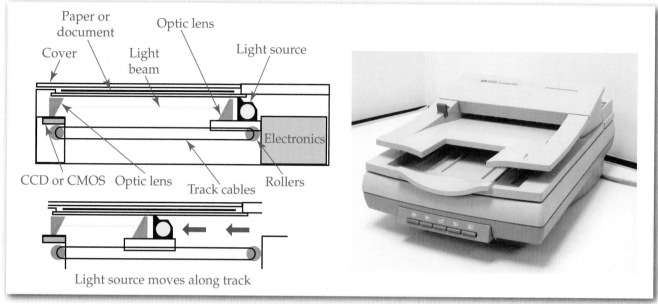

Figure 7-25. Digital cameras are similar to scanners in that they both use either a charge-coupled device (CCD) or CMOS technology to produce their images.

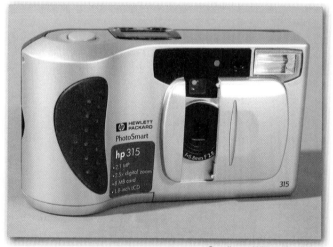

image. The digital pulses are stored in memory to be accessed by graphical software programs. See **Figure 7-26**.

The flatbed scanner uses a cable to move the light beam along the image placed on the bed of the scanner. The scanner captures the image one line at a time. After a line of the image is captured, the CCD is moved down the image a fraction to capture the next line. This process continues until the entire image has been captured.

The CCD device in a camera consists of an array of tiny windows. The entire image is captured at once rather than line by line as in the scanner application. Color filter lenses are used for color images. Each color is captured separately by incorporating a set of color filters into the lens units.

CMOS

A second type of imaging technology used for cameras and scanners is CMOS. CMOS imaging devices get their name from the fact that they are composed of CMOS transistor technology. Both CCD and CMOS convert light into electronic signals that can be transmitted to a computer or storage device for retrieval or manipulation. The main difference is CMOS imaging devices can be produced in a smaller package than CCD imaging devices. At the time of this writing, neither technology has dominated the imaging device market.

Light Pen

A **light pen** interacts with a light beam that strikes a CRT monitor screen. The raster

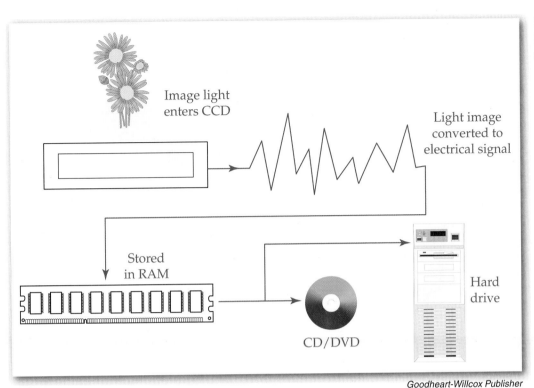

Figure 7-26.
Illustration of a graphic stored as impulses.

Image light enters CCD

Light image converted to electrical signal

Stored in RAM

Hard drive

CD/DVD

Goodheart-Willcox Publisher

or movement of the light across the screen is explained in detail in Chapter 8—Video and Audio Systems. For now, imagine the computer screen image as being generated by a light beam sweeping across the screen. The beam moves from left to right. After each pass of the beam from left to right, it moves down the screen just a fraction. This process continues until the beam has covered the entire screen. The process is repeated approximately sixty times a second. The light intensity of the beam changes as it crosses the screen to produce an image. The travel of the beam is a product of precise timing of horizontal and vertical electronic controls.

The light pen is plugged into an adapter card that is inserted into one of the expansion slots in the motherboard. Light pens are also available as USB devices. The end of the light pen is light-sensitive. The light pen can detect the beam from the monitor as it sweeps across the computer display screen. The screen area has a graphical user interface displayed. It can be a menu or a list of products. When the light pen touches the screen area where an image is displayed, the light beam strikes the screen and actuates the input area of the pen. It is the exact timing of the beam that

allows the light pen adapter card to convert the location of the pen into screen coordinates. The software program converts the screen coordinates into user information such as "one hamburger with cheese," or "open bay door number 2." The command can be anything associated with the image on the screen.

Light pen technology requires light generated from a CRT-type of display. Because the CRT is rapidly becoming obsolete, touch screen technology will soon replace light pen technology.

Touch Screens

A **touch screen display** is a computer display modified to accommodate input information by touch. The input area on the touch screen is activated by a touch, as the name implies, or by using a stylus.

A touch screen system requires a touch screen panel assembly, controller, port connector, and software driver. The controller can be a separate unit attached by cable to the touch screen or incorporated into the edge of the touch screen frame. The typical connection to the computer system is made through a USB port, **Figure 7-27**.

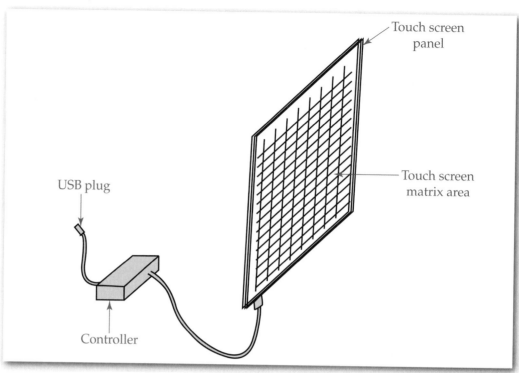

Touch screen
panel

Touch screen
matrix area

USB plug

Controller

Goodheart-Willcox Publisher

Special PCI cards may be used in place of a USB port. The PCI card can serve as a port connection to the computer and incorporate the necessary electronics to act as the system controller.

A device driver must be installed in the computer system during the installation of the touch screen. The software driver provides the necessary support for interpreting the digital signal sent by the controller. Installing the necessary driver is similar to installing a driver for any other computer input device.

Touch screens are often incorporated into a computer system when a mouse or keyboard would not be a practical input device or as a convenience for users. Touch screen applications have been applied to interactive computer communications such as those in hotel lobby information panels, manufacturing assembly line controls, hospital surgical rooms, and the food service industry. They are also used as the main input for tablets, smartphones, and similar devices. Touch screen technology falls into five major sensor categories:

- Resistance.
- Capacitance.
- Near field effect.
- Infrared.
- Acoustical wave.

All touch screen technologies operate in a very similar manner. The main difference is the touch screen surface construction and the type of electronic transmitters and receivers or sensors used.

Resistance

Touch screens that utilize the electronic principle of resistance are one of the most common and inexpensive to design. The touch screen consists of two layers of conductors separated by very tiny spacers. The first layer is a series of vertical translucent electrical conductors, and the second layer is a series of horizontal translucent electrical conductors. The two layers combine to form a matrix. The two layers are assembled into a flexible transparent cover, which fits neatly over the monitor display.

The monitor typically displays command buttons or similar graphics, which represent menu commands such as open, save, view files, and exit. When the screen is touched, a connection is made at that point in the matrix, **Figure 7-28**. Each area

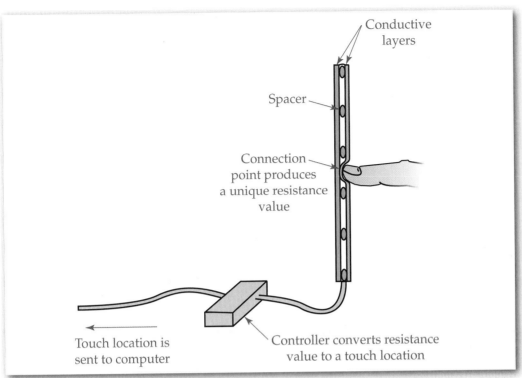

Figure 7-28.
Basic operation of a resistance touch screen.

Conductive layers

Spacer

Connection point produces a unique resistance value

Touch location is sent to computer

Controller converts resistance value to a touch location

Goodheart-Willcox Publisher

on the resistance touch screen produces a unique electrical resistance value. The electrical resistance value is interpreted by the screen controller and then passed to the computer operating system as a screen location. The digital signal is sent into the computer system through a USB port or through a PCI card designed for this purpose. Resistance touch screens work well in dusty or humid environments.

Capacitance

Capacitance touch screens operate on the principle of capacitance. See **Figure 7-29**. The touch screen is coated with a transparent metal oxide. A slight electrical charge is applied to the metal oxide, which creates an equally-distributed electrical field across the inside of the touch screen. When the screen is touched, the electrically charged field is disturbed. A drop in the electrical potential at that point in the screen is transmitted to the touch screen controller. Capacitance touch screens do not work well in a humid environment.

Near Field

Near field touch screens also operate on the principle of capacitance. However, the near field touch screen is constructed from two laminates of glass, each with a pattern of a transparent metal oxide coating. The main difference between the two technologies is that you need not touch the screen, but rather place your finger near the screen area. A finger or any other pointing device near the screen area is sufficient to disturb the electrical field between the two screen plates. Near field touch screens work well in an industrial or medical application where the user may have gloved hands.

Infrared

The infrared touch screen forms a matrix created by a row of infrared transmitters and receivers along the edges of the screen, **Figure 7-30**. The infrared transmitters are specially designed LEDs that transmit infrared light to the receivers. The receivers are light-activated transistors, which

Figure 7-29.
Basic operation of a capacitance touch screen.

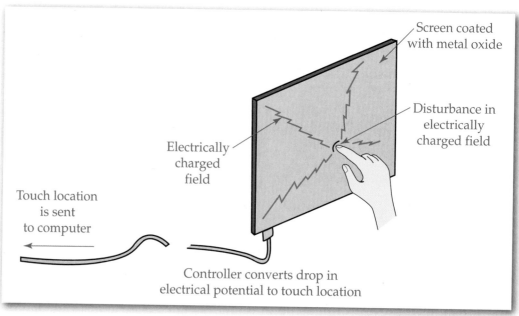

Goodheart-Willcox Publisher

Figure 7-30.
Basic operation of an infrared touch screen.

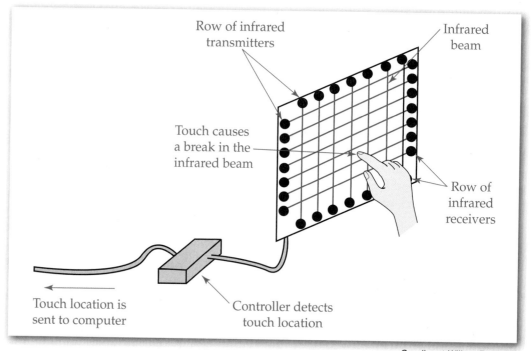

Goodheart-Willcox Publisher

act like a switch that is turned on and off by the presence or absence of the infrared light beam. When a touch interrupts the infrared beam, the receivers in that matrix area send a signal to the controller. The controller determines the touch location and sends this location to the computer.

Acoustical Wave

The acoustical wave touch screen is similar in design to the infrared screen. The acoustical touch screen, however, uses a matrix of sound waves. The edges of the panel are lined with acoustical sound wave transmitters and receivers. When an object such as a finger interrupts the sound wave, the location of the interruption is transmitted to the screen controller. The infrared and acoustical do not work well in a dusty environment.

Wireless Input Devices

Wireless input devices use either radio signal (RF) or infrared (IR) light to transfer information between an input device and a computer system. Typical wireless input devices commonly encountered are mice, keyboards, microphones, game input devices, webcams, and digitizer pads. The information in this section will be limited to how wireless input device technology correlates to common PC wireless input devices. Other wireless technologies will be introduced in later chapters.

Infrared Devices

Specifications for infrared communications have been established by the Infrared Data Association (IrDA). Infrared devices use light to establish the connection between the input device and the computer. These devices work in similar fashion as a television remote control. The one main problem with infrared controls is that they require a direct line of sight between the transmitter and receiver. The main advantage of infrared devices is that they are not susceptible to radio interference as many other wireless devices are. Infrared device communication is typically limited to only two devices. Wireless technology based on radio waves is typically used for two or more devices and does not require direct line of sight for a communications link between the devices.

Infrared connections are usually established automatically when devices are brought within one meter of each other. Microsoft operating systems use ActiveSync technology to automatically establish and synchronize a connection between infrared devices such as a PC and a personal digital assistant. Infrared devices are configured in Control Panel or Device Manager of Windows operating systems. However, if the infrared device does not exist, you will not see an option to configure the device. You can access the infrared setup and configuration

wizard in Windows Vista or Windows 8 by typing "irda" in Windows **Help and Support**, which is located off the **Start** menu.

You can only establish one infrared link between two devices, but the two devices can support more than one software application at the same time. For example, you can transfer the contents of a calendar program, a business card program, and e-mail program in one session using one common infrared link.

Several data transfer speeds are associated with infrared technology as shown in the following table. Notice that Gigabit Infrared (Giga-IR) has a data rate range from 512 Mbps to a maximum of 1 Gbps. This is because some devices that are less than 1 Gbps but higher than 512 Mbps are classified as Giga-IR.

IR Technology	Data Rate
Serial Infrared (SIR)	115.2 kbps
Fast Infrared (FIR)	4 Mbps
Very Fast Infrared (VFIR)	16 Mbps
Ultra Fast Infrared (UFIR)	96 Mbps
Gigabit Infrared (Giga-IR)	512 Mbps–1 Gbps

Each generation of IrDA infrared specifications is backward compatible with the previous version. For example, a VFIR device can communicate with a SIR device at the SIR data rate of 115.2 kbps. Infrared technology is not as popular as wireless technology because of the requirement of direct line of sight for successful transmission and reception. Wireless technology using radio frequencies is much more popular.

RF Devices

Radio Frequency (RF) devices use radio waves to communicate between the remote device and the receiver. The early radio remote control devices used the 27-MHz frequency for their wireless devices. This is the same frequency used by model remote control planes, cars, and other toys such as robots. The use of specific radio frequencies for devices is controlled by the Federal Communications Commission (FCC). It is their responsibility to assign radio frequencies and enforce rules regulating the devices using radio waves.

The radio frequency can transmit through solid material and does not need to be in direct line of sight like infrared. RF can transmit through solid objects but within limits. RF can easily pass through wood, sheet rock, glass, concrete block, and other common building materials. However, if the material is very dense, the RF may not pass through. For example, a thick concrete wall containing steel reinforcement may totally block the RF signal. Do not expect RF to pass through metal, such as metal walls or a wall covered with metal file cabinets. The metal will most likely block the RF signals.

Many RF devices are designed as proprietary devices. This means that the technology was designed by a specific company and may not be used by other manufacturers without the original manufacturer's permission. One of the drawbacks to a proprietary design is that it may not be compatible with other devices that perform a similar function. For example, a mouse designed by Logitech that uses a 27-MHz radio frequency may not be compatible with another brand of mouse receiver. This means when you replace a 27-MHz Logitech mouse, you must use another 27-Hz Logitech mouse. You cannot use a Microsoft or a Bluetooth mouse.

Wireless Technology Standards

As you study the characteristics of wireless devices, be aware that there are many overlapping RF standards, which can create a lot of confusion. For example, Logitech Fast RF is not a radio frequency standard but rather a Logitech proprietary standard developed for their brand of input devices. Fast RF is not intended to be compatible with devices manufactured by other manufacturers.

The IEEE organization developed and released a set of wireless standards for networking, which is referred to as the IEEE 802.11 wireless standard. The IEEE 802.11 standard specifies how 2.4-GHz and 5-GHz RF is used for networking devices.

ZigBee is a wireless standard used for home entertainment systems. Wireless USB (WUSB) is a standard developed by the Wireless USB Promoters Group to replace wired USB devices with wireless USB devices. Ultra-Wideband

(UWB) is an International Standards Organization (ISO) radio standard which has been adopted by several other organizations that are responsible for their own individual set of radio standards. As technology evolves, some standards are absorbed into other original standards. This adds to the confusion. The wireless technology standards covered in this section are Bluetooth, Wi-Fi, Wireless USB, and Ultra-Wideband.

A+ Note

You will most likely be asked questions about wireless technology frequencies and speeds. Keep in mind that standards for computer and electronic devices constantly change. You should always check the manufacturer's website for the very latest information about assigned RF and bandwidth.

Bluetooth

The **Bluetooth standard** was developed by a special interest group of electronics manufacturers who wanted to produce a standard way to connect low-powered devices over a short distance using the assigned 2.4-GHz frequency. Anyone can use the 2.4-GHz frequency for a wide assortment of devices. The Bluetooth organization was interested in developing a standard to be followed by manufacturers to share communication with each other's devices. For example, as a result of such technology, a cell phone could automatically transfer information between it and a computer. Bluetooth was originally designed for only very low-power devices that would transmit data over the 2.4-GHz frequency. As the demand for wireless devices expanded, so did the Bluetooth list of products. Wireless keyboards and mice conform to the Bluetooth standard.

The Bluetooth technology is slow compared to some other wireless technologies. To stay competitive, Bluetooth is constantly revising their specifications to increase data transfer speeds. The latest version, Bluetooth 3.0, can produce theoretical data transfer rates as high as 24 Mbps.

Bluetooth is often confused with other 2.4-GHz RF devices. The main difference is

Bluetooth is a design standard of how the device should operate using the 2.4 GHz-radio band. When manufacturers apply the Bluetooth standard to their devices, their devices can communicate with any other Bluetooth standard devices no matter who manufactured it. For example, a PC that uses the Bluetooth standard can communicate with any cell phone that uses the Bluetooth standard.

The Bluetooth standard specifies that all Bluetooth devices should use the same "protocol" when communicating between devices. A **protocol** as defined for use with computer and network communications is a set of rules used to govern communication between two devices. The set of rules outline information about how the data is organized that is to be exchanged between the two devices. A protocol sets the standards for such items as the following:

- How the devices are to be identified (by numbers or letters) and the exact number of characters.
- The maximum amount of data that can be transmitted at one time.
- The speed at which each of the electronic devices should operate.
- If information should be encrypted, and if so, by what method.

There are over 1200 pages in the current Bluetooth standard that manufacturers must follow to ensure compatibility with other Bluetooth devices. The Bluetooth specification as well as many other wireless specifications must adhere to regulations set by the Federal Communications Commission (FCC). There are three general wireless power classifications described by the FCC, as shown in the following table.

Class	Power in Milliwatts (mW)	Maximum Range in Meters (m)
Class 1	100	100
Class 2	10	10
Class 3	1	1

The classes are Class 1, Class 2, and Class 3. The amount of power of each classification is directly related to the maximum distance an RF device can transmit. The power output of radio devices is measured in milliwatts (mW). A milliwatt is very little energy as compared to other electronic devices.

Most common short-range, RF input devices are rated as a Class 3 device with a maximum range of 1 meter. There are some instances of Class 2 input devices. In general, the maximum distances indicated in the table are for ideal conditions. If there is a significant amount of radio interference, the maximum distance will be reduced. If the radio interference is excessive, the wireless device will fail to operate entirely.

Wireless devices will operate either in the 27-MHz range or the 2.4-GHz Bluetooth range. There are 2.4-GHz devices that are not Bluetooth. Bluetooth is a standard, not a specific frequency; although, it is assigned to use a specific frequency. When Bluetooth is used to connect to the computer receiver, the typical maximum range is approximately 6′ (1.8 meters). When using the 27-MHz frequency, the range can be significantly farther. Both the 27-MHz and the 2.4-GHz radio frequencies can be interfered with by other devices, such as cordless phones, microwave ovens, garage door openers, and baby monitors.

The wireless receiver connects to the computer either through a USB port or through a PS/2 port. Wireless devices are incorporated into many portable devices such as laptops, tablets, smartphones and cameras. If the device does not have wireless built in such as most desktop computers, the wireless connection is provided by connecting a wireless device to any available USB port.

Wi-Fi

The **Wi-Fi standard** was developed by the Wi-Fi Alliance. This group was originally organized to produce a specification for interfacing with 2.4-GHz networking devices and network applications. It closely follows the IEEE 802.11 standard. Since the original Wi-Fi standard was released, it has expanded to include cameras, webcams, laptops, phones, printers, game consoles, and many other devices that were once dominated by Bluetooth. Interestingly, Microsoft and Logitech have chosen not to include Wi-Fi as a choice for their mice and keyboard communications. Wi-Fi has similar power limitations as Bluetooth mainly because all radio equipment used in the United States must meet the FCC regulations.

Be aware that both Bluetooth and Wi-Fi devices operate at the same 2.4-GHz frequency and can interfere with each other if they are in close proximity. In addition, Wi-Fi has devices that also operate at 5 GHz, but these devices are not typical short-range input devices.

Wireless USB

One of the latest wireless specifications is the **Wireless USB (WUSB) standard**. WUSB devices use the radio frequencies between 3.1 GHz to 10.6 GHz. The WUSB standard is intended for communications between the PC and many common PC devices such as cameras, projectors, printers, scanners, and MP3 players.

In general, WUSB devices transfer more data per second than Bluetooth and Wi-Fi products. The WUSB data rate at the time of this writing is 480 Mbps at 3 meters and 110 Mbps at 10 meters. As the distance between the wireless devices increases, data throughput decreases.

There are two organizations that sponsor Wireless USB specifications: Wireless USB Promoters Group and WiMedia Alliance. The Wireless USB Promoters Group is part of the USB Implementers Forum. The WiMedia Alliance is an independent industry group. The Wireless USB Promoters Group requests that their standard users identify their products as "Certified Wireless USB" rather than with the acronym WUSB, which can lead to confusion. Both standards achieve the same data rates and are similar.

Ultra-Wideband

The **Ultra-Wideband (UWB) standard** was developed by the WiMedia Alliance and describes short-distance (10-meter) radio communication. The WiMedia Alliance is a group of industry professionals who share a common interest in developing a high-bandwidth, short-range, wireless medium specification. The UWB standard specifies the use of the 3.1-GHz to 10.6-GHz radio frequencies. The USB and FireWire cable technologies base their wireless media on the UWB specifications.

There will be more about wireless technologies presented in other chapters

throughout the textbook when subjects such as laptop computers and networking are presented.

Synchronizing the Wireless Device

A typical wireless mouse and keyboard, **Figure 7-31**, is ready to use after installing or charging the batteries. The products are usually synchronized at the factory before shipping them to retailers. Synchronizing is the operation of matching a pair of devices to each other so that they recognize each other and not other wireless devices in the same general area of use.

After a few months of use, the device batteries may fail, or radio interference from a device other than the matched keyboard and mouse may interfere. In this case, the keyboard or mouse must be synchronized with the receiving unit. Synchronization typically requires that a button on the wireless device and receiving unit be pressed so that they can identify each other and connect using the same frequency and assigned channel. **Figure 7-32** shows the instructions printed on the back of the keyboard.

The diagram shows to first press the button on the receiving unit and then to press the button on the bottom of the mouse. The two devices will establish a link as long as they are in range. The diagram indicates to wait 20 seconds for the

Figure 7-31. Wireless keyboard and mouse with installation software.

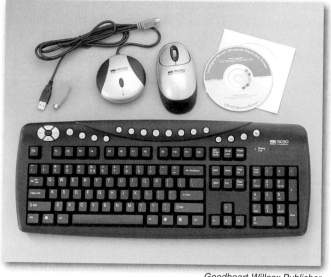

Figure 7-32. The back of this Logitech keyboard displays instructions for synchronizing the receiving unit with the mouse and keyboard.

Goodheart-Willcox Publisher

Device	Channel 1	Channel 2
Keyboard	27.095 MHz	27.195 MHz
Mouse	27.045 MHz	27.145 MHz

Wireless Device Failure

The most common reason for wireless input device failure is battery failure. A battery will last six months on average. You can expect more or less battery life depending on how much the device is used each day. Also, some batteries provide energy longer than others. Rechargeable batteries last much longer. They can often be used for up to five years or more before requiring to be replaced.

You may need to clean an optical mouse as a routine maintenance or troubleshooting problem. First, clean the optical lens area using a dry lint-free cloth or use dry compressed air designed for this purpose. If this fails to clean the unit, check the manufacturer's website or product literature to see what chemical cleaners, if any, are safe to use on the unit.

Another common reason for failure is radio interference. Many other electronic devices use the same radio frequency that is assigned to wireless devices. For example, baby monitors, garage door openers, microwave ovens, wireless phones, and more.

Many times you can counter the effects of radio interference by using a different assigned channel. Some wireless devices have several different channels to choose from when configuring the device. If radio interference is suspected as a cause for wireless connection failure or very low data rates, you may want to change the assigned channel. You can locate the exact method to change an assigned channel by checking the device documentation or the manufacturer's website. There will be much more about wireless technology in later chapters. The following are general steps to take when troubleshooting wireless input devices.

1. Turn the device off and then back on.
2. Plug the USB receiver into another USB port.
3. Restart the computer.
4. Replace the batteries.
5. Download and reinstall the device driver or check for an updated driver.

synchronization to occur and then to repeat the process for the wireless keyboard. **Figure 7-33** shows a close-up of a synchronization button located on the bottom of a keyboard. As you can see, the button is labeled "CONNECT."

Some devices do not have a synchronization button or special sequence to follow to synchronize the receiver and keyboard or mouse. They automatically synchronize when the device is turned on.

Most mice and keyboards have at least two possible channels for communication. For example, Microsoft uses the assigned channels and frequencies indicated in the following table to match the receiver with the keyboard and mouse.

Figure 7-33. Close-up of the CONNECT button which is pressed when synchronizing the keyboard with the receiving unit.

Goodheart-Willcox Publisher

Managing Input Devices

Input devices can and will fail. When they do, there are several quick and easy ways to investigate the possible reason for failure. The most common Microsoft tool used to inspect input devices is Device Manager. Devices and Printers can also be used.

Device Manager

Device Manager provides information about input devices and other hardware, **Figure 7-34**. It is an excellent tool to determine if an input device is properly installed. A problem with an input device is indicated by special symbols such as a red *X* and yellow exclamation mark. Device Manager also allows you to obtain driver details and update the driver.

To view the properties of a device, right-click the device name and select **Properties** from the shortcut menu. The **Properties** dialog box for the device will display. The options under the **Driver** tab are **Driver Details**, **Update Driver**, **Roll Back Driver**, **Disable**, and **Uninstall**. See **Figure 7-35**. Notice that the option to roll back the driver appears dimmed as compared to the other options. This is because you cannot roll back the device driver for this device. You can only roll back a device driver when a previous driver has been installed. Windows 8 added a new tab called **Events** for HID-compliant devices. The **Events** tab displays a historical log of activities related to a specific device. For example, the events log might contain the date and time of when a device was configured, stopped, started, or failed. Having a record of events that directly affect a device is invaluable when attempting to solve a device problem.

Figure 7-34.
Device Manager is a great place to start troubleshooting an input device.

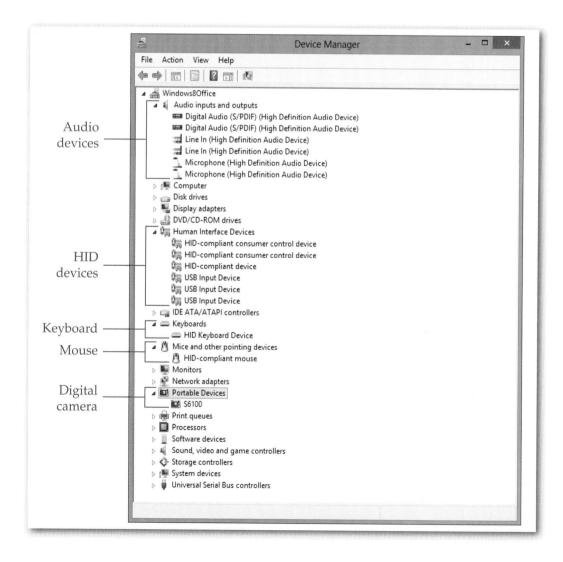

Figure 7-35. Driver details for an audio device.

Devices and Printers

Devices and Printers provides a centralized location to add or remove devices, select a default printer, view device properties, and more. It is available in Windows 7 and Windows 8. **Figure 7-36** shows a list of options that are available after right-clicking a device. Notice the long list of options. There are typically less options to select from on other devices.

In Windows 7, Devices and Printers can be accessed from the **Start** menu. In both Windows 7 and Windows 8, it can be accessed through **Control Panel | Hardware and Sound | Devices and Printers**. The Devices and Printers in **Figure 7-37** shows icons of the devices associated with a particular Windows 7 configuration. Some of the devices shown are a UPS unit, a monitor, an input tablet, and a wireless receiver. Notice that the

Figure 7-36. List of options revealed when right-clicking a device in **Devices and Printers**.

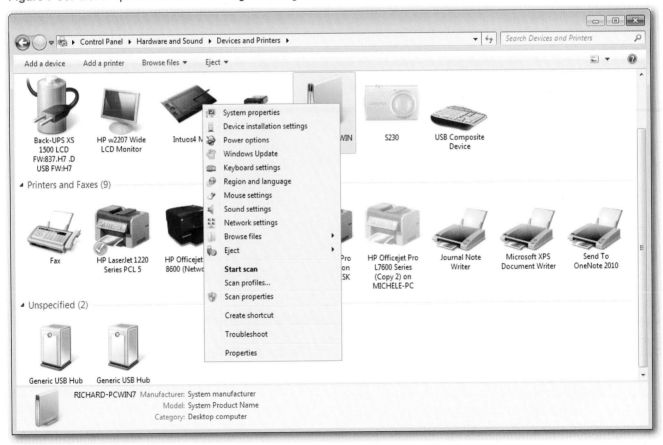

Figure 7-37.
An example of devices shown in **Devices and Printers** for a particular Windows 7 computer.

icon of the S230 digital camera appears dimmed. This means the device was installed and used in the past but at this time is not connected to the computer.

The USB Composite Device represents two or more devices configured through the same input device. In this example, it means that the wireless keyboard and wireless mouse are attached through the same receiver installed on one of the USB ports. This is just one possible example of a group of wireless devices connected to a computer workstation.

Ease of Access

The Ease of Access feature is designed to make the user experience better for people with disabilities or for those who might have difficulties using a mouse or keyboard or viewing a screen. Ease of Access options exist on all editions of Microsoft Windows. **Figure 7-38** shows the options available for user configuration in the Ease of Access Center. Some of the configuration options available that are directly related to mouse and keyboard input devices are as follows:

- **Turn on Mouse Keys:** When a mouse is not available or too difficult to use, the arrow

keys on your keyboard or the numeric keypad can be used to move the pointer.

- **Turn on Sticky Keys:** Instead of having to press a combination of keys all at once, such as when you must press [Ctrl] [Alt] [Delete] to access Task Manager, you can use one key by turning on Sticky Keys and adjusting the settings.

- **Turn on Toggle Keys:** Toggle Keys will play an alert each time you press the [Caps Lock], [Num Lock], or [Scroll Lock] keys by accident.

- **Turn on Filter Keys:** Configures Windows to ignore keystrokes that occur in rapid succession or keystrokes that are held down for several seconds unintentionally.

- **Underline keyboard shortcuts and access keys:** This option makes keyboard access in dialog boxes easier by highlighting the access keys for the commands or options in them.

- **Prevent Windows from being automatically arranged when moved to the edge of the screen:** This option prevents Windows from automatically resizing and docking along the sides of your screen when you move them there.

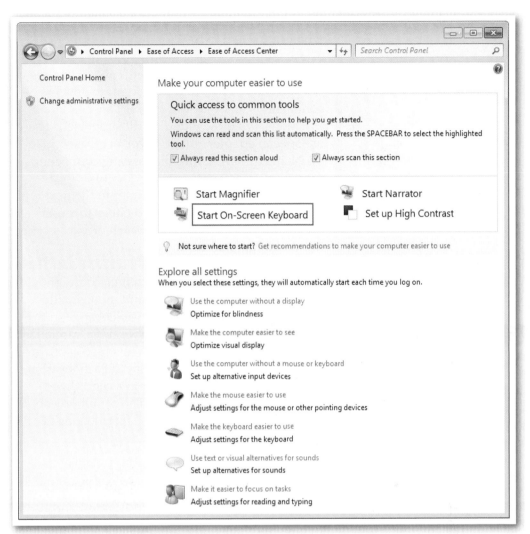

Figure 7-38.
Windows 7 Ease of Access Center.

Several audio and visual enhancements will be discussed in the next chapter.

 Sticky keys are often turned on by accident by users who hold a key down for a certain amount of time.

KVM Switch

A **Keyboard-Video-Mouse (KVM) switch** is used to share a mouse, keyboard, and monitor with two or more computers or servers. Without a KVM switch, each computer or server would require its own mouse, keyboard, and monitor. The individual computers are connected through special cables designed for the KVM switch. Some variations of KVM switches can also share devices such as speakers. KVM switches are typically found in server rooms.

The KVM switch in **Figure 7-39** contains USB, video, and audio connections. The black connections are USB and used for the mouse and keyboard. The green connection is for audio. The blue connection is for a 15-pin VGA connector, which is used for video.

 The 15-pin VGA connector is also referred to as DB-15, HDB-15, and HDDB-15. The "HD" in these connector names represents "high density."

Figure 7-39. KVM switch and cables.

Goodheart-Willcox Publisher

The switch connects directly to the master keyboard, mouse, and monitor. The cables connect to each individual computer. Older KVM switches used PS/2 connections for keyboards and mice. The VGA DB-15 connection is still found on most KVM switches. There can be some video compatibility problems associated with

KVM switches designed for VGA technology when connected to high-definition monitors. These monitors sometimes use pins to exchange information with the computer. These pins are not assigned between the HDMI and DB-15 connections and may not support special video functions, but basic video is still supported. There are special adapters made to correct these video problems by simulating the missing connection pins.

Switching from one computer to the next with a KVM switch is accomplished either through push buttons located on the switch or via assigned key combinations on the keyboard.

A special KVM switch called KVM over IP (iKVM) uses a network to exchange commands from a centralized keyboard and mouse with individual computers and servers located on the network. Each computer or server has a specialized video capture card installed. The video capture card captures the screen display at each location and transmits the image back to a centralized iKVM-designated computer. The computer can then send keyboard and mouse instructions to each computer via the network connection.

Chapter Summary

- HID is a set of standards written for hardware device drivers to ensure compatibility between hardware devices and computers.

- Keyboard scan codes are interpreted by the BIOS and sent to the CPU as an ASCII character.

- An optical mouse uses a light beam, receiver, CMOS digital camera, and microprocessor to derive its relative direction of movement and speed.

- A bar code reader uses a light source transmitter and receiver to read bar codes; the digital camera and scanner both depend on either the CCD or CMOS technology to capture images.

- The major touch screen technologies are resistance, capacitance, near field effect, infrared, and acoustical wave.

- Bluetooth, Wi-Fi, and IEEE 802.11 use the 2.4-GHz radio frequency; Wi-Fi and 802.11 use the 2.4-GHz and 5-GHz radio frequency; UWB and WUSB use the 3.1-GHz to 10.6-GHz radio frequencies.

- Device Manager, Devices and Printers, and the Ease of Access Center can be used to manage computer input devices.

Review Questions

Answer the following questions on a separate sheet of paper. Please do not write in this book.

1. What does the acronym HID represent?
2. What is the purpose of the HID set of standards?
3. What are the four types of keyboard switches?
4. How is a keyboard scan code generated and interpreted?
5. Scan codes are always equal to ASCII codes. True or False?
6. How does an optical mouse operate?
7. What are the three most common ways to connect a keyboard or mouse to a computer?
8. What is the commonly used IRQ setting for a mouse connected to a PS/2 port?
9. Which IRQ is used for a USB mouse or USB keyboard?
10. What two items does a bar code reader use to read bar codes?
11. What do a scanner and camera use to capture images?
12. What is a CCD?
13. Identify five touch screen technologies that are incorporated into the touch screen matrix.
14. What type of touch screen would you use in a dusty environment?
15. What type of touch screen would you choose for a medical surgical room where the staff commonly wears rubber or latex gloves?
16. What is the main advantage of RF over infrared technology?
17. What common radio frequency does Bluetooth and Wi-Fi use?
18. What standard is associated with wireless keyboard and mouse devices?
19. List four devices that can interfere with a wireless RF device.
20. What frequencies are supported by the UWB specifications?
21. In the **Properties** dialog box for a device, what does it mean when the **Roll Back Driver** option appears dimmed?
22. What Windows feature is used to make the user experience better for people with disabilities?

Sample A+ Exam Questions

Answer the following questions on a separate sheet of paper. Please do not write in this book.

1. Which two connection ports are most commonly associated with keyboards? Select all that apply.
   a. 15-pin D shell
   b. PS/2
   c. USB
   d. LPT1

2. Which type of device is most commonly associated with HID?
   a. Laser printer
   b. LCD display
   c. Mouse
   d. Portable device battery

3. A wireless optical mouse was installed properly and worked fine for two months. Now it fails to respond. The user has tried rebooting the computer, but the mouse still does not work. What is *most likely* the cause of failure?
   a. An incorrect driver
   b. A recent Windows update
   c. The battery
   d. Radio interference from the keyboard

4. Which best defines a keyboard scan code?
   a. A keyboard scan code is a signal generated when a key is struck on the keyboard. It determines what symbol is displayed on the monitor.
   b. A keyboard scan code is a signal generated by the keyboard scan generator. It checks what key is being pressed and then generates the corresponding ASCII symbol.
   c. A keyboard scan code is a binary code that records the duration that a key is held down.
   d. A keyboard scan code is generated by the CPU and then sent to the keyboard to identify which key is being pressed.

5. The physical design of a keyboard is referred to as what?
   a. Ergonomics
   b. Ecology
   c. Carpalmatics
   d. Physiology

6. Which of the following items is best for cleaning a keyboard?
   a. Glass cleaner
   b. A solution of 50% alcohol and 50% water
   c. Dry compressed air
   d. Any vacuum cleaner

7. Which technology does an optical mouse use?
   a. Wireless radio communications model
   b. Magnetic wheel that converts a light signal into digital pulses
   c. CMOS technology similar to digital camera technology
   d. Friction surface detection matrix

8. Which frequency is typically associated with Bluetooth and Wi-Fi devices?
   a. 2.4 GHz
   b. 24 MHz
   c. 5 GHz
   d. 5 MHz

9. Which is the correct path to access the mouse configuration speed setting on a Windows 7 computer?
   a. **Start | Mouse | Settings**
   b. **Start | Control Panel | Hardware and Sound | Devices and Printers | Mouse**
   c. **Start | Control Panel | Pointing Device**
   d. **Start | Control Panel | Device Manager | Settings**

10. What similar light-sensitive devices do scanners and digital cameras use to acquire an image? Select all that apply.
    a. OCR
    b. CMOS
    c. ADC
    d. CCD

Suggested Laboratory Activities

Do not attempt any suggested laboratory activities without your instructor's permission. Certain activities can render the PC operating system inoperable.

1. Change the keyboard properties, such as the **Repeat rate** and **Repeat delay** settings, to see the effects on the keyboard.

2. Try installing a second language for the keyboard in Windows.

3. Open the **Mouse Properties** dialog box and change the appearance of the tail, click speed, and type of icon used for the mouse pointer.

4. Explore the Ease of Access Center to familiarize yourself with the available options.

Video and Audio Systems

8

After studying this chapter, you will be able to:

- Recall the characteristics common to all monitors.
- Explain the basic operation of a CRT, an LCD, and a gas-plasma monitor.
- Carry out general procedures for troubleshooting a video display.
- Use the generally-accepted guidelines to properly clean a display.
- Compare video adapter card types.
- Carry out a video card installation.
- Use the **Appearance and Personalization** dialog box to change the display properties.
- Identify computer monitor and home theater center connection types.
- Explain how data compression works.
- Explain analog-to-digital conversion.
- Explain the operation of microphones and speakers.
- Carry out a sound card installation.
- Recall common codecs and their characteristics.
- Select components to create a customized configuration to meet customer specifications.

A+ Exam—Key Points

The CompTIA A+ exam requires candidates to select components for a customized computer based on customer needs. You should be able to evaluate a computer system and decide if it is best for general computer use, graphic design work, audio and video editing, gaming, and similar applications.

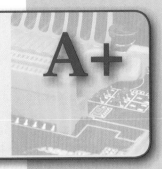

Key Terms

The following key terms will become important pieces of your computer vocabulary. Be sure you can define them.

active-matrix display
Advanced Video Coding (AVC)
alternating-frame rendering
aspect ratio
bitmap (BMP)
buffering
candela
cathode ray tube (CRT)
codec
color palette
color/graphics adapter (CGA)
contrast ratio
deflection yoke
degaussing
digital-to-analog converter (DAC)
dot pitch
electron guns
enhanced graphics adapter (EGA)
extended graphics array (XGA)
field
gas-plasma displays
home theater PC (HTPC)
inverter
LED monitor
liquid crystal display (LCD)
monochrome
Moving Picture Experts Group (MPEG)

multicolor/graphics array (MCGA)
multimedia
musical instrument digital interface (MIDI)
native resolution
organic LED display (OLED)
passive-matrix display
persistence
pixel
pixel pitch
polarized light
raster
refresh rate
resolution
response time
run-length encoding (RLE)
sampling
Scalable Link Interface (SLI)
shadow mask
split-frame rendering
super VGA (SVGA)
thin film transistor liquid crystal display (TFT-LCD)
vector graphics
video graphics array (VGA)
viewing angle

Video and audio systems are covered in this chapter, including computer displays, video cards, sound cards, and computer home entertainment systems. This chapter is critical to designing and evaluating a high-performance computer system or a computer-based home entertainment system. You will be introduced to common Microsoft operating system tools that will assist you in evaluating and designing a high-performance computer system. The video system is by far the most influential module that determines computer performance.

Video System and Display Aspects

The video system of a computer consists of two main components: the display (monitor) and the adapter. The video adapter is often called a *video card* or *graphics card*. There are some references made to legacy video systems in this chapter. Many of these legacy systems are no longer manufactured. This brief information, however, will help you understand the development of the computer video system as well as help you identify obsolete systems when you encounter them. There are still a number of these old technologies in existence. Being unable to identify them can be extremely frustrating and embarrassing to any technician.

> **Danger !**
>
> Do *not* open a computer monitor case for any reason. Inside a computer monitor you may encounter well over a thousand volts. A monitor should only be opened by a trained and qualified electronics technician.

Before examining monitor types and video cards, we will begin our discussion of video systems with color display values and resolution. Resolution greatly affects the quality of the picture produced as well as the price you will pay for the unit.

Color Display Values

The color display quality is determined by the number of bits used to represent the individual colors of red, green, and blue. The number of bits used to represent each color can determine the possible number of color shades. A byte contains 8 bits. This means that there are a total of 256 possible combinations of 1s and 0s in a byte. This means that an 8-bit color pattern can reproduce 256 intensities of a specific color. By mixing the intensities of red, blue, and green, other colors can be produced.

Figure 8-1 lists common standard color display values, expressed in bits. As the number of bits increases, so does the number of possible colors produced.

The color mix guide in **Figure 8-2** shows the application of 256,000 color intensities and the total spectrum of color produced by the monitor. This illustration is a screen capture taken from

Figure 8-2. With this color mix guide, you can display 256,000 color intensities and the total spectrum of color produced by the monitor.

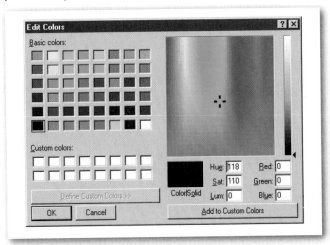

the **Edit Colors** dialog box from Microsoft's Paint program. Paint can be accessed through **Start | All Programs | Accessories**. Using the **Edit Colors** dialog box, you can create your own pallet of colors beyond the standard colors. By moving your mouse across the sample of colors in the display, the amount of red, blue, and green that make up the custom color is varied. In the bottom-right corner are three numeric text boxes. Each box contains the value of the color used to make the color indicated under the cursor. The values correspond to the 8-bit range (0 to 255). This is an example of a 24-bit color system.

Display Resolution

The term **resolution** refers to the amount of detail a monitor is capable of displaying. This term is also used to describe the detail produced by printers, digital cameras, and any similar type of graphic equipment. High resolution equals finer, better detail than low resolution. See **Figure 8-3** for a comparison of resolution patterns. The image in Figure 8-3A has a higher resolution than that in Figure 8-3B.

Resolution is measured in pixels (picture element). A **pixel** is the smallest unit of color in a screen display. Think of it as a small dot. A typical VGA system has a resolution of 640 × 480. This means a VGA display has a screen layout of 640 pixels by 480 pixels or a total of 307,200 pixels.

Figure 8-1. Common standard color display values.

Color Display Value	Number of Colors
8-bit	256
16-bit (True color)	65,536
24-bit (True color)	167,777,216
32-bit (True color)	4,294,967,296
48-bit (Deep color)	281,474,976,710,656

Goodheart-Willcox Publisher

Figure 8-3. A comparison of resolution patterns. A—The image is displayed at a relatively high resolution (600 dpi). B—The same image is shown at a low resolution (72 dpi).

A   B

Goodheart-Willcox Publisher

Some of the most common resolutions are listed in **Figure 8-4**.

When PCs first came to the marketplace, most displays were monochrome display adapter (MDA) monitors. **Monochrome** technology displayed only one color, usually amber or green. The video adapters for these monitors were designed to display text only, not graphics. Graphics required a good deal of memory, and at that time large amounts of memory were too expensive for most users. Early computers were used for business and research, not for entertainment. The screen resolution was 720 × 350, which presented a very sharp, clear image for text only.

In 1981, IBM introduced the **color/graphics adapter (CGA)**. This video standard offered two resolutions: 320 × 200 in four colors (from a choice of sixteen colors) and a higher resolution of 640 × 200 in two colors. Another company offered the Hercules adapter card. It met the requirements of graphics programs (such as AutoCAD) that the IBM adapter could not fulfill. The Hercules adapter card resolution was 720 × 348.

In 1987, IBM introduced the **enhanced graphics adapter (EGA)**. The EGA system could display 16 colors in 640 × 200 or 320 × 200 resolution on a standard IBM color monitor. In monochrome, it could display a 640 × 350 resolution. When the EGA was attached to an

Figure 8-4.
Chart of common resolutions.

Resolution	Acronym	Designation
640 × 480	VGA	Video graphics array
800 × 600	SVGA	Super video graphics array
1024 × 768	XGA	Extended graphics array
1280 × 1024	UVGA	Ultra video graphics array
1400 × 1050	SXGA	Super extended graphics array
1600 × 1200	UXGA	Ultra extended graphics array
1920 × 1200	WUXGA	Wide ultra extended graphics array

Goodheart-Willcox Publisher

enhanced color monitor, it could display 16 colors (from a choice of 64) in a resolution of 640 × 350.

The **video graphics array (VGA)** is the baseline for video adapters. The VGA standard was first introduced in 1987 with the IBM PS/2. VGA is the true minimum standard for video monitors at a resolution of 640 × 480 and 16 colors. Up to 256 colors can be displayed, but the resolution is reduced to 320 × 200.

The VGA palette contains 262,144 (256k) different colors. A **color palette** is a collection of possible different colors usually in degrees or shades, which can be displayed on a monitor. The palette contains a large variety of possible colors, but the total number of colors in the palette cannot be displayed at the same time on a monitor. For example, a video system such as VGA that can display up to 256 colors in the 320 × 200 mode can only use 256 colors from the total 262,144 colors possible in the palette.

Think of the color palette as the total number of tubes of color an artist has available to purchase from a supplier. While there may be 262,144 colors in the store, the artist can only afford to buy 256 tubes. Thus, the actual number of colors used for the painting is limited to the 256 colors. In the same way, while there are 262,144 colors that can be displayed in VGA, the video adapter can only support 256 of the total number at one time.

Also in 1987, the PS/2 display adapter 8514 was also introduced. It had better resolution than VGA and offered more colors. It supported a resolution of 1024 × 768 pixels with 256 colors. There were some disadvantages to the system, however. First, the system plugged into IBM micro-channel architecture. Second, to take full advantage of its capabilities, an 8514 color display monitor had to be used. This PS/2 display adapter was replaced by the IBM XGA standard. It is interesting to note that EGA, VGA, and the PS/2 adapter 8514 came out at about the same time. However, only VGA survived the consumer marketplace.

Another standard of the time was **multicolor/ graphics array (MCGA)**. The MCGA adapter could support CGA, and also provided up to 64 shades of gray when more color variations than the standard CGA were required to be displayed.

Tech Tip

When a computer system detects a malfunction, it will start in safe mode, which only supports the minimum video standard of VGA. The VGA mode driver is located in the first 1 MB of memory, while more sophisticated drivers require memory above the first 1 MB. Windows 8 requires a minimum resolution of 1024 × 768, which is much higher and requires more memory.

Super VGA (SVGA) supports 16 million possible colors and various resolutions such as 800 × 600, 1024 × 768, 1280 × 1024, and 1600 × 1200. The exact number of colors that can be displayed at the same time on an SVGA monitor is determined by the amount of memory. The higher the memory, the higher the number of colors produced.

In 1990, IBM introduced the **extended graphics array (XGA)**. This video standard is capable of a resolution of 640 × 480 while supporting 65,536 colors and 1024 × 768 with 256 colors. It also supports all of IBM's older graphic standards.

A+ Note

Windows 8 requires a minimum resolution of 1024 × 768, or Extended Graphics Array (XGA). Previous versions of Windows still support the original 800 × 600 resolution, or Super VGA (SVGA).

The UVGA, SXGA, UXGA, and WUXGA screen resolutions naturally evolved from the original VGA and XGA screen resolutions. They are all capable of producing over 16 million colors and are capable of supporting the high-definition television (HDTV) standard of resolution. When you see a display that is very wide, it will be usually UXGA or WUXGA. These resolutions are normally used to match the very wide display units.

Tech Tip

You will see the label Ultra VGA used in advertising. Ultra VGA is not a true standard but rather a marking terminology that is used by manufacturers to describe their video adapters and monitors in an enhanced description.

A+ Note

The A+ Certification exams will often contain a question referring to the VGA resolution. This is because VGA is the default resolution during the safe mode startup process.

When the Windows operating system starts in safe mode, the screen resolution changes to 640 × 480, the original VGA standard. Compare the 640 × 480 resolution, **Figure 8-5**, to the standard 1024 × 768 XGA resolution, **Figure 8-6**. Notice how much larger the desktop icons appear when in the VGA screen resolution of safe mode. There will be more about safe mode in Chapter 15—PC Troubleshooting.

Types of Video Displays

There are a number of different types of display systems for computers. The two most common types are the cathode ray tube (CRT) and the liquid crystal display (LCD). See **Figure 8-7** and **Figure 8-8**. As the television industry merges computer and television technology into a single display unit, it will no longer be possible to distinguish a computer monitor from a television. Because of this, the gas plasma display will also be discussed in this chapter. This section covers the basic operation and principles of all three display

Figure 8-5.
Windows Vista in safe mode. The resolution is 640 × 480, which is the resolution of the original VGA standard.

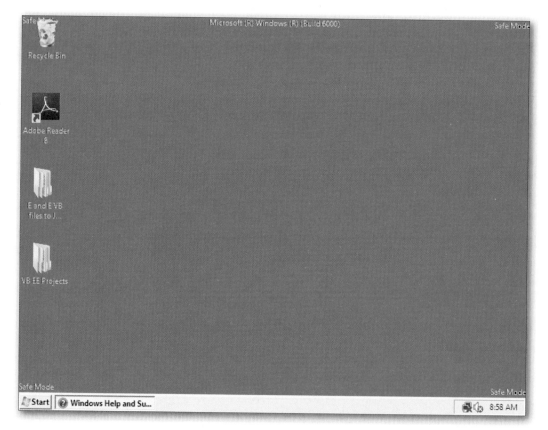

Figure 8-6. Windows Vista desktop in 1024 × 768 XGA resolution.

Figure 8-7. CRT display used with a desktop computer.

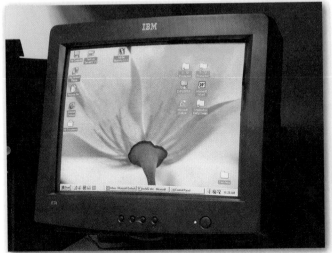

Goodheart-Willcox Publisher

Figure 8-8. The LCD monitor, because of its thin profile, takes up less desktop space than the CRT.

Goodheart-Willcox Publisher

technologies and the terminology with which they are commonly associated.

Cathode Ray Tube Displays

A **cathode ray tube (CRT)** is a glass tube in which electrons are used to produce a picture. A beam of electrons sweeps across the glass tube, exciting phosphorous dots in the screen. To understand how a CRT monitor works, you must first understand some basic electricity concepts. A brief discussion of electron theory will help you understand how the flow of electrons can create an image on a screen.

When electrons flow through a wire, similar to a filament in a lightbulb, heat and light are produced. The filament is placed inside a glass-enclosed vacuum. A vacuum contains no oxygen. Oxygen is needed for supporting fire, thus the vacuum prevents the destruction of the filament by burning. The vacuum prevents the wire from burning while producing the heat and light.

This is the most you usually need to know about a lightbulb. But, in addition to the heat and light, a cloud of electrons forms around the filament. The greater the electron flow through the filament, the larger the cloud of electrons. The movement and direction of the cloud of electrons can be controlled by a magnetic field. By shaping a magnetic field into a ring, the electron cloud can be shaped into a beam of electrons. The beam direction can also be deflected by magnetic fields. The formation of an electron beam and the action of deflecting the direction of the beam are the underlying principles behind producing an image on a CRT monitor and on a CRT-based television. See **Figure 8-9**.

Danger ! A CRT is under a vacuum condition. When broken, the pieces of glass will at first be sucked into the glass envelope and will then burst into the surrounding area. Severe damage to personnel can occur from a monitor tube bursting.

Figure 8-9. CRT-based televisions and CRT computer monitors use the same electronic principles to produce images.

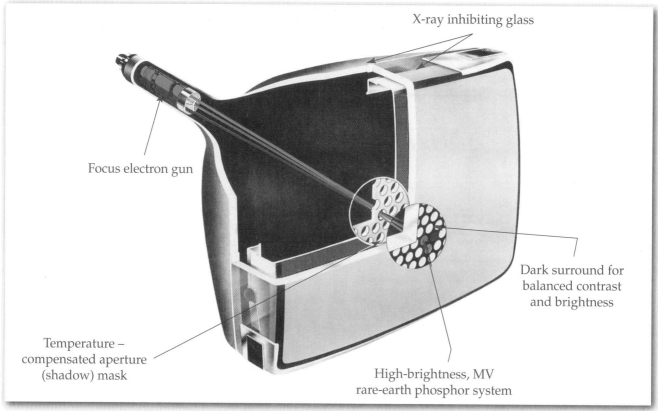

X-ray inhibiting glass

Focus electron gun

Dark surround for balanced contrast and brightness

Temperature – compensated aperture (shadow) mask

High-brightness, MV rare-earth phosphor system

Three **electron guns** are located at the back of the CRT. Electron guns produce the electron beam, which sweeps across the inside of the monitor screen. The CRT **deflection yoke** area contains electromagnets used to deflect the electron beam in a CRT. The intensity of the magnets can be changed to deflect the electron beam horizontally and vertically. The deflection yoke controls the location where each of the three electronic beams strikes the screen area.

The beam then passes through a metal mesh called a **shadow mask**. The shadow mask is designed as a pattern of triangular or rectangular holes. The shadow mask pattern of holes limits the area of the screen the electron beam can strike. The design of the shadow mask holes produces a much sharper image than would be produced without the shadow mask. The shadow mask determines the dot pitch of the monitor. The beam passes through the shadow mask and strikes the inside of the display screen.

The screen area is coated with phosphorus material. The phosphorus material is spread across the screen of the monitor in a pattern of red, blue, and green. When the electronic beam strikes the red, green, or blue phosphorus material, the phosphorus material emits a glow of light in the corresponding color. The intensity of the electron beam is directly related to the intensity of color produced in the area struck by the beam. The phosphor-coated areas continue to glow after the electron beam ceases to strike the area. The

continuation of the glow after the beam leaves the area is called **persistence**. The persistence of the color glow must last long enough so it does not disappear before the electron beam strikes the phosphor again. By mixing the intensities of the three colors, a complete spectrum of colors can be produced. See **Figure 8-10**.

As you can see in the illustration, the color white is produced when each of the three colors is at equal intensity. The color black is produced when there is complete absence of intensity. Varying the degree of intensity of the three-color combinations produces other color hues.

Cathode ray tubes, or picture tubes, can suffer from color fade or discoloration caused by remnant magnetic fields on the tube. The correction of the remnant magnetic field is called **degaussing**. CRT monitors have a degaussing feature built in. The user simply presses a button mounted somewhere on the monitor to degauss the unit.

Monitor Size

Sizes of CRT monitors are similar to CRT-based television sets. The length of a diagonal drawn from one corner to the opposite corner determines the size of a monitor. See **Figure 8-11**. Standard CRT monitor sizes are 14″, 15″, 17″, 19″, and 21″. The actual viewing area is approximately 10% less than the diagonal measurement, though it varies from monitor to monitor.

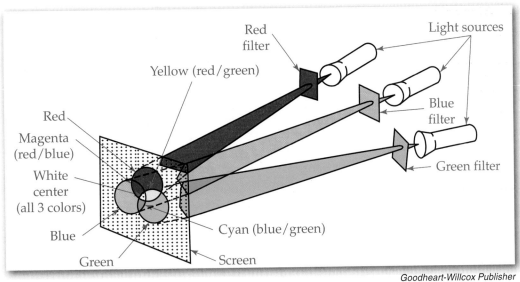

Figure 8-10.
Red, green, and blue are the basic colors used in a CRT.

Goodheart-Willcox Publisher

Figure 8-11. Computer display screen sizes are measured on the diagonal.

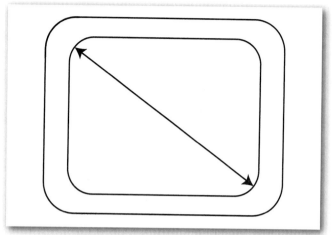

Goodheart-Willcox Publisher

A+ Note

Most PC systems use a three-row 15-pin D-shell connector for the monitor. The game port is usually a two-row 15-pin D-shell connector. The A+ Certification exams may ask a question about identifying one of these two ports on the PC.

Dot Pitch

The **dot pitch** is the distance measured in millimeters between two color dots on the screen. It is a measurement that reflects the quality of the image displayed. Generally, if the monitor has a smaller dot pitch than another monitor, it produces a higher quality (sharper) image. An acceptable standard dot pitch is from 0.28 mm to 0.25 mm. The dot pitch cannot be adjusted. It is manufactured into the screen.

Refresh Rate

The rate at which the beam sweeps across the screen is called the **refresh rate**. The refresh rate of most computer monitors can be adjusted in **Control Panel** using the **Display Properties** dialog box. Often, screen flicker can be corrected by increasing the refresh rate. A high refresh

rate is good for someone who must spend long hours in front of a computer display because it reduces eyestrain when using a CRT display. The downside of a high refresh rate is that it takes away from CPU time that could otherwise be used for processing information. Windows operating systems provide many user configuration options for the display.

> ### Tech Tip
> The original definition of the term *refresh rate* referred to CRT monitors, which produces images based on raster. LCD monitors still use the term *refresh rate*, but the definition means the rate at which the entire image is reproduced. An LCD monitor does not use raster.

The **Screen Resolution** dialog box provides links to other configuration windows, **Figure 8-12**. These windows list information about the display and video adapter and present options for configuring the display and video card properties. The **List All Modes** dialog box lists values such as screen resolution, color depth, and refresh rate. The refresh rate is expressed as Hertz (Hz) and is a measurement of electrical frequency. You can think of Hertz as a unit of measurement to express the number of times an electrical characteristic occurs. When used in the **List All Modes** dialog box, Hertz expresses the refresh rate of the display and adapter.

Raster Display

The electronic beam sweeps across the screen horizontally from left to right. The sweep of the beam is called a **raster**. The sweep from left to right is repeated each time lower on the screen until the bottom of the screen is reached. This method of producing a picture on a monitor is called *raster display*. A complete sweep of the entire screen area is called a **field**. The entire field is completed sixty times each second.

Not all monitors make one continuous sweep vertically down the screen. Some complete the process in two steps. First, all of the odd number lines are swept, and then all of the even lines are swept. This method of producing a complete frame is called *interlacing*. Some display units,

Figure 8-12. Windows 7 **Screen Resolution** dialog box and options. The **Properties** dialog box for the monitor and graphics card is accessed through **Screen Resolution | Advanced settings**. The **List All Modes** dialog box is accessed through **Screen Resolution | Advanced settings | List All Modes**.

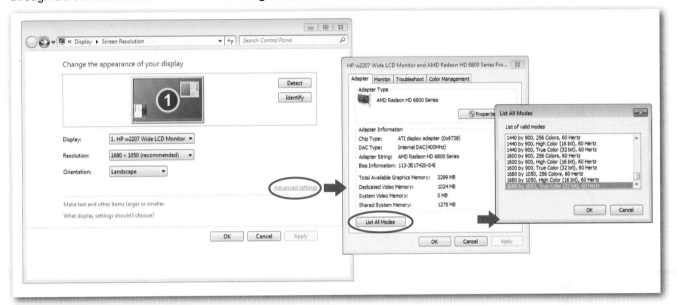

especially LCD panels, use a technique known as *progressive scan*. Progressive scan displays the image on the monitor line by line in sequence from top to bottom.

When a display specifies progressive scan, it uses the lowercase *p* and for interlacing it uses the lower case *i*. For example, 1080p means a 1080 resolution, progressive scan; 1080i means 1080 resolution, interlacing.

Warning ! The typical PC technician should never disassemble a monitor. If for some reason it is required, never wear an anti-static wrist strap when working on a monitor. You must avoid grounding yourself. The CRT can contain voltage in excess of 20,000 volts even when unplugged! The CRT tube can retain a high-voltage charge for some time, similar to a capacitor.

Liquid Crystal Displays

The most common flat-panel display is the **liquid crystal display (LCD)**. The liquid crystal display operates on two principles. The first is polarized light. The second is the effect of an electrical voltage applied to a crystal structure.

A typical light beam is composed of numerous waves of light. The waves of light travel in parallel but at different wave angles. When a thin slot is cut in a material such as metal, only light waves with an angle matching the slot can travel through the slot. The light that travels through the slot is polarized light. **Polarized light** is light energy composed of light beams with a matching wave angle.

The second principle is based on the effect of electrical voltage applied to a crystal structure. When an electrical voltage is applied to a crystal, the crystal changes shape slightly, or twists. The degree of twist is directly related to the amount of voltage applied to the crystal. Light normally passes through the crystal in a straight line. When a light is shone through a crystal and voltage is then applied to the same crystal, the angle of the light wave changes as it passes through the crystal. These two principles, polarized light and voltage effect on crystals, is the basis of how all LCD displays work.

How Liquid Crystal Displays Work

To fully understand how the typical liquid crystal display works, follow along while referring to **Figure 8-13**. The LCD panel is constructed of several thin layers of material. A thin fluorescent

Figure 8-13. The liquid crystal is used to twist the light wave.

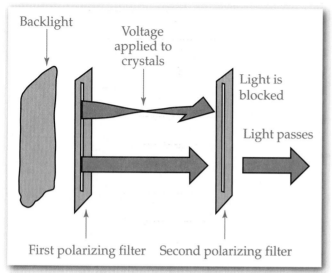

Goodheart-Willcox Publisher

backlight is used as the source of light energy for the display. When the backlight strikes through the first layer, only light waves with an angle matching the slot can pass through the filter. The light waves that pass through the slot are polarized light because they all have a matching wave angle.

The polarized light passes through the array of crystals. Each crystal has a transistor connected to it. The transistor acts similar to a dimmer light switch, which can be turned on in varying degrees. The amount of voltage applied to each crystal by the individual transistors determines the amount of twist in each crystal. Any crystal that has voltage applied to it causes the angle of the light beam to change as it passes through the crystal. The amount of change in the light wave angle is determined by the amount of voltage applied to each crystal.

The second filter is used to screen out light waves that are no longer polarized. The amount of change in each light wave determines how much of the polarized light can pass through the second filter. For example, a light beam passing through a crystal with a maximum voltage applied will have its angle changed to the extent that none of the light energy will pass through the second filter. This creates a dark pixel image on the display. A light beam passing through a crystal with no voltage applied will not have its angle changed

and will therefore pass through the second filter. This creates a pixel image at full brightness. The amount of light and dark pixels directly relates to the applied voltage at each crystal.

Backlighting

The liquid crystal display requires some form of backlighting. The two sources of backlighting are Cold Cathode Fluorescent Lamp (CCFL) and light-emitting diode (LED). The Cold Cathode Fluorescent Lamp is similar to the fluorescent tubes you see in office and school lighting, only much smaller and thinner.

A CCFL consists of a glass tube filled with a gas. Each end of the tube has an electrode. When high voltage is applied to the two electrodes, an electrical circuit is created through the gas in the tube. The electrons flowing through the gas-filled tube create light. Normally, a computer monitor or television has a 120-Vac electrical supply. When no such supply is available and the portable device is required to be energized by a power source such as a battery, an inverter is required. An **inverter** is an electronic device that converts the low voltage (12–18 Vdc) from the portable battery to a much higher voltage required by the CCFL, **Figure 8-14**. The CCFL may require as much as 1,200 Vac for initial lighting and on average as much as 800 Vac to maintain the light. The voltage range during normal operation, including dimming, can be as low as 200 Vac.

Another type of backlight used for portable devices is light-emitting diode (LED). An LED is an electronic device that emits light when a dc voltage is applied to it. **Figure 8-15** shows the construction of a single LED light.

LED Displays

A portable LCD screen that uses an LED backlight is often referred to as an **LED monitor**, or *LED TV*. An LED monitor is still a form of an LCD monitor. The only difference in the product names "LCD monitor" and "LED monitor" is that an LED monitor uses a set of LEDs as the source of backlighting rather than a CCFL.

LED backlighting is typically assembled in one of two ways. Either a series of LEDs are located along all four edges of the display or a matrix of LEDs is spread across the back of the

Figure 8-14. High-voltage ac is required to conduct electricity through the CCFL gas tube, thus creating light. An LCD panel for a portable device requires an inverter to change the low-voltage dc battery power to a much higher ac voltage.

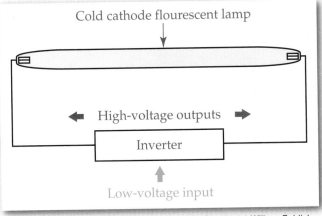

Cold cathode flourescent lamp

High-voltage outputs

Inverter

Low-voltage input

Goodheart-Willcox Publisher

Figure 8-15. An LED backlight is made up of multiple LEDs. An LED is an electronic device that emits light when a dc voltage is applied.

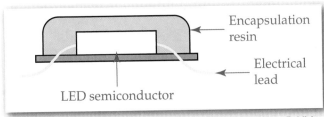

Encapsulation resin

Electrical lead

LED semiconductor

Goodheart-Willcox Publisher

display. CCFL display assemblies typically consist of two CCFLs: one at the top of the display and the other at the bottom. Only one inverter is required for the two CCFLs.

A much thinner display can be created using LED backlighting. The LED assembly is much more compact as compared to the CCFL/inverter assembly. Also, the LED backlighting is less fragile as compared to CCFL. The CCFL uses a glass tube whereas the LED is encapsulated in a resin bubble. The LED is the preferred technology for portable devices such as phones, tablets, and some laptop computers because the display can be fabricated much thinner than with CCFL and it can better resist physical damage.

When troubleshooting LCD display problems, one of the most common reasons for LCD failure

is a bad inverter. The inverter can be replaced, but in most cases, the entire display is simply replaced because of the age of the display unit. Inverter failure is indicated by a black or very dim display that cannot be brightened. Another problem is when an individual transistor fails in the display. The characteristic of a failed transistor is a persistent black or white spot on an LCD display. This type of problem cannot be fixed. The display must be replaced.

A dark area on a display is an indication of a section of backlight failure. The exact location would be directly related to the type and arrangement of the backlight. For example, a backlight arrangement in a matrix may have a failure of one small section, resulting in a dark area at the location of the small section of backlighting. An edge type of backlight may result in one section of the edge producing a dark area. This condition is not easily corrected and may result in replacing the entire display.

Organic LED Displays

An **organic LED display (OLED)** is a new technology and can create the thinnest display made today. The name *organic* means that the construction of the LED is from carbon-based materials rather than crystalline structures used for traditional electronic components. Living things are carbon based and referred to as organic, hence the term *organic* as applied to electronic components. The impression of organic LED has led some people to believe that the LED material is made from living organisms, which is not true.

The biggest advantage of OLED devices is they can be much thinner than devices of previous technologies. The OLED can be mounted on flexible plastic or flexible thin metal. Also, the displays are much more durable than those of previous technologies. This makes the typical protective layer of glass optional. See **Figure 8-16** and note how thin the television display is. The same OLED technology applied to the television display is also being used for tablets, phones, and computer displays.

Another term you will encounter is *active-matrix organic light-emitting diode (AMOLED)* when reading about OLED displays. The active matrix is composed of TFT technology and used to

Figure 8-16.
LG OLED television. Notice how thin the LG OLED television is in the side view.

Front view   Side view

LG Electronics, Inc.

select and electrify individual pixels in the OLED display. Active-matrix displays, passive-matrix displays, and TFT technology are explained in the following sections.

Passive-Matrix Display

There are two types of electrical circuitry used to energize the crystal area of a liquid crystal display: passive and active, **Figure 8-17**. A **passive-matrix display** consists of a grid of semitransparent conductors that run to each crystal. The crystals are used as part of the individual pixel areas. The grid is divided into two major circuits: columns and rows. Transistors running along the top and the side of the display unit head the columns and rows. A ground applied to a row and a charge applied to a column activates a pixel area. The voltage is applied briefly and must rely on screen persistence and a fast refresh rate. Because current must travel along the row and column until it arrives at the designated pixel, response time is slow.

Active-Matrix Display

In an **active-matrix display**, each pixel in the grid has its own transistor. The active-matrix provides a better image than the passive-matrix.

The active-matrix image is brighter because each cell can have a constant supply of voltage.

The most common active-matrix display is the **thin film transistor liquid crystal display (TFT-LCD)**. Often, this type of display is referred to simply as a TFT display. The TFT display consists of a matrix of thin film transistors spread across the entire screen. Each transistor controls a single pixel on the display. There are over one million transistors in a display, three transistors at each pixel area, one transistor for each color pixel, **Figure 8-18**. The liquid crystals in the TFT display are energized in a pattern representing the data to be displayed.

The conventional television has used the CRT to display images because the original LCD design had limitations that could not compete with larger display units. As the size of the display unit grew to over 18″, problems developed with the brightness of the display and in converting the analog television signal to a digital signal and to a wide-angle viewing area without image distortions. These problems were solved with the introduction of thin film transistor LCD technology. The advantages of LCD over legacy CRT displays are the following:

- LCDs can be constructed much smaller and are lighter in weight and thinner in design than CRT displays.

Figure 8-17. In an active-matrix display, each cell in the grid has its own transistor. The active-matrix provides a better image than does the passive.

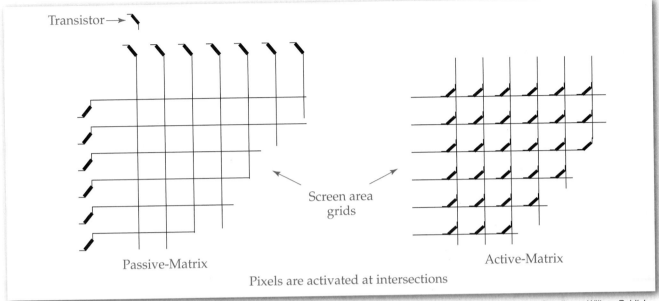

Goodheart-Willcox Publisher

- LCDs are more economical to run because they require less power.
- LCDs generate less heat.
- LCDs create more detailed images.
- LCDs produce less electromagnetic interference (EMI).

Contrast Ratio

Contrast ratio is a numeric expression in the form of a ratio that describes the amount of contrast between the darkest and lightest pixel in the image. The higher the ratio, the better the colors will be represented on the display unit. This is a very important display characteristic that correlates closely to the overall quality of the display. For example, a display with a high contrast ratio will be able to do a better job of displaying finer details of an image. Contrast ratios typically range from 500:1 to 1000:1. A contrast ratio of over 800:1 is considered a high-quality display.

Brightness

Brightness in an LCD is produced by backlighting. The maximum amount of brightness produced in the display is determined by this

Figure 8-18. Each pixel area on the TFT display consists of three transistor-controlled color fields. The three color fields—red, green, and blue—are combined to form various shades and hues of color.

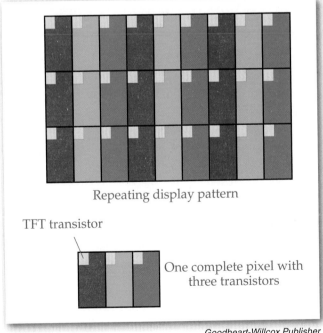

Goodheart-Willcox Publisher

light source. Brightness levels typically range from 200 cd/m² (candela per square meter) to 500 or more cd/m². A **candela** is a light measurement based on candle illumination. Many people confuse light measurement with watts or wattage. Wattage is a measurement of electrical energy, not light energy. While electrical energy often directly relates to the amount of light produced, there is not a direct correlation between electrical energy and light when comparing different light technologies such as the case of incandescent and fluorescent light. For example, a fluorescent light and an incandescent light use two different electrical technologies for generating light. The amount of power consumed measured in watts does not accurately represent the amount of light provided when comparing different technologies.

Brightness is also a main factor for determining if the monitor will adequately display an image in a bright environment such as an outdoor area.

Viewing Angle

The **viewing angle** is a measurement of the angle at which a person can adequately see an image on a display without it looking excessively distorted. As a person's angle to the screen increases, the image displayed becomes increasingly washed out until the image disappears. See **Figure 8-19**.

The viewing angle of early models of LCD panels was quite limited and could not compete with CRT screens. Today, the viewing angle is of less concern because almost all LCD panels have a very acceptable viewing angle. The actual viewing angle of a display varies from manufacturer to manufacturer, but the minimum viewing angle is typically 150°. Top-of-the-line displays have a viewing angle of 170° or more. To match the viewing angle of a CRT, the viewing angle of the LCD panel must be at least 170°.

Pixel Pitch

Pixel pitch is similar to CRT dot pitch. Pixel pitch is the distance between two same color pixels on the display area. In other words, pixel pitch is the distance between two red pixels or two green pixels. Each color pixel is composed of three pels, one pel for each of the three colors

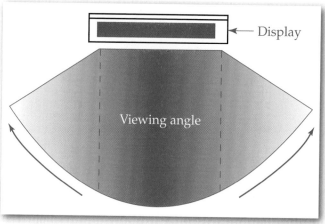

Figure 8-19. The viewing angle defines the locations where the screen can be viewed comfortably without distortion. As the angle of view increases, the image appears increasingly washed out until the image disappears.

Goodheart-Willcox Publisher

that compose a pixel. Pixel pitch is expressed in millimeters (mm).

Native Resolution

An LCD is capable of displaying a number of different resolutions. The **native resolution** is the resolution that matches the pixel design of the display. For example, if a display has a native resolution of 1280 × 1024 then it will display images best at 1280 × 1024. If a resolution other than the native resolution is chosen, an image will appear slightly blurred in some areas. The LCD is manufactured with a set number of pixels. Because a set number of actual pixels are used to generate an image, the display will operate as a bitmap device, its image blurring when the scale is changed. When a screen resolution other than native is selected, the display controller must either add or remove pixels from the image before it is displayed on the screen. The process of adding or removing pixels causes the image to appear slightly blurred. This is especially true when displaying a much higher or much lower resolution image.

See **Figure 8-20** and compare the screen resolutions. The top image is the recommended or native resolution of 1650 × 1050. The bottom image is the non-native resolution of 1280 × 800. Notice how much the non-native resolution distorts the images. Pay particular attention to

Figure 8-20.
Comparison of native resolution to non-native resolution. Native resolution (top) produces a much sharper image as compared to non-native resolution (bottom).

the way the screen text "Change the appearance of your display" is distorted and blurred. The native resolution produces the sharpest image with the least distortion of the original images and text.

Response Time

The **response time** is the amount of time it takes a TFT pixel to display after a signal is sent to the transistor controlling that pixel. Response time is measured in milliseconds (ms). A typical response time ranges from 15 ms to 40 ms. The lower the response time, the better the quality of the display unit. A quick response time is required for quality animation. A high response time can cause a slight flicker or breaks in the animation presented on the screen. It is interesting to note that the CRT is better at displaying animation or full motion video than the early designed LCD. LCD monitors today can have refresh rates many times faster than legacy CRT displays and produce much better animation.

Monitor Size

The monitor size of an LCD is measured in a similar fashion to a CRT screen—in a diagonal line across the front panel of the display. The big difference between the LCD monitor and the CRT monitor is no display size is lost to the area around the perimeter of the screen. As you recall from earlier in the chapter, a CRT monitor has an actual image display smaller than the screen's measured size. An LCD screen size is the same as the image to be displayed. There is no display size loss. A 16″ LCD monitor can and will display a 16″ image, while a 16″ CRT monitor will display less than the measured size.

Aspect Ratio

Aspect ratio refers to the ratio of the display area's height and width. A typical CRT screen is based on the television standard ratio of 4:3. The width is represented by the number 4 and the height is represented by the number 3. A newer wide-aspect ratio became a standard

with the introduction of HDTV. The wide-aspect ratio found on most LCD panels is 16:10. See **Figure 8-21** for a comparison of the two aspect ratios.

The wide-aspect ratio width allows more information to be displayed on the monitor and matches the HDTV standard for display systems. The development of the wide-aspect ratio has created a need for newer video resolution standard identification. The new identifications allow a user to select a resolution that more closely matches the design of the monitor. The resolution standards designed for wide-aspect ratio use the prefix "W" to describe the modified standard resolution. For example, an XGA resolution based on the traditional 4:3 ratio is identified as WXGA when it is modified for the 16:10 ratio.

Gas-Plasma Displays

Gas-plasma displays are flat-panel displays that operate on the principle of electroluminescence. Electroluminescence is the display of light created when a high frequency passes through a gas to a layer of phosphor, resulting in the release of photons. The electrical energy from releasing photons is better known as producing light. A gas-plasma display consists of millions of tiny cells sandwiched between two glass plates. See **Figure 8-22**. Each cell contains an inert gas and is coated with a phosphorous material of red, blue, or green.

Transparent electrodes run horizontally behind the front panel on top of the cells. Address electrodes run vertically along the rear glass panel beneath the cells. When an address electrode

Figure 8-21.
The aspect ratio is an expression of the relationship of height to width of the screen area. The aspect ratio for HDTV screens is wider than traditional screens.

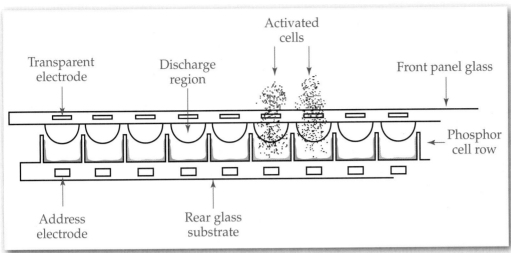

Figure 8-22.
Gas-plasma technology.

Transparent electrode

Discharge region

Activated cells

Front panel glass

Phosphor cell row

Address electrode

Rear glass substrate

Goodheart-Willcox Publisher

and its corresponding transparent electrode are energized, the gas, in an exited plasma state, releases an ultraviolet light. The ultraviolet light strikes the phosphorus coating inside the cell causing the cell to release a light corresponding to its color. By varying the pulses of current, the entire light spectrum can be duplicated such as orange, yellow, and brown.

The top electrode is called the row electrode and the bottom electrode is called the column electrode. A column and row electrode forms a junction point. Each junction point conforms to a memory address. The microprocessor sends information to the memory address and to the monitor. The junction points become energized in a pattern reflective of the computer memory pattern.

The biggest difference between an LCD and a gas-plasma display is the gas-plasma display does not require a backlight. Each cell in a gas-plasma display generates its own light. For this reason, a gas-plasma display can be manufactured much thinner than an LCD, with the exception of the OLED display.

Troubleshooting Video Displays

Troubleshooting displays is quite simple since there are no serviceable parts inside CRT or LCD monitors. You simply replace a suspected monitor

with another. Before changing the monitor, you should do the following:

- Check if the monitor is turned on.
- Check if the power cord is plugged in.
- Check if the wall outlet has voltage.
- Check the video cable between the computer and the display unit.

If after changing the monitor you still have a problem, you should check the video card. First, reseat the video card in its slot. Sometimes an oxidation builds up on the card edge connections. Reseating the card will remove the oxidation, and the card will begin to work again. If reseating the card does not produce the desired results, simply replace the video card.

Many motherboards incorporate the video chipset directly on the motherboard; there is no video card in any slot. When this is the case, simply install a video card into any available slot that is compatible with the video card. This will not always work because when the video chipset is built in as part of the motherboard and it is defective, it may prevent another video card from working. It will mainly depend on the type of electronics failure in the chipset. Also, be aware that other items such as a telephone modem or network card could prevent a computer system from completing the POST and thus make it appear as a video problem. There will be more about this type of scenario in Chapter 15—PC Troubleshooting.

Before replacing the video card, you should reinstall or update the video card drivers. Drivers often become corrupted and many times replacing the drivers or updating the drivers corrects the problem.

> ## A+ Note
>
> On the A+ Certification exams there is always at least one question on how to troubleshoot a display unit. The tips in this section should provide sufficient information to answer most questions concerning troubleshooting the display unit.

Cleaning Video Displays

There is always much debate and conflicting methods for cleaning displays. Always consult the manufacturer documentation. The following information contains the generally-accepted guidelines for properly cleaning displays.

Never clean a display while it is energized. Always unplug the electrical supply before cleaning the display.

Clean the display area using a dry lint-free soft cloth designed for screen display cleaning to remove dust. For more persistent smudges, use a slightly dampened lint-free soft cloth. Never use detergent to clean the plastic display case surface. Detergents will often leave a white residue on the surface after drying. CRT monitors have a glass covering while LCD monitors do not. An LCD monitor uses a plastic cover and can be easily damage by chemical solutions, except ones designed specifically for cleaning LCD displays.

Never use a paper towel to clean an LCD monitor. Paper towels are often made with course fibers which can scratch a plastic LCD screen. Use only soft lint-free cloth.

Never spray liquid directly on the display. Too much spray causes the liquid to run down the display and enter the monitor through the seam along the edge of the screen. When the liquid enters inside the monitor, it can short out the electronic components.

Never use the following chemicals to clean a monitor: acetone, ethyl alcohol, ammonia, products containing chlorine or chloride products.

> ## A+ Note
>
> The A+ Certification exams usually have a question about proper cleaning of display units.

Never locate a display unit in direct sunlight such as when placed in front of a window. Direct sunlight will cause excessive heat buildup inside the display. This may damage the electronics. Also, direct sunlight can damage plastic cases, resulting in yellowing or fading of colors. The direct sunlight can also cause the plastic case to become brittle, which may cause the case to crack.

Place the display unit in an area of relative low humidity. High humidity in the range of 80% to 100% can damage electronic components. Avoid moving devices in and out of drastic temperature changes with high humidity present. This is often the case with laptop computers. When moving laptops, try to keep the laptop inside a carrying case designed for the laptop. This will provide some temperature and humidity control.

Video Adapter Cards

Monitors can attach to a computer in one of two ways. The monitor can plug into a video adapter card, which is inserted into a PCI, PCI-X, PCIe, or AGP slot on the motherboard. They can also attach directly to the motherboard, which incorporates the same electronic components found on a video adapter card.

The heart of the video adapter card is a specialized chip known as a digital-to-analog converter. The **digital-to-analog converter (DAC)** converts the digital signal from the computer to an analog signal that is displayed on the computer's monitor. The DAC can consist of one single chip or three chips, one chip for each color. The card also contains RAM, ROM, a video processor, and BIOS. The entire video adapter card is similar to a complete computer that has been specialized for video display.

A VGA monitor uses a 15-pin D-shell connector to connect to the video card or to the video port on the motherboard. **Figure 8-23** shows a diagram of a standard VGA 15-pin D-shell connector. The chart next to the diagram lists the function of each pin on the connector. The 15-pin VGA D-shell is also identified as an HD-15, a DE-15, and a DB-15.

Video adapter cards are installed in PCI, PCI-X, PCIe, or AGP slots on the motherboard. As you can see in **Figure 8-24**, the PCIe design produces the highest throughput of the three technologies. Although, note that PCIe, because it transfers information in a serial fashion, is expressed as bits per second (bps), not bytes per second (Bps).

Video performance also depends on the amount of available memory that can be used to create and process images. When the graphics controller is incorporated into the motherboard, the controller uses the RAM that is installed on the motherboard for video images. This means that the motherboard RAM must be used for all software functions that require RAM as well as for video performance. When a video adapter card is used, the performance is greatly increased. The total effect on video performance is determined by how much RAM is incorporated into the video adapter card. As a general rule, the more video RAM incorporated into the video adapter card, the better the overall video performance. Other factors that influence video performance are the version of operating system, the motherboard chipset, and the video adapter card BIOS.

AGP

The Accelerated Graphics Port (AGP) is a slot used strictly for AGP adapter cards. It is designed with graphics as a priority, using a computer's memory to work more effectively with graphics. It also operates at a faster bus speed than standard PCI slots.

You will rarely encounter AGP except when servicing older equipment. When AGP is incorporated on a motherboard, there will be only one AGP slot. The AGP slot looks similar in design to the PCI slot, only in reverse. It is slightly shorter than a PCI slot, and it is usually a different color. To readily identify the AGP slot, look for the slot

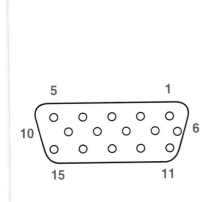

Pin Number	Function
1	Red video
2	Green video
3	Blue video
4	Monitor ID 2
5	TTL ground test pin
6	Red analog ground
7	Green analog ground
8	Blue analog ground
9	Plugged hole
10	Sync ground
11	Monitor ID 0
12	Monitor ID 1
13	Horizontal sync
14	Vertical sync
15	Monitor ID 3

Figure 8-23.
Standard VGA 15-pin connector diagram. In this arrangement, pin 5 is used for testing the monitor. Some manufacturers use pins 4, 11, 12, or 15 to identify or detect the type of monitor connected to the motherboard. Pin 9 is usually missing by design; other pins may be missing as well if not used by that particular manufacturer.

Figure 8-24.
Comparison of video adapter card bus types.

Bus Type	Throughput in MBps	Speed in MHz	Width in Bits
PCI	127.2	33	32
PCI 2.1	508.6	66	64
AGP	254.3	66	32
AGP 2×	508.6	66 × 2	32
AGP 4×	1,017.3	66 × 4	32
AGP 8×	2,034.4	66 × 8	32
PCI-X 1.0	1,060.0	133	64
PCI-X 2.0	2,150.0	266	64
PCIe 1.0	2,000	NA	NA
PCIe 2.0	4,000	NA	NA
PCIe 3.0	8,000	NA	NA

Note: The throughput for PCIe is expressed in MBps for comparison to other bus types. PCIe is a serial bus and the other bus types are parallel.

Goodheart-Willcox Publisher

closest to the CPU and offset from the alignment of the PCI slots.

PCI-X

PCI Extended (PCI-X) was designed as the successor to the PCI bus. You can see the increase in throughput in Figure 8-24. These are theoretical speeds for PCI-X and can be much slower when the bus is shared with other types of devices. PCI-X is not used by many video card systems but may still be encountered occasionally in older systems.

PCIe

PCIe ×16 is the preferred video card technology. The PCIe standard has evolved from PCIe 1.0 to PCIe 4.0 with each producing faster graphic performance than the previous version. PCIe ×16 provides approximately twice the graphics data throughput as AGP ×8. PCIe ×16 has basically replaced all other video card standards such as PCI and AGP. You may wish to review the information concerning PCI-X and PCIe bus types in Chapter 3—Motherboards.

Multiple Video Cards

Computers can be configured with two or more video cards to increase overall video

performance. This is most desirable for graphic-intensive applications such as games, Computer-Aided Design, and video editing. The increased performance is due to the parallel processing power of joining the two video cards together. The two or more video cards share the workload by using either split-frame rendering or alternate-frame rendering.

A frame is a single image similar to a single digital photo. Video, movie, and game animation consists of a series of single digital images referred to as frames. When using **split-frame rendering**, each card is responsible for half of the frame image. If four cards are used, each card is responsible for one-fourth of each image.

The second method is **alternating-frame rendering**. This method is as the name implies. Each card is responsible for rendering every other frame. If four cards are used, each card is responsible for one fourth of the total frame image. Some cards are capable of both split-frame rendering and alternate-frame rendering.

SLI

Scalable Link Interface (SLI) is a proprietary video card system owned by the NVIDIA Corporation. The original SLI system required that both cards be identical. This meant that each video card was to have a matching Graphics Processing Unit (GPU) and the same amount of RAM and bus speed. Today, SLI no longer requires identical video cards. However, when the video cards do not match, the best performance is based on the slower of the two cards.

Figure 8-25 shows two NVIDIA GeForce 8800 video cards installed in an SLI configuration. Notice the SLI bridge connector at the top of the cards.

Originally, the acronym SLI was introduced as Scan-Line Interleave by the 3DFX company. When 3DFX sold the technology to NVIDIA, NVIDIA renamed the acronym to Scalable Link Interface.

ATI CrossFire

ATI CrossFire is the multiple card technology introduced by ATI Technologies Inc., which is now owned by AMD. Two or more cards are configured for the computer. The two cards do not need to match but must be compatible. One card is referred to as the master and the second card is referred to as the slave. Both SLI and CrossFire must be installed in matching PCIe types of slots. For example, you cannot use one card in a PCIe

slot and the other in an AGP slot. You must use two PCIe ×16 slots.

In theory, using two video cards would produce an overall video rate of double, but in reality, an overall 170% to 180% increase is typically achieved at best. There is some software overhead that must be implemented that reduces the theoretical doubling speed and the speed of other processes running in the background.

Videos for installing an SLI video card or a CrossFire system are available on the NVIDIA and ATI AMD websites, respectively. To access these videos, conduct a search using the keywords, "SLI install how to" or "CrossFire install how to."

Installing a Video Adapter Card

Installing a video adapter card is easy. The steps that follow are generic in nature, but there should not be much variation in installation between different cards.

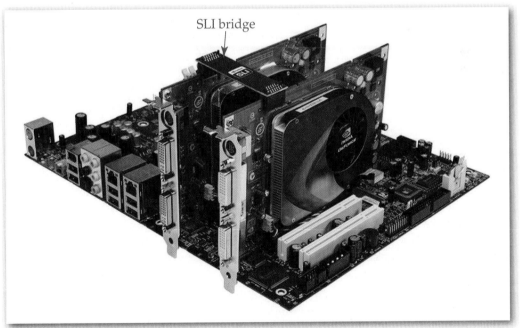

SLI bridge

Figure 8-25.
Two NVIDIA GeForce 8800 video cards installed in an SLI configuration.

NVIDIA Corporation

Caution ! Before beginning any installation of hardware, always back up critical computer files. It is very easy to accidentally destroy data on a computer. Sometimes drivers do not work the way they should, causing the computer system to lock up. In the course of recovering the system, most anything can happen. The worst-case scenario is losing hard drive data. Always back up the hard drive or critical data before working on a PC.

Steps for installing an adapter card:

1. Back up all computer files.
2. Power off the computer and unplug the power cord from the wall outlet.
3. Read the installation procedures and specification sheet that came with the adapter card. Verify that your new card is compatible with the type of display unit being used.
4. Take normal electrostatic discharge (ESD) precautions.
5. Before attempting to insert the video adapter card into the expansion slot, check for debris in the slot.
6. Insert the card by applying even force to the top of the card. Do *not* rock the card into the slot.
7. Connect the monitor to the new card and turn on the PC. The card will be automatically detected. If not, check the support link at the card manufacturer's website.
8. If Windows cannot find its own driver when the system attempts to detect the card, it will ask you to supply a new driver. The driver should have been packaged with the adapter card as a disc. It is also a good idea to check the card manufacturer's website for any patches or upgrades needed for the driver. Prepackaged drivers will often be dated. The most up-to-date drivers can be downloaded from their websites.
9. As the drivers are loading, follow the screen prompts to complete the installation.
10. A message box will display on the screen when the installation is complete. If a problem occurs, a message will appear saying that the installation is not complete. Reread the installation procedures. Also, check for bent pins on the video adapter cable connector. A pin can easily bend when assembling the system. Another area to check is your computer's BIOS. In particular with an older computer, you may need to upgrade the BIOS on the motherboard to use your new card. If problems still persist, check both the card manufacturer's and the motherboard manufacturer's website. Some motherboards have a video adapter integrated into the circuit board. If this is the case, you may have to disable the integrated system before the new adapter board will work. It is always a good idea to consult the website of the motherboard manufacturer for the latest updates before you begin.
11. If all has gone well, you should be able to close the case and reboot the system.

Personalizing Display Properties

In the Windows operating system, many adjustments can be made to the appearance of the display. **Figure 8-26** shows two main areas of the **Appearance and Personalization** dialog box that affect the way items appear on the display. The two areas are personalization and display.

The **Personalization** dialog box allows the user to select themes for appearance, desktop backgrounds, sound effects, and the screen saver. The **Display** dialog box allows the user to configure screen resolution, select the way text appears, and also connect to an external display. The configuration options are very similar in Windows Vista, Windows 7, and Windows 8. Windows XP configuration options are not as similar and are presented somewhat differently to the user.

In Windows Vista, Windows 7, and Windows 8, the various display adjustments are made through several dialog boxes accessed through **Control Panel | Appearance and Personalization**. In Windows XP these adjustments are made in the **Display Properties** dialog box. The **Display Properties** dialog box can be accessed through **Control Panel | Appearance and Themes | Display**.

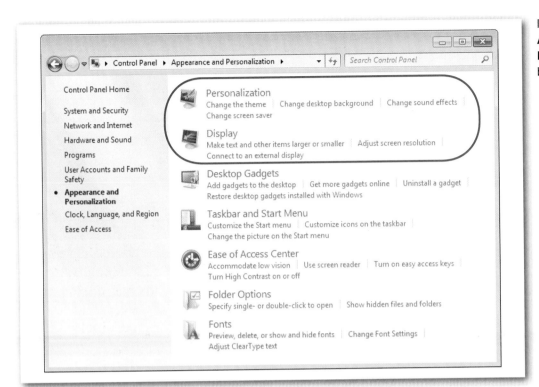

Search Control Panel

Figure 8-26.
Appearance and Personalization dialog box.

Television and Computers

Computer and television technology has rapidly merged since the development of high-definition television (HDTV) and the availability of flat-panel display technology such as TFT and gas-plasma. It is not unusual for a display unit to be designed to serve as both a television and a computer monitor, **Figure 8-27.** The merger of the two technologies has produced many conflicting standards within the television and computer industry. This conflict in standards has resulted in a variety of connector designs used to connect various displays to computers and television receivers. **Figure 8-28** shows some of the connection designs associated with computer and television systems.

All of the connection designs carry the acronym DVI, which stands for Digital Visual Interface. The DVI-I is a combination-type connector designed for both digital and analog connections. The DVI-D is designed for a digital only connection. It can be used to connect devices that support compatible digital resolutions. The DVI-A is used with digital-to-analog conversion. It is not commonly used today because of rapid

Figure 8-27. This flat-panel, gas-plasma TV is capable of both television and computer applications.

ViewSonic Corp

advances in digital video and the fading out of analog systems.

The references to DVI-D single link and DVI-D dual link relate to the amount of bandwidth that can be transmitted by each connection design.

Figure 8-28.
Various connection designs and a DVD-D connector.

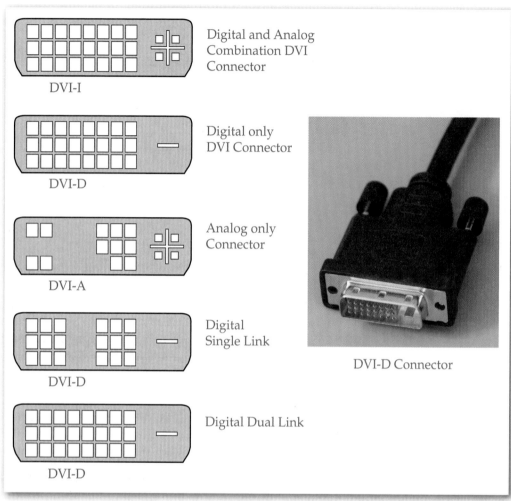

DVI-I — Digital and Analog Combination DVI Connector

DVI-D — Digital only DVI Connector

DVI-A — Analog only Connector

DVI-D — Digital Single Link

DVI-D — Digital Dual Link

DVI-D Connector

The single link can carry a bandwidth equal to 165 MHz, which is the matching bandwidth for HDTV. It is capable of producing a maximum resolution of 1920 × 1080 at 60 Hz. The dual link can carry twice the bandwidth of the single link and can produce a resolution as high as 2048 × 1536.

Some video adapter cards provide several connection types to choose from. **Figure 8-29** shows an older video adapter card with a variety of video display ports: DVI-I, S-Video (TV), and VGA (DB-15). Newer video cards also have a variety of video ports which represent the latest video port technology. In **Figure 8-30**, DVI-D, DVI-I, and HDMI ports and a DisplayPort are shown. DisplayPort was developed by the VESA organization as an open royalty-free display connection. The main advantage of DisplayPort is that it is royalty-free, whereas HDMI charges

royalties such as 10,000 dollars plus 4 cents per unit.

Some video adapter cards are manufactured to support two monitors at the same time. Webpage designers often require more than one display unit while designing webpages. By having more than one display connected to the computer station, they can view the webpage they designed at different resolutions.

High-Definition Television

High-definition television (HDTV) displays have become the center of home entertainment systems and have created a demand for computer displays that are compatible with the same resolution and aspect ratio as HDTV. The display resolutions and overall physical shape of the viewing area are designed to support HDTV

Figure 8-29. This video card is equipped with a variety of video display ports.

S-Video   VGA   DVI-I

Goodheart-Willcox Publisher

Figure 8-30. Video card with a mini-HDMI, DVI-D, and DVI-I port and a DisplayPort.

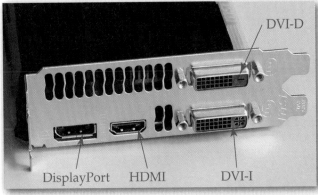

DVI-D

DisplayPort   HDMI   DVI-I

Goodheart-Willcox Publisher

as well as other media center options, such as watching movies and editing video and digital photography.

HDTV Resolution

Original analog television resolution is approximately equal to 720 × 480. The two most common HDTV formats are 720 and 1080. The 720 format is nothing more than an enhanced original analog television resolution of 720 × 480. True HDTV resolution requires a display resolution of at least 1080 × 720. The latest resolution for high-definition television is Ultra high-definition television (UHDTV) which has a resolution four times greater than HDTV. UHDTV is available in two formats at this time: 4K UHDTV and 8K UHDTV. Look at the following table of a comparison of the formats.

Format	Resolution	Pixels
HDTV	720 × 480	345,600 pixels
True HDTV	1080 × 720	777,600 pixels
4K UHDTV	3840 × 2160	8.3 Megapixels
8K UHDTV	7680 × 4320	33.2 Megapixels

Note: The 8K UHDTV is also known as the Super Hi Definition TV.

To produce HDTV on a computer system you need to have a monitor resolution set at 1920 × 1080 pixels. You can display HDTV at other resolution values, but 1920 × 1080 is recommended for the minimal HDTV experience on a digital display such as an LCD monitor.

The original screen resolution for HDTV was based on analog television signals that used raster scans and produced 480 or 720 separate lines counted vertically across the television screen. Today, 1920 × 1080 is considered the native resolution for HDTV and is often referred to as simply 1080 HDTV using only the second number of the screen resolution.

VGA vs. Digital Signals

VGA is a legacy analog video signal connection. VGA uses three separate analog signals that represent the three colors red, green, and blue. An analog signal is used for the original television terrestrial signals (radio waves), but the connectors are found on older types of devices.

Digital signals differ from analog signals in that they are broadcast using similar technology as analog signal. However, the data is carried in a series of square waves rather than sine waves. The digital (square) signals represent the ones and zeros associated with binary digital code. The progression from analog signals to digital signals was made because digital signals can carry more information than analog signals using the same radio bandwidth.

Windows Media Center

Today, more and more computers are being set up as a media center in the home. By adding a television tuner either as an expansion card or as a USB device, the computer is able to receive analog and digital television signals. Windows XP first introduced a home entertainment application called Windows Media Center which allowed the user to record and playback television, tune in radio station content, as well as view DVD movie content, play CD music, and view digital images from digital cameras in an album format.

Windows Media Center is incorporated for free into Windows Vista and Windows 7 and is available as an add-on in Windows 8. The add-on is not free at the time of this writing. Windows Media Center allows users to watch, pause, and record HDTV; play music; watch DVDs; enjoy photos; and more, **Figure 8-31**.

To receive television signals, you need to install and configure a TV tuner for your computer. The TV tuner can be installed internally or externally. **Figure 8-32** shows an example of a TV tuner card designed to fit into a PCIe ×1 expansion slot inside a computer case.

The TV tuner card comes with drivers and application software, a remote control, and a receiver. You will need to connect the TV tuner card to an antenna or to a television Cable box.

There are also TV tuners designed to connect to a PC externally via a USB port.

Home Theater PC

A **home theater PC (HTPC)** is a customized computer used to enhance the television viewing experience. The HTPC has all the capabilities of a typical PC plus additional software/hardware to support multimedia recording and playback.

Generally, a television has good sound quality, but a user may wish to create a theater-quality sound system by adding a sound card to the HTPC. A sufficient number of speakers is also added to create a surround-sound environment for the best possible listening pleasure. In addition to a sound card, you need to use a computer system and Internet access that adequately supports video streaming.

To best understand video streaming you can compare video streaming to downloading. When you download a file, you establish a connection with a remote resource on the Internet and then download the entire file before opening it to view or hear the contents. With video streaming, you can actually view the contents of the file while streaming the content. The quality of video streaming is based on the ability of the computer system or Smart TV and the quality of the material to be viewed. For video to be streamed smoothly

Figure 8-31.
Windows 7 Media Center.

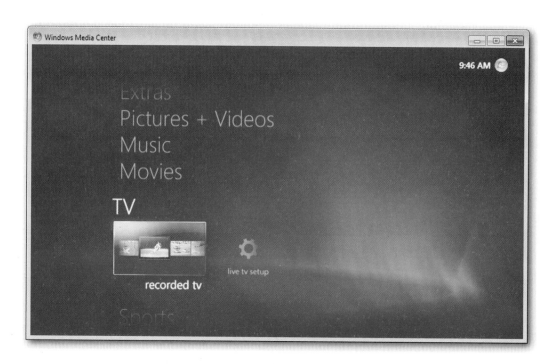

Figure 8-32.
A TV tuner card with
a remote control,
receiver, and driver and
application software.

Goodheart-Willcox Publisher

and without interruption, the minimum Internet access speeds should be used:

- 2.3 Mbps for standard-definition (SD) video.
- 2.3 Mbps–4.5 Mbps for high-definition (HD) video.
- 4.5 Mbps–9 Mbps for HDX video.
- 9 Mbps for 3D high-definition (HD) video.

High-definition video has a 720p resolution. HDX is full high-definition video, which consists of 1080p resolution video and high-definition audio. Other things that can affect the amount of bandwidth needed for video streaming is the type of codec (compression type) used and the number of users downloading over the same shared Internet connection.

Smart TVs

Smart TVs are televisions with additional features built-in, such as support for Internet access, a Wi-Fi connection, and software applications. The software applications provide features such as Internet browsing and searching, e-mail client services, video conferencing when a webcam is installed, streaming videos music, and more. The software applications can vary greatly according to the brand of Smart TV, Internet provider, and equipment provided. Smart TVs go by many other names such as interactive television (iTV), hybrid TV, and Internet TV.

A home theater can be created from many different options and features. In the future, televisions may become the sole solution. Modern televisions are based on PC technology. In fact, there is very little difference between a television display and a computer except for the installation of operating system and software. A Smart TV may soon incorporate a full computer operating system as well as high-end video and audio, thus creating a complete entertainment system in one package. Soon it will difficult to distinguish between a Smart TV and a computer system.

Home Theater Boxes

Home theater boxes are special consumer appliances that provide the same services as a Smart TVs, such as Internet services, video recording, and software applications, in one specialized box. Other features that may be included are DVD or Blu-Ray read/write burner, surround sound, and more. The features provided vary by manufacturer and by price. A typical home theater box connects directly to a television and to the Internet.

Home Theater Center Connection Types

A home theater center can consist of many different electronic devices connected together. The system may consist of a high-definition LCD or plasma television, cable TV, antenna or satellite source of signal, speakers, DVR, and a computer. The equipment that comprises a complete home theater center may involve a wide variety of cable connections. You need to be able to identify each type and understand its capabilities.

The signal that is supplied by the local cable television company or through a satellite dish system typically connects to the initial receiver in the home from a single coaxial cable. Another option is wireless cell access, the same type of connection used for wireless cell service. Original media systems consisted of a single coaxial cable that connected to a cable box and then another single coaxial cable to the television. Today, the single coaxial cable that supplies the cable television signal or satellite disc signal is separated into multiple audio and video signals which are processed by much more sophisticated equipment. The overall product is enhanced audio and video that requires a variety of connections and cables.

You need to be aware that audio cables, such as the cable used for speakers, is low frequency—less than 20 kHz. It does not require shielding from interference or cause interference the way video signals do. The speaker wiring does not use a carrier wave. It simply transmits the sound pattern as an analog signal.

Video signals are typically either UHF or VHF, each of which are high frequency in the hundreds of megahertz range. Hence, video cables must be shielded to protect the video signal from interference and to prevent the video cable from broadcasting radio wave interference to surrounding devices. Coaxial cable is used for video signals while unshielded cable is used for speakers. The speaker wires have a much larger core conductor diameter when compared to RG-6 cable, which is a type of coaxial cable. The large diameter ensures less signal loss as the audio signal travels the length of the cable.

Composite Video

Look at the cables in **Figure 8-33**. Composite video, Figure 8-33A, resembles component video connections and cables, Figure 8-33C. Notice that composite video uses an RCA-type connector similar to component video; however, it uses only one cable for the video signal and two more for stereo sound. The composite video cable uses a larger diameter cable (the one with the yellow connector) for video. The larger diameter cable is an RG-59 coaxial cable. The other two cables are used for audio and do not use coaxial shielding. Composite video provides a better signal than F-type or RF cable connections but does not provide a signal as good as S-Video or component video.

S-Video

S-Video, Figure 8-33B, is a four-pin round connector that delivers separate signals for video signal chrominance (color) and luminance (brightness). It is a very simple way to connect components together because there is no way to misconnect the audio and video cables. S-Video supports better signal quality than composite video, but not as well as component video.

A nine-pin version of S-Video is used for video in and video out (ViVO) configurations, **Figure 8-34**. The nine-pin connector allows for video to be streamed in both directions. A four-pin connector is used for applications that only require video in one direction. Many video computer cards have the nine-pin S-Video connector, which is used commonly for video editing. The video is copied to the computer from the source, edited on the computer, and then sent back to the source.

Component Video

The component video connection, Figure 8-33C, consists of three RCA connectors typically identified as Y, Pb (Cb), Pr (Cr). Component video connections are also referred to as RGB because the colors are used to identify the cables and also represent the color generated at the source for each video cable. See Figure 8-33E. Component video is found on high-performance devices and produces a better quality picture than

Figure 8-33. Various home entertainment center connections and cables. A—Composite video. B—S-Video. C—Component video. D—Audio. E—Home entertainment center connections.

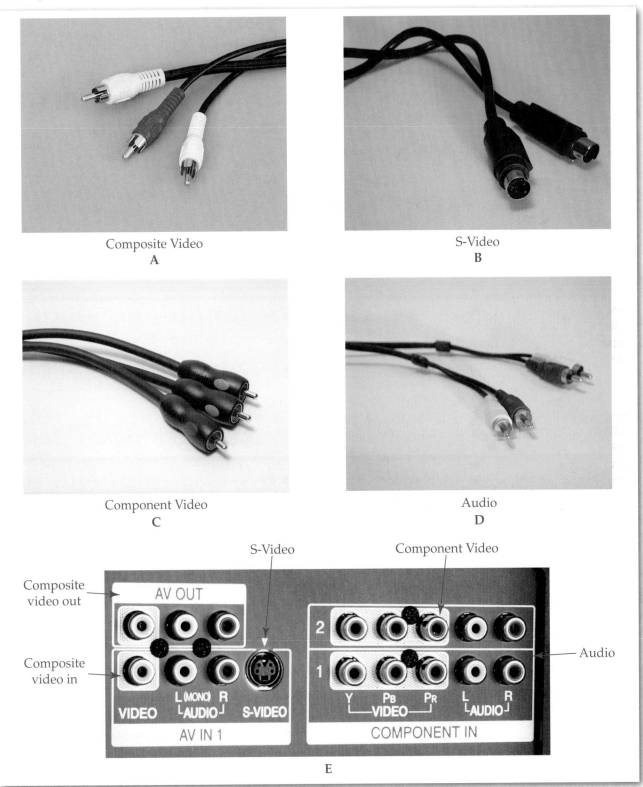

Composite Video
A

S-Video
B

Component Video
C

Audio
D

E

Figure 8-34.
An S-Video adapter with a nine-pin Video connector on one end and a combination 4-pin S-Video, component video, and composite video connection on the other end.

9-pin S-Video

Composite Video

4-pin S-Video

Component Video

S-Video and composite video. The cables used are constructed from flexible coaxial cable. Each individual cable consists of a single conductor surrounded by a dielectric and a shield to protect it from receiving or generating interference. Component video does not carry the audio signal. Audio signals are typically supplied through two separate ports using cable, Figure 8-33D, similar to the component video and composite video cables.

HDMI

The High Definition Multimedia Interface (HDMI) connector is used to supply video and audio in an uncompressed, all digital signal format. See **Figure 8-35**. Only one cable assembly is needed between devices such as satellite receivers and the HDTV. HDMI supports an enhanced HDTV format and Dolby 5.1 using a single shielded cable. HDMI, Figure 8-35A, can support a digital audio signal as high as 192 kHz, a digital video signal as high as 350 MHz, and a data signal as high as 10.2 Gbps.

At the time of this writing, HDMI provides the best picture and sound quality available. The HDMI uses the xvYCC standard, which is an enhanced color standard that exceeds the HDTV standard. The xvYCC is short for Extended YCC Colorimetric for Video Applications. The term *colorimetric* means identification of colors using three sets of numbers representing red, green, and blue. This standard was designed to enhance

the viewing experience and can support 1.8 times as many colors as existing HDTV signals. The xvYCC standard is also designed to support Blu-Ray technologies for Digital Video Disc (DVD) and newest video game technology. The HDMI connector is commonly found on many high-end computer video cards.

Sony/Philips Digital Interconnect Format

Sony/Philips Digital Interconnect Format (S/PDIF) is a special proprietary digital audio connection/cable. The connector/cable can be in one of two formats: coaxial with an RCA connector or fiber-optic with a TOSLINK connector. Fiber-optic connections are sometimes simply identified as "optic" connections rather than S/PDIF or TOSLINK.

TOSLINK

The TOSLINK optical connector, Figure 8-35B, is a proprietary connection developed jointly by Sony and Phillips. The TOSLINK cable is used quite often for home theater equipment. The TOSLINK cable is fiber-optic with a glass or plastic core. Fiber-optic cable ensures a high-quality transfer of audio signals because it is immune to radio and magnetic interference. The fiber-optic cable light signal is not susceptible to interference emitted from other cables and radio signal sources. The TOSLINK connector

Figure 8-35. HDMI and TOSLINK connectors and connections. A—HDMI. B—TOSLINK. C—HDMI, TOSLINK (optical), and RS-232 connections on the back of an HDTV system. The RS-232 connection connects to a diagnostic device that is used to troubleshoot the high-definition television.

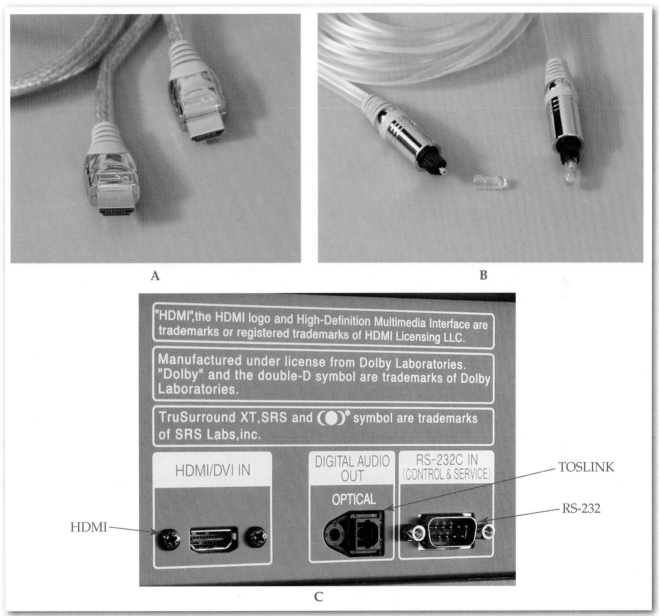

is protected from damage by plastic end pieces. The connectors are susceptible to damage from scratches or even dust collected on the ends.

RF and F-type

RF and F-type connections in general provide the poorest quality video images when used between home entertainment center devices. They are generally used only with old technologies to support connections between devices. The RF and F-type cables are a standard coaxial cable consisting of a solid or stranded copper core conductor, **Figure 8-36**. The core conductor is surrounded by a thick insulator material. The insulator material is covered by a conductive mesh or foil referred to as the shield. The shield protects

Figure 8-36.
Coaxial cable with
F-type connector.

F-type
connector

Insulator

Shield

Solid core
conductor

Goodheart-Willcox Publisher

the core conductor from outside electromagnetic interference.

RF and F-type cables provide the poorest signal quality transfer between home entertainment devices. Other cabling technologies, such as component video, S-Video, and HDMI, provide better signal support.

Do not confuse the use of transferring a signal between devices with bringing in the raw signal that comes directly from a satellite or Broadband Cable television. The other types of cabling other than coaxial are not typically used to bring a raw signal into a complete system. The exception is fiber-optic cable, which is now being introduced in many areas to bring the raw signal into a final destination. The following table compares video connection technologies.

Video Connection Type	Quality Comparison
HDMI	Best
Component Video	Excellent
S-Video	Good
Composite Video	Poor
RF	Poor

Graphic Coding

There are many different methods used to code the data of an image. The different coding methods are designed to either compress the content or preserve the quality. Compression is used to reduce file size and reduce total amount of time it takes for file transfer. Preserving the quality is needed to produce high quality final image after file transfer or image manipulation.

Bitmapped Graphics

One of the standards is the **bitmap (BMP)**, also referred to as a *raster image*. A bitmap (BMP) is a graphics standard for uncompressed encoding of images. A display screen or printed image is made from thousands or millions of pixels. As discussed earlier, a pixel is the smallest screen element. The number of bits used to encode the pixel determines the color and shades of that color.

For example, an 8-bit code is capable of 256 different binary number patterns. Each of the binary number patterns can represent a different color or shade of gray. On a color monitor, each pixel is actually a combination of three different colors: red, blue, and green. Each color has an 8-bit binary code that can represent 256 shades of the color. The three individual 8-bit colors combine to form a 24-bit code that represents the actual color of the pixel image. The 24-bit color code is referred to as true color and can produce over 16 million colors when mixed together.

Vector Graphics

Vector graphics is based on a series of mathematical formulas that can be converted into geometric shapes representing the image to be displayed. Vector graphics are typically produced by drawing programs, not by photographic images. One main advantage of vector images is they can be resized or scaled without losing the quality of the image. When a bitmap image is enlarged or reduced in size, the number of pixels must be increased or decreased accordingly. This means adding or removing pixels, which distorts the original image. The software program performing the bitmap conversion must decide what color to add as the image is increased. It chooses the pixel color closest to the original pixel. When the image is reduced, the software erases an existing pixel.

Since vector graphic images use mathematical formulas to represent the lines in the figures, the picture retains its original picture quality no matter which size it is changed to. The lines that compose the image are simply multiplied or divided by the applied scale factor. For example, all the line segments and circle diameters are multiplied by 2 for a drawing that is to be increased in scale by 200%.

A vector drawing could scale an infinite number of times and never lose its quality. In comparison, a bitmap image that was resized only a few times would become completely distorted.

Software programs that produce bitmap images are often referred to as *paint programs*. Software programs that produce vector images are often referred to as *draw programs*.

Vector image technology is used in critical drawing applications such as Computer-Aided Design (CAD) and in many different animation software programs. Bitmap is mostly associated with photographic images. It is important to note that you can convert a vector image to a bitmap image, but you cannot convert a bitmap image to a vector image.

Graphic Compression

Graphics applications require a lot of memory space for storage. Even a small graphic can require several million bytes of memory depending on the resolution and the number of colors used to create the graphic. To decrease the amount of memory space needed, image data can be compressed. There are many different compression methods. However, they all use similar techniques to accomplish the compression.

A close inspection of a typical graphic reveals the color pixels repeated many times sequentially in an area of the picture. **Figure 8-37** shows a series of apple images. Each successive photo in this series looks progressively closer at the apple to expose the pixel pattern of colors. In the first image, you see what appears as very subtle variations of shades of green and red. As the picture is enlarged, you can see that many of the pixels are the same color. These repeating pixels of the same color are the secret to file compression. Instead of describing every pixel, a compressed file can describe a series of similar pixels with a short piece of code.

For a file compression technique to be effective, it must convert the same information stored in the image but use less memory space. This image was saved as a Windows true color image, meaning that the image pixels are each composed of three 8-bit bytes. Consequently, each picture element shown uses 24 bits to represent the pixel. Look at the magnified images of the apple. Notice several continuous rows of pixels. If a row has 20 pixels, it would require 60 bytes of information.

One compression method worth looking at is run-length encoding. **Run-length encoding (RLE)** replaces a series of repeated pixels with a single pixel and the length of the series (run). The longer the runs and the greater number of runs there are, the greater the compression that will be achieved.

Figure 8-38 shows a comparison of labeled binary codes. The first set of binary codes represents the color white for 20 pixels. The second set of binary codes shows a condensed version of the same information.

In the compressed file, the first byte gives the location of the first pixel. The next three bytes represent the color white, which is equal to decimal 255 (or binary code 11111111). The color white is composed of equal parts of red, blue, and green. Thus, the color is coded as three bytes, all consisting of eight 1s. The last byte of information contains the number of times necessary to repeat

Figure 8-37. What appears to be finely detailed can be broken down into a series of pixels, some of which repeat.

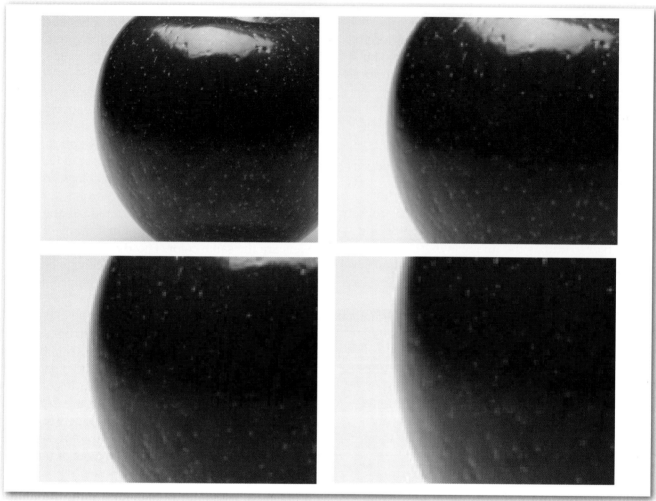

the pattern of white pixels. In the example, the last byte represents the decimal number 20. As you can see, the size of the compressed file, containing only 6 bytes, is very small in comparison to the original file that required 60 bytes of data.

Looking again at Figure 8-37, you can see many different colors that form a repeating pattern in the image. Each of these areas can be encoded the same way. This is the basic concept of compression. There are many different programs available to compress files. While they all do not work exactly as demonstrated, they do work in a similar fashion. File compression techniques are used not only for graphics but also for other forms of data such as sound files. Some compression techniques can achieve a compression ratio as high as 12:1.

 **Tech Tip**

The most commonly encountered photo compression format is JPEG, also identified as JPG.

Audio is the second half of the multimedia experience. All PCs come with a small internal speaker, but that is not enough for most users. Fancy sound cards, subwoofers, and microphones have become standard equipment on many systems. The first step in learning audio systems is to understand sound itself and how it is created. The next step is to see how audio devices interface with the PC.

The color white is equal to equal color parts of red, green, and blue.

Red	Blue	Green			
11111111	11111111	11111111	11111111	11111111	11111111
11111111	11111111	11111111	11111111	11111111	11111111
11111111	11111111	11111111	11111111	11111111	11111111
11111111	11111111	11111111	11111111	11111111	11111111
11111111	11111111	11111111	11111111	11111111	11111111
11111111	11111111	11111111	11111111	11111111	11111111
11111111	11111111	11111111	11111111	11111111	11111111
11111111	11111111	11111111	11111111	11111111	11111111
11111111	11111111	11111111	11111111	11111111	11111111
11111111	11111111	11111111	11111111	11111111	11111111

Original file information needed for the row of white pixel images.

10010011 11100111   11111111 11111111 11111111   00010100

Location of first pixel   The three colors   Repeat (length of run)

Compressed file information for same section.

Goodheart-Willcox Publisher

Figure 8-38. Compression techniques can tremendously reduce the amount of code used to store an image or text. Here repeated data is reduced from 60 bytes to 6 bytes.

What Is Sound?

Sound is comprised of vibrations that are put into motion through a medium such as air or water. We are most familiar with air as the medium. The air itself actually carries a vibrating wave action. If you place a piece of tissue paper in front of a speaker, you can see it move from the sound vibration. If you are anywhere near some cars that have megawatt speakers turned up very loudly, you are familiar with the "feel" of sound.

If all air is removed and only a vacuum exists, there would be no sound. A vacuum is completely empty. There is no medium to carry the vibrations produced that we call sound. This concept can be demonstrated by placing an alarm clock inside a sealed, glass container. In this experiment, air is removed from the container.

When the alarm goes off, it cannot be heard. There is no medium present to transport the pattern of vibrations called sound, **Figure 8-39**.

The human ear can detect sounds from approximately 20 Hz to 20 kHz. This is known as the frequency response range of the human ear. Vibrations above or below this range go undetected by human ears.

Figure 8-39. The alarm can be set off in a vacuum, but no sound will be transmitted.

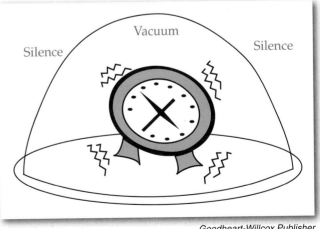

Goodheart-Willcox Publisher

Sampling

Measuring an analog signal at regular intervals is called **sampling**. Sampling is required before converting an analog signal into a digital signal. The quality of any type of analog-to-digital conversion is based primarily on the sampling rate and number of bits used to represent the height or voltage level of the signal. Sampling rates are incorporated into many different technologies. Weather radar units, security systems based on voice and image identification, and automatic piloting of aircraft are only a few examples.

A high frequency of sampling (frequent samples taken) results in a better quality of sound. **Figure 8-40** shows two different sampling rates taken from the same wave. See how the resultant waves differ with high and low sampling rates by comparing the reconstructed analog wave shapes.

A high sampling rate gives a better representation of an analog signal shape. In the illustration, an analog wave shape is sampled at two different rates. When the two wave shapes are reconstructed by connecting the points of sampling, you can see that the higher sampling rate gives a shape closer to the original analog wave shape. The quality of the sampling is directly affected by the sampling rate and by the number of bits used to indicate the height of the signal at the sampling points. The size of the file storing the signal data needed to reconstruct the sound wave also increases proportionately with the sampling rate.

Several factors affect the choice of sampling rates. Sampling rates vary depending on what is being recorded. Music would require a high sampling rate in comparison to a simple voice recording. The quality of sound may not be an issue when leaving voice mail. However, most listeners are fairly discriminating regarding the quality of their music.

Audio Resolution

The original sound card was an 8-bit card. Today, most quality sound cards are 16-bit. You can record a better image of the original sound using a 16-bit rather than an 8-bit card. A system based on 8-bit sound is limited to using 256 levels, or binary codes, to store a binary image of the

Figure 8-40.
A higher sampling creates a more accurate reproduction of the original waveform.

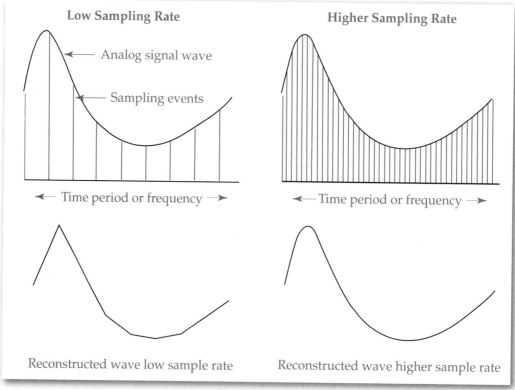

Low Sampling Rate   Higher Sampling Rate

Analog signal wave

Sampling events

← Time period or frequency →   ← Time period or frequency →

Reconstructed wave low sample rate   Reconstructed wave higher sample rate

sound wave sample. A 16-bit sound card can use 65,536 binary codes to store the sound wave pattern during each sampling. The 16-bit system can save a more detailed representation of the analog sound wave pattern than an 8-bit system.

Think in terms of graphic picture resolution. A better graphic image can be produced using 16 bits, rather than 8 bits, per pixel. Look back to Figure 8-40 where sampling rate and reconstructed analog wave shapes are illustrated. In the illustration of sampling rates, the height of the sample is measured in bits. A more detailed graph can be reconstructed by using more bits for the initial readings taken.

Audio resolution is based on two key factors: sampling rate and number of bits used to represent the analog sound. Sampling rate is how often a sample or snapshot of the sound is taken. The number of bits used to represent the analog sound determines the sensitivity of the analog measurement represented as a voltage level. Together these two quantities determine the quality of the sound captured and played back.

The original sound card was 8-bit which meant that there were 256 possible levels of audio sound level that could be captured during each momentary sampling period. A 16-bit card can capture 65, 536 discrete levels of sound. A 24-bit card can capture 16,777,216 discrete levels of sound. Today, most quality sound cards are 16-bit, 24-bit, and higher. The more bits used to record the audio image of the sound, the better the quality of the sound.

A typical sampling rate is 44.1 kHz. This is equal to 100 times per second for 16-bit and 96 kHz for 24-bit. A 24-bit sound card with a sampling rate of 99 kHz will record 4 bytes of data 99,000 times a second. A 24-bit 96 kHz sampling rate will result in 33 MB of storage for a one minute recording. As you can see, audio recordings require a significant amount of data storage.

MIDI Files

Musical instrument digital interface (MIDI) is a file standard developed for music synthesizers. Synthesized music is electronically simulated music sounds rather than recorded sounds. A chip, or set of chips, can produce the sounds of many instruments, **Figure 8-41**. To play music, input through the chips is made from a database containing information such as the type of instrument to play, the actual note to play, the length of sound, and any special effects such as an echo chamber effect. The music is actually a sequence of coded instructions sent to the chips that make the sounds. An advantage of MIDI is that it is a universal file format. A disadvantage is that many MIDI audio systems sound like artificial music to the ear. After all, they are artificial sounds produced by chips rather than real instrument recordings.

MIDI can be created electronically by connecting a PC to a sound synthesizer or keyboard, **Figure 8-42**. The keyboard has selector

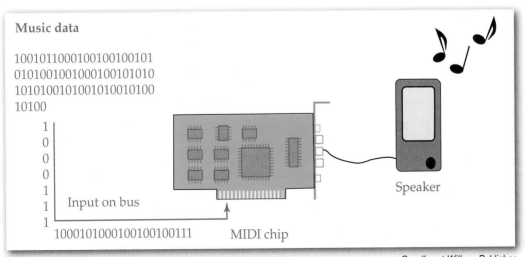

Figure 8-41.
A MIDI chip is capable of reproducing sound from a selection of instruments that are stored in its memory.

Figure 8-42. A typical keyboard (left) with its MIDI interface (right).

Goodheart-Willcox Publisher

switches from which the user can select dozens of different instruments. A song can be recorded in MIDI data format to be saved and played back on the PC. Once the sound track is saved, it can be manipulated to add special effects. A single musician can create music similar to a complete orchestra of instruments.

Audio Devices

There are numerous audio devices for the PC. They include both input devices, such as the microphone, and output devices, such as the

speaker. Most of these devices are tied into the PC through the sound card.

Microphone

A microphone is a simple electronic device used to convert sound waves into electrical energy. The microphone converts the air vibration that strikes it into voltage levels that are in direct proportion to the strength and frequency of the vibrations. The electrical energy is analog in nature. **Figure 8-43** shows sound waves striking a microphone and their conversion to digital data.

Figure 8-43.
An analog sound signal is turned into an analog electrical signal by a microphone and then into a digital electrical signal by a sound card.

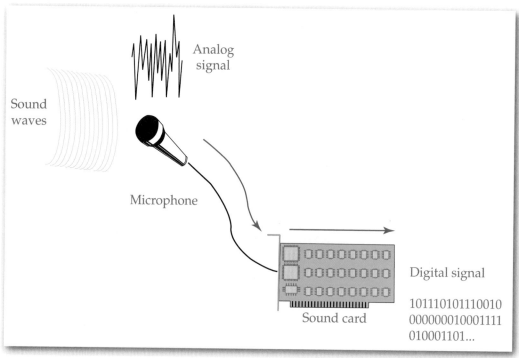

Goodheart-Willcox Publisher

When the signal reaches the sound card, the analog electrical signal is converted to a digital signal, which allows it to be stored in RAM, on a hard drive, or on a CD. When the sound is stored as a digital code, it is often referred to as a *wave* file because it usually has a .wav file extension. A one-minute .wav file can vary in size from 500 kB to over 20 MB depending on variables. Some of these variables are the speed of the sampling frequency, whether monaural or stereo sound is being recorded, whether 8-bit or 16-bit sampling is used, and what compression technique is being used (if any).

Speakers

A speaker converts electrical energy to sound energy. Look at **Figure 8-44** to see a digital sound passing through a sound card and out through a speaker. To listen to stored digital code, the code is sent through the sound card and is then converted to an analog electrical signal. As the electrical energy varies in strength, the speaker cone vibrates at a rate proportional to the analog electrical signal.

Take note of the 120-volt power converter. The power converter is used to power the amplifier inside the speaker. The speaker amplifier takes

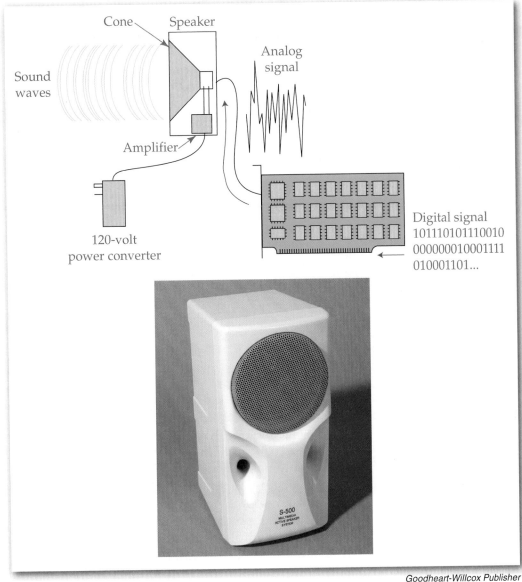

Figure 8-44.
The sound card changes a digital signal back into an analog electrical signal. This electrical signal is used to produce sound by the speaker.

the small analog signal it receives from the sound card and powerfully reproduces it. A typical sound card cannot provide ample power to drive a speaker. Most sound cards only produce approximately 2 watts of energy. This is sufficient to drive only a headphone set, not a desktop speaker. When a speaker has its own built-in amplifier, it is called an *active speaker*. A speaker without amplification is called a *passive speaker*.

A sound system can be installed wirelessly rather than using traditional cabling. A wireless system typically is composed of a set of wireless speakers, a wireless remote control, and a wireless transmitter, **Figure 8-45**. The number and type of speakers used depends on the user and application. The user may wish to install a simple two-speaker system or a multiple-speaker system to create a 3D sound system. A remote control can be used to control system volume from anywhere in range. The wireless transmitter connects to sound devices such as an MP3 player, a television, a CD/DVD system, or any other type of sound device. The transmitter in the example connects

to sound sources through a cable port in the back of the transmitter. The front of the transmitter is designed to cradle a sound source, such as a MP3 player.

Wireless sound systems are not always the best choice for high-quality sound systems. All radio wave-based technology can suffer from interference because the operating frequency of a wireless speaker system is also shared by many other types of devices. The federal government assigns radio devices to specific radio frequencies or bands also known as channels. The 900-MHz radio band is used for such items as wireless microphones, wireless speakers, baby monitors, home security systems, home intercom systems, amateur ham radio, cordless headphones, wireless utility meters, some medical equipment, and many types of industrial equipment used to produce heat for sealing packages and drying items such as glue. As you can see, there are many different items that could interfere with a wireless sound system.

The advertised range for wireless speaker systems is typically 150 to 300 feet. The advertised ranges are under ideal conditions such as direct line of sight between the transmitter and speaker receivers. Ideal conditions are seldom encountered in application because any building material such as wood, drywall, concrete, and brick reduces radio signal strength. Radio interference reduces the signal strength and the distance the signal can travel. It also distorts the radio signal and causes poor sound quality. As you can see, there can be many concerns for a wireless speaker system. To ensure the best sound delivery to speakers and other sound devices, cable is the preferred media.

Figure 8-45. Wireless speakers are an easy way to install a speaker system because there is no need to run speaker cables.

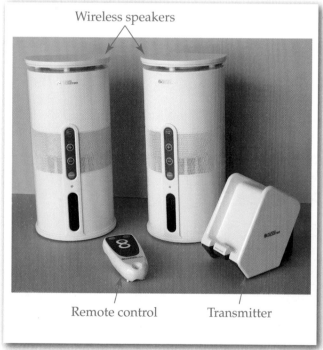

Wireless speakers

Remote control   Transmitter

Sound Cards

Most sound cards purchased today are PCI adapter cards. This means they are Plug and Play technology. All system resources (IRQ, DMA, I/O port addresses, memory addresses) are automatically detected and assigned. Older 8-bit adapter type cards will most likely require system resources to be manually assigned through software or physically assigned by setting jumpers or dip switches. System conflicts are quite common for older cards.

Always check the system resource assignments when problems arise, especially after newer hardware has been installed into an existing system. Software diagnostic programs included in most operating systems can diagnose conflicts. Windows 98 and higher versions have diagnostic software to assist you with conflicts with system resources. These tools can be accessed through **Start | All Programs | Accessories | System Tools | System Information**. **Figure 8-46** shows the **Microsoft System Information** dialog box. It can assist you when solving system resource conflicts. You can use this window to analyze conflicts arising from system resource assignments.

Video Capture Device

A video capture device is used to send audio and video from a device such as a VCR or camcorder to a PC. It can also be used to capture live video from a device such as a television or game. Most video is copy protected, but high-quality professional capture devices can still transfer copy-protected media. **Figure 8-47** shows

a video capture device with a variety of video and audio connectors on the input side of the capture card and a USB connector on the output side. Other video capture devices have other connection types such as HDMI. The video capture device also requires a software application programmed especially for the device.

Installing a Sound Card

Installing a sound card before Plug and Play could be very frustrating. The source of frustration came from system resource assignments. There was almost a guarantee of a system resource conflict appearing with legacy sound cards. Multimedia cards use all areas of system resources. Before installing any legacy sound card, review the IRQs, DMA, memory addresses, and I/O port address topics covered earlier in the textbook.

Although Plug and Play should eliminate most conflicts, there can still be problems, especially when upgrades are performed. As new technologies evolve, there will be the need

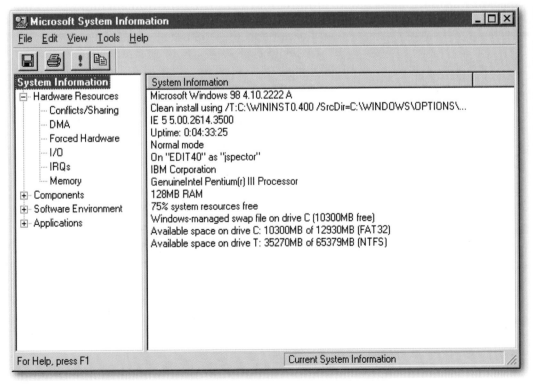

Figure 8-46.
The **Microsoft System Information** dialog box can be used to help troubleshoot conflicts. It shows the IRQs, DMAs, and I/O port addresses a computer's components are using.

Figure 8-47. A video capture device is used to transfer data from a multimedia device to a computer in digital format.

Goodheart-Willcox Publisher

to upgrade current technologies. In other words, Plug and Play operates well now, but a new technology will appear in the future that will also require Plug and Play to be upgraded or redesigned. The following steps are used for the installation of a typical sound card:

1. Back up all computer files before installing a sound card.
2. Power off the computer and unplug the power cord from the wall outlet.
3. Read the card installation procedure and specification sheet.
4. Take normal electrostatic discharge (ESD) precautions.
5. Check for debris in the expansion slot.
6. Insert the card into the slot by applying even force to the top of the card. Do *not* rock the card into the slot.
7. Check if there are any cables that might interfere with the sound card. Voltages can be induced by wires in close proximity to the sound card. This can distort the sound quality. Keep cables away from sound cards.
8. Connect the speakers to the computer and connect the speaker's power supply to the speakers. Turn the speakers on before powering on the computer.
9. Check for the latest drivers at the sound card manufacturer's website.
10. Power on the computer.

The card should be auto detected if it is Plug and Play. You may have to supply the driver for the new adapter card when the system detects the card. The Windows operating system may not have the correct driver for the card. A driver is typically packaged with the sound card on a CD or DVD. Always check the manufacturer's website for the latest patch or upgrade for the driver. Follow the screen prompts to complete the installation.

If all has gone well, you should be able to turn off the power, install the cover, and then reboot the system. If the installation failed, reread the installation procedure. Check for simple things first. For example, is the power supply module for the speakers plugged in? Or, is there a bent pin at one of the connection points? Check if the volume is turned up. You may also need to upgrade the BIOS on the motherboard. Check the website of the motherboard manufacturer and the sound card manufacturer for the latest updates.

A variety of ports associated with a typical modern sound card is shown in **Figure 8-48**. The microphone input port can also be used for other forms of input such as an MP3 device or most any sound source device. There are also four speaker outputs used to create 3D surround sound systems. Lastly, there are two optical ports: one for input and the other for output. These ports are designed to work with S/PDIF or TOSLINK connectors associated with fiber-optic cable connections.

You can also add a sound device through a USB port. **Figure 8-49** shows a Sabrent Sound Box, which is connected through a computer USB port. Portable computers such as laptops do not allow for the installation of sound cards. The Sabrent Sound Box is an ideal solution for upgrading the sound for a portable device such as a laptop. This particular device comes with two cables: a USB cable for connection to the computer system and an S/PDIF. The S/PDIF cable can be used in the S/PDIF input or output ports on the side of the sound box. The other ports are RCA for connections to the speaker system and headphone and an input device port such as a microphone or MP3 player.

Figure 8-48. A typical sound card has a variety of connection ports supporting input and output to and from sound devices such as a microphone, MP3 player, and speakers.

Microphone input   Speaker connections   Optical input and output

Goodheart-Willcox Publisher

Figure 8-49. A sound box can be installed through a USB port on the computer. It eliminates the need to open the computer case.

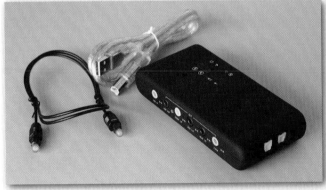

Goodheart-Willcox Publisher

Multimedia

A format that includes interaction with audio and video is referred to as **multimedia**. Attempts to create and play multimedia files more quickly and clearly has been one of the major driving factors in the computer industry. The computing power needed to render three-dimensional images and the storage needed to store or even play movies have caused the processing speeds of CPUs and the RAM considered "minimum requirements" on PCs to increase over the last few years. The greatest recent changes in PC operating systems are changes to how they handle multimedia.

Codecs

A term frequently used in compression is *codec*. It is a contraction of the two words *compression* and *decompression*. A **codec** is any hardware, software, or combination hardware and software that can compress and decompress data. The term is used most often in the video industry and telecommunications. Some examples of software codecs are MPEG, QuickTime, AVC, ATSC, DVB-T, MP3, and many more. When setting up properties for audio and video equipment using Windows, the many compression techniques will be referred to as choosing a method of codec.

MPEG Formats

The **Moving Picture Experts Group (MPEG)**, (pronounced *empeg*), is an organization made up of professionals from all areas of the motion picture industry. The goal of the organization is to develop a standard format for recording motion picture video and sound. Together they developed data compression standards and file formats for storing both audio and video data. The two main original formats are MPEG-1 and MPEG-2. MPEG-1 is similar to videotape quality. MPEG-2 is a higher quality compression used for PC CD video, Digital Versatile Disc (DVD) (also called Digital Video Disc), and HDTV.

The MP3 standard (short for MPEG layer 3) is used for music. It is a derivative of the MPEG-2 standard. (To avoid confusion, MP3 is also a well-known website, but the site takes its name from the format.) MPEG-4 came out in 1999 and is still the main standard used today. There are several more MPEG standards under development.

Advanced Video Coding (AVC) is a video compression standard used for high-definition video. It is also referred to as *H.264/MPEG-4*. You can see why the preferred acronym is AVC. The AVC standard is used in applications such as digital television, DVD and Blu-Ray disks, and Internet video streaming. There are many different broadcast compression codecs used for terrestrial broadcast systems. Terrestrial broadcast systems transmit video over radio wave from a transmitter to an antenna receiver. The term *terrestrial system* is used to classify radio wave transmission systems that do not use satellite or Cable systems. The original radio wave systems were all referred to as terrestrial systems. Cable and satellite systems were not in existence at the time of the first radio wave communication systems.

There are many different television standards and compression standards used throughout the world. The standard used in the United States is Advanced Television Systems Committee (ATSC). It is used for high-definition television broadcasts. The standard used in Europe is the Digital Video Broadcasting—Terrestrial (DVB-T). In the United States, additional compression standards are Digital Video Broadcasting (DVB) and Cable Digital Video Broadcasting (DVB-C). DVB is an open source set of standards and compression technique.

Satellite-based video communications is based on Digital Video Broadcasting and is referred to by the acronym DVB-S. The *S, T,* or *C* represents the communication media satellite, Cable, and terrestrial, respectively. There are many more standards and compression techniques. Each type of media has its own set of standards.

Tech Tip

An error message will be produced if you are trying to play or burn a multimedia file and the player does not have the correct codec configured. You may need to download a particular codec to successfully play or burn a multimedia file.

MPEG-7 and MPEG-21 are standards designed to work with existing MPEG standards and do not actually provide enhanced compression. MPEG-7 is used to identify locations of content, thus allowing faster retrieval. For example, when you play a DVD movie you will be presented with a list of chapters or scenes to choose from. MPEG-21 provides multimedia on demand and protects the digital rights. In other words, MPEG is used to manage the distribution of video while providing copyright infringement protection. MPEG-7 and MPEG-21 are open standards so that any manufacturer can ensure compatibility of these features for their media and their media players.

Buffering

Buffering is a technique used to play a downloaded file without skips or quiet spots during playback. When downloading music from a site, it must travel hundreds or even thousands of miles from the source to your PC. Unless you have a high-bandwidth connection such as a T1, Cable, or high-speed wireless such as 3G or 4G, you will have difficulty maintaining a steady stream of data from the other site. In Chapter 13—Modems and Transceivers, more detailed information about various connection mediums, such as T1 lines and high-speed wireless is presented.

Data is sent across the Internet to your PC in packets that average 1,500 bytes each. As noted earlier, data for sound is quite large. A music sample may be constructed from thousands of the 1,500-byte packets. The data does not arrive as a consistent series of packets. Many data packets will even arrive out of their original order. The reason the data packets can arrive out of order is that the data route to and from the site is constantly being updated. The Internet is composed of various types of media, both cable and wireless. Much of the media becomes congested with data traffic. At times, data packets are rerouted to achieve a faster transmission rate. If a quicker route is discovered by the transmission system while data is transferred, the balance of the data will be transmitted through the new route, **Figure 8-50**. If another route is discovered or the present one becomes very busy, an alternate route is chosen. As the routes continue to change, some of the packets arrive out of the original order.

In addition, the steady stream of packets can be momentarily stopped due to congestion on the lines. In the last few years, the dramatic increase in video and audio data packets has created a lot

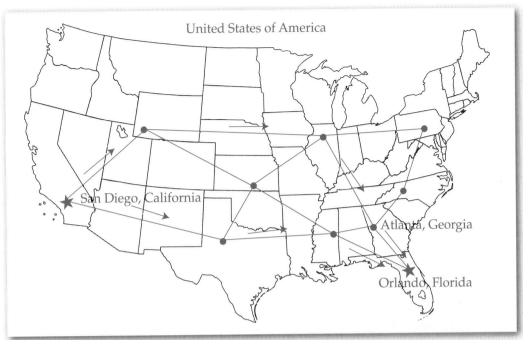

Figure 8-50.
Different routes for data flow. The shortest route is not always the quickest.

Goodheart-Willcox Publisher

of traffic on the data lines resulting in an apparent slowdown of the entire system. A good example of these seemingly slow systems can be seen on many college campuses where scores of students are downloading music and video files from the Internet at one time.

The packets must be reassembled at their destination. Buffering collects all the downloaded data and reassembles it in its original order. It then provides a steady stream of data. In the case of downloading a song, the act of buffering means the song data is downloaded into RAM. It is then assembled and transferred to the player. The player plays the song from a steady stream of data located in RAM rather than from the site. With buffering, there are no interruptions in the continuous stream of music.

Audio and Video Players

To access sound and video tracks recorded on the PC or taken from the Internet, you need a player which is often called a *plug-in*. A player is used to decode compressed multimedia files converting them to audio and video. Players can convert more than one type of compression, but when a new or enhanced compression format is developed, you will need to download an updated version of the player. See **Figure 8-51**.

A large variety of media players are available through the Internet at no charge. Some of the players are only designed to allow you to play through the Internet browser. They will not actually record. The quality of the multimedia presentation is directly related to the quality and capacities of the computer system you use. However, upgrading a single component on an existing system may not show any real improvement. Too often, novices assume that upgrading the CPU or adding more RAM will greatly improve the performance. A system needs to be studied as a whole before a decision is made about enhancing multimedia performance. For example, upgrading the CPU and adding more memory will do little to improve the quality of the multimedia performance if the system uses an 8-bit sound card. A major improvement may have resulted by simply replacing the sound card with a 16-bit PCI sound card.

Figure 8-51.
Microsoft includes Windows Media Player with its operating systems.

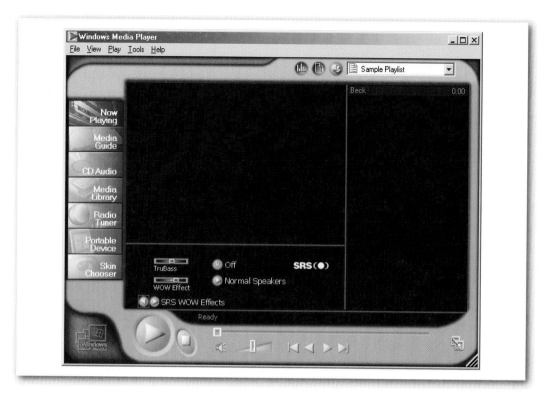

Building a Custom Computer System

When building a custom computer system, you should keep in mind how performance is affected by the five major components. If you want to build a high-performance system you need to have a good graphics adapter and plenty of memory available. To have plenty of memory available, you will need to use a 64-bit operating system. You can use Performance Information and Tools to evaluate a system before making a purchase of similar computers for an office environment or personal use. The base score generated by the tool will provide information to you concerning the ability of the system to support software applications such as CAD, 3D gaming, or video editing. You can also use this tool to identify problem components which may be upgrading or replaced to improve the system performance.

Selecting PC Components

Selecting components to build a customized computer system is based on the tasks the computer is being designed to accomplish.

Tasks such as sending and receiving email, web browsing, and word processing can be accomplished by most standard computers whether they are a desktop, laptop, or portable device such as a tablet. But when real performance is needed for video-intensive applications such as CAD, gaming, and video editing of both movies and high-quality digital imaging, it is common to have a technician design a custom computer system or provide information about which off-the-shelf computer system will meet the performance needs.

The two most important questions to ask first are "What will the computer be used for?" and "How much are you willing to spend?" No other computer component is more important than the computer video system when high-performance video is required. A good computer can be upgraded easily by adding a high-performance video card. High-performance video cards require their own electrical power connection. When upgrading to a high-performance video card, you may also need to replace the power supply with one that can supply more electrical power. Check the video card manufacturer's website for the recommended size of power supply required to support the video card. Some items to consider when building a custom PC are the following:

- **Motherboard/chipset and processor:** The processor and motherboard chipset work together as a team.
- **Power supply:** The two components that use the most electrical energy are the CPU and high-performance video card(s).
- **Video card:** Select by amount of video memory and type of video ports needed (DVD-I, HDMI, etc.).
- **Display:** LED, OLED, or gas-plasma; Internet and wireless connections.
- **Sound card:** Internal or external, number of channels, S/PDIF ports.
- **TV tuner card:** Interior or exterior.
- **Mass storage:** Size of disk storage.
- **Number and type of ports required on motherboard:** HDMI, S/PDIF, RJ-45, etc.
- **Special application software requirements:** CAD, webpage editors, multimedia editing, and 3D video.

Many websites such as NewEgg, TigerDirect, Intel, AMD, and NVIDIA provide information that can be used to custom design your computer system. There are also countless videos provided on YouTube on this topic.

Video Performance Information and Tools

Overall video performance is determined by the video adapter and RAM used to support video. When the video card does not have sufficient RAM, it will utilize part of the RAM installed on the motherboard. To assist you in evaluating a computer system, Windows provides Performance Information and Tools, **Figure 8-52**. This tool determines the overall performance of a computer system and identifies performance capabilities of five major components: processor, RAM, graphics, gaming graphics, and primary hard disk. To access this tool, simply enter the term "Windows Experience" into the **Search** box and look for the result "Check the Windows Experience Index" or right-click **Computer**, select **Properties** from the shortcut menu, and then select

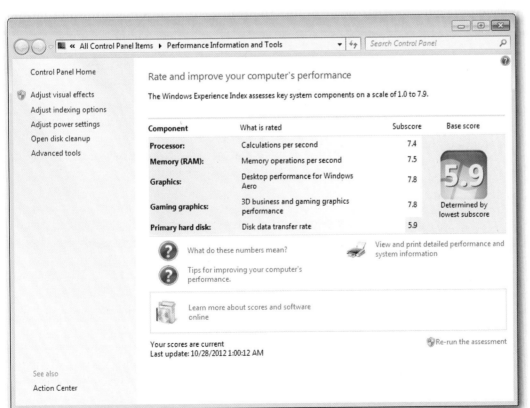

Figure 8-52.
Windows Performance Information and Tools provides a way to determine the overall performance of a computer system and of five major components.

Performance and Information Tools. Windows Experience Index was first introduced with Windows Vista.

Windows Experience Index

The Windows Experience Index is a numeric rating based on the five major components. The Windows experience scales are from 1.0 to 7.9. While each component has a subscore, the overall rating or base score is based on the lowest component score.

In Figure 8-52, the lowest individual subscore is 5.9. The 5.9 subscore is based on the disk data transfer rate. There are two different graphics subscores. The first is "Graphics" and the second is "Gaming Graphics." The graphics subscore is based on the graphics adapter or the graphics chipset incorporated into the motherboard. The second graphics index, "Gaming Graphics," is based on the performance of the graphics total available graphics memory. The graphics subscore is 7.8, and the gaming graphics subscore is 7.8. These two scores do not always match. The reason the example subscores match is the computer is equipped with a high-performance video card.

A computer with a much lower base score and two different subscores for graphics and gaming graphics is shown in **Figure 8-53**. This computer has an adequate video card but not as good as a high-performance video card. In this example, the overall base score is 4.2, based on the gaming graphics index.

Performance Details

The **View and print detailed performance and system information** link in **Performance Information and Tools** produces a window similar to the one in the **Figure 8-54**. Notice how much more detailed information is provided about the system. Notice how the information in the **What is rated** column is replaced by the **Details** column, which provides more information about each component, such as the video card type, total graphics memory, dedicated graphics memory, shared system memory, which version of Microsoft DirectX is installed, and more.

Tech Tip

Windows 32-bit systems are limited to 4 GB of RAM. This is a total amount of RAM including the RAM located on the video card. A 64-bit system does not have this same limitation and is a better choice for high-performance video systems.

Figure 8-53.
The graphics and gaming graphics subscores are based on the video adapter and RAM used to support the video system.

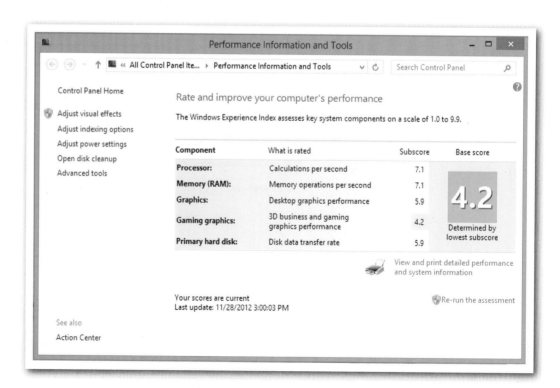

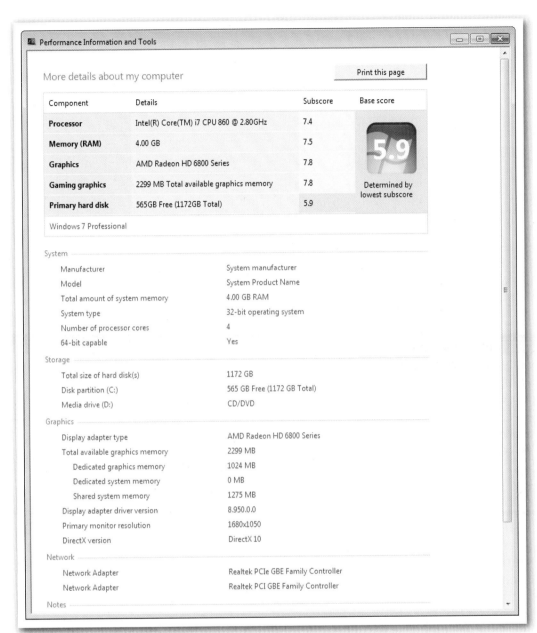

Figure 8-54.
Details for the five major components in **Performance Information and Tools** can be revealed by selecting the **View and print detailed performance and system information** link.

Microsoft Base Score Recommendations

The following table is a guide as to what can be expected from a computer system in regards to the Windows base score. The ranges are approximations. The levels are to serve as a general guide.

Base Score	Capability
2.0–2.9	General computing such as business applications, word processing, Internet browsing, and email. Not adequate for Windows Aero or multimedia applications.
3.0–3.9	Can support Aero and most, but not all, Windows video features. Can play digital TV but may not support high-definition television (HDTV).
4.0–5.9	Can support all Windows visual features and easily supports running multiple software applications simultaneously.
6.0–7.9	Will support intense graphic applications such as multiplayer games, 3D gaming, and recording and play back of HDTV content.

Improving Performance

Computer performance can be improved by adjusting visual effects in the **Performance Options** dialog box, **Figure 8-55**. To access this dialog box, right-click **Computer**, select **Properties** from the shortcut menu. Select **Advanced system settings** and then the **Advanced** tab. You can also go through **Control Panel | System | Advanced System Settings | Advanced** tab. Certain visual effects require more system resources than others. For example, Windows transparency and other visual effects like animate controls take more system resources. The **Performance Options** dialog box provides four major options to choose from that can help system performance:

- **Let Windows choose what's best for my computer**.
- **Adjust for best appearance**.
- **Adjust for best performance**.
- **Custom**.

Figure 8-55. You can use the **Performance Options** dialog box to select which options will provide the very best appearance or very best performance.

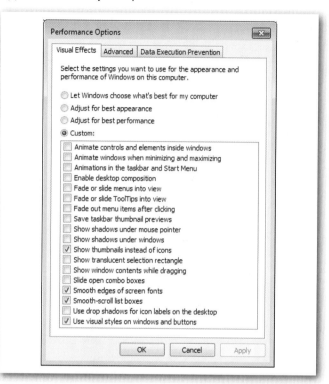

The **Let Windows choose what's best for my computer** option allows the operating system to evaluate the computer and then select appropriate visual options to produce a balance between the best-looking visual effects and maintaining good system performance.

The **Adjust for best appearance** option adjusts the computer to produce the very best possible visual effects but sacrifices performance.

The **Adjust for best performance** option turns off all visual effects to provide the best computer performance possible.

The **Custom** option allows the user to select which visual effects to enable and disable.

To see how the appearance is affected by choosing between best appearance and best performance look at **Figure 8-56**. It shows a comparison of two desktops, one with all visual effects enabled, Figure 8-56A, and the other with visual effects disabled, Figure 8-56B. The two appearances are the result from selecting **Adjust for best appearance** or **Adjust for best performance**, respectively.

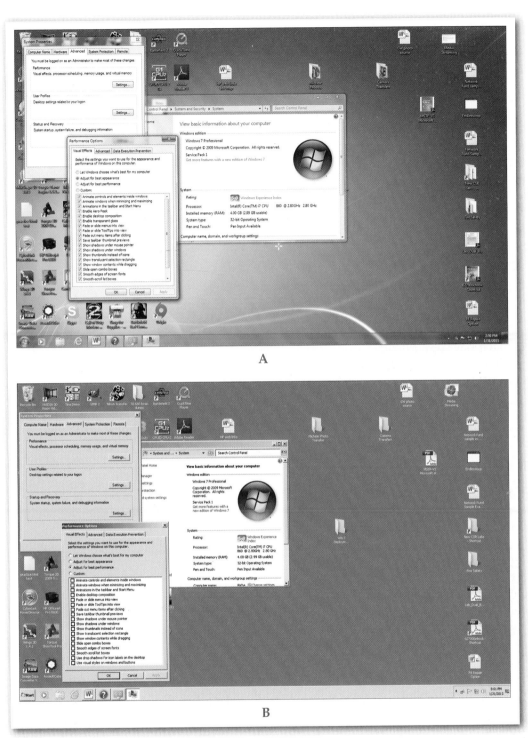

Figure 8-56.
Choosing between best appearance and best performance in the **Performance Options** dialog box. A—Windows visual effects enabled by selecting **Adjust for best appearance**. B—Windows visual effects disabled by selecting **Adjust for best performance**.

Notice how plain the presentation of Windows is in 8-56B as compared to that in Figure 8-56A. The transparency in Figure 8-58B is removed as well as other visual effects. Figure 8-56A has all the visual effects enabled.

DirectX Diagnostic Tool

Microsoft operating system provides the DirectX Diagnostic Tool to perform a quick check of the computer video and audio systems, **Figure 8-57**. You can run the DirectX Diagnostic

Figure 8-57.
The DirectX Diagnostic Tool is used to make simple checks of the computer audio and video systems.

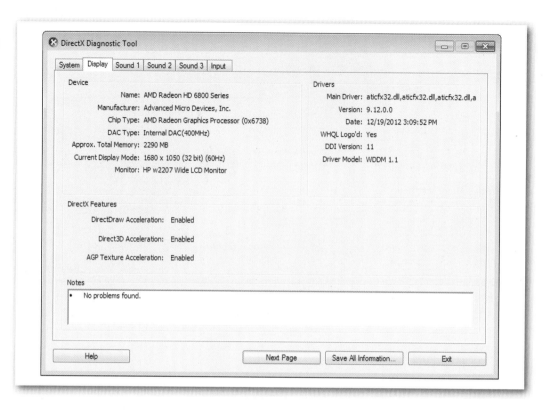

Tool from the command prompt by entering dxdiag. When running Windows XP, Windows Vista, and Windows 7, you can access and run the DirectX Diagnostic Tool by entering DirectX into the **Search** box. Windows 8 will not produce the DirectX Diagnostic Tool when you conduct

a search from the **Search** box, but it will run the DirectX Diagnostic Tool when entered at the command prompt. There will be more about DirectX later in Chapter 15—PC Troubleshooting.

Chapter Summary

- Color display values and display resolution are aspects common to all monitors.
- CRT monitor operation is based on a stream of electrons striking the phosphor coating inside the CRT; an LCD display operates on the principle of polarized light and the effect of an electrical voltage applied to a crystal structure; a gas-plasma display operates on the principle of electroluminescence.
- Troubleshooting a monitor involves checking power to the monitor and the cable between the computer and the display unit.
- Clean a monitor display area with a dry lint-free soft cloth.
- The PCIe ×16 video adapter card has replaced all other video card standards such as PCI, PCI-X, and AGP.
- Installing a video card involves inserting the card in the proper motherboard slot and installing the latest video card driver.
- **Appearance and Personalization** is used in Windows Vista, Windows 7, and Windows 8 to change the display properties.

- Typical home theater connection types are composite video, S-Video, component video, HDMI, S/PDIF, TOSLINK, and RF and F-type.
- Compressing a file is a technique that summarizes redundant information contained in a file.
- A microphone converts sound waves into electrical energy, and a speaker converts electrical energy into sound energy.
- Analog-to-digital conversion takes a periodic sample of the voltage levels in an analog signal and stores them in digital format.
- Installing a sound card involves inserting the card into the motherboard slot, installing the latest drivers, and connecting the speakers to the card and to a power supply.
- Common codecs are MPEG, QuickTime, AVC, ATSC, DVB-T, and MP3.
- The two most important questions to ask before building a custom PC is "What will the computer be used for?" and "How much are you willing to spend?"

Review Questions

Answer the following questions on a separate sheet of paper. Please do not write in this book.

1. What is a pixel?
2. Which type of standard display has the highest resolution?
   a. VGA
   b. XGA
   c. SVGA
   d. WUXGA
3. Which type of standard display has the lowest resolution?
   a. VGA
   b. XGA
   c. SVGA
   d. WUXGA
4. What is the screen resolution for XGA?
5. What is the screen resolution for WUXGA?
6. What screen resolution is used when Windows XP or Windows Vista is in safe mode?
7. How is CRT monitor size determined?
8. The distance between two color pixels on a CRT screen is called _____.
9. Dot pitch is measured in _____.
10. The smaller the dot pitch the (better, worse) the screen resolution.
11. What is raster?
12. Describe the difference between progressive scan and interlacing.
13. What are two common sources of LED backlighting?
14. What is the function of an inverter?
15. Why is the term *organic* used to describe organic LED displays?
16. What is the difference between an LED and an OLED display?

17. Which display technology produces the thinnest displays?
18. What is the difference between passive and active matrix?
19. Define the term *contrast ratio* when describing LCD displays?
20. What is the unit of measure for the brightness for an LCD display?
21. What is native resolution?
22. What affect does a high response time have on animation?
23. Why does a gas-plasma display not require a backlight?
24. If you are troubleshooting a computer with a video display problem, what should you do before changing the monitor?
25. What should you use to clean an LCD display?
26. What chemicals should never be used to clean a monitor?
27. Which motherboard slot type will produce the fastest graphics?
28. What does the acronym SLI represent?
29. What ATI technology is similar to NVIDIA SLI?
30. What should you do first before installing a video card on a customer's computer?
31. When using **Appearance and Personalization**, what does the **Personalization** dialog box allow the user to select?
32. When using **Appearance and Personalization**, what does the **Display** dialog box allow a user to do?
33. What does the acronym DVI represent?
34. What is the difference between downloading and streaming?
35. Which type of connector is commonly associated with fiber-optic sound port connections?
36. What type of image retains its quality after resizing?
37. Explain how a picture image is compressed.
38. How does analog-to-digital conversion work?
39. What two factors determine the quality of converting an analog signal into a digital signal?
40. A microphone converts _____ into electrical energy.
41. A speaker converts electrical energy to _____.
42. What steps should be taken when installing a sound card?
43. What is codec?
44. What is the purpose of a codec?
45. Which is an example of a codec?
    a. MPEG
    b. TCP
    c. TIFF
    d. DirectX
46. What are the two most important questions to ask before building a customized computer?
47. Which single component is the most important when building a customized computer designed for high performance?

48. What other computer component may need upgraded when upgrading to a more powerful high performance video card?

49. What is the name of the tool used to generate a Windows Experience Index?

50. Which five key components are measured to create the Windows Experience Index subscores?

51. What is the range of scores for the Windows Experience Index?

52. How is the overall rating or base score determined for computer system?

53. What is the difference between the graphics subscore and the gaming graphics subscore?

54. What are the four major selections listed in the **Performance Options** dialog box which can affect the computer system performance?

55. What Microsoft tool can be used to perform a quick diagnostic of the audio and video system?

Sample A+ Exam Questions

Answer the following questions on a separate sheet of paper. Please do not write in this book.

1. When a legacy PC boots in safe mode, which video mode is *most likely* used by the system?
   a. VGA
   b. SVGA
   c. XGA
   d. CGA

2. Which of the following is the best definition of dot pitch?
   a. The distance between two color dots measured in pixels
   b. The distance between two color dots measured in inch fractions
   c. The distance between two color dots measured in millimeters
   d. The distance between the diagonal of the screen corners measured in millimeters

3. Which item may need to be replaced after upgrading the video card in a computer system?
   a. CPU
   b. HDD
   c. Power supply
   d. Motherboard RAM

4. Which component will have the most influence on the performance of a 3D video game?
   a. CPU
   b. Graphics card
   c. HDD
   d. Display unit

5. Which type of connector port is used for fiber-optic connections carrying sound data?
   a. RJ-45
   b. HDMI
   c. DVI-D
   d. S/PDIF

6. What is the function of a laptop inverter?
   a. To change black and white images into color
   b. To change the digital data signals into analog data signals
   c. To convert low-voltage dc into high-voltage ac
   d. To convert analog music input into digital data signals

7. Which example would provide the best quality for a sound recording?
   a. An 8-bit, high-frequency sampling rate
   b. A 16-bit, high-frequency sampling rate
   c. An 8-bit, low-frequency sampling rate
   d. A 16-bit, low-frequency sampling rate

8. The term *codec* best relates to which of the following?
   a. Sound quality measurement
   b. Picture quality measurement
   c. A compression and decompression technique
   d. A sound transmission media type

9. A music file is being downloaded and played at the same time. The music starts, stops, and skips repeatedly. What is *most likely* the reason?
   a. Insufficient amount of RAM. The amount of memory should be increased.
   b. The modem speed needs to be increased to 112 baud.
   c. This is a normal effect caused by low download speeds.
   d. The DMA channels are blocked by too much bus traffic.

10. The smallest picture element on a monitor display is called what?
    a. Raster element
    b. Pixel
    c. Byte mark
    d. Color element

Suggested Laboratory Activities

Do not attempt any suggested laboratory activities without your instructor's permission. Certain activities can render the PC operating system inoperable.

1. Make sound recordings and experiment with changing the sampling rates.

2. Use Control Panel to install and modify the properties of a digital camera input system.

3. Create a new set of sounds for closing, opening, and maximizing windows. To do this in Windows XP, access **Control Panel | Sounds, Speech, and Audio Devices | Sounds and Audio Devices** and select the **Sounds** tab. In Windows Vista, Windows 7, or Windows 8, access through **Control Panel | Hardware and Sound | Sound** and select the **Sounds** tab.

4. Open Performance and Information Tools by entering "performance" in the **Search** box and selecting **Performance and Information Tools** from the list of results. For Windows 8, access the **Search** box through **Charms Bar | Search**. View the base score for the computer, and then click the **View and print detailed performance and system information** link to open and view the detailed performance and system information.

5. Locate and identify the driver for the monitor. This information should be provided in the video adapter's **Properties** dialog box.

6. Open Control Panel and view the various options that are available for configuring the appearance and personalization of the computer display.

7. Explore the options for selecting a new desktop background. In Windows Vista and Windows 7, enter the term "background" in the **Search** box. In Windows 8, enter the term "background" in the **Search** box after selecting the **Charms Bar | Search** and then the **Settings** option.

8. Design a high-performance multimedia computer system by selecting individual hardware components. Try to provide the best video and audio while staying within a $2,000.00 budget for the entire system.

9. Open a command prompt and enter the dxdiag command to run the Windows DirectX Diagnostic Tool. Look at the information provided about the computer video and sound system.

10. Use a digital camera to create a unique desktop wallpaper for your assigned PC. Make it a "computer techie" theme.

11. Install a new multimedia system, including a newer sound card, video card, and CD-ROM drive, in an older PC. Before starting, make sure the PC is upgradeable. Check the PC and multimedia manufacturers' websites for hardware concerns, such as BIOS support.

Magnetic and Solid-State Storage Devices

9

After studying this chapter, you will be able to:

- Explain how magnetic principles are applied to data storage.
- Explain disk geometry.
- Identify disk partition systems.
- Recall common file systems and their characteristics.
- Use Disk Defragmenter and Chkdsk.
- Carry out a PATA, a SATA, and an eSATA hard drive installation.
- Compare SAS and SCSI technologies.
- Recall the uses of Solid-State Drives and their advantages over disk and disc storage devices.
- Use Computer Management to create a Virtual Hard Disk.

A+ Exam—Key Points

This entire chapter is important for CompTIA A+ exam preparation. Hard drive installation and replacement is one of the most common jobs for a PC technician and is weighted heavily on the A+ exam.
You must be very familiar with the Disk Management tool in Windows Computer Management as well as with the various actions that can be performed on a hard drive, such as creating a partition, formatting a partition, extending a partition, adding an additional hard drive, and creating a simple or dynamic disk. Be sure to familiarize yourself with the hard drive terminology listed in the Key Terms.

A+

Key Terms

The following key terms will become important pieces of your computer vocabulary. Be sure you can define them.

active partition	logical unit number (LUN)
actuator arm	low-level format
AT Attachment (ATA)	Master Boot Record (MBR)
basic disk	Microsoft Reserved Partition (MSR)
benchmark tests	multiple zone recording (MZR)
cluster	New Technology File System (NTFS)
cylinder	parallel ATA (PATA)
defragment	primary partition
disk signature	proprietary recovery partition
dynamic disk	protective MBR
EFI System Partition (ESP)	read/write head
encrypted file system (EFS)	Resilient File System (ReFS)
Enhanced Integrated Drive	SCSI ID number
Electronics (EIDE)	sectors
extended file allocation table	Serial ATA (SATA)
(exFAT)	Serial Attached SCSI (SAS)
FAT16	Small Computer System Interface
FAT32	(SCSI)
floppy disk	solid-state disc caching
floppy disk drive	Solid-State Drive (SSD)
GUID Partition Table (GPT)	tracks
high-level format	virtual file allocation table (VFAT)
Integrated Drive Electronics (IDE)	Virtual Hard Disk (VHD)
interleave factor	volume mount points
logical drive	

This chapter will prove to be one of the most important units covered in the entire textbook. It will give you incredible insight as to how an operating system organizes, stores, and retrieves data. This information can prove invaluable when troubleshooting system failures. You will also learn about the operation of magnetic storage systems, such as hard drives, floppy disks, and tape systems as well as Solid-State Drives. These topics are critical for a computer technician and for CompTIA A+ Certification preparation.

Magnetic Storage Devices

Magnetism has been used to record data for many years. Magnetic storage devices have been the mainstays of the PC industry. This section covers the operation of magnetic storage devices:

hard drives, floppy drives, and tape drive systems. First, electromagnetic principles are explained to provide the proper foundation for understanding how magnetic storage devices work.

Electromagnetic Principles

To understand complex devices like hard drives and other disk drives, you first need some background in electromagnetic principles. These principles allow hard drives and floppy disks to store volumes of data. However, these principles also place restrictions on their use and construction.

Converting Data into Magnetic Patterns

Electrical energy can produce magnetism, and magnetism can produce electrical energy.

This principle is the basis of magnetic storage device operation. A fine layer of iron oxide covers the data storage area of a typical storage device such as tape or a disk platter. Iron oxide is easily magnetized when it is exposed to an energized conductor. A conductor is any material that allows for the easy flow of electricity. Any energized conductor is surrounded by a rotating magnetic field. The direction of the rotation determines the north and south characteristics of the magnetic field. The direction of rotation around the conductor is determined by the direction of current in the conductor.

Look closely at **Figure 9-1**. It shows the relationship of current direction and the magnetic field surrounding a conductor. The conductor is wound around the top of the magnetic **read/write head**—the mechanism that records information to and reads information from a magnetic medium.

At the bottom of the magnetic head, there is a gap. This gap is used to transfer the magnetic energy to the oxidized surface of a floppy disk, hard disk, or magnetic tape. All magnetic recording devices use this same principle.

A digital signal is composed of rising and falling voltage levels. These rising and falling voltage levels produce a changing current direction. As the current (digital signal) changes direction through the conductor wound around the read/write head, the magnetic field at the gap changes. As the digital signal flows through the read/write head, a magnetic pattern is impressed on the iron oxide. The magnetic pattern represents the digital pattern sent to the read/write head. This is how data is stored on a magnetic disk or tape.

Converting Magnetic Patterns into Data

To read the data back from a disk or tape, an electrical signal is generated from the magnetic patterns. Electrical energy can be produced by the motion of a magnetic field near a conductor.

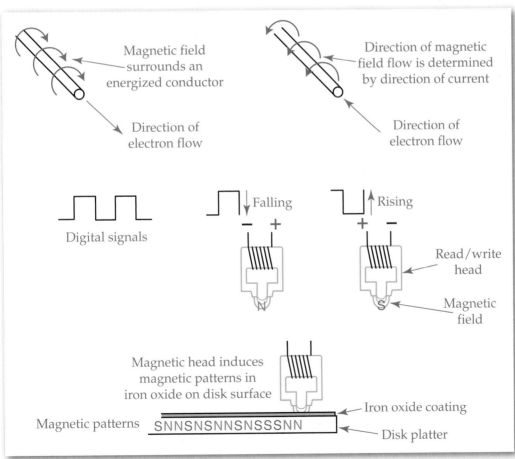

Figure 9-1.
Current flowing through a conductor produces a magnetic field (top). This field is concentrated in a magnetic read/write head (middle). The read/write head is then used to create patterns on a disk or tape surface (bottom).

Magnetic field surrounds an energized conductor

Direction of electron flow

Direction of magnetic field flow is determined by direction of current

Direction of electron flow

Digital signals

Falling

Rising

Read/write head

Magnetic field

Magnetic head induces magnetic patterns in iron oxide on disk surface

Iron oxide coating

Magnetic patterns   SNNSNSNNSNSSSNN

Disk platter

See **Figure 9-2**. The direction of the current produced in the conductor is directly related to the north and south property of the magnetic field.

As you now know, a magnetic disk has a magnetic pattern along its surface. As the magnetic pattern on the surface of the disk passes rapidly under the read/write head, electrical energy is produced in pulses. The electrical pulses that are generated match the pattern on the magnetic code stored on the disk. The pulses of electrical energy are very small, so an amplifier circuit is needed. The amplifier magnifies the electrical energy produced from the magnetic patterns stored on the media to a level high enough to be used by the computer circuitry and components. The amplifier is integrated into the electronic circuitry on the media drive's circuit board.

Hard Disk Drive

A typical hard disk drive, also referred to as a *hard drive*, consists of several platters in a stack. The platters can be made from glass, aluminum alloy, or even ceramic. The top and bottom of the platter are coated with a thin film of metal oxide. The metal oxide records the magnetic patterns introduced to the disk platter by the read/write head. The read/write head is located at the end of an **actuator arm**, which is a device that moves the head over the disk.

At one time, the read/write head was constructed of very small wire coils. Read/write head technology has now evolved to such microscopic size that the same technology used to manufacture chips is also used to create the head. The read/write head can produce extremely compact magnetic patterns exceeding 10,000 bits per inch.

The hard disk drive is simple in design but very impressive when you consider the tolerances within which it operates. The read/write head does not actually touch the platter. Instead, it rides over the platter on a cushion of air. The distance from the surface of the disk platter is only about 0.001 microns, **Figure 9-3**. Since the head travels so closely to the platter, the platter must be absolutely flat and free of defects. Any defect on the surface of the platter would destroy the read/write head on contact.

Hard drives have filters to catch any microscopic particles that might be produced during normal read/write operations. Remember that the actuator mechanism is mechanical and will produce some particles through friction between the moving parts.

Figure 9-2.
The magnetic patterns stored on a disk platter are converted to electrical pulses representing the data stored on a disk. As the platters spin rapidly under the read/write head, the magnetism creates electrical energy in the read/write head.

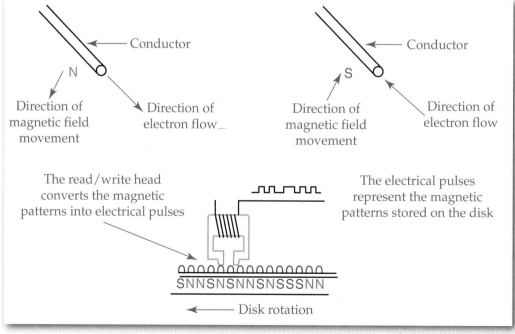

Figure 9-3. The read/write head floats just above the spinning disk of a hard drive.

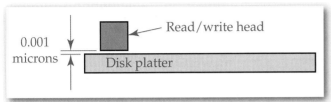

Hard drive speeds are listed as 5400 rpm, 7200 rpm, 10,000 rpm, and 15,000 rpm. In general, the faster the hard drive, the less storage space and the greater the electrical power consumption. The faster a drive spins, the more wind resistance the disk platter encounters, thus more electrical energy is required to spin the platter at the higher rpm. To overcome the wind resistance, platter diameter is reduced. This results in less storage space. So you can see that a faster disk may be compromised by the total amount of storage space available. Also, there is a direct correlation between speed and price. In general, a faster drive is usually more expensive.

The 5400-rpm and 7200-rpm drives are most commonly encountered in PC devices. Replacements for the 5400-rpm drive must come from existing stocks because it is no longer in production. After the existing stocks are gone, 7400-rpm drives will be used for replacements. The 10,000-rpm and 15,000-rpm drives are the most expensive and can be found in laptop devices. The following table summarizes the characteristics of the commonly encountered hard drive speeds.

RPM	Characteristic
5400	Reduced performance and reduced power consumption. No longer manufactured new. Only offered as a replacement part.
7200	Good performance and good storage capacity at low cost.
10,000	High performance and reduced storage capacity. More costly than 7200 rpm.
15,000	High performance and reduced storage capacity. Most costly.

A+ Note

You may encounter a question related to custom computer design or disk drive replacement. The question will relate to disk drive rpm and cost. In general, when the rpm is faster, the performance is better and the cost is higher. You would want a high rpm disk for large amounts of storage when cost is not a factor.

Floppy Disk and Drive

A **floppy disk** is a soft magnetic disk used for storing small to moderate amounts of information **Figure 9-4**. It is similar in design to the hard drive except that the disk media is readily accessible. Think of a floppy drive as an unsealed hard drive package. In the hard drive system, the data is stored on platters. In the floppy drive system, the data is stored on removable diskettes.

Figure 9-4. Early floppy disks were very flexible, earning them the name "floppy." They evolved to hard shells that have little flexibility.

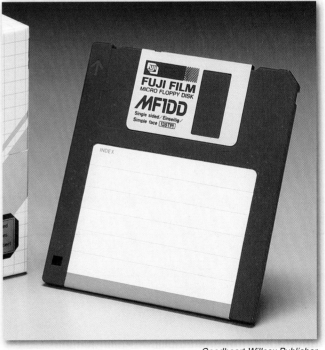

The original disk media was a thin, Mylar (plastic) disk covered with metal oxide. It was stored inside a paper jacket when not in use. This media was easily exposed to the environment, and data was often lost due to improper handling. Users were taught not to touch the disk media with bare hands and to avoid laying the disk down without the protective jacket. These early disks were easily damaged.

The floppy disk, as we know it, has evolved from a large 8″ disk, to a 5 1/4″ disk, and to the standard 3 1/2″ disk. The early 8″ and 5 1/4″ diskettes were packaged in a hard paper or thin layer of cardboard or plastic. The 3 1/2″ diskette was designed with a durable plastic case surrounding the entire disk media, **Figure 9-5**. However, the diskette inside the package is still "floppy," giving the medium its name. The protective case and the data media are supplied as a single unit rather than as two separate pieces. This protects the data on the media when not inserted in the floppy disk drive. The original floppy disks could easily be bent or warped resulting in failure of the disk inside the disk drive. Data on the 3 1/2″ diskette is protected from dust and lint particles. The older style floppy disk was exposed to contaminants, even when properly stored.

With the improvement of manufacturing capabilities, the physical size of diskettes steadily decreased while the amount of storage available

on a diskette greatly increased. The table in **Figure 9-6** lists the three common storage capacities for the 3 1/2″ floppy. The 1.44-MB format is the widely accepted format.

The **floppy disk drive** reads and writes to floppy disks, **Figure 9-7**. The floppy disk drive is almost completely obsolete and only found on legacy devices.

Figure 9-8 shows power and cable connections for a floppy disk drive. The data cables for floppy drives have a twist near one of the connectors. The connector near the twist is attached to the drive unit. The other end of the cable connects to the floppy disk drive port on the motherboard.

Figure 9-6. Floppy disk capacities.

Physical Size	Type	Capacity
3.5	Double density	720 kB
3.5	High density	1.44 MB
3.5	Extra-high density	2.88 MB

Goodheart-Willcox Publisher

Figure 9-7. Typical floppy disk drive.

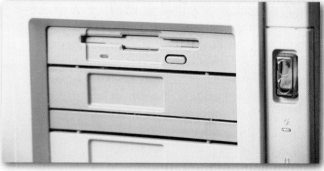

Goodheart-Willcox Publisher

Figure 9-5. The features of a typical floppy disk.

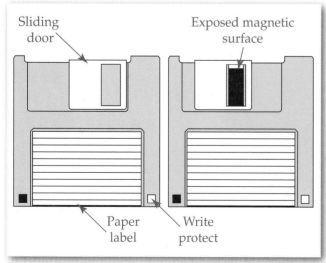

Sliding door

Exposed magnetic surface

Paper label

Write protect

Goodheart-Willcox Publisher

Figure 9-8. Cable and power connections for a floppy disk drive.

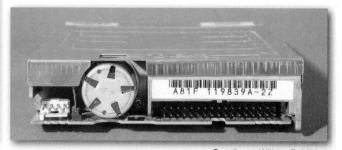

Goodheart-Willcox Publisher

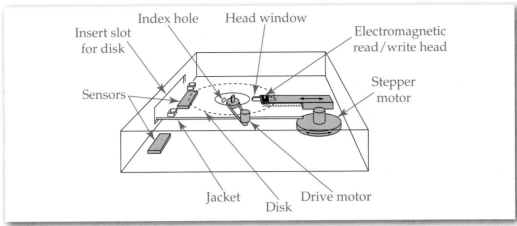

Figure 9-9.
Parts of a floppy disk drive.

Goodheart-Willcox Publisher

Figure 9-9 diagrams a typical floppy disk drive. The operation of a floppy drive is simple. The disk spins inside the drive at 300 rpms. A read/write head, similar to the one discussed with hard drives, moves across the disk's surface through an opening in the disk cover called the *head window.* The read/write head moves into position over one of the concentric tracks on the disk to read or write as necessary. A track is part of the disk geometry and is covered later in this chapter.

Repairing a floppy drive is practically obsolete. The replacement of a 3 1/2″ drive is so inexpensive that labor costs for a typical disk repair far exceed replacement.

of data and have long been used for backing up large amounts of data. Tape drives were also the preferred method of sending data from one location to another before the full development of the Internet, **Figure 9-10**.

A storage tape is created by covering a plastic tape with a thin flexible coating of metal oxide, similar to the coating on floppy disks and hard disk platters. A read/write head transfers data to and from the tape. The data is stored on the tape as a long series of magnetic pulses. The principles used to store and retrieve data on a hard drive also apply to the magnetic tape system. **Figure 9-11** shows a typical tape cartridge.

A+ Note

Even though floppy disk drives and disks are old technology, the CompTIA A+ exams may include simple questions related to these devices, as long as they are listed in the test objectives. Customers don't always have the very latest computers. This is another example of why it is important to always check the latest test objectives located at the CompTIA website.

Figure 9-10. Typical tape drive.

Goodheart-Willcox Publisher

Tape Drive

Magnetic tape storage was the earliest removable storage media used with computer systems. Tapes can hold a tremendous amount

Figure 9-11. Large storage tapes are often used to back up systems. This tape can hold 30 GB of data.

Goodheart-Willcox Publisher

The one main disadvantage of using tape is that the data must be read sequentially. That is to say you must start at the beginning of the tape and search through the data sequentially until you find what you need. Hard drives, floppies, and CD-ROMs allow you to access data anywhere on the disk without having to pass through all of the data saved previously. Still, for inexpensive, dependable backups of large data systems, the tape has been the preferred media. However, with the development of CD-RW and DVD disc systems, tape drives have diminished in popularity. CD-RW and DVD give the advantages of both large storage capabilities and random access. Tape systems will continue in industry as conversion from tape to disc continues, but they will soon be obsolete.

> **Tech Tip**
>
> The importance of system backups cannot be overemphasized. Once total loss of data or programs has been experienced, the need to back up becomes obvious. Most cases of data loss revolve around the failure of a hard drive that contained all original data. While operating system software can be reinstalled, original data can be lost forever. Data recovery techniques are not always successful, and they are certainly more time-consuming than replacing files with copies from a backup disc or tape.

Disk Geometry

The surface of the disk is divided into sections that are used as storage areas for data. The layout of the sections on the disk surface must be recognized by the computer operating systems. The sections used to record data on a disk drive are described in terms such as *sectors*, *clusters*, *tracks*, and *cylinders*, **Figure 9-12**.

Tracks are a set of concentric circles where data is stored on a disk. The tracks are subdivided into physical sections called **sectors**. The term **cluster**, also referred to as *allocation units*, describes file storage space and usually consists of one or more sectors. The smallest sector or cluster size is 512 bytes.

> **Tech Tip**
>
> A *sector* is a "physical" description of a portion of a track. A *cluster* is a "logical" file storage unit, which may span several sectors.

While a floppy disk is a single layer, a hard disk drive consists of a stack of platters. Each platter has its own tracks, clusters, and sectors. A **cylinder** is a vertical collection of one set of tracks. There is one cylinder for every stack of tracks. The read/write heads move across the platters in unison. All tracks are written to simultaneously. Thus, data files are stored in cylinders for fast access.

When writing to a disk, each head writes data to the disk sequentially. Head 1 writes data on the first available sector on the top surface of platter one. When another sector is needed, head 2 writes data on the bottom of the top platter. Head 3 writes data on the top of the second platter, and so on. This scheme of data recording is continued using the read/write heads in sequence until all the data has been recorded. Thus, the data of a single file can be spread over several disk platters.

A typical cluster size range is from 4 kB to 32 kB. It is important to note that the size of the cluster is directly related to the size of the hard disk drive when using certain file systems, such as FAT12, FAT16, FAT32, and NTFS. These file systems are discussed in detail later in this chapter.

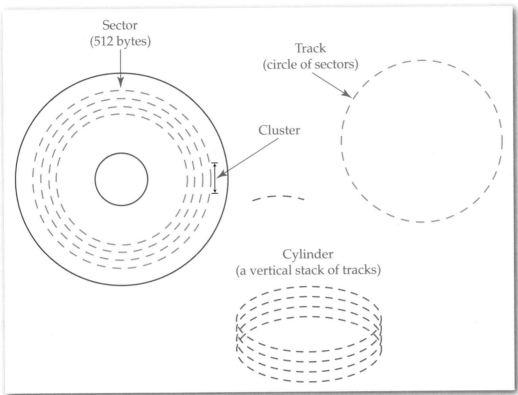

Goodheart-Willcox Publisher

Figure 9-12.
Typical disk geometry. Disks can be subdivided into sectors, tracks, cylinders, and clusters.

Data or a typical program stored on disk will span many clusters. There needs to be an organized way to keep track of all the clusters of data on a disk. The computer needs to know where clusters of a particular data group begin and end. The computer must also know which clusters on a disk are already being used for storage and which clusters are available for storage. The **GUID Partition Table (GPT)** and the **Master Boot Record (MBR)** contain information about the disk partition areas, such as the number of bytes per sector, number of sectors per cluster, number of clusters per track, number of tracks, total number of clusters, number of read/write heads, and the type of storage media (floppy disk or hard drive). It also contains the boot software program used to access or transfer control of the computer system to the operating system. When present, the MBR is located as a hidden protected area on the first sector of the hard disk drive. When present, the GPT is located as a hidden protected area in each individual partition.

Disk geometry is created in three major steps: low-level format, partitioning, and formatting. First, a low-level format is performed on the hard drive at the factory. Next, the hard drive is partitioned. Finally, the disk partition is formatted. This format is also referred to as a high-level format. Another step, which is unique to the Windows operating system, is initialization. When a disk is initialized, the type of partition (MBR or GPT) is selected. There will be more about these topics in this chapter. Some media only requires formatting and does not require partitioning. Partitioning is unique to hard drives, not floppies or optical disks.

Low-Level Format

The low-level format scans to detect bad sectors on the disk platters. Bad sectors are identified and are not used during the high-level format process. The **low-level format** is a process that determines the type of encoding to be done on the disk platter and the sequence in which the read/write heads will access stored data. The sequence is referred to as the *interleave factor*.

Interleave factor describes the way the sectors are laid out on a disk surface. Many times you will see an illustration showing sectors laid out side by side. In reality, they are staggered across the tracks, **Figure 9-13**. If the actual sectors were in sequential order side by side, disk access would be slow. At the end of each cluster or sector is information about the location of the next sector or cluster. If the sectors were side by side, the read/write head would pass the next sector before the location information could be processed. This means the disk would need to make a complete revolution before the data could be read from the next sector. By staggering the sectors across the disk track area, a hard drive's data access rate is optimized. When the read/write head passes over the end of the sector, all information about the location of the next storage sector can be processed before the read/write head reaches it. This means the disk read/write head does not need to wait for a complete disk revolution to read the stored data in the next data storage sector.

The interleave factor is unique to each disk design. It takes into account disk rpm, the speed of data transfer across the bus, and the speed of transfer through the chips and the read/write head. Because these factors differ greatly from manufacturer to manufacturer, the interleave factor also varies greatly. The interleave factor is only important for performing a low-level format. The low-level format arranges the locations of the sectors on the disks. The high-level format is performed after a drive is partitioned and identifies the sector locations and constructs the

file tables. File tables and formatting are covered later in this chapter.

Multiple Zone Recording

Early disk drive geometry provided an equal number of sectors on the innermost and outermost tracks. To improve storage capacity of the platters, a new method of sectoring the tracks was developed. Because there is wasted space in the outer tracks on the platter, multiple zone recording was developed. **Multiple zone recording (MZR)**, also called *zone bit recording*, provides twice as many sectors in the outermost tracks as compared to the innermost tracks. See **Figure 9-14**.

Disk Partition Systems

Computer technology is constantly evolving. The hard drive partition system has become quite complicated in recent years because of the need to accommodate large disk drives and to design a better system of protection for critical boot files. Because of this, there are two different Microsoft disk partition styles used for hard disk drives: Master Boot Record (MBR) and GUID Partition Table (GPT). The MBR and the GPT identify the location of the partitions on a hard disk drive. The type of partition used is directly related to the type of firmware designed to work with the

Figure 9-13.
The interleave factor describes the pattern in which sectors are laid out on a disk. Sequential sectors are not side by side.

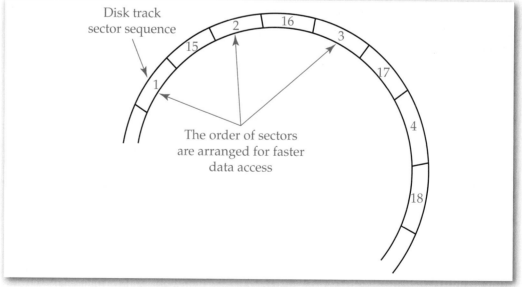

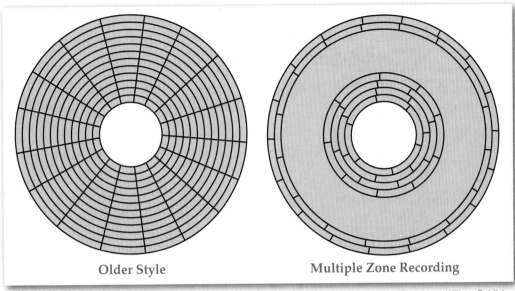

Older Style   Multiple Zone Recording

Figure 9-14.
Multiple zone recording allows for more sectors on the outer tracks of a disk. The disk on the left reflects the older style for setting up sectors on a hard drive. Inner and outer tracks contain the same number of sectors. The disk on the right shows multiple zone recording. There are more sectors on outer tracks than inner tracks with multiple zone recording.

Goodheart-Willcox Publisher

motherboard: BIOS or UEFI. The type of partition is decided when the disk is first initialized.

The operating system performs the initialization. When a hard disk drive is initialized, MBR or GPT is selected and configured or written on the hard disk drive so the drive can then be partitioned. Before GPT, partition style was never a choice, so it did not require user input.

> **Tech Tip**
>
> Storage devices such as hard disk drives and Solid-State Drives must be automatically detected by the system firmware. A failure of the firmware to detect and list the device is a symptom of complete failure of the device electronic circuitry or a loose cable. For cable failure, reconnect or replace the cable. For electronic circuit board failure, replace the entire device.

When a disk is partitioned, it is divided into separate storage areas. The separate storage areas are often referred to as logical drives. A **logical drive** is not a physically separate drive even though it appears to the user as a separate drive. See **Figure 9-15**. In this screen capture, a 10-GB hard drive has been partitioned into several areas. Notice how many hard drives are displayed. You can see five hard drives indicated by the letters C, D, E, F, and G. These are five logical hard drives created from one large physical hard drive.

Another reason for partitions is security. In Figure 9-15, drive C is set up as a network share. The hand under the drive is the symbol for a shared drive in Windows XP. Vista and later use an icon of two people side by side.. The term *shared* means that the drive can be used or shared by other computers on the network. The other drives on this computer are not shared and cannot be accessed by other users on the network.

When multiple partitions are created on a hard drive, only one of the partitions is designated as the active partition. The **active partition** is the partition from which the operating system will boot. It is the designated boot disk for the system.

The minimum amount of space a file can occupy is a cluster. By partitioning a hard drive, smaller cluster sizes can be used. The size of clusters on a hard drive is directly related to the size of the hard drive. Larger hard drives have larger clusters. The hard drive can have clusters as large as 64 kB. With 64-kB clusters, even if a file size were only a few hundred bytes total, the entire 64-kB cluster would be required for storing the small file. Examine **Figure 9-16**.

Since the cluster size is directly related to partition size, you can have more efficient use of disk space by using more than one partition. For example, a 20-GB hard drive formatted with FAT32 as one partition will contain 16-kB clusters. The same 20-GB hard drive formatted with FAT32 but divided into two equal partitions will contain

Figure 9-15.
Windows Explorer showing a 10-GB hard drive partitioned into 5 logical drives, C through G.

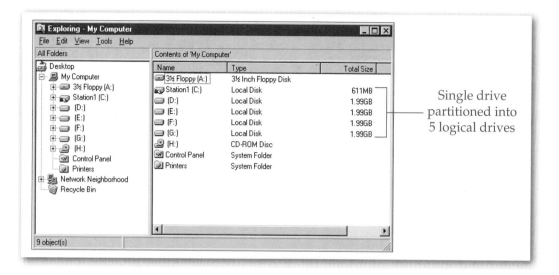

Figure 9-16.
Comparison of cluster utilization of disk storage area for a 9-kB file. The 4-kB cluster format wastes only 2 kB of storage space when storing the file. The 32-kB cluster format wastes 23 kB of space.

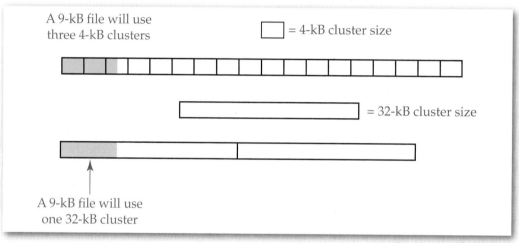

Goodheart-Willcox Publisher

8-kB clusters. Partitioning improves the efficiency of disk storage space.

The size of the cluster is also dependent on the file system used. The chart in **Figure 9-17** details cluster size in relation to hard drive size and the file system used. Note the NTFS cluster sizes compared to FAT16 and FAT32. The NTFS system uses much smaller cluster sizes than FAT16 and FAT32. This results in better use of hard disk space.

MBR Partitions

The Master Boot Record (MBR) contains partition information and a small amount of executable code that starts the computer operating system. In a FAT16 or FAT32 formatted

system, the file allocation table (FAT) contains information about where each file starts on the disk. In a system formatted as NTFS, a master file table (MFT) contains similar information. See **Figure 9-18**.

An MBR-based hard drive can contain up to four primary partitions or three primary partitions and one extended partition, **Figure 9-19**. The extended partition can contain additional logical drives. Only one extended partition can exist on a disk drive. An extended partition can only be created on an MBR-based disk.

All hard disk drives must contain at least one **primary partition** to contain operating system, boot, and data files. The primary partition can contain the system files or the boot files or a combination of both. According to Microsoft,

Volume or Partition Size	FAT16 Cluster Size	FAT32 Cluster Size	NTFS Cluster Size
7 MB–16 MB	2 kB	NA	512 bytes
17 MB–32 MB	512 bytes	NA	512 bytes
33 MB–64 MB	1 kB	512 bytes	512 bytes
65 MB–128 MB	2 kB	1 kB	512 bytes
129 MB–256 MB	4 kB	2 kB	512 bytes
257 MB–512 MB	8 kB	4 kB	512 bytes
513 MB–1024 MB	16 kB	4 kB	1 kB
1025 MB–2 GB	32 kB	4 kB	2 kB
2 GB–4 GB	64 kB	4 kB	4 kB
4 GB–8 GB	NA	4 kB	4 kB
8 GB–16 GB	NA	8 kB	4 kB
16 GB–32 GB	NA	16 kB	4 kB
32 GB–2 TB	NA	NA	4 kB

Figure 9-17. Comparison of cluster size for FAT16, FAT32, and NTFS. NTFS allows the smallest cluster for larger partitions. This data is based on the Windows 2000 Resource Book.

Goodheart-Willcox Publisher

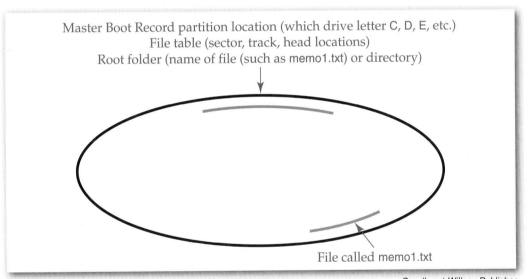

Master Boot Record partition location (which drive letter C, D, E, etc.)
File table (sector, track, head locations)
Root folder (name of file (such as memo1.txt) or directory)

File called memo1.txt

Figure 9-18. Three pieces of information are necessary to locate a file on a disk: the drive letter (to locate the drive the data is stored on), the name of the file or directory, and the cluster locations of the file.

Goodheart-Willcox Publisher

Figure 9-19. Possible partitions in an MBR-based system.

MBR	Primary	Primary	Primary	Primary

MBR	Primary	Primary	Primary	Extended Logical Logical Logical Logical

Goodheart-Willcox Publisher

the Windows "system files" are used to start the computer, and the "boot files" are used to run the operating system after the boot sequence is completed.

There can be a lot of confusion about the locations and purpose of partitions, especially since the development of the UEFI firmware and the System Reserved partition. Early disk systems using the MBR partition style often used the terms *primary partition, active partition, system partition,* and *boot partition* to mean the same partition because they were all located on the same partition most of the time. Today, the boot and system partition can be two different partitions. To determine the exact location of these designated areas on a specific computer, inspect the partition status located in the Disk Management tool of Computer Management. See **Figure 9-20**.

The partition status is how Microsoft identifies the role of specific partitions and the location of some critical files. The typical partition

Figure 9-20. Windows 7 disk partitions. A—Windows 7 basic disk partitions. B—Windows 7 basic disk partitions with an EFI System Partition (ESP).

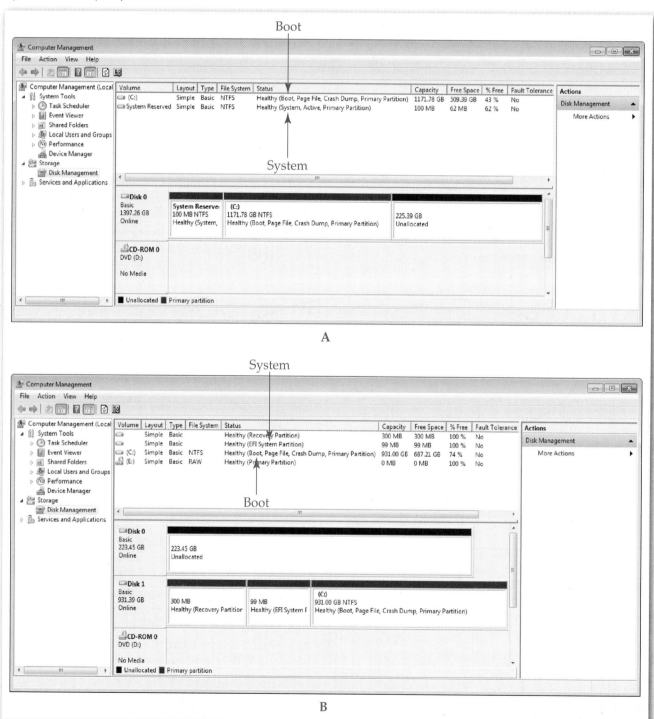

statuses are Primary, Active, Boot, System, Page File, and Crash Dump. Often, the purpose of a partition is identified by the status. For example, a drive that is marked with the Active status is an active partition. It is where the files required to start loading the operating system are located. It is not necessarily designated as drive C but will also appear as the System Reserved partition. The System Reserved partition is discussed in detail later in this chapter.

The partition marked as Active is the designated partition used to hold the files required to start loading the operating system. There is usually only one designated active partition. A typical MBR-based drive will not have a System Reserved partition, so the C partition is typically the active partition. A GPT-based drive will have a System Reserved partition, and it is the active partition. When an EFI System Partition (ESP) exists, it serves the same function as the active partition but is not necessarily identified as "Active" in the partition status. The EFI System Partition (ESP) is covered later in this chapter.

The Page File status indicates the location of the page file. The page file is a portion of the hard drive that is used to augment the system RAM. The Crash Dump status is the location where the operating system attempts to write information when a system failure happens. The file is called the *crash dump,* and the default location is the system root, which is usually drive C.

The System status indicates a system partition and is where the hardware-specific files needed to load the operating system are located. Some of the information stored on the system partition is directly related to the locations of other partitions, security tools such as BitLocker, and sometimes recovery tools.

The Boot status indicates the boot partition. The boot partition is the location of the vast majority of the operating system files as compared to the system partition. Many people and resources use the terms *system partition* and *boot partition* interchangeable because in reference to earlier computer systems, the system and boot files were typically located on the same partition. The confusion starts when you have multiple partitions or a System Reserved partition present. Then, the files can be located on different partitions.

Tech Tip

One of the most confusing Microsoft naming schemes is the way Microsoft identifies the status of the boot partition and system partition. The DOS operating system designated the boot and system partitions the opposite as they are identified today.

Take a minute or two to compare the locations of the active, primary, page file, crash dump, and especially the system and boot in Figure 9-20. Pay particular attention to which partition they are located in.

GPT Partitions

You should recall from Chapter 2 that Unified Extensible Firmware Interface (UEFI) firmware uses a GUID Partition Table (GPT). GUID represents *Globally Unique Identifier.* The GPT-based partition systems do not have the same limitations as an MBR-based partition system. You may create 128 primary partitions on a disk system initialized with GPT.

Another advantage of GPT is that it can handle large hard disk drives better than MBR. The MBR can support hard disk drive storage sizes of up to 2 terabytes (TB). GPT is designed to support hard disk drive storage sizes of up to 18 exabytes (EB). An exabyte is approximately equal to one million terabytes. GPT was first introduced with Windows XP 64-bit edition and Windows Server 2003. The following table compares MBR and GPT partitions.

MBR	GPT
Supports a maximum of four primary partitions.	Supports a maximum of 128 primary partitions.
Can support a 2-TB partition size.	Can support an 18-EB partition size.
Has no backup partition table.	Has backup partition table.

Figure 9-21 illustrates some possible partition arrangements you may encounter. Notice the addition of the Microsoft Reserved Partition (MSR), also called the System Reserved. Added are the proprietary recovery partition and EFI System Partition (ESP). The partitions are

Figure 9-21.
Possible GPT partition arrangements.

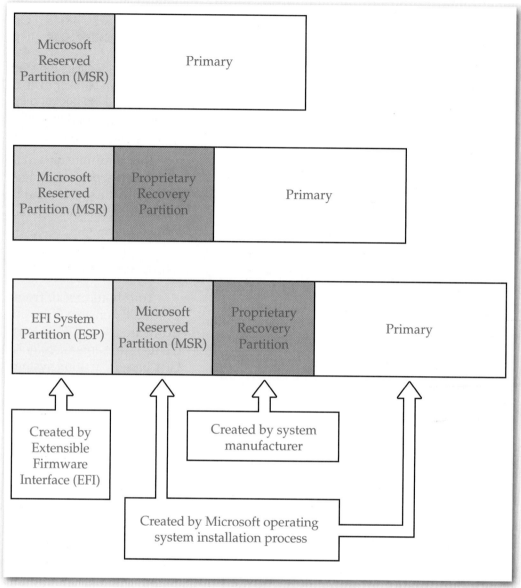

Goodheart-Willcox Publisher

arranged in Microsoft's recommended sequence, but the exact order may vary according to where the system manufacturer places the proprietary recovery partition.

EFI System Partition (ESP)

A computer system with UEFI firmware will create an **EFI System Partition (ESP)** and requires a GUID Partition Table (GPT). The acronym EFI stands for Extensible Firmware Interface. The ESP is a special area of the hard disk drive intended for use solely by the firmware and typically contains files and data required to boot the computer system. Only one ESP is required per computer no matter how many physical or logical disks are installed. A BIOS-based computer can create an MBR or a GPT partition; UEFI firmware is not required. Hence, the appearance of the ESP is determined by the presence of UEFI and GPT. That is why not all GPT arrangements will show an ESP.

Tech Tip

The acronym EFI represents "Extensible Firmware Interface" and the acronym ESP represents "Extensible Firmware Interface System Partition." However, these acronyms are often used interchangeably when discussing disk partitions.

The ESP can be created by firmware or by the Microsoft DiskPart utility. At this time, the ESP cannot be created using the Disk Management tool in Computer Management or in the Microsoft Management Console (MMC). When present, the ESP typically contains the required boot files: NTLDR, HAL, and boot.txt. Additional files, such as hardware drivers, may also be contained in the ESP. Generally, the ESP is a hidden partition that can only be viewed using the UEFI software-created utilities. The proprietary recovery partition may be hidden as well but not always.

Microsoft Reserved Partition (MSR)

The **Microsoft Reserved Partition (MSR)**, or *System Reserved Partition,* is required for GUID partition tables. The Windows installation program creates an MSR partition if one does not already exist. In **Figure 9-22**, an MSR partition appears in the Disk Management tool in Computer Management. The MSR partition is labeled "System Reserved."

Primary Partition

When the primary partition and the MSR partition are present, the primary partition will contain the boot files and the MSR partition will contain the system files. The primary partition is created by the Microsoft operating system during the installation process.

When an EFI System Partition (ESP) is created, it takes priority over the MSR and the primary partition and is required for booting the computer. The ESP partition is typically 100 MB. The MSR partition is typically 128 GB.

Removing the ESP or the MSR partition can cause boot failure. The failure is directly related to

Figure 9-22. Notice that there is no partition letter assigned to the MSR partition, which is identified as "System Reserved."

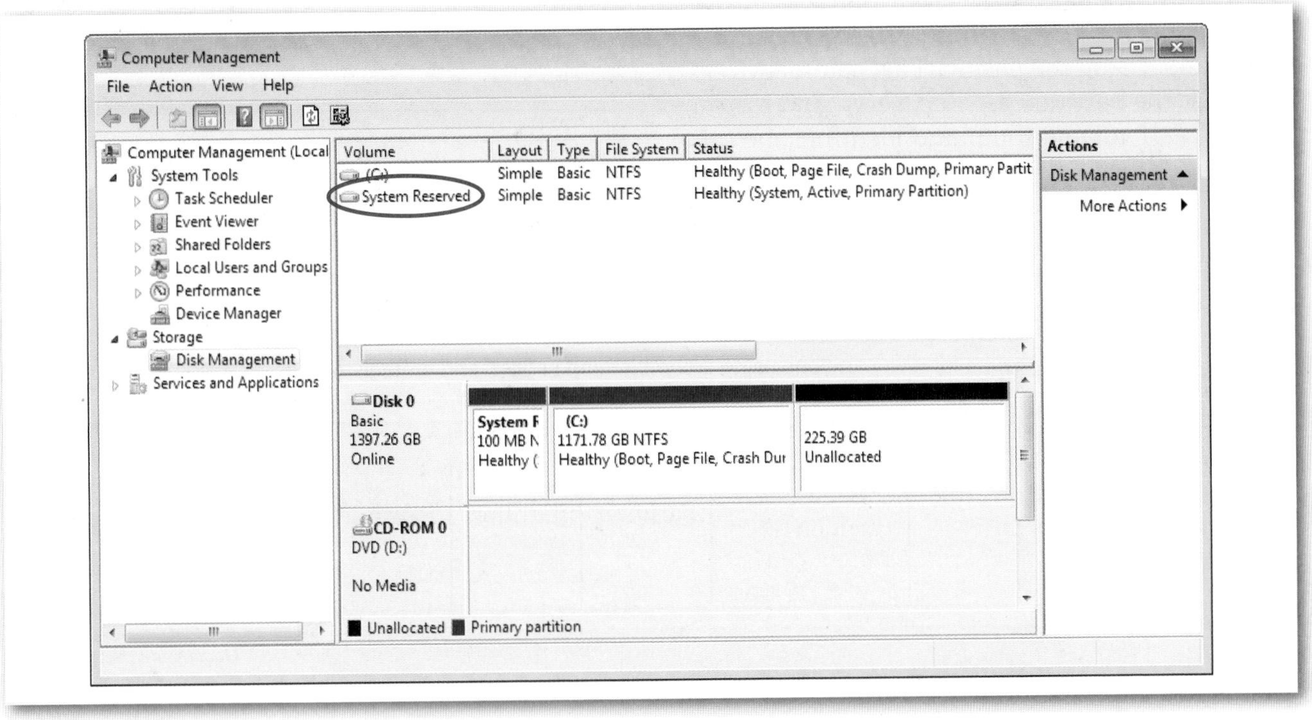

the fact that the partition table and required boot files will be missing.

Proprietary Recovery Partition

The **proprietary recovery partition**, also known as the *Original Equipment Manufacturers (OEM) partition*, is an optional partition created by the system's Original Equipment Manufacturer (OEM). This partition usually contains recovery tools, a copy of the operating system files, and any other program files that the manufacturer selects as necessary to completely recover a computer from a catastrophic failure. For example, all Windows operating system files used for installing the operating system might be placed in the recovery partition. The recovery partition may also contain software application files, copies of hardware drivers, and anything else necessary to completely restore the computer to its original condition at time of purchase.

The recovery partition is used to recover a computer system by the computer owner either through a tech support conversation, e-mail, or with a message textbox displayed at time of failure. The user simply selects a key such as [F12] to start the automated recovery process. This type of recovery often, but not always, results in the loss of all user files such as documents, pictures, and music.

The proprietary recovery partition is identified as the PQSERVICE partition on some computers. Using the DiskPart **list** command identifies the partition as "Recovery," and running the DiskPart **volume** command identifies the same partition as the "PQSERVICE" volume.

UEFI Specification Partition Terminology

The UEFI standard was developed as a guide for standardizing the way the partitions are arranged and where the critical files will be stored in the partitions. The UEFI standard allows computer software application tools, utilities, and operating systems to follow a standard way of arranging partitions and locating critical files. See **Figure 9-23**.

You may see a protective MBR located on a GPT-partitioned hard drive. The **protective MBR** is used to protect the GPT when legacy software tools are used to explore or repair the MBR. The legacy tools could interpret a missing MBR as an unpartitioned disk. Restoring an MBR could then render a GPT system unbootable.

The UEFI standard calls for the protective MBR to be located first on the hard drive followed by the primary GPT. The GPT primary partition is used by 64-bit systems to identify the system partitions. The GPT is essential to the identification of the GPT-type partitions. A backup of the GPT partition information is stored in a separate partition called the backup GPT.

A computer can contain two or more physical disks. The disks can be a mixture of both GPT- and MBR-based disks. A single physical hard disk drive cannot have both a GPT and an MBR because the system can only have one place to boot from.

> **Tech Tip**
> You can convert an MBR disk to a GPT disk or a GPT disk to an MBR disk, but all data on the disk will be lost.

Figure 9-23. UEFI specification for disk partitions using a combination of GPT and protective MBR.

Protective MBR	Primary GPT	EFI System Partition (ESP)	Partition	Partition	Partition	Backup GPT

The EFI System Partition (ESP) contains the boot loader program. After completing the POST, the control of the computer is passed from the UEFI firmware to the boot loader program. The boot loader program starts the proprietary operating system such as Windows or Linux, and then loads the remaining portions of the operating system.

After the ESP, there is one or more partitions used to contain operating system files required to run the program and store data files.

As you can see, there is conflicting terminology used to identify and explain the function and purpose of the disk partition system. This is quite common in computer-related fields when a new technology is released, especially before a standard is adopted by all parties. During the transition, you will encounter hybrids of the new and older technologies mixed together. The terminologies will conflict because of different sources of information emerging at the same time. Also, be aware that companies sometimes create their own terminology and present the information in a manner that will lead you to believe that they invented it first. This is a typical marketing technique used by software and hardware companies.

Unfortunately, not all hard disk drives conform to this arrangement nor do all manufacturers of hardware and software use the same terminology as presented in the standard. As a result of the lack of a strict standard adoption, you will encounter several variations of partition arrangements. The variations are caused by the desire of OEMs to install a recovery partition to support system recovery for their computer operating systems.

Another main factor for the various partition arrangements that do not adhere to the UEFI standard is many OEMs released computer systems into the market place before the standard was fully adopted by all major OEMs. You will often encounter this lack of total uniformity to a specific standard in the computer industry. In the free marketplace, manufacturers are always rushing to introduce their own improved technology rather than wait for a standard to be fully adopted. As a result, you will encounter many systems that are hybrids of the standard and the legacy technology.

Initializing a Disk

When a new hard disk drive is first installed on a computer that supports UEFI, it must be initialized before it can be partitioned. The Microsoft Support website states that disk initialization writes a signature to the disk. A **disk signature** identifies the disk type and properties so that the Microsoft operating system can utilize the disk. In addition to the disk signature, the type of partition style is selected and created during initialization. The two partition styles are MBR or GPT.

During a clean installation of Windows for a new computer system, the GPT partition is automatically selected as GPT. When an additional hard drive is installed in the system and detected, the **Initialize Disk** dialog box will automatically appear, **Figure 9-24**. Notice that there are two choices of initialization presented in the dialog box: **MBR (Master Boot Record)** and **GPT (GUID Partition Table)**. As the dialog box indicates, the GPT partition style is not recognized by early versions of Windows, and it is recommended for partitions larger than 2 TB.

During your computer laboratory activities, you will often install a hard drive that has been used one or more times by previous students. When this is the case, you will not see the **Initialize Disk** dialog box because the hard disk drive has previously been initialized and the partition style (MBR, GPT) has previously been selected.

Figure 9-24. A new disk must be initialized and a partition style selected.

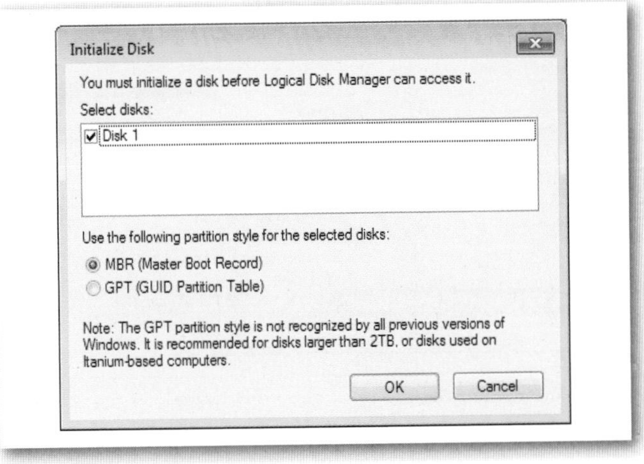

When a physical disk that has not been initialized is viewed through the Computer Management tool, it will be labeled as "Unknown" and as "Not Initialized," **Figure 9-25**. Also, note the partition labeled "System Reserved." The System Reserved partition, also called the Microsoft Reserved Partition (MSR), has no assigned partition letter.

The MBR is located at sector one, cylinder zero, head zero. It is created when a disk is initialized as MBR. **Figure 9-26** shows the critical files pattern on a MBR-based hard disk. This pattern is standard for FAT16 and FAT32 file systems. Other compatible systems have followed this design to maintain downward compatibility.

As stated earlier, a hard drive can be divided into two or more partitions. Having one hard drive with multiple partitions simulates having multiple hard drives. In an MBR-based system, each partition has its own boot record, but one partition must contain the master boot record. The master boot record is located on the partition that is used to boot the operating system. See **Figure 9-27**.

A bad sector or cluster anywhere on a disk simply causes a loss of that particular file. Often, parts of a file can be recovered using a third-party utility program, such as Norton Utilities. When the MBR is corrupted or infected by a virus, access to the entire disk is lost. The MBR may be recoverable if precautions have been taken. One

Figure 9-25. A disk will be identified as "Unknown" until it is initialized, partitioned, and formatted.

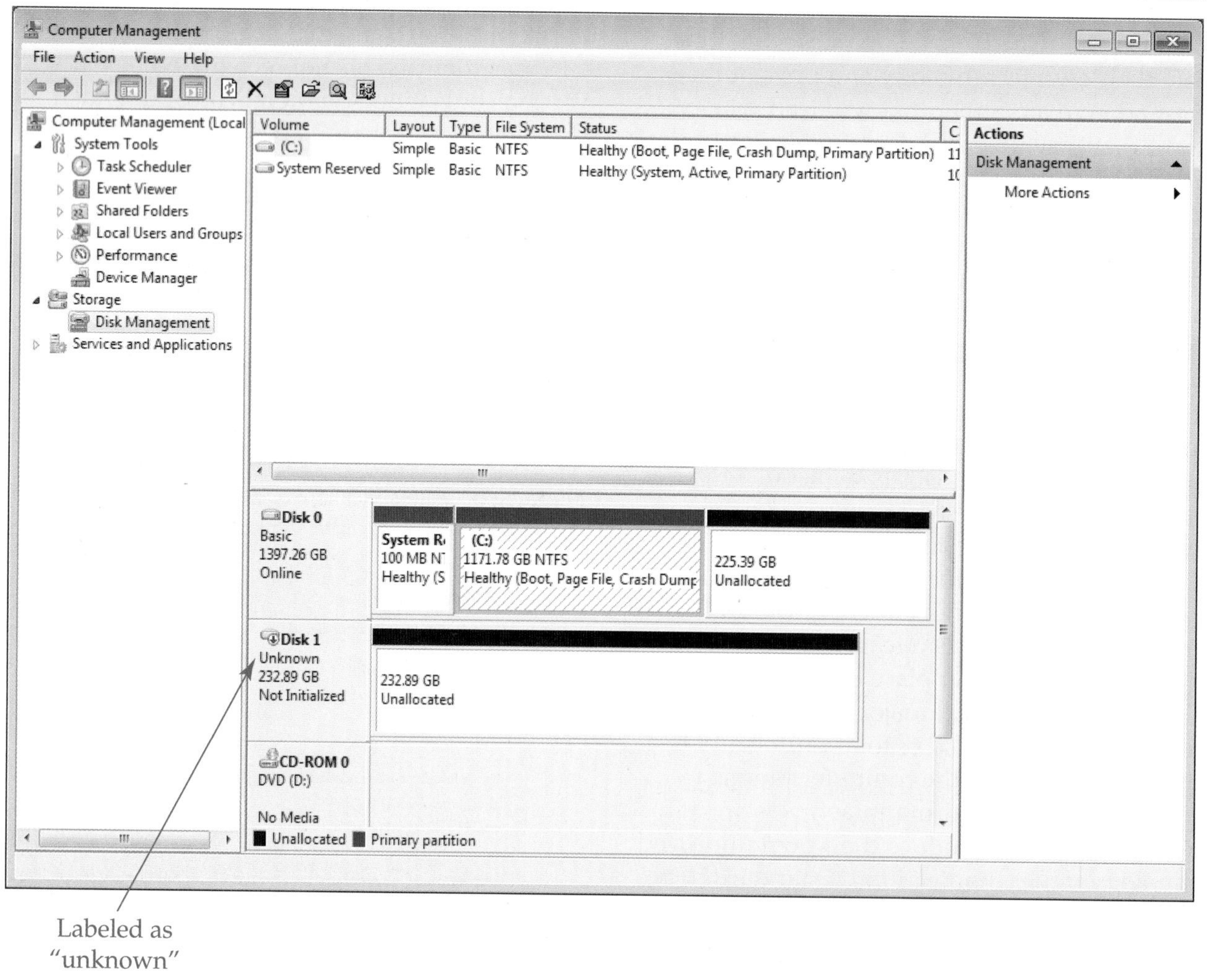

Labeled as "unknown"

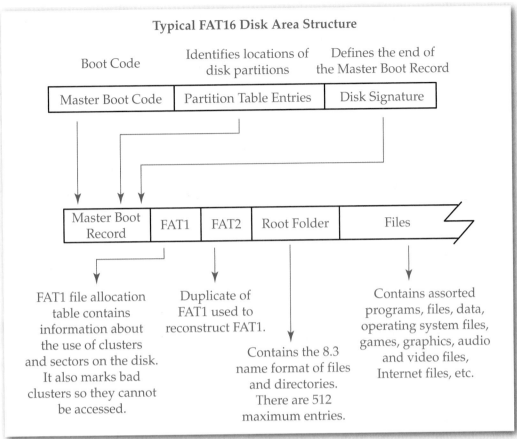

Goodheart-Willcox Publisher

Figure 9-26.
Layout of a typical FAT16 and FAT32 system.

method of recovery is to have a copy of the MBR saved on disk or flash memory so that it can be reinstalled to replace the corrupted sector that contains the MBR.

Tech Tip
There can be a lot of confusion concerning proper terminology of the Master Boot Record. Often, the MBR is referred to as the *boot record*, *boot sector*, *master boot sector*, and *boot program*. This text uses terminology as defined by Microsoft in the *Microsoft Resource Kit*.

A GPT-based system is much less likely to fail due to corruption as compared to an MBR-based system because of its redundant partition tables. In **Figure 9-28**, notice that a complete copy of the primary GUID partition table header and GUID partition entries is copied to another location. The backup is used to rebuild the original primary

GUID partition header table and GUID partition entries if the primary becomes corrupted. Also, notice the protective MBR is included in the partition structure.

To understand the progression to GPT after MBR we must first look at some of the limitations of MBR. MBR was introduced after the file allocation table (FAT) file system. This system used a table to organize files and directories and to locate them on the disk. While an excellent system at the time, it is now quite obsolete for today's large hard drives. The exception is the new extended file allocation table (exFAT) file system, which is covered later in this chapter.

Tech Tip
Windows Vista, Windows 7, Windows Server 2003, and later can read, write, and boot from a GPT-based disk. Windows XP can only read or write data.

Figure 9-27.
A disk drive can be divided into many sections called partitions. Each partition is identified with a drive letter such as C, D, E, up to the drive letter Z.

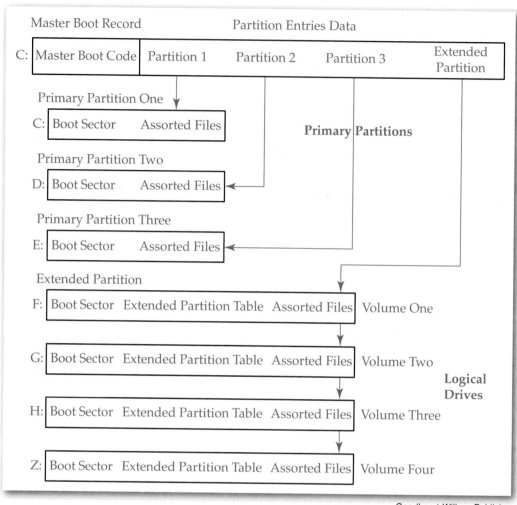

Partitioning a Disk

Fdisk was a command-line tool used in early DOS operating systems to partition a hard disk drive. Later, Microsoft incorporated an emulator of the fdisk command into the Windows operating systems. The fdisk command only works with FAT16 and FAT32 systems and not with an NTFS system. Modern operating systems incorporate partitioning and formatting utilities into the operating system. These utilities are accessed through either the command prompt using the DiskPart command-line utility or through Disk Management. Early operating systems required that the hard drive be partitioned and formatted before you ran the operating system installation program. Modern operating systems incorporate the creation of the system partition(s) and formatting the partition(s) as part of the operating system installation process.

DiskPart Utility

The DiskPart utility was first introduced in Windows 2000 Server and Windows XP. It is used to manage disk partitions and volumes from the command prompt. DiskPart has replaced the functions served by the **fdisk** command. Disks, partitions, and volumes are managed using the Disk Management tool in Computer Management, but there will be times when you will need to use the DiskPart utility, especially when you cannot access Computer Management. This may happen for example, during some troubleshooting operations while trying to recover a failed operating system.

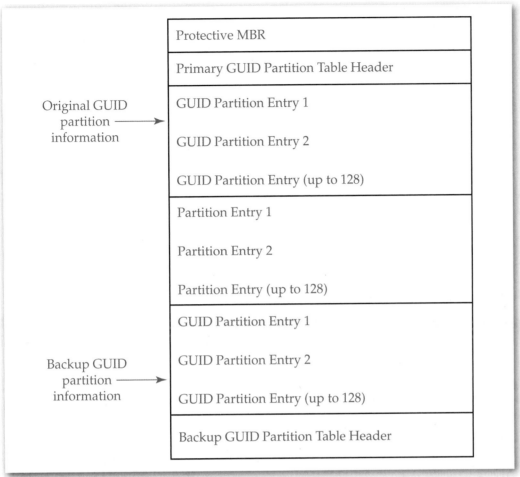

Goodheart-Willcox Publisher

Figure 9-28.
Backup GUID partition information.

Diagram labels (top to bottom):

Protective MBR

Primary GUID Partition Table Header

GUID Partition Entry 1

GUID Partition Entry 2

GUID Partition Entry (up to 128)

Partition Entry 1

Partition Entry 2

Partition Entry (up to 128)

GUID Partition Entry 1

GUID Partition Entry 2

GUID Partition Entry (up to 128)

Backup GUID Partition Table Header

Original GUID partition information → (points to the GUID Partition Entries below the Primary header)

Backup GUID partition information → (points to the GUID Partition Entries above the Backup header)

Tech Tip

Windows Vista and later operating systems no longer recognize the **fdisk** command.

Figure 9-29 lists the commands revealed from the command interpreter after issuing the DiskPart **help** command. Only a partial list of commands is shown in the figure.

The DiskPart utility is much more complex than the Fdisk utility. Commands typically use two or more words in the command-line syntax. Also, be aware that you must select the partition, disk, or volume before you can carry out many of the commands. **Figure 9-30** shows an example of the sequence used to view the details about a selected partition.

First the command **diskpart** is entered to start the DiskPart utility. Next, the **select disk 0** command is entered to focus the DiskPart utility on the hard disk drive identified as Disk 0. The DiskPart utility responds with a text message that reads, "Disk 0 is now the selected disk."

Next, the command **select partition 1** is entered. The DiskPart utility responds with the message "Partition 1 is now the selected partition."

Finally, the command **detail partition** is entered. The result is detailed information about partition 1. You can also use the DiskPart commands **list disk**, **list volume**, and **list partition** to reveal information about the disk(s), volume(s) partition(s) as seen in **Figure 9-31**.

The first command, **list disk**, provides basic information about Disk 0, the first and only disk in the system. The second command, **list volume**,

Figure 9-29.
Issuing the **help** command in the DiskPart utility displays a list of DiskPart commands.

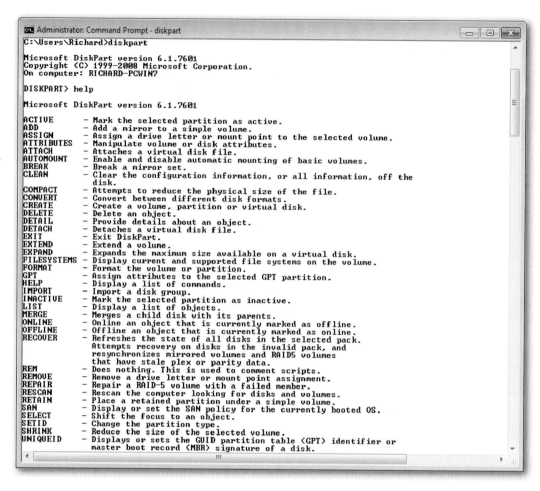

Figure 9-30.
The DiskPart utility. Notice that the object (such as hard drive, partition, and volume) to be viewed must first be selected with the **select** command (**select disk 0**, **select partition 1**). The **detail** command (**detail partition**) can then be used to display information about the object.

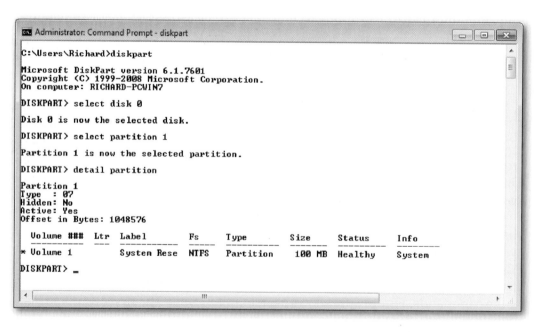

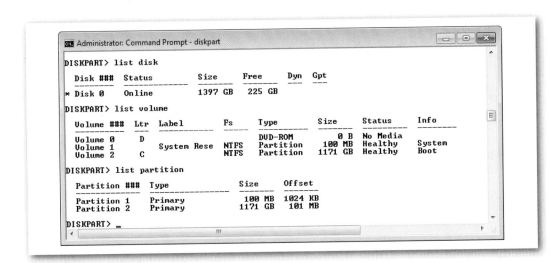

Figure 9-31.
Examples of the **list disk**, **list volume**, and **list partition** DiskPart commands.

identifies three volumes that exist on Disk 0. Notice that Volume 1 does not have a drive letter assigned and has been identified or "labeled" as the "System Rese" or System Reserved disk. The System Reserved disk contains the required boot files used to boot the computer after POST and then load the remaining operating system files located in Volume 2 (drive C). There is more information about DiskPart command available at the Microsoft TechNet website. You can find this information by conducting an Internet search using the key words "Microsoft TechNet DiskPart."

Disk Management

The preferred easy-to-use Disk Management tool is located in Computer Management or through the Microsoft Management Console (MMC). The Disk Management tool provides easy access to all installed disk drives and allows information to easily be displayed about each drive and its partition(s). You can view the drive type, the file system used, and the status of each drive. **Figure 9-32** shows an example of Windows 7 Disk Management accessed through the Computer Management utility. Notice the items listed in the shortcut menu. The shortcut menu displays when you right-click the mouse on a selected partition.

The Disk Management tool is very similar in all versions of Windows operating systems. In addition to displaying information about the disk system, it contains tools that allow you to extend or shrink the size of a partition, add additional drives and partitions, format the partitions, change the drive letters, allocate the amount of space each user can use (disk quota), convert a basic disk to dynamic disk, and run Chkdsk and Disk Defragmenter. When an option in the shortcut menu is not available, it will appear in light gray letters, or appear dimmed.

Each of the valid options in the shortcut menu will start a wizard that will walk you through the configuration of the hard disk drive or partition. For example, to resize a partition, you simply right-click the partition you wish to resize and then select the **Extend Volume** option. A wizard provides information about the process and requests information about the size to extend the volume. The other configuration options, such as **Format**, **Shrink Volume**, **Delete Volume**, **Add Mirror**, provide wizards as well. You simply need to be familiar with the terminology to successfully complete the disk configuration option selected. Computer Management provides an extensive help menu with detailed information about all the Disk Management configuration options. **Figure 9-33** shows additional disk configuration options available under the **Actions | Disk Management** menu.

Accessing the Computer Management is accomplished by right-clicking **Computer** (Windows Vista, Windows 7) or **My Computer** (Windows XP) located off the **Start** menu and then selecting the **Manage** option from the shortcut menu.

Figure 9-32. The Disk Management tool in Computer Management can be used to display information about the disk system and to perform maintenance-related tasks such as extend or shrink the size of a volume, delete a volume, and format the partitions.

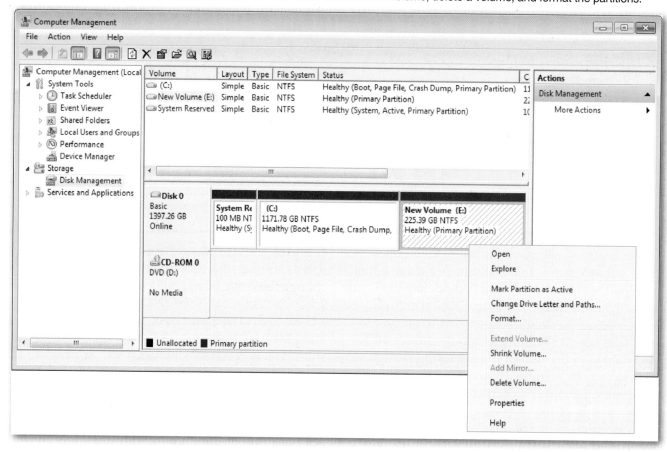

Figure 9-33. Some of the options available under the **Actions** I **Disk Management** menu selection are **Refresh**, **Rescan Disks**, **Create VHD**, and **Attach VHD**.

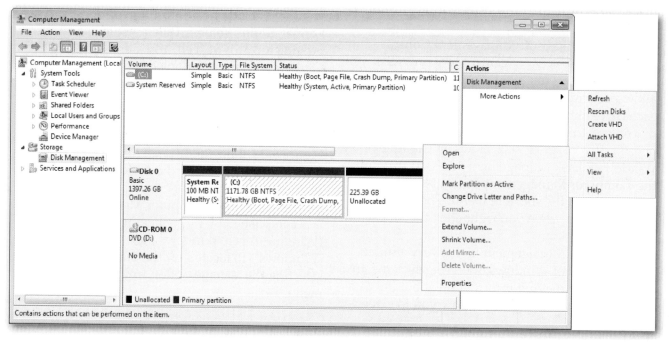

For Windows Vista and Windows 7, you can also access **Computer Management** through **Control Panel | Administrative Tools**. For Windows XP, the path is **Control Panel | Performance and Maintenance | Administrative Tools | Computer Management**.

For Windows 8, enter "Disk Management" into the **Search** box and look under **Settings**, or enter "Disk" into the **Search** box and then look for "Create and format hard disk partitions" located under **Settings**. When using the term "Disk" in the **Search** box, you will see all Apps available to be used with disk configuration such as Create a recovery drive, Manage BitLocker, Defragment and optimize your drives, and more.

A customized console can be created with Microsoft Management Console (MMC). Typing MMC or MMC.exe into the **Run** dialog box of Windows XP or the **Search** box of later Windows versions will generate a blank MMC that can be customized to include the tools you want. The MMC will be explored more in the related lab activities. There is also a lot of information about the MMC in **Help and Support**, which is located off the **Start** menu. You can also do an Internet search using the key terms "Microsoft MMC."

> **Tech Tip**
>
> To access Computer Management from a command prompt, enter **compmgmt.msc**. To access the Microsoft Management Console, enter **mmc.exe**.

Figure 9-34 shows two hard disk drives installed on the same computer and identified as Disk 0 and Disk 1. Disk 1 in the example contains a 300-MB recovery partition, a 99-MB EFI System Partition (ESP), and a 931-GB primary partition. Disk 0 is an example of a new hard drive just added to the system and not yet partitioned and formatted. Before a new hard drive is partitioned it is identified as "Unallocated."

> **A+ Note**
>
> Be sure you know how to access the Microsoft Management Console and Computer Management from the command prompt as well as through Control Panel before taking the A+ exam.

File System Formats

After a hard disk drive is partitioned, it must be formatted. The file system format or structure is determined by the type of file system selected when formatting a system partition or volume. The most commonly encountered file system formats are NTFS and some variation of FAT. The FAT file variations are FAT16, FAT32, and exFAT. Original FAT file systems, such as FAT12, FAT16, FAT32, are basically obsolete and are seldom encountered on desktop and laptop systems. You can still encounter the FAT and exFAT file system used for some USB storage devices and small portable electronic device storage systems. FAT and exFAT are used when small storage capacity is required because FAT has less overhead than the NTFS file system. The smaller overhead makes it ideal for small storage systems.

FAT16 and FAT32

There are several forms of FAT systems. The original DOS and the original release of Windows 95 used **FAT16**. The "16" represents the number of bits used to identify stored data. The maximum storage area for a FAT16 system is limited to 2 GB.

As demand for greater storage capability evolved, the **FAT32** system was designed. Starting with Windows 95 OSR2, this new FAT was available. FAT32 uses 32 bits to identify stored data, and its upper limit for storage is theoretically 2 TB (terabytes). However, Windows 2000 limits the size to 32 GB. Windows 95 OSR2 and later Windows 9x operating systems can use either FAT16 or FAT 32.

Figure 9-34. Disk 1 contains a 300-MB recovery partition, a 99-MB EFI system partition, and a 931-GB primary partition. Disk 0 is labeled "Unallocated," which means it has not been partitioned or formatted.

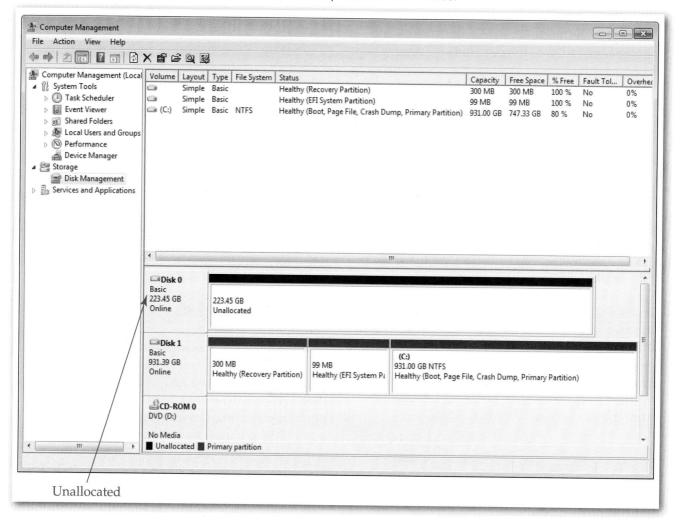

Unallocated

FAT16 has a limit to the number of files (512) that can be contained in the root directory. The root directory identifies the files and directories by name. It also identifies files that are associated with various directories and their location on the disk. It stores information such as the file extension, file attribute, time, date, and location of the first cluster.

This does not imply that a hard disk storage unit can only contain 512 files. It means that there can be only 512 unique names of files and directories in the root directory of a FAT16 file system. There can be more files on the hard disk by the use of directories and subdirectories. A directory in the root directory appears as a single file, but it can have an unlimited number of files contained under it as files and subdirectories.

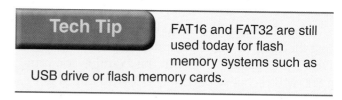

Tech Tip   FAT16 and FAT32 are still used today for flash memory systems such as USB drive or flash memory cards.

VFAT

Virtual file allocation table (VFAT) is not a truly independent file allocation table system but rather a method of programming related to the existing FAT16 root directory. This programming allows the FAT16 to appear to have long file name capabilities similar to FAT32. The long file names span over several normal eight-point-three (8.3) file name spaces on the FAT16 file allocation table, thus allowing the system to reflect long file names. This system is used for operating systems prior to Windows 95 OSR2. The VFAT system of storing file names in its root directory significantly reduces the total number of root directory files it can handle. NTFS and the Windows 2000 dynamic disk system have long file name capabilities without limiting the number of files that can be listed in the root directory.

exFAT

The **extended file allocation table (exFAT)** file system is a proprietary Microsoft design for portable devices such as USB flash drives and flash memory cards. The exFAT file system can also be used to format external hard disk drives when attached through a USB port.

The SD Association has chosen exFAT as the default file format for their Secure Digital Extended Capacity (SDXC) memory card, which is used in portable devices such as cameras and tablets. The exFAT file format extends the memory card capacity from the previous 32 GB to 2 TB.

NTFS

The **New Technology File System (NTFS)** was designed specifically to operate with the Windows NT operating system. Microsoft Corporation realized the limitations of FAT that included a 2-GB size limit for a volume on a hard drive and for large cluster sizes. NTFS was designed to ensure that much larger hard drives could be accommodated. The maximum hard drive volume that can be used with NTFS is 16 EB (exabytes). NTFS also limits the size of clusters, which results in less wasted space on the hard drive. NTFS uses a master file table (MFT) in similar fashion as the FAT file system uses a file allocation table to locate files.

NTFS supports long file names for user convenience and security access features that are not available in FAT systems. NTFS is compatible with FAT16 but not with FAT32. Windows 2000 further developed the NTFS with additional features and called its file system *dynamic disk*. NTFS was originally more commonly found on a file server or an NT workstation than on a typical PC. However, with the introduction of

Windows XP, Microsoft moved the home user to an NTFS-based file system.

Since the introduction of the dynamic disk file system, the NTFS name has been changed to NTFS5.0. The original NTFS is now called NTFS4.0. This can lead to a lot of confusion. Technical literature written during and before the year 2000 uses the terms *NTFS* and *dynamic disk*, while literature produced post 2000 uses NTFS4.0 and NTFS5.0. Today, the preferred term is simply *NTFS* for either NTFS4.0 or NTFS5.0. The only distinction is when technical information uses the term *dynamic disk* in relation to NTFS5.0. Microsoft uses the term *dynamic disk* in their own literature when describing NTFS, but publications that originate outside of Microsoft use *NTFS5.0*. In addition, Microsoft refers to FAT16, FAT32, and the NTFS4.0 as *basic disk systems*.

Encrypted File System

The **encrypted file system (EFS)** is the native encryption system used with NTFS. NTFS uses a file encryption key (FEK) to encrypt and decrypt the file contents. A single file, folder, or a complete data drive may be encrypted. A common way to use EFS is to create a folder in a directory and then set the properties of the folder to encrypt. After the folder is set for encryption, any file that is dropped into the folder will be encrypted. The encryption and decryption process is transparent to the authorized user of the file. EFS is an ideal security measure that can prevent confidential data from being accessed by unauthorized users.

The compression and encryption features in Windows operating systems can be accessed by right-clicking the item to be encrypted (file, folder, or data drive), selecting **Properties**, and then **Advanced. Figure 9-35** shows the **Advanced Attributes** dialog box.

You cannot encrypt a file that is compressed. EFS is only available in Windows Professional and Ultimate editions and not in Home editions.

There is one shortcoming of EFS. It cannot encrypt the entire hard disk drive where required system files are located and any hidden partitions. Microsoft now offers BitLocker as an application which permits the encryption of the entire hard disk drive, even the boot files and hidden partitions. The advantage of using BitLocker is

Figure 9-35. The **Advanced Attributes** dialog box can be used to encrypt or compress a file in an New Technology File System.

File systems often derive their names from the amount of available space used to identify the clusters in binary form and to store the value in the file allocation table. The file allocation table binary code space is as follows:

$$FAT12 = 2^{12} \text{ entries}$$
$$FAT16 = 2^{16} \text{ entries}$$
$$FAT32 = 2^{28} \text{ entries}$$
$$exFAT = 2^{70} \text{ entries}$$

FAT32 only uses 2^{28} of the available 2^{32} possible entries. It saves the rest as spares for future development.

that it provides for extreme security by preventing unauthorized access to a disk system. Another application of BitLocker is called BitLocker To Go, which allows the entire contents of a flash drive to be encrypted.

NTFS Compression

NTFS supports its own file compression system. The NTFS file compression allows you to compress a single file, a folder, or an entire volume. Like file encryption, file compression is transparent to the user. A compressed file opens and closes in a fashion typical to an uncompressed file. The only time file compression is obvious to the user is during the initial compression of a large folder or volume. An entire volume could take hours to compress. After it is compressed, the time it takes to open and close is comparable to an uncompressed volume.

Compression does not always achieve the desired effect. For example, if a user is trying to create more disk space by compressing graphic files, they may notice very little difference in file size after compression. Most graphic file systems, such as JPEG and GIF, already use a file compression technique. Additional compression has little or no effect on the file size. Also, be aware that files that are compressed may be difficult or impossible to recover after a complete system failure.

Disk Quotas

There are a number of important advantages to NTFS as compared to FAT file systems. Disk quotas can be set using NTFS. That means when a hard disk drive is shared by several users, each user can be allocated a portion of the disk for storage and cannot use more space than they have been allocated. This prevents one user from using up all the disk space for photos and such.

Dynamic Disk

Dynamic disk was first introduced with Windows 2000 Professional and provides many more disk configuration options as compared to basic disk. **Basic disk** refers to the traditional FAT16, FAT32, exFAT, and NTFS file storage system. Dynamic disk is based on NTFS technology, but with significant improvements. It has improved disk security as well as lifted restrictions normally associated with NTFS.

One of the biggest advantages to dynamic disk as compared to basic disk is that dynamic disk can span a volume (partition) across multiple physical disks while basic disk cannot. This means that you can keep increasing the size of a volume (partition) by adding additional disk drives.

You can install a basic disk file system on your computer and convert to dynamic disk at any time without losing data, but you probably will not be able to reverse the operation without losing data. Microsoft recommends against reversing the process, though there are some third-party utilities that claim they can do the job. Use them at your own risk.

You can change a basic disk to a dynamic disk either through Computer Management, Computer Management Console (MMC), or at the command prompt with the DiskPart utility. At the command prompt, you would access the DiskPart utility and then select the disk you wish to change into a dynamic disk. After selecting the disk, you would enter the command **convert dynamic**. When converting a basic disk into a dynamic disk, existing partitions on the disk will become simple volumes.

With dynamic disk, the traditional method of allocating additional space on a large disk system by using partitions and additional logical drives is no longer needed. Dynamic disk treats the entire disk as one large volume of data. It appears seamless to the user. The usual long list of additional drive letters such as R, P, S, and Z is no longer required to appear on the screen to the user. Instead, a system of volume mount points can be established. This gives the user an illusion of one long continuous file structure.

Volume mount points allow a volume or additional hard disk drive to be attached to a directory structure. Traditionally, adding a new hard disk drive required a new partition and new directory assigned such as E or F. With the volume mount point feature, a new volume or disk can be attached to an existing directory.

See **Figure 9-36**, which shows four screen captures of a partition that was created using NTFS dynamic disk and then assigned to a folder. In Figure 9-36A, the **New Simple Volume Wizard** dialog box allows you to "browse" to a folder rather than assign a partition or volume letter. Look at the summary in Figure 9-36B. You will see that the new partition has been assigned to location C:\Artwork.

When looking at the Windows Explorer directory shown in Figure 9-36C, you will see a shortcut on drive C that leads directly to the Artwork folder. There is no partition letter assigned. Lastly, looking at Computer Management in Figure 9-36D, you can see that no drive letter has been assigned to the new volume.

When the new partition/volume is created, it is spliced into an existing file structure rather than

appears as a separate drive with an individual drive letter. Basic file systems are limited in the number of drives that can be installed and in the maximum number of partitions that can be created. The maximum number of partitions is equal to the letters of the entire alphabet minus the letters used for assignment to floppy drives, CD/DVD drives, and other disk drives. Since the volume mount point technology does not require a separate drive letter, there is no practical limitation to the number of drives assigned to a system. This is especially important on network systems.

Storage Spaces

Storage Spaces is a new feature introduced in Windows 8. Storage Spaces allows a group of two or more drives to be configured into a pool of storage devices. All data stored on the original storage drive is automatically written to a second or third storage drive within the pool, thus preventing the loss of data caused by disk storage failure. The technique of writing duplicate data to two separate drives is referred to as *disk mirroring*. Writing data to three drives is referred to as a *three-way mirror*.

You can access Storage Spaces by entering "Storage" or "Storage Spaces" in the Windows 8 **Search** box and then selecting the **Settings** Search category. The results will appear on the left. You can also access it through **Control Panel | System and Security**, Figure 9-37.

The Storage Spaces wizard will prompt for information about the desired configuration, such as the storage name, resiliency type, and storage size. The term *resiliency* as applied to mass storage is the ability of a computer system to recover from data loss caused by a disk or storage system failure.

Look at **Figure 9-38**. Notice that the storage name is "Storage space" and the assigned drive letter is F. The chosen resiliency type is **Two-way mirror**. A two-way mirror means that the data will be duplicated across two separate drives. The other options available are **Three-way mirror** and **Parity**. Parity resiliency storage is when data is written across all three drives but in a special way. The first two drives each contain the actual data, and the third contains a parity bit. Hence,

Figure 9-36. When using NTFS dynamic disk, a new partition can be assigned to an existing file folder in the directory structure. There is no need to assign a volume letter to the new partition.

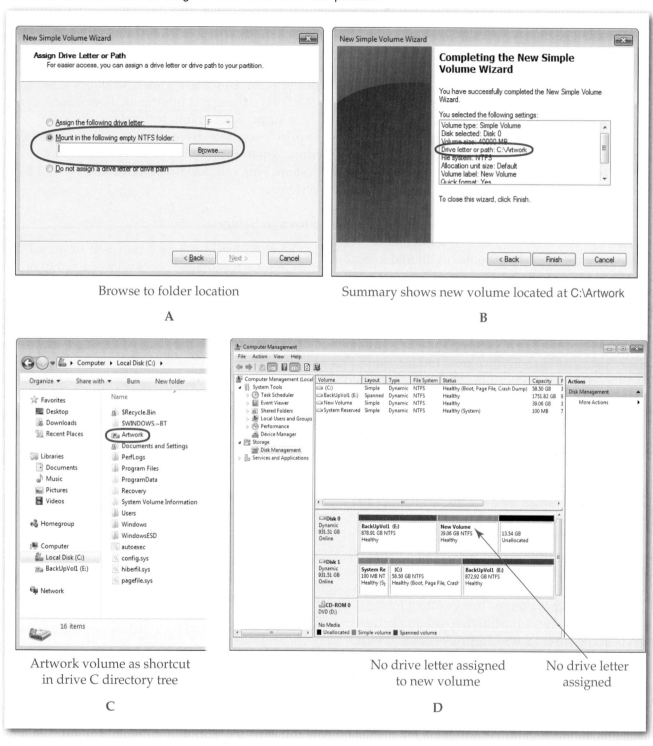

Browse to folder location

A

Summary shows new volume located at C:\Artwork

B

Artwork volume as shortcut
in drive C directory tree

C

No drive letter assigned
to new volume

No drive letter
assigned

D

the name "parity" used to describe the disk storage selection. The parity bit is calculated from the data on the first two drives. If any one drive fails, the parity bit can be used to automatically rebuild the missing data and a new drive after it is installed. There will be more about mirror and parity resiliency configurations in Chapter 17—Network Administration.

Figure 9-37. Windows 8 Storage Spaces can be accessed through **Control Panel | System and Security**.

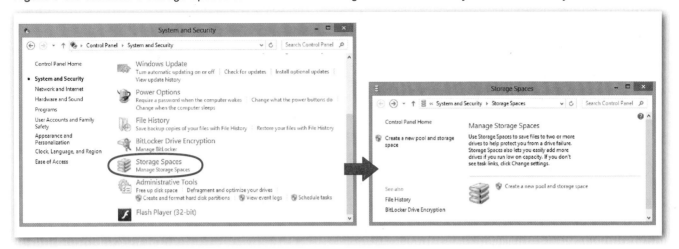

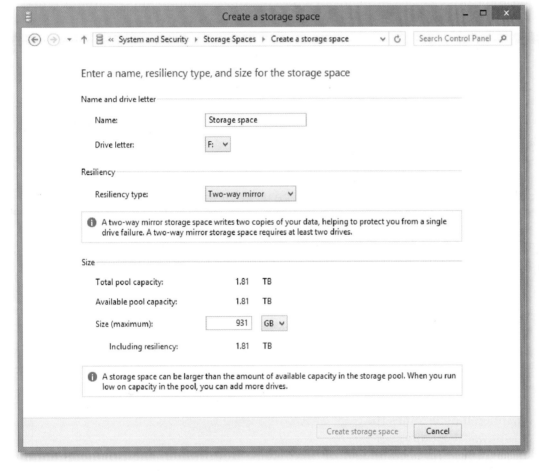

Figure 9-38. Storage Spaces refers to the duplication of data across two or three drives as "resiliency."

ReFS

Resilient File System (ReFS) is the newest Microsoft file system. It has many improvements over other file systems, but the most outstanding feature is its resiliency. The term *resiliency* as applied to ReFS refers to the file system's capability to recover after a major catastrophe such as a power outage or system failure. With previous versions of file systems, such as FAT or NTFS, a power failure or a system failure would corrupt the file system. Power outage or system failure during the time the operating system is writing data to a file causes the file writing process to stop before the file is properly closed. Remember that a file can require two or more clusters or sectors to hold its contents. Each cluster or sector reserves its last byte of storage for data identifying the location of the next storage segment. Any interruption in the write process ends the write and leaves the cluster or sector without the address of the next storage segment, thus corrupting the file.

The Resilient File System maintains copies of file contents on two or more disks. When a file corruption error is detected, ReFS replaces the corrupt file with a good copy. The entire process of detecting and replacing corrupt data is transparent and requires no user intervention.

While Microsoft provides other means of duplicating file content, ReFS is the only method that continually runs in the background. You can say that it is continually checking for data errors and making continuous data backups. ReFS is intended for use on a network server designed for data storage only and not intended to be used as a file system for hosting an operating system on a server or personal computer. Because of the continuous data-checking feature used with ReFS, an operating system would be slowed down considerably and would appear too sluggish by a user.

At the time of this writing, ReFS is limited to the Windows Server 2012 and is not available for Windows 8 or earlier systems. Windows Server 2012 is also referred to as Windows Server 8.

Formatting a Disk

Before a floppy or hard disk can be used to store data, it must be formatted. This type of format is referred to as a **high-level format**. This format prepares a disk to receive data in a systematic, organized manner. It determines the file table type, checks the physical condition of all sectors, marks bad sectors so that they cannot be used to store data, and identifies the operating system being used. A low-level format actually destroys all data on a disk. While a high-level format is said to destroy all data, in actuality, the sectors/clusters still contain the original data. It erases only the contents of the file table so that no file name is associated with the data clusters.

Data can be recovered after a high-level format takes place. The collection of clusters that contain the file data can be identified and given a file name using third-party tools. Also, certain third-party disk editor utilities can display the ASCII contents of a file after the disk has been formatted or the file deleted.

The **format** command is seldom issued from the command prompt today. When a hard drive requires to be formatted, the Disk Management tool in Computer Management is typically used. For removable storage such as flash memory, the format process is carried out through a format tool. You can locate the portable storage device using Explorer and then simply right-click on it and select the **Format** option.

When formatting storage media, Windows offers two format methods: quick and full. See **Figure 9-39**. The quick format simply erases the FAT. It is used on a disk that has already been formatted once. Rather than prepare the entire disk surface for storage, only the file table and the root directory are changed. This is much quicker than the full formatting process, which prepares the entire disk. The full format erases information across the entire disk and checks for bad sectors. The full formatting process typically would be used for an unformatted disk. This process was useful when floppy disks were sold

Figure 9-39. When formatting a floppy disk, there are two formatting options: **Quick (erase)** and **Full. Quick (erase)** can only be used on a floppy that has been previously used or formatted. Most floppy disks are now formatted by the manufacturer.

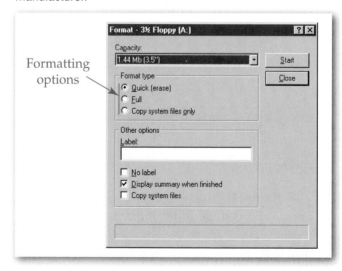

Formatting options

unformatted. Since disks are now formatted during manufacture, this process is not needed as often.

The file system on a floppy disk is similar to that on a hard disk with the exception of partitions. A floppy disk cannot be partitioned. As with hard drives and tapes, floppy disks must be formatted before they can be used to store data. Most disks are preformatted when purchased.

Figure 9-40 shows the available file system choices when formatting a removable disk. The choices are NTFS, FAT, FAT32 (Default), and exFAT. Notice that FAT is only a choice for small drives less than 4 GB, Figure 9-40A. For drives 4 GB or larger, FAT is not an option, Figure 9-40B.

File systems use part of the storage space for file tables and such known as "overhead." NTFS requires much more overhead as compared to the FAT file system. The modern flash memory systems are often formatted with exFAT rather than NTFS. The exFAT file system can theoretically support 64 zetabytes (ZB), or 1,073,741,824 billion terabytes, but Microsoft recommends a limit of 512 TB.

Tape uses a format similar to disks. A file allocation table is used to keep track of sectors on the tape. A tape must also be formatted before it can be used. Formatting a tape is similar to

formatting a disk except that it takes a great deal of time because of the tape's large capacity. Tapes are generally preformatted when they are purchased, saving hours of valuable time. Some of the top-of-the-line tape systems can format a tape as they are being used.

A+ Note

On the A+ exam, you may be asked a question related to quick and full formatting. A quick format only erases the file name in the file allocation table and does not erase file data. A full format when using Windows Vista erases all file data. The full format in earlier Windows systems did not erase all data.

Disk and File Maintenance

Disk drives require some routine maintenance to enhance performance. Two common tools used to perform disk maintenance are Disk Defragmenter and Chkdsk. First you must understand how files become fragmented.

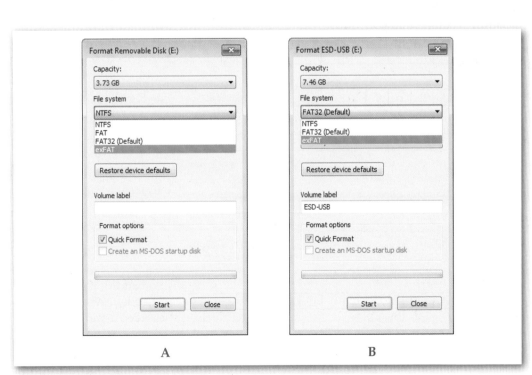

Figure 9-40.
The file format selection is directly affected by the size of the USB storage device. A—FAT is a choice for drives less than 4 GB. B—FAT is not listed as an option because the drive to be formatted is 8 GB.

Disk Defragmenter

File fragmentation is a common occurrence on disks. Files are assigned to disks by clusters. A file is fragmented when the clusters used for data storage are not consecutive. File fragmentation occurs through normal disk activities such as saving new files, erasing files, opening files, and adding additional data to files.

Figure 9-41 illustrates a possible sequence of events leading to fragmented files on the hard drive. The first three files saved (A, B, and C) show no file fragmentation. Each file is stored in a consecutive series of clusters. When file B is erased, it creates an opening in the sequence of clusters, which can now be used for the storage of new data. When file D is saved, it uses the two clusters left open by the deletion of file B as well as three additional clusters. File D is a fragmented file because the clusters used to store the data are not sequential. Next, file C is opened and used by the computer. As file C is used, it grows in size. When file C is saved back to the disk, it uses the four original clusters and two additional

clusters at the end of the file system. File C is now fragmented also.

The more often files are opened, modified, closed, or erased from a disk, the more fragmented the system becomes. The more fragmented a file becomes, the longer it takes to load and use the file. It is more difficult for a data recovery utility to identify the cluster sequences of fragmented files. As part of routine file maintenance, a hard drive should be defragmented (defragged) on a regular basis with the Disk Defragmenter utility. When you **defragment** your hard drive, the computer moves the clusters around so that all files have their clusters organized sequentially. The Windows Disk Defragmenter utility is located at **Start | All Programs | Accessories | System Tools | Disk Defragmenter**.

Windows 8 also has a disk defragmenter program called Optimize Drives. It is located in **Control Panel | Administrative Tools | System and Security**.

Figure 9-42 shows the **Local Disk (C) Properties** dialog box and the schedule for Disk Defragmenter program. Disk Defragmenter is

Figure 9-41.
Through the repeated saving and deletion of files, fragmentation occurs.

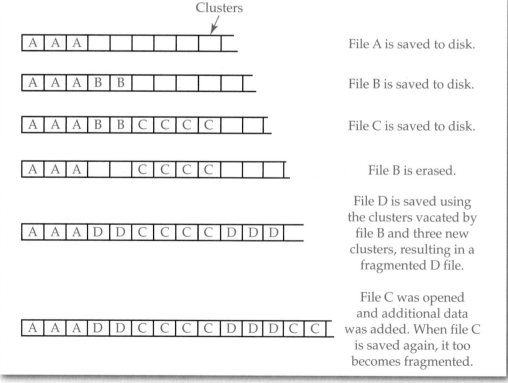

File A is saved to disk.

File B is saved to disk.

File C is saved to disk.

File B is erased.

File D is saved using the clusters vacated by file B and three new clusters, resulting in a fragmented D file.

File C was opened and additional data was added. When file C is saved again, it too becomes fragmented.

scheduled by default for every Sunday at 1:00 A.M. The scheduled time and date can be reconfigured.

Chkdsk

Chkdsk is a utility that checks and repairs the integrity of the file system on a hard drive. Disk problems such as bad sectors, lost clusters, cross-linked files, and directory structure errors can be detected and repaired automatically. Chkdsk can be run from the command prompt or from the GUI. **Figure 9-43** shows the results of the **chkdsk** command run on a Windows XP computer from the command prompt.

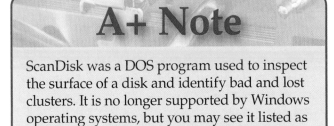

A+ Note

ScanDisk was a DOS program used to inspect the surface of a disk and identify bad and lost clusters. It is no longer supported by Windows operating systems, but you may see it listed as an answer on the CompTIA A+ Certification exam as a distracter for the **chkdsk** command.

When the Chkdsk utility is run from the command prompt, it will identify but not repair problems found. To automatically repair problems found, the **chkdsk** command must be run with the **/r** switch.

To run the Chkdsk utility as part of a GUI, simply access the Windows Explorer view of the desired drive or partition you wish to test. Then, right-click the partition or drive and select **Properties** from the shortcut menu. You will see the drive's **Properties** dialog box similar to that in **Figure 9-44**.

Under the **Tools** tab, click the **Check Now** button to check the partition or drive. A dialog box appears with two options: **Automatically fix file system errors** and **Scan for and attempt recovery of bad sectors**.

The Chkdsk utility will run as a GUI. When completed, the results will be displayed in GUI format similar to the Windows Vista screen capture in **Figure 9-45**. Notice the reference to "Chkdsk" listed in the results. The results are very similar to when Chkdsk is run from the command prompt.

Figure 9-42. Disk Defragmenter is accessed through the **Properties** dialog box of the drive and by clicking the **Defragment now** button. By default, Disk Defragmenter will automatically run at a scheduled time.

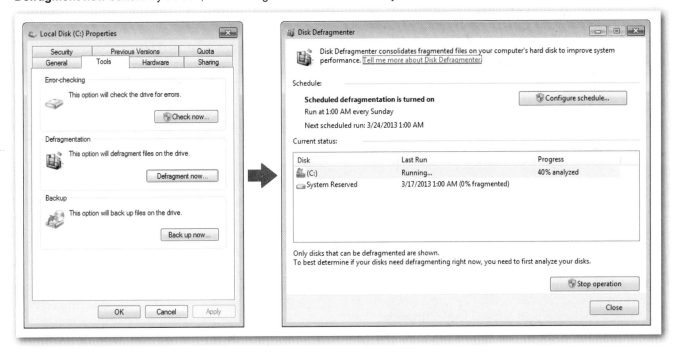

Figure 9-43.
The results of the
chkdsk command
run on a Windows XP
computer.

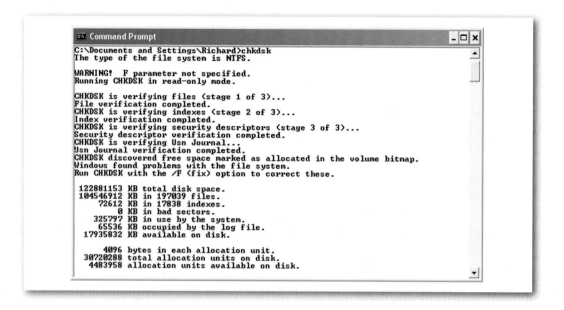

```
C:\Documents and Settings\Richard>chkdsk
The type of the file system is NTFS.

WARNING!  F parameter not specified.
Running CHKDSK in read-only mode.

CHKDSK is verifying files (stage 1 of 3)...
File verification completed.
CHKDSK is verifying indexes (stage 2 of 3)...
Index verification completed.
CHKDSK is verifying security descriptors (stage 3 of 3)...
Security descriptor verification completed.
CHKDSK is verifying Usn Journal...
Usn Journal verification completed.
CHKDSK discovered free space marked as allocated in the volume bitmap.
Windows found problems with the file system.
Run CHKDSK with the /F (fix) option to correct these.

 122881153 KB total disk space.
 104546912 KB in 197039 files.
     72612 KB in 17838 indexes.
         0 KB in bad sectors.
    325797 KB in use by the system.
     65536 KB occupied by the log file.
  17935832 KB available on disk.

      4096 bytes in each allocation unit.
  30720288 total allocation units on disk.
   4483958 allocation units available on disk.
```

Figure 9-44. Chkdsk can be run from the GUI by right-clicking the drive, selecting **Properties** from the shortcut menu, selecting the **Tools** tab, and clicking **Check Now**.

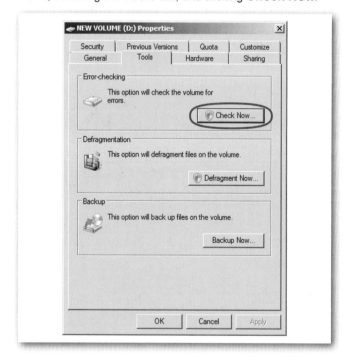

Chkdsk must have exclusive control of the volume it is checking. This is a problem when attempting to run Chkdsk on the default boot partition when it contains the complete operating system. A message will appear indicating that Chkdsk cannot be run at this time, but it can be scheduled to run automatically when the

computer is restarted. When the computer is restarted or shut down and started at a later time, the Chkdsk utility will automatically start up and run on the boot partition.

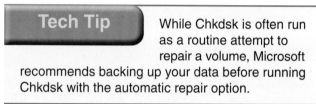

Tech Tip
While Chkdsk is often run as a routine attempt to repair a volume, Microsoft recommends backing up your data before running Chkdsk with the automatic repair option.

Performance Measures

Benchmark tests are performance tests that are conducted to compare different hardware and software. Industry journals and third-party organizations often do comparisons to rate the quality of hardware and software. Many times these same performance tests are conducted by the manufacturer and then used in advertisement campaigns. Always check who conducted the performance test. Based on this information, the results of the test should be viewed with caution.

Hard drive performance is judged on such items as *access time, latency,* or *seek time.* Access time, latency, and seek time mean the same thing when it comes to performance. These terms refer to the amount of time taken to position the read/write head over the proper sector. This is usually measured in microseconds.

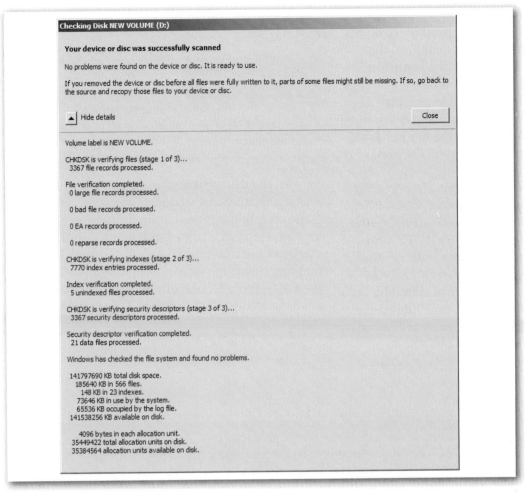

Figure 9-45.
GUI results of the **chkdsk** command.

Another standard of measure is data transfer rate. This rate refers to the speed of transfer of data to and from the disk. The actual time it takes must include the fact that cache memory is used to give the appearance of higher transfer rates. Disk data transfer rates are usually measured in megabytes per second (MBps).

The fastest and easiest way to compare disk drive systems is to load the two drives that are to be compared with a Windows operating system. Place one or two typical software applications in the system's Startup folder so that they launch when Windows opens. The two systems should then be booted. Compare the length of time it takes to boot and load the software systems. Any technician can perform this simple test. When comparing two devices, all other hardware must be equal. The only variation can be the actual piece of hardware or software being compared in the test.

PATA and SATA Hard Disk Interface

IBM introduced the first hard drive in 1957. It was constructed of fifty 24-inch platters with a total storage capacity of 5 MB. IBM would not sell the hard disk, but, at that time, it could be leased for approximately $35,000 per year. The entire disk drive system was physically enormous by today's standards. It was as big as a refrigerator box. Today's hard disk has a thousand times more storage space at a fraction of the size and cost.

Early PC hard drive controller circuitry was mounted on an adapter card and installed into an ISA slot. A cable ran from the adapter card to the hard disk drive. A second hard disk drive standard was introduced by IBM and was used with the MCA slot. It was used to interface with the MCA bus system. It is now obsolete.

As the hard disk drive became more popular, the card was integrated into the hard drive device so that the adapter card and physical hard disk drive became one unit. This was the beginning of a third standard called the **AT Attachment (ATA)**, developed for the 80286 model. The original ATA was a 16-bit data transfer system using a 40-pin cable connector that attached to the motherboard and to the circuit board mounted on the hard drive.

Parallel ATA (PATA) is an interface standard for the connection of storage devices. PATA is in use today and is referred to as *IDE* or *EIDE*. The term **Integrated Drive Electronics (IDE)** came from the adapter card being integrated into the hard drive device. **Enhanced Integrated Drive Electronics (EIDE)** was a term introduced by Western Digital Corporation, a major hard drive manufacturer. EIDE hard drives originally used a

new ATA standard known as ATA-2, Fast ATA, or Fast ATA-2.

Tech Tip
Since the development and release of the SATA standard, the traditional acronym ATA is now often referred to as PATA, representing "parallel ATA."

All the different terminology around the ATA/IDE drive connection can prove very confusing. Some manufacturers didn't wait for new standards to be implemented and came out with similar sounding names. Other manufacturers have changed the requirements for their standard. The requirements for EIDE have changed many times. Refer to **Figure 9-46** for ATA standards.

Figure 9-46. ATA standards.

Drive Specification	Features
ATA-1	The original ATA design released in 1988 used a 40-conductor ribbon cable and featured a master, slave, and cable select option. It also used a programming technique to automatically identify itself to the BIOS system during setup.
ATA-2	Released in 1996, it allowed other storage devices to be connected to the bus system, not just hard disk drives. It allowed disks up to 8.4 GB to be accessed easily. It was also called Fast ATA because it featued faster DMA data transfer speeds than ATA-1.
ATA-3	A revised ATA-2 that allowed password protection for hard disk drive security and a few other minor changes.
ATA-4	A 1998 revision that allowed data transfer rates as high as 33 MBps. It is also referred to as UDMA/33 and Ultra ATA/33. ATA-4 also introduced an optional 80-conductor ribbon cable for the standard 40-pin connector. This modification reduced electrical effects that limited data transfer rates. The ATA-4 specification also integrated the ATAPI standard, which allows for the attachment of CD-ROM, tape drives, and other forms of mass storage devices that required an ATAPI interface.
ATA-5	Introduced in 1999 with a standard 80-conductor ribbon cable. The 80-conductor ribbon cable allowed for transfer rates as high as 66 MBps as long as the motherboard is designed to take advantage of the ATA-5 design. If not, the transfer rate is only 33 MBps. The ATA-5 is also referred to as UDMA/66.
ATA-6	ATA-6, released in 2000, offers transfer rates as high as 100 MBps. An 80-conductor ribbon cable is again used with this design. If the motherboard is not designed for the ATA-6 specification, then the highest transfer speed will probably be 33 MBps.
ATA-7	ATA-7, also known as ATA/133, is the latest and fastest version of the ATA series. It is capable of producing a transfer data rate of 133 MBps. ATA-7 was introduced in 2005 and uses Ultra DMA 133 and an 80-conductor data cable.

Some ATA designs use an adapter board inserted into the PCI slot to take advantage of higher data transfer speeds. When using the expansion slot to upgrade to a higher ATA standard, check if the motherboard chipset will support the higher ATA standard. Otherwise, the desired higher transfer speed of the newer ATA design may not be reached.

Tech Tip

Many people still refer to the ATA design as IDE or EIDE, so when you are in the field talking to other technicians, remember that they are talking about the connection to the mass storage devices other than SCSI.

When working with computers, be aware that computer repair shops as well as your own classroom laboratory may have many old devices and cables in supply storage areas. Be sure you are using the correct cable to match the technology. **Figure 9-47** shows two types of ATA cable. One has 40 conductors and the other has 80 conductors. You must use an 80-conductor ATA data cable to

support the higher data rates of ATA-5, ATA-6, and ATA-7. ATA-6 reaches 100 MBps. ATA-7, also known as ATA-133, is capable of reaching data speeds of 133 MBps. ATA was replaced by PATA technology.

Serial ATA (SATA) was developed to overcome the limitations of the ATA drive. The SATA 1.0 maximum transfer rate is 150 MBps and as high as 600 MBps for SATA 3.0. See **Figure 9-48** to see the standard data rates for SATA 1.0 through SATA 3.0. The table expresses the data rates in both gigabits and megabytes. SATA is a serial device. Serial device data rates are expressed in bits. Bytes is the common measure used for parallel devices such as the original ATA hard disk drive. The chart uses both serial and parallel rates so that SATA technology can be more easily compared to other technology data rates.

SATA has a higher performance than ATA because it moves data to the motherboard in a series of packets in a similar fashion to USB and FireWire. The ATA transfer rate is slower because it is limited to the clock frequency of the motherboard and to the effect of induction caused by the design of the flat ribbon cable. The SATA design can achieve a higher data rate because it generates its own frequency for the data transfer, and its cable is designed to reduce the effects of electrical induction. As you recall from earlier chapters, induction can limit the frequency of data traveling through a conductor, reducing data transfer speeds.

SATA was originally designed for internally-connected PC devices. Later, the eSATA standard was developed for connecting external SATA devices. eSATA has the same data rates as corresponding SATA generations. The difference is eSATA provides a SATA connection and electrical power to an external device.

Figure 9-47. ATA drive cables come with 40 and 80 conductors. You must use an 80-conductor cable to meet the ATA-5, ATA-6, and ATA-7 data rates.

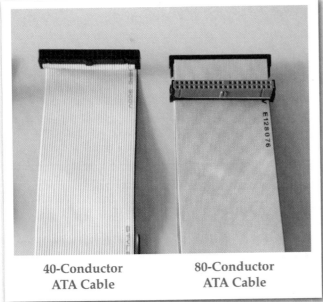

40-Conductor ATA Cable   80-Conductor ATA Cable

Goodheart-Willcox Publisher

Figure 9-48. SATA data rates.

Standard	Gigabit/Second	Megabyte/Second
SATA 1.0	1.5 Gbps	150 MBps
SATA 2.0	3 Gbps	300 MBps
SATA 3.0	6 Gbps	600 MBps

Goodheart-Willcox Publisher

PATA Drive Installation

Figure 9-49 illustrates two drives, one slave and one master, connected to a motherboard using an IDE interface connection point. Typical motherboards provide two sets of connections identified as IDE0 and IDE1. They provide two channels of communication to hard drives and to other devices such as CD-ROM, CD-RW, or tape drive systems. Each channel can provide an interface with the computer bus system for two hard drives, creating a total of four separate physical drives. Each channel consists of one drive designated as a master and the other designated as a slave. Moving jumper settings on the hard

Figure 9-49. Illustration of two PATA hard drives connected to a motherboard. Two hard drives are connected as shown. One hard drive is the master and the other is the slave.

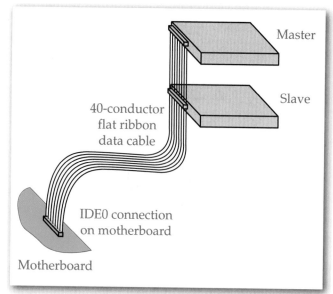

drive sets the designation of master and slave. See **Figure 9-50**.

When two or more drives are installed on the same PC system, one drive must be designated the slave and the other the master. The jumper settings are required because the two drives share the same communication cable. Failure to configure one device as master and the other as slave can result in hard drive failure. Think about the partitions in the hard drive system. When the PC is booted, it must be able to differentiate between the two or more drives. How can the BIOS system search out the active boot partition if it cannot tell the difference between the two hard drives installed on the same PC? By making one the master and the other the slave, one drive becomes the extension of the other. The BIOS system can now differentiate between the two drives and try each one out as it searches for the master boot partition.

Tech Tip

Before you replace a suspected bad hard drive, verify that the hard drive is actually bad. Try installing the suspect drive in another PC to verify it is indeed bad. There are many items, such as the data cable, the EIDE on the motherboard, or a boot sector virus, that would make the hard drive appear to be defective.

SATA Drive Installation

The SATA drive uses a thin, flat or round cable with 7 conductors and a 7-pin cable connector. This is quite a reduction in cable width compared to the width of the 40-conductor and 80-conductor ATA cables. Because of the width

Figure 9-50. Jumper settings for a Western Digital Caviar 24300 drive. Moving the jumper identifies the drive as a master or slave.

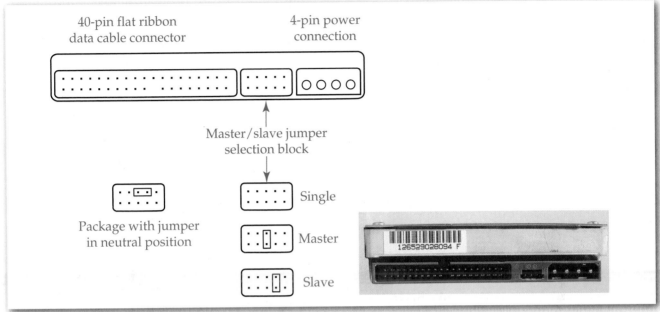

40-pin flat ribbon
data cable connector

4-pin power
connection

Master/slave jumper
selection block

Single

Master

Slave

Package with jumper
in neutral position

Goodheart-Willcox Publisher

reduction, the SATA cable is much easier to route inside the computer chassis.

See **Figure 9-51**. Three of the seven conductors in the illustration are identified with the letter *G*, which represents ground. The pair of conductors used to transmit data are marked DT– and DT+. The pair of conductors used to receive data are marked DR– and DR+. The pairs of cables and the grounds are twisted together to reduce the negative effect of electrical induction on the data transfer rate.

The SATA cable connectors are keyed to prevent a user from incorrectly connecting the cable to the motherboard or to the hard drive. The SATA cable is connected to the motherboard at locations identified such as SATA 0 and SATA 1, **Figure 9-52**.

The SATA drive is designed with only two sets of connectors: power and data. See **Figure 9-53**. There are no master/slave jumper pin connections to worry about. Each device is automatically set as master. There is no slave in the SATA design.

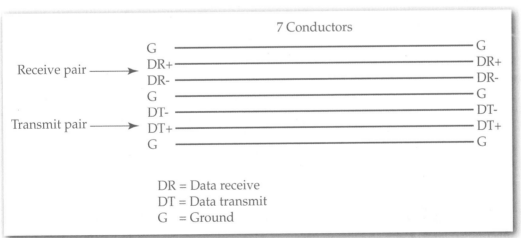

7 Conductors

Receive pair →

Transmit pair →

G — G
DR+ — DR+
DR- — DR-
G — G
DT- — DT-
DT+ — DT+
G — G

DR = Data receive
DT = Data transmit
G = Ground

Figure 9-51.
The SATA cable consists of seven conductors—two sets of transmit and receive pairs and three separate grounds.

Goodheart-Willcox Publisher

Figure 9-52.
SATA connections on a motherboard.

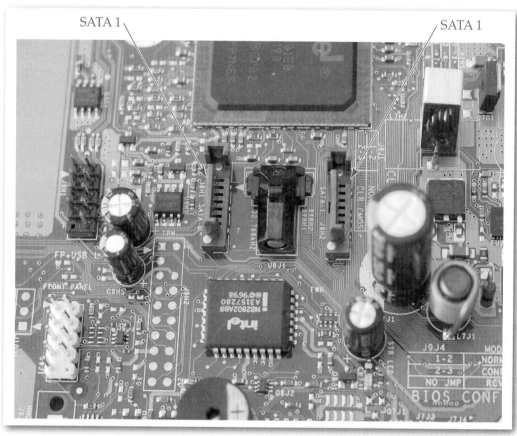

SATA 1

SATA 1

Goodheart-Willcox Publisher

Figure 9-53.
SATA drive and cables. A SATA drive has only two connectors: a data connector and a power connector.

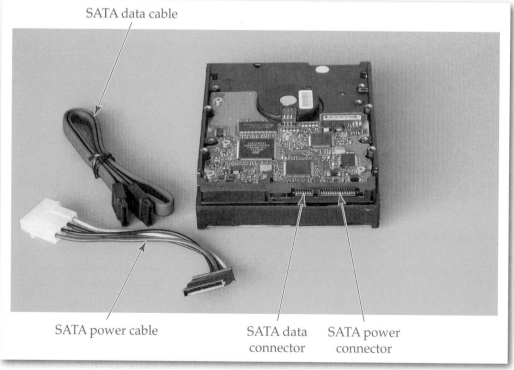

SATA data cable

SATA power cable

SATA data connector

SATA power connector

Goodheart-Willcox Publisher

An existing computer system may be upgraded to SATA by using a SATA host adapter card. The host adapter card is installed in an available PCI slot. The SATA drive is then connected to the host adapter card using a SATA cable. When using a host adapter card, you must check that the BIOS and motherboard will support the SATA technology. Even if SATA is supported, the motherboard BIOS may report the SATA drive as a SCSI drive. The SATA system should perform normally even if it is identified as a SCSI drive. Also note that only one SATA drive can be connected on a SATA cable. This means that each motherboard SATA connection can only support a single SATA device.

> **Tech Tip**
>
> During the early implementation of SATA, regular ATA drives were fitted with a bridge adapter and a SATA conversion chip at the manufacturer and then marketed as SATA drives.

eSATA Drive Installation

SATA drives can also be connected from the exterior through specially-designed SATA bays. **Figure 9-54** shows a SATA bay used to connect a SATA drive to a computer system from outside the case. SATA bays are also referred to as hard drive docks, docking stations, and docking bays.

The SATA drive is simply inserted into the drive bay. You do not need to turn off the computer power before inserting the SATA drive because it is designed as a "hot swap" device. The term *hot swap* is used to identify devices that can be connected or disconnected from a computer without the need to turn off the computer power first.

SATA bays can be added to an existing computer using any empty drive bay in the front of the computer case. The electronics incorporated into the bay case allow the SATA device to be hot swappable.

The SATA drive adapter kit in **Figure 9-55** allows for an internal SATA drive to be connected to an external USB port on a computer. A USB

Figure 9-54. SATA drive bay used to house a SATA drive. The drive can be inserted or removed without the need to turn off the power to the computer. A—Drive bay door closed. B—Drive bay door open.

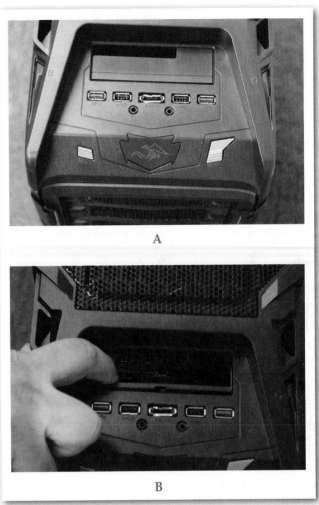

A

B

Goodheart-Willcox Publisher

to PATA or SATA drive adapter can be used to connect any device designed to be installed internally in a computer to an external USB port. For example, a PATA drive can be connected to an external USB port and then accessed by the computer after a reboot. The typical adapter kit comes with a power supply that converts 120-Vac power to 12 Vdc required by the drive. The adapter is designed with a 40-pin PATA connector and a SATA connector which connect to the computer through a USB port. The adapter is not limited to hard drives but can also be used for internal devices such as a CD or DVD drive.

Figure 9-55. SATA/PATA external adapter.

SATA or PATA connector   Power supply

Goodheart-Willcox Publisher

Figure 9-56. SATA expansion port.

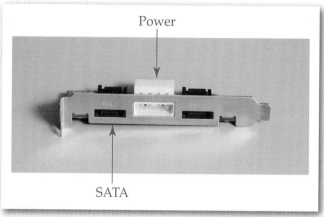

Power

SATA

Goodheart-Willcox Publisher

Figure 9-57. An adapter for converting a standard 12-Vdc Molex connector to supply power to two SATA devices.

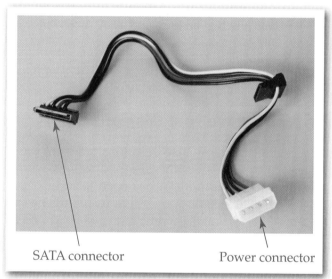

SATA connector   Power connector

Goodheart-Willcox Publisher

There are also other products designed to support exterior connections of internal devices. In **Figure 9-56** you can see how an external port and 12-Vdc power supply connector can be added to an exterior slot on the computer case. After the exterior SATA port is installed, a SATA device and power can be connected to the expansion port. The power connection adapter in **Figure 9-57** connects SATA devices to a 12-Vdc, 4-pin peripheral power connector (Molex connector).

A+ Note

Be able to identify a cable type when presented with a picture or drawing of a connector or port such as PATA, SATA, and eSATA.

SCSI Interface System

Small Computer System Interface (SCSI) (pronounced *skuzzy*) uses an adapter board and connects up to seven devices on one flat ribbon cable. This is the standard system used by Macintosh/Apple and many UNIX mainframe systems to connect peripherals. Because it was fairly expensive, SCSI technology was slow coming to the PC market. It was first used in the IBM market for file servers that required a lot of disk storage. File servers are like super PCs that control network systems. They are covered in more detail in later chapters.

The SCSI standard was developed, in part, to remedy compatibility problems between PCs and aftermarket hardware. Original market concerns created proprietary systems in early PCs. PC upgrading and expansion was a challenging task because of the compatibility issues. SCSI was designed to eliminate some of these issues by creating a standard that was available to all manufacturers.

The SCSI system was also designed to free the CPU from the burden of processing all data transactions. SCSI interfaces with a PC through an intelligent controller card inserted into the expansion bus. A SCSI bus cable connects the SCSI card to a series of devices. These devices, as directed by the controller card, can communicate freely along the bus cable, eliminating the need for the CPU's involvement.

Figure 9-58 shows a typical SCSI-1 installation. The SCSI-1 standard allows for eight devices at maximum to be connected to a SCSI-1 cable. One of these is the host adapter card. The ID numbers assigned range from 0 to 7 (eight numbers total). SCSI-2 allows for 16 devices (host adapter included) to be assigned.

A+ Note

The quantity of SCSI devices allowed can make for a tricky question on the A+ Certification exams. When asked how many devices can be connected to a SCSI-1 cable, the correct answer is eight. However, eight may not be one of the multiple-choice answers. In that case, the answer is seven. Examine how the question is worded. Eight devices can be connected to the cable. Seven devices can be connected to a host adapter card. In various reference materials, you will see it written that seven devices can be connected to a SCSI-1 cable. This is written because the host adapter card is understood to be a necessary part of the installation. Read and answer the question carefully.

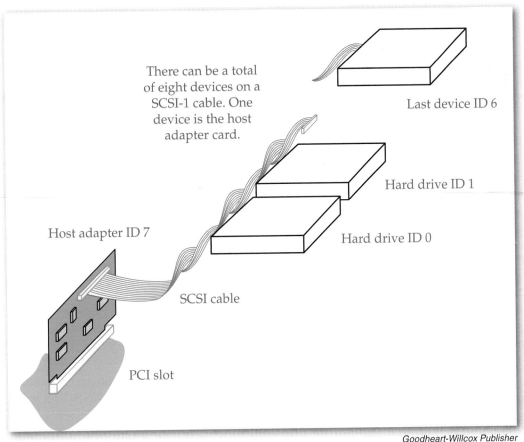

There can be a total of eight devices on a SCSI-1 cable. One device is the host adapter card.

Last device ID 6

Hard drive ID 1

Hard drive ID 0

Host adapter ID 7

SCSI cable

PCI slot

Figure 9-58.
Typical SCSI-1 setup. There can be a total of eight devices including the adapter card.

There are many styles of SCSI that have developed over the years. The main three classifications are SCSI-1, SCSI-2, and SCSI-3, **Figure 9-59**. There are variations of these three SCSI styles that can easily be confusing. Some of the names are Wide SCSI, Fast SCSI, Fast Wide SCSI, Ultra SCSI, Ultra2 SCSI, and Wide Ultra2 SCSI. When selecting SCSI hardware to install or replace, you must exercise caution. Though SCSI was originally created to help solve compatibility problems, many of the SCSI systems are still not compatible with each other. The problem lies in the many proprietary variations.

You must be careful to match the device to the proper SCSI technology. *SCSI-1* uses an 8-bit system and supports data transfer rates as high as 5 MBps. It was the first SCSI technology. It uses a 25-conductor flat ribbon cable. *SCSI-2* is similar to SCSI-1, but it uses a wider, 50-conductor connector and supports up to 7 devices on one cable. *Wide SCSI* uses a wider cable with 68 conductors, hence the name "Wide SCSI." Wide SCSI can transfer 16-bits of data at one time. *Fast SCSI* uses an 8-bit bus similar to SCSI-1, but has a much higher transfer rate of 10 MBps. There are also Fast-20, Fast-40, and Fast-80 SCSI systems. The last two digits of the name reflect the speed of data transfer in megabytes per second (MBps). The speed of each can be doubled by the use of a Fast Wide device. Hence, a normal SCSI that is 10 Mbps will become 20 Mbps when employed as a Fast Wide SCSI.

> **Tech Tip**
> Be careful when checking the speed of a device. When abbreviated, *megabits per second* is *Mbps* while *megabytes per second* is *MBps*. The small change in the case of the "b" means a very large change in the speed of the device.

Advantages of SCSI

One advantage of SCSI is that SCSI devices can be connected inside or outside the computer case, leaving some flexibility for the user. IDE and EIDE are designed to install hardware inside the case. SCSI also has very high data transfer rates. Older SCSI hard drives were much faster than IDE hard drives. (New EIDE drives have closed that

gap.) Most SCSI devices are also fully compatible with the Windows Plug and Play specification making installation simple. Some older SCSI systems may not be Plug and Play compatible.

A big advantage of SCSI in a multitasking environment is its ability to disconnect the communication between devices when the device is not needed, thus conserving resources. For example, when a tape is rewinding, it does not need to maintain its connection to another device. SCSI can disconnect the communication to and from the tape for a period of time and then go back and check if it is ready for additional communication.

In the SCSI technology system, equipment can be easily exchanged. At the most, the driver may need to be upgraded. To a SCSI host adapter, all hard drives look the same, as do other SCSI devices such as printers and optical drives. Of course, the total capacity of the drives may differ. There is no need for slave and master arrangements as there is with IDE/EIDE. Each device is given its own unique ID number.

SCSI ID

SCSI devices must have a unique **SCSI ID number**, which is used to identify that device. The ID range for the typical SCSI-1 is from 0 to 7 (eight ID numbers). When two devices attempt to control the SCSI bus at the same time, the device with the highest number takes control.

While any device connected on the SCSI cable can have any ID number assigned, there are some common assignments. The host adapter is usually assigned the number 7, and hard drives are usually assigned 0 and 1. The host adapter is usually given the highest priority number. These are normal SCSI assignments, but they are not mandatory nor a recognized standard. It is simply a general practice.

The original SCSI limit of eight devices was first expanded by the use of SCSI bus extenders. The bus extenders were integrated circuit cards that connected as SCSI devices. They allowed an additional seven devices to be connected within a SCSI system. See **Figure 9-60**. As the SCSI-1 system was expanded, an additional system of identification was needed. The additional devices connected to the SCSI extender are identified using a **logical unit number (LUN)** from 0 to 7.

Figure 9-59. SCSI standards.

Controller	Maximum Number of Devices	Typical Devices	General Information
SCSI-1	8 (host adapter plus 7 devices)	Hard drive, CD-ROM, scanner	Low transfer rate, 5 MBps
SCSI-2	Fast SCSI: 8 (host adapter plus 7 devices) Fast Wide SCSI: 16 (host adapter plus 15 devices)	Hard drive, CD-ROM, CD-RW, DVD, tape drive, scanner	Fast SCSI: 10 MBps Fast Wide SCSI: 20 MBps
SCSI-3	16 (host adapter plus 15 devices)	Hard drive, CD-ROM, CD-RW, DVD, tape drive, scanner	Various speeds from 20 MBps to 160 MBps

Goodheart-Willcox Publisher

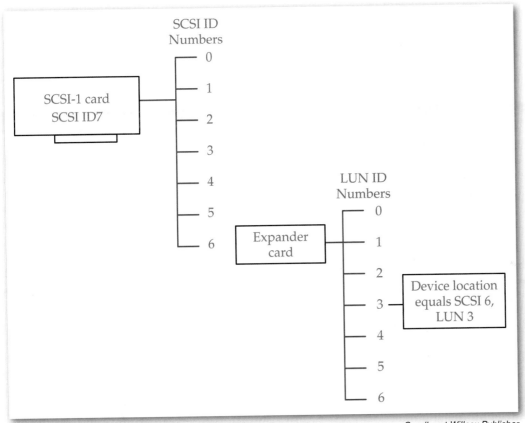

Figure 9-60.
The SCSI limit of seven devices can be expanded by using expander cards. Each expander card allows an additional seven devices to be connected to the SCSI system. A LUN number is assigned so the system software and BIOS can identify each of the additional units.

Goodheart-Willcox Publisher

Expanders can also be found in some SCSI-2 systems. They may be referred to as *expanders*, *repeaters*, and *regenerators*. The use of a LUN ID is not limited to only SCSI storage drives. LUN IDs are often used to identify nonstorage devices connected on a common SCSI cable, such as SCSI-compatible CD-ROM, DVD, and tape drives.

SCSI ID Jumpers

Older SCSI systems used jumpers to identify devices. **Figure 9-61** illustrates how a set of pins and jumpers might look on a SCSI device. The pins are actual electrical connections, and the jumpers are used to make an electrical connection across the pairs of pins. The jumpers are set in

Figure 9-61. SCSI binary patterns.

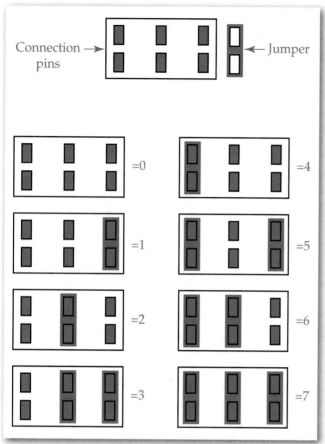

Goodheart-Willcox Publisher

the binary pattern that represents the SCSI ID number. If you have trouble interpreting the jumper patterns, you may wish to review Chapter 1—Introduction to a Typical PC, which illustrates and discusses binary numbers.

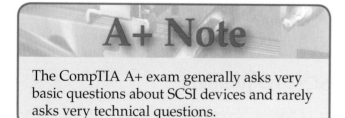

A+ Note

The CompTIA A+ exam generally asks very basic questions about SCSI devices and rarely asks very technical questions.

LVD and HVD

SCSI systems communicate using two different voltage levels identified as High Voltage Differential (HVD) and Low Voltage Differential (LVD). HVD uses 5 volts for a high and 0 volts for a low. LVD uses 3.3 volts for a high and 0 volts for a low. The high-and low-voltage levels are represented by a binary 1 or 0 respectively. The advantage of HVD is that data can be transmitted on longer cables than on LVD. HVD can transmit data on cables up to 25 meters long while LVD is limited to cables 5 meters long.

The SCSI Trade Association website has excellent reference material, such as detailed charts of SCSI connectors. Also, Adaptec and other hard drive manufacturers contain SCSI information.

SCSI Commands and Terminology

In the SCSI system, there are two classifications of hardware that relate to communication between SCSI devices. They are targets and initiators. The SCSI host adapter card is usually the *initiator*, while the devices connected to the SCSI bus (printers, hard drives, tape drives, and other SCSI devices) are usually the *targets*.

SCSI has its own set of commands, which are used to control the flow of data and the communications between targets and initiators. There are also nine special control signals used in a SCSI system. They are as follows:

- **C/D (Control/Data):** This control signal allows the target to signal if it will return a command or data to the initiator. The initiator will wait for the data or command.
- **I/O (Input/Output):** This indicates whether the target will be sending or receiving on the data bus.
- **MSG (Message):** The target uses this control signal to send error messages or status conditions back to the initiator.
- **REQ (Request):** This control signal allows the target to obtain data from the bus.
- **ACK (Acknowledge):** This is a reply signal sent after the REQ signal. It acknowledges the REQ signal and takes control of the bus.
- **BSY (Busy):** This control signal lets other devices know that a device is busy.
- **SEL (Select):** This control signal is used to select a target device.

- **ATN (Attention):** This control signal informs the target that a message is coming.
- **RST (Reset):** This control signal resets all devices on the bus system.

These signals are sent on wires inside the complete cable assembly. By placing a high- or low-voltage level on the wire, a signal is sent between initiator and target devices. Additional wire in the cable assembly supplies data and power. These commands are invisible to the user.

SCSI Cable

SCSI cables are designed in many variations, **Figure 9-62**. The cable is either single-ended or differential. A single-ended cable simply carries the signal from the initiator to the target. Each wire carries the signal to the target and to a common ground. There is a terminating resistor located at each end of the cable to absorb stray signals.

In the other design, called *differential*, a pair of wires is used for each signal transmitted. By using a pair, the signal travels simultaneously from the initiator to the target and from the target to the initiator. This transmission cancels the effects of electrical noise generation. The system still uses terminating resistors at each end to absorb the signals. The main advantage of the differential design is that it can be used for greater distances, up to 25 meters. In high-speed data transmissions, single-ended cable may be required to be as short as 1.5 meters.

SCSI Termination

Each end of the SCSI cable must be terminated immediately after the last device on the end of the cable. Without the terminators, data would be garbled. The high-speed transmission of data through the cable would produce an effect similar to radio broadcast waves. These waves would echo and return to the ends of the cable causing the data to be garbled.

Cable termination is classified as either active or passive. *Passive termination* uses resistors to terminate the cable on each end. Passive termination is powered through the cable itself and is good for short runs of up to one meter. Passive termination works well for cables limited to the inside of the PC case. *Active termination* requires the use of an external power supply. It uses a voltage regulator and resistors to control the amount of voltage transmitted inside the cable and to absorb the signals at the end of the cable. The active terminator allows greater lengths of SCSI cable to be used. It is typically used for cable runs outside the computer case to connect devices such as flat bed scanners.

Figure 9-62. Typical SCSI device and cabling. The back of this SCSI CD-RW drive has two SCSI cable connectors. The photo on the right shows the ends of a cable connector. Compare the cable connector on the left (SCSI) to the cable connector on the right (parallel).

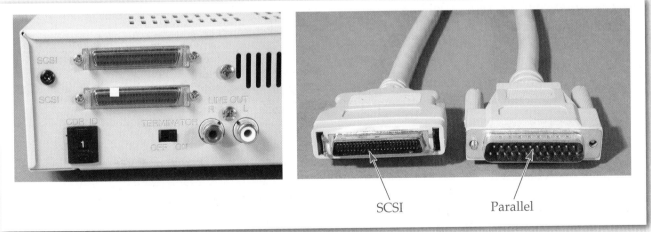

SCSI   Parallel

Goodheart-Willcox Publisher

SCSI Bus Operation

The first part of communication on the SCSI bus is the control of the bus. The control of the bus can only be attempted while there is no active BSY or SEL signal on the bus. Both BSY and SEL must be idle. Only one device can communicate on the bus at a time, so the device must gain exclusive control of the bus. The device that has control is the *initiator*. When a device is attempting to take control of the bus, it is called the *arbitration phase*. Once a device (the initiator) has taken control of the bus, it identifies the target device. Identification of the target device is called the *selection phase*.

The individual devices negotiate the control of the SCSI bus. When two devices attempt to take control of the bus at the same time, the device with the highest assigned ID number wins control. This is the reason that the host adapter is usually assigned the highest number. In a SCSI-2 system, the host adapter is usually assigned the number 7.

The initiator sends a BSY signal a SEL signal. After the initiator has transmitted data or a command, it then releases the BSY signal. The target then receives the data and issues a BSY signal until a reply with data or a command such as ACK is transmitted. The following steps are an example of how a typical communication might take place between two devices:

1. The system checks that the bus is idle with no BSY or SEL signal.
2. Arbitration takes place until the device chosen as the initiator takes control.
3. Selection of the target takes place.
4. The target device acknowledges the communication link.
5. The target notifies the initiator that it is ready to receive data.
6. The data is transferred to the target device.
7. Status of the data transfer is maintained. For example, are there any errors?
8. A message indicating all the data has been transferred is sent.
9. The bus is released to all devices.

Tech Tip

When putting a SCSI system together with multiple devices, one device at a time should be installed after the host adapter card is installed. Using this method, it is easy to isolate a problem with an individual device if it arises during assembly. Also, note that all devices on your SCSI chain must support (or not support) parity. Some SCSI devices use parity and others do not.

Serial Attached SCSI

Serial Attached SCSI (SAS) is the latest development for SCSI technology. Serial attached SCSI is similar in design to SATA. A SAS host adapter card can connect to two types of drives: SAS and SATA. There are many different types of SAS cable designs which are mostly proprietary. Some SAS cables look similar to SATA cables.

Figure 9-63 shows a SAS cable that consists of a SAS connector, a SATA connector, and a 4-pin peripheral power connector (Molex connector). The SAS connector connects directly to a SAS hard drive. The SATA connector connects to the

Figure 9-63. A SAS hard drive cable with a SAS connector, a SATA connector, and a power connector.

Power connector SATA connector

SAS connector

motherboard SATA port. The power connector provides 12 Vdc to the drive.

Figure 9-64 shows a SAS cable that supports multiple SATA drives connected to a SAS host adapter. Look closely at the red cable assembly. This cable is equipped with one mini-SAS (mSAS) and four SATA connectors. The four SATA connectors connect to SATA disk drives or to SATA Solid-State Drives. The single mSAS connector attaches to a SAS host adapter card located in a PCI or PCIe slot inside the computer. This particular cable is designed for RAID arrangements. RAID is a disk configuration that provides redundancy to prevent data loss when a disk device fails. There will be much more about RAID in Chapter 17—Network Administration.

SAS can achieve data transfer rates as high as 6 Gbps. Note that SAS data rates are expressed in gigabits per second (Gbps), not gigabytes per second (GBps). Gbps is used as a measurement for serial data transfers. Since SAS transfers data in a serial fashion, Gbps is technically correct. For comparison to other SCSI standards, 6 Gbps is equal to 375 MBps. This is more than twice as fast as the 160-MBps transfer rate associated with the SCSI-3 standard. While SCSI devices still exist in network storage environments, SAS devices have made SCSI a legacy device.

SAS disk arrays create large storage pools for networks. A typical PC user does not require the use of SCSI or SAS arrays. These arrays are employed commonly to support network server storage. A SAS switch provides multiple disk connections and one Ethernet port. The Ethernet port allows the switch to be connected to a network system. Mini-SAS cables are often used with SAS switches. They connect between the switch and other storage devices or network servers. The following are some advantages of SAS technology as compared to SCSI:

- Higher data transfer speeds.
- Can be used to create arrays containing 65,000 devices through the use of expanders.
- Does not require termination like SCSI.
- The cost of installation can be reduced because SAS host adapters can connect to SATA storage devices.

Solid-State Drives

A **Solid-State Drive (SSD)** uses flash memory chips in place of disks and discs for storage. The advantage of SSD over disk and disc storage devices is SSD transfers data quicker, uses less power, is silent, and does not have any moving parts which can wear out in time. SSD does not have latency issues when accessing a data location as do storage devices that use disks or discs. Also, computers that use an SSD from which to boot the operating system boot faster than disk systems.

The most commonly found place for SSDs is in the portable computer or laptop models. SSDs weigh less than and are much smaller in physical size than traditional laptop storage drives. This helps to make the laptop and portable device lighter and thinner. The SSD uses both ATA-6 and SATA data interfaces. Some computers use a combination of mechanical disk storage and Solid-State Disk storage. When a mechanical disk drive is used in combination with a solid-state disk drive, the principle of solid-state disk caching is typically applied.

Solid-State Drives are much quicker than traditional hard drives, but at the time of this writing, SSD are much more expensive. To increase the performance of a computer system, an SSD is often used in combination with a hard

Figure 9-64. SAS cable with four SATA connectors and one mini-SAS (mSAS) connector.

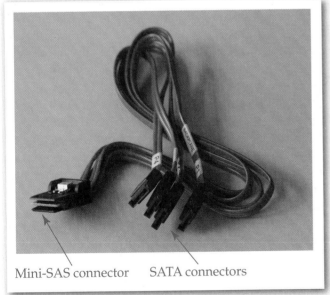

Mini-SAS connector   SATA connectors

Goodheart-Willcox Publisher

drive. This allows overall performance to be improved without completely replacing the low-cost hard drive with a much higher-cost SSD.

The SSD is used to augment the hard drive system in desktop computers by providing a temporary storage space for frequently accessed files or programs. When the SSD is used as a temporary storage location for frequently accessed files or programs, the technique is referred to as **solid-state disc caching**. The SSD is used to store frequently accessed files and programs to allow for quicker loading. The computer operating system keeps track of which programs and files are commonly accessed, and it stores an up-to-date copy on the SSD. After the computer finishes its boot sequence, the file or program loads much quicker as compared to a computer system that relies solely on a hard drive for file and program storage. **Figure 9-65** shows how an Intel motherboard identifies a SATA port used specifically for solid-state disc caching. Solid-state disc caching is referred to by Intel as Smart Response Technology (SRT).

Figure 9-65. Intel motherboards provide a special SATA port to support SSD caching.

SSD Caching port

Goodheart-Willcox Publisher

You may see a question about a problem installing a new SSD on an older computer system. The correct answer to remedy the problem will most likely relate to upgrading the motherboard BIOS. An old system may not recognize an SSD.

Virtual Hard Disk

A **Virtual Hard Disk (VHD)** is a file that behaves exactly like a physical hard disk. The ability to create a VHD from Computer Management was first introduced in Windows 7. Refer to Figure 9-33 to see the **Create VHD** and **Mount VHD** options. Selecting the **Create VHD** option will open the dialog box shown in **Figure 9-66**.

After creating a VHD, it must be mounted. The action of "mounting" the VHD makes it

available for access. The VHD can be used as a backup location for the existing operating system. For example, the VHD can be used for a complete backup of the entire operating system and important files. Later if needed, it can be used to recreate the original operating system and files much in the same way a recovery partition is used to reinstall an operating system after a system failure.

Another way the VHD is used is to run another operating system. For example, after a new operating system has been installed on a computer it is discovered that the new operating system will not support an older software application or hardware device such as a printer. A VHD can be created and the legacy operating system can be installed in the VHD, thus allowing the older software application or legacy hardware device to function.

A VHD can also be used to test a new operating system. For example, you can create a VHD and then install a newer operating system on a computer system and test it out before replacing the existing operating system. You could create a VHD on a Windows 7 computer and then install Windows 8 into the VHD. The VHD can be made bootable so that the VHD containing the Windows 8 system becomes the boot partition or drive.

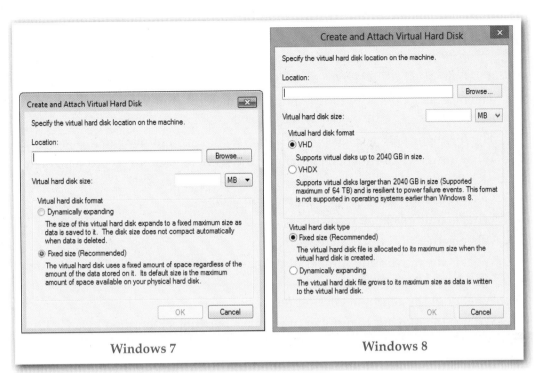

Figure 9-66.
Windows 7 and Windows 8 **Create and Attach Virtual Hard Disk** dialog boxes.

Windows 7

Windows 8

Chapter Summary

- Magnetic storage devices operate on the principle that electrical energy can produce magnetism and magnetism can produce electrical energy.
- The hard drive is divided into sectors, cylinders, tracks, and clusters.
- Hard drives can be divided into multiple partitions to simulate additional drives.
- FAT16, FAT32, exFAT, NTFS, and ReFS are common file systems.
- Disk Defragmenter is used when files become fragmented under normal disk operations; Chkdsk checks and repairs the integrity of the file system on a hard drive.
- When two PATA drives are installed on the same cable, one drive must be designated the slave and the other the master; SATA drives do not have master/slave jumper pin connections and only one drive can be installed per cable.
- SAS technology can achieve higher data transfer rates than SCSI and does not require termination.
- Solid-State Drives transfer data quicker, quieter, and use less power than disk or disc storage devices, and they do not have any moving parts which can wear out in time.
- The Computer Management utility is used to create and mount a Virtual Hard Disk.

Review Questions

Answer the following questions on a separate sheet of paper. Please do not write in this book.

1. The magnetic polarity produced by a conductor is directly related to the direction of _____ through the wire.
2. The magnetic patterns left on a disk represent _____ numbers.
3. What terms are used when describing the sections used to record data on a disk drive?
4. What is another term used for allocation units?
5. What is multiple zone recording?
6. When is the MBR or GPT created?
7. What is the maximum number of primary partitions identified by a standard MBR-based hard disk drive?
8. What does the acronym GPT represent?
9. What is the maximum number of primary partitions identified by a GPT?
10. What is the largest partition size supported by MBR?
11. What is the largest partition size supported by GPT?
12. What does the acronym ESP represent?
13. What does the acronym EFI represent?
14. What is responsible for creating the ESP partition?
15. What drive letter is assigned to the System Reserved partition?
16. What files are typically located in the ESP partition?
17. What does the acronym MSR represent?
18. Which optional partition is created by the OEM?
19. What is the purpose of the PQSERVICE partition?
20. What command-line utility has replaced the functions of the **fdisk** command?
21. Which operating systems no longer recognizes the **fdisk** command?
22. How is the first physical disk identified when the **list disk** command is issued from the DiskPart utility?
23. What DiskPart command is used to list the volumes located on the disk?
24. What are two ways to access Disk Management in Windows Vista and Windows 7?
25. What is the maximum size hard drive that can be formatted using a FAT16 file system without more than one partition?
26. What file system is used for portable devices such as USB flash drives and flash memory cards?
27. On which file system can EFS be used?
28. What is Microsoft's newest file system?
29. What is the purpose of Windows 8 Storage Spaces?
30. What Windows utility is used to format a hard drive?
31. What is the purpose of Disk Defragmenter?

32. What is the purpose of Chkdsk?

33. What switch must be used with the **chkdsk** command that will enable it to automatically make repairs to the disk?

34. What is the maximum data transfer rate of SATA 3.0?

35. What is the maximum number of physical hard drives that can be installed on a typical PC with two IDE channels?

36. How many drives are designated as master on a PC with two channels and four physical hard drives?

37. How many SATA drives can be connected to a SATA cable?

38. How many hard drives can be installed on a type SCSI-1 interface?

39. How many devices can be attached to a SCSI-1 cable?

40. How many devices can be attached to a Fast Wide SCSI-2 cable?

41. What types of drives can connect to a SAS host adapter card?

42. What is the highest data rate a SAS drive can achieve?

43. List four advantages of SAS drives over SCSI.

44. In what applications are Solid-State Drives commonly used?

45. List four advantages of Solid-State Drives over disk and disc storage devices.

46. What is a Virtual Hard Disk?

47. What Windows utility is used to create a VHD?

Sample A+ Exam Questions

Answer the following questions on a separate sheet of paper. Please do not write in this book.

1. You install a new second hard drive to increase the total storage capacity of a PC. Both hard drives are installed on the same PATA data cable. When you boot the system, the computer displays the BIOS information and the RAM test on the screen. After the RAM test is completed and passed, the PC hangs up. What is *most likely* the problem?
   a. The BIOS needs to be upgraded to match the new hard drive.
   b. A virus has been introduced into the system from the new hard drive.
   c. The jumper settings identifying master and slave are incorrect.
   d. The two drives' positions are reversed on the data cable.

2. Where in a FAT16 file system is the MBR located?
   a. In the first disk sector
   b. In the last disk sector
   c. The exact location varies according to the number of cylinders.
   d. An MBR is only on a hard disk system formatted for NTFS4.0.

3. Which of the following file systems is the default file system used for a Windows Vista clean install?
   a. FAT16
   b. FAT32
   c. VFAT
   d. NTFS

4. Which FAT file system is used for flash drives of 32 GB or larger?
   a. FAT12
   b. FAT16
   c. FAT32
   d. exFAT

5. A certain file consists of 12 sectors. The sectors are not contiguous but rather divided into two separate areas on the disk. Which of the following technical terms is used to describe this condition of file storage?
   a. Cross-linked sectors
   b. File fragmentation
   c. Multiple-zone recording
   d. Multiple-sector storage

6. Which of the following technologies is *not* used for disk storage?
   a. ATA
   b. IDE
   c. SCSI
   d. DDS

7. What is the size in bytes of the smallest typical disk sector?
   a. 256
   b. 512
   c. 1024
   d. 2048

8. What is the maximum number of hard drives that can be installed on a Wide SCSI-2 configuration?
   a. 5
   b. 9
   c. 15
   d. 24

9. Which is the correct path to Computer Management on a Windows 7 operating system?
   a. **Start | All Programs | Accessories | System Tool | Disk Management**
   b. **Start | right-click Computer | Manage**
   c. **Start | Control Panel | Hardware and Sound**
   d. **Start | right-click Computer | Properties | Device Manager**

10. What is the maximum number of hard disk drives that can be installed on a single motherboard PATA port?
   a. One
   b. Two
   c. Three
   d. Eight

Suggested Laboratory Activities

Do not attempt any suggested laboratory activities without your instructor's permission. Certain activities can render the PC operating system inoperable.

1. Using a lab PC identified by your instructor, experiment with the **fdisk** command. Try to set up multiple partitions on one physical drive. Also, try to create FAT32 and FAT16 file systems. Boot the system before formatting any of the partitions to observe the error generated. Format the same hard drive and reboot the system to observe the error generated. Now format the partition using the **/s** switch, which installs system files to the partition. Boot the system once more to see if any errors are generated. Remember, the **fdisk** command is available but cannot be used on an NTFS file system. The **fdisk** command can only be used from the command prompt and can only be used on Windows Vista or earlier operating systems.

2. Install a second hard drive on the same PATA cable as the original drive. Configure the jumpers as needed to identify the slave and master drive.

3. Install a second SATA hard disk drive.

4. Access the Seagate website. Download any hard drive utilities that are available. There are usually hard drive utilities that will identify the type of hard drive installed, perform diagnostics, or allow access to hard drives too large for DOS and older BIOS systems.

5. Open the Storage Spaces wizard and view the options available. You will need to use a Windows 8 computer and have a second hard disk drive available, preferably one that connects through a USB port as an external drive.

6. Access the firmware Setup utility and find information about the hard drive configuration. See if the drive is auto detected or assigned a number. See if there is information about the number of heads, cylinders, and sectors. See if you can find controls to change the boot order (which boots first: floppy, hard drive, or CD/DVD drive). Do *not* make any changes to the Setup utility without your instructor's approval.

Optical Storage Technology

10

After studying this chapter, you will be able to:

- Explain how data is stored and retrieved using CD storage devices.
- Explain how data is stored and retrieved using magneto-optical storage devices.
- Compare CD and DVD construction.
- Compare HD-DVD and Blu-ray Disc storage technologies.
- Carry out an optical storage device installation.
- Identify digital rights management technologies and their characteristics.
- Identify the most common problems encountered with an optical storage system.

A+ Exam—Key Points

For the CompTIA A+ exam, you should know the differences between CD, DVD, and Blu-ray Discs and be familiar with the different storage capacities of disc types and disc compatibility. You should also know the various ways optical storage devices can be added to an existing computer system.

Key Terms

The following key terms will become important pieces of your computer vocabulary. Be sure you can define them.

access time
Advanced Access Content System (AACS)
Advanced Access Control System
Advanced Video Codec High Definition (AVCHD)
AT Attachment Packet Interface (ATAPI)
Blu-ray Disc (BD)
Blu-ray Disc Plus (BD+)
Blu-ray Disc Recordable (BD-R)
Blu-ray Disc Recordable Erasable (BD-RE)
CD-ROM File System (CDFS)
colored books
Compact Disc Read-Only Memory (CD-ROM)
Compact Disc-Recordable (CD-R)
Compact Disc-ReWritable (CD-RW)

constant angular velocity (CAV)
constant linear velocity (CLV)
data transfer rate
digital rights management (DRM)
Digital Versatile Disc (DVD)
High Sierra format
High-bandwidth Digital Content Protection (HDCP)
ISO 9660
ISO image
lands
magneto-optical (MO) drive
numerical aperture (NA)
packet writing
photocell
pits
Universal Disk Format (UDF)
Volume Table of Contents (VTOC)

Optical data storage began with the CD-ROM. It revolutionized the methodology for storing and retrieving data. Great amounts of data could be stored in much smaller physical areas. The CD-ROM paved the way for economical computer storage of music, graphics, and video. This chapter discusses and explains CD and DVD technology associated with the PC.

CD

In 1978, Philips and Sony Corporations developed the **Compact Disc Read-Only Memory (CD-ROM)**, an optical disc able to store large amounts of data. Compact Disc (CD) technology was originally developed to replace plastic records and tapes used in the music industry and not directly for computer storage, **Figure 10-1**. The first CD-ROMs were large 12″ platters. By 1982, the 4.72″ platter became the standard.

Tech Tip

Note that spelling *disc* with a *c* is a common practice to indicate optical disc media. Spelling *disk* with a *k* is used to indicate magnetic disk media, such as floppy disks and hard disks.

To see the layers built into a CD-ROM, see **Figure 10-2**. A typical CD-ROM is composed of a polycarbonate (plastic) wafer approximately 1.2 mm thick. The base of the wafer is coated with an aluminum alloy. This is where the actual data is encoded. A final layer of polycarbonate is used to seal the aluminum alloy layer. A label is then placed on the top of the CD. The data is read from the bottom of the CD, not the label side. Data is recorded on the aluminum alloy as a series of pits and lands.

The **pits** are holes etched into the disc in order to record data. **Lands** are the flat areas between the pits in a compact disk. The lands reflect the light of the laser beam. The pits disperse the light rather than reflect it. Digital data is recorded to the CD as a series of pit and land sequences. The

Figure 10-1. Typical CDs. CDs can hold 650 MB to 700 MB of information.

Goodheart-Willcox Publisher

pits and lands convey the binary values of 1 and 0. Changes from lands to pits and pits to lands create 1s. Lack of change for defined periods of time creates 0s.

Most CD-ROMs are mass-produced using a laser to etch the surface of a disc known as the *master*. The master is then used to "stamp out" copies of the original data pattern onto many more plastic discs. The mass-produced discs are copies of the original. The plastic disc is then coated with a thin film of aluminum reflective material. The aluminum material follows the pits and lands etched into the plastic. An additional layer of plastic seals the aluminum material, and the outside is given a smooth finish to allow the laser light to pass freely through the surface.

A CD-ROM drive uses a laser diode to read the disc, **Figure 10-3**. The laser diode produces

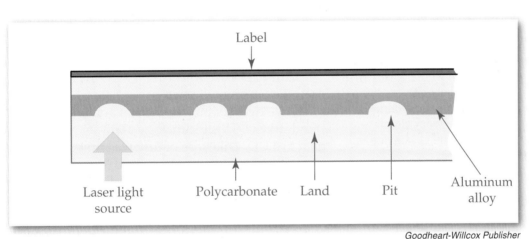

Goodheart-Willcox Publisher

Figure 10-2. Cutaway view of a typical CD-ROM.

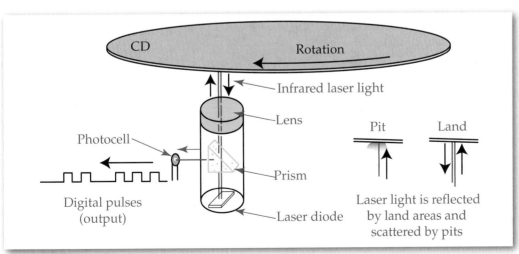

Goodheart-Willcox Publisher

Figure 10-3. A laser diode sends a beam of light through a prism and onto the CD. If the light hits a land, the light is reflected. Pits disperse the light. The reflected light travels through the prism, which sends some of the light to a photocell. The photocell turns the light into digital electrical pulses.

a laser light when energized. The laser produces a low-energy infrared beam. A servomotor in the drive follows commands issued by software to position the beam on the spiral path of pits and lands on the disc. The pits defuse the light, while the lands reflect the light. The reflected light strikes a photocell, which is sometimes referred to as a photo detector. A **photocell** is an electronic component that changes light energy into electrical energy.

The light reflected off the CD produces a pattern that replicates the data stored on the disc. The light is reflected to the photocell where it generates electrical pulses. These electrical pulses are reproduced as a digital signal (on or off), and they represent the binary codes used to encode the data on the CD. Once the information stored on the CD is converted to digital signals, it can be utilized by the computer system. A typical CD-ROM contains between 650 MB and 700 MB of information.

| Warning ! | Permanent damage can result to the retina of the eye when working with any laser source. There are specially-designed safety glasses for working on lasers. As a computer technician, you should *never* work directly on the parts inside a CD device. The CD device is considered a field replacement unit. |

The CD data is organized somewhat differently than that on a hard drive platter. The CD uses a spiral technique to record data rather than dividing the platter into separate tracks, **Figure 10-4**. By using a spiral technique, it is possible to increase storage capacity. There is no wasted space as is found on the conventional hard disk platter.

Two major advantages of optical storage over magnetic storage are capacity and the stability of stored data. Using the same physical amount of storage area, much more data can be stored using optical systems than magnetic systems. Optical systems are also more stable than magnetic systems. Magnetic systems such as floppy disks and hard drives maintain data for approximately 5 to 8 years before they must be refreshed (written again). Optical storage does not have this limitation. There is debate over how long a CD can

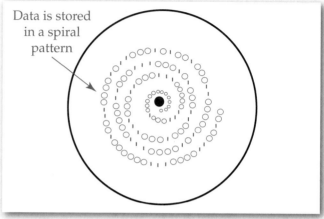

Figure 10-4. CDs store data differently than hard drives. CDs do not use sectors.

Data is stored in a spiral pattern

Goodheart-Willcox Publisher

last before it degrades to a point where it cannot be read. Some estimate 10 to 25 years. Other estimates put the life span of the discs at over 100 years.

CD-R

Compact Disc-Recordable (CD-R) is an optical storage media that uses photosensitive reflective dye to simulate the pits and lands of a standard CD. This technology allows you to write data to a CD. This type of disc was first called CD-WORM (CD-Write Once Read Many). With CD-R, data *can be* erased and the disc *can be* written to again. However, it cannot be written to a previously recorded sector. A previously recorded area *cannot* be recorded on again. When an area on the CD is said to be *erased*, the data is actually still present. It simply can no longer be accessed. Consequently, every time a file is updated on a CD-R, the existing file is made inaccessible and a new section of the CD-R is used to store the newest version of the file.

A CD-R is designed with a photosensitive transparent organic dye layer placed against an aluminum alloy layer inside the CD. The photosensitive layer reflects light in its natural state. Thus, in its natural state, it appears as one long land to the CD reader. **Figure 10-5** shows a typical CD-R disc. When exposed to the recording laser light, the photosensitive layer changes from a reflective state to an opaque state. Instead of reflecting light, it absorbs the light from the laser similar to the pits used in the standard CD.

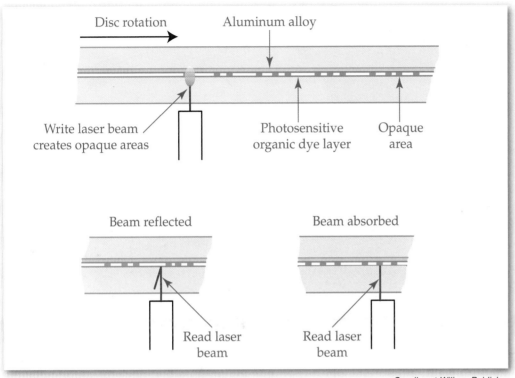

Goodheart-Willcox Publisher

Figure 10-5.
One laser is used for writing to the CD-R while a second laser is used for reading.

Note that with these discs you can actually see where you have recorded your data. With the mass-produced CDs, the entire disc has universal shine. With CD-R discs, the area that has been recorded reflects light differently than the unrecorded area, **Figure 10-6**.

CD-R drives have been replaced by CD-RW drives. You will still encounter the CD-R drive in existing PCs for some time, but virtually all new PCs come with combination CD-RW and DVD recordable systems.

CD-RW

Compact Disc-ReWritable (CD-RW) an improvement over the CD-R technology, featuring special discs that can be erased and rerecorded. It allows the same sections of a CD to be written to many times instead of only once. A special polycrystalline structure is sandwiched inside the plastic platter, **Figure 10-7**. The polycrystalline is a composite silver-indium-antimony-tellurium layer.

This technology uses a laser beam that has two states of heat intensity: low and high. When the polycrystalline structure is exposed to the high heat 932°F–1292°F (500°C–700°C), it loses its reflective quality. When the low-power beam of the laser 392°F (200°C) is applied, it changes the surface back to a reflective quality. By applying the high- and low-beam heat effects on the polycrystalline structure, the reflective quality of the disc can be arranged (and rearranged) into a state similar to the land and pit technique. This means that previously recorded areas of the disc can be rewritten to, allowing for a data-recording media similar to a hard drive or floppy disk. The CD-RW has become a cost-effective media for low-volume data backups.

Compatibility issues have, at times, plagued the CD industry. Older CD players will often not be able to play new CDs, in particular CD-RWs. This lack of recognition is related to the intensity of the light used to represent the lands and pits on newer discs. The original CD standards required that the CD reflect at least 70% of the light striking the land. With the pits, no more than 28% of the light could be reflected. On the modern CD-RW, the land areas reflect no more than 15% to 25% of the light striking the surface of the land. This is well below the early standard of 70%.

Today's CD and CD-RW systems can read older technologies and make adjustments for the

Figure 10-6.
Notice the change in the appearance of the CD-R disc. Data has been recorded on the inner circle.

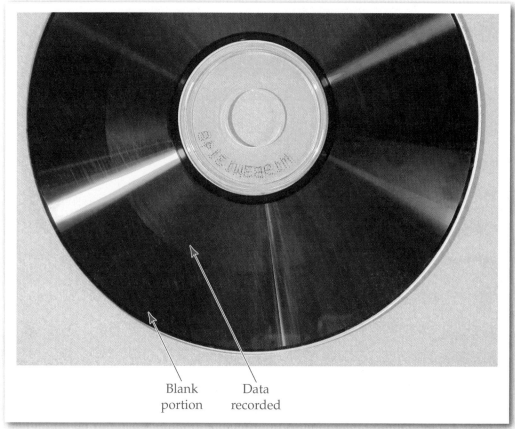

Blank portion   Data recorded

Goodheart-Willcox Publisher

Figure 10-7.
With the CD-RW process, firing a laser at its high intensity causes the disc to lose its reflective quality. The firing of a low-intensity beam returns the reflective quality to the material.

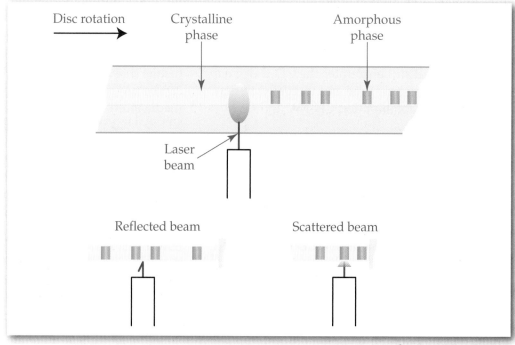

Goodheart-Willcox Publisher

various light-reflective intensities. However, the older technologies cannot make these adjustments. Consequently, a CD-RW made on a PC today, may not be readable by a CD system that is not CD-RW capable. Typically, only a CD-RW can exchange data with another CD-RW.

CD Specifications

Two of the most common CD specifications are data transfer rate and access time. The **data transfer rate** is a measurement of how much data can be transferred from the CD to the PC random access memory in a set period of time. This standard is usually given in kBps or MBps. If a manufacturer claims a transfer rate of 1 MBps, they are claiming that the CD can transfer a steady stream of data at 1 megabyte per second. Data transfer rate is more important if you transfer a lot of data from a CD on a continual basis. Playing games off a CD is one use where you would like a high data transfer rate.

Tech Tip　Be careful when reading manufacturers' claims. Sometimes, they use the numbers based on compression techniques rather than true data transfer time. Another method of producing a higher-than-normal transfer figure is by incorporating software that uses the hard drive as a buffer to cache information from the CD system. With this type of software, any CD drive will appear to be faster and any CD system can be used this way.

The access time for a CD is measured in much the same way as it is for a hard disk. The **access time** is the amount of time that passes between the issue of the read command and the point in

time when the actual first data bit is read after it has been located on disc. Because the amount of time delay varies according to where the data is physically located on the CD, the rating is usually an average. If you run applications where you periodically access a CD, access time becomes a more important time factor.

When upgrading a CD drive, be sure of what you are trying to achieve. Consider why you are upgrading. A better access time and transfer rate will not deliver a significant difference in performance to the average user. However, if the drive is being used as part of a CD tower in a network system, it can make an important difference in the performance. The table in **Figure 10-8** shows a comparison of CD drive access and data transfer rates.

Note that CD drives are commonly advertised as 40X, 48X, or 52X. This naming convention is relative to the speed at which the disc is spinning, with 1X set by the speed at which the early CD-ROM drives turned.

There are two methods of reading data from a CD: constant linear velocity and constant angular velocity. **Constant linear velocity (CLV)** was used on earlier CD drives. It varied the speed at which the CD was spinning to keep points on the inside and outside of the disc spinning at a constant linear velocity. To better understand this concept, we must look at the relationship of data location on the disc and the speed of disc rotation. **Figure 10-9** shows the relationship between the speed of rotation on the surface of a disc and the distance from the center of the disc.

All points on the surface of a disc that is spinning at a constant speed rotate at the same rpm. However, the farther any point is from the center, the faster that point will move. The point farther from the center has a longer distance to travel to complete its revolution, yet it has the same amount of time in which to complete it. Thus, data patterns at the outer edge of a CD move more quickly than data patterns in the center of the disc. CLV technology maintains the same speed of data transfer by varying the speed of the disc. When reading data from the outer areas of the disc surface, the rpm is reduced. When reading data from the inside areas, rpm is increased. By varying the speed of the spinning disc, a steady stream of data flow is maintained.

Figure 10-8.
Table showing the access times and the data transfer rates of a selection of speeds of CD drives. The *X* represents the base speed of the original music CD. For example, a 24X CD spins 24 times faster than a 1X CD.

Speed	Access Time	Data Transfer Rate
1X or Single-speed	600 ms	150 kBps
2X	320 ms	300 kBps
3X	250 ms	450 kBps
4X	135– 180 ms	600 kBps
6X	135–180 ms	900 kBps
8X	135–180 ms	1.2 MBps
10X	100–150 ms	1.6 MBps
12X	100–150 ms	1.8 MBps
16X	100–150 ms	2.4 MBps
24X	100–150 ms	3.6 MBps
32X	100–150 ms	4.8 MBps
40X	50–100 ms	6.0 MBps
48X	50–100 ms	7.2 MBps
52X	50–100 ms	7.8 MBps
60X	50–100 ms	9.0 MBps
72X	50–100 ms	10.8 MBps

Note: The access time and data transfer rates indicated in the chart are intended as a guide for comparison. Actual drive access times and data rates will vary widely by manufacturer.

Goodheart-Willcox Publisher

Figure 10-9.
Although the rpm of a CD remains constant, the speed of the CD varies from point to point. A point farther out on the disc has a longer distance to travel per revolution. Consequently, the point moves at a faster speed.

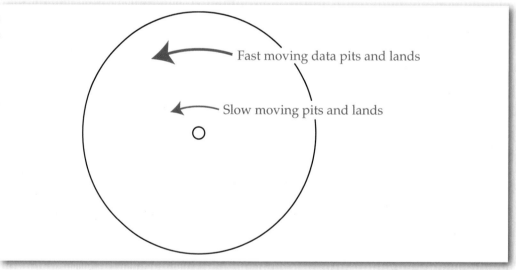

Fast moving data pits and lands

Slow moving pits and lands

Goodheart-Willcox Publisher

Modern drives use constant angular velocity technology. **Constant angular velocity (CAV)** maintains the same rpm regardless of the data location. These drives permit the data flow rate to change. With CAV technology, there is no more lost time while the CD drive adjusts its speed. Thousands of revolutions could be wasted with

the CLV method while the drive sped up or slowed down to the proper speed.

CD Formatting

Without some standard method for coding CDs, data recorded on one CD device would be unreadable to a CD device made by a different manufacturer. Producers of CD technology foresaw these problems and met to set some standards for the industry. The first set of standards became what is known as the *High Sierra format*. This format was later modified into ISO 9660. This format is the worldwide standard for CD-ROMs. An additional format, UDF, was developed for packet writing of information. **Packet writing** records data in small blocks similar to the way hard drives store data. This format was developed primarily for the CD-RW and DVD systems.

High Sierra Format

The **High Sierra format** is a standard for compact discs. It was created so that CDs could be read on any CD device. The format got its name from the meeting place at the High Sierra Hotel near Lake Tahoe. CD industry representatives were interested in combining their efforts to achieve a common format they could all share. All members would benefit if they could use their CDs on any type of CD device.

The following explains the standard in simple terms. The first section of the spiral path or sector on the CD identifies the CD as the media and synchronizes the CD with the drive mechanism. The disc also identifies the directories of data on the volume. The CD contains a Volume Table of Contents (VTOC). The **Volume Table of Contents (VTOC)** is a data structure that tells the CD drive how the data is laid out on the disc. It is similar to the file table on a hard drive.

The spiral path of data on the CD does have sectors and clusters, but there is no need of tracks since the disc consists of one long spiral. The CD also contains a directory. The directory is used for organizing the data stored on the CD.

ISO 9660

In 1988, the High Sierra format was transformed into **ISO 9660**. The two standards are identical in content. However, the exact formatting is different. The ISO 9660 format is the CD format used today. An interesting note to the ISO acronym is that it is also a Greek word. *Iso* in Greek translates to mean "equal." The ISO 9660 is also called **CD-ROM File System (CDFS)**.

The ISO 9660 is a file system structure very similar to FAT16 but with many improvements. There is no limit to the size of the root directory, and it can contain up to eight levels of files and directories. Look at the example that follows:

F:\LEV1\LEV2\LEV3\LEV4\LEV5\LEV6\LEV7\
LASTFILE

The root directory is F:\ and then there are seven levels of subdirectories ending with the file LASTFILE.

ISO 9660 supports long file names. However, if you intend to use it with an operating system like DOS, you must use the 8.3 file naming convention. The ISO standard for CDs allows only uppercase letters, digits, and the underscore when naming a file or directory. Remember, DOS allows the use of many special symbols in the name. CD files are stored by sectors, usually 2,048 bytes long, but the sectors can be made larger or smaller. The exact size of a sector can be different depending on if the disc is providing header information or error correction. The sector data size is 2,048. With header information, it is 2,352. The sectors are numbered consecutively starting with sector zero.

An **ISO image** makes an exact copy of the contents by copying all sectors containing data and ignores the file system being used. For example, if you need an exact copy of an operating system, creating an ISO image will copy all sectors containing data and will ignore the file system being used.

Only Windows Vista Business edition and Ultimate edition or later are capable of creating an ISO image. All earlier Microsoft operating systems cannot create an exact ISO image of a disk without the use of a third-party software package, such as Nero 8 Ultra Edition or Roxio Easy Media Creator 10 Suite. ISO disc images are a common way of distributing software operating systems and an excellent way to back up a computer system.

UDF

The Optical Storage Technology Association (OSTA) was formed by manufacturers to create a file system structure that could be used for CD-RW, magneto-optical, and DVD technology. The file system structure accepted for CD-RW, magneto-optical disc, and DVD technology is **Universal Disk Format (UDF)**. UDF defines the new file system structure. It is the successor to the ISO 9660 file structure.

The greatest improvements of the UDF file system structure is that it allows for a bootable disc. One of the reasons CD-RW discs cannot be read by CD-ROM technology is the way the UDF file structure is organized.

Disc System Standards

Disc system standards are outlined in a series of specifications referred to as the **colored books**. Each set of specifications is classified by book color. The *red book* specifications describe the physical properties of compact disc audio and graphics. The *yellow book* describes the requirements of using CD technology for computer data storage systems. The *green book* describes the specifications of interactive CD technology (CD-i). The *orange book* describes recordable CD media. The *white book* is used for video standards. The *blue book* is an expanded version of music standards referred to as *CD Plus* or *Enhanced Music CD*.

The CD standards contain information about the physical description of sectors and overall physical dimensions as well as data formats, data encoding, disc compression, light reflection intensities, and error-correction techniques. The standards allow for compatibility between different manufacturers in the industry.

Magneto-Optical

A **magneto-optical (MO) drive** combines magnetic and optical principles to store and retrieve data on a CD-like disk. The MO disk is constructed of a magnetically-sensitive metal crystal that is sandwiched between two plastic disks.

When writing to the MO disk, a laser heats the plastic surrounding the metallic crystal. This allows the crystal to change its orientation on the disk when exposed to the magnetic field of the write head. When the plastic cools, the metallic crystal is aligned along the disk track representing the binary information, **Figure 10-10**.

To read the data from the disk, the CD is spun while the laser is focused on the track. This time the laser uses much less power and simply provides light to be reflected back to the photodiode. The reflected light is slightly polarized by the magnetic domain. The direction of the polarization represents the bit pattern stored on the disk. For example, a north pole orientation may represent a binary one, while a south pole orientation may represent a binary zero.

DVD

Digital Versatile Disc (DVD), also known as *Digital Video Disc (DVD)*, is a standard that was pushed by the motion picture industry so that it could release films on CD, thus replacing early tape systems. DVD obtains its higher storage capacity than CD by using a shorter wavelength

Figure 10-10.
The crystals on a magneto-optical disk are fixed until the plastic around them is heated with a laser. During this heating process, the crystals are susceptible to having their orientation on the disk changed to store data.

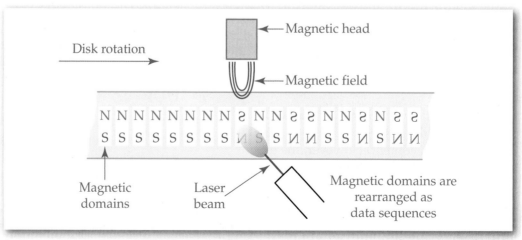

Goodheart-Willcox Publisher

Figure 10-11. Comparison of disc technology land and pit size and track spacing.

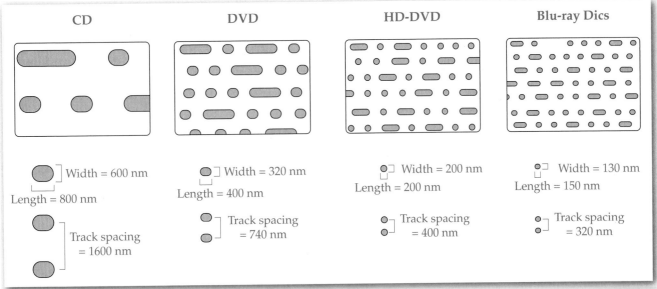

Goodheart-Willcox Publisher

of light to record and play back data. Look at **Figure 10-11** to see a comparison of CD, DVD, HD-DVD, and Blu-ray Disc land and pit spacing. As disc technology advanced from the CD-ROM to the Blu-ray, the land and pit areas and the distance between the spiral track became more compact. There is a direct correlation between storage media compact structure and the total amount of storage provided by each media type. The table in **Figure 10-12** lists the various DVD speeds and data transfer rates.

Another factor is the wavelength of the laser used to record data. As the wavelength becomes shorter, it is possible to write data in smaller and closer lands and pits. DVD uses a shorter wavelength red light as opposed to the infrared light used by CDs. The wavelength continues to be progressively shorter until it reaches Blu-ray.

Look at **Figure 10-13** to see a comparison of CD, DVD, HD-DVD, and Blu-ray laser wavelengths as well as approximate storage capacity for a single-layer disc and the depth of the laser penetration into the disc. The wavelength of the red CD laser is 780 nm. The red DVD laser is 650 nm. HD-DVD and Blu-ray Disc both use a blue laser wavelength of 405 nm, but the depth is different at 0.6 mm for HD-DVD and 0.1 for the Blu-ray Disc.

The DVD Forum developed DVD-RW standards, which are not compatible with

DVD-RAM developed by manufacturers that did not wait for a standard to be developed. DVD-ROM was developed mainly to focus on multimedia in order to store video and sound on the same disc space. DVD-ROM is a playback-only media and cannot be used to record. DVD-RAM is made to be written to and played back many times. It features the random access of data.

Figure 10-12. Comparison of DVD speeds and data transfer rates.

DVD Speed	Data Transfer Rate
1 X	1.32 MBps
2 X	2.64 MBps
3 X	2.64 MBps
4 X	5.28 MBps
5 X	6.6 MBps
6 X	7.93 MBps
8 X	10.57 MBps
10 X	13.2 MBps
12 X	15.85 MBps
16 X	21.13 MBps

Note: This chart is for comparison purposes. DVD 1X is approximately equal to the CD 9X data rate.

Goodheart-Willcox Publisher

Figure 10-13.
Comparison of disc technology laser wavelengths and depth penetration.

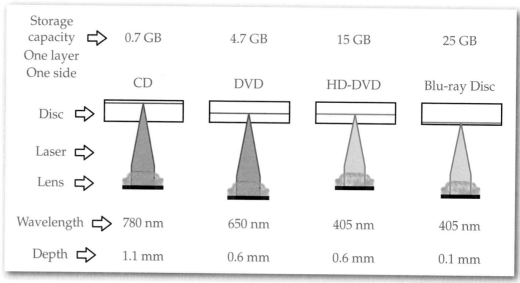

Goodheart-Willcox Publisher

DVD Structures

The DVD comes in several structure styles to increase data storage capacity. See **Figure 10-14** for a drawing of DVD structures.

The 4.7-GB single-sided, single-layer DVD structure consists of a single layer of reflective film that contains the pit and land areas representing stored data. It is similar in construction to the typical CD. However, the 4.7-GB DVD storage

capacity far surpasses the CD's 650-MB capacity, **Figure 10-15**.

The 8.5-GB single-sided, dual-layer structure contains two reflective film layers, a gold layer and a silver layer. For this technology to operate, the laser beam is run at two different intensities. The first layer is gold. When the laser is run at high intensity, this layer is partially transparent to the laser beam. This allows the data on the second layer, the deepest

Figure 10-14. Different DVD structures allow for a variety of storage capacities. DVDs can store up to 17 GB of data.

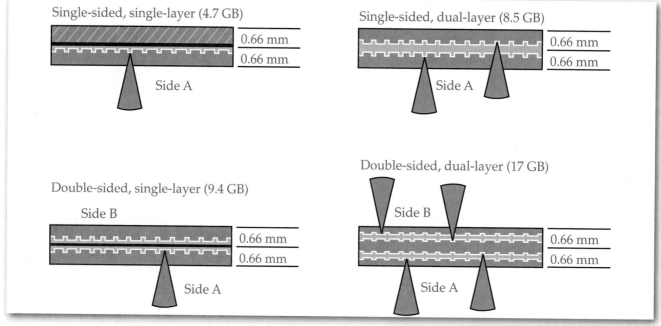

Goodheart-Willcox Publisher

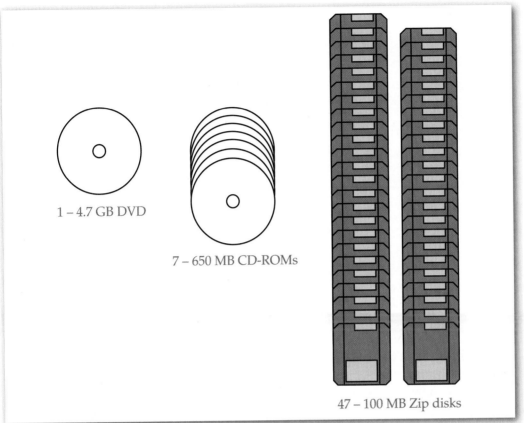

Figure 10-15.
The storage capacity of a DVD is a significant increase above the CD, and a tremendous increase above the old storage king, the Zip disk.

1 – 4.7 GB DVD

7 – 650 MB CD-ROMs

47 – 100 MB Zip disks

Goodheart-Willcox Publisher

silver reflective film, to be read. When intensity is lowered, it cannot penetrate through the gold reflective layer. The gold layer data is read when the beam is in low-intensity mode.

The 9.4-GB double-sided, single-layer disc structure is accessed from both sides. Think of the 9.4-GB double-sided, single-layer disc as two 4.7-GB discs back-to-back. The double-sided disc works with a DVD drive that has two lasers, one to read the top and another to read the bottom of the disc. If the DVD drive has only one laser, the disc must be turned over to read the other side.

The 17-GB disc is dual-layer for each disc joined together for a total of four layers. It is similar to two 8.5-GB dual-layer, single-sided discs joined back-to-back. The same technology of a gold layer is applied to this disc structure. Again, as with the 9.4-GB double-sided disc, there must be two lasers or the disc must be turned over to access data on both sides of the disc. A 13.2-GB disc is double-sided with a dual-layer on one side and a single layer on the other side. This type of disc is referred to as a mixed-layer disc.

In a race to have the first double-sided, dual-layer discs available to the public, some compatibility problems developed. The manufacturers did not wait for a standard to be fully developed and implemented. Usually, if the disc is referred to as 17-GB DVD-RAM, it is not compatible with 17-GB DVD-RW. DVD technology capacities are based on the number of sides and number of layers used to record data.

Look at the table in **Figure 10-16**. Notice the DVD can record to either one side only or both sides. When both sides are used for recording media, it is referred to as double-sided. The acronyms used to describe single-sided and double-sided are SS and DS, respectively. The number of layers used to record varies from a single layer to up to four layers. The acronyms associated with layers are single-layer (SL), dual-layer (DL), and mixed-layer (ML). Hence, a disc may be described as a DVD DS/DL or double-sided, dual-layer disc. These acronyms are often used in disc drive device specifications and tables to identify which disc formats the drive supports.

Figure 10-16. DVD technology comparison.

DVD Technology	Descriptive Acronym	Sides	Layers	Description	Approximate Capacity
DVD-5	SS/SL	1	1	One side, one layer	4.7 GB
DVD-9	SS/DL	1	2	One side dual-layer	8.5 GB
DVD-10	DS/SL	2	2	Both sides single-layer	9.4 GB
DVD-14	DS/ML	2	3	One side dual-layer, one side single-layer	13.2 GB
DVD-18	DS/DL	2	4	Both sides dual-layer	17 GB

Goodheart-Willcox Publisher

Advantages of DVD

In addition to the obvious advantage of tremendous storage capacity, there are several other advantages to DVDs and DVD drives. One of the best advantages of purchasing a DVD drive is its downward compatibility with CD technology. A DVD drive will read most older CD technologies in addition to the new DVDs. DVD players have no trouble reading CD-ROMs; however, some players may have difficulty with CD-Rs and CD-RWs. The newer DVD players should be able to handle all the older CD technologies. Unfortunately, older CD technology drives will not read DVD discs because the laser intensities are different.

Another advantage of DVD is that video cards can incorporate MPEG standards of decompression directly onto the adapter card. This eliminates the use of the processor to decompress the files. This means faster overall performance.

DVD Compatibility Issues

Manufacturers raced to release DVD technology to dominate the market, and the consumer was therefore left with enormous compatibility issues. Consequently, there are several DVD standards that are not compatible with each other. This is a common cause of customer complaints about making a DVD on one DVD recorder and not being able to access it on another. Presently, there are two formal organizations dictating standards: DVD+RW Alliance and DVD Forum. Interestingly, some manufacturers, for

example Sony and Ricoh, are members of both organizations. The following section covers DVD format standards for both groups.

DVD-R

DVD-R is a write once DVD recordable format introduced by the DVD Forum. The DVD-R format is compatible with most DVD players. DVD-R comes in two types: general use and authoring. The authoring type is a higher quality than the general use type. The DVD-R type must match the recorder being used for the initial writing, but it can be read back on either type.

DVD-RW

DVD-RW is a ReWritable format introduced by the DVD Forum. DVD-RW can be reused over 1000 times. Most DVD players will read DVD-RW, but not all. It is not as compatible as the DVD-R format.

DVD+R

DVD+R was introduced by the DVD+RW Alliance and functions similar to DVD-R. There are some minor differences that are sufficient to prevent compatibility with the DVD-R format. It is also interesting to note that DVD+R is not compatible with all DVD+RW players. Most DVD players support both DVD+R and DVD+RW formats.

DVD+RW

DVD+RW is similar to DVD-RW except for minor differences in the format structure. One of the main differences is that DVD-RW was designed to allow drag-and-drop file exchange, which earlier formats did not support. The drag-and-drop capability is often referred to as the Mount Rainier drag-and-drop support. The Mount Rainier version is also referred to as +MRW.

> **Tech Tip**
>
> Early DVD players will have the most problem reading the variety of formats available. Today, it is common to purchase a DVD player that cannot only read, but can also write in any of the mentioned formats.

DVD-RAM

DVD-RAM is used primarily as a video format but originally was designed as a data storage format. One problem with DVD-RAM is it will not work in a standard DVD-ROM player.

> **A+ Note**
>
> There will most likely be a question requiring you to select the correct disc media type based on its ability to record data and on the acronyms R, RW, and ROM.

HD-DVD and Blu-ray Disc

The demand generated by high-definition television (HDTV) and movie industries for better video recording media has led to the development of two disc formats: HD-DVD and Blu-ray Disc (BD). **Blu-ray Disc (BD)** is a new high-definition video and data format developed jointly by the Blu-ray Disc Association, which was started by Sony. The HD-DVD standard was abandoned in 2008 because it failed to compete successfully with the Blu-ray standard. Blu-ray and large-capacity DVD is the preferred format of the movie industry.

The DVD Forum approach is to preserve as much previous DVD design technology in order to ensure downward compatibility while increasing storage capacity. The Blu-ray Disc Association is more concerned with achieving the greatest possible storage capacity while not necessarily ensuring downward compatibility with previous CD and DVD designs. The Blu-ray Disc Association does encourage downward compatibility, but does not require it in its specifications for the design of Blu-ray devices. Modern Blu-ray recording devices are backward compatible with CD and DVD technology. A modern Blu-ray disc recording system is capable of burning a Blu-ray Disc as well as CD or DVD.

A standard CD can store approximately 650 MB of data, and a DVD disc can store 4.7 GB of data, which is far less than what is required to record movies and television programs in HD format. However, single-layer HD-DVD has a capacity of 15 GB, and single-layer Blu-ray Disc has a capacity of 25 GB. The storage capacity doubles for dual-layer disc formats. For example, dual-layer HD-DVD can store 30 GB, and dual-layer Blu-ray Disc can store 50 GB. See **Figure 10-17** for a comparison of the various disc technologies.

Notice that HD-DVD and Blu-ray Disc use the same laser wavelength of 405 nm; however, they are incompatible. The main difference between HD-DVD and Blu-ray Disc technology is the laser lens numerical aperture (NA) setting. The **numerical aperture (NA)** is a numerical expression for the way the light is gathered and focused into a single point. The Blu-ray Disc NA setting is 0.85. HD-DVD is 0.65. As a result, the tracks written on a Blu-ray Disc can be spaced closer than those on an HD-DVD disc. Also, the Blu-ray laser does not penetrate the disc structure as far as an HD-DVD laser. This also allows for more tracks per disc surface. See **Figure 10-18**.

The Blu-ray Disc surface is sealed using a much more scratch-resistant material than CD and DVD discs. The harder disc surface is required because scratches would more easily prevent the reading of data from the smaller and closer disc tracks used in Blu-ray. As with DVD, there are several different formats of HD-DVD and Blu-ray Disc. These are listed and described in **Figure 10-19**.

The HD DVD-R is a record-only disc that will soon become obsolete and difficult to find. The HD DVD-R is available in a single-layer capacity of 15 GB or a dual-layer capacity of 30 GB.

Figure 10-17. Disc technology comparison.

	CD	DVD	HD-DVD	Blu-Ray Disc
Storage Capacity	0.65 GB	4.7 GB	15 GB	25 GB
Approx. Data (1X) Transfer Rate	0.15 MBps	1.32 MBps	4.36 MBps*	4.29 MBps*
Video Resolution	Varies	720 × 480	1920 × 1080	1920 × 1080
Wavelength	750 nm (infrared)	650 nm (red)	405 nm (blue-violet)	405 nm (blue-violet)

*HD-DVD and Blu-ray Disc data transfer rates are typically specified in bits per second (bps), but are presented here in bytes per second to simplify their comparison to CD and DVD data transfer rates. The bits per second data transfer rate is 36.5 Mbps for HD-DVD and 36 Mbps for Blu-ray Disc.

Goodheart-Willcox Publisher

Figure 10-18. The numerical aperture (NA) and the depth of laser penetration of Blu-ray Disc allows for more disc tracks than HD-DVD. Notice the difference in track pitch between HD-DVD and Blu-ray Disc and the depth of penetration of each laser.

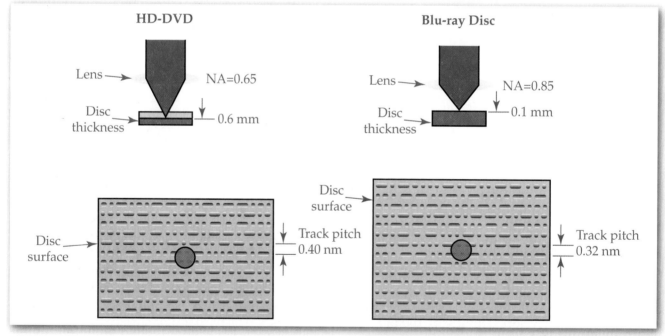

Goodheart-Willcox Publisher

Blu-ray Disc Recordable (BD-R) can only be recorded to once and is available in single-layer 25 GB and dual-layer 50 GB. **Blu-ray Disc Recordable Erasable (BD-RE)** discs are single-layer Blu-ray discs that allow you to add to and back up your data, music, or video to approximately 1,000 times.

A+ Note

Remember that Microsoft does not support recording to Blu-ray Disc. A third-party software application is required and usually comes with the Blu-ray Disc burner.

Formats	Storage Capacity	Description
HD DVD-R	15-GB, single-layer 30-GB, dual-layer	Record only. Used for distribution of media such as movies. Legacy standard abandoned as a movie media since 2008.
BD-R	25-GB, single–layer 50-GB, dual-layer	The disc can only record once.
BD-RE	25-GB, single–layer 50-GB, dual-layer	The disc can be used to record, erase, and rerecord. Used for distribution of media such as movies.

Figure 10-19.
HD-DVD and Blu-ray
Disc formats.

Goodheart-Willcox Publisher

Disc Drive Interface

There are several ways to interface disc drive technology with existing PC technology. PATA and SATA are commonly used for internal connections while USB and eSATA are used for external connections. The main advantage of an eSATA device is that the device does not need a separate power source. FireWire can be found on legacy computers, but replacement FireWire devices are hard to find.

> **Tech Tip**
>
> The technology name "PATA" commonly used today was referred to in the past by several other legacy terms such as *IDE*, *EIDE*, *ATAPI*, and *ATA*.

The IDE port on a motherboard was designed as a hard drive interface. As CD technology became popular, the IDE system was modified to accept a CD upgrade; hence, the development of **AT Attachment Packet Interface (ATAPI)**. ATAPI is the interface used for standard IBM PC AT and compatible systems for accessing CD devices. ATAPI drives are also referred to as *Enhanced IDE* drives or *EIDE*.

The connection points on an optical drive are similar to a hard disk drive with the addition of an audio analog and digital output connection. When connecting to a SATA optical drive, a separate audio analog and digital output is not necessary. **Figure 10-20** shows the back and front view of a PATA optical drive. **Figure 10-21** shows a SATA optical drive. The power and data connection cables are similar to the ones found on SATA and PATA hard disk drives.

The difference between the legacy hard drive and the legacy optical drive is the audio analog and digital output connections. The CD or DVD analog connection connects to the sound card. This connection provides sound from the disc drive to the sound card. The digital connection can be connected to an audiotape or other recording device for direct data transfer to the device.

Installation of CD and DVD technologies can also be made using SCSI. SCSI was the preferred method for high data transfer rates, but SATA is the preferred method and the most common and works well for most consumer PCs.

Comparing the SATA optical drive with the PATA optical drive, you see that there is a more complex set of connections required for the PATA optical drive. The PATA drive required an EIDE connection, also known as an *ATA connection*. Note that master/slave selection jumpers must also be installed if the optical drive is to share a channel with another EIDE (PATA) device such as a hard drive or another optical drive. It is recommended that EIDE channels not be shared with an optical drive if possible. Sharing the same channel with the optical drive can cause some unusual problems.

Many legacy motherboards have both PATA and SATA data connectors. You may encounter a problem or you may have a conflict when attempting to use both types of devices. Device configuration of motherboards with both PATA and SATA connections depend on the motherboard firmware. Refer to the motherboard documentation to see if there are any possible conflicts. The computer industry made the transition from PATA to SATA a bit later with optical drives than with hard disks. This can lead

Figure 10-20. PATA optical drive. A—PATA optical drives are more complicated to install than SATA optical drives because of all the various connection ports required for power, data, and analog and digital audio data. B—PATA optical drives can be equipped with drive controls incorporated into the front panel of the drive.

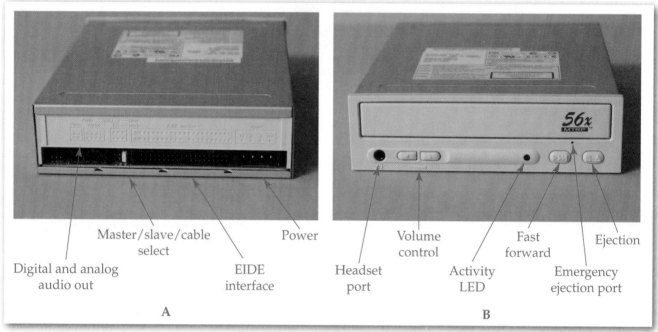

Goodheart-Willcox Publisher

Figure 10-21. Blu-ray SATA drive. A—Modern optical drives such as this Blu-ray drive have limited controls in the front of the drive. They use a software interface to control the functions of the drive such as volume, fast forward, and reverse. B—SATA optical drives are much simpler to install than PATA drives. SATA optical drives only require power and data/control connections.

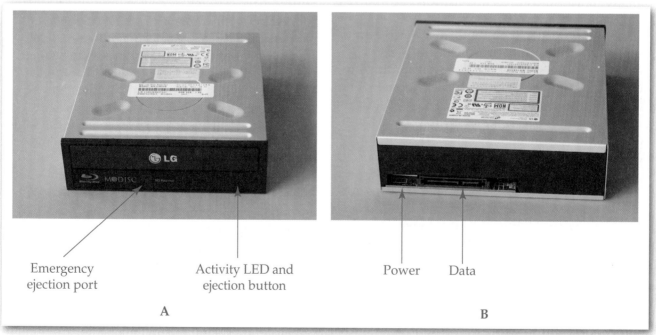

Goodheart-Willcox Publisher

to problems when working with older computer systems. One way to resolve an issue with older systems is to use an external optical drive connected through a USB port.

> **Tech Tip**
> Some SATA optical drives such as Blu-ray are not detected or automatically configured by the Windows operating system, especially on legacy computer systems. This is because the motherboard firmware may need to be upgraded. Often a motherboard can be two or more years old even in a newly-purchased computer system. When a new technology is developed, the system firmware often has a problem detecting the new technology and requires a firmware upgrade.

Digital Rights Management

Digital rights management (DRM) is any technology that ensures copyright protection for digital media such as digital music and video. DRM is used by online stores and media providers, such as Sony movies. Some online stores provide download services that use DRM to prevent illegal copies of media from being distributed.

DRM has a specific permissions set that control how the media can be used. For example, you can have a permission set to allow two copies of the media to be made to disc; allow you to install the media on two different devices; or sync the media between two devices. The number for each of the examples are simply an example of how many times the media can be copied or synchronized, when in reality, the media provider determines the maximum number of copies, devices, or number of synchronized devices. The media user rights are often referred to as media license.

DRM is constantly evolving because it is continually compromised, resulting in unauthorized duplication of media. Since DRM rapidly changes, you need to check for the very latest on a regular basis.

Advanced Access Control System

The **Advanced Access Control System (AACS)** standard was designed as a digital rights management system for media content distribution. The AACS restricts access to and copying of optical discs, such as CDs, DVDs, and Blu-ray Discs. The specification was publicly released in April 2005, and the standard has been adopted as the access restriction scheme for HD-DVD and Blu-ray Disc.

High-Bandwidth Digital Content Protection

High-bandwidth Digital Content Protection (HDCP) system encrypts the data sent by a high-definition content player such as Blu-ray or HD-DVD to other devices such as a television or computer monitor via a physical connection. The idea is to prevent copying copyrighted media content as it travels across cables. The Blu-ray Disc is reproduced with a lower resolution whenever a full HDCP-compliant link is not used, thus producing a low-quality copy.

Advanced Video Codec High Definition

Advanced Video Codec High Definition (AVCHD) is a proprietary specification developed jointly by Sony and Panasonic. The AVCHD standard allows using recordable DVDs, memory cards, non-removable solid-state memory, and hard disk drives as recording media. See **Figure 10-22**.

The AVCHD format allows high-definition video to be burned to a standard DVD disc, which can then be played in a Blu-ray Disc player at high-definition resolution. This means that a Blu-ray Disc burner is not required to burn a high-definition recording when using devices compatible with AVCHD format technology such as computers, video recorders, and similar devices. At the time of this writing, only Panasonic and Sony cam recorders use AVCHD technology, but many different brands of Blu-ray Disc recording devices are capable of using AVCHD.

Figure 10-22. Advanced Video Codec High Definition is a protection feature that prevents unauthorized duplication of disc content.

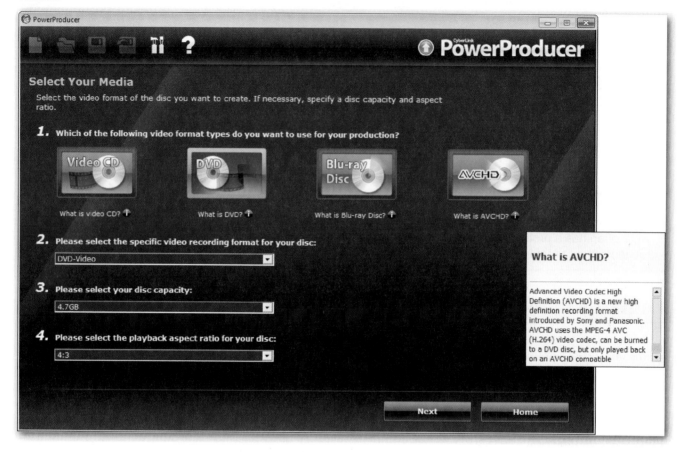

Advanced Access Content System

The **Advanced Access Content System** is another standard used for content distribution and digital rights management. Developed by a consortium of media corporations, the standard uses a security system based on a set of encryption keys that must be used to play the media. An encryption key is a special series of letters and numbers used to encode content. Another key is used to decode the content. The encryption keys are constantly updated to prevent them from being compromised by unauthorized personnel. There will be much more about encryption in Chapter 14—Physical and Digital Security.

Region Code

Region codes have been developed and assigned to specific media disc and disc players to protect digital content on DVD. The region code is configured to play only discs authorized by the content provider for that region. The region code allows the content creator or distributor to control the price and the release date of the media, such as a movie, according to the physical location or country.

To change the current region, right-click the DVD drive located in Windows Explorer and then select **Properties** from the shortcut menu. When the **Properties** dialog box appears, select the **Hardware** tab and then select the DVD drive from the list under **All disk drives**. Click the **Properties** button. The **Properties** dialog box for the CD or DVD drive will appear. Select the **DVD Region** tab to access the region codes. Notice in **Figure 10-23** that Windows allows you to change the region a total of five times.

In Windows, the video format that is selected by default is based on the **Region and Language**

Figure 10-23. Path to Windows 7 **DVD Region** tab. CD and DVD players can be encoded to play only in specific regions.

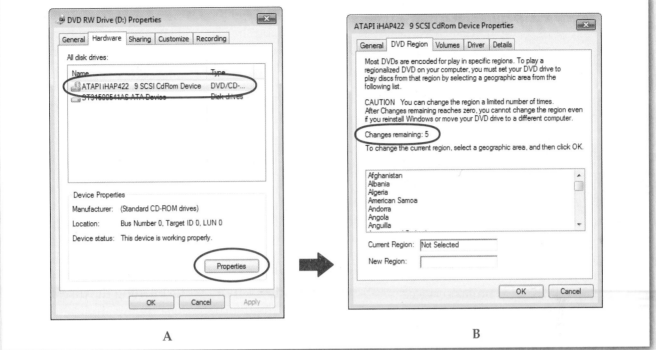

A   B

settings in Control Panel and is selected during the installation of the operating system.

BD+

Blu-ray Disc Plus (BD+) is another standard used with Blu-ray Disc digital rights management systems and performs the same type of protection as DVD region codes. Developed by Cryptography Research Inc., Blu-ray Discs are digitally encoded with a region code (A, B, or C, sometimes referred to as 1, 2, or 3), that allows the disc to play only in a Blu-ray player with the same region code. Windows operating systems do not incorporate a region code for Blu-ray. In fact, Microsoft does not directly support Blu-ray Disc functions. Blu-ray Disc support requires a third-party software application when a Blu-ray device is installed on a computer that uses a Windows operating system.

Troubleshooting CD, DVD, and BD

There are many reasons for failure of the optical disc system to write or read disc data. In this section, we will look at some of the most common problems encountered with optical disc systems.

Failure to Eject

Optical drives do fail mechanically or physically become jammed and fail to properly eject disc media. For this reason, they are equipped with a small access hole in the front panel of the drive. A paper clip can be inserted into the small hole to release the lock mechanism. The drive tray and disc will be partially ejected. This will allow you to retrieve the disc from the failed system. See **Figure 10-24**.

Copy Control Protection Problems

Copy Control is a type of protection that is used to control the number of copies (if any) that can be made. For example, television DVD recorders can be designed to allow the user to make a single copy of a movie or some other type of television program once. The single copy can be played back at a later time but only on the same device or another device that has been equipped with the same type of copy protection. Typically, this code is associated

Figure 10-24. Optical storage drives are equipped with an emergency ejection system. You simply insert a paper clip into the emergency ejection hole in the front panel of the drive.

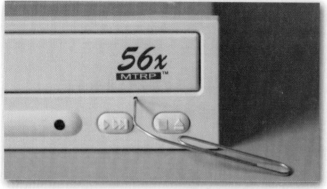

Goodheart-Willcox Publisher

with digital video recorders (DVRs) used with television systems such as TiVo, Verizon FiOS, HBO, SHOWTIME, and similar services.

You may be wondering why Copy Control protection has been included in a computer service and repair book when it mostly deals with DVR and television provider protection schemes. Many entertainment systems use computers as the heart of the system. You need to have an understanding of why clients are having what they perceive as a problem moving recorded materials between television DVRs and computer systems as well as other devices.

Three common flags are used for Copy Control protection. A flag is a short program code that identifies the type of copy protection assigned to the recorded media. The three common Copy Control protection flags are the following:

- Copy Freely.
- Copy No More or Copy Once.
- Copy Never.

Copy Freely means the content is free to copy as many times as you desire. When identified with a Copy Freely flag, you can generally record the content on one type of device and play it on another type of device. For example, a Copy Freely flag on a DVR-recorded movie should be able to be viewed on a PC and vice versa.

Copy No More and *Copy Once* mean you can make a single copy of the media and no more and then play back the media. You cannot copy the media a second time or play the media in a different device. For example, you can make a copy of a television show on your DVR for playback

later. That copy cannot be copied or even played on another device that is networked to the DVR.

The *Copy Never* flag allows you to copy the media, but has several stringent restrictions as far as using the copy. For example, you may make a single copy of a movie but must play it back within 90 minutes. You can only make a single copy similar to Copy Once. The Copy Never tag is commonly used with Pay-Per-View (PPV) content.

Disc Recording Problems

Disc burning can be affected by computer system resources such as hard disk drive space, memory, and CD/DVD drive speed. The function of burning a disc typically requires RAM and hard disk storage. When using a computer that has limited resources, you should not engage in any other activity while burning the disc. Do not access the Internet, run software applications, or allow the screen saver to run. Any other activity can cause a disc burn function to fail.

Failure to Finalize or Close a Disc Session

In general, a disc must be finalized or the disc session closed before it can be played on another optical device. Microsoft uses a disc recording feature known as Live File System, which allows you to continually record on disc media, such as CD-R, DVD-R, DVD+R, DVD-R DL, or DVD+R DL, as long as you continue to use it on the same computer. But, if you try to use the disc on another optical device without finalizing the disc or closing the disc session, the disc will fail.

Finalizing the disc means that the disc has closed the process of writing more data to the disc. Other data, such as a menu or table of contents and directory data have been written to the disc, and the disc has been enabled to play on other systems. Approximately 20 MB of disc storage space is used each time a disc is finalized. In general, once a disc has been finalized, it may not have any more data written on it. There are software applications that will allow you to record digital information again on the disc but only in the unused region of the disc. Closing a disc session means that the current recording has been temporarily stopped and you can access the data on the disc from the device that made the recording. The disc session has not been finalized.

When writing data to a CD/DVD, Windows provides you with two options: Live File System (**Like a USB flash drive**) and Mastered (**With a CD/ DVD player**), **Figure 10-25**. The Live File System allows you to save, edit, and delete files on the disc at any time. Mastered will not allow you to change the contents of the files after burning. Mastered is permanent, while Live File System is not permanent. When you eject a disc that was written to with the **Mastered** option, it is automatically finalized. When you eject the disc that was written to with the **Live File System**, it is not finalized. The session is simply closed. More data can be added to the CD or DVD.

Before you can use a recordable optical disc formatted with the Live File System format in a different computer, you need to close the disc session. The disc session is closed by default when you eject a recordable optical disc. You can change the close session settings for both multi-session and single-session capable discs by opening **Computer** and right-clicking the disc burner. Select **Properties** from the shortcut menu. A **Properties** dialog box for the drive will appear. Click the **Recording** tab and then click the **Global**

Figure 10-25. Windows provides two choices when writing data to a CD or DVD drive: Live File System and Mastered.

Settings button to open the **Global Settings** dialog box. See **Figure 10-26**.

The options in the **Global Settings** dialog box allow you to finalize a recording session when the disc is ejected. If you do not want to automatically close the recording session when the disc is ejected, simply click the appropriate check box to remove the check mark. The check mark means the session will be finalized.

Figure 10-26. A disc session must be closed before it can be read by another computer. The **Global Settings** dialog box allows you to change if a disc session is automatically closed when ejected.

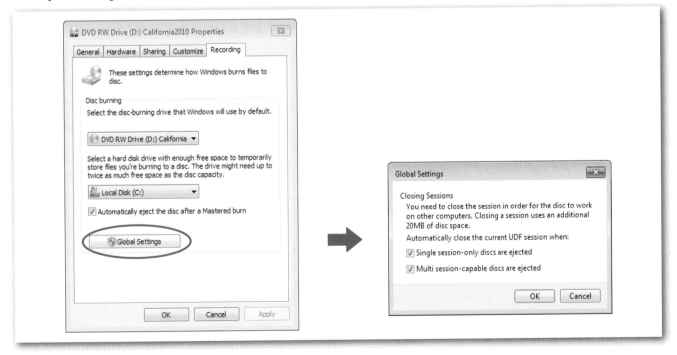

Tech Tip

The Volume Table of Contents (VTOC) is added when a disc is finalized. Without the VOTC, the new device cannot locate data on the disc.

Physical Defects

Dirt scratches or dust on the recording media can prevent a successful burn. Handle recording media by the edges so that you do not leave fingerprints on it. Do not lay the media down on a surface that can scratch the disc.

Wrong Media

A user might attempt to use the wrong type of media in an optical drive; for example, inserting a DVD into a CD drive or a Blu-ray Disc into a DVD drive. Most Blu-ray recorders are backward compatible and can write to all DVD and CD formats such as DVD-RW, DVD+RW, DVD-R, and DVD+R.

Burning Speed Too Fast

When burning a disc that is to be used on the same optical device, recording speed is not that critical. When burning a disc to be used on another optical device or for distribution, speed can be an issue. You could burn a disc at a recording speed too high to be read by another optical device.

Too Many Repeated Writings

ReWriteable media has a range of maximum recording events. Most will not record over 1000 times; some types, even less. This sounds at first as more than you would ever need, but when used in an application such as a security system, a 1000 recordings is not unusual. The disc could be recording video camera data over and over for days, months, and even years. Sooner or later, the media will reach its range of maximum number of recordings.

Laser Failure

Lasers that are used to burn data to a disc can fail after a period of time. They can also become weaker with time until they reach a point that they start to fail to make a successful burn, leaving many points of corrupt data on the disc. There is no economical way to repair a media laser. You simply replace the optical recording device.

Firmware Update

As time progresses, new recording techniques are applied to optical storage devices. When a new feature, such as a new codec or a new compression technique is used, the optical storage device may not work and require a firmware update. When a firmware update is needed, it should be downloaded from the optical storage device manufacturer along with the directions for performing the upgrade. A typical optical device firmware upgrade is similar to performing a computer motherboard firmware upgrade. An optical device firmware upgrade usually requires downloading the new firmware to disc. Then, the optical device is rebooted with the disc. The firmware is usually automatically installed. The only real danger is if the upgrade operation is interrupted by a power outage or by the disc being ejected. The upgrade can fail, leaving the optical device completely inoperable. The device would have to be sent to a service center for repair. Most of the time, the cost of repair is prohibitive, and it is more economical to replace the optical recording device.

Failure to AutoPlay Disc

The way media such as audio CD, movie disc, and blank disc react when placed into the disc device can be configured through **Control Panel | Hardware and Sound | AutoPlay**, **Figure 10-27**. The **AutoPlay** dialog box will display and allow you to configure how the media will react when inserted into a drive. **Figure 10-28** shows the **AutoPlay** dialog box from a Windows 8 operating system, but it is similar in other versions of Windows.

Options such as **Take no action**, **Burn an Image using ImgBurn**, or **Ask me every time** are just three of the options available. When a third-party software application is installed along with the device driver, other options often appear using the software application name.

Figure 10-27.
The default settings for media can be changed through **Control Panel I Hardware and Sound I AutoPlay**. After selecting **AutoPlay**, you will see a detailed list of options for the different types of media.

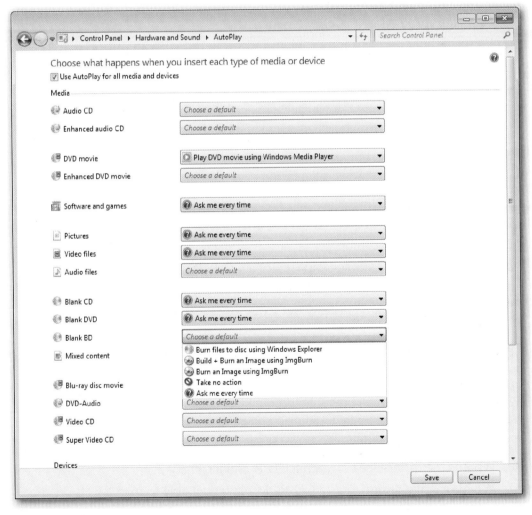

Figure 10-28.
The **AutoPlay** dialog box allows you to configure how media such as a blank disc reacts when placed into the optical disc drive.

Chapter Summary

- CD technology uses laser light reflected from the CD disc to generate electrical pulses that represent the data stored on the disc; patterns known as land and pit areas represent data stored on a CD-ROM.

- Magneto-optical drives use a combination of laser and magnetic properties to store data; the magnetic properties are used to polarize reflected light from the magneto-optical storage disc.

- DVD offers the same flexibility that a CD has, only at much higher storage density.

- HD-DVD and Blu-ray Disc use the same laser wavelength of 405 nm; however, the HD-DVD NA setting is 0.65 and the Blu-ray Disc NA setting is 0.85.

- PATA and SATA are commonly used for internal disc drives; USB and eSATA are used for exterior connections.

- Digital rights management (DRM) is any technology used to ensure copyright protection for digital media.

- Some of the most common problems encountered with an optical disc system are failure to eject, Copy Control protection, disc recording problems, not finalizing the disc, physical defects, and using the wrong media in an optical device.

Review Questions

Answer the following questions on a separate sheet of paper. Please do not write in this book.

1. How do pit and land areas affect the laser light?
2. What does a photocell do?
3. What is the typical storage capacity of a CD-ROM?
4. What precaution should be taken when working around lasers?
5. How does the track on a CD differ from the track arrangement on a hard drive?
6. Why must a CD-R use a new section of the CD to store a file after the file is modified?
7. What other CD acronym could be used in place of CD-WORM?
8. How does a typical CD-RW have the ability to reuse the same areas for storage of data?
9. What is the difference between a CD-ROM and a CD-R?
10. What is the difference between a CD-R and a CD-RW?
11. Why is a drive designed as a CD-ROM player *not* able to read a CD-RW disc?
12. What does data transfer rate mean when used in specifications?
13. What does access time mean when used in specifications?
14. What does the "X" represent on a CD drive when printed as 24X?
15. What is High Sierra format?

16. Magneto-optical drives operate on what two principles to store and retrieve data?

17. Of what is a magneto-optical disk constructed?

18. What two factors give DVD a higher storage capacity than CD-ROM?

19. What is the typical storage capacity of the smallest capacity DVD disc?

20. What does DVD DS/DL mean when reading optical drive specifications?

21. Which DVD technology provides approximately 17 GB of storage capacity?

22. What is the wavelength of Blu-ray Disc?

23. What is the wavelength of HD-DVD?

24. Which stores more information, HD-DVD or Blu-ray Disc?

25. What is a numerical aperture?

26. Which disc technology provides the most storage capacity?

27. What is the storage capacity of BD-R single-layer?

28. What is the storage capacity of BD-R dual-layer?

29. What acronyms are used to identify legacy motherboard ports that are similar to PATA?

30. What connection is available on a PATA optical drive but is not available on a SATA optical drive?

31. It is recommended that a hard drive share the same EIDE channels with an optical drive. True or False?

32. What is Digital Rights Management (DRM)?

33. What DRM technology encrypts the data sent by a high-definition content player such as Blu-ray or HD-DVD to other devices such as a television or computer monitor via a physical connection?

34. What DRM technology uses a security system based on a set of encryption keys?

35. What is the purpose of a region code?

36. What should be done last before moving a recorded DVD to another optical device for playback?

37. What two options does Windows provide when writing data to a CD/DVD device?

38. When burning a disc to be used on another optical drive or for distribution, burn speed can be an issue. True or False?

Sample A+ Exam Questions

Answer the following questions on a separate sheet of paper. Please do not write in this book.

1. After upgrading an existing computer CD drive to a Blu-ray recordable device, the Blu-ray recorder is not detected correctly by the operating system or BIOS. What is *most likely* the cause of the problem?
   a. The Blu-ray recorder has been connected to the wrong type of motherboard port.
   b. The motherboard BIOS needs to be updated.
   c. The Blu-ray recorder is defective.
   d. The Blu-ray recorder drivers have a virus.

2. Which is true about MO disk technology?
   a. The read/write head uses intense magnetic fields to change the arrangement of the magnetic particles embedded in the disk drive.
   b. The read/write process uses laser technology to heat the plastic surrounding the magnetic storage particles being written to.
   c. The laser head is used to melt the reflective material embedded in the plastic disk leaving a bit pattern matching the data.
   d. The read/write head cuts small notches, which represent binary data, into the surface of the plastic disk. The individual notches reflect laser light, which is then interpreted as data by the BIOS system.

3. Which are the standards for CD file storage? (Select two.)
   a. UDF
   b. CDUF
   c. CDRW
   d. CDFS

4. The amount of storage on a typical single-layer Blu-ray Disc is equal to _____.
   a. 650 MB
   b. 15 GB
   c. 25 GB
   d. 50 GB

5. A DVD fails to eject from a DVD recorder because of mechanical failure. After repeatedly attempting to eject the disc through the user interface, how would you proceed to remove the disc from the recorder?
   a. Disassemble the optical disc after removing it from the computer.
   b. Use a small flat-tip screwdriver to pry open the disk tray.
   c. Insert one end of a paper clip into the emergency eject port of the front panel of the optical disc recorder.
   d. Reboot the computer and the disc will be automatically ejected.

6. Which of the following technologies offer the greatest storage capacity?
   a. DVD+R
   b. Dual-layer HD-DVD
   c. BD single-layer
   d. BD dual-layer RE

7. Which two options are available for recording to a DVD-RW in Windows 7? (Select two.)
   a. Mastered
   b. Live File System
   c. Blue book
   d. Yellow book

8. Which type of optical disc requires a third-party software application to record media when using a Windows 7 operating system?
   a. CD+R
   b. DVD+R
   c. DVD RW
   d. BD

9. A couple brings in their laptop computer and complains that when they make a video disc using their Blu-ray recorder on the laptop, they cannot play the video on their older desktop PC that has a CD player. What is *most likely* the cause of the problem?
   a. The Blu-ray is copy protected and cannot be played back on another player.
   b. The Blu-ray player has a much more powerful laser and has burned the disc severely, preventing playback on the older player.
   c. The BIOS on the desktop must be upgraded to match the laptop DVD player/recorder.
   d. The density of the Blu-ray Disc is too high to be read by the older CD player.

10. What is the purpose of the VTOC on an optical disc?
   a. Its function is similar to a FAT. It describes how the data is laid out on the disc.
   b. It controls the volume level on the disc so that it will not blow the speaker system during playback.
   c. It controls the speed of the compact disc to make it compatible with other systems such as DVD.
   d. It is a special identification data flag that protects against copyright infringements.

Suggested Laboratory Activities

Do not attempt any suggested laboratory activities without your instructor's permission. Certain activities can render the PC operating system inoperable.

1. Format and then copy a file to an optical disc. You can go to the optical storage device manufacturer's website and access information about the steps necessary to record data.

2. Install an optical storage device into a PC. After installation, test the optical storage device by accessing data from an existing optical disc.

3. Check the Hardware Compatibility List (HCL) at Microsoft's website to see if all CD and DVD drive systems are compatible with Windows XP, Windows Vista, Windows 7, and Windows 8 operating systems.

4. Open **Device Manager** and see what the system resource assignments are for an existing optical storage device.

5. Download a driver for an optical storage device from a manufacturer's website.

Printers 11

After studying this chapter, you will be able to:

- Explain the operating principles of a laser printer.
- Explain the operating principles of an LED printer.
- Explain the operating principles of an inkjet printer.
- Explain the operating principles of a dot matrix printer.
- Explain the operating principles of a color thermal printer.
- Explain the operating principles of a dye-sublimation printer.
- Explain the operating principles of a solid ink color printer.
- Identify the common features of all-in-one products.
- Carry out a printer installation.
- Use the print queue window to view and manage print jobs.
- Carry out a printer memory upgrade.
- Identify and diagnose common printer faults.
- Explain how fonts are generated and installed.

A+ Exam—Key Points

For the A+ Certification exam, you should be able to discriminate between printer types, such as laser, inkjet, thermal, and impact. The exam usually features a few questions about the function of the major parts of the laser printer, such as the primary corona wire. Study the major parts and the steps of the laser printer process. You should also understand how printer drivers are installed and how to solve common printer problems.

Key Terms

The following key terms will become important pieces of your computer vocabulary. Be sure you can define them.

bitmap font	network printer connection
CMYK	paper jams
color thermal printer	paper train
dot matrix printer	pitch
dye-sublimation printer	points
electrophotographic process (EP)	print queue
font	print spooler
HP network re-discovery port monitor	printer
	printer driver
inkjet printer	solid ink printer
LED printer	spooling
local printer	vector font
local printer connection	Web Services for Devices (WSD)
network printer	

A **printer** is an electromechanical device that converts computer data into text or graphic images printed to paper or other presentation media. PC technicians are responsible for the installation, setup, modification, and troubleshooting of printer systems. A PC technician is not usually responsible for making physical repairs to the electromechanical parts of the printing engine, but a good knowledge base of the electromechanical operation of printers can prove valuable when troubleshooting a printer system. The electromechanical repair of printers is a specialization area. In this chapter, you will learn the basic operation of the most common styles of printer.

Laser Printer Operation

Traditional printing is based on wet ink applied to paper using several different processes. Laser printing uses a process called the electrophotographic process. The **electrophotographic process (EP)** is a combination of static electricity, light, dry chemical compound, pressure, and heat. To better understand this process and the role that the major parts of the laser printer perform in the printing process, view the step-by-step series of illustrations shown in **Figure 11-1A** through **Figure 11-1G**. A black-and-white laser printer is shown here.

Step 1. Processing

Processing is sending the data (text or image) to the printer. The processing stage relies on the correct printer driver software being installed. The **printer driver** converts specific file types to electronic signals that control how the image or document is printed on the paper. For example, the electronic signals control the quality of the image or document, number of copies, and overall size of the image or document. In addition to controlling how the document or image is printed, the print driver provides alert messages for low toner or ink, paper jams, and many other functions. See **Figure 11-1A**. When data is sent to a printer, it first passes through a **print spooler** which is a software program that temporarily stores the data in RAM or an area on the hard drive. Print spooling is discussed later in this chapter.

Figure 11-1A. Processing.

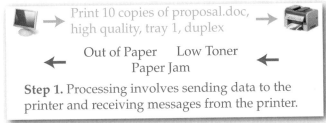

Print 10 copies of proposal.doc, high quality, tray 1, duplex

Out of Paper   Low Toner
Paper Jam

Step 1. Processing involves sending data to the printer and receiving messages from the printer.

Goodheart-Willcox Publisher

Step 2. Charging the Drum

The primary corona wire is charged to approximately –6000 volts. The high voltage creates an electrical condition known as corona. The corona is a static charge surrounding a high-voltage conductor. The primary corona wire is in close proximity to the drum. The primary corona wire applies a large negative charge of approximately –600 volts to –1000 volts to the surface of the drum. See **Figure 11-1B**.

Figure 11-1B. Charging the drum.

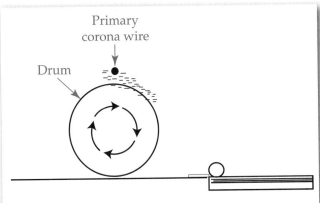

Primary corona wire

Drum

Step 2. The primary corona wire charges the surface of the drum with a negative charge of approximately –600 to –1000 volts.

Goodheart-Willcox Publisher

Warning ! The laser printing process uses extremely high levels of voltage. Never attempt to repair or disassemble a laser printer. Repairing a laser printer requires special training and safety precautions. PC technicians do not normally replace printer parts other than toner cartridges.

Step 3. Exposing the Image

The image is exposed or written to the drum using laser light. The laser light changes intensity according to the light and dark patterns encoded by the data describing the image. A rotating pentagon-shaped mirror reflects the laser beam horizontally across the surface of the drum. See **Figure 11-1C**.

After each horizontal trace is complete, the drum rotates by a small increment and the next trace begins. A typical laser printer makes 300 to 1200 increments of rotation per inch. The drum is coated with a light-sensitive photoconductive material. The special coating on the drum conducts electricity when struck by intense light. As the laser beam is reflected across the drum, the areas struck by the beam become conductive and lose most of their negative static charge. For example, when a typical image or business letter is to be printed, the white areas of the image are struck by the laser beam while the dark areas, such as letters and lines, are not struck by the laser light. The parts of the drum that are not exposed to the light retain the 600-volt to 1000-volt negative charge.

Figure 11-1C. Exposing or writing the image.

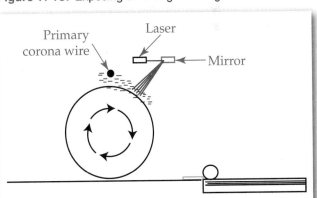

Primary corona wire

Laser

Mirror

Step 3. A laser beam pulses to a spinning mirror which reflects light across the negatively-charged drum. The laser light draws the outline of the image to be produced.

Goodheart-Willcox Publisher

Step 4. Developing the Image

As the drum turns, the image created by low and high static charges on the drum pass by the toner cartridge. The toner is attracted to the static charge on the drum. Think of toner as a form of very fine plastic dust particles. See **Figure 11-1D**.

A roller is incorporated in the toner cartridge to assist with dispersing the toner from the cartridge. The image to be printed is now formed on the drum.

Figure 11-1D. Developing the image.

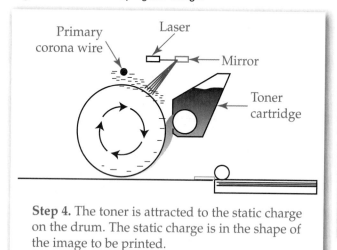

Step 4. The toner is attracted to the static charge on the drum. The static charge is in the shape of the image to be printed.

Goodheart-Willcox Publisher

Step 5. Transferring the Image

As the drum continues to rotate, the paper is fed under the drum. A set of rollers called pickup rollers lift one sheet of paper at a time from the paper tray. The paper is fed into position under the drum. A device known as a separator makes sure only one sheet of paper is sent into the drum area. The separator is located at the edge of the paper tray near the pickup rollers.

Just before the paper passes under the drum, it is given a positive charge by the transfer corona wire. See **Figure 11-1E**. The transfer corona wire works much like the primary corona, only using the opposite charge. The paper now has a

positive charge of static applied to its surface. As the positively-charged paper passes under the negatively-charged toner on the drum, the toner is attracted to the paper. (As you should remember from a basic physics class, opposite charges attract.)

Figure 11-1E. Transferring the image.

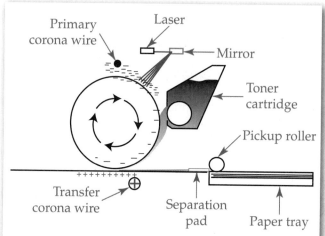

Step 5. The paper is fed into position by the pickup roller. The paper receives a positive charge from the transfer corona wire. The positively-charged paper attracts the toner from the drum, creating the image.

Goodheart-Willcox Publisher

Step 6. Fusing the Image

There is no longer a need for the static positive charge on the paper. A static brush contacts the paper and drains off any charge remaining on the paper. If the charge was not removed from the paper, the paper would stick to the negatively-charged drum and would also make the paper difficult to handle after leaving the printer.

Covered with a dry toner image, the paper passes through the fuser. The fuser consists of a pair of rollers, one of which is heated to a very high temperature. As the toner-covered paper passes through the fuser rollers, the heat and pressure melt the toner, fixing it to the paper's surface. See **Figure 11-1F**.

Usually, a quartz lamp is used to produce the high temperature of the fusing unit. The lamp generates a temperature of over 356°F (180°C). As a safety precaution, there is usually a temperature sensor installed near the fusing unit. This sensor will shut off power to the fusing unit if the temperature gets too high.

Figure 11-1F. Fusing the image.

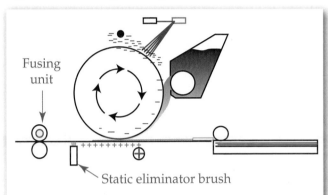

Step 6. The static eliminator brush removes the static charge from the paper. The fusing unit rollers heat the toner and paper until the toner melts and bonds to the paper.

Goodheart-Willcox Publisher

Warning !

The area around the fusing unit in the printer can cause severe burns when touched. Never attempt to work inside a laser printer unless it has been off for at least 15 minutes.

Step 7. Cleaning the Drum

The drum must be prepared before the next image can be printed. A cleaning unit removes any toner that might still be on the drum. The unit consists of a simple rubber scraper or blade that removes any residual toner left on the drum. The particles of toner are collected inside the cleaning unit container. See **Figure 11-1G.** The blade or scraper is specially designed not to scratch the drum surface. Any scratches on the drum would remove the photosensitive finish. This would cause poor quality printed images.

Figure 11-1G. Cleaning the drum.

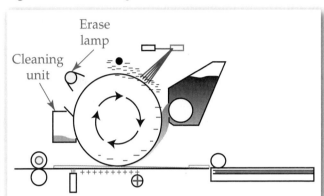

Step 7. The cleaning unit removes any residual toner that might remain on the drum. The erase lamp shines a bright light on the drum to remove any remaning charge. The drum is now ready to begin the process over again.

Goodheart-Willcox Publisher

A high-intensity light is also beamed onto the drum to remove any remaining charge from the drum's surface. The drum is now ready to be charged again by the primary corona wire, and the printing process can be repeated. **Figure 11-2** shows all the parts together.

Note that in the example of the laser printing process, the drum illustrated was negatively charged. The same process can occur using opposite polarities. Different manufacturers use different charging levels and polarities to create the same printing process that was shown in our example.

These principles of operation employed in the black-and-white laser printer can also be applied to a color laser printer. A color laser printer uses four separate print engines, one for each of the major colors. The major colors used in a color laser printer are blue, red, yellow, and black. Often, blue is represented by the color cyan and the red is represented by the color magenta.

Figure 11-2.
Shown are the vital parts of the laser printer in relation to each other. This illustration shows a negatively charged drum. Some printers place a positive charge on the drum and a negative charge on the paper. The process is the same but with the polarities reversed.

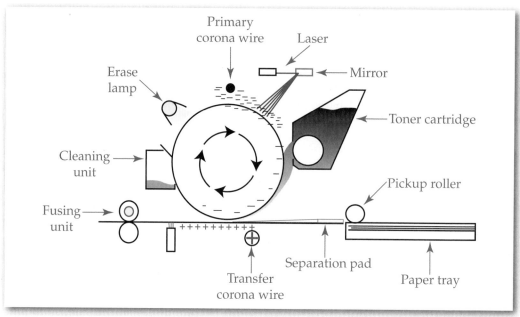

Goodheart-Willcox Publisher

A+ Note

The printing process for laser printers often appears on the CompTIA A+ exam. The exact term used to identify the process of using a light beam to create an image on the drum changed from *writing* to *exposing* and could change back again in the future. The exact terminology is determined by a team of subject experts who review and write the objectives. The next team of subject experts very well could change the term back to *writing* because it is used in the CompTIA Printing and Document Imaging (PDI+) Certification exam objectives.

LED Printer Operation

LED printer operation is very similar to laser printer operation. The main difference between a laser printer and an LED printer is the **LED printer** uses an array of light-emitting diodes (LEDs) rather than a laser to write the image to the drum. Using an array of LEDs instead of a laser eliminates several moving parts required by the laser printing process. By reducing the number of parts, the LED printer can claim better reliability because there are fewer mechanical parts to fail. Also, LED printer manufacturers claim that a more compact-size printer can be produced. The printer is actually more reliable mechanically because of fewer moving parts, but there is no great reduction in physical size when comparing a laser printer to an LED printer.

Color Inkjet Printer Operation

An **inkjet printer** uses specially designed cartridges that spray a fine mist of ink as they move horizontally in front of a sheet of paper. Some inkjet printers are commonly referred to as *bubble jet printers*.

The inkjet printhead is the part that fires the ink onto the paper. The construction of an inkjet printhead is fairly simple. Ink must be forced out

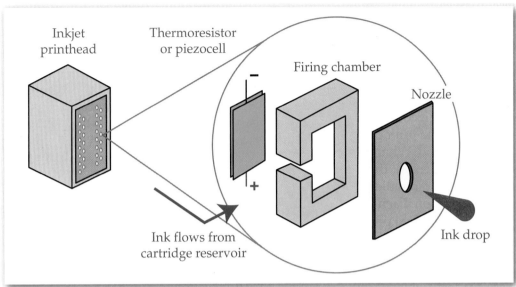

Figure 11-3.
Exploded diagram of typical color inkjet printhead.

Inkjet printhead

Thermoresistor or piezocell

Firing chamber

Nozzle

Ink flows from cartridge reservoir

Ink drop

Goodheart-Willcox Publisher

of the printhead. The two most common types of inkjet printers use either a *thermoresistor* or *piezocell crystal* to produce a force that fires a drop of ink through a nozzle directly onto the paper.

Figure 11-3 is an exploded view of a single nozzle and its major parts: nozzle, firing chamber, and (in this model) thermoresistor. The ink flows into the firing chamber from the ink cartridge reservoir. An electrical pulse from the computer enters the thermoresistor and the ink in the firing chamber is instantly heated to over 1112°F (600°C). The extreme heat expands the ink in the chamber, causing it to fire through the nozzle and onto the paper. As the chamber cools, a vacuum is created that draws more ink into the firing chamber from the ink cartridge reservoir. An inkjet printer can fire its chamber many times a second.

The single ink droplet is quite small. A typical low-cost inkjet printer can produce 720 × 720 dots per square inch (dpi). High-quality inkjet printers can produce a dpi of 1200 × 1200 and higher.

A piezocell could be used instead of the thermoresistor. A piezocell is a crystal that deflects or bends when energized by an electrical pulse. The bending is so rapid, it is often described as vibrating. When a piezocell is used in place of the thermoresistor, the piezocell flexes every time an electrical pulse is sent. When the piezocell crystal flexes, the ink drop is fired through the nozzle. When the electrical pulse stops, the crystal returns to its original shape. This creates a vacuum in the firing chamber (like with the thermoresistor), which draws more ink into the chamber.

A color inkjet printer uses four hues of ink: cyan, magenta, yellow, and black. This is a standard combination of colors often referred to simply as **CMYK**. Note that the letter *K* is used to signify black rather than *B*, which is used for blue in the RGB (red, green, blue) system. See **Figure 11-4**. These colors are standard in the printing industry. They can be mixed to make other hues such as green, orange, brown, and gray.

Dot Matrix Printers

The **dot matrix printer** derives its name from the pattern, or matrix, of very small dots it prints to create text and images. Dot matrix printers were some of the earliest printers. They are now much

Figure 11-4. CMYK stands for cyan, magenta, yellow, black. These are the colors used for ink printing. They can be mixed to produce a broad spectrum of colors.

Cyan Magenta Yellow Black

Goodheart-Willcox Publisher

less common and tend to be used only for special purposes.

The dot matrix printhead consists of a line of small metal rods called print pins, **Figure 11-5**. In appearance, the metal rods look much like a series of small nails. An electrical coil, called a solenoid, controls each print pin. When energized, the solenoid creates a magnetic field. The print pin is constructed with a magnet at one end. When the solenoid is energized, the magnetic end of the pin is attracted to the coil and the print pin rapidly moves forward, striking an ink ribbon. Each energized solenoid causes that individual print rod to strike the ribbon, leaving a dot of ink on the paper.

To form a letter, such as the letter *A* in the illustration, a series of electrical pulses is sent to the printhead. The pulses are coded in a sequence that forms the letter *A* on the paper as the entire printhead moves horizontally across the paper.

The two most common printhead styles are 9-pin and 24-pin.

Tech Tip

Dot matrix printers were also known as *impact printers*. Impact printers are a special classification of printers that use a mechanical device to strike an ink ribbon to create a character or image.

Dot matrix printers are quite slow and noisy. To achieve finer detail, the printhead may have to make multiple passes on the same line. Dot matrix printers are used primarily for spreadsheets and other text applications in businesses. When graphics with fine detail are desired, other printers such as inkjet or laser are typically used.

Dot matrix printers require special paper referred to as "impact" or "dot matrix paper." The paper has a series of holes running along the edges. The printer has a set of spiked gears at each

Figure 11-5.
Dot matrix printhead close-up. Dot matrix printers generate a pattern of dots to create images.

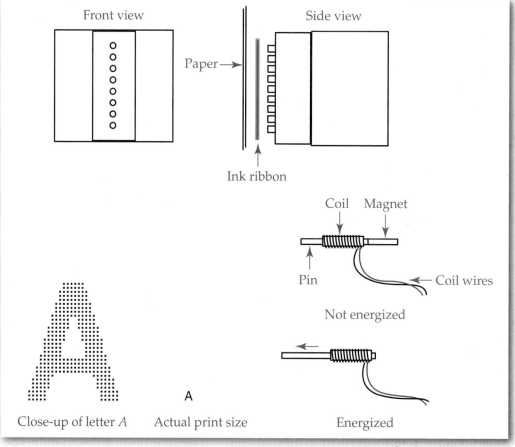

side of the printer that insert into the paper edge holes. When the printer is printing, the spiked gears advance the paper. Improper alignment of the paper with the spiked gears can cause a paper jam to occur during the print operation.

Printed documents with only partial letters are a sign of a faulty printhead. One or more pins in the dot matrix printhead are not firing properly. Another sign of a faulty or damaged printhead is the appearance of horizontal lines across the document. A printhead pin is most likely stuck in the struck position, thus causing the pin to drag across the ribbon and paper.

Overall poor quality text on the document typically indicates the ribbon is worn and out of ink and needs to be replaced. If replacing the ribbon does not correct the problem, the printhead may be damaged or loose.

Dot matrix paper jams are typically caused by a small piece of paper or foreign object lodged in the gears or rollers. Many times, the bit of paper or foreign object can be removed with a paper clip shaped as a hook. If the paper clip hook fails, you will have to disassemble the dot matrix printer.

Check the printer manufacturer's website for detailed information about dot matrix disassembly, printer ribbon, and printhead replacement as well as cleaning and recommended maintenance practices.

Caution ! Be sure the printer power cord is disconnected before performing any type of physical repairs on a printer.

Color Thermal Printer Operation

Color thermal printer operation is based on the principle of applying color by heating a special ribbon that is coated with a wax-like material. Heat is used to melt the wax. The wax is then sealed to the surface of the paper by Teflon-coated rollers. See **Figure 11-6**.

The heating unit consists of an array of small heaters that melt the wax in small dots. The small dots of heated wax represent the data sent from

Figure 11-6. Sketch of a color thermal printer.

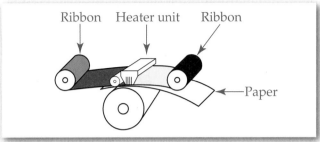

Goodheart-Willcox Publisher

the PC to the printer. The paper must be run through the process four separate times. Each time the paper is run through, a new color is added to the paper. The colors are cyan, magenta, yellow, and black (CMYK). The process is similar to the dye-sublimation process described in the next section. The difference is that in dye sublimation the color actually penetrates the paper, while in thermal print operation the color is printed to the surface of the paper.

Color thermal printers are used for high-quality presentation drawings and illustrations. Many corporations use them for special applications such as CEO reports to the board when color photos and charts are required. They are not commonly found in home use. These printers produce high-quality print but at a relatively high cost per sheet since they use special paper and expensive color wax supplies. Color thermal printers are not used for mass copies, just high quality.

Dye-Sublimation Printer Operation

A **dye-sublimation printer** produces near photo quality printed images by vaporizing inks, which then solidify onto paper. *Sublimation* is a scientific term that means changing a solid material into a gas.

The major parts used in the dye-sublimation process are the drum, transfer roll, and heater, **Figure 11-7**. A special paper is mounted directly on the drum. The transfer roll is a long sheet of plastic material coated with CMYK colors. As the drum rotates, the plastic transfer sheet (roll) passes under the drum and across the heater.

Figure 11-7. The important parts of a dye-sublimation printer.

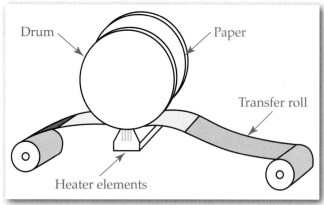

Drum

Paper

Transfer roll

Heater elements

Goodheart-Willcox Publisher

The heater consists of thousands of tiny heating elements arranged in a close array. These elements heat up in patterns representing the data patterns sent from the computer system. The heating elements can heat to 256 different temperature levels, which cause the dye to be transferred at 256 different levels of intensity.

The drum rotates four times. During each revolution of the drum, a different color passes from the transfer roll into the paper. The color is absorbed into the fibers as opposed to coating the top of the paper. The four colors sublimate to the paper and combine to create over 16 million colors.

Dye-sublimation printers and materials are very expensive. However, the dye-sublimation process gives much higher resolution and better color representation than the laser or inkjet processes.

Solid Ink Color Printer Operation

A **solid ink printer** uses solid ink cartridges similar to wax. The printhead consists of four long rows of many individual nozzles. Each of the four rows produces one of the CMYK colors. The four colors are heated and flow into individual reservoirs. As the paper passes by the printheads, the nozzles are fired, releasing a fine mist of color to the paper.

An advantage of the solid ink color printer is that it uses ordinary paper for its process. However, printer and ink supplies are expensive when compared to laser and inkjet supplies.

All-in-One Products

In recent years, manufacturers have introduced all-in-one products, especially for home and small office use. The all-in-one units are a combination of four common office devices that rely on printing techniques to accomplish their tasks: printer, fax, copier, and scanner. The all-in-one devices are a cost-effective way to purchase office equipment. The downside is that when the all-in-one device fails, typically you cannot use any of the devices.

Printer Installation and Configuration

Printers connect to computers in several different ways. They can be connected to the computer directly, wirelessly, or through a wired network. A USB connection is the preferred method of connecting a printer directly to a computer. Wireless connections include Infrared, Bluetooth, and IEEE 802.11 wireless. A connection to a printer made through the Internet is also possible.

The most common printer connections used today are USB, RJ-45 (wired network connection), and wireless. FireWire is also an option but only with older Apple computer systems. When connected directly to a computer, the printer connection is referred to as a **local printer connection**. When connected by other means than a direct connection to a computer, the connection is referred to as either a **network printer connection** or *shared printer connection*.

Printers can also be connected to through web services such as HP ePrint and Apple AirPrint. Web printer services are designed for portable devices such as smartphones, tablets, and laptops. The printer must be a web service enabled printer to use the service. You must obtain an email address for the printer from the web print service provider. After an email address is obtained for the printer, you can then send an email with an attachment to the printer over the Internet. The email attachment contains the item to be printed, such as a document or photo.

Google Cloud Print services also provides web service printing used with HP, Apple, Dell,

Epson, Kodak, Samsung, or any print or mobile device capable of accessing cloud storage. You can configure the print service using a Google account. After the printer has been identified, you can send documents and photos stored on your Google cloud storage service to your printer using the Internet.

Local Printer Installation

The term **local printer** refers to a printer that connects directly to a PC. The printer is local to that particular computer. Not all printers are local printers. A printer can be connected to a PC through a network and shared by many different PCs. This type of connection is covered later.

Most printers are automatically detected and configured. However, not all printer configurations are simple. Sometimes, the printer configuration must be accomplished manually. A technician must become familiar with the setup options and properties available for printer systems. Be aware that the users you serve are easily frustrated by inoperable equipment or by new computer equipment that does not perform to expectations. Knowledge can generate confidence

in the user and lessen some frustrations during setup or repair.

Manual printer installation begins with opening the **Printers and Faxes** dialog box in Windows XP, the **Printers** dialog box in Windows Vista, and the **Devices and Printers** dialog box in Windows 7 and Windows 8.

In Windows XP, the **Printers and Faxes** dialog box is accessed through **Control Panel | Printers and Other Hardware** in the Category view. In the Windows Vista, the **Printers** dialog box can be accessed through **Control Panel | Hardware and Sound | Printers**. In Windows 7 and Windows 8, it is accessed through **Control Panel | Hardware and Sound | Devices and Printers**. **Devices and Printers** is located directly off the **Start** menu in Windows 7.

After accessing the **Printers and Faxes**, **Printers**, or **Devices and Printers** dialog box, any printers for which the PC has been set up will appear in the window. See **Figure 11-8**. Notice the **Add a printer** option. The **Add a printer** option is activated to add a new printer to the PC. This Add Printer option takes you through the installation procedure. When activated, the **Add Printer** dialog

Figure 11-8.
In Windows 7, the **Devices and Printers** dialog box displays printers and fax devices available to the PC.

box appears, **Figure 11-9**. To install a local printer, select **Add a local printer**. A dialog box like that in **Figure 11-10** will appear and prompt you to select a printer port.

Selecting a Printer Port

The number of ports to choose from when manually configuring a printer port can be very confusing. Microsoft maintains backward compatibility with older printers, and as a result, you will still see choices of printer ports listed as COM and LPT. COM is a legacy serial port, and LPT is a legacy parallel port. Some printer manufacturers write their own proprietary software applications for automatically configuring a printer port. Those proprietary ports can show up in the list of available printer ports.

Figure 11-9.
The Add Printer wizard provides two options: **Add a local printer** and **Add a network, wireless or Bluetooth printer**.

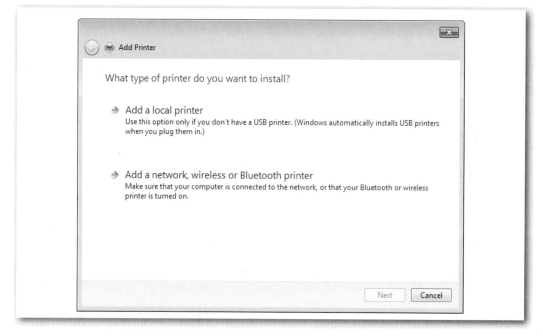

Figure 11-10.
There can be a wide variety of old and new technology printer ports to choose from when manually configuring a printer.

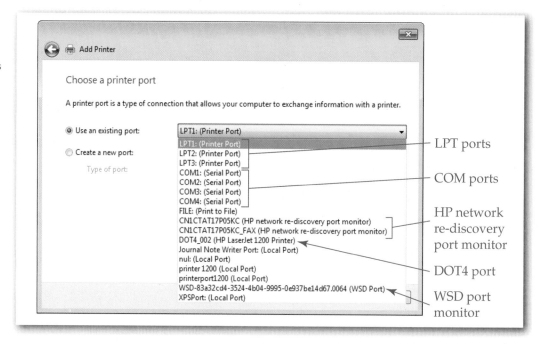

COM ports are serial ports and are seldom used. There are usually four COM ports identified as COM1, COM2, COM3, and COM4. COM1 and COM3 share the same IRQ assignment, and COM2 and COM4 share the same IRQ assignment. Look at the table in **Figure 11-11** to see the assigned IRQ and port memory address for each COM and LPT port.

LPT is a parallel port used to connect to a printer or other device that requires a parallel connection. It, too, has an assigned IRQ and a port memory address. LPT ports are still in use to some extent for printers. Businesses, government, and educational institutions often use equipment like printers much longer than home users.

Tech Tip

The older method of using COM and LPT ports is mentioned here so that you will be familiar with the technology if you run into it on the A+ Certification exam. Also, some older printers are still in use and the configuration options still exist.

The preferred cable connection for local printers is USB. When USB is used to connect to a printer, the port may be identified as a DOT4 port as shown in Figure 11-10. This port is a virtual port, not an actual physical port in the sense that COM and LPT ports are. The DOT4 port provides two-way communications between the printer and the computer. This allows the printer to send messages to the computer indicating things such as "out of paper" or "toner/ink low."

Figure 11-11. COM and LPT ports and their resources.

	IRQ Assigned	Port Address	Comment
COM1	4	3F8h-3FFh	Serial port
COM2	3	2F8h-2FFh	Serial port
COM3	4	3E8h-3EFh	Serial port
COM4	3	2E8h-2EFh	Serial port
LPT1	7	378h-37Fh	Parallel port
LPT2	Any available	278h-27Fh	Parallel port

The lowercase letter *h* signifies a hexadecimal number.

Goodheart-Willcox Publisher

Look again at Figure 11-10 and notice the port beginning with "WSD." The **Web Services for Devices (WSD)** is a printer port monitor service developed by Microsoft and first introduced in Windows Vista. The WSD printer port monitor allows printers and computers to discover each other when connected on a home or office network. The printer must be WSD-compliant to allow for communications between the printer and computer(s) on the network.

The **HP network re-discovery port monitor** is a wireless port used to support connections to a wireless printer. When the printer is an all-in-one printer with a fax, a second HP network re-discovery port monitor will appear in the list. Network discovery protocols and applications are covered in much more detail in the chapters concerning networking.

Device Manager can be used to look at available printer devices that are installed. **Figure 11-12** shows three types of connections available on a particular Windows 7 computer: IEEE 1284.4 (USB), ports COM and LPT, and WSD printer port monitor. The types of printer devices and connections listed vary according to the type of printer connected to the computer and the way the printer is connected. For example, a wireless connection to a printer may only show as a WSD Print Provider. There will be no **Ports (COM & LPT)** entry if the computer motherboard does not have these ports available. After the port is selected, the wizard will search for a printer.

Selecting a Printer and Printer Driver

Usually, the wizard will automatically identify the correct printer. If the wizard fails to correctly identify the correct printer, you will need to select the printer yourself. **Figure 11-13** shows the list of printer manufacturers and printers that are displayed. The dialog box shown is from Windows 7, but it will look very similar in other Windows operating systems. Notice the **Manufacturer** and **Printers** lists that are used to identify the printer for which the drivers must be installed. A printer driver contains the code necessary to allow the computer to communicate to the printer. Without the correct driver, the printer may operate incorrectly or may not operate at all. When you attempt to print without

Figure 11-12. The three types of printer connections appearing in this Device Manager are USB, ports COM and LPT, and WSD printer port monitor.

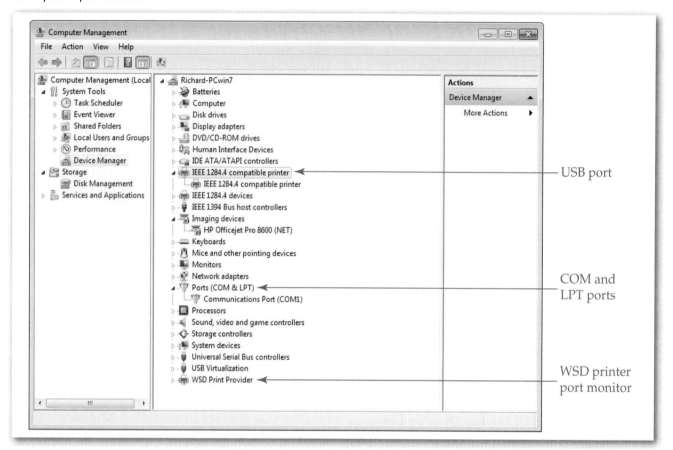

— USB port

— COM and LPT ports

— WSD printer port monitor

Figure 11-13. The Add Printer wizard offers a selection of manufacturers to choose from. First choose the manufacturer. Next, pick out the model of printer you are installing.

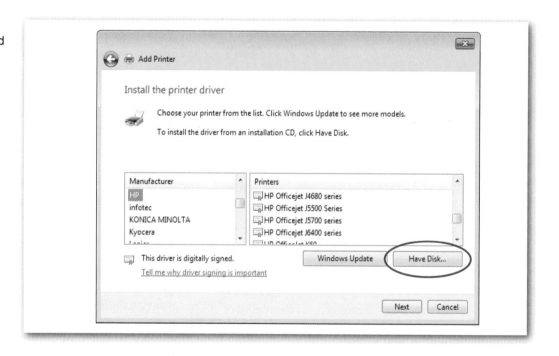

shows how a shared printer appears in a Windows 7 directory tree under Network.

In Windows 7 and Windows 8, you can use the **Devices and Printers** dialog box to determine if a printer is shared. Look at **Figure 11-19** and compare how the selected printers are identified as either network or as a shared local printer.

A network printer is represented by an icon resembling a cable connection at the bottom of the **Devices and Printers** dialog box, Figure 11-19A. It also is labeled as "Network Connected" to the right of the icon.

The printer in Figure 11-19B is configured as a shared local printer. It is connected to the computer via a USB cable. The fact that the printer is configured as a shared printer is indicated by the icon of two people side by side.

To share a local computer in Windows XP, the Add Printer wizard is used. This wizard has an option for sharing the printer in a network. In Windows Vista, when the Printer Sharing option in the Network and Sharing Center is enabled, the operating system automatically searches for local printers and configures them as shared printers.

Figure 11-19. Network printer and shared local printer identified in Windows 7 **Devices and Printers** dialog box. A—Network printer. B—Shared local printer.

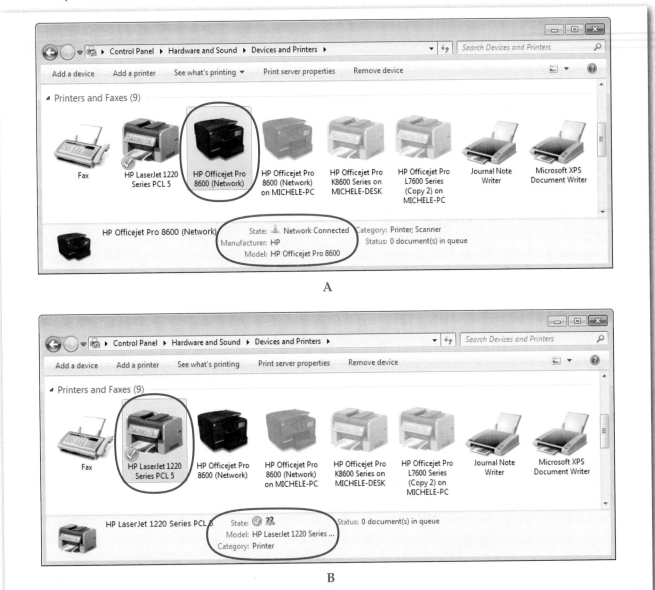

For Windows 7 and Windows 8, the network sharing options for devices such as printers are accessed through **Network and Sharing Center | Change advanced sharing settings**. This will open the **Advanced sharing settings** dialog box.

The Windows 7 HomeGroup feature automatically configured a printer as a share for members of the HomeGroup, **Figure 11-20**. Sharing has become much easier over the years with each new operating system. A more detailed study of sharing will be covered in Chapter 19—SOHO Networking.

Tech Tip

To access a printer that has been configured as a local printer and then shared, the computer that the printer is connected to must be turned on.

Print Spooling

In early computer systems, no other operation could be accomplished until the computer finished printing. Today, when a file is sent to the printer, other activities can be performed on the PC without waiting for the printer to complete its job. This is accomplished through a technique called spooling. Many input/output (I/O) devices and operations use spooling to temporarily store data, freeing up CPU resources and allowing other activities to be performed on the PC. When a printer uses spooling, it stores the data to be printed in a buffer. This list of print jobs waiting to be completed and their status is also referred to as the print queue (pronounced like the letter Q). The printing operation can be completed in the background while the user performs other tasks on the PC.

Many printer jobs can be sent to the printer at the same time. The computer, rather than sending multiple printer jobs directly to the printer, sends them to the print queue. The print queue can be RAM or area on the hard drive. With the data in the print queue, the documents, or print jobs, can be accessed and printed by the printer one at a time. **Figure 11-21** shows a print queue window with multiple documents waiting "in line" to be printed. You can check the print queue at any time. It is accessed by double-clicking the icon for the printer you wish to inspect in the **Printers and Faxes** dialog box in Windows XP, the **Printers** dialog box in Windows Vista, and the **Devices and Printers** dialog box in Windows 7 and Windows 8.

Notice that the status of the current print job is shown in Figure 11-21 and is indicated as "printing." Other status possibilities are "paused" and "spooling." If the printer is shared by more than one PC, the owner of the job will be displayed.

The same print job may be repeated twice in the queue. It is very common to have many copies of the same file sent to a print queue as a result of a stalled printing process. When a page fails to print, a novice user will attempt to

Figure 11-20.
The Windows 7 HomeGroup feature provides an easy method for sharing a local printer.

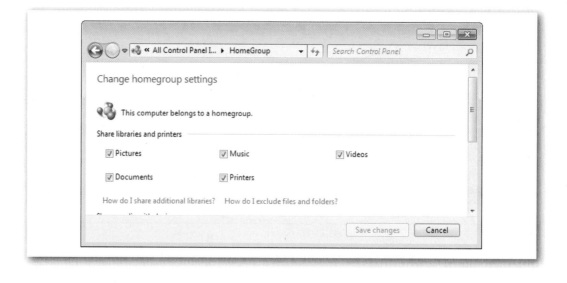

Figure 11-21. Print queue Windows and **Printer** menu.

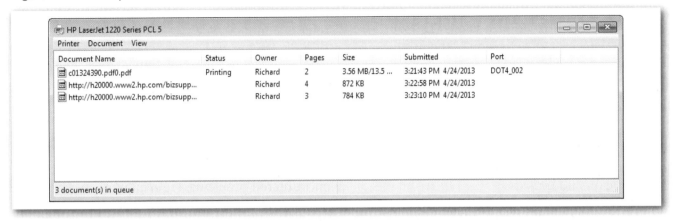

print the document several times before calling for technical support. One of the first things a technician should do when responding to a print call is to purge all the duplicate print jobs from the queue. Sometimes a printer is locked up because of a document sent by a shared user. By purging a particular user's document, the printing problem may be cleared and the remaining documents will print as they should. Look at **Figure 11-22** to see the options available from the **Printer** menu in the print queue window. You can select **Pause Printing**, **Cancel All Documents**, **Sharing**, and more.

Printer Memory

Legacy printers usually have memory in the form of SIMMs or DIMMs. Modern printers have sufficient memory to meet most printing needs, including printing photographic-quality pictures. The amount of memory with which a printer is equipped determines the resolution and size of the subject to be printed. If a printer does not have sufficient memory to print a file, it will generate an error code. Error codes are common when printing large, memory-intensive, graphic images. The exact error code will depend on the printer manufacturer and model. When a printer prints only a portion of an image, it is a sure sign of insufficient memory.

Installing more printer memory is a relatively simple task. Consult the printer documentation to determine what type of memory is recommended as the best solution for additional memory. Once the printer documentation is consulted about the appropriate memory type to use, the memory installs just as it would to the RAM banks on a motherboard. Review the "Installing RAM Modules" section from Chapter 6—Memory. The amount of memory in the printer can usually be verified by a self-test performed at the menu on the printer.

Figure 11-22. Print queue window **Printer** menu.

Flash memory ports are available on most printers, which support printing directly from the memory module, **Figure 11-23**. The flash memory becomes an extension of the printer memory and can be used to store documents and images that require frequent printing. For example, sales brochures, product information, or catalogs can be stored on a memory card and then printed as needed. You should consult the printer specifications to determine the exact type of memory the printer is compatible with.

Troubleshooting Printers

Troubleshooting printers is easy if you understand the printing process and know the function of the printer driver. The paper train and the function of printer drivers are similar for all printers. Error codes are designed by printer manufacturers to help you with the troubleshooting process.

Interpreting Error Codes and Messages

Error codes produced on some printer LCD displays provide a frequent source of confusion. Some errors generated are straightforward such as "Paper Jam" or "Refill Paper Tray." Other errors are cryptic and require decoding. They simply refer to a number such as "40 ERROR" or "22 ERROR." Some of these errors can be translated by using the owner's manual. Other times, you may need to access the manufacturer's website for more information.

Many printer manufacturers include printer diagnostic software. The diagnostic software can determine problems such as paper jams, no paper, low toner/ink, and most other commonly encountered problems, **Figure 11-24**.

Some of the codes are not published for the general public. The manufacturers feel these repairs involve work beyond the typical user's expertise. For example, a defective fuser which requires a replacement fuser module may simply generate an error code with a statement such as "Contact ABC.inc" where "ABC.inc" is the printer manufacturer.

Printer manufacturers also provide diagnostic software applications over the Internet. For example, HP provides diagnostic services for many of their products, **Figure 11-25**.

Diagnosing General Printer Problems

Many general printer problems are created by the user. For example, incorrect colors, paper jams, blank areas, printer offline, and other problems are user-created problems. The user may not fully understand how to configure a printer or the fact that a local printer needs the computer to be turned on to work. This section will present some of the most commonly encountered problems usually created by the user. The problems presented here may apply to any printer type.

Incorrect Colors

A color printer printing the incorrect color is a sign that the print cartridges are installed incorrectly. Ink cartridges have a particular order in which they must be installed. Also, be aware that a printer may not correctly match the color that appears on the monitor. Windows provides the **Color Management** dialog box, **Figure 11-26**, which is accessed through the printer **Properties** dialog box. The color can be adjusted to better

Figure 11-23. Printers can print directly from devices such as USB flash memory and flash memory cards.

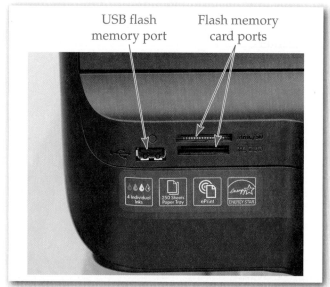

Figure 11-24. The HP Officejet Pro 8600 webpage provides information such as printer status, ink levels, wireless status, and more.

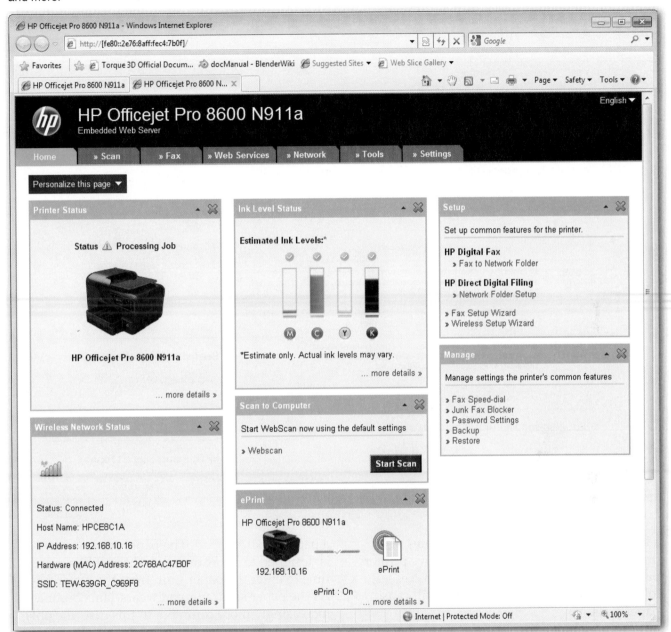

match what is being printed to what appears on the monitor or digital photos.

Blank Areas in Printing Job

If blank areas are appearing on the printing job, there is a good chance the wrong paper length has been selected at setup. Check if there is a mismatch in paper length.

Paper Jams

Paper jams occur when a printer pulls one or more sheets through its mechanism and the paper becomes wedged inside. They are a very common problem associated with most printers. There are many causes of paper jams, but with proper care, most jams can be avoided.

Paper quality is an important issue when it comes to paper jams. Low-quality paper produces

Figure 11-25. HP provides several printer diagnostic software applications for download.

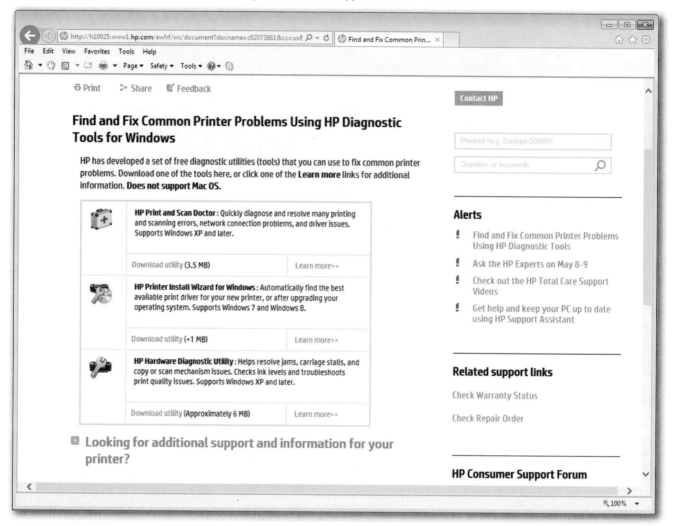

a lot of paper lint. Paper lint accumulates in all printers. Accumulation around sensitive printer parts can cause jams. Also, paper with creases, folded corners, and damaged edges will cause paper jams.

Another issue is moisture. When paper arrives from an outside storage area that is not climate controlled, condensation (moisture) can be created due to the change in temperature. This can make the paper damp. Damp paper is almost sure to jam in a printer. Paper should be stored at the same room temperature and humidity level as the printer for approximately twenty-four hours.

Another common cause of paper jams is worn parts along the paper train. The **paper train** is the route that the paper follows through the printer. The train consists of several rubber rollers and a paper separator pad. The paper separator pad is designed to allow only one sheet of paper at a time to enter the paper train from the paper tray. As the paper separator pad wears, jams become increasingly more common. In this case, the only remedy is to replace the separator pad. Worn pickup rollers can also cause jams. Sometimes, cleaning the rollers or removing paper lint can solve the problem. Other times, the pickup rollers have to be replaced. See **Figure 11-27**.

The direction of paper can influence the number of jams created in the printer. Most paper is manufactured with a natural curve. Typically, the outside wrapper of the paper will indicate the side of the stack of paper that should be used first in any printer or copy machine. The wrapper is often marked with an arrow. However, not all

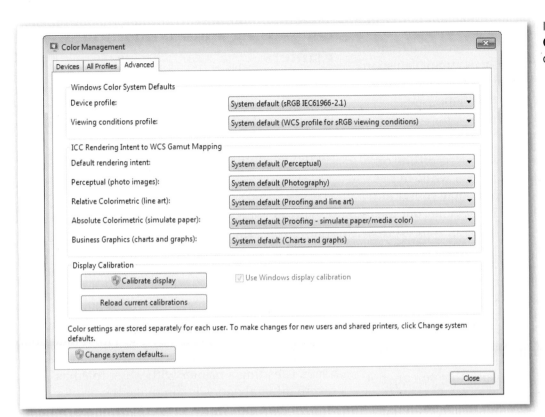

Figure 11-26.
Color Management
dialog box.

Figure 11-27. Printer maintenance kits for the paper train provide the most common parts that require periodic replacement. Shown are the separation pad, transfer roller, and pickup roller.

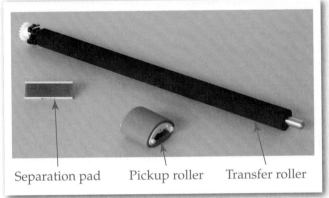

Separation pad   Pickup roller   Transfer roller

Goodheart-Willcox Publisher

paper packages are marked with an indicating arrow. If you are experiencing a definite curl to the finished printed page, check for markings on the paper wrapper for the correct positioning of the paper into the paper tray.

Tech Tip   One way to avoid paper jams is to discard the first sheet of paper where the fold of the wrapper comes together. Many times this sheet of paper contains glue residue from the sealing process. The glue can collect inside the printer on the rollers and separator as well as on the fusing unit or drum. *Always* discard the first sheet from a new package of paper.

Printer Trips the Circuit Breaker

If the circuit breaker trips when the printer is running, it is a good sign that electronic or other parts of the printer are failing. However, you must remember that a printer uses heat to fuse the toner to the paper. A printer may draw as much as 15 amps of current while processing a page. If the printer is on the same circuit as another piece of heavy-load equipment, the two running at the same time can trip a breaker. A coffeepot, copy machine, toaster oven, and microwave are good examples of equipment that may be found on the same circuit breaker as the printer. The combination of these types of equipment sharing the same breaker as the printer can cause frequent breaker trips. Check carefully. A circuit can span more than one room. The overloaded equipment may not be near the printer location.

Printer Is Offline

A printer can have power but be offline or on standby. A printer cannot print while in the offline mode. An offline printer may sound like too simple of a problem or too obvious, but the problem often occurs. When giving support over a telephone, the power source and whether the printer is offline should be checked first. Don't be surprised if the person on the other end of the telephone does not exactly know what you mean by "offline."

Cannot Access Local Printer

There are two main reasons that you are not able to connect to a local printer configured as a shared printer. The first reason is you do not have permission to access the printer. When a printer is configured as a shared local printer, the host computer must be configured to allow other users to access the printer. The host computer can configure the local printer to be accessed by everyone or only by specific people or computers.

The second reason you may fail to access a local printer remotely is the host computer is turned off or in sleep mode or the printer is turned off.

Cannot Access Network Printer

The first reason not to be able to access a network printer is you do not have permission to access the printer. On some networks, printer access is determined by the network administrator. The network administrator selects the persons and computers that can access the network printer.

The second reason is the network printer may be turned off or in offline mode. There will be more about network problems as related to devices in Chapter 19—SOHO Networking.

Diagnosing and Maintaining Inkjet Printers

Inkjet printers are one of the most commonly used home printers. They are simple in design, but there are several commonly encountered problems and some simple maintenance routines you should be familiar with.

Inkjet Printer Cleaning Guidelines

Inkjet printers operate on the principle of controlling a fine mist of ink to print images on the paper. Because of this printing technique, the mist of ink often collects on the inside and outside of the printer case. To remove ink deposits from the outside of the printer case, you should use a soft cloth and water. If the case will not clean properly with water, you may use a mild detergent diluted in water. The water should be distilled water. Cleaning a printer with water that has severe mineral deposits can make the printer case look worse than before it was cleaned. Never clean a printer case with alcohol or any form of strong commercial cleaners. Harsh chemicals will ruin many plastics.

> ## A+ Note
>
> The A+ Certification exam will most likely only list water or very mild detergent as the correct answer.

Most printer designs have been engineered to allow for some accumulation of ink inside the printer. In general, you should never attempt to clean the inside of the printer with alcohol or any commercial solvents. Alcohol, solvents, and water can damage the electrical components inside the printer. The only areas inside the printer that may require cleaning are the print cartridges. The printer should only be turned off after the printing process has completed. When the printer has finished printing, the ink cartridge is returned to "home" position. The home position is engineered to cover the ink ports to prevent them from drying out. Inkjet ports often dry out because of long periods of nonuse.

A small, fine brush or an anti-static vacuum should be used to remove paper dust and lint. Do *not* use compressed air to remove dust. The compressed air may actually force the dust deeper inside the printing mechanism and cause more harm than good.

Never attempt to lubricate parts inside the inkjet printer. Lubricants can cause an increased buildup of dust and lint inside the printer. Lubricants can also damage electronic components.

These are general guidelines to follow and may vary somewhat when working with specific printers. The best policy is to download a copy of maintenance and cleaning instructions for the exact printer model from the manufacturer's website.

Automated Calibration and Head Alignment

Inkjet printer calibration and head alignment and head cleaning are performed to ensure the best quality printed image possible. **Figure 11-28** shows a maintenance screen from the utility software for an HP Officejet Pro 8600 printer.

When **Align Printer** is selected, the head alignment is performed automatically without user intervention. The printer prints lines on a

test paper and shines a light beam onto the paper. The light is reflected back to a sensor. The amount of light reflected back to the sensor is directly correlated to the physical properties of the ink line. The two physical properties are color and line width. The printer automatically calculates the physical attributes of the lines on the paper to determine if they are within acceptable tolerances. If the printhead is not correct, the printer will automatically make adjustments to align it. Printhead alignment is routinely performed after replacing ink cartridges. **Figure 11-29** shows an HP Officejet Pro 8600 printhead alignment test sheet.

Another test performed is print quality diagnostics. **Figure 11-30** shows the diagnostic sheet for an HP Officejet Pro 8600. The top of the diagnostic sheet is used to visually check if the printhead is properly aligned. You would visually check to verify that the lines are straight and that the corners of the box where the lines meet are properly aligned. Any gaps or overlapping at the corners indicate a problem with the printhead alignment.

A thin white line appearing across the color bars indicates that there is a problem with the ink

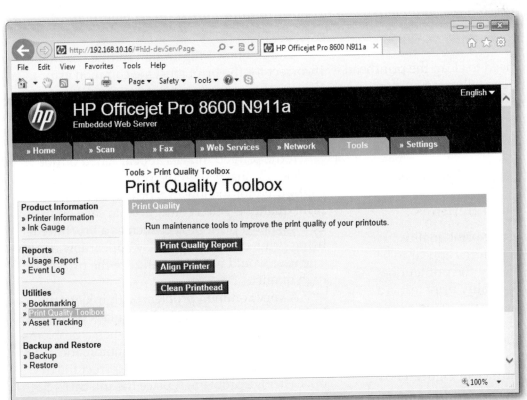

Figure 11-28.
Inkjet print quality, alignment, and printhead cleaning can all be implemented through printer software.

Figure 11-29. Printhead alignment is performed by printing a pattern of lines on paper and then shining a light on the paper which is reflected back to a light sensor to verify or correct printhead alignment.

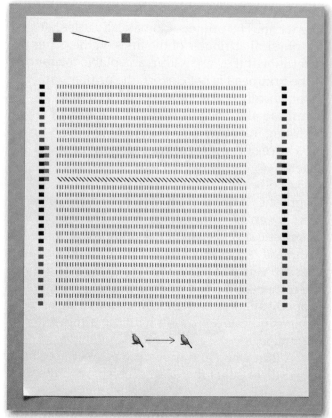

Goodheart-Willcox Publisher

Figure 11-30. The print quality diagnostic sheet is used to determine if the printer needs printhead alignment and to diagnose if there is a problem with the ink cartridges.

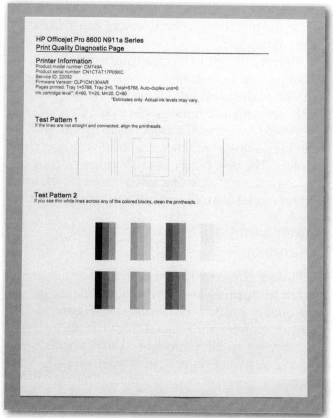

Goodheart-Willcox Publisher

cartridges. You would need to clean the printhead to correct the problem. The following are some other problems associated with the ink cartridges but that may be due to incorrect printer settings:

- Print is smeared.
- Color bars are faded.
- Color bars appear jagged along the edges.

Incorrect Inkjet Printer Settings

If the printer passes the print quality diagnostics and the test patterns appear to be correct, it does not mean that the printer does not have a problem. The quality print test is a self-diagnostic test and does not reflect user configuration settings. For example, a document or image that appears too light or low quality can be caused by user configuration. Look at the printer configuration settings in **Figure 11-31**.

The printer configuration settings could be incorrect for the print job. One common error is the use of the wrong type of paper setting. For example, if you are using high-quality, glossy photo paper and the printer is configured for plain copy paper, the ink will most likely smear.

If the printed images appear faded or not sufficiently sharp, then the printer might be configured for too low of a print quality. Low print quality is often configured to save on ink. Later, when a print project such as a brochure is being printed, the images may appear low quality. The user would need to configure the printer for high quality.

A very common problem with inkjet printers is the ink cartridges dry out from lack of use over a long period of time. To correct such a problem, clean the printhead by using the automatic cleaning function. If this fails to correct the dry ink cartridge problem, replace the ink cartridge.

Figure 11-31. If the printer passes the self-test and you still have a problem with the appearance of the document or image, check the user configuration settings for the printer.

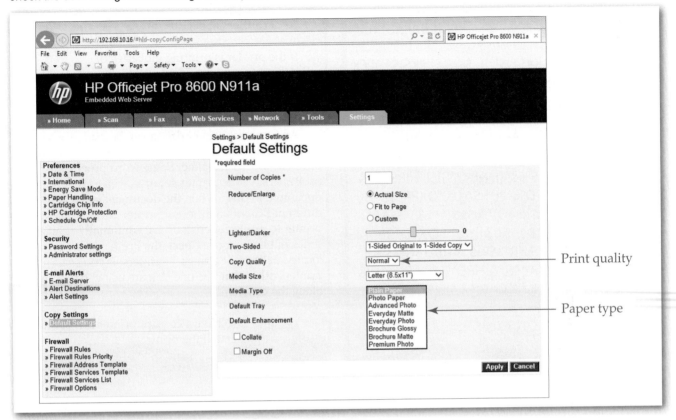

Diagnosing Laser Printer Problems

Laser printers are one of the most common printers you will encounter, especially in the office environment. Understanding the complete printing process of the typical laser printer based on the electrophotographic process will give you a quick insight to the problem. Most printers are equipped with a self-test program as part of a diagnostic routine. Running the printer self-test can eliminate many printer faults.

The following covers ten of the most common problems you may encounter with a laser printer. Examine them along with their causes and solutions.

Printing Gibberish

If the printer is printing gibberish or unintelligible symbols, **Figure 11-32**, but prints fine during the self-test, you probably have the wrong printer driver loaded or a corrupted driver.

An incorrect printer driver can be loaded when a user attempts to use a disk from another PC with a different printer installed. Some word-processing packages save the document along with the printer setup to the disk. When the document is loaded on a different PC with a different printer, it can cause the printer to print gibberish or just continually print a series of blank pages. Check **Printers and Faxes** (Windows XP), **Printers** (Windows Vista), or **Devices and Printers** (Windows 7 and Windows 8). If you see printers other than the one you are using, this is most likely the problem.

You may also have a corrupt printer driver and may need to reinstall the printer driver. A computer "hiccup" can corrupt a driver. Reinstalling the printer driver will correct this problem. Reinstalling the driver is done just like the initial installation, using the Add Printer wizard. The computer will install the new driver over the old, corrupt driver.

Figure 11-32. If your printed page looks like this, there is likely a problem with your printer driver.

```
$$%34693%@%&&#^&bsr    ]]]]]]]]]]]]]]]]]]]]]]]]]
#^tbsss$%^^%#$#%$%^%%^%&LK$J^$%JYS}
}}}$@L#K!!K@#LL$K#$T)$U))_$        #KS)$%)LFX
)$I)$#  )#$L      )$##@)#^&B%PO("R
@!@RGXR^*&*)%Y%^%&&R(T)(+{&^@$^%^%E
R^*^R<LTG*&T<A#$^E&I&R*KFEA$^%E&HEW$
#^%DB$%&%4985)(*&(()*)(Q@LJ9984jlk
094/94"3434W%$))$E)$I)@LR_%%+@<V<
%)$#########)I$#$%&*()_&E<?""})_(%#R$%*(&
:$*&L(MN?){"_W^((D%^*(*E$^JJ&*O)(PAE$^^%
*P_VHJ*%&K<M?":"?><O)*%$#&(**>&T%$#^*&
&())?><R$%E$%O*&#^%*&)(*&^%Q%*D*$B^&(
*@R****D^U^E&I^%*R*KS%$*&T(IAY$Q@$%*(*
JYR#^%E(*&(OYT$A^%(*&(HRE^%&(I^R*%*UI&
^O$%*D%&%&Y^%*IKM^%^&^)%%%%%%%%
%%%%%%%%%%
```

Goodheart-Willcox Publisher

Figure 11-33. When toner cartridges run low, the printed page will show insufficient toner coverage.

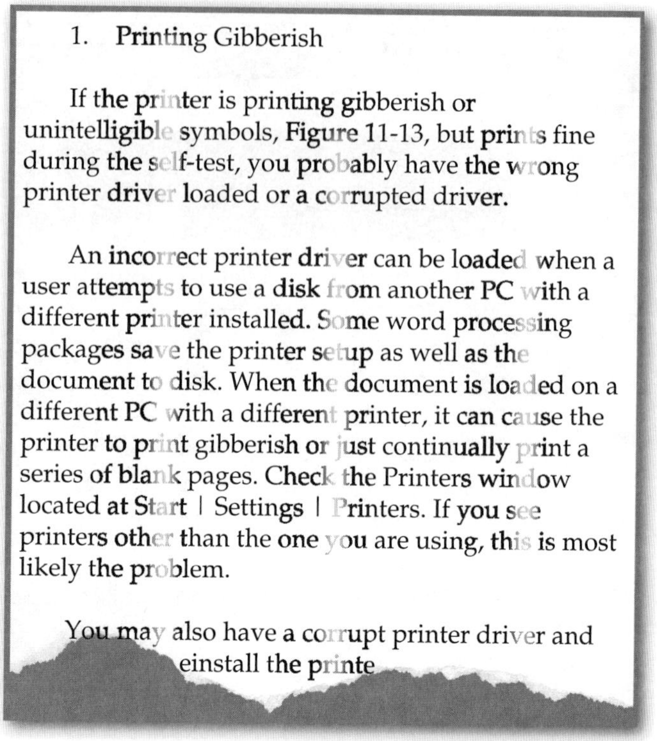

1. Printing Gibberish

If the printer is printing gibberish or unintelligible symbols, Figure 11-13, but prints fine during the self-test, you probably have the wrong printer driver loaded or a corrupted driver.

An incorrect printer driver can be loaded when a user attempts to use a disk from another PC with a different printer installed. Some word processing packages save the printer setup as well as the document to disk. When the document is loaded on a different PC with a different printer, it can cause the printer to print gibberish or just continually print a series of blank pages. Check the Printers window located at Start | Settings | Printers. If you see printers other than the one you are using, this is most likely the problem.

You may also have a corrupt printer driver and einstall the printe

Goodheart-Willcox Publisher

Pages Have Light Streaks

If pages are printing light images or have light streaks vertically down the page, **Figure 11-33**, the printer is low on toner. Remove the toner cartridge, shake it gently from side to side, and then reinstall it. If the quality of the printed pages improve, replace the toner cartridge.

Pages Print Solid Black

When pages print solid black or if there is a great deal of gray in the areas that should be white, the most likely problem is the toner cartridge is seated improperly, allowing toner to dump on the paper, **Figure 11-34**. It is also possible that the toner cartridge is defective. Fixing an improperly-seated toner cartridge is as simple as removing the cartridge and replacing it correctly.

Although less likely, there is also the possibility that the laser may not be working or the mirror may be defective. The primary corona wire could also be at fault. When the primary corona wire is at fault, there is no initial charge

Figure 11-34. If extra toner appears on a page, you should first check if the toner cartridge is seated correctly.

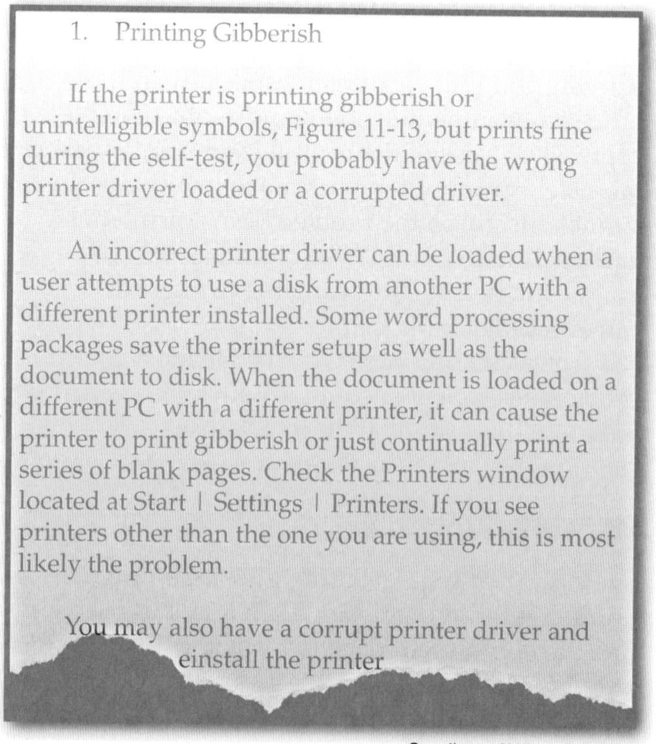

1.   Printing Gibberish

If the printer is printing gibberish or unintelligible symbols, Figure 11-13, but prints fine during the self-test, you probably have the wrong printer driver loaded or a corrupted driver.

An incorrect printer driver can be loaded when a user attempts to use a disk from another PC with a different printer installed. Some word processing packages save the printer setup as well as the document to disk. When the document is loaded on a different PC with a different printer, it can cause the printer to print gibberish or just continually print a series of blank pages. Check the Printers window located at Start | Settings | Printers. If you see printers other than the one you are using, this is most likely the problem.

You may also have a corrupt printer driver and einstall the printer

Goodheart-Willcox Publisher

placed on the drum. Remember that the polarities used depend on the manufacturer. The polarities used determine if the page prints totally black or totally white. You must first determine whether the laser on the printer writes the images or writes the background. If any of these parts have gone bad, a qualified technician needs to be contacted.

Pages Print Blank

Always check the easy things first. A common error that causes blank pages occurs when the toner cartridge is changed. Often users fail to remove the sealing tape that keeps the toner slot closed during shipping and transfer. If you are getting blank pages, always remove the toner cartridge first to ensure that the sealing tape has been removed.

The wrong driver or a corrupt driver can also cause blank pages. If only alternate pages or just the first page is blank, it is probably a printer setup problem. The printer configuration is the place to look. Try reconfiguring the printer to correct the first page from being blank or alternate pages printing blank.

If all the pages of the print job are blank, the transfer corona may be at fault. Without a charge on the paper, it cannot attract toner from the drum. A qualified technician must be called for this problem.

Poor Print Quality

With poor quality prints, first check that the toner cartridge is not low on toner or completely empty. Also, check if the printer is set up for economy or draft mode. The economy or draft mode is used to conserve toner. This option usually can be accessed in the printer setup window of the operating system and through the printer menu options controlled by the buttons on the printer. Usually, any settings on the printer will override settings created with the operating system interface.

Toner Smears on Paper

As stated earlier, always check the simplest thing first. With toner smears, the easiest thing to check is if the printer was loaded with the wrong type of paper. Some printers require special paper. If there are multiple types of printers at a location,

there is a chance the wrong type of paper may have been placed into the paper tray.

However, when toner smears across the paper when touched, **Figure 11-35**, it is a good indication that the fusing unit is out. With the fusing unit out, the toner is never melted to the paper.

Printer Acts Completely Dead

If a printer acts dead, check if the printer is offline. If there is no response, check the printer cables, as they may have become loose. Of course, never forget to check the power cable and to make sure there is power at the outlet. A dead printer can also be a driver problem.

Printed Characters are Fuzzy

With fuzzy printing, check the type of paper loaded into the printer. If the wrong type of paper is used, the toner may scatter outside the character outline.

Constant Dark or White Spots

If you find dark or white spots that appear in the same place on multiple printed sheets, it is likely that the drum is scratched. With a scratch on the drum, it may not be able to hold toner or it may hold toner on the spot at all times. Replacement drums can be purchased and installed fairly easily for most laser printers.

Figure 11-35. If toner is not sealed properly to paper, it smears easily.

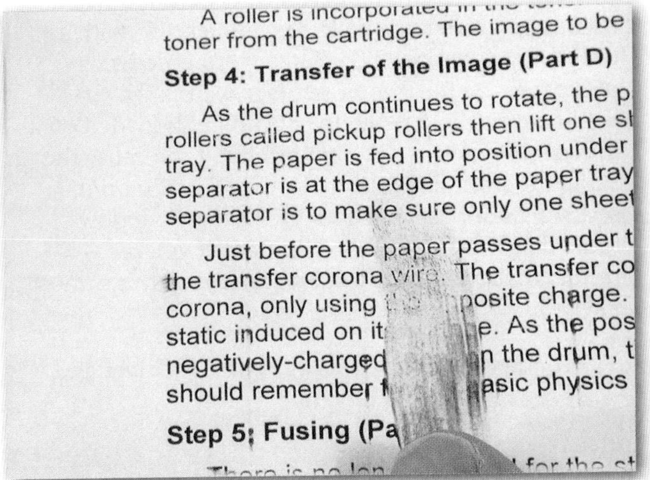

A roller is incorporated in the toner from the cartridge. The image to be

Step 4: Transfer of the Image (Part D)

As the drum continues to rotate, the p rollers called pickup rollers then lift one sl tray. The paper is fed into position under separator is at the edge of the paper tray separator is to make sure only one sheet

Just before the paper passes under t the transfer corona wire. The transfer co corona, only using the opposite charge. static induced on it e. As the pos negatively-charged n the drum, t should remember asic physics

Step 5: Fusing (Pa

Ghost Images

A ghost image is a second image that appears on the paper in the background of the image you are trying to print, **Figure 11-36**. A ghost image is usually a sign that the erase lamp is burnt out. When the erase lamp is out, the image of the last print run will remain on the drum.

Diagnosing USB Printer Problems

The USB connection has become the standard cable connection for printers, thus replacing the parallel cable and earlier serial connections. While USB is easy to install and typically configures automatically, there are several problems commonly associated with this type of connection.

Insufficient Or No Electrical Power

It is most important to mention that you should always check for the simplest and easiest solution first when dealing with printer problems.

Figure 11-36. Ghost images appear when the image from a previous print is not erased from the drum.

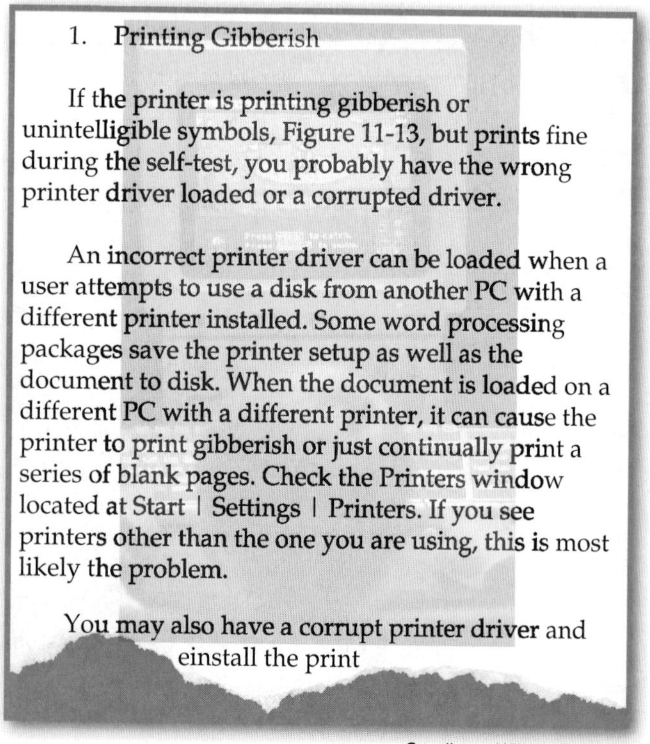

1. Printing Gibberish

If the printer is printing gibberish or unintelligible symbols, Figure 11-13, but prints fine during the self-test, you probably have the wrong printer driver loaded or a corrupted driver.

An incorrect printer driver can be loaded when a user attempts to use a disk from another PC with a different printer installed. Some word processing packages save the printer setup as well as the document to disk. When the document is loaded on a different PC with a different printer, it can cause the printer to print gibberish or just continually print a series of blank pages. Check the Printers window located at Start | Settings | Printers. If you see printers other than the one you are using, this is most likely the problem.

You may also have a corrupt printer driver and
einstall the print

Check if the printer is turned on and is online. An LED generally indicates power to a printer. If the LED is lit, the USB port selected for the printer connection may not be providing sufficient electrical power to operate the printer. While the majority of electrical power is supplied to the printer through its own electrical plug, the USB cable also provides a small amount of energy required to run the printer. This problem is easily remedied by installing a powered USB hub capable of supplying the higher electrical power needed by the printer.

Conflicting Devices

USB devices are not supposed to conflict, but this is in theory only. Occasionally, conflicts do arise and are generally caused by either the BIOS/UEFI setup or the USB device driver. One of the devices may be programmed to take over the bandwidth of the port, causing the other devices to go into a hibernation state or simply lock up.

Microsoft furnishes basic device code to developers to use and modify for their USB devices. Microsoft will also test the software and the hardware compatibility for a small charge. If the device passes Microsoft testing, the device is added to the Microsoft Hardware Compatibility List (HCL) for the operating system version for which it was tested. However, some manufacturers develop their own driver software and only refer to the Microsoft guidelines. For whatever reason, they do not submit their code for testing or it is tested after the release of the hardware device. If a problem is found, the manufacturer will simply provide a "patch" at their website.

To troubleshoot a USB device, remove all other USB devices from the port that the printer is connected to. This will help eliminate the possibility of a conflict between the devices connected to the same port.

Check the Device Manager for a problem with the USB port indicated by an exclamation mark or question mark. These symbols indicate that the printer is not properly recognized or configured. The software drivers, BIOS/UEFI, or both may need to be upgraded. Check the printer manufacturer's website for more information.

Toner Spills

Toner will be spilled from time to time, especially when replacing toner cartridges. Toner is composed of extremely small particles, usually a combination of carbon and polyester resin. Since the particles are so small and the toner is designed to permanently adhere to paper and similar products, there are some precautions that should be observed.

Small spills should be cleaned up with an approved vacuum cleaner. An approved vacuum cleaner designed for toner spills is made with a dust-tight motor. Normal household vacuum cleaners do not have dust-tight motors and can create static discharge inside the vacuum cleaner housing. A static discharge can cause an explosion of toner particles, especially since one of the main ingredients is carbon. Approved toner vacuums also have a conductive hose. The conductive hose is designed to prevent static discharge created from the moving parts inside the vacuum.

The approved vacuum typically has a High-Efficiency Particulate Air (HEPA) filter. The HEPA filter can filter out smaller particles than a normal household vacuum cleaner. Attempts to vacuum toner spills with a normal household vacuum will produce a cloud of toner particles that could cause harm when breathed.

Danger ! Do *not* use a standard household vacuum cleaner to remove toner spills. Only an approved vacuum expressly designed to clean toner spills should be used.

Small toner spills on hard surfaces such as tile can be swept with a broom. Be sure to use a slow, sweeping action so not to create a cloud of toner dust. Never use hot water to wipe or mop a toner spill. Hot water will set the toner, causing a permanent stain. This is especially true for clothing. Try to always remove loose toner from clothing before washing. Use only cold water to wash clothing covered with toner.

Spills on a printer case can be removed with a soft dry cloth. Toner can be removed from case areas that are difficult to clean with a cloth by using a small paintbrush. Again, slowly brush the areas as not to create a cloud of toner dust.

For information about any special precautions or dangers associated with toner and other chemical products, you can consult the Material Safety Data Sheet (MSDS) for that specific product. By law, all chemical products must have an MSDS available on request to answer all questions about how the product should be handled. This includes safe handling and cleanup. Printer toner is considered safe when handled in the intended manner.

Products associated with technical equipment, such as printers, generate billions of tons of waste which can be harmful to our environment. To reduce the impact on our environment, most manufacturers such as Xerox and Hewlett Packard have recycling programs that allow a consumer to recycle toner and ink cartridges as well as other consumables. You can view the manufacturer's website to obtain information about their recycling program.

Windows Printer Troubleshooter

Windows provides the Printer troubleshooter feature through its Help and Support software. The Printer troubleshooter helps solve printer problems. This feature can be accessed by entering the keywords "printing troubleshooting" in the **Search** text box of Help and Support. This series of screen captures shown in **Figure 11-37** are from Windows 7, but each operating system has a similar Printer troubleshooter tool. The exact sequence of troubleshooting Windows will vary according to the problem and possible solutions.

The Printer troubleshooter conducts a series of tests such as checking the printer spooler for errors and checking for the latest drivers. The troubleshooter may offer a solution and allow the user to apply the solution automatically. Finally, additional resources are offered to help find a solution, if needed. Some of the additional help features are requesting help from a friend through the Remote Assistance feature. Remote Assistance allows you to send an email or instant message to a friend and give the friend limited control of your computer as a way to let them fix the print problem for you. You can also perform a system recovery, which will allow you to reset your

Figure 11-37. Windows provides the Printer troubleshooter wizard, which takes the user automatically through a series of steps that automatically detect the problem, offer solutions, and offer additional help.

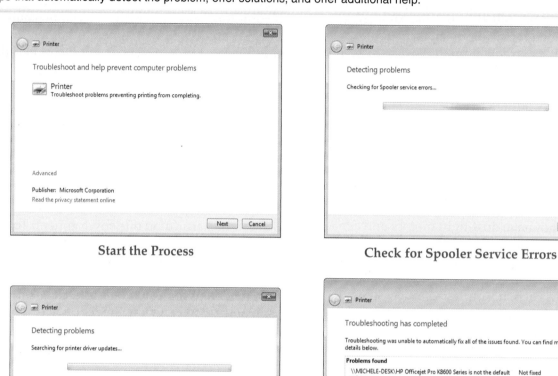

Start the Process

Check for Spooler Service Errors

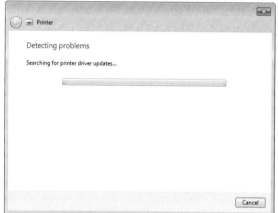

Search for Updated Print Drivers

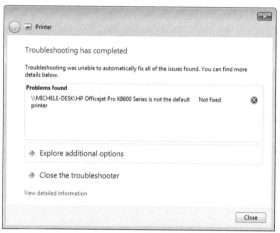

Troubleshooting Completed

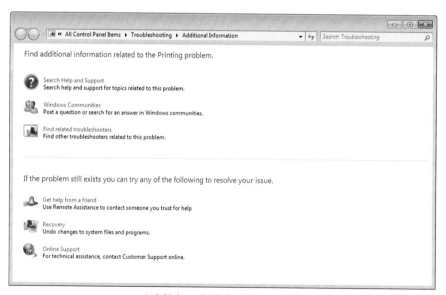

Additional Help Resources

computer system settings to an earlier time. Also, there is an option for online support and technical assistance from Microsoft. There will be much more about these options later in Chapter 15—PC Troubleshooting.

Tech Tip
Windows Help and Support provides a lot of easy-to-understand step-by-step instructions for most of the print installation and configuration needs. Be sure to check the Help and Support feature when trouble-shooting a printer problem or before performing a printer configuration that you are unfamiliar with.

Fonts

A **font** is a design for a set of symbols, usually text and number characters. A font describes characteristics associated with a symbol such as the typeface, size, pitch, and spacing between symbols. Look at **Figure 11-38**.

The two main classifications of fonts are *bitmap* and *vector*. A **bitmap font** uses a pattern of dots to represent each letter. The bitmap images of the text are stored in memory. As you type, the bitmap images are placed on the screen by a process similar to a cut-and-paste process. Each and every different font requires a different bitmap pattern. A bitmap font must also use a separate bitmap for each size of the letter.

A **vector font** is also referred to as an *outline font*. A vector font draws the outline of the letter rather than storing a separate bitmap pattern for each font. The angles, turns, and distances are calculated for each character. A vector font is easily scaled to larger or smaller sizes because the letter is based on an algorithm.

A bitmap font looks better than a vector font when displayed on low-resolution devices such as monitors. On high-resolution devices, such as some printers, vector fonts look better than bitmap fonts.

The physical size of a font is described in points and pitch. The height of a letter is measured

Figure 11-38. Samples of common typefaces and point-sizes.

Sample Fonts

This is a sample of Times New Roman 8 point font.

This is a sample of Times New Roman 12 point font.

This is a sample of Times New Roman 18 point font.

This is a sample of Courier 8 point font.

This is a sample of Courier 12 point font.

This is a sample of Courier 14 point font.

This is a sample of Brush Script 16 point font.

This is a sample of Brush Script 20 point font.

This is a sample of Tahoma 10 point font.

This is a sample of Tahoma 14 point font.

This is a sample of Myriad 10 point font.

This is a sample of Myriad 16 point font.

This is a sample of Myriad 16 point italic font.

This is a sample of Myriad 16 point bold font.

in **points**. The width is measured in **pitch**. Each point is equal to 1/72 of an inch.

Vector fonts are used with Page Description Language (PDL). Common PDLs are Adobe PostScript and Microsoft TrueType. A page description language treats everything on a page as a graphic image. The PDL translates the picture on the monitor into a set of printer codes that will exactly duplicate the image seen on the screen. This is often referred to as "what you see is what you get" (WYSIWYG).

Figure 11-39 shows all the ways the Microsoft Word program can manipulate a font.

The manipulation feature is typical in most word-processing packages. Available fonts can be viewed in Windows XP by accessing **Start | Control Panel | Appearance and Themes** and then selecting **Fonts** located under **See also** in the side panel.

In Windows Vista, Windows 7, and Windows 8, available fonts are located under **Start | Control Panel | Appearance and Personalization | Fonts**, **Figure 11-40**. The **Font** folder and available fonts are shown in **Figure 11-41**. You can print a sample of the selected font by right-clicking the folder and selecting **Print** from the shortcut menu.

Figure 11-39.
A sample of the Arial typeface printed from **Control Panel | Appearance and Personalization | Fonts**.

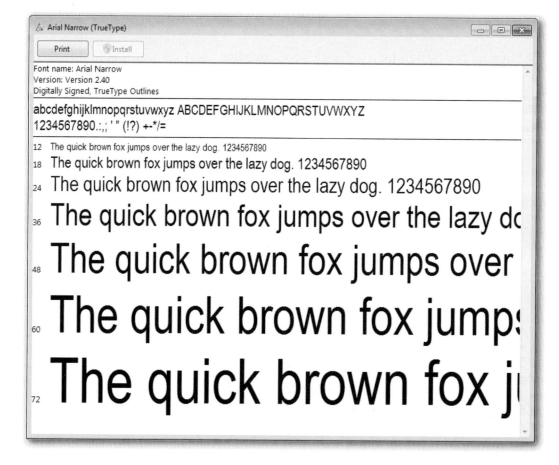

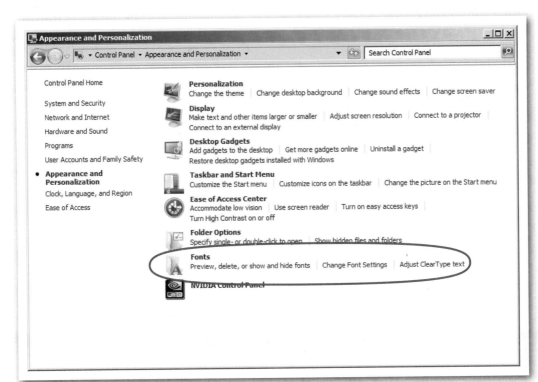

Figure 11-40.
In Windows Vista, Windows 7, and Windows 8, available fonts are located under **Start | Control Panel | Appearance and Personalization | Fonts**.

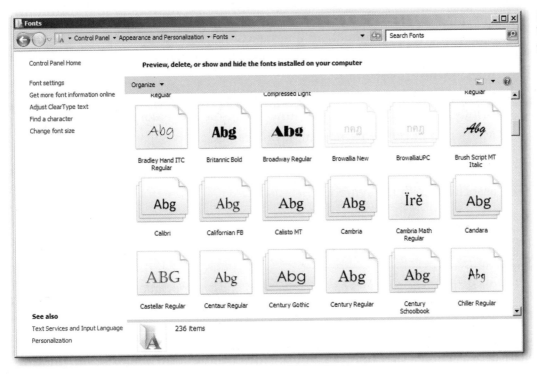

Figure 11-41.
Windows available fonts.

Chapter Summary

- The seven laser printing stages are processing, charging the drum, exposing or writing the image, developing the image, transferring the image, fusing the image, and cleaning the drum.

- LED printers use an array of light-emitting diodes to write an image to the drum.

- Inkjet printers use either a thermoresistor or a piezocell crystal to produce the force needed to spray a fine mist of ink onto paper. Use water or a mild detergent to clean a printer case.

- Dot matrix printers use a printhead consisting of small metal rods which when affected by the magnetic field of an energized solenoid, strike an ink ribbon and leave a dot of ink on paper.

- Color thermal printers operate on the principle of applying color by heating a special ribbon that is coated with a wax-like material, which is sealed to the surface of the paper by Teflon-coated rollers.

- Dye-sublimation printers print images by vaporizing inks, which then solidify onto paper.

- Solid ink printers use solid ink cartridges similar to wax and a printhead that consists of four long rows of many individual nozzles, each row producing one of the CMYK colors.

- All-in-one products are a combination of printer, fax, copier, and scanner.

- A printer can be connected directly to a computer, wirelessly, through a wired network, or through an Internet connection.

- The print queue window can be used to check the status of a print job and to manage the print job.

- Before installing more printer memory into a printer, you should first consult the printer documentation to determine what type of memory is recommended.

- Many printer problems are simple and can be easily solved by users or technicians.

- A font is a design for a set of symbols. A font describes the characteristics associated with the symbol.

Review Questions

Answer the following questions on a separate sheet of paper. Please do not write in this book.

1. Place the following steps in the correct order.
   a. Toner is attracted to the drum.
   b. The static brush removes the charge from the paper.
   c. The laser writes the image on the drum.
   d. The transfer corona charges the paper.
   e. The fusing section melts the toner.
   f. The drum is erased of all charge.
   g. The primary corona wire places a charge on the drum.
2. What is another term used to describe the "writing" stage of the laser or LED printing process?

3. Which part of a laser printer applies a static charge to the drum?

4. The LED printer uses an array of _____ to write the image to the drum.

5. Inkjet printers use either a(n) _____ or _____ to produce a force that fires a drop of ink through a nozzle directly onto the paper.

6. What are the four common colors associated with an inkjet printer and what letter is used to represent each color?

7. What is an impact printer?

8. The heating unit in a color thermal printer consists of an array of small _____ that melt the wax in small dots.

9. A dye-sublimation printer produces near photo quality printed images by _____ inks, which then solidify onto paper.

10. A solid ink printer uses solid ink cartridges similar to _____, which when heated flow into the individual reservoirs of the printhead.

11. An all-in-one product is a combination of what four devices?

12. List four ways a computer can connect to a printer.

13. Which connection is typically used to connect a computer directly to a printer?

14. Name three types of printer wireless connections.

15. How is a network printer indicated in Windows 7 Devices and Printers?

16. How is a shared printer indicated in Windows XP?

17. What is Web Services for Devices (WSD)?

18. What is the HP network rediscovery port monitor and what is it used for?

19. What new feature in Windows 7 will assist a user in creating a shared printer for home installation?

20. Describe what spooling does.

21. What is the print queue?

22. How do you access the print queue in Windows 7 and Windows 8?

23. What is the first thing you should do before installing printer memory?

24. An error code appears on the printer panel that you are not familiar with. What should you do?

25. A paper jam constantly occurs when using a printer. This is a recent problem. What might be the cause?

26. What are the two common reasons that you are unable to connect to a local printer configured as a shared printer?

27. A user comes back from a long vacation and now their inkjet printer is no longer working. What is *most likely* the problem and how do you remedy it?

28. A color laser printer that is shared by other users was working fine yesterday. Today, the printer is producing faded or low-quality images of pictures. What is *most likely* the problem?

29. After a laser printer prints a page of text, the toner smears when touched. What is *most likely* the problem?

30. What is the difference between a bitmap font and a vector font?

31. The height of a font is measured in _____.

32. The width of a font is measured in _____.

Sample A+ Exam Questions

Answer the following questions on a separate sheet of paper. Please do not write in this book.

1. What type of printer uses piezoelectric technology?
   a. Laser
   b. Dot matrix
   c. Dye-sublimation
   d. Inkjet

2. What type of printer uses pins driven by a solenoid striking a ribbon to make dots conforming to letters, symbols, and pictures?
   a. Laser
   b. Dot matrix
   c. Dye-sublimation
   d. Inkjet

3. Which type of printer uses thermoresistors to force the ink from a reservoir?
   a. Laser
   b. Dot matrix
   c. Dye-sublimation
   d. Inkjet

4. In the electrostatic process, the term *fusing* can best be described as which of the following answers?
   a. The protective device installed in electrostatic laser printers to prevent electrical overload of the circuits
   b. The transfer of toner to the paper to construct the printed image
   c. The bonding of the toner to the paper
   d. A special module that prevents the voltage from exceeding the 600-volts positive charge

5. Which of the following includes all the correct processes in correct order for electrostatic printing?
   a. Processing, charging the drum, exposing or writing the image, developing the image, transferring the image, fusing the image, cleaning the drum.
   b. Processing, charging the drum, transferring the image, exposing or writing the image, developing the image, fusing the image, cleaning the drum.
   c. Processing, cleaning the drum, charging the drum, transferring the image, developing the image, charging again, exposing or writing the image, fusing the image.
   d. Processing, exposing or writing the image, charging the drum, developing the image, transferring the image, fusing the image, cleaning the drum.

6. The acronym LPT represents which of the following?
   a. Local printer transferring-port
   b. Line printer terminal
   c. Local printer terminal
   d. Line port terminal

7. What does the printer term *spooling* mean?
   a. It describes the mechanical device that holds the ribbon in place on a dot matrix printer.
   b. It is a method of connecting a local printer to an area network printer group.
   c. It is the method used to store print jobs waiting to be processed in an orderly fashion.
   d. It is a method of determining the amount of rotation or "print spooling" required for blank spacing between lines of text in a document.

8. Which item is required for inkjet printhead alignment?
   a. Compressed air
   b. Flat tip screwdriver
   c. Toner wrench
   d. Software application

9. A paper comes out of a laser printer, and its printed surface is completely black. What is *most likely* the cause?
   a. The toner cartridge is seated improperly.
   b. The charge is too low on the drum.
   c. The laser is defective.
   d. The fuser is overheating the paper.

10. A laser printer prints a page, and the document smears when touched. What is the *most likely* cause of the image smear?
    a. The primary corona is defective.
    b. The transfer corona is defective.
    c. The toner is damp.
    d. The fuser is defective.

Suggested Laboratory Activities

Do not attempt any suggested laboratory activities without your instructor's permission. Certain activities can render the PC operating system inoperable.

1. Install and set up a local printer.

2. Practice downloading a printer driver.

3. Set up a printer to print to paper in landscape orientation.

4. Send the same print job to a printer three or four times. Open the print queue window and look for a listing of files being printed. Stop the file printing process and purge the duplicate files.

5. Try printing to a printer while it is turned off and observe the error code.

6. Go to a major printer manufacturer's website and access information about how to care for the printer. What is the routine maintenance that should be performed?

7. Using a laser printer or inkjet that cannot be salvaged, carefully disassemble the printer and identify all the major parts. You may try to use the manufacturer's website to assist you. Do not be surprised if you cannot find information about the disassembly process. Usually, the manufacturer does not want persons who are not fully qualified to disassemble their printers.

8. Add memory to an existing printer. Go to the manufacturer's website for step-by-step instructions. Do *not* attempt to disassemble a working laser printer without instructions on how to access the memory chips. Attempting to access the memory chips without knowing how can result in damaging the printer's plastic assembly.

9. Draw out the step-by-step electrostatic printing process. When presented, this is one of the most commonly missed questions on the A+ Certification exams by PC technicians.

10. Go to the HP website and download a list of common error codes associated with an HP4L printer.

11. Go to a major printer manufacturer and obtain a copy of a toner MSDS. Look over the sheet to see what precautions are recommended when handling toner.

Laptops and Mobile Devices

12

After studying this chapter, you will be able to:

- Compare and contrast laptops, tablets, and smartphones.
- Identify portable PC parts.
- Use Windows **Power Options** to configure power management features.
- Compare and contrast mobile operating systems.
- Identify the features of Windows Mobility Center.
- Compare and contrast the IEEE 802.11 standards.
- Compare and contrast methods of securing mobile devices.
- Identify the ways data can be transferred between a mobile device and a full-size PC.
- Carry out a laptop upgrade.
- Use common laptop troubleshooting practices to evaluate and repair a faulty laptop.
- Carry out a laptop disassembly.
- Use common preventive maintenance tips to maintain a laptop.

A+ Exam—Key Points

The CompTIA A+ exam has many questions relating to mobile computing devices. You need to be prepared to answer questions related to mobile device connectivity, synchronization, remote backup services, and securing mobile devices.

Key Terms

The following key terms will become important pieces of your computer vocabulary. Be sure you can define them.

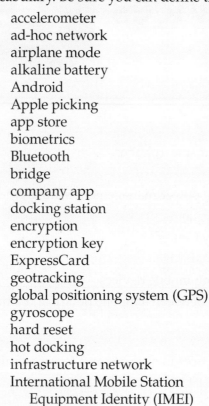

accelerometer
ad-hoc network
airplane mode
alkaline battery
Android
Apple picking
app store
biometrics
Bluetooth
bridge
company app
docking station
encryption
encryption key
ExpressCard
geotracking
global positioning system (GPS)
gyroscope
hard reset
hot docking
infrastructure network
International Mobile Station
    Equipment Identity (IMEI)

iOS
jailbreaking
lithium-ion (Li-ion) battery
lithium-ion polymer (Li-poly)
    battery
multi-touch
nickel-cadmium (NiCd) battery
nickel-metal hydride (NiMH)
    battery
passcode lock
PCMCIA card
port replicator
remote wipe
rooting
security key
security set identifier (SSID)
smart card
subscriber identity module (SIM)
synchronization
TouchFLO
Windows CE
Windows RT
wireless access point (WAP)

The portable PC is a computer that is designed to go wherever the user needs it. There are a variety of portable PCs on the market. They go by names such as laptops, notebooks, tablets, and smartphones. All modern portable PCs are battery-powered devices that use some type of flat-panel screen technology to keep weight and power consumption to a minimum. For this chapter, we will consider laptops as compact portable desktop devices and consider tablets and smartphones as mobile devices, **Figure 12-1**.

Portable PCs generally have computing power equal to full-size PCs; although, they are more expensive than the equivalent full-size model. However, as their numbers have increased, their price per unit has come down. When electronic devices are manufactured in limited numbers and with the latest technology, the prices are always higher. The classic electronic calculator is an excellent example. The first calculators, which provided only basic mathematical functions, cost

Figure 12-1. The three commonly-encountered portable devices used for computing are laptops, tablets, and smartphones.

Goodheart-Willcox Publisher

$325 or more. Now, a small-size calculator, which can perform nearly any desired mathematical function, preprogram math formulas, and plot graphs on an LCD screen, can be purchased for much less. This same trend is in progress with portable electronic devices such as tablets and smartphones.

Many of the technologies directly related to laptop and mobile devices, such as networking, security, modems, email, and cloud services, are covered in detail later in the textbook.

Mobile Devices

Mobile devices, such as tablets and smartphones, are simply smaller computers as compared to desktops and laptops. Mobile devices are designed to be lightweight and compact and Internet ready wherever you are at in the world. There are many unique features associated with mobile devices that make them quite different than their desktop counterparts, for example, the use of accelerometer and gyroscope technology. First, let's consider the differences between mobile devices and laptops.

Laptop and Mobile Device Comparison

To better understand the difference between a mobile device and a laptop, look at the following comparison chart.

	Laptop	Tablet	Smartphone
CPU	High performance	Low performance	Low performance
Hard drive	Yes	No	No
Storage size	Large (500 MB or more)	Small	Smallest
Optical read/write device	Yes	No	No
Standard keyboard	Yes	Yes/No	No
Repair/replace parts	Yes	No	No
Upgrade	Yes	No or limited	No

Tech Tip   You may encounter the terms *palmtop* and *netbook*, which are also used to describe small mobile devices.

Laptops have CPUs that are capable of supporting intense software applications such as 3D games, drawing programs, and office suites. Tablets and smartphones cannot support intensive software applications. The CPU in tablets and smartphones are RISC processors and are typically soldered permanently into the device circuit board. The CPU is not upgradable or replaceable in a mobile device such as a tablet or smartphone.

Laptops commonly have 500 MB and more of storage space and have either hard drives or Solid-State Drives (SSDs), or a combination of both. Tablets and smartphones have much less storage space as compared to laptops. They have no traditional disk drive system. Instead, they have flash memory chips embedded into the motherboard. Since the storage space is limited, mobile devices often augment storage space by using flash drives, Secure Digital (SD) cards, and cloud storage.

Figure 12-2 is a screen capture of an Android tablet file directory. Mobile devices typically have a very simple directory structure because of limited storage space. The device in Figure 12-2 is using an SD card and a flash drive.

CD, DVD, and Blu-ray Disc devices are common for laptops but physically impossible to design as an internal device for tablets and smartphones.

All laptops have standard keyboards while tablets and smartphones do not because of their physical size limitations. Tablets and smartphones generally use an on-screen keyboard simulator. Tablets can also have optional peripheral equipment added, such as a standard keyboard. The standard keyboard peripheral is added to the device usually by Wi-Fi, Bluetooth, or mini-USB connection.

Laptops have many parts that can be easily replaced, such as hard drives, Solid-State Drives, batteries, and memory. Tablet and smartphone replacement parts are almost non-existent. Typically, tablets or smartphones need to be exchanged or sent back to the manufacturer for repair.

Figure 12-2. Android tablet file directory. Tablets have limited storage, but additional storage space can be provided through flash drives, Secure Digital (SD) cards, and cloud storage.

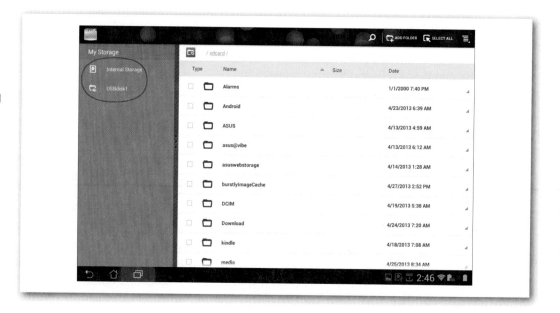

The overall advantage of tablets over laptops is they are lightweight and use less electrical energy, so they can typically perform for longer periods of time as compared to a laptop. The tablet is best for mobile users who want to use applications for Internet surfing, email, chat, social media applications, and games. Mobile devices are not designed for CPU-intensive software applications such as computer aided design (CAD), webpage design, and 3D game playing and design.

As electronic components evolve and become more and more compact and powerful, the distinction between tablets and laptops will blur. Today's average laptops are more powerful than the average desktops of five to six years ago. No doubt, the tablets of the future will become as powerful as laptops are today, **Figure 12-3**.

Figure 12-3. An Acer tablet running the Android operating system.

Goodheart-Willcox Publisher

Accelerometer and Gyroscope

Accelerometer and gyroscope technology provide the means of input for a mobile device based on changes in physical position. A mobile device equipped with accelerometer and gyroscope can produce the same effects as a joystick does for a desktop or laptop computer. The mobile device itself becomes an input device.

In electronics terminology, an **accelerometer** is an electromechanical device that measures acceleration forces. A **gyroscope** measures the vertical and horizontal orientation. Together, these two electronic devices provide data related not only to speed but also to the physical orientation of a device. These two technologies are the magic behind many interactive games. For example, a device with an accelerometer allows the user to move the device like a steering wheel in a driving software application.

Global Positioning System

The **global positioning system (GPS)** was developed by the Department of Defense (DoD) and relies on a series of satellites in geocentric orbit. A geocentric orbit is when satellites are set at an altitude that matches the rotation of the earth. The altitude to achieve geocentric orbit is approximately 22,369 miles (36,000 kilometers) from the Earth's surface, according to NASA. By matching the rotation of the earth, the satellite is always above the exact same spot on earth. These satellites are the reference points used to find the location of a GPS-enabled device. A radio wave is transmitted to and from a group of satellites. The time it takes for the radio wave to travel between three or more satellites and the GPS device is measured. The GPS-enabled device uses the measurements between the device and the three satellites to calculate the exact location of the GPS-enabled device. The location is expressed in longitude and latitude coordinates. The longitude and latitude coordinates are then plotted on a digital map such as Google Maps.

Geotracking is when a device is tracked by another device. For example, you can track the location of a mobile device and display the location on a map. This option is used to locate friends, children, and even lost mobile devices.

Cloud Services

Cloud services are computer services such as storage and application software from a remote location on the Internet. Cloud storage services provide a way for mobile devices with limited physical storage space to store data such as documents, photos, music, and videos. The mobile device can access the cloud storage from anywhere in the world as long as Internet service is available. For example, Google Cloud Storage is compatible with Android, iPhone, BlackBerry, and Windows phone.

Another great feature is that data on most cloud storage locations are automatically backed up. If you lose your phone or tablet, a copy of your work still exists on the cloud. When you replace your device, you can access your data on the cloud.

Limited storage on mobile devices is one of the driving forces supporting cloud services. Cloud services are offered by Google, Microsoft, Apple, ASUS, and a wide assortment of other laptop, smartphones, and tablet manufacturers and camera companies. Cloud storage services can augment computer storage. **Figure 12-4** shows a

screen capture of Google Drive. Google Drive is a cloud service that automatically synchronizes documents and more between multiple devices.

App Distribution

An **app store** is a location that provides software applications for portable devices such as smartphones and tablets. Apple App Store, Amazon Appstore for Android, Microsoft Store, and Google Play for Android, are just a few of the many app distribution services available.

Applications are written for specific operating systems. For example, an Apple app is designed to run only on Apple products, not Android. Android applications are designed to run only on Android products. The same is for Microsoft apps. Users will "jailbreak" an operating system to allow it to run other applications.

Bluetooth Standard

Bluetooth is the name of a standard developed for short-range radio links between portable computers, mobile phones, and other portable devices. The standard was created by many of the world's leaders in mobile computing equipment. It is a royalty-free standard enabling major manufacturers to develop compatible equipment. PCs, personal digital assistants (PDAs), and mobile phones using the Bluetooth standard are able to communicate with one another. A small transmitter and receiver are incorporated into the devices. They transmit data and commands on a 2.45-GHz radio band. Bluetooth standards support data transfer speeds as high as 1 Mbps. Actual speed, however, is 700 kbps to 800 kbps. The Bluetooth classifications are the following:

- **Class 1:** 100 meters or 300 feet range. Used primarily in industry.
- **Class 2:** 10 meters or 33 feet range. Most commonly found in mobile devices.
- **Class 3:** 1 meter or 3 feet range.

Connecting a Bluetooth device to a computer or mobile device is referred to as pairing. Typically, you simply press a button on one Bluetooth device, such as an earpiece, and the mobile device automatically connects another Bluetooth device, such as a smartphone, **Figure 12-5**. Sometimes you

Figure 12-4. Google provides cloud storage services that allow you to store documents and synchronize your devices.

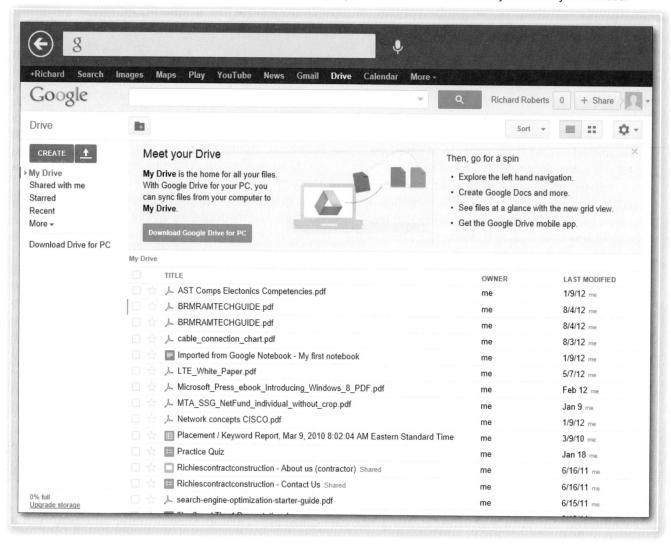

will need to enter a security pin which is usually only three or four digits in length.

There are some common problems encountered with Bluetooth and wireless devices such as no connection or intermittent connections. If you are experiencing no Bluetooth connection, check if the device has Bluetooth or wireless enabled. This is especially true for mobile devices because depending on the design, some are easily disabled unintentionally. Often you can avoid wireless and Bluetooth interference simply by moving to a new location, sometimes as short as a few feet. Intermittent connections are usually the result of interference or reaching the maximum distance that the connection can maintain. Some Bluetooth devices only have a range of a few feet.

Figure 12-5. A Bluetooth earpiece and microphone device can be paired to a mobile device that has Bluetooth enabled, such as a smartphone.

Goodheart-Willcox Publisher

Portable PC Parts

A portable PC functions very similarly to a full-size PC. However, alterations have been made to the design of the portable PC to allow it to be carried easily, used anywhere, and connected quickly to other PCs and networks. To allow this functionality, laptop computers are equipped with some parts that full-size PCs don't have (large storage batteries). Laptop computers also have had other common PC components altered significantly (such as the mouse). In addition, to keep laptops adaptable like their full-size counterparts, PCMCIA and ExpressCards were developed. PCMCIA and ExpressCards allow new devices to be added to laptops easily. However, USB ports have made PCMCIA and ExpressCard less common in new laptop models.

Batteries

Batteries are a vital part of portable computing, **Figure 12-6**. There are four major types of batteries found in use for portable computers:

- Alkaline.
- Nickel-cadmium (NiCd).
- Nickel-metal hydride (NiMH).
- Lithium-ion (Li-ion).

The type of battery is extremely important when selecting a portable PC. It determines the number of hours a PC can be used independently, and it also greatly affects the weight of the PC. All four types of batteries are rechargeable.

The **alkaline battery** is a common battery found in small devices such as TV remote controls and some of the older palmtops. They are not used much today with computers.

The **nickel-cadmium (NiCd) battery**, also called *NiCad* for short, was a standard, rechargeable computer battery used for many years. It is one of the least expensive batteries. However, NiCad has some drawbacks. NiCad batteries can take up to 12 hours to fully recharge. Also, older NiCad batteries are subject to a phenomenon known as *memory effect*. When NiCad battery-powered equipment is recharged before the battery is completely drained, the battery operates for a shorter time before it appears to be completely discharged. Batteries that are not fully drained cannot be fully recharged. They show a "memory" of previous use. For example, a battery should last four hours, but the equipment is only run for one hour and then recharged. With future uses, the battery appears completely drained after one hour. This is not a problem with today's batteries.

All batteries have limits to the number of recharges. For NiCad, the average number of recharges is approximately 1000. This number of recharges can last an average user up to 2 1/2 years. Cadmium is a very toxic material, which presents a problem with the disposal of spent batteries.

Figure 12-6.
This laptop battery is lithium-ion which is the most commonly encountered type of battery for mobile devices.

The **nickel-metal hydride (NiMH) battery** is a second generation of rechargeable battery used for portable computers. An improvement over the NiCad battery, the NiMH battery can store up to 50% more charge time than a NiCad battery. It does not have the memory effect problem, so it can be recharged anytime during its discharge cycle. The NiMH battery has a shorter number of total recharges then NiCad. It can usually only be recharged about 500 times.

The **lithium-ion (Li-ion) battery** has the highest electrical potential of all the batteries discussed here. As with NiMH batteries, lithium-ion batteries also do not suffer from a memory effect. Lithium-ion is both lightweight and compact, making it the most popular battery type used for laptop computers. Lithium-ion batteries contain no poisonous metals and are relatively safe for the environment. The only disadvantage to lithium-ion batteries is that they are more expensive than their counterparts.

The **lithium-ion polymer (Li-poly) battery** is the latest version of the lithium-ion class of battery which uses a polymer or polymer gel as the electrolyte. They are also known as *Li-po* or *Li-poly* batteries. Lithium-ion polymer can be made much thinner than when using a thin metal foil case. The polymer version is very popular for mobile devices such as smartphones because it can be fabricated thin and lightweight. The disadvantage is that it cannot support high current. Thus, it cannot be used to power equipment that requires a lot of electrical power.

Most rechargeable batteries are regulated because of the hazardous waste materials they contain. The exact method of disposal varies according to local government authority such as cities, counties, state, and the federal government. Almost all states have adopted their own set of guidelines that exceed the federal regulations. Following is a list of common battery types and why they can be dangerous:

- **NiCad batteries:** NiCad batteries contain the toxic metal cadmium.
- **Mercury batteries:** Mercury batteries contain the toxic metal mercury.
- **Lithium-ion batteries:** Lithium-ion batteries contain lithium, which is highly reactive with water. (Not all lithium-ion batteries are considered a waste hazard.)

- **Lead-acid and lead-gel batteries:** These batteries contain the toxic metal lead.

In most areas, there is a recycling facility that takes old batteries and either recycles them or sends them to another facility for recycling.

If a battery is rechargeable, it is usually recyclable. Do *not* attempt to disassemble a battery for recycling. It takes a highly-skilled and trained individual and special safety equipment to disassemble a battery for recycling.

> **Warning !**
> - *Never* attempt to incinerate a battery.
> - Never attempt to solder wire leads to a battery.
> - *Never* short circuit (connect the positive and negative terminal with a wire or any conductive material) a battery. Batteries can explode or catch fire.
> - *Never* puncture, crush, or physically damage a battery. Some battery vapors are hazardous.

As a PC technician, you and your company will encounter more than the average number of recyclable batteries. You must adhere to all laws and regulations when disposing of batteries. The regulations vary according to the amount of batteries accumulated over a set period.

Docking Station

A **docking station** is an electronic cradle that provides power for a laptop, allowing users to turn the laptop into a full-size PC. The laptop slides into the docking station and snaps into place. Once in place, the laptop can operate from the power provided by the docking station rather than from a battery or a battery charger. Some docking stations contain slots for expansion devices and bays for additional storage devices. Many times, the docking station automatically connects the laptop to the company network or the Internet.

Docking stations essentially allow users to turn their laptops into full-size PCs when portability is not necessary. By connecting to the docking station, you can easily connect a full-size keyboard, mouse, or other less portable equipment to your laptop.

Normally, a portable computer needs to have the desired configuration identified while docking or undocking. For example, a laptop is equipped with an LCD screen but a docking station may use a CRT screen as a display. When the laptop is connected to the docking station, the video must be configured for the CRT display. When the laptop is removed from the docking station, it must be reconfigured for the LCD screen. Windows XP and later automatically configures the laptop video. Windows XP introduced a feature called hot docking. The **hot docking** feature allows users to dock or undock their laptop computer without the need to change hardware configurations. Windows XP and later automatically detects when a portable computer is placed into or removed from a docking station.

Keyboard

A digital keyboard on the display is used to enter text into a mobile device. Most mobile devices are also equipped with a voice-recognition app. Look closely at the top right corner of **Figure 12-7**, and you will notice a symbol of a microphone. When the microphone is selected, you can simply talk to the device and your voice will be converted to text. The voice-to-text feature

is not always accurate, and a virtual keyboard is still often required to enter the correct text.

Look at **Figure 12-8** and you will see a tablet equipped with an optional keyboard. The keyboard is actually a docking station designed to work with this particular tablet. In addition to providing a keyboard for user input, it also provides a touch pad. Additional features of the docking unit are USB port, Secure Digital (SD) card reader, and a 40-pin proprietary port used for charging the battery and synchronizing the tablet with a PC. **Synchronization** is the act of matching data between two devices. When used for synchronizing, the cable is disconnected from the 120-Vac plug (charger). The end of the cable that plugs into the charger has a USB plug. The USB plug is used to connect to a PC while the 40-pin plug at the other end of the cable is used for the tablet.

Compare the ASUS tablet in **Figure 12-9** with the same ASUS tablet in Figure 12-8, which is equipped with a keyboard accessory. Notice how the screen information is displayed vertically no matter which way the physical screen is turned. This is an example of the gyroscope working inside the tablet to maintain the same view no matter which way the tablet is turned.

Figure 12-7.
A virtual keyboard can be used to enter text on a mobile device.

Figure 12-8. The ASUS tablet is equipped with an optional keyboard. The keyboard is actually a docking station. After the tablet is docked into the keyboard docking station it resembles a laptop.

Goodheart-Willcox Publisher

Figure 12-9. A typical ASUS tablet without attached keyboard.

Goodheart-Willcox Publisher

Tablets can be made so thin that they cannot accommodate ports the way a laptop does. A keyboard accessory provides a standard-size USB port as well as a flash card port. The keyboard is also equipped with a small, flat rechargeable battery, which provides additional electrical power for the tablet.

Multiple Screens

Mobile devices are small by nature, and as a result, a user can have difficulty viewing the contents of the display. You can connect a second monitor to your Windows computer if the video card supports such a feature. All laptops and most portable devices do support a second monitor, but not all. In **Figure 12-10** you can see the options to duplicate or extend the monitor as well as use a projector with the device.

A shortcut key combination to access the external display is [Windows logo key] [P]. After using the key combination, the **Screen Resolution** dialog box will appear and look similar to that in **Figure 12-11**. You can also access this dialog box through Control Panel.

Once the **Screen Resolution** dialog box is accessed, a second monitor can be detected and identified. Most times, the operating system will automatically detect the second monitor.

To configure a second display, you would open **Control Panel** and then select **Adjust Screen Resolution** located under the **Appearance and Personalization** category. This path is the same for Windows Vista, Windows 7, and Windows 8. For Windows XP, open **Control Panel**, select **Appearance and Themes**, and then select **Display**.

> ## A+ Note
>
> The CompTIA A+ exam often asks for the correct path to detecting an external display.

Once you have made sure that your video card can support a second monitor, follow these steps to add the additional monitor:

1. Turn off your computer and monitor.
2. Connect the second monitor to the unused video port.

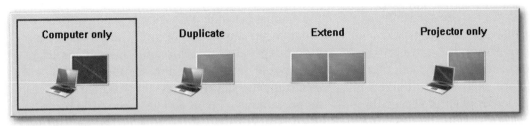

Figure 12-10.
Laptops and mobile devices are designed to duplicate the display, extend the display, or easily connect to a projector.

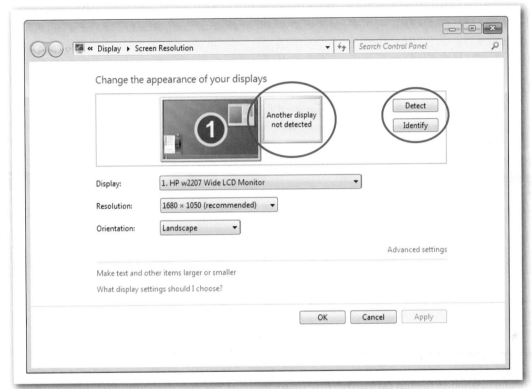

Figure 12-11.
Windows **Screen Resolution** dialog box. Notice the **Detect** and **Identify** buttons, which automatically detect and identify a second monitor.

3. Plug the second monitor into an electrical power source and turn it on.
4. Turn on your original monitor and computer. Windows should automatically detect the second monitor. You may be prompted to install driver software for the monitor. If you cannot connect to a projector or second display, do the following:

- Make sure the monitor or projector is turned on and plugged into the correct video port on your computer.
- Make sure you have selected the correct video input port on the second monitor or projector. Many display devices such as televisions have options for multiple inputs and must be selected through a remote control or buttons located on the display device.

- As always, check the manual for the monitor or projector. You can download the manual from the manufacturer's website.

Port Replicator

A **port replicator** is an external computer device that provides additional ports to be used by a computer system. The most common computer systems to use a port replicator are notebook computers and other portable devices. Portable devices typically have a very limited number of ports available due to their compact design. For the same reason, it is often difficult or impossible to add additional ports by using expansion cards. Adding a PCI card to a laptop or tablet is not a practical solution. A port replicator solves the problem of adding additional ports.

A port replicator allows for the addition of devices such as a printer, camera, joystick, external CD or DVD drive, monitor, extra hard drive, external modem, scanner, keyboard, mouse, or any other digital device used by a full-size PC. In many ways, the port replicator serves the same function as a docking station. The use of a port replicator is not limited to just small digital devices. You can also use a port replicator to add additional ports that are not usually found on a typical computer, such as SCSI ports. It is also important to note that a USB hub designed to add additional USB ports can also be classified as a port replicator.

Portable Motherboards

Portable PC motherboards do not follow a standard form factor, **Figure 12-12**. The form factors are proprietary. To help keep the PCs small, most portable PCs incorporate the processor directly into the motherboard. The processor is often purposely set to run at a lower speed than it is capable of if installed in a full-size PC. The reason for the slower speed is to reduce heat in the portable PC. Portable PCs leave little room for cooling because of the compact design. They incorporate large, flat heat sinks inside the case, but there is not sufficient room for a full-size cooling fan.

Touch Pads

Laptops today come with touch pads, **Figure 12-13**. Touch pads are also referred to as *trackpads*. Touch pads are a standard feature for most laptop computers. The touch pad works on the same principles as a touch screen.

Figure 12-12.
Laptops, such as this unit, have the same internal components as full-size PCs. However, the layout of a laptop is very different to keep size and weight down.

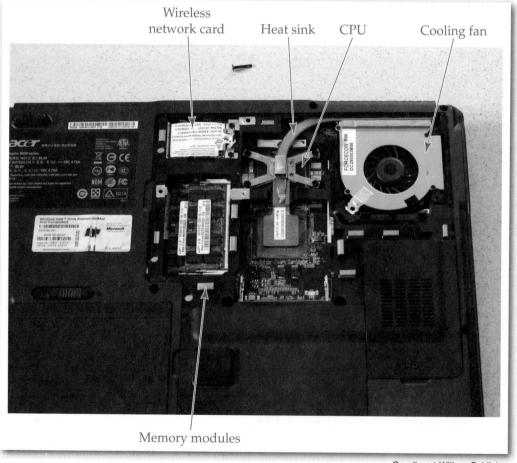

Goodheart-Willcox Publisher

Figure 12-13. A touch pad is an input device that serves the same function as a mouse.

Goodheart-Willcox Publisher

Touch Screens

Tablets and smartphones use touch-technology for the user interface, **Figure 12-14**. A touch screen reacts to a person's touch or gestures to launch apps (applications) or navigate the directory structure. Tapping on any of the application icons launches a particular app. The screen can zoom in or out by using figure gestures such as pinching two fingers together or spreading them apart. Using two or more fingers to zoom in or out is a form of multi-touch action. **Multi-touch** describes the action of touching any surface-sensing device, such as a tablet touch screen or touch pad, with two or more fingers. Finger gestures can also be used to open or close an application, perform scrolling, flip or rotate windows, and more.

TouchFLO is another term used in similar fashion as multi-touch. It was first introduced with the HTC corporation smartphones interface. The objects on the display move according to the direction a finger is moved across the display surface.

Most mobile devices require calibration. Input devices such as pen, stylus, or speech require some calibration because each user is unique. **Figure 12-15** shows **Pen and Touch** dialog boxes used to calibrate an input stylus for a drawing tablet. The first dialog box, Figure 12-15A, configures the input pen or stylus. The second, Figure 12-15B, configures pen or stylus gestures. The last, Figure 12-15C, calibrates handwriting. Together, these three windows are used to configure and calibrate the gestures and handwriting of the individual user.

Infrared Devices

Data can be transferred between computer devices using infrared beams of light. This was once a common way to transfer data, but today it has limited application. Infrared was used to transfer data from full-size PCs to laptops or mobile devices and vice versa. The infrared beam of light is broadcast from an infrared transmitter

Figure 12-14. The Android tablet, as well as other Android mobile devices, uses a touch screen as the user interface.

Figure 12-15. Windows 7 **Pen and Touch** dialog box. A—**Pen Options** tab. B—**Flicks** tab. C—**Handwriting** tab.

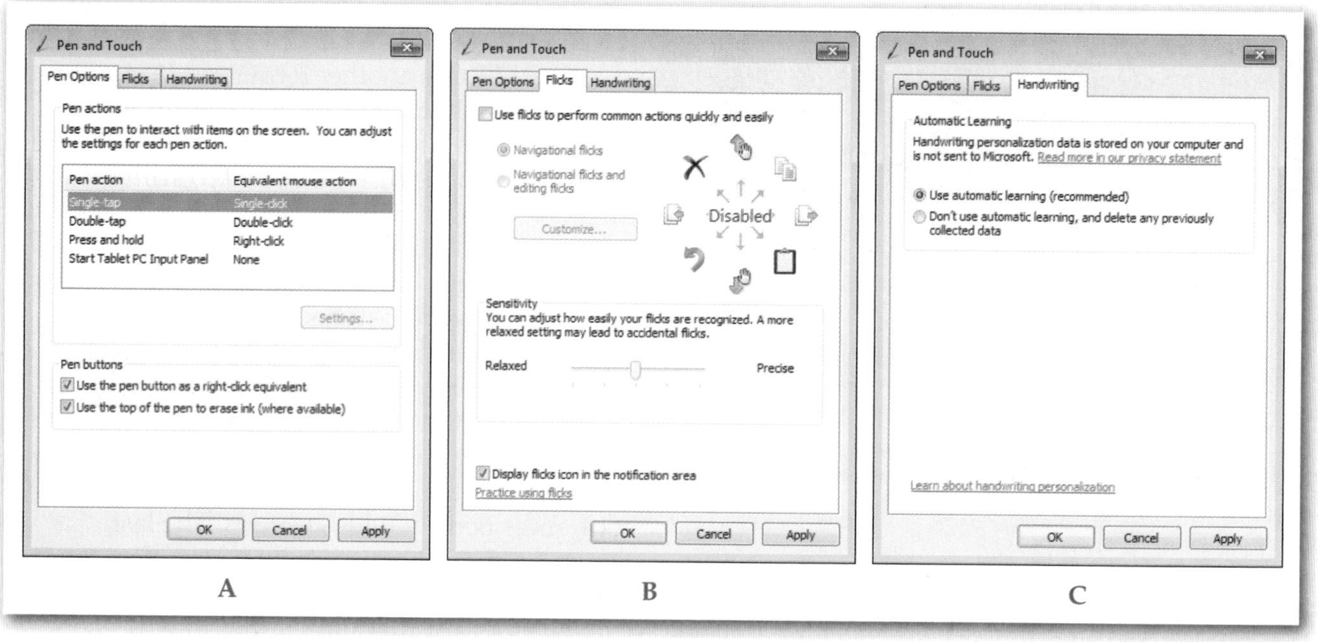

A   B   C

located on one PC to another PC. Infrared ports can also transmit to other equipment, such as a printer. Today, infrared transfer is seldom encountered because most portable devices are equipped with Bluetooth and Wi-Fi abilities. Wi-Fi and Bluetooth outperform infrared and do not require direct line of sight to work.

The infrared port is sometimes referred to as an *IrDA transceiver port*. The IrDA stands for Infrared Data Association, a group responsible for a set of standards for infrared data transmission. The term *transceiver* is used because it implies a device that cannot only transmit a signal but can also receive a signal. Think of *transceiver* as a combination of the words *transmit* and *receive*.

Printers and many other devices that are not designed with infrared ports can be modified to accept the infrared signals. An infrared port can be added to existing equipment typically through a USB port.

The infrared light beam is pulsed in patterns representing the data transferred. Transfer rates as high as 115 kbps are typical through a standard serial port. Speeds as high as 4 Mbps can be achieved going directly to and from infrared transceivers.

PCMCIA Cards

The Personal Computer Memory Card International Association (PCMCIA) designed a set of standards for adding memory and expanding a portable PC through the use of devices resembling thick credit cards. These cards are called PCMCIA cards. A **PCMCIA card** is designed to add memory or expand a portable PC. The PCMCIA card is often referred to as simply a *PCM* or *PC card*. It is installed in a PCMCIA slot on the side of the portable PC. These slots are used in place of expansion slots as the way to install additional devices. As with USB connections, many PCMCIA cards are hot swappable (can be swapped without powering off the computer).

All PCMCIA cards have the same rectangular (85.6 mm by 54 mm) shape, but they vary in thickness, **Figure 12-16.** Their thickness classifies the cards. There are three classifications of cards:

- **Type I:** 3.3 mm thick. These cards are used primarily to add memory to the portable PC.
- **Type II:** 5.0 mm thick. These cards are usually used to add modems and network cards to the portable PC. The cards are equipped with either RJ-11 or RJ-45 connectors. The RJ connectors look like telephone jacks.

Figure 12-16. A PCMCIA wireless network card.

Goodheart-Willcox Publisher

Figure 12-17. An ExpressCard wireless network card.

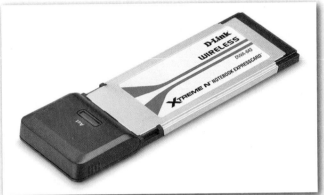

D-Link

- **Type III:** 10.5 mm thick. These cards are designed to support hard drives or to support external CD, DVD, or tape drives.

There is a selection of slots to go with the cards. A Type I slot can hold one Type I card. Type II slots can hold one Type II card or two Type I cards. Type III slots can hold one Type III card or one Type I card and one Type II card. All of the smaller cards fit into larger slots on their own.

Type IV cards are in the works, but they have not been ratified by the PCMCIA consortium at this time. Type IV cards are expected to be 16 mm thick. They will be used for large-capacity hard drives.

ExpressCards

The **ExpressCard** is rapidly replacing the PCMCIA card as the choice for laptop computers because it can achieve high data rates, **Figure 12-17**. ExpressCards can be used for modems, analog and digital television tuners, wireless network cards, exterior SATA connections, and to expand the PCIe bus to connect other devices.

The card is available in two widths: 34 mm and 54 mm. Examine **Figure 12-18** to see what each width looks like. The exact choice of width is based on the type of device the card incorporates.

ExpressCards are designed to connect internally to the USB 2.0 bus, USB 3.0 bus, or the PCIe bus. When using the USB 2.0 bus, the data rate for the ExpressCard is 480 Mbps. It is approximately 5 Gbps for USB 3.0.

Wireless Devices

Most laptops come with a wireless device incorporated into the motherboard or as an add-on. The exact type of wireless technology will vary. When the wireless device is not already incorporated into a laptop, a PCMCIA card, an ExpressCard, or a USB device is used to provide wireless network support.

Special Function Keys

Portable PCs typically have special keyboards not found on the standard keyboard associated with desktop PCs. The keyboards are made very compact and also incorporate special function keys typically associated with laptop needs.

The special function keys typically are activated by pressing the [Fn] key in combination with other function keys identified in blue, **Figure 12-19**. The [Fn] key in Figure 12-19A is positioned on the left side of the keyboard. The function keys in Figure 12-19B are positioned on the right side of the keyboard. These function keys share the key space with the arrow keys. Other special function keys are located along the top or along the right side of the keyboard.

Many times a new laptop user will inadvertently hit a combination of keys which causes unexpected results while typing a document. They may turn off the sound, put the laptop in sleep mode, change the brightness of the display, automatically connect or disconnect from the Internet, and more. The user may make the same mistake several times, causing the user to

Figure 12-18.
ExpressCards come in two widths: 34 mm and 54 mm.

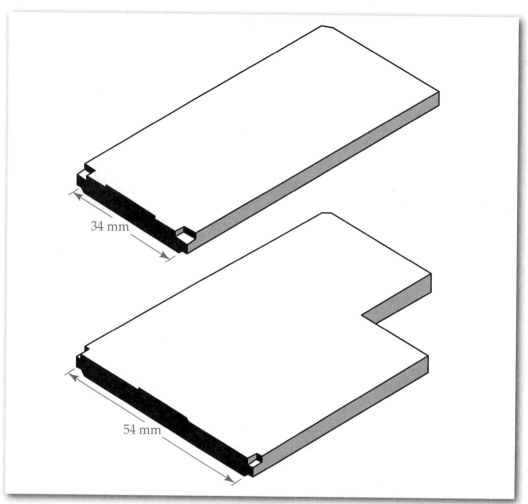

34 mm

54 mm

Figure 12-19. To access special laptop functions, simultaneously press the [Fn] key and the desired function key. A—The [Fn] key. B—Function keys.

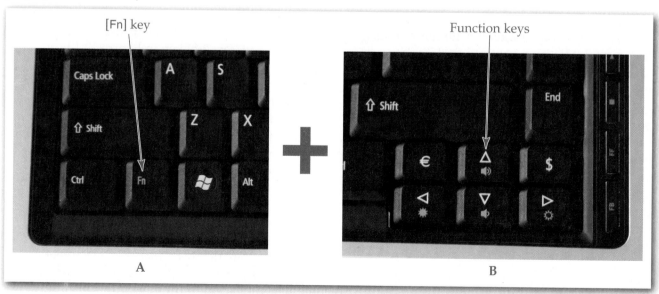

think that something is wrong with the laptop. At times, a new user will repeatedly make the same mistake and think the laptop has a virus. The user calls tech support to resolve the problem, and if misdiagnosed, the laptop may be packaged and sent to a repair depot needlessly.

In addition to special function keys, many laptops have physical switches that control wireless access, Internet access, sound, and more. The switches can be placed along the top of the keyboard or along the outside edge of the laptop. The problem with physical switches along the outside edge of laptop computers is that they can be switched off accidentally, for example, while being placed into a backpack. The accidental moving of the switch to an off position can confuse the user and cause them to think they have a problem with the laptop operating system or some component such as the wireless card.

Power Management

Power management is a very important aspect of laptop computers. Configuring the power management incorrectly can reduce the battery power length of time considerably. The power management configuration reduces the amount of power used by the three major power consumption devices: display, CPU, and hard drive.

APM and ACPI

Automatic Power Management (APM) and Automatic Configuration and Power Interface (ACPI) are industry standards for automatically configuring power on portable devices. The difference is APM was first available in Windows 95 and was incorporated as a BIOS configuration option to conserve electrical power. The simple APM design powered down the computer after a predetermined amount of inactivity. It also included a suspend or sleep switch typically located at the front of the computer case. APM was enabled by default and could not be accessed directly by the operating system. APM is no longer used.

ACPI replaced APM as a natural evolution in power management. It was first introduced in Windows NT and Windows 98 operating

systems. ACPI has many more advanced options not found in the original APM. ACPI is not limited to managing power consumed by the display and CPU. ACPI can manage the power of any hardware device added to a computer. For example, it can power down a device that is not being used after a short period of time, such as a modem, wireless card, or network card. It also includes features to awaken or bring devices automatically out of the power-down state when needed. For example, a network card in a sleep state can be awakened by network activity directed to that particular network card while ignoring all other network activity.

ACPI also provides a feature referred to as soft-off which allows the computer to be turned off by the software. Previous to this add-on feature, the computer had to be manually turned off with a switch. Some companies did design a proprietary soft-off switch before the ACPI standard. Another feature of ACPI is support for a switch that can be used to place the computer automatically in sleep mode. All the features associated with ACPI are controlled by the BIOS. The configuration is stored in CMOS. ACPI allows the operating system to directly control the power configuration features. Microsoft has incorporated energy configuration features in all their products.

> **Tech Tip**
> Power management is not limited to portable devices. Desktop systems also have power management configuration options to conserve electrical energy.

Windows Vista and Later Power Management Options

Microsoft Vista and later power management options are based on preconfigured power plans, or power profiles. The power plans are a way to choose between long battery life and computer performance. They are located in **Control Panel | Hardware and Sound | Power Options**.

See **Figure 12-20**. Notice that there are three power plans available in Windows Vista and later: balanced, power saver, and high performance. The *balanced power* plan equally emphasizes battery

Figure 12-20.
Windows 7 **Power Options** dialog box.

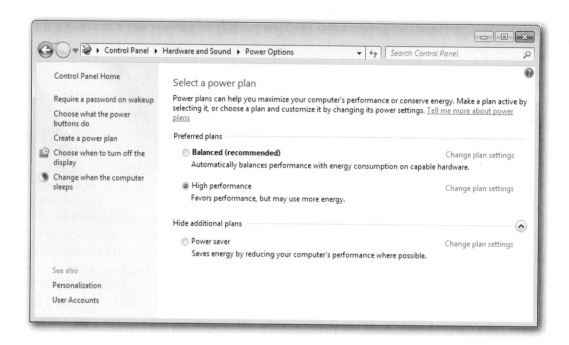

conservation and system performance. The *power saver* plan slows the performance of the CPU and lowers the backlighting of the LCD display. Both actions save considerable electrical energy. High performance sacrifices battery life but allows for top computer performance. Best performance is often required for intense activities such as viewing movies, playing graphic-intense computer games, and editing photos.

Other power management features allow you to configure the power buttons and password protection. The settings for these features are located in **Control Panel | Hardware and Sound | Power Options | System Settings**.

See **Figure 12-21**. Notice that you can select how the laptop will react when the power button or the sleep button is pressed or when the laptop lid is closed. The options for each are **Do nothing**, **Sleep**, **Hibernate**, and **Shut down**. The **Do nothing** and **Shut down** options are straightforward. They should need no further explanation, but **Sleep** and **Hibernate** do require some explanation.

The **Sleep** option saves all documents and folders that are in use at the time sleep is invoked. When the computer is awakened, the same open files automatically reappear on the desktop. Sleep mode has very little drain on laptop battery.

The **Hibernate** option saves your open files and current work to the hard drive, and when the PC is awakened, it reopens the files and current work. The hibernate mode uses less battery life than sleep mode. The main difference between sleep mode and hibernate mode is where the open files and current work are saved. Sleep mode saves the files and current work in RAM, and hibernate mode saves the files and current work to the hard drive. Hibernate mode takes longer to recover from than sleep mode because sleep mode stores the files in RAM. Open files and work can be lost when a laptop is placed in sleep mode and the power is disconnected, such as when removing the battery or during battery failure with no ac plugged in. In Figure 12-21, notice that each of the selections is correlated to when the laptop is supplied battery power or ac power.

Tech Tip

Some computers have a hybrid sleep feature that saves working files to both RAM and the hard drive while in sleep mode. The computer still has fast recovery when awakened and also has protection against data loss due to lost power or battery failure. Hybrid sleep requires a BIOS that supports this feature.

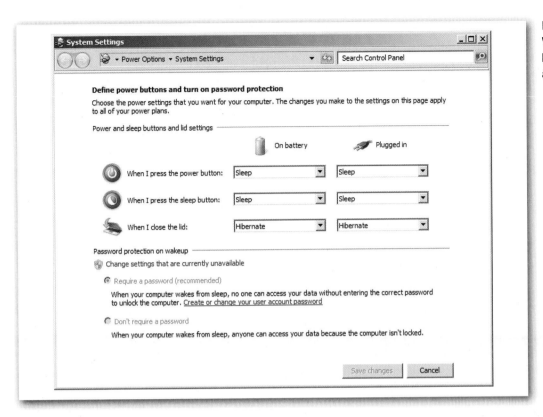

Figure 12-21.
Windows 7 power button, sleep button, and lid settings.

Another Windows power management feature is password protection. Password protection is provided as an option for scenarios such as when closing the lid of the laptop and leaving the area. Anyone could awaken the laptop from sleep mode by simply opening the lid of the laptop. The password option is used to ensure security against unauthorized access to the laptop. When the password option is configured, the computer requires the password to be entered after bringing the computer out of sleep mode.

The main reason for a power management option not to be available is a BIOS or hardware device that does not support that feature. For example, an older video card may not allow the **Sleep** option to be selected because the software drivers do not support sleep mode.

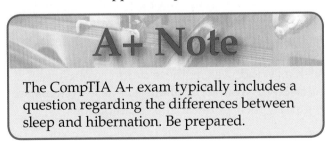

A+ Note

The CompTIA A+ exam typically includes a question regarding the differences between sleep and hibernation. Be prepared.

Windows XP Power Management Options

Windows XP power management options are quite a different layout when compared to those in Windows Vista. Look at **Figure 12-22**. Notice that Windows XP includes a hibernate feature (under the **Hibernate** tab). The Windows XP hibernate feature provides the same effect on the system as the Windows Vista hibernate feature. Also, power schemes in Windows XP are similar to Windows Vista power plans in that they are preconfigured power configurations.

Mobile Operating Systems

Laptops use standard operating systems just like desktops, but mobile devices such as tablets and smartphones require special operating systems. The operating systems used on mobile devices are very compact and provide minimal software applications referred to as apps. There are many operating systems designed for mobile devices, but the two dominate mobile operating systems are Android and iOS. Mobile operating

Figure 12-22. Windows XP **Power Options Properties** dialog box.

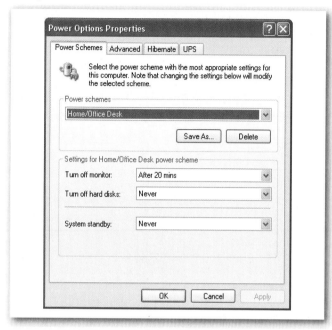

systems are designed to be much more compact than traditional operating systems. They are designed this way because mobile devices have limited hardware abilities. A desktop PC or laptop has much better performance in comparison to a mobile device. Desktops and even laptops can have very powerful CPUs, large amounts of memory, large hard drive storage, and powerful graphics processors. Mobile devices have much more conservative hardware. They are designed to consume as little electrical power as possible while still maintaining some decent performance.

iOS

All Apple devices run the proprietary mobile operating system **iOS**. The iOS is used on Apple iPhone, iPad, iPod touch, and other Apple products. Apple only allows iOS to be used on their mobile products. When iOS is used on other manufacturer's products such as smartphones, the iOS is not allowed to be customized. This is in sharp contrast to Android, which allows manufacturers to modify the code for the Android operating system.

Android

Android was originally developed by a company called Android Inc., which was bought by Google Inc. Google retained the name Android for the operating system. Android is derived from the Linux open source operating system. Open source means that the programming source code is not secret but freely available for viewing so that anyone can modify the code.

Android differs from Apple iOS in that different hardware manufacturers can customize Android to meet their individual needs. The developers for the various companies can customize Android for their particular device. For example, the Android operating system on a Samsung tablet does not exactly match the Android operating system installed on an ASUS tablet.

Windows RT

Windows RT is designed to run on the ARM processor. Windows RT is a lightweight version of Windows 8. It comes preinstalled on PCs and tablets that are powered by ARM processors. Windows RT is not available to the general public as a download for purchase.

Windows CE

Windows CE is designed as a compact Windows operating system to be used on devices that have limited hardware. The Windows CE program is similar in appearance to any of the Windows operating systems. It has a Control Panel and uses the registry system to control devices and users. Files and directories are arranged in the same way. Windows CE also supports a number of third-party software programs.

Windows CE is not just for computers. It is also installed in some stereos, telephones, and other electronic items where programmable features such as memory storage are desired. When programmed through an operating system such as Windows CE, these units are often referred to as smart appliances. These systems are regularly incorporated into common toys.

Windows CE will not run correctly on a standard PC because it is designed to work on RISC processors. Remember from Chapter 4—CPU that a RISC (reduced instruction set computer) CPU is designed to run on a minimal instruction set. Windows CE is not designed to support graphics-intensive programs.

Microsoft has developed a stereo system for cars called AutoPC, which uses the Windows CE operating system. It is a voice-controlled car stereo that can check and read email, dial a cellular phone, and give directions to the driver's destination.

Windows Mobility Center

The Windows Mobility Center was introduced with Windows Vista. This feature contains a collection of the most common utilities and configurations used by laptops. **Figure 12-23** shows a typical **Windows Mobility Center** dialog box. As you can see, the most commonly used configurations are readily available, such as Volume, Battery Status, and Wireless Network. Configurations like Presentation Settings will not appear unless the computer has previously been configured for a projector. See **Figure 12-24** for a description of each feature.

The Brightness configuration controls the brightness of the LCD monitor. Often, computer hardware manufacturers modify the Windows Mobility Center to incorporate their own special mobile service.

Wireless Connections

A wireless connection is commonly used to connect a laptop or mobile device to a full-size PC or to join a small network. A wireless connection can be made using radio waves. A much more detailed description of wireless networking is covered later in this textbook. This section covers terminology related to wireless data transfer.

Ad-Hoc Network

When a wireless network is formed between two or more wireless devices, such as a workstation and a notebook, it is called an **ad-hoc network**, **Figure 12-25**. You can think of an ad-hoc network connection as a direct cable connection that uses radio waves as the connection media rather than cable.

Wireless Infrastructure Network

Another classification of wireless connection is called **infrastructure network**. An infrastructure network differs from an ad-hoc network in that it contains a wireless access point (WAP). A **wireless access point (WAP)** is a device that supports communications between wireless devices and a hard-wired network system, **Figure 12-26**. A wireless access point is often referred to as a bridge. A **bridge** is a device that is used to connect two dissimilar networks. In this example, the wireless access point is bridging the connection between the hard-wired network and the wireless network.

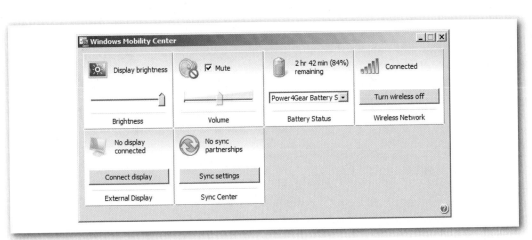

Figure 12-23. Windows 7 Mobility Center.

Figure 12-24. Common Windows Mobility Center features and their description.

Windows Mobility Center Feature	Description
Battery Status	Allows you to modify the battery usage by selecting a different power plan for the laptop.
Brightness	Controls the brightness of the LCD monitor.
External Display	Used to automatically set up a second or third display. An external display is often connected to a laptop PC via a cable or docking station.
Presentation Settings	Allows you to preconfigure presentation settings, such as the volume or which projector to use if more than one projector is typically connected. The projector can be automatically detected through a wizard, or you can enter the URL or a UNC address of the projector. After the presentation settings are configured, you can simply access the present configuration and start your presentation immediately without a further configuration.
Sync Center	Maintains the very latest version of a file or collection of files that are commonly transferred between the laptop and another device. This feature is only available in Windows Vista Business and Windows Vista Ultimate editions. Sync Center is short for Synchronize Center.
Volume	Allows you to adjust the portable laptop speaker volume.
Wireless Network	Displays the status of a wireless network connection. Also includes an option to enable and disable the wireless network adapter.

Goodheart-Willcox Publisher

Figure 12-25.
Some devices are connected together by radio waves in an ad-hoc network. An ad-hoc network can consist of 2 to 64 wireless devices.

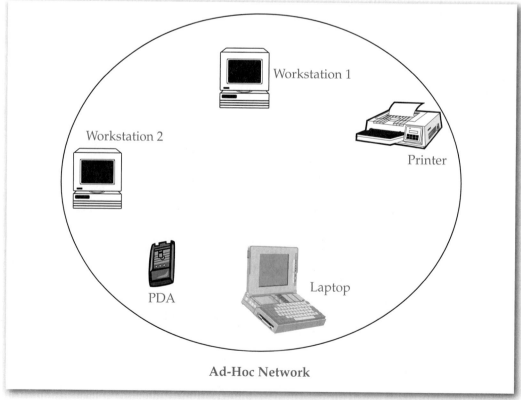

Goodheart-Willcox Publisher

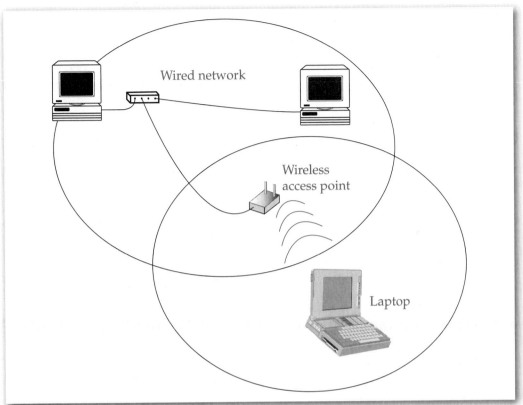

Goodheart-Willcox Publisher

Figure 12-26. A wireless access point acts as a bridge between the wireless device and the wired network system.

Radio Waves

Radio waves are used to deliver or exchange information all over the world. To prevent radio waves from interfering with each other, radio frequencies are regulated by the FCC. The FCC assigns specific radio frequencies to various types of equipment. For example, toy remote control cars are typically 27 MHz and 40 MHz. When you tune your car radio, you are actually selecting a radio frequency. When you select a radio station such as 104.5 FM, you are tuning the radio receiver to a transmitted carrier wave of 104.5 MHz. The carrier wave is a set frequency, which is used to carry the information from the transmitter to the receiver.

Radio Signal Interference

Radio signal interference is a radio wave transmission that corrupts a desired radio wave signal. Some common sources of wireless computer communication devices are wireless telephones, medical equipment, microwave ovens, and cell phones. While all electronic equipment generates some interference, these specific devices share the same radio wave frequencies that wireless network cards use, approximately 2.48 GHz. Other electrical devices and appliances containing electrical motors can also cause problems.

A wireless connection rated at 300 Mbps may actually be only 100 Mbps or as low as 1 Mbps or less. Another major factor that affects wireless communication is the distance between the source and destination. As the distance between the source and destination increases, the throughput decreases. This is because the greater the distance of the transmitted radio signal, the weaker the signal becomes. As the signal becomes weaker, it is more susceptible to radio interference.

On average, the maximum advertised distance for IEEE 802.11b wireless devices is approximately 250 meters indoors and 450 meters outdoors. There is no definitive maximum distance because of the variables that affect radio waves. Realistic distances for wireless transmissions will be much shorter distances than advertised because wireless systems rarely operate in ideal environments.

Another factor that affects radio signals is physical objects in the radio wave area. Objects placed directly between the source and destinations weaken the radio signal. The most common object that affects radio signals are building partitions, file cabinets, furniture, fireplaces, appliances, and similar objects. The density and material these objects are made from affect the signal. For example, a wall constructed of concrete block will weaken a signal more than a wall constructed of sheet rock. A metallic partition commonly used to create an office cubicle will block a radio signal. A wireless connection to exchange data directly between a notebook computer and a PC should not be affected by building structures. If you are using a notebook on a patio to access an Internet connection through a PC inside the home, the distance and building materials will affect the signal to a great extent. Windows and wireless device manufacturers have utilities that allow you to monitor the wireless network. **Figure 12-27** shows the strength of the wireless signal displayed as a bar graph. The speed of the data is also displayed as 39 Mbps.

Figure 12-27. Wireless Network Connection Status dialog box. The bar graph displays the strength of the signal.

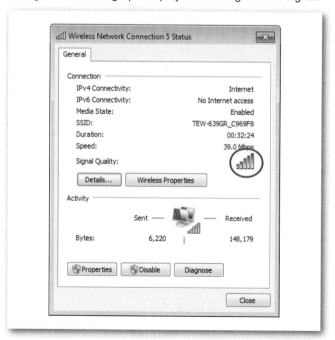

Wireless Standards

The IEEE organization has developed and released several standards that deal specifically with wireless communication. The standards serve as guidelines for how the equipment should function. Remember that standards are developed so that equipment developed by different manufacturers can communicate with each other. The wireless standards 802.11, 802.11a, 802.11b, 802.11g, and 802.11n recommend characteristics and specifications for wireless networking. Some of the items specified are frequencies, maximum bandwidth, and communication procedures.

The original 802.11 standard was first developed to standardize wireless devices that would transmit data at 1 Mbps and 2 Mbps. The frequency, or radio band, assigned to 802.11 by the FCC is 2.48 GHz. It was a very short time before 802.11 had to be modified to provide for higher data rates and was soon followed by 802.11a and 802.11b. Although both standards were released at the same time, 802.11b became the de facto standard for small office and home wireless devices.

The 802.11a standard specifies a frequency of 5 GHz and a maximum bandwidth of 54 Mbps. While 802.11a has a much higher bandwidth than 802.11b, it has less range, approximately half that of 802.11b. It is not backward compatible with 802.11.

The 802.11b standard allows for data transmission rates at 1 Mbps, 2 Mbps, 5.5 Mbps, and 11 Mbps. The 11 Mbps throughput, however, is only achieved at optimal conditions. Optimal conditions are short distances with no radio interference and only two devices. As distance increases between two wireless devices, the bandwidth drops drastically. Building materials and furnishings can also interfere with radio wave transmissions. Other devices such as portable phones, microwave ovens, wireless industrial communication control devices, and wireless medical devices assigned to the same frequency, can generate radio interference. 802.11b is backward compatible with 802.11 and is assigned the same 2.48 GHz frequency.

The 802.11g standard was the next to be developed. It operates at the 2.4 GHz frequency with a maximum transmission rate of 54 Mbps. It is compatible with 802.11a and 802.11b.

The 802.11n standard is referred to as Multiple In Multiple Out (MIMO) device. As the name *MIMO* implies, the device is capable of multiple input and output transmissions at the same time. Data rates standard for 802.11n are a maximum of 450 Mbps according to the Wi-Fi organization. You will see devices identified as 802.11n compliant with data rates as high as 600 Mbps. In reality, you would most likely achieve a data rate lower than 300 Mbps, but much faster than 802.11g. The high data rate meets the data throughput requirements for high-definition video streaming. The 802.11n standard is backward compatible with 802.11a, 802.11b, and 802.11g.

Wireless technology has not fully developed to one set of de facto terminology to describe the wireless systems. Do not be surprised to see that terms vary among manufacturers. For example, Basic Service Set (BSS) may be listed as Independent Basic Service Set (IBSS). Also, be aware that the specified frequency of a standard will vary. For example, 802.11b may be presented as 2.5 GHz, 2.4 GHz, and 2.45 GHz. The frequency for 802.11a may be presented as 5 GHz, 5.1 GHz, and 5.8 GHz. In actuality, the frequency is not one set frequency, but a range of frequencies. The following table lists the assigned frequency ranges.

Wi-Fi Technology	Frequency Band	Bandwidth or Maximum Data Rate
802.11a	5 GHz	54 Mbps
802.11b	2.4 GHz	11 Mbps
802.11g	2.4 GHz	54 Mbps
802.11n	2.4 GHz, 5 GHz	450 Mbps

A 802.11n device can support wireless connections at both 2.4 GHz and 5 GHz. In general, wireless technologies are classified as 2.4 GHz and 5 GHz. The actual frequency ranges are almost never used in product identification.

Security

Security is a high priority at all times, especially when dealing with portable PCs. The portable PC may contain important company information such as customer lists, contract information, proposed business ventures, and other sensitive communications. Information for connecting to the company network may also be contained on the hard drive. Security is even more important for portable PCs issued to people in police departments, the FBI, or the CIA. As you can see, laptop security is a vital issue.

Encryption

Encryption is used as part of the security system. **Encryption** is a way to code data that cannot be converted back to meaningful words without an encryption key. The **encryption key** is not a physical device but rather a mathematical formula for substituting values in strings of data. For example, a text-based code could be developed based on the number five. The data in a file would be stored with every letter changed to one that is four places further in the alphabet. See **Figure 12-28**.

The message is rewritten in code and then stored. To read the message, you would need the code. This is a simple example. A true encryption code is more complex.

BitLocker and BitLocker To Go

Microsoft BitLocker and BitLocker To Go is an encryption feature that allows the user to encrypt the entire hard drive, including the operating system. BitLocker was introduced in Windows Vista. BitLocker To Go was introduced in Windows 7. The main difference between BitLocker and BitLocker To Go is BitLocker To Go is designed to be used with removable storage media such as a flash drive or a portable hard drive.

NTFS vs. FAT

NTFS is designed with many more improvements as compared to FAT16, FAT32, or exFAT. A typical security system using FAT16 or FAT32 allows for only two types of file access when shared: full access and read only. These options are set when a file or directory is shared. NTFS4.0 and NTFS5.0 allow more choices when file and directory security are set up. There are many options to choose from when a file

Figure 12-28.
Very simple encryption code.

Sample message:

THIS IS THE TIME FOR ALL GOOD MEN...

Change the position of all letters by four positions in the alphabet.

A B C D E F G H I J K L M N O P Q R S T U V W X Y Z
E F G H I J K L M N O P Q R S T U V W X Y Z A B C D

Coded message:

X L M W   M W   X L I   X M Q I   J S V   E P P   K S S H   Q I R...

Goodheart-Willcox Publisher

share is created. These options are referred to as permissions.

For example, a Windows system using FAT16, FAT32, or exFAT can only set file access options to either full access, read only, or no access. With full access capabilities, another user can do anything to the file that the file originator can do. The user can delete the file completely, copy the file, or create a new file. When the NTFS system is used, access to the shared file can be controlled through more precise options. These options include read only, modify, read and execute, write, and list files. The people who have the right to modify or delete the file can be tightly controlled.

Tech Tip

A FAT system can be set up with similar file restrictions used for NTFS when running the NT operating system. However, the file restrictions are lost when the files are transferred to another directory or operating system.

The strongest security feature for NTFS is its encryption capabilities. NTFS allows for file encryption. FAT does not. This means that a low-level disk editing utility can be used to access the contents of a hard drive formatted with FAT. NTFS system files are protected.

Figure 12-29 shows a text file that was created and saved to the hard drive of a FAT system and viewed through the Norton Disk Editor. The Norton Disk Editor program is used to inspect the disk storage system and reveal the contents of the clusters byte by byte. In Figure 12-29, you can

see the contents of a file located at cluster 291,629. The Norton Disk Editor reveals the contents as ASCII code on the right side of the screen and as hexadecimal codes on the left side.

Notice the hexadecimal number 73 in the center field of hexadecimal numbers. The number 73 is equal to the ASCII character code for the letter s. If you count the hexadecimal position locations, you can see that the hexadecimal code 73 occurs at the fourth, seventh, and eleventh position in the line of hexadecimal characters. These three locations correspond to the location of the ASCII text for the letter s on the right.

With NTFS, you could not view the file system this way. NTFS has encryption capabilities built into the system. The files created by the user can be saved as encrypted files that would have no meaning to the person opening them in Norton Disk Editor.

Another feature of NTFS that makes it more suitable than FAT and exFAT for portable PCs is NTFS uses smaller cluster sizes when formatting the drive. Portable systems generally have less storage space available than full-size PCs because of their physically smaller storage drives, **Figure 12-30.** The smaller NTFS cluster sizes result in less wasted space on a hard drive, making it the preferred storage file system for portable PCs.

Smart Cards and Biometrics

Use of a smart card is another clever way to protect your laptop. A **smart card** is identical in size and feel to a credit card. Smart cards store information on a chip located within the body of the card. These chips can hold a variety of

Figure 12-29. An unencrypted text file viewed through a disk editor. The ASCII code can be read and translated.

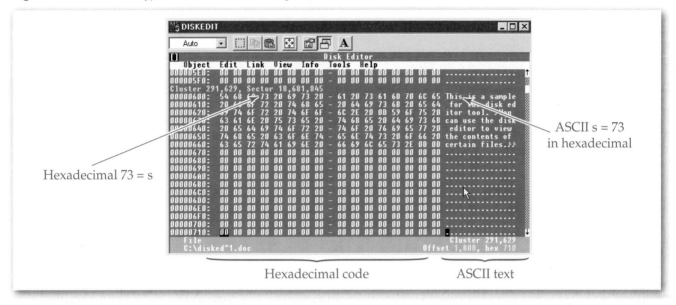

Hexadecimal 73 = s

ASCII s = 73 in hexadecimal

Hexadecimal code   ASCII text

Figure 12-30. The form factor of a laptop hard drive is much smaller than that in a desktop PC hard drive.

PC hard drive   Laptop hard drive

Goodheart-Willcox Publisher

information. They can be used commercially for retail or vending operation. They can be used with pay phones or for gaming. With portable computers, they work very well for security. A smart card setup can be used to allow you to access the laptop (or full-size PC). Without the card, the computer cannot be accessed. The smart card works in conjunction with a smart card reader, which is placed in the PC. The typical smart card connects through a USB port Type II

PCMCIA card slot. The smart card is supported by all the latest Microsoft operating systems and by many other operating systems.

Biometrics is the science of using the unique physical features of a person to confirm their identity for authentication purposes. For example, a person can use their fingerprint or eye color patterns to log on to a computer system. **Figure 12-31** shows a laptop with a built-in biometric device. The biometric device is a fingerprint reader that is used to verify the identity of the user at logon.

Figure 12-31. This IBM ThinkPad computer has a fingerprint reader that is used to verify the identity of the user at logon.

International Business Machines Corporation

Wireless Configuration for Mobile Devices

Mobile devices use wireless technology to access the Internet and networks. In **Figure 12-32**, you can see the **Settings** windows of an Android tablet with options for Wi-Fi and Bluetooth access. You would identify the wireless network by the SSID and then enter the security key to gain access to the secure network. Many locations do not use secure access so there is no need for a security key.

Wireless Network Security and Encryption Types

There are currently three major types of wireless network security: Wired Equivalent Privacy (WEP), Wi-Fi Protected Access (WPA and WPA2), and 802.1x.

Wired Equivalent Privacy (WEP) is an old network security method and not recommended because it can be cracked. WEP is still available because some old devices only have WEP encryption. WEP requires you to set up a security key. The **security key** encrypts the information that one computer sends to another computer across the network. When you manually configure a wireless network connection to a secured network, you must supply the security key. The security key is also known as a passphrase and many times is simply referred

to as a *password* or *passcode*. When manually connecting to an unsecured network you need not supply any security key.

> ## A+ Note
>
> On the CompTIA A+ exam, you may see any of the following terms used in questions related to wireless security: *security key*, *passphrase*, *passcode*, or *password*.

There are several variations of Wi-Fi Protected Access such as WPA-Personal, WPA2-Personal, WPA-Enterprise, and WPA2-Enterprise. WPA requires a user to provide a security key. WPA2 is more secure than WPA. With WPA-Personal and WPA2-Personal, each user is given the same passphrase. WPA-Enterprise and WPA2-Enterprise are designed to be used with an 802.1x authentication server, which distributes different keys to each user. 802.1x is typically used to connect to a workplace network that contains a network server. The network server authenticates a user security key. 802.1x can work with WPA, WPA2, or WEP keys.

Figure 12-33 shows the dialog box used when manually connecting to a wireless network. The network name is the broadcasted name of the wireless access point and is also known as the

Figure 12-32.
The Android **Settings** window has options for Wi-Fi and Bluetooth configurations.

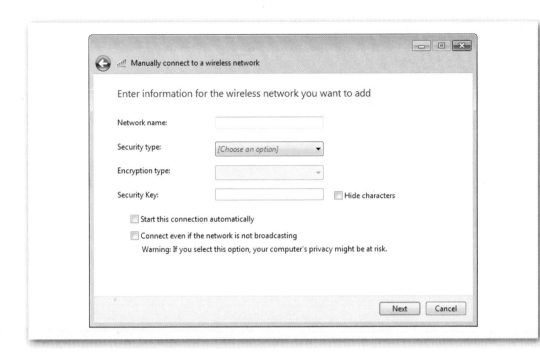

security set identifier (SSID). The wireless access point may be either secured or unsecured. When the wireless access point is secured, each device connecting to it must match the security type, encryption type, and security key. Some of the possible security types are WEP, WPA2-Personal, WPA-Personal, WPA-Enterprise, and 802.1x. After selecting the security type, you would next select the type of encryption. The two common encryption types are AES and TKIP.

The last bit of information is the security key. The security key is a set of numbers and case-sensitive letters that must be the same for all devices. The exact number of characters and the range of letters vary according to the encryption type being used.

Look at **Figure 12-34** and **Figure 12-35** to see some rules associated with a particular type of encryption and correlated security key. The dialog box allows you to hover the mouse pointer over the textbox to see the rules. Also, if you enter a security key incorrectly, a message box will appear telling you what the rule is for a specific type of security key.

Some wireless access points are configured not to broadcast their name or SSID. In the case of such a configuration, you would need to provide the name or SSID of the wireless access point to connect to it.

Securing Mobile Devices

Mobile devices can be expensive and often contain user personal or business data. Portable devices should always be secured immediately after purchasing. Mobile devices can be secured in many different ways. The exact method used is determined by the type of device, the operating system used, and the service provider.

Passcode Locks

The **passcode lock** is typically a set of numbers used as a password. The numbers must be entered in correct sequence to access the device. Another method that is similar to a password is a picture password. When using a picture password, the user can select an image such as a picture. After selecting the picture, the user then selects three gestures related to the picture to use as a key to unlock the device. The term *gesture* is used because the user can tap three locations or slide their finger to three different locations on the picture. **Figure 12-36** shows the Windows 8 PC settings for configuring a password, picture password, and PIN.

Figure 12-34.
WEP security key
description.

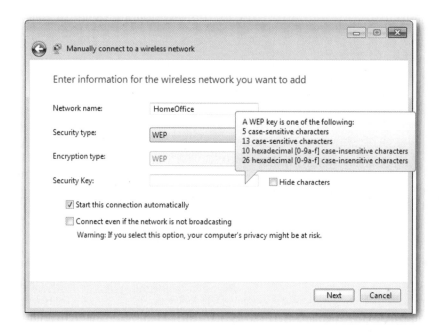

Figure 12-35.
WPA2-Personal
security key
description.

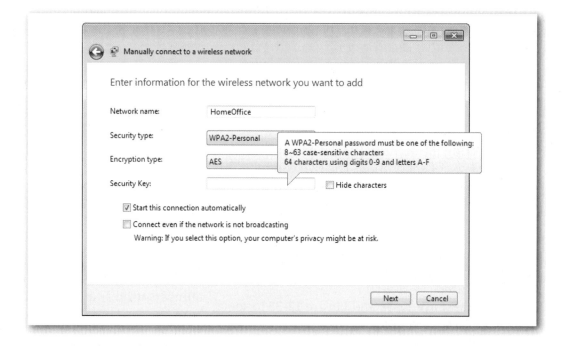

Device Access Failure

Devices typically are configured to limit the number of attempts to access the device. For example, if a person fails to correctly enter the PIN for an Android device, the person will have to wait a set period of time before the device will allow access to be reattempted. Continued failure will cause permanent denial of access until the device is sent back to the factory to be restored.

Some devices provide an option to perform a "hard reset." A **hard reset** returns the device to its original condition and removes all user data, passwords, and apps. The hard reset typically requires the user to perform some sort of button combination while booting the device. For example, the user must hold down the sleep/wake button and Home button until the device reboots. Devices sent back to the factory for reset result in complete data loss. Some systems allow the user

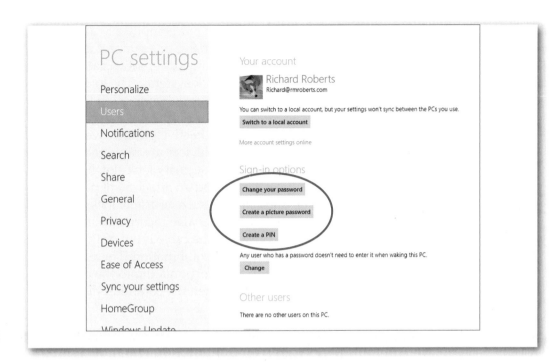

to reset the device by performing synchronization with a PC or a cloud service.

Jailbreaking and Rooting

The boot process used for mobile devices is designed to prevent users from having complete control over the device. The mobile device owner can change many device configurations but does not have unlimited abilities by default. For example, the owner of an Apple product cannot install certain applications that are not specifically designed for the Apple device. The term **jailbreaking** describes the process of overcoming the operating system's user limitations. After jailbreaking, the user can modify the operating system and applications.

The term **rooting** applies to Android devices. When you "root" an Android device, you take complete control of the device without limitations. Rooting provides the user with unlimited configuration abilities to the mobile device. The word *rooting* is associated with the Linux operating system, which is the operating system from which the Android was derived or modeled after. Linux has a security system based on a hierarchy of users. The user who controls the entire system is referred to as the "root user." Other users are simply referred to as "users" and

are considered limited users because they do not have the same privileges as the root user. The most powerful user of Linux operating system can control the root. Hence the term *rooting*.

Tech Tip

The terms *jailbreaking* and *rooting* are often used to mean the same thing. The terms *super user*, *privileged user*, and *root user* are used when describing the person who controls the device.

Apple Picking

Apple picking is the method of stealing a user's mobile device while they are using it. The word *apple* is used in the term because of Apple devices being stolen in this manner. The thief simply runs by a person and snatches the device right out of the person's hand while he or she is using the device.

Security Policy

A mobile device security policy consists of apps that call for the user to follow specific procedures such as use a password to access the device. The security policy can also require the password to be complex, such as be at least eight characters long and contain at least one letter, number, and special character. Some security policies are encapsulated into company apps.

Company Apps

A **company app** is an application that ensures and enforces security policies on a mobile device. The app may be designed to allow the company to disable the SD card, encrypt internal storage, and remotely delete all mobile device content and settings, thus rendering it useless to a thief. Some synchronization services such as Google Sync allow an individual user to remotely "wipe" their mobile device. Most mobile devices have some sort of **remote wipe** application that allows the user to wipe all user information, data, and settings when the device is stolen.

Settings Menu

Apple, Android, and Windows mobile devices all have a menu item called "Settings" that is used to configure the device. Settings is similar to Windows Control Panel. Typical options under Settings are theme, email accounts, internet sharing, lock screen, Wi-Fi, Bluetooth, location, brightness, and speech. The exact step-by-step procedure is outlined at the manufacturer.

Airplane Mode

Every mobile device capable of supporting wireless communication is required to have an airplane mode. When the device is placed in **airplane mode**, wireless services are disabled so that the device cannot send or receive telephone calls or text messages. Airplane mode disconnects cellular, Wi-Fi, Bluetooth, GPS, and location services. If allowed by the aircraft operator and applicable laws and regulations, you can re-enable Wi-Fi and Bluetooth while in airplane mode. When in airplane mode many functions are supported that do not require connection services such as games and music.

Physical Locks

Not all security is software related like encryption and passwords. There is also a physical aspect to security. Cable locks are available that can physically secure your computer to a fixed object such as a table, desk, or even part of the building. There are many different variations of physical security lock systems. The locking mechanism can be either a combination lock or simply a key. The cable is typically a flexible steel cable coated with a protective plastic cover. Many laptops and portable devices are designed with a hole referred to as a security lock slot. Not all devices have a hole, and an attachment point must be made another way such as a steel lock attached with epoxy. Some locks also incorporate an alarm which goes off when the cable is cut or the lock is removed without the combination. There are also alarms that can be incorporated into the computer. The alarm goes off when the computer device is removed from a designated area.

Exchanging Data with Full-Size PCs

Laptops and other portable devices exchange data with full-size PCs for a variety of reasons. One very common reason is to exchange information between home and work computers. For example, when someone brings work home from the office or from a road trip or takes work into the office from home or from a road trip.

Direct connection between a PC and a laptop can be accomplished with a serial null modem cable, parallel null modem cable (also known as a parallel link interlink cable), USB link cable, crossover network cable, infrared ports, and wireless connection. Infrared is hardly used today. The preferred cable is a USB link cable. Null modem cables are still available but seldom encountered because of the lack of serial ports on modern computers. **Figure 12-37** shows how a null modem cable is wired. Both serial and parallel null modem cables are difficult to find today.

The most common methods used to exchange data are USB link cable, wireless, or a small network system using a hub and two network cables.

The USB link cable is a special USB cable with matching connectors on each end. The center or one end typically contains an integrated chip which allows the two devices to exchange data. A regular USB cable extension will not allow the direct exchange of data.

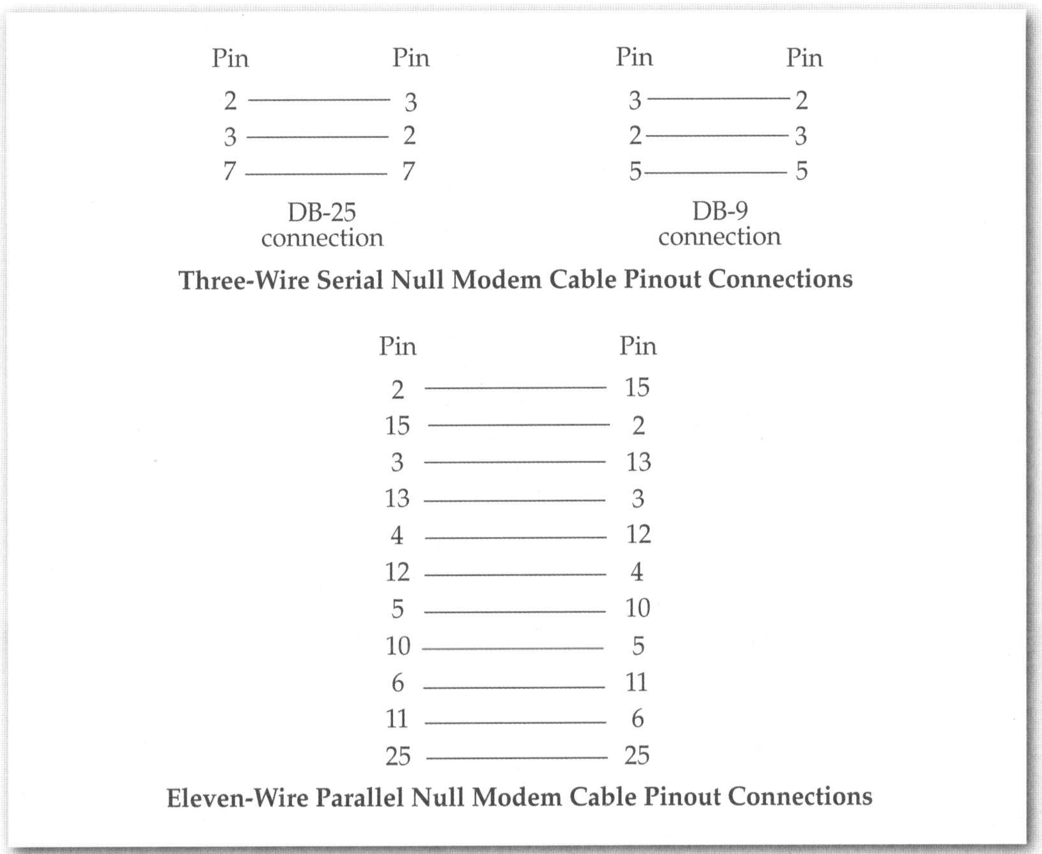

Three-Wire Serial Null Modem Cable Pinout Connections

Pin		Pin		Pin		Pin
2	——	3		3	——	2
3	——	2		2	——	3
7	——	7		5	——	5

DB-25 connection   DB-9 connection

Eleven-Wire Parallel Null Modem Cable Pinout Connections

Pin		Pin
2	——	15
15	——	2
3	——	13
13	——	3
4	——	12
12	——	4
5	——	10
10	——	5
6	——	11
11	——	6
25	——	25

Figure 12-37. A null modem cable is designed by switching the transmit and receive connections on one end of the cable. This allows data from the transmit connection on one computer to be sent to the receive connection on the other computer.

Goodheart-Willcox Publisher

Wireless is fine for exchanging small amounts of data, but for large volumes of data, a USB link cable works better. Wireless often suffers from radio interference, and Bluetooth devices have a very limited data rate.

The best way to exchange large volumes of data is to create a small network using a network hub or switch. Speeds in the range of 1 Gbps to 10 Gbps can be nearly achieved in a small network system. Networks systems such as this are presented in later chapters that cover networking. See **Figure 12-38** for a quick comparison of direct data exchange methods.

Figure 12-38. Comparison of direct data exchange methods.

Media	Theoretical Data Rate	Comments
Infrared	115 kbps–4 Mbps	Uses a direct line of sight but is immune to radio and magnetic interference.
Network cable	10 Mbps–10 Gbps	Excellent for large volumes of data exchange.
Parallel null modem	500 kBps–2 MBps	Rate too low to be used today.
Serial null modem	115 kbps	Rate too low to be used today.
USB link cable	USB 2.0, 480 Mbps USB 3.0, 4.8 Gbps	Excellent for high volumes of data exchange.
Wireless (Bluetooth, Wi-Fi, WiMAX)	700kbps–300 Gbps	Wireless devices vary greatly because of all the various standards. They are not immune to radio interference.

Goodheart-Willcox Publisher

Direct Connection

In Windows XP, you can create a direct connection using the New Connection Wizard located at **Start | All Programs | Accessories | Communications**. Refer to **Figure 12-39**.

As you can see in the New Connection Wizard, the fourth option is **Setup an advanced connection**. This option allows you to connect two computers using a serial, parallel, or infrared port.

Since almost all modern laptops have built-in wireless technology, Windows Vista and later no longer have a direct connection option. To configure a direct connection in Windows Vista and later, you need to use either an ad-hoc wireless connection or a small network connection using wireless or cable media. You can still connect two Windows computers using a USB link cable because the USB link cable comes with required support software on disc. Transfer cables, like the USB link cable, are often used to transfer system and user settings between two computers.

Look at **Figure 12-40** to see the Set Up a Connection or Network wizard. This wizard is accessed in Windows Vista by opening the **Start** menu, right-clicking **Network** and selecting **Properties** from the shortcut menu, and then clicking **Set up a connection or network**. In Windows 7 and Windows 8, simply open the **Networking and Sharing Center** and then select

Figure 12-39. The Windows XP New Connection Wizard can be used to set up a direct connection.

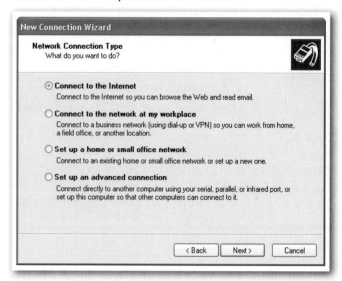

Set up a new connection or network. You can also enter "connection" into the **Search** box and then select **Set up a connection or network** from the search results.

As you can see, there is no option for a direct cable connection as in Windows XP and earlier operating systems. Wireless and cabled networking are the preferred methods of direct data exchange in Windows Vista and later.

Figure 12-40. Windows Vista and later operating systems provide the Set Up a Connection or Network wizard that will assist you in creating a network or establishing a connection.

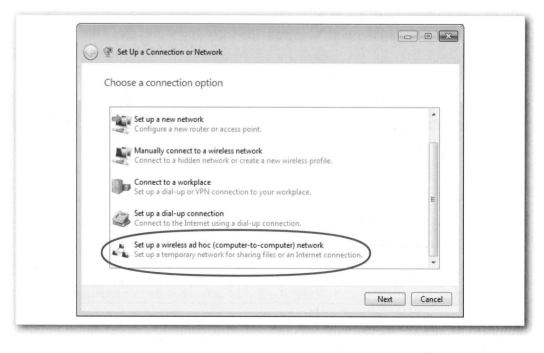

Briefcase

Briefcase is a Microsoft program that is designed to exchange files between laptops and full-size PCs while keeping the most recent version on both devices. For example, you want to take several files to work on while away from the office. You can simply copy the file to a removable storage device or use Briefcase. Briefcase determines which file has the latest changes, and it issues warnings about updating a file before action is taken. Briefcase is not supported in Windows 8.

Briefcase can be copied across a network or loaded to a USB flash drive. To use Briefcase, simply copy the files you wish to work on into the Briefcase folder, **Figure 12-41**. You can simply

Figure 12-41. A new Briefcase folder is created by selecting **Briefcase** from the Windows Explorer shortcut menu and then selecting **New**.

drag each file into Briefcase folder, and then drag the folder onto a USB flash drive. Take the PC home, complete your work, and then reverse the operation. Briefcase is no longer supported in Windows 8.

Sync Center

Windows Vista continues to support Briefcase but has added a feature called Sync Center. Sync Center is supported in all Windows Vista and later versions, including Windows 8. The Sync Center is designed especially for mobile device data exchange to ensure that the very latest file version is available and not confused with an older file version. The Sync Center only works with files that are configured for sharing in a network environment, even a small home network containing only two devices. Once the desired folder is set up as a share, the file can be synchronized using the Sync Center. This will enable the latest version of the file to always be available for use by either device.

The Sync Center is shown in **Figure 12-42**. Notice that it allows folders and files to be accessed, viewed, and modified offline. You can synchronize the contents of a folder used by two or more computers or portable devices so that the very latest version is always available for use.

Synchronization of Mobile Devices

The term *synchronization* when applied to mobile devices is the matching and/or exchanging of data between two or more devices. For example, a smartphone's email account can be synchronized with other devices such as a tablet and a PC. Opening and reading or deleting email on one particular device will automatically occur on all other synchronized devices. The mobile device manufacturer provides an app which can be downloaded onto a PC and then used to access the mobile device, **Figure 12-43**. After the app is downloaded and installed, you then connect to the phone using a USB cable equipped with a standard USB connector at one end and a mini-USB connector on the other end.

After synchronization, you will be able to view the mobile device in the Windows directory structure. Look at **Figure 12-44** to see how Windows Phone is now a part of the PC directory structure. A set of folders also appear on the right side of the Windows Explorer window. The most common connection types used to support mobile device synchronization are Wi-Fi, Bluetooth, and USB ports.

Upgrading the Laptop

Laptops can be upgraded easily. Memory and hard drive upgrades are not difficult. Some of the internal parts for laptops are smaller and more delicate than their full-size PC versions, so handle all parts with care. The CPU upgrade is usually not an option because of the design. Upgrading a CPU is a very difficult task, even for an experienced electronics technician.

Figure 12-42. Windows Vista Sync Center.

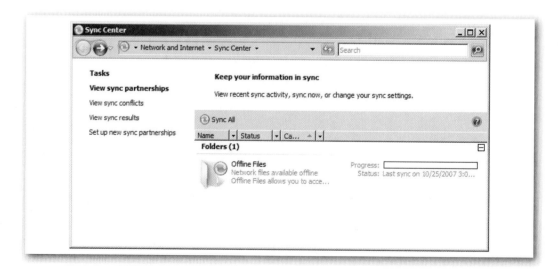

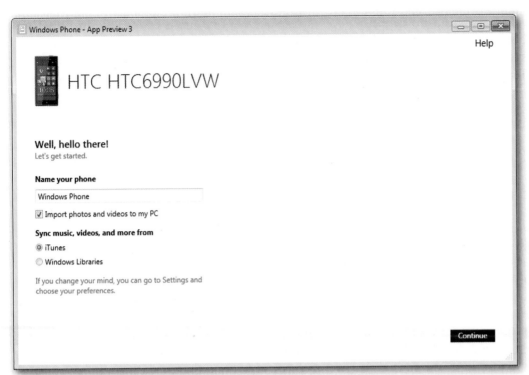

Figure 12-43.
Windows Phone sync setup.

Figure 12-44. The Windows phone appears in the Windows computer directory structure.

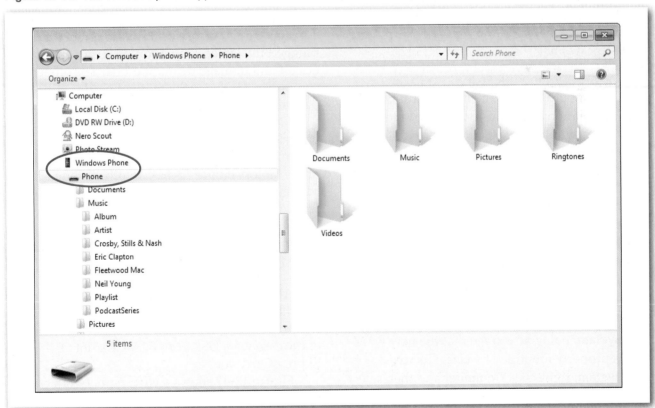

By now, you are aware that most computer repairs are required because of software or operator error. Third-party downloads and add-ons can cause a system lockup or crash. Most repair techniques related to software or operator error that are used for a full-size PC work equally as well on portables.

Upgrading Memory

Adding or replacing memory is a very common laptop upgrade. The memory modules for laptops are accessed through panels under the laptop. Laptops use SO-DIMM. The *SO* represents "Small Outline." Installing SO-DIMM is not difficult, but you should consult the manufacturer's documentation before performing the memory replacement or upgrade. The following lists the general steps for replacing or upgrading SO-DIMM memory in a laptop.

1. Before performing any hardware replacement or upgrade, remove the laptop battery and unplug the power cord or adapter.
2. Remove the retaining screw(s) that hold the memory access panel in place.
3. Either gently pull the retaining clips from each end of the memory module or rotate the memory module to a 30° to 45° angle. (You should consult the manufacturer's information about this procedure before attempting to remove and replace the memory.)
4. Align the memory module key notch to ensure the correct direction and alignment of the memory module into the memory socket.
5. Gently press the memory module into the socket until it is seated evenly and snuggly.
6. Replace the memory module access panel and replace the retaining screw(s).
7. Replace the power cord and battery.
8. Power on the computer and check the **System** dialog box to see that the new RAM is properly identified by size. (To access **System**, right-click **Computer** and then select **Properties** from the shortcut menu.) If not, you may need to reseat the memory module. Be sure to remove the battery and the power cord. Most of the time, a memory upgrade or

replacement failure is caused by improperly seating the memory in the socket.

Replacing an Internal Hard Drive

The hard disk drive can be accessed either under an access port on the bottom of the laptop or through the side of the laptop. See **Figure 12-45**. When installed in the side, Figure 12-45A, the hard drive typically has at least one screw to keep the hard drive in place. When it is located on the bottom of the laptop, it may have several screws, Figure 12-45B. Replacing the physical hard drive is an easy task. You must use a form factor designed for laptop computers. Desktop computer hard drives are much too large to fit inside a laptop.

Replacing the Battery

Before performing any repairs on a laptop computer, you should first remove the battery and disconnect any ac source of power. Some areas of the motherboard are still energized by battery power or by ac through the power adapter even when the laptop is turned off. Working inside a laptop with a battery or the ac adapter still plugged into an ac source could cause a short circuit and damage the motherboard or other components because the motherboard is still partially energized.

Figure 12-46 shows two common ways batteries are mounted in a laptop configuration. In some models, the battery slides out of the side of the laptop, Figure 12-46A. In other models, the battery is removed from the bottom of the laptop, Figure 12-46B. For both configurations, a latch is used to secure the battery in place.

Replacing a Wireless Card

Almost all laptops have a wireless card installed inside the case. Older laptops use wireless devices connected through the exterior of the case via a USB port, PCMCIA slot, or ExpressCard slot.

Figure 12-47 shows a wireless network card installed inside an Acer laptop. It is held in place by a bracket. There are also two wires, one black and one white, that run from the card through the inside of the case into the LCD display housing

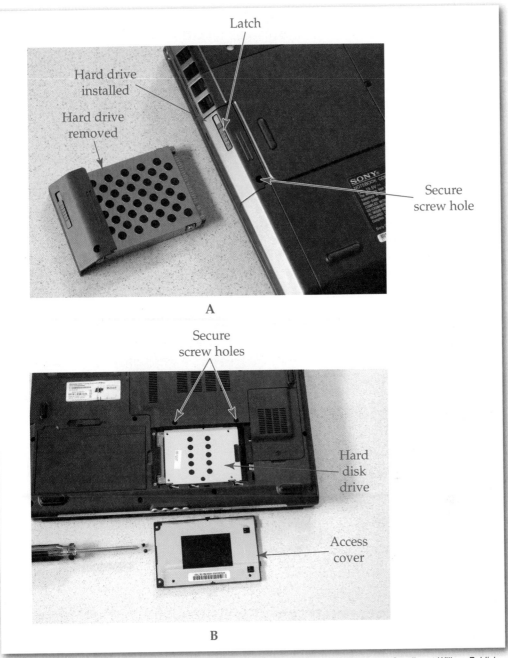

Goodheart-Willcox Publisher

Figure 12-45. Laptop hard drive removal. A—The Sony laptop hard drive is removed from the side access panel of the laptop. B—The Acer laptop hard drive is removed from the bottom of the laptop.

where the antenna is installed. A common error by new technicians is forgetting to reconnect the wires running from the card to the antenna.

Replacing the CPU

Replacement of the CPU is not an easy task. You should never attempt to replace the CPU without first studying the manufacturer's manual on that particular laptop model. The replacement of the CPU often requires a tedious disassembly of the cooling fan and heat sink and may involve the removal of other parts. Looking at **Figure 12-48**, you can see that the CPU is covered by the heat sink assembly and may also require the removal of the cooling fan before removing the heat sink.

Figure 12-46.
Laptop battery removal.
A—The battery snuggly
fits inside the back of
this Acer laptop and
is held in place by a
spring latch. B—In this
image, a spare battery
is resting beside the
installed battery of a
Sony laptop computer.
This laptop uses a
latch to hold the battery
in place. The battery
is inserted from the
bottom of the case.

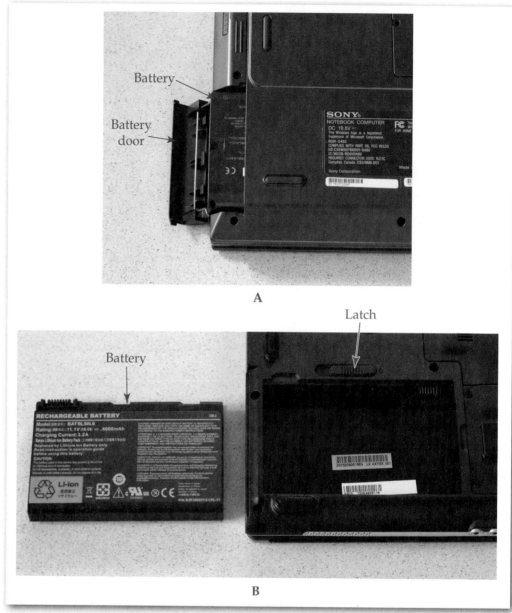

Goodheart-Willcox Publisher

Replacing the SIM Card

A **subscriber identity module (SIM)** or
subscriber identification module is an integrated
circuit that is used to securely authenticate a user's
identity for a mobile device. Look at **Figure 12-49**
to see what a SIM card looks like. A red circle is
drawn around the actual SIM card that is installed
in the mobile device.

Each card has a unique **International
Mobile Station Equipment Identity (IMEI)**
which identifies the mobile device and the user.

The SIM card typically contains the personal
information of the user and data such as address
book, phone numbers, and text messages. When
you configure a mobile device with a password
or PIN, the password or PIN is also stored on the
SIM card. Each card has a unique identification
number that is matched to the user. The card
must be activated by the carrier service before the
device can be used.

Mobile devices are rarely upgraded or
repaired in the field. Mobile devices typically
need to be returned to the manufacturer for repair

Figure 12-47.
A wireless network card installed inside a laptop PC. Notice the black and white wires that connect the network card to the antenna.

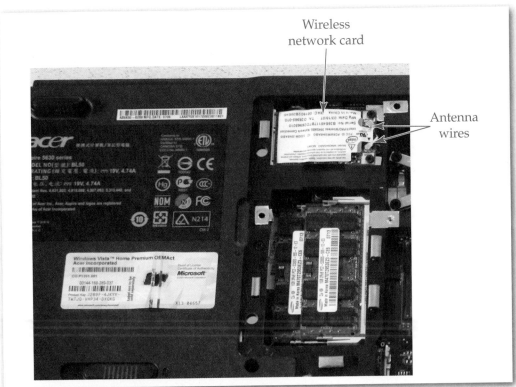

Wireless
network card

Antenna
wires

Goodheart-Willcox Publisher

Figure 12-48.
To replace a laptop CPU, the heat sink and possibly the cooling fan needs to first be removed.

Heat
sink

Cooling
fan

Goodheart-Willcox Publisher

Figure 12-49. A SIM contains the personal information of the user and data such as address book, phone numbers, and text messages.

Goodheart-Willcox Publisher

and/or replacement. One common task that can be performed is installing or replacing a SIM card.

Removing a SIM card is an easy operation. The SIM card is usually located under the battery on some mobile devices or easily accessed by inserting a paper clip into the SIM card ejection port. Look **Figure 12-50** to see the steps for removing a SIM card from a mobile device. First, you locate the ejection port. Then, you straighten a paper clip and insert it into the SIM ejection port and remove the SIM card. You should follow electrostatic discharge (ESD) rules while handling a SIM card.

Tech Tip
The SIM card is a serviceable item. It can be replaced if damaged or corrupted, but some SIM cards are programmed to only work with a specific service provider or a set of specific devices.

Troubleshooting the Laptop

There are some very common laptop troubleshooting practices you need to be familiar with. This section is brief and intended only as an introduction. For more in-depth troubleshooting, check Chapter 15—PC Troubleshooting.

Tech Tip
Be sure to remove the battery from a laptop or portable device before attempting any repairs that involve disassembly of the unit. A screwdriver tip can short circuit the motherboard, even when the laptop is turned off. This is because the battery still supplies power to parts of the motherboard.

Symptom 1:

No power LED or other LEDs are lit when the laptop is plugged into an ac power source.

Items to check:

This is an indicator that a major power problem has occurred in the laptop, most likely

Figure 12-50. A SIM card is removed from this particular device using a paper clip.

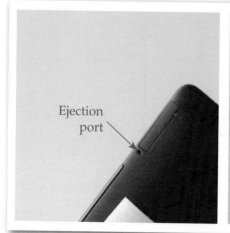

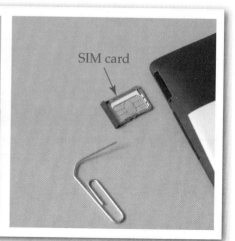

on the motherboard. Laptops do not have a power supply as desktops do. The power input is incorporated into the motherboard. The laptop uses dc power. You may try changing the ac adapter first. Be sure to use an adapter that matches the voltage and current output. Also, be aware that not all adapter plugs are physically the same size and shape.

If the motherboard is at fault, the laptop should be returned to the laptop manufacturer for motherboard repair issues. Most technicians do not repair laptop motherboards. If the laptop is out of warranty, the motherboard should be replaced.

Symptom 2:

The laptop seems to boot, but there is no display.

Items to check:

When the laptop boots and the display appears black, gray, very dim, or discolored, it is a symptom that the backlight is defective or the LCD inverter has failed. Active-matrix LCD displays used two main parts to produce the required backlighting: a florescent lamp and an inverter. A florescent lamp, also referred to as the Cold Cathode Fluorescent Lamp (CCFL), produces the light necessary for the LCD display. The inverter is a small circuit board that converts the low dc voltage to a much higher ac voltage. An inverter may produce anywhere from 500 Vac to over 1000 Vac from a 12-volt to 18-volt laptop battery. LEDs are also used for backlighting, but they do not require an inverter.

Symptom 3:

Slow laptop, and too many popups.

Items to check:

The laptop is infected with spyware. Install and run a reputable antispyware program.

Symptom 4:

Laptop freezes and will not respond, even to the power button.

Items to check:

Unplug the power cord and remove the battery from the laptop. Replace the battery and power cord, and the laptop should reboot and respond normally.

Symptom 5:

Laptop is booting slower and slower over time.

Items to check:

Typically, too many programs and downloads have been installed on the computer. The programs are all loaded at startup into RAM, thus slowing the overall boot time and slowing computer performance. Remove unnecessary programs from the laptop. You can also stop many programs from loading during startup by running the System Configuration Utility (msconfig.exe) and selecting which programs to load at startup. Using the System Configuration Utility is covered in Chapter 15—PC Troubleshooting.

Symptom 6:

A blue screen appears during the boot process and an error message appears on the screen.

Items to check:

This symptom is typical of a major problem. The easiest way to remedy this problem is to completely reinstall the Windows operating system. Be aware that a complete reinstall may cause you to lose all data and files stored on the laptop. This is a major reason why you should frequently back up valuable data!

Symptom 7:

The laptop acts strangely.

Items to check:

When the laptop "acts strangely" and unpredictable results occur when certain programs or certain actions are taken, it is a good sign that the laptop has a virus or malware. The computer may randomly stop running, automatically shut down, or take you to a website you did not intend to launch. All these symptoms are usually a good indicator that a virus has infected the computer. Install and run an antivirus program.

Symptom 8:

Incorrect characters appear on the screen.

Items to check:

A very common client complaint is that the laptop prints characters on the screen when the number keys are pressed. Again, this is very common, especially for new users. The most likely cause is that a function key or function key combination has been pressed, setting the default state of the keys to characters rather than numbers. Also, be aware that laptop keyboards often have many more special function keys than the traditional full-size keyboard. This causes many other problems for users who are not familiar with that particular laptop keyboard or who have recently changed from a desktop system to a laptop.

Symptom 9:

Battery not charging.

Items to check:

Sometimes the obvious is overlooked. Make sure there is electrical power (120 Vac) at the plug that the laptop or mobile device is charging from.

Check for loose connections. Many times a cable appears to be plugged in but is not making good electrical contact. Simply disconnect and reconnect all plugs.

Symptom 10:

Ghost cursor.

Item to check:

When a mouse cursor moves on its own it is often referred to as a ghost cursor. It seems to be haunted. This condition is generally associated with a wireless mouse and is usually the result of the mouse being too far from the radio receiver, the batteries becoming weak, or a combination of both. Change the batteries in the mouse and move the receiver closer to the mouse. Some wireless receivers plug directly into a USB port on a computer that may be too far from the mouse. They have cords that can plug into the USB port on one end and the wireless receiver on the other end which allows the receiver to be placed closer to the mouse. The same is true for a wireless keyboard.

A+ Note

Be sure you are familiar with the disassembly of a laptop computer. Download a copy of the laptop repair manual and study the procedure for at least two different types of laptops. This will prove to be a valuable aid if you are planning to take the CompTIA A+ exam.

Disassembling the Laptop

Before attempting to disassemble any laptop or mobile device, always consult the manufacturer's website for the correct sequence and procedures. Laptops can be very difficult to disassemble and could cause the device to be damaged. Always use a system to keep track of the location of any screws removed while disassembling the device. Some laptops have over 24 screws that must be removed to replace a critical part. A digital camera and a small multi-bin storage container can be a big help during disassembly. The screw threads are usually the same, but not always, and the length of screws can also vary.

Do *not* attempt an upgrade such as installing a better optical drive without first checking the manufacturer's website. At the website, you can find information about upgrade requirements such as upgrading firmware.

Some laptop and mobile device manufacturers offer special training and certification for their products. After training, your place of business or employment can become an authorized repair location.

Laptop Preventive Maintenance

Preventive maintenance of laptops and portable devices are always outlined in the user manual that comes with the device. They are very common for all such devices. The most common preventive maintenance tips are as follows:

- Never store a portable device or laptop in direct sunlight. Direct sunlight can harm the plastic case, causing it to yellow and make the plastic brittle, which can cause the case to easily break when dropped.
- Never leave a portable device in a car. Extreme heat can damage the components, such as the motherboard capacitors. Extreme cold can cause condensation problems when taking the portable device from a very cold car into a hot and humid environment, causing water to condensate inside the case. Condensation can damage motherboard components.

- Never use harsh chemicals to clean the case, especially the screen area.
- Do not spray liquids directly on the screen area as they can drip down and enter the display at the display edge. This can damage the inverter or other components. When you must use a spray, spray the liquid directly on a soft cloth and then use the damp (not wet) cloth to wipe the screen.
- Clean the keyboard with compressed air or a small paintbrush. Never use liquid or sprays directly on the keyboard. The keyboard is mounted over the motherboard, and any

liquid that seeps through the keyboard will wet the motherboard components and cause a short circuit.

A+ Note

To better prepare for the A+ Certification exams, download one or two laptop manuals and review the information about preventive maintenance and common repairs. Check the Gateway support website for a list of laptops and available manuals.

Chapter Summary

- Laptops contain many modules than can be easily upgraded; mobile devices such as tablets and smartphones do not.
- Laptop computers are equipped with some parts that full-size PCs don't have such as a battery, touch pad, and ports for PCMCIA cards and ExpressCards.
- Portable computers and mobile devices rely on energy management software to lengthen the life of the batteries.
- Mobile devices such as tablets and smartphones require special operating systems such as iOS, Android, Windows RT, and Windows CE.
- The Windows Mobility Center contains a collection of the most common utilities and configurations used by laptops such as Volume, Battery Status, and Wireless Network.
- IEEE 802.11n transmits at 2.4 GHz and 5 GHz and is backward compatible with 802.11a, 802.11b, and 802.11g.
- Some of the ways to secure a mobile device are encryption, passcode locks, security policies, company apps, and physical locks.
- The common way to create a direct connection between a PC and a laptop is with a USB link cable, wireless, or a small network system using a hub and two network cables.
- Upgrades such as installing more memory and replacing the hard drive and battery can be performed on a laptop.
- Some very common laptop troubleshooting practices can help you evaluate and repair a faulty laptop.
- A digital camera and a small multi-bin storage container can be used to keep track of the location of any screws removed while disassembling a laptop.
- Some common preventive maintenance tips are to never store a portable device or laptop in direct sunlight; never use harsh chemicals to clean the case; and do not spray liquids directly on the screen area.

Review Questions

Answer the following questions on a separate sheet of paper. Please do not write in this book.

1. Tablets and smartphones use _____ processors, which are typically soldered permanently into the device circuit board.
2. How can storage space be expanded in tablets and smartphones?
3. How can a standard keyboard be attached to a tablet?
4. Name four types of batteries commonly associated with portable PC products.
5. Which type of battery has memory effect?
6. Which battery is the preferred choice for portable PCs?
7. What is the most lightweight and compact battery?
8. What is the function of a docking station?
9. What device can be used to provide additional ports for a portable or compact digital device?
10. List five devices that can be connected through a port replicator.
11. What type of PCMCIA card is used for hard drives?
12. What type of device is associated with a Type I PCMCIA card?
13. Which type of PCMCIA card is the thickest?
14. What are the two ExpressCard widths?
15. What is the data rate of an ExpressCard using a USB 2.0 bus?
16. What is the data rate of an ExpressCard using a USB 3.0 bus?
17. What are the three power schemes available in the Windows Vista and later **Power Options** dialog box?
18. What is the difference between sleep mode and hibernate mode?
19. What is hybrid sleep?
20. What are the two most common smartphone operating systems?
21. What is the name of the Apple mobile operating system?
22. What is the name of the Google mobile operating system?
23. What is the main difference between iOS and Android source code?
24. What features can be accessed or configured through the Windows Mobility Center?
25. How does distance affect wireless device communications?
26. What is the frequency and the maximum bandwidth associated with IEEE 802.11g devices?
27. According to the Wi-Fi organization standards, what is the frequency and bandwidth associated with IEEE 802.11n devices?
28. What items can interfere with radio wave communications?
29. Why is security so critical for a portable PC?
30. Which provides better security, WEP or WPA?
31. What two pieces of information do you need to connect a smartphone to a wireless network?

32. What is jailbreaking?
33. What is rooting?
34. What is airplane mode?
35. What is the name of the Windows XP through Windows 7 program that synchronizes the contents of a folder shared between two computers?
36. List three common connection types used to support mobile device synchronization.
37. What should be removed from the laptop before replacing or upgrading parts?
38. What type of memory is used in a laptop?
39. Why is it difficult to upgrade the CPU in a portable PC?
40. What should be checked if the laptop seems to boot, but there is no display?
41. What should you do if the laptop freezes and will not respond, even to the power button?
42. What should you check if the battery is not charging?
43. What should you do before attempting to disassemble any laptop of mobile device?
44. Why should you never store a portable device or laptop in direct sunlight?
45. Why should you never spray liquids directly on the screen area?
46. With what should you clean a laptop keyboard?

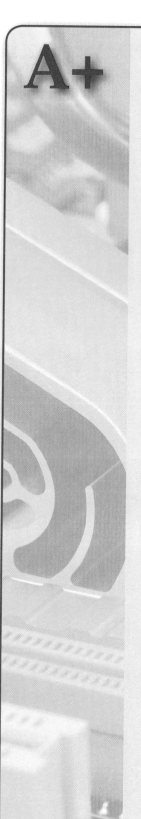

Sample A+ Exam Questions

Answer the following questions on a separate sheet of paper. Please do not write in this book.

1. Which term is used to describe bypassing the security on an iOS, thus allowing an unauthorized app to be installed?
   a. Jailbreaking
   b. Highjacking
   c. Rooting
   d. Drafting

2. Which type of memory is most commonly used for laptop computer RAM?
   a. SIMM
   b. SO-DIMM
   c. EPROM
   d. DIMM

3. What two pieces of information are required to connect to a secure wireless access point? Select two.
   a. MAC address
   b. SSID
   c. Security key
   d. Authorization code

4. Which is the best example of battery memory effect?
   a. A battery supplies the same level of voltage when connected to various types of laptop computers because it remembers the voltage level required the last time it was used.
   b. A battery loses its charge after the amount of time lapse of its last usage, even if the battery is designed to last longer.
   c. A battery is designed to remember the total length of warranty and will cease supplying voltage after the expiration date.
   d. A battery remembers the orientation of the connection polarity after being removed from the case for reinstallation at a later date.

5. Which type of battery would you *most likely* find in a new laptop computer?
   a. Lithium-ion
   b. Alkaline
   c. NiCad
   d. Nickel-metal hydride

6. Under which Windows 7 Control Panel option would you *most likely* find the option to configure a second display monitor?
   a. System and Security
   b. Ease of Access
   c. Programs
   d. Appearance and Personalization

7. Which statement is true for proper disposal of a laptop battery?
   a. It must be disposed of by incineration to protect the environment.
   b. You must follow local, state, and federal guidelines.
   c. Any container that is lined in plastic can be used.
   d. Lithium-ion batteries do not need to be disposed of because they can be recharged indefinitely.

8. Which situation best describes an ad-hoc network?
   a. An Ethernet network with two wireless access points: one for WAN and the other for LAN service
   b. A notebook PC connected to a full-size PC transferring files by radio signal
   c. A group of computers using radio waves to communicate through a centralized access point on a 1000BaseT network
   d. A network consisting of several access points each using a different frequency

9. What is the maximum data transfer described by the IEEE 802.11b standard?
   a. 2 Mbps
   b. 5 GHz
   c. 11 Mbps
   d. 54 GHz

10. Which form of wireless security requires an authentication server?
    a. WEP
    b. WPA
    c. 802.1x
    d. Bitlocker

Suggested Laboratory Activities

Do not attempt any suggested laboratory activities without your instructor's permission. Certain activities can render the PC operating system inoperable.

1. Set up a laptop PC to access your home or school PC.
2. Transfer a file from a laptop to a full-size PC using a direct cable connection.
3. Set up and configure a free cloud storage service for a computer and then access it from a mobile device.
4. Inspect the wireless encryption configuration associated with a wireless device.
5. Explore the power management settings on a typical portable PC. Be sure to record the settings before making changes.
6. Set up a portable PC for use by multiple users. Each user should have their own password and they should be able to retain their personnel desktop settings. For example, change the desktop display so each user has a different desktop.

Modems and Transceivers

13

After studying this chapter, you will be able to:

- Recall the characteristics of the public telephone system.
- Recall the characteristics of telephone wiring systems.
- Carry out a typical telephone modem installation and configuration.
- Recall the characteristics of ISDN, DSL, cable, and satellite.
- Explain the basic operation of a multiplexer and demultiplexer.
- Recall the characteristics of mobile broadband.
- Carry out a residential Internet connection installation and configuration.
- Use McAfee Internet Connection Speedometer to determine Internet connection speed.
- Use common troubleshooting practices to diagnose modem problems.

A+ Exam—Key Points

A variety of questions related to modems of all types, including telephone modems, will appear on the CompTIA A+ Certification exam. You may think that telephone modems are old technology, but many locations have only telephone service rather than high-speed Internet service. You should practice configuring a telephone modem so that you are familiar with the terminology associated with the device. Also, you should look at the latest troubleshooting information located on Internet service provider websites such as Comcast, Verizon Wireless, Bright House Networks, and CLEAR.

Key Terms

The following key terms will become important pieces of your computer vocabulary. Be sure you can define them.

bandwidth
baud rate
cable modem
Code Division Multiple Access (CDMA)
Data Over Cable Service Interface Specification (DOCSIS)
demarcation point
demultiplexer
digital subscriber line (DSL)
DSL modem
eMTA modem
Global System for Mobile Communications (GSM)
integrated services digital network (ISDN)
Internet service provider (ISP)
Long Term Evolution (LTE)

multiple input multiple output (MIMO)
mobile broadband
mobile hotspot
modem
multiplexer
protocol
router
T-carrier lines
telephone jack
tethering
universal asynchronous receiver-transmitter (UART)
Universal Mobile Telecommunications System (UMTS)
USB modem
WiMAX

One of the basic functions of the modern PC is communication with other computers, usually through Internet access. In this chapter, you will learn about the modem, basic residential telephone system wiring, modem installation, and communications software setup. Some of the material covered here will be seen again in the chapters discussing the basics of networking.

Modems allow you the freedom to surf the Internet, connect with others through e-mail, send pictures around the world, take part in conference calls, and participate in many other activities relating to communications. While the modern modem is a Plug and Play device, there is still much to learn about modems and modem-related issues. We will begin this chapter with a brief description of the public telephone system and residential telephone wiring.

Public Telephone System

To understand the complete communications model, we must first take a look at the standard telephone system. The public telephone system has been serving the general public for over 100 years.

As telephone system technology evolved, it has retained its own downward compatibility to existing equipment. The original telephone system was designed to transmit voice as an analog signal across the country and world. This system only had to be able to accommodate the frequency spectrum of sound associated with voice communications. The voice frequency spectrum for the telephone industry operated between 200 Hz and 4,000 Hz. This frequency spectrum is more than adequate for carrying voice. However, it is not adequate for high-speed modem connections. High-speed connections demand higher bandwidth. This is the main reason why people switch to cable television carriers for Internet access. The cables used for cable television can carry much higher frequencies than the simple twisted-pair telephone cable. This large bandwidth allows for much more information to be transported in shorter spans of time.

The **bandwidth** of a cable or device is the range or limit of frequency that the electronic cable or component is designed to carry. For example, a cable with a bandwidth of 4 kbps is designed to carry a maximum frequency of 4 kbps. Note that bandwidth is also used to describe a portion of the frequency spectrum. For example, television channels use a bandwidth of 6 MHz for each channel. This means that each channel has a frequency range of 6 MHz.

Telephone technology has made tremendous advances over the years, but the downward compatibility issue has made it difficult to implement all the latest technologies. The main bottleneck of the entire telephone system is the last few hundred feet of connection that serve each building, especially in private homes. Most of the public telephone network system (PTNS) is constructed of high-speed fiber-optic cables, microwave transmitters and receivers, digital equipment, and computerized telephone control units. While all of these major parts of the telephone network system are composed of cables and media that have high data transfer rates, the last few hundred feet of twisted pair from the main system to the individual connection point severely limit the speed of data transmission.

> **Tech Tip**
>
> The public telephone system is often referred to as POTS, which is an acronym for *plain old telephone system.*

Residential Telephone Wiring System

The typical residential telephone wiring system is simple in design while a system for a commercial enterprise is somewhat more complicated. The simple residential wiring system consists of two to four wires running throughout the residence and connecting to telephone jacks. See **Figure 13-1**.

The telephone wiring in a residential dwelling is typically a #22 copper conductor run in a daisy-chain fashion throughout the residence. Older homes may have a two-wire system, but four-wire systems are most common. Two wires are the minimum number used for one telephone to communicate with another telephone. The pair of connections are referred to in telephone technician terminology as the "tip and the ring." The additional two wires from the four-wire system can be used for an additional phone or to connect to electrical power for phone lighting or other electrical device on the phone.

Phone lighting does not use 120 volts. A transformer is used to step the voltage level down to 12 volts, which is used to light the keypad. The voltage level at the telephone jack is considered low voltage. It reaches an approximate 48 volts when the phone is ringing. This voltage can be felt by touch, but is not considered deadly. To see how a typical phone line might be run through a home, look at **Figure 13-2**. As you can see, the cable runs through the residence from room to room. This is the usual style, but each individual jack could have its own run of cable from a junction box. The daisy-chain style is preferred because it uses less cable, which means it is less expensive.

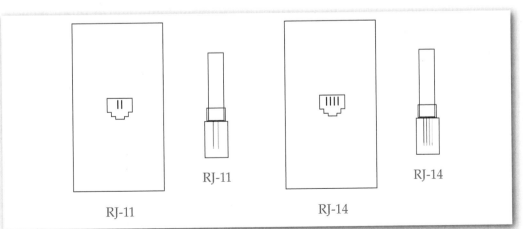

RJ-11

RJ-11

RJ-14

RJ-14

Figure 13-1.
RJ-11 and RJ-14 connectors look very similar. The difference in classification is determined by the number of electrical contacts inside the connector. An RJ-14 has four contacts for four wires, and an RJ-11 has two contacts for two wires.

Figure 13-2.
The telephone jacks in a home are run using one common line.

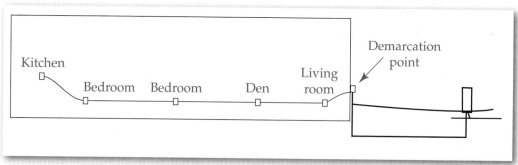

Goodheart-Willcox Publisher

Warning !

Never work on a telephone line when there is a storm in the area. Lightning strikes can travel many miles across a telephone system and exit anywhere along the system. You could be injured during a lightning storm.

A **telephone jack** is where the telephone line connects to the cabling. This is a standard connection used to attach devices such as modems and telephones to the wiring system. The telephone jack is usually an RJ-11 or an RJ-14. Since the deregulation of the public telephone system some years ago, the wiring inside the residence is typically the responsibility of the owner and not the local telephone company. A **demarcation point** is where the telephone company system ends and the residence ownership begins.

A+ Note

For the CompTIA A+ exam, you should know the difference between an RJ-11 and an RJ-14 telephone connection.

Modems

A **modem** is an electronic device that converts serial data from a computer to an audio signal for transmission over telephone lines and vice versa. The term *modem* is a contraction of two words: *modulator* and *demodulator*. It is derived from the field of electronics. A modem can be integrated into the motherboard, it can be

installed in the form of an adapter card, or it can even be connected outside the computer case as a peripheral device. A modem must be used to transmit data across traditional telephone lines. The modem simply converts a digital signal into an analog signal, and then transmits a signal across telephone lines. Another modem on the receiving end converts the analog signal back to a digital signal. See **Figure 13-3**.

Tech Tip

A modem is sometimes referred to as a transceiver. A transceiver is an electronic device that not only transmits data but also receives data.

Two computers can communicate using modems. The modem converts the digital signal from the computer system to an analog signal that can be carried over telephone lines. When the analog signal reaches the destination PC, the modem converts the analog signal back to a digital signal. Some common uses for modems are to gather information across the Internet, to connect to an office PC from home, to connect to a home or office PC from a laptop while on the road, and to establish a connection to a mainframe computer system. Examples of modem applications include sending and receiving facsimiles (faxes), pictures, and music or having a simple telephone conversation online.

Modem Construction

The modem is simple in construction and only requires a few electronic components. See **Figure 13-4**. The main chip is the **universal**

Figure 13-3. These two computers are connected by a modem. The signal coming from the first computer is digital until it passes through its modem. The modem converts the digital signal to an analog signal and passes it through the phone lines. The second computer's modem receives the analog signal and converts it back to a digital signal that the computer can read.

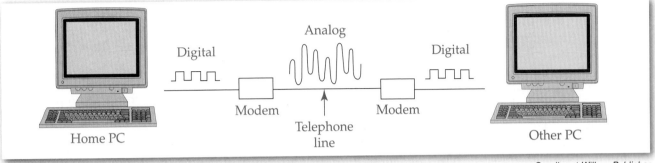

Goodheart-Willcox Publisher

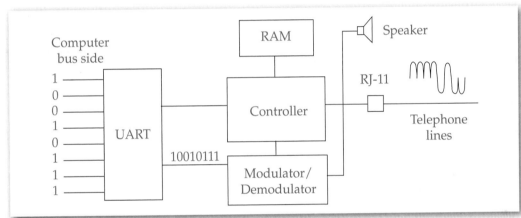

Goodheart-Willcox Publisher

Figure 13-4. There are only a few major components in a modern modem. The UART is the most important.

asynchronous receiver-transmitter (UART). The main purpose of the UART is to change parallel data to serial data and vice versa. Data moves as bytes on the computer bus system. The telephone uses a single wire to communicate in one direction. Thus, the byte, which is a parallel arrangement of data, must be converted into a series or single string of data bits.

The modem must also change the data into a form that can be transmitted across telephone lines. Digital data from the computer system cannot travel across typical phone lines because of its high frequency and wave shape. To operate over traditional phone lines, the digital signal must be modulated. This means that the digital signal is changed into an analog signal and its frequency is slowed down. The rate of data flow inside the computer is far too high to pass through traditional phone lines.

The rate of the analog frequency that a modem transmits at is known as the **baud rate**. When the original modem was designed, the baud rate and data transfer rate were very close. Today, the baud rate and data rate are two distinct speeds. Baud rate reflects the actual analog signal rate. However, now there are a number of modulation techniques that can get a higher data transfer rate from the same baud rate. Some of these techniques include frequency-shift keying (FSK), Quadrature Amplitude Modulation (QAM), and phase-shift keying (PSK). These systems of encoding are very difficult to fully understand without an adequate electronics background. For now, just know that these techniques allow data to be a multiple of a single baud rate. For example, a baud rate of 900 bits per second (bps) can be changed to a data rate of 1800 bps or 3600 bps. Even bits per second is not the actual data speed. The actual data speed is increased by data compression techniques as well. Compression techniques were introduced in Chapter 8—Video and Audio Systems.

In addition to the components that produce signal modulation, modems need a memory chip component. The data flow from the computer bus is too fast to transmit directly through the modem. Data must be stored in the modem and transmitted more slowly. This is the job of a simple RAM chip incorporated into the modem. The RAM chip holds large chunks of data and sends it at a slower rate, a rate the modem can handle. When a modem receives data, the same action takes place in reverse. The data received is stored in RAM until the computer bus system is ready to receive it.

Modems also come with an audio device, such as a small speaker. This speaker allows you to hear the audible tones dialed by the modem when activated. This will assist you when troubleshooting. The speaker allows the user to hear the tones used in the transmission of data, usually at startup. When you connect to the Internet through your modem, you can hear the modem dial out to your Internet service provider. If you don't hear any tones when the modem is dialing out, the modem may be set up incorrectly or the modem may have failed. However, some people turn off the sound to the modem, so lack of sound does not always indicate a problem.

The job of coordinating the entire operation of the modem is left to the control chip. The controller chip controls the flow of data and the interaction of all the parts of the modem. It is similar to a minicomputer and is often referred to as a microcontroller.

Modem Connection Process

There are several steps that must be performed to make and maintain a connection to another computer. The act of connecting to another computer using a modem is often referred to as modem negotiation. Often, these steps can be observed on an exterior modem through the use of lights (LEDs). The process of making the connection is a series of signals and commands, which include the following:

- Data Terminal Ready (DTR).
- Data Set Ready (DSR).
- Transmit Data (TD).
- Receive Data (RD).
- Carrier Detect (CD).
- Request to Send (RTS).
- Clear to Send (CTS).

A software program commands a modem with a *Data Terminal Ready (DTR)* signal, which tells the modem that the user wishes to make a connection to another location. If the modem is ready, it sends a Data Set Ready (DSR) signal back to the software. Both signals must be present before any data can be transmitted. Next, the PC sends a Transmit Data (TD) signal to the modem. This commands the modem to dial a particular phone number. The modem replies with a Receive Data (RD) signal and proceeds to open a connection on the phone line, which is referred to as "off the hook." A series of electrical pulses flows from the modem through the telephone line. This is the same as dialing a number. When the other modem receives the hailing signal, it responds to the originating modem. The modem now uses a Carrier Detect (CD) signal to let the originating PC know that a carrier signal has been received from the modem. An example of this conversation is shown in **Figure 13-5**.

There are many different modem styles and software systems, so the two modems now communicate back and forth trying to establish a common ground for exchanging data. The communication includes such matters as the transmission speed, the number of stop and start bits, and the type of parity that will be used. The handling of half-duplex and full-duplex must also be resolved. Data speed or baud rate must be the same for both modems. The absolute base speed is 300 baud, but normally it will be above 1200 baud. Start and stop bits must be established.

Data sent across telephone lines by a modem is sent in packets. A single bit is used to mark the beginning of a packet, and either one or two bits are used to mark the end of the packet. Look at **Figure 13-6**.

The type of parity must also be agreed on. There are three options: no parity, odd parity, and even parity. Parity is a way to check the accuracy of the data packet being sent. When the number of bits inside the data packet is added up, it will equal an odd or an even number. The systems agree to send an additional bit that represents

Figure 13-5. Modems send signals back and forth to set up a conversation.

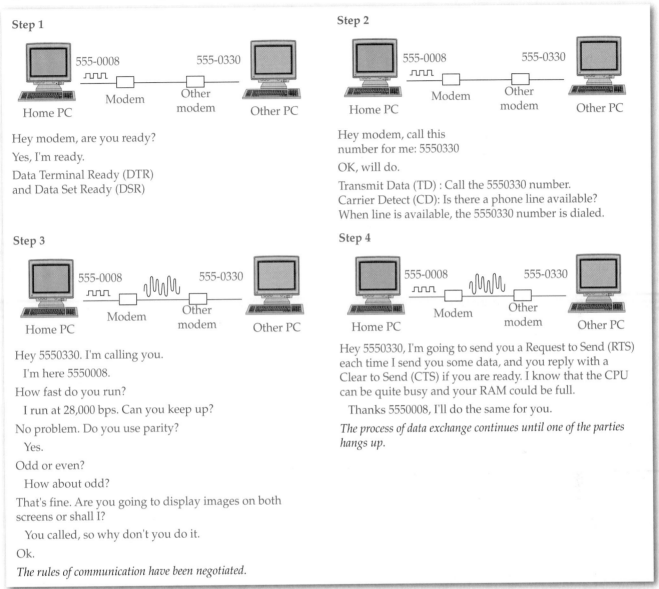

Step 1

555-0008   555-0330

Home PC   Modem   Other modem   Other PC

Hey modem, are you ready?

Yes, I'm ready.

Data Terminal Ready (DTR) and Data Set Ready (DSR)

Step 2

555-0008   555-0330

Home PC   Modem   Other modem   Other PC

Hey modem, call this number for me: 5550330

OK, will do.

Transmit Data (TD) : Call the 5550330 number.
Carrier Detect (CD): Is there a phone line available?
When line is available, the 5550330 number is dialed.

Step 3

555-0008   555-0330

Home PC   Modem   Other modem   Other PC

Hey 5550330. I'm calling you.

I'm here 5550008.

How fast do you run?

I run at 28,000 bps. Can you keep up?

No problem. Do you use parity?

Yes.

Odd or even?

How about odd?

That's fine. Are you going to display images on both screens or shall I?

You called, so why don't you do it.

Ok.

The rules of communication have been negotiated.

Step 4

555-0008   555-0330

Home PC   Modem   Other modem   Other PC

Hey 5550330, I'm going to send you a Request to Send (RTS) each time I send you some data, and you reply with a Clear to Send (CTS) if you are ready. I know that the CPU can be quite busy and your RAM could be full.

Thanks 5550008, I'll do the same for you.

The process of data exchange continues until one of the parties hangs up.

Goodheart-Willcox Publisher

Figure 13-6. Typical modem data packet. Surrounding the data is a start bit, stop bit, and parity bit.

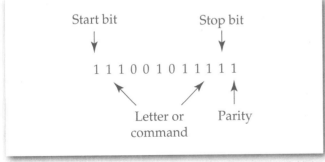

Start bit   Stop bit

1 1 1 0 0 1 0 1 1 1 1 1

Letter or command   Parity

Goodheart-Willcox Publisher

either an odd number or an even number. A zero can represent odd or even parity and the same is true for a one. The receiving system adds up the bits in the data and compares that number to the parity bit to check for errors.

The last item to resolve is the half- and full-duplex condition. The two communicating systems must agree which system will be responsible for half-duplex transmission and which will be responsible for full-duplex transmission. The terminal responsible for full-duplex is responsible to display data on the screen for both PCs. The other PC need not be responsible. If this condition is not in agreement, neither system will display the data on the screen, or both systems will display data on the screen. This means the data will be displayed twice on each screen.

After all the responsibilities have been negotiated between systems, messages can begin to be transmitted. The modem sends a Request to Send (RTS) signal asking if the other modem is ready to receive data. It replies with a Clear to Send (CTS) signal. The two computers can send data back and forth in continuous operation and actually both can transmit data over the line at the same time.

Many of these commands and activities can be monitored when using a modem connected outside the PC unit. The exterior type of modem has a series of lights that indicate different stages of activities. **Figure 13-7** is a list of typical light abbreviations and their meanings.

The entire operation of the modem is a combination of coordinating the operating system software, modem controller chip, and UART chip. The entire process seems complicated, but in effect it appears transparent to the typical user. The user simply clicks an icon and connects.

Modem Signaling Standards

Data sent between two modems must use some type of communication standards after the initial process of setting up communication rules. The standards are used for data compression techniques and error correction after an error has been detected. When there were only a few telephone companies operating, this was not an issue. The Bell Telephone Company developed a set of standards known as the Bell standards. Bell 103 was the first widely accepted standard used for modems operating at 300 baud. Later, Bell 212A was the accepted standard for 1200 bps. After deregulation of the telephone companies in America, a number of standards were used.

A dominant standard was the *International Telecommunications Union (ITU)*. This was not actually a single standard but rather a collection of standards. The standards resolved issues such as volume, minimum and maximum tone sound, and synchronous or asynchronous transmissions. As the speed of modems increased, new standards had to be developed based on the new techniques and technical parameters. Communication is now a worldwide event and involves standards from Europe also. As computer network systems evolved, another set of standards was developed called the *Microcom Networking Protocol (MNP)*. This was developed in the mid-1980s. This set of standards deals mainly with the rules of communication between two computers.

In addition to the standards, a system is needed for telephone data communication between two points. A modem standard is developed so that two modems can communicate effectively. After a communications standard is established, the modem must have a way to determine data and command codes. A system is needed to show how the electrical pulses and fluctuations will be used to represent data. A modem simply transports packets as a series of electrical fluctuations. A protocol is needed to represent the data and how it is to be encoded. You can think of a protocol as the organized manner and the rules used to represent the data

Figure 13-7.
External modem light abbreviations and meanings.

Abbreviation	Meaning
AA (Auto Answer)	Ready to accept incoming calls automatically.
CD (Carrier Detect)	The modem has detected a carrier signal.
HS (High Speed)	The modem is operating at its highest speed.
MR (Modem Ready)	Modem is ready to operate; the power is on.
OH (Off Hook)	Same as taking the receiver off the telephone hook.
SD (Send Data)	Data is being received at the other modem.
TR (Terminal Ready)	Modem indicates it has received a (DTR) from the software package.

being transmitted. Some common communication protocols are Kermit, ASCII, Zmodem, Ymodem, and Sealink. There will be much more information about protocols later in this textbook when covering network fundamentals.

Telephone Modem Installation

A telephone modem adapter can be installed inside a desktop computer, or a USB telephone modem can be added to a computer using any available USB port. A typical modem adapter card comes with a telephone cable equipped with RJ-11 connectors and a disc containing drivers and appropriate telephone modem software applications, **Figure 13-8**. The USB telephone modem kit comes with a telephone cable, a USB cable, and a disc containing software drivers and software applications for the modem, **Figure 13-9**. A USB telephone modem makes a nice addition to a computer tech troubleshooting tool bag. You can check the telephone dial-up connection without replacing an existing internal telephone modem.

Tech Tip

A telephone modem is also referred to as a *dial-up modem.*

Figure 13-9. A USB telephone modem is connected as an exterior device using any available USB port.

Goodheart-Willcox Publisher

A telephone modem comes with two RJ-11 ports, one labeled "Line" and the other labeled "Phone," **Figure 13-10**. The port labeled "Line" connects to the incoming telephone line. The port labeled "Phone" connects to a line telephone. Since there will most likely be only one telephone wall jack at the computer location, the dual-port design allows the user to use the telephone and the dial-up connection without the need of a special adapter.

Figure 13-8. A telephone modem adapter card is installed into a PCI slot of a desktop computer.

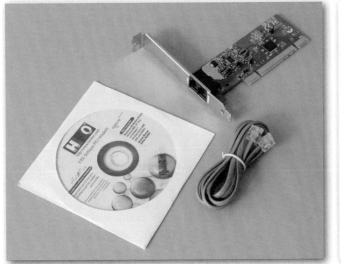

Goodheart-Willcox Publisher

Figure 13-10. A typical telephone modem has two RJ-11 ports, one labeled "Line" and the other labeled "Phone."

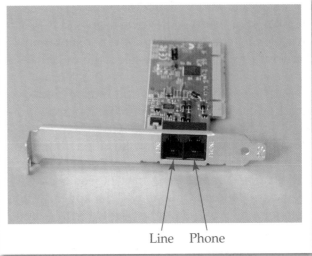

Goodheart-Willcox Publisher

Telephone Modem Dialing Properties

There are many different properties associated with a telephone modem. Plug and Play modems are easy to install. But, as easy as it is to install a Plug and Play modem, there will be times when you will need to be familiar with the various property settings associated with the telephone modem and modem connections to the Internet. During troubleshooting scenarios, you may need to reconfigure a telephone modem or talk a customer through various changes and verifications when performing customer support.

When a new telephone connection is first set up, you will use the **My Location** dialog box. When configuring an additional modem location, you will use the **New Location** dialog box, **Figure 13-11**. The **New Location** dialog box looks very similar in Windows XP, Windows Vista, Windows 7, and Windows 8 and requires information about several items. These items are described in **Figure 13-12**.

The **Area Code Rules** tab reveals how the area code should be entered. For example, what number(s) or prefixes are to be used and in what sequence. The **Calling Card** tab, shown in **Figure 13-13**, allows you to select the calling card company you wish to use with the dial-up connection. As you can see, you must include a calling card account number and a personal identification number (PIN).

In Windows XP, the **New Location** dialog box is located through **Start | Control Panel | Phone and Modem Options** when in the **Classic** view. The **Phone and Modem Options** will not appear in the **Category** view of the **Control Panel** if a telephone modem has not been installed. After a telephone modem has been installed on the computer, it will

Figure 13-11. The **New Location** dialog box allows you to examine and change settings for your modem.

appear and be accessed through the **Control Panel | Printers and Other Hardware | Phone and Modem Options** in **Classic** view. The **Phone and Modem Options** dialog box is similar in Windows XP, Windows Vista, Windows 7, and Windows 8.

In Windows Vista, you can access **Phone and Modem Options** through **Start | Control Panel | Hardware and Sound | Phone and Modem Options**. You may also access **Phone and Modem Options** using the **Classic** view setting of **Control Panel** to reveal the **Phone and Modem Options** icon. In Windows 7 and Windows 8, access the dialog box through **Control Panel | Phone and Modem**. Control Panel should be set to **Classic** view (**Small icon** or **Large icon** view).

Tech Tip

If a telephone modem is not installed, you will not be able to access the modem configuration setting through the Control Panel **Category** view in Windows Vista, Windows 7, or Windows 8. You will only be able to access the modem configuration dialog box through the Control Panel **Classic** view.

Figure 13-12.
New Location dialog box properties and description.

Property	Description
Location name	A name that identifies the location to which the modem will connect. This is very important if there are more than one dial-up connection, such as one to your Internet service provider and one to your work location.
Country/region	Country or region of the location you are calling from.
Area code	The area code of the telephone line you are calling from, not to.
Dialing rules	Special numbers required to place an outside call. For example, a number such as *9* or *1* may need to be dialed before a connection outside the facility can be established.
Call waiting	Used to disable call waiting. Some service providers require that you disable the call waiting feature. The local telephone provider will supply the required number(s) to disable the call waiting feature.
Dial using	Options are **Pulse** or **Tone**. Pulse phone dialing is used with the rotary dial phone. In the U.S., touch-tone dialing is used almost everywhere.

Goodheart-Willcox Publisher

Figure 13-13. Beneath the **Calling Card** tab is a list of many calling card companies with which to use your dial-up connection. Notice that you must also enter your account number and personal identification number (PIN).

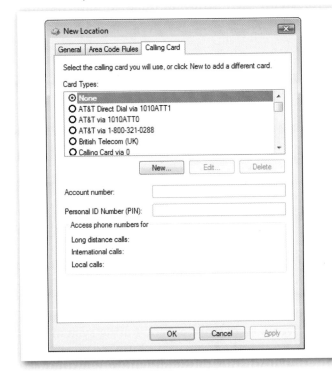

Windows Dial-up Internet Connection Features

Windows Vista drastically changed how network and Internet connections are made. The Windows Vista and later operating systems automatically detect installed devices such as modems and network connections and then automatically start the appropriate wizard to help a user configure the device. However, when Windows fails to automatically detect an installed device, it modifies the dialog input boxes and wizards according to which devices are detected. For example, if a telephone modem has not been installed or configured, Windows will not display an option for the device. Look at the differences between the dialog boxes shown in **Figure 13-14**. Notice the option **Show connection options that this computer is not set up to use**. After selecting this option, the dialog box displays other devices that can be configured for Internet access, such as a dial-up modem or ISDN. Therefore, the option to configure a dial-up connection is displayed, even though it was not automatically detected. The **Dial-up** option allows you to manually configure a dial-up connection if the Windows Vista operating system has failed to automatically detect the modem.

Figure 13-14.
Windows Vista and later modifies the dialog input boxes and wizards according to which devices are detected as installed. A—The **Dial-up** option is hidden because the operating system did not detect the modem. B—With **Show connection options that this computer is not set up to use** selected, the **Dial-up** option is displayed.

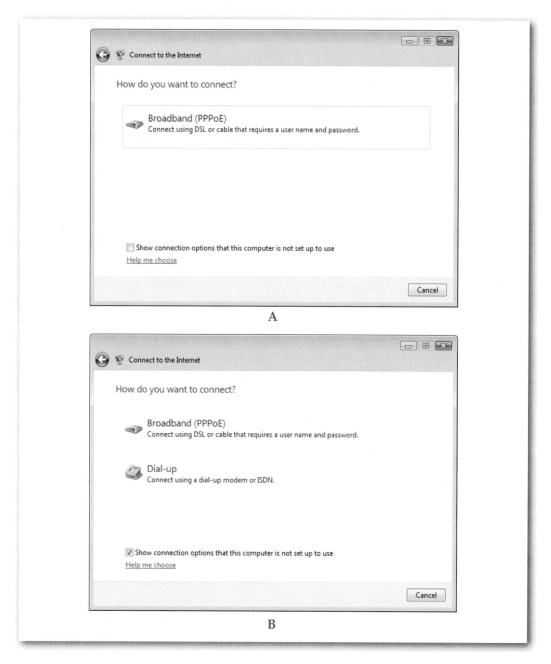

Figure 13-15 shows the typical information required to establish a dial-up connection to an Internet service provider. An **Internet service provider (ISP)** provides a connection to the Internet, and it usually provides many other services as well. Services such as e-mail, tools, and space to set up your own website, search engines, and local information are provided by most ISPs. The three items of required information are the Internet service provider telephone number, a user name, and a user password. The Internet connection can be shared by selecting **Allow other people to use this connection**.

Some of the features that were standard in earlier versions of Windows operating systems have been absorbed into other setup programs. For example, a direct telephone dial-up feature is no longer available, but the same service can be provided through the Connect to a workplace wizard.

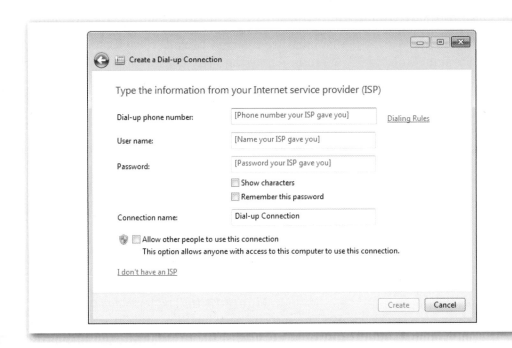

Figure 13-15.
The **Create a Dial-up Connection** dialog box solicits the user for required information to establish a connection with the Internet service provider.

Tech Tip

Many times a feature not seen in Control Panel can be viewed and accessed by changing the default Control Panel view to **Classic**. For example, **Phone and Modem Options** is directly available under **Classic** view but not in the **Category** view, which is the default view.

Integrated Services Digital Network

Integrated services digital network (ISDN) is a standard that allows a completely digital connection from one PC to another. Like the regular dial-up service, ISDN uses phone lines to transfer data. Although, to use ISDN services, you must be within approximately 3 1/2 miles of the actual digital equipment of the telephone company. To use ISDN lines for communication, you must use a terminal adapter (TA) rather than a modem. A terminal adapter is like a modem, only it does not need to convert signals back and forth between analog and digital. The signal stays digital. Terminal adapters come in the form of adapter boards or exterior devices that connect directly to the serial port.

ISDN can be used to carry voice and digital information simultaneously. Traditional phone lines only allow voice or data. They cannot handle both at the same time. On a standard ISDN line there are three channels: one D channel and two B channels. The D channel is designed to carry control signals and operates in a range of 16 kbps to 64 kbps. The two B channels are used for voice and data and can carry data at speeds up to 64 kbps. The two B channels can be combined to carry data up to 128 kbps.

ISDN provides services for businesses as well as for private use. The price is much higher for digital service than for traditional phone lines. This makes its use prohibitive for many private users.

Digital Subscriber Lines

A **digital subscriber line (DSL)** provides high-speed Internet access over telephone lines and has become one of the most popular methods for connecting to the Internet. There are many different variations of DSL available, such as ADSL, HDSL, VHDSL, and SDSL. In this textbook, we will use the acronym DSL to represent the technology in general and will not address any particular type of DSL.

A DSL can provide a constant connection to the Internet and can be used to send and receive both voice and data over the same line. Regular telephone lines are designed to carry low-frequency voice communications in a range of 0 kHz to 4 kHz. DSL telephone lines are designed to carry much higher frequencies at 25 kHz to 1 MHz. The higher frequencies can be used for high-speed Internet access. DSL is not available in all areas, and it is more expensive than regular telephone line service.

The maximum distance DSL can span is limited by the high frequencies it uses. The typical maximum distance for DSL ranges from 1,000′ to 18,000′ measured from the DSL modem to the telephone central office. The exact limit depends on the type of DSL used and any special equipment such as loading coils or media such as fiber-optic cable that might exist on the telephone line.

A loading coil is used to amplify analog voice signals. It will not amplify a DSL signal. In fact, the loading coil reduces or blocks the higher frequency DSL signal. The media might also change between the subscriber location and the central office. For example, the copper conductor cabling may change to fiber-optic cabling at some point, which will prevent the application of DSL. DSL technology is applied only to copper wiring, not fiber-optic.

The actual physical attributes of the copper core in the cable is another factor that determines the maximum distance DSL can be applied. The cable copper core length, diameter, and number of twists per foot in the cable pairs affect the actual distance and throughput of the DSL

service. The diameter of the cable is expressed in a measure referred to as AWG, which is the acronym American Wire Gage. The three common diameters range are 22, 24, and 26 AWG. The 22 AWG is the largest diameter, and the 26 AWG is the smallest diameter. The smaller the diameter of the cable and the greater the number of twists in the cable pairs, the shorter the distance the cable can span and the lower the frequency it can carry. The most significant factor affecting DSL performance is the cable overall length.

DSL Types

There are many types of DSL systems. They vary in upstream and downstream bandwidths as shown in **Figure 13-16**. The term *downstream* is used to describe the data flow direction from the carrier or provider's site to the customer. The term *upstream* is used for the data flow direction from the customer to the carrier.

ADSL is the original DSL service and is commonly used by Internet service providers for residential services. ADSL2+ is an improved version of the original ADSL and has greater service distances and higher data rates. VDSL is a high-speed, short-distance DSL service that is typically used for short runs from the home or office to a higher speed fiber-optic cable service. VDSL2 and VDSL2+ are the latest DSL service technologies which provide combined voice, video, and data to support high-definition television (HDTV).

SDSL and HDSL are both symmetric services, which mean that the upstream and downstream

Figure 13-16.
DSL types and their upload and download speeds. Typical maximum distances are also listed.

DSL Type	Upstream	Downstream	Maximum Distance
ADSL	800 kbps	1.5 Mbps–8 Mbps	12,000–18,000
ADSL2+	2 Mbps	24 Mbps	5,000
HDSL	1.544 Mbps	1.544 Mbps	15,000
SDSL	1.544 Mbps	1.544 Mbps	10,000
VDSL	1.5 Mbps–2.3 Mbps	13 Mbps–52 Mbps	1,000–4,500
VDSL2	1 Mbps–16 Mbps	30 Mbps	4,000
VDSL2+	2 Mbps	24 Mbps	5,000
RADSL	1 Mbps	7 Mbps	1,000–18,000
G.lite ADSL	192 kbps–2.3 Mbps	192 kbps–2.3 Mbps	14,000

data rates match. Services that start with the letter *A* are asymmetric. This means the upstream and downstream data rates do not match. SDSL is a basic service, while HDSL is a high-speed data rate form of DSL.

RADSL stands for Rate Adaptive DSL. *Rate adaptive* means the connection is shared and the actual connection speed will vary depending on the number of persons using the service. When more people are using the service, the actual connection speed drops in increments. For more information on the various DSL technologies, visit your local area service provider's website.

> **Tech Tip**
>
> When comparing information about xDSL from other sources, you will see that data rates and maximum distances will vary greatly. This is because some sources only reflect their company's technologies. A major factor is the electrical characteristics of the copper wire.

DSL Modem and Cables

A **DSL modem** allows for high-speed Internet access over existing phone lines. It is also referred to as a DSL transceiver. A typical DSL modem is shown in **Figure 13-17**. Also shown are a power adapter, telephone cable, and Ethernet cable. The power adapter converts the standard 120 Vac to 12 Vdc needed to power the modem. The telephone cable connects to the back of the DSL modem to the telephone wall jack using RJ-11 connectors. The Ethernet cable is a standard Cat 5 or Cat 5e cable. The Ethernet cable connects to the back of the DSL modem and then to the network adapter card installed in the PC, **Figure 13-18**. Some DSL modems use a USB cable to connect to the PC's USB port. No network adapter is required to be installed in the PC if a USB cable is used.

An additional device called a *filter* may be required if there is other equipment connected to the same telephone line used for Internet access. Other equipment types are fax machines or telephones. Fax machines and telephones can be plugged into the same DSL line as the PC,

Figure 13-17. DSL modem, cables, and power adapter.

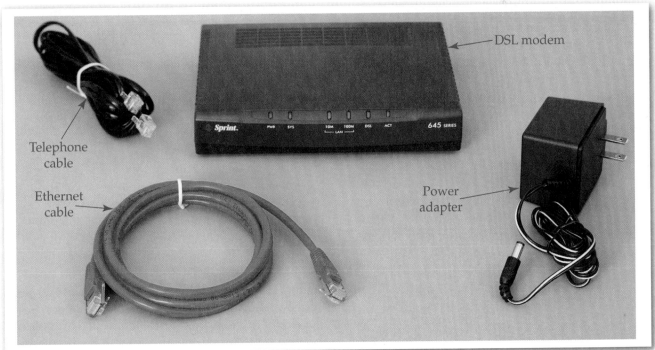

Figure 13-18.
The DSL modem is connected between the DSL telephone line and the network card on the PC.

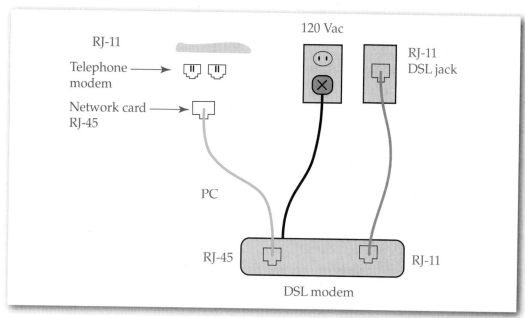

RJ-11

Telephone → modem

Network card → RJ-45

120 Vac

RJ-11 DSL jack

PC

RJ-45   DSL modem   RJ-11

Goodheart-Willcox Publisher

but they must do so through a filter. The filter prevents lower frequency signals to and from these devices from interfering with or corrupting the higher frequency signals used for the Internet connection. A filter is never installed in the line between the DSL modem and the PC because it will block the high frequency signals used by the Internet connection.

DSL is a point-to-point connection. This means it will provide a steady bandwidth and will not fluctuate like other broadband connections. For example, cable television access used for Internet connections are shared by other connections in the local neighborhood. Cable television bandwidth varies according to how many other people are accessing the Internet using the shared cable.

Both cable Internet access and DSL can be used to support multiple devices such as other computers or gaming consoles. A device called a *router* or *gateway* is installed after the modem, or the modem can be a combination of router and modem. The router can distribute additional connections using cable or wireless radio signals.

Cable

Cable Internet service provides high-speed Internet access using lines designed for cable

television. It uses a cable modem to connect you to the Internet without having to dial in. It can provide you with a continuous connection. Your connection will not time out for lack of use like it may with a dial-up Internet service provider. ISPs set a time-out value so they can take back the IP address and make it available to other users. With a cable Internet service, you have your own IP address. IP addresses are discussed later in this chapter.

DSL and cable provide much more bandwidth than a 56 k telephone modem. DSL has several different speed options running from 250 kbps to over 1.5 Gbps. One drawback of cable is that its Internet bandwidth varies greatly depending on the number of users accessing the Internet through the shared connection. Thus, as more people access and use data-intense services, such as video and audio downloading, your data speeds will slow. You can expect 300 kbps to 500 kbps on average from each of the Internet services, despite their claims of speeds in the very high Mbps range. In some cases, you can expect speeds as high as 1.5 Mbps or slightly higher. Another drawback of cable Internet service is there is often only one choice of cable service provider per neighborhood. So, if you are unhappy with your service provider, your options are limited.

Cable Media

There are two major types of cable television media used for access: fiber-optic cable and coaxial cable. See **Figure 13-19**. Coaxial cable consists of a solid copper conductor surrounded by thick insulating material. An outer conductor is made of braided copper or a foil jacket surrounding the insulating material. An insulating jacket, used to provide physical protection to the cable assembly, covers the entire assembly. Special coaxial cable connectors are crimped onto the ends. Coaxial cable is easily spliced or extended. Coaxial cable has a maximum data transfer speed of 350 MHz. Originally a conventional telephone line was used to establish the connection to the Internet, and then the coaxial cable was used to download from the Internet. Today, coaxial cable is currently a two-way data transmission system and does not require a separate telephone to establish the connection.

Fiber-optic cable consists of a glass or plastic core. Each core material, glass or plastic, is quite small in cross-sectional area and is very flexible. Fiber-optic cable transmits light rather than an electrical signal through the core. Fiber-optic cable has many advantages over coaxial cable or any type of copper core cable. It is lightweight, resistive to corrosion and water, and immune to electrical interference. It also provides excellent security because it is almost impossible to tap into. One very big advantage of fiber-optic cable is that it is immune to strikes by lightning. When lightning strikes traditional metal core cable, a high current can run through the cable and damage sensitive electronic equipment, including computers and monitors. Fiber-optic cable can also be run for longer lengths with less signal loss than conventional copper core cables.

The downside of fiber-optic cable is essentially price. Fiber-optic cable is expensive to install. Also, special equipment is required for splicing the cable.

Fiber-optic cable through the television company is usually divided into many different channels. Each channel uses a 6-MHz channel to transmit each separate television channel or network, such as ABC, CBS, or NBC. The same principle is used for Internet connections. Two channels, each 6 MHz, are provided to transmit data to and from the Internet. Currently, there is not a single standard for cable modem specifications. You must check with the local ISP cable company to see what type or brand of cable modem you will need. One standard that has been established for cable modems is called **Data Over Cable Service Interface Specification (DOCSIS)**. This standard allows any DOCSIS cable modem to communicate with any other DOCSIS cable modem. Also, you will need to install a cable splitter.

Figure 13-19. Coaxial cable and fiber-optic cable comparison. A—Coaxial cable. Note the center conductor surrounded by layers of insulation. B—Fiber-optic cable. Fiber-optic cable has several outer layers. The layers protect the cable and reflect the light down the cable.

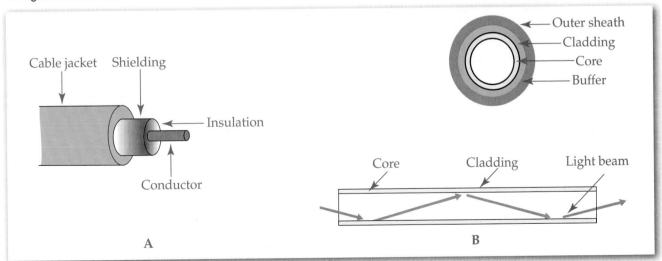

Cable Modem

A **cable modem** is a transceiver similar to a DSL modem and allows existing cable television coaxial cable to be used for Internet access. Look at the cable modem connection in **Figure 13-20**. The cable modem is installed between a splitter and the PC. The cable splitter divides the signal between your modem and your television. Remember, the same cable provides both television and Internet access. In this configuration, the coaxial cable can supply a television signal to the television as well as provide Internet access for the PC. The cable television coaxial cable connects to the cable modem from the splitter. An Ethernet cable or USB cable is used between the cable modem and the PC. More than one PC can use the cable Internet connection if a router or gateway is installed. The router or gateway need not be a separate device. Some cable modems are a combination modem and router.

DSL and cable modem ISPs typically include a setup CD. The setup CD automatically configures the connection to the ISP. The DSL and cable modem require an IP address before making a connection to the Internet.

eMTA Modem

The acronym eMTA stands for Embedded Multimedia Terminal Adapter. An **eMTA modem** combines the functionality of a DOCSIS cable modem and a phone adapter in one device. This device allows a service provider such as Comcast to provide both Internet access and telephone service to a customer using one device and one cable. The eMTA modem is usually provided by the service provider, but it can be purchased to avoid rental fees. The only requirement is that the eMTA modem be compatible with the service provider requirements.

Satellite

Satellite systems can be used for Internet access and are ideal for remote locations when a home or office is located a great deal away from city services. Satellite Internet service typically costs more to set up than other residential forms of service. You typically must either buy the satellite equipment for several hundred dollars or rent it.

The data rates for satellites vary greatly. The common downstream speed varies from 512 kbps

Figure 13-20. The cable modem is installed between a splitter and the PC. The splitter separates the cable television signal from the Internet signal.

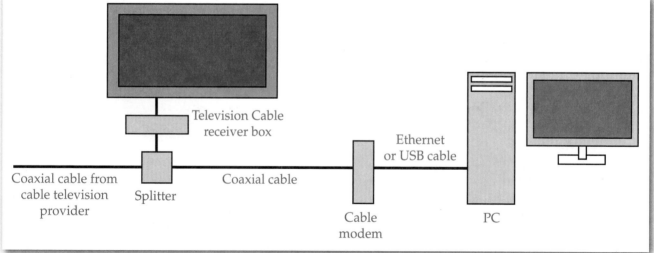

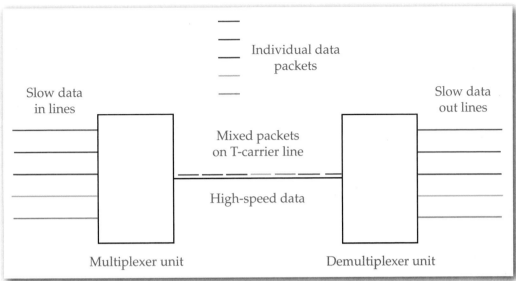

Figure 13-21.
A multiplexer organizes slower speed data and voice signals into a series of higher speed data packets. The packets are converted back to a lower speed at a demultiplexer unit.

Individual data packets

Slow data in lines

Slow data out lines

Mixed packets on T-carrier line

High-speed data

Multiplexer unit

Demultiplexer unit

Goodheart-Willcox Publisher

to 1.5 Mbps. The common upstream data rates vary from 128 kbps to 256 kbps. The satellite provides a constant connection to the Internet in similar fashion to xDSL and cable systems. Satellite systems are line-of-sight systems, which mean they must have an unobstructed direct view to the source. Trees and buildings can obstruct the satellite receiver from the source. The satellite system is also susceptible to weather conditions, such as heavy rain storms.

T-Carrier Lines

T-carrier lines were first introduced in 1993 by AT&T. They are designed to carry voice and data. The lines have the ability to carry data at a much higher rate than traditional phone lines. An important part of the T-carrier line system is the use of a multiplexer and a demultiplexer. A **multiplexer** is a special electronic device that controls the flow of data and voice over a T-carrier line. Think of it as a funnel that combines lower frequency lines together to take advantage of the higher frequency transmission rates of the T-carrier. Look at **Figure 13-21** to view a multiplexer and T-carrier.

As you can see in the illustration, there are several low-speed lines tied into the multiplexer. As data is transmitted through the multiplexer, it is reorganized into smaller packages called *data packets*. The multiplexer sends the data packets

through the T-carrier in an organized manner. The data packet then travels at the maximum speed of the T-carrier. At the opposite end of the T-carrier there is a **demultiplexer** that reverses the process. It rearranges the packets back into their original structures and releases them to lower data rate lines. Businesses, government, and educational institutions are the primary customers who lease T-carrier lines. The levels of T-carrier lines are identified in the list in **Figure 13-22**.

An additional label, called a *fractional T-1*, is a T-1 line that is only partially issued to a customer. Think of a fractional T-1 line as a line shared among different parties who, individually, do not require full T-1 line capacity.

Mobile Broadband

Mobile broadband is a wireless Internet connection based on mobile phone technology. *Broadband* is an electronics term and is a classification of a communication with a bandwidth in excess of 256 kbps. When you see the term *broadband* used in the context of mobile devices, this is a general reference to any form of wireless communication that supports data rates at or above 256 kbps. **Figure 13-23** shows a USB modem that allows a laptop or similar device to connect to the CLEAR mobile broadband service through a USB port. The USB device is a mobile broadband modem.

Figure 13-22. T-carrier identifications.

| T-1 = 1.544 Mbps or 24 voice channels |
| T-2 = 6.312 Mbps or 96 voice channels |
| T-3 = 44.736 Mbps or 672 voice channels |
| T-4 = 274.176 Mbps or 4,032 voice channels |

Goodheart-Willcox Publisher

Figure 13-23. USB mobile broadband modem.

Goodheart-Willcox Publisher

A **USB modem** is a tiny mobile broadband device that plugs into any laptop with a USB port. It allows the laptop to connect to the Internet using a mobile broadband service. Some companies refer to their USB modems as *laptop sticks* or *data cards*. Some USB modems can also be used as storage devices similar to a USB flash memory device. USB modems with storage capacity often include installation manuals, software applications, and required drivers. No separate installation disc is needed.

Tech Tip   There are several different definitions of broadband speed. For example, the FCC's definition of high-speed access is at least 3 Mbps downstream and 768 Mbps upstream. The IEEE defines broadband as having instantaneous bandwidths greater than 1 MHz and supporting data rates greater than 1.5 Mbps.

Sharing Mobile Broadband Connections

There are two general methods used to share mobile broadband access. The first is to share the connection through a mobile broadband-equipped device such as a smartphone, tablet, or laptop. The second way is to use a dedicated device that makes a connection to the mobile broadband provider and then shares the connection using Wi-Fi or network cables. In general, a network device used to connect to the Internet and share the Internet connection with other devices in the home or office is called a **router**. A mobile broadband router is used to connect wirelessly to a cell service. Many times the mobile broadband router is called other names by the service provider such as *jetpack* or *wireless pocket router*.

Tethering

Connecting a mobile device to another device is called **tethering**. Mobile broadband services are provided by communication companies such as Verizon Wireless, Sprint, and AT&T. A single device can be configured to share access to mobile broadband services. For example, a smartphone can share its mobile broadband service with other devices such as computers or tablets. You can create and share an Internet connection using a smartphone or a tablet that is equipped with cell phone access such as 3G or 4G. Sharing an Internet connection through a mobile broadband device is also referred to as *tethering*. Look at the **Figure 13-24** to see the Internet sharing configuration on a Windows 8 phone.

The connection to the Internet is made using the Windows 8 phone. The connection between the mobile devices is using Wi-Fi technology. This particular device can be configured to share its Internet connection with up to eight other devices. To connect to the smartphone Internet share, you need two things: the broadcast name (SSID) of the wireless network and a password. The password is also referred to as a *security key, passphrase,* or *passcode*.

Another way of sharing an Internet connection is through the use of a dedicated device that is especially designed to connect to the Internet wireless broadband service and then

Figure 13-24. Windows 8 phone Internet sharing configuration. Mobile devices can be configured to share their Internet connections with other devices.

Goodheart-Willcox Publisher

Figure 13-25. A mobile hotspot can provide shared Internet access to other Wi-Fi—capable devices from any location that has compatible mobile broadband service.

Goodheart-Willcox Publisher

distribute the connection to other devices. This type of device is referred to as a hotspot or a mobile hotspot.

Mobile Hotspots

A **mobile hotspot** is a portable wireless router that allows multiple devices to share a common Internet connection, **Figure 13-25**. The mobile hotspot connects to a mobile broadband service and then shares the connection with other devices using Wi-Fi, **Figure 13-26**.

Some mobile hotspots have mobile broadband capability built into the device and are typically marketed by the mobile broadband service provider. Other mobile hotspot devices that are not mobile broadband enabled use a USB modem to establish a connection to the mobile broadband service provider. After a broadband connection is established with a service provider, the connection can be shared to other devices using either Wi-Fi or network cable connections.

You can also create a mobile hotspot through devices such as tablets. **Figure 13-27** shows an Android tablet configuration option for creating a

mobile Wi-Fi hotspot. Some tablets are equipped with a SIM card that allows the tablet to share a mobile broadband connection with other devices.

3G and 4G

The acronyms *3G* and *4G* represent third generation (3G) and fourth generation (4G) when used in respect to mobile broadband systems. There have been four major generations of mobile wireless technology starting with the first mobile wireless communication device, the walkie-talkie. A radical change in the development of portable wireless communication that requires all new electronic concepts and parts is referred to as a generation. A generation of portable wireless communication devices is not compatible with devices from previous generations. You cannot upgrade a device from one generation to be compatible with devices in the next generation.

3G and *4G* are not technical terms and are not specifications but rather an entire set of various standards and electronic technologies. The terms *3G* and *4G* are used in advertisement and marketing of broadband wireless portable devices. In fact, when used in advertisement and marketing, 3G or 4G may be based on entirely different sets of mobile radio communication standards depending on the service provider.

Figure 13-26. A portable wireless router wireless converts broadband radio wave frequencies and format to Wi-Fi frequency and format.

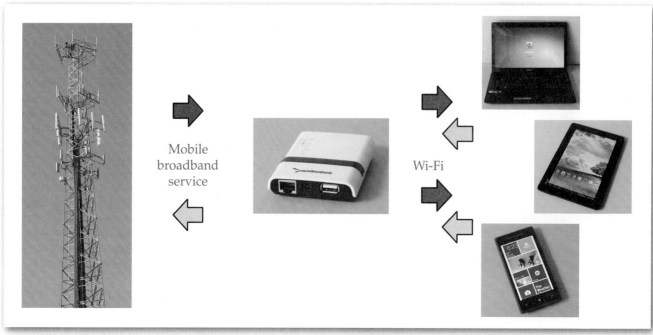

Mobile broadband service

Wi-Fi

Goodheart-Willcox Publisher

Figure 13-27. Most tablets have a configuration option for tethering or creating a mobile Wi-Fi hotspot.

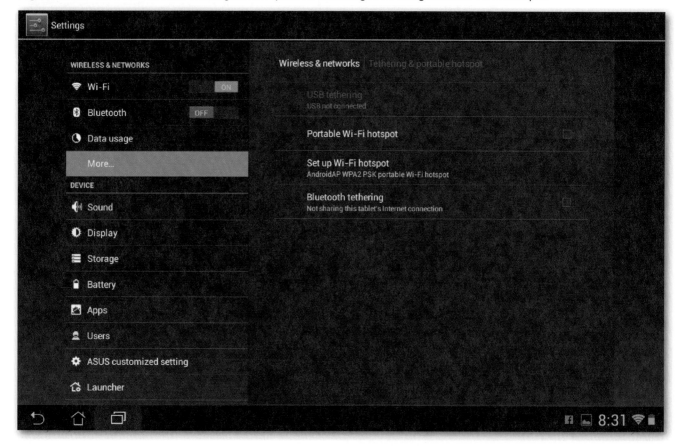

In general, with respect to devices and services classified as 3G and 4G, 4G is far superior as compared to 3G. You can download or upload a great deal more data with 4G as compared to 3G.

Broadband Data Rates

Data rates vary greatly between broadband service providers and technologies. Data rates vary a great deal when comparing 3G to 4G. In general, 4G is significantly faster than 3G but there are many factors that can directly affect data rates. At best, the true data rates are much lower than actual advertised data rates. For example, you will see data rates as high as 100 Mbps uplink and 50 Mbps downlink for 4G LTE wireless. In actuality, the average user data rates are 5 Mbps to 12 Mbps downlink and 2 Mbps to 5 Mbps uplink. The reasons for the difference is radio interference, distance from the service provider, and how many users are accessing the service at the same time.

Radio interference can be a real problem for both 3G and 4G service. There are so many devices that rely on radio technology that the air is simply full of signals generated from many different sources. The distance from the service provider can also affect the data rate. The farther the mobile device is from the service provider, the lower the data rate. This is caused by the fact that the radio signal becomes weaker the further it travels, thus causing a loss of data generally in direct proportion to the distance.

Lastly, the total numbers of users sharing the same frequency can cause a fluctuating data rate. Since the frequency is a shared medium, there is a direct correlation between the number of users sharing the frequency and individual user download and upload data rates. Another factor that affects data rates is location, which is directly related to the data rate factors mentioned before. A mobile device might work great in a city like Atlanta but seem to operate sluggishly in another city. This is because of all the factors previously mentioned. The following is a table of approximate data rates recommended for use of different services.

Application	Description	Data Rate
Multimedia messaging	A combination of texting and attached image.	8 kbps–64 kbps
Video telephony	Telephone with a live video feed.	64 kbps–384 kbps
General web browsing	Webpage viewing from a simple static webpage to a dynamic webpage with animation.	32 kbps–1 Mbps
Video and audio streaming	Viewing both video and audio media, such as television or movies, with modest resolution.	32 kbps–2 Mbps
High-definition video streaming	Viewing both video and audio media, such as television or movies, with excellent resolution.	4 Mbps and higher

The table contains suggested or recommended data rates for good performance. You can still obtain some of these services with lower data rates, but the performance will be poor. Verizon Wireless advertises the following data rates, which are based on an independent third-party test:

- **4G Long Term Evolution (LTE):** Download speeds of 5 Mbps to 12 Mbps and upload speeds of 2 Mbps to 5 Mbps.
- **3G Evolution Data Optimized (EVDO):** Download speeds of 600 kps to 1.4 Mbps and upload speeds of 500 kbps to 800 kbps.

Metered Bandwidth Consumption

Most mobile broadband service providers charge users by the amount of bandwidth they consume. For example, a mobile broadband service provider may sell a service plan based on consuming 2 GB of bandwidth per month at $40.00 per month, but an additional 1 GB may cost an additional $15.00. In other words, it is like an electric bill. The more you consume, the more it will cost you.

Because most plans charge for additional usage, many wireless mobile devices have some type of metering so that you can view your total consumption. Some devices will also send you a text alert to let you know when you are getting close to exceeding your total bandwidth allocation. The following table can be used as a general guide to relationship between mobile broadband total consumption and the application used.

Consumption	E-mail	Music	Video
1 GB	250	3 hours	2 hours
4 GB	2,000	15 hours	8 hours
10 GB	10,000	30 hours	20 hours

Note: Based on Verizon Wireless customer information.

Assigned Frequencies

Wi-Fi has definite assigned frequencies such as 2.4 GHz and 5 GHz, depending on which standard is applied such as 802.11a, 802,11b, 802,11g and 802.11n. There is no one assigned radio frequency for mobile communications, but rather several different assigned frequencies that can be used by service providers. Some commonly-encountered frequencies are 700 MHz, 800 MHz, 850 MHz, 900 MHz, 1,700 MHz, 1,800 MHz, 1,900 MHz, and 2,100 MHz. Many devices can work on multiple frequencies. A device that can work on two frequencies is referred to as a dual-band device. One that can work on three frequencies is called a tri-band device, and one that works on four, a quad-band device.

Figure 13-28 shows the choices related to the configuration of the operational mode for a Verizon Wireless cell phone. The choices are Global mode; LTE and CDMA; and LTE, GSM, or UMTS. What do all these acronyms mean? It can be very confusing because cell phone and mobile broadband technology is worldwide and applies to many different standards and electronics technologies. When accessing mobile broadband services, you may need to match the technology to the device before you can obtain service. For example, you may need to configure the device for LTE and CDMA mode before the device will access the mobile broadband service. The following sections describe the most common operational modes to help you better understand the specifications of mobile broadband equipment and services.

Figure 13-28. Cellular telephone devices provide several options to match the type of cellular service.

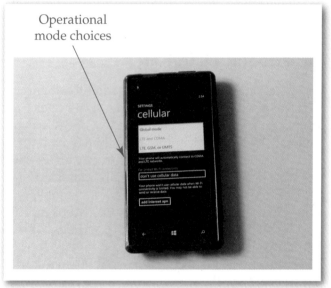

Operational mode choices

Goodheart-Willcox Publisher

Global System for Mobile Communications

Global System for Mobile Communications (GSM) was originally an analog wireless communication system used for voice communications or wireless telephones. Later, GSM evolved into a wireless digital communication system for transmitting mobile voice and data. The European Telecommunications Standards Institute (ETSI) developed the standards for the second generation (2G), which became the defacto standard all over the world. There are some other standards, but they only account for a small percentage of all wireless communications and need not be mentioned here. These standards are maintained by the GSM Association, a group of cellular network operators and associated companies.

Universal Mobile Telecommunications System

Universal Mobile Telecommunications System (UMTS) is a 3G standard developed by the 3rd Generation Partnership Project (3GPP). UMTS is a component of the International Telecommunication Union (ITU) set of communication standards. UMTS also incorporates the electronics technology of CDMA.

Code Division Multiple Access

Code Division Multiple Access (CDMA) is one of the electronic techniques used to encode digital information when using radio as a medium. CDMA greatly increases the amount of data and number of users that can be carried on a single radio channel. Major carriers Sprint and Verizon Wireless mainly use CDMA technology, while AT&T and T-Mobile use GSM technology. All of these carriers also support 3G networks.

Long Term Evolution

Long Term Evolution (LTE) is an evolution of the GSM and UMTS standards. LTE is considered 4G and has the highest advertised data rates. LTE is the best choice for streaming music, videos, and high definition. However as mentioned earlier, the advertised data rates and the actual data rates vary greatly.

WiMAX

WiMAX is a wireless technology similar to Wi-Fi but has a much greater range, and the radio broadcast direction can be controlled. Wi-Fi is limited to a few hundred feet at best, but WiMAX can be used at distances of 30 miles for fixed stations and 3 to 10 miles for mobile stations. Some factors that affect the distance and throughput are terrain, weather, and large buildings. A Wi-Fi broadcast signal is typically omnidirectional, meaning it broadcasts in a 360° radius from the transmitter. A WiMAX broadcast signal can be shaped to transmit in point-to-point, omni, or sector. Omni means the radio wave is broadcast in all directions (360°). Point-to-point means the radio wave is broadcast in a narrow beam or direct line of sight. A sector broadcast is a portion of the 360° broadcast, such as 60°, 90°, or 120°. The patterns are produced according to the type of antenna selected. See **Figure 13-29**.

The data rates for WiMAX are approximately 46 Mbps for downlink and 7 Mbps for uplink but may vary according to interference, distance, location, number of users, and other factors.

The assigned frequencies range from 2 GHz to 66 GHz. The most commonly applied frequencies at this time are 3.5 MHz, 5 MHz, 7 MHz, 8.75 MHz, and 10 MHz. Other frequencies may be assigned by the FCC in the future because WiMAX is relatively a new form of wireless broadband.

Figure 13-29. WiMAX can shape the broadcast pattern of the radio waves.

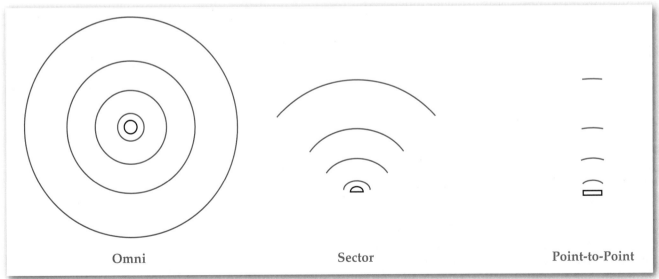

Omni   Sector   Point-to-Point

Multiple Input Multiple Output

Multiple input multiple output (MIMO) is a device that uses multiple radio channels to transmit and receive data to increase the overall data rate. MIMO is a method employed by many different wireless technologies. You can think of it as a device that uses two or more parallel channels to communicate, thus doubling the data rate. When a device has multiple antennas, it is almost always a MIMO device. Look at the wireless router in **Figure 13-30**.

A device with two or more antennae is always a sign of MIMO technology being used, but not all devices have visible antennae. Many devices hide the antennae inside the case of the device to make it more aesthetically pleasing.

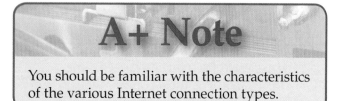

A+ Note

You should be familiar with the characteristics of the various Internet connection types.

Setting Up a Residential Internet Connection

A residential Internet connection can be easily set up. The term *residential* is used because setting up an Internet connection for a network

Figure 13-30. A device with two or more antennae is always a sign of a MIMO-enhanced device.

Goodheart-Willcox Publisher

system is different. The requirements for a large network are covered later in this textbook. Most of the residential setup is done using a setup wizard program, but even the setup wizard will need some information from you.

Most ISPs provide a disc to assist you in automatically connecting with their services. Running these discs starts a wizard that helps you set up your connection to the Internet. In addition, most PCs purchased today have setup software for several ISPs loaded onto the desktop. These ISPs can be added quickly by clicking the associated icon on the display. Usually, all this will work automatically. At times, you may be required to do some configuring manually. This is especially true in a business environment or in a PC with a security system such as a firewall.

For a typical home PC, you will need to enter the telephone number of the ISP, your user ID such as JonesB, and a password issued by the ISP. Other items that you may need to enter are the name of the e-mail server accessed at the ISP location and type of e-mail protocol being used, such as POP3. These last two items are usually provided by the ISP. You might also need to select the type of protocol used to transmit data to the ISP over the telephone line, such as PPP or SLIP. Typically, PPP is used.

When you are setting up your Internet connection, you may be required to input a choice of protocol. A **protocol** is a set of rules much like the rules that are used by two modems. The standard protocol used for the Internet is TCP/IP, which stands for Transmission Control Protocol/Internet Protocol.

A special number referred to as a TCP/IP or an IP address will be assigned to the modem. The Internet communicates using the IP address to identify a website or device as opposed to using the site name (such as www.g-w.com) that you are used to seeing in a web browser. Software converts the numeric ID (IP address) into the name of the site you are trying to reach. There will be much more about TCP/IP and Internet device identification later in the textbook.

Since you are connecting to the Internet and expect other websites and people to respond to you, your PC also will have an IP address. If you use a dial-up ISP, the IP address you use may not be permanent. Rather, the address is newly issued each time you access the Internet through your ISP. This allows the ISP to have a smaller number of IP addresses and distribute them to users as they need them. The phone number dialed as you access the Internet is just the phone number of the ISP used by your PC. It is not your IP address.

McAfee Internet Connection Speedometer

A good free utility to test the actual speed of the Internet media is the McAfee Internet Connection Speedometer, **Figure 13-31**. The McAfee Internet Connection Speedometer tests the transfer of data packets for both upstream and downstream connections and then displays

the result in the dial. In Figure 13-31, you can see that a 600 kB file was used to test the connection and the average speed obtained was 2,000 kbps. The McAfee Internet Connection Speedometer is one the best free utilities available to test your connection speed.

Troubleshooting Modems

Troubleshooting procedures for Internet service devices are very similar for all devices. Most commonly, the modem in question requires some form of reset such as power off and then power on. The following troubleshooting information should be considered as a general guide. You should always visit the service

Figure 13-31. The McAfee Internet Connection Speedometer is an excellent utility to determine the speed of your Internet connection.

provider's website for detailed troubleshooting information.

Telephone Modem Troubleshooting

Use the following suggestions when troubleshooting a telephone modem:

- Always check the modem connections first. Do *not* waste valuable time until you check the most obvious and the most common problem. People tend not to check cabling unless told to do so. A modem connection can be easily disturbed by vacuum cleaners, plugging in other equipment, or moving furniture. Always check the cable first.
- For Windows XP, Start **HyperTerminal** and type **AT** at the command prompt to see if the modem responds. The response should be "OK." The OK response tells you that communication between the PC system and modem is working. Do *not* disassemble the PC.
- Try dialing a local or test telephone number. Use the computer's Phone Dialer, **Figure 13-32**, to call the phone number of a phone on a neighboring desk. The phone should ring.
- Check the call-waiting function on the modem or dialer setup.
- Check if there is a time-out feature being used for the modem. Some modems cut off after a set time period of no activity.
- Check the telephone cable and telephone line. Faulty wiring along the telephone cable can be the cause. Try plugging in a standard telephone.
- Check with the phone company if any lines are out. Look for communications vehicles in the area of the company or residence with a modem problem. If you are called to a business for a modem problem and you see a communication vehicle sitting beside a ditch on your way there, it may save you a lot of frustration troubleshooting the modem if you stop and ask a few questions.
- If the modem is connecting but you are receiving or transmitting gibberish, then you probably have a software issue. Check the manufacturer's website for last minute upgrades and patches.
- Always assume that someone has already attempted to correct the problem before you were called. You may have to correct several problems before you detect the original one.

DSL Modem Troubleshooting

Use the following suggestions when troubleshooting a DSL modem:

- Check the status lights on the DSL modem.
- Check the cable connections at the DSL modem, computer, and the telephone wall jack.
- Reboot the computer.
- Reboot the DSL modem by disconnecting the power to the DSL modem, wait for 30 seconds

Figure 13-32.
Windows Phone Dialer can be located by entering the term "phone dialer" into the **Search** box for Windows Vista, Windows 7, and Windows 8.

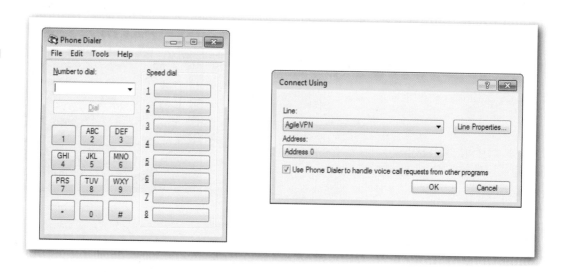

or more, and then reconnect the power to the DSL modem.

- Call your service provider for further assistance.

Cable Modem Troubleshooting

If the cable modem has a reset button, press and hold it for five seconds before releasing. If it doesn't have a reset button, try power-cycling it. The following steps can be used to power-cycle your modem:

1. Shut down your computer.
2. Unplug the cable modem from the electrical outlet.
3. Leave the cable modem unplugged for at least 10 seconds.
4. Plug the cable modem back into the electrical outlet and wait 30 seconds or more and then restart your computer.
5. Check your cable service provider for possible outage.

eMTA Modem Troubleshooting

Resetting an eMTA modem is similar to resetting a cable modem, but with one distinct difference. The eMTA modem typically has a reset button not found on cable modems. Eventually, all units, both cable modem and eMTA, will have a reset button provided.

To reset the eMTA mode, press the reset button on the back of the eMTA with a pen or other pointed, nonmetallic object. Keep the button pressed until the lights in the front of the device go off and then release the reset button. The unit will reset itself but it could take up to five minutes. If the reset does not correct the problem, you should call the service provider.

Mobile Broadband Modem Troubleshooting

Troubleshooting a mobile broadband modem is easy in contrast to troubleshooting a telephone modem. In most cases, you simply unplug the device and wait one to two minutes and then simply plug it back in. If it is a USB device, remove it from the USB port and then wait and reinsert it. If it is a hotspot device, disconnect it from the electrical power, wait a few minutes, and then plug it back in. Because mobile wireless broadband is actually a form of network, other methods of testing the connection are explained in the networking section of the textbook. Some devices do have troubleshooting software applications that will guide you through some tests. Also, service providers have troubleshooting steps and frequently asked questions (FAQs) listed at their websites, typically under a support webpage.

Wireless Hotspot Troubleshooting

Use the following steps when troubleshooting a wireless hotspot:

1. Verify that you are in your service provider coverage area.
2. Power the unit off for 30 seconds and then turn it back on.
3. Check if the SIMM is inserted properly.
4. Verify device status and signal strength as displayed by the device LEDs.
5. Check if "work offline" mode has been enabled.
6. Open **Windows Network and Sharing Center** and disable the Wi-Fi connection and then reconnect to the Wi-Fi hotspot network.

Chapter Summary

- The public telephone network system (PTNS) is constructed of high-speed fiber-optic cables, microwave transmitters and receivers, digital equipment, and computerized telephone control units.

- A residential telephone wiring system consists of two to four wires running throughout the residence and connecting to telephone jacks.

- To add a telephone modem, a telephone modem adapter card can be installed inside a desktop computer or a USB modem can be connected externally to a USB port.

- ISDN is a completely digital connection that uses a terminal adapter rather than a modem and phone lines to transfer data.

- DSL provides high-speed Internet access over DSL telephone lines.

- Cable Internet service provides high-speed Internet access over lines designed for cable television.

- Satellites are line-of-sight systems that can be used to provide a constant connection to the Internet.

- A multiplexer organizes slower speed data and voice signals into a series of higher speed data packets; a demultiplexer converts the packets back to a lower speed.

- Mobile wireless broadband is a term used to describe wireless Internet connections based on mobile phone technology.

- Most ISPs provide a disc with a wizard program to assist you in setting up a residential Internet connection.

- Actual Internet connection speeds can be determined by running the McAfee Internet Connection Speedometer.

- Troubleshooting procedures for Internet service devices are very similar for all devices in that the modem in question requires some form of reset.

Review Questions

Answer the following questions on a separate sheet of paper. Please do not write in this book.

1. Name several specific tasks that can be done by using a modem.
2. From what type of media and devices is the public telephone network system constructed?
3. What is the main factor that limits the speed of data transfer over the residential telephone system?
4. What is the designed frequency spectrum for voice communication over traditional telephone lines?
5. What does a simple residential wiring system consist of?
6. What is the difference between an RJ-11 and an RJ-14 connector?
7. What is a demarcation point?
8. What is the most important task of a telephone modem?

9. Describe the difference between baud rate and data rate.

10. Describe the difference between a protocol and a standard.

11. On a telephone modem, the port labeled (Line, Phone) connects to the incoming telephone line, and the port labeled (Line, Phone) connects to a line telephone.

12. What Windows dialog box is used to configure modem dialing properties?

13. To use ISDN, you must be within how many miles of the actual digital equipment of the telephone company?

14. How many channels does a standard ISDN line have?

15. Which ISDN channel is designed to carry control signals?

16. Which ISDN channels carry voice and data?

17. What is the typical maximum distance for DSL measured from the DSL modem to the telephone central office?

18. Which two versions of DSL are the latest DSL service technologies designed to provide combined voice, video, and data to support high-definition television (HDTV)?

19. Describe two drawbacks of using cable Internet service.

20. Give five advantages that fiber-optic cable provides over coaxial cable and typical telephone wiring.

21. What is an eMTA modem?

22. What type of Internet access system is ideal for remote locations when a home or office is located a great deal away from city services?

23. Explain the operation of a multiplexer and demultiplexer.

24. What configuration term describes connecting a mobile wireless device such as a smartphone to another device?

25. What is another name for a mobile hotspot?

26. What are the two latest generations of mobile wireless technology?

27. What factors affect the data rate of 3G and 4G services?

28. Are mobile broadband data rates consistent from city to city?

29. What data rate is needed for high-definition video streaming to perform successfully?

30. What are two main differences when comparing WiMAX to Wi-Fi?

31. How does WiMAX control the pattern of the broadcast area?

32. How does MIMO technology incorporated into a wireless device affect data rates?

33. What three pieces of information do you typically need when setting up a residential Internet connection?

34. What is the McAfee Internet Connection Speedometer?

35. What is the first thing you should check when troubleshooting a telephone modem?

36. What are the standard steps to troubleshooting a wireless broadband modem?

A+

Sample A+ Exam Questions

Answer the following questions on a separate sheet of paper. Please do not write in this book.

1. Which statement best describes the operation of a modem?
   a. A device that converts digital signals from the PC bus system to analog signals that are transmitted across telephone lines
   b. A device that transmits digital signals across telephone lines
   c. A device that converts analog signals from a USB port to digital signals that are transmitted across telephone systems
   d. A device that sends digital signals across various network systems until a digital signal reaches a predetermined PC connection

2. Which of the following has the slowest data transfer rate?
   a. ISDN TA
   b. DSL modem
   c. Cable modem
   d. Dial-up modem

3. Which is an example of tethering?
   a. Using a USB cable to connect two PC desktops together
   b. Sharing a mobile telephone Internet connection with a tablet
   c. Connecting two or more devices to the same UPS
   d. Following a person closely as they enter a secure area

4. What should you do first when you lose a cable modem connection?
   a. Shut the modem down, wait 10 or more seconds, and then restart the modem.
   b. Select a recent system restore point on the first computer that connects to the cable modem.
   c. Go to the outside of the building and disconnect the cable modem cable. Wait two minutes and then reconnect the cable modem.
   d. Replace the cable modem with a known good cable modem.

5. What factors affect the data rate of 3G and 4G services? Select all that apply.
   a. Radio interference
   b. Distance from the service provider
   c. How many users are accessing the service at the same time
   d. Which software application you are using

6. Which connection type is typically found in a residential telephone jack outlet?
   a. RJ-45
   b. RJ-11
   c. BNC
   d. AT-45

7. Which connection type is typically found between a PC and a DSL modem?
   a. RJ-45
   b. RJ-11
   c. BNC
   d. AT-45

8. What would *most likely* affect the bandwidth of a cable Internet connection?
   a. The amplitude of the signal modulation
   b. The number of subscribers sharing the cable line
   c. The distance from the cable modem to the cable provider
   d. Changes in media between the subscriber location and the central office
9. What is the maximum bandwidth using an ISDN line?
   a. 56 kbps
   b. 1.54 Gbps
   c. 128 kbps
   d. 256 kbps
10. A T-1 line is capable of reaching what data transfer speed?
    a. 56 kbps
    b. 1.54 kbps
    c. 1.544 Mbps
    d. 2.56 Mbps

Suggested Laboratory Activities

Do not attempt any suggested laboratory activities without your instructor's permission. Certain activities can render the PC operating system inoperable.

1. Enter the term *dialer* into the Windows **Search** box and observe the results.
2. Enter the term *telephone* into the Windows **Search** box and observe the results.
3. Inquire about what types of Internet service are available in your area. The services to inquire about are DSL, ISDN, cable modem, and satellite. Use the Internet to inquire about availability in your area.
4. Download and read a DSL and cable modem user manual. Pay special attention to the modem's ports, physical installation, software configuration, and troubleshooting.

Physical and Digital Security

14

After studying this chapter, you will be able to:

- Implement appropriate security practices for securing the physical area of a computer system and disposing of and destroying critical data.
- Implement security best practices for securing a workstation.
- Recall the purpose and characteristics of common Microsoft security applications.
- Classify malware by their action or description.
- Recall the purpose and characteristics of a firewall.

A+ Exam—Key Points

The topic of security has become a major portion of the A+ Certification. A vital part of the exam is identifying the type of malware when presented with a brief description. You must also be familiar with common security practices as outlined in this chapter. Practice with all the common Microsoft security applications and be familiar with the various configuration options for each.

Key Terms

The following key terms will become important pieces of your computer vocabulary. Be sure you can define them.

adware
authentication
back door virus
botnet
browser hijacker
cookie
data miner
denial-of-service (DOS) attack
dialer
dumpster diving
firewall
grayware
hard disk drive (HDD) password
hoax
keylogger
logic bomb
macro virus
malicious software
man trap
MBR virus
Measured Boot
multi-factor authentication
password virus
pharming

phishing
polymorphic virus
port number
power-on password
principle of least privilege (POLP)
privacy filter
radio-frequency identification (RFID)
rootkit
sanitation
service
shoulder surfing
social engineering
spam
spyware
stealth virus
tailgating
Trojan horse
Trusted Boot
Trusted Platform Module (TPM)
virtual smart card
virus signature
worm

The focus of this chapter is the secure practices and common best practices of securing the computer system, user identify, and critical computer data. The topic of computer security can fill an entire textbook. The CompTIA organization has a certification just for security called Security+. Computer system security is a vast and detailed subject that cannot be completely covered in a single chapter. This chapter presents the most common security elements required to adequately secure a computer system and prepare you for A+ Certification exam.

Security is both physical and digital in nature. Physical security refers to securing the computer using physical means, such as physical locks and security devices. The term *digital* in relation to security refers to controlling security through the use of software applications such as antimalware, antispyware, firewall, authentication, and user privileges and permissions.

A+ Note

CompTIA uses the term *digital security* in the A+ Certification Exam Objectives to include all aspects of security that are not considered physical security. Digital security encompasses software applications or programs designed to secure the access to the computer system and data. Digital security begins with user authentication.

Physical Security

Physical security is the practice of protecting the computer system by securing the computer physical area. First and most importantly, you need to secure the physical location by controlling access to the computer system and data storage areas.

As simple as it sounds, you should always lock doors that access the computer and data storage areas. However, even a locked door can be compromised. One such method of compromising a secure area is tailgating. **Tailgating** is when an unauthorized person closely follows an authorized person into a secure area. It can be prevented in high-security areas by the use of a man trap. A **man trap** is a physical configuration that allows only one person access at a time. The man trap can be as simple as a turnstile or a double set of entry doors allowing only room for one person to enter at a time. A man trap design based on a double set of entry doors can incorporate other security access features, such as biometrics, PIN key entry, radio-frequency identification (RFID), or proximity card, all of which are covered later in this section. A man trap can also be enforced using a security guard.

Securing the Physical Area

The simplest way to secure the physical area of the computer(s) or areas containing sensitive data is the common door lock. The area can be protected by a traditional door lock which requires a traditional metal key to gain access. Electronic door lock systems can be used to provide additional security measures as compared to traditional door locks. For example, an electronic door lock system can be equipped with a radio frequency identification (RFID) system and a push button system for entering a PIN number.

Many different types of identification badges and key fobs are designed to interact with RFID security systems. Each badge or key fob is unique so that each can be assigned to a specific user. Both device types produce unique radio signal patterns that activate an electronic lock. A user simply waves the assigned badge or key fob past the reader. The system can also be programmed to require each user to wave the badge or key fob past the reader and then enter a PIN into the keypad. The combination of PIN and RFID is an example of multi-factor authentication, which is covered later in this chapter. The PIN is an example of something the user knows, and the badge is an example of something the user has.

There are many different hardware devices that can be used for user authentication. Some of the many different hardware authentication systems use specially designed badges or tokens referred to as *key fob, RFID badge, RSA token,* and similar names.

Radio-Frequency Identification

Radio-frequency identification (RFID) is an electronic system that uses radio waves to identify objects or people. RFID can be incorporated into a hardware device for authentication of personnel. An RFID system consists of an RFID transponder and an RFID reader. The transponder is also referred to as an RFID tag, an RFID badge, or a key fob. Look at **Figure 14-1** to see an example of an RFID reader and transponders.

> **Tech Tip**
>
> The term *fob* is believed to be based on the word that means "an object other than keys placed on a key ring."

There are two major classifications of RFID transponders: passive and active. An *active RFID transponder* uses a battery to produce radio wave power, and a passive transponder does not. The *passive RFID transponder* uses the radio wave power received from the reader. **Figure 14-2** illustrates the main parts of a passive RFID system.

The RFID reader consists of an electronic circuit board containing the processor, antenna, and other electronic components. The passive RFID transponder consists of an antenna and an integrated circuit. Each transponder is encoded with a unique series of numbers. It is also assigned to a person; hence, each person is represented by a unique number code. The RFID reader contains all the electronic components necessary for transmitting and receiving radio waves and for decoding radio waves from transponders.

The RFID reader can be programmed to respond to transponders in ways such as sounding an alarm for an unauthorized transponder or opening an electric door lock for an authorized one. The RFID reader can be programmed to store

Figure 14-1.
An RFID reader and assortment of RFID key fobs and badges, also known as *RFID transponders*.

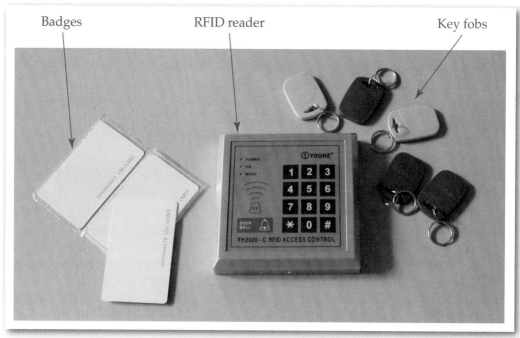

Goodheart-Willcox Publisher

Figure 14-2.
Passive RFID system principle parts identification.

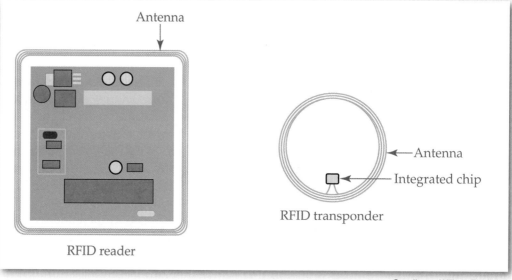

Goodheart-Willcox Publisher

information or transmit information to a computer system, which then records the reader's activity. A complete list of personnel who have entered a facility or area and at what time can be recorded and stored in a database. The database can be reviewed later to pinpoint the possible source of a security breach. Also, the RFID reader can be programmed to only allow certain transponders to access the area on specific days and at specific

times. The abilities of the RFID reader vary by different models and manufacturers.

The electronic theory of RFID system operation is simple. See **Figure 14-3**. The RFID reader constantly emits short radio wave pulses. When the transponder is brought into close proximity of the RFID reader, the pulsing radio waves emitted from the RFID reader antenna cross over the transponder antenna, creating

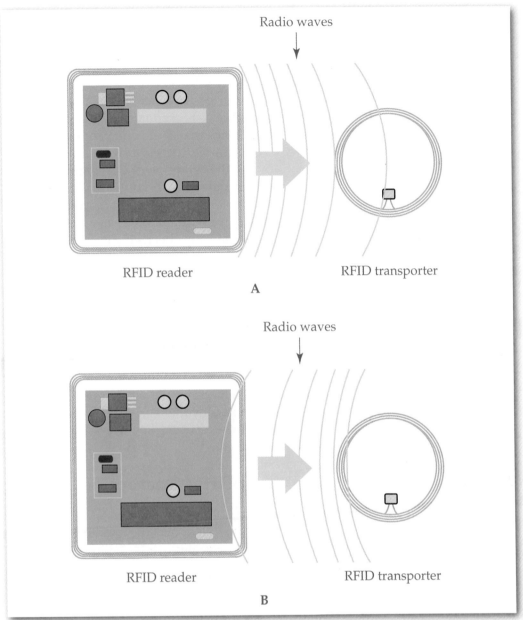

Radio waves

RFID reader

RFID transporter

A

Radio waves

RFID reader

RFID transporter

B

Goodheart-Willcox Publisher

electrical energy in the transponder antenna. This energizes the transponder's integrated chip. When the RFID reader radio wave pulses subside, the transponder's integrated chip transmits a short radio wave pulse to the RFID reader. The transponder's radio wave pulse represents a unique series of binary numbers. If the transponder's unique code matches a preprogrammed code, the person using the transponder is admitted to the area. If not, the person is denied admittance.

A passive transponder has a much shorter range when compared to an active transponder. An active transponder would be used to monitor personnel movement inside a facility. The movement of a person could be tracked simply by being in proximity of the reader. The person would not need to swipe the transponder close to a reader.

A+ Note

You may see the term *RSA token* listed in the CompTIA A+ Certification Exam Objectives as related to security. The letters *RSA* are the initials of the founder of RSA Security LLC. The security company developed an RFID system which used a transponder identified as an "RSA token." If you encounter the term *RSA token* on the exam, just think of an RFID transponder.

Smart Cards and Virtual Smart Cards

Smart cards are used along with a PIN or password. The card is inserted into a reader or scanned, and then the user enters a PIN to gain access to the computer system. Windows 8 is the first Microsoft operating system to introduce a virtual smart card application. A **virtual smart card** is not a physical card but rather a card simulation created by a combination of software and electronic integrated circuit. The virtual smart card utilizes the Trusted Platform Module (TPM), which is an integrated chip discussed in the following section. Chances are if the computer uses UEFI firmware, it has a TPM incorporated into the motherboard. If there are multiple users for a single computer, each user can have his or her own virtual smart card.

A virtual smart card has two advantages over a physical smart card. First, virtual smart cards are more convenient than physical smart cards because they are always present and cannot be lost or misplaced. Second, there is no cost of purchasing a physical smart card reader and a smart card for each user. As long as the motherboard is equipped with a TPM and the computer is running the Windows 8 operating system, the virtual smart card system is free.

Trusted Platform Module

The **Trusted Platform Module (TPM)** is an integrated chip that is incorporated into the motherboard and has the ability to create and store cryptographic keys. The keys protect information such as file contents, passwords, and

PINs. The TPM standard was developed by the Trusted Computing Group (TCG) organization. TPM is at the very heart of Windows BitLocker Drive Encryption and virtual smart card system security.

The TPM is also used as part of a security system that checks a computer for changes during the boot sequence that could compromise the system. For example, the TPM stores an encrypted description of the condition of the computer system relating to the BIOS configuration and any changes to the startup programs and files. Normally, a drive with the BitLocker feature enabled automatically checks the computer TPM for the PIN or key during the boot operation. If no security concern or problem has been detected, the computer continues its normal boot sequence. If a change to the computer startup files or BIOS has been detected, the TPM will require a special recovery key to unlock the encrypted system. The recovery key is created when the BitLocker feature is first enabled on the computer. The security check made by the BitLocker feature and TPM goes noticed by the user. The user is only prompted for the recovery key when a security problem is detected.

BitLocker Drive Encryption

BitLocker Drive Encryption is a Microsoft security feature that allows the user to encrypt an entire hard drive, **Figure 14-4**. BitLocker stores the encryption key in the TPM. When a TPM is not incorporated into the motherboard, BitLocker can store the encryption key on a flash drive. What makes BitLocker unique as compared to NTFS file encryption is BitLocker will encrypt the entire drive, not just directory files like NTFS file encryption. Also, BitLocker protects the data against theft. For example, if someone removes a hard drive protected by BitLocker and then attempts to access the drive, that person will be prompted for a PIN or encryption key. The drive contents will not be able to be accessed. This is also true when an unauthorized person attempts to access the BitLocker secured drive from across a network system.

BitLocker To Go is another version of BitLocker introduced with Windows 7. BitLocker To Go allows for the encryption of portable storage

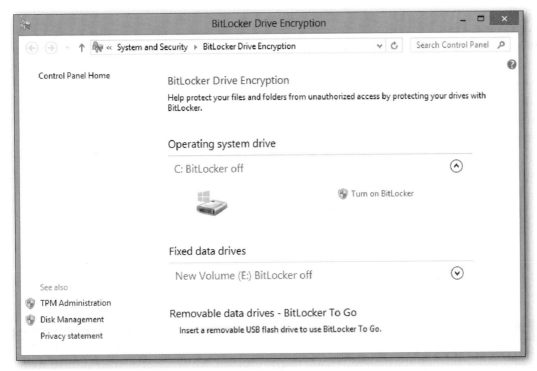

Figure 14-4.
Windows BitLocker Drive Encryption encrypts the contents of an entire hard drive. BitLocker To Go can encrypt removable data drives.

devices, such as external USB hard drives or USB flash drives. Files on a USB drive can be encrypted and then the drive removed and taken to another computer. The files can be opened as long as the PIN is known.

BitLocker is included in Windows Vista and Windows 7 Ultimate and Enterprise editions and Windows 8 Professional edition. BitLocker and BitLocker To Go are not available for Windows Home editions.

Trusted-Boot and Measured-Boot Security

Trusted Boot and Measured Boot are security features integrated into the Windows 8 operating system. While these security features at first appear very much the same, the differences are apparent when directly related to required hardware. For example, Trusted Boot requires UEFI firmware. Measured Boot does not, but it can be implemented on a system that utilizes UEFI firmware. Also, Measured Boot is designed to work with a Trusted Platform Module (TPM). The following table compares Measured Boot and Trusted Boot.

Security Feature	Trusted Boot	Measured Boot
Automatic system update required	Yes	No
Inspect OS boot loader to determine changes or replacement	Yes	Yes
Scan boot path and BIOS code	No	Yes
TPM required	No	Yes
UEFI firmware required	Yes	No

Trusted Boot

Trusted Boot is a Windows 8 security feature that checks the integrity of the operating system during the boot process and only allows digitally-signed software to boot and run on the computer. Trusted Boot is also referred to as *Secure Boot* and *UEFI Secure Boot*. It requires UEFI firmware rather than BIOS and is designed to prevent malware, such as root kits, from hijacking the boot operation and taking over the computer.

Tech Tip

Secure Boot is an open-source security application, not a Microsoft proprietary application.

If a software application is not approved by Microsoft, it will not be installed on a computer that uses Trusted Boot. This type of security is common to other operating systems and devices such as Android and Apple devices. If you want to install a third-party application on a device using the Trusted Boot feature, you would first need to jailbreak or root the device, thus becoming the overall system administrator. After bypassing the Trusted Boot feature, you can then install unauthorized software applications. This is a classic example of the way security features are compromised soon after they are developed. Bypassing the operating system protective feature on an Apple device is called *jailbreaking*. For an Android device, it is called rooting. There is no name for bypassing the Microsoft Trusted Boot associated with Windows 8 as of yet, but it can be assumed it will be either rooting or jailbreaking.

Measured Boot

Measured Boot works with the Trusted Platform Module (TPM). It verifies the successful launch of the operating system and then stores the information in the TPM. This information is then used to validate computer integrity, which is required before remote services, such as cloud computing, are enabled. The remote service accesses the information stored in the TPM and verifies that the computer contains no malware and that it is safe to allow the computer or device to join the cloud service or the network.

The Measured Boot feature is required for cloud computing and other types of remote services. It ensures that (1) the computer or device is equipped with an up-to-date antimalware software application, (2) the antimalware application was initialized, and (3) the computer is virus free. Measured Boot is used to limit the spread of malware across the Internet to servers. This is an essential feature for cloud computers and remote server access.

Trusted Boot and Measured Boot both ensure that the operating system is not infected with malware. These security features go unnoticed by computer and device users. The only time a user may become aware of these features is when denied access to a remote website or cloud service due to the lack of a security feature. For example, a user may attempt to connect to a cloud service and be denied because the computer does not have up-to-date antimalware software or up-to-date operating system security patches installed. To learn more about Trusted Boot and Measured Boot, conduct a search using the entry "Microsoft Trusted Boot Measured Boot."

Privacy Filters

A **privacy filter** is a device that attaches to a display and limits or reduces the viewing angle, thus reducing the risk of unauthorized viewing of the display unit. Computer and mobile device screens are designed to enable the user to have the greatest possible viewing angle. While providing a wide viewing angle is convenient for the user, it poses a security risk because it allows unauthorized persons to also view screen contents. Unauthorized viewing of the display to gain information is referred to as **shoulder surfing**.

Dumpster Diving

Dumpster diving is the act of inspecting a user or company's garbage to locate sensitive information. There are times when physical documents must be secured and disposed of properly. Physical documents should be stored in locked areas or in file cabinets equipped with locks. When a document is no longer needed, it should be destroyed and not simply thrown into the trash. For example, medical records contain patient information that often include home addresses, phone numbers, credit card numbers, insurance data, and other sensitive information concerning the patient. The documents contain information that can be used for identity theft.

Documents that are no longer needed, which contain personal information and sensitive data, should always be destroyed and not just thrown away. Documents should be shredded, and if possible, burned. There are service companies that specialize in the destruction of documents. Even in this modern age of digital systems, almost half of all security breaches occur from improperly stored and improperly disposed of paper documents.

Disposal of Computer Equipment

Computer equipment is often replaced or updated which results in the disposal of the original equipment. For example, all the PCs in a company department could be updated with new PC models and all of the old PCs could be donated to a charity or school or some other organization. The old equipment could even be auctioned off to members of the public. The old computer systems could contain user identity information such as Social Security numbers, addresses, and more. Think of all the data collected by banks, medical offices, credit card companies, police departments, personal departments, education facilities, and department stores. Sensitive material is not just limited to personal information. Computer equipment also may contain company secrets related to manufacturing and design.

The old equipment data storage system should be completely wiped clean or made secure by destroying the media. How the data is erased or destroyed will be based on company policies and individual users. Removal of data from a storage media such as a hard drive is referred to as **sanitation** or *sanitized*. One way to erase data from a hard drive and allow it to be used again without risk is to perform a low-level format. Low-level format utilities are available through hard drive manufacturers, such as Seagate or through third-party software companies. A low-level format completely erases data stored on a hard drive by writing a series of binary zeros across the entire drive, no matter which operating system (Microsoft or Linux) created the directory and file structure. In contrast, the Windows **Quick Format** option does not completely erase the data. The **Quick Format** option only erases file names and leaves the data in the file which can be recovered by third-party tools.

Low-level formatting can take a long time, especially for large storage systems. Some faster methods of destroying data which do not take a great deal of time are drilling a hole through the storage media, degaussing the media, and physically destroying the media using a hammer. Drilling a hole through a hard drive will shatter the disc, rendering the drive unusable. Degaussing the drive is a matter of bringing a degaussing tool in close proximity of the hard drive. A degaussing tool is a very strong electromagnet that will erase all data on the hard drive. When you use a degaussing tool, you will *not* be able to reuse the hard drive.

Authentication

At the very heart of computer security is authentication. **Authentication** is the process of verifying the identity of the user. The most commonly used form of authentication is the user account password.

Passwords

The best passwords are complex and composed of a mixture of letters (both uppercase and lowercase), numbers (*0–9*), and special symbols ($ % & ( ) { } [ ] + = < >). The special symbols that can be used as part of the password depend on the operating system. There may be a maximum and minimum length for the password as well. Passwords should not be names or words found in a dictionary. Strong passwords are created using combinations of words and other symbols that do not make sense to a typical person when used together. Strong passwords are complex as compared to weak passwords, which are simple. Weak passwords are typically names or words found in a dictionary. See **Figure 14-5** for a list of examples.

Letters can be replaced by symbols, such as the dollar symbol ($) for *S*, the caret symbol (^) for *A*, or the left bracket symbol ([) symbol for *C*. The use of symbols improves the security of a password. Many hackers attempt to crack passwords by using a database of dictionary words. Each entry in the database is systematically substituted for the password until the correct word is found or the database is exhausted. The use of symbols and numbers negate the use of a dictionary database as a password breaker.

Figure 14-5. A complex password combines numbers, letters, and special symbols in a way that has no meaning to a typical person. Common names, words, and phrases make poor passwords.

Complex	Simple
Night$tar1	Star
Brend^01	Brenda
Dog$uper5	BigDog
Pa$$word_1	Password
Acce$$005	Access
Mountain_Blue3	Bluemountain
Rock{123}Surf	RockSurf
[h^rle$_01	Charles

Goodheart-Willcox Publisher

Protecting Your Password

Even a secure password can be jeopardized. A password can be jeopardized by intentionally or unintentionally telling someone your password or by creating a password that is easy to guess. The following are suggestions for protecting your password:

- Never let anyone watch you enter your password.
- Never reveal your password to anyone or transmit a password in an e-mail.
- Never reveal your password to a supervisor or system administrator.
- Do not use a hint feature for a password such as (My dog's name).
- Do not use the "remember password" feature found in programs such as Outlook, Eudora, Netscape, or many websites.
- Never write down a password.
- Do not give your password to someone temporarily.
- Do not give your password to a PC technician.
- Change passwords often, at least every four to six months.
- Never use words found in any dictionary as a password.
- Passwords should contain numbers, special characters, and uppercase and lowercase letters.

A+ Note

The A+ Certification exam often has test items on password protection. Always select the answer that most closely conforms to the rules listed in this chapter.

System Configuration Passwords

The operating system typically prompts for a user name and password at logon. This is the last step in a complete system boot. But there can be other passwords configured for a computer. For example, the BIOS/UEFI can be configured with a password to restrict access to BIOS/UEFI configuration changes. The user must present a password before changes can be made.

Another type of BIOS/UEFI password is the computer user password, also known as the *power-on password*. The **power-on password** is prompted for during the POST and before loading the operating system. The power-on password prevents booting from external devices such as flash drives or external hard drives.

In addition to the two BIOS/UEFI password possibilities, there is a third type of hardware password known as the **hard disk drive (HDD) password**. The HDD password is also known as the *drive lock password* or *hard disk drive lock password*. The user is prompted for a logon password in a similar manner to a BIOS/UEFI user password. The HDD password is unique to the hard drive, not the computer. It is intended as additional protection for when a hard drive is stolen. The HDD password prevents unauthorized access to the data stored on the hard drive.

Screen Saver Password

A user should log off from the computer system when away from the computer, but most people forget to log off. Microsoft has an option that allows the computer to be protected when a user steps away from the computer. The screen saver program has an option that when enabled, requires the user to log on to the computer using a password. The exact amount of time required to force a user logon screen varies. See **Figure 14-6**.

Figure 14-6. The screen saver settings can be configured to require a user to log on using a password after the computer has been unattended for a period of time.

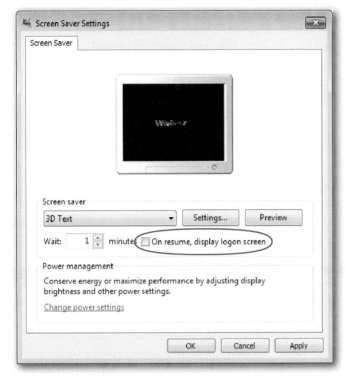

Figure 14-7. A USB biometric fingerprint reader can be added to an existing computer system using any available USB port.

Goodheart-Willcox Publisher

Multi-Factor Authentication

Multi-factor authentication is a combination of two or more authentication techniques. The techniques of authentication are divided into three categories: something you know, something you have, and something you are.

- **Something you know:** Password, PIN, or pattern.
- **Something you have:** Smart card, key fob, or ID card with magnetic strip.
- **Something you are:** Biometric identifier (fingerprint, retinal eye scan, voice recognition, or facial recognition).

Biometrics is the use of a physical attribute for authentication. Some common biometric devices are fingerprint scanner, palm scanner, and retinal eye scanner.

Figure 14-7 shows a biometric fingerprint reader. This particular biometric fingerprint reader can be installed on any computer device that has a USB port. Once installed, the device creates a virtual hard drive partition that only gives access to the user who configured the fingerprint scanner. The combination of a user password and a biometric device is an example of multi-factor authentication.

The exact method(s) of authentication required depends on the desired level of security for protecting the computer system and storage data. You would expect the common home user to need no more than password protection. A bank, investment company, or the Pentagon would most likely require more than a simple password.

User Accounts

Of all the methods to achieve authentication, none is more often used than the user account. The user account, which consists of a user name and password, is assigned during the installation of the computer operating system. Another way the computer user account is created is after a computer is purchased by a user. When a user purchases a computer, the user account is created the first time the user boots the new computer. A user account can also be created by a network administrator. That type of user account is covered in detail later in the textbook. A user account created and stored on a computer is referred to as the *local user account*. A user account created for a network is referred to as the *domain user account* or *network account*.

User accounts determine a user's privilege. Another term you will encounter is *permission*. User account privilege and permission are two different aspects of computer security. By Microsoft definition, permissions apply to objects while privileges apply to user accounts. In other words, the term *privilege* applies to a user's ability to make changes to the computer configuration or to install a software program. *Permission* applies to a user's ability to access an object such as a particular file. The term *rights* is also used to describe user permissions and privileges such as the right to access a specific file or folder. The three terms *permissions*, *privileges*, and *rights* are often used interchangeably.

The user name and password are controlled under the local computer **User Accounts** dialog box. In Windows XP, it is accessed through **Control Panel | User Accounts**. In Windows Vista, Windows 7, and Windows 8, it is accessed through **Control Panel | User Accounts and Family Safety | User Accounts**. **Figure 14-8** shows the **User Accounts and Family Safety** category, which allows you to add or remove user accounts, configure passwords, and configure family safety features. Windows XP does not include options to configure family safety features.

User accounts are created in the **User Account** dialog box which appears in **Figure 14-9**. The User

Account Control (UAC) feature is incorporated into the user account and determines which permissions or privileges are assigned to the user. The UAC assigns permissions to the user account, which in turn determines what the user can do to the computer system, such as install a software program.

Microsoft operating systems come with a set of built-in user account assignments that vary somewhat according to the operating system version. The three computer user account assignments starting with Windows Vista are administrator, standard, and guest. Windows XP is the only version that has a limited account. The limited account does not have as many privileges as the Windows Vista and later standard account.

Windows XP User Accounts

- **Computer administrator:** Create, change, or delete a user account; install programs and access all files; and make system wide changes.
- **Limited:** View files you created, view files in the Shared Documents folder; change or remove own password; and change your own theme, picture, and desktop settings.
- **Guest:** Check e-mail and use the Internet. Cannot make any changes to the system configuration or install software and hardware. Typically used as a temporary account.

Figure 14-8.
User Accounts and Family Safety provides options to add or remove user accounts, configure passwords, and configure family safety features.

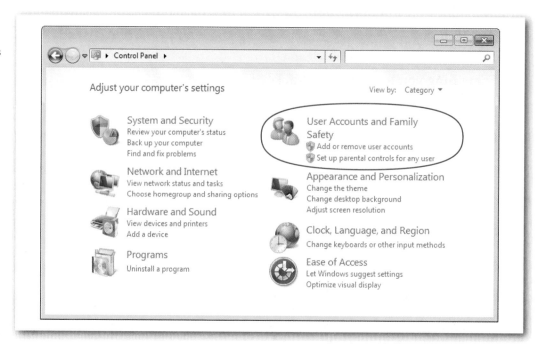

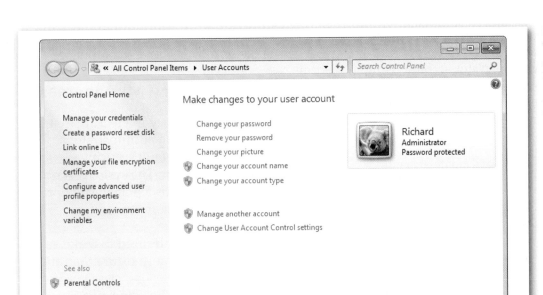

Figure 14-9.
The **User Account** dialog box is used to create, delete, or modify user accounts on the local computer.

Windows Vista and Windows 7 User Accounts

- **Administrator:** Create, change, or delete a user account; install programs and access all files; and make system-wide changes. While performing system changes, the administrator may be required to provide the administrator password.
- **Standard:** Designated for everyday use and is not as powerful as the administrator account. If you want to make changes to the computer configuration that affect other users of the computer, such as installing software or changing security settings, you may need to provide the administrator password.
- **Guest:** Check e-mail and use the Internet. Cannot make any changes to the system configuration or install software and hardware. Typically used as a temporary account.

Windows 8 User Accounts

- **Administrator:** Create, change, or delete a user account; install programs and access all files; and make system-wide changes. While performing system changes, the administrator may be required to provide the administrator password.
- **Standard:** Designed for everyday use and is more restrictive than the administrator account.

- **Guest:** Check e-mail and use the Internet. Cannot make any changes to the system configuration or install software and hardware. Typically used as a temporary account.

In Windows 8 and Windows RT when you create an administrator, a standard, or a guest account, you can choose two ways to sign in: local account or Microsoft account. With a local account, you can sign in with a user name (with or without a password) and you can access files, settings, and apps on just your local PC. With a Microsoft account, you sign in with an e-mail address as your user name. Signing in with an e-mail address and password lets you access your favorite apps and your unique settings and preferences on any PC.

Two common security recommendations concerning user accounts in all Windows versions are changing the default user names and disabling the guest account. The guest account is disabled by default. You can enable the guest account through the **User Account Control** dialog box.

Changing default user names generally refers to the built-in Administrator account. The built-in Administrator account is disabled by default beginning with Windows Vista. Earlier operating systems, such as Windows XP, enabled the Administrator account by default. This is now considered a security risk since anyone in the world would know that the built-in Administrator account name is "Administrator." If the

Administrator account had a weak password, the computer system could easily be compromised. You can restore the Administrator account using the Local Security Policy editor, as long as you use a password that meets the minimum complexity rule for passwords.

> **Tech Tip**
>
> Always create at least two user accounts with administrative privileges. If you only have one account with administrative privileges and that account becomes corrupt, you may not be able to access the computer system and thus lose access to all computer files and directories.

Principle of Least Privilege

The **principle of least privilege (POLP)** is a security principle that states a user should only have sufficient privileges to complete their work task. In other words, not all users need to have full administrative privileges. If a user account is compromised while the user is performing routine tasks and the user has been assigned full administrative privileges, then the entire computer system is vulnerable because the unauthorized person is equal to the Administrator. Microsoft as well as security experts recommend that all users including the system Administrator use a standard or limited user account when performing day-to-day tasks on a computer.

Local Security Policy Management

The Local Security Policy is a feature that allows a computer user with administrator privileges to modify the default security configuration of a computer. The system security configuration is described as a policy. The Local Security Policy sets the parameters of user permissions.

Permissions can be configured to make computer system features more secure than their default settings. For example, user passwords can be enforced to be more secure using a Password Policy. In **Figure 14-10**, the **Local Security Policy** editor has the security settings for **Password Policy** expanded, showing the security settings that can be configured for the user password to enhance security. The settings related to password security are **Enforce password history**, **Maximum password age**, **Minimum password age**, **Minimum password length**, **Password must meet complexity requirements**, and **Store passwords using reversible encryption**. These security options are not enabled by default. Through the **Local Security Policy** editor, these options can be enabled, thus forcing all users to follow enhanced security password best practices.

The **Local Security Policy** editor also allows you to change the default name of the built-in

Figure 14-10.
The Windows **Local Security Policy** dialog box allows the system user with the administrative privilege to make changes to the default security settings of the computer system.

Administrator account or guest account. To access the **Local Security Policy** editor, enter **secpol. msc** into the **Search** box for Windows Vista, Windows 7, or Windows 8. The **secpol.msc** file is a Microsoft Management Console snap-in application and is only available for Windows editions such as Professional, Ultimate, and Enterprise. It is not available in Home editions.

Figure 14-11 shows the **Security Options** section of the **Local Security Policy** editor. The first policy listed relates to the Administrator account status. **Figure 14-12** shows the dialog box

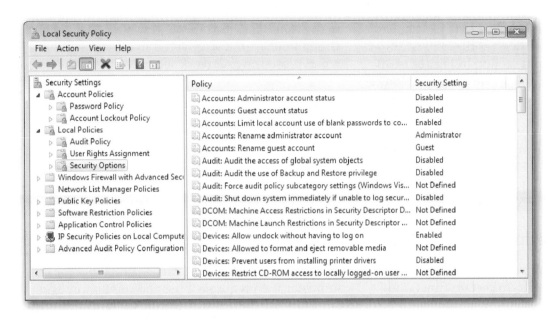

Figure 14-11.
Local Security Policy editor with **Security Options** expanded.

Figure 14-12. Local Security Policy editor dialog boxes related to the built-in Administrator account status. A—The built-in Administrator account is disabled by default ever since Windows Vista. B—The Administrator account cannot be enabled except by a user with equal to administrator privileges. The password policy must also be configured to require complex passwords.

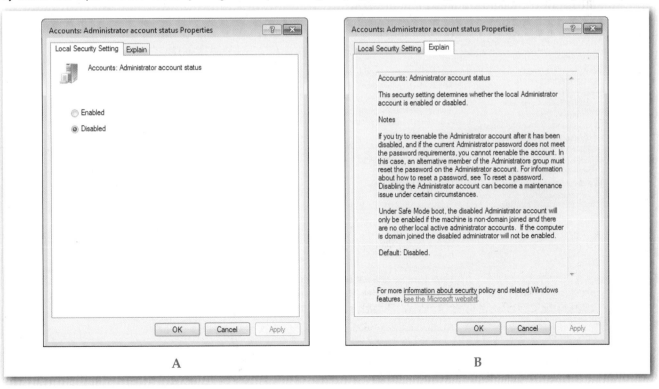

presented for restoring the Administrator account as well as an explanation concerning enabling and disabling the Administrator account.

The **Local Security Policy** editor provides a vast array of options to increase or decrease computer system security, for example, security features concerning network access, software restrictions, hardware device restrictions, and more. To see an example of just how restrictive some of the policies are, look at the expanded **User Rights Assignment** section in **Figure 14-13** and take note of the **Back up files and directories** option. Any user can be restricted from making copies of any file or directory on the computer system. It is common to configure computers to restrict users from making copies of sensitive computer information. **Figure 14-14** shows the dialog boxes presented when the **Back up files and directories** option is selected.

Local Group Policy Management

Users have a set of permissions by default that allows them to perform certain functions on a computer. The assigned permissions can be changed through the **Local Group Policy** editor. This tool is similar to the **Local Security Policy** editor. The **Local Group Policy** editor is available in all editions of Windows operating system except the Home editions. To start the **Local Group Policy**, enter **gpedit.msc** into the **Search** box in Windows Vista, Windows 7, and Windows 8 or in the **Run** dialog box in Windows XP. The **Local Group Policy** editor is covered in a later chapter when presenting network security.

Social Engineering

Social engineering is the act of manipulating people to get then to divulge confidential information about the computer system. Social engineering can come in the form of a phone call, an e-mail, or even direct in-person contact. For example, a person could call, e-mail, or show up in person and present themselves as a company technician working on a network problem or investigating a network security problem. The impostor then requests a user account name and

Figure 14-13. The Local Security Policy editor provides a policy to restrict the ability to copy files or directories to other media such as USB attached storage devices.

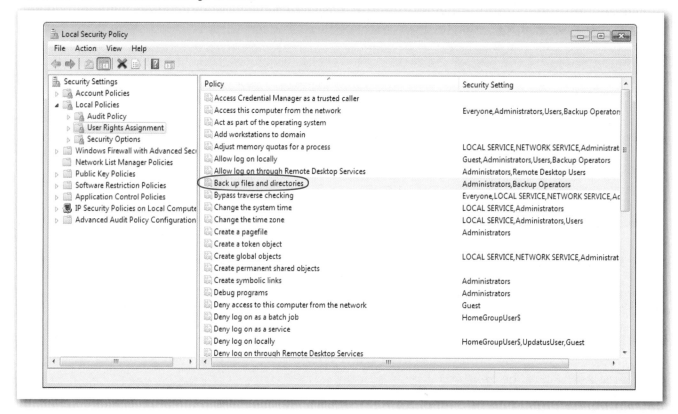

Figure 14-14. Local Security Policy editor dialog boxes for the **Back up files and directories** option. A—**Local Security Setting** tab. B—**Explain** tab.

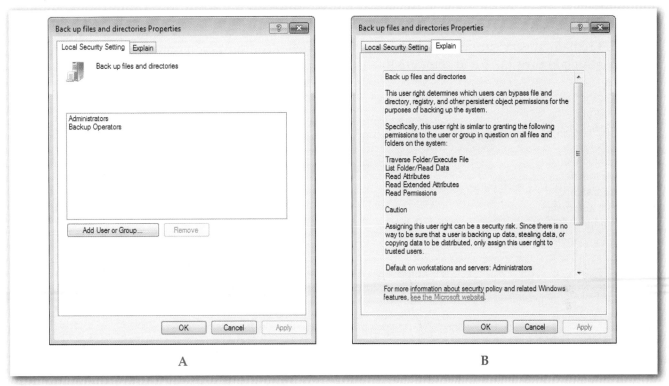

A

B

password in order to conduct an inspection of the local computer system. If the user account information is given to the impostor, the entire system can be compromised. The only real protection from social engineering is through user security education.

User Security Education

One of the best methods of securing computer systems and data is to educate the user. Never assume that a user understands security concepts. Users need not understand how to configure the Local Security Policy editor and Local Group Policy editor or how to allow a specific program to pass data through a firewall. Users *do* need to understand how to create a complex password and why it is important. They also need to understand the dangers of opening certain e-mail attachments and why they must follow company security policy such as never giving their password to anyone, not even the computer technician. The user must be educated about how social engineering can be used to compromise the computer system.

All companies need to conduct security education on a regular basis. All new employees should be trained about security and company policies based on security standards before they begin working with the computer system. Even the most secure hardware and software system can be accessed or compromised because of a user not following or understanding effective user security.

Microsoft Security Applications

Security has been a primary concern for computer users over the years. As a result, Microsoft has developed many different software applications used for computer security. Many of the tools come preinstalled while others can be downloaded from the Microsoft website. Enabling Windows Update will keep the computer system patched and using the very latest version of the free tools.

Action Center and Security Center

The Windows Security Center was first introduced in Windows XP Service Pack 2 (SP2) and remained very similar in Windows Vista. Examine **Figure 14-15** and compare the Security Center for the two operating systems. The Windows Security Center monitors security features such as the status of the firewall, virus or malware protection, automatic updates, and other security configuration options related to operating system applications.

Figure 14-15.
The Windows Security Center provides a centralized location for monitoring the status and configuration of the firewall, automatic updates, virus protection, and more.

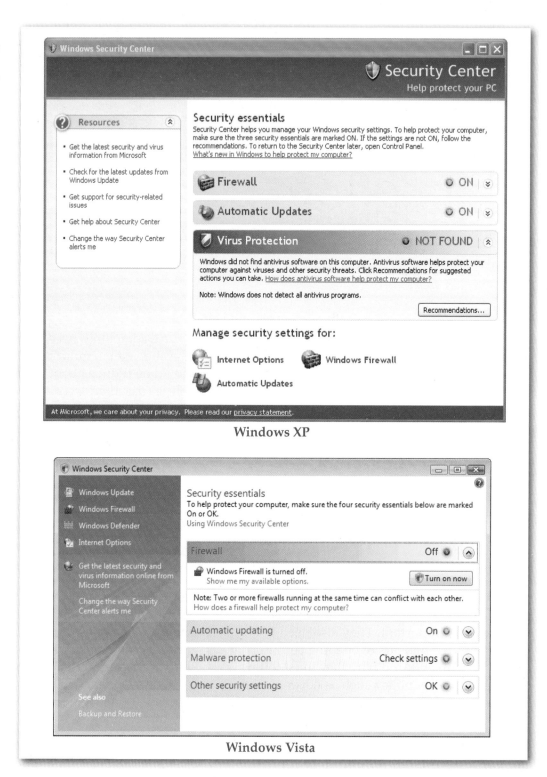

Windows XP

Windows Vista

Windows 7 introduced the Action Center, **Figure 14-16**, which incorporates the features of the Windows Security Center. The Action Center contains two major sections: **Security** and **Maintenance**. The **Security** section presents the status of security items such as the network firewall, Windows Update, virus protection, spyware, Internet security settings, User Account Control, and Network Access Protection. The **Maintenance** section provides the status of detected computer problems, backups, and updates. The Action Center **Maintenance** section is covered in Chapter 15—PC Troubleshooting.

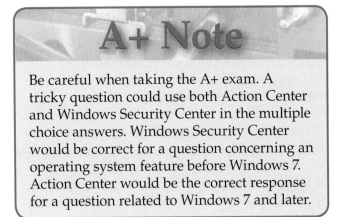

A+ Note

Be careful when taking the A+ exam. A tricky question could use both Action Center and Windows Security Center in the multiple choice answers. Windows Security Center would be correct for a question concerning an operating system feature before Windows 7. Action Center would be the correct response for a question related to Windows 7 and later.

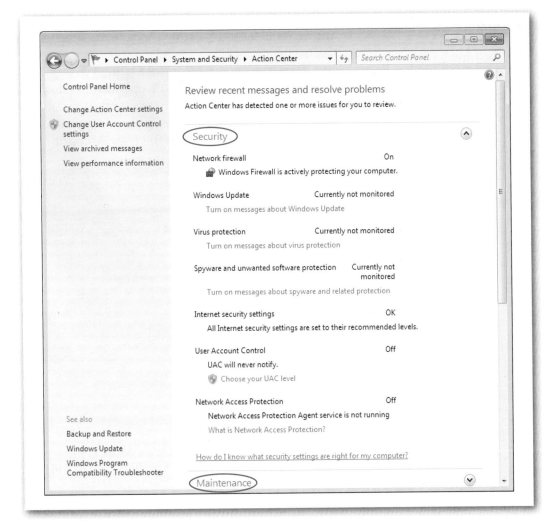

Figure 14-16.
The Windows Action Center provides a centralized location to view the status of security-related features such as network firewall, Windows Update, virus protection, and spyware.

Network Access Protection Agent

The Network Access Protection Agent, when running, indicates that the latest important updates concerning security are installed. Before the computer is allowed to join a network that requires the latest updates to be installed, the Network Access Protection Agent checks that the computer has the latest updates. This feature is not required for general network connections, such as those to most Internet sites. However, it can be required to connect to some Internet locations, such as when connecting to a company network as an employee working from a remote location.

User Account Control

Users often complained about the lack of security associated with Windows XP. The default user in Windows XP was equal to the system administrator. Other user accounts added to the computer were by default equal to the built-in Administrator, unless **Limited** was selected when creating the account. That is why the standard user account was introduced in Windows Vista and the built-in Administrator account was disabled by default. Also in answer to user complaints, Microsoft developed the User Account Control (UAC), which was first introduced in Windows Vista and has continued to be a vital part of all Windows operating systems.

The original Windows Vista version of the UAC was quite annoying to the user. Each time a change to the computer configuration was being made, the user was prompted for the administrator password. As a result, Windows Vista was not a popular operating system and many computer manufacturers offered to substitute Windows XP operating system in place of Windows Vista.

Because of the public criticism of Windows Vista, Microsoft designed the next operating system to be less restrictive by default. Thus, Windows 7 does not have near as many annoying security-enabled prompts as Windows Vista. It allows the user to fine-tune the security level of the user account.

The **User Account Control Settings** dialog box is used to control how the operating system will notify you of potentially harmful programs attempting to make changes to your computer system. **Figure 14-17** shows the User Account Control set to default.

Figure 14-17.
The **User Account Control Settings** dialog box allows you to select the type of notification to produce on the screen based on the slide selector range of **Always notify** to **Never notify**.

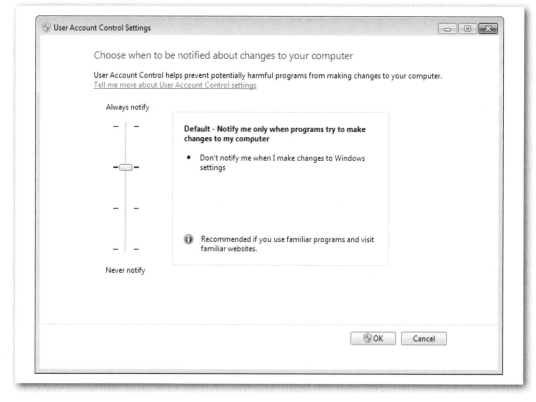

The **User Account Control Settings** dialog box has four setting adjustments: **Always notify me**, **Notify me only when apps try to make changes to my computer (default)**, **Notify me only when apps try to make changes to my computer (don't dim my desktop)**, and **Never notify me**. The following table describes each setting.

UAC Setting	Description
Always notify me	The UAC will notify you when apps try to install software or make changes to the computer configuration or when you make changes to Windows settings. This setting is recommended if you routinely install new software and visit unfamiliar websites.
Notify me only when apps try to make changes to my computer (default)	The UAC will only notify you when apps try to make changes to your computer. It will not notify you when you make changes to Windows settings. This is the default setting and is recommend for users who use familiar apps and visit familiar websites.
Notify me only when apps try to make changes to my computer (don't dim my desktop)	This level is the same as default level except that the desktop will not dim during the notification. Choose this setting only if it takes a long time to dim the desktop on your computer.
Never notify me	The UAC will never notify you when apps try to install or make changes to your computer configuration. This setting is not recommended.

The **Notify me only when apps try to make changes to my computer (default)** and **Notify me only when apps try to make changes to my computer (don't dim my desktop)** settings are the same, except that the latter of the two will not dim the desktop during notifications. Some computers have an annoying long delay when they dim the screen at the default setting, so Microsoft created the same security setting with an option that will not dim the screen when the notification appears. The **Never notify me** setting is selected when users do not ever want the security warning messages to appear on their screen. This setting is not recommended.

Parental Controls

Parental Controls was first introduced in Windows Vista. In Windows 8, it was renamed Family Safety. This feature monitors and limits a user's computer and network activity. Look at **Figure 14-18** to see the Windows 7 **Parental Controls** dialog box. The Parental Controls three main configuration options are **Time limits**, **Game**, and **Allow or block specific programs**. The **Time limit** option is used to configure which days of the week and which hours of the day the user account is allowed to use the computer. The **Game** option sets the user account gaming practices by game rating or content. The **Allow or block specific programs** option allows the user account to be restricted from running specific software applications.

Windows 8 added enhanced restrictions limiting the access to the Windows Store. Parental Controls is a very powerful feature, but most parents are not even aware of its existence. Parental Controls need not be limited to children. It can also be used to control computer activities by other adults.

Microsoft Security Tools

Originally, operating systems such as Windows did not incorporate any security software applications. Security software applications had to be installed separately. Ever since Windows XP, Microsoft has incorporated several different security tools into its operating systems or has provided these tools as an add-in program. You can still install additional security tools, which is both recommended and often done.

A+ Note

Even though the CompTIA A+ Certification is advertised to be vendor neutral, it is still Microsoft Windows oriented. Therefore, you should be familiar with all the various Windows security features.

Figure 14-18.
Windows Parental Controls is used to limit and monitor user account activity on the computer or network.

We will now look at several of the Microsoft security tools available for Windows XP through Windows 8. These tools do not provide the same level of protection that commercial antimalware software provides. These tools are provided by Microsoft so that the computer has minimal protection, rather than no protection at all.

Microsoft Malicious Software Removal Tool

All versions of Windows from Windows XP to Windows 8 include the Microsoft Malicious Software Removal Tool (MSRT). The MSRT is designed to remove malicious software from your computer. Even if you know the name and location of the malware file, removing the file by simply selecting the file with the mouse and placing it in the **Recycle Bin** or deleting it will not remove most malware. Most malware is designed to reinfect the computer unless all parts of the malware are removed. The malware can remain resident in RAM and reinfect the computer periodically even after the original file has been removed.

The Microsoft Malicious Software Removal Tool is installed and updated every month by default if the computer has automatic updates enabled. There is also an option to download and install a copy of the tool manually.

Microsoft releases an updated version every month, which can be configured to automatically download and run. It is important to emphasize that the MSRT does not replace an antimalware product. The MSRT does not prevent the installation of malware; it only removes known versions of malware. It is strictly a post-infection removal tool. You should always install an up-to-date antimalware product designed to work with the edition of the operating system. Commercial antimalware software tools are designed not only to remove existing malware but to also detect potentially dangerous malware before it infects a computer.

Windows Defender

Windows Defender is included in all versions of Windows starting with Windows XP. It is designed to protect the PC against spyware. Windows Defender is installed by default in Windows Vista, Windows 7, and Windows 8, but not in Windows XP. There is a free version for Windows XP that can be downloaded and installed. **Figure 14-19** shows the default dialog box for Windows Defender in Windows 7, and **Figure 14-20** shows the default dialog box in Windows 8. The Windows 8 Windows Defender is an enhanced version in that it provides malware protection in addition to spyware protection.

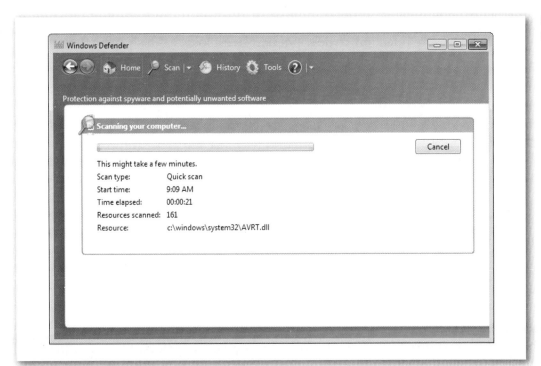

Figure 14-19.
Windows 7 Defender.

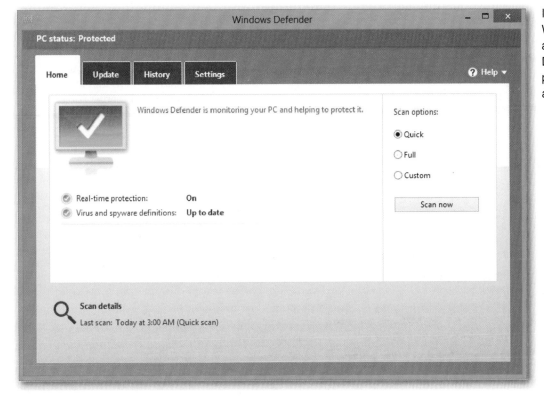

Figure 14-20.
Windows 8 Defender is an enhanced version of Defender in that it also provides protection against malware.

Microsoft Defender Offline

Microsoft Defender Offline (WDO) is one of Microsoft's most powerful malware scanner.

WDO is available for download. It is a standalone software application and runs independently of the operating system. As part of your technician tool kit, you should download a copy and save it to a USB flash drive. You can then use it to check a client's computer for suspected malware infection.

SmartScreen

SmartScreen is an additional safety feature incorporated into Windows 8 and Windows RT. It is designed to protect the computer system from new malware that antimalware software most likely hasn't detected. SmartScreen was originally designed for Internet Explorer, but now it is included in Windows 8 and Windows RT.

SmartScreen checks an application when it is downloaded from the Internet and warns the user based on the reputation of the Internet source. If the source of the app is known to distribute malware intentionally or accidentally, a warning message will be displayed on the screen. **Figure 14-21** shows the SmartScreen configuration. SmartScreen can be accessed through **Control Panel | System and Security | Action Center**.

Microsoft Security Essentials

Microsoft Security Essentials detects and removes malware such as viruses, spyware, worms, and similar unwanted software. It does not detect or remove cookies. Most Internet browsers do have options to protect against or handle cookies. Microsoft Security Essentials does not perceive cookies as a security threat. It is compatible with Windows 7, Windows Vista, and Windows XP and is available as a free download.

Microsoft recommends Microsoft Security Essentials as a replacement product for Windows Live OneCare. Microsoft originally introduced Windows Live OneCare as an antimalware solution but discontinued distribution in October 2009 and then discontinued support for Live OneCare in April 2011. If a computer is running Windows Live OneCare, it must be uninstalled before installing Microsoft Security Essentials. Microsoft recommends uninstalling other antimalware and antispyware before installing Security Essentials. Running more than one antimalware or antispyware application on a computer will greatly reduce its performance.

Microsoft Security Essentials can be used for small businesses that have a maximum of 10 PCs. If your business has more than 10 PCs, Microsoft System Center 2012 Endpoint Protection should be used instead.

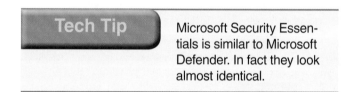

Tech Tip

Microsoft Security Essentials is similar to Microsoft Defender. In fact they look almost identical.

Figure 14-21.
Windows 8 and Windows RT introduced SmartScreen, which warns about the potential hazard of downloading a particular application or app based on the reputation of the Internet source.

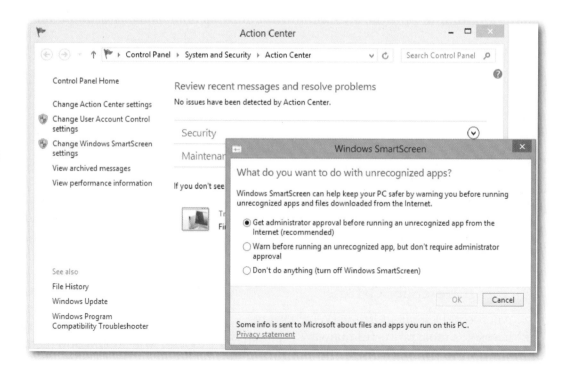

Microsoft Safety Scanner

Microsoft Safety Scanner checks the computer system for all forms of malware. It is not installed by default but is free to download and run on any Microsoft operating system. The Microsoft Safety Scanner is a standalone program that only runs when activated by the user. It does not provide constant protection by running in the background of the operating system. The Microsoft Safety Scanner is compatible with other malware scanners and can coexist on a system that has an active malware scanner already installed. It has a limited life span and must be downloaded again after approximately ten days.

Microsoft Active Protection Service

Microsoft Active Protection Service (MAPS) automatically reports malware to Microsoft. There are two levels of membership: basic and advanced. Basic membership sends information to Microsoft about the malware, where it came from, and whether the actions taken to remove the malware were successful. Advanced membership provides the same information but in addition it sends information about where the malware is located on the computer, its file name, how the malware operates, and its impact on the computer system.

MAPS is a voluntary program. You can choose to not participate. The option not to participate is located under the **Settings** tab of **Windows Defender**. MAPS is installed automatically with a basic membership configuration when you install Windows Defender or Windows Security Essentials. MAPS is part of the Microsoft SpyNet program. SpyNet is a volunteer membership program designed for users to report malware.

> **Tech Tip**   Microsoft also uses the acronym MAPS to represent the Microsoft Assessment and Planning kit.

As you can see, Microsoft has many security software applications integrated into the operating system or available for download. Many have overlapping features making them quite confusing to distinguish. Take time to explore the

Microsoft webpage dedicated to security. Simply enter the search terms "Microsoft Security" into a web browser and look for results that link you to the Microsoft website.

Windows Update

Microsoft provides a service called Windows Update, which automatically checks for operating system updates. Its options allow you to configure how the system should respond to updates. The Windows Update service is accessed through **Start | All Programs | Windows Update** in all versions of Windows except Windows 8. See **Figure 14-22**. Windows Update can be accessed through **Control Panel** in all versions of Windows or by conducting a search using the entry "update."

Figure 14-22. Windows Update is located directly off the **Start** menu in most operating systems and can also be accessed through **Control Panel**.

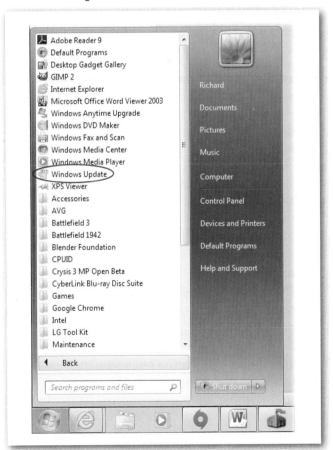

Figure 14-23.
Windows Update provides information about updates as well as options to modify how and when to check for updates and to view the update history.

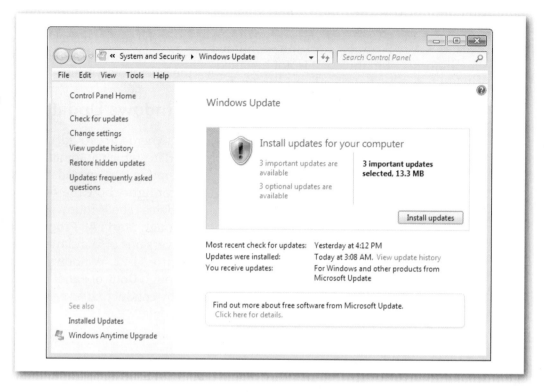

After the Windows Update service is selected, a dialog box similar to that in **Figure 14-23** will appear. The **Windows Update** dialog box provides information about the current status of the computer updates as well as a number of related options. You can configure a time and day of the week to automatically check for updates. You can also run a check for updates at any time by selecting the **Check for updates** option. You have the option to select all updates or only important updates to install. When updates are not installed, they are saved as hidden updates that can be installed at a later date if desired. Windows Update provides the following options for handling updates:

- **Install updates automatically (recommended)**.
- **Download updates but let me choose whether to install them**.
- **Check for updates but let me choose whether to download and install them**.
- **Never check for updates (not recommended)**.

Microsoft recommends the automatic download and installation of all updates. Many network administrators do not choose to automatically download and install updates for two main reasons. First, downloading and installing updates while performing other tasks can greatly depreciate computer performance and make the computer appear sluggish. Second, there are times when a particular update can adversely affect a software application or a hardware device not on the Microsoft approved list. Updates are often tested by a network administrator before installing them on a network of computers. The updates are tested to ensure compatibility with all network computer hardware and software applications.

Security Auditing

Computer activity can be monitored with Windows Event Viewer. The Event Viewer records activity related to security events such as failed logon attempts, which can indicate an attempt of unauthorized computer access. Look at the Event Viewer in **Figure 14-24**. The Event Viewer has indicated a series of "Audit Failure" events or failed logon attempts from a computer named *Richard-PCwin7*. It also lists the time it occurred and an event ID. The event ID can be used to find out more about the cause of this type of failure. You can simply double-click the event and a window will appear providing more information. Event Viewer is covered in Chapter 15—Troubleshooting.

Figure 14-24. Event Viewer showing a logon failure event.

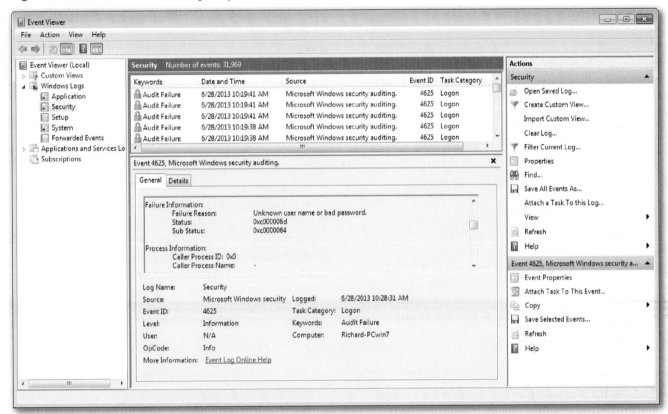

Malicious Software

Malicious software, also called *malware* is written for the express purpose of modifying a computer's configuration or causing damage to the computer system. There are many different categories of malicious software, such as virus, worm, root kit, and more. In this section, basic information relating to all forms of malicious software is presented.

A virus is typically written to duplicate itself and, in the process, cause problems and possible permanent damage to a computer. It usually has three phases: infection, replication, and execution.

The infection arrives from a source such as a flash drive, CD, e-mail, or network connection to a computer, such as the Internet. Replication is when the virus duplicates itself to other programs, files, drives, or other computers on a network. If a virus continually replicates itself, it can easily use all available disk space. Execution can take many forms. Some are harmless and just annoying. Others can be very destructive. They can erase files and lock up hardware.

Viruses are said to have *signatures*. A **virus signature** is a combination of characteristics that include such things as its length, file name(s) used, mode of infection or replication, the areas of the system that are attacked, the type of software programs that are attacked, and the name or length of the file attachment. A virus signature describes a particular virus. These signatures are what antimalware software use to catch viruses on your computer.

Malicious software cause a tremendous amount of destruction and aggravation. Sooner or later, you will encounter a virus or worm. You must have a knowledge base to deal with these threats. This may be one of the most important chapters you read.

Malware Classifications

Most malicious programs (malware) that infect computers are referred to as viruses. The term *computer virus* has taken on a very broad definition with the public. However, the software companies that develop antimalware software programs have developed a variety of classifications. These classifications vary somewhat from company to company. In addition to a virus, there are other malicious programs called *worms*. Each program has its own features. Common classifications of computer infections are Trojan horse, logic bomb, macro, worm, password, back door, and hoax. While some classes will seem similar, there are sufficient variations in their style to allow a classification system to be used. Note that there are many viruses and worms that are composed of the features of multiple classifications.

Worm

While many viruses attach themselves to other programs to slip into your computer, worms operate on their own. Technically speaking, a worm is not a true virus. A virus replicates itself on one computer and infects files on that particular computer. A **worm** is a destructive program that contaminates files on the infected computer and spreads to other computers without prompting from the user. Spreading to other computers is what makes it different from a virus. Worms are also referred to as bacterium viruses by some authorities.

It is important to note that worms are self-replicating. Once infection takes place, the worm replicates or transmits itself to other computers without user intervention. A classic example of its reproduction is through an e-mail application. When a worm is sent as a file attachment, it replicates itself by using the list of contacts in the user's e-mail database. The recipients of the e-mail inadvertently infect the people on their lists. The infection rate is exponential. See **Figure 14-25**. The infamous Melissa and I Love You viruses are both worms.

Figure 14-25. E-mail is the most common method of transmitting a worm. Using this method, the worm multiplies at an exponential rate.

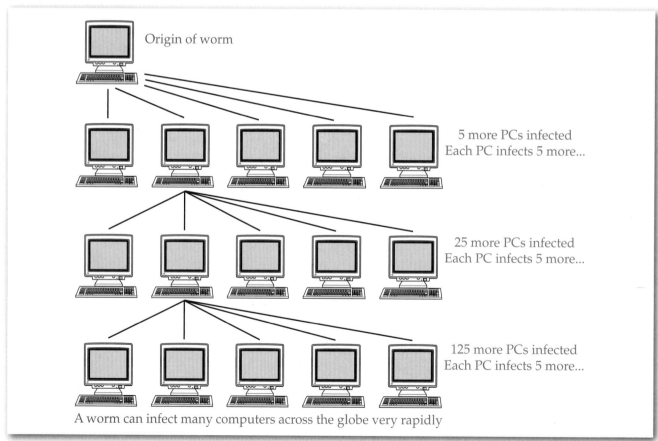

Origin of worm

5 more PCs infected
Each PC infects 5 more...

25 more PCs infected
Each PC infects 5 more...

125 more PCs infected
Each PC infects 5 more...

A worm can infect many computers across the globe very rapidly

Trojan Horse

The Trojan horse classification is named after the Trojan horse from Homer's *Iliad*. In the legend, the Trojans leave a huge wooden horse to the city of Troy, presumed as a gift that symbolized the end of the Trojan War. The horse was taken inside the walls of the city. However, the horse was hollow and filled with Greek soldiers. In the secret of night, the Greek soldiers climbed out of the horse, attacked the guards, and opened the gates to the city. This allowed additional Greek soldiers to enter and defeat the city of Troy. The city was captured and burned to the ground. The virus acts very much like the Trojan horse in the legend.

The **Trojan horse** class of virus appears as a gift. It may be a free download of a program such as a game or utility program, an e-mail attachment, or some other item that is attractive to a user. When opened, the virus activates. Some cause immediate damage. Others wait until a later date. The Trojan horse can have a harmless outward appearance. It often advertises itself as a utility to assist with some sort of computer operation. Since the Trojan horse is disguised, users may not realize that they have infected their computer. After a time, unusual operations or glitches appear in the computer. The hard drive may be erased or overwritten, leaving no space for other files to be saved. There are too many possible symptoms of Trojan horses to list them all, but you can expect many unusual operations on the computer and may not recognize the problem until damage has been done.

Macro Virus

A **macro virus** is named after the macro software-programming tool. It is a virus created using a macro programming language, and it is attached to documents that use the language. A standard macro program is designed to assist a computer user by converting repetitive tasks into one simple key code or name. Macros can record a set of user keystrokes and then save the set of keystrokes under a file name. When needed, the set of keystrokes can be easily loaded any time. For example, a set of keystrokes used to create a template that will be used over and over again can easily be created using the macro feature in Microsoft's Word program. A typical letter heading including a company's name, address, phone number, and contact person is an example. When loaded, the macro automatically recreates the keystrokes, producing the desired information.

This same method is used to create some virus programs. They are often distributed as e-mail attachments. Once a computer is infected, the virus attaches itself to any new file created with the infected software application. Macro viruses are very common. In fact, macro viruses are estimated to account for 75% of all viruses.

MBR Virus

An **MBR virus** attacks the master boot record (MBR) of a hard drive and is considered extremely destructive. When activated, the virus plants hexadecimal codes in the master boot record, rendering it useless. This results in hard disk failure. Damage is usually limited to only the master boot record, which can be rebuilt if backups have been made. Many antimalware programs perform MBR backups as part of their installation and require a floppy or flash drive to save necessary records for rebuilding the system.

> **Tech Tip**
>
> One point of particular interest is the **fdisk/mbr** command used to repair the MBR. Certain known virus programs, such as the Monkey virus, actually move the location of the MBR. Applying the **fdisk/mbr** command will not remedy the problem. It will most likely do more damage when the command reconstructs the MBR with a damaged file and saves the damaged file as the backup copy.

Logic Bomb

A **logic bomb** is a destructive program that is slipped into an application and is dormant until some event takes place. The event could be the arrival of some date or time; the entering of a certain number, word, or file name; or the number of times the application is loaded. The idea behind the design of a logic bomb is for it to wait for a period of time, allowing it to spread to other computers before releasing its payload of destruction.

Back Door Virus

A **back door virus** is designed to go undetected and leave a "back door" or "hole" in the security system of a computer or network. The back door virus is not designed to be directly destructive like the typical virus or worm. Rather, it is used to breach security systems. Once the back door is created, the computer file system can be accessed in spite of password and other standard security setups. Back doors are usually associated with network systems but can also be used on a single computer.

Password Virus

A **password virus** is not designed to destroy a system or replicate itself. Rather, like the back door virus, it is designed to breach security. These viruses steal passwords. The passwords are stolen and then redirected to another location possibly, on some other system on the Internet to be accessed later. Often, the system that is housing the stolen passwords is not even aware that it is being used to hold stolen material.

A password virus is closely associated with a back door virus, and both may be used in combination. The password virus and back door virus are designed for illegally accessing networks, though either can be used to access a single computer when it is connected to the Internet.

Stealth Virus

A **stealth virus** hides from normal detection by incorporating itself into part of a known, and usually required, program for the computer. The signature of a stealth virus is difficult to acquire unless the original computer system has an antimalware program installed when new. When the antimalware program is installed on a clean computer, the program monitors changes in all files, especially those susceptible to a stealth virus. For example, if the important files change in length, it is a sign that it has been infected with a stealth virus.

Polymorphic Virus

To resist detection, a **polymorphic virus** changes as it evolves. It can randomly change its program length and the location or type of file it chooses to infect. By constantly changing its profile, it can go undetected by antimalware programs that compare the signature or profile of the known virus. The most modern and dangerous viruses use both polymorphic and stealth characteristics to protect themselves.

Hoaxes

A **hoax** is not actually a virus. Instead, a hoax, as the name implies, is a false message spread about a real or unreal virus. These messages could be classified as pranks. While hoaxes do not directly damage the computer or destroy files, they are not harmless.

Hoaxes can cost money through the loss of production time. If a hoax warns of a virus such as a logic bomb that will activate at 12:00 on June 5, people who believe the hoax will stop working and use antimalware software to clean their computer before resuming work. It may take some time before they find out that the message was just a hoax and that no real virus exists. If this message spreads through a large corporation, thousands of computers could be shut down. Another trick used by hoaxes is to pick the name of a legitimate file used by a computer's operating system and claim that it is a virus. You are then warned to delete the file. Many people lost their ability to read long file names when one of these hoaxes passed through.

A hoax is considered harmful because it too can cause losses. While the damage is not usually directed to the computer or data system files, money is lost in the form of labor costs. The best way to prevent against being fooled by a hoax is to visit one of the websites of an antimalware software manufacturer. These sites have pages dedicated to discussing common hoaxes.

Rootkit

A **rootkit** consists of a collection of software programs that installs on a computer and allows an intruder to take administrative control. What makes a rootkit so difficult to detect and remove is that it boots and runs before the operating system does. This allows it to take over the computer before the operating system can. It is similar to having two operating systems installed on the computer running simultaneously.

Rootkits are difficult to remove and often require a step-by-step manual removal procedure. At times, the only way to eliminate a rootkit is to do a complete low-level format of the hard drive. You may even need to flash the system BIOS or firmware.

There are four classifications of rootkit identified by the location it resides in: firmware rootkit, boot rootkit, kernel rootkit, and driver rootkit. The *firmware rootkit* replaces or overwrites the computer firmware. This type of rootkit exists during the computer system POST. The *boot rootkit* replaces the operating system bootloader file, which is used to start or load the operating system. The *kernel rootkit* replaces part or all of the operating system kernel. The *driver rootkit* replaces entirely or partly a legitimate trusted driver file used to support hardware.

You can now see why it is so difficult to detect and repair a computer system infected by a rootkit. Earlier in this chapter, security measures such as Trusted Boot and Measured Boot were introduced. These measures are incorporated into the computer system and are mainly designed to detect malware such as a rootkit. Computers equipped with UEFI and a Trusted Platform Module (TPM) are the best at detecting and preventing rootkits.

Botnet

One common virus is the **botnet**. Botnet is also referred to as a *robot network*. The term *bot* means "robot" when used in variations of the name. A botnet is a collection of infected computers that are controlled by a source computer. The collection of robot networks can be used to simultaneously send out spam or newsletters to millions of computers connected to the Internet. This type of arrangement can also be used to create a **denial-of-service (DOS) attack**. A denial-of-service attack is when a network server or web server is flooded with requests to the point that it cannot fulfill the requests. This causes the requests to time out. A web server would appear to the requester as being out of service, and in the practical sense, it is.

Grayware

The exact definition of **grayware** depends on which antimalware manufacturer website you

visit. In general, grayware refers to a collection of malware that is not regarded as very dangerous, but rather more of a nuisance. Examples of grayware are pop-up ads, adware, joke programs, spyware, and data mining software. Examples that are not considered grayware are Trojans, MBR viruses, and destructive worms. Grayware does slow computer performance because it often uses the Internet connection to send information back to the originator or collection point.

Spam

Spam is unsolicited junk e-mail or junk electronic newsletters. Spam is responsible for drastically reducing the bandwidth of the Internet. Millions of pieces of spam are circulating the Internet at any given moment. Spam is illegal in most countries, but it is difficult to stop when coming from a country that does not have laws against spam. Also, many times spam is distributed by taking over a computer and using the computer as a source of spam e-mail. For example, a malicious software package can be downloaded and installed on an unsuspecting user's computer. The computer is under the control of a hacker and is used for other purposes, such as forwarding e-mail spam. The computer is therefore considered as a *zombie*.

Keyloggers

A **keylogger** is malware that after being installed on a computer keeps track of all keys pressed by the user. It records the keystrokes in a file, which can later be retrieved. The data collected from the keylogger program can be accessed remotely and then used to learn the user logon name, password, and other confidential information. Keylogger programs are often distributed through Trojans attached to e-mail.

Adware

Adware is so named because it is designed to support advertisements such as popups and may also gather information about the user. Adware is also referred to as *spyware* by some antimalware software programs.

Adware most commonly infects computers through free downloads such as screen savers, free trial software programs, and file sharing programs. Adware is not overtly destructive as many malware programs are. However, adware can cause computer performance to suffer. The adware program often sends data to the originating source to keep track of the user's Internet habits. Computer performance suffers because while the user is trying to use the Internet and search the web, the adware program may keep sending information to the source, thus reducing bandwidth.

The right to use adware on the computer is typically stated in the end user license (EUL) agreement that most users never read. When you click the **I agree** button while installing the software, you have agreed to let the company spy on you or gather information about you and your browsing habits. This is completely legal. Many antimalware programs do not remove adware. You should install an additional program designed specifically for removing adware and spyware. Two very common free versions are Ad-Aware by Lavasoft Corporation and Spybot—Search & Destroy by software programmer Patrick Kolla. Windows Defender also combats adware and spyware.

> **Tech Tip**
>
> Be aware that some antiadware software companies make agreements with some software distributors not to remove their adware. Do not be surprised to find that if you run two different antiadware software packages on a computer that you obtain different results.

Spyware

Spyware is designed to track a user's habits such as their web browsing habits. Spyware is often included as part of a free download software package. Many software companies include spyware as part of the trial or free software package. The main difference between spyware and adware is that spyware is considered malicious or illegal because you have not given your consent to install the program on your computer. Spyware and adware can be used to generate popups on a computer as you surf the Internet. Some forms of spyware may monitor the user's keystrokes and read cookie contents stored on the computer.

Data Miner

Data miner is another name for spyware. Data miners gather information about a user's web browsing habits. This information is used for marketing purposes. Data miner programs are classified as spyware by most antimalware organizations. Data miners are also considered a form of grayware. Data miner programs are often embedded into downloaded software, especially free applications or trial versions of software. It is usually legal because when the software or trial version is downloaded, the user agreement often states that the software will be using a data miner to gather information about the use of the product and the user's browsing activities. When users select the **I agree** button at the end of the license agreement, they give permission to the company to mine data from their computer or simply put, to be spied on.

Browser Hijackers

A **browser hijacker** is a program that changes the browser configuration, such as by replacing the default home page or default browser. The new browser was not intentionally installed by the user. Some forms of browser hijackers are identified as adware by some antimalware software packages. Some browser hijacker programs simply install undesired icons or modify the toolbar. The purpose is to take users to a website they did not intend to connect to or view.

Dialers

A **dialer** is a program that automatically disables a telephone modem that is dialing a number and automatically switches to another phone number. The new phone number is typically an expensive (900) number. The user unknowingly is creating a very expensive phone bill.

Phishing

Phishing (pronounced *fishing*) is an e-mail used to impersonate a legitimate company or institution, thus fooling the user into believing the e-mail is from some trusted source. The phishing e-mail requests information from the user, such as the user name, password, account number, Social Security number, or some combination of personal information. A very common phishing scam is to send millions of e-mails that look like legitimate e-mails from eBay requesting that the user confirm personal information, such as the user name, password, and account number. If the user responds to the bogus e-mail, then his or her account is compromised by the criminal. Phishing is also considered a form of social engineering.

Pharming

Pharming is the deceptive practice based on poisoning a Domain Name Service (DNS) server with an incorrect IP address for a website. Pharming is also referred to as DNS cache poisoning or simply as DNS poisoning. All websites have a name address known as a domain name and a numerical address known as the IP address. DNS servers are located all over the Internet at different levels. For example, each Internet Service Provider (ISP) is responsible for running a DNS server at their location. When you request a web page, such as www.rmroberts.com, your request is sent to the local ISP. When it reaches the local ISP, the IPS's DNS server matches the domain name to the domain name's IP address, such as 65.254.254.34. It is the IP address that is then used to find and connect to the requested website.

Pharming takes place when the domain name requested is realigned with a different IP address. When this happens, any requests through the DNS server is redirected to the counterfeit or bogus website. For example, you request to connect to a company selling computers. The bogus website is an exact replica of the real site. When you find the computer you want at a great price, you purchase the computer by providing your name, address, credit card information, and more. What has happened is the bogus website has collected all your information needed to use your credit card anywhere in the world. Pharming is a very sophisticated method of identity theft and is relatively new.

The pharming strategy takes place on a remote computer so that traditional antimalware, antispam, and other malware protection programs cannot prevent pharming. Pharming can only be prevented at the DNS server by ensuring that the DNS server is using protection mechanisms.

Cookies

A **cookie** is a small text file used to send information about a user to a server. Cookies were originally designed to assist users in finding topics or information on a server that they should be interested in. For example, if a user browses a website and purchases a fishing pole, a cookie is generated and stored on the user's computer. The next time the user visits that particular website, information is displayed relating to fishing poles, such as wading boots, fishing lures, and any related fishing merchandise that might be on sale. The cookie and the text information stored in it identify the special interest of the user.

A+ Note

Questions related to malware can be very tricky on the A+ exam. More than one answer can appear to be correct when identifying a specific malware by description. It is sometimes difficult to identify the correct response when the multiple choice answers are social engineering, spam, and phishing. Read the question carefully.

Creation of Viruses

By understanding something of how a virus is created, you may better be able to detect a virus. Viruses are created in a number of different ways using many different programming tools. For example, one common way viruses are created is through macros. As discussed in the section on macro viruses, a macro is a short program written to save keystrokes. Macros are written in macro language programs, such as Visual Basic or similar programming tools. They were developed to help users. However, the same techniques used to save you time can also be applied for destructive purposes.

Programming software such as Visual Basic, C++, and ActiveX are commonly used tools to develop viruses and worms. Even the simple macro editor that comes with Microsoft Word can be used. There are websites that will even sell password, back door, and worm programs. They are advertised "for educational use only."

Most virus and worm paths can be tracked. They can often be traced backward to the original source, especially when delivered by e-mail. Look at **Figure 14-26**. Notice how the e-mail properties can be revealed to expose the real e-mail address, e-mail server name, and originating IP address. Once the TCP/IP address is known, a trace can begin. The ISP can revoke access to any user who violates privacy or harasses another computer site. Remember that accessing another person's computer without their express permission and distributing a virus is a crime.

Malware Prevention

Keeping a computer free of viruses can be a task. Most malware can be prevented, but with new malware appearing all the time, it is difficult to prevent them all. Worms make use of existing program security flaws. For worms, there is no other protection than to avoid all contact on networks and the Internet. For most people, this is not an option.

> **Tech Tip**
>
> A virus or worm designed to crack an e-mail list is specific to a particular e-mail software package. Since each e-mail system has a unique program design, malware must be designed especially for that e-mail software package. This means other e-mail software packages cannot be cracked by the same virus or worm.

Most malware infections can be prevented following some simple practices. Additional practices will help keep the damage to a minimum if you are infected. The following suggestions will help keep your computers and networks safe:

- Always use a firewall to protect your computer from Internet access.
- Always install an antimalware program to combat malware.
- Never open unsolicited e-mail or e-mail attachments.
- Never reveal your password to anyone or transmit a password in an e-mail.
- Never respond to any e-mail that requests your password, account numbers, Social Security number, or any other information that could put you at risk.

Figure 14-26.
The source information of an e-mail can be revealed in Microsoft Outlook through **Message Options**. This dialog box is accessed by opening the e-mail and then clicking **View | Message Options**.

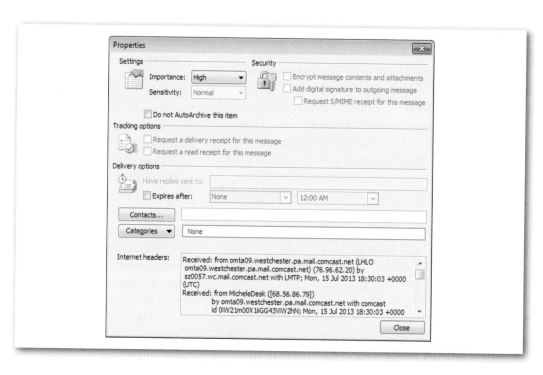

- Don't accept file attachments on e-mails from unknown sources. It is true that you can still get a virus from a known source. This happens when friendly sources do not know that they are spreading a virus. However, your chances are lessened by accepting attachments from only known sources. Regular acceptance of file attachments from completely unknown sources will almost surely cause a problem sooner or later.
- Never load a file from media that you have not checked first with up-to-date antimalware software. The number of infections that have occurred by simply exchanging discs or flash drives (especially games) is enormous.
- Before giving a file to anyone, check the storage media using an antimalware program.
- Encrypt your important files. Encrypted files are usually useless to another user without the encryption key. Even if you have files stolen, minimal damage is done.
- Always perform regular daily backups of important files. Not all malware can be stopped before doing damage to a computer system. Performing regular backups are your best insurance against a malware disaster.

If you have any doubts about taking the time to protect yourself or taking the time to back up your files, consider the following questions regarding your options if a virus destroys your files.

1. Do you have the discs to reload everything, from your operating system to your leisure programs?
2. How much time would it take to reconstruct everything on your computer?
3. How many of the items on your computer are one of a kind?
4. Are there important documents on your hard drive? Do you have term papers, legal papers, financial data, income tax forms, and other unique items stored on your computer?
5. Do you have any hard copies of this information?
6. What happens to you if you are responsible for a corporation?
7. How much would the corporation lose if the

computer was wiped out? Could it lose a list of thousands of customers? Could it lose a 200-page catalog sitting on the hard drive or file server?

Tech Tip Cloud service providers run antimalware to protect user data. Cloud storage is an excellent choice for backing up critical files.

After thinking about the individual or corporate losses, it is easy to see the benefits of protecting your computer and backing up all important files.

Malware Removal

While preventing the arrival of a virus or worm is ideal, there is a good chance that at some point you will encounter an infected computer. Remember that a virus or worm is simply a program designed to annoy, amuse, or destroy. You eliminate a virus that has never been run as you would any unwanted program. You delete it. Place it in the Recycle Bin and then empty the Recycle Bin.

However, once the virus has been activated (run on your computer), it can be a much more complicated task. The removal of some viruses and worms is as easy as locating and erasing the file containing the virus. In most cases, removal often involves removing various files, installing a software patch, and adjusting registry settings. Most antimalware manufacturers provide a small downloadable program that does many of these tasks automatically. When a widespread virus is first discovered and publicized, your first move should be to go to the website of your antimalware provider and check its alert bulletins for a description and remedy.

The first step in virus removal is to identify the virus. Just because a computer is acting strangely does not mean it has contracted a virus. Any number of things can produce the same effects of known viruses. Check your antimalware software manufacturer website for information about the particular virus characteristics. The characteristics of a virus, or its signature, can be found there. This will give you a complete description of the virus and what it does. This includes its symptoms and size, where it is generally located, how it spreads, and what areas of the computer system are affected. Most viruses and worms have hidden, system, or read only file attributes set to help protect it.

The next step is the actual removal. Usually, antimalware manufacturers provide a removal tool, which is an executable program you download and run. The executable program does all the complicated steps for you. Behind the scenes, it removes all the infected files, and, if need be, corrects any altered registry settings. If there is no removal tool available, you can usually find step-by-step instructions on the Internet. You will have to manually delete all infected files. If registry changes are needed, you must open the registry program and make the alterations as specified. You must be extremely careful when altering the registry. If you make a typo in your registry alteration, great trouble may ensue.

A virus may make additional copies of itself so that it can reinfect your computer if the original virus file is erased. For example, it can attach itself automatically to any drive when files are saved to that drive. This means that while the bug has not been detected and you save a file to a flash drive, CD/DVD, or to a network hard drive, the virus also saves a copy of itself to the same media. When media such as a flash drive or CD/DVD is used to load a file to a hard drive or to RAM, the virus tags along, loading itself as well. This is one way many viruses spread. As part of eliminating a virus, all CDs and flash drives must be scanned. This is the only way to ensure the complete removal of the virus.

Tech Tip   When an antimalware program identifies a virus or malware item but fails to remove it successfully, try running the computer in safe mode and then start the antimalware program.

Legal Aspects

Legal punishment for the creation and distribution of a virus is severe. In addition,

individuals can be held liable for the cost of financial losses suffered by any corporation harmed by the virus. The FBI National Computer Crime Squad (NCCS) has classified computer crimes into certain categories. These categories include the following:

- Intrusions of the public phone system.
- Major computer network intrusions.
- Network integrity violations.
- Privacy violations.
- Industrial espionage.
- Pirated software.
- Other crimes committed by using a computer

In addition to the federal crime statutes, most states have their own crime statutes that are comparable to the federal statutes. Computer crimes are not taken lightly. An example of harsh consequences can be seen in the cases of a number of young students who have used new computer systems to break these laws. The final outcome is usually simple. While the students serve no time for their mistakes, their entire computer systems have been confiscated, and they may be banned from using a computer for five years or more.

You may be wondering why there are laws dealing with intrusion into the public telephone system. The public telephone system provides a medium for a tremendous amount of Internet use. Many hackers have attempted to gain, or have successfully gained, access to telephone company records. This has allowed them to use other people's identifications when accessing the Internet for illegal purposes. Illegal access to the public telephone system carries severe penalties.

The last classification, "other crimes committed using a computer," is a catchall. If a computer crime is not specifically listed, then the act of any criminal nature committed using a computer will fall under this statute. This law is important because people who are determined to do damage or illegally use computer systems invent new crimes on a continual basis.

Mistaken Identifications (or Oops)

Many times a problem occurs on a computer and the computer software automatically assumes it to be a virus. Some technicians automatically assume that many difficult-to-solve problems are caused by a virus. However, users do make errors when using their computers and often the results can appear similar to problems caused by a virus. A classic problem is when a user accidentally hits a key combination that has devastating effects. For example, a key combination struck in error can cause an entire manuscript to disappear. When the key combination [Ctrl] [A] is struck in Microsoft Word, the entire text document is highlighted. The very next keystroke will replace all text in the document with the next letter typed. A major disaster has now occurred, and the computer user may have no idea that he or she actually caused the problem. It would be easy to assume that a virus has attacked the computer system.

A follow-up phenomenon is the repeat of the keystroke error. Once a mistake is made, human nature allows that person to repeat the same mistake again. Since the technician will probably never view the error in progress and will only get a verbal description of the situation, it may be difficult to diagnose the problem. A frantic description of time lost on a document does not make for easy computer diagnosis. The assumption is that it must be a virus. A few simple steps can help if the user has not tried to repair the error first. Typing [Ctrl] [Z], the shortcut combination for undo, can save the day if the user has not typed too many additional keystrokes before you arrive.

Users often assume a virus has attacked their computer as things go wrong. However, there are many different reasons that a computer can exhibit unusual actions. Possibilities include power glitches, magnets too close to the computer or monitor, network glitches, and more. A strong magnetic field can completely erase computer disks. When this happens, it will probably be reported as a virus.

Firewall

No chapter concerning computer security would be complete without covering the firewall. A **firewall** is a hardware device or software application that protects the computer from unauthorized access or malware delivered through a network or Internet connection. This section will provide you with a short introduction to firewalls. More information is provided in Chapter 18—WAN.

To fully understand the digital mechanics of how a firewall operates, you need detailed knowledge about protecting a network system by blocking access to specific ports or by filtering IP addresses, packet contents, services, and protocols. The details of these topics require you to understand the basics of network and Internet address systems and network protocols. For now, the firewall will be introduced in general terms rather than detailed technical specifics of how the firewall works based on packet contents and Internet addresses.

Windows operating systems include a firewall that protects the computer from unauthorized access from a person or some types of malware. If a computer never connected to a network system and the Internet, there would be no need for a firewall. Since many programs rely on an Internet connection, a firewall is basic for a computer. For example, many programs check for system updates or require an Internet connection to perform normal duties such as checking e-mail, engaging in social media, or playing an online multiplayer game. There is a constant flow of information in the form of data blocks called *packets* to and from the computer. Each packet contains a port number in addition to the data.

A **port number** is a number in the range of 0 to 65,535. All software applications that use a network system use assigned port numbers to identify the software application or service. The software application is identified by a port number so that the packet can be delivered to the intended software application.

The flow of packets to and from a computer on a network requires that each packet contain a port number; hence, the flow of data can be controlled by blocking specific port numbers or ports. The term *port* is used when referring to a specific destination. Most port numbers or ports are blocked by default but some remain open to allow special software applications called services to function. A **service** is a software application that performs specific network functions such as assigning network addresses or supporting remote access to the computer desktop.

There are times when you may need to block or unblock a specific port. For example, a firewall is set up to block all ports that are not absolutely essential. A person wishes to participate in a game online. The game "Rainbow Six" requires the use of TCP ports 2346, 2347, and 2348 for Internet gaming. These ports can be opened by entering their numbers in the firewall service properties dialog box. Opening these ports allows data to pass through the firewall, allowing two computers to communicate freely during a gaming session. View the Microsoft Knowledge Base Article 307554 online to see other port addresses associated with common games and services.

The firewall for Windows was first introduced with Windows XP Service Pack 2 (SP2) and was called the Internet Connection Firewall (ICF). Later versions of Windows refer to it as Windows Firewall. Since the introduction of the first Windows Firewall, each new operating system included a more advanced version. There are also many third-party utilities that can be used to increase computer network and Internet security. **Figure 14-27** shows the Windows 7 version of Windows Firewall.

Notice in the screen capture that the Windows 7 Firewall has two broad categories of default configuration: **Home or work (private) networks** and **Public networks**. Public networks are Internet access locations such as airports, coffee shops, or other similar public locations. Private networks are those that support Internet access in homes or business offices. Public networks are the most vulnerable to attacks and as such have the most restrictive default configuration which blocks all port access except for vital ports. Home or private networks are less restrictive because they typically do not connect directly to the Internet. Private networks usually have some sort of security device, such as a router or a firewall that provides protection to the computers and network system. When using a public location, the computer user has no control over the Internet access being provided, thus there is no insurance that the connection is protected by a security device or how strict the security configuration settings are.

Figure 14-27.
Windows Firewall automatically checks information coming from the Internet or a network. Then, it either blocks it or allows it to pass through to the computer.

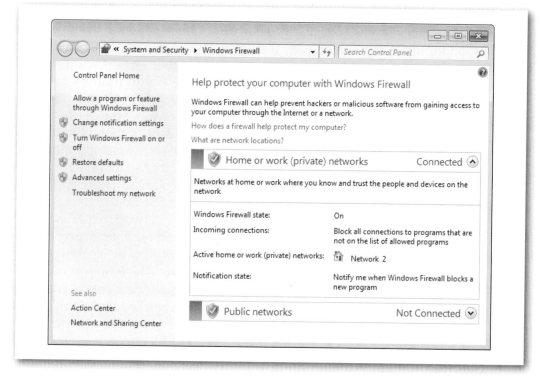

Chapter Summary

- Security practices for securing the physical area of the computer and data storage areas include locking access doors, implementing a man trap, and incorporating biometrics, a PIN key entry system, radio-frequency identification (RFID), or proximity cards.

- Best security practices include enforcing complex passwords, using multi-factor authentication, and implementing the principle of least privilege.

- Microsoft antimalware security tools include Microsoft Malicious Software Removal Tool, Windows Defender, Microsoft Defender Offline, SmartScreen, Microsoft Security Essentials, Microsoft Safety Scanner, and Microsoft Active Protection Service.

- Common classifications of malware are Trojan horse, logic bomb, macro, worm, password, back door, hoax, rootkit, and botnet.

- A firewall is a hardware device or software application that protects the computer from unauthorized access or malware delivered through a network or Internet connection.

Review Questions

Answer the following questions on a separate sheet of paper. Please do not write in this book.

1. What is tailgating?
2. How can tailgating be prevented?
3. What is the simplest method of implementing a man trap?
4. What types of security features can a man trap incorporate to make it more secure?
5. How is a smart card used?
6. What two advantages does a virtual smart card have over a physical smart card?
7. What technology must be incorporated into the computer motherboard for a virtual smart card to be used?
8. What technology must be incorporated into the computer motherboard for a Windows BitLocker Drive Encryption to be used?
9. What is the best practice for disposing of physical documents containing personal information and sensitive data?
10. List four ways data can be destroyed on a hard drive before disposal?
11. What are the characteristics of a complex password?
12. When is it all right to reveal your password?

13. Match the authentication category to its example. The authentication categories can be used more than once.
    A = Something you know.
    B = Something you have.
    C = Something you are.
    a. _____ PIN
    b. _____ fob
    c. _____ fingerprint
    d. _____ password
    e. _____ smart card
    f. _____ retinal eye scan

14. Which category in the Windows 7 Control Panel allows you to create a new user account?

15. Which Windows operating systems allow you to sign in to a computer system with an e-mail address?

16. Why should you create at least two user accounts with administrative privileges?

17. Which operating system first disabled the built-in Administrative account by default?

18. What is the Local Security Policy?

19. What Windows XP through Windows Vista security feature monitors the status of the firewall, virus or malware protection, automatic updates, and other security configuration options related to the operating system applications?

20. What Windows 7 security feature is similar to the Windows Security Center?

21. What is the most common way to eliminate or disable annoying messages that appear when a standard user attempts to make changes in the computer configuration?

22. Which version of Windows includes an enhanced version of Windows Defender?

23. What is the difference between Microsoft Security Essentials and Windows Defender for Windows 7?

24. What Microsoft application allows you to monitor security events such as unsuccessful logon attempts?

25. What are the three major stages of a computer virus?

26. How is a worm different than a virus?

27. How can replication harm a computer system?

28. What is a Trojan horse virus?

29. Define *macro*.

30. What is a polymorphic virus?

31. What is a hoax virus?

32. What two technologies incorporated into a computer system offer the best protection against rootkits?

33. What is a botnet?

34. What is grayware?

35. Name five types of malware that can be referred to as grayware.
36. What is a zombie?
37. What is a keylogger?
38. What is the difference between adware and spyware?
39. What effect does data miner and adware programs have on a computer?
40. What is phishing?
41. Why can't antimalware software prevent pharming?
42. What steps can you take to prevent malware infections?
43. What are the six major categories of computer crime as identified by the FBI?
44. What is a firewall?
45. In relation to Windows 7 Firewall, what defines a public network?
46. In relation to Windows 7 Firewall, what defines a private network?

Sample A+ Exam Questions

Answer the following questions on a separate sheet of paper. Please do not write in this book.

1. Which is the *least likely* way to contract a virus?
   a. Loading a game program on a computer from a flash drive given to you by a trusted friend
   b. Downloading a file from a reputable Internet site
   c. Connecting to another computer on a corporate network
   d. Loading a new operating system from a DVD taken directly from a sealed shrink-wrapped box

2. Which of the following is the *best* password to use to prevent possible compromise or intrusion?
   a. Secret
   b. Big$tar_5
   c. President Roosevelt
   d. Password

3. Worms are typically spread by which of the following methods?
   a. E-mail attachments
   b. Exchanged flash drive contents
   c. The system BIOS whenever two computers connect together on the Internet
   d. Exclusively by text editor programs

4. Which application would you run to enhance password security in Windows 7?
   a. msconfig.sys
   b. secpol.msc
   c. ipconfig
   d. sysconfig

5. Which accounts are disabled by default in Windows 7? Select all that apply.
   a. Administrator
   b. Standard
   c. Guest
   d. Limited

6. The characteristics that describe the uniqueness of a virus are referred to as a
   _____.
   a. signature
   b. reputation
   c. payload
   d. morphic synopsis

7. Which management tool is used to change default user permissions?
   a. User Account Control
   b. Local Security Policy
   c. BitLocker
   d. Windows Defender

8. Which malware type changes the DNS server address of a legitimate website and replaces the IP address with a bogus website?
   a. Phishing
   b. Zombie
   c. Trojan horse
   d. Pharming

9. Which management tool is designed to prevent unauthorized access to a computer through an Internet connection?
   a. Windows Defender
   b. BitLocker
   c. Windows Firewall
   d. Local Security Policy

10. Which technique or software program is based on poisoning the DNS database of a DNS server?
    a. Rootkit
    b. Phishing
    c. Pharming
    d. Data mining

Suggested Laboratory Activities

Do not attempt any suggested laboratory activities without your instructor's permission. Certain activities can render the PC operating system inoperable.

1. Visit some antimalware manufacturer websites. Download and install trial versions of their antimalware program.

2. Visit the SANS organization website. Enter the term "SANS.org" into an Internet browser to find it.

3. Visit the EICAR website and download their antimalware test file.

4. Download the latest security patch for Microsoft e-mail. While at the Microsoft website, look for other patches to update security for your computer.

5. Visit the Lavasoft website and install and run the free version of Ad-Aware.

6. Visit the Microsoft computer security webpage. You can find it by conducting an Internet search using the key terms "Microsoft security webpage."

7. Visit several different antimalware websites and scan their virus encyclopedias.

PC Troubleshooting

15

After studying this chapter, you will be able to:

- Implement common sense practices when troubleshooting a PC.
- Identify the three stages of computer operation.
- Recognize common startup problems and identify their causes.
- Recognize common hard drive failures and identify their causes.
- Recognize common mechanical problems and identify their causes.
- Use a variety of troubleshooting modes and utilities to recover from a system startup failure.
- Use the appropriate diagnostics utility given a specific problem.
- Recall the boot sequence for Windows XP and later.
- Recall basic data recovery methods.
- Implement appropriate practices when preparing to upgrade or install an operating system.
- Implement preventive computer maintenance.
- Interpret the CompTIA A+ troubleshooting steps.

Key Terms

The following key terms will become important pieces of your computer vocabulary. Be sure you can define them.

archive bit	Microsoft Dynamic Link Library (DLL)
blue screen error	
clean room	registry keys
differential backup	startup problem
hive	system image
incremental backup	user mode
kernel mode	

Troubleshooting a PC requires a combination of the technician's knowledge, intuition, and experience. Microsoft Windows operating systems include many diagnostic tools as standard programs. Many diagnostic tools are also available from third-party vendors that can assist in the troubleshooting process. Third-party vendor programs range from freeware and shareware to systems costing several thousands of dollars. The more expensive programs include a diagnostic board that plugs into the PC's expansion slots.

Most problems can be diagnosed without expensive diagnostic tools. The value of these tools is they can be used to save time and money when trying to identify problems that may be caused by two or more components. For example, it can be difficult to determine if a problem is caused by a troublesome CPU or a bad motherboard. When this situation arises, a simple solution is to substitute a known or good CPU for the suspect CPU. However, this substitution alone can be very expensive.

Common Sense Practices

Remember, when troubleshooting and repairing PCs that "time is money." Always take the quickest and easiest path first. When troubleshooting, there are some common sense practices you should follow:

- Determine the major area at fault.
- Determine what action occurred just prior to failure or problem.
- Proceed carefully.
- Write down settings before you change them.
- Think the problem through.

Determining the Major Fault Area

The first step is to try to determine what major area is the most likely source of the fault. There are three major fault areas to be considered:

- Hardware failure.
- Software failure.
- User-generated problems.

The most common error or problem is the user-generated problem. Some users like to tinker with Control Panel, and others will try to solve their problems alone. Users with a little technical knowledge can be the most dangerous. They often attempt to fix a problem before calling the technician. When this happens, you may very well be faced with more than one problem. First, the original problem likely still exists, and then there are additional problems created by the user. Repairing computers in a school setting can be the most frustrating. Some students love to experiment on the settings on a school's computer before trying the activity on their home computer.

What Happened Last?

It is critical to determine from the computer user what the last action on the computer was prior to the problem occurring or before computer failure. Often, the last action taken by the user can lead the technician directly to the problem. Find out if the user recently installed some new software. Perhaps, there has been a recent hardware upgrade to the problem PC. Has the user recently downloaded a file from the Internet? Ask as many questions of the user as possible. This can save valuable time.

Proceed Carefully

Do not rush when diagnosing problems. Operating in a hurry will lead to sloppy work. This can create new problems or cause you to overlook something important. In contrast, do proceed in a methodical yet constant pace. Customers will not appreciate a technician who is standing around drinking coffee, talking, socializing, or any other activity that appears to be a nonproductive use of energy. Customers are typically paying a premium price for service and are losing the use of their computers while they are inoperable. Don't waste their money, or, next time there is a problem, someone else will be called.

Write Things Down

Do not rely on your memory alone while troubleshooting. Before you change a setting, write down the current setting. If you are going to delete a file, write down the file name. You can make the problem much harder to find if you create another problem along the way. If a problem is not cleared after changing a setting or deleting a file, you should return the system file or setting to the way you found it. Do not simply move on and try something else.

Think the Problem Through

Don't try operations out of desperation. Desperate technicians will often run the same test twice knowing the results from the first test were valid. These are acts of desperation, and they occur when a technician is stumped.

When you run out of tests—*stop and think* about the situation. Writing things down in a list helps. Make two lists. First, make a list of what you know is not the problem. Then, make a list of possible problems that could still exist. Check the website of the manufacturer of the PC, the BIOS, and the operating system. Corrections could be posted for the exact symptoms you are encountering. Many times, a problem is discovered that affects a particular setup or particular combination of hardware and software programs.

Don't hesitate to contact the manufacturer of the hardware or software in question by e-mail with a description of the problem. Most questions will be answered in 24 to 48 hours at no cost for the service. You can get much faster replies by calling, but that service is seldom free.

Your fellow technicians are another very important source of information. As you progress in the PC repair world, you will make many friends. It is a standard practice to share information with a colleague who may have encountered a similar problem. A peer may have a quick and easy answer to a problem that you have not encountered before. Other times, simply discussing the problem with a peer can be quite helpful. Explaining the problem forces you to summarize the situation and describe it in logical terms. Just the act of verbalizing the problem may allow you to solve it. Never be embarrassed to use this form of assistance.

Troubleshooting Overview

There is no one foolproof method to troubleshooting. There are too many variables that can cause a computer to fail, but there are recommended procedures that can be used to help you organize your approach to solving a computer problem. The causes of failure discussed are not all inclusive and should be interpreted as a guide to solving a computer-related problem or complete system failure.

When troubleshooting computer problems, the first thing you must do is isolate the problem. You must determine if it is a hardware problem, software problem, or user-generated problem. This is easier said than done. The best way to go about this is to decide when the problem is occurring. In other words, at what stage of computer operation is the problem occurring? Did the failure or problem happen during the POST (power-on self-test), during the loading and initialization of the required operating system files, or after the logon and running the services and application software?

This section discusses the common causes of failure related to the three stages of computer operation. The first stage is the POST. The second stage is loading the required operating system files and initializing the hardware system. The third stage is after the logon. It comprises loading the startup programs and running applications and services.

First Stage

If the problem occurs during POST, it is most likely a hardware failure. In this stage, no operating system software or application software has been loaded. The POST may fail to complete if a damaged hardware device fails POST or fails its own diagnostic routine. For example, a telephone modem that has been damaged during a thunderstorm may cause the computer to lock up during the POST or immediately after.

If you just built the computer system and it fails to successfully boot the first time during POST, chances are you have improperly installed the RAM, CPU, or CPU cooling device. A high-speed CPU that has an improperly installed cooling fan and heat sink may generate excessive heat in a few seconds, causing the computer to freeze while performing the POST. Improperly seated RAM may also cause the computer to fail during POST. When memory is improperly seated, a beep code typically will be issued, indicating a problem with RAM. Go back and reinstall these devices and remove all unnecessary devices, such as adapter cards that are not required for system operation, and reboot the system. If the problem still persists, you can either substitute parts to determine which hardware device is causing the failure or use a third-party utility that uses a POST card to diagnose the problem.

Firmware POST Codes

The firmware (BIOS or UEFI) produces specific error codes or POST codes that can be used as a diagnostic tool. POST codes are not universal and can vary quite a bit depending on the manufacturer of the computer, motherboard, or firmware. A beep code is used to indicate failures before the video system is initialized and when there is no display on which to print screen messages. After the video is enabled, a message will appear on the screen during or immediately after the POST indicating the problem by either an alphanumeric code or short message.

Some computers indicate a successful POST with a single beep while others do not. Some BIOS/UEFI firmware allow the single beep to be disabled because some users are annoyed by the beep. To identify the problem, you must consult the computer, motherboard, or firmware manufacturer. A series of short and long beeps on a Dell computer indicates a problem that does not necessarily match the same series of beeps on an ASUS computer. One thing you can be sure of is if you hear a series of beeps it is an indication of a major hardware failure.

PC-Doctor POST Card

A very popular third-party utility suite used by repair centers is PC-Doctor Service Center 8. The complete PC-Doctor Service 8 kit is shown in **Figure 15-1**. The kit includes all the software and hardware you need to thoroughly test all

Figure 15-1. The PC-Doctor Service Center 8 is a complete kit for diagnosing computer hardware.

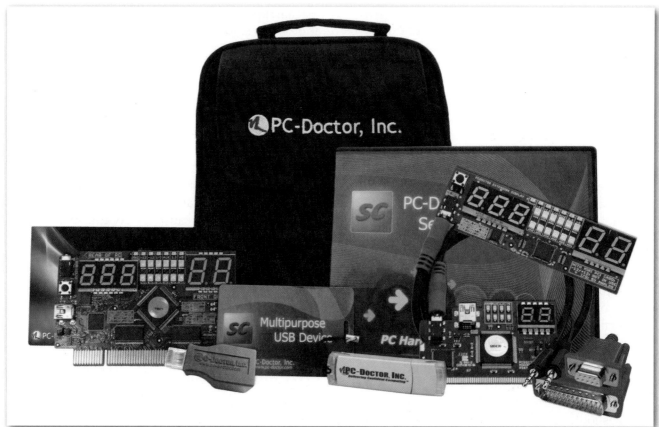

computer hardware components. PC-Doctor is used by Dell Computers to perform computer diagnostics in the service department.

The PC-Doctor POST card, **Figure 15-2**, is inserted into any PCI slot and used to diagnose errors during POST caused by hardware failure such as the CPU, RAM, or the motherboard. A POST error code is displayed on the LEDs. The technician can then match the code to the diagnostic chart in the user manual. Without a POST card, a technician would have to substitute the CPU, RAM, and motherboard with a known good component. Part substitution can be time-consuming and expensive. The technician runs the risk of damaging a part during the substitution process.

For more information on problems that can occur during the POST stage, see the following chapter sections: Typical Startup Problems, Hard Drive Failures, Additional Mechanical Problems, and Boot Sequences.

Second Stage

If the problem occurs during the second stage—operating system loading and initialization—the problem is most likely related to a corrupt operating system file or a driver. You can identify when stage two starts by observing the screen display. Many computer systems display the results of the POST as it occurs. You

will see on the screen the RAM check verified and the hard disk drive and other devices that are present identified. Soon after the POST turns over loading the operating system to the boot strap program, you will see a progress bar appear on the screen. When you see the progress bar, you know that the second stage has begun and the operating system has successfully loaded the system kernel. The operating system then initializes the hardware devices.

Failure during the second stage is usually the result of a corrupt system file (required operating system file) such as ntldr or failure to properly detect and initialize a piece of hardware such as the sound card. It can also be caused by a corrupt hardware driver.

The fastest way to repair a system failure that occurs during the loading and initialization of the operating system is by reinstalling required system files. Simply insert the installation CD/DVD and then reboot the computer. When the installation CD/DVD boots, follow the screen prompts. For more information on problems caused by hard drive failure that can occur during the second stage, see the Hard Drive Failures section. Detailed troubleshooting methods for this stage are covered in the Recovering from System Startup Failure section.

Third Stage

System logon is the end of the second stage. Keep in mind that not all operating systems require a logon. The third stage is when the desktop first appears. During the third stage, startup programs, services, and applications are loaded. The most common problems that can occur during this time are usually due to corrupt or incompatible drivers and files.

File Corruption

Files can be corrupted in various ways, such as by virus attacks and hardware failures. For example, an intermittent RAM failure can also corrupt files if the file contents are transferred or copied during the time of RAM failure. Files are corrupted when stored in an area of the hard drive that has a bad sector. All data saved to the bad sector is lost, thus corrupting the contents of

Figure 15-2. PC-Doctor PCI POST card.

PC-Doctor, Inc.

the complete file. Files can also be corrupted by an unexpected power outage or shutting down the computer system while installing updates.

Overwritten DLL File

Certain files, such as a DLL file, can cause a system failure when inappropriately applied in a software program or when they become corrupt. A **Microsoft Dynamic Link Library (DLL)** file is an executable file that can be called and run by Microsoft software applications or by third-party software programs. Rather than write code from scratch each time a new software application is written, programmers can simply call a DLL from within the program they have written and run the function they need automatically. One DLL can be used by more than one software program at the same time. By reusing the same code contained in the DLL, a programmer saves time and the computer uses less memory and disk space. The term *dynamic* is used because the file can be loaded, run, and then unloaded from computer memory when no longer needed.

One of the major software problems in the past is when a user loads a software application from a disc that contains the necessary DLL files to run a software application. All too often, the DLL file on the software disc overwrites the existing DLL residing on the computer. If an older DLL file overwrites a newer DLL file, an error can occur when the user starts an application other than the one just loaded. A classic example is when a user loads an older version of a software game on a computer that has other games requiring the similar DLL file. While the older game runs perfectly, one or more of the other games may now run incorrectly or may not run at all.

DLL files usually have a .dll file extension such as in mon.dll. Sometimes the DLL will have an .exe file extension. Look at **Figure 15-3** to see the search results for files with the .dll extension. There are 16, 643 files that have a .dll extension on this particular computer. As you can see, there are thousands of possible DLL files that can be used as part of multiple software applications and hardware drivers.

Figure 15-3. DLL files are called by software applications to perform common tasks. There are over 16,000 DLL files listed in this particular Windows 7 installation.

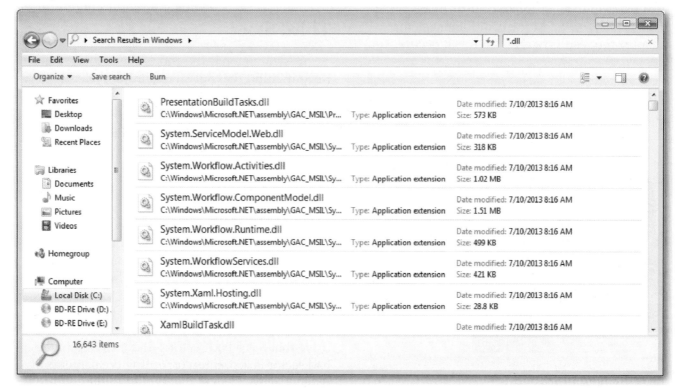

Blue Screen Error

The system may experience a blue screen error commonly referred to as the *Blue Screen of Death (BSoD)*. A **blue screen error** is a blue screen that appears with an error code and then freezes the system. Microsoft also refers to blue screen errors as *fatal errors*, *stop errors*, and *stop error messages* because the system is not recoverable at the time of the error. The system must be restarted before you can attempt to remedy the problem. Some of the most common causes for blue screen errors include the following:

- Defective hardware, such as memory chips and video adapter cards.
- Corrupt files on the hard drive.
- System BIOS settings that are beyond the capabilities of the hardware.
- Third-party software containing bad code.
- Bad code in the Windows operating system.

The error codes displayed on the blue screen can be quite cryptic. You should copy the error code and use it as a reference when searching Microsoft's Support website.

The most appropriate utility for diagnosing a problem after the logon is the System Configuration Utility (msconfig.exe). This and other utilities for diagnosing problems during this stage are covered in the Recovering from a System Startup Failure and the Windows Diagnostic Utilities section. You may also check out the "Demystifying the Blue Screen of Death" Microsoft TechNet article for detailed information. To find it, search the Internet for "Demystifying the Blue Screen of Death."

Tech Tip

A malicious software program (virus or worm) can attack a computer at any time, not just after the system logon. For example, if the MBR is corrupted by a virus, the computer will fail before switching from text mode to graphic mode.

Typical Startup Problems

Startup problems are a tough class of computer error that you are likely to run into. A startup problem causes the computer to lock up during the boot process. These problems occur too early in the PC operation to be solved by system diagnostic tools. This section details some of the most common and catastrophic boot problems you may encounter while starting the PC. Each of the following problems is described as a symptom. Possible solutions are provided as a guide. The list of symptoms is condensed and centers on the problems encountered before the boot process is completed. Keep in mind that there are hundreds of possible computer symptoms. What follows are a few of the most common system hardware failures during the boot.

Think about the boot process and the steps involved. System boot failures involve the power supply, CPU, hard drive (boot device), RAM, BIOS, CMOS, system configuration, loading of drivers, and the loading of the operating system. Now let's look at some of the most common hardware problems and their symptoms during the boot process.

When reading the list that follows, assume that there is one hard drive labeled C and a disc drive labeled D. Note that these are recommended procedures, not absolute procedures. Also, viruses can imitate some of the described symptoms. Always check for the presence of a virus on the hard drive.

Tech Tip

When troubleshooting a PC, always attempt the simplest tests first. Then, move on to the more complex and labor-intensive tests.

Symptom 1:

There is no power light, no fan running, and no sound of boot operation. It appears that the PC is completely dead.

Items to check:

Before you open the case, make sure the PC is plugged in. Next, check the power from the wall outlet or power strip, or both. Be sure there is power to the unit. If you have power, then the likely problem is the computer's power supply. Open the case and test the power supply outputs. Replacing the power supply is generally more cost-effective than fixing a broken one.

Symptom 2:

The power light (LED) is on and the fan is running, but there is no activity. The system appears dead.

Items to check:

Check the power supply for a power good signal. The power good signal is sent to the BIOS system to signal that the power supply is on and ready.

If the power supply passes the power test, try reseating the RAM and the CPU. The CPU or RAM may not be making a good electrical connection in their sockets. First, try reseating the RAM because it is much easier to remove and reinsert than the CPU. The CPU and RAM operate on very low voltages. A slight oxidation buildup on one of the device pins that is operating at 3.3 volts or less is sufficient to render the CPU or RAM dead. Cleaning the oxidation will bring it back.

If you perform all of the listed operations and the system still fails to activate, you probably have a defective motherboard.

Symptom 3:

The system tries to boot. There are two or more beeps, and then nothing (no video). The fan is running, and there is a power light.

Items to check:

Make sure the monitor is plugged in correctly (both the data plug and the power cord). Check the video card. Try reseating the card. Also check the RAM. Remove the RAM and then reinsert it. If those actions do not help, try to decode the beep error code. If you have the manual that came with the motherboard, start there. Newer manuals often come as a PDF file on disc as opposed to the traditional paper booklet. If there is no manual, look up the BIOS chip manufacturer on the Internet. First, copy all information from the BIOS chip or motherboard and then check the manufacturer's website.

Symptom 4:

A setup error is indicated on the screen.

Items to check:

This is probably a CMOS setup problem. Access the BIOS Setup utility by using the key combination indicated on the screen. If no key combinations are given, try those you are familiar

with. Some popular combinations can be found in Figure 3-44 from Chapter 3—Motherboards. You can also look up the keystroke combination for accessing the BIOS at the BIOS manufacturer's website.

Normally, CMOS settings do not change. However, sometimes when you install a new hard drive and the drive is automatically detected, the settings change. Also, if the battery used to hold the CMOS data is going bad, you could lose the settings. The date and time not matching the true date and time is a good indication that your battery is going bad.

Be sure to write down the existing CMOS settings before making any changes. This is extremely important if you are going to try something like the **Return to default settings** option. When that option is selected, many settings will change instantly, and you will not be able to tell which settings have changed or what they changed from. Check the manufacturer's website for the correct CMOS settings for your particular model of PC.

Sometimes people get curious and go into the Setup utility to see what it looks like. They also make changes either intentionally or accidentally. What makes it worse is they generally deny doing so.

Symptom 5:

The PC powers on, but there is no drive activity.

Items to check:

Check the system CMOS settings. Make sure the drive is identified. The drive and the number of cylinders, heads, and sectors should be identified in the Setup utility. In addition, while the PC is booting, the hard drive manufacturer and hard drive model number will often flash on the screen when the BIOS detects it. If the drive is not detected during the boot, the screen will flash something similar to "No hard disk drive."

You should also check the connections between the power supply and the hard drive and the motherboard and the hard drive. They should be tight.

If all that checks out, boot the system with a recovery disc or the operating system installation disk. From the command prompt, see if you can access the hard drive.

Symptom 6:

There is normal boot activity, lights and sounds, but no video.

Items to check:

Check if the monitor is plugged into the computer and that the monitor has power. Swap the monitor for one that is known to be good. If the system fails to generate a display, you probably have a bad video adapter card. Try reseating the video adapter card. If the system will still not display, change the video adapter card or try another video port. Many video cards have two or more ports.

Symptom 7:

The computer attempts to boot to the wrong device.

Items to check:

This can be caused by several issues. The device boot order is controlled by the BIOS/UEFI setup configuration. An inexperienced user may have changed the boot order while trying to install a program from disc and never returned the boot order to the correct sequence. Another possible reason is the computer had an external storage device, such as a hard disk drive attached to a USB port, and was configured to boot from this device. The device has been removed and now the computer is looking for the device during a normal boot. Inspect the Setup utility configuration and correct as necessary.

Symptom 8:

The computer continually reboots on failure.

Items to check:

Some computers can be configured to reboot on a detected error. Disable this option to stop the continuous reboots and then diagnose the cause of the failure. Also, Windows provides an option in the **Startup and Recovery** dialog box that can configure the way the computer reacts on an error. The **Startup and Recovery** dialog box is accessed through **System Properties | Advanced** tab and by clicking the **Settings** button in the **Startup and Recovery** section. The option to automatically restart the computer is the default setting in Windows. **Figure 15-4** shows that the **Automatically restart** option is enabled.

Figure 15-4. The **Startup and Recovery** dialog box is set by default to continuously reboot when a system error is encountered.

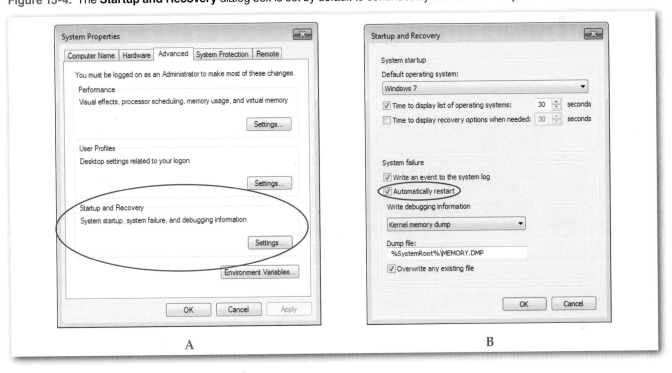

A   B

Symptom 9:

The system crashes or reboots for no apparent reason.

Items to check:

Check the power supply and cables. Make sure they are all tight. Check for excessive heat on the CPU and memory chips. Make sure all DIMMs are seated properly. Try reseating the CPU. Also, check the BIOS/UEFI configuration to verify the correct amount of RAM.

Symptom 10:

A burn smell or smoke is coming from the computer.

Items to check:

When the smell of smoke is detected, and at times visually observed coming from inside a PC case, you most likely have a defective power supply. While not required, a power supply suspected of severe electrical damage can be easily removed from the computer and opened and inspected. Severe electrical damage is very easy to identify. The power supply in **Figure 15-5** shows the following signs of severe damage caused by a failed capacitor:

- An imperfection in the side of the capacitor that appears like a dent or bulge.

Figure 15-5. Typically, a suspected damaged power supply can be verified by visual inspection.

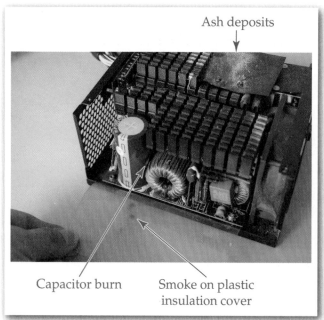

Ash deposits

Capacitor burn   Smoke on plastic insulation cover

- A smoke stain on the clear plastic insulation cover that protects the electrical parts from the metallic cover.
- A deposit of ash from the electrical fire created by the defective capacitor.

You don't have to be an electrical engineer to tell this power supply is bad. If all of that hardware checks out, the motherboard is most likely defective or there is a problem with the hard drive. Swapping the hard drive with one you know is working should show where the problem lies. If the hard drive is causing the problem, check for a virus or a corrupt operating system. Always think about the last thing that occurred on the PC before the problem developed. For example, did you or your client recently install a new software program? The following section looks at hard drive failures in more detail.

Hard Drive Failures

Hard drives fail more often than would be thought. Any component that is an electronic and a mechanical combination will fail after a period of time. In addition, hard drives can fail because of software issues. A corrupt MBR can cause hard drives to be unresponsive. It is important for you to determine more than if a hard drive is bad. You must also determine why it is bad. A bad hard drive or a corrupt MBR will generate a screen message, such as one of the following:

- Invalid partition table.
- Error loading operating system.
- Missing operating system.

If any of these error messages appear, you most likely have a hard drive problem. To check, try booting the system from a bootable disc or a bootable USB drive. If the system boots normally, this will verify a hard drive problem.

Mechanical Hard Drive Failure

Mechanical parts wear out. A sure sign of an upcoming mechanical hard drive failure is an unusual sound coming from inside the computer when it is being accessed (a read or write operation is being done). The sound may be high-pitched whining or clanking. The strange sound coming from the hard drive is mechanical in origin and cannot be repaired. Replacing the bad hard drive is the only solution.

The only guaranteed method of fully recovering from a hard drive failure is by regularly backing up data. You can always reinstall a collection of software when replacing a hard drive, but the data will be lost unless a recent backup has been made. Users should be instructed to back up data regularly, but it is even more important when a hard drive makes strange sounds. Data should be backed up immediately, and a technician should be called to prepare for the crash. The technician should have parts on hand and be prepared to replace the hard drive.

MBR Failure and Recovery

Hard drives can also fail because of corrupted files and data. The most important area of the hard drive is the master boot record (MBR). If the MBR is damaged, the hard drive will not support the booting process. However, you will still be able to boot from a bootable floppy or CD/DVD. Once you boot from the floppy or CD/DVD, try to look at the hard drive by entering the dir C: command at the command prompt, **Figure 15-6**. If you can view the files on the hard drive, then you are in a position to do a repair. You probably will be able to remedy the situation. As a precaution, back up all data immediately.

You will not be able to back up the files in every situation. But, if you can see files on the hard drive, you should be able to back up important data to some kind of data storage media. Generally on an older system, you will be forced to copy files to a disk. Though, on some newer systems, you may be able to access the drive via an existing network connection.

A computer with a bootable CD/DVD allows for a quicker and easier backup of system files. You can boot the PC using a system restore CD/DVD. The CD/DVD is placed in the drive and loads all necessary files to boot the PC. In addition, you may load a driver to support the CD/DVD. After the drivers are loaded for the CD/DVD, you can copy files that need to be backed up.

If the hard drive has MBR-based partitions, avoid using the **fdisk/mbr** command unless it is as a last resort. The **fdisk/mbr** rewrites the boot code portion of the MBR. The last two bytes in the MBR contain partition and volume information. If the last two bytes in the MBR were deleted by a virus, all partition information will be lost when you use the **fdisk/mbr**. Two situations are made worse by this command. One situation is when you have a multiple boot system using at least two partitions. The **fdisk/mbr** command can make the second partition inaccessible as well. It overwrites the partition table, the boot sector, and the file allocation table. This essentially erases any record of the other partitions. The second situation affects some older computer BIOS systems that cannot access large disk drives. A third-party tool called an *overlay program* is used to remedy the large disk access problem. The **fdisk/mbr** command can overwrite the information used by the overlay program to allow large disk support. This can further complicate or compound the program.

Many third-party software systems can repair an MBR, especially if the software is installed

Figure 15-6.
Examine the hard drive through the command prompt. If you can see the files, you should be able to repair the drive and save the data.

before the problem develops. Software recovery systems make a copy of all vital information, including creating a copy of the MBR. When an error occurs, the recovery software can use the copy to recover the damaged system. In addition, third-party software systems can be used to inspect, copy, and modify bytes in each sector of the hard drive. This is a very powerful tool, but using it can be time-consuming.

The **fdisk** command is no longer available in Windows 7 and later operating systems, but a Windows 7 computer can still use an MBR when a new drive is added. Another case of Windows 7 using an MBR is when Windows 7 was installed on a computer that formally had an MBR.

For Windows 7, you can use the **bootrec.exe** command from the Windows Recovery Environment (WinRE) to recover an MBR. You can also use the **bootrec.exe** command to recover an MBR in Windows Vista. At the command prompt, enter **bootrec.exe /fixmboot** and the MBR will be repaired. You can access the command prompt through the **System Recovery Options** menu, which is covered later in the chapter. The **bootrec.exe** file is not available in Windows 8.

A GUID partition has a protected backup of the partition located on the hard drive. It automatically rebuilds the GUID partition table on failure. Also, the Windows operating system has an option to create an image of the entire disk, including the GUID partition table. The image can be used to recover the entire computer system.

Additional Mechanical Problems

A number of other mechanical faults can cause problems in PCs. Boards, cards, and cables can go bad, but these occurrences are not all that common. You will find that, along with hard drive failure, most other mechanical problems arise from two areas: improper hardware upgrades and accumulation of dust in the system.

Problems After Hardware Upgrades

Many possible system failures can occur after a hardware upgrade. The first thing to check

when a system fails to boot is the power and cable connections. Many times while working inside the case, cables are pulled loose. So, the first things to look for are free-hanging cables. However, cable problems are not always caused by cables that were not reconnected. Sometimes when a cable is pulled loose, the user will inadvertently replace the cable incorrectly. The cable may be off one pin, or a pin may be damaged. Data cables can also be pinched when systems are reassembled.

Another major problem occurs when mixing different generation technologies together inside the same PC. When a PC has been upgraded several times, problems do arise. An older BIOS chip may not be able to recognize a certain new memory module or see the new hard drive that has been installed. Check the system resources for conflicts using Device Manager or the Microsoft System Information utility.

Dust Accumulation

The accumulation of dust inside a PC is typical. The type of environment in which the PC operates, as well as its age, determines how much dust has accumulated. Large amounts of dust can cause heating problems by blocking air filters and by collecting on processor heat-sink fins and fan components, preventing the proper dissipation of heat. The dust acts like an insulator and holds the heat to the CPU rather than allowing the cooling fins to dissipate it. The dust can clog air filters and render a fan inoperable.

Remove dust carefully using a can of compressed air or a special vacuum cleaner designed for PC cleaning. Standard vacuum cleaners generate a tremendous amount of static electricity, which is very dangerous to computer chips. Use only vacuum cleaners made specifically for electronic equipment.

Danger ! Removing dust from a CRT can be dangerous. Do *not* attempt to open and remove dust from inside a CRT without special training. There are dangerous voltage levels inside a CRT case that remain even after the CRT has been disconnected from electrical power.

Recovering from System Startup Failure

Recovering from a system startup failure requires the technician to have advanced skills. Many of the utilities described in this section should not be used by the inexperienced user because they can cause additional problems if not used correctly. To become an experienced technician, you should practice using these utilities in the lab before attempting to use them on a customer's PC. You can also download extensive information about each of the utilities from the Microsoft Support website.

Advanced Boot Options

There are a number of different modes you can boot your computer into other than the normal mode that your PC boots into by default. The other modes are used for troubleshooting the computer. You can force your computer to boot into these other modes. They are useful if your computer has any of the following symptoms:

- System stalls for an unusually long period of time.
- Printer problems (as a last resort only).
- Video display problems.
- Computer shuts down or locks up for no apparent reason.
- Intermittent error conditions.

Pressing the [F8] key during the boot process in Windows XP, Windows Vista, and Windows 7 halts the boot process and displays the **Advanced Boot Options** menu. These choices vary somewhat depending on the operating system you are using. A typical Windows operating system lists the following options:

- **Safe Mode.**
- **Safe Mode with Networking.**
- **Safe Mode with Command Prompt.**
- **Enable Boot Logging.**
- **Enable Low-Resolution Video (640 × 480).**
- **Last Known Good Configuration (advanced).**
- **Directory Services Restore Mode.**
- **Debugging Mode.**
- **Disable Automatic Restart on System Failure.**

You will likely use the **Safe Mode** menu option on a frequent basis. In this option, only the essentials are used to start the system, giving you a chance to diagnose the computer. Safe mode disables Windows device drivers and starts the display in standard VGA mode. When in safe mode, each corner of the monitor screen displays the message "Safe Mode."

Safe mode will start automatically if Windows detects a system startup failure. Safe mode allows you to establish a probable cause of the computer problem. For example, if the problem no longer exists while the computer is running in safe mode, the problem is most likely not caused by basic drivers or system files. If the computer problem still exists while in safe mode, you most likely need to perform a system refresh. If the system refresh does not clear the problem, then you most likely need to perform a system reset. The following is a description of each startup mode.

- **Safe Mode with Networking**: Starts the computer with a network connection, which means the network adapter will be enabled.
- **Safe Mode with Command Prompt Only**: Starts the computer with only the essential drivers as if in safe mode. It does not load the graphical user interface. The command interpreter is loaded, and the command prompt appears, allowing commands to be issued.
- **Enable Boot Logging**: Creates a file called ntbtlog.txt, which lists all the drivers that are installed during startup. It is useful in identifying any drivers that did not load.
- **Enable Low-Resolution Video (640 × 480)**: Loads a low-resolution driver for the video system.
- **Last Known Good Configuration**: Uses the last set of registry data before the system failed. This selection assumes that a change occurred in the configuration of the computer system, which resulted in the system failure.
- **Directory Services Restore Mode**: An advanced option used in conjunction with a Windows domain that utilizes Active Directory services.
- **Debugging Mode**: Starts the computer in advanced troubleshooting mode and

is intended only for the most advanced technicians.

- **Disable Automatic Restart on System Failure**: Prevents the computer from restarting when an error is detected and causing a continual reboot loop.

Windows XP, Windows Vista, and Windows 7 use the [F8] key to launch the **Advanced Boot Options** menu, **Figure 15-7**. This menu is slightly different in appearance in Windows XP.

The option **Repair Your Computer** at the top of the menu list is not a default option. It is only available for operating systems that have the recovery disc installed on a hard drive partition. This is usually performed by the computer manufacturer to reduce the number of service requests. The user can be guided through the recovery process very simply when this option is available. The **Repair Your Computer** option provides a list of recovery tools that can be used to repair startup problems, run diagnostics, or restore your system. These are the same options that appear when using an installation disc for recovery.

- **Startup Repair**: Automatically fix problems that are preventing Windows from starting, such as missing or damaged system files. Startup repair cannot fix problems such as hardware failures or remedy virus problems.
- **System Restore**: Restore Windows to an earlier point in time.
- **System Image Recovery**: Recover your computer using a system image you created earlier.
- **Windows Memory Diagnostic**: Check your computer for memory hardware errors.
- **Command Prompt**: Open the command prompt.

Windows 8 Startup Settings

Windows 8 replaced the **Advanced Boot Options** menu with the **Startup Settings** menu. Many of the options available in the Windows 8 **Startup Settings** menu are similar to those in the **Advanced Boot Options** menu of previous Windows versions, but there are significant changes. For example, Windows 8 requires pressing [Shift] [F8] while the computer is booting to access a boot options menu. Previous versions only required pressing [F8].

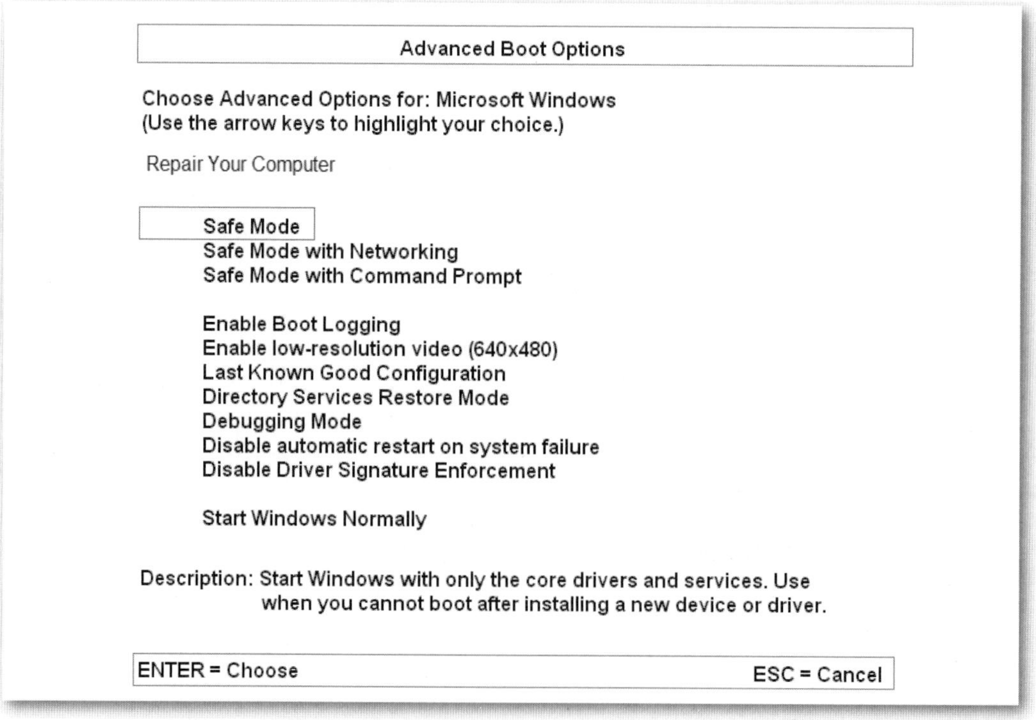

Figure 15-7.
Windows XP, Windows Vista, and Windows 7 provide the **Advanced Boot Options** menu to assist with troubleshooting and recovering from a failed system.

```
                    Advanced Boot Options

Choose Advanced Options for: Microsoft Windows
(Use the arrow keys to highlight your choice.)

   Repair Your Computer


      Safe Mode
      Safe Mode with Networking
      Safe Mode with Command Prompt

      Enable Boot Logging
      Enable low-resolution video (640x480)
      Last Known Good Configuration
      Directory Services Restore Mode
      Debugging Mode
      Disable automatic restart on system failure
      Disable Driver Signature Enforcement

      Start Windows Normally

Description: Start Windows with only the core drivers and services. Use
            when you cannot boot after installing a new device or driver.


   ENTER = Choose                              ESC = Cancel
```

Because of the newer high-performance computers and the fact that Windows 8 has been designed to boot faster than previous versions, it can be difficult if not almost impossible to boot the Windows 8 computer to a boot options menu using the [Shift] [F8] key. The short time interval between POST and loading the operating system has been greatly reduced. Therefore, Microsoft allows access to the **Startup Settings** through the **PC Settings** screen (**Charms Bar I Settings I Change PC Settings**).

Pressing [Shift] [F8] while the computer is booting will allow you to boot the computer to a boot options menu, but this option works only on very slow computers. The amount of time that Windows 8 waits for [Shift] [F8] is very short, and as a result it almost never works. It can be done, but it can be difficult to catch the timing just right. On the bright side, Windows 8 detects most errors and either automatically repairs them or presents the user with an option to start in safe mode.

Accessing Windows 8 in Safe Mode

To start Windows 8 in safe mode other than pressing [Shift] [F8], you will need to change the computer configuration through the **System Configuration** dialog box or access the **Startup Settings** menu and select **Enable Safe Mode**. Accessing the **Startup Settings** menu is discussed in the following section.

To access the Windows 8 **System Configuration** dialog box, go to the desktop and then press the [Windows logo] [R] key combination to produce the **Run** dialog box. Enter **msconfig**.

Tech Tip

The Windows logo] [R] key combination produces the **Run** dialog box in all versions of Windows.

You may also access the **System Configuration** dialog box by entering **msconfig** in the Windows 8 **Search** box. You can also enter **msconfig** at the command prompt. No matter which method you use, you will see the **System Configuration** dialog box similar to the one in **Figure 15-8**. Enable the **Safe boot** option to allow the computer to start in safe mode.

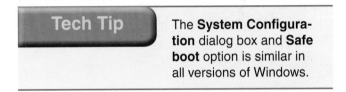

Tech Tip

The **System Configuration** dialog box and **Safe boot** option is similar in all versions of Windows.

A typical Windows 8 safe mode desktop is similar in design as that in earlier Windows versions. The Windows **Help and Support** screen will appear automatically with information about safe mode in Windows Vista and later as shown in **Figure 15-9**.

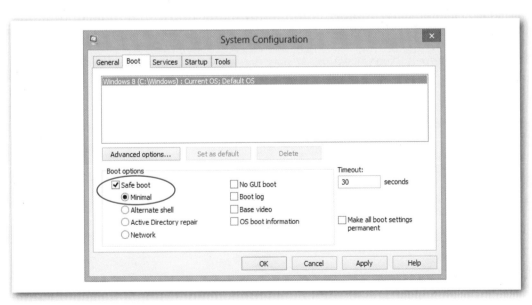

Figure 15-8. The Windows 8 **System Configuration** dialog box can be used to start the computer in safe mode by selecting the **Safe boot** option.

Figure 15-9. The Windows 8 safe mode desktop is black. "Safe Mode" is displayed in each corner. Windows Help and Support is also displayed.

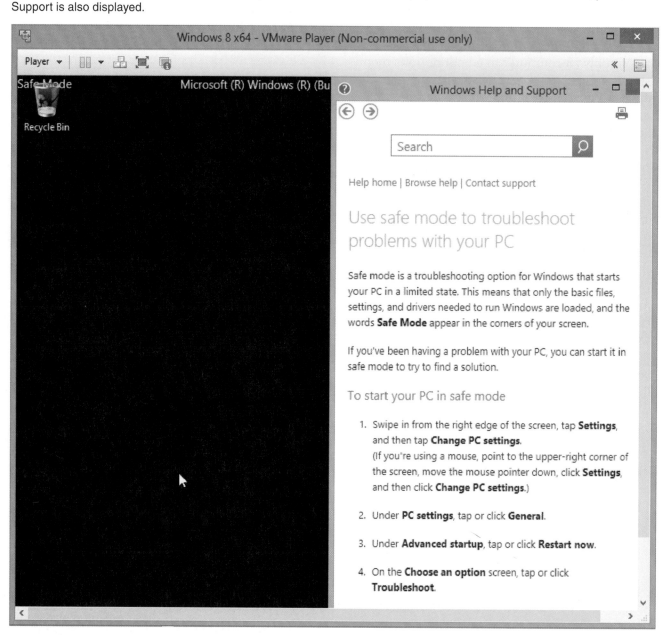

Accessing Windows 8 Startup Settings

The **Startup Settings** menu is accessed through a series of menus that provide various options to repair the PC. This section follows the path to **Startup Settings** as well as discusses each menu and option along the way.

First, access **Change PC settings** (located in **Charms Bar | Settings | Change PC settings**), **Figure 15-10**. The **PC settings** dialog box will appear. Select **General** as shown in **Figure 15-11**, and then click **Restart now**. A dialog box similar to the one in **Figure 15-12** will appear with the following options:

- **Continue**: Exits **Advanced startup** and returns to the Windows 8 operating system.
- **Troubleshoot**: Select to continue with the troubleshooting process and to configure the PC for an advanced startup method.
- **Turn off your PC**: Turns the PC off.

Tech Tip
Another way to access the **PC settings** menu is to enter "Advanced Startup" or "Safe Mode" in the Windows 8 **Search** box with **Settings** selected.

Figure 15-10. The **Change PC settings** option is located under the **Settings** charm.

Figure 15-11. The **Advanced startup** option is used to start a computer from a disc or USB drive, change Windows startup settings, or restore Windows from a previously created system image.

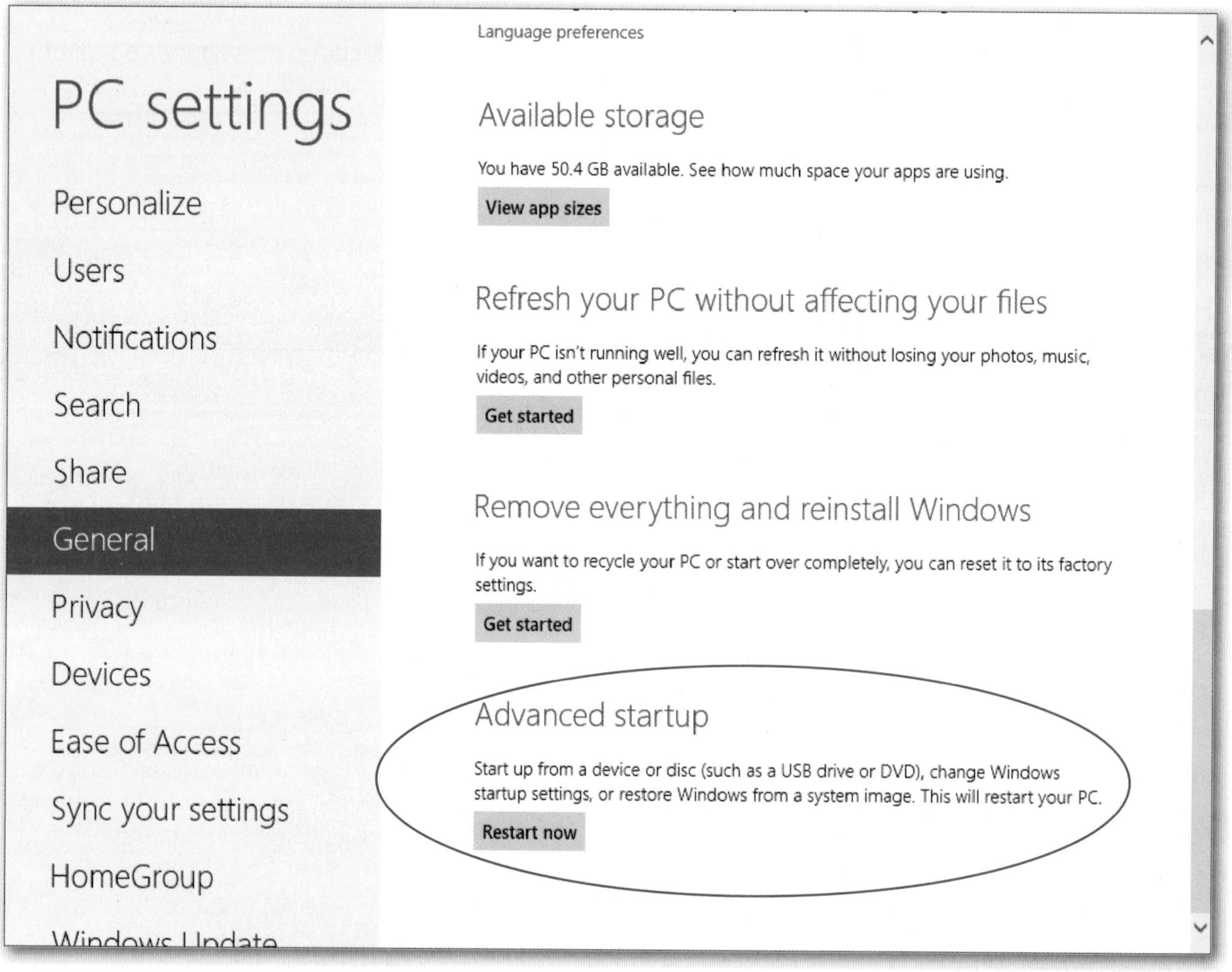

Language preferences

PC settings

Personalize

Users

Notifications

Search

Share

General

Privacy

Devices

Ease of Access

Sync your settings

HomeGroup

Windows Update

Available storage

You have 50.4 GB available. See how much space your apps are using.

View app sizes

Refresh your PC without affecting your files

If your PC isn't running well, you can refresh it without losing your photos, music, videos, and other personal files.

Get started

Remove everything and reinstall Windows

If you want to recycle your PC or start over completely, you can reset it to its factory settings.

Get started

Advanced startup

Start up from a device or disc (such as a USB drive or DVD), change Windows startup settings, or restore Windows from a system image. This will restart your PC.

Restart now

Figure 15-12. The **Choose an option** dialog box provides three options: **Continue**, **Troubleshoot**, and **Turn off your PC**.

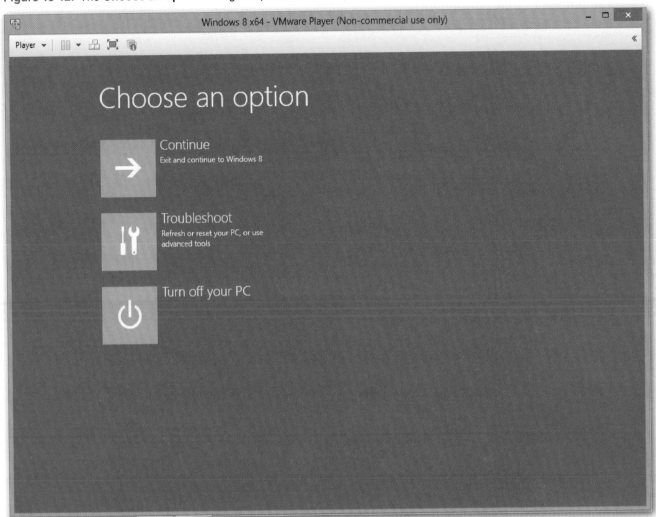

Select the **Troubleshoot** option. Three more options are presented, **Figure 15-13**. The three options are **Refresh your PC**, **Reset your PC**, and **Advanced options**.

Refresh your PC reinstalls the critical operating system files without disturbing personal files, such as documents, photos, and software programs.

The **Reset your PC** option completely formats and reinstalls the operating system, causing all files and software applications to be lost. This is an excellent reason to perform regular system backups and another reason to use cloud services for storage and software applications. Performing a system reset will still allow you access to all cloud storage and software applications. You may be required to access them with a user account name and password that was established when the service was originally configured. Also, be aware that Microsoft states that you can still download and install any of the software applications purchased previously through the Windows Store.

Figure 15-13. The **Troubleshoot** dialog box provides three additional options: **Refresh your PC**, **Reset your PC**, and **Advanced options**.

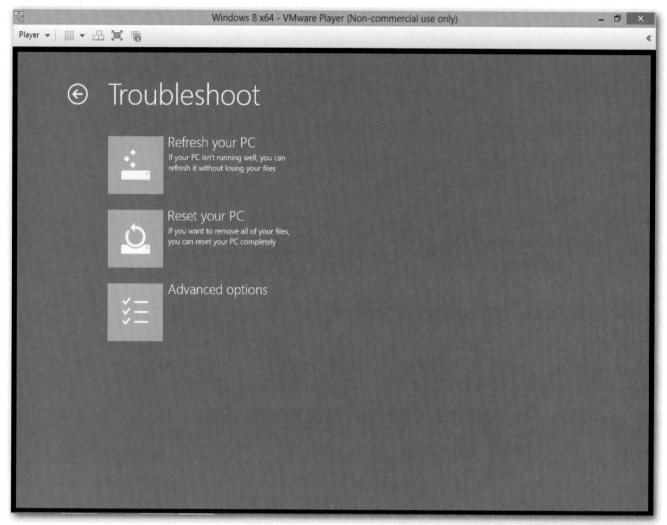

To get to the **Startup Settings**, select **Advanced options**. The menu shown in **Figure 15-14** will appear with five advanced troubleshooting options:

- **System Restore**: Uses a restore point recorded at an earlier time. System Restore does not make any changes affecting your personal folders, but any software application installed after the selected restore point was created may be affected.
- **System Image Recovery**: Requires that a previous image of the system was saved to media such as a disc or to a partition on the computer or on the network. The system

image could be one created by the OEM and stored on a partition or created earlier by the computer user.
- **Automatic Repair**: Searches for problems that may keep Windows from loading correctly, and then it automatically performs a repair. This option usually is performed to repair basic drivers.
- **Command Prompt**: The system command prompt.
- **Startup Settings**: Produces many more options similar to those in the **Advanced Boot Options** menu in earlier Windows versions.

Figure 15-14. The **Advanced options** menu provides five more recovery methods to choose from: **System Restore, System Image Recovery, Automatic Repair, Command Prompt**, and **Startup Settings**.

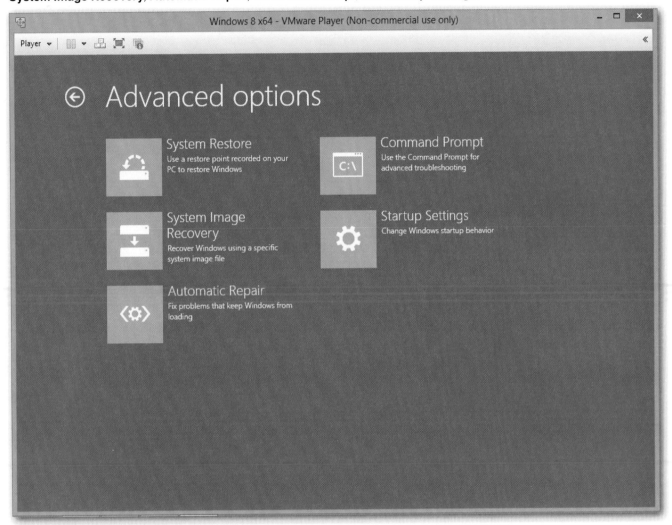

Tech Tip

Some original equipment manufacturers (OEMs), such as ACER, incorporate into the Windows 8 **Advanced options** menu an option to access the UEFI system configuration on startup without the need to press a special key when booting the computer.

The **Startup Settings** screen produces a list of startup options, **Figure 15-15**. Many of these options are the same as the safe mode options of previous versions of Windows. On this screen, however, you can only select one of two options: the **Back** arrow, which returns you to the previous screen and the **Restart** button. When you click the **Restart** button, you will be presented with ten

more options as shown in **Figure 15-16**. Again, these options are similar to those in the **Advanced Boot Options** menu of previous Windows versions. Function keys are used to select the options. Once a function key is pressed, the computer will reboot into the Windows mode selected. The following lists the function keys and a description of each menu option:

- [F1], **Enable debugging**: Starts Windows in an advanced troubleshooting mode and is intended for IT professionals with some programming experience.
- [F2], **Enable boot logging**: Creates a file called ntbtlog.txt which lists all the drivers that are installed during startup. It is useful in identifying any drivers that did not load.

Figure 15-15. Windows 8 **Startup Settings** screen.

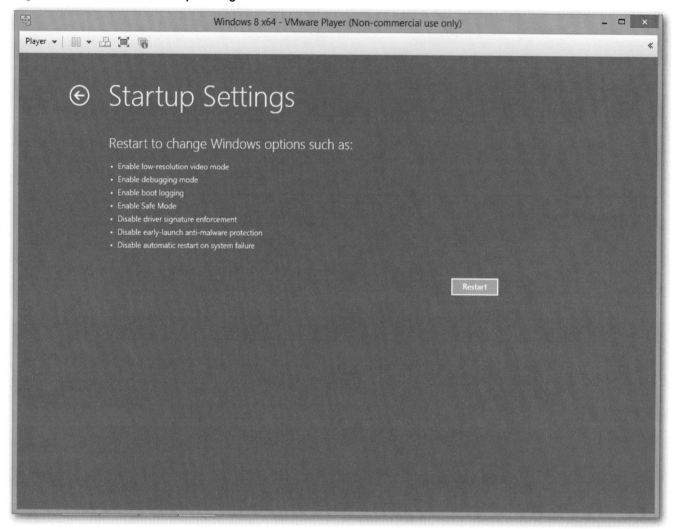

- [F3], **Enable low-resolution video**: Resets the video to a low-resolution configuration setting.
- [F4], **Enable Safe Mode**: Starts Windows with a minimal set of drivers and services.
- [F5], **Enable Safe Mode with Networking**: Starts Windows with a minimal set of drivers and services. Networking is enabled. This is helpful if you wish to access other computers on the network.
- [F6], **Enable Safe Mode with Command Prompt**: Starts Windows with a minimal set of drivers and services and provides a command prompt.

- [F7], **Disable driver signature enforcement**: Allows drivers without Microsoft approved signatures to be installed.
- [F8], **Disable early launch anti-malware protection**: Prevents the loading of an anti-malware protection driver, which can also allow malware to be installed.
- [F9], **Disable automatic restart after failure**: Prevents Windows from automatically restarting when a failure is detected. The automatic restart option can cause a computer system to continuously reboot.
- [F10], **Press F10 for more options**: Produces a menu with an option to launch the Windows Recovery Environment.

Figure 15-16. Many of the Windows 8 **Startup Settings** options are the same as those in the **Advanced Boot Options** menu of previous Windows versions.

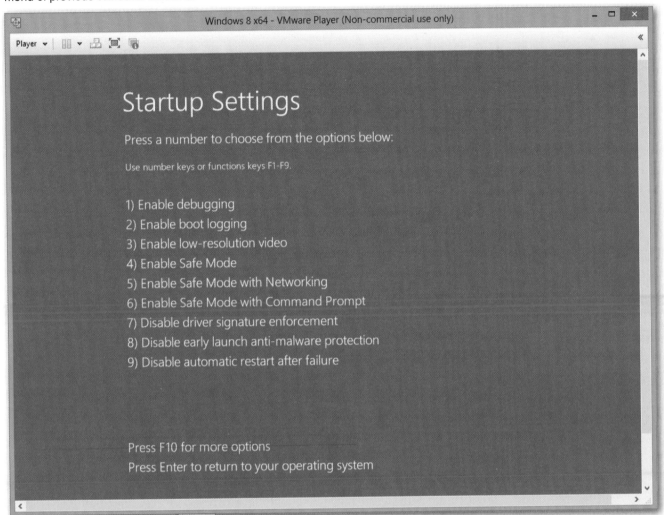

Tech Tip Microsoft states that BitLocker needs to be disabled on a tablet or PC if you wish to access the **Startup Settings** menu.

Selecting [F10] produces a screen with an option to launch the Windows Recovery Environment. See **Figure 15-17**. The **Launch recovery environment** option takes you back to the previous menu options: **Continue**, **Troubleshoot**, and **Turn off your PC**. Pressing [F10] returns you to the **Startup Settings** menu.

Tech Tip In some scenarios, the Windows Recovery Environment (WinRE) automatically tries to repair the system. WinRE can be triggered by two successive failures to start Windows, for example by two successive unexplained shutdowns within approximately two minutes of a completed boot operation or a secure boot error.

Troubleshooting requires experience and knowledge. The options you should try and in what order depend on the problem and area of the

Figure 15-17. The **Startup Settings** menu has two options: **Launch recovery environment** and **Press F10 for more options**.

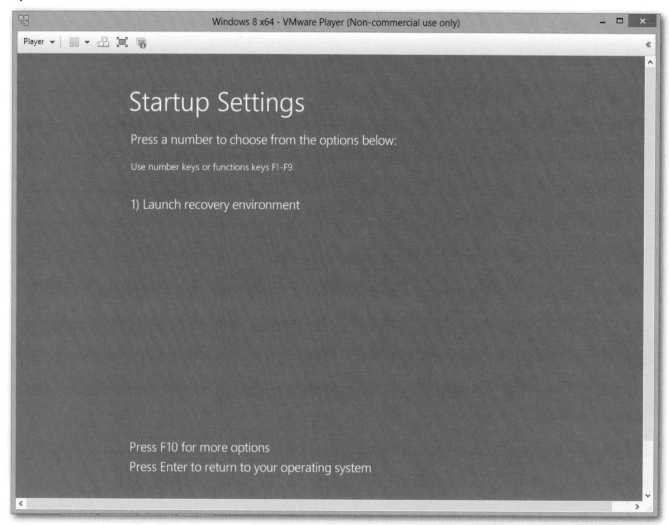

computer in which it has occurred. For example, successfully running the computer in safe mode and observing that the computer problem no longer exists indicates the problem is most likely not caused by basic drivers or system files. If the computer problem still exists while in safe mode, you most likely need to perform a system refresh. If the system refresh does not clear the problem, you most likely need to perform a system reset.

System Restore

System Restore is a feature available in all Windows operating systems and can be used to restore a system to a previous working state,

Figure 15-18. The actual look of the dialog boxes can vary according to which operating system you are using, but the main system restore principles and characteristics are the same. Restore points are backups of system settings and configurations. The restore point can be used to correct a computer problem. The computer system can be reverted to an earlier time when the computer system was working properly.

System restore points can be created manually, but most of the time they are created automatically when changes to the system settings and configuration are made, such as when new drivers, programs, or hardware are installed. Anything that significantly changes

Figure 15-18.
System Restore allows
a computer to be
returned to an earlier
system configuration.

the operating system configuration is recorded
as a system restore point. System restore points
are not affected by changes in stored data such
as documents, pictures, and videos. As a safe
practice, Microsoft recommends manually creating
a restore point when changing configurations,
such as when adding hardware or installing
software. If something is done to the system that
results in improper operation, the System Restore
feature can be used to return the system to its
previous state.

System Restore is accessed through **Start | All
Programs | Accessories | System Tools | System
Restore**. The path is the same for Windows XP,
Windows Vista, and Windows 7. In Windows 8,
simply conduct a search using the term "system
restore" or open **Control Panel | System and
Security | System | System protection**.

Figure 15-19 shows the way Windows 7
displays the system restore points. The date, time,
and purpose of the system restore point is listed.

Tech Tip

If a problem developed
after installing a new or
updated device driver,
use the **Roll Back Driver** option in Device
Manager instead of System Restore.

Recovery Console

The Recovery Console is a last resort recovery
utility available in Windows XP. Recovery Console
is also referred to as *command console* and *repair
console*. The Recovery Console is used when a
problem is so severe, you cannot access the safe
mode startup option. Recovery Console is not a
GUI utility. It is a command line interface utility.
Commands are issued at the Recovery Console
command prompt. The commands are very
similar to the old style DOS commands issued at
the DOS prompt. Many of the commands you are
probably familiar with, but there are some new
ones. The chart in **Figure 15-20** is a partial listing
of the many commands available in Recovery
Console.

Recovery Console looks very much like the
Windows command line interface, but it is not the
same. Recovery Console is not installed by default.
Unless the computer system has been previously
configured to run Recovery Console from the
hard drive, you must use the installation CD to
start the Recovery Console. To do this, insert the
installation CD into a bootable CD-ROM drive.
You may need to configure the BIOS settings to
allow the CD-ROM drive to be the first device in
the boot sequence.

Figure 15-19.
Restore points provide a method to restore a computer to the way the system was operating at a previous date.

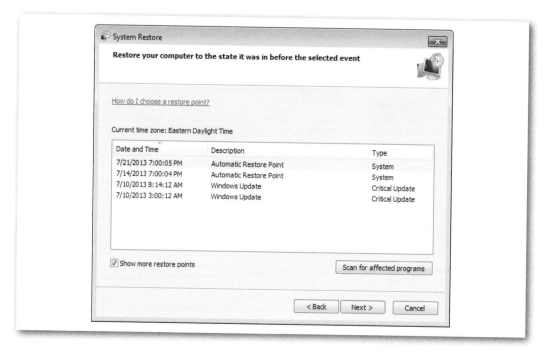

Figure 15-20. Text-based commands available in Recovery Console.

Command	Description
attrib	Clears or sets file attributes.
bootcfg	Used to recover multiboot system failures and to reconfigure the boot.ini file.
cd or **chdir**	Changes directory or folder location.
chkdsk	Checks for and may repair bad disk sectors, and checks the surface of the disk.
copy	Copies a file.
del or **delete**	Deletes a file.
dir	Displays the contents of a directory.
disable	Disables a service or driver.
diskpart	Manages the partitions on a disk.
enable	Enables a service or file.
exit	Closes the Recovery Console.
expand	Extracts a compressed file known as a cabinet (.cab) file.
fixboot	Writes a new boot sector on a partition.
fixmbr	Repairs the master boot record.
format	Formats a partition, volume, or logical drive.
help	Displays a list of Recovery Console commands.
listsvc	Lists all available services and drivers.
logon	Lists all Windows 2000 and XP systems and lets you log on to one pariticular system.
md or **mkdir**	Creates a directory or folder.
rd or **rmdir**	Removes a directory or folder.
ren or **rename**	Renames a file.

When the PC boots to the installation program, press the [R] key to repair the system and the [C] key to enter Recovery Console. Pressing [R] key will command the Recovery Console to perform an automatic recovery of the system similar to the **Last Known Good Configuration** option. Pressing [C] key displays the Recovery Console command prompt. You can issue commands from the command prompt or copy a missing file from a floppy disk to the operating system directory. The Recovery Console is a last resort utility and should only be used by technicians with advanced troubleshooting experience. Windows Vista has redesigned the Recovery Console into a much more sophisticated utility called the Windows Recovery Environment. It is discussed in the following section.

Windows Recovery Environment

The Windows Recovery Environment (WinRE) is a vast improvement over earlier startup repair utilities developed by Microsoft for their operating systems. It is launched by booting to the Windows Vista or Windows 7 installation DVD. A dialog box will prompt you to select the keyboard layout and regional preferences, such as language. The next screen presents an option to perform a system repair and looks similar to that in **Figure 15-21**.

Look closely in the lower left-hand side of the dialog box and you will see an option to **Repair your computer.** The letter *R* is underlined, which represents the fact that you can simply press the letter *R* on the keyboard to start the

Figure 15-21. The Windows Recovery Console is accessed by booting to the Windows Vista or Windows 7 installation DVD and selecting **Repair your computer**. This dialog box is similar for both Windows Vista and Windows 7.

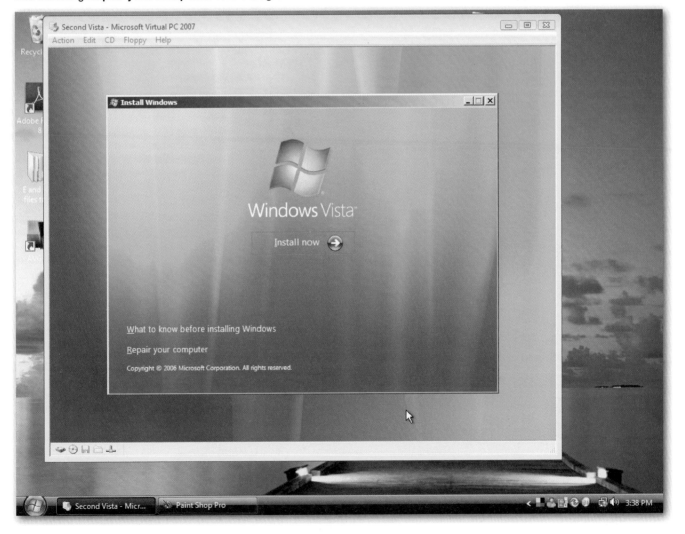

repair process. This feature is a standard option in repair scenarios because the mouse might not be working, and you may only have use of the keyboard.

The first dialog box to appear requests that you to identify the drive or partition to repair.

Look at the screen capture in **Figure 15-22** to see the first dialog box as it appears in a repair scenario. The second dialog box to appear prompts you to select the type of repair, as shown in **Figure 15-23**. The five options include:

- **Startup Repair**.
- **System Restore**.
- **Windows Complete PC Restore**.
- **Windows Memory Diagnostic Tool**.
- **Command Prompt**.

The **Startup Repair** option searches for and replaces corrupt or missing system files. **System Restore** provides access to the System Restore utility from which you can restore the system to a point in time that the system was working. The **Windows Complete PC Restore** option makes an image of the hard drive including files such as

Figure 15-22. Windows Recovery Environment (WinRE) prompts for the operating system to repair.

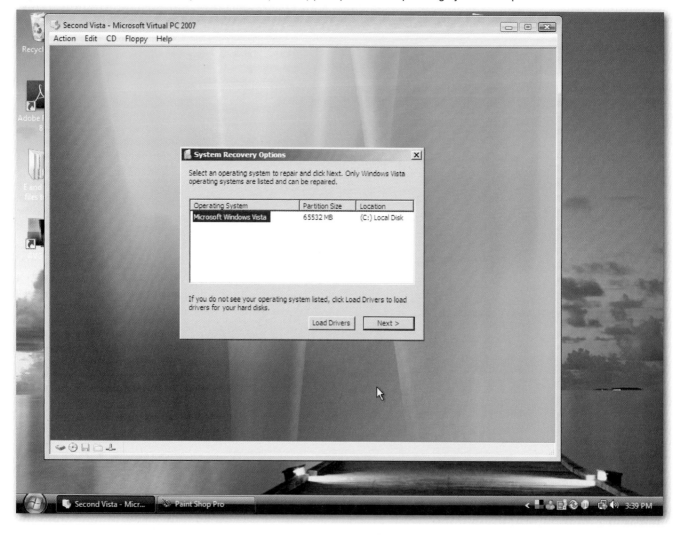

the MBR, which normally cannot be accessed or copied without the use of third-party tools. This option is only available in Windows Business, Ultimate, and Enterprise editions. It is not available in the Home versions. It is the most complete restoration option. It replaces the entire collection of operating system files as well as all data. You can even restore the complete system to a brand new computer if the original computer cannot be recovered.

The **Windows Memory Diagnostic Tool** option, of course, loads the Windows Memory Diagnostics Tool. The **Command Prompt** option provides access to the command prompt from which you can use command line utilities to repair the system.

Some computer manufacturers pre-install System Recovery Options. To access System

Recovery Options in a pre-installed system, you would press [F8] during the boot process and then select **Repair Your Computer** from the **Advanced Boot Options** menu.

WinRE will launch if a boot failure is detected. When the computer starts, the Windows boot loader stores a binary code indicating the boot process has started. The binary code is normally cleared before the Windows logon screen is displayed. If the boot fails, the binary code is not cleared. The next time the computer starts, the binary code is detected and the operating system assumes that a boot failure occurred on the previous startup attempt. This action causes the boot loader to launch WinRE instead of the operating system.

Figure 15-23. Windows Recovery Environment tools.

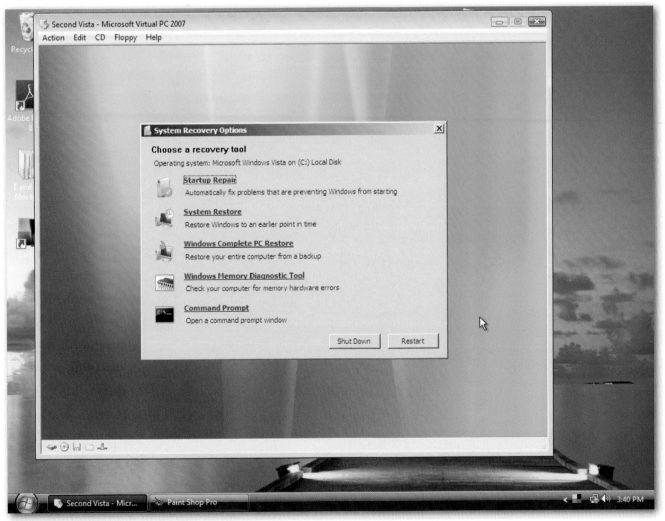

Automated System Recovery

Automated System Recovery (ASR) is a Windows XP utility. The ASR utility automatically restores critical files that were backed up by the Backup utility. The ASR wizard can be accessed through the menu options of the Backup utility and through many third-party troubleshooting utilities. When ASR is used in conjunction with the Backup utility, it is possible to restore critical system files and data files. The Backup utility is available through **Start | All Programs | Accessories | System Tools | Backup**. The Backup utility can also be accessed by running the command **NTbackup** from the **Run** dialog box.

Windows Vista and later continues to offer system backups through the Backup and Restore Center. However, it does not use the acronym ASR when referring to the newest backup and restore system. Be aware that there are differences between the backup features of the Windows editions. Windows Home Basic and Windows Home Premium do not have a feature for creating a complete PC backup image. Windows Home Basic and Home Premium do include a feature for backing up personal files.

Windows 8 Recovery Options

Windows 8 incorporates several new options for recovery after a computer system failure. Look at **Figure 15-24** to see the two options located in the **PC settings** dialog box under **General**. These options are **Refresh your PC without affecting**

Figure 15-24. You can refresh your PC without affecting your files or you can completely reinstall Windows 8 to factory condition.

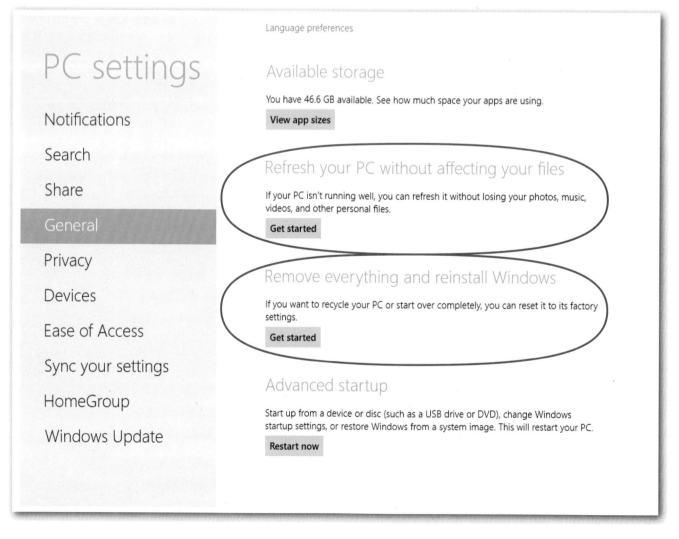

your files and **Remove everything and reinstall Windows**. The first option refreshes your PC without affecting your files. All the system files required to run the operating system are replaced without destroying personal files or installed software applications. The second choice removes all files by formatting the partition and then reinstalling the Windows 8 operating system. The only software applications that will not be harmed are those installed from the Windows Store. Any other software applications will need to be reinstalled from the original source (disc or website location) after the Windows reinstall process.

Windows 8 Recovery Partition

Recovery partitions help restore a computer system back to its original condition. Recovery partitions are not new and have been used by OEMs for many years. A recovery partition typically is a separate partition on a hard drive that contains all the files necessary to reinstall the operating system. Some are designed to simply format the C partition and reinstall the operating system, thus deleting all valuable user files such as documents and photos. Some are designed to reinstall the operating system without formatting the partition, thus saving valuable user files. However, it may fail to repair the computer system because of a hidden virus contained in one of the user files.

Microsoft first incorporated a recovery partition feature called Refresh your PC in Windows 8. To check if a recovery partition has been created for the computer, access the command prompt with administrator privileges and enter **recimg /showcurrent**. The status of the refresh image will be displayed on the screen.

To create a refresh image, first create a folder for the recovery partition by entering **mkdir C:\ RefreshImage** at the command prompt. Then, create the refresh image by entering **recimg -CreateImage C:\RefreshImage**. Notice that the default drive selected for the image is C. You could use another partition or even a flash drive for the location of the refresh image. You can even copy the refresh image folder to a flash drive or DVD.

You can also create a recovery partition or drive by entering "recovery" into the Windows 8 **Search** box. Notice that when "recovery" is entered in the **Search** box, several recovery options are listed as shown in **Figure 15-25**. Select **Create a recovery drive**. This option will create a set of recovery files, which can be stored on an external drive, a CD/DVD disc, or a USB flash drive.

Microsoft System Configuration Utility

With the Microsoft System Configuration Utility (msconfig.exe), also referred to as *Msconfig*, you can perform a diagnostic startup or select specific services and applications not to load. Using the process of elimination, you can determine which service or application is causing the problem. The System Configuration Utility is used to eliminate items that can cause a problem during the startup of the computer system and after user logon. This is one of the most common and useful troubleshooting utilities provided by Microsoft as part of the operating system.

Figure 15-26 shows the Windows XP and Windows 7 version of System Configuration Utility. This utility is very similar in Windows Vista, Windows 7, and Windows 8. The Windows XP version of the System Configuration Utility reflects the legacy operating system. Look closely at the tabs in the Windows XP version and you will see references made to system.ini, win.ini, and boot.ini, which are system files unique to the Windows XP operating system. Windows Vista and later operating systems do not depend on the .ini files.

> **Tech Tip**
> The exact look of the System Configuration Utility may change after installing service packs.

The **General**, **Services**, **Startup**, and **Tools** option tabs are similar in all versions of the System Configuration Utility. When used in troubleshooting startup problems, you can select

Figure 15-25. Windows 8 provides many options for recovering the computer system after a system failure, but it is important to create a recovery drive before a failure occurs.

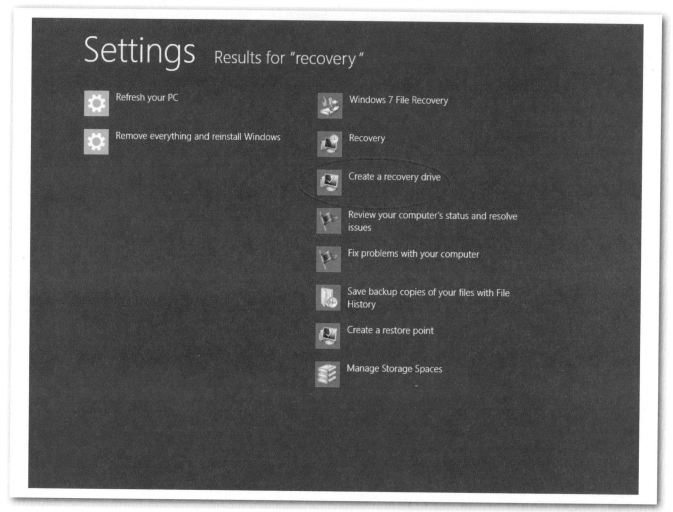

the **Startup** tab and use the **Diagnostic startup** option, which loads only the basic devices and services necessary to start the operating system. You can also select the **Selective startup** option, which provides a more selective diagnostic startup. It allows you to choose between system services and startup items. For a very detailed selection of which services and applications may be allowed to load and run on the system, additional tabs are provided, such as **Boot**, **Services**, and **Startup**.

When you suspect the source of the computer problem to be directly related to a startup program or service, the System Configuration Utility is your best choice to isolate the suspect program or service. **Figure 15-27** shows the **Startup** tab, and **Figure 15-28** shows the **Services**

tab. You can disable one or more of the suspect startup programs and services and then restart the computer. Once you discover the program or service causing the problem, you can take corrective action, such as uninstalling the program or service.

Computer problems that appear after the user logon are usually directly related to a startup program or service. Disabling all services and startup programs will quickly confirm if one of the many services or programs is causing the problem. If disabling all services and startup programs clears the problem, you can enable programs and services one by one or in a group until you isolate the offending program or service. You can also use the information displayed in Event Viewer to coordinate which service

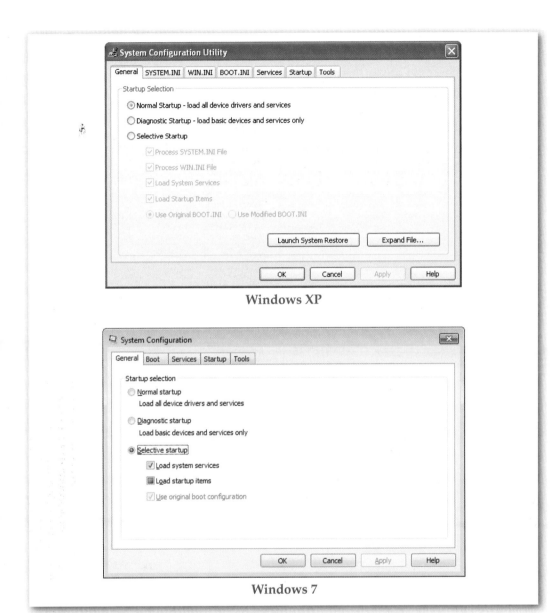

Figure 15-26.
The System
Configuration Utility is
a very handy tool for
solving PC problems
that occur after system
logon.

or program to disable. Also notice the **Hide all Microsoft services** option in Figure 15-28. Most of the time, Microsoft services will not be the cause of a computer problem. The cause of the problem is more likely a third-party software application service. You can quickly eliminate all the Microsoft services at once by selecting this option.

Other tools available for troubleshooting are located under the **Tools** tab, **Figure 15-29**. You can launch tools such as Event Viewer, Registry Editor, System Restore, Command Prompt, and Action Center. The exact listing of tools depends on which operating system you are using.

Microsoft System Information

Microsoft System Information (msinfo32.exe) displays detailed information about the hardware and software in the system. **Figure 15-30** shows the System Summary of a Windows 7 computer. More detailed information can be viewed by expanding the directory in the left pane. All Windows versions can run System Information through the **msinfo32** command. It can also be launched in other ways, such as through **Start | All Programs Accessories | System Tools | System Information** or by conducting a search using the entry *msinfo32*.

Figure 15-27.
The System Configuration Utility can be used to disable one or more suspect startup programs.

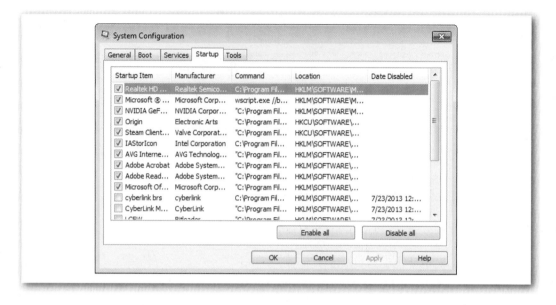

Figure 15-28.
The **Hide all Microsoft services** option is a quick way to remove from view all Microsoft services running on the computer.

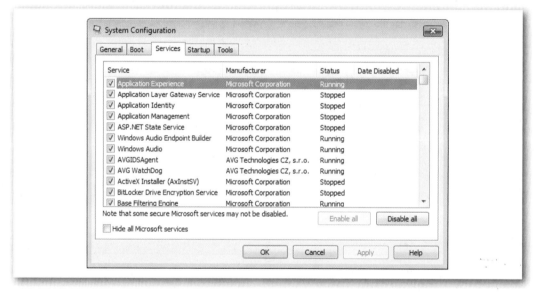

Figure 15-29.
The System Configuration Utility can be used as a centralized location for launching other troubleshooting tools.

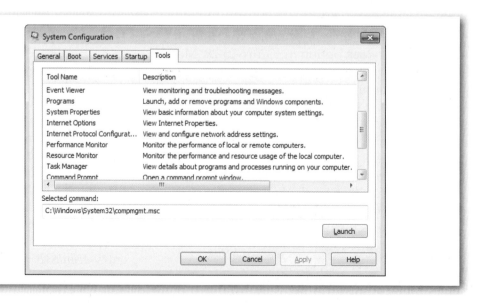

Figure 15-30. System Information contains a collection of information about the computer hardware, components, and software environment.

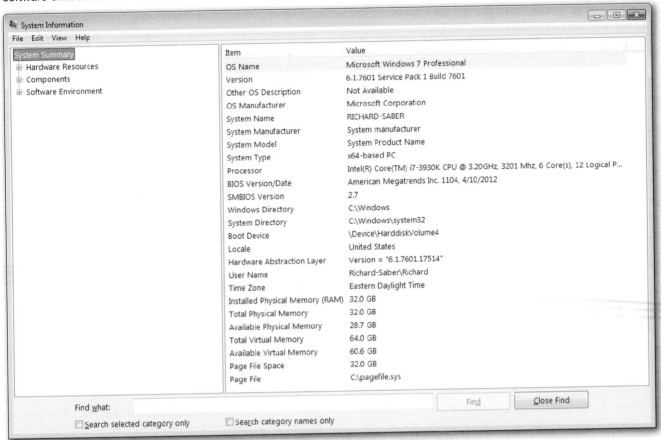

Hardware devices, system resources, software, and Internet program settings can be displayed from this location. You can readily determine conflicts in system resources and locate most startup problems. Microsoft System Information is a great way to identify hardware without the need to open a computer case.

Reinstall the Operating System

If you cannot repair the system using the utilities provided, you will need to reinstall the operating system. Reinstalling an operating system is the very last resort to recovering from a system startup failure. When reinstalling the operating system, first try to perform a system upgrade or a system refresh rather than a clean install or a system reset. This will allow you to retain the data files that reside on the hard drive. Performing a new installation rather than a system

upgrade wipes out all existing files on the hard drive, thus losing all data files.

Over the years, Microsoft has changed terminology relating to system upgrades and clean installs, and the same terminology is not used consistently by technical information or operating system options. Early Microsoft operating system use the term *clean install* to mean the operating system partition would be formatted, thus wiping out all user data files. The term *system upgrade* meant that only the operating system would be replaced and personal data files would remain intact. Starting with Windows 7, the term *upgrade* sometimes means performing a backup of all important user files and then formatting the operating system partition, thus wiping the partition clean before installing the upgrade of the operating system. Microsoft uses the terms *reset* and *refresh* when addressing the Windows 8 operating system. Be sure you know how the user files are going to be affected before performing a system install, reset, refresh, or upgrade. Always consult the Microsoft website if you are unsure of the effect on the computer system.

Many computer repair shops only allow a limited amount of time to repair a computer system before the computer is wiped clean and a new copy of the operating system is installed. This is because repair to computer systems can be labor-intensive which results in a large bill for the customer. The customer may not want to pay hundreds of dollars to repair a computer. Instead, the customer may prefer that the technician simply wipe the system clean and reinstall the operating system or a newer operating system. Many times this will be less expensive than a lengthy troubleshooting repair.

Tech Tip

Some problems can be intermittent and be a hardware problem related to a loose connection or excessive heat. For example, partially blocked airflow could cause heat to slowly build inside a computer and the memory modules to overheat. Once the memory module has overheated, the system locks up. Always be aware of "what happened last" when troubleshooting a computer.

Windows Diagnostic Utilities

Most Microsoft operating systems incorporate the same troubleshooting utilities. You need to become familiar with these utilities to save time when troubleshooting a system problem. Let's see how they might be helpful.

Dr. Watson

Dr. Watson (drwtsn32.exe) is a standard Windows XP troubleshooting utility used to diagnose software fault problems. Dr. Watson collects information about the computer system during and just before a software application fault. It tracks down the program that caused the fault and reports the part of the memory and the program in which it occurred. This information can be used when contacting product support.

Dr. Watson does not load automatically. To activate Dr. Watson, enter **drwatson** in the **Run** dialog box. The Dr. Watson diagnostic program will appear as an icon in the system tray (bottom right taskbar area). You can then right-click the icon to open it. You can also access Dr. Watson through **Start | Programs | Accessories | System Tools | System Information**, click on the **Tools** menu, and then choose **Dr. Watson**.

By accessing **View** from the menu and selecting **Advanced View**, you can view the drivers, startup programs, and many more items, **Figure 15-31**. Dr. Watson can also write

Figure 15-31.
The Advanced View in Dr. Watson can be shown by selecting the **View** menu and selecting **Advanced View**. Running Dr. Watson places an icon in the system tray. You can activate the program from there.

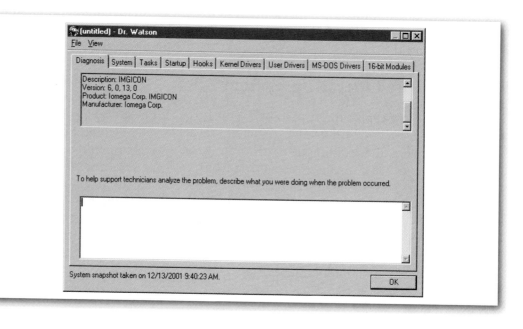

to a log to save errors and fault descriptions. These descriptions can be used when contacting technical support. Dr. Watson cannot diagnose a system hang or lockup condition.

Starting with Windows Vista, Dr. Watson has been replaced with Windows Vista Problem Reports and Solutions. This utility is discussed later in this section.

DirectX Diagnostic Tool

DirectX is a software development tool used for multimedia applications. It allows programmers to directly access many Windows built-in features. A poorly written program using DirectX can cause severe system hangs or crashes. The DirectX Diagnostic Tool (dxdiag.exe) looks at every DirectX program file on the computer, **Figure 15-32**. You can look for non-Microsoft approved program labels here. If a file is Microsoft approved, you should not have a problem. That cannot be said for other programmers' tools.

DirectX program files are abundant. They are used for game development and all types of multimedia programs. The DirectX Diagnostic Tool is incorporated into all Windows operating systems but has gotten much more sophisticated.

System File Checker

The System File Checker (sfc.exe) can be run to check for corrupt, changed, or missing files from Windows-based applications. It can be used to restore system files. In Windows XP and later, you can launch the System File Checker by entering **sfc /scannow** at the command prompt. See **Figure 15-33**. The **sfc /scannow** command scans all protected system files and replaces incorrect versions with correct versions. System File Checker is also incorporated into the **Advanced Boot Options** menu. When **Repair Your Computer** is selected, the System File Checker is run automatically.

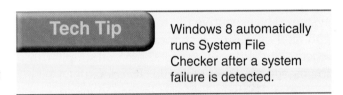

Tech Tip

Windows 8 automatically runs System File Checker after a system failure is detected.

Registry Editor

Registry Editor is a Microsoft software tool that is used to view and modify the system registry

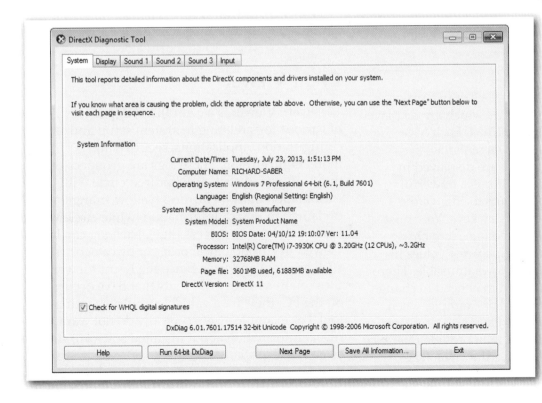

Figure 15-32. The DirectX Diagnostic Tool checks for problems with DirectX files. This check shows no problems.

Figure 15-33.
System File Checker can be used to check the integrity of system files.

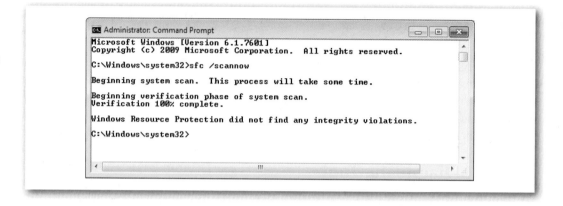

files. There are several versions of the tool available depending on which operating system you are using and if you are running a 32-bit or 64-bit operating system. The executive file for 32-bit Windows XP and later operating systems is regedit.exe and regedt32.exe. Running regedt32.exe will simply run the regedit.exe executable file. The default 64-bit version of Registry Editor is launched using regedit.exe and is included with 64-bit versions of Windows. When the 64-bit version is launched, it will display both 64-bit keys and 32-bit keys.

Tech Tip
Microsoft Register Server (regsvr32.exe) is a command-line tool used for adding or removing DLLs and ActiveX controls to or from the system registry. Using Microsoft Register Server will avoid generating system error messages.

The Registry Editor consists of five major groupings referred to as *hives,* which are displayed in the left pane. See **Figure 15-34**. Each **hive** contains folders referred to as **registry keys**. Values for each registry key are displayed in the right pane. Registry Editor is a powerful tool, which allows technicians to change the values associated with registry keys. You must use extreme caution when you use it to change registry values. Missing or incorrect values in the registry can make Windows unusable. There are times when a technician may need to change the values of registry keys. For example, when a new virus is released and causing a problem with a computer, Microsoft may provide reference material as to how to remove the virus. The

information may also contain directions for changing or deleting registry values. Changing the system configuration should be done through Control Panel or through Microsoft utilities designed for that purpose. In general, you should not make changes to the computer system using the Registry Editor.

Tech Tip
You should never attempt to repair the registry files directly. An error made in the registry files can render the computer system inoperable. You may have to completely reinstall the system onto a clean hard drive. Simply loading the software over the corrupt registry would do no good. The new installation would inherit the previous corrupt settings.

Event Viewer

Event Viewer is a centralized depository of various logs relating to system setup and configuration, applications, security, and more, **Figure 15-35**. These logs are grouped into summaries such as Error (red circle with exclamation mark), Warning (yellow triangle with exclamation mark), Information (white circle with blue *i*), and Audit success (key). Each log can be viewed in chronological order or by categories such as event and user. Since the Event Viewer log files retain a history of events that have occurred on the PC, they are a valuable troubleshooting tool. For example, users typically do not want to reveal information about installed software such as games, especially if gaming software is against company policy. A technician can quickly view a

Figure 15-34. Windows 7 Registry Editor.

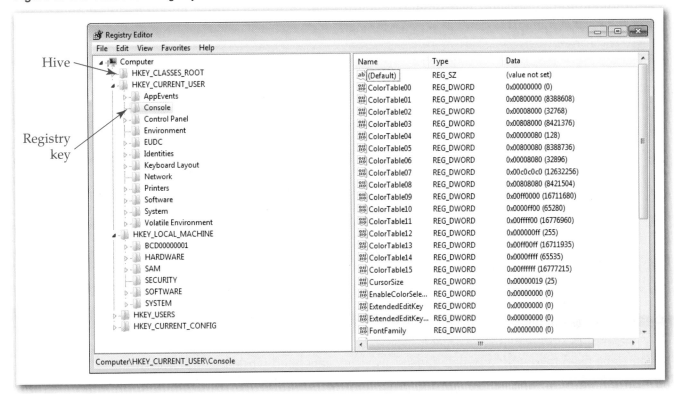

Figure 15-35.
Event Viewer collects information about events that happen relating to the computer system and it stores a description of the event in a log. The content of the log can be viewed through Event Viewer.

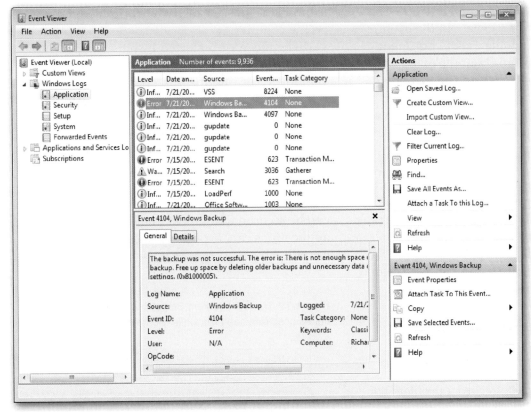

Figure 15-36.
Detailed information about an event is shown in the **Event Properties** dialog box and is accessed by double-clicking the event.

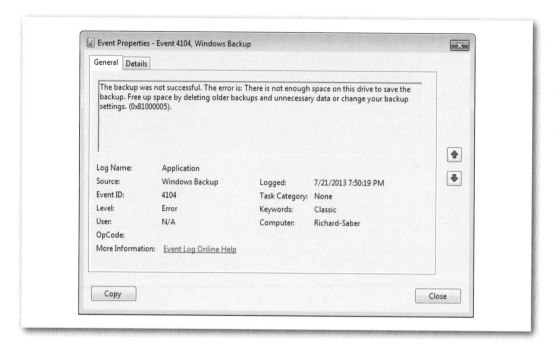

list of software changes and obtain objective data that can be used to identify possible causes of system problems.

Specific types of events can be selected from the list of Windows logs located in the left pane of Event Viewer. The individual events (located in the middle pane of Event Viewer) can be opened to reveal details about the event, **Figure 15-36.** Notice that more information about the event can be accessed through the **Event Log Online Help** option. To find more about the extensive capabilities of the Event Viewer, use Windows Help and Support.

There can be many different log files on a computer system, not just the ones discussed in this section. Software and hardware manufacturers write their own log file collection programs to assist them (and you) in determining problems that may have occurred during the installation of their hardware or software package. The log files can be used to relay information to technical support personnel by e-mail or telephone. Sometimes these files can be accessed remotely by technical support personnel.

Problem Steps Recorder

Problem Steps Recorder is available in Windows 7 and Windows 8 and is designed as a screen capture tool to record a problem as it is occurring. A series of screen captures are generated while the utility is running. After the problem recorder is stopped, comments can be added and the recording session saved as a zipped (compressed) file in the MIME HTML (MHTML) format. The file can then be sent by e-mail to a technician or help desk for viewing. The technician can see exactly what problem occurred on the computer.

The recorder is started by entering **psr** into the **Search** box located off the **Start** menu for Windows 7 or into the **Search** box in the **Charms Bar** menu in Windows 8, and then selecting **Steps Recorder** from the results.

The Problem Steps Recorder is a very simple and intuitive tool. As you can see in **Figure 15-37**, it has controls for recording, pausing, or stopping the recording. You name the file as you would for any other program. Not all types of problems can be recorded, but most involving software applications can, especially ones which generate cryptic error messages that users cannot interpret.

Figure 15-37. The Problem Steps Recorder tool creates a series of screen captures while recording computer problems.

Remote Assistance

Remote Assistance was first introduced with Windows XP and continues to be a part of all Windows operating systems. It allows a user to invite another user to access his or her computer and assist in repair. The user needing help sends an e-mail invitation to another person, such as a technical support person. Technical support can then repair the system while chatting with the user.

Remote Assistance should not be confused with Remote Desktop. Remote Desktop allows a user to connect directly to his or her computer from another location. For example, a user could connect to the office computer from a home computer. The user would have complete control over the office computer just as if he or she were sitting at its keyboard. Remote Assistance is a temporary connection, and a person must be present at both locations.

Figure 15-38 shows the Remote Assistance and Remote Desktop options listed in the **System Properties** dialog box. Remote Desktop

Figure 15-38. Two remote access programs are available in Windows XP Professional: Remote Assistance and Remote Desktop. The Windows XP Home edition only includes Remote Assistance.

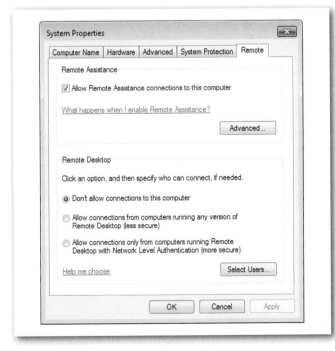

can only be initiated from a computer running Windows Professional and Ultimate editions. Any versions of Windows can return the connection to the computer that starts the Remote Desktop connection. For example, you can start a Remote Desktop connection session from any location running Windows Professional and then access the Windows Professional computer system from another computer running Windows Home Basic. There are no such restrictions for Remote Assistance.

Windows Vista Problem Reports and Solutions

The Windows Vista Problem Reports and Solutions utility identifies problems as they occur on the system and can be used to automatically find solutions. Problems are automatically reported to Microsoft via the Internet. If a solution is known, it is sent to the computer. An icon that represents the Security Center is located in the notification area of the taskbar. Double-clicking the icon expands the message about the problem and provides links to solutions and other information. A complete history of all problems and solutions can be archived for future use and diagnostics. This is a great improvement over previous versions of error reporting utilities. The path to this utility in Windows Vista is **Start | Maintenance | Problem Reports and Solutions**.

Starting with Windows 7 Problem Reports and Solutions is now part of Action Center. See **Figure 15-39** and **Figure 15-40**. You can use Action Center to review important notifications about security and maintenance settings that need your attention, get information about specific system settings, and perform recommended maintenance tasks. You can also find helpful links to troubleshooters and other tools that can help fix problems.

The Action Center is accessed by clicking the **Action Center** icon (flag), which is located in the notification area on the taskbar. When a problem occurs on your computer that you need to address, you will see a notification. When you hover over the icon, you'll see all the recent notifications.

Figure 15-39.
Windows 7 Action
Center.

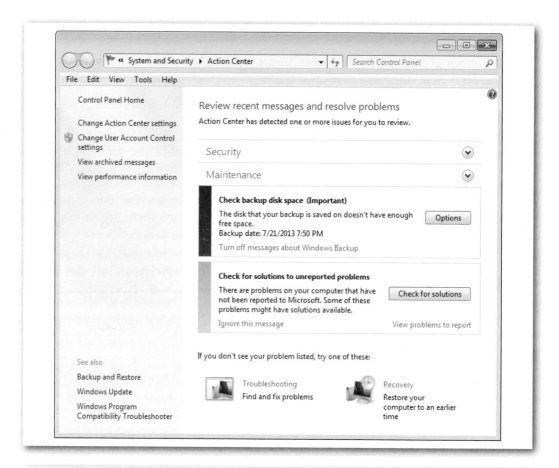

Figure 15-40.
The Action Center
allows you to check for
solutions for problems
encountered on the PC.

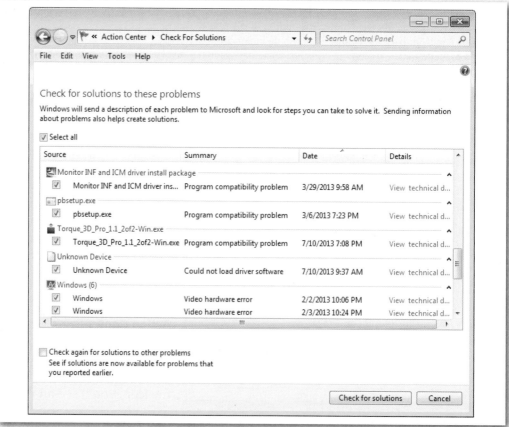

Figure 15-41. A flag with a red circle with an *x* indicates a serious problem has been resolved and you should open the Action Center to view the solution.

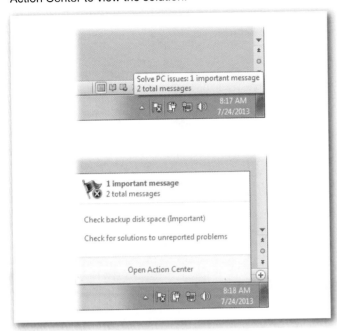

See **Figure 15-41**. A red circle with an *x* indicates a message about a serious problem, such as an application failure. A black clock means there is a scheduled task running in the background. A yellow exclamation point represents informational issues, which are less serious than those indicated by a red circle with an *x*. A blue *i* is used to indicate general information about the system and is not serious.

Windows Performance, Resource, and Reliability Monitors

Windows Vista and later include performance, resource, and reliability monitors, which provide detailed information about performance issues and system reliability. Performance Monitor can be configured to collect data about the computer system and specific hardware devices. **Figure 15-42** shows Performance Monitor running and collecting data about a computer system.

Resource Monitor allows you to observe the effects of specific programs and services on computer hardware and resources. In **Figure 15-43**,

Figure 15-42. Performance Monitor examines how programs affect the computer's performance.

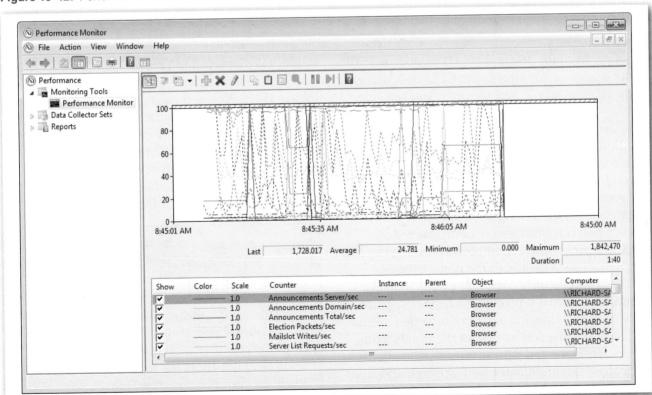

Figure 15-43. Resource Monitor allows you to view the performance of computer systems and resources such as the CPU, memory, disk, and network system.

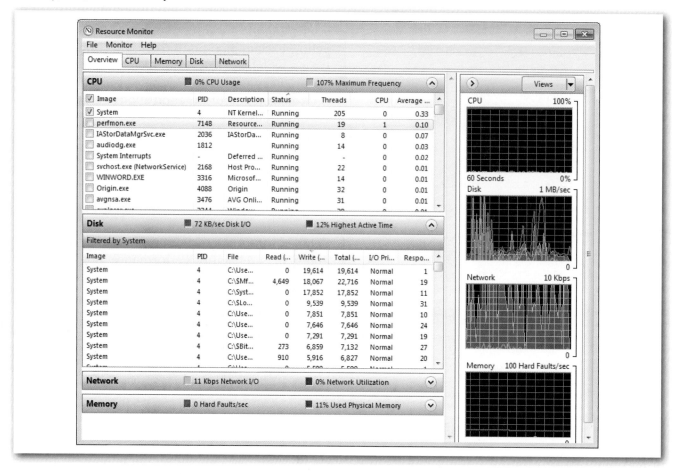

Resource Monitor displays charts of system performance as it relates to the CPU, disk drive, network connection, and memory. You can select services and programs to monitor by clicking the box next to the service or program.

Both Performance Monitor and Resource Monitor are very sophisticated tools and generally beyond the abilities of a typical PC technician. They are designed more for interpretation by an engineer or system designer, but even a technician can see that if a chart is constantly maxed out, there is a problem with the corresponding device.

Reliability Monitor, as the name implies, monitors and records computer events that affect computer stability. It produces a historical graph appearing as a linear calendar of recorded events and indicates the seriousness of the events using icons such as the red *x* for severe, a yellow triangle with an exclamation mark for warnings, and a blue *i* for information. The effect on computer stability is displayed in graphic form on a scale from one to ten, with ten being the most severe. See **Figure 15-44**. Notice the descriptive details beneath the chart. This tool is similar to Event Viewer, but as you can see, much more compact and easier to interpret. Reviewing the reliability history will help locate the origin of computer problems. Reliability Monitor is another great addition to the technician's assortment of troubleshooting tools.

A+ Note

Be sure you familiarize yourself with all the various diagnostic tools available in the Windows operating systems. Open the Microsoft Configuration Utility (**msconfig.exe**) and select the **Tools** tab to see a list of some of the most common diagnostic tools.

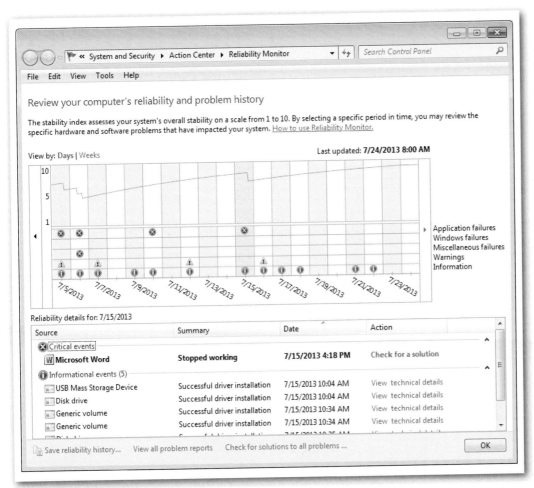

Figure 15-44.
Reliability Monitor
shows the history
of all problems that
have occurred on the
computer.

Figure 15-45. In Windows Vista, Reliability Monitor is accessed through Reliability and Performance Monitor. In Windows 7 and Windows 8, Reliability Monitor is accessed through the Action Center.

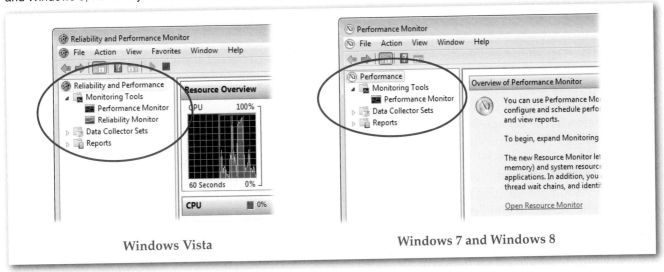

Figure 15-46. The Reliability Monitor is accessed through **Action Center | View reliability history**.

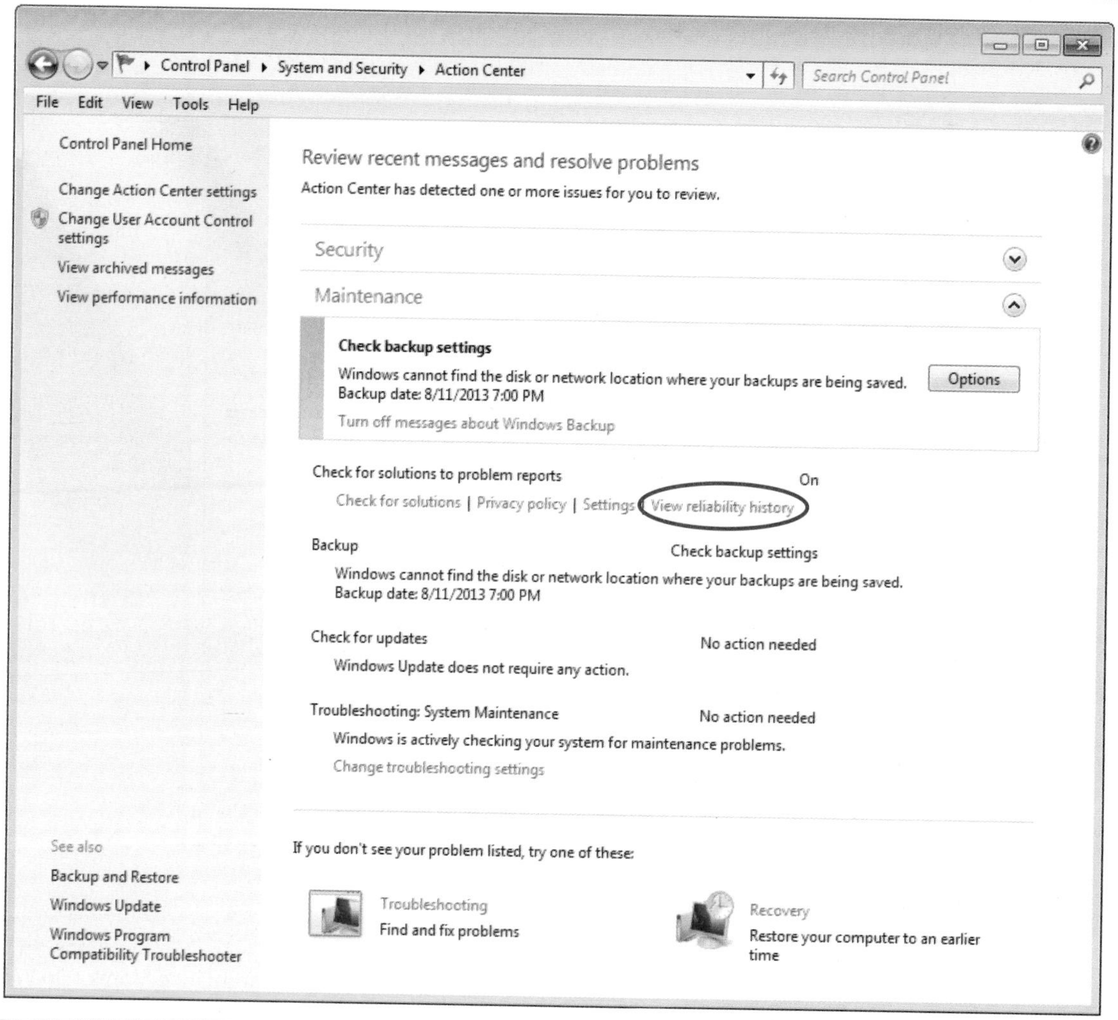

In Windows Vista, Reliability Monitor is located in the **Reliability and Performance Monitor** dialog box, **Figure 15-45**. It is listed under **Monitoring Tools** along with Performance Monitor. To access Reliability and Performance Monitor, enter **perfmon** in the **Search** box.

Reliability Monitor in Windows 7 and Windows 8 is no longer listed as a separate tool, but rather as a chart listing reliability issues. The Reliability Monitor history is accessed through **Control Panel | System and Security | Action Center**. See **Figure 15-46**.

Windows Memory Diagnostics Tool

Memory problems can be difficult to identify because they can occur intermittently. For example, if a computer slowly overheats after an extended period of time, RAM could stop working or cause software program errors. Often, a technician may completely reinstall the operating system only to have a random error reoccur. Windows Vista first introduced the Memory Diagnostics Tool, which diagnoses memory module problems. If the Memory Diagnostics Tool detects a problem with a section of RAM, it automatically restricts the use of the RAM cell locations. This allows the computer to be used until the RAM is replaced.

In all versions of Windows, the Memory Diagnostics Tool is accessed through **Control Panel | Administrative Tools**. You can also start the Windows Memory Diagnostics Tool from the command line by entering **mdsched** at the command prompt. The command prompt needs to be opened with administrative rights in order to run the Memory Diagnostics Tool from the command line.

Figure 15-47 shows the **Windows Memory Diagnostics Tool** dialog box. Notice that the test can be performed immediately or scheduled to run the next time the computer is started. The **Windows Memory Diagnostics Tool** in progress looks similar to that in **Figure 15-48**. Notice that the status of the memory diagnostics appears on the screen in text mode, not graphic mode. The progress of the tests is presented as a bar graph and as a numerical percentage. Any problems identified are also presented on the screen.

The Windows Memory Diagnostics Tool can also be run from the **Memory Diagnostics Tool** option on the Windows Vista and Windows 7 installation DVD. See **Figure 15-49** for a chart of diagnostic utilities and the operating systems in which they are available.

Boot Sequences

A good understanding of the startup process is an essential part of troubleshooting. It is, therefore, imperative that you study the boot sequence of all standard operating systems and compare the differences. One way to accomplish this is to study the programs associated with the

Figure 15-47. The Windows Memory Diagnostics Tool was introduced with Windows Vista.

Figure 15-48. A recreation of the Windows Memory Diagnostics Tool in progress.

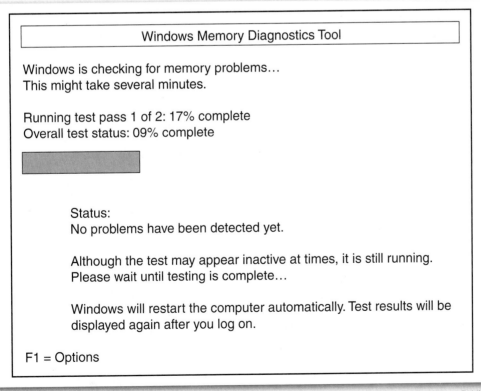

Figure 15-49.
Windows diagnostic
utilities and related
operating systems.

Diagnostic Utility	Windows XP	Windows Vista	Windows 7	Windows 8
DirectX Diagnostic Tool (dxdiag)	Yes	Yes	Yes	Yes
Dr. Watson (drwtsn32)	Yes	No	No	No
Event Viewer	Yes	Yes	Yes	Yes
Microsoft System Information (msinfo32)	Yes	Yes	Yes	Yes
Performance Monitor	Yes	Yes	Yes	Yes
Problem Step Recorder	No	No	Yes	Yes
Recovery Console	Yes	No	No	No
Refresh Your PC	No	No	No	Yes
Registry Editor 32-bit (regedt32)	Yes	Yes	Yes	Yes
Registry Editor 64-bit (regedit)	Yes	Yes	Yes	Yes
Reliability Monitor	No	Yes	Yes	Yes
Reset Your PC	No	No	No	Yes
Resource Monitor	No	Yes	Yes	Yes
Roll Back Driver	Yes	Yes	Yes	Yes
Safe Mode	Yes	Yes	Yes	Yes
System Configuration Utility (msconfig)	Yes	Yes	Yes	Yes
System File Checker	Yes	Yes	Yes	Yes
System Recovery Options menu	No	Yes	Yes	*
System Restore	Yes	Yes	Yes	Yes
Windows Recovery Environment	No	Yes	Yes	Yes

*Microsoft redesigned access to the System Recovery Options menu for Windows 8.

Goodheart-Willcox Publisher

boot disk created for each system. The boot disk contains the files necessary to boot the computer as well as some of the various enhancement files. Not all files on a boot disk are necessary for booting the system.

Tech Tip

The term *boot disc* is still used today for any disc that is intended to start the computer system. Technically, the term *boot disc* means a disc capable of running as a minimal system by itself. In Windows Vista and later, the boot disc is referred to as a *startup disc*, *recovery disc*, or a *system repair disc*.

The following table compares the boot sequences of the various Windows operating systems. Notice that they are all similar in that they begin with the POST.

Windows XP	Windows Vista, Windows 7, and Windows 8
POST	POST
Initial startup phase	Initial startup phase
Boot loader phase	Windows Boot Manager phase
Detect and configure hardware phase	Windows Boot Loader phase
Kernel loading phase	Kernel loading phase
Logon phase	Logon phase

Tech Tip
There is a lot of information at the Microsoft TechNet website about how to recover the operating system. Each operating system is slightly different, and it is imperative that you review the information at the Microsoft website before attempting any system recovery.

Power-On Self-Test (POST)

When a computer has power first applied to the motherboard by pressing the power switch, the BIOS or UEFI will start the boot process with a quick check of hardware components to verify that all hardware devices listed in the firmware configuration database (CMOS) are present and appear to be in working order. The firmware configuration settings are typically automatically detected or manually modified when the computer is first assembled and started the very first time. The BIOS/UEFI has a default configuration that will start most computers without a problem, but not always. Some BIOS/UEFI configurations require technician modification. The hard drive is automatically detected and configured by the BIOS/UEFI and typically does not need to be modified by the technician. All configuration data is then stored in the CMOS memory.

The BIOS/UEFI is independent from the operating system. All systems today use either BIOS or UEFI as the first computer software routine to run on the computer. Since the power-on self-test (POST) is independent of the operating system, it is safe to assume that there is a hardware problem if the computer fails during the POST or the POST generates an error message or a series of beeps. You can research the error message or beep codes at the BIOS or motherboard manufacturer website. You can also do an Internet search using the contents of the error message as the key terms. The following is a partial list of the system hardware checked during the POST:

- CPU system clock.
- CPU registers.
- Keyboard controller.
- Video controller.
- RAM.
- Disk controllers.
- Motherboard bus.
- Adapter card ROM.

Tech Tip
The POST can only display error messages after the video has been tested and verified. The system can fail or lock up before the video has been verified and thus give no screen error message.

When POST is complete, some adapters such as video cards or hard drives may carry out their own firmware diagnostics routine. This is independent from BIOS diagnostics.

The United Extensible Firmware Interface (UEFI) is a new approach to the BIOS system. The original BIOS program was first developed in the late 1970s. Before BIOS, each computer manufacturer had to have a matching operating system designed especially for that computer. After the BIOS was developed, you could run a variety of operating systems on the same computer. The BIOS was responsible for linking the communications between the operating system and the PC hardware. Extensible Firmware Interface (EFI) was first introduced by Intel, but now a large group of computer hardware manufacturers are involved with creating a set of standards of design for EFI. The group organization is the United EFI (UEFI), thus EFI is now referred to as UEFI. It can be installed to work directly with the BIOS or as a replacement for the BIOS. UEFI is required on computers in order to use a GUID Partition Table (GPT). Expect the transition from BIOS to UEFI to be gradual, not abrupt.

> **Tech Tip**
>
> UEFI was not supported by the Windows Vista operating system at the time of Windows Vista's original release. However, it was supported starting with the release of Windows Vista Service Pack 1.

The BIOS is limited in size and typically has less than 1 MB of ROM. It also uses 16-bit drivers. UEFI is not limited in size and can load 32-bit and 64-bit drivers before the operating system is loaded. UEFI can also load and run applications during the POST without the loading of an operating system. For example, a diagnostic utility or disaster recovery tool, or even a virus check program, can be run before the operating system is loaded. This is an extreme difference when comparing BIOS systems to UEFI based systems.

BIOS is not governed by any collective organization, and there is no one set of standards controlling the design of BIOS code. The United EFI (UEFI) organization has designed the EFI to be vendor neutral. This means no one operating system or no one BIOS manufacturer can control the firmware coding. All source code is open and shared so that all software and hardware designers have full access to the EFI coding.

Initial Startup Phase

For the initial startup phase in a BIOS-based system, the POST completes and then looks for the boot device where the master boot record (MBR) is stored. The BIOS configuration determines the order for the computer system to locate the next boot device. The boot device could be the floppy drive, hard drive, CD/DVD drive, or USB flash drive. The exact order can be changed in the BIOS Setup utility and stored in the CMOS memory. In general, the computer uses the hard drive as the boot device. Exceptions are when a boot disk is

used to start the computer or when an installation CD/DVD is used to install an operating system or recover the system.

After identifying the location of the MBR, the BIOS loads the MBR into RAM. For Windows XP, the BIOS loads the ntldr file into RAM, and for Windows Vista and later, it loads the Windows Boot Manager (bootmgr).

Keep in mind, you cannot use a non-bootable CD, DVD, or floppy to start the computer. When a non-bootable media is encountered during the boot sequence, an error message will appear on the screen. Some possible errors include the following:

- Non-system disk.
- Missing Ntloader (ntldr).
- Hard disk errors.

In a UEFI system, a GUID Partition Table (GPT) is used instead of an MBR to locate partitions on a physical disk(s). This table overcomes the partition limitations imposed by the MBR. Before GPT, Microsoft operating system partitioning was based on the limitations of the MBR. Partitions could consist of four primary partitions or three primary partitions and one extended partition subdivided into logical partitions. This is an archaic partitioning system, which evolved from the DOS file system. The maximum number of partitions that can be supported by the Microsoft MBR partition is 128. Since the GPT partitioning system does not have the same limitations of MBR-based partitions, you can have almost an unlimited number of partitions using GPT. UEFI does not require a GPT and can be used with a partition system based on MBR. Also, UEFI can use a disk system that contains both GPT and MBR partitions.

Since the boot sequence is different for Windows XP as compared to Windows Vista and later, the rest of this section is organized by Windows XP and Windows Vista and later. Each operating system boot sequence discussion continues from the initial startup phase to the last phase.

Windows XP Boot Sequence

A Windows XP computer starts with the POST, loads the BIOS program, and looks for the boot sector and the MBR. Once the BIOS has loaded the ntldr file into RAM, it turns control over to it for the boot loader phase. During this phase, ntldr loads the program startup files from the boot sector. Part of loading the startup files is detecting the preferred operating system. This information is stored in the boot.ini file.

Note that in a BIOS-based system, the operating system provides a boot manager to select which operating system to boot to after the POST has been completed. Often there are compatibility issues when multiple operating systems reside on the same computer and use a boot manager designed by one of the operating systems, such as Windows or Linux. The UEFI has designed and implemented a boot manager that allows the selection of the operating system to load during the POST. The intention is to prevent incompatibility issues caused by a boot manager designed by an operating system rather than one designed by the UEFI.

Once Windows XP is selected as the operating system, ntldr calls the ntdetect.com file. This file detects the hardware in the PC system. After the hardware detection is complete, the boot process loads the operating system kernel (ntoskrnl.exe) and the hardware abstraction layer (hal.dll). The Windows XP operating system does not allow software programs direct access to the system hardware the way that traditional Windows programs allow. The hal.dll is a machine language program that serves as the go-between for software and hardware. The hal.dll makes it possible for the computer system to be hardware and device independent. It supports many different CPU platform designs. In other words, the PC does not have to be an IBM clone. It could use a processor such as Digital's Alpha processor. The ntoskrnl.exe file is the heart of the operating system. It initializes the hardware system and drivers. It controls and oversees the entire operating system and the processing of instructions and files.

The entire boot process is not considered complete until the user logs on. After log on, the system changes to the user mode of operation. There are two modes of operation: user mode and kernel mode. **Kernel mode** is an automatic mode of operation that oversees the system resources and processor actions. This is an automatic mode requiring no user intervention. **User mode** is the actual user interface with the operating system. It is very restrictive in the sense that many areas are not accessible by the user or user programs. This environment is what makes NT-based operating systems such a stable system, compared to other earlier Microsoft Windows products. The stability is due to software and users not being allowed to manipulate hardware resources and features.

A+ Note

Students often ignore the oldest operating systems when preparing for the A+ exam. Always check the latest CompTIA A+ Certification Exam Objectives and spend time studying the oldest operating system listed.

Windows Vista and Later Boot Sequence

Starting with Windows Vista, ntldr has been replaced by the Windows Boot Manager (bootmgr) and Windows Boot Loader (winload.exe). Ntdetect is incorporated into the kernel. Windows Vista and later also uses Boot Configuration Data (BCD) in place of the boot.ini file. This section begins with the Boot Manager phase.

Boot Manager Phase

The Windows Boot Manager (bootmgr) is used to select which operating system to load when more than one operating system is present on a computer. If more than one operating system is installed on a computer, a screen similar to the one in **Figure 15-50** will appear. The Windows Boot Manager screen does not appear if only one operating system is installed on a computer. However, the Windows Boot Manager still runs even if it does not appear on the display. The default for the boot manager is 30 seconds, but the delay is reduced to approximately two seconds when only one operating system is present. It is during this two-second interval that the [F8] key can be pressed to interrupt the boot process causing the **Advance Boot Options** menu to appear. The **Advanced Boot Option**s menu is

Figure 15-50.
The Windows Boot Manager menu will appear by default if there are multiple operating systems on the computer.

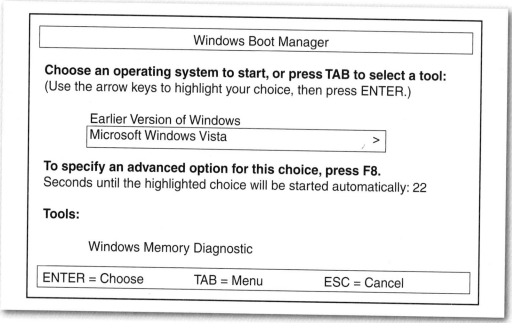

```
┌─────────────────────────────────────────────────────────────┐
│  ┌───────────────────────────────────────────────────────┐  │
│  │               Windows Boot Manager                    │  │
│  └───────────────────────────────────────────────────────┘  │
│                                                             │
│  Choose an operating system to start, or press TAB to       │
│  select a tool:                                             │
│  (Use the arrow keys to highlight your choice, then press   │
│  ENTER.)                                                     │
│                                                             │
│           Earlier Version of Windows                        │
│           Microsoft Windows Vista              >            │
│                                                             │
│  To specify an advanced option for this choice, press F8.   │
│  Seconds until the highlighted choice will be started        │
│  automatically: 22                                          │
│                                                             │
│  Tools:                                                     │
│                                                             │
│           Windows Memory Diagnostic                         │
│  ┌───────────────────────────────────────────────────────┐  │
│  │ ENTER = Choose    TAB = Menu    ESC = Cancel          │  │
│  └───────────────────────────────────────────────────────┘  │
└─────────────────────────────────────────────────────────────┘
```

Goodheart-Willcox Publisher

similar to the one in Figure 15-7. The Windows Boot Manager passes control to the Windows Boot Loader.

Tech Tip

Windows 8 changed from simply pressing [F8] to pressing [Shift] [F8], but this key combination often does not work because the system simply boots much too fast to interrupt the system. Windows 8 typically requires modifying startup in the **Advanced startup** menu accessed through **PC settings** as presented earlier in the chapter.

Boot Loader Phase

In this phase, the Windows Boot Loader first loads the kernel (ntoskrnl.exe) into RAM, but does not execute it yet. The Windows Boot Loader file is determined by the type of firmware used, BIOS or UEFI. A BIOS-based system uses winload.exe, and a UEFI-based system uses winload.efi. Next, the hardware abstract layer file (hal.dll) is loaded into RAM as well as the system registry hive. Certain key services are started to support various device drivers that are required during the boot process. Lastly, the kernel (ntoskrnl.exe) is executed and takes over operation of the computer system.

Kernel Loading Phase

After the kernel (ntoskrnl.exe) is executed, the kernel and hardware abstract layer (hal.dll) work together to communicate with software applications, drivers, and hardware. Driver files that do not require user security clearance are typically loaded. For example, the driver and services required to minimally run the printer are loaded at this time.

The kernel and hardware abstract layer work together to process information stored in the registry. This information is required to complete the boot process. The kernel also creates a new registry key which contains information about the drivers and devices loaded so far and through the rest of the boot operation. This information is used for the **Last Known Good Configuration** boot option when troubleshooting the system or attempting to recover from a system failure. The kernel then loads the Session Manager (smss.exe) and the boot process switches from text mode to graphic mode. A progress bar appears at the bottom of the screen. The Session Manager continues to run in the background until the computer is shut down.

The Session Manager starts and runs an abbreviated version of Chkdsk and determines if the system volumes and partitions are in working order. The Session Manager is also responsible for loading the page file or virtual memory. The page file supplements the amount of RAM installed on the computer.

Microsoft does not allow third-party software applications to directly access hardware and certain operating system files. But when access is needed by the third-party software applications, the Session Manager manages the activities. If the startup process fails here, you will see a blue screen error. Recall that a blue screen error is a full-screen text message describing the error on a plain, blue background. There will be a cryptic error code that can be used to conduct a search at the Microsoft website to find the most likely cause. Microsoft has a very extensive collection of troubleshooting information at their TechNet website. The last phase of the startup process is the logon phase.

Logon Phase

In this phase, the windows logon file (winlogon.exe) is executed, and the Windows **Logon** dialog box appears. A user typically enters his or her logon name and password to proceed to the operating system desktop.

After a successful logon, the lsass.exe file loads and runs. This file is the Local Security Authority (LSA). Then, the service subsystem file, services.exe loads and runs. The exact services loaded and started are determined by the computer's configuration and the user's credentials. Only the services the user is allowed to access will start. If there is only one default user and the computer is not connected to a network with a server, the user will be able to access and run all services for the computer. If a user has a limited account, the user will only be able to run services allocated by the system administrator.

Startup programs are loaded and run at this point. Any problems such as the computer locking up or the desktop taking a long time to appear are associated with the startup files and services. If a user installs many programs over a period of time, the appearance of the desktop after completing logon will take more time.

After a successful logon, the boot process is considered a success. The registry is updated and will become the registry reference for the "Last Known Good Configuration." A failure of the system after logon is usually a sign of a failed service or a software startup application. One of the best utilities for analyzing failures after logon is the Microsoft System Configuration Utility (msconfig.exe). Services and software applications that might be causing the problem can be selected and isolated from startup with this utility.

> ## A+ Note
>
> Be prepared to identify the executive file of a specific program associated with the boot operation. (For example, ntoskrnl.exe when asked for the name of the operating system kernel file.)

Data Recovery Techniques

Many times, data on a nonfunctioning hard drive is not actually lost, although it cannot be directly accessed. Think about the causes of failure for a hard drive. They include the electronics board mounted on the hard drive, the mechanical parts inside the drive, or simply a boot sector failure. If you can still see the directory of files on drive C when using a boot disk, startup disc, or recovery disc, chances are excellent for recovering the data.

One of the most common ways to recover data is with software. There are a number of third-party programs out there designed to read disks that have failed to boot to an operating system. **Figure 15-51** shows a disk being accessed by Norton Disk Editor. It can examine the disk and display the sectors in your choice of ASCII, binary, or hexadecimal code. Sections can then be copied to another disk.

Mechanical and electronic repairs should be left to the specialist. Many businesses specialize in this type of data recovery. An electronic circuit board controller mounted on the drive could fail. It can be replaced, but it takes a skilled electronics technician. The circuit conductors are very fragile and easily broken. Also, hard drive platters can be removed and installed on other drives. However, it takes special tools, training, and a clean room

Figure 15-51.
Data on a hard drive that stops working can often be accessed using special software. Here a file is being viewed in the Norton Disk Editor.

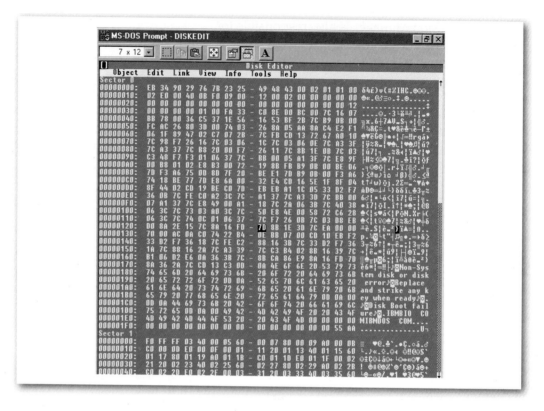

(which is not just a room that is clean). A **clean room** is a room where dust and foreign particles have been completely eliminated.

Preparation for Installing or Upgrading an Operating System

Before installing a new operating system, several appropriate practices should be followed for the ideal setup:

- Check for viruses.
- Defrag the drive.
- Read the readme.txt file if one exists.
- Check the operating system's website for latest updates, known installation problems, hardware compatibility lists, patches, and updates.

If you are upgrading an existing system, be sure to back up data. You are probably tired of hearing "back up the data," but it is the *only way* to rebuild a destroyed system. There are two commonly accepted methods of backing up files: *incremental* and *differential*.

The difference between the two is determined by the archive bit. The **archive bit** indicates if a file has been backed up. This issue is important on large data systems where backups are performed daily to ensure against data loss.

An **incremental backup** is an operation that backs up select files that have changed since the last backup of files. In this instance, the archive bit is reset. An incremental backup requires a disc or tape for each daily backup. When performing an incremental backup, only the changes in data since the last incremental or last full backup are copied. A copy of the last full data backup plus each incremental backup in sequence must be used to reconstruct an entire collection of data, **Figure 15-52.** When performing a **differential backup**, all the data changes are copied since the last full backup. Only one disc or tape is needed to perform the differential backup because it copies all changes in data since the last full backup was performed. To restore the data, you need only the last full backup and the last differential backup.

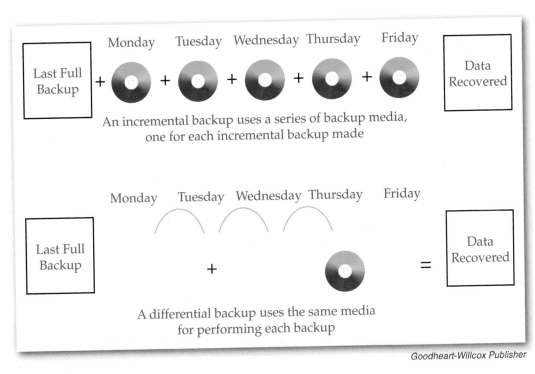

Monday   Tuesday   Wednesday   Thursday   Friday

Last Full Backup +

An incremental backup uses a series of backup media, one for each incremental backup made

Data Recovered

Monday   Tuesday   Wednesday   Thursday   Friday

Last Full Backup + = Data Recovered

A differential backup uses the same media for performing each backup

Figure 15-52. The incremental method requires the complete set of discs or tapes plus the last full backup to restore the system data. The differential method requires only the last differential backup made plus the last full backup to restore the system.

Goodheart-Willcox Publisher

With a differential backup, the archive bit is *not* reset.

The reason for selecting an incremental or differential backup is based on the amount of time and disc or tape space required for each type of backup. Since the incremental backup only copies changes from the last incremental backup, there is less data to copy. This results in a shorter time period required to perform the backup. A differential backup copies all data changes since the last full backup. This can require a significant amount of storage space and time if there is a great number of days between full backups. These differences may seem insignificant at first, but when you are talking about the large volumes of data that some corporations generate, you can be talking about significant periods of time and backup storage space.

Preventive Maintenance

Performing routine maintenance on the PC can help prevent future problems and improve system performance. Some of the most common but often overlooked routine maintenance items are listed in this section. Many of the items can be scheduled to perform automatically.

System Backups

Backups should be performed as part of routine system maintenance. You may not be able to repair a failed computer system, but you can at least restore critical data after installing a clean copy of the operating system. If the system has been configured to perform automatic backups, check if the backups are being performed. The automatic backup configuration may have been turned off or has been corrupted. You can verify that the backup job has run at the scheduled time and that the backup was successful by checking the backup log. Most backup programs keep a backup log, which is accessible through the program's main menu. You should occasionally verify that the data could be read and restored from the backup tape. If you have installed a patch, however, you should verify that you could still restore data. Microsoft has many problems with their DLL files. A DLL file used in the restore process could develop a problem after a system patch is installed.

A+ Note

You may be asked, "What is the best data protection against viruses or malware?" When you see *system backup* as an answer, it is usually the correct response. The term *best data protection* can be deceiving. Antivirus software does not protect files such as documents. It detects and removes or quarantines malware but does not restore lost data. Only a system image or backup will protect the data after a malware attack.

System Image

Windows includes a utility to create a system image. A **system image** is an exact replica of a hard drive partition including all personal and operating system files. The system image can be used to repair a computer system to an exact copy the day the system image was created. The main difference between making a system backup and creating a system image is the selection of files and folders. A system backup allows you to choose which files and folders to back up, but a system image does not allow you to choose which files and folders to copy.

Figure 15-53 shows the options available to create a system image, create a system repair disc, and automatically back up the computer. A system repair disc contains a collection of system recovery files and produces a system recovery menu. The exact look and collection of files is determined by the operating system for which it is created.

You should make a system image immediately after the initial configuration of a new computer system. You should also periodically create a new system image after major changes to a computer system such as the installation of a new software application. A system image is vital to computer system recovery after a major system failure.

Figure 15-53.
A system image and a system backup are two best options for protection from malware that damage or destroy system files and folders. A system repair disc can be created and used to start a computer that fails to complete the boot sequence.

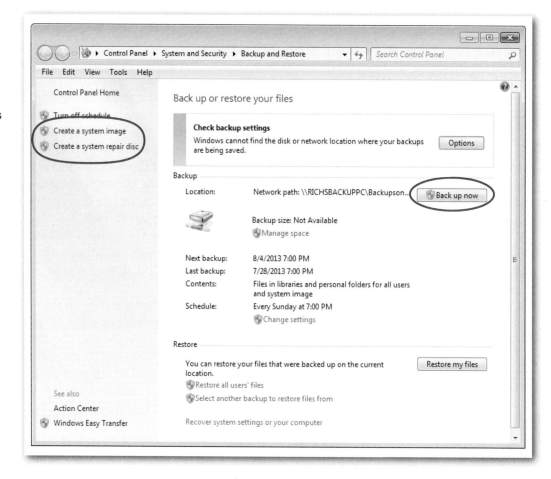

System backups can be performed on a routine basis such as once a week at a particular time. The backup should be located at another location such as a network drive.

Disk Cleanup Utility

The Disk Cleanup utility can be used to regain hard drive space such as that consumed by temporary files, files sitting in the Recycle Bin, unused Windows components, unneeded installed programs, and restore points created by System Restore. Some of the temporary files that Disk Cleanup allows you to remove are downloaded program files, temporary Internet files, and offline files. The Disk Cleanup utility performs the functions of other Windows programs, such as Recycle Bin and Add or Remove Programs. From this one utility the Recycle Bin can be emptied, saving you the extra steps of accessing **Recycle Bin** and clicking **Empty Recycle Bin**. Windows components and installed programs can be uninstalled, rather than accessing Add or Remove Programs.

The Disk Cleanup utility can be used to remove all but the most recent restore points created by System Restore. System Restore automatically backs up system information. This information can be used to restore a computer to a previous operational state. Depending on factors such as how much hard drive space is available, how much hard drive space is allocated to System Restore, and the amount of activity on the hard drive, System Restore can save one to three weeks of system information in restore points.

Disk Defragmenter Utility

As you recall from Chapter 9—Magnetic and Solid-State Storage Devices, files can become fragmented over time by opening, closing, and deleting them and by changing their contents. These activities can cause a file to be segmented and stored in various clusters across the hard drive. The Disk Defragmenter utility rearranges all files on your hard drive into a continuous series of clusters. This results in better disk performance. The Disk Defragmenter utility should be run at least once per month depending on the amount of file activity on the system, and

especially run after using the Disk Cleanup utility. Also, be aware that running Disk Defragmenter on a large disk, can take a very long time. Schedule to run the Disk Defragmenter when you do not need to use the computer for an extended period of time.

Chkdsk

Windows XP and later use Chkdsk to inspect the hard drive and correct errors in the file structure, such as bad sectors, lost clusters, cross-linked files, and directory errors. Some computer problems can be solved and performance improved by making sure that the hard drive has no errors.

Figure 15-54 shows the **chkdsk** command and its results. The **chkdsk** command with an **/F** switch (**chkdsk /F**) is used to fix errors automatically as they are located during the disk inspection. The **chkdsk** command with the **/R** switch (**chkdsk /R**) is used to locate bad sectors on the disk and recover readable information. Chkdsk can also be accessed through the hard drive **Properties** dialog box as shown in **Figure 15-55**. Notice the option for error-checking and the **Check now** button.

To access the **Properties** dialog box for a hard drive, right-click the drive that you want to check, click **Properties**, and then click the **Tools** tab. Under **Error-checking**, click **Check now**. If you select to automatically repair disk errors and the disk is in use, you will be prompted to reschedule the disk check for the next time you restart the computer.

> ## A+ Note
>
> ScanDisk is an earlier version of a disk checking program similar to Chkdsk. You may see ScanDisk as a distraction answer on the A+ Certification exam.

Install Patches

Check for the latest software patches for your operating system. Patches should be installed on a regular basis, especially as a matter of security.

Figure 15-54.
The **chkdsk** command is used to check the hard drive for disk errors.

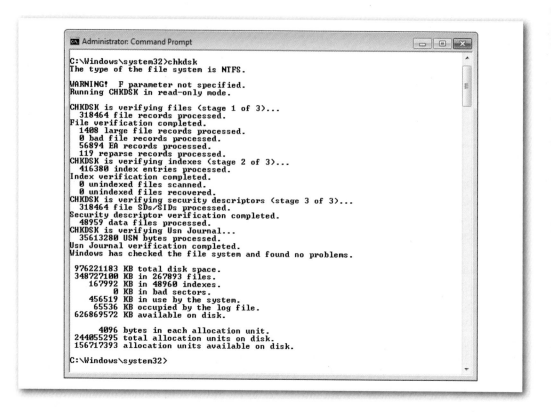

Figure 15-55. The hard drive **Properties** dialog box has an option for checking the disk for errors and correcting them if necessary.

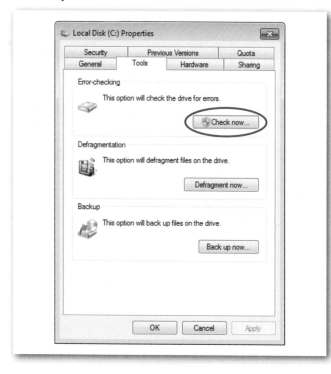

Many operating system security problems are discovered after the release of an operating system. Checking for and installing patches on a regular basis will keep the security level high on the computer system. Some patches can have adverse effects on your computer system. Be sure to back up your system files before installing a patch.

Virus Protection Updates

Virus protection software requires updates on a regular basis. Your virus protection can fail to protect your system if it does contain the latest virus definitions. Check the company website of your virus protection software for the latest virus information and updates.

Clean the Physical System

Routinely check and clean the cooling system on the computer. The cooling system includes the power supply fan(s) and the fans located on critical components such as the CPU, chipset, memory modules, and video cards. Also, remove dust accumulations from passive heat sinks located in the same areas. Dust should be removed using a static-free vacuum cleaner.

Also, be sure to remove dust and debris from the keyboard, mouse, and monitor screen. Do not use chemicals when cleaning the plastic parts of a computer system or the screen area. First, attempt to clean the plastic parts with a dry, soft, lint-free cloth. If that doesn't clean the area, try a damp cloth, and as a last resort, you may use a mild cleaning solution. Keep water away from electronic components inside the computer and computer vents. Avoid the use of any harsh chemicals for cleaning the computer and computer components.

Two Microsoft websites provide extensive information that will be very valuable when troubleshooting computers. The first site, Microsoft Support, is designed for the average computer user, and the second website, Microsoft TechNet, is designed for advanced technicians or IT professionals. Save both links in your Internet Browser because you will most likely be using them often to assist you in troubleshooting computer problems.

CompTIA A+ Troubleshooting Objectives

The CompTIA A+ Certification Exam Objectives list a sequence of actions related to troubleshooting. These objectives are a common source for at least one troubleshooting question on the A+ Certification exam. The objectives are quit ambiguous and need some explanation. Also, be aware that exact sequence and objective phrasing may change when the exam is updated. The troubleshooting steps are taken from the 220-802 CompTIA A+ Certification Exam Objectives in domain 4 and are the following:

1. Identify the problem.
2. Establish a theory of probable cause (question the obvious).
3. Test the theory to determine cause.
4. Establish a plan of action to resolve the problem and implement the solution.

5. Verify full system functionality, and if applicable, implement preventive measures.
6. Document findings, actions, and outcomes.

To better prepare you for any questions that may appear on the exam related to these objectives, each step has been expanded and a more detailed explanation given.

Identify the Problem

The first step to the troubleshooting process is to correctly identify the problem. You must gather information from the user. The following are typical questions that you should ask as a technician.

- What is the computer doing or not doing?
- When did the problem first occur?
- Did you recently install a software application?
- Can you demonstrate the problem for me?

Do not be surprised if a user is not totally truthful with you. A user will most likely not tell you they attempted do something against company policy or something they know was wrong. For example, if the last thing a user did before the problem began was attempt to install a game or a software application, the user may fear losing his or her job.

While not listed as a separate step, you should perform a backup (if possible) before you begin attempting to correct the problem or making any changes to the computer system. After backing up the system, look in Event Viewer to see what changes have occurred. This may prove to be a better source of information than the user. For example, if the user attempted to install a software package, it will be listed in one of the events logs or the reliability history as an informational event. If the customer has caused the problem, do not make the customer feel uncomfortable about it. Simply tell them, "This type of problem happens all the time," and then go on to repair the system.

Also, always get a customer's permission before performing major corrections to the computer system such as replacing a motherboard or reinstalling the operating system, which could wipe out all previous software packages that the customer installed.

Establish a Theory of Probable Cause

Once you have gathered sufficient information from the user about the problem and have backed up the system files, you can form your theory about the probable cause. Recall the information presented earlier in the chapter about the three stages of system operation: hardware failure, software failure, and user-generated problems. Determine when the problem occurs. It will help you establish a theory of probable cause.

Test the Theory to Determine Cause

Test your theory with corrective actions related to what you believe is the cause of the problem. If you do not correct the problem, you need to establish another theory of probable cause. Again, take corrective actions. Repeat the sequence of establishing a theory and performing corrective action until the problem is solved.

Establish a Plan of Action

Establishing a plan of action to resolve the problem and implementing the solution relates to more than repairing the computer. You need to ensure that the problem will not occur again. The plan of action may be as simple as replacing the power supply. In the last step, you tested the possibility that the power supply was defective. You changed out the original power supply for one that is in known working order. The change fixed the problem. Now you can notify the customer that a new power supply is needed and provide a price quote for repair. If the customer gives permission, you can go ahead and order the replacement and repair the computer.

To prevent a recurrence of the problem, you can ask if the customer has surge protection or a UPS unit. The installation of a surge protector or UPS can help prevent losing a power supply in the future due to power surges. You need to also establish the fact that a power supply can still fail due to wear and tear or old age.

Verify Full System Functionality and Implement Preventive Measures

To verify the system functionality, you should not only check the system yourself, but also have the customer try out the computer system. You need to establish that the computer is actually fixed to the customer's satisfaction.

Implementing preventive measures can be any number of procedures ranging from installing a UPS unit for surge protection to customer education. The education for the customer should be as simple as possible and not condescending in nature. You should never make customers feel stupid about something they did if they are the cause of the problem. For example, if the computer failure happened because of a recent driver update, show the customer how to "roll back" the driver. This will go a long way to win over a customer's confidence in you. It's not all about making money from customer repairs. The customer who brought in a computer in for repair will most likely not attempt a repair, even if it as simple as rolling back the driver. The customer will respect the fact that you are willing to show how to make the repair, and it will also make the customer confident that you are not out to inflate the repair bill. A good customer relationship is the most valuable asset that a computer repair business can have.

Document Findings, Actions, and Outcomes

Documentation of the findings, actions, and outcomes is standard practice in the computer system repair industry. One of the main reasons for documenting the computer system repair is so another technician can see what has been done to the system. For example, the original technician does not come in because of illness and another technician has to take over the repair or provide a status report to the customer. The documentation will prove to be vitally important. Customers are not going to be happy when they call about the computer repair and the only answer they get is, "I don't know. The person working on it is not here." Another reason for documentation is when the computer system returns at a later date for the same problem. This happens far too often.

Troubleshooting becomes easier with experience. There will be times when you can immediately identify the source of a problem and other times it will not be so easy. This is especially true with an intermittent problem. Do not hesitate to ask for help from other technicians or from sources such as the manufacturer website and the Internet in general. Always consider the source of information. There is a lot of bad information about computer repair on the Internet, especially in chat rooms or discussion groups. Many times,

the solutions you find from questionable sources will cause more problems rather than fix the system. With time, dedication, and study, you will become an excellent technician.

A+ Note

One or two questions are typically taken directly from the exam objectives related to the troubleshooting order, such as what do you do first and what do you do last.

Chapter Summary

- When troubleshooting, determine the major area at fault, determine what action occurred just prior to failure or problem, write down settings before you change them, go slowly, and think the problem through.

- The three stages of computer operation are the POST, the loading and initialization of the required operating system files, and after the logon when services and application software are loaded and running.

- Common startup problems involve the power supply, CPU, hard drive (boot device), RAM, BIOS, CMOS, system configuration, loading of drivers, and the loading of the operating system.

- Hard drives have a high failure rate because mechanical systems have a higher failure rate than electronic systems.

- Besides hard drive failure, most other computer mechanical problems arise from two areas: improper hardware upgrades and accumulation of dust in the system.

- Windows XP, Windows Vista, and Windows 7 can be started in several different modes by pressing [F8] before the Windows logo appears; similar modes are available in Windows 8 through **PC settings**.

- Some of the diagnostic utilities included in Windows are the DirectX Diagnostic Tool, Readability Monitor, Event Viewer, and Resource Monitor.

- The major boot sequence phases for Windows Vista and later are POST, initial startup, Windows Boot Manager, Windows Boot Loader, kernel loading, and logon.

- One of the most common ways to recover data from a failed hard drive is with software.

- Before installing a new operating system, always check for viruses; defrag the drive; read the readme.txt file; and check the operating system's website for latest updates, known installation problems, hardware compatibility lists, patches, and updates.

- Performing regularly scheduled maintenance can prevent future problems and improve system performance.

- The A+ Certification exam troubleshooting steps are identify the problem; establish a theory of probable cause; test the theory to determine cause; establish a plan of action to resolve the problem; verify full system functionality; and document findings, actions, and outcomes.

Review Questions

Answer the following questions on a separate sheet of paper. Please do not write in this book.

1. List five common-sense practices you should follow when troubleshooting a computer.
2. What are the three major fault areas?
3. What are the three major stages of computer operation?
4. What is *most likely* the cause of a failure during POST?
5. If there are no power lights and the fan is not running, which is *most likely* the cause?
   a. Power supply
   b. Motherboard
   c. Hard drive
   d. CMOS settings
6. If there is normal boot activity, lights and sounds, but no video, which is *most likely* the cause?
   a. Power supply
   b. Monitor
   c. Hard drive
   d. CMOS settings
7. When booting a computer after POST, an "invalid partition table" message is generated. What is *most likely* the cause?
   a. Power supply
   b. Monitor
   c. Hard drive
   d. CMOS settings
8. What is a sure sign of an upcoming mechanical hard drive failure?
9. What command can be used in Windows 7 to recover an MBR?
10. What two areas of mechanical problems can arise other than hard drive failure?
11. You can start the PC in safe mode after pressing _____, except for in Windows 8.
    a. [Ctrl] [Alt] [Del]
    b. [F8]
    c. [F3]
    d. [Ctrl] [Shift] [Del]
12. How does safe mode differ from a normal boot process?
13. How can you access the Advanced Boot Options menu in Windows XP, Windows Vista, and Windows 7?
14. What key combination sometimes allows access to a boot options menu in Windows 8?
15. What keyboard combination produces the **Run** dialog box in all versions of Windows?

16. How do you access the Windows 8 **System Configuration** dialog box from the **Run** dialog box?

17. Which utility will allow you to change the boot configuration to start a Windows 8 computer in safe mode?
    a. System Configuration
    b. System Information
    c. Device Manager
    d. System File Checker

18. What three options are listed under the Windows 8 **Troubleshoot** menu?

19. Which two repair options will reinstall critical operating system file(s) without disturbing personal files such as documents, photos, and software programs? Select two.
    a. **Reset your PC**
    b. **Refresh your PC**
    c. **System Image Recovery**
    d. **Automatic Repair**

20. Which Windows 8 **Troubleshoot** menu item will return the PC to brand new condition but will format the partition and destroy all saved files?
    a. **Reset your PC**
    b. **Refresh your PC**
    c. **Advanced options**
    d. None of the above.

21. What are the six options listed in Windows 8 **Advanced options** menu?

22. Which Windows 8 **Advanced options** menu item installs a previous image of the computer system?
    a. **System Restore**
    b. **System Image Recovery**
    c. **Automatic Repair**
    d. **Startup Settings**

23. Which **Advanced options** menu item is used to repair basic drivers that are keeping Windows from loading correctly?
    a. **System Restore**
    b. **System Image Recovery**
    c. **Automatic Repair**
    d. **Startup Settings**

24. Which **Advanced options** menu item will restore your computer to an earlier time and not change any personal documents, pictures, or videos?
    a. **System Restore**
    b. **System Image Recovery**
    c. **Automatic Repair**
    d. **Startup Settings**

25. Which **Advanced options** menu item requires that a complete copy of every storage sector of the entire computer system be made prior to a recovery attempt?
    a. **System Restore**
    b. **System Image Recovery**
    c. **Automatic Repair**
    d. **Startup Settings**

26. Which **Startup Settings** menu item would you choose to stop the computer from continuing in a startup and restart loop?

27. Which file contains the boot log entries?

28. What needs to be disabled on a PC or tablet if you wish to access the **Startup Settings** menu according to Microsoft?

29. What troubleshooting utility is available in Windows XP that can be used when you cannot access the GUI interface or safe mode?

30. How do you start the Windows Recovery Environment in Windows Vista and Windows 7?

31. What are the five Windows Recovery Environment options?

32. What is the Windows XP ASR utility?

33. What utility can be used to eliminate services and applications while troubleshooting a computer problem?

34. What program allows you to directly access the registry files?

35. What tool will create a screen capture of a problem while it is happening?

36. What happened to Windows Vista Problem Reports and Solutions in later versions of Windows?

37. Which four hardware resources are monitored by the Resource Monitor?

38. What Windows utility starting with Windows 7 provides a historical graph of computer problems?

39. What is the first boot sequence step in all Windows operating systems?

40. What does the Windows XP ntldr file do?

41. What is the name of the Windows XP kernel file?

42. What is the final phase to the boot process in Windows XP?

43. In Windows Vista and later, what two files have replaced ntldr?

44. What is the name of the Windows Boot Loader file when the computer has UEFI firmware?

45. What is the name of the Windows Vista and later kernel file?

46. What is the final phase of the Windows Vista and later boot process?

47. What are three typical causes of failure for a hard drive?

48. What are four things you should do before installing a new operating system?

49. What is the difference between an incremental backup and a differential backup?

50. List eight things to perform during regular system maintenance.

51. Which option in Backup and Restore will create an exact backup of all files and folders including system files?

52. What command prompt command is used to automatically inspect and repair disk errors? (Include the command switch.)

53. What switch used with the **chkdsk** command is used to locate bad sectors on the disk and recover readable information?

54. What is the last thing you should do when troubleshooting a system according to the CompTIA A+ Certification Exam Objectives?

55. Which stage of the CompTIA A+ troubleshooting process consists of asking the client a series of questions?

Sample A+ Exam Questions

Answer the following questions on a separate sheet of paper. Please do not write in this book.

1. How do you access safe mode in Windows 7 while the system is booting?
   a. Press the [Del] key.
   b. Press the [F8] key.
   c. Press [Ctrl] [Alt] [Del].
   d. Hold down the [Windows logo] key.

2. Which of the following typically causes a failure during the POST?
   a. Corrupt operating system boot files
   b. A printer driver
   c. A critical hardware device
   d. A software application

3. Which two files are required to load the Windows 7 operating system? Select two.
   a. ntldr
   b. bootmgr
   c. autoexec.bat
   d. ntoskrnl.exe

4. What is the name of the Windows 7 kernel?
   a. ntldr
   b. ntoskrnl.exe
   c. ntdetect.com
   d. service.exe

5. Which command is used to detect and automatically fix errors on a Windows 7 hard drive?
   a. **chksk/f**
   b. **fmbr**
   c. **scandisk**
   d. **msconfig32**

6. Which is the recommended way to back up the system registry files in Windows 7?
   a. Insert the Windows 7 installation CD into the CD drive. Reboot the computer and then select **Backup registry** from the menu.
   b. The Windows 7 registry is backed up each time the operating system is started.
   c. Open **Control Panel** and then double-click the **Registry Backup and Restore** icon.
   d. Create a restore point.

7. How do you access the System Restore feature in Windows 7?
   a. **Start | All Programs | System Restore**
   b. **Start | All Programs | Accessories | System Tools | System Restore**
   c. Right-click **Computer**, select **Properties** from the shortcut menu, and then select the **System Restore** tab.
   d. **Start | All Programs | Accessibility | System Restore**

A+

8. Which command can be run to view and manually edit the system registry in Windows 7?
   a. **msconfig**
   b. **sysconfig**
   c. **regediting**
   d. **regedt32**

9. Which command can be issued to open the Windows 7 System Configuration Utility?
   a. **sfc**
   b. **sysconfig**
   c. **msconfig**
   d. **regedit**

10. What would be used to diagnose a problem that occurs during the POST phase of the system boot operation?
    a. A POST card
    b. A multimeter
    c. System Configuration Utility
    d. A DOS disk

Suggested Laboratory Activities

Do not attempt any suggested laboratory activities without your instructor's permission. Certain activities can render the PC operating system inoperable.

1. Launch msinfo32.exe. View all the information related to the system.

2. Launch msconfig.exe. Look at all the options available that can be used to diagnose a system problem. Try stopping the loading of a specific software application and observe the results.

3. Access the **Advanced Boot Options** menu in Windows XP, Windows Vista, or Windows 7. Press the [F8] key during the boot to access the menu, and then select **Safe Mode** to observe the effect on the operating system. See what files and programs can be accessed and run during safe mode.

4. Using a specific workstation designated for experimentation by your instructor, try several of the following tests:
   - Remove the data cable from the hard disk drive and boot the system to observe any error messages.
   - Perform a complete PC backup using Windows Vista or Windows 7. The backup utility is located at **Start | All Programs | Maintenance | Backup and Restore**.
   - Run **regedt32** in Windows XP and inspect the contents of the registry. Do *not* make any changes to any of the contents.
   - Run **regedit** in Windows Vista, Windows 7, or Windows 8 and inspect the contents of the registry. Do *not* make any changes to any of the content.
   - Open the **Problem Reports and Solutions** in Windows Vista located at **Start | All Programs | Maintenance | Problem Reports and Solutions**. After opening the utility, explore the features available, but be careful not to select the **Clear solution and problem history** option.
   - Open Windows 7 or Windows 8 **Action Center** located in **Control Panel | System and Security**.
   - Open **Administrative Tools** in Windows Vista, Windows 7, or Windows 8 and look at all the various tools available for system repair.

5. Visit the Microsoft TechNet website and look at all the available features for technicians.

6. Visit the AMI, Phoenix, and BIOS Central websites and look at the information about BIOS beep codes.

7. Run the Windows Memory Diagnostics Tool (mdsched.exe) from the command prompt in Windows Vista, Windows 7, or Windows 8.

Introduction to Networking

16

After studying this chapter, you will be able to:

- Recall the benefits of a network.
- Compare the client/server and peer-to-peer administrative models.
- Recall the characteristics of a LAN, MAN, WAN, and PAN.
- Recall the characteristics of common network topologies.
- Explain how networks communicate.
- Identify common network cabling materials.
- Select the proper cable tool for a specific task.
- Recall the characteristics of basic network equipment.
- Carry out a typical network adapter card installation.
- Compare a diskless workstation and thin client.
- Recall the three most common network operating systems.
- Match the OSI model layer to its function.
- Recognize common IEEE 802 standards.

A+ Exam—Key Points

Be sure you can identify the layers of the OSI model and identify the various network topologies. You also should be familiar with network protocols and network cable media.

Key Terms

The following key terms will become important pieces of your computer vocabulary. Be sure you can define them.

active hub
adapter teaming
Automatic Medium Dependent Interface Crossover (Auto-MDIX)
backoff interval
bus topology
cable crimper
cable tester
cable tracer
Carrier Sense Multiple Access with Collision Avoidance (CSMA/CA)
Carrier Sense Multiple Access with Collision Detection (CSMA/CD)
client
client/server network
coaxial cable
cross talk
dedicated server
diskless workstation
Ethernet network
fail-over
fiber-optic cable
hub
hybrid topology
insulation displacement connector (IDC)
load balancing
local area network (LAN)
loopback plug
media access code (MAC) address
mesh topology
metropolitan area network (MAN)
Multiple Input Multiple Output (MIMO)
network

network interface card (NIC)
network media
network operating system (NOS)
node
Open Systems Interconnection (OSI) model
packet
passive hub
peer-to-peer network
personal area network (PAN)
plenum
Power over Ethernet (PoE)
protocol suite
punch down tool
query
ring topology
rollover cable
router
segment
sequence number
server
spatial multiplexing (SM)
star topology
switching hub
thin client
tone generator
topology
twisted pair cable
Wake-on-LAN (WOL)
wide area network (WAN)
Wi-Fi Protected Setup (WPS)
wireless range extender
wireless router
wireless topology

The technical support of multiple computers in the home and office requires special skills. As a technician, you must have a basic understanding of the principles and operation of networked computers. This chapter and the following three chapters will introduce you to the basic knowledge required to successfully network and support a small group of computers and related equipment. All technicians will encounter some form of a network when troubleshooting a computer system. In recent years, CompTIA has increased the percentage of questions related to networking on the A+ Certification exams.

Networks—What Are They?

A computer **network** consists of two or more computers connected together for the purpose of sharing data and resources. Networked computers can share data, hardware, programs, and provide a means of e-mail communications and video conferencing. See **Figure 16-1**.

In the illustration, there are several computers connected to a server. A server is usually the most powerful computer in the network system. It contains the network operating system (NOS) on its hard drive. The server also controls network security and communications. There are many benefits to using networks. Networks often increase the productivity, cost effectiveness, and security of an institution because they allow authorized personnel to interact and share data quickly. These benefits are worth looking at more closely.

Shared Resources

Networks provide an economical solution for sharing hardware, such as printers. Look again at Figure 16-1. A printer is connected to one of the computers. When connected as a network device, the printer can be accessed by any of the computers connected to the network. Through this arrangement, all the computers on the network share a common printer instead of each having its own single printer.

Shared Data

The main reason for installing a network system is to simultaneously share data among a large group of computer users. For example, a company that sells computer parts has sales, supply, distribution, and accounting departments. If the company did not have a network, daily operation would depend on written or verbal communication between these departments. The various departments would have to work closely and carefully to organize complex tasks such as ordering inventory for projected seasonal sales trends or reducing sales discounts to slow paying customers.

Before computer networks, this system required a large quantity of paperwork, such as customer order forms, inventory forms, and customer invoices. The completion of these forms consumed personnel time and the exchange of information could take days or even weeks depending on the size of the company. A network

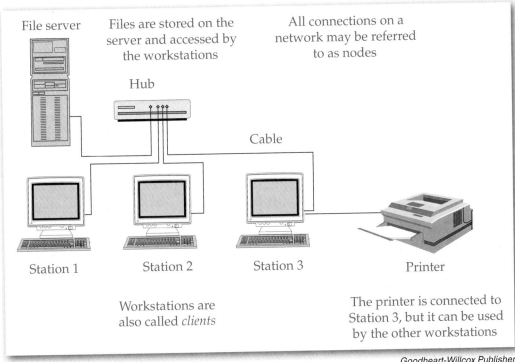

Figure 16-1.
A simple client/server network.

File server

Files are stored on the server and accessed by the workstations

All connections on a network may be referred to as nodes

Hub

Cable

Station 1

Station 2

Station 3

Printer

Workstations are also called *clients*

The printer is connected to Station 3, but it can be used by the other workstations

system alleviates the lag time required to match customer orders to warehouse inventory and distribution. The sales department has immediate access to the warehouse and distribution system of the company. Customer orders are processed instantly. In addition, there is no need to do a physical inventory of the warehouse because a running tally is kept electronically for each item in the inventory.

As soon as the sales force enters an order, the products can be pulled from the warehouse, sent to distribution, and put in the mail or loaded on a delivery truck. The invoice can be generated at the same time and automatically mailed to the customer. If the inventory levels drop below predetermined limits, the items are automatically reordered or manufactured to replenish the inventory. In addition to the above steps, a customer's information is added to the customer list, which can be used for catalog distribution.

This speed can only be achieved with a network. The inventory, billing, and distribution information is stored on the file server and shared by all who require it.

Computer System Management

A network can make the management of a large number of computers much easier. For example, distribution of new software or upgrades can be handled quicker using a network than with individual computers. Think of a large corporate network consisting of hundreds or even thousands of computers. If the word-processing application used by the company's personnel is installed in one central location and accessed by all users, it is relatively easy to upgrade or swap with a new software package. In contrast, loading software onto hundreds of computers can be very time-consuming.

Productivity

A folder of information, such as a client list containing telephone numbers, addresses, and e-mail addresses, can be easily and instantly shared by users on a network. A business's inventory can be constantly updated as orders are placed. Shipping can be made automatic.

Cost Effective

A network system is usually expensive, but when compared to the cost of individual computers needed to accomplish the same scope of work, networks can actually save money. Savings are realized through the sharing of expensive equipment and reduced labor costs.

Security

Security is a major issue in the world. A network can limit data access to only authorized personnel. Network operating system software can determine who can read, copy, or erase the contents of a file. The network can also keep a log of all files accessed, who accessed them, and from which workstation they were accessed. The hours and days of the week that a user is authorized to use the network can be controlled. The network administrator can control the appearance of a workstation display and the programs and information the user can access.

Network Administrative Models

There are two main network administrative models: client/server and peer-to-peer. We will look at both models and compare them.

Client/Server

The **client/server network** is a model in which the network is made up of computers that are either clients or servers. A **server** is a powerful computer used to manage network resources and provide services such as security and file sharing. A **client** is an individual PC or workstation that accesses a server's resources and shared files. The client/server model provides a method for centralized administration of the network.

A network administrator controls the operation of the file server, which in turn controls workstation access to the files located on the server. The network operating system software located on the file server also controls how each workstation interacts with other workstations, printers, and any devices connected to the network.

A device connected to the network is often referred to as a **node**. Nodes are connected together by a device called a *hub*. A **hub** provides a quick and easy method of connecting network equipment together by cables. The cables simply plug into the hub. A typical client/server network is represented in Figure 16-1.

Servers

The server is similar to the standard PC in design. In fact, early versions of servers were simply PCs designated as servers. Today, many small networks still use a typical PC for the network server. For large network systems, the server is an enhanced, more powerful PC. It may contain two, four, or more CPUs and ten times the amount of RAM normally found on a typical PC. The additional RAM and CPUs allow for faster information processing when connected to many workstations. The server is usually equipped with several hard drives. The server may also have a duplicate set of hard drives used for backing up the data saved on the first set of hard drives. Backup systems for servers will be covered in greater depth later in the textbook.

A network system may consist of one or more servers, each having a special function. A server with special functions is referred to as a **dedicated server**. Some types of dedicated servers are file servers, print servers, database servers, webpage servers, and administrative servers. A file server is used to store data files that can be accessed by individual workstations. A printer server coordinates printing activities between PCs and network printers. An administrative server may be used to administer network security and activities. A database server contains data files and software programs that query the data. **Query** is a term that describes locating and extracting data from a database. Microsoft SQL Server, a common server software system, is a typical database query software package.

Clients

Clients are computers connected to the client/server network and that access network resources controlled by the server. The term *client* is also used to define the software program that runs on a computer and accesses the resources on the network. For example, an e-mail client sends and receives e-mail stored on the network mail server. Clients are also cross-platform. For example, you can connect a client running a Microsoft Windows operating system, such as Windows 7, to a server running UNIX or Linux.

Peer-to-Peer

Another type of network administrative model is the **peer-to-peer network**. As the name implies, all the PCs connected together on this type of network are considered equal, or peers. A typical peer-to-peer network is represented in **Figure 16-2**. Devices on a peer-to-peer network are also connected together by a hub. On a peer-to-peer network, the workstations are typically standard PCs.

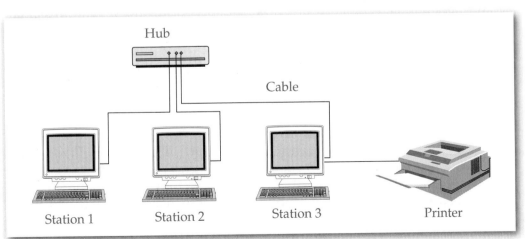

Figure 16-2.
A simple peer-to-peer network.

Hub

Cable

Station 1   Station 2   Station 3   Printer

Since a peer-to-peer network has no centralized administration, each workstation has equal administrative powers over the network. A workstation must grant permission to the other workstations before they can access its files or use its hardware. This model is usually used on very small networks of less than 25 workstations. It is very difficult to manage this type of network. For example, if all the workstations had to access a database of company customers, each user would have to be aware of the file location as well as any other needed files or software. A peer-to-peer network is inexpensive to install and simple to administer as long as it remains small. Unlike the client/server model, a peer-to-peer network requires no costly network-specific software. You can build a simple peer-to-peer network using only Windows 95 or later and minimal hardware.

Tech Tip
Approximately 45% of all networks used in the world are composed of fewer than 25 computers. This number does not include home networks.

Network Classifications

Networks are classified into four major categories. The categories are used to describe the size and complexity of the system. The four major categories of networks are the local area network (LAN), metropolitan area network (MAN), wide area network (WAN), and personal area network (PAN). These classifications are based on the physical size, management, and use of a telecommunication system, such as the telephone network.

A **local area network (LAN)** is a small network of computers contained in a relatively small area, such as an office building. It operates under a single management. An example of a LAN is a computer network in a small business office.

A **metropolitan area network (MAN)** is a group of two or more interconnected LANs operating under a single management. An example of a MAN is a network system on a university campus. It consists of a group of LANs but is limited to the campus area.

The **wide area network (WAN)** is typically a large number of computers spread over a large geographic area and under the control of a centrally-located administrator. The communication over the large area is made possible by the world's telecommunication network. The Internet is a good example of a WAN. It consists of millions of PCs spread across the entire world. A WAN is usually composed of a group of LANs interconnected through a telecommunication network. See **Figure 16-3**.

Tech Tip
Another classification of wide area network is wireless WAN (WWAN), which is based on cellular phone technology. Cellular phone access media can be used as part of a network system.

A **personal area network (PAN)** is a short-range network, wired or wireless, that connects devices such as a PC, cell phone, tablet, camera, and printer. Common media used for a PAN is typically wireless and is based on Bluetooth, 802.11, or IrDA standards. Another name for PAN is piconet.

Tech Tip
Wireless PAN is described in the IEEE 802.15 standard.

Network Topologies

The physical arrangement of hardware and cabling in a network system is referred to as the **topology**. The most distinctive identifier of topology is the computer cable arrangement. The three major topologies are the *bus*, *ring*, and *star*. See **Figure 16-4**.

Bus Topology

In a **bus topology**, a single conductor connects to all the computers on the network, Figure 16-4A. A bus topology uses less cable than the other cabled topologies and requires a 50-ohm terminating resistor at each end of the cable. The resistor

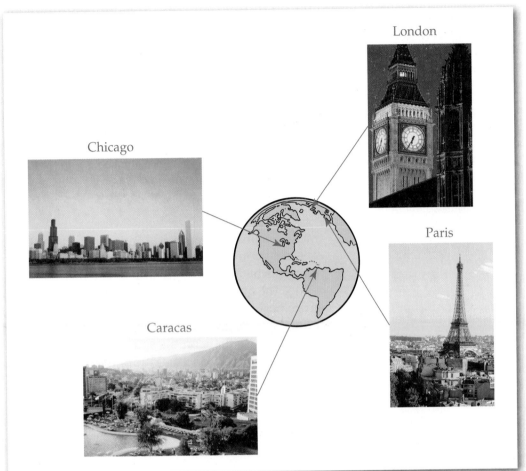

Goodheart-Willcox Publisher

Figure 16-3.
A WAN connects smaller networks around the globe.

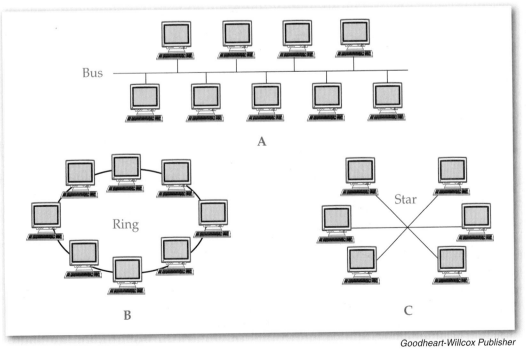

Goodheart-Willcox Publisher

Figure 16-4.
A—Bus topology. All workstations are connected to a single conductor called a backbone. B—Ring topology. All workstations are connected in series, forming a closed loop. C—Star topology. All workstations are connected to a center point such as a hub or switch.

absorbs the transmitted signals when they reach the end of the bus. Without the terminating resistors, some of the transmitted signals would be reflected back through the cables, distorting the data.

Ring Topology

The **ring topology** consists of a single cable that runs continuously from computer to computer, Figure 16-4B. The cable begins and ends at the first computer in the system. The ring must remain unbroken. Depending on the type of equipment and cable used, a ring topology can resemble a star topology, which is discussed in the following section.

Ring topology is not used for local area networks anymore, but it is still used for large metropolitan area network systems that span many miles and connect separate network systems. A double ring is used to ensure availability when one ring fails.

Star Topology

The **star topology** is a network in which cables run from each computer to a single point, forming a star, Figure 16-4C. The center of the star is usually a hub or switch. Cables from the network's computers plug into the hub or switch, which provides a common electrical connection to all the computers in the network.

Hubs are classified as either active or passive. A **passive hub** simply acts as a connection point in the star topology. Transmitted digital signals from one computer are passed to all computers connected to the passive hub and through the hub to other network sections. An **active hub** has a

source of power connected to it. When a signal is received by an active hub, it is regenerated. The active hub can be used to extend the range of a signal transmission. The passive hub does not extend the range of the transmission signal.

A **switching hub** reduces excessive data transmissions on a network. A network with an excessive number of collisions can be broken into segments by adding switching hubs. This can reduce the amount of frames transmitted over the entire network. This will only reduce the traffic if there are a significant number of transmissions between computers on the same network segment. Examine **Figure 16-5**. Imagine Station 3 is attempting to communicate with Station 1. The switching hub will not allow the data frame to be transmitted through the hub to other parts of the network. The hub directs the frame directly to Station 1.

Hybrid Topology

A **hybrid topology** is simply a mixture of star, bus, and ring topologies. Look at **Figure 16-6**. Notice the different sections of the network in the example. Hybrid is very common and often uses wireless and cellular technology.

Mesh Topology

Mesh topology is a network system in which each node connects directly to every other node on the network. This is the most reliable network topology and the most expensive because of the additional cost of cabling and equipment. A mesh is only practical when the network mission is critical and cost is not a barrier. A network consisting of multiple servers may use a mesh topology to ensure the reliability of the servers. See **Figure 16-7**.

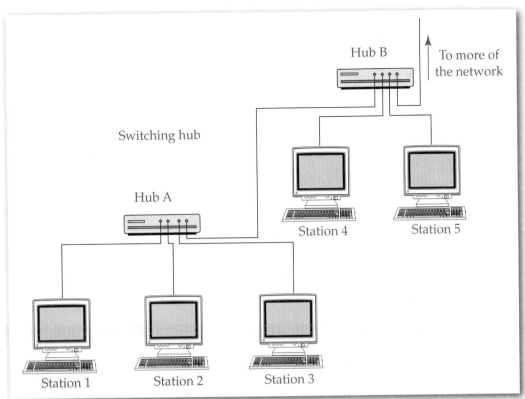

Figure 16-5.
Switching, or intelligent, hubs are used to segment the network, reducing unnecessary data traffic.

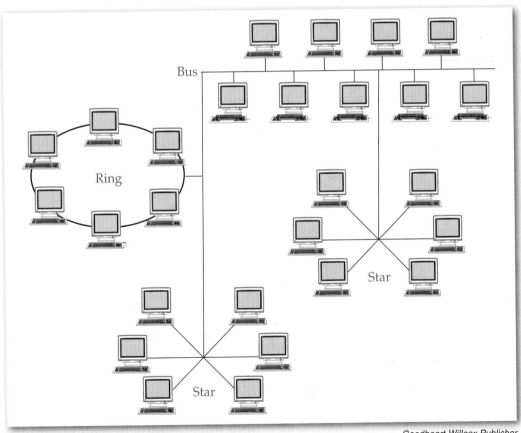

Figure 16-6.
Any mixture of topology types, even if it is only two different types, is known as hybrid topology. Shown is a network consisting of three topology types.

Figure 16-7. Mesh topology connects each node to every other node on the network.

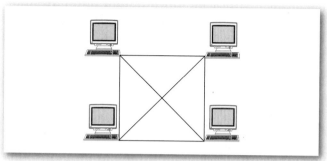

Wireless Topology

As the name implies, a **wireless topology** is a network system that uses no cabling between the computers, **Figure 16-8**. It uses either infrared light or radio transmission to communicate between network devices. Unfortunately, infrared transmissions require an unobstructed line of sight between devices to establish connections. This means that nothing can be placed between the devices that would block the light beam used for communication. Radio transmission systems

Figure 16-8.
A—Wireless topology can be used to connect mobile computers, as found in many police cars, to a stationary network. B—Wireless topology can bridge a gap between buildings where cable connection is impractical. C—A wireless topology can also be used to connect workstations to a server.

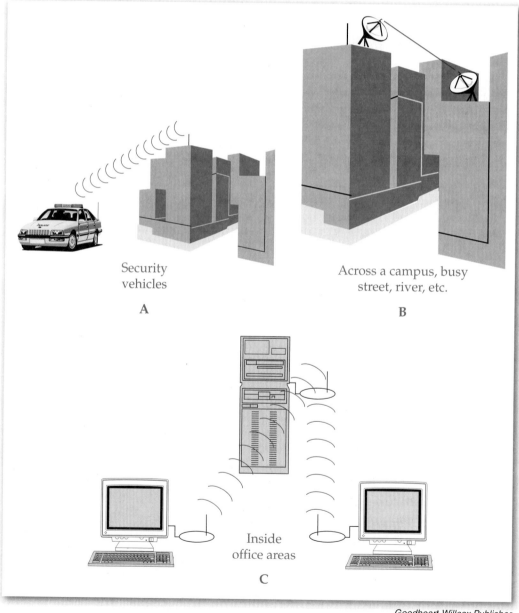

don't need a line of sight. However, they can experience difficulties caused by the building structure and other interference generated by a variety of electrical equipment, such as radios, motors, welders, and microwaves.

There are many reasons to use wireless topologies. Wireless topology can be used to connect vehicles to a network. The transmission can originate from a building antenna or even from a satellite, Figure 16-8A. Wireless technology may be used in place of conventional network cabling to bridge a gap between two buildings separated by a wide metropolitan street or a river, Figure 16-8B. Connecting two buildings with cable could be more expensive and time-consuming than installing transmitters and receivers. A wireless system can provide a quick way to reconfigure a computer arrangement, Figure 16-8C. Moving cables to rearrange computers may not be as easy. In recent years, the cellular phone system has become a large part of wireless Internet systems.

Segments

Segmenting a network is the separating of certain portions of network traffic to increase performance, security, or reliability. The term **segment** can be applied to a physical portion of a network or to a logical portion of a network, **Figure 16-9**.

In the physical sense, a segment is a section of cable between two network devices. For example, it can be the backbone or drop cables in a bus topology, the cables between nodes and hubs or between hubs and hubs in a star topology. Figure 16-9 illustrates how a network can be subdivided into three smaller sections using switches. Each switch creates a network segment or section. A bridge, switch, or router can be used to separate network devices into segments. Switches and routers are discussed in detail later in this chapter. Bridges are discussed in Chapter 18—WAN. In a logical or network operation sense, a segment is a portion of a network that shares a collision domain.

Figure 16-9. A network is segmented to increase performance, security, and reliability.

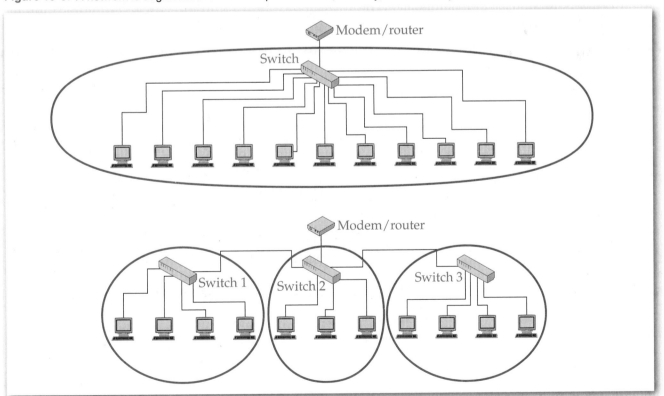

Goodheart-Willcox Publisher

Tech Tip

The term *segment* as applied to networking has changed over time and depends on the context and the source of technical information. The term *segment*, when applied to IP address, MAC addresses, physical cabling, and wireless networking, can have a contrasting definition when compared to each application. When you "segment" a network you "divide" a network according to the context of the material being presented.

Network performance for individual users is increased by segmenting a large network. Reducing the size of a network through segmenting increases the available bandwidth for each segment. For example, if a network has 100 users with equal access to a 1,000 Mbps network system, all 100 users would share the same 1,000 Mbps maximum available bandwidth. By segmenting the network into two or more logical segments, the available bandwidth is increased to 1,000 Mbps for each segment, thus increasing the available bandwidth for users. The original 1,000 Mbps network provided approximately 10 Mbps of availability for each of the 100 users. By dividing the network into two segments, the original 100 users now are divided into two groups of 50 users. Each segment has the available bandwidth of 1,000 Mbps, and each user has the available bandwidth of 20 Mbps—an increase of 100%.

Segmenting a network is a basic security measure for large networks. By segmenting a network, security is increased by separating the network into common workgroups. For example, a school network can be segmented into student, teacher, and administration workgroups. Separating workgroups physically and logically makes it harder for an unauthorized person to gain access to sections of a computer system.

Segmenting a network can improve reliability. Dividing a large computer system into many smaller systems by segmentation helps ensure at least part of the network will be up and running, even if a switch or router fails.

How Networks Communicate

For two or more computers to communicate, they must use the same system of identification and data transfer. Data is divided into smaller units called *packets* or *frames*. A **packet** is a small unit of data into which larger amounts are divided for passage through a network. Like an envelope going through the mail system, each packet contains the address of the sender and the intended recipient. When all of the packets have arrived at their destination, they are reassembled to form a complete message or file.

How Data Is Packaged

Data is sent across a network in the form of digital pulses, or rapidly changing levels of voltages. For data to be sent across a network from node to node, a common data-packaging scheme must be used. The sequence and length of the information is the key to coding and decoding the data frames.

The digital pulses represent binary and hexadecimal codes, which in turn represent the data that is being transmitted. Different network operating systems use different encoding schemes for transmitting data. In a typical data frame, the first six bytes represent the *network interface card (NIC)* to which the data is being sent. The NIC is identified by its *media access code (MAC) address*. NICs and MAC addresses are discussed more thoroughly later in this chapter.

The second six bytes represent the NIC that is transmitting the data. Again, the MAC address of the sending NIC is used. Additional blocks of encoded data may contain information such as the length of the particular packet being sent, a sequence number for the packet, and an error-checking code. Error checking is incorporated into the packet to ensure the data was not corrupted during transmission. A frame of data has a maximum length, usually approximately 1,500 bytes.

A **sequence number** is attached to each packet of data. The sequence number ensures the data will be reassembled in the exact order it was transmitted. Some network systems, such as the Internet, are very complex. The various packets of information that make up a message may not be routed through the same path and may not arrive at their destination in the same order they were sent. Packets of information arriving at different times would be garbled when reassembled. The amount of time it takes data to arrive at its destination is influenced by three major factors:

- Length of route taken.
- Type of media and equipment used to route the data.
- Amount of data traffic on that particular route.

Protocols

For computers to be capable of communicating with each other, they must use the same protocol. A protocol is a set of rules for formatting the data stream transmission between two computers or devices and for describing how to transmit data, usually across a network. Data can be transmitted between two computers in small packets or as a steady stream of data. The protocol determines the size of the packets. It also compresses the information to allow for faster transmission rates, verifies that the information transmitted is complete, and reassembles the information packets when they are received. The protocol usually has some error-checking capabilities. The following is a list of common protocols:

- NetBEUI (NetBIOS Extended User Interface).
- TCP/IP (Transmission Control Protocol/ Internet Protocol).
- DHCP (Dynamic Host Configuration Protocol).
- DNS (Domain Name System).
- LDAP (Lightweight Directory Access Protocol).
- SNMP (Simple Network Management Protocol).
- SMB (Server Message Block).
- CIFS (Common Internet File System).
- SSH (Secure Shell).
- SFTP (Secure File Transfer Protocol).
- HTTP (Hypertext Transfer Protocol).
- S-HTTP (Secure Hypertext Transfer Protocol).
- VoIP (Voice over IP).
- SSDP (Simple Service Discovery Protocol).
- LLDP (Link Layer Discovery Protocol).

The terms *protocol* and *service* can cause confusion for students. Often, both the protocol and service is identified by the same acronym, such as the DHCP protocol and the DHCP service, which adds to the confusion. However, protocols and services are not the same. Services are typically small programs. Service programs act on the information contained in the protocol. A protocol and service are directly related in that both are typically required for the computer system to function properly. Required services are programs, also known as processes, which usually start automatically and run continuously in the background.

When information is exchanged between two services, the information is assembled in a standard format identified by the protocol standard. You can think of the relationship to how a web browser and webpage content are distributed. The web browser can be considered a service. The actual code that creates the individual webpage conforms to a protocol standard. The web browser provides the service and the content is assembled in a specific manner as defined by the protocol.

Protocol Suites

A **protocol suite** is a combination of individual protocols, each designed for a specific purpose. TCP/IP is an example of a protocol suite and is identified by two of the protocols in the suite: TCP and IP.

Some protocols within a suite guarantee delivery of a data packet, while others do not. For example, if a command is issued from one computer on a local network to another on the same local network, delivery is almost guaranteed. No method of checking for delivery is absolutely necessary. If one computer sends a message to another across the United States, a method needs to be used to verify delivery.

As technology progresses, newer protocols must be added to existing suites. For example, when transmitting a collection of data, such as a large document, there is no requirement that the individual packets that represent the entire document arrive at the destination in proper sequence or with extraordinary speed. The document can be reassembled at the final destination in a reasonable amount of time. However, when transferring data, such as sound or video, the data must be received in proper sequence in a short period of time. A telephone conversation that is broken into packets and received out of order sounds garbled. Protocols constantly evolve and grow as new technologies emerge.

TCP/IP

Transmission Control Protocol/Internet Protocol (TCP/IP) is the standard default Internet protocol. It was developed for UNIX to communicate over the Internet. TCP/IP is the combination of two different protocols: transmission control protocol (TCP) and Internet protocol (IP). TCP is designed to guarantee delivery of all packets. IP simply delivers packets and assumes they are received. Originally, TCP/IP was the default protocol installed in a Windows operating system environment. Today, there are two default TCP/IP protocols: IP version 4 (IPv4) and IP version 6 (IPv6). Each version uses a unique set of numbers to identify network devices. The two IP versions are identified in Microsoft network adapter properties as Internet Protocol Version 4 (TCP/IPv4) and Internet Protocol Version 6 (TCP/IPv6). Both protocols are enabled by default and run simultaneously. IPv6 is designed to solve many of the problems associated with IPv4, such as mobile networking and automatic network device configuration.

IPv4

Internet Protocol Version 4, also known as TCP/IPv4 or simply IPv4, has been a standard network protocol for many years. The main design of the IPv4 protocol is the identification of the source computer and destination computer in the form of a 32-bit address written as a set of four decimal numbers in the range of 0 to 255 separated by a period, for example, 192.168.0.23. The IPv4 address is one way a network device is identified.

IPv6

Internet Protocol Version 6, also known as TCP/IPv6 or simply IPv6, is designed to

eventually replace TCP/IPv4. TCP/IPv6 was first introduced in Windows XP but was not enabled by default until Windows Vista. Both IPv4 and IPv6 are enabled by default for all Windows Vista and later operating systems. There will be more about IPv4 and IPv6 in the Chapter 18—WAN, which will present the differences between the two.

> **Tech Tip**
>
> There are hundreds of protocols in use which can be very confusing because they appear to perform similar functions. IPv4 and IPv6 are a classic example of two protocols that by general description seem to perform the same function, but have many technical differences between them.

LLDP

The Link Layer Discovery Protocol (LLDP) is a vendor-neutral protocol standard described by the Institute of Electrical and Electronic Engineers (IEEE). LLDP allows network devices to advertise and exchange information such as their MAC address and network function. Examples of network function are computer, switch, router, and wireless access point. The requirement of being vender-neutral ensures that any device that implements LLDP will be able to exchange information with any other device, even if the two devices are manufactured by different companies.

Because it was taking a long time for the committee to agree to a universal set of standards to determine the final design of LLDP, many venders developed their own proprietary version that closely matched the final vender-neutral standard. Each major company wanted to be the first to implement the improved features associated with LLDP.

There are several proprietary versions of LLDP protocols. The most common discovery protocols are the Cisco Discovery Protocol (CDP), Cabletron Discovery Protocol (CDP), and Nortel Discovery Protocol (NDP). The Cisco Discovery Protocol (CDP) is used for CISCO network devices. Cabletron Discovery Protocol (CDP) is designed by Enterasys Networks and is used for some Ethernet switches. NDP is used for Nortel telephone networks. Microsoft developed the Link-Layer Topology Discovery protocols.

Microsoft Link-Layer Topology Discovery Protocols

The Microsoft version of the Link Layer Discovery Protocol (LLDP) is identified by two protocols in the **Properties** dialog box for a network connection: Link-Layer Topology Discovery Mapper I/O Driver and Link-Layer Topology Discovery Responder. These two protocols work together to discover other network devices and to exchange information. The information exchanged allows network devices on the local area network to discover each other and automatically make some network configurations. For example, a Windows computer using LLTD can automatically configure itself to join an existing local area network. It can automatically discover the local area network router and will automatically create an Internet connection unless the router has security measures enabled.

The Microsoft Link-Layer Topology Discovery protocols make it possible to create a drawing of logical network device locations. **Figure 16-10** shows how a network might appear after being mapped. A solid line represents an Ethernet cable and a dashed line represents a wireless connection. Devices are identified by the logical names assigned to them during configuration. The devices that appear at the bottom of the screen cannot be placed in the map because of many different reasons. Two of the most common reasons for failing to appear in a map is the device does not support the IPv6 protocol. Another reason is the device has a security feature that does not allow it to be mapped.

In Windows 8, Microsoft added two more protocols to the **Properties** dialog box for a network connection: Microsoft LLDP Protocol Driver and Microsoft Network Adapter Multiplexor Protocol, **Figure 16-11**.

Figure 16-10. The Link-Layer Topology Discovery protocols make it possible to create a network map, identifying the logical location of network devices and the network connection type.

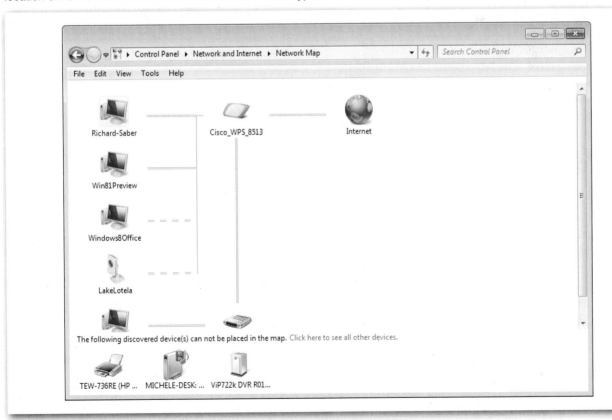

Figure 16-11. Windows 8 does not enable the LLDP Protocol Driver by default. It does enable Microsoft's own version of LLDP, the LLTD Mapper I/O Driver and LLTD Responder.

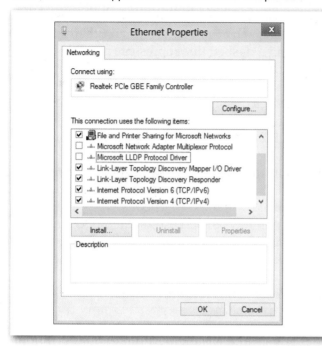

Microsoft LLDP Protocol Driver

The Microsoft LLDP Protocol Driver supports the exchange of information to the Microsoft datacenter network system. The Microsoft datacenter is a server that acts as a centralized data storage system. The Microsoft LLDP Protocol Driver is not enabled by default. In most instances, you will not need to enable either the Microsoft LLDP Protocol Driver or the Microsoft Network Adapter Multiplexor Protocol.

Microsoft Network Adapter Multiplexor Protocol

The Microsoft Network Adapter Multiplexor Protocol (MNAMP) supports load balancing and fail-over support. **Load balancing** is a process that occurs when a computer has multiple network adapters installed and then balances or divides the exchange of packets between the multiple network adapters. The two or more network adapters work as a team. The term **fail-over** is used by Microsoft to describe the process that occurs when one system fails and another system takes over. When used with network adapters, fail-over means that when one network adapter card

fails, another installed network adapter will take over the responsibilities of the failed adapter. The Microsoft Network Adapter Multiplexor Protocol is not enabled by default.

UPnP

Universal Plug and Play (UPnP) is a suite of protocols that exchange information with other devices such as printers, cameras, phones, web cameras, and similar devices. It allows these devices to connect to an existing computer, tablet, or network device with almost no effort by the user. The UPnP specification was developed by the UPnP Forum. This forum consists of hundreds of device manufacturers that want to make their devices exchange information with other devices, especially in a network with minimal user intervention. The UPnP technology is similar to the LLDP protocol.

SSDP

The Simple Service Discovery Protocol (SSDP) is another network protocol used for discovery of network services and device information. SSDP works in conjunction with the UPnP protocol and is intended for use in home office or small office networks to detect Networked Home Entertainment Devices (NHED). SSDP was developed by Microsoft and Hewlett-Packard.

NetBEUI

NetBEUI is an enhanced version of NetBIOS. NetBIOS is software that provides basic services for the transfer of data between nodes, allowing a computer to communicate with many other computers. IBM and Microsoft jointly developed the NetBIOS Enhanced User Interface (NetBEUI) protocol. This simple protocol is used for small network systems of 100 or fewer computers. The ideal small computer network system for NetBEUI consists of 25 computers or fewer. If more than 25 computers are installed on a network using the NetBEUI protocol, the system starts to slow down significantly because of user activity.

NetBEUI is now obsolete as a network protocol. Windows Vista and later versions do not provide support for NetBEUI. Windows XP supports NetBEUI, but does not install it by default. In all versions of Windows, you can still see configuration options for NetBIOS in the **Advanced TCP/IP Settings** dialog box, **Figure 16-12.**

FIP

Fast Infrared Protocol (FIP) is used for transmitting data from laptop computers to desktop PCs without the use of cables. This protocol governs the transmission of data by infrared light.

ATM

Asynchronous Transfer Mode (ATM) is a protocol used for transmitting data, voice, and video simultaneously over the same line. It rearranges the packets in such a way that the quality of the voice or video is not degraded when transmitted. Data is broken into packets containing 53 bytes each, and communicates between any two nodes in the system at rates ranging from 1.5 Mbps to 622 Mbps.

VoIP

Voice over IP (VoIP) is not just one protocol, but rather a suite of protocols. VoIP supports voice communications over an existing network system. Originally, networks were designed to exchange text-based information. Text-based information does not require high-speed network systems. As network systems evolved, network media and equipment were designed to meet the requirements for high-resolution images, movies, and music. With the increase in network bandwidth, it became possible to move telephone communications to existing networks, rather than to keep separate lines—one for networking and one for telephone conversations.

Telephone companies first combined telephone and network media before making VoIP available for residential users. Today, telephone service and movie service is combined with Internet access. These services are provided by networks designed by service providers.

The big problem that service providers needed to overcome was providing telephone conversations in real time. A delay cannot be tolerated when exchanging network packets containing voice messages. Text, movie, and television downloading does not require real-time packet transfers like telephone conversations. A movie or television show can be downloaded over a long period of time and then played back. A telephone conversation must exchange voice messages instantly without a delay between network packets.

VoIP was first introduced as an alternative telephone system for overseas calls because it was approximately half the cost of a traditional telephone connection. Later, it became very cost-effective to use as an everyday service, especially when combined by a service provider with other services, such as television and movies.

To accomplish real-time voice packet exchange, a new set of telephone protocols had to be developed that would ensure quality of service. The protocol developed was named *Quality of Service (QoS)*. This protocol assigns a higher priority to packets that contain time-sensitive information, such as voice, or than less time-sensitive packets, such as e-mail.

Figure 16-12. Even though NetBIOS is basically obsolete, you can still see configuration options for NetBIOS under the network adapter **Advanced TCP/IP Settings** dialog box.

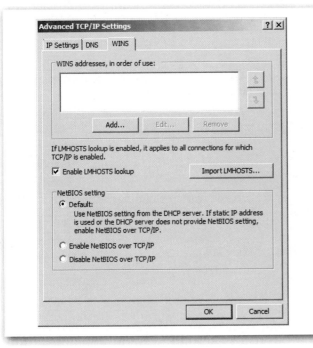

Tech Tip   QoS is not exclusive to telephone applications. This protocol is also applied to any application that requires a steady stream of packets, such as live video.

Figure 16-13 shows a typical Windows network connection **Properties** dialog box. Notice that the QoS Packet Scheduler has been installed by default. The IPv4 and IPv6 protocols combine with QoS Packet Scheduler to provide telephone service through a computer for users with an Internet connection. To learn more about VoIP, visit the government Federal Communications Commission VoIP website.

Client for Microsoft Networks

The Client for Microsoft Networks is installed by default and is used to access resources on a Microsoft local area network. In the early days of networking, there were several different network operating systems, for example Novell NetWare and Apple AppleTalk. To be able to communicate with these network systems and access resources, you needed to install a network client designed especially for the corresponding network. A NetWare client was required for Novell NetWare, and an AppleTalk client was required for Apple networks. Today, everything is compatible with Client for Microsoft Networks.

Figure 16-13. The **Properties** dialog box for a local area connection displays the protocols and services for which a network adapter is configured. Notice that the QoS Packet Scheduler has been installed.

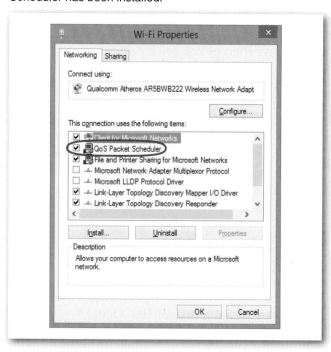

Ethernet

An **Ethernet network** communicates by broadcasting information to all the computers on the network. This is similar to a room full of people talking and one person yelling, "Bob, do you hear me?" Everyone in the room hears Bob's name being called, but only Bob will reply if he is in the room

In an Ethernet system, each computer on the network is given a unique name; no two computers can have the same name. A computer name can be most anything you desire, such as Station 1, Accounting 3, or even WildBill. Each computer in the system also has a unique hexadecimal address programmed into the network card inside the computer. The hexadecimal address is six bytes long. For example, C0 0B 08 1A 2D 2F is a hexadecimal address. See **Figure 16-14**. No other computer on the network has the same number. Using the hexadecimal number system to communicate would be difficult for humans. Therefore, a database automatically corresponds the unique number of the network card to the unique name given to the computer.

A typical session on an Ethernet network goes something like this. Using the network, Bob wants to send a message to Sue. Bob uses Station 1 to send data to Sue at computer Station 4. When Bob sends the message to Sue, he is actually sending the message to all computers on the

Figure 16-14. Close-up of a network interface card media access code (MAC) address.

network. However, only Sue's computer accepts the message. See **Figure 16-15**. Let's take a closer look to see how this happens.

Bob's computer transmits the first six bytes of data, the address of the target computer. Next, six more bytes are sent, the address of Bob's computer. Then, the message data is sent, followed by the frame check sequence. When Sue's computer receives the transmission, it recognizes its own address in the first six bytes of data and accepts the packet. When the data packet is accepted, the next six bytes, which identify the sending PC (Station 1), are decoded and stored for a return message. Next, the actual message is decoded, and then the transmission is checked for errors. If there are no errors detected, a return message is transmitted to Bob's PC to verify receipt of the message. If Bob's PC does not receive the return message, it will continue to retransmit the data packets until the return message is received.

> **Tech Tip**
>
> The act of sending a message or command to all nodes on the network is referred to as *broadcasting*. Sending a message or command to more than one, but not to all nodes, is called *multicasting*.

CSMA/CD

One inherent problem with Ethernet communications is the collision of data being transmitted across the network. When two data packets collide on the network, they both become corrupted and cannot be delivered. Ethernet networks use a protocol called **Carrier Sense Multiple Access with Collision Detection (CSMA/CD)** to control and ensure the delivery of data.

The following passage describes how CSMA/CD works. A workstation listens for data traffic on the network before transmitting data. When the network is silent, the workstation transmits data to another workstation. However, another station may choose the same lull in activity to transmit data. If the data packets from the two stations collide on the network, each station waits for a random period of time, known as the **backoff interval**, before trying to retransmit the data. The random period is a very small fraction of a second. A typical network can transmit thousands of data packets in one second. Collisions do not usually noticeably affect the performance of a properly installed network. However, a poorly designed network may operate very slowly due to excessive collisions.

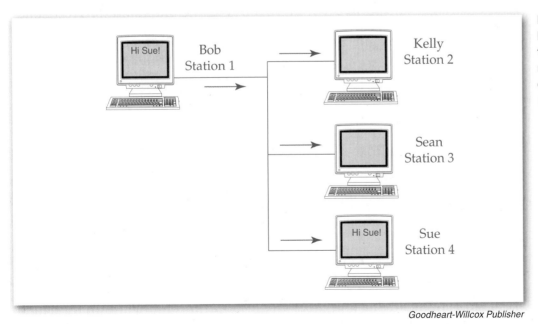

Figure 16-15.
Bob transmits to all the computers on the network, but only Sue's computer accepts the message.

Goodheart-Willcox Publisher

CSMA/CA

Wireless communication uses another type of network access called **Carrier Sense Multiple Access with Collision Avoidance (CSMA/CA)**. This access method is different than CSMA/CD in that it does not detect collisions; it avoids them. There are times when wireless networks cannot detect collisions, so the Ethernet method cannot be used as a media access method.

Look at **Figure 16-16**. In the drawing, a wireless access point and two computers with wireless adapter cards are connected to a cabled network. The limited range of the wireless network cards does not allow the two computers to communicate directly with each other. They can only communicate with the wireless access point. To prevent both computers from communicating with the wireless access point at the same time, which would cause collisions, each computer must ask permission first. A wireless network card sends a very small packet requesting permission to transmit before it sends larger packets to the wireless access point. If the wireless access point is not busy communicating with the other computer on the wireless network, it responds by giving permission for communication. The wireless access point controls all communication.

When a wireless network uses a wireless access point to control communications, the wireless network is referred to as an *infrastructure design*. The wireless access point creates a communications bridge between the cable network and the wireless network.

Tech Tip	The term *Ethernet* is used to identify the type of network system communication and also identifies a specific type of network protocol.

Network Media

Network media is the means by which an electronic signal is transmitted. An electronic signal can be transmitted via cable-based media or wireless media. Generally, there are three types of cable-based media from which to choose: coaxial, twisted pair, and fiber optic. There are also two types of wireless media: infrared and radio transmission. The radio transmission media breaks down into several different media types described in what is known as *standards*.

Figure 16-16.
Wireless systems use collision avoidance to control communication.

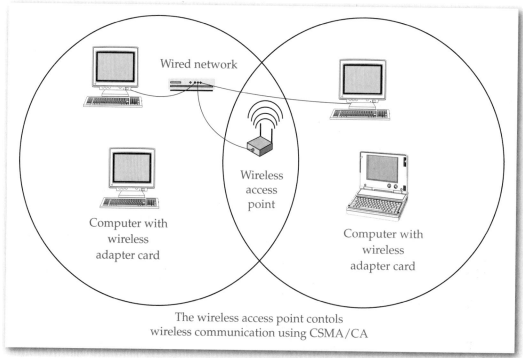

Coaxial Cable

Coaxial cable, or *coax*, consists of a core conductor surrounded by an insulator. The insulator is covered with a shield of either a solid foil or a braided wire layer. The shield protects the cable core from stray electromagnetic interference, which would corrupt the transmitted data. See **Figure 16-17**. Coaxial cable is difficult to work with and relatively expensive when compared to some of the other wiring media.

Coaxial cable uses two main types of connectors: BNC and F-type. BNC is not threaded. It simply makes a connection by pushing onto the connection post and then twisting to the right. F-type coaxial cable connectors have treads and make a much better connection. See **Figure 16-18**.

Figure 16-18. BNC and F-type coaxial cable connectors.

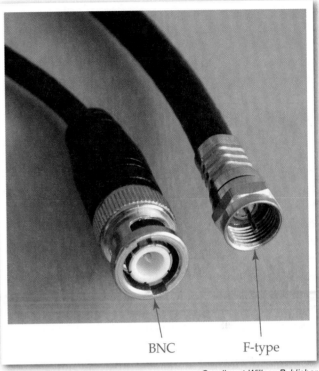

BNC   F-type

Goodheart-Willcox Publisher

> **Tech Tip**
>
> The true origin of the BNC acronym is a mystery. The terms *British Naval Connectors*, *Bayonet Nut Connectors*, *Bayonet-Neill Concelman*, *Baby N Connector*, and *BayoNet Connectors* all refer to BNCs.

RG-6 and RG-59

Coaxial cable was designed to be used as media for radio systems, hence the acronym *RG*, which represents *Radio Guide*. The acronym *RG* is still used to classify the various types of coaxial cable. Coaxial cable is classified by its electrical characteristics and best application for its use.

Two types of coaxial cable commonly encountered are RG-6 and RG-59. RG-6 is very similar to RG-59, but there are sufficient differences that make RG-6 better suited than RG-59 for high-frequency systems such as Cable TV (CATV) and satellite. RG-59 was originally used for CATV and satellite systems, but as more data throughput, more channels, and higher frequencies became standard, RG-6 became the replacement for RG-59.

> **Tech Tip**
>
> The term *coaxial cable* describes any cable that shares the same physical cable characteristics.

RG-59 is still used for some low-frequency applications such as audio systems. RG-59 does not work well in applications involving gigahertz or higher frequencies, but does work well for lower frequencies such as video and audio distribution inside a building or home. The following summarizes the applications for RG-6 and RG-59:

- RG-59 used in analog video systems.
- RG-6 is used for digital video systems.
- RG-6 supports higher frequencies than RG-59.

Figure 16-17. The structure of typical coaxial cable is shown here.

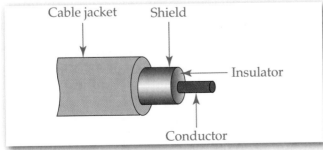

Cable jacket   Shield

Insulator

Conductor

Goodheart-Willcox Publisher

The ANSI/TIA/ EIA-570 Residential Telecommunications Cabling Standard specifies RG-6 coaxial cable for multimedia systems installed in homes.

Twisted Pair Cable

Twisted pair cable has been available for many years and was first used to carry voice transmissions by telephone companies. Today, twisted pair is the most common choice for network wiring. It consists of four pairs of conductors twisted around each other. The two broad classifications of twisted pair are unshielded twisted pair (UTP) and shielded twisted pair (STP). The physical difference is STP has a foil shield surrounding the conductors and UTP does not. The foil shield greatly reduces the effects of radio signal interference from other electrical sources in a similar manner that coaxial cable shielding helps shield the coaxial core conductor.

The common Ethernet network uses only two of the pairs in the cable. Duplex Ethernet uses all four pairs. In a typical standard Ethernet installation, the extra two pairs can be thought of as spares. When only two pairs are used for the network, the remaining two pairs are often used for telephone communication.

The twists in the pairs are necessary to eliminate cross talk between the conductors. **Cross talk** is the imposition of a signal on one pair of conductors by another pair of conductors that run parallel to it. Twisting each pair inside the cable greatly reduces the effect of cross talk. This occurs because, when twisted, the two pairs are no longer parallel to each other.

Wire sizes range from #18 AWG to #26 AWG, with #24 AWG used most often. AWG stands for American Wire Gauge, a standard method for sizing wire. The categories or classifications of twisted pair cable that follow are based on the physical design of the cable. The chart in **Figure 16-19** summarizes the maximum frequency and maximum speed of the most used twisted pair cable types.

Figure 16-19. Common twisted pair cable types and their maximum frequency and speed (bandwidth) ratings.

Category	Maximum Frequency	Maximum Speed
Cat 3	16 MHz	16 Mbps
Cat 4	20 MHz	20 Mbps
Cat 5	100 MHz	100 Mbps
Cat 5e	100 MHz	1,000 Mbps/1 Gbps
Cat 6	250 MHz	1,000 Mbps/1 Gbps
Cat 7	600 MHz	10 Gbps

Goodheart-Willcox Publisher

Category 1

Category 1 cable consists of two twisted pairs. While this design was sufficient for electrical signals representing voice transmission, it is entirely inadequate for computer networks.

Category 2

Category 2 cable consists of four twisted pairs. This design again is not acceptable for today's networking systems. It was used in some early applications that were limited to 4 Mbps. Today's networks run at a minimum of 10 Mbps.

Category 3

Category 3 cable consists of four twisted pairs, three twists per foot. This can be found on legacy networks usually rated at 10 Mbps and 16 Mbps and in many legacy telephone installations.

Category 4

Category 4 cable consists of four twisted pairs. This cable handles 20 Mbps and is only a slight improvement over Cat 3 cable. It reduces cross talk and signal loss.

Category 5

Category 5 cable consists of four twisted pairs and offers a transmission speed of 100 Mbps. It is found commonly in 10BaseT and 100BaseT installations. 10BaseT and 100BaseT are Institute of Electrical and Electronic Engineers (IEEE) network cable classifications, which are covered later in this chapter.

Category 5e

The *e* in Category 5e represents *enhanced*. Cat 5e is an enhanced version of the Cat 5 standard that provides a little less signal loss. It is designed for Fast Ethernet and Gigabit Ethernet transmissions, which are also IEEE network cable classifications. The Cat 5e standard is actually an addendum to the existing standard to expand the qualities of existing Cat 5 cable.

> **Tech Tip**
>
> Not all Cat 5 cable can reach the Cat 5e standard, but much of it can. The real difference is in the amount of cross talk permitted for Cat 5e when compared to Cat 5. The difference is only slight.

Category 6

Category 6 cable supports frequencies as high as 250 MHz and data throughput of 1 Gbps. The high data throughput is achieved by using all four twisted pairs of wiring. See **Figure 16-20** to see a physical comparison of Cat 5e and Cat 6 cable.

> **Tech Tip**
>
> Cat 6a is a new classification that can be used for 10 Gbps applications, but the maximum distance is reduced to 55 meters.

Category 7

Category 7 cable provides data transmission speeds as high as 600 MHz. It uses a different construction technique to achieve the higher transmission speeds. Cat 7 is constructed of four pairs of twisted conductors with a protective foil or a conductive braid surrounding each pair. In addition to the individual pair shields, there is an overall protective foil or conductive braid surrounding the complete assembly. See **Figure 16-21**.

Figure 16-20. Cat 6 can support a much higher data rate than Cat 5 because of the physical design of the cable. Cat 6 has a plastic spacer separating the conductor pairs.

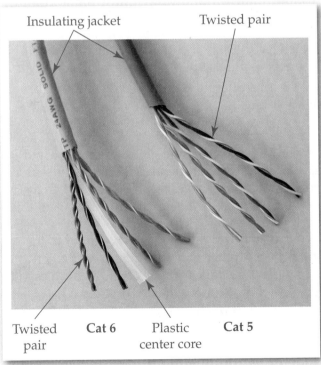

Figure 16-21. Cat 5 is constructed of four pairs of twisted conductors. Cat 6 is similar in construction to Cat 5. Unlike Cat 5 and Cat 6, Cat 7 has a shield over each conductive pair, and an overall shield between the plastic outer jacket and the individual-pair shielding.

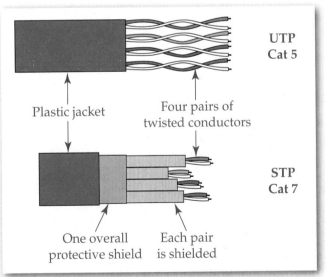

Goodheart-Willcox Publisher

Goodheart-Willcox Publisher

Fiber-Optic Cable

Fiber-optic cable, often referred to as *fiber,* contains a glass or plastic center used to carry light, **Figure 16-22.** The electronic signals transmitted from the computer are converted to a signal consisting of a fluctuating beam of light. The fiber-optic cable carries the light signal to its destination where it is converted back to an electrical signal. The use of fiber optics has many advantages over conventional copper wire systems. The advantages include increased security, greater resistance to corrosion, immunity to lightning strikes, longer transmission distances per segment, and decreased weight. Its biggest disadvantages are greater expense and the increased difficulty of field installations. It is ideal for network backbones.

The broad classifications of fiber-optic cable based on the diameter of the core are multimode and single-mode. In general, multimode fiber-optic cable has a larger core diameter than single-mode fiber-optic cable. The diameter of the core has a direct relationship to the distance the cable can carry light signals. The loss of light signal is referred to as *attenuation.* The larger the core diameter, the more light signal loss or the greater the attenuation. Single-mode fiber-optic cable has a much smaller core diameter than multimode cable. The result is single-mode fiber-optic cable can carry light signals farther than multimode fiber-optic cable.

Fiber-optic core dimensions are measured in micrometers (μm) or millionths of a meter. The size of a fiber-optic cable is expressed in two numerical values separated by a slash. For example, a fiber-optic cable identified as 65.5/125 indicates that the core diameter is equal to 65.5 micrometers and the overall core and cladding diameter is 125 micrometers. Typical multimode core dimensions are 50/125, 62.5/125, and 100/140. However, 100/140 is an older technology and is not encountered very often. A typical single-mode core is 8.3/125.

There are many different fiber-optic cable connectors in use, but there are five common fiber-optic connectors you need to become familiar with. The five fiber-optic cable connector styles are ST, SC, FC, LC, and MT-RJ. Look at the **Figure 16-23** to see the general shape of each type of connector.

The ST connector must be pushed directly in and then twisted to the right to lock in place. The SC connector pushes directly in and then snaps into place. Both connectors offer a quick way to connect and disconnect a fiber-optic cable. The FC style is designed with screw threads. The FC connector offers superior connection strength when compared to the other connectors in Figure 16-23.

The LC style of connector has a smaller form factor when compared to SC, ST, and FC styles. The LC is designed for a single cable but can be modified to form an LC duplex connector to accommodate two cables. The pair of LC connectors are held together using a clip and thus form a duplex connection.

The MT-RJ style connector is similar to the shape of a copper cable RJ connector. The MT-RJ is unique in that it incorporates two fiber cables into one assembly without the use of a clip. The MT-RJ has a small form factor and is considered a duplex connector like the LC duplex. To learn more about network cables and connectors visit the Black Box Network Services website.

Figure 16-22. Fiber-optic cable contains a glass or plastic core, which is used as a conduit for light.

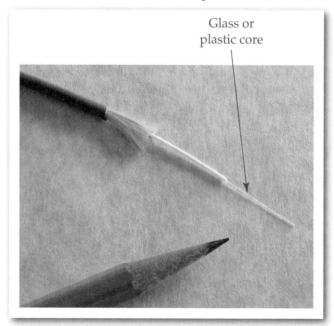

Glass or plastic core

Goodheart-Willcox Publisher

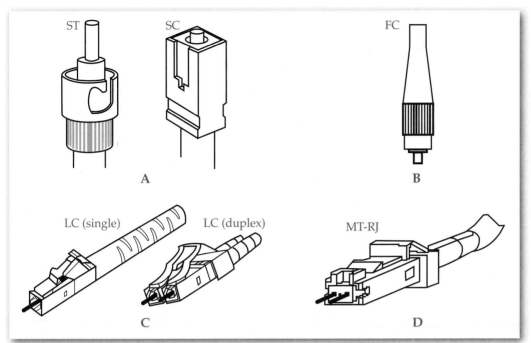

Figure 16-23.
Fiber-optic cable connectors. A—ST and SC connectors. B—FC connector. C—LC connectors. D—MT-RJ connector.

Goodheart-Willcox Publisher

A+ Note

Be sure you can identify the fiber-optic cable connection types.

Wireless

Wireless media for local area networks are based on the IEEE 802.11 standard. The two common wireless network topologies, which are referred to as wireless modes, are ad-hoc and infrastructure. *Ad-hoc* is a peer-to-peer configuration where all wireless devices can connect directly to each other. The most common ad-hoc arrangement is when a wireless laptop connects directly to a desktop that has a wireless device installed. A *wireless infrastructure* requires a wireless access point. A wireless access point is used to control the flow of data between each wireless device in the network. A wireless access point is also used to provide a connection to and from a wireless network to a wired network system. The wireless media is assigned specific radio frequencies as listed in the following table.

IEEE Standard	Radio Frequency	Frequency Range	Maximum Data Rate	Approximate Range	Comments
802.11a	5 GHz	5.15 GHz–5.825 GHz	54 Mbps	50 m	Obsolete
802.11b	2.4 GHz	2.4 GHz–2.4835 GHz	11 Mbps	100 m	
802.11ac	5 GHz	5.15–5.825 GHz	1.3 Gbps	*See note.	Backward compatible with 802.11a, 802.11b, 802.11g, 802.11n
802.11g	2.4 GHz	2.4 GHz–2.4835 GHz	54 Mbps	50 m	Compatible with 802.11b
802.11n	2.4 GHz / 5 GHz	2.4 GHz–2.4835 GHz / 5.15 GHz–5.825 GHz	300 Mbps	200 m	Compatible with 802.11a, 802.11b, and 802.11g

*Distances for 802.11ac have not been established at time of printing for this edition.

Be aware that some wireless network card manufacturers exceed the standard data rate set by the IEEE organization. However, 802.11ac is the latest wireless standard that provides the highest data rates to date. The exact data rate varies quite a bit.

Plenum and PVC

Not all cables are approved for installation in a commercial building in the area referred to as the *plenum*. The **plenum** is the space above a ceiling or raised floor and is designed to carry return air in a closed air conditioning system. Cables are often installed in the plenum space and are required to be plenum rated. The plenum rating means that if the cable burns, it will not give off harmful gases. Many cable protective jackets and insulators are constructed from polyvinyl chloride (PVC). PVC produces deadly gases when burned. Thus, any cable that contains PVC is not permitted to be installed in any building plenum area.

IEEE Network Cable Classifications

The Institute of Electrical and Electronic Engineers (IEEE) has classified network cables according to their abilities and physical description. Network cables are classified with a short description such as 100BaseT. The "100" represents the speed of transmission—in this case, 100 megabits per second. Note that the speed is rated in bits, not bytes. The "Base" refers to baseband, which means data travels across the network one message at a time rather than in multiple simultaneous messages. When the last character or characters are letters, it provides

specific information about the cable used. For example, when the last letter is a *T*, the name denotes twisted pair with a maximum distance of 100 meters. An *F* represents fiber-optic cable. The table in **Figure 16-24** lists the specifications of some common cables.

Ethernet Twisted Pair Wiring Standards

The two standard wiring configurations for Ethernet twisted pair cable are 568A and 568B. The only real difference in the connections is the color of the conductors inserted into the pin areas. There is no real electrical difference between the two standards, only the color arrangement of the conductors. Compare the two standard arrangements for the 568A and 568B connectors in **Figure 16-25**.

Ethernet twisted pair cables have two common classifications of assembly: straight through and crossover. A straight-through cable is used to connect a computer with a hub, and a crossover cable is used to connect a computer with a computer. The straight-through cable is constructed with each numbered pin connecting to the matching numbered pin on the opposite end of the cable. Look at the wire map in **Figure 16-26**. Notice that in the straight-through wiring, pin 1 connects to pin 1, pin 2 connects to pin 2, and so on.

When a two-workstation Ethernet network is configured, a crossover cable must be used for the network cards to communicate. A crossover cable has two pairs (four individual conductors) that are cross-connected. Cross connecting cable

Figure 16-24. IEEE network cable classifications and specifications.

Category	Classification	Data Rate	Maximum Segment Length	Minimum Segment Length	Cable Type
10 Mbps	10BaseT	10 Mbps	100 m	0.5 m	Cat 3, 4, and 5
Fast Ethernet	100BaseT4 100BaseTX	100 Mbps 100 Mbps	100 m 100 m	0.6 m 0.6 m	Cat 3, 4, and 5 Cat 5
Gigabit Ethernet	1000BaseT	1,000 Mbps	100 m	0.6 m	Cat 5e
10 Gigabit Ethernet	10GBaseT 10GBaseT	10 Gbps 10 Gbps	55 m 100 m	0.6 m 0.6 m	Cat 6 Cat 6a

pairs 1 and 2 with 3 and 6 allows a transmit signal from one computer to be sent to the receive pins of a network card on the other computer. This allows the computers to communicate without a hub. A crossover cable is not needed when a hub is used because the circuitry at each access port crosses the connection internally. Therefore in this situation, a straight-through cable is used. Network devices and Ethernet adapters that incorporate the Auto-MDIX feature do not require the use of a crossover cable.

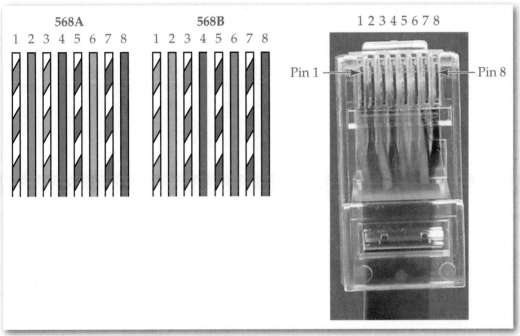

Goodheart-Willcox Publisher

Figure 16-25.
The only difference between the 568A and 568B wiring standard is the arrangement of the conductors as identified by jacket color.

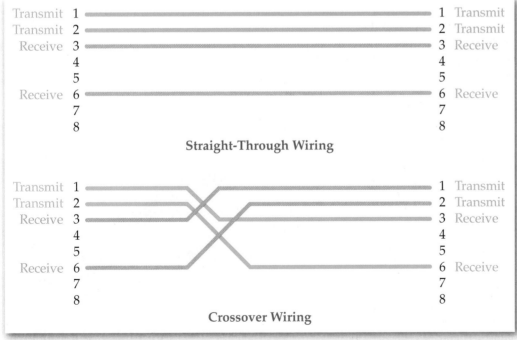

Goodheart-Willcox Publisher

Figure 16-26.
A crossover cable switches the position of cable pair 1 and 2 with cable pair 3 and 6.

Auto-MDIX

Automatic Medium Dependent Interface Crossover (Auto-MDIX) is a standard first introduced by Hewlett-Packard. Auto-MDIX is an electronic chip technology incorporated into the IEEE 1,000 gigabit Ethernet standard for network devices such as switches and network adapters. The Auto-MDIX device automatically reassigns the pin functions so that a crossover cable is no longer required for communication. To verify that a network device is Auto-MDIX compliant, look at the device specifications. Not all devices are Auto-MDIX compliant, especially if they are quite old.

Rollover Cable

A **rollover cable** is a special cable in which the pin order is completely reversed on the opposite end of the cable. For example, pin 1 connects to pin 8, pin 2 connects to pin 7, and so on. The Cisco console cable is wired like a rollover cable. The pin numbers are reversed, but the main difference is a rollover cable uses an RJ-45 connector on each end. A Cisco console cable uses an RJ-45 connector on one end and a DB-9 serial connector on the other. Rollover cables connect a PC to a network device, such as a router. The router can then be programmed by the PC.

Power over Ethernet (PoE)

The **Power over Ethernet (PoE)** provides a means to supply small amounts of electrical power to network devices such as a camera, IP phone, wireless access point, speakers, and phone or PDA charger. The amount of power delivered is approximately 13 watts at 48 volts. The cable used for PoE must be rated as Cat 5 or better. The Cat 5 cable consists of 4 twisted pairs. Two pairs of cables are used for network communication and one pair is used to supply the electrical power.

Another more electronically-sophisticated method is used for gigabit networks in which all cable pairs are used to carry network communication. Electrical power is supplied using two of the existing cable pairs that provide network communication. A more technical explanation of how PoE works is beyond the scope of this textbook. To learn more about the electronic aspect of PoE, visit the Power Over Ethernet website. For a detailed explanation, visit the Texas Instrument website and search its technical documents for Power over Ethernet.

A common PoE application is providing building and area security when electrical power is not readily available. Using PoE is very cost-effective compared to installing electrical circuits to power devices such as cameras.

Cable Tools

There are a variety of cable tools you need to be familiar with. Not all tools are made exactly the same, and the exact construction can vary quite a bit between different manufacturers.

Cable Crimper

A **cable crimper** is a tool designed to crimp (squeeze) an RJ-45 connector onto the end of a twisted pair cable, thus making the electrical connections between each of the eight conductors and the connector, **Figure 16-27**. The individual RJ-45 connector pins align with each conductor of the twisted pair cable, **Figure 16-28**.

A standard crimper usually incorporates a cable stripper and a cable cutter. The overall cable jacket is first removed using a cable stripper, but there is no need to remove the insulation from the individual wires. The crimper presses the pins through the insulation and into direct contact with the copper core or each wire, **Figure 16-29**.

Figure 16-27. A cable crimper is designed to crimp (squeeze) an RJ-45 cable connector onto the end of a twisted pair cable.

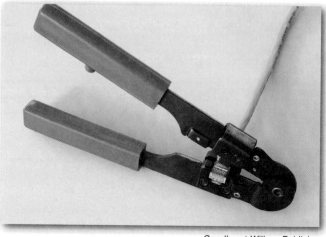

Figure 16-28. Top view of an RJ-45 connector and close-up of individual wires aligned with individual connector pins.

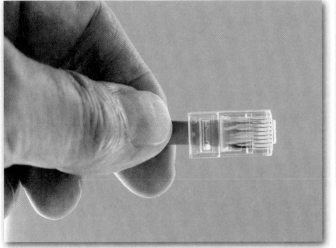

Goodheart-Willcox Publisher

Figure 16-30. Cable cutter and wire stripper.

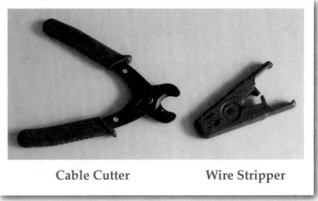

Cable Cutter   Wire Stripper

Goodheart-Willcox Publisher

Figure 16-29. The RJ-45 connector pins are pressed through the cable insulation and into direct contact with the individual wires.

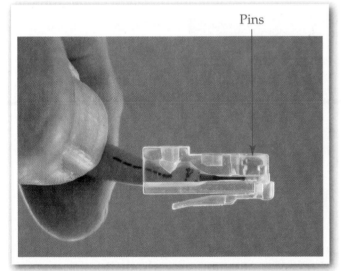

Pins

Goodheart-Willcox Publisher

Cable Cutter and Wire Stripper

Figure 16-30 shows two more tools commonly associated with cables, a cable cutter and wire stripper. A cable cutter can cut through a variety of cable types such as twisted pair and coaxial cable. The cable stripper shown in Figure 16-30, is designed to remove the outer jacket from a cable.

Punch Down Tool

A **punch down tool** is used for inserting twisted pair conductors into a slotted post called an **insulation displacement connector (IDC)**. See **Figure 16-31**. IDCs are found on patch panels and punch down blocks. A punch down tool is also used for inserting wires into RJ-45 keystone modules. A keystone module snaps into a keystone wall plate, allowing RJ-45 cables to be terminated at wall outlets.

The punch down tool is an impact tool because it has an internal spring-loaded mechanism that snaps the wire into place in the IDC. The spring mechanism ensures that the required pressure is reached for inserting the wire. The tool not only inserts the wire into the slot, but it also trims excess conductor. The tip of the tool is referred to as a blade. The blade comes in two standard sizes: 66 and 110. The numbers 66 and 110 represent punch down block types.

Cable Tracer and Tone Generator

A **cable tracer** and **tone generator** both allow a technician to trace the exact location of cable runs inside walls, ceilings, or under floors to identify unmarked cables. The tone generator attaches to one end of a cable and transmits an analog or digital signal through the cable. The cable tracer receives the signal and produces a tone if it is in close proximity to the cable. When a cable fault is encountered, the signal ends or changes pitch.

Figure 16-31. A punch down tool inserts twisted pair conductors into a special termination block called an IDC. A—The tip of the punch down tool inserts the wire into the connector and trims off excess wire. B—The punch down tool inserts the insulated individual conductors into IDCs on patch panels and punch down blocks.

Figure 16-32. A cable tester is used to check the wiring assembly of a network cable.

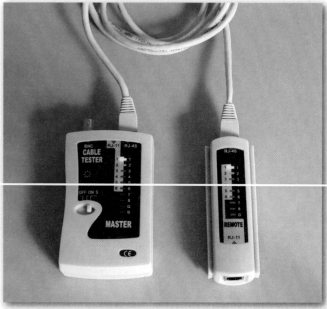

Goodheart-Willcox Publisher

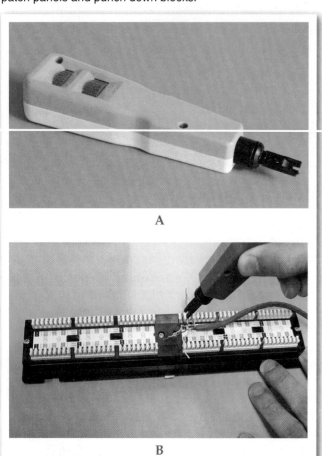

Goodheart-Willcox Publisher

Tech Tip   The BICSI organization is a not-for-profit organization that trains and certifies installers for voice, data, and video distribution systems. A BICSI certification for network cable installer would enhance your job résumé. To learn more about BICSI, visit the organization's website.

Cable Tester

A **cable tester** is used to test newly-made and existing network cables. The complete cable tester consists of two devices: master and remote. The master is a battery-equipped device that transmits a signal on each cable wire. The remote receives the signals. A light will flash for each cable wire, indicating it is properly wired. The cable tester in **Figure 16-32** can test twisted pair and coaxial cable. It is equipped with a BNC connector, RJ-45 ports, and RJ-11 ports. The RJ-11 ports are for testing telephone cable.

Loopback Plug

A **loopback plug** is used to test an Ethernet network card. The plug or cable is inserted into the RJ-45 port on the network adapter. The plug simulates an actual network because it completes the electrical circuit between the transmit and receive pins. The **ping 127.0.0.1** command is then issued at the command prompt to complete the test. You then observe the link and activity lights on the network adapter. A normal network card periodically sends out network packets to probe the network for other devices, thus generating network activity.

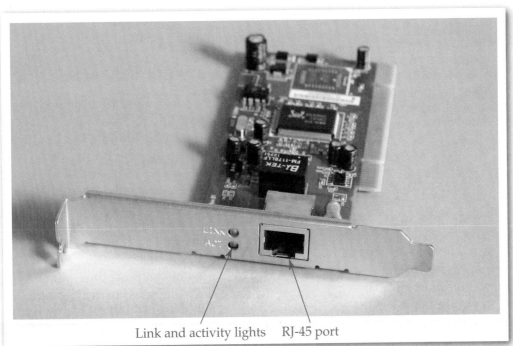

Link and activity lights   RJ-45 port

Goodheart-Willcox Publisher

Figure 16-33. Network adapter designed to fit into a motherboard expansion slot.

Network Equipment

A variety of devices are used to create networks. The most common network devices used in a home or small-office network are network interface cards, wireless network interface cards, switches, routers, and wireless routers.

Network Interface Cards

A **network interface card (NIC)**, also called a *network adapter card* and *Ethernet card*, connects media, usually twisted pair, to individual network devices such as workstations, file servers, and printers. Network adapter cards come in a variety of designs. For example, the adapter in **Figure 16-33** is designed to be installed into a motherboard expansion slot. Network adapters integrated into the motherboard can fail and are not typically repairable. A network adapter card can be installed into a motherboard slot to replace the existing integrated network adapter. Another replacement alternative is a USB to Ethernet adapter, **Figure 16-34**. The adapter simply plugs into any available USB port and provides an Ethernet RJ-45 connection.

Network adapters are not only installed to replace a failed integrated network adapter, but also to upgrade an existing system. For example, a legacy computer may have a network adapter rated for 100 Mbps. To upgrade the computer for higher network performance, an adapter rated for 1,000 Mbps can be installed either into a motherboard slot or via the USB port. A wireless network adapter can also be installed.

Figure 16-34. Network adapter designed to connect to any available USB port.

USB connector   RJ-45 connector

Goodheart-Willcox Publisher

Simply upgrading a computer network adapter may not increase network performance if the other devices, such as the router or Cable modem maximum rating, are less than that of the network adapter. Network performance is limited to the slowest network device.

As discussed earlier, each network adapter card has a unique **media access code (MAC) address**. A MAC address is a hexadecimal number programmed into the card's chip. Refer to Figure 16-14. The address is composed of twelve digits divided into two equal sections. The first six digits identify the card's manufacturer. The second six-digit sequence is a number assigned by the manufacturer and is different on every card produced. No two network adapter cards can have the same MAC address on the same network. The network uses the MAC address to identify the different nodes on the network. If two cards match, the network cannot communicate properly with either card. The MAC address functions like telephone numbers in a telephone system. If two people had the same telephone number, each one might receive calls that were unintended for the other.

The Mac address is often referred to as the *physical address* because it is physically burned into the card. Names used to identify computers or network nodes are referred to as the *logical address*. A typical PC has both a physical address assigned through the network adapter card and a logical address assigned by the technician when the NIC is installed. For example, a computer may have a physical address of 0020AF012AB3 and a logical address such as Station 12.

The MAC address is also referred to as the *data link control (DLC) identifier*. In the IEEE 802 standard, the data link layer of the OSI model is subdivided into the logical link control (LLC) layer and the media access control (MAC) layer. The MAC layer communicates directly with the network while the LLC layer uses a protocol such as Address Resolution Protocol (ARP). ARP is part of the TCP/IP protocol suite. The ARP resolves the MAC address to a computer name, such as Station 1. Using the computer name Station 1 is more convenient than trying to remember the hexadecimal code number for the node.

Powerline Network Devices

Powerline network devices are designed to extend a network by using the existing 120-volt electrical wiring system, **Figure 16-35**. Extending an existing network using powerline network technology requires two powerline network devices. Each device is equipped with an RJ-45 Ethernet port and a standard 120-volt plug. The RJ-45 Ethernet ports are used to connect to network equipment such as a router, computer, or other network device. The network packets are carried over the 120-volt powerline. Some powerline devices are designed to be used as a hub, providing typically four RJ-45 Ethernet ports at one of the devices.

Advertised data rates are as high as 500 Mbps, but this is rare in practice. The very nature the 120-volt power cable design does not allow it to support advertised speeds. In reality, the actual speed is much lower and network communication may not work at all for long runs of cable. The actual length of an electrical cable run can be

Figure 16-35. Powerline network devices extend a network over existing 120-volt power wiring.

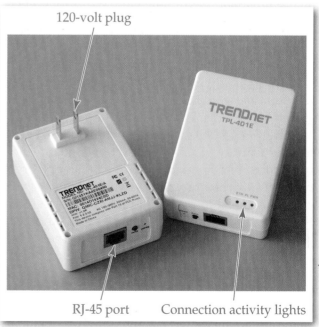

120-volt plug

RJ-45 port   Connection activity lights

Goodheart-Willcox Publisher

deceiving because the cables are hidden in the walls. Also, be aware that some electrical distribution systems, especially in commercial buildings, use transformers to step down the voltage to the 120-volt level. A transformer will not support the high frequencies associated with network transmissions.

Hubs

A hub is a device that connects network equipment together quickly and easily. See **Figure 16-36**. The hub in this figure has eight RJ-45 ports for quick connection of twisted pair cable.

Hubs may be cascaded to provide more connections or to segment a network (as with switching hubs). See **Figure 16-37**. Compare the daisy-chain arrangement to the cascading arrangement. When a network is expanded, the daisy-chain arrangement can be used to add additional computers to the network. The problem is that most systems are limited to only four hubs connected in this manner. After four hubs, the signal is degraded and data may have to be retransmitted many times before it can be received at its destination. The regeneration of data causes a delay in the delivery of the packets. If the delay is too long, the packet is discarded.

The preferred arrangement is the cascading style. By connecting the hubs in a cascading arrangement as in the illustration, the number of hubs the signal travels through is limited to two. The cascade arrangement allows a greater number of PCs to be connected without traveling through four hubs.

When hubs are cascaded, a crossover cable may be needed. Some hubs are equipped with a selector switch that eliminates the need for a crossover cable. By changing the selector switch to the uplink position, port eight is reconfigured as the uplink port for a cascading hub configuration.

Switches

You can think of switches as intelligent hubs. A switch is equipped with more sophisticated electronic components than a simple hub. The hub broadcasts packets to every one of its RJ-45 ports, thus transmitting packets to each device connected to the hub. If the hubs are cascaded, the packets are transmitted to more devices. A switch only forwards packets to the intended network device. As stated earlier, each network device has an assigned MAC address. The electronic design of the switch allows it to match each MAC address with a corresponding port, thus only forwarding the packet to the intended device. Because of the way the switch is designed, overall network traffic is greatly reduced.

Switches were once considered very expensive, but today they are competitively priced with hubs. This has caused switches to be used in place of hubs. In fact, in small networks, a hub is seldom encountered.

Some switches are referred to as *smart switches* or *managed switches*. Smart switches and managed switches have more capabilities than ordinary switches. They have many of the same capabilities as routers.

Routers

A **router** supports communication between different types of networks, for example a home network and the Internet. Routers are very common in homes and small offices. A router is more electronically sophisticated than a switch and can be configured to perform many more tasks than a switch. Specific router ports can be designated to function in a particular way.

Home and small business routers commonly incorporate a wireless access point, thus making the router the central device for both the wired

Figure 16-36. A typical hub. The RJ-45 ports allow twisted pair to be connected. Various LEDs make the hub's current status visible at a glance.

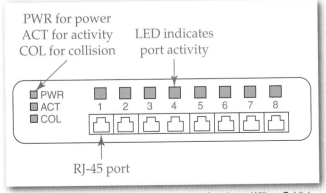

Figure 16-37. By arranging the network in a cascading hub configuration, data must pass through a maximum of two hubs to reach its destination. With the daisy-chain configuration, data may have to pass through as many as four hubs to reach its destination.

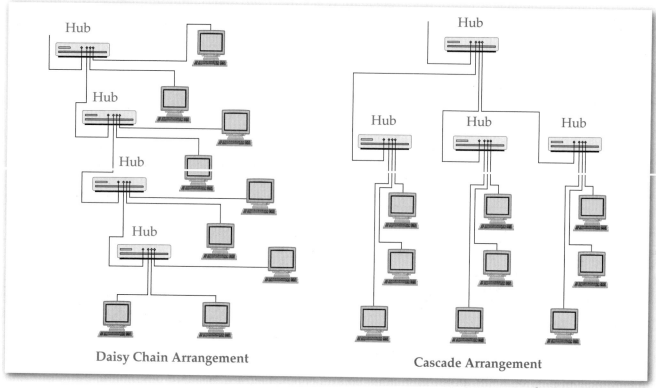

Daisy Chain Arrangement

Cascade Arrangement

portion and the wireless portion of the network. Most home routers are limited to only four RJ-45 ports. The total number of ports can be increased by connecting a hub or switch to one of the router ports. You should avoid adding additional routers because they could cause network conflicts. For example, routers have the capability to issue IP addresses to the local area network devices by default. Using two routers in a network could cause problems with issuing IP addresses. Some Cable modems have router capabilities. There will be more about switches and routers in Chapter 18—WAN.

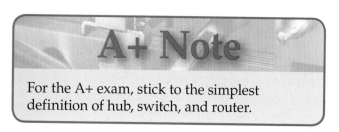

A+ Note

For the A+ exam, stick to the simplest definition of hub, switch, and router.

Wireless Routers

Wireless routers are commonly used in homes and small offices as a centralized distribution point for wireless and wired connections to computers and mobile devices, **Figure 16-38**. The **wireless router** is a combination of wireless access point, switch, and router. Some wireless routers also incorporate a Cable modem.

Tech Tip

The exact name of a device will vary somewhat depending on the manufacturer and intended purpose of the device.

Figure 16-39 shows the connections on the back of a wireless router. The RJ-45 port labeled "Internet" connects directly to a DSL modem or Cable modem, allowing access to the Internet service. The USB port can also be used to connect to a DSL modem or Cable modem.

Figure 16-38. A wireless router with three antennae is a good indication that it has the MIMO feature.

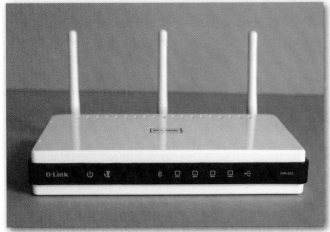

Goodheart-Willcox Publisher

The reset button is used to restore the router to its original factory settings. For example, if the router security password (passphrase or security key) is forgotten, the reset button can be used to erase the existing security password and return it to the factory default. Users often forget their security password, and the only way to gain access is by using the reset button. The reset button is recessed below the case surface and can only be pressed by inserting a paper clip into the hole. The reset button is designed so that it will not be accidentally pressed. To reset the router, the button is held for a short period of time, usually for about ten seconds.

You should always configure a wireless router with security encryption key to prevent unauthorized access. This is especially true for routers installed in apartments or in closely-spaced housing. Anyone can easily access an unsecure wireless router and gain access to your network. Once someone gains access to your network, that person can also use your Internet connection. The effects of accessing the Internet through your or your client's router can have devastating results. Additional charges could be billed to the owner if the total bandwidth is exceeded. The unauthorized user could download copy-protected materials such as games. To the Internet provider, it appears that the owner of the router has downloaded the copyrighted materials, not the unauthorized user. Always protect access to the wireless router.

WPS

Wi-Fi Protected Setup (WPS) is a standard developed by the Wi-Fi Alliance and intended to make it easy to configure secure access to a wireless router. Many wireless routers or other devices are WPS compliant. When a device is WPS compliant, it will typically come with a preprogrammed WPS Personal Identification Number (PIN), which consists of a series of numbers or letters, or combination of both. There are two common configuration methods for using the WPS feature: the WPS push button method and the software wizard method.

When using the software wizard method to connect a device to a wireless router, you may be prompted to enter a WPS PIN. The PIN is not the security key or passphrase. It simply makes it

Figure 16-39. Wireless routers provide connections to wireless and Ethernet cable devices.

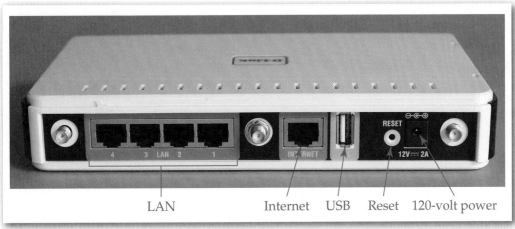

LAN   Internet   USB   Reset   120-volt power

Goodheart-Willcox Publisher

easy to configure a secure connection between the router and a network device. The WPS PIN may be requested during the automatic configuration process.

Figure 16-40 shows several options for configuring the WPS feature. The first method requests that you press the WPS button on the client device and then press the Software button located in the wizard display. The second method requests that you enter the client PIN into the wizard text box. The third method is to enter the router PIN on the client device.

Another option is to configure the security manually, which requires the network name (SSID), selecting the encryption type (WPA2/ WPA mixed mode), and entering the passphrase. Notice in Figure 16-40 that the passphrase for the router is shown (at the bottom of the screen)

as "56nlwwsywocjcb." There will be more about wireless encryption in Chapter 19—SOHO Networking.

Another method to automatically configure the secure connection to a wireless router is by pressing a WPS push button on the router and the client device. In most instances, you simply press a WPS button physically located on the router (if equipped) and then you have a time period of approximately two minutes in which to press the WPS button on the client device. The client device might have a physical WPS button or software application that generates the WPS connection negotiation with the router.

You may also be presented with an option to copy the setup configuration to a USB flash drive and then use the flash drive to configure other devices without the need to use a WPS push button or wizard.

Figure 16-41 shows the location of a WPS PIN. It is located on a sticker on the bottom of the router. There are many advantages to using the WPS feature, but there are some disadvantages too. The following lists the advantages and disadvantages of using WPS.

Figure 16-40. The Cisco Wi-Fi Protective Setup provides several different methods for automatically configuring WPS.

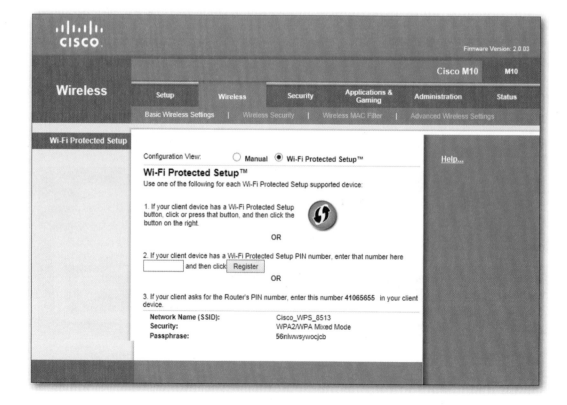

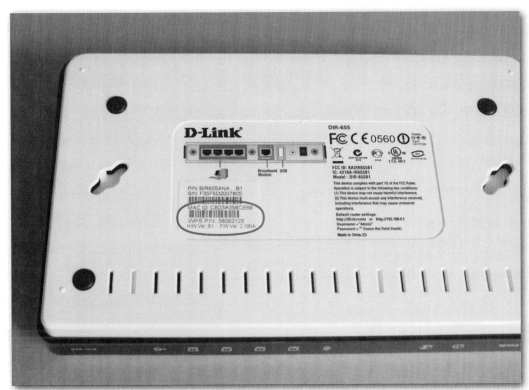

Figure 16-41.
The MAC ID and WPS PIN can be often located on the bottom of the wireless router.

Advantages of WPS

- Automatically configures the network connection to the wireless router or wireless access point without needing to know the SSID or the security key (passphrase).
- The security key (passphrase) is randomly generated and complex, which makes it more difficult for an unauthorized user to guess.
- WPS has been supported in all Windows operating systems since Windows Vista.

Disadvantages of WPS

- Each wireless device must be WPS compliant to take advantage of the feature. If a device is not WPS compliant, it can still be configured manually.
- Manual configuration can be difficult because the security key (passphrase) consists of a long series of random letters and numbers, making it difficult to remember and often resulting in typing errors.

MIMO

Multiple Input Multiple Output (MIMO) is a wireless technology that uses two or more streams of data transmission to increase the data throughput and range of the wireless network. Two of more streams of data transmitted in the same frequency channel is referred to as **spatial multiplexing (SM)**. MIMO is an integral part of the 802.11n standard. Some manufacturers have incorporated MIMO into the latest revisions of their 802.11g devices to take advantage of producing higher data rates.

Prior to MIMO, wireless access points and devices sent a single stream of data between the transmitter and receiver. MIMO uses two or more antennae, thus allowing for two or more streams of data to be transmitted simultaneously. For example, an 802.11n wireless device that transmits data at 100 Mbps can apply MIMO and raise the data rate to 200 Mbps. The latest 802.11n standard is 300 Mbps. By utilizing MIMO technology, the data rate can be raised to nearly 600 Mbps.

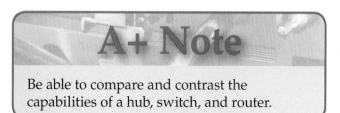
Wireless Adapter Cards

There are many different wireless network adapter designs available to choose from. The wireless network adapter in **Figure 16-42** is designed to be installed inside a desktop computer in an available motherboard expansion slot. The card is equipped with a wireless antenna. The disadvantage of this wireless design is the antenna is located on the backside of the desktop computer which may affect the wireless range, **Figure 16-43**. Since the placement of the antenna is at the back of the computer case, the office or home wall and the computer case and monitor may block the radio signals, thus reducing the overall range of the network adapter. Some wireless cards of this type have replacement antennae that consist of a flexible coaxial cable with an antenna that can be placed on the desk or wall. The cable antenna replaces the shorter original antenna.

There are many different USB wireless network adapters to choose from. **Figure 16-44** shows a mini and a micro USB wireless network adapter. These styles can fit into any available USB port on the computer. In the figure, a full-size

network adapter card is placed beside the two USB wireless adapters for the purpose of scale. As you can see, the mini and micro are quite small in overall dimensions.

Figure 16-43. The placement of a wireless network adapter can greatly affect the overall range of the wireless adapter.

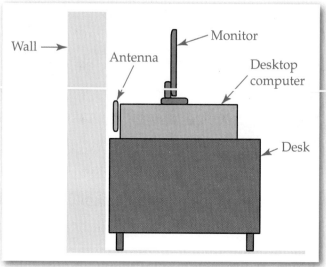

Goodheart-Willcox Publisher

Figure 16-44. A mini and micro USB wireless network adapter placed next to a full-size network adapter card.

Mini USB wireless network adapter

Micro USB wireless network adapter

Goodheart-Willcox Publisher

Figure 16-42. Some wireless adapter cards are designed to be installed inside a desktop computer in an available motherboard expansion slot.

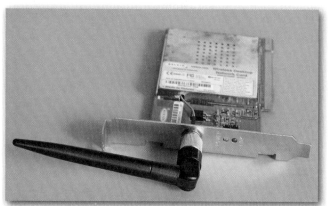

Goodheart-Willcox Publisher

A USB wireless network adapter is equipped with a much longer antenna than normal wireless network adapters. The increased antenna size directly affects the overall range of the wireless adapter, **Figure 16-45**. Another advantage is the USB cable extension that comes with the wireless adapter. The cable allows the adapter location to be easily changed without moving the computer. A slight change in wireless antenna or device location can greatly affect the range of the wireless adapter. Notice the driver disc that accompanies this particular wireless adapter. In many cases, the wireless drivers must be installed first before connecting the adapter. This is also true for other wireless devices, such as wireless access points and wireless routers.

The IEEE 802.11 standards do not express distances for wireless adapter cards. The actual distance is a direct reflection of the output power of the wireless adapter expressed in watts.

Figure 16-45. This particular USB wireless adapter has an increased range because of the larger antenna.

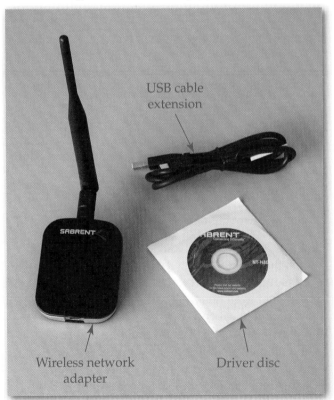

USB cable extension

SABRENT

Wireless network adapter

Driver disc

Goodheart-Willcox Publisher

Distances are subject to many factors such as physical objects and sources of radio interference. Some examples of physical objects are building walls, partitions, metal storage cabinets, and metal buildings. Some common sources of radio interference are microwave ovens, electric welding machines, cordless phones, electrical power lines, radio transmitters, portable radio equipment, baby monitors, wireless surveillance equipment such as cameras, and garage door openers.

Wireless Range Extenders

A **wireless range extender** extends the range of the wireless network. Another name for a wireless range extender is wireless repeater. The range extender in **Figure 16-46** does not provide a set of RJ-45 ports as a router does. You do not directly connect network cables to the range extender with one exception. Some wireless range extenders are equipped with an RJ-45 or a USB port to provide a way to configure the range extender directly from a computer. This particular wireless range extender uses a WPS button to connect with the main wireless router.

Wireless range extenders are affected by building materials and placement. Building material such as metal, concrete, and some types of glass adversely affect them. The placement of wireless devices in relationship to each other and the angle of a wall separating the devices can also greatly affect the wireless range. Look at **Figure 16-47** to see how placement can greatly affect the wireless signal strength when penetrating a wall at an angle of only a few degrees. When two devices such as a router and mobile device are at an angle that closely matches the length of the wall, the overall distance through the wall material is greatly increased. This is the same effect as attempting to penetrate a wall several feet thick. The signal will be greatly degraded.

Electrical devices such as appliances, ceiling fans, 2.4GHz cordless phones, microwave ovens, and similar devices generate electrical interference that can degrade the wireless device range. Try to keep wireless devices at least three feet from all electrical appliances.

Figure 16-46.
A wireless range extender extends the overall range of a wireless network.

Goodheart-Willcox Publisher

Figure 16-47.
A wireless signal can be greatly degraded by the angle transmission through a wall.

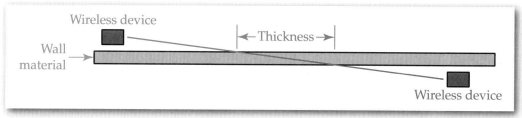

Goodheart-Willcox Publisher

A+ Note

The A+ exam has many questions requiring knowledge about wireless networking, both ad-hoc and infrastructure. Be sure to memorize the data rates and assigned frequency for each of the IEEE wireless standards.

Installing a Typical Network Interface Card

When selecting a network interface card that inserts into a motherboard expansion slot, choose a card that matches the motherboard slot type and one that matches the speed of the network.

Anti-static precautions must be taken when handling a NIC, just as with any static-sensitive device. Firmly push the NIC into the appropriate expansion slot. After it is installed, boot the computer. If you are using Windows XP or later, the operating system will most likely automatically detect the new hardware item, assign system resources, and install the proper driver. If the operating system does not detect the card automatically, you will have to install the drivers manually.

Device manufacturer websites provide complete instructions for installing a particular network adapter. Some devices also come with a CD/DVD that contains detailed instructions.

When installing a relatively new device as compared to the computer system, you may encounter a problem with the computer's ability to detect the device. In most cases when installing a new technology device into an older computer system, you must install the driver first before physically installing the device. Network adapters differ greatly physically but most have similar configuration options, such as Wake-on-LAN and adapter teaming.

Wake-on-LAN

Wake-on-LAN (WOL) is a network adapter feature that allows the adapter to wake the computer from sleep or hibernation when network activity is detected. It can even power on a computer. Wake-on-LAN is also referred to as Remote Wake-Up (RWU). This feature can be configured as either enabled or disabled. Often, it is disabled for security purposes and enabled for remote network administration by network system administrators. For the computer to be completely Wake-on-LAN capable, the network adapter, operating system, and the computer BIOS/UEFI must support the feature. For Windows, the Wake-on-LAN is enabled by default in desktop computers but disabled in laptops, **Figure 16-48**. The wake-up message sent to the network adapter is referred to as a *magic packet* by Microsoft and Intel.

Adapter Teaming

Another new feature is adapter teaming. **Adapter teaming** allows two or more network adapters to share the network load and ensure network reliability. The number of packets is divided between the two or more network adapters, which increases network performance and improved reliability. If one network adapters fails, another is still working. **Figure 16-49**.

Figure 16-48. Wake-on-LAN options for an Intel network adapter card.

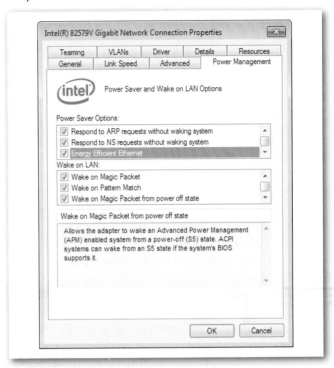

Figure 16-49. Adapter teaming allows two or more network adapters to share the network load and improve network connection reliability.

Network Adapter Speed and Operation Mode

Network adapter speed and mode of operation are automatically detected and configured. Most network adapters are capable of supporting many different network speeds such as 10 Mbps, 100 Mbps, and 1,000 Mbps. The network adapter automatically detects other device speed capabilities and adjusts the speed of the adapter to correspond. Network adapters also automatically configure the mode of operation, **Figure 16-50**. There are two modes of operation: half duplex and full duplex. A network adapter configured for half duplex can send or receive network packets, but not simultaneously. When configured for full duplex, the network adapter can send and receive packets simultaneously.

Many other options are available for most network adapters. Only the most common options were introduced here. To learn more about network adapter configuration options, visit a network adapter manufacturer website such as Intel.

Figure 16-50. The speed is automatically negotiated by the network adapter as well as full-duplex or half-duplex mode of operation.

> **A+ Note**
>
> Be prepared to answer a question about full-duplex and half-duplex mode of operation and the Wake-on-LAN feature.

Diskless Workstations

A **diskless workstation** is a workstation that runs without a floppy drive or hard disk drive. Some do have small-capacity hard drives, but they are used solely as a cache rather than for data storage. The diskless workstation relies on the file server's hard drive for application software and data storage. As you know from previous study, the hard drive contains the bootstrap program needed to boot the workstation. A diskless workstation is booted from the interaction of the NIC and the file server. The NIC is equipped with a BIOS ROM chip, which contains the boot code needed to boot the workstation and connect to the network file server.

There are some very strong advantages to diskless workstations. Diskless workstations provide extremely good security. Without a disk system for employees to use, there is no way for data files to be electronically duplicated at the workstation. In addition, diskless systems eliminate the possibility of acquiring viruses from portable storage media, such as flash drives and CDs/DVDs.

Another consideration is the overall cost of installation. By eliminating the cost of hard drives, floppy drives, and CD/DVD drives, there can be substantial savings, especially when installing several hundred or thousands of PCs in an enterprise system. Another real advantage is administration of the PCs. Because all workstations are dependent on the file server for their application software, thousands of diskless workstations can be upgraded at the same time. This results in a tremendous savings in labor costs of installing software on individual computers. The only real disadvantage is when the network is down, all workstations are affected.

Thin Client

A **thin client** is a computer that has minimal hardware resources. The typical thin client relies on other computer equipment such as network servers or the cloud as a resource for running software applications and processing data. For example, a computer intended for use by a bank employee who simply services customer accounts does not require top-of-the-line hardware such as a large hard disk storage system, very fast processor, extreme video card, or any other hardware associated with high-performance computer systems. Since the bank employee will most likely only need to access information stored on a network server and record transactions, a thin client is perfect. Thin clients that rely on cloud resources are also referred to as cloud computers or cloud clients.

Thin clients reduce the cost of equipment and software. Software applications that are run from the cloud or from a server save overall cost. Rather than install multiple copies of a software application on each computer, a single software application can be accessed through cloud services or from an application server.

In the context of discussing the term *thin client* to describe a minimal hardware system, a standard-size computer system is often referred to as a *fat client*.

Network Operating Systems (NOS)

The most common network operating systems today are Linux Server (many different versions), Windows Server (many different versions), and OS X Server. The **network operating system (NOS)** provides communications between computers, printers, and other intelligent hardware on the network. A network need not consist of a single brand of hardware or software. For example, a network may consist of Linux Server, Windows Server, and client operating systems, such as Windows 7, Windows Vista, and SUSE Linux Enterprise Desktop.

The NOS is also composed of software programs that provide security, user identity, remote access, and sharing for printers and other devices. Without the NOS, a network would be a useless collection of parts.

After completing your studies for computer service and repair, you might consider specializing in a specific server operating system such as Microsoft Server or Linux Server. Mastering a server operating system will greatly enhance your technical credentials.

OSI Model

The **Open Systems Interconnection (OSI) model** was a joint effort of international members to standardize network communication systems. The OSI model is a seven-layer model used to describe how hardware and software should work together to form a network communication system. The OSI model consists of the following:

- Layer 1—Physical.
- Layer 2—Data.
- Layer 3—Network.
- Layer 4—Transport.
- Layer 5—Session.
- Layer 6—Presentation.
- Layer 7—Application.

Physical Layer

The physical layer is the most basic layer of the model. It consists of the cable and adapter cards. The structure of this layer determines how electrical signals are carried between the devices on a network.

Data Link Layer

The data link layer describes the network's level of operation at which the raw data is packaged for transfer from one network card to another. It packages binary numbers (1s and 0s) into frames or packets for transmission between nodes.

Network Layer

The network layer is responsible for routing packets of data from one network card to another across a large network. Routing provides a means of preventing or limiting congestion on large networks. It can also prioritize the transmission of data. As data is transmitted from one computer to another, several different routes may be used. If the equipment senses too much traffic along one cable section, the data can be transmitted along a different route to avoid the congestion.

Transport Layer

The transport layer's main responsibility is to ensure the data received from a transmission is reliable. It sequences the packets of data and reassembles them in their correct order. The individual data packets that compose a single file or message may arrive by very different routes when transmitted over many miles. Also, the packets of data may not arrive in the same sequence in which they were transmitted, requiring reassembly into the correct order. This correct reassembly is especially important in the transmission of graphic images.

Session Layer

The session layer is the layer at which a connection is established between two different computers. This layer also provides system security based on computer and user name recognition. The session layer and transport layers are sometimes combined. The session layer also resolves compatibility problems between dissimilar systems, such as a PC and a Macintosh or a mainframe.

Presentation Layer

The presentation layer ensures character code recognition. It is responsible for converting the character codes from the originating computer to another form that can be recognized by the receiving computer. An example would be converting ASCII codes to EBCDIC codes. Extended Binary Coded Decimal Interchange Code (EBCDIC) is a character code widely used on mainframe computers while most PCs use the American Standard Code for Information Interchange (ASCII) character code.

Application Layer

The application layer manages network processes such as file transfer, mail service, and file-server database access. Thus far in your study of PCs, when you hear the term *application* you think of application software, such as word processing, spreadsheets, and graphic programs. These are not the same applications referred to in the OSI model. In the OSI model, the application layer strictly applies to network applications, such as web browser and e-mail software. The application is designed as a communication interface for the user. Think of the application layer as a network browser.

The OSI model clearly demonstrates the complexity of transmitting data from one computer to another and should be used as a model for a well-designed protocol. Not all software companies follow the strict guidelines of the OSI model. Many systems were already in place long before the model was developed and adopted. Some protocol systems combine two or more layers into a single unit. It is important to remember that the OSI model is simply a guide for future protocol development.

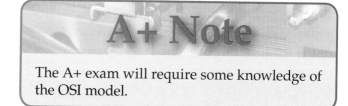

The A+ exam will require some knowledge of the OSI model.

Network Devices Defined by OSI Model

Network devices are defined by which part of the OSI model they align with. The best definitions of the common three network devices encountered, router, switch, and hub, are based on how they deliver network data. Destination or device location is based on MAC address or IPv4 and IPv6 assigned addresses. The following table lists the layer to which a standard hub, router, and switch belong.

Device	OSI Layer	Description
Router	Layer 3	Direct packet destination based on IPv4 and IPv6 addresses.
Switch	Layer 2	Direct packet destination based on MAC address.
Hub	Layer 1	Simply provides network connections.

The definition of specific devices gets clouded as more capabilities are added and then advertised by manufacturers. A smart switch and managed switch are good examples.

IEEE 802 Standards

The Institute of Electrical and Electronic Engineers (IEEE—pronounced *I triple E*) is a professional organization that continually develops standards for the networking and communication industry. The organization consists of scientists, students, commercial vendors, and other interested professionals within the industry. The IEEE's network standards are identified with an 802 prefix. Specific standards are listed here:

- IEEE 802.1 Bridging and network management.
- IEEE 802.2 Logical Link Control and Media Access Control.
- IEEE 802.3 Ethernet (CSMA/CD).
- IEEE 802.4 Token Bus (disbanded).
- IEEE 802.5 MAC layer for Token Ring (inactive).
- IEEE 802.6 Metropolitan Area Networks (disbanded).
- IEEE 802.7 Broadband LAN using coaxial cable (disbanded).
- IEEE 802.8 Fiber-optic token-passing network (disbanded).
- IEEE 802.9 Integrated voice and data (disbanded).
- IEEE 802.10 Interoperable LAN security (disbanded).
- IEEE 802.11 Wireless LAN and mesh (Wi-Fi certification).
- IEEE 802.12 Demand priority (disbanded).
- IEEE 802.13 Not Used.
- IEEE 802.14 Cable modems (disbanded).
- IEEE 802.15 Wireless PAN.
- IEEE 802.16 Wireless Broadband (WiMAX certification).
- IEEE 802.16e Mobile Broadband.
- IEEE 802.17 Resilient Packet Ring.
- IEEE 802.18 Radio Regulatory Technical Advisory Group.
- IEEE 802.19 Wireless Coexistence Technical Advisory Group.
- IEEE 802.20 Mobile Broadband Wireless Access.
- IEEE 802.21 Media Independent Handoff.
- IEEE 802.22 Wireless Regional Area Network.

Many of the standards are inactive or disbanded because there is no need for a standard any longer or another organization or entity has assumed responsibility for the standard. For example, Token Ring is no longer a viable choice of network media and is no longer in need of an up-to-date set of standards, so it is now inactive. Data Over Cable Service Interface Specification (DOCSIS) is an international organization that is now the recognized authority for Cable modem standards.

The specifications outlined in the IEEE 802 standards are not to be thought of as laws. They are a set of recommended practices that are designed to ensure the quality of a network system. However, if a contract to install a network system refers to the IEEE 802 standards, they should be thought of as law. If a new network is required to meet the IEEE 802 standards and problems arise because the standards were not followed, the installation contractor or designer of the network system can be held liable. The IEEE 802 standards will be referred to constantly throughout your studies of network systems. The most up-to-date information on the IEEE 802 standards can be obtained at IEEE Standards Association website.

Chapter Summary

- The benefits of using a network are the ability to share data and hardware, providing a centralized location to manage computer systems, increased productivity, and security.

- The client/server model is centrally administered; the peer-to-peer model is not.

- The four major categories of networks listed from smallest to largest are PAN, LAN, MAN, and WAN.

- The three major network topologies are star, ring, and bus.

- Data transmitted on a network is broken down into packets or frames, which contain the address of the PC sending the data, the address of the intended recipient, an error-checking program, and a sequence number.

- The three common types of cable-based media are coaxial, twisted pair, and fiber optic.

- The most common tools used by the network technician are the cable crimper, cable cutter, wire stripper, punch down tool, cable tracer and tone generator, cable tester, and loopback plug.

- Some basic equipment used in a network are network adapter cards, hubs, switches, routers, wireless routers, wireless adapter cards, and wireless range extenders.

- When installing a typical network interface card, take proper anti-static precautions and firmly push the adapter into the appropriate expansion slot in the motherboard.

- A diskless workstation relies on the file server's hard drive for application software and data storage; its NIC is equipped with a BIOS ROM chip, which contains the boot code needed to boot the workstation and connect to the network file server.

- A thin client is a computer that has minimal hardware resources and typically relies on other computer equipment such as network servers or the cloud as a resource for running software applications and processing data.

- The most common network operating systems are Linux Server, Windows Server, and OS X Server.

- The OSI model consists of seven layers: physical, data, network, transport, session, presentation, and application.

- The IEEE 802 standards are a set of recommended practices that ensure the quality of a network system.

Review Questions

Answer the following questions on a separate sheet of paper. Please do not write in this book.

1. What are the advantages of using a computer network system?
2. How does a large network server differ from a typical PC?

3. Name three types of dedicated servers.

4. How does a client/server network differ from a peer-to-peer network?

5. Six computers connected together in your classroom without the presence of a server would *most likely* be classified as a _____-to-_____ network.

6. Your instructor has a computer that is connected to a powerful computer in another building. This would *most likely* be classified as _____/_____ network.

7. What are the four major classifications of networks used to describe the size and complexity of a network system?

8. The Internet would be best described as a _____.
   a. LAN
   b. MAN
   c. WAN
   d. PAN

9. Rank LAN, MAN, WAN, and PAN by their typical sizes, from smallest to largest.

10. What are the three major classifications of network topologies?

11. A bus topology segment is often called a _____ or _____.

12. Define a segment for a typical ring and a typical star topology.

13. What does a typical frame of data contain?

14. What three things affect the time it takes for data to arrive at its destination?

15. What is the purpose of the QoS protocol?

16. Where would you *most likely* encounter RG-59 and RG-6 coaxial cable?

17. What are the two broad classifications of twisted pair?

18. What is the purpose of the foil shield in STP cable?

19. In twisted pair cable, what is the purpose of twisting conductors into pairs?

20. What are the major advantages of fiber-optic cable systems?

21. What are the major disadvantages of fiber-optic cable systems?

22. What technology replaced the use of a crossover cable?

23. You want to install a remote web camera outside a business for security purposes but there is no available electrical power at the outside location. What feature or specification would you look for concerning the camera?

24. What is the common Ethernet network connector associated with UTP cable?

25. What is the purpose of a punch down tool?

26. What is the purpose of a loopback plug?

27. What could you use to extend a home network without using Ethernet cables or wireless devices?

28. What wireless technology allows a user to configure a secure connection between two wireless devices using only a push button?

29. What are three advantages of Wi-Fi Protected Setup (WPS)?

30. What two factors may increase the range of a wireless device?

31. Name three factors that can adversely affect wireless device range.

32. When selecting a network adapter card that inserts into a motherboard slot, what characteristics should you match to the motherboard and the existing network?

33. What is the name of the network adapter feature or specification that enables a network administrator to turn on a computer remotely?

34. Which type of workstation relies on the file server's hard drive for application software and data storage?

35. Which type of workstation has minimal hardware resources and typically relies on other computer equipment such as network servers or the cloud as a resource for running software applications and processing data?

36. What are the three most common network operating systems?

37. Which layer of the OSI model is mainly concerned with network cables and connectors?
    a. Application
    b. Session
    c. Transport
    d. Physical

38. Which layer of the OSI model is mainly concerned with routing packets of data from one network card to another across a large network?
    a. Application
    b. Session
    c. Network
    d. Physical

39. Which IEEE standard describes Ethernet CSMA/CD?
    a. 802.3
    b. 802.5
    c. 802.11
    d. 802.15

40. Which IEEE standard describes wireless local area networks?
    a. 802.3
    b. 802.5
    c. 802.11
    d. 802.15

Sample A+ Exam Questions

Answer the following questions on a separate sheet of paper. Please do not write in this book.

1. Which of the following statements best defines a peer-to-peer network?
   a. A group of computers in which each has control of its own resources
   b. A group of computers controlled by one central computer
   c. A group of computers in which one is designated the control unit and the rest are defined as peers
   d. A group of computers in which each computer has the ability to remove any other computer from the group

2. A network limited to one particular floor of an office building would *most likely* be classified as a _____.
   a. LAN
   b. MAN
   c. WAN
   d. CAN

3. Which cable type is the most susceptible to radio interference?
   a. UTP
   b. STP
   c. Fiber optic
   d. RG-6

4. Which protocol is designed to allow network devices to advertise and exchange information?
   a. FTP
   b. LLDP
   c. POP3
   d. SMTP

5. What feature allows for automatic security configuration between two wireless devices?
   a. WPA
   b. WEP
   c. WPS
   d. Adapter teaming

6. The unintentional transfer of data between individual wires inside a network cable, such as Cat 5e, is called _____.
   a. impedance
   b. attenuation
   c. cross talk
   d. broadcast storm

7. Which of the following best represents a network card MAC address?
   a. 123.202.16.24
   b. 1673452
   c. 00 A1 23 12 C2 F1
   d. CF12D

8. A web browser program would be located at which layer of the OSI model?
   a. Presentation
   b. Application
   c. Session
   d. Network

9. Which of the following protocols is associated with transferring data using infrared light?
   a. TCP/IP
   b. MIMO
   c. FIP
   d. ATM

10. Cat 5e provides less signal _____ than Cat 5 cable.
    a. strength
    b. loss
    c. quality
    d. cost

Suggested Laboratory Activities

Do not attempt any suggested laboratory activities without your instructor's permission. Certain activities can render the PC operating system inoperable.

1. Construct a small peer-to-peer network using two or more PCs and a switch.
2. Make a Cat 5 or Cat 5e cable for connecting a PC to a switch or hub.
3. Install a network card.

Network Administration

17

After studying this chapter, you will be able to:

- Implement the various types of file sharing available in Windows XP and later.
- Identify the characteristics of centralized and decentralized network administration.
- Identify the features of Windows Server 2012.
- Recall the general procedures and tools used for installing multiple copies of an operating system and application software onto multiple computers.
- Identify the most common RAID levels and their characteristics.
- Differentiate between Microsoft Storage Spaces and Storage Pools.

A+ Exam—Key Points

The CompTIA A+ Certification exam does not go into great depth with regards to networks, but the exam will test your basic knowledge of network administration. You should be prepared to answer questions like the following:

- Who controls system logons?
- Who controls system security?
- How do you log on to a workstation?
- How do you set up a peer-to-peer share?

Also, be prepared to identify differences between share permissions and security (NTFS) permissions.

Key Terms

The following key terms will become important pieces of your computer vocabulary. Be sure you can define them.

Access Control List (ACL)
Active Directory
answer file
deployment image
domain
domain user account
fault tolerance
group
HomeGroup
Libraries
local user account
network administration

network administrator
Public Folders
RAID
Security Accounts Manager (SAM)
Security Identifier (SID)
share
Simple File Sharing
user
unattended installation
Windows Automated Installation
    Kit (WAIK)

Network administration is the use of network software packages to manage network system operations. The central focus of network administration is network security and coordination of shared resources on the network. In this chapter, the fundamentals of network administration are covered. It is important to have a basic understanding of network operations when troubleshooting PCs that are connected to a network. You must be able to determine if the problem is PC-related or network-related. This chapter is not intended to prepare you for the Network+ Certification exam, but it will help you begin the process of achieving such additional certification if you desire.

Network administration in the corporate world is a vast subject requiring years of study and experience. To be competent in a single networking software package can take years. Home and small business networks are becoming more popular every day. Therefore, it is imperative that you have a basic understanding of peer-to-peer networks.

Windows Server is also introduced in this chapter. A complete understanding of Windows Server administration would take a complete course of study. This chapter only introduces the very basic concepts you need as a PC technician.

The main purpose of networking computers and hardware is to share data and equipment. The shared data is in the form of documents, music, videos, and pictures. The shared equipment

are devices such as printers, network storage devices, and Internet access devices, such as cable modems. Sharing is accomplished in one of two administrative models: peer-to-peer or client/server. These two administrative models were introduced in the previous chapter. This chapter explores them in detail.

Peer-to-Peer Network Administration

Peer-to-peer (P2P) networks are common, especially in home and small business offices. These networks can be set up easily and administered to allow users to share files, printers, hardware, and Internet connections. You can set up a peer-to-peer network using any Windows PC operating system. Windows PC operating systems typically limit the number of concurrent connections from 10 to 20 users, depending on the operating system edition. Larger networking systems require a client/server operating system.

Tech Tip

Windows 7 and later allow up to 20 concurrent connections to a shared resource. Prior to Windows 7, a maximum of ten concurrent connections were allowed, with the exception of Windows Vista Home edition which only allowed five.

Administrative functions in a peer-to-peer network are not highly organized and are best described as decentralized. In a decentralized administrative system, no one person controls the network. All users have equal rights on the network, and each user usually controls access to their own files and hardware.

To create a peer-to-peer network, all that is required is an operating system that supports peer-to-peer networking and a network adapter card for each PC participating in the network. Ever since Windows XP, creating a peer-to-peer network with Windows is very easy. In fact, Microsoft has continued to make peer-to-peer networking easier with each new edition of an operating system.

Peer-to-peer is also referred to as a *workgroup network*. Computer membership configuration to a workgroup or domain is selected when the Windows operating system is first installed. A computer is configured for membership to a workgroup by default. You can view the name of the workgroup or domain by opening the **System** dialog box. In **Figure 17-1** you can see how the name of the workgroup appears. Notice that membership to a workgroup or domain can be changed and the workgroup renamed.

Network and Sharing Center

The Network and Sharing Center is a centralized location in Windows Vista and later that provides links to many related networking tools and wizards and displays the current network status. From the Network and Sharing Center, you can view the status of the network connection and the name of the local area network, access and change the network adapter configuration and sharing settings, add and configure new network connections, and more. Look at **Figure 17-2** and compare the Network and Sharing Center for Windows Vista, Windows 7, and Windows 8.

As you can see, the Network and Sharing Center user interface has changed with each edition of Windows. The Network and Sharing Center performs most of the same, but not all, networking tasks throughout all three versions of

Windows. For example, the option **View full map** or **See full map** no longer exists in Windows 8. The Windows Vista **Sharing and Discovery** section was changed to **Change your networking settings** in Windows 7 and Windows 8. The Windows Vista version allows you to directly change file, folder, and printer sharing settings. Windows 7 and Windows 8 provides the **Change advanced sharing settings** link in the left pane, which takes you to the **Advanced sharing settings** dialog box and allows you to configure the sharing settings. The **Advanced sharing settings** dialog box is covered later in this chapter.

> ## A+ Note
>
> The A+ exam always has several questions about shares, permissions, and user accounts.

Local User Account

The **local user account** is configured on the workstation and controls access to specific resources on that specific workstation. You can have multiple local user accounts, one assigned to each user of that particular workstation. Local user accounts are created in the **User Accounts** dialog box. This dialog box is accessed in Windows XP through **Control Panel | User Accounts** and in Windows Vista, Windows 7, and Windows 8 through **Control Panel | User Accounts and Family Safety | User Accounts**.

For added security in a peer-to-peer, or workgroup-based, network, a user account should be set up for each user on each computer that the user plans to log on to and use. The main characteristics of a local user account include the following:

- Associated with a peer-to-peer, or a workgroup-based, network.
- Needed to access resources at the local computer.
- Authenticated through the computer at which the account is created.
- Maintained on the computer at which the account is created.

Figure 17-1. The name of the workgroup a computer belongs to can be viewed in the **System** dialog box. This dialog box allows you to change membership to a workgroup or domain and to rename the workgroup.

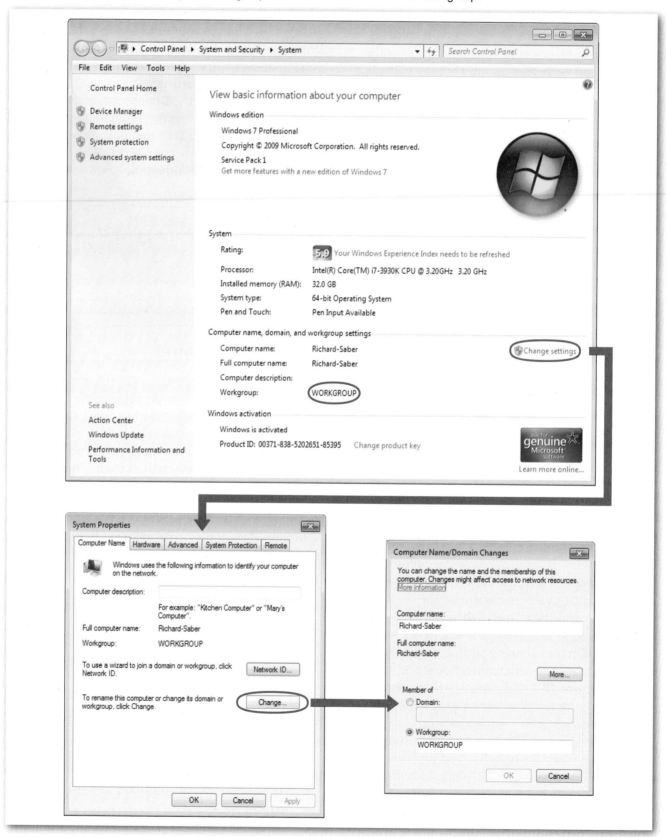

Figure 17-2. The Network and Sharing Center provides a centralized location to view the current status of the local area network and provides links to many related network configuration tools and wizards.

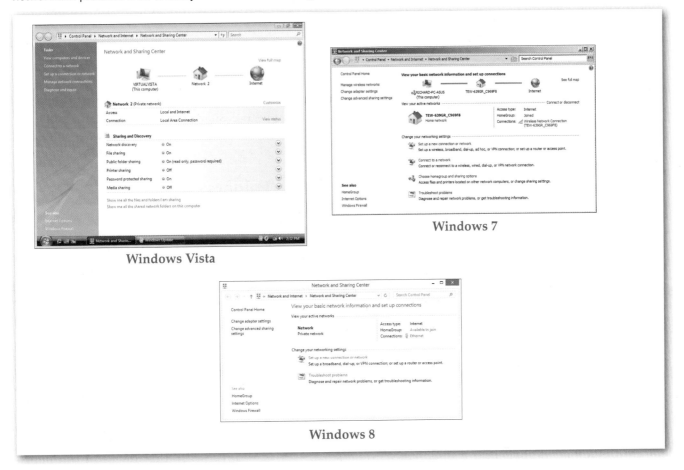

Windows Vista

Windows 7

Windows 8

Windows PC Shares

A share is an object that is shared across the network, such as a file, hard drive, DVD drive, printer, or scanner. Sharing has changed quite a bit from the early days of computing. The way to configure shared objects can vary according to which operating system you are using. As Windows operating systems evolved, Microsoft introduced new sharing techniques such as Simple File Sharing in Windows XP, the Public Folders feature in Windows Vista, and HomeGroup and Libraries in Windows 7. All Windows operating systems also use advanced (classic) file sharing. In advanced file sharing, the user configures a folder as a shared resource and selects who can access the folder and with what permissions. The basic concepts of advanced sharing still continue today for all Windows operating systems. Each major operating system sharing method is explored in the following sections.

Simple File Sharing

Windows XP introduced the Simple File Sharing feature. Simple File Sharing is enabled by default and designates the Shared Documents folder as a shared resource.

The Simple File Sharing feature can be enabled and disabled through the **Folder Options** dialog box and by selecting or deselecting the **Use simple file sharing** option. This dialog box is accessed through **My Computer | Tools | View tab | Folder Options**, Figure 17-3.

Figure 17-3. Windows XP introduced the Simple File Sharing feature. It can be enabled and disabled in the **Folder Options** dialog box.

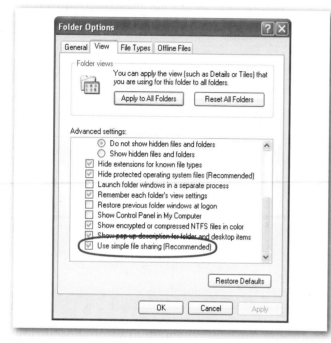

The Windows Home Edition only uses Simple File Sharing. Therefore, it does not have an option to enable and disable this feature.

When Simple File Sharing is enabled, a Shared Documents folder is automatically created. See **Figure 17-4**. Notice that the Shared Documents folder contains the My Music folder and My Pictures folder by default. New Folder was created by the user. Additional items, such as other folders and documents, can be added to Shared Documents to be automatically shared with other users. When an item is shared in Windows XP, an open hand icon is used to show the resource is shared, **Figure 17-5**.

Public Folders

Windows Vista, Windows 7, and Windows 8 uses a feature similar to Simple File Sharing called **Public Folders**. When the Public Folders feature is enabled, the Public folder located under C:\Users\ is configured as a share. Beneath the Public folder are the following subfolders:

- Public Desktop.
- Public Documents.
- Public Downloads.
- Public Music.
- Public Pictures.
- Public Videos.
- Recorded TV.

The Public folder and its subfolders are created by default; however, sharing is not enabled.

Figure 17-4.
When Simple File Sharing is enabled, a **Shared Documents** folder is created and appears under **Other Places** in the left pane of Windows Explorer.

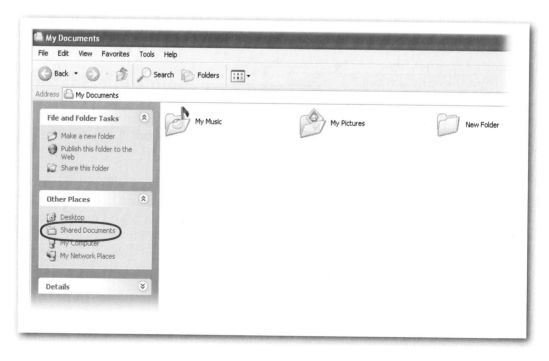

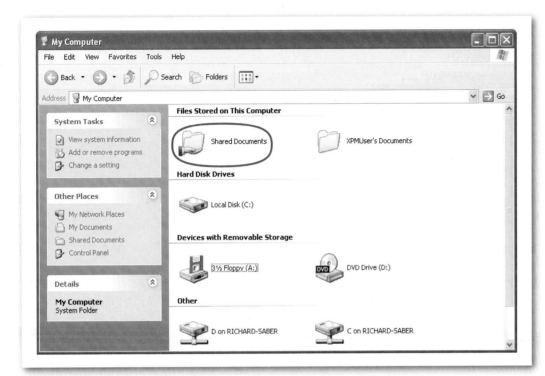

Figure 17-5.
An open hand indicates
a shared resource in
Windows XP.

Figure 17-6 shows the default location of the Public folder. Notice the icon next to it. A shared folder in Windows Vista appears with a two-people icon. Earlier Windows operating systems identified a shared folder with an open hand under the folder.

Figure 17-7 shows the subfolders beneath the Public folder. Once the Public folder feature is enabled, the contents of the Public folder and its subfolders can be shared with other users of the same computer or with anyone on the local area network.

The sharing of other folders can be simplified by enabling the Sharing Wizard. The Sharing Wizard is activated when a user right-clicks a file or directory to be shared and selects **Sharing**. It guides a user through setting up the share, such as selecting the users with whom to share the file or directory and selecting the permission to assign them. The Sharing Wizard is enabled through the **Folder Options** dialog box and by selecting **Use Sharing Wizard (Recommended)** option. In Windows Vista, access the **Folder Options** dialog box through **Windows Explorer | Tools | Folder Options**. For Windows 7, it is accessed through **Windows Explorer | Organize | Folder and search options**, and for Windows 8 it is accessed through **Windows Explorer | View | Options | Change folder and search options**.

> **Tech Tip**
>
> In Windows Vista and later, users who do not have permission to access a shared folder will no longer be able to see the folder. In previous versions of Windows, it was possible to view a shared folder even when you did not have permission to access the folder.

HomeGroup and Libraries

The HomeGroup and Libraries features were introduced in Windows 7 and are used to automatically configure sharing between Windows 7 and Windows 8 computers in a local area network. A **HomeGroup** is a group of PCs that can share libraries and printers. The PCs must run Windows 7, Windows 8, or Windows RT to participate in a HomeGroup. Windows 8.1 does not include Libraries by default. **Libraries** are a virtual collection of folders and files from different locations displayed as a single virtual folder. The library folders and files are displayed

Figure 17-6.
A two-people icon by
a folder indicates the
folder is shared.

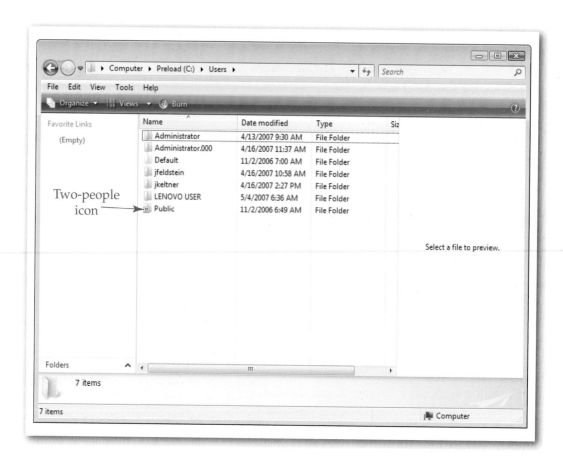

Figure 17-7.
Default folders within
the **Public** folder.

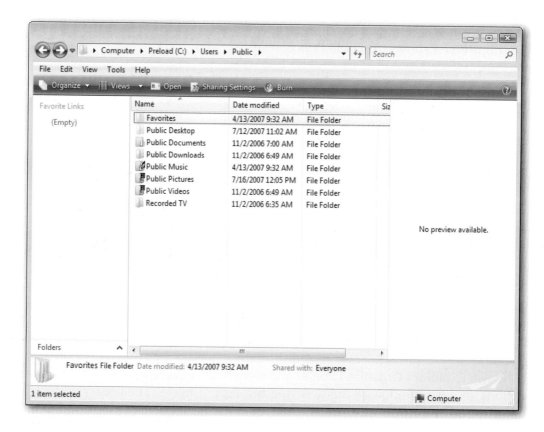

as a single collection on the computer, but they are actually located on other computers. When you share libraries with a HomeGroup, all folders within the Libraries folder (including the Public folders) are shared. For example, if you share the Documents library, this shares the My Documents and Public Documents folders.

Using Libraries

There are four default libraries (Documents, Music, Pictures, and Videos), but additional libraries can be created. For example, a collection of a specific type of document, such as work documents, can be added to the library. The user can then move between a desktop computer and a laptop or tablet and have virtual access to the collection of work documents created on the original computer.

The user has complete access to these files. All that is required is that the user set up a user account on each computer with the same account name and password. The Library then identifies the user's files on all computers in which the user has an account and it puts them together as a virtual collection on each computer.

The HomeGroup and Libraries features are not supported in Windows Vista and Windows XP. Sharing between Windows 7 or Windows 8 and previous versions of Windows is achieved through advanced (classic) file sharing.

The HomeGroup feature is available in all editions of Windows 7. However, in Windows 7 Starter and Windows 7 Home Basic, you can join a HomeGroup, but you cannot create one. Windows XP and Windows Vista computers cannot join a HomeGroup, but you can still share files with Windows 7 and Windows 8 computers by using the advanced sharing method.

Creating a HomeGroup

To create a HomeGroup, your computer must be running Windows 7 Home Premium or Windows 8. When the operating system is first installed, you will be prompted to create a HomeGroup and to write down the security password for joining other computers to the HomeGroup. You have an option not to create a HomeGroup during the operating system installation. If you do not create a HomeGroup at

time of installation, you can create a HomeGroup later by going through the Network and Sharing Center.

Look at **Figure 17-8** to see the types of objects that can be configured for automatic sharing. The folder objects are pictures, music, videos, and documents. The Documents folder is not shared by default. It must be selected before it can be shared with members of the HomeGroup. There is also an option to share printers. In this example, you see another HomeGroup has been automatically detected and there is a **Join now** button, which allows users to join the HomeGroup if they know the password. The password can be viewed through **Control Panel** on the computer that created the HomeGroup.

Look closely at the options available under **Other HomeGroup actions**. These options will guide you through the most common tasks associated with maintaining a HomeGroup. When you select the **Change advanced sharing settings** option, the **Advanced sharing settings** dialog box will appear and you will see two options: **Home or Work** and **Public**, **Figure 17-9**.

When either one of these two options is selected, a complete list of configuration options is revealed. **Figure 17-10** shows the configuration options for the Home or Work profile. The configuration options for the Home or Work profile are as follows:

- Network discovery.
- File and printer sharing.
- Public folder sharing.
- Media streaming.
- File sharing connections.
- Password protected sharing.
- HomeGroup connections.

The Public profile is shown in **Figure 17-11**. Notice that it has the same configuration options as the Home or Work profile, except for HomeGroup connections. The Public profile has no option for HomeGroup connections because HomeGroup is disabled in the Public profile.

Password Protected Sharing

In Figure 17-11, notice the options to enable and disable password protected sharing: **Turn on password protected sharing** and **Turn off password protected sharing**. When password protected

Figure 17-8. A HomeGroup allows you to easily share resources, such as pictures, music, videos, documents, and printers.

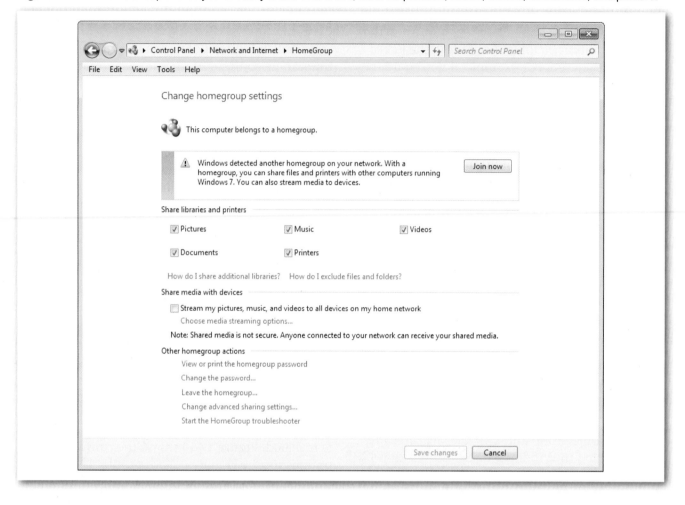

Figure 17-9. Advanced sharing settings dialog box.

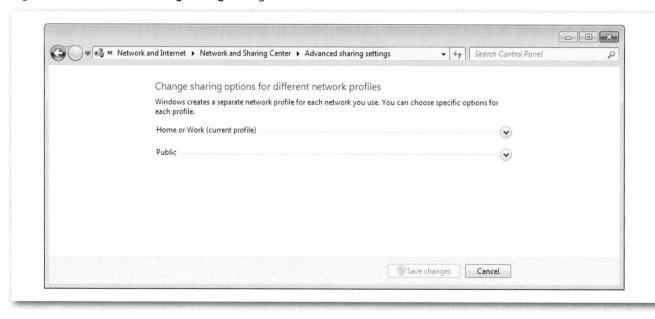

Figure 17-10. Configuration options for the Home or Work profile.

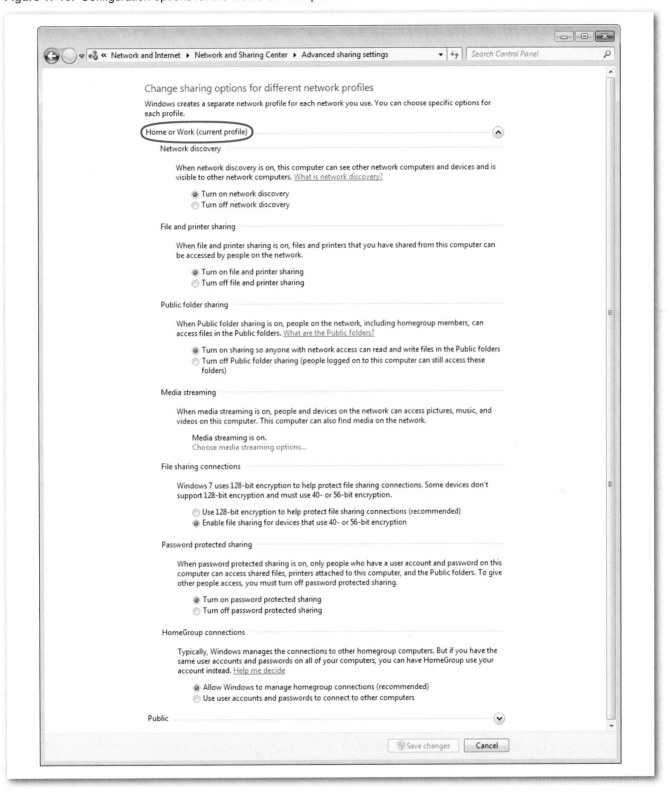

Figure 17-11. Configuration options for the Public profile.

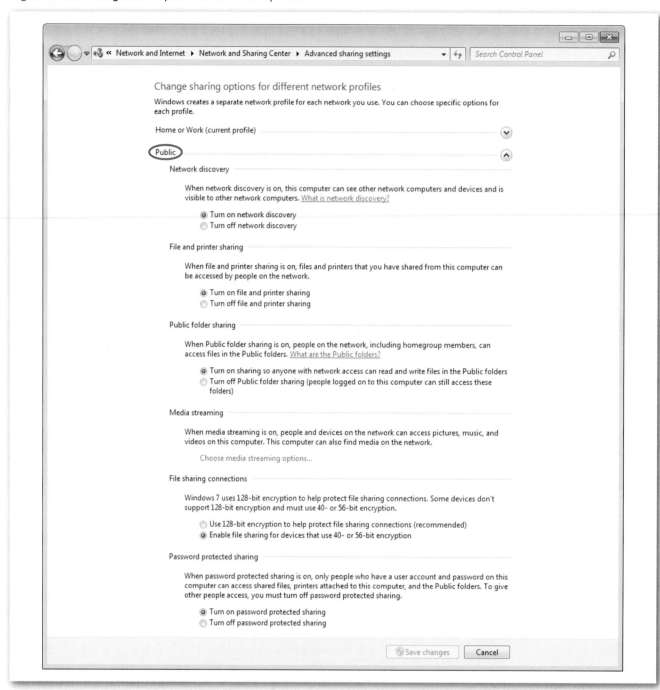

sharing is enabled, users on other computers will not be able to access shared folders on that computer, including the Public folder(s). To access the shared folder from a different computer, the user must have a local user account on the computer with the shared resource. To provide access to a shared resource, you must do one of the following:

- Configure each computer with the same user account name and password.
- Enable password protected sharing.

Remember, when you disable password protected sharing, everyone on the network can access the shared resource and no user account or password is required.

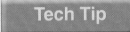

Tech Tip   It is very important that you set passwords for shares, especially if the same workstation will be connecting to the Internet.

Network Discovery

Notice the **Network discovery** option in Figure 17-10 and Figure 17-11. Network Discovery makes setting up and configuring a network easy as it automatically detects and configures a network and sets up a share and Internet connection. This feature was introduced in Windows Vista and continues to be supported by Windows 7 and Windows 8. It is directly related to the network location chosen when connecting to a wired network, a wireless network, or remotely across the Internet to a work location.

Windows 7 can be configured for three network locations: home, work, and public, **Figure 17-12**. Network locations are also referred to by Microsoft as network profiles. The following describes each location:

- **Home network:** A home location and all computers on the network are trusted.
- **Work network:** A work location and all computers are trusted. This may also be used for a home office.
- **Public network:** A public area, such as a coffee shop, airport, or hotel. Other computers on the network are not trusted.

There is a fourth network location known as a domain network. A domain network typically uses a network server to control access to the network. It is configured and controlled by the network administrator and is not a location indicated in the three choices in the **Set Network Location** dialog box.

The HomeGroup feature is disabled for domain network locations. You cannot create a HomeGroup while you are connected to a domain, but you can join a HomeGroup and access shared resources in the HomeGroup.

Windows 8 provides two choices of network location Public and Private, unless the Windows 8 computer is connected to a domain.

Changing the network location is simple in Windows 7. Open the **Network and Sharing Center** and click the current network location.

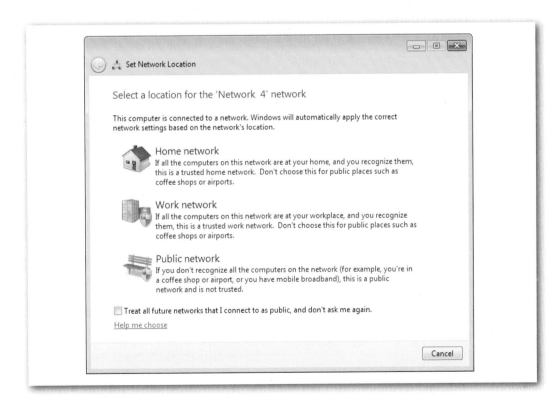

Figure 17-12.
The three network locations for Windows 7 are home, work, and public.

See **Figure 17-13**. The **Set Network Location** dialog box will appear, providing you with three choices of network locations: **Home network**, **Work network**, and **Public network**.

Changing the network location in Windows 8 is quite different than in Windows 7. The network location is changed by clicking the **Network Connections** icon located in the notification area of the taskbar. This will open the **Networks** menu. Right-click the network connection and select **Turn sharing on or off** from the shortcut menu. You will be prompted with two options: **No, don't turn on sharing or connect to devices** and **Yes, turn on sharing and connect to devices**. See **Figure 17-14**. Selecting the first option will set the location to Public. The second option will set the location to Private.

Advanced File Sharing

All Windows operating systems have the ability to use the advanced file sharing options. Advanced file sharing provides much more detailed options that are not used in Simple File Sharing and HomeGroup. These options, however, are not intended for the novice user.

To set up advanced sharing in Windows XP, right-click the folder to be shared. A shortcut menu will appear, **Figure 17-15**. Select the **Sharing and Security** option. The **Properties** dialog box will open to the **Sharing** tab. The **Sharing** tab

exposes options for enabling folder sharing, naming the share, selecting the number of users allowed to access the shared folder, and viewing and configuring folder permissions. See **Figure 17-16**. To set permissions, you can click the **Permissions** button or select the **Security** tab. Clicking the **Permissions** button will take you directly to the **Security** tab.

A folder's **Properties** dialog box will have a different appearance and options than when Simple File Sharing is disabled. Compare Figure 17-16A (Simple File Sharing disabled) to **Figure 17-17** (Simple File Sharing enabled). Notice that there is no **Security** tab to select user permissions when Simple File Sharing is enabled. The security options are very limited when using Simple File Sharing. You can only select the following options:

- **Make this folder private**.
- **Share this folder on the network**.
- **Allow network users to change my files**.

When the folder is made private, only the owner of the folder has access to it. Not even the system administrator can access the folder. When the folder is configured as a share on the network, everyone has access to the shared folder contents. They can read the contents but not change the file contents. When the option to allow network users to change files is selected, all network users can access and change the contents of the folder. As you can see, the term *simple file sharing* is very appropriate.

Figure 17-13.
To change the network location of your computer in Windows 7, click the current network location in the **Networking and Sharing Center**. The **Set Network Location** dialog box will appear with the choices **Home network**, **Work network**, and **Public network**.

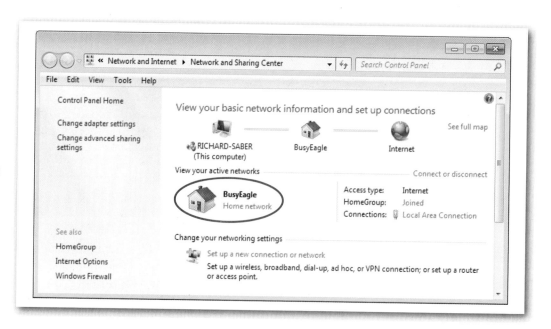

Figure 17-14. Changing the network location in Windows 8. Selecting **No, don't turn on sharing or connect to devices** changes the network to the Public location setting. Selecting **Yes, turn on sharing or connect to devices** changes the network to the Private location setting.

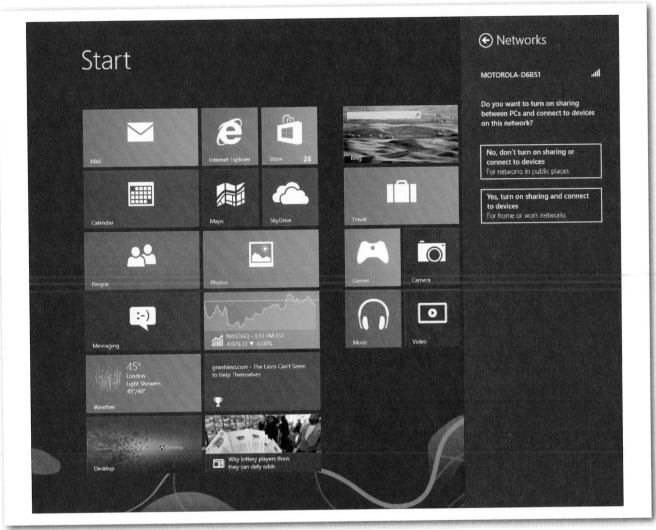

Figure 17-15. To share a folder in Windows XP using advanced file sharing, right-click the folder to be shared and select the **Sharing and Security** option.

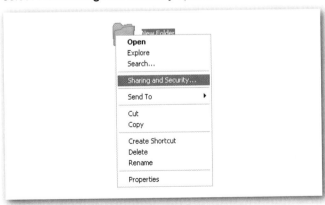

Tech Tip

Windows XP Home edition has Simple File Sharing enabled by default. Windows XP Professional uses advanced (classic) file sharing when connected to a network domain.

A+ Note

Be familiar with how to disable Windows XP Simple File Sharing. You should also know that you cannot view file share permissions when Simple File Sharing is enabled.

Figure 17-16. Setting up advanced file sharing in Windows XP. A—The **Sharing** tab exposes options to share the folder and select the number of users allowed to access the folder. B—The **Security** tab allows you to configure folder security permissions such as full control, read, write, and more.

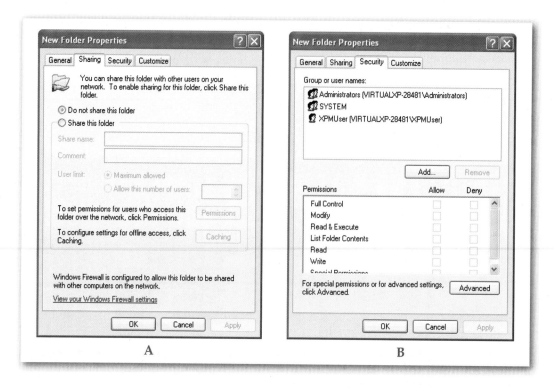

Figure 17-17. When Simple File Sharing is enabled, there are less folder sharing options and no **Security** tab, thus no selection of folder permissions.

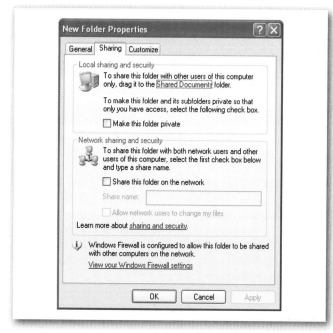

Figure 17-18. Setting up advanced file sharing in Windows Vista and later. Clicking the **Advanced Sharing** button on the **Sharing** tab of a folder's properties dialog box opens the **Advanced Sharing** dialog box.

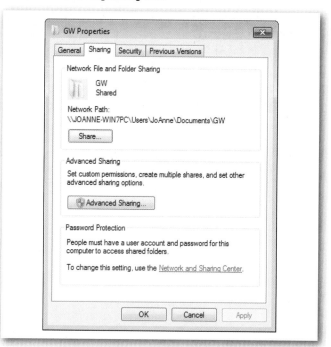

To set up advanced sharing in Windows Vista, Windows 7, and Windows 8, right-click the folder to be shared. From the shortcut menu, select **Properties** and then the **Sharing** tab, **Figure 17-18**.

Click the **Advanced Sharing** button. The **Advanced File Sharing** dialog box will appear, similar to that in **Figure 17-19**. Select the **Share this folder** option,

Figure 17-19. Advanced Sharing dialog box. Clicking the **Permissions** button opens the **Permissions** dialog box.

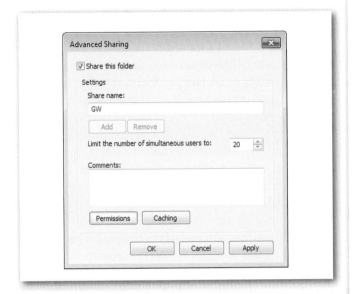

Figure 17-20. Permissions dialog box.

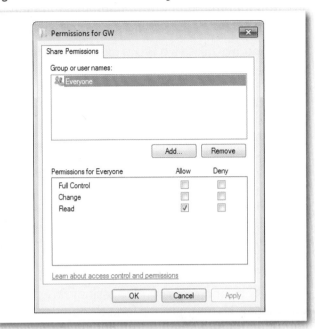

and then click **Permissions**. In the **Permissions** dialog box, **Figure 17-20**, you can select the group or users with whom to share the folder as well as select permissions. The following table

summarizes which sharing features belong to each Windows operating system.

Feature	Windows XP	Windows Vista	Windows 7	Windows 8
Centralized Network Tool	My Network Places	Network and Sharing Center	Network and Sharing Center	Network and Sharing Center
Simple File Sharing	Yes	No	No	No
Public Folders	No	Yes	Yes	Yes
Shared Folders	Shared Documents	Public Documents, Public Downloads, Public Music, Public Pictures, Public Videos, Recorded TV	Public Documents, Public Music, Public Pictures, Public Videos	Public Documents, Public Music, Public Pictures, Public Videos
HomeGroup	No	No	Yes	Yes
Libraries	No	No	Yes	Yes/No Win 8.1
Advanced file sharing	Yes	Yes	Yes	Yes

Note: Windows 8.1 no longer supports the Libraries feature.

Share Permissions and Security Permissions

Windows uses two types of file and folder permissions: Share permissions and Security permissions. Security permissions are also referred to as NTFS permissions. Shared folders have a combination of share and security permissions.

Share permissions apply to users who access the resource over the network. Share permissions do not apply if a user logs on locally to the computer. Security permissions can only be applied to resources that are located on a volume/partition that is formatted with the NTFS file system.

Look at **Figure 17-21** for a comparison of share permissions and security permissions. You will only see three permissions for a resource when the resource has a FAT partition. These permissions are full control, change, and read. NTFS partitions support a wider range of permissions.

When a user logs on to a computer, he or she is assigned a unique **Security Identifier (SID)**, which is an identification code used to determine what Share and Security permissions have been assigned to the user. Every user, group, and computer has a unique SID assigned. In an Active Directory domain controlled by a Windows server, an **Access Control List (ACL)** database is used to match a user SID to the resource and then allow or deny access to it. During a local computer logon, the user logs on using the local user account in the **Security Accounts Manager (SAM)**, a registry file used to maintain the user account database on a computer. A local logon grants access only to that particular computer's resources. Local user and group SAM membership is used to manage access to local resources. A user is issued a security token after a successful logon. This token contains security information based on the SID. The contents of the security token is compared to the SAM or ACL, which determines if the user has the correct permissions to access a shared resource.

Tech Tip

When you share a folder, the Everyone group is given the read permission by default.

Figure 17-21.
The partition format style determines which set of permissions can be assigned to a shared resource. A—Permissions for a share formatted with FAT. B—Permissions for a share formatted with NTFS.

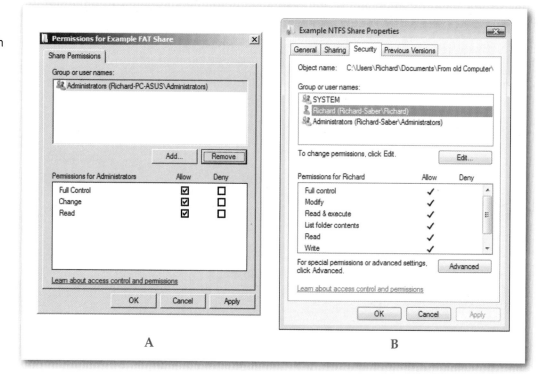

Figure 17-22. When the Network folder is expanded in Windows Explorer, all devices connected to the network are shown.

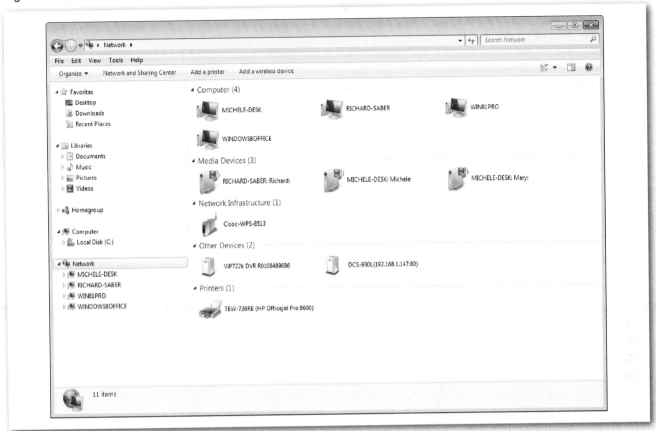

Accessing a Shared Resource

You access a shared resource by first opening Windows Explorer and expanding the Network folder which is located in the left pane. This will expose all the network locations, such as other computers, external drives, network storage, and devices.

Figure 17-22 shows the Network folder expanded and a list of computers, media devices, network infrastructure devices, and other devices. The other devices can be most anything that is accessible through the network, such as remote cameras and television interface devices.

To access the shared resource, you simply navigate to the network device through Windows Explorer and then double-click the device icon. You can also right-click and then select **Open** from the shortcut menu. You will then be presented with a **Windows Security** dialog box prompting you for a user account name and password for the

remote location, **Figure 17-23**. The user account name and password control access to the network device. A failure to access the device is caused

Figure 17-23. When accessing a shared resource, you will be presented with a **Windows Security** dialog box prompting you for a user account name and password for the remote location.

Figure 17-24.
A message box similar to this one typically appears after a failed logon attempt to a network resource.

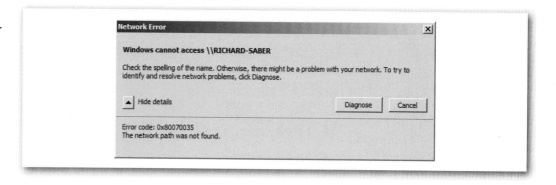

by improper credentials (no user account for the device) or a failure of the network infrastructure, such as a bad cable or the device being offline. A network connection failure usually generates a message box similar to the one in **Figure 17-24**.

Look again at the **Windows Security** dialog box in Figure 17-23. Notice that there is a **Remember my credentials** option. This option is used to save your logon name and password (credentials). When checked, the next time you access the share, you will not need to supply a user account name and password. When you access a network share and do not check the **Remember my credentials** option, you can still access the network resource for several hours without the need to enter your user name and password.

Network share access in a network domain does not require individual user accounts for each network resource. The user account credentials are activated when you log on to the domain.

Centralized Network Administration

This part of the chapter introduces you to the client/server network administration model also referred to as the *domain network model*. The client/server network model is based on administration of the network being controlled by a centralized server and administrator. This type of network has a server which controls the user authentication.

All files pertaining to users, groups, and computers connected to the client/server network are contained in the file server. A network may be composed of many file servers sharing the burden of the network system. In the early Windows NT networks, one file server was known as the

primary domain controller and the others were called *backup domain controllers*. The primary domain controller (PDC) kept the master record of all user accounts, and the backup domain controllers (BDC) kept backup copies of the user accounts. The redundancy helped to protect against losing information about the users if the primary domain controller should fail or crash. In today's systems, all servers can be configured with equal responsibilities. They no longer require the notation of *primary* and *backup*.

> **Tech Tip**
>
> The terms *primary domain controller* and *backup domain controller* have become legacy terms. The newer network operating systems technologies do not require a primary domain controller or a backup domain controller, except when the network incorporates legacy network systems. Often, you simply see the term *domain controller* which implies a primary domain controller.

The most commonly encountered network operating systems used for managing large networks are UNIX, Linux, and Windows. Each of these systems will be briefly introduced.

UNIX

UNIX is the oldest of the four server operating systems. It was written in the C programming language and was mainly intended for use on minicomputers. One of the things that made it so popular was that it was not computer specific. In the early days of computers, operating systems were written specifically for certain computer types. You could only use an operating system on a specific brand and model of computer. Today, you can run most software across the boundaries of different manufacturers with relatively few restrictions.

UNIX was adopted by IBM and became the standard operating system for its RISC-based systems. UNIX is still used on many mainframe computers and enterprise servers. The original UNIX operating system required a mainframe computer to meet the operating system hardware requirements. Early PC models did not have sufficient hardware to support the UNIX operating system. Today, many variations of UNIX exist, such as the numerous Linux versions that are designed to run on a PC. Today's PCs have more computing power than the early mainframe computers.

Novell NetWare/SUSE

Novell NetWare was developed by Novell. It was a popular network operating system in the 1980s and into the 1990s. The early versions of NetWare were very complex to use because they were only equipped with a command line interface. To perform functions, commands had to be typed in at the command line rather than issued by clicking an icon. Later versions incorporated a graphical user interface (GUI), and you could simply point and click to access its features. In 2004, Novell acquired SUSE Linux and offered as an alternative to NetWare, the SUSE Linux Enterprise server. Today, Novell no longer exists as the original Novell NetWare Company. Novell was acquired by The Attachment Group in 2011. The Attachment Group provides client software for UNIX and existing NetWare systems and offers SUSE Linux as a server operating system.

> **Tech Tip**
>
> The term *platform* is often used as a synonym for *operating system*.

Microsoft Windows Server

Microsoft has provided a wide variety of Windows Server operating systems. It introduced the Windows NT Server in 1993, which was the first server operating system that featured a GUI. Prior to Windows NT, server operating systems only used a command line interface. You had to type commands at a prompt when configuring the server, such as adding or configuring user accounts. As you can imagine, when Microsoft introduced the GUI, the Windows Server operating system gained in popularity. Some other network operating systems, such as Novell, were slow to embrace the GUI and consequently lost the dominance of the server operating system market. Today, Microsoft provides more server operating systems than any other company.

The next significant development Microsoft made to the operating system was Active Directory, which is still part of the Microsoft Server operating systems. Windows 2000 Server (introduced in 2000) was the first server operating system designed on the Active Directory technology. This technology removed many restrictions imposed by the Windows NT domain file structure limitations.

Early network systems were limited in their size as compared to today's large network systems. It was difficult to configure file servers for multiple servers present in a network system. **Active Directory** allows files and information to be easily shared across large enterprise networks. Active Directory technology is based on the Lightweight Directory Access Protocol (LDAP). With the implementation of Active Directory, a user or group member can simply log on once and have complete access to resources across the entire system. With Windows NT Server, users had to be authenticated for each individual domain, and trust relationships needed to be set up between network domains.

> **Tech Tip**
>
> Active Directory is typically taught as an entire course. Microsoft has a certification just for Active Directory design and configuration.

Linux

Linux is one of the latest network operating systems to be fully developed. Because the source code is available to the public, there are many different Linux operating systems available. Linux has become very popular because its source code is readily available to the public, and it is relatively inexpensive compared to other network operating systems.

Most software companies guard their source code and only release sufficient information about the code to allow third-party developers to write software to enhance their product. By having the complete listing of source code for the Linux operating system, programmers can write any feature they desire into the networking software. Anyone with reasonable programming skills can use the open source code to build a network operating system of their own specifications. Even though major software companies now build networking software packages based on Linux, the pricing remains very reasonable.

However, complete access to source code does have a price. In this case, it is security. If you have complete access to the source code, so does every interested hacker in the world. To abide by the Linux software copyright regulations, if you use the Linux source code to develop your software system, you must allow access to any and all modifications to the code when you market it. As far as security goes, everyone has a road map to your system's operations when the source code is freely distributed.

Linux is used as the programmable operating system for many electronic products, such as digital recorders, television systems, music systems, and telephones. Many network models incorporate a Linux server and a server of another network operating system. For example, the front-end server (the part that allows users to access the network) uses a standard high-security package such as those provided by UNIX or Windows Server. This provides the security that the network must have. To cut operating cost, a Linux system is used as a mail server or web server.

Network Administration Models

Each major software vender uses its own terminology to describe its network organization. They are all similar for the most part, and terminologies can be easily transferred from one system to another without losing their intended

meanings. The terminology used in this chapter is primarily based on the Microsoft network systems. Concentrating on one system in generic fashion will be less confusing than explaining different systems in one unit.

Centralized networks are organized administratively into sections. These sections are called *domains*, *groups*, and *users*. The **domain** is an organized collection of all groups and users on the network. A **group** is a collection of users organized together by similarities in their job tasks. A **user** is an individual who may use the network system resources.

> **Tech Tip**
>
> The term *domain* has two meanings: one for the early Windows Server models and another when used to discuss Internet locations. A domain in Windows Server terminology means "a collection of computers." When discussing the Internet, the term *domain* refers to a classification of a site, such as .com or .org or to represent the Internet site.

Domains

The entire network organization is usually referred to as a domain. For example, ABC Inc. may be a domain. The entire organization is one whole unique network system. Inside the domain are groups of users with related tasks, such as the personnel in the accounting and sales departments. Each of these groups is composed of individual users, such as John Doe in accounting and Jane Doe in sales.

Groups

The next level in the network organization is the group. Groups are workers who share common responsibilities and can be thought of as a set. For example, the payroll, marketing, research, design, and administrative departments of a corporation could easily form five distinct groups of network users. The workers within the group usually require similar system resources (files, software, printers, etc.) to perform their jobs.

Users

The individual user is at the bottom of the network organization. A user is an individual who uses the network system. Each user is assigned an account, which includes all available information about him or her. The account, which contains such information as the user's password, user name, restrictions, and the group(s) he or she belongs to, is kept in a database on the file server. Each user must have an account before he or she can use the network system. Once the user has an account, he or she can be granted full use of the network and can be given access to any area of the network by the system administrator. The user usually belongs to one or more groups, but may belong to no group at all.

System Administrator

When talking about a system administrator, or network administrator, we are talking about the centralized model of network administration, the client/server model, rather than the peer-to-peer model. The **network administrator** is one person (or more) who has the highest security rating on the network. The network administrator is responsible for delegating authority all the way down to the user level. The other users on the network can exercise only the authority granted to them by the network administrator.

Delegating Administrators

The network administrator controls all aspects of the network. However, in a large organization with thousands of users spread all over the country, it would be difficult, if not impossible, for one person to perform all the duties associated with running a network. For this reason, the network administrator usually grants limited administrative powers to a middle management level of administrators. The middle management people take care of routine duties, such as adding or deleting users from the network, setting up printers to be shared, setting up specific files or programs to be shared, and doing routine data backup.

Logging on the network involves identifying the user by name and password. The user name identifies the individual and the password verifies his or her identity. The network administrator issues the user name and the user's initial password. The administrator can give permission to users to change their logon password following the first successful logon. This is the typical password administrative scenario used.

Choosing User Names

The typical format for a user name is the user's last name followed by the underline symbol and ending in the first letter of user's first name. For example, the author's user name would likely be Roberts_R. There are many different naming styles, but once a naming style is chosen, it should remain consistent as new user accounts are added to the network. Inconsistent naming styles can easily lead to confusion. Windows 8 and Windows Server 2012 allow users to use their email address as a logon name.

Creating Passwords

Passwords should be complex, which means they are created from numbers, uppercase and lowercase letters, and special symbols. You should review Chapter 14—Physical and Digital Security for information about complex passwords and password security.

Default Users and Groups

Server operating systems typically have a set of default users and groups. These are the most common users and groups required in most server systems. Default users and groups save time when setting up a server.

Some of the most common users are as follows:
- Administrator.
- User.
- Guest.

Some of the most common groups are as follows:
- Print Operators.
- Backup Operators.
- DHCP Administrators.
- Domain Administrators.

The exact title of the user or group account will vary according to the operating system used. Each group can have specific permissions set, which dictates what the members of the group can do, access, or modify. Users are simply added to each group and the users are restricted to the permissions of the group.

Additional users and groups can be added to meet the needs of the environment. For example, in a school setting, a group named *Teachers* and another group named *Students* can be set up on the server. A user named *Teacher* and another user named *Student* can be added to the user list. All students can log on using the user name *Student*. The student would be restricted according to the permissions set in the group called *Students*. The same scenario can be applied to the teachers. Each teacher can log on using the user name *Teacher*. The teacher would be restricted according the permissions set in the group named *Teachers*.

Assigning Resources at the Group Level

If the company has several hundred or thousands of employees, the amount of time required to set up individual shares for each employee would be unreasonable. Although access to system resources can be granted to individual users, network administrators can save a great deal of time by assigning resources to groups rather than to individual users. In this case, each group can be allowed access to the normal software programs, files, and hardware required by that group. When it is necessary to add new users to the network, it is quicker and simpler to assign a new individual to an existing group than it is to authorize each individual to use specific network resources.

As you just learned, networks are organized by domains, users, and groups. These groups are often formed from the different divisions or departments in the corporate structure. Although all of these departments are part of the same company and may have many common needs, they each will likely have special needs based on their different job requirements. For example, all departments will need some sort of word-processing package but only a few would need access to the accounting software or payroll database. Each group's needs and security requirements must be determined individually.

Even when resources are assigned at the group level, each employee must still have an account.

Domain User Account

When the computer is configured as part of a domain, the user is configured with a **domain user account**. The domain user account provides access to network domain resources and to resources on the workstation. Domain security is configured to control access at the domain level, which means configuring user access for multiple computer and network resources. The software system used by Microsoft to control access to the network system at the domain level is called *Active Directory Domain Services (AD DS)* or simply *Active Directory*.

When a user account is part of a network administrative security database, the user of that account can do the following:

- Be authenticated through the domain server.
- Access resources anywhere in the network domain.
- Log on through any computer in the domain.
- Access resources anywhere in the domain.

The domain user account is created on the network server. The domain user account can be created at the server or remotely from a workstation. Even when the domain user account is created from the workstation, the domain user account is created and controlled by the domain server, not the workstation. The domain user account controls access to network resources and access to the workstation. The domain user account is an example of a single sign-on user account. The user can then access resources throughout the network without the need to supply a password again.

A Quick Tour of Windows Server 2012

We will now take a quick tour of a typical Windows Server 2012 system. The following paragraphs illustrate differences between a simple peer-to-peer network and a much more sophisticated network system. This will be a quick tour, not an in-depth study of Windows Server 2012. It is intended to introduce you to some of the capabilities and features of a network operating system. A complete study of any Windows Server system would require a complete textbook of its own. Remember, a network that uses Windows Server is a client/server network.

Windows server operating systems parallel the look of the current Windows style and features of the Windows PC operating systems of the same era. For example, Windows Server 2008 looks very similar to Windows Vista and Windows 7. The Windows Server 2012 desktop and Start screen look very similar to the Windows 8 desktop and Start screen. **Figure 17-25** shows the Windows 2012 desktop and Start screen.

Figure 17-25. Windows Server 2012 GUI. A—Desktop. B—Start screen.

A

B

User Management

The Active Directory Users and Computers management utility is used to enter or examine information about users, groups, domains, and other objects in the Active Directory structure. See **Figure 17-26**. The right pane contains a listing of the names and descriptions of the network's built-in users and groups.

From the Active Directory Users and Computers window, you can add or delete users and groups. Microsoft is famous for providing software wizards to assist users with their tasks, and Microsoft Server 2012 is no exception. Microsoft provides several wizards, such as the New Object wizard shown in **Figure 17-27**, to assist the network administrator. This wizard helps add users to the network in a systematic way, ensuring that no important security features are inadvertently left out.

After a domain user is created, the user account will have a **Properties** dialog box, **Figure 17-28**. Everything needed to be known about a user is displayed in the user **Properties**

dialog box. The user **Properties** dialog box can also be used to configure user properties, such as password security and group memberships.

Security Features

Many standard security features are incorporated into Windows Server. These include password, account lockout, and time policies. The security features associated with the user account are set to a minimum level of security, but when needed, a network administrator can alter the default settings.

Password Policy

The Windows Server creates a default password policy that sets the standards for domain user access. The default settings can be altered by the administrator. **Figure 17-29** shows the Windows Server 2012 **Create Password Settings** dialog box, which allows an administrator to alter the password policy for all domain users.

Figure 17-26.
Information about Active Directory objects is displayed in the **Active Directory Users and Computers** window.

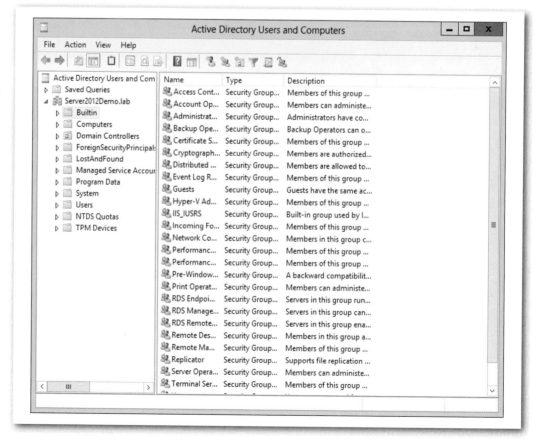

Figure 17-27. When adding users to the network system in Windows Server 2012, the user is created using the New Object wizard. A—The first dialog box to appear during the creation of a new user in the network system. B—User password settings are entered in the second dialog box. C—The last dialog box allows you to verify the new user's settings.

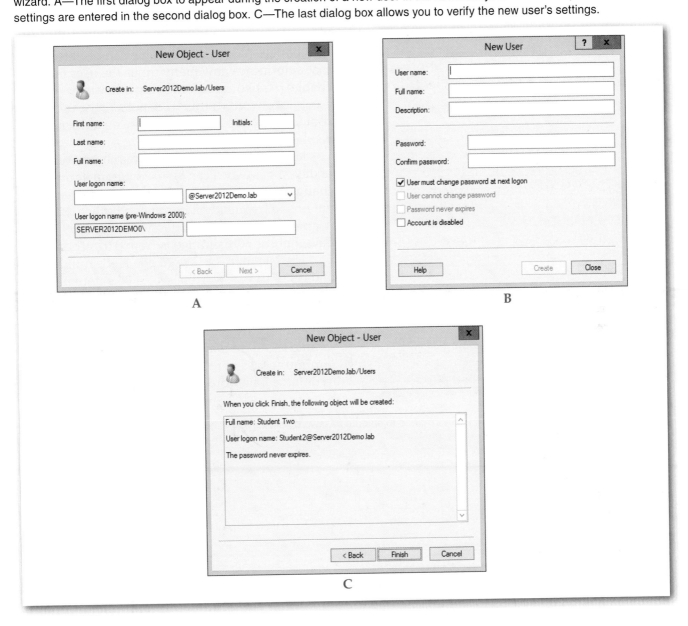

The domain password policy is in contrast to the password policy used to access the server locally. The **Local Security Policy** dialog box is used to configure local computer access or, in this case, the server. In short, the Local Security Policy sets the configuration of security features for password access to the computer (server), and the Active Directory Domain Services (AD DS) password policy configures the security settings for access to the network domain. **Figure 17-30** shows the **Local Security Policy** dialog box, which looks very similar to the Windows 7 or Windows 8 **Local Security Policy** dialog box.

Notice that selecting **Password Policy** from the left pane of the **Local Security Policy** dialog box reveals six password policy features on the right. The following security features are listed:

- Enforce password history.
- Maximum password age.
- Minimum password age.
- Minimum password length.
- Password must meet complexity requirements.
- Store passwords using reversible encryption.

Figure 17-28. Everything that needs to be known about a user can be viewed through the user's **Properties** dialog box.

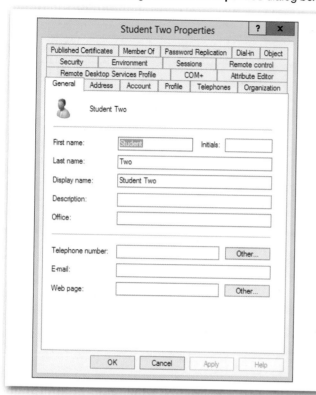

Enforce password history determines how old passwords are remembered by the system. Password controls can be set to require a user to use a different password every time he or she changes passwords. A value can be entered that determines how many times the user must change passwords before being allowed to repeat an old password. If this were not set, the user could simply flip-flop between two passwords, weakening system security.

Maximum password age is maximum number of days a password can be used before it must be changed. Passwords should be changed frequently but not so frequently it becomes a bother to the user. The recommended password age is 30 to 90 days, but the actual range is from 0 to 999 days.

The **Minimum password age** is the number of days old a password needs to be before it can be changed. **Minimum password age** is a required feature when using the password history policy. Values range from 0 to 998 and must be set at a value less than maximum. If there were no minimum password age and a value was set in **Enforce password history** that determined

Figure 17-29. The Windows Server can be configured to enforce password policies that directly affect all domain user passwords.

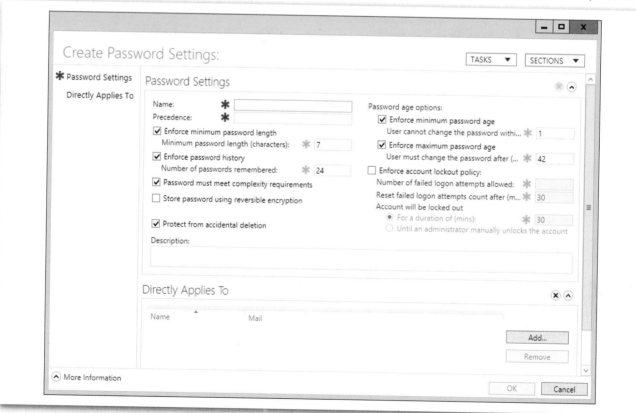

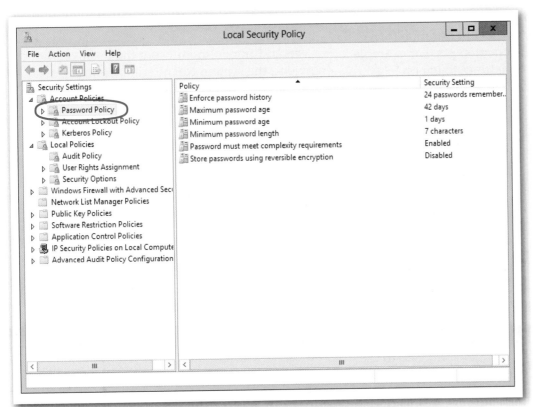

Figure 17-30.
A password security policy can be configured for access to the server in similar fashion to the password policy used on a simple computer system.

a user must change a password seven times before being allowed to reuse an old password, a user could change his or her password to meet the maximum password requirement and then immediately change the password back to the original. For example, if a user's original password was "MyPassword_1," the user could create a series of passwords based on the last digit, such as "MyPassword_2," "MyPassword_3," and so on. When the password series reached the value set in **Enforce password history**, the user once more could use the original password, "MyPassword_1." Setting the minimum password age feature to as little as one day will prevent a user from cycling through all their old passwords at one sitting.

Minimum password length sets the minimum length a password can be. Enforcing passwords of six characters or more can increase security. The length of a password is directly related to the how secure the password is. The longer the password, the longer it takes to "crack." It can also, however, be more difficult to remember. The length of the password must provide a reasonable amount of security and not be too difficult or complex to use.

Microsoft and most security experts recommend a password of at least 6 characters. A longer password of at least 12 characters is not unreasonable. As the length of the password increases and if the complexity requirements of the next section are met, a lengthy password could be difficult to use. Just remember that the password must be at least 6 characters in length to be considered a minimally secure password.

The **Password must meet complexity requirements** prevents a user from choosing a password that is easily compromised by cracking tools such as dictionaries. Complex passwords require a minimum length and the use of an assortment of letters, numbers, and special symbols in the password. A complex password is extremely difficult to compromise.

Store passwords using reversible encryption hides the user password by encrypting the characters so they cannot be seen by unauthorized probes of the security database.

Account Lockout Policy

The **Account Lockout Policy** dialog box accessed through **Default Controller Security**

Settings | Account Policies allows the system administrator to select a lockout duration for a set number of failed logon attempts. For example, if a person attempts three times to log on to a network system and fails, the system locks the user out for a period of time. The time can range from 0 to 99,999 minutes. The idea is to cause a reasonable delay between login failures to prevent a "dictionary attack" by an unauthorized person. Even a delay of a few minutes will ward off most attacks.

Time Policy

The time (days and hours) a user may access the network can be easily controlled through an individual's **Properties** dialog box, In **Figure 17-31**, logon hours are configured so that the user can only access the network system from 6:00 a.m. to 8:00 p.m. Monday through Friday. At any other day or time, the user will be denied access to the network. This security feature prevents someone from accessing the network with a stolen user name and password during a business's off hours. One option of this feature forces users off the system when their time expires. Another option allows them to continue (or finish) working in their current program or document but does not allow them to open any new files or services.

Figure 17-31. Logon Hours dialog box. A user's access to the network can be limited to certain days of the week or hours.

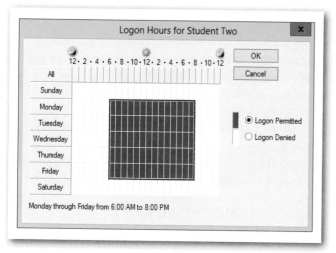

Monitoring the System

In addition to monitoring the users on the network, the system can monitor itself, record events in the system log, and alert the system administrator to potential problems. Various features available in Windows Server allow the network administrator to observe and track system performance. The features are discussed in the following sections.

Event Viewer

The Event Viewer in Windows Server displays recorded events that occur on the server. Look at **Figure 17-32**. Notice that this Event Viewer looks similar to the Windows PC version of Event Viewer. It also serves the same function. Events that are directly related to security, applications, the operating system, and more are recorded and can be viewed later. Event Viewer is a handy tool to use when analyzing system failures and security breaches.

Performance Monitor

The administrator can use the Performance Monitor utility to monitor the performance of some of the computer system components. The main difference between the Performance Monitor for Windows Server when compared to the Windows PC version is the server version provides options to diagnose Active Directory performance issues. In **Figure 17-33,** the Performance Monitor is displaying the CPU activity. The usage is expressed as a percentage from 0 to 100. The administrator can use this tool to diagnose various network problems, such as network congestion or failing hardware.

You will find many of the same tools in the server version of Windows as compared to the PC version. By learning to use the Windows PC version of tools and utilities, you have already gained a valuable insight into the Windows Server.

Permissions

A network security system maintains a database of security information on all network

Figure 17-32. The Event Viewer in Windows Server has the same look as the personal computer version of Event Viewer and serves the same function.

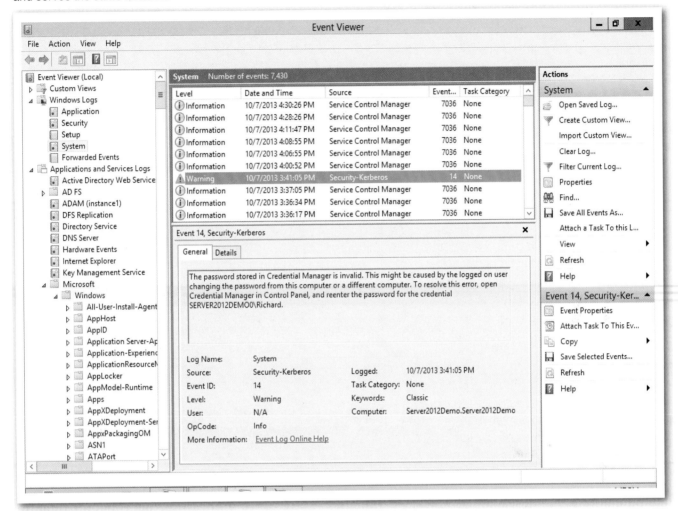

users. The exact terminology used to describe the individual features varies somewhat according to the network operating system software used. The database stores information such as the group(s) the user belongs to and their access rights to files and drives. The administrator can alter, copy, delete, or simply read the contents of a profile. There are many aspects to the individual user profile. In **Figure 17-34**, you can see that each share has a **Properties** dialog box that controls who has permission to access the network share. This dialog box can be used to add or remove users and change the individual user permissions.

In the **Advanced Security Settings for Network Share Students** dialog box, **Figure 17-35**, you can see part of the default restrictions assigned to users accessing the shared network folder called

"Network Share Students." This network share has been created to allow students to store files and folders on the network. It was created by the network administrator who has full control over the share. Student One has been assigned limited permissions to only read and execute files stored in the share. As you can see, the network administrator can place strong limits on a user to ensure a secure network environment. The administrator can limit a user's access so that the user may only run the programs and access the files authorized by the network administrator.

Access to shares can also be controlled by the **Permission Entry for Users** dialog box. As you can see in **Figure 17-36**, the share permissions are very similar to the ones encountered in peer-to-peer Simple File Sharing.

Figure 17-33. The Windows Server Performance Monitor can be used to analyze not only the server hardware performance but also Active Directory problems.

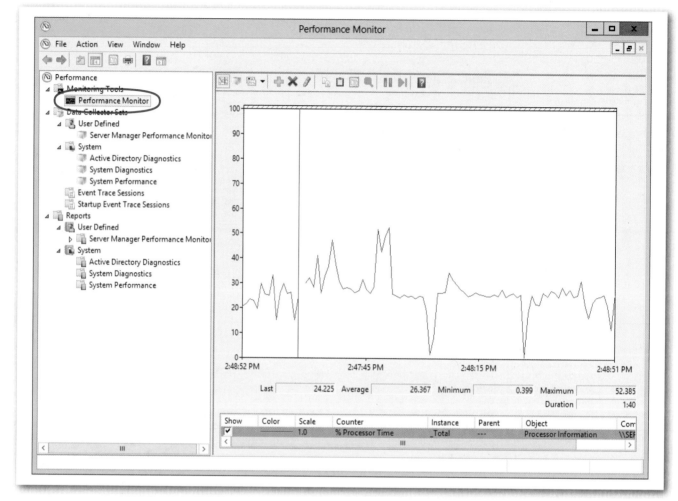

Permissions can be assigned to individual users or groups. Look at **Figure 17-37**. When permission is assigned to a group, all members of that group are assigned the permission. It is common in network domains to assign a specific set of permissions to a group as related to a resource rather than assigning permissions for each individual. If a group of people share the same resource on a network, it is easier to assign individuals to a group and then assign permissions to each individual user. For example, in a school setting a Homework folder, Tests folder, and Assignment folder could be created. The collection of folders could be placed in another folder called Student Resources. The network administrator could then create a group called Students. The Student group would then be assigned the read permission for the Student

Resources folder. All folders inside the Student Resources folder would also have the read permission. Another group of users called *Teachers* can be created and teachers could be assigned to the Teacher group. The Teacher group could then be given the full control permission. That way, any and all teachers assigned to the Teacher group would have full control over the entire collection of student resources. Assigning group permissions is the most efficient way to manage large numbers of users and large numbers of resources.

Joining a Windows Server Domain

Computer membership configuration to a HomeGroup, workgroup, or domain is first selected when the Windows operating system

Figure 17-34. The server provides a centralized location to manage network share permissions.

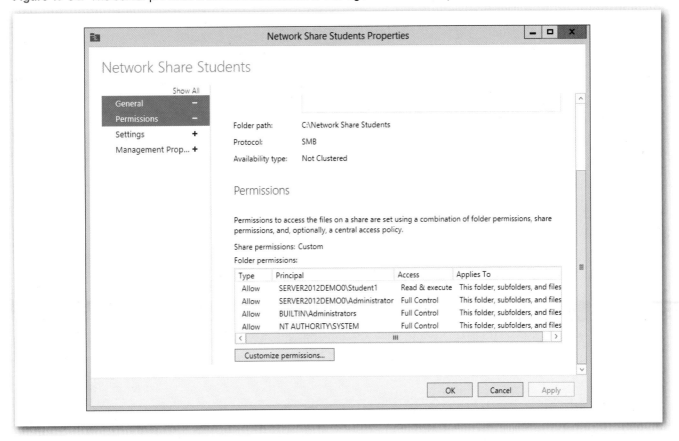

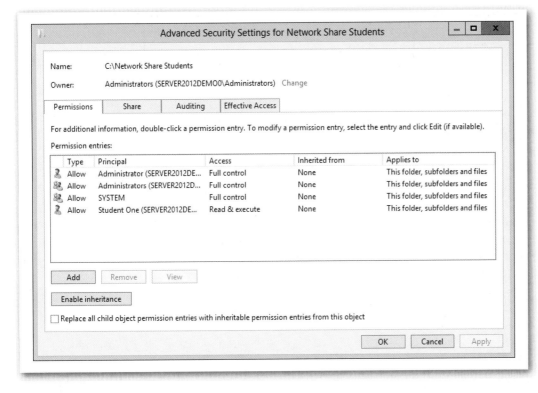

Figure 17-35.
Each server share has
an **Advanced Security
Settings** dialog box
which is used to
configure who has
permission to access
the network share, add
clients, and more.

Figure 17-36. Basic user permissions are similar to the ones encountered in peer-to-peer Simple File Sharing.

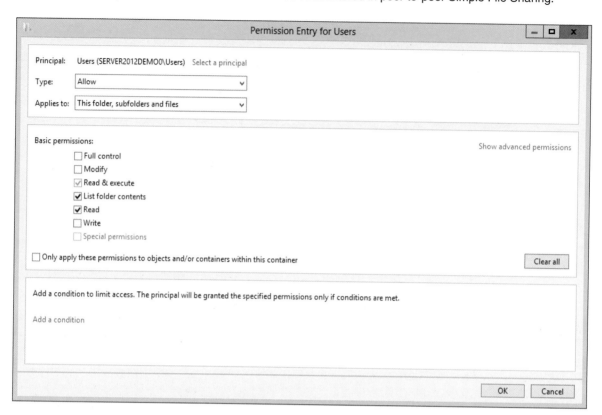

Figure 17-37.
Assigning users to groups and then assigning permission to the group is the most efficient way to manage large numbers of users on a domain network.

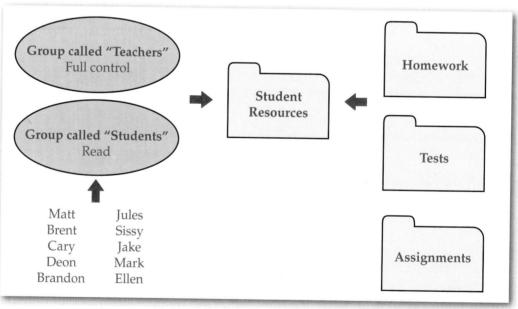

is first installed. The default configuration for the Windows operating system is as a member of a workgroup. Starting with Windows 7, the computer may also be a member of a HomeGroup. Domain membership can be created during the operating installation process, but it is not typically configured for home computer use.

Tech Tip
The domain network administrator can configure the domain policy to prevent joining a HomeGroup.

The membership configuration can be changed at any time after the operating system has been installed by opening the **System Properties** dialog box and clicking the **Change** button. The **Computer Name/Domain Changes** dialog box will open, allowing you to rename or change the computer domain or workgroup membership. See **Figure 17-38**.

Working with computers that are part of a HomeGroup or workgroup is quite different from working with computers that are part of a network domain, which require a different understanding of user account limitations.

Tech Tip
Home editions do not provide the option to join a network domain. Home edition membership is limited to workgroup or HomeGroup. Also, computers running Windows RT or Windows 8 cannot join a domain. You can only join a domain if your PC is running Windows 8 Pro or Windows 8 Enterprise.

Network Unattended Installation

When working with small networks, the technician is often required to install new operating systems or perform upgrades. For a very small network system, it is acceptable to perform manual installation at each and every computer. As the size of the network grows, this becomes a time-consuming task. A better method of deployment is performing an automated installation of a new operating system or upgrade of an operating system through an **unattended installation**. Microsoft refers to the operation of massive installation as "deployments," and

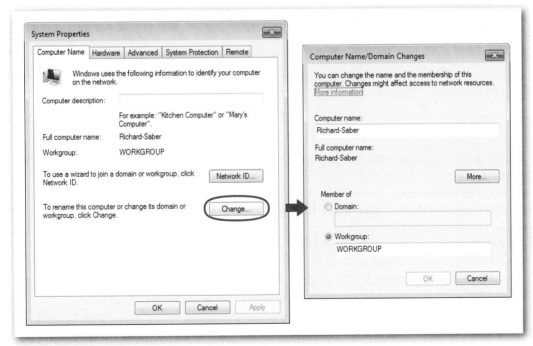

Figure 17-38.
Changing membership from a workgroup to a domain.

it provides a complete set of tools designed for installing multiple copies of the operating system and application software onto multiple computers.

This section will familiarize you with the unattended installation. To further enhance your knowledge and become an in-depth expert in mass deployments, please visit the Microsoft TechNet website. There is extensive material written about performing unattended installations and remote network installations.

> ## A+ Note
>
> For the A+ exam, you do not need an expert's level of knowledge about the unattended installation tools and methods mentioned in this chapter. The unattended installation questions are targeted at a general knowledge level. In contrast, Microsoft does require expert level knowledge of unattended installation procedures for the Microsoft Windows operating system certifications.

Look at **Figure 17-39** to see the three computer designations discussed in the unattended installation process. In an unattended installation, there is a technician computer, a reference computer, and target or destination computers. The target or destination computers either contain no operating system or contain operating systems that will be upgraded.

Reference Computer

A reference computer is a model computer representing what a typical desktop used in the organization should look like. Microsoft also refers to the reference computer as the "master computer" in some of its documentation. The reference computer has the operating system installed as well as software applications, such as Microsoft Windows Office and any required hardware drivers that might be needed that are not contained on a typical Windows installation DVD. The reference computer is used to create a **deployment image** which is an exact copy of all the files contained on the hard disk drive of the reference computer.

Technician Computer and WAIK

The technician computer contains all the various software tools used to configure the deployment image. The Windows Automated Installation Kit (WAIK) is installed on the technician computer. In some system configurations, there is no need for a keyboard or monitor located at the reference computer. A device known as a Keyboard-Video-Mouse (KVM) switch can be used.

Performing an Unattended Installation

The general steps for creating and performing an unattended installation are as follows.

1. Download and install the Windows Automated Installation Kit (WAIK) at the technician computer.
2. Create a reference computer (master computer) containing the operating system and software applications.
3. Create an answer file.
4. At the technician computer, run the System Preparation Tool (Sysprep) to prepare and create a deployment image of the reference computer.
5. Create a bootable Windows system media (bootable ISO) such as a CD, DVD, or USB flash drive or copy the image to a network location to be used for distribution of the image.
6. Distribute the system media. At the destination computer, insert the distribution media and then press [Ctrl] [Alt] [Del] to boot the computer and start the unattended installation process.

While the list of key steps makes the distribution process sound simple, in reality it is not. The successful distribution of the operating system using an unattended file takes many hours of preparation, but it is far less than manually installing the operating system and software at each computer.

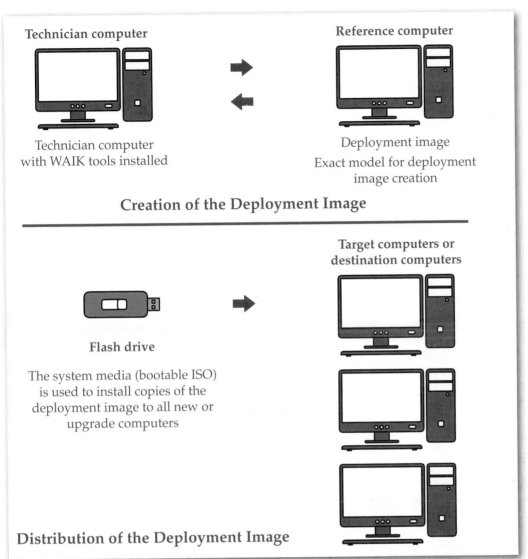

Goodheart-Willcox Publisher

Figure 17-39. Massive deployment machines are identified as the technician computer, reference computer, and target or destination computer.

Technician computer

Technician computer with WAIK tools installed

Reference computer

Deployment image
Exact model for deployment image creation

Creation of the Deployment Image

Flash drive

The system media (bootable ISO) is used to install copies of the deployment image to all new or upgrade computers

Target computers or destination computers

Distribution of the Deployment Image

Installing the Windows Automated Installation Kit

The **Windows Automated Installation Kit (WAIK)** is a collection of tools that support the Windows deployment process. The kit is a collection of software applications that are used to make an exact copy of all content located on a computer hard disk drive. To become expert in the use of the WAIK takes many hours of training, study, and practice. Microsoft provides hundreds of pages of documentation concerning the Windows automated deployment strategy and deployment techniques.

Creating a Reference Computer

The reference computer is the model of what all the computers in the network should look like when the distribution of the operating system is finished. It will contain the operating system and other software, such as Microsoft Office and hardware drivers.

It is advisable, but not required, that the reference computer should have the same hardware components as the destination computers. If the corporation requires a variety of computers, several reference computers can be created. For example, computer hardware and software requirements used for accounting and sales departments can vary greatly when compared to the art department. A reference computer should be created for the accounting department and another created for the sales department.

Creating an Answer File

The answer file is what truly makes an automated installation process possible. The **answer file** is a text-based document that is used in conjunction with the Sysprep tool to configure the unattended destination computer. It is created by using the Windows System Image Manager (Windows SIM) tool and contains all the answers to questions that are normally encountered during an operating system installation procedure. It also contains a series of commands that will perform such activities as preparing the partition when required. The answer file can automatically supply information for the configuration, such as the name of the computer, time zone, language, network domain, and other configuration information. It can make the installation possible without human interaction, thus the term "unattended installation."

The answer file can also be configured to make the user answer specific questions during the first time the computer boots, for example, when a new owner of a computer first boots his or her brand-new computer. Some typical new owner questions that may require user intervention are the user name and password, language, and time zone. The answer file can be very simple or very complex, depending on the environment where the computer will be located and the need of any additional driver software applications. Microsoft provides samples of answer files to make the creation of the file less complicated.

Running Sysprep and Creating Deployment Image

When the operating system is first installed on the reference computer, a user account is created and the computer is named. Also, a product key is generated and other security features, such as Security identifiers (SID) and product ID, which make the computer unique. Before copies of the reference computer can be distributed to multiple computers, all unique information must be removed. The Sysprep tool (sysprep.exe) removes all system identification and security features associated with an individual user account and computer, thus creating a deployment image. The deployment image contains all the files associated with the reference computer, except the unique configuration information is removed. You can think of the reference computer as a generic computer with an operating system and other software applications and drivers but no user account, computer name, product key, or security identifier.

Creating a Bootable Windows System Media

The deployment image can be burned to a disc or copied to a USB flash drive or to an exterior USB storage drive and then used for distribution to computers. The deployment image can also be stored on a network share and used for distribution across the network to new or upgrade computers. When used for installation to new computers having no operating system, the Windows Preinstallation Environment (WinPE) is used to start the installation process from the new computer. WinPE is a minimal Windows operating system similar to the legacy DOS boot disk. It can boot and run a computer but does not provide a GUI. It only responds to text-based commands. WinPE is required to start the blank destination computer when performing and unattended installation from a network share. WinPE contains a set of generic drivers that supports most commonly used hardware devices.

Distributing the System Media

At the destination computer, insert the distribution media and then press [Ctrl] [Alt] [Del] to boot the computer and start the unattended installation process. You can make multiple copies of the distribution media and start the installation process at multiple locations. In most cases, you will not need to be in attendance at the computer locations while performing the installation. You can return after a period of time to retrieve the distribution media and verify the installation was successful.

Before performing the actual distribution of the system media, you should first run a test to verify the system media will install properly and confirm that the finished destination computer will perform as desired.

This was a short introduction to how an unattended installation is performed, and you have become familiar with the general concepts. This should be sufficient for the CompTIA A+ exam. For Microsoft certification, much more knowledge is required than presented here.

RAID Systems

Fault tolerance is a system's ability to recover after some sort of disaster. The hard drive could fail, the operating system could crash, a user could accidentally erase some files, and many more things could happen. Networks have the ability to recover from these types of disasters. There are many fault tolerance methods available. The two most common methods of fault tolerance are the use of RAID and the use of tape backup. In this section, we will explore common RAID configurations used with Microsoft servers.

A **RAID** is a system of several hard drive units arranged in such a way as to ensure recovery after a system disaster or to ensure data integrity during normal operation. RAID is the acronym for Redundant Array of Inexpensive or Independent Disks. The translation of the acronym varies between the use of the word *inexpensive* and *independent*. The exact translation is not important, but the concept behind RAID technology is. There are four forms of RAID associated with Microsoft servers: Level 0, level 1, level 5, and level 10. **Figure 17-40** illustrates the first three forms.

Level 0

Level 0 is called striped without parity. A striped set is two or more areas across two or more disks to which data is written or from which data is read. The main purpose of a striped set is to speed up the data read/write process. Data is recorded more quickly when it is being written simultaneously to multiple disks. When data

is recorded in a striped set, the data is equally divided, and equal portions of the data are written to each hard disk drive.

A striped set spreads the data across two drives or volumes. Data is written alternately to each drive or volume in 64-kB blocks of data. When two separate hard drive controllers are used, one for each drive, the read and write times are faster than those of a single drive. The disadvantage to this RAID arrangement is that there is no data protection. When one of the drives fails, all data on that drive is lost. To prevent the loss of data, the arrangement for data storage must use parity. Parity, as you recall, is a technique used to ensure data is correct. See Figure 17-40A.

Level 1

RAID level 1, or disk mirroring, requires two hard drives. One drive keeps an exact copy of all data on the other drive. This way if one drive fails, all its data can be retrieved from its duplicate. See Figure 17-40B.

Level 5

RAID level 5 can use from 3 to 32 hard drives of equal partition size to form what is called a striped set with parity. Parity is used to reconstruct data lost on either of the two hard drives that are used to store data. For example, data is duplicated on two hard drives and the third is used to store the parity of the two. Parity is staggered across all drives when a minimum of three are used. See Figure 17-40C.

Remember from previous units, parity is the sum total of two bytes of data added together. The two bytes will be either odd or even. By reversing the operation, the missing data can be reconstructed using the value stored in the parity section. It is important to remember that none of the techniques discussed are infallible. Anything can happen to destroy data. Regular backups are the only way to ensure some degree of fault tolerance.

Level 10

RAID level 10 is also referred to as RAID 1+0. It is a combination of RAID 0 and RAID 1, hence

Figure 17-40.
Three forms of RAID used on a Microsoft server. A—RAID level 0 offers no data protection. It is used to speed up the read/write process. Data is spread across more than one volume in 64 kB blocks. B—RAID level 1 uses at least two volumes to store an exact duplicate of data. If one drive fails, the other still contains an exact copy of the data. C—RAID 5 is a striped set with parity. Parity is used to reconstruct data lost on any of the volumes.

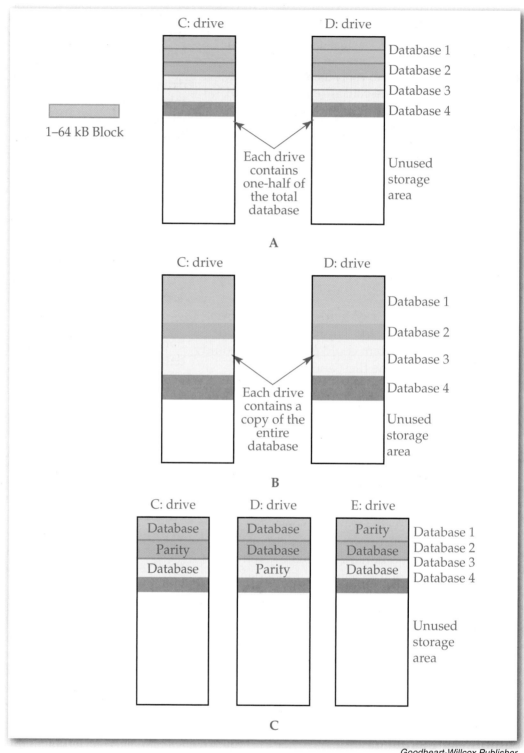

the name RAID 1 + 0 or RAID 10. RAID 10 is a combination of mirroring and striping. It provides the redundancy of two hard drives in a mirror configuration and the speed of a striped set of disks. RAID 10 provides the fastest storage data rate with the added redundancy feature but at a higher cost than the other RAID levels.

Storage Spaces and Storage Pools

Microsoft introduced two more storage technologies known as Storage Spaces and Storage Pools. Storage pools are a collection of physical disks that act as one large storage device or configured to represent multiple storage units. Storage Spaces is a virtual disk created from the free space in a storage pool.

Storage Spaces provides three storage layouts similar to RAID types. The storage space can be configured as a Simple (RAID 0), Mirror (RAID 1), and Parity (RAID 5). The minimum number of disks required for each type of storage pool matches the same requirements of RAID.

Storage spaces that provide protection, such as mirror and parity, automatically rebuild themselves after failure. When the failed hard drive is replaced, the server rebuilds the storage pool using the data in the remaining disks.

Chapter Summary

- The Simple File Sharing feature is available in Windows XP; the HomeGroup and Libraries features are available in Windows 7 and Windows 8; and the Public folders feature is available in Windows Vista and later. Windows 8.1 no longer supports the Libraries feature.

- A centralized administration network system has a single and central network authority that controls all aspects of the network system; administrative functions in a peer-to-peer network are not highly organized and are best described as decentralized.

- Windows Server 2012 is similar in design as Windows 8 and has many standard security features as well as utilities to manage users and monitor the system.

- Windows Automated Installation Kit (WAIK) is a collection of tools that support the Windows deployment process.

- RAID is a way to ensure data integrity and fault tolerance through the use of multiple drive volumes.

- Storage pools are a collection of physical disks that act as one large storage device, and Storage Spaces is a virtual disk created from the free space in a storage pool.

Review Questions

Answer the following questions on a separate sheet of paper. Please do not write in this book.

1. Who controls a peer-to-peer network?
2. Who controls the access to shares on a peer-to-peer network?
3. What is the Network and Sharing Center and in which Windows versions is it available?
4. What is a local user account?
5. What type of user account is created on an individual computer that is used in a workgroup-based network and is not part of a network domain?
6. Where is the local user account information stored?
7. What is a share?

8. Which operating system first introduced Simple File Sharing?

9. Which operating system first introduced Public Folders?

10. Which operating system first introduced HomeGroup?

11. Which editions of Windows can create a HomeGroup?

12. Which editions of Windows can join a HomeGroup?

13. What are the three network profiles identified by Microsoft Windows 7 operating system?

14. What two types of file and folder permissions does Windows use?

15. What is another name for security permissions?

16. What is the difference between share permissions and security permissions?

17. What is a domain?

18. What is a group?

19. What are the responsibilities of a network administrator?

20. What type of user account is created for a user who is a member of a network that uses a server to control access to network resources?

21. What is the name of the Microsoft software system that controls domain level security and membership?

22. What is the name of the utility in Windows Server that allows an administrator to enter or examine information about users, groups, domains, and other objects in the Active Directory structure?

23. What is a lockout policy?

24. What Windows Server utility is a handy tool to use when analyzing system failures and security breaches?

25. Which editions of Windows do not provide an option for domain membership?

26. What are the three computer designations in an unattended installation process?

27. What does the acronym WAIK represent?

28. Which tool is used to remove the security identifier and computer name?

29. What does the WinPE acronym represent?

30. What is WinPE used for in relation to an unattended installation?

31. What are the four forms of RAID associated with Microsoft servers?

32. Which two RAID types does RAID 10 mimic?

33. What are Microsoft Storage Pools?

34. What is Microsoft Storage Spaces?

Sample A+ Exam Questions

Answer the following questions on a separate sheet of paper. Please do not write in this book.

1. Which of the following is the best password to use to prevent possible compromise or intrusion?
   a. secret
   b. Big$tar_5
   c. President Roosevelt
   d. Password

2. Which is *not* a typical Windows share permission?
   a. Read
   b. Full control
   c. Partial
   d. Change

3. What does a user need to access a network system? Select all that apply.
   a. User name
   b. Password
   c. Group membership
   d. A security clearance

4. Who determines a user's rights on a client/server network?
   a. Each computer user determines the user rights for their own workstation.
   b. Users set their own individual rights based on their total system knowledge.
   c. The network administrator sets individual rights on the network system.
   d. All users automatically have full rights to use the entire network when they are issued an account on the network.

5. In a Windows Server network, user accounts are set up in _____.
   a. Active Directory Users and Computers
   b. Performance Monitor
   c. Event Viewer
   d. User Share Setup

6. In a Windows network system, the user password is changed _____.
   a. in the **Active Directory Users and Computers** dialog box
   b. in the **Account Policy** dialog box
   c. at the user's workstation under the **Change Password** icon in **Control Panel**
   d. A user password can never be changed once it is issued.

7. Which program can be used to monitor user activity on a computer system?
   a. Event Viewer
   b. Net Monitor
   c. Performance Monitor
   d. Net Movement

8. Which program would you select to check the total amount of activity through the CPU?
   a. Net Monitor
   b. Performance Monitor
   c. CPU Monitor
   d. CPU Pole Watch

9. When using Windows, a collection of users who have similar tasks and are consequently assigned the same user rights are generally referred to as a _____.
   a. group
   b. covey
   c. pod
   d. corporate entity

10. In a centralized network with user logon controlled by the server, the entire business network is usually referred to as a _____.
    a. corporate entity
    b. select pod
    c. domain
    d. group

Suggested Laboratory Activities

Do not attempt any suggested laboratory activities without your instructor's permission. Certain activities can render the PC operating system inoperable.

1. Set up a client/server network. Choose one PC to be the server. All other PCs must log on through the server to gain access to the network.

2. Use an existing network to do the following:
   a. Add a new user to the network.
   b. Restrict the time of day a particular user can access the network.
   c. Set a time limit, by days, during which a user may use the network.
   d. Display a list of users and groups on the network system.
   e. Change an existing user's password.
   f. Set up a minimum password length.

Wide Area Network (WAN)

After studying this chapter, you will be able to:

- Identify the various methods of TCP/IP addressing.
- Identify equipment associated with a WAN.
- Use common diagnostic utilities associated with networks.
- Explain the physical structure of the Internet and how a web browser locates a webpage.
- Use e-mail client software or a webmail program to set up an e-mail account.
- Recall common Internet protocols and their characteristics.
- Identify cloud service terminology and characteristics.
- Implement basic knowledge of networking when troubleshooting network problems.

A+ Exam—Key Points

The A+ Certification exam requires knowledge of the basic operation of network systems. In recent years, CompTIA has greatly expanded the network portion of the exam objectives. Be sure you are able to distinguish between DNS, WINS, and DHCP services because you will definitely encounter one or more questions directly related to these topics. You may also be asked to identify an example of an IP address and a subnet mask. You will most likely be asked several questions related to common network protocols and port address assignments.

Key Terms

The following key terms will become important pieces of your computer vocabulary. Be sure you can define them.

Address Resolution Protocol (ARP)
Anything as a Service (XaaS)
Automatic Private IP Address (APIPA)
brouter
circuit switching
Class A network
Class B network
Class C network
Client-side virtualization
Common Internet File System (CIFS)
community cloud
Domain Name Service (DNS)
dynamic addressing
Dynamic Host Configuration Protocol (DHCP)
emulator
File Transfer Protocol (FTP)
gateway
hybrid cloud
Hypertext Markup Language (HTML)
Hypertext Transfer Protocol (HTTP)
hypervisor
Internet Corporation for Assigned Names and Numbers (ICANN)
Infrastructure as a Service (IaaS)
Internet Control Message Protocol Version 6 (ICMPv6)
Internet Message Access Protocol (IMAP)
IP address
IPSec

Kernel-based Virtual Machines (KVM) client
Messaging Application Programming Interface (MAPI)
Multipurpose Internet Mail Extensions (MIME)
octet
Packet Internet Groper (PING)
packet switching
Platform as a Service (PaaS)
Post Office Protocol 3 (POP3)
private cloud
proxy server
public cloud
registrar
repeater
Secure Shell (SSH)
Secure Sockets Layer (SSL)
Server Message Block (SMB)
Simple Mail Transfer Protocol (SMTP)
Simple Network Management Protocol (SNMP)
Software as a Service (SaaS)
static IP addressing
subdomain
subnet mask
switch
telnet
time to live (TTL)
Uniform Resource Locators (URLs)
webmail
Windows Internet Naming Service (WINS)

Wide area networks (WANs) are network systems that cover a large geographical area. They require additional networking equipment and different protocols than local area networks (LANs). WANs use routers, bridges, hubs, and more.

When you think about wide area networks, you must think globally. Many corporations include thousands of computers in their network system. These systems often stretch across countries or even continents. The networks used by organizations like the United States Postal Service, the combined armed forces, an international bank, and a state school system, are all examples of wide area networks. Many of these networks are connected to the Internet.

You may wonder how the Internet or WAN handles the volume of data packets generated by all those users. It may seem like all the traffic would slow the Internet to a snail's pace, since there are packets of information being sent everywhere.

In this chapter, the basic concepts of wide area network operation are introduced along with the technologies that make WANs possible. The types of equipment, protocols, and techniques required by a WAN are examined. This chapter will provide you with an overview of how data is delivered over the Internet, the world's largest WAN. You will learn how e-mail gets to its destination and how your web browser can locate a particular webpage in the Internet's endless tangle of cables, routers, and computers. Some of the subjects in this section are vast enough to fill textbooks of their own. The purpose of this chapter is to help you gain a basic understanding of how a WAN operates and to explain some of the technical terminology associated with wide area networks, including the Internet.

TCP/IP Addressing

The TCP/IP protocol is the secret to communicating over the Internet and over other WANs. It was designed for the Internet and is the dominant protocol for data exchange on a typical LAN, MAN, or WAN. TCP/IP addressing is a method of identification used to identify every node or host on a network. The terms *host* and *node* are used interchangeably to identify individual PCs, printers, and network equipment that may require an address. *TCP/IP addressing* and *IP addressing* are also interchangeable terms.

ICANN

Internet Corporation for Assigned Names and Numbers (ICANN) is a nonprofit organization that monitors the use of domain names, IP address, and related protocol. The Internet uses the TCP/IP protocol to route data packets all over the world. Every network has a unique IP address assigned to it. An **IP address** is a numeric identifier regulated and assigned through the organization known as ICANN.

ICANN operates under the direction of the Department of Commerce. It is responsible for regulating the Internet, overseeing the issue of domain names, and assigning IP addresses to them. A user does not directly contact ICANN for an IP address or domain name. The user places an application through a **registrar**, a private sector

company to which users apply for an IP address or domain name . The registrar is regulated by ICANN, which allocates IP addresses much like the way the government issues telephone area codes to long distance carriers and telephone companies. IP addresses must be similarly regulated or there would be chaos in the computer world.

> **Tech Tip**
>
> The Internet Corporation for Assigned Names and Numbers (ICANN), under the supervision of the Department of Commerce, has assumed the name and responsibilities of InterNIC. Currently, InterNIC is a website that provides services and information about Internet assigned names and numbers.

IP Addresses

An Internet Protocol (IP) address is assigned to nodes on a network for the purpose of identification. The term *host* or *node* represents network equipment that requires an IP address for communication. Examples of hosts are computers, servers, network printers, routers, and gateways. The IPv4 address was designed originally for Internet access and communications between Internet-connected devices. Networks did not always access the Internet. Originally, very few computers accessed the Internet, and IP addresses were not required. Instead, local area networks used the MAC address to identify a host. Today, a computer that does not access the Internet is rare. By default, all computers starting with Windows Vista are automatically configured to use two types of IP address: IPv4 and IPv6.

IPv4 was introduced in 1981 and has been used to identify computers in large networks such as a WAN. With the rapid expansion of the Internet in the 1990s, there were too many computers and network devices requiring an IP address. Therefore, the IPv6 address standard was introduced to provide a larger pool of IP addresses to accommodate the increasing number of computers. An IPv5 was under development, but it was abandoned and was never accepted as an alternative to IPv4.

An IPv4 address consists of four sets of decimal numbers in the range of 0 to 255. Each set of decimal numbers is derived from an octet, an 8-bit binary number. An example of an IP address is 183.24.202.17. An IPv6 address consists of eight groups of hexadecimal numbers. Each set is in the range of 0 to FFFF. An example of an IPv6 address is fe80:c21d:bc 23:acf4:578:34da:f0b2:dc56. The IPv4 format is x.x.x.x where the *x* represents decimal numbers in the range of 0 to 255. The IPv6 format is x:x:x:x:x:x:x:x where the *x* represents hexadecimal numbers in the range from 0000 to FFFF. Look at **Figure 18-1** to see an IPv4 and IPv6 address assigned to the same network adapter in Windows Vista.

Notice that each set of decimal numbers in the IPv4 address is separated by a period. In the IPv6 address, each set of hexadecimal numbers is separated by a colon. A double colon is used in an IPv6 address as an abbreviated form of an all zeros entry. For example, the IPv6 address fe80:0:0:0:ac32:0:0:ffe4 can be written as fe80::ac32:0:0:ffe4. A series of zero can be replaced by a single set of double colons. However, you can only replace one string of zeros, not two sets. Also, notice that each network card has an assigned MAC address.

Windows Vista is the first operating system to assign to a computer both the IPv4 and IPv6 address by default. Earlier operating systems used only the IPv4 address and the MAC address. Windows XP was the first operating system that would allow you to assign an IPv6 address to a network adapter, but it was not configured by default.

> **Tech Tip**
>
> IPv4 provides a total of 4,294,967,296 possible addresses, while IPv6 provides a total of 340,282,366,920,938,463, 463,374,607,431,768,211,456 possible IP addresses.

Advantages of IPv6

IPv6 provides many advantages and improvements when compared to the limitations of IPv4. The main improvements of IPv6 over IPv4 are a much larger pool of Internet and network addresses, reduced broadcast traffic, better security, and improved quality of service.

Larger Pool of IPv6 Addresses

The main reason IPv6 was implemented was to increase the number of available Internet addresses. An IPv4 address is equal to 32 bits or approximately 4,000,000,000 billion addresses. IPv6 uses 128-bit addresses, which is approximately equal to 340,000,000,000,000,000, 000,000,000,000,000,000,000 possible addresses.

Figure 18-1.
By default, Windows Vista and later assign IPv4 and IPv6 addresses to a network card.

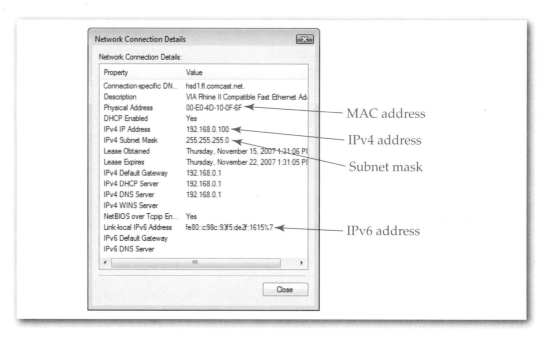

As you can see, the possible number of unique addresses seems inexhaustible. However, when the IPv4 standard was developed, it was also thought that the total number of IPv4 addresses were inexhaustible.

Reduced Broadcast Traffic

IPv4 utilizes the Address Resolution Protocol (ARP) to resolve IPv4 addresses to media access code (MAC) addresses. A unique MAC address is assigned to each network adapter card. IPv6 uses the Neighbor Discovery (ND) protocol, which is carried inside a series of Internet Control Message Protocol (ICMP) packets on the local area network. Basically, ND will eventually replace ARP broadcasts. This will significantly reduce network traffic on the local area network. A lot of network traffic is caused by a constant repetition of ARP requests generated on a network system by various software applications. The software applications constantly verify the presence of other devices. At this time, the implementation of both IPv6 and IPv4 by default does not result in total reduced local area network traffic.

Improved Security

IPv6 incorporates IPSec to provide better security than IPv4. **IPSec** is a collection of protocols that encrypt and authenticate each packet that uses an IP address over the Internet. The reason IPv6 has improved security is that IPSec is mandatory for use with IPv6 and only optional for IPv4.

Better Quality of Service

Quality of service refers to a protocol's ability to deliver certain packets in a timely fashion. For example, a long text document can have delays between packets because the delays do not affect the content of the text document. Packets that contain live video or audio must not have delays between the packets. A long delay between packets can result in a choppy conversation with parts of speech missing. IPv4 does have a quality of service feature, but when using a security protocol such as IPSec, the delivery of packets is slowed. The IPv6 standard significantly improves quality of service and does not let IPSec security cause long delays

between packets, thus ensuring a better quality of service. IPv6 has a new feature built into the header called the *flow label field*. The flow label field contains information that identifies the packet as special and allows routers to stream the content of the IPv6 packet, even when encrypted with IPSec. Also, the IPSec standard is incorporated into the IPv6 standard making it native, while IPSec is optional for IPv4. IPSec was developed after IPv4 standard and is handled as an optional add-on feature, thus creating more overhead.

Support for Network Discovery

The **Internet Control Message Protocol Version 6 (ICMPv6)** is a protocol and a service for exchanging messages between network neighboring nodes on the same link. This is the basis of the Network Discovery protocol, which allows a computer system to identify other devices connected to the same section (subnet) of a local area network. Network Discovery allows for automatic configuration of network devices and the discovery of routers attached to the local area network.

IPv4 Network Class

For the purpose of assigning IP addresses, IPv4 networks are divided into three classifications: Class A, Class B, and Class C. Large networks are assigned a Class A classification. A **Class A network** can support up to 16 million hosts on each of 127 networks. Medium-sized networks are assigned Class B status. A **Class B network** supports up to 65,000 hosts on each of 16,000 networks. Small networks are assigned a Class C classification. A **Class C network** supports 254 hosts on each of 2,000,000 networks. IPv4 networks are assigned an IP address based on their network classification. Look at **Figure 18-2.**

In the table, you can see that the class of the network determines the numeric value of the first octet in its IP address. The range for a Class A network is from 1 to 127; the range for a Class B network is from 128 to 191; and the range for a Class C network is from 192 to 223. IP addresses for Class A networks use only the first octet as the network address. The remaining three

Figure 18-2.
The attributes of IPv4 networks are listed here by class.

Table of TCP/IP Classes			
	Class A	**Class B**	**Class C**
Format	net.host.host.host	net.net.host.host	net.net.net.host
Subnet	255.000.000.000	255.255.000.000	255.255.255.000
Range of 1st Octet	1–127	128–191	192–223
Total Hosts per Network	16,777,214	65,534	254
Total Number of Networks	126	16,384	2,097,152
Typical Address	122.57.103.147	135.200.137.102	198.45.103.67

Goodheart-Willcox Publisher

octets define hosts on the network. The first two octets of a Class B network IP address identify the network. The remaining two octets identify hosts on the network. A Class C network uses the first three octets to identify the network and the last octet to identify hosts. For example, a typical Class C network might have a TCP/IP address of 201.100.100.12. The network is identified as 201.100.100, and the host is identified as 12.

IPv4 Subnet Mask

An organizational network may be divided into several smaller networks. These networks within networks are known as *subnets*. A **subnet mask** is used to determine what subnet a particular IP address refers to.

When the subnet mask is encountered, it is usually viewed in decimal form in a series of four three-digit numbers. At first glance, a subnet mask may appear identical to an IP address. However, a subnet mask is distinguishable from an IP address because it begins with one or more octets of 255. An IP address cannot begin with 255. The subnet mask can be used to identify the class of network, but is really intended to allow the network address to be broken down into smaller subnetworks.

The octets of a subnet mask correspond to octets in the IP address. The actual numbers found in a subnet mask depend on the class of the network and the number of subnetworks it is divided into. The subnet mask is combined with the IP address using the bitwise "AND" operation, the details of which are beyond the scope of this textbook. The resulting address is the subnet

address. For now, just remember that the subnet mask is used to identify any subnetworks at a network address. IPv6 does not require the use of a subnet mask. IPv6 incorporates a subnet mask function as part of the assigned IPv6 address. There is no need for a separate IPv6 subnet mask.

Running Ipconfig

Information about the computer IPv4 and IPv6 address, MAC address, and network adapter can be obtained by running the **ipconfig** command from the command prompt. **Figure 18-3** shows the results of running **ipconfig** from the Windows Vista command prompt.

Adding the **/all** switch to the **ipconfig** command will reveal even more detailed information about the network adapter. In **Figure 18-4**, you can see detailed information concerning the DHCP configuration, DHCP and DNS server assigned IP addresses, NetBIOS over TCP/IP, and more.

A+ Note

Make sure you know the difference between the information produced by the **ipconfig** and **ipconfig /all** commands.

DHCP

Originally, computers on a network had to have their IP addresses assigned manually as part of the routine to get a PC ready to communicate on

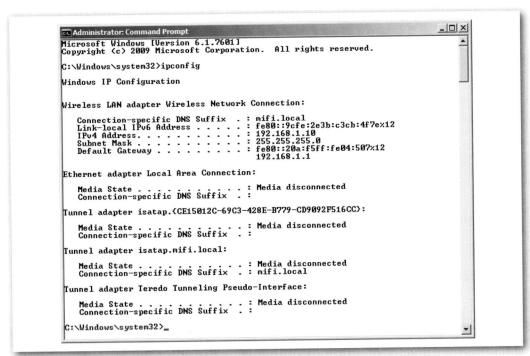

Figure 18-3.
The **ipconfig** command reveals information about the network adapter, such as the assigned IPv4 address and subnet mask, as well as the IPv6 address, MAC address, and default gateway.

a network and over the Internet. When IP addresses are assigned manually, the process is referred to as **static IP addressing**. This is a time-consuming operation if hundreds or even thousands of hosts are on a network. A log of computer names, locations, MAC addresses, and the assigned IP addresses must be recorded. IP addresses on each host must be unique. Using the same IP address on more than one host causes communication conflicts, and thus erratic behavior.

Most network systems are configured using a DHCP service. **Dynamic Host Configuration Protocol (DHCP)** was written to replace the manual setup of IP addresses on a network. When a server runs DHCP, the IP addresses are assigned automatically to the hosts. The act of automatically assigning IP addresses is known as **dynamic addressing**. The DHCP server is given a pool, or list, of IP addresses. Each host is assigned an address from the pool as it logs on to the network. The IP address is issued to each host temporarily. The address is released after a period of time and may be reissued to another host later.

Tech Tip

The DHCP service can be provided by a router or server.

A static IPv4 and IPv6 address can be assigned to a network adapter. Static IP addresses are often used for network devices such as servers, routers, and printers. A static address ensures that the same IPv4 or IPv6 address will be used for the device.

A DHCP assignment does not guarantee the same IPv4 and or IPv6 address will be assigned to the device. This can cause problems, especially for devices that host webpages. A computer uses a cache to store webpage names resolved to IP addresses. A webpage hosting device, such as a web server, requires a static IP address because a computer will cache the webpage server address. If the webpage server constantly changes its assigned IPv4 and or IPv6 address because it is configured for DHCP, then the computer seeking the webpage will display an error and not be able to connect to the destination based on the older IP address.

Automatic Private IP Address

A computer requires an IP address to communicate, even on a local area network. When a IPv4 DHCP address cannot be issued to the computer, the computer automatically issues an Automatic Private IP Address (APIPA) to itself, so it can communicate with other computers and

Figure 18-4.
Using the **/all** switch with the **ipconfig** command reveals even more detailed information about the network adapter assignments.

equipment on the local area network. The APIPA range is from 169.254.0.1 to 169.254.255.254. An **Automatic Private IP Address (APIPA)** is an IP address that is automatically issued to a computer when a DHCP address cannot issue an IP address.

When the DHCP problem is resolved, the computer drops the Automatic Private IP Address, and the DHCP server automatically issues an IP address to the computer. These actions are automatic and transparent to the user. The user is never aware of what is happening. Typically, the user cannot access the Internet until the problem is solved with the DHCP server.

Alternate IP Address

Windows has a configuration option which allows the computer to be configured with an alternate IPv4 address. This configuration is for computers, such as laptops, that are used at home on a peer-to-peer network and at work as part of a client/server network. See **Figure 18-5**.

When a computer is configured with the alternate IP address, it cannot use APIPA. IPv6 has no alternate IPv6 configuration option. IPv6 does not require an alternate IP address because it automatically generates its own IPv6 address in similar fashion that IPv4 generates an APIPA.

Figure 18-5. The **Alternate Configuration** tab of the **Internet Protocol Version 4 (TCP/IPv4) Properties** dialog box allows a computer to be configured with a static IPv4 address.

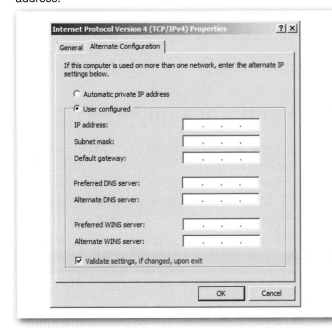

Link-Local IPv6 Address

There can be more than one IPv6 address assigned to a network adapter in contrast to IPv4 which only assigns one IPv4 address. Microsoft uses the term *link-local* in reference to the IPv6 address assigned to support communications on the local area network. The link-local addresses serve the same function as IPv4 Automatic Private IP Addresses (APIPAs). The IPv6 link-local address always starts with FE08. Link-local IPv6 addresses are automatically assigned and are required for the Network Discovery feature. Without a link-local IPv6 address, Network Discovery will not function. This is why Microsoft operating systems automatically configure link-local address "FE08" for network devices.

WINS

On a typical Windows network, each computer has its own name, such as "Station1" or "BillC." The **Windows Internet Naming Service (WINS)** a software service that resolves the computer name to the equivalent IP address on the network. DHCP servers assign IP addresses to

hosts from a pool of IP addresses. The same host may have a new IP address each time it logs on to the local network. To correlate a computer name to its current IP address, WINS works closely with the DHCP server.

WINS is not required for computers later than Windows 2000 but still remains as a configuration option for the network adapter. Today's operating systems rely on DNS rather than WINS to resolve computer names to IP addresses.

DNS

The **Domain Name Service (DNS)** is a service that translates domain names to IP addresses. The DNS service is used across the Internet, assisting computers in identifying and talking to each other. Similar to WINS, instead of translating computer names to IP addresses in the network, DNS translates domain names. DNS is also used in smaller network systems to match computer and network services to IP addresses. When a user inputs a user-friendly name, the DNS service resolves the name to a computer or device. Domain names are easier to remember than actual IP addresses.

When a domain name is entered, the DNS service searches its database for the matching IP address and connects the user to that address. Web addresses are entered into a browser or search engine and then passed and copied throughout the Internet by routers. Once a domain is located, the Internet Service Provider (ISP) server retains a copy of the domain name and corresponding assigned IP address in a database. When a DNS query is made from a corporate domain, a copy of the domain name used in the query is saved on the corporation domain server as well.

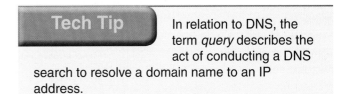

In relation to DNS, the term *query* describes the act of conducting a DNS search to resolve a domain name to an IP address.

Another copy of the resolved DNS query is saved on the computer that initiated the search. The copy of the query is referred to as the *DNS cache*. The DNS resolver cache is a list of recent domain queries saved on the local computer. When a query is made, the computer first looks in the DNS cache before conducting the query on the ISP and the Internet to see if a record has been saved.

Figure 18-6 shows the results of issuing the **ipconfig /displaydns** command, which displays the content of the DNS cache. The host computer name is Richard-Saber. The name is appended with "mshome.net" which turns the host computer name into a domain name. The operating system automatically appends the computer or other local area network devices with a domain name so that the assigned IP address can be resolved to the user-friendly computer or network device name by the DNS service. Some commands directly related to DNS are listed in the following table.

Ipconfig Command	Description
ipconfig /displaydns	Displays the contents of the DNS client resolver cache.
ipconfig /dnsflush	Flush and reset the contents of the DNS resolver cache. This command is used for trouble-shooting when the DNS cache is suspect. The DNS resolver cache is emptied, forcing the computer to use the next available Internet DNS server to resolve the DNS query.

Tech Tip

The computer DNS cache is referred to as *client-side DNS*.

A+ Note

One or more questions are always asked about DHCP and DNS. WINS is often used as a distractor.

Special WAN Equipment

A typical WAN must handle a tremendous amount of packet traffic. To accomplish this, some special equipment must be used to route data to and from hosts across the WAN. Wide area networks also consist of a variety of media, equipment, and protocols. Certain pieces of equipment are used in a network environment when all the hosts are using the same protocol to communicate. Other types of equipment are used when a mixture of protocols are used. For example, protocols designed for satellite transmission and telephone systems do not directly match the Ethernet and TCP/IP suite of protocols. The protocols need to be translated to other protocol formats.

In **Figure 18-7**, you can see a variety of media and devices that support communication between people and places, such as satellites, radio towers (cells), laptops, tablets, desktop PCs, and more. There are also a mixture of different networking protocols, such as Ethernet, Bluetooth, and Frame Relay. All these separate technologies work together even though the data packets created by each system differ. For the many different protocols to communicate with each other, special

Figure 18-6.
The DNS cache is displayed. The host computer domain name is richard-saber. mshome.net.

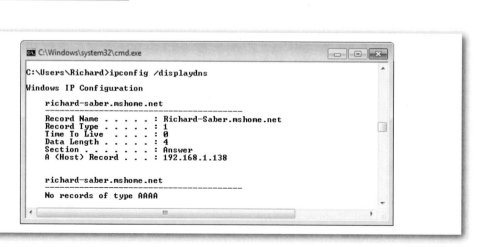

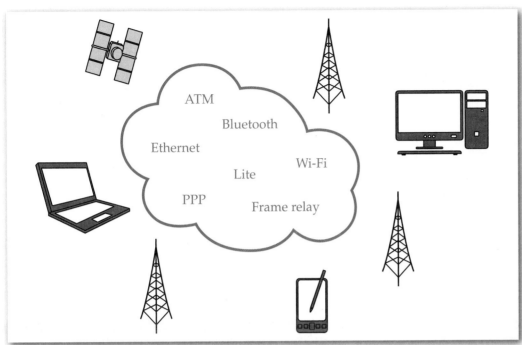

Goodheart-Willcox Publisher

Figure 18-7.
The wide array of networking media and technologies are complex and require a wide variety of specialized equipment.

hardware and software must be used. This section covers the major types of equipment and briefly explains the function of each in a network environment.

Repeater

A **repeater** is a piece of equipment that regenerates a weak digital signal. Network cable standards recommend a maximum cable length to prevent the loss of data signals. For example, the maximum recommended length for a typical Ethernet cable (Cat 5 and Cat 6) is 100 meters. For farther distances, a repeater must be installed. A repeater is often incorporated into other devices such as switches and routers to send data across many miles. A repeater receives a signal, reshapes it to its original form, and transmits it over the cable. See **Figure 18-8**.

Figure 18-8. A—Digital signal is transmitted. The only values in the signal are 1s and 0s. B—As the signal approaches its maximum transmission distance, the "shoulders" of the signal are slumped, creating graduated values (analog) in the transmission. Also note the crests of the signal are no longer at maximum height. C—The repeater restores the signal to its original strength and shape.

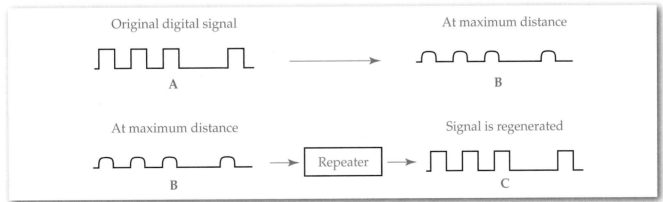

Goodheart-Willcox Publisher

As a digital signal travels farther from its source, it degrades, eventually becoming unintelligible. At great distances, a network adapter cannot distinguish between the 0s and 1s transmitted through the cable. A repeater receives the degraded digital signal and reshapes it to its original form.

A+ Note

A repeater is often referred to as an amplifier. Technically speaking, an amplifier increases the original signal strength rather than reshaping the signal to its original form. On the A+ Certification exam, the only correct answer may equate a repeater with an amplifier. In this case, choose the answer that implies that a repeater works like an amplifier.

Bridge

A bridge is a piece of equipment that joins two dissimilar network segments. For example, a bridge may connect an Ethernet twisted pair cable network to a Satellite dish or fiber-optic network. The bridge simply passes packets from one system to the other regardless of the protocol. The bridge maintains a list of MAC addresses that are connected to it so it can filter out data packets. For example, if two network segments are connected by a bridge, the bridge can be programmed to pass only data packets that match the MAC address of hosts on the other side of the bridge. By doing this, data traffic is minimized. See **Figure 18-9**.

Router

A router connects networks together and controls the flow of exchanged data packets. The term *routing* means moving a packet of data from a source to a destination. A router performs much more complex tasks than a bridge. A router not only connects hosts together on a WAN, it also determines the best route to use. The router calculates the "cost" of a number of different ways to connect the hosts together and uses the least expensive method. The cost is based on the use of leased lines and equipment, the time to transmit, and the distance.

In **Figure 18-10**, you can see that the function of the router is to determine the least "expensive" route from one host to another. In networking, the term *expensive* refers to the cost of routing data through a network system. Distances between the source and destination in a network system are measured by routers. Each pass of data through a router is referred to as a *hop*. The more hops required to meet a destination, the more expensive the route.

Figure 18-9.
A bridge limits the number of hosts affected by data broadcasts. The bridge passes or blocks data based on the MAC address in the destination address in the packet header. If a large network were constructed without bridge techniques, the constant broadcast of data packets would slow the entire network.

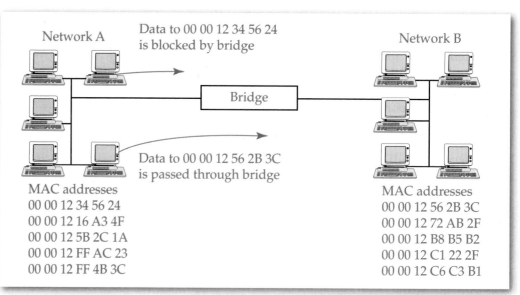

Goodheart-Willcox Publisher

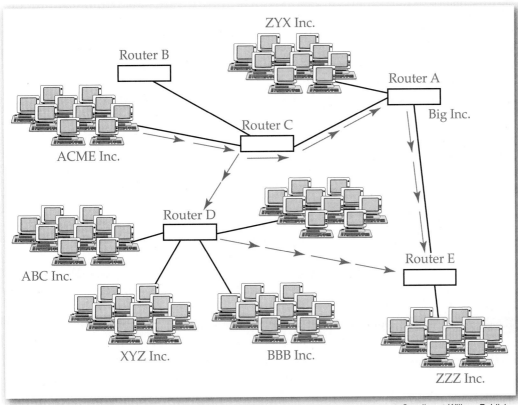

Figure 18-10. Routers send data traffic across the entire world. They also select the least expensive route to use. As you can see, there are several routes that can be chosen to send a data packet from ACME, Inc. to ZZZ, Inc.

Goodheart-Willcox Publisher

A router adds information to the data frame surrounding the data packet. The information expands the identification of the packet's origin, its destination, and its route.

Routers are available in two styles: static and dynamic. A static router is programmed with a database of IP addresses, subnet masks, and network IDs. It does not broadcast information on a constant basis. A dynamic router communicates with other routers on the network. Dynamic routers constantly exchange data about each other's location and database tables. See **Figure 18-11** for a quick comparison of bridging and routing.

Brouter

A **brouter** is a combination router and bridge. A brouter applies the best characteristics of both systems. A bridge can pass network data packets that do not contain an IP address but does contain a MAC address. The router forwards packets based on IP address rather than MAC address.

Figure 18-11. This table offers a short comparison of routers and bridges.

Bridge	Router
Forwards broadcast traffic	Blocks broadcast traffic
Uses MAC addresses	Uses IP addresses
Does not add to packet information	Adds to packet information
Forwards packets to unknown addresses	Blocks packets to unknown addresses

Goodheart-Willcox Publisher

Switch

A **switch** filters data packets and forwards them between network segments. Switches are usually intelligent hubs, meaning they can determine on which side of the switch a packet's destination is located.

There are two types of switching communication used for computer networks: packet switching and circuit switching. **Packet switching** divides data into packets, which can take a variety of routes to get to their destination. **Circuit switching** makes a permanent connection for the duration of the transmission, and data is transmitted in a steady stream. For example, when you make a dial-up connection with a modem, a circuit switch is closed to keep the modem in constant connection on the telephone line. On the network, the packet switching method is used rather than a permanent connection for the duration of the call.

Gateway

A **gateway** is a networking device that translates information between two networks that use different protocols to communicate. Think of a gateway as a communications translator because it translates commands and data from one protocol to another or from one format to another. For example, a gateway may be required to translate protocols for Voice over IP (VoIP). H.323 is a telephone protocol used to support VoIP over traditional telephone equipment, but it must be converted when it connects to a standard Ethernet TCP/IP network system. There are a variety of modems used today, such as cable modems, telephone modems, DSL modems, wireless modems (hotspots), and more. Most of the time devices translate TCP/IP to another protocol such as PPP.

A gateway may be a special piece of equipment or a software package loaded onto a server or a router. It is important to understand that a network server can provide more than one service. For example, a computer can serve as a gateway, a proxy server, a firewall, and a file server. The exact name used for the server is relative to the network service being discussed.

Proxy Server

When dealing with Internet service, you may hear the term proxy server. A **proxy server** is a computer server that hides all the PCs in the LAN from direct connection with PCs outside of the LAN. This provides a better security service than

if each PC had direct access to outside the LAN. The server acts as a go-between for the distant sites and the user behind the server. The proxy server relays the requested information for the client, leaving the client anonymous to the outside network. Users outside of the network from locations across the Internet cannot communicate directly with the computer located behind the proxy server. The function of the proxy server is often incorporated into cable, DSL, and other network modems and with network devices such as routers.

The proxy server makes accessing the web more efficient for the network clients by caching frequently requested webpages. By caching the frequently accessed web information, the process of accessing distant webpages is expedited.

Firewall

The term *firewall* refers to a barrier that prevents direct contact between computers outside the organization and computers inside the organization. A firewall can be strictly software or a combination of software and hardware. All data communications to and from the organization are routed through the proxy server, and the firewall software decides whether to forward the data.

One way a firewall determines to block or pass a network connection is by the assigned port number of the packet. A port number identifies which program or service can utilize the information or command contained inside the network packet. For example, a packet with an assigned port number of 80 is to be sent to the web browser program/service and then opened by the appropriate web browser program, such as Internet Explorer.

Port numbers are assigned according to three ranges:
- System ports (0–1023).
- User ports (1024–49151).
- Private ports (49152–65535).

System ports are also called *well-known ports* and range from 0 to 1023. These port numbers are assigned by the Internet Assigned Numbers Authority (IANA) and cannot be used except for their intended purpose.

User ports, also known as *registered ports*, range from 1024 to 49151 and are assigned by the IANA for use by software companies such as Microsoft or CISCO systems. The private company requests the reservation of the port number for use with one of its software programs and then IANA assigns the port number to the company software service.

Dynamic ports, also known as *private ports*, range from 49152 to 65535 and are not assigned by IANA. Anyone can write a software application to use this range of port numbers. You will often encounter games that use port numbers in this range to support online game communication and management. Network system managers select which ports to block to prevent unauthorized use of the Internet connection. **Figure 18-12** lists some of the most common port number assignments used.

In **Figure 18-13**, you can see some of the many assigned port numbers viewed through **Windows Firewall with Advanced Security** in Windows 7 and Windows 8. Notice the list of services or programs, the assigned port numbers, and the status, such as enabled.

Double-clicking a particular service or program listed in **Windows Firewall with Advanced Security** produces a dialog box similar to the one in **Figure 18-14**. This particular dialog box shows the DNS properties for this particular computer. As you can see, it is used to enable and allow

Figure 18-12. Common port numbers and protocols or services.

Port Number	Protocol or Service
21	FTP
23	Telnet
25	SMTP
53	DNS
80	HTTP
110	POP3
143	IMAP
443	HTTPS
3389	RDP

Note: This table contains the most common port numbers that are used in questions for the CompTIA A+ exam. Always check the CompTIA website for the very latest complete set of port numbers.

Goodheart-Willcox Publisher

connection for this service. The DNS port number assigned is 53. Only port number 53 can be used for the DNS service. The DNS service is what is known as a core network service and cannot be changed or reassigned. The Microsoft operating system prevents the changing of core network port numbers. Other network port assignments for programs such as games are easily reassigned or disabled.

Figure 18-13. Port numbers of software programs and services can be viewed through **Windows Firewall with Advanced Security**.

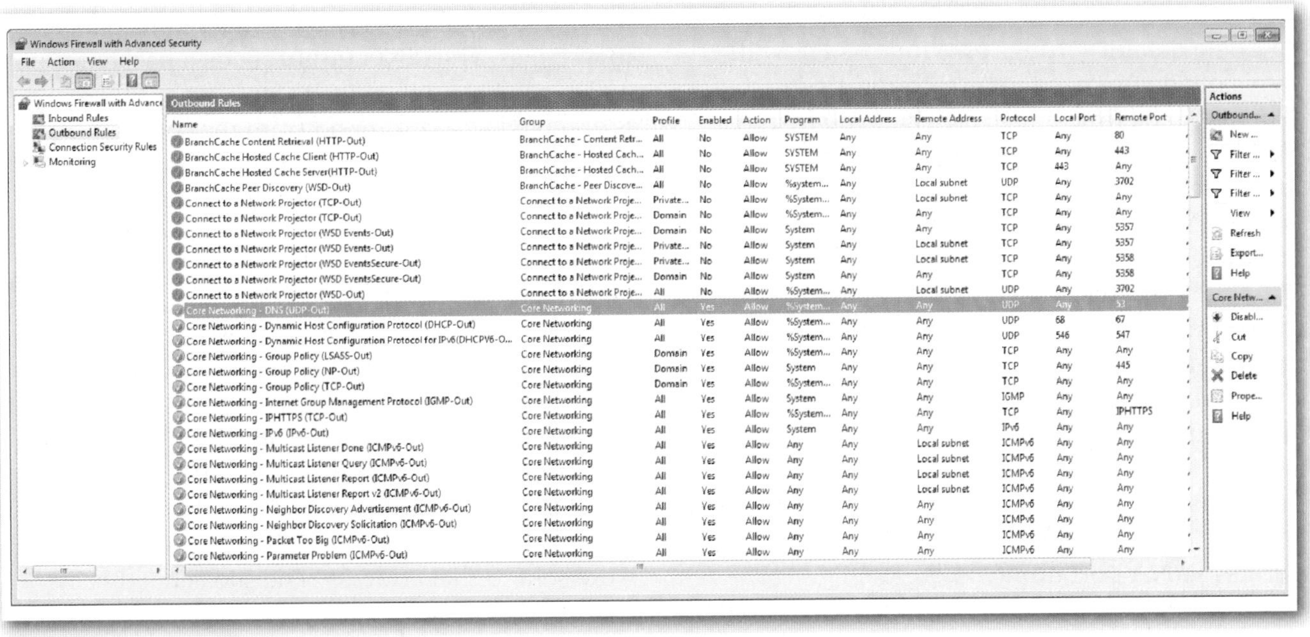

Figure 18-14. In **Windows Firewall with Advanced Security**, the **Properties** dialog box for a service or program provides options related to the port number, such as **Allow the connection**, **Allow the connection if secure**, and **Block the connection**.

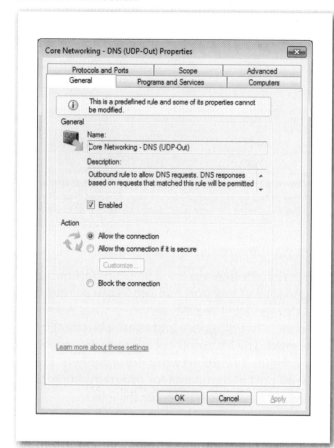

A firewall can be either a dedicated piece of network equipment or a software package. For example, Windows Firewall is a software package. Some network devices, such as routers or wireless access points, are also referred to as a *firewall* because they can also limit port connections.

Network Diagnostic Utilities

Standard utility programs are very handy when troubleshooting networked PCs. PING and tracert are the most common network diagnostic utilities used from the command prompt. In most cases, troubleshooting the network will be a combination of running troubleshooting wizards, issuing commands at a command prompt, and automatic detection by the operating system. Many network diagnostics are now built into the operating system. When an error is detected, it is either automatically diagnosed and corrected or a message appears informing the user that a problem exists and prompts the user for some type of action. We will now look at the most common troubleshooting commands issued from the command prompt and how they are used to diagnose network problems.

PING

The **Packet Internet Groper (PING)** is a utility that is often used to verify network connections to websites. The PING utility sends a packet to a distant site and then waits for a reply. PING is executed as a command from the command prompt. At the prompt, you simply type **ping** followed by the IP address or its URL name, such as www.yahoo.com. **Figure 18-15** shows the results of issuing a **ping** command to the Yahoo website. If you are on a network with a firewall, this test may not work. The **ping** command may be blocked by the firewall. Check with the network administrator.

When the Yahoo site was pinged, www.yahoo.com was automatically resolved to an IP address. You can see the IP address listed as 69.147.114.210. After the IP address was determined, four packets with 32 bytes of data were sent to that address. The site echoed back

The default settings of Windows Firewall typically do not need to be reconfigured. There will be times, such as when you install a particular software program, when you will be prompted to allow the assignment of a particular port number from the dynamic port range. The message usually does not request a particular port number but rather asks permission to allow the program to communicate through the firewall. If permission is granted by the system administrator or equal, then one or more port number(s) is assigned to that particular software program or service. A complete listing of all assigned port numbers is located at the IANA website. To find it, you can conduct an Internet search using the key terms "IANA port numbers."

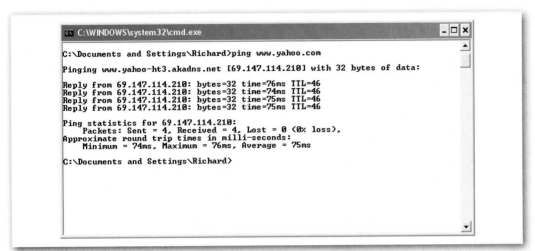

Figure 18-15.
A ping performed on www.yahoo.com.

with four replies. The average round trip to the site and back was 75 milliseconds. The **time to live (TTL)** is the length of time the data in a packet is valid. Packets are transmitted with the TTL setting recorded in the packet's header. This tells the network to disregard the packet after the set TTL time. If the destination did not exist, the ping would circulate the Internet forever. The Internet would soon become burdened with millions of ping packets circulating the Internet. The TTL feature limits the maximum time that the ping packet can circulate the Internet looking for the destination.

There are a number of switches that can be used with the **ping** command. The additional switches for the **ping** command can be viewed by issuing **ping /help** or **ping** at the command prompt.

A handy way of checking the network card to see if it is responding to TCP/IP transmissions is to "ping" the card. This is also referred to as a *loopback test*. The IPv6 loopback address is the reserved IP address of the network interface card. It is used to test if an IP address is configured for the network interface card and if the network interface card is functioning normally. The loopback address for IPv4 is 127.0.0.1. The loopback address for IPv6 is 0:0:0:0:0:0:0:1 or ::1. Note that the double colon eliminates fields containing only zeros.

To perform a loopback test for the IPv4 protocol, enter **ping 127.0.0.1** at the command prompt. The same command for IPv6 is **ping ::1** or **ping localhost**. The "::1" represents the IPv6 localhost address. To specify the localhost ping for IPv4, you must use the **ping -4 localhost** command. See **Figure 18-16**.

Tracert

The tracert utility is short for trace route. Tracert is more advanced than the PING utility. Like PING, it sends a packet out and waits for a reply. In addition to the information that PING provides, tracert displays information about the route that was taken to the destination. See **Figure 18-17**. As with the **ping** command, depending on how the firewall is configured, this test may not work on a network.

The **tracert** command is issued from the command prompt. In Figure 18-17, the **tracert** command reveals the actual route taken by the data packet. Among the information provided are the name of the router at comcast.net, the names of the routers at various cities, and the names of the different telephone carriers. The utility also displays the time it takes each packet to reach its destination. This feature is extremely useful in locating bottlenecks along the route.

Many third-party software developers offer utilities that further enhance the tracert function. NeoTrace is a commercial product developed and distributed by McAfee. It is a powerful diagnostic and investigation tool. The program traces the route to any destination over the Internet and returns information about the hosts on the route taken. The information includes registered details of each host along the route, such as address, telephone number, e-mail address, and IP address. See **Figure 18-18**. The information can be displayed as a detailed listing similar to a spreadsheet and as a graphical display in which the route is displayed on a map.

Figure 18-16.
When issuing the **ping localhost** command in Windows 7, the localhost is identified with the IPv6 localhost address or ::1.

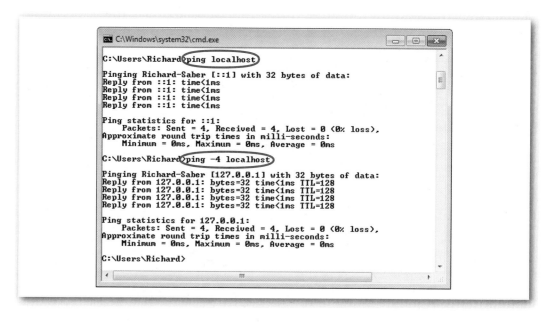

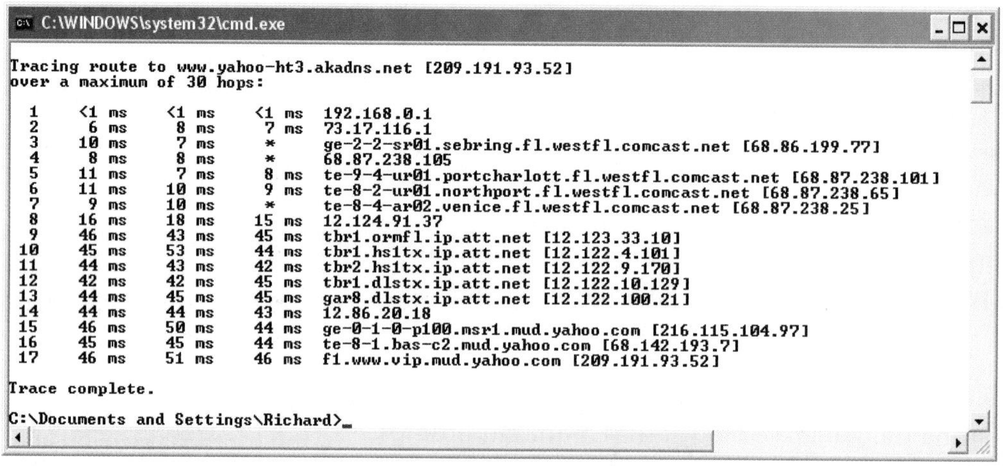

Figure 18-17.
The tracer utility is used here to trace the network path to www.yahoo.com.

Pathping

The pathping utility is an enhanced combination of the PING and tracert utilities. When issued from the command prompt, it performs in a similar fashion to tracert, but with additional information. Look at **Figure 18-19**.

After pinging the path to the destination and displaying the results similar to tracert, pathping continues to ping the destination with additional test packets. After 400 seconds, the additional information is displayed, indicating what percent of the additional test packets reached the destination. This test is much more thorough than tracert because it tests the connectivity to the final

destination over a longer period of time. Some network problems are intermittent and may not be revealed by a simple ping or a tracert.

After completing a trace of the route from the source computer to the destination, the pathping utility continues to send diagnostic packets. A series of additional packets are continuously sent for a period indicated at the end of the original tracert. In Figure 18-19, the time value is 450 seconds, or approximately 7 1/2 minutes. Pathping is used to detect intermittent connection problems or bottlenecks in the traffic flow. This is the main advantage the pathping utility has over the tracert utility.

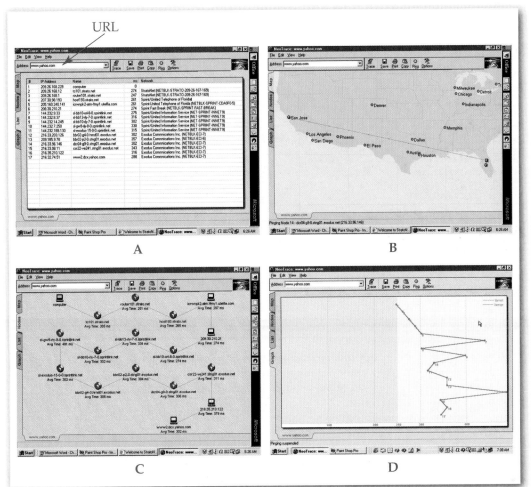

Figure 18-18.
A—The network path
to www.yahoo.com
displayed in NeoTrace
using the **List** tab.
B—The network path
to www.yahoo.com
displayed using
NeoTrace's **Map** tab.
C—The network path
to www.yahoo.com
displayed using
NeoTrace's **Nodes**
tab. D—The network
path displayed using
NeoTrace's **Graph** tab.

Nslookup

The nslookup utility is used to diagnose
Domain Name Service (DNS) server problems.
In the command line, you can use either the IP
address or the URL of the domain being tested.
The **nslookup** command queries the nearest DNS
server and displays the information contained
in its DNS database for the corresponding IP
address. **Figure 18-20** shows the nslookup utility
resolving the IP address 66.94.234.13. Notice that
Yahoo is matched to the IP address. You can also
perform an nslookup on the name of a server and
to obtain the assigned IP address.

Netstat

Netstat (network statistics) displays network
connections and is used to diagnose network

connection and traffic problems. Netstat is
issued from the command prompt. **Figure 18-21**
shows the results of the **netstat** command issued
without a switch. The results show the active TCP
connections by address. You can also see which
computers have a current connection established
in the local area network. The following table lists
the common **netstat** command switches.

Netstat Command	Description
netstat -a	Displays all connections and "listening" ports.
netstat -r	Displays routing tables.
netstat -e	Displays Ethernet statistics.
netstat -s	Displays statistics by protocol.
netstat -n	Displays IP addresses and port numbers in numerical order.

Figure 18-19. The pathping utility used on www.yahoo.com.

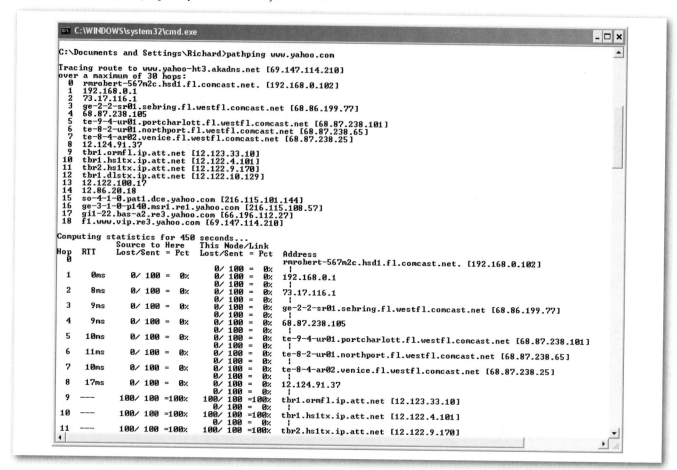

Figure 18-20.
The nslookup utility
resolving the IP
address 66.94.234.13.

Nbtstat

Nbtstat is used for troubleshooting NetBIOS name resolution problems. The function of a network adapter configured for NetBIOS over TCP/IP is to resolve NetBIOS names to IP addresses. Microsoft originally used NetBIOS names for network computers and devices. The

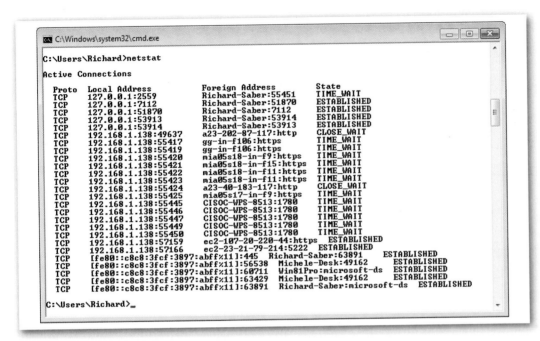

NetBIOS naming convention used a maximum of 15 characters for a name. The name as well as a code was assigned to each device on the network. The two-letter code identified the type of device, such as a computer, server, or workgroup.

NetBIOS names are resolved through network mechanisms, such as WINS broadcast and DNS server queries. NetBIOS is not required for computers starting with Windows Vista, but the commands related to NetBIOS, such as **nbtstat,** are still valid on later Windows operating systems. Some of the more common switches used for **nbtstat** are listed in the following table.

Nbtstat Command	Description
nbtstat -c	Displays the contents of the NetBIOS name cache.
nbtstat -n	Displays names of all devices registered through broadcasts by NetBIOS applications.
nbtstat -r	Displays NetBIOS names resolved by using broadcasts on the local area network.
nbtstat -S	Displays the current network NetBIOS sessions and the status of each.

Figure 18-22 shows the results of the **nbtstat -n** command. **Figure 18-23** shows the results of the **nbtstat -r** command. The results are NetBIOS names resolved by using broadcasts on the local area network.

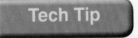

Tech Tip

The last operating system to depend on NetBIOS was Windows XP, so any operating system later than Windows XP will produce limited results when issuing the **nbtstat** command.

Net Services

Net services are a set of commands that can display and manage local user accounts, shared folders, and start or stop services. The set of net services commands are entered at a command prompt. Commands are entered as two or more words. For example, **net view** displays a list of computers that are members of the local area network or domain, **Figure 18-24.** Some of the more common net services commands are listed in the table on page 773.

Figure 18-22.
This is an example of the **nbtstat -n** command, which provides a list of NetBIOS name assignments for the local computer and the workgroups they belongs to.

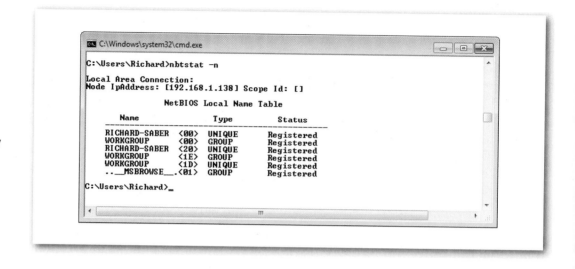

Figure 18-23.
This is an example of the **nbtstat -r** command results, which lists the computer names on the local area network resolved by broadcast.

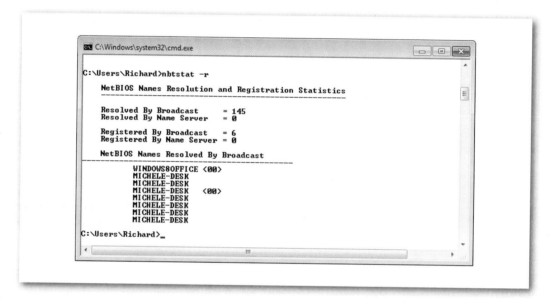

Figure 18-24.
The **net view** command displays a list of local computers connected on the local area network.

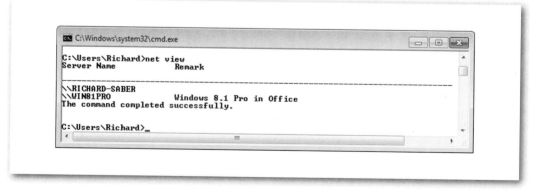

Net Services Command	Description
net view	Displays computers connected to the local area network.
net share	Displays information about local shares.
net user	Displays information about the local device users.
net accounts	Displays information related to the local user account, such as password configuration options.
net groups	Displays information related to local computer groups.
net stop	Stops a network service.
net start	Starts a network service.
net print	Manages print jobs.
net statistics workstation	Displays workstation network statistics.
net statistics server	Displays server network statistics.

These are just a few of the many net services commands available. To learn more about Microsoft net services commands, visit the Microsoft TechNet website. You can find it by conducting an Internet search using the key terms "Microsoft TechNet net command."

ARP

Address Resolution Protocol (ARP) is a protocol used to resolve IPv4 addresses to physical addresses. Physical addresses are also referred to as *MAC addresses*. There is also a command called **arp,** which when issued displays the contents of the ARP cache as seen in **Figure 18-25**. The ARP cache holds a list of IPv4 addresses correlated to MAC addresses. IPv4 relies on the ARP cache to locate other devices on the local area network. IPv6 does not use ARP to resolve MAC addresses to IP addresses. IPv6 communicates directly with other local area network devices without the need to identify the MAC address. The IPv4 protocol has to convert IPv4 addresses to MAC addresses in order to communicate on the local area network. The ARP command can be used to verify that the IPv4 protocol is properly identifying devices by MAC address.

Windows XP Net Diagnostics

A utility developed by Microsoft and first introduced in Windows XP is Net Diagnostics. Net Diagnostics is easily accessed by running **msinfo32.exe** from the **Run** dialog box at the **Start** menu. Once the **System Information** dialog box opens, select **Tools** from the main menu, and then

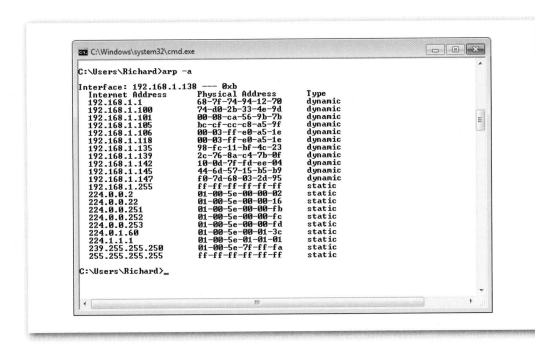

Figure 18-25.
The results of issuing an **arp -a** command.

select **Net Diagnostics**. Another way to access Net Diagnostics is through **Help and Support**.

Once the Net Diagnostics tool is run, it displays information about the network system. In **Figure 18-26**, you can see items that fail tests are displayed in red as "FAILED" and items that pass tests are displayed in green as "PASSED." Critical items are automatically tested, and information can be revealed, such as the MAC address, IP address, DNS host name, and WINS server. The Net Diagnostics utility combines the PING, tracert, and other utilities into one tool.

Windows Vista and Later Diagnostics

Windows Vista and Windows 7 have incorporated a visual representation to indicate a network problem. Windows 8 does not support this feature but does have automatic detection of network problems. Look at **Figure 18-27**. You can

see how a problem with the Internet connection is indicated in the Network and Sharing Center. A bright red *X* is placed across the Internet cable symbol between the local area network (Network 2) and the Internet connection device, such as a router or gateway. In **Figure 18-28**, there is no local area network. The computer connects directly to the Internet through a cable modem or other Internet access device.

Windows also provides other network troubleshooting tools or wizards. Looking again at Figure 18-28, you can see an option in Network and Sharing Center called **Troubleshoot problems**. This option is available in Windows 7 and Windows 8 and produces a list of troubleshooting tools similar to the ones in **Figure 18-29**.

Windows Vista has an automated troubleshooting wizard in the Network and Sharing Center also, but it is identified by the **Diagnose and repair** option. This wizard does not provide choices as in Windows 7 and Windows 8.

Figure 18-26.
Windows XP Net Diagnostics tool.

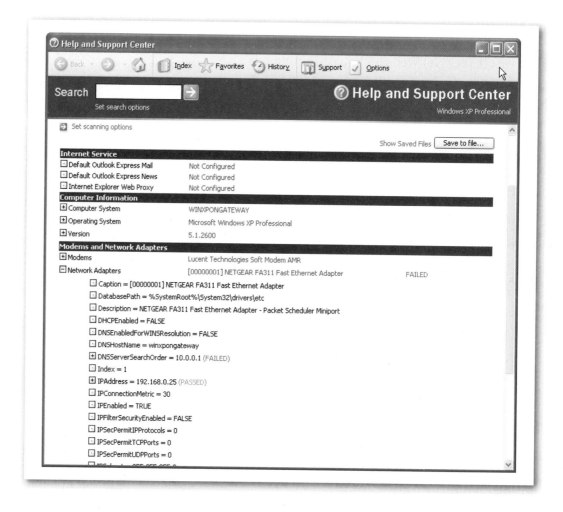

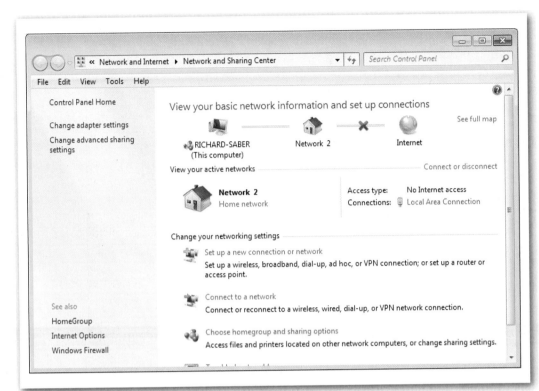

Figure 18-27.
The Network and Sharing Center indicates a problem with the Internet connection by placing a red *X* on the network cable icon before the Internet symbol.

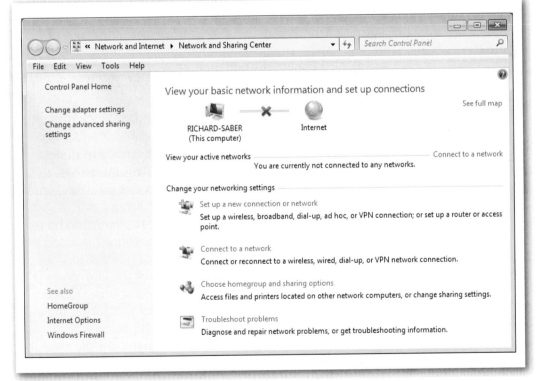

Figure 18-28.
In this scenario, the computer connects directly to the Internet.

Figure 18-29.
Troubleshooting wizards available in Windows 7 and Windows 8.

The Windows Vista wizard simply runs and diagnoses the network and Internet connections generally.

The diagnostic wizards for the Windows operating system incorporate a series of diagnostic programs that are similar to the ones run from the command prompt. The wizard interprets the results and then displays a message on the screen related to the diagnosed problem. In **Figure 18-30**, you not only see the most likely cause but also possible solutions to remedy the problem. As operating systems evolve, they incorporate more and more automatic network connection problem detection systems and also automatically correct problems.

The Internet Structure

No discussion about WAN systems would be complete without a discussion of the largest WAN in the world, the Internet. This section will give you a brief historical background of the Internet and its development, and it will make you aware of how complex the Internet really is.

Development of the Internet

The Internet has actually been in existence since the 1960s and grew from a simple project of the Advanced Research Project Agency (ARPA). The project was designed to test the feasibility of communication between computers over telephone lines. The first experiments were very simple but also very impressive. The original experiments contained only four hosts. Today there are millions.

Later, ARPA was absorbed by the United States military, renamed DARPA, and operated by the U.S. Department of Defense (DOD). As the network grew, the National Science Foundation became involved by awarding grants to many different universities and private companies to develop a communications model for what is now called the Internet.

In 1985, some of the centers connected by the DARPA network's 56-kbps backbone included Cornell University, the National Center for Supercomputing Application at the University of Illinois, the Pittsburgh Supercomputing Center in Pittsburgh, the University of California in San Diego, and Princeton University in New Jersey. This backbone is viewed by many people as the true beginning of what was to become the Internet. Over the next several years, many more universities, private companies, and research centers connected to the line. Within three years, the increased traffic forced the original 56-kbps backbone to be replaced with a T-1 line that could

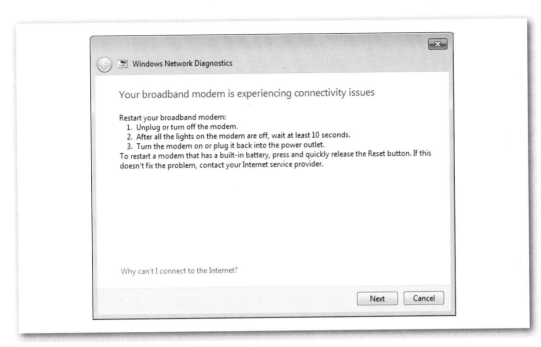

Figure 18-30.
A message box with information about the probable cause of the network failure will appear after running diagnostic wizards.

carry 1.544 Mbps. The new line connected six diverse regional networks in the United States, including the National Center of Atmospheric Research in Colorado, the original computer centers previously listed, and the Merit site at the University of Michigan.

Merit played a significant role in further developing the Internet. In 1990, Merit, IBM, and MCI started a nonprofit organization called Advanced Network and Services, Inc. (ANS). Its major goal was to manage the National Science Foundation backbone and continue to upgrade it. IBM and MCI both contributed four million dollars to the venture. The backbone was expanded to 16 major sites connected by a T-3 line, which could carry 43 Mbps. A T-3 line consists of 672 lines, each with a capability to carry 64 kbps.

By 1993, the National Science Foundation bowed out of the Internet management business. They designed a series of Network Access Points (NAPs) for private companies to connect to the backbone. Private companies could develop their own networks and then tie directly into the backbone, but only at a NAP. Originally, four locations were designated to serve as access to the backbone. The four locations were San Francisco, operated by Pacific Bell; Chicago, operated by Ameritech; New York, operated by Sprint (the actual NAP is located in Pennsauken, New Jersey, not New York); and Washington DC, operated by Metropolitan Fiber Systems. As demand grew, more locations were added.

Merit was chosen to maintain a database of information about the Internet and act as the arbitrator for disputes. The Internet then came into full power, based on the original ARPA backbone project. Private communications companies constructed their own backbones as well. Some companies constructed MANs in large metropolitan areas. The MANs were designed to allow businesses to have access to high-speed backbone systems spanning the US.

Growth has continued at an astounding rate. The Internet consists of fiber-optic and copper cables, wireless devices, infrared devices, satellites, and millions of miles of old telephone lines. The Internet grows so fast and is so diverse, there is no map of all the lines and connections in existence. Individual companies do have information regarding connection and traffic lines, but they only have what is limited to their direct control. There are over 4,500 companies making changes to the Internet daily, making it impossible to create an up-to-date and all-inclusive map of the Internet.

The diversity arises from the Internet's practice of sending data along the shortest route between two points. Most Internet providers have agreements allowing each to access the other's backbones and parts of their individually constructed networks. If these agreements were not arranged, access to the Internet would be very limited.

For example, one customer may use ABC as their Internet provider and another customer may use XYZ as their Internet provider. The two companies are located across the street from each other. However, if it were not for mutually beneficial agreements set up between the two companies, the data sent by one customer to the other customer might very well be routed hundreds or even thousands of miles to a national backbone before making a return trip to the other provider's lines.

There are thousands of agreements in place between providers to lease line access from one another. In this manner, the route taken by data is considerably shortened. This is one of the main reasons there are so many routers used on the Internet. The routers are constantly updated either manually or automatically to find the least expensive route between two points on the Internet. In short, the Internet is a network of networks that are all interconnected, forming a huge spider web of communication circuits.

You might want to conduct an experiment to see how the lines in your own geographic area are accessed. Use the tracert utility to trace the route to some point close by, such as a local business's website. You may be surprised to see exactly how far the data must travel. The NeoTrace utility will map the exact route for you.

Domain Names and URLs

Uniform Resource Locators (URLs) are the global addresses for websites all over the Internet. InterNIC was the government agency first responsible for issuing uniform resource locator addresses and domain names. The first part of the URL identifies the protocol used and the second part identifies the domain name.

Many people confuse domain names with URLs because they appear so similar. The domain name is an alphanumeric name that identifies one or more IP addresses. The domain name is combined with the protocol type to form the URL.

For example, for the URL ftp://www.download.com/freestuff.exe, download.com is the domain. The file freestuff.exe is located at that domain and can be accessed using the FTP protocol. For the URL http://www.ace.com/index.html, the domain is ace.com. The file, index.html, is a webpage that is accessed using the HTTP protocol.

The **Domain Name System (DNS)**, as mentioned earlier, is a system used to identify domain names of sites on the Internet and resolve them to their IP addresses. When you enter a URL in your web browser, a query is sent to a local resolver, a database of domain names and matching IP addresses. The query requests a matching IP address for the domain name that you entered. The resolver transmits the requested IP address to your computer, and you are then seamlessly connected to the requested site. If the resolver's database does not contain the requested IP address, it forwards the query to the next resolver in the network. This continues until the IP address is located and you are connected to the requested site, or until all of the resolvers are searched without success, resulting in an error message.

Originally and until 1995, InterNIC issued domain names and matching IP addresses. Then, the InterNIC commercialized the system, turning it over to the private sector. Today, InterNIC retains the control of the system. However, it has delegated the responsibility of dealing with the public to the not for profit organization known as *Internet Corporation for Assigned Names and Numbers (ICANN)*. ICANN in turn handles the day-to-day operations associated with issuing private sector companies. However, you can access a list of authorized domain name registration companies from the InterNIC site. Domain name suffixes are assigned according to the domain's function. **Figure 18-31** lists some common suffixes found in domain names.

Tech Tip   InterNIC is the registered service mark of the U.S. Department of Commerce, which licensed the use of the name InterNIC to ICANN.

Figure 18-31. The top portion of this table lists common domain suffixes and the types of organizations that use them. The bottom portion of this table contains some of the latest domain suffixes and the types of organizations that use them.

Domain	Type of Organization
.com	Commercial business
.edu	Educational
.gov	Government
.mil	Military
.net	Host or gateway
.org	Organizations usually, but not necessarily, nonprofit
.aero	Global aviation authority
.arts	Art and cluture
.asia	Pan-Asia and Asian Pacific region
.biz	Restricted to business
.info	Information services
.jobs	Human resources management community
.mobi	Mobile products
.museum	Museums and related areas
.name	Individual personal names
.nom	Individuals
.pro	Reserved for licensed professionals
.rec	Recreational and entertainment
.store	Merchants
.travel	Travel industry
.web	Web activities

Goodheart-Willcox Publisher

Subdomains

Subdomains create a third level to a website. A **subdomain** is a division of a group of networks. Subdomains function in a similar manner to folders in a file system and offer another way to organize a website. For example, http://www.RMRoberts.com is the regular URL without a subdomain. In http://staff.RMRoberts.com, "staff" is the subdomain for the RMRoberts.com website. The website is organized as follows: the .com represents the first-level domain, RMRoberts represents the second-level domain, and staff represents the third-level domain.

The website hosting company determines if you can create a subdomain. Web hosting companies vary on this issue, but most do allow subdomains. Some web hosting companies provide free website hosting. Free website hosting typically provides the user with a subdomain.

Subdomains allow you to create shorter URL addresses, which are easier to remember. For example, a subdomain can be www.backups.rmroberts.com. This subdomain points to a file location deeply embedded into the website, which requires a longer URL, such as www.rmroberts.com/resources/teachers/labactivities/backups.

Subdomains can be password-protected and can be accessed by designated company employees or affiliate companies. Subdomains can be used to create departments within the organization such as Finance, Engineering, blog or forum, help, and FAQ.

E-mail Communications

E-mail has become one of the most popular uses of the Internet. You can send messages anywhere in the world via the Internet. Originally, e-mail was little more than a system to exchange ASCII text files. It is now a complete communication system that allows for not only text-based messages but also attached files. Any type of file can be attached, including reports, spreadsheets, database information, photos, illustrations, animations, and sound. There are numerous e-mail software packages available. The e-mail software packages encapsulate the available Internet e-mail protocols and greatly enhance the user interface.

Setting up an E-mail Account

To set up an e-mail account, you must have certain information. First, you need to know your user name and password. You also need to know the name and type of mail server being used for incoming and outgoing messages. Common e-mail protocols include *Post Office Protocol 3 (POP3)*, *Internet Message Access Protocol (IMAP)*, *Hypertext Markup Language (HTML)*, and *Simple Mail Transport Protocol (SMTP)*. A protocol is required to communicate with a mail server that is hosting the e-mail software and the Internet connection.

Figure 18-32 shows the **Add New Account** dialog box, which is used to create a new e-mail account in Microsoft Outlook. Your Internet Service Provider (ISP) will provide your user name, password, and e-mail server name(s). Providers usually have this information on an automatic installation disc. If they do not, you can contact them to get the information. Once the account is established, there are many features you need to understand.

The mail server usually stores all e-mail communications until the user retrieves them. In a strict network environment, e-mails can be delivered directly to the individual PCs. Once you log on to your ISP, you can open your e-mail account, which is stored on the server, and access your personal e-mail. E-mail protocols vary according to the way they manage e-mail messages and interact with the e-mail server.

POP3

Post Office Protocol 3 (POP3) is a common e-mail protocol used to download e-mails (incoming) from an e-mail server. POP3 mail servers hold incoming e-mail messages until you check your e-mail. When you check your e-mail, the e-mail message and e-mail attachment(s) are downloaded to your computer. When the e-mail transfer is complete, the original e-mail is deleted from the POP3 mail server.

Tech Tip Some e-mail services do provide an e-mail storage option for its POP3 server, but this is not generally the case.

SMTP

Simple Mail Transfer Protocol (SMTP) is an e-mail protocol used to upload and transfer e-mail messages (outgoing) between e-mail servers. SMTP servers send e-mail to the Internet and transfer e-mail between mail servers. For home user applications, the SMTP mail server is located at the ISP. In business applications, the SMTP mail server may be at the ISP or located on the business network. The SMTP server handles outgoing e-mail and is used in conjunction with a POP3 or IMAP incoming mail server.

IMAP

Internet Message Access Protocol (IMAP) is an e-mail protocol used to access e-mail from a server. IMAP mail servers allow you to view e-mail message content without the need to download the e-mail. This allows you to preview, delete, and organize e-mail messages while they are still on the mail server. Also, copies are stored

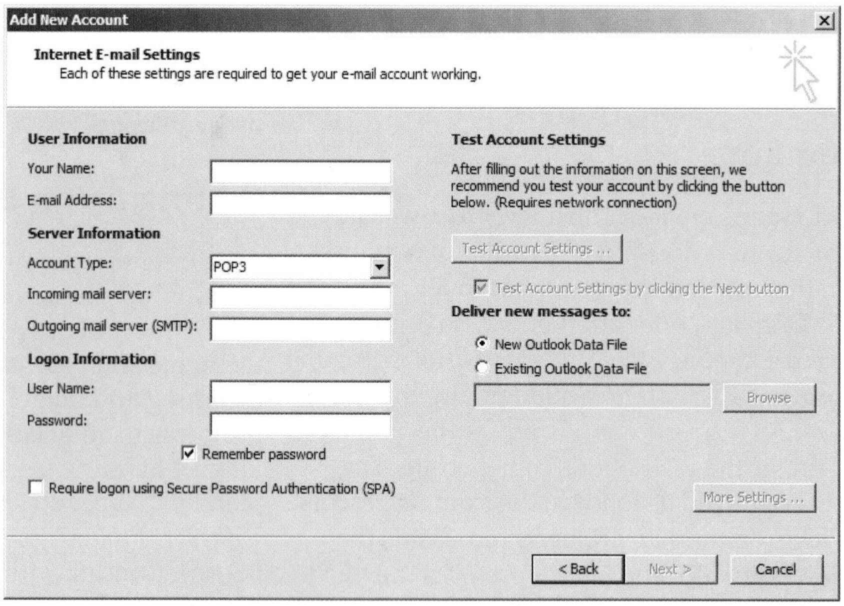

Figure 18-32.
To set up an e-mail account, you need to configure the user e-mail client name, e-mail address, e-mail account type, incoming mail server, outgoing mail server, user name, and password.

on the server until you choose to delete them. If you have a number of computers or networking devices that are capable of accessing your e-mail account, each device will see the same e-mail content. When using POP3 with several different devices, e-mail will download to each device. You will need to read and delete the e-mail from each device as needed. IMAP is most common for business e-mail accounts.

MAPI

Messaging Application Programming Interface (MAPI) is Microsoft's proprietary e-mail protocol and is very similar to IMAP. MAPI provides greater functionality than IMAP for Outlook e-mail clients interacting with a Microsoft Exchange Server. It does not work for anything else. You would commonly encounter MAPI on an enterprise or business network that is running Microsoft Exchange Server. MAPI is used with the Microsoft Outlook client along with Microsoft Exchange Server.

Accessing a MAPI mail server requires a virtual private network (VPN) connection. This is because the ports (communications channels) that MAPI uses are otherwise blocked for security reasons.

Tech Tip

In Microsoft Outlook, you may simply see the connection option **Microsoft Exchange Server** rather than **MAPI**. Microsoft Exchange Server is the same as MAPI.

Webmail

Webmail is typically a free e-mail service, such as Gmail, Outlook.com, or Yahoo! Mail, based on using a web browser to access e-mail, hence the name "webmail." Webmail is also referred to as *HTML e-mail*.

When you configure webmail, you do not need to supply the outgoing or incoming mail server or select an e-mail type. You simply choose an available e-mail address for your account and select an available user account name and password. The downside of webmail is that it is usually inundated with commercial advertisements. Also, webmail service providers have been suspected of collecting user information and selling it to marketing services.

Sending an E-mail

To send an e-mail, you must type in the address of the recipient, such as jsmith@acme.net. See **Figure 18-33**. Each e-mail user has a unique address. Two or more users can have the same alpha name on the same network, but they are usually given a numeric extension to maintain the uniqueness of the address, such as jsmith23@acme.net. A message is then typed into the message space and the **Send** button is clicked, sending the e-mail to its destination. The menus provide the user with many options, including delete and save. There are some options that are unique to e-mail, such as reply, reply to all, resend, and attach file.

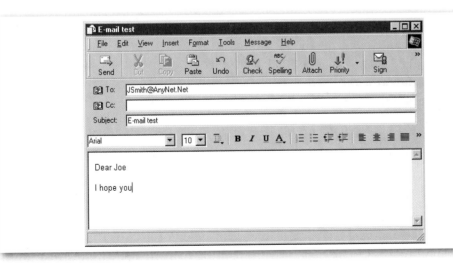

Figure 18-33.
The three most important pieces of information to enter when creating an e-mail are the recipient's e-mail address, the subject of the e-mail, and the message.

MIME and S/MIME

When a non-text file is attached to an e-mail message, it must be converted to a form that can be handled by text-oriented e-mail protocols. The **Multipurpose Internet Mail Extensions (MIME)** standard is a specification for formatting non-text-based files for transmission over the Internet. MIME is used for graphics, audio, and video. A newer version of MIME is S/MIME. The *S* stands for *secure*. S/MIME allows the sent message to be encrypted and signed with a digital signature, or certificate. Methods used to ensure S/MIME security are discussed in the following section.

Digital Signatures and Encryption/Decryption Keys

Three components are required to digitally (electronically) sign and encrypt a message: a public key, a private key, and the appropriate encoding software. To obtain a public and private key, you must first apply for a digital ID from a third-party software vendor. You make an application using e-mail, and then the certifying authority verifies your identity.

Your digital ID provides you with two digital keys. One key is a private key, which you keep entirely to yourself. The private key can be used to sign your e-mail and also encrypt messages. The receiving party will be warned if a signed message has been tampered with. It also verifies your identity to the recipient. The other key is a public key, which you distribute to people you wish to communicate with. The public key allows others to decode messages encoded with your private key. It also allows them to encode messages that can only be decoded by your private key.

When you digitally sign an e-mail, software compresses the message contents to a few lines of text known as a *message digest*. The message digest is then encoded using the sender's private key. The resulting data is the sender's *digital signature*. The digital signature is then added to the end of the message.

The receiver can decode both the signature and the message using the sender's public key. When the signature is decoded, it results in the same message digest used to create it. When the

message is decoded, it results in the same data used to create the message digest, and therefore the signature. If the receiver compresses the message, and the resulting message digest does not match the message digest extracted from the key, the recipient knows that the message has been altered.

A+ Note

The A+ exam always has several questions about e-mail protocols. Remember, SMTP sends e-mail to a mail server. POP3 and IMAP download e-mail from the mail server.

Internet Protocols

Hundreds of protocols have been developed over the years. Protocols began as simple programs that carried out commands and transported plain ASCII text files but have evolved into sophisticated programs. In the strictest sense, protocols are software programs that establish a set of rules to allow two entities to communicate. As protocols evolve, they take on the appearance of application software and are classified as such. As technology evolves, there will always be new protocols, usually built on top of the older protocols to keep the downward compatibility of the system.

Protocols are assembled into packages of data containing addresses and data or commands. Protocols are designed to either encapsulate or be encapsulated by other protocols. When you connect to a distant webpage, several protocols work together to complete the transaction. Each protocol serves a special purpose and multiple protocols are required to complete the task. A request for an Internet webpage requires several different protocols, such as Ethernet, IP (IPv4 or IPv6), TCP, and HTTP. Each protocol has a distinct responsibility for the successful downloading of a single page of HTML code.

Ethernet contains the MAC address of the source and destination device. Ethernet also encapsulates IPv4 or IPv6, which contains the source and destination of IPv4 or IPv6 address.

IP encapsulates TCP, which contains the port address of the source and destination. TCP also encapsulates the HTTP, which contains the HTML data. See the following table for a summary of what each protocol contains.

Protocol	Contains
Ethernet	MAC address of the source and destination device.
IP	IPv4 or IPv6 address of the source and destination device.
TCP	Port address of the source and destination. Also, encapsulates HTTP.
HTTP	HTML code data for the browser to interpret the webpage.

Ethernet

Ethernet is both a protocol and a networking standard. The Ethernet standard describes the network system as related to media and function. The Ethernet protocol is designed to encapsulate other protocols and carry them to and from devices located on an Ethernet network based on the MAC address of the source and destination device.

IP

The Internet Protocol (IP) communicates across the Internet and contains the destination and source IP addresses. Currently, there are two IP protocols used: IPv4 and IPv6. The IP protocol routes packets containing other protocols across the Internet through a series of routers.

TCP and UDP

Transmission Control Protocol (TCP) and User Datagram Protocol (UDP) are the two main protocols associated with the TCP/IP protocol suite. TCP is described as a connection-oriented protocol, and UDP is described as a connectionless protocol. In other words, TCP establishes a connection between two network devices and maintains that connection until the purpose of the connection is completed. For example, connecting to an Internet server and downloading the content from the server using TCP requires the computer and server to establish a connection and maintain the connection until all the content has been downloaded. After several packets are downloaded, a TCP packet is sent to the source to confirm that the connection is still established. If a packet does not return to the source device, the process to establish a connection will once more begin. In comparison to UDP, TCP generates a lot more network traffic because it must establish and maintain the connection between the two devices.

UDP does not establish a connection with the destination device. UDP simply sends a command or data to the destination and assumes that it will be delivered to the destination. It does not guarantee delivery of the packet.

UDP might seem like a terrible way to send information, but it is used for applications in which speed is more essential than ensuring packet delivery. For example, when sending time-sensitive material, such as live streaming music or video, using UDP is more efficient than TCP. UDP sends the packets of data directly to the destination and does not check if they arrived intact. TCP establishes a connection and a series of packets between the destination and source to ensure the connection is maintained. The additional packets cause latency between the two devices and cause small breaks in live music or live video. Both TCP and UDP use port numbers to determine the destination of the packet.

HTTP

Hypertext Transfer Protocol (HTTP) is a standard protocol used to transport webpage content across the Internet. **Hypertext Markup Language (HTML)** is a programming language used to create webpages and is often confused with HTTP. Simply put, HTTP delivers webpage content written in HTML code. Look at **Figure 18-34**. The top is a screen capture that shows what HTML code looks like. This code does not appear to the page viewer. A web browser interprets the HTML code and then displays what the code instruction tells the browser. The bottom half of Figure 18-34 shows what the HTML code instructed the browser to display. It shows a photograph of a dog and the text "This is an example of an HTML webpage."

Figure 18-34. An example of HTML code (top) and the code interpreted and displayed (bottom).

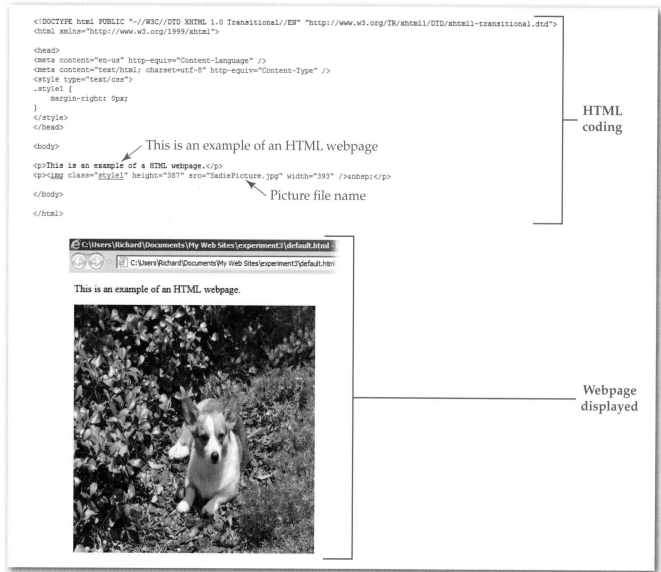

HTML coding

Webpage displayed

HTTPS

HTTPS is a combination of HTTP and Secure Socket Layer (SSL) protocols. While HTTP is fine for browsing the Internet, it does not provide a secure connection for exchanging information such as credit card numbers. HTTP was never intended to be used for transmitting secure information such as business transactions involving personal identification and money. **Secure Sockets Layer (SSL)** is a protocol developed by Netscape Navigator to make HTTP-based Internet business transactions secure.

The combination of HTTP and SSL provides a secure connection to the Internet site using encryption. When used, the website URL location will be HTTPS:// as shown in **Figure 18-35**. The "S" in the HTTPS represents "secure" as in Secure Socket Layer. The "https" indicates that you are connected to the distant webpage using a secure connection provided by the SSL protocol. SSL can be used with any protocol in the TCP/IP suite, not just with HTTP.

Figure 18-35.
You can tell if a webpage connection is secure by the "https" code located at the beginning of the URL.

SSH

Secure Shell (SSH), also known as *Secure Socket Shell*, is a protocol that provides secure access to a remote computer. The connection between both computers is encrypted and authenticated using digital signatures, a password, or both. The main difference between SSL and SSH is SSL does not require a user name and password to log in while SSH typically does. You will encounter SSH in applications such as a remote administrative logon for a secure server or network device such as a router. SSH uses port 22, and SSL uses port 443.

FTP

File Transfer Protocol (FTP) is a protocol used for transmitting files across the Internet. A special FTP is called *anonymous FTP*. Many sites accept anonymous FTP, which simply means you can access the files for downloading without using a secret password and identity. FTP is commonly used to upload and download files between a computer and a web hosting server. There are two variations of FTP that add security features: FTPS and SFTP. FTP over SSL (FTPS) is a combination of FTP with SSL or TLS encryption. Secure FTP (SFTP) is based on Secure Shell (SSH) technology. The two protocols, SFTP and FTPS appear to be the same and are often confused with each other, but they are two different security schemes.

Telnet

Telnet is a protocol that allows a user to log on to a remote computer and download or upload files. It is often referred to as a terminal emulation protocol because it causes a PC to act as though it is a terminal connected to a mainframe computer. Telnet is part of an entire suite of protocols inside the TCP/IP protocol. It is often used to connect two dissimilar systems, such as a PC running Microsoft Windows and a UNIX mainframe. Telnet is commonly used to program remote routers on wide area networks. It can also be used to control other computer operations remotely.

SNMP

Simple Network Management Protocol (SNMP) is a protocol that collects information about network devices and configures network devices, such as servers, printers, switches, and routers. SNMP is a standard as defined by the Internet Engineering Task Force (IETF). Because the SNMP packets have a design standard, different companies are able to create software packages based on SNMP to create tools that monitor devices and can make configuration changes when necessary.

CIFS

Common Internet File System (CIFS) is a network file-sharing protocol developed for early Microsoft operating systems. Microsoft developed CIFS as an open source standard and then submitted the standard to the Internet Engineering Task Force (IETF) so anyone could use it royalty-free. CIFS was designed as a file sharing protocol that utilizes the HTTP protocol to support sharing files across the Internet. CIFS was designed mainly as a file sharing protocol but can also support printing across the network.

SMB

Server Message Block (SMB) is a network file-sharing protocol that supports file sharing for client/server applications. The term *server* is not limited to what is commonly known as a *dedicated network device*. When there is no server such as in a workgroup configuration, any computer configured to share files can act in a server role. In the context of the SMB protocol, a server is any device that provides services, such as a shared file.

SMB is considered a dialect of CIFS. SMB has been used by Microsoft for many years and has many design revisions. There have been three major revisions of SMB since Windows 2000 and Windows XP. SMB 3.0 is used for Windows 8 and Windows Server 2012 as the main protocol used to support file sharing. The following table provides a brief summary of the evolution of CIFS and SMB.

File Sharing Protocol	Operating systems
CIFS	Windows NT
SMB 1.0	Windows 2000, Windows XP, and Windows Server 2003
SMB 2.0	Windows Vista and Windows Server 2008
SMB 2.1	Windows 7 and Windows Server 2008 R2
SMB 3.0	Windows 8 and Windows Server 2012

Cloud Services

Cloud computing is becoming a popular alternative to manually configuring a SOHO network. Cloud services allow you to share a pool of resources such as storage, application software, and specialized services, such as instant messaging, e-mail, and database support. The term *cloud* is synonymous with the Internet symbol used in network drawings. The "cloud" in network drawings represents the remote location of the service on the Internet location rather than the individual user's computer.

In a SOHO configuration, each computer has the entire software application, such as Microsoft Office, installed on it. Each computer has complete access and control over the use and configuration of the software application. The user can also store files on the computer as related to the software application. For example, a computer user might have Microsoft Office installed on the computer and store all generated data, such as documents, on the same computer.

In a cloud-computing setting, the user installs a very small software application that allows the user to access the larger software application on the cloud service location. In this scenario, the user computer is referred to as a *thin client*. A thin client depends on the software application at the remote location to do most of the work. The user has the option to store the document on the Internet cloud location or on his or her computer.

The cloud service can be provided free of charge or as a pay service. Free services generally provide fewer services and have less storage space as compared to pay services. There are many cloud service providers, such as Google, Apple, Microsoft, Android, Amazon, VMware, and IBM, as well as private companies.

Cloud Service Characteristics

The five characteristics of cloud service that have been identified by the National Institute of Standards and Technology (NIST) are on-demand self-service, broad network access, resource pooling, rapid elasticity, and measured service. These common characteristics are used to identify cloud services as compared to traditional on-site network systems.

On-Demand Self-Service

The cloud service is readily accessible and requires no real expertise or on-site technical support personnel as in a traditional network model. A network technician is not required to set up the cloud service. A cloud service is a self-service oriented system.

Broad Network Access

The cloud by its very nature can be accessed from most anywhere through a variety of devices such as, but not limited to, workstations, laptops, PDAs, cell phones, and tablets. Cloud services are accessed by thin client software. Thin client software is a minimal software application and does not require a hardware device designed with a large amount of RAM or a high-speed CPU.

Resource Pooling

The real strength of cloud service is resource pooling and resource sharing. Computer resources such as documents, pictures, videos, and other types of files can be easily shared with other members of the cloud service. In addition to sharing resources, the cloud provider typically provides software applications appropriate for the type of cloud membership. For example, word-processing, database, e-mail, and digital photo software applications may be provided as a service. The cloud member need not install the software application on his or her device but rather connect to the cloud host as a thin client. A thin client can connect to the cloud hosting service and use the software application on the remote server.

For example, the word-processing application need not be installed on the cloud member's computer or portable device. The actual software application is installed on the cloud hosting server. The cloud member has a relatively very small software application installed on his or her personal device, which supports communication with the cloud host provider's software application. The advantage of the software application being installed on the cloud service server is that the software application will be available no matter which device the user decides to use. The cloud member can run the software application from his or her desktop, tablet, or cell phone. Another advantage is the cloud hosting provider is responsible for updating the software application, for making backups, and providing the necessary technical support.

When software applications are provided through cloud services, it is often referred to as *virtualization*. The software appears to the user as though it is installed entirely on the user's PC or portable device, when in reality, the software application is installed on the cloud server. The user is utilizing the features of the software application through the thin client, thus the "virtualization" of the software application.

Rapid Elasticity

Cloud services can be rapidly expanded or contracted as needed. For example, when more server disk space is required for the storage of additional documents or images, the additional space can be added instantly. In a traditional on-site network model, a technician would have to allocate more space or even add additional hardware, such as additional disk drives for storage.

Measured Service

The cloud service can be measured to match the pricing of services. For example, the amount of storage space, bandwidth, or number of user accounts can be used to determine pricing for the service. The amount of resources consumed by the user(s) can be monitored and reported.

Cloud Infrastructure

Cloud infrastructure allows users to access a network cloud service. There are four major cloud infrastructure, or deployment, models identified by NIST for cloud deployment: private cloud, community cloud, public cloud, and hybrid cloud. Any combination of the first three infrastructure models is considered a hybrid cloud. The main difference in the cloud infrastructure models is who may become a member of or access the cloud structure and who is responsible for maintaining the cloud service.

Private Cloud

A **private cloud** is an infrastructure model typically designed for exclusive use by an organization, such as a private corporation, government organization, or an educational organization like a university. A private cloud is operated exclusively for the organization, but the service may be provided by a third-party vendor. A private cloud does not require the infrastructure or support to be exclusive to the private party. Only access to the private cloud is exclusive.

Community Cloud

A **community cloud** is a shared infrastructure of users who share a common interest or concern. You can think of Facebook, Twitter, or similar services as a community cloud. A community cloud can also be shared by several different organizations that support a common interest, such as a collection of individual schools or businesses that operate under different authorities. For example, the Department of Defense (DOD) might set up a cloud service to provide and exchange information exclusively to a group of private defense contractors that are all involved in building a new aircraft for the DOD.

Public Cloud

A **public cloud** is an infrastructure open to the general public. It may be used by individuals, business organizations, or educational organizations. The main difference between a private cloud and a public cloud is a public cloud is typically hosted by a cloud service provider. The cloud service provider determines membership. A private cloud is built exclusively for a private entity, such as a corporation, and provides services exclusively for that entity. The private cloud can be hosted either by the private entity network server or from a cloud service provider. When the private

cloud is provided by a cloud host service provider, the cloud access is controlled by the private entity.

Hybrid Cloud

A **hybrid cloud** is simply a combination of two or more of the other cloud infrastructures: private cloud, public cloud, and community cloud.

Service Models

The main purpose of a cloud is to provide services to its clients. The four classifications of service to consumers are Software as a Service (SaaS), Platform as a Service (PaaS), Infrastructure as a Service (IaaS), and Anything as a Service (XaaS). The services are typically designed to run on minimal computer devices, such as smartphones, tablets, laptops, and desktop computers.

Software as a Service

Software as a Service (SaaS) is a cloud service model that provides software applications to a user either through a thin client software application or through a web browser. For example, web-based e-mail can be provided as a cloud service. All that is needed to use the cloud-based e-mail is a compatible web browser. Another example is running software such as a Microsoft Office application from the cloud. Microsoft Office applications are quite large, and many cannot be installed on a portable device that has minimal processing power, storage space, and RAM. By accessing the Microsoft Office application through a cloud software service, a thin client can connect to the cloud server that is hosting the Microsoft Office application and allow the consumer to use it as though it was installed on the user's device. This is also an example of how virtualization is achieved. The software application appears to the consumer as though it is installed on their own device. The consumer uses the cloud provider's software applications.

Platform as a Service

Platform as a Service (PaaS) a cloud service model that supports programming software. The consumer deploys onto the cloud consumer-created applications using programming languages. In computer science, the term *platform* generally refers to the computer operating system. In the context of cloud service, it means that the computer programming language and programming language environment is provided. For example, Google App Engine is an example of PaaS. The Google App Engine allows users to develop software applications for Google using programming languages such as Python, Java, and PHP. In addition to the cloud hosting the consumer programming language, the PaaS cloud can also host libraries of programs and tools used in the creation and distribution of the complete software package, such as a game. This is a great way to host everything used by a large group of programmers working on the same project. The programmers can have access to the very latest version of all programs and program libraries and tools.

The consumer does not need to manage the cloud server(s), storage, and operating system, but the consumer does have control over who has access to the project and its parts. Another example of PaaS is when a database software application such as SQL Server is hosted by a cloud service provider and used by a consumer. The SQL Server software can be programmed into many different database configurations. It is not considered a general-consumer software application. SQL Server is a technically-challenging programmable database application. Platform as a Service is also referred to as *Service Platform* by some cloud providers such as Microsoft.

Infrastructure as a Service

Infrastructure as a Service (IaaS) a cloud service model that provides storage and basic networking functions, which are used by the consumer. The consumer decides what software and applications to use and does not need to worry about typical network support. The cloud provider provides all the necessary network support functions required by the consumer.

You can think of IaaS as a barebones type of service that provides the hardware required to operate a cloud, while the consumer is responsible for what will be installed and distributed on the cloud. For example, a cloud provider might provide an IaaS to a game developer. The game developer installs game(s) and controls the

distribution of the game to users. The game developer writes and distributes the game without the need to manage the cloud infrastructure, such as the servers, storage, and networking. The game developer controls who can access the games and is responsible for updating the game software.

As you can see, there are five typical cloud characteristics, three types of cloud service, and four deployment models. The cloud classifications can be somewhat "cloudy" themselves, and at times, somewhat difficult to classify according to the NIST definitions.

Anything as a Service

Anything as a Service (XaaS) is a hybrid of the first three types of services (Saas, PaaS, and IaaS) designed to meet a variety of needs. XaaS can be thought of as an "anything you want to do" type of service. XaaS is not an official NIST service standard, but the term and acronym is used by many providers. This is a prime example of how a term is coined and used by industry but in reality is not recognized as a standard by any authority. In time, it could become a de facto term used to describe hybrid cloud services. The largest cloud service providers will design a cloud service to meet anyone's needs, thus the "anything as a service" designation. Note that XaaS is also the name of a cloud service provider. Now let us take a look at a few common cloud services available today.

Microsoft Cloud Services

Microsoft offers several versions of cloud services at this time such as, but not limited to, SkyDrive, Office 365, Windows Azure, and Windows Intune. Some are free, but most are not. The fees vary in range based on the desired services and number of users. For example, the cost of the service can be based on the number of users determined by the number of unique e-mail accounts.

SkyDrive

The most popular cloud service at this time is cloud storage. Cloud storage allows the user to store documents, pictures, and more on a remote server and access the storage at anytime from anywhere using a standard web browser. Typically, all that is required is a user name and password and the user can access the storage from any type of device, such as a desktop computer, tablet, or smartphone. One such cloud storage service is Microsoft's SkyDrive. Look at **Figure 18-36**. Notice the **Sharing** option (on right side of screen), which will allows you to share a file with others.

Office 365

Microsoft Office 365 is a pay cloud service that provides storage space for files and photos and access to Microsoft software such as Word, Excel, OneNote, PowerPoint, Publisher, Access, e-mail service, calendar sharing, PC to PC calling, and video conferencing. Most individuals would not use all the features available in Office 365.

They would most likely prefer one of the smaller free services. Larger groups of consumers, such as educational institutions, small businesses, and midsize to large enterprises, would find the Office 365 service quite useful, especially since Microsoft provides the support services. This reduces or eliminates the need for a large network support group of technicians and to purchase costly software packages. This is not to say that individuals could not purchase the Office 365 service, because they can.

Microsoft Office 365 has several different plans with different combinations of software applications and services. You can select the plan based on your needs or your company's needs. For example, the needs of a corporation would be much different than a home user's needs.

Figure 18-36. SkyDrive is an example of Microsoft's free cloud service for storing documents.

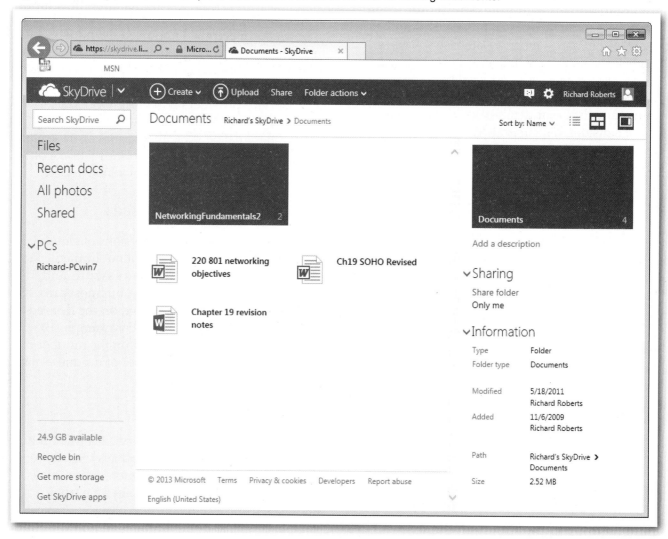

The corporation Office 365 package has all the common software applications as required in the corporate environment, such as company e-mail, voice mail, and other server applications. One such optional service is called Windows SharePoint Services. Windows SharePoint Services is designed for creating a website that will share information and documents and support collaboration between employees. This can be a private or public type of website.

Windows Intune

Windows Intune is a cloud service designed for businesses to manage and secure their business computers. Many small businesses do not have a full-time computer or network technician and simply have a designated computer person who deals with common computer and network problems. If the designated person cannot remedy the problem, he or she will contact a support provider to come to the business and remedy the problem.

Intune provides remote services to business computers and allows the designated support person to remotely perform many common computer tasks. The designated person can perform many remedies that would normally require a technician. For example, the designated person can manage malware scans and updates for all PCs from one centralized location. They can remotely monitor computers, force computer restarts, manage updates, distribute software, provide remote assistance, and manage the firewall all from one centralized location.

Windows Azure

Windows Azure is Microsoft's complete cloud service offering all variations of cloud service. Azure provides storage space for backups, website hosting, and database services and provides media services such as content streaming with content protection. You can also build, deploy, and manage applications across a worldwide network. Visit the Windows Azure website to learn more.

Client-Side Virtualization

Client-side virtualization is a software application used to create multiple operating system environments on the host machine. Client-side virtualization is closely related to cloud services. When fully implemented, a client device such as a PC, laptop, tablet, or smartphone accesses software applications, storage, and services on a remote server. There are many client-side virtualization providers, such as VMware, Microsoft Hyper-V, and Citrix XenClient.

In **Figure 18-37**, you can see the Microsoft Hyper-V client and management tools introduced in Windows 8. They are not installed by default. The Hyper-V must be installed through the **Windows Features** dialog box accessed through **Control Panel | Programs | Programs and Features | Turn Windows features on or off**. You

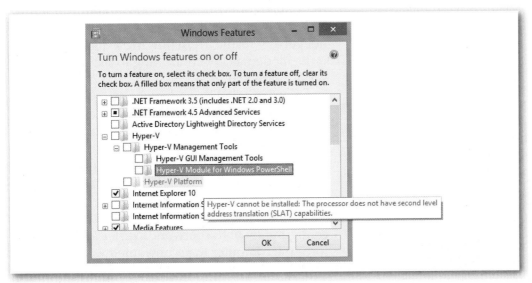

Figure 18-37.
The Microsoft Hyper-V client is included in Windows 8 but is not installed by default.

will also notice that a message has appeared stating that "Hyper-V cannot be installed: The processor does not have Second Level Address Translation (SLAT) capabilities." *Second Level Address Translation* is the technical term used by Intel and AMD for hypervisor capabilities. In other words, older CPU technology cannot support virtualization.

The client requires a CPU and firmware (BIOS/UEFI) that supports virtualization. The client also requires a hypervisor. A **hypervisor** is the technical term used to identify the software that creates the virtual machine on the client device. Hypervisor is also referred to as a *virtual machine monitor*.

Some machines are referred to as *bare metal devices*. Certain bare metal devices do not have a standard operating system installed. There are Linux-based devices that implement client-side virtualization called *Kernel-based Virtual Machines (KVMs)*, not to be confused with the acronym KVM which represents keyboard video and mouse. A **Kernel-based Virtual Machine (KVM) client** is a machine having the virtualization software installed directly on the machine hardware rather than inside a host machine operating system. A KVM client is referred to as a *bare metal device*. The term *bare metal* is used because the device does not contain an operating system.

Virtualized applications require excellent network bandwidth to operate correctly. Because the virtualized machine requires a constant exchange of data and commands with the remote service, performance is sluggish without ample bandwidth.

Emulator

The term *emulator* is often confused with the term *hypervisor*. An **emulator** is a software application that acts as an interface between the user and a software application. You can think of it as a software application designed to run another software application. It is two layers of software application. An example is Linux WINE, which is an emulator designed to make the Linux user interface look and feel like a Windows user interface.

The problem with emulators is poor performance. This is due to running two software applications to obtain the same results of running a single software application. Emulation software applications require more system resources because they are actually running two different software applications at the same time.

Network Troubleshooting

As a technician, you will be responsible for small networks commonly found in homes and small business offices. When troubleshooting equipment that is part of a large enterprise network, you must know where your responsibility for the repair of a PC ends and where the responsibility of the network administrator begins.

When troubleshooting a network, remember the basics of networking. To create a network you need cable, a properly-configured adapter card, and software support for the network. Most networking problems are simple problems, such as loose connections. When there are network system problems, check the connections.

To quickly verify that the local network is working correctly, open the Network folder. The Network folder in Windows Explorer provides a quick analysis of the local area network status, **Figure 18-38**. You can see the number of network devices currently identified as part of the local area network. If the network connection or adaptor had failed, no devices would appear in the Network folder.

The next step is to ping the adapter card (**ping 127.0.0.1** for IPv4 or **ping ::1** and **ping localhost** for IPv6) to verify that it is communicating with the TCP/IP protocol. Finally, try to connect to a known URL using the **ping** command. You will not get any results from pinging a distant host if the modem is not connecting to the Internet service provider.

Keep in mind that adapter settings can be accidentally changed, especially while exploring the network setup dialog boxes. If you are accessing the network via some type of modem, you will have to check the modem setup. For more information, review Chapter 13—Modems and Transceivers.

Problems can also result from malware programs. The malware program could change the configuration of the network adapter in an effort to force the computer to an unwanted website.

Figure 18-38. The Network folder gives a quick assessment of whether the network is working properly.

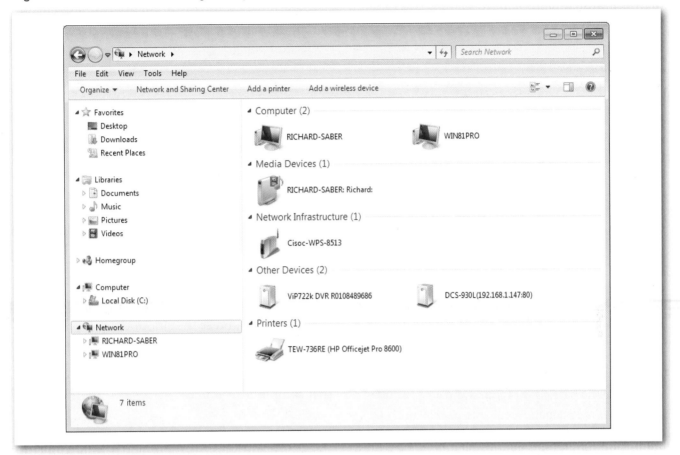

Another common problem associated with a network is difficulty logging in. Often, the user is incorrectly entering his or her name and password or is attempting to use an expired password. As a technician, you will have your own access name and password and will be capable of easily determining if the network is accessible.

Most problems you will be expected to handle as a PC technician are simple in nature. More complex issues may require the assistance of the network administrator. With experience, you will soon be able to determine when you need to consult the network administrator or the Internet service provider.

Wireless network adapters are often configured to automatically connect to the strongest wireless signal available, which can result in an unintended wireless connection and a change in assigned IP address.

Check the assigned IPv4 address to see if it is in the APIPA range starting with 169.254.

An APIPA assignment typically means there is a problem with the DHCP service. Most home networks are configured with a router that serves as a DHCP server and automatically issues an IPv4 address. When an APIPA address is assigned, it is best to reset the router.

Limited Connectivity

Microsoft Windows will present a message stating there is "limited connectivity." The message indicates the computer can connect to the local area network but not all areas of the local area network. When this happens, you can open the dialog box for the network adapter by entering **ncpa.cpl** into the **Search** box or **Run** dialog box. You can also access the network adapter **Properties** dialog box by going through **Control Panel** or through the **Network and Sharing Center**. Whichever method you use will produce the same dialog box similar to that in **Figure 18-39**. Right-clicking a network

Figure 18-39.
You can run **ncpa.cpl** to open the **Network Connections** window. You can then view the network adapter status and properties or run diagnostics when troubleshooting a network problem.

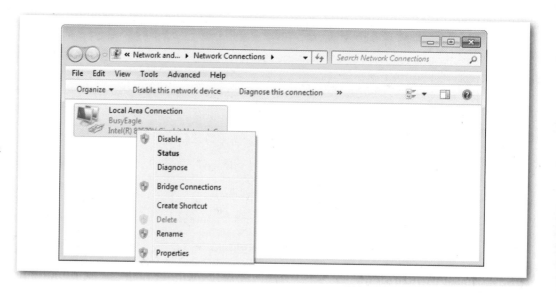

connection icon will display a shortcut menu allowing you to access the status, properties, or perform a diagnosis of the network adapter.

 **Tech Tip**   The most common way to solve most network connection problems is by either resetting the local area network router or restarting the computer.

Slow Transfer Speeds

Slow transfer speeds can be caused by several different reasons. First, the network could be congested because too many users are downloading or uploading content at the same time. This can be true not only for a local area network but also Internet access. For example, when too many users are downloading from the Internet at the same time when using a shared Internet connection, the available bandwidth for each user is reduced.

The transfer speed may seem particularly slow if an application, such as an antimalware program, is running in the background. Another reason for slow transfer rates is when a computer is automatically downloading Microsoft updates. Users will also experience slow transfer rates when they use their computer for the first time following a long period of computer shutdown, such as after returning from a vacation. When a

computer has been shut down for a long period of time, it will usually automatically connect to the Internet and search for updates for all software applications and look for new drivers. All this background activity affects the overall transfer speed of the computer system. Remember that computer resources such as the Internet connection are shared.

IP Conflict

An IP conflict occurs when the same IP address is assigned to more than one network device. This is seldom encountered today except when network devices are configured with a static IP address. Legacy network systems allowed the same IP address to be statically configured for more than one device. When the same IP address is configured twice, only one device can successfully connect to the network. The second device will fail to connect to the network. A message box will inform the user that there is a conflict with the assigned IP address. Today, a message will appear when you configure a duplicate IP address and you will not be able to complete the configuration. The message will only appear if the device that has a duplicate IP address is online. If the device with a duplicate IP address is not online, the message will not appear. After the device assigned the duplicate IP address attempts to come online, a problem will arise. That is why duplicate IP addresses are rarely encountered when all devices are assigned IP addresses through a DHCP service.

Low RF Signal

A low RF signal for a wireless device is usually caused by either distance or position. As the distance between wireless devices increases, the device connection loses signal strength. You must move the devices closer together or install a wireless range extender, which will increase signal strength between the devices. You may also opt to install a more powerful wireless device, such as a wireless USB adapter equipped with a longer antenna. This will allow it to broadcast farther and receive low RF signals better.

Low RF signals can also be caused by radio interference from many different sources. Sometimes it can be remedied by simply repositioning the RF receiver a few feet or even a few inches. Many times, the antenna orientation makes a big difference in signal strength. The wireless adapter signal strength is indicated in the wireless adapter **Properties** dialog box.

Intermittent Connectivity

Intermittent connectivity can be difficult to diagnose because of its inconsistent nature. A bad connection can only be diagnosed while the poor or no connection condition exists. If the connection is working fine, attempting to diagnose the cause of an intermittent connection is futile.

Diagnosing an intermittent connection requires analysis and experience. You are making educated guesses as to the cause if the signal is working at the time of troubleshooting. It is important to ask questions such as the following:

- When does the connection seem to go out?
- How long has this condition existed?
- Is the connection slow or completely out?

Asking questions can provide enough information for a possible solution. For example, a connection seems to go out every morning at 9:00, which is the same time most employees take an office break. Is it possible employees could be using the microwaves in the break area to heat snacks, resulting in wireless connection interference? This scenario is not to infer that all wireless interruptions are caused by microwave ovens. However, it serves as an example to help you understand the need to consider related issues. You must ask questions and gather information to come to a possible solution.

When experiencing intermittent connectivity or no Internet connectivity at all, you should also check with the Internet service provider. The ISP may be servicing its network.

Chapter Summary

- IPv4 uses four sets of decimal numbers in the range of 0 to 255, and IPv6 uses eight sets of hexadecimal numbers in the range of 000 to ffff.
- Navigation across WAN systems is enabled by network devices, such as bridges, routers, brouters, gateways, and switches.
- Some common network diagnostic utilities are PING, ipconfig, nslookup, netstat, nbtstat, pathping, tracert, and net services.
- The Internet is a collection of networks that are all interconnected by fiber-optic and copper cables, wireless devices, infrared devices, satellites, and millions of miles of old telephone lines.
- Four common e-mail protocols or services are POP3, SMTP, IMAP, and MAPI.
- IP, TCP, UDP, HTTP, SSH, FTP, Telnet, SNMP, CIFS, and SMB are commonly used Internet protocols.

- The five characteristics of cloud service that have been identified by the National Institute of Standards and Technology (NIST) are on-demand self-service, broad network access, resource pooling, rapid elasticity, and measured service.
- Remember the basics of networks when troubleshooting network problems.

Review Questions

Answer the following questions on a separate sheet of paper. Please do not write in this book.

1. What protocol is predominately used for exchanging data on the Internet?
2. What is ICANN?
3. How does the TCP/IP protocol identify individual networks on the Internet?
4. What is an octet?
5. What is an octet's numeric range expressed in decimal fashion?
6. What is the difference between an IPv4 and IPv6 address?
7. Which operating system was first to assign by default an IPv4 and an IPv6 address to each network adapter?
8. Identify the class to which a network with an address of 128.204.19.103 belongs.
9. What is a subnet mask?
10. What does the **ipconfig** command reveal about a PC connected to a network?
11. What does a DHCP server do?
12. What does the acronym APIPA represent?
13. When is an APIPA assigned?
14. What is the range of APIPA?
15. What does DNS do?
16. What is the difference between DNS and WINS?
17. What device extends the maximum length of a network cable run?
18. What is the purpose of a proxy server?
19. What is a firewall?
20. What is the purpose of a ping?
21. What command is used as the loopback check for IPv6?
22. What command is used to display DNS record information?
23. What command displays information about active TCP connections, ports, and IPv4/IPv6 statistics?
24. What command will display NetBIOS name information?
25. In Windows 7, where is the **Troubleshoot problems** option located?
26. Which operating systems have the **See full map** option available in the Network and Sharing Center?
27. What is a URL?

28. The first part of the URL identifies the _____ used and the second part identifies the _____.
29. What happens when you enter a URL into a web browser?
30. What is a subdomain?
31. Which e-mail protocol does not typically retain the e-mail message on the server after it has been accessed by the e-mail client?
32. Which e-mail protocol is used to send an e-mail message to an e-mail server?
33. What is MAPI?
34. What three components are required to digitally sign and encode an e-mail message?
35. What is a digital signature?
36. What type of addresses does an Ethernet packet contain?
37. Which is described as a connectionless protocol, TCP or UDP?
38. What is the difference between the HTML and HTTP?
39. What is the function of SNMP?
40. What protocol is a combination of HTTP and Secure Socket Layer (SSL) protocols?
41. What are the five characteristics of cloud service that have been identified by NIST?
42. What are the four classifications of cloud service to consumers?
43. What is hypervisor?
44. What is another name for *hypervisor*?
45. What hardware requirements are needed to support virtualization on a client machine?
46. Describe four factors that could affect network transfer speeds.
47. How might a computer be assigned a duplicate IP address?
48. What two factors are commonly associated with a weak RF signal?

Sample A+ Exam Questions

Answer the following questions on a separate sheet of paper. Please do not write in this book.

1. Which is an example of a typical IP address?
   a. 168.23.145.25
   b. 10 2D C4 56 DE FF
   c. JohnH@netcom.org
   d. 255.255.255.000

2. What command issued at the command prompt allows you to inspect the IP address on a Windows system?
   a. **winipconfig**
   b. **winipcfg**
   c. **ipconfig**
   d. **configip**

3. Which of the following services automatically issues an IP address to a PC when it boots?
   a. WINS
   b. DHCP
   c. IPSETUP
   d. DNS

4. Which of the following services is responsible for resolving domain names to IP addresses?
   a. WINS
   b. DHCP
   c. IPSETUP
   d. DNS

5. Which of the following equipment is used primarily to extend the length of a network cable run?
   a. Repeater
   b. Hub
   c. Gateway
   d. Router

6. What command can be used as a quick test to see if a network card is functioning properly with IPv4?
   a. **ping 127.0.0.1**
   b. **tracert 128.10.10.285**
   c. **cardTest**
   d. **NICset**

7. Which of the following is an example of a URL?
   a. JoeB@AcmeNet.Gov
   b. www.g-w.com
   c. 127.34.002.145
   d. BlakeManufacturing@setpoint.com

8. Which command would you use to check cable connectivity between a workstation named Station12 and a file server named Ntserver? (Note that the command is being issued from Station12.)
   a. **ping station12 via ntserver**
   b. **ping ntserver**
   c. **ping ntserver/station12**
   d. **ping station12/ntserver**

9. An IPv4 address consists of _____.
   a. four octets
   b. 24 binary numbers separated by three colons
   c. a group of 24 hexadecimal numbers
   d. four three-digit decimal numbers ranging from 000 to 999

10. Which is an example of a Class C subnet mask?
    a. 255.255.000.255
    b. 255.255.000.000
    c. 000.255.255.255
    d. 255.255.255.000

Suggested Laboratory Activities

Do not attempt any suggested laboratory activities without your instructor's permission. Certain activities can render the PC operating system inoperable.

1. Configure an e-mail client for Microsoft Windows 7 Outlook. (You will need to have Microsoft Office installed on the computer.)
2. Configure a Gmail account (Google e-mail.)
3. Use the Windows Help and Support to see how to set up an Internet connection.
4. Use the Windows Help and Support to see how to share an Internet connection between two or more computers.
5. Use Windows Help and Support to set up a virtual private network (VPN).
6. Set up two PCs and share a game connection. (Instructor's permission is definitely required.)

Small-Office/Home-Office (SOHO) Networking

After studying this chapter, you will be able to:

- Design a SOHO network based on the media, the number of PCs, and the type of Internet access that will be used.
- Select the best media for use in a SOHO network based on cost and building structure.
- Select an appropriate file sharing and storage media method based on overall cost for equipment and administration.
- Select an appropriate Internet access configuration based on the number of PCs and the type of network media used in a SOHO network.
- Select an appropriate level of administration for a SOHO network.
- Identify methods to secure a SOHO network.
- Construct a Windows XP SOHO network.
- Construct a Windows Vista or later SOHO network.
- Identify common problems that can occur in a new SOHO network installation.
- Recall the role of backups as related to data protection.
- Use the Remote Desktop feature to connect to a remote PC.

A+ Exam—Key Points

The A+ Certification has increased the percentage of questions pertaining to networking. This is due to the growing number of small-office/home-office (SOHO) networks. You need to be familiar with all aspects of SOHO networking. It is vital that you have some hands-on experience setting up a small network system with shared Internet access using a variety of media and equipment. You should also be familiar with setting up routers and some form of virtualization. Be prepared to answer several questions directly related to SOHO router configuration, such as MAC filter and port forwarding.

Key Terms

The following key terms will become important pieces of your computer vocabulary. Be sure you can define them.

Demilitarized Zone (DMZ)
fully qualified domain name (FQDN)
Home Phoneline Networking Alliance (HomePNA) technology
HomePNA adapter
Internet Connection Firewall (ICF)
Internet Gateway Device Discovery and Control (IGDDC)
network-attached storage (NAS)
packet sniffer
port forwarding
port triggering
powerline communications (PLC)
proxy server
single port forwarding
small-office/home-office (SOHO) network
Universal Naming Convention (UNC)
virtual private network (VPN)

Installing a network in a home or small office is one of the most common tasks for a computer technician. This chapter prepares you for that task by applying many of the concepts presented earlier in the textbook to the installation, configuration, and support of the small-office/home-office (SOHO) network. You will learn how to use common Windows network wizards to configure a SOHO network and how to troubleshoot the common problems that can occur. You will also learn about the many factors that determine SOHO network design. You will look at many of the features available on a typical network router, such as DHCP, port forwarding, port triggering, and MAC filtering.

Most of the technologies presented in this chapter have already been covered in detail in earlier chapters. This chapter brings together the information already learned and applies it to creating a home network or a small business network. The four main areas of content covered in this chapter are the following:

- Selecting network media and hardware.
- Configuring a local network system.
- Securing the network.
- Troubleshooting the SOHO network.

Designing the SOHO Network

The **small-office/home-office (SOHO) network** is a simple peer-to-peer LAN that is used to share resources and data in a home- or small-office environment. Although any computer hardware connected to the SOHO network can be shared, printers and Internet access devices are the most commonly shared.

As a computer technician, you may be called on to design and configure a SOHO network. There are several factors to consider in its design. These factors include the following:

- Type of media that will be used to connect the PCs together.
- Methods of hosting file sharing services for the SOHO network.
- Manner in which the networked PCs will access the Internet.
- Level of administration that will be used to secure resources and data.
- Methods of security that will be used to protect the network from intruders.
- Methods of securing individual workstations.

The following sections examine each of these factors as they introduce the configurations and technologies commonly used in a SOHO network.

SOHO Media

The four common choices of networking media for SOHO networks are copper cable (Cat 5e and Cat 6), wireless, existing home telephone lines, and existing power lines. The choice is based on cost, building construction, and user or installer preference. For example, copper cable is inexpensive, but the building structure may prove difficult for installing the cables. This is especially true in buildings with open spaces, high ceilings, and concrete floors. Wireless technology is easy to install, but it has some security issues. Existing telephone lines are economical and convenient but may not be suitable for an office environment. Using existing power lines is inexpensive but undesirable to many people who do not like the idea of connecting the network to 120 volts of ac power.

There are many variables to consider when determining the type of network media to use. The following sections explore each of these variables and also look at implementing a mixed network environment and using a prewired home system.

Copper Cable

Copper cable has been the choice for many years. However, the main objection to using copper cable is that it is often difficult to run the cable through the walls. To overcome this difficulty, copper cable can be used in one room and another form of network media can be used in a different room. For example, you can use copper cable in one room and wireless technology in the other. This type of network configuration is known as a hybrid or a *mixed network* environment and is discussed later in this chapter.

Wireless

Wireless is a popular choice of SOHO media. It is quick to install, and the location of the networked PCs can be easily changed. It is the ideal solution for a building that is difficult to cable. However, be aware that when using a wireless NIC to access the network, the default settings allow the network to be compromised by an intruder. The default setup configuration uses a default network group name and no data encryption. It is not difficult, though, to change the default network group name and to configure all packets to be encrypted. Doing so increases network security, **Figure 19-1**.

There are two common encryption types associated with wireless network adapters: Advanced Encryption Standard (AES) and

Temporal Key Integrity Protocol (TKIP). The encryption types also have several security types used to secure data such as WPA-Personal, WPA2-Personal, WPA-Enterprise, and 802.1x. You may wish to review Chapter 12—Laptops and Mobile Devices, which cover basic wireless security features for mobile devices.

When you use wireless media for a SOHO network, you should configure the wireless network so that only designated persons can access the network through a wireless access point.

Existing Phone Lines

Home Phoneline Networking Alliance (HomePNA) technology allows existing home telephone lines to be used for the network media. Any telephone jack can be used as a connection point for the network system. Network cables and a hub are not required for making the connections. All that is needed is a **HomePNA adapter**, a networking device that allows every telephone jack connected together physically in a building to be part of the network. When a HomePNA adapter is installed, every telephone jack is part of the network. Some HomePNA adapters, like the one in **Figure 19-2**, include two RJ-11 ports. One RJ-11 port is used to connect to the telephone jack and the other is used to connect to either a telephone or to cascade to another HomePNA device, **Figure 19-3**. Cascading HomePNA adapters is useful when there is not an adequate amount of telephone jacks for each PC.

Using existing telephone lines as network media does not interfere with telephone calls. Typical voice and sound data transmitted on a residential telephone system are of relatively low frequencies, usually between 0 Hz and 4 kHz. The HomePNA adapter uses a frequency higher than 4 kHz to transmit data across the existing telephone line. The two frequencies do not interfere with each other.

While HomePNA technology is a practical solution for homes and for some businesses, it is not recommend for commercial buildings. Most corporate offices use a private branch exchange (PBX) as the centralized point of the telephone system. Because the telephone lines for a typical PBX system run directly from each telephone jack to the PBX, a complete network circuit cannot

Figure 19-1.
The **Wireless Network Properties** dialog box provides options for configuring the wireless security type and encryption type.

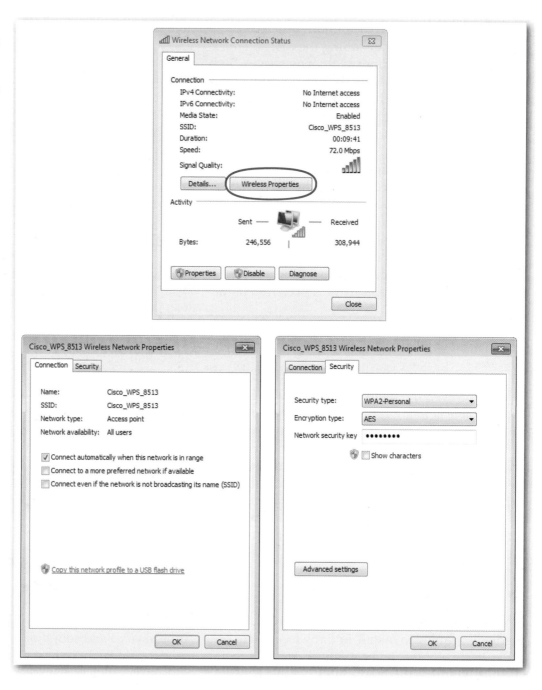

be established. The telephone lines in a home, however, typically run in a daisy-chain fashion from one telephone jack to the next, making a complete loop throughout the house.

Existing Power Lines

Powerline communications (PLC) is technology that allows existing power lines to be used as network media. A PLC adapter connects a PC to the 120-volt ac outlet, **Figure 19-4**. When a PLC network is implemented, two separate systems can operate over the same media at the same time: a 120-volt ac power source and an Ethernet network. PLC works in the same fashion as HomePNA technology by transmitting data at a higher frequency than the existing system. Data transmission on the PLC network operates at frequencies much higher than the 60 Hz of the 120-volt ac outlet.

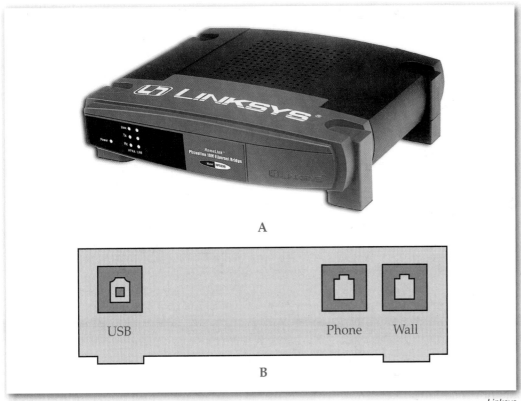

Linksys
Goodheart-Willcox Publisher

Figure 19-2.
A—This HomePNA adapter connects to a PC with a USB cable. B—Back of HomePNA adapter. This adapter includes two RJ-11 jacks: a phone port to connect to a telephone or to another HomePNA adapter and a wall port to connect to the telephone line.

Figure 19-3. A—PCs connected directly to separate telephone jacks through HomePNA adapters. Telephone jacks must share the same telephone line. B—PCs connected to the same telephone jack through cascading HomePNA adapters.

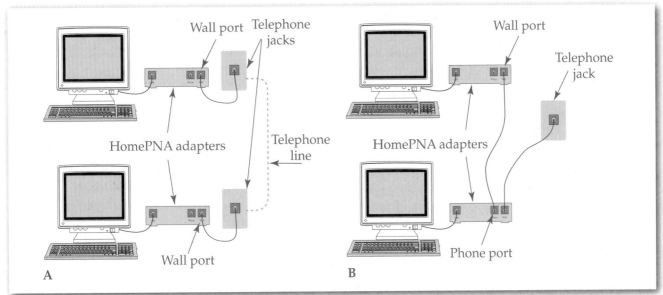

Goodheart-Willcox Publisher

Figure 19-4. This PLC adapter plugs directly into an ac outlet. Some PLC adapters have a separate power cable.

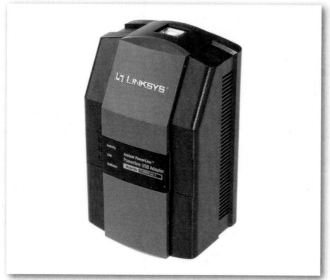

Linksys

Existing power lines have been used as a network media for some time in Europe, but have been slowly accepted in the United States. The main reason is that people have a natural fear of electricity. The idea of plugging network equipment directly into a 120-volt ac outlet leaves them somewhat concerned. However, plugging a PLC device into a 120-volt ac outlet is no more dangerous than plugging in any other electrical device. All electrical and electronic equipment used in the United States is tested for safety by the Underwriters Laboratories (UL). Any equipment designed to plug directly into the power outlet of a home is safe. After all, even the PC plugs directly into the 120-volt ac outlet, and it is safe to use.

PLC has some advantages over HomePNA technology. Typically, a room is limited to one telephone jack or possibly two, but power outlets are spaced more conveniently throughout a building. With PLC, there is a connection point for the network just about anywhere in the building.

Mixed Network Environment

It is not uncommon to have a mixed network environment. For example, a home- or small-office network may use Cat 5e cable in one room and wireless technology in other rooms. When converting from one network media to another,

a network bridge is required. A bridge connects dissimilar network media while making no decisions about packet contents, destination, or filtering. Bridges use MAC addresses to communicate. This allows all packets to pass through the bridge, no matter which protocol is used. Bridges are covered in Chapter 18—WAN.

Connecting a wireless network to another type of network always requires a wireless bridge. The wireless bridge is referred to as a *wireless access point*, **Figure 19-5**. When a router is used to combine different media and provide an Internet connection, it is often referred to as a gateway router, gateway, or simply router. The exact terminology used can vary between different vendors.

Home Prewired Systems

New homes are often prewired for all types of low-voltage communications systems, such as telephone, audio, television, and computer network systems. Communication equipment suppliers manufacture cabinets to make telephone, television, sound, and computer network system installation simple and convenient. The cabinet shown in **Figure 19-6** provides a common connection point for each home communications system. The cabinet is designed to quickly configure network cables together as needed.

Data Transfer Rates

A comparison of data transfer rates will also help in selecting the best media for the network. The table in **Figure 19-7** compares commonly used media in a SOHO network. As indicated in the table, copper cable has the only predictable data rate. Wireless, existing power lines, and existing telephone line data throughputs vary greatly. Often, vendors emphasize the maximum achievable throughput for these media, but this is not the normal throughput. Actual throughput varies because of environmental conditions. For example, a wireless network may advertise a throughput of 100+ Mbps but can only achieve that if the wireless network devices are at a close proximity, without radio interference or partitions between the transmitter and receiver. The farther apart the transmitter and receiver, the more the

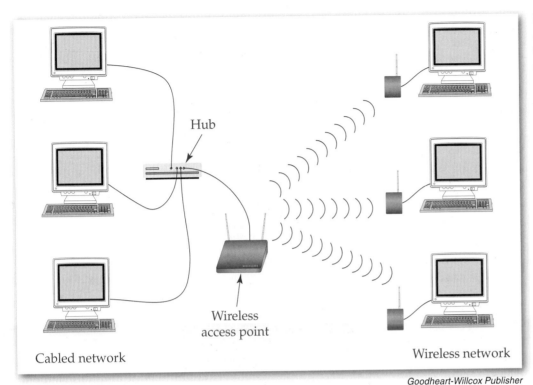

Figure 19-5.
A wireless access point functions as a bridge connecting a cabled network to a wireless network.

Hub

Wireless
access point

Cabled network

Wireless network

Goodheart-Willcox Publisher

throughput rate drops. If wireless devices must transmit through walls, the transmission rate also drops, especially if the walls are constructed of a dense material such as concrete.

PLC technology has a limited throughput because power line conductors are not designed for data transmission. Also, power line conductors may be connected to sources of interference such as electric motors. Since interference on the power line corrupts packets, the packets have to be retransmitted, thus reducing the actual system throughput.

Using the existing telephone lines is unpredictable because the older generation lines were not designed to carry high frequencies. The length of the telephone cable also reduces throughput. Cable signal losses known as *attenuation* increase directly with cable length. As cable length increases, the digital signal strength deteriorates, which results in corrupt data packets. Each packet that is corrupt must be retransmitted. The loss of data packets and the need to retransmit each lost packet causes the loss

of effective bandwidth. The length of the cable will finally reach a point where all data packets are corrupt.

Another cable length factor is cross talk. Older style telephone cable was not designed with twisted pairs. Thus, older cable is much more likely to produce cross talk even on a very short length of cable. The twists in the cable pairs are designed to counter the production of cross talk.

As you can see, the only predictable transmission rates are with traditional network cable. However, the need for a network media that overcomes building structure limitations may outweigh the disadvantages of the lower and unpredictable rates. It is, therefore, the choice of the network user or installer regarding the best media to use for the SOHO network.

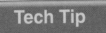 **Tech Tip** Cat 6 Ethernet cable and wireless are the two best choices for performance. Cable is more secure than wireless.

Figure 19-6.
A communications cabinet provides a common connection point for home communications systems, such as telephone, television, sound, and a computer network.

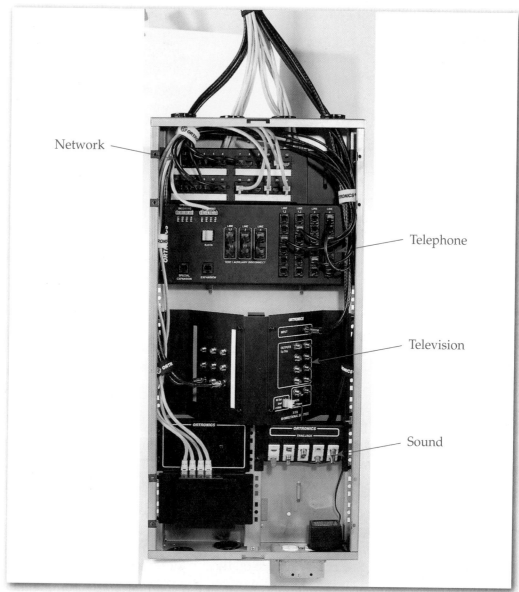

Network

Telephone

Television

Sound

Ortronics

Figure 19-7.
Data rate comparison for various SOHO network media.

Media	Maximum Data Rate	Remarks
Copper cable	10 Mbps or 100 Mbps	Predictable data rates.
Wireless (802.11a, b, g, and n)	100 Mbps or higher	Data rate is drastically effected by distance, building materials, and interference. Rates below 10 Mbps are not uncommon.
Existing power lines (PLC)	No standard	Advertised as 75 Mbps, but in reality is 4 Mbps–10 Mbps.
Existing phone lines (HomePNA)	No standard	Advertised as high as 32 Mbps, but in reality is 4 Mbps–10 Mbps.

Goodheart-Willcox Publisher

File Sharing and Storage Methods

Small networks are all about sharing. When planning a small network system, you must consider which file sharing and storage method is needed. You must also consider the overall cost for equipment and administration. Four common methods of hosting file sharing services for SOHO are NAS, dedicated computer, domain network, and cloud service. You can also use other means to share files such as e-mail and flash drives, but they are not practical methods.

Network-Attached Storage

Ideal for a small-office or home-office network, **network-attached storage (NAS)** is a form of data storage that provides a means of centralized file sharing with little administrative overhead. Some NAS storage devices are arranged in a RAID configuration to provide data protection. The NAS can be configured to provide a backup service for all local network PCs. Some NAS manufacturers provide cloud backup services.

The equipment cost of NAS can be somewhat expensive compared to using a spare computer as a shared access storage unit but less expensive than server-based sharing. In addition, the actual cost of the NAS unit is increased by the number of hard disk drives required for storage or RAID configuration. NAS units typically support a limited number of users, approximately 25 simultaneous connections. This can be considered a lot less than the total number of connections supported by a server but more than adequate for a small business office or home use.

Dedicated Computer

You can create a dedicated file storage and file sharing device from a surplus computer station. Using a computer solely for file sharing, storage, and backup can be cost-effective, especially if using a workstation that has been replaced by a newer model. You can add additional hard disk drives to increase the amount of storage space and even configure the hard disk drives into a RAID. However, configuring a centralized dedicated

computer requires specialized skills, such as the skills learned in this course.

While the single computer is less expensive than using a server or NAS, the single computer can only support a limited number of simultaneous client connections. Windows Vista and earlier operating systems only support a maximum of 10 client concurrent connections when configured as a workgroup. Windows 7 and Windows 8 support up to 20. This limited number of client connections may be more than adequate for a home or small business.

Domain Network

Creating a network domain using a server provides the best way to meet any and all client needs in a network environment. You can create a network with unlimited number of clients and have complete detailed control of all users. The big disadvantage of a domain network is that it requires specialized skills to administer. The skills needed to administer a domain network can require two or more years of schooling and experience. Also, if the network is to be available 24/7, you need a staff of at least four technicians with an administrator skill set to oversee the domain network. The cost of employees to maintain a network with 24/7 availability as well as the cost of special equipment and software to create a domain network can be very expensive.

Cloud Services

The cloud is quickly becoming the main choice for file sharing, file backup, and remote access. Many cloud services are provided for free and are easily configured, but the service is only free for a limited storage size and for the number of clients accessing it. Once this limit is exceeded, you must pay for the cloud service. While the cost may increase for the cloud service, it will not be nearly as expensive as a domain network system. The cloud service does not require specialized training to configure compared to a domain network and does not require a large number of support technicians. The support personnel and special equipment is provided by the cloud service. The cost of the technical support personnel and special equipment is shared by all cloud service customers, thus reducing the cost of creating and maintaining a single SOHO network.

The two main advantages cloud services have over a domain network is reduced cost and no need of multiple technicians with specialized training. The disadvantage is you do not have complete anonymity. Someone else always has physical access to your storage and some control over your network system. The one exception is if you create your own cloud service using your own domain network. Review the following chart for a quick comparison of NAS, cloud, domain, and dedicated computer.

Method	Advantages	Disadvantages
NAS	Easy to administer. Centralized storage. Remote access.	Equipment cost. Limited number of clients.
Dedicated computer	Similar to a domain network. Less expensive than a domain network.	Requires regular administration. Requires specialized skills. Limited number of clients.
Cloud	Easy to administer. Cost-effective. Unlimited number of clients. Remote access.	Does not have complete anonymity.
Domain	Maximum control and security. Maximum customization. Centralized administration. Unlimited number of clients. Remote access.	Can be expensive. Requires specialized skill set.

Internet Access and SOHO Design

There are several typical Internet access configurations that can be used in SOHO networks. The exact configuration depends on the building's environment and the type of Internet access device selected. The common choices of Internet access devices in a SOHO network are the telephone modem, DSL modem, cable modem, and wireless hotspots. This section covers various network configurations that use a telephone, DSL, or cable modem to access the Internet.

Internet Shared Access

When using a modem as the Internet access device, the configuration varies depending on the number of PCs that are networked. A two-PC network may be connected directly from PC to PC without the use of a hub. **Figure 19-8** shows a two-PC network that uses a modem to connect to the Internet. In this configuration, the two PCs are connected directly from NIC to NIC with a crossover cable. This is the simplest way of connecting PCs together in a SOHO network. When the computers are configured with network cards that utilize the Auto-MDIX feature, no crossover cable is required. All modern Ethernet network cables are Auto-MDIX compliant.

> **Tech Tip**
>
> A NIC is incorporated into most motherboards, which means you may not need to purchase a NIC for each computer in the network.

Notice that the PC with two network adapters is designated as the *host* because it provides the Internet connection for both PCs. A PC that accesses the Internet through the host is called a *client*.

For the host to provide Internet access, Internet Connection Sharing (ICS) must be established. ICS is Microsoft's simple application of the network address translation (NAT) standard. The NAT standard was developed by the Internet Engineering Task Force (IETF) and is described in detail in RFC 1631. NAT was specifically designed as a standard for sharing a single Internet connection and providing a type of firewall protection. NAT can support more clients than ICS and is more versatile than ICS.

The host in a typical ICS configuration may be assigned the IP address 192.168.000.001, and the clients may be assigned IP addresses in sequence starting at 192.168.000.002. Setting up an ICS is covered later in this chapter.

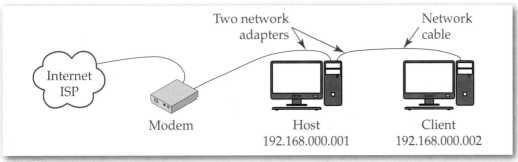

Figure 19-8.
Two-PC network with shared Internet access. No router, switch, or hub is required.

Goodheart-Willcox Publisher

Tech Tip

Different router manufacturers may use a wide variety of default IP address assignments for the router such as 192.168.0.1, 192.168.100.1, and 192.168.1.1. However, they all start with the first two octets of 192.168.

Tech Tip

In general, the term *host* describes any computer that provides a service. The term *client* describes a computer that uses the service provided by the host. In the example of an ICS system, the host provides Internet access to the client computers.

Another SOHO Internet access arrangement is that in **Figure 19-9**. Notice that the three PCs are connected together using a switch or hub. This is a typical Ethernet cable arrangement. Again, note that the PC connected to the Internet is the host, while the other two are considered clients. When a client sends a request to access the Internet, the host automatically connects to the Internet service provider (ISP). The host must be turned on for the clients to access the Internet.

Tech Tip

NAT is designed for IPv4 and is not required for IPv6.

Figure 19-10 shows a typical SOHO Internet access arrangement when a router with wireless access capabilities is used. The router acts as a wireless access point and as the main connection point for the Ethernet network cables. In this arrangement, the router is the host, providing Internet access to all the devices in the local area network.

Figure 19-9. Shared Internet access using a switch or hub to share the Internet connection from the host.

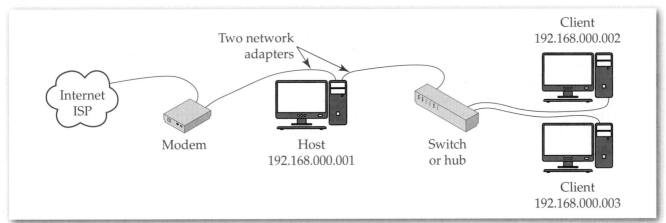

Goodheart-Willcox Publisher

Figure 19-10.
Routers can provide a common connection point for Ethernet network cables and serve as a wireless access point.

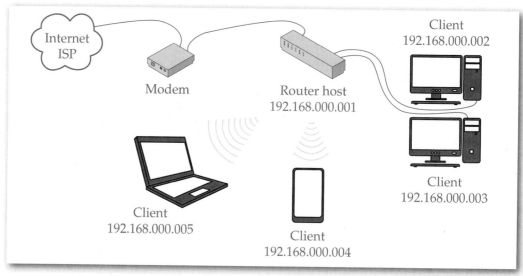

Goodheart-Willcox Publisher

> **Tech Tip**
>
> The router is a complete small computer system. It contains a CPU, memory, and software.

Some network devices provide the combined function of DSL modems and router and provide both Ethernet network ports and wireless access, thus eliminating the need for multiple devices.

Mobile Hotspot

A mobile hotspot provides a direct connection to an ISP through mobile broadband service. The hotspot can provide 3G and 4G wireless Internet connections. For a SOHO network or business applications that must have 24/7 Internet access, a mobile hotspot can be installed as an Internet access backup option. For example, when using a cable modem for Internet access, you could use a mobile hotspot as a backup system. If the cable modem goes down because of cable failure, you can switch to a mobile hotspot to maintain the Internet access until the cable is repaired.

SOHO Administration

SOHO network administration can be as simple or as complex as you wish to make it. Since the SOHO network is a peer-to-peer network, you need not have any real administrative hierarchy.

Everyone using the network can have equal access to all files and programs on the network. However, this can be disastrous. With everyone having equal access, anyone can change the properties of any PC in the network. A better scenario is to have a single administrator with limited authority delegated to other users. The administrator can determine how much control other users have over hardware and software by setting up local and share-level security.

Local security is implemented by creating a local user account on each PC. The local user account allows the user to log on to a single computer where the user account has been created. Remember that a peer-to-peer network uses the workgroup model of security. This model of security maintains a security list at each PC and requires that a local user account be set up at every PC the user will access locally.

Local security protects system settings on a PC. Any changes the user makes to the desktop or to a program is stored in the user's personal settings on that PC. These changes do not affect other local users.

Share-level security protects resources accessed from across the network by requiring a password to access the share or by limiting its access. For example, network users may only have read access to files on another PC, or they may not be able to access the files at all unless they know the password.

Even in a home network, local and share-level security should be implemented to avoid disastrous situations. To reinforce how important security is, let us look at a typical home network in which no security has been implemented.

Two parents use one of the PCs and two children, ages 10 and 16, use the other. Each PC has been set up with a single user account. A color printer is attached to the parent's PC and is shared to allow the children to print to it from their computer. Drive C on the parent's computer is also shared and allows full access to all files. Both of the parents use their PC for work-related activities and for personal finances.

The children use their PC for school assignments and use the color printer to print their school assignments and the graphics they find on the Internet. They also use their PC for their favorite pastime, computer games. The children are constantly downloading sample gaming software and exchanging software games with their friends. The children often need to use the PC at the same time. When this happens, one of them uses the parent's PC.

As you are probably sensing, severe problems are likely because of this casual setup. With everyone using the same local user account, anyone using a PC can make changes on it. For instance, the children could delete important files on their parent's PC, such as banking information. They could even delete important files from across the network if share-level security has not been set up on the parent's local hard drive. Also, one of the children can download a game on their parent's PC and then change the PC's default settings to optimize the game. Or, by simply installing the computer game, a DLL file or some other file can possibly be overwritten. This would lock up, or crash, the PC.

> **Tech Tip**
>
> Other security practices to keep in mind are to use passwords that are complex, containing uppercase and lowercase letters, numbers, and special symbols. *Never* use a password that matches any word found in a dictionary or a person's name. *Never* leave the password blank. *Always* encrypt important data so even if it is accessed, it will be of little use to the intruder.

SOHO Security

PCs in a SOHO network are vulnerable to attacks from outside the LAN if the LAN is connected to the Internet. The Internet is "public" media. Users from anywhere in the world could access a networked PC through the Internet connection or intercept a PC's message content. There are several ways to set up security to protect the SOHO network from intruders and to protect data as it travels across the Internet. Two common security implementations that should be configured for the SOHO network are a firewall and a virtual private network (VPN).

Firewall

In Chapter 18—WAN, you learned that a firewall protects a LAN by blocking access to specific ports or by filtering out IP addresses, packet contents, services, and protocols. For example, a firewall can filter out echo requests. This stops a site that is being probed with the **ping** command from displaying its IP address via echo.

There are times when you may need to block a specific port or open a port. For example, a firewall is set up to block all ports that are not absolutely essential. A person wishes to participate in a game online. The game "Rainbow Six" requires the use of TCP ports 2346, 2347, and 2348 for Internet gaming. These ports can be opened by entering these numbers in the firewall service properties dialog box. Opening these ports allows data to pass through the firewall, allowing two computers to communicate freely during a gaming session.

The firewall must be configured to allow file and printer sharing. Windows automatically configures the correct port numbers in the firewall when you first set up a file share or printer share. If you are not using a Windows-based firewall, you could encounter problems related to blocked ports.

Windows XP comes with a standard firewall called the **Internet Connection Firewall (ICF)**, software that can be configured to keep unauthorized users from accessing the network. Windows Vista and later simply refer to the firewall as Windows Firewall. There are also many third-party utilities that can be used to increase SOHO security. Using the Network Setup Wizard to install ICF is covered later in this chapter.

Originally in Windows XP, it was advisable to only enable one computer firewall. Installing a firewall on more than one PC in a Windows XP SOHO network adversely affected shares, thus preventing the network's main purpose. Today, Windows Firewall automatically controls the opening of ports for the support of Microsoft software applications and does not adversely affect the network. Each computer should have the Windows Firewall enabled.

Starting with Windows Vista, the firewall is automatically configured according to the type of network location you select when configuring the network. The firewall settings, or profiles, are automatically configured for different network locations such as Domain, Private, and Public during the network configuration. For example, when configuring a new network connection, you are prompted for the type of location you are in. When you select the new network location, such as Home network, Work network, and Public network, the firewall configuration is automatically configured to match the new network location. **Figure 19-11** compares the network location settings with the profiles used by the firewall. The network profiles shown are used for Windows Vista and Windows 7. Windows 8 simply identifies two types of firewall network profiles: Private and Public.

Virtual Private Network (VPN)

A **virtual private network (VPN)** is a security configuration that ensures data sent across the Internet is not intercepted, read, or modified. It does this by creating a private tunnel between the destination and source PC and encrypting packet contents. As the term *tunnel* implies, all the messages are exchanged privately as though they traveled through the public space of the Internet encapsulated in a security tunnel that no one else can see into or access, **Figure 19-12**.

A VPN should be created to ensure security when communicating across the Internet through an ISP. A VPN can also be created if you are permanently connected to the Internet via a cable modem or DSL modem.

Normally, because data is encoded in plain ASCII text, the content of a typical packet is completely viewable through a packet sniffer. A **packet sniffer** is a utility that captures packets on a network and displays their entire contents. When a VPN connection is made, all the contents of the packet are encrypted except for the destination address. The destination address remains readable so it can travel across a series of Internet routers to reach its final destination. The VPN is transparent to users at the destination and the source.

The two main security connection protocols associated with a VPN connection are Point-to-Point Tunneling Protocol (PPTP) and Layer 2 Tunneling Protocol (L2TP). These protocols also incorporate other protocols, such as IPSec, IKE, and CHAP, to further enhance their security features.

Be aware that some ISPs do not allow VPN connections through their system. The ISP filters out protocols associated with VPNs. To determine if you can use a VPN, check with the ISP.

Windows XP users experienced many problems implementing a VPN. The problems were caused many times by the Windows XP Internet Connection Firewall (ICF) and by the Windows XP implementation of Internet Connection Sharing (ICS). The more modern operating systems and more sophisticated firewalls have eliminated most encountered problems. When configuring a VPN connection on the more modern operating systems, the firewall is automatically configured to permit the VPN connection. **Figure 19-13** shows the VPN wizard in Windows 7, which allows you to configure a VPN connection between two computers.

The most typical problem associated with a VPN is incorrectly entering the destination address. The address can be either a fully qualified domain name (FQDN), or an IP address.

Wireless Router Security

Wireless networks are much more a security risk than a wired network. In a wired network, access is not readily accessible by the very nature of the network media. Cables are typically inside the building structure, which means to gain access to the physical media, an unauthorized person would need to be inside the building. A

Figure 19-11. The Windows Firewall automatically configures the appropriate ports based on the type of network location. A—Network location settings. B—Windows Firewall profiles.

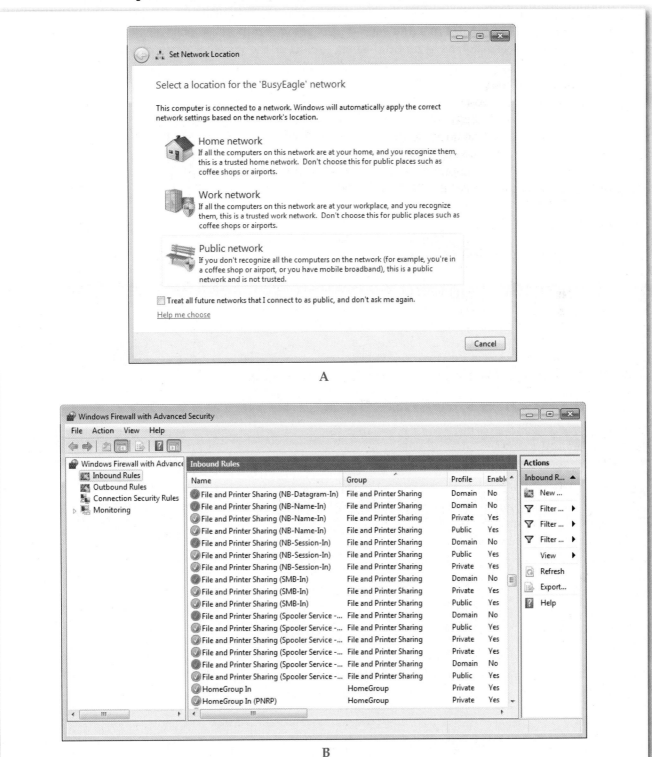

wireless network can be accessed from outside the building. Hence, no physical access to the building is required. Apartment buildings, hotels, and some commercial buildings may have a variety of separate areas, such as individual units, special rooms, and private office areas. These separate areas result in easy access to one or more wireless network systems. However, there are some common security best practices that can help secure the wireless network system.

Figure 19-12.
A virtual private network (VPN) creates a private tunnel between the destination and source PC. The data flowing between the two PCs cannot be interpreted by other computers on the Internet.

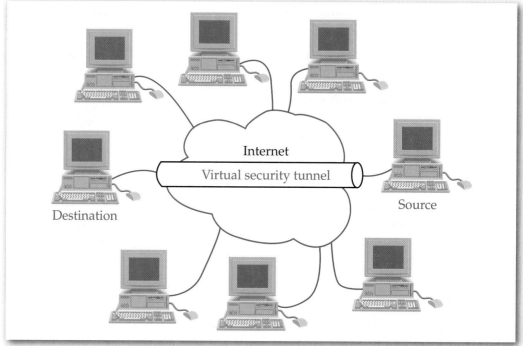

Goodheart-Willcox Publisher

Figure 19-13.
Windows provides a simple VPN wizard that automatically configures a VPN connection between two computers.

Change Default Names

Wireless access points and routers have default device names, as well as default administrator names and default administrator passwords. As a result, an unauthorized person could simply view available networks with a wireless device and spot any wireless routers that are using a default assigned name. After identifying the default router name, he or she can then conduct a simple Internet search to find the default administrator name and password to gain control of the wireless router. To prevent access to the router, the default name of the router, the default administrator name, and password should be changed. Also, wireless routers have a configuration option to not broadcast the router SSID. While stopping the broadcast will not secure the router 100%, it will prevent most unauthorized persons from discovering the presence of the wireless router. The following table lists the default SSID and administrator name and password for some major brands of routers.

Router Brand	SSID	Administrator Name
Linksys	linksys	admin
D-Link	dlink	admin
Netgear	NETGEAR	admin
Cisco	Cisco	Cisco

Router Brand	Administrator Password	IP Address
Linksys	admin	192.168.1.1
D-Link	admin	192.168.1.1
Netgear	password 1234	192.168.0.1
Cisco	Cisco	192.168.0.1

Enable MAC Filtering

One of the best ways to secure a wireless network is by applying MAC filtering to the wireless network router. MAC filtering is a router configuration that accepts or rejects connections based on device MAC addresses. To enable MAC filtering in the Cisco software shown in **Figure 19-14**, you simply select **Enabled** and **Permit PCs listed below to access the wireless network**. Then, you enter each computer's MAC address. To reveal a computer's MAC address, simply enter **ipconfig /all** at the command prompt and then look for the physical address entry.

Disable SSID Broadcast

Basic wireless security measures call for disabling the wireless router SSID broadcast, **Figure 19-15**. When disabled, the wireless router will not appear to users looking for a wireless connection. While this security measure is effective for preventing an average user from discovering the existence of a wireless router, it will not prevent the discovery of the wireless router from a trained technician using a protocol analyzer or some other sophisticated software application.

Demilitarized Zone (DMZ)

Network security often involves configuring a **Demilitarized Zone (DMZ)**. This term originally referred to an area between two opposing military forces. In network security application, the DMZ is an area of a network system that is intentionally created to be less secure than the main network system and is directly accessible from the Internet. A demilitarized area is less secure than a secure, occupied area. The less secure area is used to support network systems such as web servers, mail servers, FTP servers, and VoIP servers. These types of servers all have one thing in common—they must allow for access from outside the network and are not protected behind the local network firewall.

The DMZ is exposed to access from outside the secure network. In **Figure 19-16**, you can see all that is required to configure the DMZ is to supply the incoming source IP address and the destination IP address. The default setting of the source address is **Any IP Address**, which means any outside computer can connect to or pass data to the designated destination IP address. The destination IP address is the location of the device, which is a member of the local home or office network.

The DMZ option is often used for home systems to support activities such as gaming or video conferencing. The DMZ destination typically has all ports opened, which exposes the destination to the Internet and is a security risk. Two methods of router configuration that support the function of a DMZ are port forwarding

Figure 19-14. A router can be configured to accept or reject device connections based on device MAC addresses.

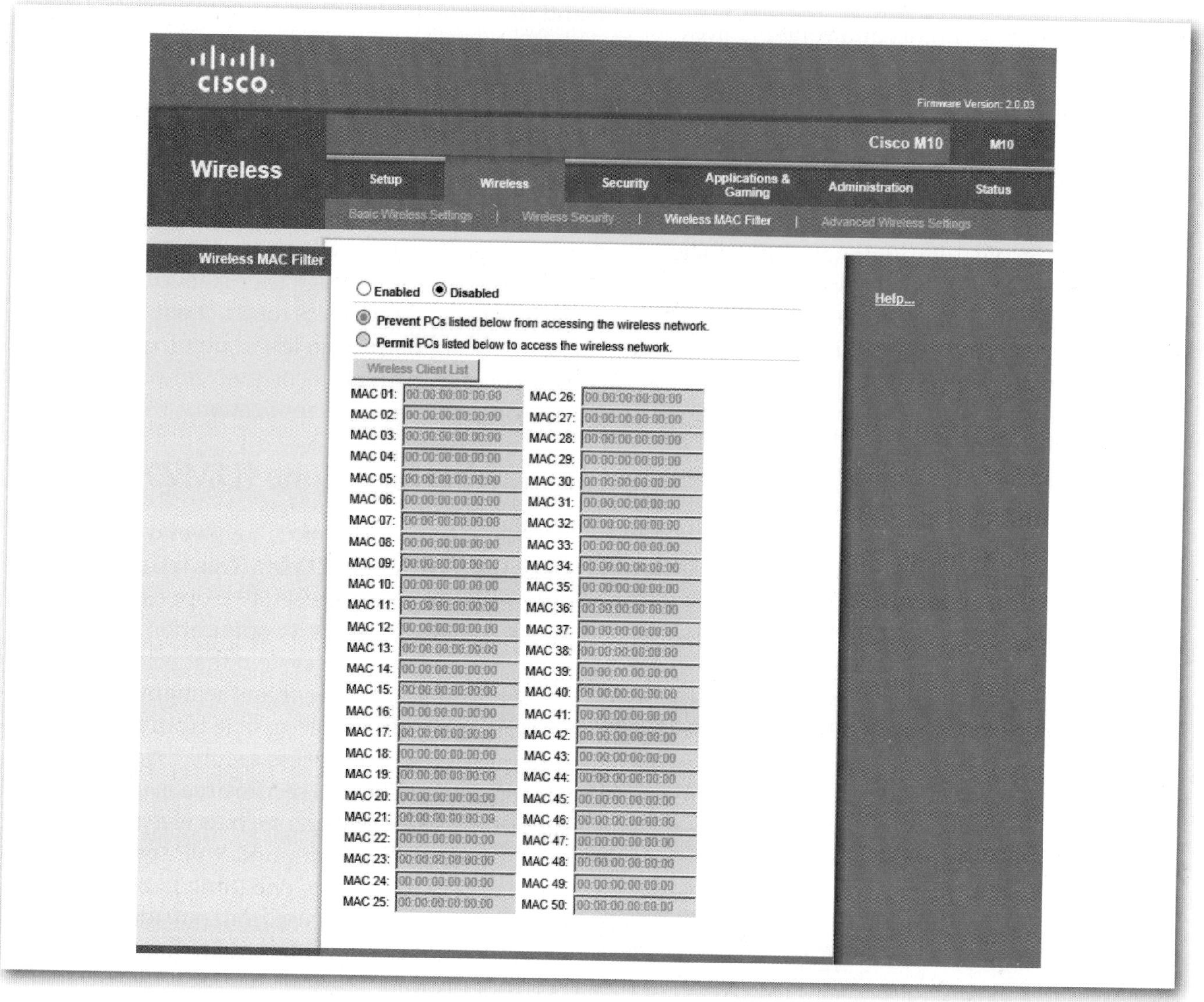

and port triggering. Although they are similar in function, there is a distinct difference. Port triggering is dynamic and is used to temporarily open a port. It is not affected by a change of IP address, such as when a DHCP server issues a new IP address to the device. Port forwarding is static and is used to maintain a connection for applications, such as a web server, or to play games that use the Internet.

Port Forwarding

Port forwarding, also referred to as *port mapping*, is a router configuration set to forward packets to a destination computer/server by allowing specific ports to remain open to the destination. For example, a router configured for port forwarding can be configured to direct all inbound traffic on port 80 from the Internet to a designated web server. Look at **Figure 19-17**. To configure port forwarding, you simply input a software application name and then identify a range of port numbers and the protocol type (TCP or UDP, or both). You also identify the IP address of the computer. Cisco recommends that you assign a static IPv4 address to the computer. If the computer is configured for a dynamic IPv4 address, the DHCP service may change the assigned IPv4 address of the computer. This will result in the port forward configuration needing to be reconfigured for the new IPv4 address.

Figure 19-15. Wireless routers have an option to disable the SSID broadcast.

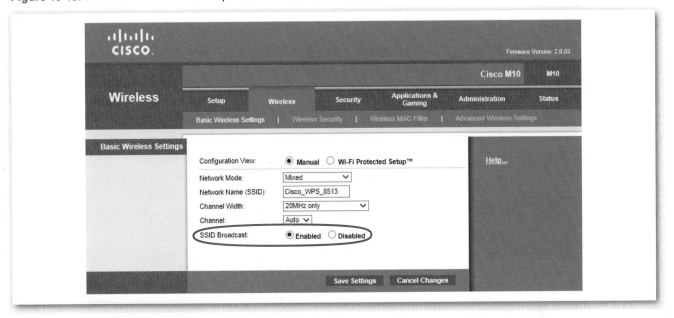

Figure 19-16. Cisco routers provide a configuration option for creating a home network DMZ.

Port Triggering

Port triggering is a router configuration that monitors outbound traffic by port number. When data passes from the outgoing port, the designated inbound port automatically opens. For example, a router can be configured to detect outbound traffic on port 3300 and then automatically open port 3100 on a designated IP address for inbound traffic in response. After the connection is terminated, the port is closed. The router remembers the IP address of the computer that sent the outgoing data on a particular port. The outgoing data triggers the opening of an inbound port. The incoming data is then sent to the computer identified by the outgoing data IP address.

Figure 19-17. Port forwarding allows a range of port numbers to be opened in the firewall for a particular computer or network device.

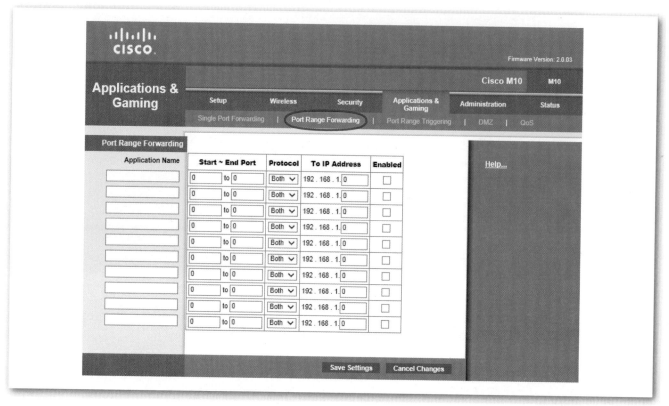

Port triggering is dynamic and does not require a static IP address. Take a look at **Figure 19-18**. As you can see, an IP address is not required. Only the software application and the ports need to be identified. The trigger range is the list of ports that can trigger the opening of the matching forwarded port.

Single Port Forwarding

Single port forwarding is a router configuration that works in similar fashion as port forwarding, however, a single designated IP address is identified instead of all IP addresses in the local area network. When single port forwarding is configured, one particular computer or server is designated by IP address. In **Figure 19-19**, a single designated IP address for each external and internal port and protocol is identified.

As you can see, the router is capable of controlling the opening and closing of specified ports and directs the inbound and outbound traffic to and from a single IP address or a range of IP addresses. Port forwarding and port triggering

provide much more security than the creation of a DMZ. A DMZ opens all ports to the Internet.

DHCP Configuration

SOHO routers provide an option for DHCP services, which means the router will automatically issue IP addresses to the network devices. In **Figure 19-20**, the router setup software has an option for enabling the DHCP service. The default settings for this particular router are assigned IP address 192.168.1.1 and subnet mask 255.255.255.0. The router is capable of issuing 50 IP addresses in a range from 192.168.1.100 to 192.168.1.149.

The router also has the capability to issue reserved or static IP addresses to specific network devices. For example, some devices, such as printers, web cameras, and network storage, may require a static IP address. The router can "reserve" an IP address for any device that requires a static IP address. **Figure 19-21** shows a router option to reserve DHCP assignments. The router identifies all existing network devices and

Figure 19-18. Port triggering is the temporary port opening of an inbound port, which occurs only after data is sent through a particular outbound port.

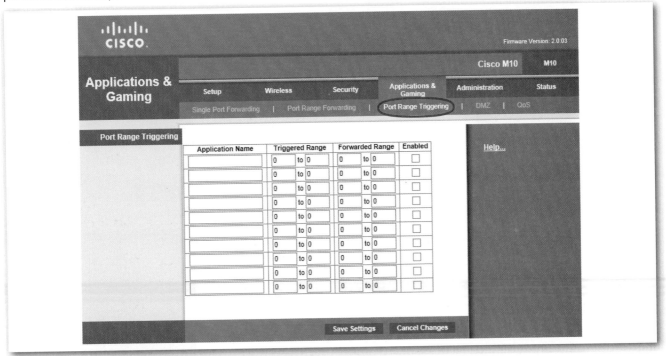

Figure 19-19. Single port forwarding designates one particular destination by IP address.

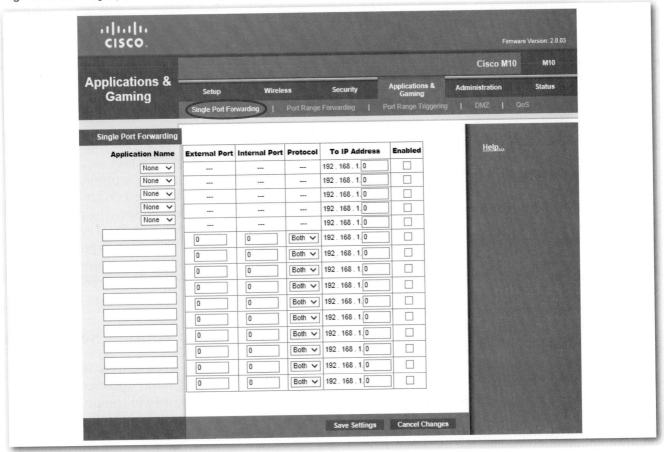

Figure 19-20. Routers have the capability to automatically issue IP addresses to local network devices.

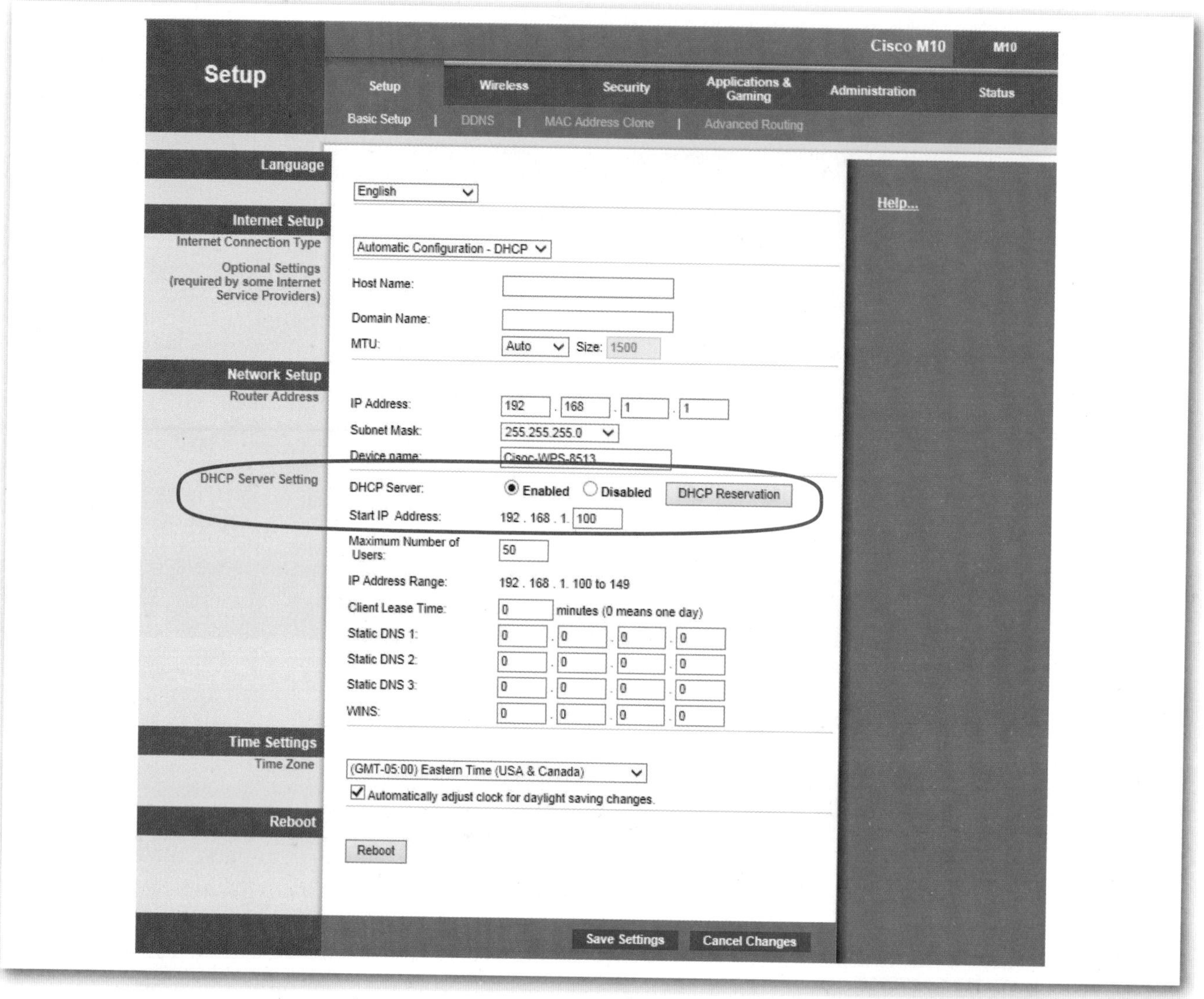

their IP and MAC addresses. All you do is select the device. There is also an option to manually add a device by entering the client name, assigning an IP address, and entering the MAC address.

Proxy Server

A **proxy server** serves as an intermediary between the Internet and a network client computer. The most common proxy server is a web server proxy, which stores webpage content that is frequently accessed by network users. For example, if a company has employees that must access company content at a remote site, the proxy server can store content that is frequently accessed

by the users. This way, the content can be accessed much faster from the proxy server, and there is no need to access the remote site. The principle is the same as with a webpage cache. The webpage appears to be accessed faster than when actually downloading the remote location content. A proxy server can also improve security by applying a filter that prevents specific ports from being used.

Using Policies to Harden Security

The Local Security Policy Editor (secpol.msc) and Local Group Policy Editor (gpedit.msc) can be used to increase the security of computers in the SOHO network. The Local Security Policy Editor is a subset of the Local Group Policy Editor.

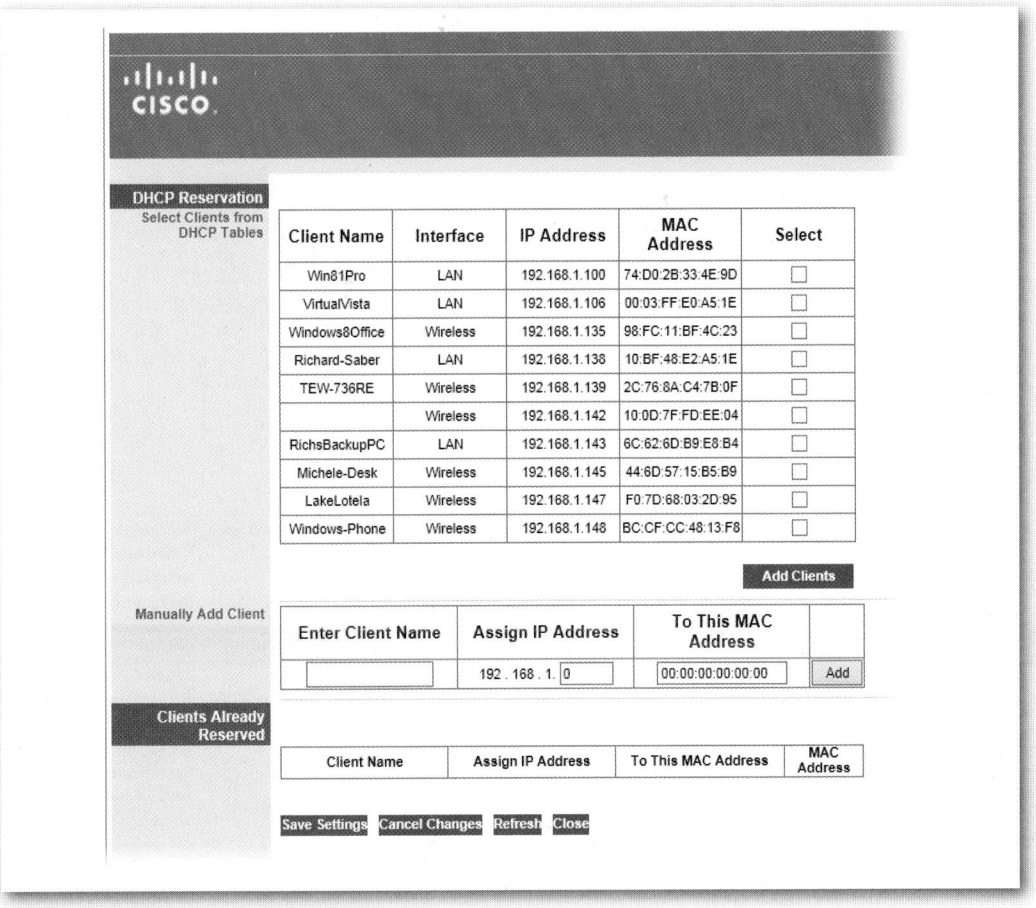

Figure 19-21.
Specific IP addresses can be reserved, which means a device such as a printer or a web camera is given a static IP address assignment.

The Local Security Policy Editor is run on each computer that is a member of a workgroup. When computers are part of a workgroup, each computer has its own local group policy. When a computer is a member of a domain controlled by a server, the Local Group Policy Editor is run and configured at the server. The policy is applied from the server to all computer users typically by group membership.

In **Figure 19-22**, you can see the wide array of security policies available for configuration. Under Windows Components, there is a long list of Windows features that can be restricted through policies.

Surfing the Internet through Internet Explorer can cause serious security problems for a network. The network administrator can set policies to restrict the downloading of files that contain ActiveX controls, prevent bypassing smart screen filter warnings, control the Internet Settings configuration, and more. A system administrator should add restrictions to the computer system but not to the extent of hampering the user so the user has difficulty completing his or her assigned tasks. When a particular problem arises, such as visits to unsafe websites, the administrator can configure a policy to raise the minimal level of the Internet Settings configuration of Internet Explorer, thus eliminating the problem.

In a domain network, policies are controlled through the domain server and it is not necessary to configure each workstation individually. When network domain users complain that a Windows feature is missing from their workstation, it is usually the result of a group policy configuration restricting the use of some feature. Windows components, such as Instant Messaging, Game Explorer, Remote Desktop Services, and Internet Explorer configuration options (Home Page, Disabling Wireless Connect Now, and such) are commonly disabled through the Local Group Policy Editor.

To open the Local Group Policy Editor, enter **gpedit.msc** in the **Search** dialog box. The .msc

Figure 19-22. The Local Group Policy Editor can harden the security of workstations on the network.

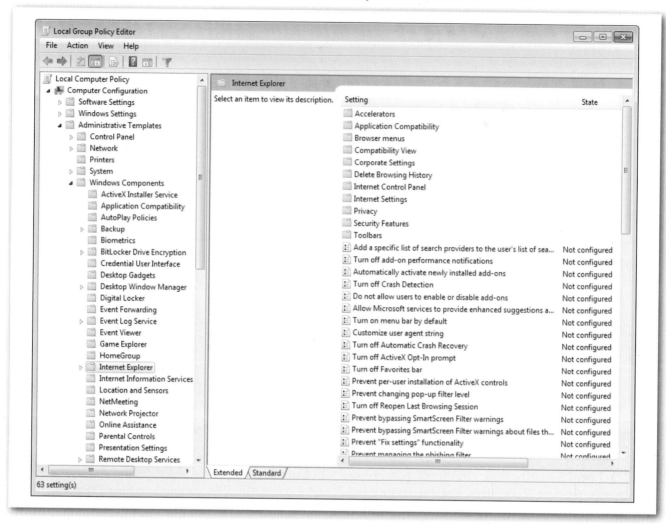

extension must be added to the program name. To open the Local Security Policy Editor, enter **secpol.msc** in the **Search** dialog box. Again, the .msc must be added to the program name.

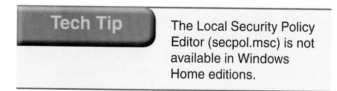

The Local Security Policy Editor (secpol.msc) is not available in Windows Home editions.

Configuring the SOHO Network with Windows XP

The Network Setup Wizard makes it easy to set up a Windows XP SOHO network. It includes

a series of dialog boxes that ask for information about the network. The wizard can be accessed through **Start | Settings | Control Panel | Network Connections | Setup a home or small office network**. **Figure 19-23** shows the first dialog box of the Network Setup Wizard. The Network Setup Wizard helps you to share an Internet connection, enable the Internet Connection Firewall (ICF), and enable file and printer sharing.

The Network Setup Wizard is easy to use if you are familiar with networking hardware and terminology. However, if you have never set up a network before, it is easy to provide the wrong information. As an aid, the Network Setup Wizard includes a checklist which assists in setting up a SOHO network. See **Figure 19-24**. The checklist can be printed and carried with you until you become comfortable with setting up networks.

Share an Internet Connection

One of the main tasks of configuring a SOHO network with Internet access is setting up Internet Connection Sharing (ICS). ICS can be configured manually or automatically. When configured automatically, choose from the Network Setup Wizard menu **This computer connects directly to the Internet. The other computers on my network connect to the Internet through this computer**. See **Figure 19-25**. When activated, a series of prompts appear on the screen. Answer the series of questions presented in the dialog boxes.

Using the Network Setup Wizard is by far the easiest method for setting up Internet Connection Sharing. Even a novice can usually configure ICS by responding to the series of dialog boxes. A technician will also use the wizard to set up ICS, but he or she must know how to configure the same connection manually to be able to perform and understand the results of troubleshooting an ICS installation.

After the computer has been set up and configured, you can make a disk that will automatically set up the clients for you. You can make the client disks by simply inserting the Windows XP installation CD. When the first screen appears, select **Additional tasks** from the menu and follow the prompts. A client disk will

Figure 19-23. Network Setup Wizard welcome screen.

Figure 19-24.
This checklist, provided by Windows XP, is a valuable aid for setting up a SOHO network.

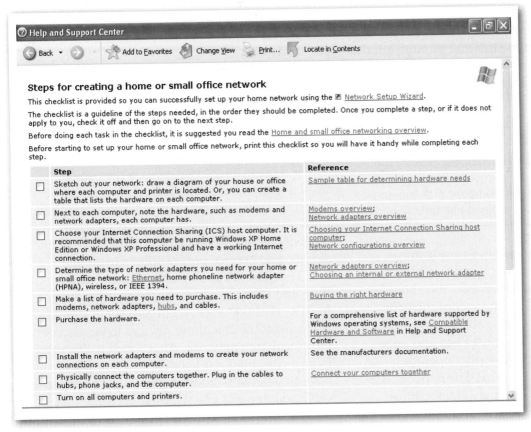

Figure 19-25. The Network Setup Wizard prompts for an Internet connection method.

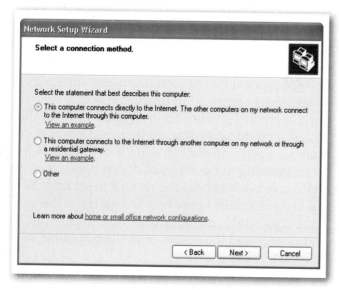

be made on a floppy or other portable storage media such as a flash drive, which can be inserted into each client PC. The portable storage media will automatically configure the client with the appropriate IP address and necessary protocols. If, however, the clients are running Windows XP, you may as an alternative run the Network Setup Wizard on those computers and choose **This computer connects to the Internet through another computer on my network or through a residential gateway**. The wizard will automatically configure the client with the appropriate IP address and protocols.

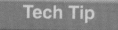

Tech Tip   Originally, Windows XP used floppy disk for the purpose of setting up network clients because the floppy disk was the main portable storage media at that time.

When adding computers running an operating system later than Windows XP, you do not need to use the client disk. You should disable Windows XP ICS and reconfigure the shared network access using the newest version of operating system. Windows Vista and later operating systems support earlier operating systems, such as Windows XP. The network ICS created with Windows XP may block critical ports, thus preventing later operating systems

from functioning properly on the network. Also, for Windows XP to join the new network shared Internet access and to support file sharing with other network computers, the default workgroup name must be changed to "Workgroup" or the workgroup name used in the newer operating system. Some versions of Windows XP use MSHome as the workgroup name. If the Windows XP workgroup name does not match the other computers, the computers will not be able to share network resources with each other.

Another network connection sharing technology is Internet Gateway Device Discovery and Control (IGDDC). **Internet Gateway Device Discovery and Control (IGDDC)** is designed to discover and control network gateway devices such as routers. IGDDC monitors and configures Internet connection settings from any computer on the local area network that is running Windows.

For example, when you configure a wireless adapter to support ICS on a computer that has Network Discovery enabled, IGDDC is also enabled. When IGDDC is enabled, the Internet Gateway Device icon will appear in the Network folder located off the **Start** menu. Look at **Figure 19-26** to see the **Internet gateway device** icon. The **Internet gateway device** icon appears in the Network folder of every computer in the local area network.

The advantage of using IGDDC is that any computer on the local area network can manage the Internet gateway device. Any Windows operating system including all legacy systems back to Windows 95 can access the Internet through the Internet gateway device.

In **Figure 19-27**, you can see the options available for sharing the Internet connection through a wireless network adapter. The wireless network adapter is the designated Internet gateway device. Notice that you can select which service and service port numbers to enable.

The network router must support Universal Plug and Play (UPnP) technology, otherwise IGDDC will not work. UPnP is a set of standards and a protocol that allow devices to be discovered on a local area network. Also, when configured from a computer workstation, the computer must have two network adapters, such as one Ethernet cable adapter and one wireless network adapter. If there are not two network adapters in the

Figure 19-26. When Internet Gateway Device Discovery and Control is enabled, the Internet gateway device icon appears in the Network folder.

computer, the **Sharing** tab will not appear as seen in Figure 19-27.

Internet Gateway Device Discovery and Control is an ISO/IEC organization standard. It is not supported on all routers at the time of this writing. The IGDDC protocol also provides a means for configuring port forwarding.

Set up Internet Connection Firewall

In Windows XP, the Internet Connection Firewall (ICF) is automatically enabled on the computer that connects directly to the Internet or has ICS installed. When ICF is enabled, it not only protects the computer on which it is configured, but also the other computers on the network. The ICF monitors all communications from the Internet by inspecting the source and destination of each packet sent to the network.

The combination of port number and IP address determines if the packet may pass to the network or be discarded. The firewall can also filter packets based on services. Services are identified by port numbers.

Once ICF is enabled, it can be configured manually by accessing the **Network Connection** folder, right-clicking the firewall-enabled connection, and selecting **Properties**. From the **Properties** dialog box, select the **Advanced** tab and then click the **Settings** button. A dialog box like that in **Figure 19-28** will appear, displaying a list of services that can be filtered by the firewall. To select a service, click the box next to the service. A check mark will appear in the box. If the service exists on another computer in the network, you must enter that computer's name or IP address in the **Service Settings** dialog box, **Figure 19-29**. To access the **Service Settings** dialog box, highlight the service to be configured and click the **Edit** button.

Figure 19-27. When Internet Gateway Device Discovery and Control sharing is configured, you can select which service you wish to allow through the shared connection and also enable or disable ports for added security.

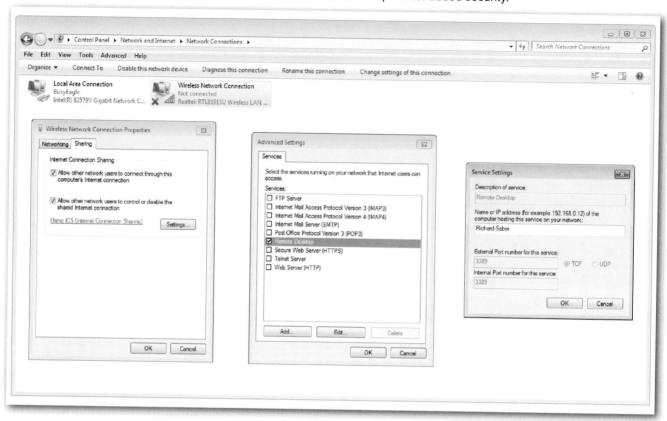

Figure 19-28. Various common network services can be filtered for added security.

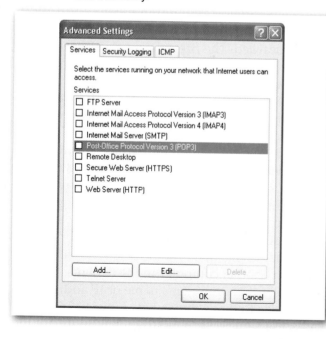

Figure 19-29. Service Settings dialog box set to filter the POP3 service on a computer named "infinity-soyo."

In Figure 19-29, the computer hosting the POP3 service is identified by its name, "infinity-soyo." Notice how the POP3 email service corresponds with port 110 indicated in the text box. Port 110 is the default port number for the POP3 service.

A service that is not listed in the **Advanced Settings** dialog box may be added by clicking the **Add** button. In this case, the description of the service, the name or IP number of the computer hosting the service, and the external and internal port number for the service must be added.

Share Folders and Files in Windows XP

Windows XP introduced Simple File Sharing but also retained the advanced file sharing feature. All Windows operating systems since Windows XP have maintained the ability to use the advanced file sharing options. To use advanced file sharing, partitions must be formatted with NTFS. For a detailed discussion of Simple File Sharing and advanced file sharing, see Chapter 17—Network Administration.

The main purpose of networking users is sharing. Permissions as related to sharing folders and files can be very complicated. As presented earlier in the textbook, there are two different types of permissions that can be set for a folder: share permissions and NTFS permissions. Share permissions are a set of legacy permissions dating back to FAT16 and FAT32 systems and are used to ensure backward compatibility with older systems. Share permissions only apply to folders, and NTFS permissions can apply to both folders and individual files. NTFS permissions provide much more detailed control of shared resources and are also referred to as security permissions. Share permissions and NTFS permissions are shown in **Figure 19-30** and **Figure 19-31**, respectively.

Since two different permissions (share and NTFS) can be assigned to a share, there can be conflicts between the two. Remember, the most restrictive permission takes precedence and will be enforced. For example, if the share permission of a folder is set to full control for the User group and the NTFS permission is set to read, then the User group can only read the contents of the folder and cannot make changes.

Figure 19-30. Share permissions.

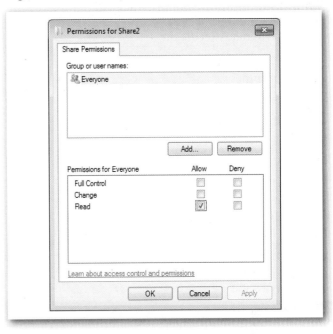

Figure 19-31. NTFS permissions.

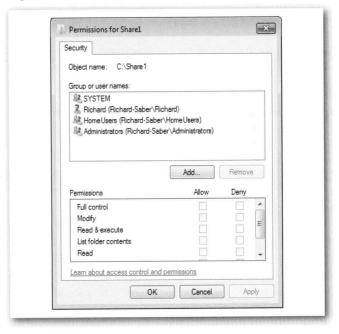

Microsoft recommends managing folder access by setting share permissions for the Everyone group to full control and using NTFS permissions to set more restrictive permissions to manage users. Share permissions apply only to network shares and do not limit access to local user accounts. NTFS permissions control user access locally and remotely from the network.

Special Permissions	Full Control	Modify	Read & Execute	List Folder Contents (folders only)	Read	Write
Traverse folder/execute file	x	x	x	x		
List folder/read data	x	x	x	x	x	
Read attributes	x	x	x	x	x	
Read extended attributes	x	x	x	x	x	
Create files/write data	x	x				x
Create folders/append data	x	x				x
Write attributes	x	x				x
Write extended attributes	x	x				x
Delete subfolders and files	x					
Delete	x	x				
Read permissions	x	x	x	x	x	x
Change permissions	x					
Take ownership	x					
Synchronize	x	x	x	x	x	x

Special NTFS permissions are commonly used for detailed control of access to folders and files located on a file server. The special permissions are full control, modify, read & execute, list folder contents, read, and write. See the table above for a quick comparison of access limitations for NTFS permissions.

The following table will help you better understand the role of permissions and how they might be applied to the design of a collection of SOHO shared folders. The designated Drop folder is used by Microsoft as a location for a folder used to transfer data files or folders from one person to another person or group of persons. The title of the folder can be most anything and does not have to be "Drop."

Folder Type	Share Permissions	NTFS Permissions
Public folder: Default folder on Windows.	**Change:** Permission assigned to the Users group.	**Modify:** Permission assigned to the Users group.
Drop folder: A type of folder used to "drop" files or folders into, such as homework assignments. Only an instructor or group management account can read contents.	**Change:** Permission assigned to the Users group. **Full Control:** Assigned to the instructor or group manager.	**Write:** Permission assigned to the Users group that is applied to the Drop folder. **Full Control:** Permission assigned to the group manager or instructor.
Application folder: Contains software applications or programs.	**Read:** Assigned to the Users group.	**Read, Read & Execute, and List Folder Contents:** Permissions assigned to the Users group.
Home folder: A folder created for each user and intended for access only by that particular user.	**Full Control:** Assigned to each user on his or her home folder.	**Full Control:** Assigned to each user on his or her home folder.

Share a Printer in Windows XP

Sharing a printer on a local network is similar to sharing a folder. If the printer is already installed, access the **Printers and Faxes** folder through **Start | Control Panel | Printers and Other Hardware | Printers and Faxes** and right-click the printer. Select **Sharing**.

In the **Sharing** dialog box, select **Share this printer**. The first eight characters of the printer's name will automatically display in the **Share name** box. You may change this to a more descriptive name. You may also add additional drivers for users running different versions of Windows. This will enable the correct version of the printer driver to be automatically downloaded to a user's system when the user adds the shared printer. If you do not choose to add the additional drivers, users will be required to provide the drivers themselves, either from the installation CD or from the Windows cabinet files.

You can also set up user privileges on the network to determine who may reconfigure the network printer. To assign printer privileges, you must be logged on as the network administrator.

To connect a computer to a networked printer, access the **Printers and Faxes** folder through **Start | Control Panel | Printers and Other Hardware | Printers and Faxes**. You can then use the Add Printer Wizard to add a printer to the local computer or connect to a printer in the network, **Figure 19-32**.

The next screen in the wizard, **Figure 19-33**, displays two choices: **Local printer attached to this computer** and **A network printer, or a printer attached to another computer**. The first choice is for connecting a printer directly to the PC. When a printer connects directly to the PC it is referred to as the *local printer*. The second choice is for connecting the PC to a printer located on another PC using a network connection. Select the second choice: **A network printer, or a printer attached to another computer**. A dialog box will appear similar to the one in **Figure 19-34**.

Figure 19-33. To set up access to a network printer, select **A network printer, or a printer attached to another computer**.

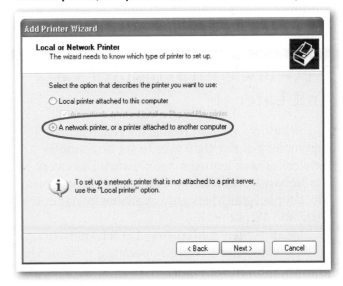

Figure 19-34. To specify a network printer, you may browse the network for it, enter its UNC path, or enter its URL path.

Figure 19-32. Add Printer Wizard welcome screen.

You now have three choices: **Browse for a printer**, **Connect to this printer**, and **Connect to a printer on the Internet or on a home or office network**. Pay particular attention to the way the printer path is displayed in the examples. The first example, under **Connect to this printer**, uses the **Universal Naming Convention (UNC)**. A UNC is a path format that identifies the server and its share and uses backslashes to separate the server name from the share name. The second example, under **Connect to a printer on the Internet or on a home or office network**, uses a URL to indicate the path. A URL uses forward slashes and must be used to indicate the path for a share on the Internet or on a network that uses Active Directory as the directory service.

Configuring the SOHO Network with Windows Vista and Later

Windows Vista introduced a few features that make it easier than ever to set up a small network. These features are Network Discovery, the Network and Sharing Center, and People Near Me. People Near Me is only available in Windows Vista and Windows 7.

Ideally when configuring a SOHO network, all PCs would use the latest operating system. This provides for the easiest installation. Unfortunately, this is not always the case. Many SOHO networks are constructed with various operating systems and equipment. Incorporating legacy computer systems with modern ones can be challenging but can be done if carefully thought out.

If setting up a SOHO network in a mixed operating system environment, use the PC with the latest or most up-to-date operating system as the host or as the computer that will share other resources, such as a printer. Typically, the latest operating system will have the technology available to support older operating systems. It will also have a wizard that assists in configuring the network.

Network and Sharing Center

The Network and Sharing Center displays in one centralized location all aspects concerning the local area network. This feature allows you to view the local area network, configure sharing options, and control the Network Discovery feature. The Network and Sharing Center is accessed through **Control Panel | Network and Internet**. You can also access the **Network and Sharing Center** by right-clicking the **Network Connection** icon in the taskbar.

View the Network Adapter Card Status

In Windows Vista, selecting the **View status** option in **Network and Sharing Center** reveals information about the network adapter, such as connection status, connection speed, number of bytes sent and received, and more. This feature in Windows Vista is very similar to the Windows XP **Local Area Connection Status** dialog box. Review **Figure 19-35** to see the Windows Vista **Local Area Connection Status** dialog box. To view the status of the network connection in Windows 7 and Windows 8, click the network **Connections** entry located in the **View your active networks** section.

Figure 19-35. The Windows Vista **Local Area Connection Status** dialog box reveals information about the computer's local area connection.

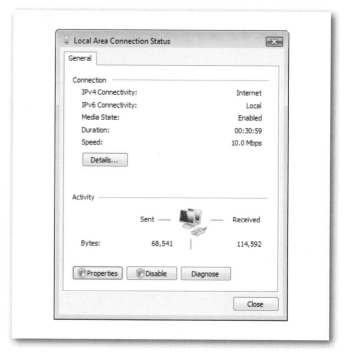

Figure 19-36. Clicking the **Details** button in the **Local Area Connection Status** dialog box opens the **Network Connection Details** dialog box.

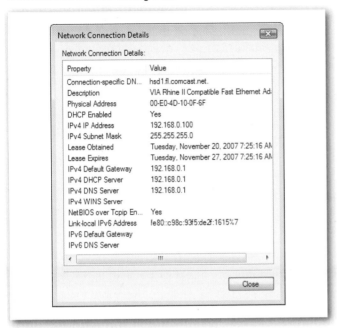

Figure 19-37. The Windows Vista **Local Area Connection Properties** dialog box.

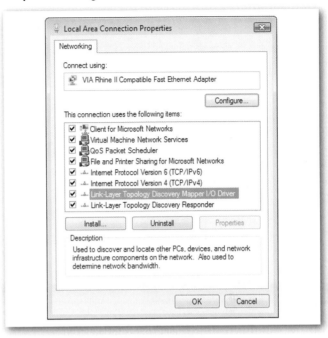

Selecting the **Details** button in the **Local Area Connection Status** dialog box reveals details about the connection. Look at **Figure 19-36** to see an example of the details of a typical network connection. This feature is similar in Windows XP.

Notice that the **Network Connection Details** dialog box displays all technical information about the network adapter, such as the IPv4 address, IPv6 address, physical or MAC address, and DNS suffix. You are already familiar with these details from the previous chapter.

Selecting the **Properties** button on the **Local Area Connection Status** dialog box reveals the familiar **Local Area Connections Properties** dialog box, which is similar to the one designed for Windows XP and earlier operating system. See **Figure 19-37** for an example of the Windows Vista **Local Area Connection Properties** dialog box. Notice the Link-Layer Topology Discovery Mapper I/O Driver and Link-Layer Topology Discovery Responder listed under the **This connection uses the following items** section.

Configure a New Network Connection

All three versions (Windows Vista, Windows 7, and Windows 8) of the Network and Sharing Center have an option for configuring a

new network connection. See **Figure 19-38A** and **Figure 19-38B**. After the option for creating a new network connection is selected, another dialog box appears, prompting you to select a particular type of network configuration choice. You can set up a new network or connect to an existing network, create a VPN, set up a dial-up connection, or create or manage a wireless access point or router. Look at **Figure 19-39** to see the choices for the three different Windows operating systems.

After selecting the type of network configuration you want, a series of dialog boxes will appear, prompting you to make configuration choices. After the first network configuration is complete, it becomes even easier to add additional computers to the local area network. The Windows discovery protocols and UPnP automatically detect network devices, such as routers, and configure the connection. Typically, the only question you will be prompted to answer is, "Do you wish to join an existing HomeGroup if one has already been created?"

Joining a network domain that is controlled by a server is more complicated. Joining a network controlled by a domain requires a user account created for the domain network as discussed in Chapter 17—Network Administration.

Figure 19-38A. Windows Network and Sharing Center is a centralized location that is used to start the network configuration wizard for creating various types of networks.

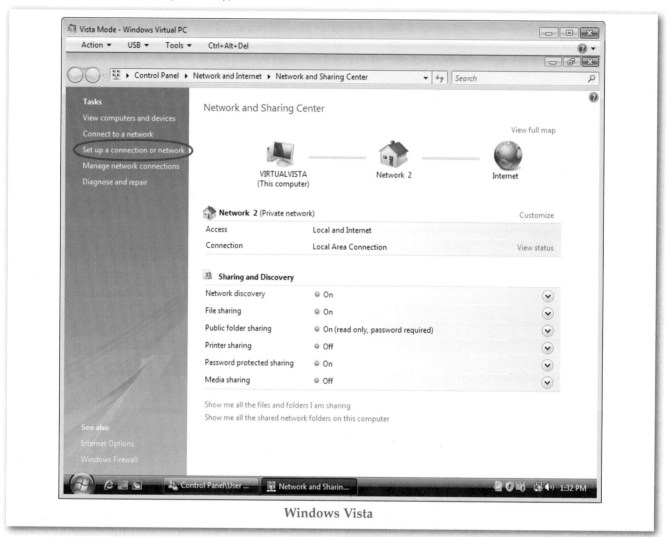

Windows Vista

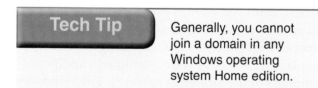

Generally, you cannot join a domain in any Windows operating system Home edition.

Share a Printer in Windows Vista and Later

Configuring a printer share in a Windows Vista and later SOHO environment is very similar to configuring a file or folder share. The exact method of configuring a printer share will be determined by the number of clients you wish to share the printer with and the amount of control you wish to have over the printer.

The two basic ways of installing a shared printer are attach a printer to a PC and then share access through the PC or connect the printer to the network as a stand-alone printer.

Sharing a printer that is connected to a PC has one major problem. The computer must be on for other clients to use the printer. This can also be an advantage if you wish to limit access to a special printer, for example, if a home has multiple users and you want to limit the access to the printer. A home with young children often finds the printer is completely out of paper or ink when you need to use it.

Figure 19-38B.

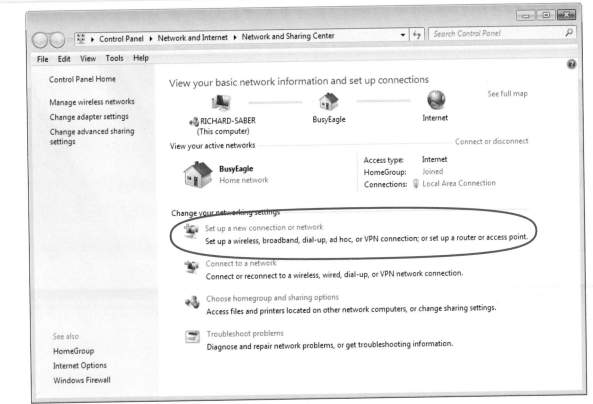

Windows 7

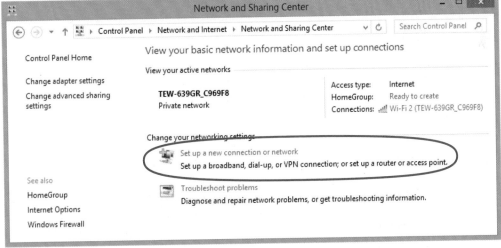

Windows 8

Figure 19-39. The **Setup a Connection or Network** dialog box is very similar in Windows Vista, Windows 7, and Windows 8.

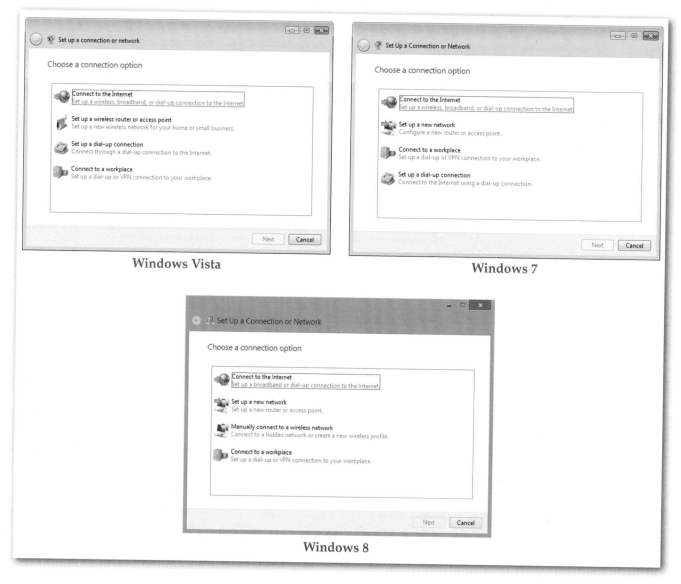

Windows Vista

Windows 7

Windows 8

A network printer provides access to all users on the network and does not require a single dedicated PC. The network printer can be configured for password access to prevent unauthorized access.

When a network is set up as a HomeGroup, printers and certain files are automatically shared to all members of the HomeGroup. This is one of the advantages of using the HomeGroup option when setting up the computer. You can also share the printer by right-clicking the printer, selecting **Printer properties**, the **Sharing** tab, and the **Share this printer** option.

In **Figure 19-40**, you can see what a typical set of printer share permissions look like. The printer share permissions are quite different than shared folder permissions. Printer permissions are designed to match the function of a network shared printer. Other network devices, such as a DVD, have share permissions similar to folder share permissions.

When configuring a network printer as a share, you must provide some information for the configuration. A default name will be listed, but it can be changed to a name that identifies the printer location. This is helpful if there are

Figure 19-40. Shared devices, such as printers, have a special set of share permissions that can be assigned to users.

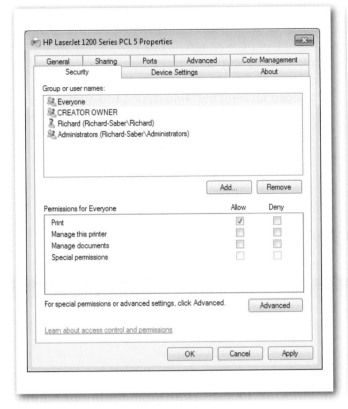

Figure 19-41. You have an option to provide drivers to computers running different operating systems.

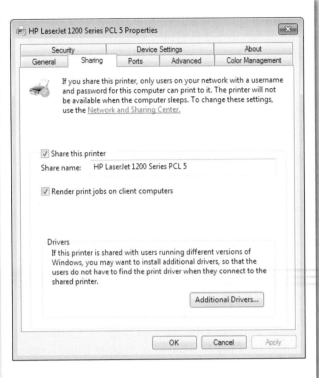

many people sharing access to the printer and the printer is located in another room. For example, you may want to identify the printer as "Art Department LaserJet1200." This name identifies the department where the printer is located and the type of printer it is. You could also include the room number or the building number for a large network system.

If you select the **Sharing** tab of the printer **Properties** dialog box, you will see the **Render print jobs on client computers** option, **Figure 19-41**. Selecting this option directs the processing print job to the client computer and not to the computer that the printer is connected directly to. The advantage to this is the computer/server which is connected directly to the printer will not be bogged down by print requests from other computers.

Offline printing is supported, which means that the client computer can send a print job to the printer computer/server even when not connected.

When the connection is reestablished, the print job will automatically be spooled to the printer and then print.

In Figure 19-41, notice the option to install additional drivers. When a printer is configured as a local printer and shared to the network, the print driver installed matches the local computer. If a computer accesses the shared printer and does not have the exact same driver as the local printer, then a driver error will likely occur. For example, if the local computer connected to the printer has a 64-bit Windows 7 operating system, the driver for the printer will be a 64-bit version. If the shared printer is accessed by a 32-bit version of Windows Vista, the printer job will fail because the Windows Vista operating system is 32-bit and the printer driver is 64-bit. Selecting the **Additional Drivers** option will install additional drivers, making the network printer compatible with other versions of operating systems.

Share Files and Folders in Windows Vista and Later

Sharing in Windows Vista and later has been made very simple for the local area network. Windows Vista introduced the Public Folders feature. It is similar to Windows XP Simple File Sharing and is used in Windows 7 and Windows 8 as well. The HomeGroup and Libraries features are also used in Windows 7 and 8. For detailed information on Public Folders, HomeGroup, and Libraries, see Chapter 17—Network Administration.

Again, the Network and Sharing Center provides an easy way to manage shared folders, files, and printers. For Windows Vista, you simply open the **Network and Sharing Center** and then select the corresponding feature you wish to enable or disable. Look again at Figure 19-38 and examine the Windows Vista **Sharing and Discovery** section. The following is a description of each sharing option available through the Windows Vista Network and Sharing Center.

- **File sharing**: Enable and disable file sharing.
- **Public folder sharing**: Automatically configure the Public folder for sharing on the network or disable it.
- **Printer sharing**: Enable and disable printer sharing.
- **Password protected sharing**: When password protection is enabled, a user must have a local user account on the local computer and a password to access the Public folder, files, and printer attached to the local computer. When password protected sharing is disabled, all people have access to the shared file, Public folder, and printer.
- **Media sharing**: Provide devices and people access to shared music, pictures, and videos on the local computer. It also allows the computer to locate the same types of resources from other locations on the local area network.

At the bottom of the Windows Vista **Network and Sharing Center**, there are two options: **Show me all the files and folders I am sharing** and **Show me all the shared network folders on this computer**. These options are very handy when you need to identify which resources are shared. It might seem strange, but all too often it is difficult to determine which resources are shared and which are not.

In Windows 7 and Windows 8, file and printer sharing can be managed by selecting the **Change advanced sharing settings** option in the Network and Sharing Center. See Figure 19-38. The **Advanced sharing settings** dialog box will appear, providing options to turn printer and file sharing on and off and to either allow Windows to handle HomeGroup connections or use user accounts and passwords to connect to other computers. **Figure 19-42** shows the Windows 8 **Advanced sharing settings** dialog box.

> **Tech Tip**
>
> All users need a network location to share information with each other, and all users need a network location that is private for their own personal storage that is accessible only by that particular user.

Enable Shared Folder Caching

The caching feature for shared folders makes it possible to access shared contents when the share is not available or the shared device location is offline. The caching feature is also referred to as *offline sharing* and is not enabled by default.

The share caching feature can be very helpful when using a portable device such as a laptop computer or tablet, which is frequently disconnected from the network system. You can work with cached files in a similar manner as when you are connected through the network. When you reconnect to the network, the file is synchronized so that any changes you make are updated to the network file. Synchronization allows you to save your version of the file to the network, keep the other version, or save both.

Share caching is easy to configure. See **Figure 19-43**. You simply open the shared folder's **Properties** dialog box and then click the **Advanced Sharing** button. The **Advanced Sharing** dialog box appears, which allows you to select the **Caching** button. The **Offline Settings** dialog box appears with options to choose which files will be available for offline caching.

Figure 19-42. The Windows 8 Network and Sharing Center **Advanced sharing settings** dialog box allows you to enable and disable file and printer sharing. The Windows 7 dialog box is similar, but has a few more features.

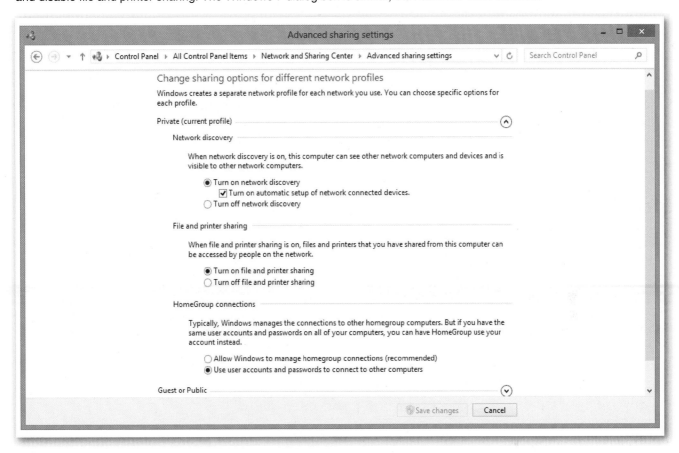

Enable Disk Quotas

Disk quotas are an important configuration option for shared storage disk space. Users tend to use much more space on shared media and often save anything whether it is important or not. It does not take long to use up an entire disk when multiple users are storing information, pictures, videos, music, and more. To prevent one or more users from using too much disk storage space, each user can be assigned a maximum amount of storage space, which is referred to as a *disk quota*. Look at **Figure 19-44**. The default setting is **Do not limit disk usage**. When enabled, disk space can be limited and a warning can be issued to the user when he or she is close to exceeding the allocated disk space.

Enable People Near Me

People Near Me is a feature introduced in Windows Vista and carried on into Windows 7, but not Windows 8. When enabled, the People Near Me feature dynamically discovers when other users are on the local area network. You can send an invitation to join a user in Windows Meeting Space to have a collaboration activity. Look at **Figure 19-45** to see the **People Near Me** dialog box. Notice that under the **User Information** section, you enter your name as you want it to appear. You can also make a picture of yourself available. In the **Options** section, you can allow Windows to automatically sign you in when Windows starts.

Figure 19-43. The caching feature for shared folders makes it possible to access share content when the network share is not available.

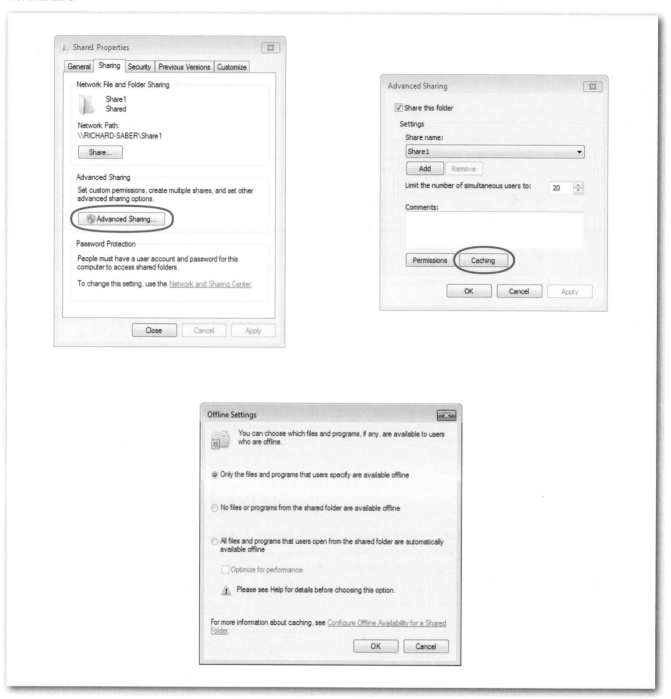

Figure 19-44. Disk quotas allow you to limit the amount of disk storage space a network user can utilize.

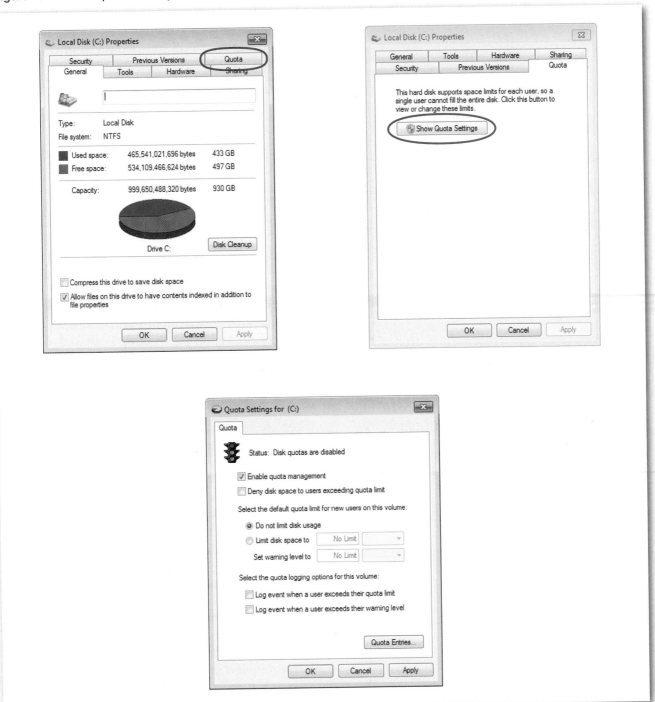

Figure 19-45. The People Near Me feature allows you to make yourself available for a meeting or other collaborative activity over the network.

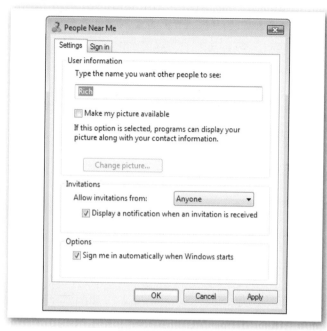

On the **Sign in** page, **Figure 19-46,** you can sign in or out of People Near Me. Notice that the privacy information states that your name, the computer name, and IP address are made visible by default to all people in the local area network.

Figure 19-46. The **Sign in** page of the **People Near Me** dialog box allows you to sign in and out of People Near Me.

After the People Near Me feature is enabled, a utility such as Windows Meeting Space can be used to hold a social or business collaboration meeting. **Figure 19-47** shows the Windows Meeting Space utility. With this utility, you can see the features available for the meeting. You can include handouts, which are actual files on your computer. This feature allows you to create a temporary share on your computer limited to the people in your meeting. You do not need to set up permissions or shares in the traditional way. This is a very user-friendly sharing method.

You control who can be part of the meeting by sending out an invitation. People in the local area network are automatically listed. Placing a check mark in the box beside their name will automatically put them in the list of invitations. Requiring a password to join the meeting is optional.

You can also share your entire desktop in the meeting. When the desktop is shared, the desktop background will appear black on the host computer. This will make it obvious to you that your desktop is being shared. Look at **Figure 19-48** to see an example of how the desktop appears when shared for a meeting.

You can end the meeting at any time or stop the sharing at any time during the meeting. People Near Me and Windows Meeting Space are standard in all versions of Windows Vista except Windows Vista Home Basic. Windows Meeting Space is not available in Windows 7. People Near Me is available in Window 7 Home Premium or better.

As you can see, everything concerning networking in Windows Vista and later is centralized and redesigned for an average user with limited technical skills. Windows Vista makes networking and collaboration much easier than previous operating systems.

Troubleshooting the SOHO Network

Once you have installed and configured your SOHO network, you may find that you cannot access certain resources or that access is slow. This section covers the most common problems that can occur with a new SOHO network installation.

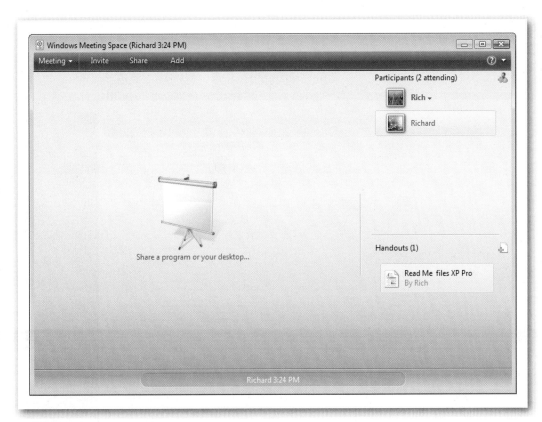

Figure 19-47.
The Windows Meeting Space utility allows you to conduct meetings over the network.

These problems involve firewall installation, VPN and firewall conflicts, improper ICS host configuration, and hardware and software incompatibilities.

Internet Access Is Sluggish

The shared Internet connection can be extremely slow or sluggish if someone on the network is downloading pictures or sound files. Files containing graphics or sound clips are excessively large when compared to text files. Since the bandwidth of the local network is shared by everyone connected to the network, large file transfers can reduce the network response time for everyone connected. This problem can be eliminated by blocking the ports associated with the large file transfers. For example, the music download site Napster uses TCP port 6699. If excessive use of Napster is reducing network performance, simply filter out port 6699.

Cannot Access Resources on the Network

Installing the Internet Connection Firewall (ICF) on a Windows XP computer that is not the Internet Connection Sharing (ICS) host can cause communications problems by blocking transmissions. Users will not be able to share a file with other Windows XP PCs on the network or access the shared Internet connection on the ICS host. To solve this problem, only configure ICF on the ICS host. Windows Vista and later do not have this problem.

A firewall and VPN on the same SOHO network can also cause access problems. Microsoft does not recommend a firewall and VPN on the same SOHO network. Use one at a time, not both at the same time. An ISP typically assigns only one IP address to a user location. If a computer is configured as a VPN, all other computers in

Figure 19-48. During a meeting, a black desktop indicates the desktop is shared.

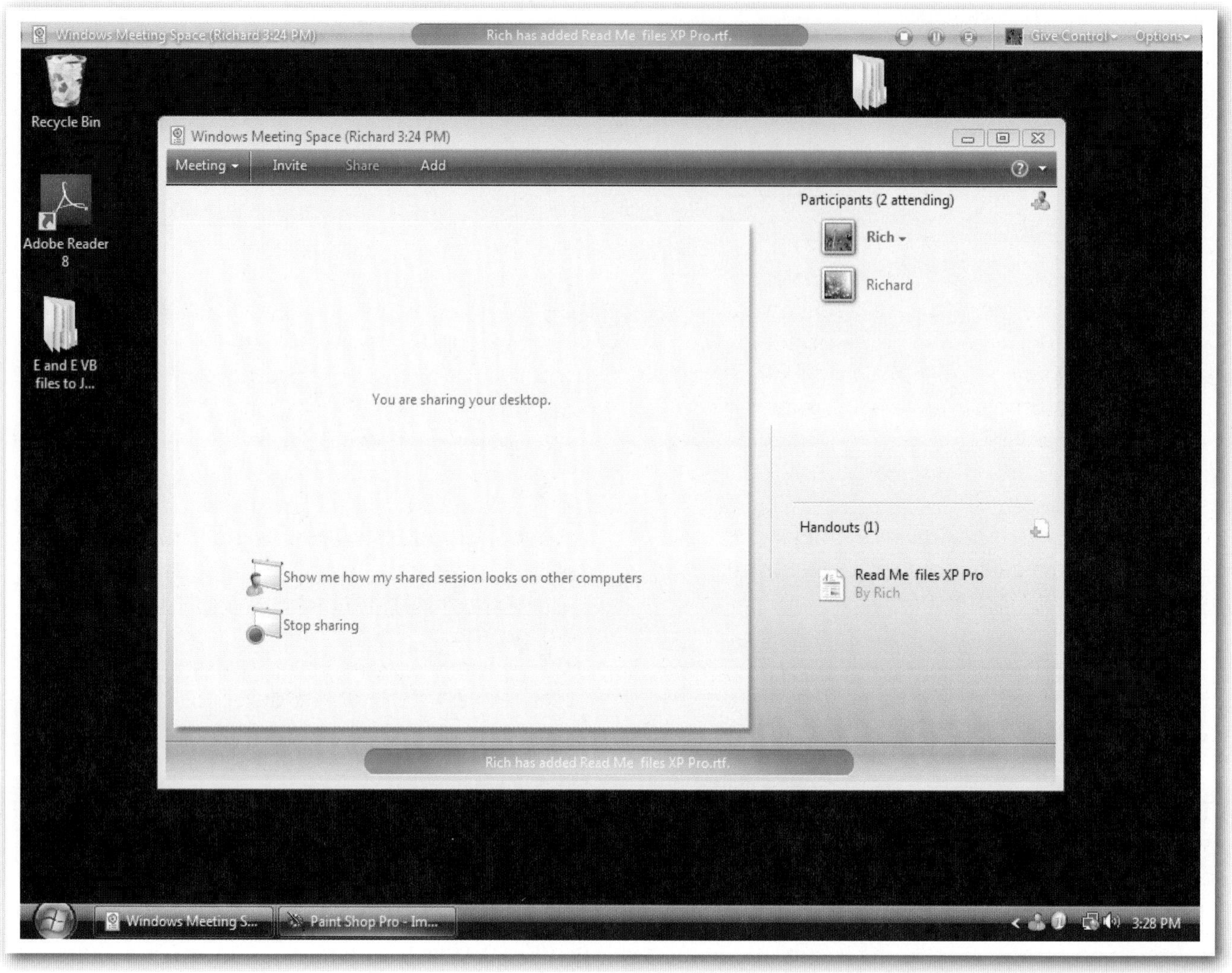

the network will be blocked from accessing the Internet. If the Internet connection is already made to the ISP, the VPN computer will not be able to access the Internet and complete its connection to the VPN destination.

Some routers will perform multiple duties and support several functions or services simultaneously. For example, a router can provide shared Internet access and support a VPN connection at the same time. This is another example of the superiority of a router used in a small network system. Otherwise, you will need to separate the computer using the VPN from the rest of the network.

Setting up a PC with a different protocol than the other PCs on the network will prevent that

PC from accessing resources on the network. This can often happen when the network is set up with a mixture of old and new computers. The older computers may be configured by default with the NetBEUI protocol while the newer computers are configured with TCP/IP by default. There may also be a conflict in the names of computers in a network of mixed operating systems. NetBIOS only allows 15 characters in the name. Modern computer systems assign additional names to computers that conform to the NetBIOS 15-character rule. This allows the modern system to be backward compatible with legacy systems. The first thing to check on a new network is the correct spelling of the workgroup, computer, and share name.

Cannot Access the Internet Through the ICS Host

You should not use any form of server software on any of the local workgroup workstations. For example, a small network system is growing in size and eventually needs to switch to a client/server model. A combination file server and web server is installed in the existing network. The installation of the server and web server by an inexperienced technician can cause severe network communication problems. A server is typically configured as a DHCP server or DNS server, which will interfere with ICS host on the network. Remember, the ICS wizard automatically configures IP addresses. If the server is configured for DHCP or DNS, it will also attempt to issue IP addresses, which will cause intermittent access problems or even complete failure of the ICS feature.

Incompatible Hardware or Software

Incompatibility can be a real problem. Check the hardware compatibility list before setting up a SOHO network. If a device that is not on the Hardware Compatibility List (HCL) is installed and is incompatible, any unexpected occurrence might happen. The device may try to constantly broadcast, or simply communicate in only one direction. It might respond to text-based commands such as **ping** and **tracert** but not communicate at a higher level. If a network is composed of mixed computers (computers with various types of hardware and operating systems), some of the computers may support communication with the legacy device and some will not. Anything might happen when using devices that have not been thoroughly tested.

Tech Tip
Not all devices not listed on the HCL will cause problems. Many function perfectly.

Network Path Not Found Message

Receiving the error message "Network path not found" is common. It can be caused by one of several typical reasons:
- The network path was typed incorrectly.
- The network connection does not exist.
- The network location does not exist.
- You do not have permission to access the network location.

When making a new network connection, it is common to incorrectly type the network location or leave out the proper punctuation. You can ping the network location to verify that you have correctly typed the network path and that all network media (cable and wireless) and devices are working properly. Verifying the network location with the **ping** command will rule out the first three reasons listed.

Another common reason for generating the "network path not found" error message is the user does not have permission to access the network location share or device. Network share or location permission can be easily verified through the network administrator.

Tech Tip
Port numbers 137, 138, 139, and 445 must be open in the firewall to access a shared folder.

Regular Backups

The best method of prevention of shared data loss is regular backups. Antimalware may or may not prevent data loss. Equipment failures do happen. Damage to stored data can result from disasters, such as a fire, a flood, or even a disgruntled employee. The only way to protect against data loss is through regular routine backups. The very best protection from natural disasters is a backup location far away from the network site. This is one of the advantages of cloud service backup locations.

Remote Desktop

Remote Desktop is a very handy feature which allows a user to access and take control of one computer from another. The computer you are connecting from is referred to as the *client* and the computer you are remotely connecting to is referred to as the *host*. For example, you could access your work computer (host) from your home computer (client) and then perform tasks just as though you were sitting at your work computer. You would have access to all of your programs, files, and network resources at work from your home computer.

> **Tech Tip**
>
> The Remote Desktop feature is an example of a VPN application. To use the Remote Desktop feature, TCP port 3389 must be open in the firewall.

Figure 19-49 shows the display of a Remote Desktop connection. The user has opened the Documents folder located on the remote computer. The user can then open a particular document and make changes to it or do anything as if he or she were sitting at the remote computer location.

Accessing a remote computer using the Remote Desktop Connection program is easy. You simply enter the name of the remote computer and the name of the user account configured on the remote computer, **Figure 19-50**. During the establishment of the connection, you are prompted for the user account password.

The computer name is your choice, such as "Windows8Office," for a connection on the local network. For a connection using the Internet, you must supply a **fully qualified domain name (FQDN)**. The FQDN is a combination of both the computer name and the domain name. A fully qualified domain name includes the host (computer) name, the domain name, and all the higher-level domains. For example, the fully qualified domain name of a computer named "Windows8Office" located at www.RMRoberts.com would be www.Windows8Office.RMRoberts.com or Windows8Office.RMRoberts.com. The "www"

Figure 19-49. Remote Desktop allows you to access your computer remotely.

Figure 19-50. To establish a Remote Desktop connection, you must enter the computer name and the user name. You will be prompted for the account password when connecting to the remote computer.

Figure 19-51. After the first time a Remote Desktop connection is established, the logon dialog box will be presented with the user account name and computer name already completed.

is optional. You can also use the remote computer IP address in place of the computer name.

Tech Tip

Be aware that TCP port 3389 must be open to allow a Remote Desktop connection.

After the first time a Remote Desktop connection is established, the logon dialog box will be much simpler. **Figure 19-51** shows a Remote Desktop logon dialog box after a previous connection has been established. Only the user password needs to be entered.

Remote Desktop should not be confused with Remote Assistance. Remote Assistance provides access to a computer by sending an invitation to another person to help with a computer problem. For example, a user can send a request for remote assistance to another user by sending the user an email with a Remote Assistance attachment. The person receiving the email with the Remote Assistance request attachment can access the sending person's computer. The difference is that for Remote Assistance, the user must be present at the computer being accessed, but for Remote Desktop the user is not present at the computer being accessed. Another difference is that when using Remote Assistance, the person requesting assistance can limit access to the computer and also disconnect the Remote Assistance connection at any time.

As you can see, this chapter provides not only new material, but also refreshes your learning of material already covered. The new material and the previously-learned material directly apply to SOHO design and support. All you need now is experience.

Chapter Summary

- Some of the factors to consider when designing a SOHO network are the type of media that will be used to connect the PCS together, the manner in which the networked PCs will access the Internet, and the level of administration that will be used to secure resources and data.

- Typical media used in a SOHO network are copper cable, wireless, existing phone lines, and existing power lines.

- Four common methods of hosting file sharing services for SOHO are NAS, dedicated computer, domain network, and cloud service.

- Common choices of Internet access devices in a SOHO network are the telephone modem, DSL modem, cable modem, and wireless hotspots.

- The best scenario for SOHO administration is having a single administrator with limited authority delegated to other users and setting up local and share-level security.

- Some ways to secure a wireless router are changing the default SSID, login name and password; disabling the SSID broadcast; configure encryption; and enabling MAC filtering.

- In Windows XP, the Network Setup Wizard helps you to share an Internet connection, enable the Internet Connection Firewall (ICF), and enable file and printer sharing.

- Windows Vista and later includes the Network and Sharing Center, which displays in one centralized location all aspects concerning the local area network.

- Common problems that can occur in a new SOHO network installation are the Internet access is sluggish, networked resources cannot be accessed, Internet cannot be accessed, incompatible software and hardware, and receiving the "Network path not found" message.

- The best way to protect against data loss is through regular routine backups.

- Using Windows Remote Desktop, you can access your work computer (host) from your home computer (client) and then perform tasks just as though you were sitting at your work computer.

Review Questions

Answer the following questions on a separate sheet of paper. Please do not write in this book.

1. Explain some of the limitations associated with each of the SOHO network media.

2. Explain why the use of telephone lines as a means of networking an office might not work.

3. What is the name of a network device that connects two different types of network media?

4. What are four common methods of hosting file sharing services for a SOHO network?

5. What is the big disadvantage of a SOHO network created as a domain network rather than as a HomeGroup or peer-to-peer network?

6. What Internet access devices are commonly used for a SOHO network installation?

7. What does the acronym NAT represent?

8. How can local security be implemented in a peer-to-peer network?

9. How does share-level security protect resources accessed from across the network?

10. Describe two instances of when a VPN should be created.

11. What are the two main security connection protocols associated with a VPN connection?

12. What are some ways to secure a wireless router?

13. How does MAC filtering work?

14. What is a DMZ?

15. What is the difference between port forwarding and single port forwarding?

16. How would you secure an office computer to prevent users from installing new software? (Select the best answer.)
    a. Open the BIOS/UEFI Setup utility and select the disable software installation option.
    b. Run **secpol.msc** and select the option to prevent a user from installing software.
    c. Open **Control Panel** and then select **User Accounts**. Change all computer users to guest accounts.
    d. Open **Control Panel** and then select the security option **Lock Down PC**.

17. Windows XP includes the _____ to assist in the configuration of a SOHO network.

18. What are the two different types of permissions that can be set for a folder?

19. What is the main difference between share permissions and NTFS permissions?

20. A user has been assigned two different permissions to a particular folder: an NTFS permission set to full control and a share permission set to read. Which permission will take affect for the user?

21. Permissions can be applied to a printer. True or False

22. What is the path to the Network and Sharing Center?

23. What might cause a network to perform sluggishly?

24. List four common reasons the error message "network path not found" might be generated when trying to access a shared resource.

25. What is the best method of prevention of shared data loss?

26. What Windows feature would you use to create a connection between your home and work PC and to access any of your work files?

Sample A+ Exam Questions

Answer the following questions on a separate sheet of paper. Please do not write in this book.

1. Which technology would provide the best protection against unauthorized access from the Internet?
   a. Standard V92 modem
   b. Firewall
   c. A good Internet access password for modem access
   d. Antivirus program

2. Phil has been mistakenly assigned to two different user groups: Teacher and Student. The Teacher group has full control over the folder named Grades. The Student group has only read permissions. How will this affect Phil when he tries to access the Grades folder?
   a. Phil will not be able to access the Grades folder.
   b. Phil will be able to read the contents of the Grades folder.
   c. Phil will have full control over the Grades folder.
   d. Phil's user account will be automatically locked out until the share permission conflict is resolved.

3. What is the typical IPv4 address assigned to an ICS host?
   a. 123.145.000.001
   b. 192.168.000.1
   c. 127.000.000.1
   d. 255.255.255.255

4. A small SOHO network has been set up in a local insurance company, which consists of four Windows 7 Professional workstations. Jim has successfully created a local user account on Workstation_1 for his own use. All workstations belong to the same workgroup. Jim is unsuccessful at logging on to the other workstations. What is *most likely* the problem?
   a. Jim does not have a local user account set up on Workstation_2 through Workstation_4.
   b. The network cabling has been disconnected from Workstation_2 through Workstation_4.
   c. Share-level security must be configured on Workstation_2 through Workstation_4.
   d. A user on a peer-to-peer network may not log on to more than one PC at a time.

A+

5. Carlos is working late at the office. The office consists of eight computers configured as a peer-to-peer network. The office manager's computer is an ICS host and has a telephone modem installed to access the ISP. The system was installed two months ago and has worked well. Everyone has shut down their computer and has gone home except for Carlos. Carlos attempts to access his email before leaving but finds he cannot access the Internet. What is *most likely* the problem?
   a. The IP address supplied to the ICS host by the ISP has changed.
   b. The connection cannot be established because the ICS host has been shut down.
   c. The Internet Connection Firewall is configured to prevent Carlos from accessing Internet port 110.
   d. The ISP does not provide telephone support after 6 p.m.

6. Which technology allows existing power lines to be used as network media?
   a. VPN
   b. PLC
   c. ICS
   d. HomePNA

7. A(n) _____ ensures that data sent across the Internet is not intercepted, read, or tampered with.
   a. PLC
   b. firewall
   c. ICS
   d. VPN

8. A router that is used to combine different media and to provide an Internet connection is often referred to as a(n) _____ router.
   a. bridge
   b. access
   c. Internet
   d. gateway

9. Which wireless router feature will prevent unauthorized access to the router?
   a. Disabling the SSID broadcast
   b. Configuring the router for 802.11n frequency
   c. MAC filtering
   d. Port forwarding

10. Which option is used to secure a workstation by preventing clients from accessing specific Windows features?
   a. BitLocker
   b. Local Group Policy Editor
   c. Firewall
   d. Port filtering

Suggested Laboratory Activities

Do not attempt any suggested laboratory activities without your instructor's permission. Certain activities can render the PC operating system inoperable.

1. Set up a SOHO network with a shared Internet connection.
2. Configure a printer share on the SOHO network you set up in Activity 1.
3. Open Windows Firewall and view the various configuration settings.
4. Configure a VPN across a peer-to-peer network. Use a packet sniffer to see if it can view the contents of the data packets flowing through the VPN.
5. Design a SOHO network for a home that consists of three bedrooms, an office, and a game room. Each bedroom will have one PC, and the office and game room will each have a printer. There will be one Internet access point located in the office area. The access point is a DSL line. Make a drawing of the layout. Make a list of materials and costs based on current prices.

Customer Support, Communication, and Professionalism

20

After studying this chapter, you will be able to:

- Explain common customer support organization models.
- Use proper communication skills in the workplace.
- Identify the traits that exhibit a professional image.
- Identify the key steps related to handling a prohibitive content or prohibitive activity incident.

A+ Exam—Key Points

The CompTIA A+ exam contains questions related to proper communication and professionalism. You will most likely encounter questions related to customer relations, such as communicating clearly with the customer, listening to the customer, and conveying to the customer a positive attitude.

Key Terms

The following key terms will become important pieces of your computer vocabulary. Be sure you can define them.

call center
chain of custody
customer support
depot technician
emoticons

help desk
live support
professionalism
teamwork

This chapter covers the basic skills necessary to function in a customer- or client-related environment. Not all computer jobs require you to meet and work with customers and clients. However, most jobs do require working with customers and clients on a regular basis. You probably assume you already know how to deal with people. There are some specific skills required to keep customers and clients happy that you may not be aware of.

In this chapter, you will be introduced to specific support scenarios. You will learn about the forms of conduct that have been accepted as an industry standard. You may be the most skilled technician in the company, but if you do not deal with people in a professional and courteous manner, you will most likely lose your job or be banned from dealing with customers and clients. You will also never be raised to a position of leadership or management, and all other career options may become limited. The importance of learning the skills in this chapter cannot be emphasized enough. Reading, understanding, and being able to put into practice the skills covered in this chapter may determine your future in a computer-related career.

Customer Support

Simply put, **customer support** is the delivery of customer assistance, customer training, and customer services. This section provides an overview of customer support. In it, you are given the big picture of how the organization models work together to resolve customer and client computer problems. You will learn how different levels of support can be distributed across these models and will be made aware of the level of customer interaction typical of each model.

Customer Support Organization Models

There are several customer support organization models that are recognized as standard. Some of these models are help desk, call center, small business, service counter, depot technician, and corporate enterprise support. The exact model of your company and how you fit within that model depends on three main factors:

- The number of people requiring support.
- The product being supported.
- The customer location (local or global).

Some organizations are a combination of several models working together as a team. For example, a help desk service may be outsourced to a foreign country such as India. This help desk may work closely with an organization in the United States that performs the actual physical work. In the following sections, several of the most common support organization models are presented.

Help Desk

A **help desk** is a central point of contact that provides technical support to clients. The clients may be company employees or customers. The usual method of contact is by telephone or e-mail. Examples of organizations that typically provide help desk support are Internet service providers (ISPs), hardware and software manufacturers, corporate businesses, and educational and government institutions.

The help desk is the first level of support used to resolve common computer hardware and software problems. In most instances, a service request and repair ticket is generated from the first moment of contact with a client.

The help desk can be a dedicated, single location or part of a larger organization, such as a call center, **Figure 20-1**. For example, a large company such as Dell could outsource its first level of support to a call center. If the call center cannot immediately resolve the problem, the support request is forwarded to the next level of support, which may be a technician located at Dell. The technician is trained to handle more difficult problems requiring intervention by a person with much more expertise.

Call Center

A **call center** is typically a large collection of support people located in a common facility equipped with telephones and computer network support. Many call centers provide support for more than one company or product. The center may be located anywhere in the world.

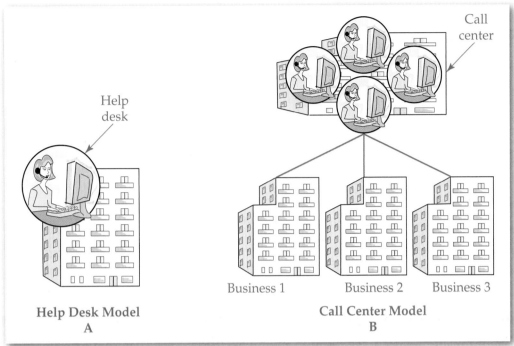

Figure 20-1.
Help desk model and call center model. A—In the help desk model, the help desk is part of the company. B—In the call center model, the help desk is a part of a call center. The call center provides support to many different businesses.

Call center employees do not necessarily have technical skills required for repairing computer-related problems. They are more likely trained to read prepared scripts correlated to the most common general problems. If they cannot adequately fix the problem, the support request is forwarded to the next level of repair technician. This repair technician is usually located at the company who manufactures the equipment or writes the software.

Small Business Service Counter

Small businesses are the backbone of the American economy. Over half of all American employment opportunities are in small businesses. You will very likely start your career in a small business environment. You may even start your own small business. In the small business environment, you will meet face-to-face with customers on a regular basis. Good customer relation skills are a key factor to your success.

The customer may be at the counter to make a purchase, request assistance in a purchase, or solicit technical support for an item purchased at the vendor location. In the small business environment, a service technician will most likely fulfill multiple roles for the employer. He or she may be responsible for selling computer hardware and software and related materials. The service technician may also be responsible for technical support and for answering customer questions in person, by telephone, or through e-mail. He or she may be dispatched to a customer location to install or troubleshoot computer equipment or provide training.

Depot Technician

A **depot technician** is one who performs repair work usually covered by warranty. The depot technician receives the hardware item after the client has contacted customer support through a call center or help desk or if the problem is not immediately resolved by the first contact. Once the equipment arrives at the depot, it is assigned to a technician for inspection and for repair or replacement. A depot technician has very limited customer contact or no customer contact at all.

Corporate Enterprise Support

In the large corporate environment, technical support services can be composed of many people working as a team. Typically, an employee contacts a help desk. The help desk technician generates a repair or incident ticket, **Figure 20-2**. If the help desk technician fails to assist the fellow employee

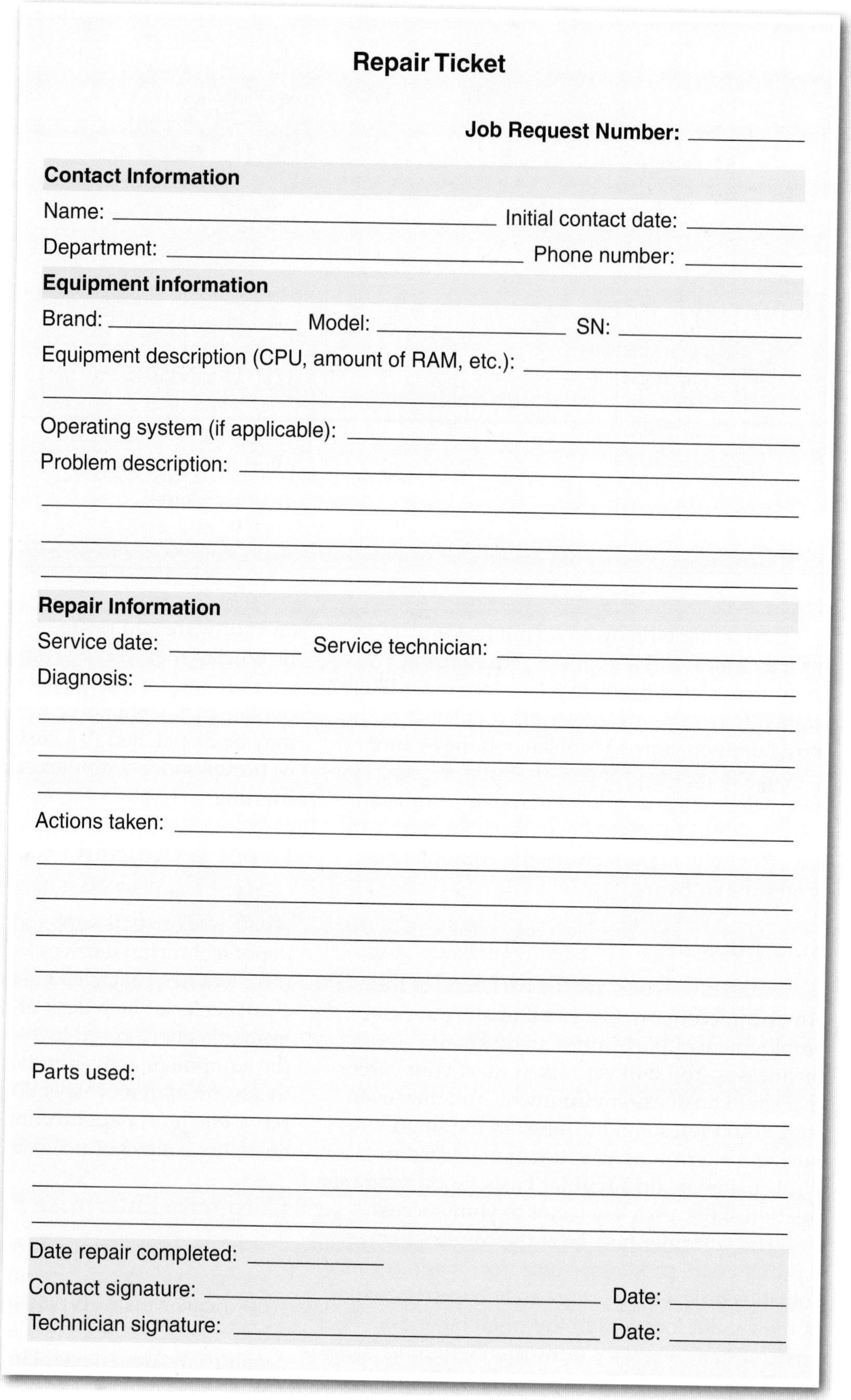

Repair Ticket

Job Request Number: ________

Contact Information

Name: ________ Initial contact date: ________

Department: ________ Phone number: ________

Equipment information

Brand: ________ Model: ________ SN: ________

Equipment description (CPU, amount of RAM, etc.): ________

Operating system (if applicable): ________

Problem description: ________

Repair Information

Service date: ________ Service technician: ________

Diagnosis: ________

Actions taken: ________

Parts used:

Date repair completed: ________

Contact signature: ________ Date: ________

Technician signature: ________ Date: ________

Goodheart-Willcox Publisher

Figure 20-2.
This shows an example of a repair ticket for the corporate environment.

to make the necessary adjustments to the item, the ticket is then assigned to a technician who will report to the employee's location.

At the location, the technician will either repair or replace the piece of equipment in question. This organizational model is found where there are sufficient numbers of computers and related equipment to justify the cost of a full-time staff dedicated to this function.

Support Software

There are many different software packages designed to keep track of service requests and

the final results. This is typically how service is organized and tracked. For example, when a customer or client first contacts the help desk with a service request, the call is logged, **Figure 20-3**. This includes adding the date and time and a description of the problem. The software will typically generate a repair ticket.

The help desk technician may resolve the problem immediately or may dispatch a technician to the client's location. The copy of the repair ticket is distributed to the technician who will report to the physical location of the problem.

On resolving the problem, the technician completes the ticket by adding the procedure used

Figure 20-3. HelpSTAR ServicePRO provides a complete system for reporting and tracking service requests.

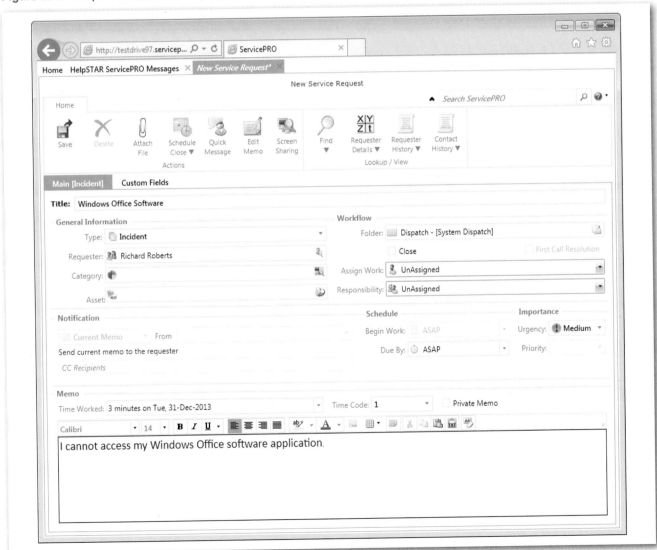

to resolve the problem. Any hardware or software that needs to be provided or has been provided to remedy the problem is also listed. A follow-up of the incident can be reviewed at the end of the day to ensure all problems have been resolved and that no incident has been left unresolved.

Levels of Support

There are typically three levels of support within an organization, **Figure 20-4**. Level-one support is the initial technical support contact. This is typically made with technical support from a help desk, website, or call center. Most problems can be corrected at this level.

Level-two support is when the problem is elevated to a person with more experience or expertise than the first person contacted. While level-one support handles most problems, the person at level one typically answers technical support questions from cue cards or a software program that has answers available for the most common customer problems and questions. Level-two support is provided for problems that are much less commonly encountered or more unique in nature. For example, a new software application that has just been released to the public may be conflicting with another software application. The problem is so new that there is no or very limited information. The level-two support technician works closely with the customer to solve the problem. The technician may need to recreate the problem before being able to find a procedure for correcting the problem.

Level-three support is typically provided outside the immediate technical support location. For example, a third-party company, such as

Microsoft and IBM, provides level-three support when a problem cannot be solved locally by level-one or level-two support. This is often a combined effort to solve a customer problem and is coordinated by the original support team member who is a level-two member at the home company. Level-three support may involve software programmers and engineers. Consumers are generally never involved with level-three support personnel.

Most level-one technical support is free, at least for a limited time. The highest level of support is typically not free and is set up on a cost-per-incident basis or through a service contract. It may also be based on a specific number of incidents or minutes of live support. **Live support** allows a customer or client to talk directly to support personnel for technical assistance, rather than use an FAQ list or web page.

Outsourcing

Customer support is often outsourced to a company that specializes in technical support. The outsource company may reside in the United States or be located overseas. The main reason for outsourcing is cost of the support service, of which the major cost is employee wages. It is often less expensive for a company to use a call center located in a foreign country because the wages may be far less than if the same service was provided locally.

A software or hardware company may find it more cost-effective to outsource level-one support and opt to provide level-two support on a local basis. All common or routine problems encountered by customers or clients can be answered by the outsource service. Problems requiring a level-two technician are reserved for the company at the local location or authorized service centers scattered across the United States and around the world.

For example, the ABC Laptop manufacturer has all client and customer support requests directed to an 800 number or to e-mail support. The first level of support is provided by the outsource company XYZ Corporation located in Bombay, India but authorized to represent the ABC Laptop manufacturer company in the United States. The XYZ Corporation handles all routine

Figure 20-4. The levels of support through which a problem can flow.

Support Level	Description
Level one	Help desk, website, or call center.
Level two	Supervisor over the level-one response team.
Level three	Supervisor (level two) working with third-party support from a larger company.

Goodheart-Willcox Publisher

calls and provides help to customers. They cover the basic problems and talk customers through the process of verifying the following:

- Power LEDs are lit.
- All cables are connected.
- Memory has been reset.

They may also talk the customer through the procedures for using the support CD to reinstall the operating system and through other basic tasks. If the problem cannot be resolved, the outsource support company forwards the problem to the ABC Laptop manufacturer. This is when more sophisticated troubleshooting diagnostics are required or the actual physical replacement of hardware items. The customer is provided an address to send the laptop to or a pickup ticket for FedEx, UPS, or similar service. The laptop is then sent to the ABC Laptop manufacturer for diagnostics and repair.

Frequently Asked Questions (FAQs)

Most businesses have a Frequently Asked Questions (FAQs) section posted on their website. The FAQ section is designed as the name implies, to answer the most commonly asked customer questions and inquiries. This is a valuable tool that can help save many hours of customer support. It is especially valuable if the company or business does not have a technical staff available 24/7. Large companies typically have a very extensive FAQ section on their website. One such company is HP. See **Figure 20-5**.

Microsoft also provides information for many common customer questions. Look at the Microsoft Support page in **Figure 20-6**. All Microsoft products are listed as well as common questions and tasks organized by category. You simply select the category of product and then select from a list of common topics. This site is designed for general users with minimal technical expertise. Microsoft provides both written and video demonstrations for many of the most common Microsoft customer questions.

You can also find the information to most common technical support questions by simply conducting an Internet search using terms such as "Microsoft Tech Support" followed by the product or issue such as "wireless networks." You then look for the browser search results with a link

directed to a Microsoft Support or TechNet site. **Figure 20-7** shows one such search result related to viewing and connecting to a wireless network.

Companies save thousands of dollars in manpower by posting answers to the most commonly asked customer questions. They also satisfy customer needs all around the globe by providing customer support 24/7. It is interesting to note that many companies provide the very same information that could be found on the Microsoft Support website. However, some companies have personalized the information for their customers.

Communication Skills

Communication skills are an area of customer support in which computer technicians will most likely have the greatest room for improvement. Communication with a customer is not limited to just the actual conversation. It includes other aspects, such as body language and attitude. Although both of these communication skills are unspoken, they present a clear message to customers about your level of willingness and concern for fixing their problems. This section discusses various aspects of communication—specifically verbal communication, body language, attitude, listening skills, telephone skills, and writing skills.

Verbal Communication

The secret to a successful business is repeat customers. The secret to having repeat customers is customer satisfaction. Customers are satisfied when you are helpful, courteous, and express a genuine sincerity when dealing with their problems and complaints. This may sound like a simple task, but one slip of your tongue while you are frustrated could mean the difference between success and failure in customer relations.

When communicating with customers and clients, always speak clearly and concisely. If you can avoid it, never use technical jargon and acronyms. You may think using such language makes you sound smarter or more knowledgeable. In reality, it can break down the confidence of the customer by making him or her feel less knowledgeable. The customer or client should feel comfortable while engaged in a conversation with you.

Figure 20-5. HP provides a printer installation FAQ webpage which addresses the most common questions concerning printer installation.

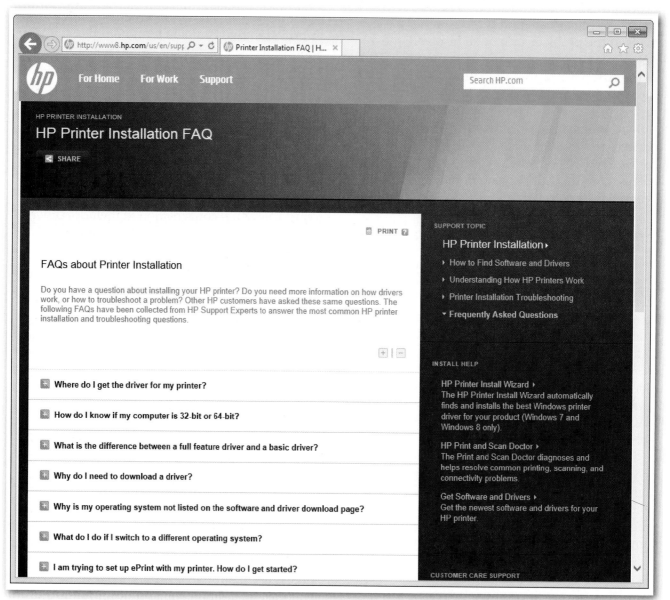

Figure 20-6. Microsoft provides extensive technical support for all of its products with information addressing the most common customer questions.

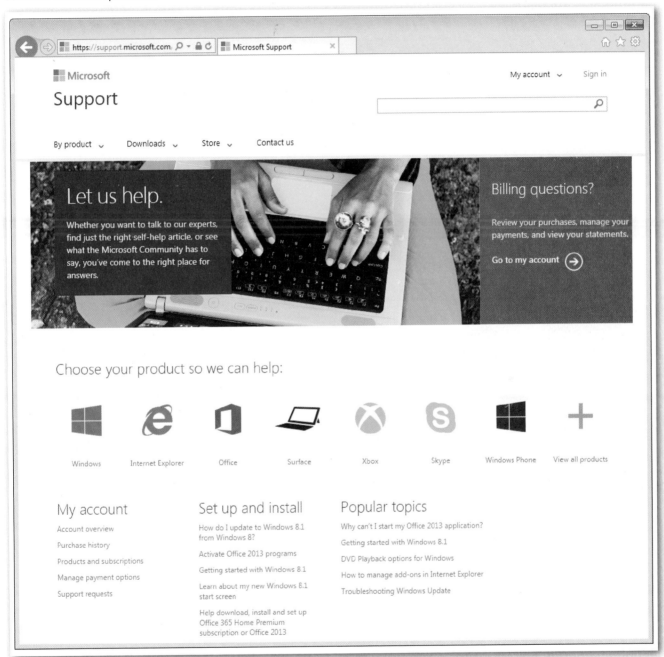

Figure 20-7. Microsoft provides written and video technical support for common customer questions such as how to view and connect to wireless networks.

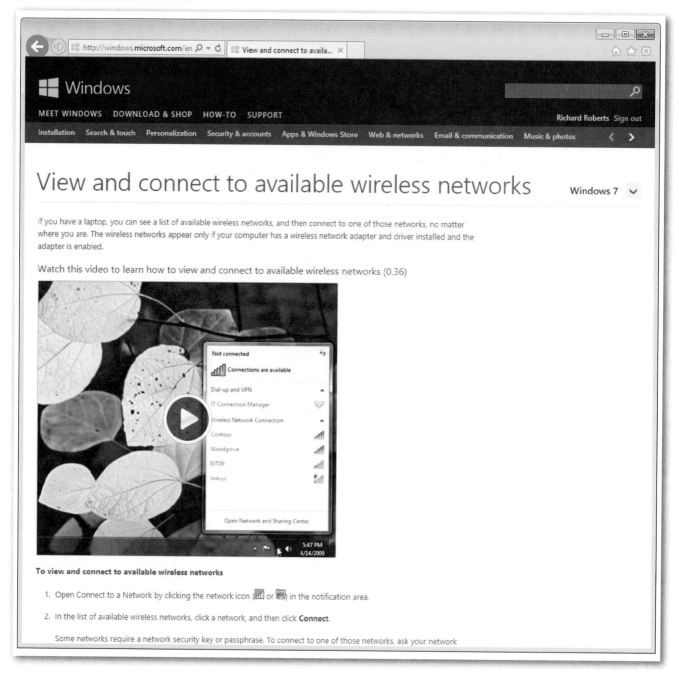

Always begin your conversation with a warm greeting. For example, "Good morning, what can I do to be of service to you?" While engaged in conversation with customers or clients, use positive words to establish a "Can do!" attitude. Use reinforcing statements such as, "Don't worry, I'll have this fixed in no time," or "This is a very common problem. Lots of people have

trouble at first." Do whatever you can to build their self-esteem and their confidence in both you and your company. The following are some good and bad examples of statements used when communicating with a customer or client:

Good examples:
"Yes, we can fix that."
"No problem, we can handle that."

"Yes, we fix that type of problem all the time."

"If you have any more problems, don't hesitate to call."

"You are no bother. This is what I am here for."

Bad examples:

"I hope we can help you."

"I've never fixed that type of problem before."

"I don't know, but I'll try."

"I'll be busy later, so let's get this finished now."

Body Language

Body language and mannerisms can say more than the spoken word and reveal your true feelings. For example, as an employee you may say, "How may I help you?" However, if you continue to work on a customer's computer and avoid eye contact with the customer, you are sending the nonverbal message, "I am very busy right now and really do not have time for your problem." If you greet a person with a smile or handshake, you warmly say nonverbally, "I am open to your problem." On the other hand, if you greet the customer with arms folded across your chest and a scowl on your face, you are sending the nonverbal message, "Keep out." The following are some body language key points to keep in mind:

- Smile.
- Maintain eye contact with the customer while listening, **Figure 20-8**.

Figure 20-8. By maintaining eye contact with the customer while listening, you tell that customer you are truly interested in helping him or her with the problem.

auremar/Shutterstock.com

- Face the customer squarely.
- Never look away from the customer or stare off at a distant point while conversing.
- Do not fold your arms across your chest or take a defensive posture.

Always face people directly and squarely. Do not turn away while addressing a person or engage in other activities when you should be giving your complete attention to the customer. If you are alone in a shop and must answer a phone, always apologize and ask if you can return the call at a better time. All customers appreciate they are being given fair attention. If you do, ask to return a call at a better time because you are helping another customer. Return the call.

Attitude

Attitude is easily perceived by a customer but is very hard to define in objective terms. Everyone knows a good attitude or a bad attitude when they experience it. It is critical to your success to always maintain a positive attitude while working with people. Without it, you may not have a job. It does not take long to earn a reputation for your attitude—good or bad.

For this chapter, the best definition of *attitude* is a subjective judgment of character made by the customer based on the perception of how the technician presents himself or herself and meets the customers' needs.

Show the customer that his or her problem is your main concern. You do this by asking probing questions such as, "How long have you had this problem?" Never be judgmental or indicate that the customer caused the problem, even if the customer did. You will use training techniques and suggestions to help the customer avoid the problem in the future.

Avoid distractions. A customer or fellow worker will feel you are not interested if you do not give him or her your full attention. For example, when working on a project, always stop your work to talk to a customer. This will give the customer a feeling of importance and show that you care about his or her problem. It will also keep you from making an error on your project because you are distracted. In making customers feel important, you will gain their confidence.

Listening Skills

Listening skills are the most important trait listed by employers in recent surveys conducted to identify the trait most desired in customer support. They all agree that employees who work with clients and customers must have excellent listening skills. Listening seems like such a simple task. So why do not all people have good listening skills? Many people, especially the type of personalities that gravitate toward the computer field, are often bright and articulate and may already be thinking ahead of the customer. Avoiding this habit will keep your customers from feeling inadequate. The following are a list of guidelines to put into practice:

- Always maintain eye contact while listening.
- Avoid distractions while listening. Do not try to perform other tasks while the customer or client is talking to you. Focus on the speaker.
- Never eat or drink while talking with a customer.
- Always allow customers or clients to complete their sentences. Never cut them off or interrupt them, anticipating what they are going to say.
- Restate the problem to the customer or client. This will ensure that you understand the issue or problem.

Check out the International Listening Association website, which is dedicated to listening skills. There you will find many interesting facts, such as only seven percent of the meaning in a conversation is transmitted by actual words.

Telephone Skills

Many of the same skills used in face-to-face communication also apply to telephone support. Always speak clearly and concisely and avoid trade jargon, slang, and acronyms.

Never engage in other activities while talking to the customer or client. A person can always tell when someone is not focused on his or her conversation. When you are engaged in another activity, like working on a computer while talking to the customer on the telephone, the customer will be able to tell you are not fully engaged with the conversation. This will generate a feeling that you are not truly concerned with his or her problem or need and will probably irritate the customer.

Always avoid talking on a speakerphone, as this only confirms that you are not paying attention to the caller. You are a technician. If you must be "hands free," get a headset. At least this way, the customer will feel that he or she is the focus of your conversation. Unless it is necessary to use the keyboard or remotely access the customer's computer, keep your hands off the keyboard. Customers can hear that you are using the keyboard and will nearly always conclude that it does not have to do with his or her problem.

Smile while on the phone, **Figure 20-9**. It might sound crazy, but it actually works. A person on the other end of the telephone conversation can actually perceive when a person is happy on the telephone. This is interpreted as a feeling that the support person is pleased to hear from the customer and wants to help. A good idea is to hang a mirror near the telephone with a sign that says "Smile!"

Figure 20-9. Smiling while on the telephone can help you convey that you are pleased to hear from the customer and want to help.

Again, avoid using acronyms, jargon, or sophisticated technical terminology. Customers are not typically sophisticated computer users and are frequently intimidated by your conversation. Always use language that anyone can understand, no matter what his or her technical background. You do not impress customers with technical terms. If you want to impress a customer, use terms that express your sincere desire to help with his or her problem.

Writing Skills

Writing is a part of all customer support technician duties. As a customer support person, you will either write by hand on repair tickets or enter into a computer the specifics about a repair. Content typically consists of a description of the problem and the repair procedure used to fix the problem. Often, your writing and documentation of specific problems and the method used to fix the problem will become valuable company information for problems encountered in the future.

When creating written communications, always use appropriate grammar and correct spelling. All word-processing packages and software programs that require written responses have spell checkers and usually grammar checkers. Use them! Do not disable them or ignore them. When writing, use sentences limited to 15 to 20 words. Avoid long, run-on sentences.

Always be polite in your correspondence, and never use sarcasm. Sarcasm is always inappropriate because the customer or client may very well misinterpret your intent. Sarcasm is based on familiar personalities, and you are not familiar with all who might read your correspondence.

Many help desk support software packages contain sections to support e-mail directly from within the software package. You will need to respond to customer and client e-mails. E-mail correspondence is covered in the next section.

Another function of customer support may involve writing training manuals or a set of procedures for a company. Often, part of a contract of installing computer equipment and software involves training the customers on how to use the equipment. Many times technical support personnel must write training packages to support

the customer. You may very well find yourself responsible for part of the written package.

E-mail

Customer support may require a great deal of time answering e-mails from customers and clients. When writing e-mails to customers and clients, avoid computer jargon, acronyms, and abbreviations, just as you would in spoken language. Communicating in writing with other technicians is not the same as communicating in writing with customers and clients. While it might be perfectly all right to use an acronym or abbreviation on a customer repair ticket, you should avoid acronyms and abbreviations when communicating with customers.

Auto Responders

Using an e-mail auto responder can show customers or clients that you care about them and their problems. E-mail auto responders are e-mail programs provided by e-mail service providers that create an automatic response to a received e-mail. The auto responder gives the illusion that someone has just read the e-mail sent by the customer or client and will be answering the request very soon. The auto responder allows for an instant reply 24 hours a day, 7 days a week. An auto responder can also be used to notify customers that you are out of the office for a brief time. Some e-mail client software, such as Microsoft Outlook, will allow you to set up an auto response, **Figure 20-10**.

E-mail Acronyms and Emoticons

E-mail acronyms are very popular with all of the electronic communications devices, but they are never to be used in customer support e-mail. E-mail acronyms became especially popular when phone text messaging started because they save a lot of keystrokes. You may receive e-mail acronyms or emoticons from customers, but you should never respond in these terms. The following are some e-mail acronyms:

- **LOL**: Laugh out loud.
- **BTW**: By the way.
- **TIA**: Thanks in advance.
- **IOW**: In other words.

Figure 20-10. Microsoft Outlook has a tool called the Out of Office Assistant, which is used to send an auto reply to senders.

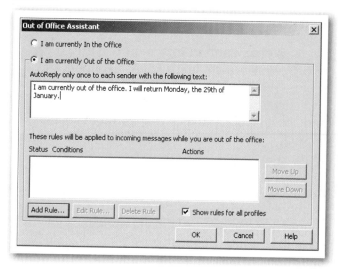

Emoticons are cartoon face characters made from keyboard symbols, used to express emotions in e-mails, letters, and text messaging. The following table lists some common emoticons.

Emoticon	Emotion
:)	Smile or happy
: o	Shock.
: (	Frown or sad.
;)	Wink.

If you have trouble communicating with customers using e-mail, practice regularly in a business format. Try sending a few e-mails every day to friends and relatives. Writing e-mail messages daily will sharpen your skills. Use the principles previously mentioned. The following is a list of key points you should always remember when communicating through e-mail with customers and clients:

- Check your e-mail regularly.
- Keep the e-mail brief.
- Do not use e-mail emoticons.
- Limit the size of file attachments. This is especially true if the customer is using a 56-k telephone modem.
- Never use all capital letters in an e-mail to emphasize a word or phrase. If you must emphasize a word or phrase, use italics or an asterisk, for example, **this is very important. Do not use bold or underline. This can be misinterpreted as a link.
- Never ever send sensitive or inappropriate information in e-mail.
- Do not send personal greetings, jokes, or other materials that are not suitable for the work environment.

Professionalism

Professionalism is a businesslike characteristic reflected in a person and work environment. In relation to a person, it is identified in a person's attitude and dress. In the work environment, it is identified in its décor and general atmosphere. This section explores various aspects of professionalism in an employee and work environment.

Professional Image

Businesses and their employees are often judged by a customer 's first impression of them. For example, if a technician looks professional, the customer feels confident in the technician. If the technician looks sloppy, dirty, unkempt, or bizarre, the customer or client might have a less than confident feeling about the technician.

Dressing appropriately means dressing professionally. In the work environment, there are two distinct types of acceptable dress: formal business and business casual. For women, formal business attire usually includes a suit with a skirt or slacks and a blouse. For men, formal business typically means a suit or sport coat with a collared shirt and tie (or just a collared shirt and tie) and a pair of dress slacks and leather shoes.

See **Figure 20-11**. However, as a computer technician, business casual is appropriate attire. Business casual generally means a polo shirt (often with a company logo) or collared shirt with no tie, dress or casual slacks, leather shoes, and in rare cases, tennis shoes, **Figure 20-12**. Some computer technicians believe they are entitled to wear torn or tattered blue jeans, T-shirts, tennis shoes, flip-flops, or sandals. These are never acceptable forms of business attire. Remember your casual attire may reflect a casual attitude. You are a trained professional; dress like one.

Figure 20-11. This IT person is wearing formal attire.

OPOLJA/Shutterstock.com

Figure 20-12. This IT person is wearing casual business attire.

wavebreakmedia/Shutterstock.com

Many businesses provide shirts for their support staff. When shirts are provided, the dress code is clearly stated to the employees. If the dress code is not clearly stated, then it is assumed. When working in the area of customer support, a polo shirt is most appropriate, but be aware that some companies require a dress shirt and tie to be worn when dealing with customers and clients at their locations.

As a computer technician, you will likely be crawling on the floor or reaching behind desks. Unisex (the same for both men and women) dress is typically the best and safest choice. Women should never wear short dresses or revealing clothing if they have to work in this environment. The following are some tips that should become a part of your own professional image:

- Dress professionally. Clean, neat slacks and a shirt with a collar are much more appropriate than a T-shirt with a slogan. This is especially true if the T-shirt has a controversial slogan or image printed on it.
- Hair should be neat and clean. Hair with spikes or wild colors might be cool to you, but it is entirely unprofessional in the workplace.
- Speak to customers in a professional manner. Never use profanity or inappropriate language or terms, even as a way to emphasize certain points.
- Do not eat, drink, or smoke while dealing with a customer.

Many students feel that if they have exceptional technical skills, they will never be fired. Nothing could be further from the truth. More employees have lost their jobs because of their unprofessional manner than from technical incompetence. An employer will tolerate an employee with average technical skills, but will not tolerate an employee who conducts himself or herself in an unprofessional manner. When employers contact other professionals for hiring recommendations, they typically request someone who can work well with people rather than request the "smartest" or most technically able person. The most important thing to the employer is an employee's image and personality. Employers rarely, if ever, call a second time if a nonprofessional person comes in for an interview.

Customers' Confidential Materials

Computers are used by a wide range of people and contain a wide assortment of information. Customer devices may contain confidential information, such as bank account balances, private written correspondence and private e-mails, customer client lists, Social Security numbers, medical information, and business information.

Customers and clients expect privacy. Violating their privacy is a breach of trust which will cause at least the loss of future business and may very well damage your business reputation. A breach of confidentiality may also result in legal action. For example, patient medical records are considered confidential and are protected by federal and state laws. The same is true for intellectual properties such as inventions, formulas, and some forms of business data such as customer personal and financial information.

Some businesses require computer support personnel to sign a nondisclosure agreement before working on the business computers or before being hired as a business employee. The agreement provides for the legal protection of proprietary information such as customer lists, trade secrets, financial information, business strategies, and intellectual property. Violating the agreement can result in job loss and financial punishment. In short, a computer technician has no reason to be viewing customer or client personal information except if requested by the customer or client, such as during data recovery.

Work Environment

The store or work location image is also critical and is often a direct result of the employees' efforts to maintain a professional image. The work environment must represent a professional atmosphere. If the work environment is to be visited by customers and other employees, it should be maintained so as not to be offensive to others. For example, you may enjoy a particular style of music while you are working; however, it may not be the choice of many customers. The customer should not be offended by loud music of any generation. You should avoid music in the work environment where customers may be present, except for soft, neutral background music.

Also, be aware that listening to music through earphones is offensive to many people. You should be concentrating on the customer or client. This also applies to working at a client's workstation and in the corporate environment as a whole. The following are some tips to help you maintain a professional environment in your workplace:

- Keep your location and workstation clean and well organized.
- Never keep food containers, cups, and general trash on counters or work areas.
- Do not play music that is not in the mainstream or blast music of any kind.
- Do not let friends "hang out" around the store or workspace. The workplace is not a social club.
- Do not display inappropriate posters, pictures, or signs. You may think they are fun or entertaining, but not all customers share your view.

Handling Difficult Situations

When a client is angry and upset, the client will vent his or her emotions toward the person who represents the company or problem. Dealing with difficult people requires patience and composure. Do not take complaints personally. Never react to a difficult customer, but rather listen and respond with empathy. *Empathy* means that you show by your words that you understand the other person's feelings and his or her situation. There is likely always a situation that would warrant a statement like, "I can understand how this problem is frustrating you."

A coworker or other customer might normally be very pleasant and fun to be around until a situation causes that person to be very angry. While in an angry state, the person may say things that he or she normally would never say to another person. Arguing with an upset person will only make things worse.

Your job is to defuse the situation by letting the customer vent. When responding to the customer, use a calm assuring voice. What you want the customer to do is talk to you and calmly explain the issue. At an opportune time, simply say, "Let's see what I can do to resolve this problem." When you start to work on the problem, or to tell the customer what you are planning to do, check if it is all right with the customer.

If the customer continues to vent, find out what will make the customer happy. For example, a customer may have brought his or her computer to the shop several times for the same problem. It may or may not be the same problem, but that is the customer's perception. Find out what will make the customer happy by asking, "What do you think it will take to make you satisfied?"

The customer may want his or her bill adjusted or to not be charged for the present repair. If you are not authorized to waive the costs, simply say, "I'll see what we can do for you," and then check with your supervisor. If a person is upset, it will only become worse if the person thinks that he or she is not being taken seriously.

Is the Customer Always Right?

There is a very old business saying: "The customer is always right." Well, this is true most of the time, but there are times when this motto just does not apply. When the customer or client wishes you to do something unethical or illegal, he or she is wrong. For example, a customer may request you write a receipt for more value than the actual cost of the repair. Or, a customer may ask you to violate some copyright law. Do not do it.

How about when a customer uses foul language in a loud tone and threatens you? Can you really make that person happy? You never need to fear for your life or bodily harm. If the customer threatens you, you should politely ask the person to leave, and if the customer will not, call the police or security. What if the customer is intoxicated and becomes abusive? Again, this customer should be asked to leave, and if he or she refuses, call the police. An intoxicated or violent customer is not only a threat to you and the business, the customer is also a threat to any other people who enter or are present at the business.

Follow-Up

A follow-up helps to build a good relationship with the customer or client. Perform a follow-up after you have had a break in contact with the customer or client. For example, after a customer's problem has been fixed, follow up a few days after completing the repair to see if the customer is satisfied and all went well. This technique improves service and builds a client's trust. Customers and clients love the fact that someone is checking if the problem was handled in a timely fashion and if he or she was dealt with professionally.

Your Word

One of the most important assets you have is your word, and it costs you nothing. Your word or promise can make or break your client relationship. Be a person of your word. Your word should be your bond. Suppose you tell a customer you will contact him or her with a repair estimate the next day, but you run into a problem with a vendor. The vendor does not respond to your inquiry, so, in turn, you do not have the customer estimate ready. If you told the customer you would call the next morning, do so, even if it is to say you do not have the estimate yet. It is important that you be a person of your word.

Keep your promises. If you say you will be there in the morning, be there. The client may have rearranged his or her schedule to accommodate you. If you have a problem, call ahead, and always apologize. How often have you been given a date and been required to sit home all day to have a service done. Do not allow this type of behavior to become your business signature.

Contracts

If a company is large, it may be necessary to create a written document or contract to be sure everyone has the same expectations. The contract should contain a description of the work to be performed, the estimated or actual cost, the estimate of completion time, and other terms agreed on. By having a customer signature prior to work, you always protect yourself against a misinterpretation of expectations. A client or customer should always receive exactly what they agreed to—maybe more, but never less.

Teamwork

Teamwork is two or more people working toward a common goal. For example, the goal of customer support is customer satisfaction. When you work as part of a team, you place the common goal of the team (customer satisfaction) above your own individual goal(s), such as recognition and promotion. Teamwork is an essential component of a successful business.

As a team member, you must be willing to help other team members and to share your own expertise and knowledge with others. For example, a customer calls and asks about the status of his or her computer. If the person assigned to repair the computer is out of work that day, you should check the job ticket to review the status of the repair. It could be ready for pickup or awaiting parts. You should try to help the customer even if it is not your assigned repair. Make a note of the customer call and record your actions. For example, you might write a note on the ticket such as, "Customer called and asked the status of the repair. I informed him it was awaiting parts and should be ready in a day or two." Then, sign the note.

When working as a member of a team, you should be willing to share your knowledge with other team members. Knowledge is not just limited to technical issues. It also covers company procedures or any other bit of knowledge that might help another team member perform his or her duties.

Job Protection

A common, yet unattractive trait in the business world occurs when a person will not share his or her individual knowledge with another team member. The concept is referred to as "job protection." This happens, for example, if one person is the only person that knows how to perform specific tasks and is not willing to share this information or train another person. The person thinks that he is secure in his position with the company if he is the only person who knows how to perform that task.

In reality, this type of person is actually jeopardizing his or her position with the company. The company management or owner will not like the fact that an employee is not willing to share knowledge for the good of the company. If the person is unwilling to share knowledge or to help other team members, he or she will most likely find him or herself looking for other employment. Remember that working as a team requires supporting other team members, especially by sharing knowledge and reinforcing good work products. If you are not willing to function as a team member, then you will most likely not be a member of the team very long.

Helping Team Members

You must be willing to do more than just what you have been assigned. For example, a collection of repair tickets might be divided between team members. Each member is assigned four tickets each. If you finish your repairs before anyone else, you should not assume that you are done for that day. You should see if you could help someone else with his or her assigned work.

Employers do not like to see employees that are doing just enough to get by or wasting company time. Employers love to see employees going above and beyond their assigned duties. When you finish your assigned tasks, you should immediately inform your supervisor and volunteer to help other team members with their assigned duties. This will impress your employer and also be appreciated by fellow team members. Remember, the company goal is to repair all the customers' computers, not just the ones assigned to you that particular day.

A+ Note

There will often be one or two questions related to professionalism on the CompTIA A+ exam. While one would think that the subject of professional dress would be obvious, there are students who always seem to try to justify their own inappropriate dress as suitable for working on computers. Remember that you are not simply working on a computer but are representing your employer.

Dealing with Prohibited Content/Activity

When a technician services and repairs a computer or is maintaining the network system, he or she may very likely encounter prohibitive content or a prohibitive activity. It is the technician's responsibility to report all illegal activity and content to his or her immediate supervisor, and in some cases, directly to law enforcement.

Prohibitive content and activity can be any one of numerous activities and content. A few examples, but not limited to the following, include anything illegal, malicious, harassing, invasive of personal privacy, libelous, pornographic, offensive, and infringes on copyright. It is not just the data or the network system being compromised. Organizations can be held responsible for the actions of their employees or members of the organization. For example, if harassing e-mails are discovered and no action is taken, the victim may choose to obtain an attorney and file a lawsuit claiming he or she has been forced to work in a hostile workplace environment. If the company has not taken any corrective actions, it can be held legally responsible for the actions of the employee creating and distributing the harassing e-mails.

Any person engaged in prohibitive activity or dealing in prohibitive content can be prosecuted for criminal activity by the legal system, and at the very least, be fired by his or her employer or be issued a written reprimand for a minor offense.

The following is a list of common prohibited activities and content. However, this is not a complete list of all prohibited activities and content.

- Engaging in illegal activities such as gambling.
- Distributing spam.
- Soliciting or distributing personal information.
- Collecting information from a minor.
- Engaging in harmful, malicious, harassing activity or discriminating against, bulling, or humiliating other people.
- Accessing a person's computer or area of a network without authorization.
- Interfering with or interrupting a network service.
- Intentionally uploading viruses or other malicious programs.

Companies, schools, and government agencies often include a long sample list in their company conduct or policy books. Also, most organizations have policy and procedure books that detail how a security incident is to be handled and provide examples of forms which must be completed for any incident that occurs. The procedure for handling incidents can be broken down into three general steps:

1. Identify exactly what happened when the unauthorized activity or prohibitive material was discovered.
2. Write a complete detailed description of the incident and the procedures you followed.
3. Document the chronological order of the handling of evidence from the time it is first discovered until it reaches trial or final conclusion.

A security event form can be used for the first step and possibly the second step of the procedure. See **Figure 20-13**. If additional information must be documented and the security event form does not provide enough space, additional written documentation can be added to the form.

A routine incident typically does not require much detailed written information. For example, when a malware, such as a worm, attacks a computer or network system, a simple remedy may be provided by one of the many antivirus vendors. The malware is removed and normal operation is restored. In contrast, an incident involving theft or breach of security causing the loss of sensitive data may require much more detailed information than a routine incident. You should provide as much detail as possible in the documentation. Normally, additional pages may be required to record all pertinent facts concerning the incident. If the incident results in legal action by law enforcement, you may need to recall important facts about the incident at a much later date. It is not unusual for a technician to be called in for a legal deposition or to testify at a date one to two years after the incident has occurred. Memories fade, and the only way to be accurate and detailed about the incident is to record as much detail as possible when the incident first occurs.

Once law enforcement becomes involved in an event, the responsibility for handling the

Figure 20-13. An example of a Computer Security Event form.

Computer Security Event Form

Person who reported incident:

Name _____   Title _____   Department _____

Phone _____   E-mail _____

Location of incident: Building _____   Room _____

Time incident was reported: Date _____   Time _____

	Virus/Malware		Social Engineering		User Account Compromised
	Hoax		System Misuse		Network Intrusion
	Theft/Loss		Physical Security Violation		Other

Virus/Malware: Describe virus/malware in general terms and the impact on the system.

Technical or Physical Vulnerability: Describe the nature and effect of the incident in general terms.

Equipment loss or stolen: Provide details of data or equipment loss or stolen.

Host/Network Information

IP Address	Host Name	MAC Address

Suspected Source of Intrusion or Unauthorized Activity.

Source IP Address	Resolved IP Host Name	Application used to verify.

evidence or chain of custody will become their responsibility. They most likely will collect the original incident report, so you should make a copy for your records.

Experience is the best teacher for determining whether an incident is considered routine or very serious. This is why, as a new technician, you will rely on your supervisor's judgment of how to proceed after the initial report is created. Large companies and organizations always have policies established as to how to handle all of the most common security incidents. Be sure to review your company's security policy publications so you know how to respond to an incident.

When you use your employer's equipment, such as computers and the network system, you no longer have the right to privacy as you do when using your own computer at home. Employers have the right to monitor employee activities on the company computer as well as the network system.

First Response/Incident Response

The first response is to identify exactly what happened when the unauthorized activity or prohibitive material was discovered. A security incident could be discovering phishing e-mail, malware, unauthorized access to a user account, deletion of data, or any activity that is considered a security incident or the unauthorized use of organization equipment. Many organizations routinely run software applications that detect security problems and breeches. Organizations can also monitor employee activities on a network or workstation and generate reports containing the date, time, and type of activity. For example, there are software applications that monitor user Internet activity and record the locations visited, the amount of time at the location, and even the type of transaction conducted at a location, such as a purchase or e-mail and chat room activity. It is normal for an organization to have employees, students, or other users of the computer system to sign agreements describing permissible network and workstation conduct. After the incidence is properly identified or classified, the incident must be documented.

Documentation

You should write a complete detailed description of the incident and the procedures you followed. Most companies and large organizations have established policies and procedures for reporting an incident, as well as forms to be completed by the technician or person reporting the incident. For example, when an incidence occurs, such as when a technician discovers the presence of malware on an employee workstation or an employee reports a company laptop missing, the company has established procedures to follow. A security event form, like that shown in Figure 20-13, is used to record information directly related to the security event. The collection of all security events can be reviewed later and serve as the basis for making decisions affecting security, such as a change in established policies and procedures.

Chain of Custody

A **chain of custody** is a method of preserving the evidence, tracking the exchange of evidence, and ensuring the integrity of the evidence. You cannot simply collect evidence and leave it on your desk or in some other unsecure area where anyone can tamper with it. A chain of custody is documentation of the chronological order of the handling of evidence from the time it is first discovered until it reaches trial or final conclusion. The chain of custody ensures that the evidence is as close as possible to its original condition when it was first discovered and secured. The chain of custody form, **Figure 20-14**, tracks the evidence, such as listing every person who took possession of it, the time and date it was taken, and the method used to securely store it.

The evidence collected can be in different forms. For example, the evidence of a security breech may be simply a copy of the event captured by a software application such as Microsoft Event Viewer or by a commercial product. In the case of a software application, a copy can be made to a flash drive or disc. The flash drive or disc is then sealed in a labeled evidence bag and secured in a locked file drawer or cabinet that only you have access to. Another example is the unauthorized use of a company cell phone or tablet. The device can be confiscated and secured until it is needed as evidence of the incident.

Security Training

It is important that all members of the organization, not just the security team and technicians, be trained as to how to respond

874 Computer Service and Repair

Figure 20-14. An example of a Computer Evidence Chain of Custody form.

Computer Evidence Chain of Custody

To be completed by initial collector

Evidence collected by (name): _____

Date/time collected: _____

Description of evidence:_____

_____

Collection method (operating system, utility, commands, etc.):

_____

_____

Where is evidence originally stored? _____

How is evidence originally secured? _____

Collector signature:_____

Evidence copy history:

Date	Copied By	Copy Method	Disposition of original and all copies

Transfer History:

Date	Released by (print name, sign)	Received by (Print name, sign)	How is evidence secured?

Goodheart-Willcox Publisher

to a security incident. All members of the organization must be made aware of what is considered unacceptable activity when using the organization's devices and network. The most common response from members of an organization when questioned about an unauthorized activity is "I didn't know that I wasn't allowed to do that" or simply, "I didn't know."

A+ Note

The CompTIA A+ exam requires knowledge of how to respond to a security incident. Questions may require knowledge of chain of custody, how to respond to an incident, and what constitutes an incident.

Chapter Summary

- A help desk or call center is usually the first contact point for service and can belong to a single company or be part of a call center; a call center typically provides support for more than one company or product.

- Effective communication skills include various aspects of communication, both verbal and nonverbal.

- Professionalism in relation to a person is identified in a person's attitude and dress; in the work environment, it is identified in its décor and general atmosphere.

- The key steps for handling a prohibited activity or content incident are to identify exactly what happened when the unauthorized activity or prohibitive material was discovered, write a complete detailed description of the incident and the procedures you followed, and document the chronological order of the handling of evidence.

Review Questions

Answer the following questions on a separate sheet of paper. Please do not write in this book.

1. What is customer support?
2. Explain the difference between the help desk model and call center model.
3. Which level of support is provided when the problem is elevated to a person with more experience or expertise than the first person contacted?
4. Is it permissible to use acronyms when communicating with customers? Explain why or why not.
5. What are the key points of body language you should use?
6. What is attitude?
7. Why is sarcasm inappropriate in communications?
8. What are emoticons?
9. What are the key points in communicating with customers and clients through e-mail?
10. What two elements are required to deal with difficult people?
11. Why is it important to perform a follow-up?
12. What is the goal of the customer support team?
13. Give at least five examples of prohibited activity or content as related to computer use.
14. What are the three major steps for handling a prohibited activity or content incident?

Sample A+ Exam Questions

Answer the following questions on a separate sheet of paper. Please do not write in this book.

1. Which is an example of level-one support?
   a. A software engineer at Microsoft
   b. A hardware engineer at Apple
   c. The FAQ section of a customer support website
   d. A live conversation with a level-one supervisor

2. It is 9:00 a.m. and you are repairing a customer's computer that must be ready by 3:00 p.m. because it was promised to the customer. The phone suddenly rings, and you answer to find that it is a new customer calling about a problem with her computer. Which is the best way to deal with customer support on the telephone?
   a. Do nothing except focus on the customer and her problem. You should write down key points during the conversation, starting with her name.
   b. You should continue to work on the computer repair while listening to the customer. This is the most efficient use of time and your supervisor will be pleased.
   c. Have the customer call back later after another employee comes into the shop.
   d. Tell the customer you are in the middle of an important repair and that you will return her call later in the day. Take down the customer's name and telephone number.

3. Which is the most expensive element of customer service?
   a. Employee wages
   b. Support software
   c. Support hardware
   d. Technical support articles and website access

4. The company you work for performs computer system repairs in addition to selling new computers and hardware. A repair ticket is completed at the time of repair. The status of the repair is also recorded on the ticket. Some notes recorded on the ticket describe when the repair was completed or when parts were ordered for the repair. Mr. Smith dropped his computer off at your company computer shop three days ago. The repair was assigned to Joe and he is not in at the moment. You answer the phone and find Mr. Smith is calling to find out the status of the repair of his computer. What is the most appropriate response to Mr. Smith's inquiry?
   a. Tell Mr. Smith his computer is being worked on by Joe who is not in today and that Joe will call him back when he returns.
   b. Tell Mr. Smith to hold for a minute while you check the status of the repair ticket.
   c. Tell Mr. Smith you are not the one that has been assigned to his repair and to call back later.
   d. Tell Mr. Smith to come by the shop and pick up the computer. The computer is most likely repaired, but if it isn't, you can have it repaired before he gets there.

5. Analyze the following image. Then, match the body language with the conveyed meaning.

Lucky Business/Shutterstock.com

 a. It's really good to hear from you!
 b. How may I help you?
 c. I don't have time for your problem.
 d. I'm open to your problem.

6. When is it proper to use all uppercase letters in an e-mail?
 a. When emphasizing an important point
 b. When making a list of steps in sequential order
 c. When listing parts in an e-mail
 d. Uppercase is never appropriate in an e-mail.

7. An irate customer calls and complains about how she brought her computer home to find it has the same problem it had before she brought it in for repair. What is the first thing you should do?
 a. Smile so that the customer will sense your willingness to help her.
 b. Let the customer finish speaking and venting her anger.
 c. Interrupt her by asking her what it will take to make her satisfied.
 d. Hang up, and hope she will call back when she is in a better mood.

8. A customer brings into the shop a computer exhibiting a problem you have never encountered before. Which of the following responses would be most appropriate?
 a. Yes, we can fix that.
 b. Yes, we fix that type of problem all the time.
 c. I've never fixed that type of problem before.
 d. I don't know if I can fix it, but I'll try.

9. You need to explain the cause of a boot failure to a customer. Which of the following explanations would build the customer's confidence in your company?
 a. A virus corrupted the MBR
 b. A virus corrupted the master boot record
 c. A virus corrupted the boot sector, which stores partition information
 d. A virus corrupted an area of the hard drive that is required for startup

10. A customer uses profane language because you will not write a receipt for more value than the actual cost of the repair. You can tell that the customer is intoxicated. What is the first thing you should do?
   a. Write the receipt for the amount he specifies.
   b. Politely ask him to leave.
   c. Call the police.
   d. Respond with empathy.

Suggested Laboratory Activities

Do not attempt any suggested laboratory activities without your instructor's permission. Certain activities can render the PC operating system inoperable.

1. Check out the FAQ or support sections of the Dell, HP, and Microsoft websites.

2. Write a step-by-step procedure for checking the IP address of a Windows Vista, Windows 7, and Windows 8 computer. This step-by-step procedure would be used for customer support when, for example, a customer calls an ISP for a connection problem. Through the procedure, the customer should be able to check if there is an appropriate IP address assignment, not one such as 0.0.0.0 or 169.254.12.34. (IP address 0.0.0.0 means that a connection has not been established. IP address 169.254.xxx.xxx means that the Automatic Private IP Addressing (APIPA) feature has assigned the IP address, instead of a DHCP server.) Make the procedure as clear as possible.

3. Write a step-by-step procedure to have a customer ping a server located at www.helpdesk1.com. Include what to do next if the ping is successful or unsuccessful.

4. Write a step-by-step procedure for using System Restore on a Windows 7 and Windows 8 computer.

CompTIA A+ Certification Exams Preparation

After studying this chapter, you will be able to:

- Recall the requirements for taking the CompTIA A+ Certification exams.
- Recall the format of the CompTIA A+ Certification exams.
- Identify strategies for preparing for the CompTIA A+ Certification exams.
- Evaluate your readiness for taking the CompTIA A+ Certification exams.

A+ Exam—Key Points

Always check the CompTIA website for the latest news concerning the A+ Certification exams. The requirements for the exams frequently change. Typically, CompTIA reviews the exams at least once a year, and minor changes are made to the examination objectives. Major changes to the examination objectives occur approximately every three years following the release of the latest Windows operating system. The testing format also changes from time to time. While every attempt is made to provide you with the latest information in this textbook, changes do occur after the release of the textbook. Your best source of exam information is the official CompTIA website, www.comptia.org. You can also check www.RMRoberts.com for additional information about the CompTIA A+ Certification exams and to download additional free practice exams.

Key Terms

The following key terms will become important pieces of your computer vocabulary. Be sure you can define them.

CompTIA A+ Certification exam domains

examination objectives

If you are reading this chapter, you are probably near the completion of your course. You have gained a basic knowledge of computer service and repair and have acquired many skills by performing the lab activities. You have certainly reached a milestone in your education in computer service and repair. Your next step, should you decide to make computer service and repair a career, is to become certified. Certification proves to a potential employer that you have the knowledge and skills needed to perform the typical job duties and tasks of a PC service technician.

A+ Certification Exams

The **CompTIA A+ Certification exam** consists of two tests: CompTIA A+ 220-801 and the CompTIA A+ 220-802. The CompTIA A+ 220-801 exam measures the fundamentals of computer technology, and the CompTIA A+ 220-802 exam measures the skills related to more advanced topics in computer technology. You must pass both exams to receive the CompTIA A+ Certification. The A+ Certification is valid for three years. You can keep your certification current through the CompTIA Continuing Education Program.

The CompTIA A+ Certification exams measure a candidate's competency equal to an entry-level IT professional with the equivalent knowledge of at least 12 months experience in the lab or field. Knowledge required to pass the exams is based on the ability to assemble components according to customer requirements; install, configure and maintain devices, PCs, and software for endusers; understand the basics of networking and security; and properly and safely diagnose, resolve, and document common hardware and software issues while applying troubleshooting skills. Successful candidates will also provide appropriate customer support and understand the basics of virtualization, desktop imaging, and deployment.

CompTIA provides exam objectives on its website, www.comptia.org. The **examination objectives** are derived from industry surveys that determine the actual job requirements of a PC service technician and are categorized according to **domains**, or topic areas. The CompTIA A+ Certification Exam Objectives are *not* a comprehensive listing of all exam content. The objectives are to be used as a guide to the general test content. There can be material on the test not included in the exam objectives. The following tables list the domains measured by each exam and the extent to which the domains are represented.

CompTIA A+ 220-801	
Domain	**Percent of Exam**
PC Hardware	40%
Networking	27%
Laptops	11%
Printers	11%
Operational Procedures	11%
Total	100%

CompTIA A+ 220-802	
Domain	**Percent of Exam**
Operating Systems	33%
Security	22%
Mobile Devices	9%
Troubleshooting	36%
Total	100%

CompTIA A+ exam content is constantly being reviewed and updated. The exams can change from the list of original objectives. The CompTIA organization always includes a disclaimer as part of the exam objectives which basically says that the exam objectives are subject to change without notice. This means that you should always check the CompTIA website for the very latest test objectives before taking the exam.

A+ Note

Always check the CompTIA website for the very latest information on the CompTIA A+ Certification Exam Objectives.

CompTIA A+ 220-801 Exam

CompTIA A+ 220-801 covers the fundamentals of computer technology; the installation and configuration of PCs, laptops, and related hardware; printers; basic networking; and operational procedures. Any student who has paid attention to the instructor and has performed the required laboratory activities, thus meeting the expected level of experience, should not have much trouble passing the CompTIA A+ 220-801 exam. As long as the student has covered all test objectives, he or she should be fine.

Most students do not cover all test objectives. In fact, they cover the areas they like or think are important but do not cover other objectives that they think are not interesting. For example, most students can explain the principles of overclocking a system usually in greater depth than is required on the exam. In contrast, most students do not understand printers well enough to pass the printer portion of the exam. You need to study all test objectives.

The networking portion of the exam has been greatly expanded from 15 to 27 percent. This is a significant increase compared to the old CompTIA A+ 220-701 exam. A lot of networking fundamentals are covered on this exam. Those students who have not performed routine network configurations and had at least 60 hours of direct instruction will have difficulty with test items related to networking.

CompTIA A+ 220-802 Exam

CompTIA A+ 220-802 covers operating systems, security, mobile devices, and troubleshooting. These domains require a more in-depth knowledge of computer systems than those for the CompTIA A+ 220-801 exam. The CompTIA A+ 220-802 exam is, therefore, much harder than the first exam. It covers a lot of material and requires some hands-on experience. Many questions, but not all, are in scenario format, requiring you to think and apply knowledge and make decisions based on the given situation. Always read the questions carefully.

The first domain of the CompTIA A+ 220-802 exam is Operating Systems. This domain can prove to be quite difficult, especially when you are required to contrast the different operating system features. You will need to have a good understanding of the configuration options and features of all Windows operating systems for the last ten years. This exam covers all of the commonly encountered editions of Windows operating systems. Be aware that when a new Windows operating system is released, it takes CompTIA approximately one year before adding additional questions for the newest operating system.

Some areas of the exam can be quite difficult and require memorization. For example, questions appear on the test requiring you to correctly identify which operating system edition can be upgraded to another operating system edition. Another difficult area is correctly matching operating system features to the correct operating system and edition.

There are also command prompt questions requiring you to match the correct command and switch to the desired result. For example, which command and switch is used to automatically inspect a hard disk drive and automatically repair errors? The Operating System domain is quite extensive and accounts for 33 percent of the exam objectives.

Security and troubleshooting questions will also prove to be difficult. Many of the troubleshooting questions will most likely be a scenario type of question. The scenario-based question will require you to make an analysis based on given facts or characteristics of the problem.

You may encounter questions that have two possible correct answers, but CompTIA only wants you to choose one. When there are two correct answers, you will need to pick the one that is the most correct or the most reasonable. For example, you could be asked, "What is the best way to protect a computer from malware?" Two good possible answers would be install an antivirus (antimalware) protection suite and the other answer could be to perform regular routine backups. Would you know which is the best or most correct answer? If not, you need to study more and focus on the term *protect*. Ask yourself, "What are you protecting and is there anything that is close to foolproof protection?" The Troubleshooting domain is the largest and represents 36 percent of the exam objectives.

A+ Note

CompTIA A+ certifications issued after 2011 are valid for only three years. You can keep your certification current through the Continuing Education Program.

Certification and Exam Requirements

CompTIA recommends that a test candidate have at least 12 months of hands-on lab or work experience. The 12 months is a recommendation, not a requirement. In fact, anyone is eligible to take an A+ Certification exam. There are no prerequisites. However, work experience alone does not ensure that a candidate will pass the exams. Formal training provides the best opportunity for passing.

There are some candidates who do pass the exams by using self-study techniques, but this is rare. Your best preparation for passing the exams is a combination of structured classroom-related experiences and hands-on laboratory activities that reinforce classroom training and textbook studies.

When you feel you are ready to take an A+ Certification exam, you must make an appointment to test at a registered testing center. When reporting to the testing center, you must show two proofs of identification. One is typically a photo ID and the other is a document with your signature, such as a credit card. Always check the requirements for identification before reporting to the testing center.

After proving your identity, you will be assigned a workstation in the testing area at which you will take your exam. You will not be allowed to bring any reference material into the testing area. You are provided with scrap paper on which you may want to do a quick "brain dump" of any material you think you may have problems remembering during the exam. Do *not* waste your time by writing down exam questions to share with others who are studying for the exam. You must turn this paper over to the proctor (exam attendant) before you leave the testing center.

Exam questions are not scored, or *weighted*, equally. This means that exam questions are worth different amounts of points. It is impossible to determine the exact weight of a question because CompTIA does not reveal it. However, the weight of one question compared to another is often rather obvious. A question that asks you to identify a component carries less weight than a question that asks you to apply analytical thinking. For example, a question that asks which component on a motherboard is responsible for processing instructions carries less weight than a question that asks you to identify the order of the Windows XP boot process.

The usual number of questions for each exam is 90 but can vary because CompTIA sometimes adds additional questions that do not count toward the score. The additional exam questions are field-test questions. By answering them, you are helping CompTIA develop new exam questions. Field-testing ensures the question has been clearly written and the correct answer is clearly indicated in the list of answers. If an experimental exam question is too difficult to understand or does not have a clear, correct answer, it is evident to CompTIA by a higher than average number of incorrect responses to the question. These questions are rewritten and tested again before becoming a valid exam question.

Each exam has a time limit of 90 minutes. The passing score for the CompTIA A+ 220-801 exam is 675 (on a scale of 900). For the CompTIA A+ 220-802 exam, it is 700 (on a scale of 900).

Question Format

All questions are presented by computer and fall into one of two formats: multiple-choice and performance-based. A vast majority of questions on the CompTIA A+ exams will be in multiple-choice format. Most questions will have four answers to choose from, but there may be a few questions that require you to choose multiple answers from more than four choices. For example, you may be asked to choose the three best answers from a list of six possible answers.

In addition to multiple-choice questions, you will most likely encounter two or three performance-based questions. Performance-based questions ask you to complete a task rather than select the correct answer as in a multiple-choice question. An example of a performance-based question for a CompTIA A+ exam is to enter the command to check the assigned IP address of a computer. Another example is to arrange the given list in the correct order for installing an additional PATA drive, such as the following list:

- Power off the computer.
- Format the PATA drive.
- Power on the computer.
- Install the drive.
- Partition the drive.

The CompTIA website provides sample questions to help you determine if you are ready to take the test. The sample is also provided to help you know what to expect during the test. The CompTIA website also provides a link to more information about performance-based questions and provides a sample of what you might encounter.

A+ Note

The A+ Certification exams are graded on a scale from 100 to 900. A minimum score of 675 is needed to pass the CompTIA A+ 220-801 exam, and a minimum score of 700 is needed to pass the CompTIA A+ 220-802. Because each question is weighted, it is difficult to translate these passing scores into a percentage.

Exam Preparation

To successfully prepare for an A+ Certification exam, you must design an exam preparation strategy. A few possible strategies are presented. Using them will increase your chances of passing an A+ Certification exam on your first attempt.

Establish a Study Schedule

Establish a realistic study schedule. Use a calendar and write in the dates and times for study. You will know best how much time to allocate. You can also ask your instructor for input on how many hours of additional study you might need before taking the exam. Having a planned schedule for study allows you to set times for other activities, such as movies, dates, family plans, and television. If you have a set study schedule, you will most likely think twice about those other activities and will schedule your study time around them.

Get Hands-On Experience

Hands-on experience provides you with many of the required skills that are tested on in the A+ Certification exams. You should spend as much time as possible practicing many of the skills that are tested. For example, you should practice setting up and formatting partitions on a hard drive, rather than just reading and memorizing procedures. For many of the skills tested, there is no substitute for hands-on experience. The series of lab activities designed to accompany this textbook should provide you with many of those skills. It is highly recommended you practice performing the lab activities and review the questions at the end of each lab. Many of the lab review questions are designed to prepare you for an A+ Certification exam. Begin your review at the beginning of the lab manual. Often, students forget the basics that were covered early in the course.

Read a Variety of Computer-Related Material

It is helpful to read a variety of computer-related material. Sometimes reading the same topic in a different book or manual can illuminate the information in a new way or can commit better to memory. Some materials you should read, besides this textbook, are installation manuals, Readme files, and instructional websites.

Textbook Material

Review the textbook material covered in the course. Just as it was suggested for the lab activities, start your review at the beginning of the textbook. Do you still remember the definition of multitasking? Review all tests, end of chapter Review Questions, pop quizzes, and classroom handouts.

Installation Manuals

Installation manuals are vast sources of excellent study material. Seagate, D-Link, Sony, HP, Microsoft, and many other manufacturers have a lot of valuable information directly related to the exam in their installation manuals. You can learn by reading the installation manual for a hard drive, a network adapter card, or a multimedia card. An installation manual for a motherboard will contain a lot of valuable information, especially for setting up the BIOS configuration and for BIOS terminology which you may encounter on the test. Download at least one Intel and one ASUS motherboard manual. An installation manual reinforces what you have already learned in the course by showing you how that knowledge is applied. Most of these manuals can be downloaded from the Internet. Simply go to the manufacturer's support page on their website, locate the desired manual, and download the PDF file.

Readme Files

The Readme files that accompany an installation CD/DVD contain valuable study material. Search the operating system installation disc for the document containing the installation information. Also, check the operating system's website for information about the installation. Many exam content items have been derived directly from this source of information.

Instructional Web pages and Websites

There are hundreds of web pages available to assist you in learning more about computer technology. Seeing the same material presented in a different format by a different writer can be extremely helpful, especially when learning difficult concepts. For example, if you have difficulty learning the differences in RAID types, you could search the Internet for "RAID" or "RAID types." You will find many sources about RAID, including short tutorials.

Create a Study Guide

A great technique to use in preparing for the A+ Certification exams and reviewing for the course is to make your own study guide. Teacher handouts are convenient, but are seldom studied in-depth by the average student. There are also many study guides located on the Internet. Some are free, and some are costly. Some commercial and free study guides contain material that is no longer required for the exam or is not included in the examination objectives. To increase your retention of the subject matter, it is recommended that you make your own study guide. One suggested method of creating a study guide is to list the examination objectives on a sheet of paper, leaving ample space in which to write your own notes between the content items.

A better way to copy the examination objectives is to use a word processor. Add an ample amount of space between the content items listed. When studying, write in by hand the information you have collected about each objective and content item. See **Figure 21-1**. Using this method will not only give you a set of notes matching the exact exam objectives, it will serve as an excellent study tool.

When filling in your study guide, be aware that many content items are listed under more than one objective. When you see a content item that is listed more than once, look for key words in the related objective that identify the desired information for that content item. For example, if a USB port is listed under more than one objective, one occurrence may be under an objective that is concerned with the USB port's identification and characteristics and the other occurrence may be concerned with troubleshooting. Write your notes about the content item according to the specifics of each objective.

Join or Form a Study Group

A group formed of individuals that are serious about preparing for the A+ Certification exams can be an excellent way to prepare. Here are some general guidelines to follow:
- Stay on task.
- Set a regular schedule of dates, times, and duration. (Every day is best, but not always possible.)
- Write practice exam questions for each other.
- Share resources such as sample exams or websites that support your studies.

Figure 21-1.
Sample study guide.

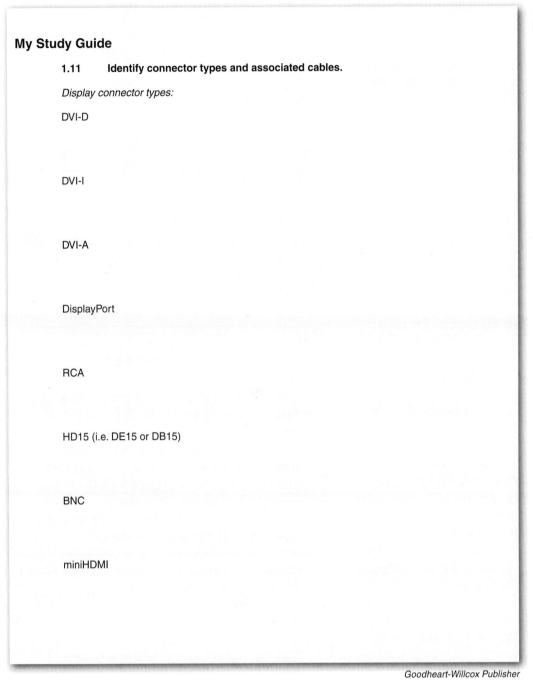

My Study Guide

1.11   **Identify connector types and associated cables.**

Display connector types:

DVI-D

DVI-I

DVI-A

DisplayPort

RCA

HD15 (i.e. DE15 or DB15)

BNC

miniHDMI

Goodheart-Willcox Publisher

A study group can make exam preparation fun and provide you with the additional motivation you need to study. The members of the study group help keep one another on task. For example, you may plan to study every night for the next two weeks for three hours each night. However, when it comes to executing the plan, you may easily find a reason not to study. When two or more of you plan to study together, each member feels more obligated to meet at the established time.

The study group can also share some of the burden of exam preparation. Each member of the study group can take a particular area covered on the exam and write a set of questions for the other members. When you meet at your regularly scheduled time, you can exchange the questions. You can also share resources such as sample exams or websites that you have found helpful in your personal studies.

One word of caution, though, is to make sure the study group functions as a study group and not as a social group. A group of friends gathered for study can quickly get off track and spend a lot of time discussing football, movies, and other events. It is critical that the study group remains focused on the task at hand—exam preparation.

Take Practice Exams

Practice exams are an excellent way to determine your test readiness and to identify weak areas. You may discover that you do not know the printing process as well as you thought. Practice exams are an important ingredient to your exam preparation strategy. You can use the practice exams to design the content for your review sessions. After taking a practice exam, identify the topics you feel you need more help in. Make a list, and then review materials covering those topics.

There are numerous websites offering free on-line or downloadable practice exams. While many are quite reputable, some are rather questionable. There are hundreds of sample exams located throughout the Internet. These exams provide only a sampling of a full test bank. Some have been found to be flawed, misleading, and definitely designed to have the student fail. The marketing idea is to show the student how little they know about the subject so that he or she may be lured into purchasing the full test bank of questions. You may take the free sample exams because they still have many good questions, but do not consider them a true measure of your ability to pass the exam.

Many students want to score a 100 percent on their A+ Certification exam. They constantly take practice exams and may continuously achieve a score that is less than 100 percent. Because of this, they never feel prepared for an A+ Certification exam. While scoring a 100 percent on a practice exam is a worthy goal, it is unrealistic for many students. To determine if you are prepared to take an A+ Certification exam, consider a passing score of 80 percent on a practice exam as a good indication. Remember that a student who does pass the exam on the very first attempt is well

prepared and confident. A student who fails an A+ Certification exam is obviously not prepared and has not been committed to a set study schedule.

Schedule a Test Date

Scheduling a test date is an excellent component to add to the established study schedule. As soon as you think you know the amount of preparation you will need, set a time and date for the exam. Do not wait until you know the material in its entirety. Chances are you will most likely never feel you know the material 100 percent. Procrastinating when setting a test date will quickly put you out of date with the material you have studied. Set a date to give yourself a deadline for preparation.

> ## A+ Note
>
> The CompTIA exam often includes questions about items not specifically listed in the exam objectives. For example, there may be a question about the OSI model as related to networking. The CompTIA exam objectives serve the purpose as a general guide and are not all-inclusive of the exam parameters. Be prepared for possible topics not precisely identified by the objective outline.

Sample CompTIA A+ 220-801 Exam

The following is a practice exam intended to simulate the type and depth of questions commonly encountered on the CompTIA A+ 220-801 exam. The sample exam is divided by domain. The real exam is not. The real exam questions do correlate closely by percentages as presented in the CompTIA A+ objectives, but the test is not divided into a defined sequence of domain areas as in this practice test. The practice test has been divided into domain sections so that you can better identify the areas in which you need additional preparation. Each group of exam questions for a domain is preceded by an abbreviated copy of the related objectives. Always check the CompTIA website for the very latest list of detailed objectives. The objective contents can change at any time.

Domain 1.0—PC Hardware

- 1.1 Configure and apply BIOS settings.
- 1.2 Differentiate between motherboard components, their purposes, and properties.
- 1.3 Compare and contrast RAM types and features.
- 1.4 Install and configure expansion cards.
- 1.5 Install and configure storage devices and use appropriate media.
- 1.6 Differentiate among various CPU types and features and select the appropriate cooling method.
- 1.7 Compare and contrast various connection interfaces and explain their purpose.
- 1.8 Install an appropriate power supply based on a given scenario.
- 1.9 Evaluate and select appropriate components for a custom configuration to meet customer specifications or needs.
- 1.10 Given a scenario, evaluate types and features of display devices.
- 1.11 Identify connector types and associated cables.

Domain 1.0—Practice Exam Questions 1–36

1. Which computer component normally contains firmware required to start the computer boot operation?
   a. Hard disk drive
   b. RAM
   c. BIOS
   d. CPU

2. An ATX12V motherboard typically has a _____-pin power connector.
   a. 12
   b. 24
   c. 16
   d. 32

3. What name is used to describe the physical shape of a motherboard?
   a. Outline
   b. Frame size
   c. Case factor
   d. Form factor

4. Which slot type provides the highest data transfer rate?
   a. PCI
   b. ISA
   c. PCIe
   d. PCI-X

5. What is the theoretical maximum data transfer rate of IEEE 802.11b?
   a. 1 Mbps
   b. 5 Mbps
   c. 11 Mbps
   d. 54 Mbps

6. What is the purpose of a KVM switch?
   a. To increase the bandwidth of an Internet connection
   b. To increase security for a home office
   c. To reduce the number of computer station input and output devices
   d. To allow more than one user to share two or more desktop computers

7. The purpose of CPU cache is to _____.
   a. temporarily store data
   b. create the digital clock signal used by the CPU
   c. synchronize IRQ signals with other motherboard components
   d. store BIOS setup configuration data

8. Which two port types are used to connect to an internal HDD? (Select two.)
   a. SATA
   b. PATA
   c. USB
   d. FireWire

9. What is another name for FireWire?
   a. RS-232
   b. RJ-45
   c. BNC
   d. IEEE-1394

10. Which partition typically has no drive letter assigned?
    a. Boot partition
    b. Active partition
    c. Reserved partition
    d. Extended partition

11. What should be applied between a new CPU and the CPU heat sink?
    a. A thin film of lightweight oil
    b. A thermal compound paste
    c. Ceramic glue to ensure a tight fit
    d. The surface area must remain absolutely clean; nothing should be applied to the surface of a CPU.

12. What is the maximum amount of RAM recognized by 32-bit Windows operating systems?
    a. 1 GB
    b. 4 GB
    c. 16 GB
    d. 1 TB

13. Which file system is associated with CD technologies?
    a. FAT12
    b. FAT16
    c. FAT32
    d. UDF

14. What type of device would connect to the motherboard port in the following exhibit?

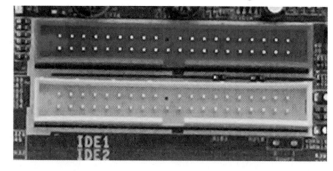

    a. CRT
    b. HDD
    c. FDD
    d. SCSI

15. Which set of voltage levels are associated with a standard ATX power supply?
    a. 3.3, 5, 12
    b. 6, 12, 18
    c. 3.3, 6.6, 18.8
    d. 3.3, 12, 24

16. Which is the correct sequence for installing a PATA hard disk drive?
    a. Install the hard drive into the drive bay, set the selection jumper to slave or master, format the hard disk drive, and create a primary partition.
    b. Partition the hard drive, format the hard drive, set the selection jumper to slave or master, and install the hard drive into the drive bay.
    c. Set the selection jumper to slave or master, install the hard drive into the hard drive bay, partition the drive, and format the partition.
    d. Install the hard disk drive into the hard drive bay, format the hard disk drive, partition the drive, and set the selection jumper to slave or master.

17. Which port is commonly used to support flash drives?
    a. PS/2
    b. USB
    c. IEEE 1394
    d. DB-15

18. How many hard drives are required for a RAID 1 system?
    a. 1
    b. 2
    c. 3
    d. Any number can be used.

19. Which CPU type is manufactured by AMD?
    a. Pentium
    b. Core i7
    c. FX
    d. Celeron

20. A customer wants to ensure her data is protected from loss caused by a power failure. She also wants to protect her data from loss caused by a hard disk drive failure. Which solution would you recommend?
    a. Install a UPS and a RAID 1 system.
    b. Install a tape backup unit and a power strip with surge protection.
    c. Install a UPS and a DVD writer, which can be used to perform daily backups.
    d. Install a dual power supply and a RAID 0 system.

21. Which PC computer component tests hardware devices and loads the boot loader program?
    a. Operating system
    b. BIOS
    c. Hard disk drive
    d. RAM

22. What is the name of the CPU feature that supports multiple paths for data processing through each core?
    a. Flash Flow
    b. Flash Bus
    c. Hyperthreading
    d. Throttling

23. Which two devices are commonly connected to the south bridge? (Select two.)
    a. Mouse
    b. Keyboard
    c. DIMM
    d. Video Card

24. What is the data rate for a USB 3.0 port?
    a. 1 GB
    b. 2 GB
    c. 3 GB
    d. 5 GB

25. Where do you change the boot order so that the DVD is the first place the computer looks for an operating system?
    a. In the Msconfig utility
    b. In the BIOS setup
    c. In **Control Panel | Admin Tools**
    d. In the boot.ini configuration file

26. What are the two power options associated with shutting down a Windows 7 laptop?
    a. Standby and Suspend
    b. Sleep and Hibernate
    c. Restart and Sleep
    d. Snooze and Nap

27. How many pins are on a DDR2 SO laptop memory module?
    a. 100
    b. 168
    c. 200
    d. 204

28. Where in Control Panel would you disable a hardware device?
    a. Power Options
    b. Administrative Tools
    c. Device Manager
    d. Devices and Printers

29. Which type of motherboard interface would you use for an SLI graphics card configuration?
    a. ISA
    b. AGP
    c. PCI
    d. PCIe

30. A client reports that his computer date and time on the taskbar is always incorrect every time he boots his computer. What is *most likely* causing the problem?
    a. The CPU is going bad.
    b. The power supply connection is loose.
    c. The BIOS battery is bad.
    d. The OS has a corrupt driver file.

31. What is the maximum amount of RAM recognized by the Windows 7 64-bit operating system?
    a. 16 GB
    b. 32 GB
    c. 128 GB
    d. 1 TB

32. How do you upgrade the BIOS?
    a. Remove the CMOS chip and replace it with the newest version from the manufacturer.
    b. The BIOS is automatically upgraded each time you install the latest Windows service pack.
    c. BIOS cannot be upgraded. You must replace the motherboard.
    d. Download the BIOS upgrade from the BIOS manufacturer and then flash the BIOS.

33. What Windows operating system feature is used to augment system RAM?
    a. Page file
    b. EFS
    c. XP Mode
    d. DMA

34. Which command line tool is used to inspect and create a partition in Windows 7?
    a. Fdisk
    b. Format
    c. Diskpart
    d. Msifo32

35. What is the default disk format option used for Windows 7?
    a. FAT16
    b. FAT32
    c. NTFS
    d. EFS

36. What is an MSDS?
    a. It protects hardware items from electrical shock.
    b. It protects technicians from electrical shock.
    c. It provides instructions about how to handle specific materials.
    d. It provides information about the proper technique to install computer components.

Domain 2.0—Networking

- 2.1 Identify types of network cables and connectors.
- 2.2 Categorize characteristics of connectors and cabling.
- 2.3 Explain properties and characteristics of TCP/IP.
- 2.4 Explain common TCP and UDP ports, protocols, and their purpose.
- 2.5 Compare and contrast wireless networking standards and encryption types.
- 2.6 Install, configure, and deploy a SOHO wireless/wired router using appropriate settings.
- 2.7 Compare and contrast Internet connection types and features.
- 2.8 Identify various types of networks.
- 2.9 Compare and contrast network devices, their functions, and features.
- 2.10 Given a scenario, use appropriate networking tools.

Domain 2.0—Practice Exam Questions 37–60

37. Which type of network cable uses an F-type connector?
    a. STP
    b. T567A
    c. Fiber
    d. Coaxial

38. Which subnet mask is associated with a Class B network?
    a. .000.000.000.255
    b. 255.255.255.000
    c. 255.255.000.000
    d. 255.000.000.00

39. Which is an example of an IPv6 address?
    a. 192.168.1.01
    b. AF 2B 12 C2 3t4 D1
    c. Fe80::2bc3:3c3b:4212:4f23
    d. 10100011011101

40. Which type of device automatically issues IPv4 addresses?
    a. WINS server
    b. DHCP server
    c. DNS server
    d. NetBIOS server

41. Which IPv4 address is an example of a APIPA address?
    a. 192.168.10.100
    b. Fe80:2bc3:3c3b:4212:4f23%12
    c. 169.254.12.43
    d. 10.10.10.1

42. Which port number is associated with DNS?
    a. 21
    b. 53
    c. 80
    d. 3389

43. Which port number is assigned to POP3 mail?
    a. 21
    b. 80
    c. 110
    d. 443

44. What type of connector is in the exhibit?

    a. STP
    b. F-type
    c. RJ-45
    d. DB-232

45. Which application would *most likely* need QoS to function properly?
    a. Telephone modem
    b. VoIP
    c. Email
    d. Instant Messaging

46. Which cable type provides no protection from EMI?
    a. STP
    b. Fiber
    c. RG-6
    d. UTP

47. Select the most accurate answer based on the information provided by the exhibit.

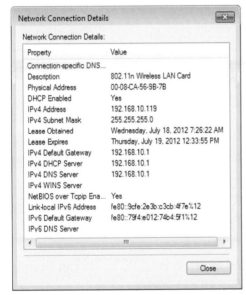

    a. The network connection has been disabled.
    b. The computer has been assigned a private IP address.
    c. The computer cannot access the Internet because it has no IPv4 WINS server address assigned.
    d. The IPv6 network address is corrupted.

48. A computer is not connecting to the Internet but is connecting to local network shares. You inspect the computer assigned IP address and see that it is 169.254.10.1. What is *most likely* the problem?
    a. The network card is defective.
    b. The WINS server is down.
    c. The DHCP server has failed.
    d. The network cable has become disconnected from the PC.

49. Which command would you use to identify a computer MAC address?
    a. **ping**
    b. **tracert**
    c. **ipconfig**
    d. **msconfig**

50. What is the loopback address associated with IPv4?
    a. 192.168.0.1
    b. 127.0.0.1
    c. 10.0.0.1
    d. 255.255.255.255

51. Which type of address must be manually configured?
    a. APIPA
    b. Static
    c. Dynamic
    d. DHCP

52. Which protocol is designed to support network file sharing?
    a. SNMP
    b. SMB
    c. SSH
    d. SFTP

53. At which two frequencies does 802.11n operate? (Select two.)
    a. 2.4 MHz
    b. 2.4 GHz
    c. 5.0 MHz
    d. 5.0 GHz

54. Which encryption type provides the least security?
    a. WEP
    b. WPA
    c. WPA2
    d. AES

55. What is the name of the technology that only lets specific wireless devices connect to a wireless access point?
    a. Channel selection
    b. MAC filtering
    c. Dynamic addressing
    d. Port forwarding

56. Which protocol is used to map all local network addresses to one single Internet address?
    a. DMA
    b. TCP
    c. NAT
    d. UDP

57. Which protocol or standard is designed to allow a user to connect a wireless device to a secure wireless device without the need to enter a passphrase or key? The device typically uses a push button.
    a. Mac filter
    b. Dynamic addressing
    c. WPS
    d. FTP

58. Which are the two major types of ISDN services available?
    a. Static and dynamic
    b. Fixed cost and variable
    c. BRI and PRI
    d. DSL and Cable

59. A home office uses a centralized network switch to connect all computers and printers using UTP cable. Which network topology would this physical arrangement most closely match?
    a. Mesh
    b. Star
    c. Bus
    d. Ring

60. Which tool can be used to measure ohms?
    a. Loopback plug
    b. Multimeter
    c. ODM
    d. Toner probe

Domain 3.0—Laptops

- 3.1 Install and configure laptop hardware and components.
- 3.2 Compare and contrast the components within the display of a laptop.
- 3.3 Compare and contrast laptop features.

Domain 3.0—Practice Exam Questions 61–70

61. What is the purpose of a laptop inverter?
    a. To reveal encrypted file content.
    b. To change a SATA drive connection to a PATA drive connection.
    c. To change a WAN connection to a LAN connection.
    d. To change DC voltage to AC voltage, which is required for the laptop backlight.

62. Which type of battery is most commonly found in laptop computers?
    a. Li-ion
    b. NiCd
    c. NiMH
    d. Lead acid

63. What does *Fn* represent on a laptop keyboard?
    a. Fast network
    b. Function key
    c. Fixed network
    d. Find now

64. What type of HDD is used internally on a modern laptop computer?
    a. 2.5 SATA
    b. 3.5 SATA
    c. 2.5 PATA
    d. 3.5 PATA

65. How many Type II PC cards can fit into a laptop access port?
    a. One
    b. Two
    c. Three
    d. Four

66. A customer complains that her laptop screen has grown very dim over time and cannot be brightened anymore. What is *most likely* causing the problem?
    a. The battery is getting weak.
    b. The charging unit is defective.
    c. The inverter is defective.
    d. The CRT pixels are burning out.

67. Which is the resolution of a WUXGA screen?
    a. 600 × 400
    b. 960 × 800
    c. 1280 × 900
    d. 1920 × 1200

68. Which type of memory module is used for laptop computer RAM?
    a. SODIMM 204-pin DDR3
    b. DIMM 240-pin DDR3
    c. SIMM 72-pin
    d. SIMM 168-pin

69. Where would you configure an additional monitor for a laptop computer running Windows 7?
    a. Administrative Tools
    b. Windows Mobility Center
    c. Device Manager
    d. Display

70. Which standard provides the lowest bandwidth?
    a. IEEE 802.11b
    b. IEEE 802.11n
    c. IEEE 802.11g
    d. Bluetooth

Domain 4.0—Printers

- 4.1 Explain the differences between the various printer types and summarize the associated imaging process.
- 4.2 Given a scenario, install and configure printers.
- 4.3 Given a scenario, perform printer maintenance.

Domain 4.0—Practice Exam Questions 71–80

71. Which step of the laser printer process uses laser light to write images on the laser printer drum?
    a. Processing
    b. Developing
    c. Exposing
    d. Fusing

72. What term is used to describe the temporary storage of a file before it is sent to a printer?
    a. Writing
    b. Spooling
    c. Imaging
    d. Share

73. Which are the two most common methods of connecting an all-in-one printer to a computer? (Select two.)
    a. USB cable
    b. RF Wireless
    c. RS-232
    d. Serial cable

74. A laser printer produces copies that easily smear when touched. What laser printer component is *most likely* causing the problem?
    a. Laser
    b. Drum
    c. Fuser
    d. Transfer corona

75. You want to install the very latest printer drivers for a customer's printer. Where would you locate the latest drivers?
    a. At the Microsoft Support website
    b. On the latest version of the Windows operating system installation DVD
    c. On the printer manufacturer's website
    d. On the DVD that accompanied the printer when purchased

76. You have a printer configured to share with your HomeGroup. The printer was working fine yesterday but today you cannot print. What is *most likely* the cause of the problem?
    a. The printer is out of toner.
    b. The printer is offline.
    c. The printer is no longer shared.
    d. The printer driver is corrupt.

77. Which would be the most common impact printer maintenance task?
    a. Replacing the impact head
    b. Replacing the ribbon cartridge
    c. Replacing the toner cartridge
    d. Replacing the pickup rollers

78. Which laser printer part is *most likely* the cause of a printer suddenly printing blank paper?
    a. Low toner
    b. Defective transfer corona wire
    c. Defective fuser
    d. Tripped electrical breaker

79. Which printer connection type requires direct line of sight to successfully transfer information from a mobile device to a printer?
    a. 802.11x
    b. Bluetooth
    c. Infrared
    d. Wi-Fi

80. Which item is required for inkjet head alignment?
    a. Compressed air
    b. Flat tip screwdriver
    c. Toner wrench
    d. Software application

Domain 5.0—Operational Procedures

- 5.1 Given a scenario, use appropriate safety procedures.
- 5.2 Explain environmental impacts and the purpose of environmental controls.
- 5.3 Given a scenario, demonstrate proper communication and professionalism.
- 5.4 Explain the fundamentals of dealing with prohibited content/activity.

Domain 5.0—Practice Exam Questions 81–90

81. Which is the proper fire extinguisher type for electrical fires?
    a. Class A
    b. Class B
    c. Class C
    d. Class D

82. What organization is responsible for developing worker safety guidelines?
    a. FCC
    b. IEEE
    c. Microsoft
    d. OSHA

83. Which is the proper way to dispose of a CRT monitor?
    a. Pack the CRT inside a cardboard box and return it to the manufacturer.
    b. Dispose of the CRT at recycling facility.
    c. Place the CRT inside a metal dumpster and then shatter the screen with a metal hammer while wearing eye protection.
    d. Seal the CRT inside a 55-gallon metal drum and then place it by roadside for regular garbage pickup service.

84. Which type of document would contain information about the safe handling of a particular toner cartridge?
    a. Shipping packing slip
    b. Invoice
    c. MSDS
    d. Original order form

85. What should you do before replacing a computer electronic component or device? (Select two.)
    a. Wipe all hand tools with alcohol to ensure all containments and oily residue are removed.
    b. Follow the recommended ESD procedures.
    c. Disconnect the electrical power.
    d. Review the BIOS setup configuration.

86. What is the best protection from electrical surges?
    a. UPS
    b. Electrostatic wrist straps
    c. ESD mats
    d. Oscilloscope

87. What should you do when dealing with customers?
    a. Talk using technical terms when discussing the computer problem so that the customer is impressed with your knowledge.
    b. Avoid using technical jargon when discussing computer problems with the customer.
    c. Explain procedures to a customer in a stern manner so that they clearly understand the importance of your work.
    d. Always avoid direct eye contact with the customer while explaining the repair procedure.

88. The tracking and documentation of computer evidence is referred to as which?
    a. Chain of custody
    b. Modus operandi
    c. Evidence buffering
    d. Evidence status

89. A customer complains that he loses power because of thunderstorms in the summer. As a result, he often loses data while working on his computer. Which is the best solution for his problem?
    a. Tell him to turn his computer off before a thunderstorm and do not use it for at least twenty minutes after the storm has passed.
    b. Tell him that power and data loss caused by thunderstorms is common. Get used to it.
    c. Tell him that he needs a better grounding system, which will result in a better electrical path for the lightning, thus avoiding the direct hit to the computer system.
    d. Tell him that he needs to use a UPS to provide surge protection and to provide constant power to the computer system for a limited time.

90. According to the troubleshooting steps outlined by CompTIA, what is the first thing you should do when troubleshooting a computer on a service call?
    a. Ask the customer probing questions to pin down what exactly is the problem.
    b. Test the 120-volt power outlet to ensure a proper voltage level.
    c. Check if the computer is still under warranty.
    d. Run a credit check on the customer to be sure he or she can pay for the service.

Sample CompTIA A+ 220-802 Exam

The following practice exam is intended to simulate the type and depth of questions commonly encountered on the CompTIA A+ 220-802 exam. The structure of the 220-802 exam is similar to the 220-801 exam except that it is considered to be more difficult. The sample exam is divided by domain so that you can better identify the areas in which you may need additional preparation. Always check the CompTIA website for the very latest list of objectives. The objective contents can change at any time.

Domain 1.0—Operating Systems

- 1.1 Compare and contrast the features and requirements of various Microsoft operating systems.
- 1.2 Given a scenario, install and configure the operating system using the most appropriate method.
- 1.3 Given a scenario, use appropriate command line tools.
- 1.4 Given a scenario, use appropriate operating system features and tools.
- 1.5 Given a scenario, use Control Panel utilities (the items are organized by "classic view/large icons" in Windows).
- 1.6 Setup and configure Windows networking on a client/desktop.
- 1.7 Perform preventive maintenance procedures using appropriate tools.
- 1.8 Explain the differences among basic OS security settings.
- 1.9 Explain the basics of client-side virtualization.

Domain 1.0—Practice Exam Questions 1–30.

1. Which is the correct file structure path by default for the My Documents folder for a user named Student1? Assume the operating system is Windows 7.
   a. C:/Windows/Student1/My Documents
   b. C:/AllUsers/Student1/Library/My Documents
   c. C:/Users/Student1/My Documents
   d. C:/Windows/My Documents/Student1

2. Which operating system supports the Windows "XP Mode?" (Select all that apply.)
   a. Windows Vista
   b. Windows XP
   c. Windows 7
   d. Windows 8

3. Which Microsoft Windows tool is used to create a disk image?
   a. Backup and Restore
   b. Msconfig
   c. Robocopy
   d. Computer Management

4. Which type of installation requires the sysprep tool?
   a. Clean install
   b. System upgrade
   c. System migration
   d. Unattended installation

5. Which is the correct order for installation of a multiple-boot system using the Windows Vista and Windows 7 operating systems? The hard disk drive has been prepared with two partitions. The first partition is primary partition C, and the second partition is D.
   a. Install Windows Vista on the primary partition C and then perform a clean installation of Windows 7 on C.
   b. Install Windows 7 on the primary partition C and then install Windows Vista on the second partition D.
   c. Install Windows Vista on the second partition D and then install Windows 7 on the primary partition C.
   d. Install Windows Vista on primary partition C and then install Windows 7 on partition D.

6. What command is used to convert partition D, which is a FAT32 partition, into an NTFS file system?
   a. **convert d:/fs:ntfs**
   b. **c: convert d:/ntfs**
   c. **convert FAT32 NTFS**
   d. **convert NTFS d:fat32**

7. Which command line tool will verify a network connection through several routers across the Internet and provide the time required for each hop?
   a. Ping
   b. Tracert
   c. Nslookup
   d. Net View

8. Which command line tool will check and verify the integrity of system files and replace them if necessary?
   a. Bootrec
   b. Sfc
   c. Fixboot
   d. Fxmbr

9. Which system tool can be used to temporarily disable certain programs from running at system startup?
   a. Sysprep
   b. Sysconfig32
   c. Msconfig
   d. Mstsc

10. Which command entered into the **Search** box will start a Remote Desktop connection?
    a. **remote**
    b. **mstsc**
    c. **regedit**
    d. **services**

11. Which operating system first introduced HomeGroup?
    a. Windows XP
    b. Windows Vista
    c. Windows 7
    d. Windows 8

12. Which operating system first introduced the Windows Action Center?
    a. Windows XP
    b. Windows Vista
    c. Windows 7
    d. Windows 8

13. Which power setting saves your work to the hard drive and takes the longest period to wake?
    a Hibernation
    b. Suspend
    c. Sleep
    d. Pause

14. Which tab in the **Internet Options** dialog box do you use to change the default home page address for Microsoft Internet Explorer?
    a. **General**
    b. **Security**
    c. **Connections**
    d. **Privacy**

15. Under which tab in the **Internet Options** dialog box do you access the Parental Controls feature and configuration?
    a. **General**
    b. **Security**
    c. **Privacy**
    d. **Content**

16. Which file types are changed when performing a system restore? (Select all that apply.)
    a. Email contents
    b. Programs
    c. System files
    d. Register settings

17. Which is *not* a user account type?
    a. Administrator
    b. Guest
    c. Standard
    d. Primary

18. What is the primary function of the DXDIAG tool?
    a. Detect network connection problems.
    b. Check the system registry for errors.
    c. Check multimedia features.
    d. Check partition fragmentation.

19. Which subnet mask is associated with a Class C network?
    a. 255.255.255.000
    b. 255.255.000.000
    c. 000.000.255.255
    d. 254.254.254.000

20. Which is the best definition of a system image created in Windows Backup and Restore?
    a. A copy of all drivers that are required to boot the computer system.
    b. An exact copy of an entire drive or partition.
    c. A copy of the operating system without user documents and settings.
    d. An exact copy of all required system files and drivers, excluding user files.

21. What is *not* shared by default when joining a Windows HomeGroup?
    a. Printer
    b. Pictures
    c. Music
    d. Documents

22. What is the default workgroup name for Windows 7?
    a. HomeGroup
    b. Workgroup
    c. Domain
    d. Windows 7

23. What does the acronym DNS represent?
    a. Domain Network System
    b. Domain Name System
    c. Dominant Network System
    d. Domain Network Services

24. Which is the correct path to **Windows Update**?
    a. Right-click **Computer** and then select **Updates** from the shortcut menu.
    b. Right-click **Computer** and then select **Manage** from the shortcut menu.
    c. **Start | All Programs | Windows Update**
    d. **Start | All Programs | Accessories | Updates**

25. What are the three network locations associated with the Network and Sharing Center?
    a. Home, Office, and Public
    b. Home, Work, and Public
    c. Home, School, and Public
    d. Home, Public, and Domain

26. What is true about the network connection based on the screen capture of the network adapter details?

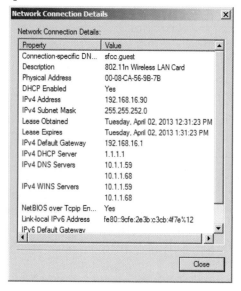

Property	Value
Connection-specific DN...	sfcc.guest
Description	802.11n Wireless LAN Card
Physical Address	00-08-CA-56-9B-7B
DHCP Enabled	Yes
IPv4 Address	192.168.16.90
IPv4 Subnet Mask	255.255.252.0
Lease Obtained	Tuesday, April 02, 2013 12:31:23 PM
Lease Expires	Tuesday, April 02, 2013 1:31:23 PM
IPv4 Default Gateway	192.168.16.1
IPv4 DHCP Server	1.1.1.1
IPv4 DNS Servers	10.1.1.59
	10.1.1.68
IPv4 WINS Servers	10.1.1.59
	10.1.1.68
NetBIOS over Tcpip En...	Yes
Link-local IPv6 Address	fe80::9cfe:2e3b:c3cb:4f7e%12
IPv6 Default Gateway	

a. The network is connected using a 100BaseT connection.
b. The computer is connected to the network using a private IPv4 address.
c. The computer is connected to the network using a public IPv4 address.
d. The computer cannot establish a connection with the DNS server.

27. Which port number is associated with Windows SMB file sharing?
a. 55
b. 110
c. 445
d. 1033

28. You are performing a remote network operating system installation across a network. The target computer has no OS installed on the hard drive. Which is required to be at the computer machine to start the operating system installation?
a. DVD drive
b. PXE
c. A copy of Microsoft Office
d. Notepad

29. What task must be performed first after physically adding a new additional hard disk drive to a Windows 7 computer?
a. The hard disk drive must be assigned a drive letter.
b. The hard disk drive must be initiated.
c. The hard disk drive must be formatted.
d. The hard disk drive must be erased.

30. Which network system provides the most secure connection between two computers across the Internet?
a. 801.11a
b. 802.11g
c. VPN
d. Workgroup membership

Domain 2.0—Security

- 2.1 Apply and use common prevention methods.
- 2.2 Compare and contrast common security threats.
- 2.3 Implement security best practices to secure a workstation.
- 2.4 Given a scenario, use the appropriate data destruction/disposal method.
- 2.5 Given a scenario, secure a SOHO wireless network.
- 2.6 Given a scenario, secure a SOHO wired network.

Domain 2.0—Practice Exam Questions 31–50

31. Which command is used to access the local group policy editor for Windows 7?
a. **poledit.exe**
b. **gpedit.msc**
c. **local.msc**
d. **grplocal.exe**

32. A user receives an email stating that there has been an attempt to access her eBay account. The email requests that the user select the link in the email and reset her password. When she opens the link, she is prompted to enter her old password before entering her new password and then confirm the new password. This is an example of which type of security threat?
    a. Rootkit
    b. Worm
    c. Phishing
    d. Piggybacking

33. Which is the best practice to prevent phishing in the corporate environment?
    a. Installing a good antivirus program.
    b. Disable the autorun feature for the disc drive system.
    c. Set the Internet browser security setting to high.
    d. Educate the user.

34. Which is the quickest way to remove or counter a rootkit?
    a. Perform a clean installation of the operating system.
    b. Scan the system registry and then restore the default settings.
    c. Start the computer system in Safe Mode and then run a good antivirus program.
    d. Install and then run a good antispam tool.

35. Which is an example of a biometric security system?
    a. RFID chip
    b. Photo ID worker badge
    c. PIN card
    d. Fingerprint scanner

36. Which is the recommended minimal length of a secure password?
    a. 4 characters
    b. 8 characters
    c. 16 characters
    d. 24 characters

37. Which example is the strongest password?
    a. BobbyYoung12345
    b. SecretPassword54321
    c. $ecurePa$$word123
    d. xcdexveaztq

38. Which is *not* a standard NTFS permission?
    a. Hide
    b. Full Control
    c. Modify
    d. Read & Execute

39. Which Windows file system(s) can use EFS?
    a. FAT16
    b. FAT32
    c. NTFS
    d. Any Microsoft Windows compatible file system can use EFS.

40. Which editions of Windows 7 support BitLocker? (Select all that apply.)
    a. Windows 7 Home
    b. Windows 7 Professional
    c. Windows 7 Ultimate
    d. Windows 7 Enterprise

41. Which Windows 7 application is designed to protect a PC against spyware?
    a. Defender
    b. BitLocker
    c. Msconfig
    d. Firewall

42. Your company is using a software application provided by another organization over the Internet. The software application uses port 2323. What would you do to allow the employees to use the software application from the organization?
    a. Change Internet Explorer security level from high to low.
    b. Establish a guest account for each local user to use only to access the software application from the other organization.
    c. Change each user's computer location from Private to Public.
    d. Configure the firewall for an exception for the software application.

43. Which Windows application would you use to see if there have been attempts by unauthorized person(s) to access a computer?
    a. Msconfig
    b. Event Viewer
    c. Device Manager
    d. Internet Explorer

44. Which is the best way to eliminate or disable annoying messages that appear when a standard user attempts to make a change in the computer configuration of a Windows 7 system?
    a. Change the user account from standard to administrator.
    b. Change the user account from standard to guest.
    c. Change the User Account Control settings to never notify.
    d. Change the Firewall setting from Public to Private location.

45. What are two advantages of using a virtual smart card in place of a physical smart card? (Select two.)
    a. A virtual smart card will provide better encryption.
    b. A virtual smart card is always available.
    c. A virtual smart card is more economical.
    d. A virtual smart card is much more secure than a physical smart card.

46. An unauthorized person entering a secure area by closely following an employee through a locked door is an example of which type of security breech?
    a. Spoofing
    b. Mascarade
    c. Tailgating
    d. Barnstorming

47. Which is the best method to prevent unauthorized access to a wireless router from an unauthorized portable computer?
    a. Change the SSID.
    b. Configure a MAC filter.
    c. Place the wireless router inside a secure closet.
    d. Use only 802.11n devices.

48. Where is the TPM located on a computer system?
    a. On the motherboard
    b. In the hard disk drive
    c. Virtually located in RAM
    d. On the network adapter

49. What is multi-factor authentication?
    a. When two or more security measures are used, such as something you know and something you have
    b. When two or more encryption keys are used to access a resource
    c. When two persons are required to enter a facility
    d. When an encryption cypher key is run two or more times during the encryption process

50. What would you do to restrict access to a specific folder to only a few select persons working in an office?
    a. Place the folder in a hidden directory and only tell specific people the location.
    b. Place the folder in a BitLocker drive and provide only specific people with the password.
    c. Set folder permissions to only allow specific persons to access the folder.
    d. Encrypt the folder and then place a copy in each person's Document folder.

Domain 3.0—Mobile Devices

- 3.1 Explain the basic features of mobile operating systems.
- 3.2 Establish basic network connectivity and configure email.
- 3.3 Compare and contrast methods for securing mobile devices.
- 3.4 Compare and contrast hardware differences in regards to tablets and laptops.
- 3.5 Execute and configure mobile device synchronization.

Domain 3.0—Practice Exam Questions 51–58

51. Which operating system is used by Apple mobile devices?
    a. Android
    b. Windows CE
    c. iOS
    d. OS X

52. Which operating system is not considered open source? (Select two.)
    a. Linux
    b. iOS
    c. Microsoft
    d. Android

53. Which two characteristics best describe the physical attributes of a tablet as compared to a desktop computer? (Select two.)
    a. Tablets have very few field service replacement parts.
    b. Tablets use AAA batteries.
    c. Tablets use flash memory rather than an HDD.
    d. Tablets have more ports than a standard desktop.

54. Matching the data on a mobile device to a laptop or desktop is referred to as which?
    a. Tethering
    b. Synchronization
    c. Matching
    d. Clouding

55. Which type of CPU would *most likely* be installed on a tablet device manufactured in 2012?
    a. ARM
    b. Core i3
    c. Core
    d. Phenom II

56. What two pieces of information are required to be identified by the user when connecting to a secure wireless device? (Select two.)
    a. SSID
    b. Passcode
    c. MAC
    d. IP address

57. Which type of connection is most commonly used to synchronize a smartphone with a desktop PC? (Select two.)
    a. RS-232
    b. USB
    c. Wi-Fi
    d. SATA

58. Which security practice is designed to protect sensitive data stored on a mobile device that is missing or has been stolen?
    a. System reset
    b. Remote wipe
    c. Pairing
    d. SSL configuration

Domain 4.0—Troubleshooting

- 4.1 Given a scenario, explain the troubleshooting theory.
- 4.2 Given a scenario, troubleshoot common problems related to motherboards, RAM, CPU, and power with appropriate tools.
- 4.3 Given a scenario, troubleshoot hard drives and RAID arrays with appropriate tools.
- 4.4 Given a scenario, troubleshoot common video and display issues.
- 4.6 Given a scenario, troubleshoot operating system problems with appropriate tools.
- 4.7 Given a scenario, troubleshoot common security issues with appropriate tools and best practices.
- 4.8 Given a scenario, troubleshoot and repair common laptop issues while adhering to the appropriate procedures.
- 4.9 Given a scenario, troubleshoot printers with appropriate tools.

Domain 4.0—Practice Exam Questions 59–90

59. What is the last step of the troubleshooting process?
    a. Establish a plan of action to resolve future problems.
    b. Document findings, actions, and outcomes.
    c. Verify full system functionality.
    d. Confirm theory and solutions.

60. After a PC has completed the boot process, you notice that the time and date are incorrect. What is *most likely* the cause?
    a. System updates have not been configured automatically.
    b. The CMOS battery has failed.
    c. The HDD is about to fail.
    d. The system is overheating because of excessive dust accumulation in the heat sink cooling fins.

61. You hear a clicking noise during the boot process and periodically while using the computer. What is *most likely* the cause of the clicking noise?
    a. HDD
    b. CMOS
    c. RAM
    d. CPU

62. During the boot process you hear multiple beeps coming from the computer. After the POST is complete, the display is blank. Where would you look to decipher the beep codes?
    a. Microsoft TechNet website.
    b. The HDD manufacturer website.
    c. The motherboard manufacturer website.
    d. The display manufacturer website.

63. A computer is approximately five months old. The user says that the computer ran fine at first but over time it seems to be responding slower and slower and it takes much longer for the computer to boot. What procedure would you try first?
    a. Check the amount of RAM and add or replace it if necessary.
    b. Make sure the antivirus program is installed, enabled, and working.
    c. Run Msconfig and then remove all unnecessary programs.
    d. Check the BIOS configuration and verify all hardware devices, especially the HDD, have been correctly detected.

64. A computer system fails to complete the POST. What is *most likely* the source of the problem?
    a. One or more of the operating system essential files are corrupted.
    b. The administrator user account has been compromised.
    c. A hardware device has had a catastrophic failure.
    d. One or more software applications installed on the HDD are corrupted.

65. A user complains that when he uses his laptop, the Internet connection is slow or intermittent. What is *most likely* the cause?
    a. The wireless network card is incorrectly configured.
    b. The wrong type of encryption is configured for the wireless access point.
    c. The laptop is configured for IPv6, not IPv4.
    d. The laptop is too far from the wireless access point.

66. Which tool would you select to make a network cable connection to a 110 termination block?
    a. Standard wire crimper
    b. Punch down tool
    c. Wire stripper
    d. Flat tip screwdriver

67. Which command would you issue from the command prompt to view the computer assigned IP address?
    a. **ping**
    b. **ipconfig**
    c. **net**
    d. **tracert**

68. Which key or key combination would you press during the boot process to access the **Advanced Boot Options** menu for Windows 7?
    a. [F8]
    b. [Ctrl] [Alt] [Del]
    c. [Ctrl] [Z]
    d. [F4]

69. How do you access the Windows Recovery Environment (WinRE) in Windows 7?
    a. Press [Ctrl] [Alt] [Del] during the POST.
    b. Press [F6] during the boot process.
    c. Place the Windows 7 installation DVD into the DVD drive and then reboot the computer.
    d. Enter **WinRE.msc** at the command prompt.

70. Which option in the **Advanced Boot Options** menu will start the computer with minimal drivers?
    a. **Safe Mode**
    b. **Last Known Good Configuration**
    c. **Disable Driver Signature Enforcement**
    d. **System Image Recovery**

71. Which selection is *not* a Windows 7 System Recovery option?
    a. **Startup Repair**
    b. **System Restore**
    c. **Windows Memory Diagnostics**
    d. **Registry Editor**

72. Which command would you enter at the command prompt to recover the Windows 7 bootmgr?
    a. **bootrec/fixboot**
    b. **fixboot/all**
    c. **fixboot**
    d. **bootrec/now**

73. A user installed an updated hardware driver for her computer and now the computer boots to a blue screen and freezes. Which method would you use to repair the computer?
    a. Reinstall the operating system using the installation DVD.
    b. Start the computer in Safe Mode and then roll back the device driver.
    c. Remove the offending hardware device and then reboot the computer.
    d. Start the computer in Safe Mode and then go to the command prompt and enter **bootrec/fixboot**.

74. Which command will produce the Windows 7 **System Configuration** dialog box?
    a. **msconfig**
    b. **regedit**
    c. **sfc**
    d. **system32**

75. Which Device Manager symbol is used to indicate a disabled device driver?
    a. Red *X*
    b. Yellow triangle
    c. Red stop sign
    d. The device will not appear in the list of devices when it is disabled.

76. Which of the following would *most likely* cause a BSOD error?
    a. Faulty or failed CPU fan
    b. Loose connection to a SATA drive
    c. Improperly-seated RAM module
    d. Misconfigured modem

77. Which command issued from the Windows 7 command prompt will check the HDD and automatically repair most errors?
    a. **chkdsk/R**
    b. **regedit/F**
    c. **chkdsk/F**
    d. **scandsk/F**

78. Which utility would you use to prevent a specific software application from loading at startup?
    a. Sysconfig
    b. Msconfig
    c. System32
    d. Chkdsk

79. Which command would you use from the Windows 7 Recovery Environment to rewrite the boot code for the MBR?
    a. **fdisk/boot**
    b. **bootrec.exe/fixboot**
    c. **fdisk/mbr**
    d. **mbr/repair**

80. You are troubleshooting a computer problem. The symptoms are three short beeps followed by two long beeps and no apparent video. What would be your next course of action?
    a. Search the Microsoft TechNet website using the key terms "three short beeps two long beeps no video."
    b. Consult the video card manual.
    c. Open **System Configuration** and then disable all startup programs.
    d. Search the motherboard firmware website using the key terms "three short beeps two long beeps."

81. Which log contains a list of all drivers that are loaded during system startup?
    a. ntblog.txt
    b. startup.txt
    c. repair.txt
    d. details.txt

82. Which command would you issue from the command prompt to view system information?
    a. **sysconfig**
    b. **msconfig**
    c. **system**
    d. **msifo32**

83. A user has recently installed a new printer driver and now the printer will not print at all. Which is the best method to recover from this issue without the possibility of changing other drivers or system file updates?
    a. Perform a clean system install and then install the latest service pack.
    b. Power off and disconnect the printer, and then power the printer back on and follow the screen prompts to install a new driver.
    c. Perform a System Restore from any recent restore point.
    d. Open **Device Manager**, select the printer, and then select **Roll Back Driver** option.

84. A Windows 7 computer fails to complete startup to the system logon. You suspect that one or more system files are corrupt. You can access the command prompt from the **Advanced Boot Options** menu. Which course of action would you choose to repair or replace system startup files?
    a. Run **fdisk/mbr.**
    b. Run **sfc/scannow.**
    c. Run **msconfig/repair.**
    d. Run **system32/repair.**

85. Which command will start the Problem Steps Recorder from the command prompt in Windows 7?
    a. **prbrec**
    b. **recorder**
    c. **psr**
    d. **problem**

86. A computer program is no longer responding. Which keyboard combination can be used to access Task Manager?
    a. [Ctrl] [Shift] [Del]
    b. [Ctrl] [Alt] [Del]
    c. [Ctrl] [F8]
    d. [Alt] [F8]

87. A laptop computer has a very dim display. Which component would you replace first?
    a. LCD inverter
    b. Video adapter card
    c. Display wiring harness
    d. Laptop battery

88. You are checking a customer's Windows 7 computer. Each time you boot the computer, you see a message on the display immediately following the POST. The message states, "Invalid partition table." Which hardware device is *most likely* the cause of the problem?
    a. CMOS battery
    b. HDD
    c. RAM
    d. CMOS

89. How do you access **System Restore** in Windows 7?
    a. **Start | All Programs | System Restore**
    b. **Start | All Programs | Accessories | System Tools | System Restore**
    c. Right-click **Computer**, select **Properties** from the shortcut menu, and then select the **System Restore** tab
    d. **Start | All Programs | Accessibility | System Restore**

90. Which item is commonly used for troubleshooting rather than substituting various hardware devices?
    a. POST card
    b. Multimeter
    c. Oscilloscope
    d. Tone generator

Scoring the Exam

Copy the following tables onto a separate sheet of paper. Use the tables to determine your readiness to take the CompTIA A+ 220-801 and CompTIA A+ 220-802 exams. Simply record in the appropriate column the number of questions you answered correctly. Then, place a *P* for "pass" in the "Pass or Fail" column if the number of questions you answered correctly is equal to or exceeds the number indicated in the "Number of Correctly Answered Questions Needed to Pass" column. Place an *F* for "fail" in the "Pass or Fail" column if the number of questions you answered correctly is less than the number indicated in the "Number of Correctly Answered Questions Needed to Pass" column. Please do *not* write in this book.

Remember, the actual exam pass or fail status is not expressed as a percentage. The exam uses a weighted calculation to determine a score from 100 to 900. A test with weighted questions means that not all questions have equal value. Some questions are worth more than others and have a special numerical value assigned to each. The exact numeric value is used to arrive at a weighted score between 100 minimum and 900 maximum.

A score of 80 or better on a practice exam indicates you are well prepared and ready to take the real CompTIA A+ exam. A passing score below 80 is considered marginal and indicates that you should do some additional preparation before taking the real exam. A score below 70 means you are not well prepared and should most definitely perform additional study.

You can look at the table and the scores you recorded to determine the areas you need to review the most. Many students perform poorly in the areas they are least interested in. For example, many students perform poorly on safety and environmental issues, printers and scanners, and security for the simple reason they spend little time studying this area and would rather concentrate on areas of more interest, such as personal computer components and operating systems.

After completing some additional study in each deficient area, take another A+ practice test. Check www.rmroberts.com for additional A+ practice exams. Also, check with your instructor for recommended sites for practice tests.

A+ Note

Never give up if you fail the exam. If you apply yourself and work hard toward your goal, you will surely accomplish the task at hand.

CompTIA A+ 220-801				
Domain	Number of Questions	Number of Correctly Answered Questions Needed to Pass	Number of Correct Answers	Pass or Fail
PC Hardware	36	25		
Networking	24	17		
Laptops	10	7		
Printers	10	7		
Operational Procedures	10	7		
Total	90	63		

CompTIA A+ 220-802				
Domain	Number of Questions	Number of Correctly Answered Questions Needed to Pass	Number of Correct Answers	Pass or Fail
Operating Systems	30	21		
Security	20	14		
Mobile Devices	8	6		
Troubleshooting	32	22		
Total	90	63		

Chapter Summary

- The examination objectives are categorized according to domains and are based on industry surveys that correlate exam content to actual job requirements.
- CompTIA recommends that a test candidate have at least 12 months of work experience. This is not a requirement.
- When reporting to the testing center, you must typically show two proofs of identification. Always check the requirements for identification before reporting to the testing center.
- The A+ Certification exams consist of multiple-choice and performance-based questions.
- To ensure success on an A+ Certification exam, establish a realistic study schedule and stick to it.
- Hands-on experience provides you with many of the required skills that are tested for on the A+ Certification exams.
- Additional study resources include installation manuals, Readme files, and instructional web pages and websites.
- Creating your own study guide will improve your overall retention of the subject matter.
- Studying with a group of individuals who are serious about preparing for the A+ Certification exams can be an excellent way to prepare.
- Taking practice exams help evaluate your weak areas.

Review Questions

Answer the following questions on a separate sheet of paper. Please do not write in this book.

1. How many exams must a candidate pass to earn the CompTIA A+ certification?
2. All questions on the CompTIA A+ exams are scored equally. True or False?
3. Which is the largest domain in the CompTIA A+ 220-801 exam?
4. Which is the largest domain in the CompTIA A+ 220-802 exam?
5. Why is having a planned study schedule beneficial?
6. Which types of computer material should you read to prepare for the A+ exams?
7. What are some general guidelines to follow when working with a study group?
8. Why is it important to set a test date as soon as you think you know the amount of preparation you will need?

Suggested Laboratory Activities

1. Form a study group of students who are serious about preparing for the A+ Certification exams.

2. Make a date to take an exam and construct a schedule of study times and dates.

3. Write practice exams for other members in your study group.

4. Make 3 × 5 flash cards with A+ Certification exam questions. Include the answers on the opposite side. Use the cards to test your knowledge.

5. Create your own study guide using the examination objectives provided by CompTIA.

6. Write your own exam questions using the examination objectives provided by CompTIA. If you have formed a study group, you can try the exam questions out on each other. You will be surprised how many questions you write will be similar to ones found on the A+ Certification exams.

Employment and Advanced Education

After studying this chapter, you will be able to:

- Plan a career in an IT field, including education, certification, and keeping up-to-date with changes in technology.
- Carry out a job search.
- Identify appropriate interview skills.

This chapter discusses ways to gain employment and ways to advance your career in the future. Because the world of technology is constantly advancing, careers in the computer technology field require continuing education. New ideas become reality every day. To keep up with the rapid changes in technology, you must form an action plan. Your plan must include strategies for keeping up-to-date with the changes in technology and using that newfound knowledge to create career advancement opportunities. See **Figure 22-1**.

Employment issues are discussed in this chapter. Although you may already be employed in a computer repair or related job, this chapter can help you better define your career goals. First, let's look at some of the many job titles found in the computer industry.

A Career Working with Computers

By successfully reaching this point in the textbook, you have probably decided whether or not to pursue a career working with computers. If you have the interest, desire, and ability, you can find a very rewarding career in the computer technology field. By completing this course, you have attained the first level of expertise. You may elect to go on for additional training in a more advanced field of computer technology. Computer technician is only one broad area in a field rich in choices. Some of the many other fields from which you can choose are the following:

- Network installation and support.
- Network administration.
- Digital electronics.
- System analysis.
- Technical sales.
- Help desk support.
- Web support.
- Computer programming.
- Computer engineering.

Figure 22-1. Once you land a job in the information technology field, you must continue to learn about new software and hardware or your skills will quickly become obsolete.

Stephen Coburn/Shutterstock.com

Because the tools of the trade are constantly changing, a computer technician must continuously learn new software, operating systems, and hardware. You can expand your knowledge to make yourself even more valuable as a computer technician or just to satisfy your own curiosity. There are no limits to your education in the field of computer technology. In fact, if you stop learning, the entire technology will soon pass you by. It would only take a few years before you would feel as obsolete as some of the equipment on which you may work. Some possible career positions are as follows:

- Analyst.
- Application developer.
- ATM engineer.
- Chief information officer.
- Customer service representative.
- Data communications engineer.
- Database specialist.
- Entry-level help desk operator.
- Industrial control engineer.
- Internet systems administrator.
- Internet website developer.
- IT consultant.
- Network engineer.
- Network hardware specialist.
- Network security specialist.
- Network support specialist.

- PC installer.
- PC support professional.
- Programmer.
- Systems engineer.
- Technical sales and marketing professional.
- Technical writer.
- Telecommunications data specialist.
- Training specialist.
- Voice over IP systems engineer.
- Webmaster.

You may be considering a career that requires a college-level education. There are many outstanding career opportunities for persons who earn a computer science or related degree. Some college-level training programs offer specialized degrees in many of the areas listed. Some colleges award credit based on technical certifications or work experience.

If you are interested in science and math in high school, you would probably enjoy studying computer science at a four-year college. Mathematics is a large part of computer-related college education. If you do not like mathematics and still want a good career, you may choose to pursue an alternative educational path.

One alternate path you may consider is the training offered in the armed forces. The various branches of the military offer many specialized areas of study in the computer technology field. The opportunities for education are very good in the military services, and valuable work experiences are gained along the way.

Another alternative educational path might be the completion of a special technical program offered at a local school, college, or technical center. These programs typically consist of advanced courses leading to certifications that are recognized worldwide. For example, Novell, Microsoft, Cisco Systems, and many other companies offer certification examinations in many advanced fields of study. One of the certifications offered by Microsoft is the Microsoft Certified Solutions Expert (MCSE). Generally for this certification, you must pass two or more exams that test your knowledge and competency of a particular Microsoft product, such as a particular Microsoft operating system. Preparing for this certification can take a significant amount of time and experience or classroom or online training, but earning the MCSE can prove to be a valuable addition to your résumé.

Each person must ask himself or herself several questions before going further into the computer arena. Have you enjoyed this textbook and the laboratory activities? The fact that you are studying computers is a good indicator of an interest in this area. Have you taken other classes in computer technology? Did you like them? Did you do well? Give serious thought to the questions before responding. Your answers may provide you with the insight you need to choose a rewarding career.

Careers in the Information Technology Industry

As we have noted, there are a wide variety of career options in the information technology (IT) industry. Computers, communications, and information systems play a major role in our daily life. Think of all the things that depend on computer systems today. For example, our communication systems—telephone, television, and radio—are all linked to computers. Hollywood studios use advanced computer graphics software to create special effects that were impossible before the advent of the computer.

The manufacturing industry uses computer-controlled robots and automated assembly lines. In the business world, computers tie a company's sales department to its accounting and shipping departments for seamless transactions. The entire banking industry relies on computers to track money exchanges, post records of interest and earnings, and compile mortgage statistics. Computer technology has also saturated the field of medicine. Surgeons can now perform computer-assisted surgeries. Patient medical records are all computerized, **Figure 22-2.** MRI scans can be transmitted instantly across a network to a specialist in a distant city for expert evaluation.

With development of each new application for the computer, many highly skilled technicians must be trained to maintain and service it. The need for people with computer technology training will continue to grow rapidly into the next century. Law enforcement, the military, and other governmental units rely a great deal on computers. Architects and engineers use

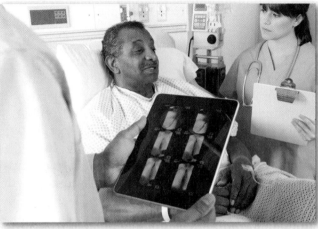

Figure 22-2. Medical records are computerized, allowing for immediate access in case of emergency, automated scheduling, and a reduced risk of misplacement.

Monkey Business Images/Shutterstock.com

computers to design structures. With computers, they cannot only design the structure but also get a realistic first-person view of the design as they take a virtual stroll through its corridors. As computer technology integrates into every aspect of our world, the need for highly trained and skilled technicians grows.

Entrepreneurs

Entrepreneurs own and operate their own businesses. According to the Small Business and Entrepreneurship (SBE) Council 2009 data, small businesses with less than 500 employees make up 99.9 percent of businesses in the United States. They also provide 49.9 percent of the jobs in America. Entrepreneurs usually start with an idea for filling a gap in the marketplace, perhaps where a new product or service is needed. Typically, a business plan is produced before a group or individual decides to open a private business. A business plan is always required if financial support is sought to open a business. This plan outlines goals for the business, an action plan, and a timetable for meeting those goals. A business plan is vital if the business is to succeed.

In addition to a sound business plan, a successful entrepreneur possesses a good knowledge of his or her business, industry, service, or product. This knowledge allows the owner to make smart business decisions.

The successful entrepreneur also has sound management skills. These skills allow the owner to successfully manage money, time, and employees. Management of each of these is critical to success, and poor management in any of these areas leads to certain failure.

Entrepreneurial skills, or the ability to think and move creatively and wisely, are also very important for the successful entrepreneur. These skills allow the business owner to control the business and move it in the right direction. Entrepreneurial opportunities are vast in the information technology industry. The tremendous growth in the market has triggered a similar growth in the demand for computer services. These highly demanded services include copmuter maintenance and repair, training, and Internet services.

Consulting is yet another growing business in the information technology industry, **Figure 22-3**. Consultants work for clients on special or individual projects. The specific job they do often depends on what work is needed. Clients pay a consultant for his or her expertise. When the job is completed, the consultant is free to move on to a new job and client.

Career Information Sources

The Occupational Outlook Handbook offers information on careers in many industries. It is published by the United States Department of Labor and the Bureau of Statistics. Most high school, community college, university, and public libraries have copies of this book. It can also be viewed online at www.bls.gov/oco. School guidance counselors, local labor markets, and one-stop offices are other outstanding sources of career information. They can help you find information on particular careers, colleges, and other programs that offer training in areas that you are interested in. These people are typically well-informed and ready to help in your search for jobs or training. Many colleges offer job information and placement services as well.

The Internet also contains a great amount of career and training information. Many private company sites list employment opportunities. Usually, the listing includes the required skills and educational levels and a brief job description with a list of duties.

Education

The educational requirements for jobs in the information technology industry vary. However, a minimum of a high school education is a solid foundation on which to build. Some high school graduates enter industry directly and receive specialized education in employer-sponsored training programs. However, many of these workers do not stop at this point. They continue to study to keep abreast of all the changes and new technologies that develop in the industry.

As discussed, specialized training can also be found in colleges, technical schools, or the military. Advanced degrees are becoming more commonplace as a means of moving ahead. Many state and private universities offer engineering and computer science degrees. Talk with your school counselor to learn locations and entry requirements.

Advanced Certification

Often, people who work in the field of computer technology have minimal certification. They must study at night for the certification exams, while working during the day in a related job. They most likely work under the supervision of another person who already has the certification. This can limit their career advancement.

Figure 22-3. Consultants are computer experts who offer their services on a per job basis.

stockyimages/Shutterstock.com

Certification is a way to advance your knowledge and career in the information technology industry. Certification combined with work experience is a way to prove your abilities to a potential employer. It is also a way to advance within a company and gain job security. As an IT professional, you will be learning the rest of your life. The knowledge base of the computer industry is ever expanding. Part of what you know now may very well be obsolete in a few years. If you did not learn another thing from this point forward, your skills would be very weak in just a few short years.

Obtaining your A+ Certification should be just the beginning for you. You should immediately start advancing toward another area of certification. The Network+ Certification is a good place to continue. This area will serve as a springboard to other more advanced certificates.

You may choose to not pursue another certification, and this decision is acceptable as long as you keep your skills up-to-date. Subscribe to and read professional journals in your area of work. Take as many courses as you can, such as digital electronics, to enhance your computer repair skills.

Home-study groups and courses are becoming commonplace. A student simply signs up from home and takes courses online. Many education websites offer such programs, but there are many other sources as well. Unfortunately, this type of study takes a lot of self-discipline. Most people do not have the drive needed to stick with this type of schooling. Another drawback is the lack of hands-on activities, which are essential to be successful in technical areas of study. Without the hands-on application, simple memorization of facts is useless. If you are already employed in a technology field and do not have time to attend school on a regular basis, home study may be best for you. You will not be looked down on for earning your certification through home study. The place you study and the method you use to learn your skills are not indicated on your certificate.

After you enter the workforce at an entry-level position, you will want to consider further developing your technical skills. If you feel you have a future with the company, you should match the certification route to the company's needs. For example, if the company network system is based on Microsoft, you should pursue the Microsoft line of certificates. If the company uses a system such as Novell, UNIX, or Linux, you should seek certification in one of these areas.

The time required to earn any certification depends on the individual's abilities. Some people are able to complete certification within a year; others lack the necessary aptitude and will never earn their certification. A good rule of thumb is at least two years experience and one year of study before attempting most advanced certifications. Let's look at some other certifications you may wish to obtain.

CompTIA Certifications

The CompTIA organization offers certification by examination in many areas. Receiving an A+ Certification from CompTIA is just the beginning. CompTIA offers advanced certificates that you may elect to pursue, such as CDIA+, Network+, Server+, Linux+, Healthcare IT Technician, Mobility +, and Cloud Essentials. The CompTIA certifications discussed in this section are limited to what a CompTIA A+ certified student might actually consider. Visit the CompTIA website for more detailed information about the various certifications.

CDIA+

The CDIA+ (Certified Document Imaging Architect) is a good, advanced certification. There is a great demand for persons with expertise in computer imaging. The CDIA+ examination tests your knowledge of imaging systems, including scanners, displays, printers, graphic file types, file conversion, and image enhancement. Typical questions include those about storage systems, transition speeds across networks, and computer performance as they relate to imaging. There is a tremendous need for technicians who can quickly and efficiently convert text pages and illustrations into formats recognized by computer systems.

Network+

The Network+ Certification tests knowledge of small and large network systems. The ideal candidate should have 9 to 12 months of networking experience. Experience alone, however, will not prepare you for the examination. You need to prepare for the test by taking an instructor-led course, a distance-learning course, or a self-study program. The test is not vendor specific. This means that the test is not based solely on a particular proprietary hardware or software system by manufacturers such as D-Link, Intel, AMD, ASUS, Cisco Systems, and Microsoft. The examination tests knowledge of the universal concepts of network systems.

Although you need to know the basics of network administration to pass the Network+ Certification exam, the knowledge is only intended as a foundation before going on to network administration certification. The Network+ Certification is recommended prior to pursuing many advanced certificates.

Many of the CompTIA certifications have similar domain objectives. When you earn one certificate, such as A+ Certification, you have also learned many of the skills tested on for other certificates, such as Network+, Cloud+, Security+, and Server+.

Server+

The Server+ Certification is designed to test a person's knowledge about network server hardware and software. The candidate is tested on installation, configuration, and diagnosis of network server hardware and network operating systems. The examination requires an in-depth knowledge of protocols, backup system standards, and system security.

Linux+

The Linux+ Certification covers the installation, configuration, and troubleshooting of the Linux operating system for the single PC and the network server. The Linux operating system is similar to the operating systems you have studied thus far. However, there are enough significant differences to warrant a separate certification. Two proprietary Linux certifications are Red Hat and SUSE, but there is also a vendor-neutral Linux certificate provided through the Linux Professional Institute (LPI), which is similar to the CompTIA Linux+ Certification. In fact, CompTIA refers to its Linux+ exam as "powered by LPI." Before taking a Linux+ exam, candidates may choose to have their exam results forwarded

to the Linux Professional Institute, thereby earning them LPIC-1 (Junior Level Linux) Certification if they achieve Linux+ Certification.

Mobility +

The Mobility+ Certification measures skills related to supporting mobile devices such as smartphones. CompTIA recommends that a candidate have at least 18 months of experience with mobile devices and Network+ Certification or equivalent knowledge. While you are not necessarily ready for this particular certification, it is one to consider for the future. If you choose to select a path to Mobility+, you should first acquire Network+ Certification.

Mobility+ should not be confused with Mobile App Security+. The Mobile App Security+ measures the skills necessary to create secure native iOS or Android mobile applications. This certification covers programming concepts and is not advised for anyone who does not have programming experience with Android or iOS programming languages.

Cloud Essentials

Cloud services have expanded rapidly in the last few years and, as a result, so has the need for persons with skills to support cloud services. The Cloud Essentials Certification measures basic knowledge related to cloud services and is designed mainly for a cloud services sales representative. This certification does not require any depth of technical knowledge as related to cloud implementation and technical support. CompTIA recommends that a Cloud Essentials candidate have at least six months of experience working for a company that represents cloud services or related IT services.

Cloud+

The Cloud+ Certification measures skills related to the implementation and support of cloud services and cloud infrastructure. This certification requires much more in-depth knowledge of cloud services than the Cloud Essentials Certification. The Cloud+ test candidate should be familiar with cloud server configuration, network storage, and virtualization technologies. CompTIA recommends 24 to

36 months of work experience in a related IT field, such as networking, network storage, or data center administration. Many cloud service providers also offer certification for their proprietary products. Some such companies are Cisco Systems, Amazon, HP, IBM, and Microsoft. Many of the other proprietary cloud certifications require passing multiple tests to obtain certification for a particular company.

Healthcare IT Technician

The Healthcare IT Technician Certification demonstrates that the successful candidate has the skills necessary to implement, deploy, and support IT systems in a healthcare setting. While acquiring A+ Certification is not required before taking the Healthcare IT Technician Certification exam, the Healthcare IT Technician Certification is intended to follow A+ Certification. The healthcare IT technician is responsible for supporting electronic healthcare record systems in healthcare locations such as a hospital. Much of the exam covers healthcare regulatory requirements and medical business operations.

Security+

The Security+ Certification measures a candidate's mastery of general security concepts. Areas covered include communications, infrastructure, cryptography, and organizational security. Candidates are recommended to have at least two years experience in networking, a good knowledge of TCP/IP, some experience in related network security, and possess the Network+ Certification. While these are recommended, they are not required before taking the exam.

This certification has rapidly become recognized internationally as an excellent verification of basic security principles and application. The CompTIA Security+ Certification may be used to award credit toward other certifications offered by companies such as Microsoft, Novell, and Symantec. You should consider the Security+ Certification if you plan to stay in information technology as a career.

PDI+

PDI stands for Printing and Document Imaging. The PDI+ Certification is recommended for persons associated with printer, scanner, copier, fax, and multifunctional machines at the entry level or at the basic level one for support personnel. The PDI+ Certification validates a candidate's abilities to install, maintain, and troubleshoot software and hardware associated with the document printing industry. The test items cover the printing process and components, scanner process and components, basic electronic components and tools, color theory, and network connectivity. Many of the same skills measured in the CompTIA A+ exams are tested for on the PDI+ exam. The biggest differences are the objectives that cover electronic components, such as electrical relays, solenoids, motors, sensors, and switches. A student that has achieved A+ Certification and has had some basic electronics training is a good candidate for this certification. Check the CompTIA website for the very latest information concerning certification credit.

Microsoft Certifications

Microsoft has had numerous certifications over time. In recent years, Microsoft has restructured the way a candidate can achieve individual certification. The most common Microsoft certifications offered are Microsoft Technology Associate (MTA), Microsoft Certified Solutions Associate (MCSA), Microsoft Certified Solutions Expert (MCSE), and Microsoft Office Specialist (MOS). These certifications are a possible next step after obtaining A+ Certification.

Two entry-level certifications you may wish to consider are Microsoft Technology Associate (MTA) and Microsoft Office Specialist (MOS). Microsoft Technology Associate is associated with operating systems, networking fundamentals, servers, and software development. Microsoft Office Specialist is associated with Microsoft software office application products such as Word, Excel, Outlook, PowerPoint, OneNote, and SharePoint. Typically after successfully passing the CompTIA A+ exams, many persons go on to achieve an MTA, usually by mastering one of the Microsoft operating systems such as Windows 8. We will now briefly look at some of the most common Microsoft certifications.

MTA

Microsoft Technology Associate (MTA) is the starting point before pursuing more advanced Microsoft certification, such as a Microsoft Certified Solutions Associate (MCSA) or Microsoft Certified Solutions Developer (MCSD); however, it is not a prerequisite. Microsoft requires that a candidate pass one exam to achieve MTA Certification. Major test areas specific to MTA Certification are as follows:

- Fundamentals of operating system configuration.
- Installing and upgrading client operating systems.
- Managing applications.
- Managing files and folders.
- Managing devices.
- Understanding operating system maintenance.

If you have completed CompTIA A+ Certification coursework and laboratory activities, you can most likely pass an MTA exam with minimal review of the test topics. The test topics can be reviewed at the Microsoft certification website. The MTA is a very minimal certification of basic knowledge associated with Microsoft operating systems and computer and networking fundamentals. Minimal hardware technical knowledge is required for the MTA. The next level of certification after the MTA is the Microsoft Certified Solutions Associate (MCSA).

 The MTA certification never expires.

MCSA

The Microsoft Certified Solutions Associate (MCSA) Certification tests a candidate's mastery of a specific area of Microsoft technology. For example, to become a certified MCSA Windows 8 support specialist, you would need to pass two exams: Configuring Windows 8 and Managing and Maintaining Windows 8. To earn the Windows Server 2012 MCSA, you would need to pass three exams: Installing and Configuring Windows Server 2012, Administering Windows Server 2012, and Configuring Advanced Windows Server 2012 Services.

MCSE

The Microsoft Certified Solutions Expert (MCSE) is the next level after completing the MCSA. Generally, you first achieve the MCSA for a given area and then pass two or more additional exams to earn an MCSE.

For example, after earning an MCSA for Server 2012, you would need to pass two additional certification exams: Designing and Implementing a Server Infrastructure and Implementing an Advanced Server Infrastructure. Passing all five examinations would earn an MCSE for Server Infrastructure. You would then be recognized as an expert in the field of server infrastructure and Windows Server 2012.

Microsoft offers more certifications over a broader range of products than any other company. Certifications include database management, software development, game development, and more.

The acronyms of certification names can be confusing, especially when an acronym matches two different certifications. For example, the newest MCSA represents Microsoft Certified Solutions Associate and the older certification, now retired, represents Microsoft Certified System Administrator. The Microsoft Certified Solutions Associate (MCSA) credential focuses on the ability to design and build technology solutions. The Microsoft Certified Systems Administrator (MCSA) certification focused on a specific job role.

MOS

The Microsoft Office Specialist (MOS) Certification proves knowledge of Microsoft Office software applications such as Word, Excel, Access, PowerPoint, Project, and Outlook. There are presently three levels of certification: Specialist, Expert, and Master. The Microsoft Office Specialist Certification is a prerequisite to the higher-level Microsoft Office Specialist Expert and Microsoft Office Specialist Master certifications.

To earn MOS Certification, the candidate must demonstrate the ability to use a software application's basic features, such as cut, copy, and paste. To earn an Expert certification, the user must be able to use all of the features included in the Specialist certification, plus more advanced features. For Microsoft Word, these features would include modifying the contents of tables, setting up automatic calculations for tables, and embedding worksheets. To earn a Master certification, you must demonstrate expert-level skill in five Microsoft Office products. You must also be able to embed information into and freely exchange information between the five products.

As a technician, why would you want to learn these products in detail? When you become a technical support person for a large or small company, people automatically think of you as somewhat of an expert in all areas of computers and system information. Automatically, they feel you are qualified to advise them about software, monitors, and even Internet service providers. For example, a person may want to know how to perform a mail merge in Word. After all, you are supposed to be the expert on computers. If you are unable to answer the question, the customer may perceive you as being poorly trained, even if the question falls outside the scope of your job.

A good way to increase your value to a company is to master popular software, such as Word, Access, Excel, and PowerPoint. You will probably be asked more questions about these products than questions about hardware, operating systems, or drivers.

Novell Certifications

Novell offers several certifications, such as Certified Novell Administrator (CNA), Certified Linux Professional (CLP), and Certified Linux Desktop Administrator (CLDA). The certifications are tied directly to Novell software products such as Novell SUSE Linux. The Novell certifications are similar to the Microsoft certifications. However, they prove knowledge of Novell network products rather than Microsoft products. You can learn more detailed information about the Novell certifications by visiting the Novell website.

CNA

The Certified Novell Administrator (CNA) Certification is awarded for the skills necessary to set up and manage user workstations and manage network system resources such as files, printers, and software. It requires that the person understand how

to monitor network performance, provide remote access to the network, and possess various other network skills. This particular certification has two learning paths: Novell Open Enterprise Server for NetWare and Novell NetWare 6.

CLP

The Certified Linux Professional (CLP) Certification proves expertise as an administrator for Novell SUSE Linux Enterprise Server. The test is a practicum exam. A practicum exam is generally a hands-on demonstration of skills. The term *practicum* has changed meaning over the years as related to the Novell certifications. The original Novell practicum exams required the candidate to actually perform configurations on a networked desktop or server. The candidate would report to a physical location that had a test network system set up solely for the practicum. Today, Novell uses a written examination referred to as a practicum exam. The test items are scenario-based problems for which the candidate must select a solution that meets the minimal requirements presented in the test item. This type of questioning is very difficult as compared to a traditional multiple choice test used for other certifications.

CLDA

Certified Linux Desktop Administrator (CLDA) is an entry-level Linux certification that measures the administration skills needed to install, configure, and manage a Linux desktop environment.

Cisco Training and Certifications

Cisco Systems provides training opportunities at high schools and colleges all over the United States. A Cisco training site is referred to as a *Cisco Networking Academy*. These academies emphasize network design, implementation, and troubleshooting using Cisco products. Cisco products are widely used for network communications. The academy courses are designed as a combination of lecture, textbook, on-line learning, and hands-on laboratory activities.

Two of the entry-level certifications are Cisco Certified Technician (CCT) and Cisco Certified Entry Networking Technician (CCENT). Some other common certifications are Cisco Certified Network Associate (CCNA), Cisco Certified Network Professional (CCNP), and Cisco Certified Internetwork Expert (CCIE). Cisco also offers many specialized certificates in areas of security, wireless network systems, and IT essentials.

Cisco has restructured its certifications in recent years and divided the areas of certification into career areas. The areas are the following:

- Networking, Network Design, and Security.
- Voice and Collaboration Solutions.
- Data Center and Storage Networking.
- Service Provider.

The certification process is then arranged in a hierarchy starting at Entry and progressing to the hardest to attain Architect. The five levels of expertise are the following:

- Entry.
- Associate.
- Professional.
- Expert.
- Architect.

The certificates are obtained by passing specific Cisco examinations. You can learn more about the certifications offered and locate the Cisco Networking Academy nearest you by visiting the Cisco Systems website.

BICSI Certifications

Building Industry Consulting Service International (BICSI) provides certification for information technology design and installation. Candidates are required to take a written and a hands-on exam to achieve the certification. The hands-on portion tests the candidate's expertise at making cable splices for copper core or fiber-optic cables, depending on the certification the candidate wishes to attain. Some of the various certifications from BICSI are as follows.

- ITS Installer 1.
- ITS Installer 2, Copper.
- ITS Installer 2, Optical Fiber.
- ITS Technician.

Other Certifications

Many other companies such as 3Com, Corel, Nortel Networks, Red Hat Linux, and Oracle have certification programs. Check their websites for in-depth information about the exams. There you will find exam outlines, study materials, schools and available training, and prerequisites.

Job Search Ideas

Finding a job can be a time-consuming and difficult task. The Occupational Outlook Handbook has excellent tips for conducting a job search. Start by talking to your parents, neighbors, teachers, and guidance counselors. These people may know of job openings that have not been advertised. Read the classified ads in the newspaper, especially the Sunday editions. Look through the Yellow Pages to generate a list of local companies, their addresses, and phone numbers. Companies are grouped according to industry in the Yellow Pages. You may see companies to contact.

City, county, and state employment services may also provide useful job leads. Private employment agencies might also provide leads, but they often charge a fee for a job placement.

The Internet is a valuable source of job information. Almost every computer-related site has a section devoted to job opportunities. You can often complete an application online. There are also many websites that will allow you to post a résumé.

Job Interviews

The three most important factors that determine your ability to land a job are your work history, technical expertise, and the job interview. A work history tells the employer a lot about you as a future employee, even if the job experiences are unrelated to the job for which you are applying. You may just be entering the IT profession, but a solid recommendation from a past employer can make the difference. A recommendation from a former employer shows that you have been a valuable and dependable employee. A person with no work history is a gamble in most employers' eyes.

Prior technical experiences can prove to be a real asset, whether they are past jobs or formal training. Other applicants may have no technical employment history or technical training. They may have simple, informal experience helping friends with their home computer and now believe they can handle the job. This is where your training and work history puts you ahead of others.

The job interview is the major factor in determining if an applicant gets the job. The job interview gives the employer a chance to evaluate the applicant through a series of questions. The way a question is answered is at times more important than the answer itself. For example, if an employer asks, "What would you do if you could not fix a computer problem?" The way you answer the question may tell the employer about your character, your confidence, and your ability to work with others. The employer is looking for certain traits in the individual he or she is about to hire. Some common traits are honesty, confidence, dependability, and the ability to work well as a team member.

While your physical attractiveness may not be important to an employer, your neat and clean appearance shows that you take pride in yourself and your work. Even if the job is a "backroom" position, dress well for the interview. Blue jeans and a T-shirt are never appropriate.

Employers may not ask the same questions of all applicants and will not usually be direct about the qualities they are seeking. The employer will ask questions to probe for the character and job-related qualities they want. For example, an employer may ask you to describe a time you had a problem with a fellow employee. How was it resolved? The answer to this question can tell an experienced interviewer a lot about the character of the applicant. Once you have secured an interview, it is important to be prepared for it. Read the following tips for a successful interview.

Preparation for the Interview

An interview is perhaps the most critical stage in a job search, and a process that you can control to a great extent. A good interview can cause an employer to overlook a lack of experience or education. On the other hand, a poor interview can cause even the most qualified candidate to be passed over. The following are a few tips to help you prepare for your interview.

- Always learn about the prospective employer and the position. Many times this information is available on the employer's website. This preparation lets the employer know you are truly interested in the company and that you possess the personal initiative to research and learn.
- Have a specific job or jobs in mind, generally at an entry level. Most companies do not begin a new employee in a high-level job until the employee has proven his or her worth to the company.
- Review your qualifications for the job. Make sure your qualifications match those desired by the employer. Do not waste the employer's time or yours by interviewing for a job that is far beyond your level.
- Prepare to answer broad questions about yourself. It is wise to practice interviewing with someone who has knowledge about job interviews. A family member or friend who regularly does hiring for a company can be a great help, even if he or she does not work in the field you are seeking. Practicing the interview will help you learn to control your natural nervousness and become more relaxed for the real thing.
- A quality résumé can make a favorable impression on an employer. Use a good quality paper and a cover sheet. Make sure you have produced an original copy that the employer may keep.
- Arrive at least 15 minutes prior to the scheduled time of your interview. Showing up late for your interview does not enhance your prospects for the job. It displays a lack of care for the job, the company, and your interview person or committee. Locate the building in

advance and figure how much time it will take to get there. Consider the traffic conditions for that time of day. Do a practice run so you will know exactly how to get to the interview and the length of time it will take you to arrive.

- If you really want that job, have a backup plan in case you have difficulty with your transportation.

Personal Appearance

The first impression you make on an employer is critical. People are summarily judged on their outward appearance. If you look and act professional, you will make a favorable impression on your interviewer and future coworkers.

- Dress appropriately and be well groomed.
- Blue jeans and a T-shirt are never appropriate. Regardless of the job conditions, men and women should always dress up rather than down for an interview. Do not dress for a party. Dress for a formal business setting.
- Smile and use a firm handshake when you introduce yourself. This shows your confidence, **Figure 22-4**.
- Do not chew gum, eat candy, or smoke at any time when you are on the company premises. This is not a social visit, and you may likely encounter your prospective supervisor on the property prior to your interview.

Figure 22-4. A neat appearance, good posture, and a firm handshake demonstrate self-confidence.

Alexandar Raths/Shutterstock.com

The Interview

Once the interview begins, your responses to questions are being actively evaluated. The interviewer is trying to determine your work ethic, attitude, intelligence, and competency based on your answers and body language. The following are tips to help you avoid creating the wrong impression on the interviewer.

- Answer all questions to the best of your ability. If you do not know the answer, simply say so. Do not try to make up an answer. Express your willingness to learn any new topics with which you may not be familiar. The person conducting the interview is an expert. You will not fool them by trying to invent an answer. Admit your limitations, and you will find the interviewer will most likely respect your honesty.
- Use proper English and avoid slang. Speak slowly and concisely. Never use foul language, even in a joking manner.
- Use good manners. Always address the persons who are conducting the interview as "Sir" and "Ma'am." Even if you are personally acquainted with your prospective employer, treat them with polite formality. Do not become complacent or presume you have the job.
- Convey a sense of cooperation and enthusiasm. Your body language will convey a lot about your personality. Keep smiling. Have a look of confidence. Sit up straight and look the interviewer directly in the eyes. Do not slump or look away as you talk.
- You can ask questions about the position and the organization, but limit your questions to operations or conditions that you do not understand. Much information regarding a job can be obtained prior to the interview, especially if the information was posted. Unless it has not been covered in a job posting, uncovered through your research, or discussed by your prospective employer during the interview, do not ask questions regarding salary.
- Remember that the interview has not ended when you start asking questions. As a matter of fact, your questions can reveal even more to the employer. Asking how many breaks

you will get during a day will send an undesirable message to the employer. It is not required that you ask questions, especially if the interview has been thorough, but do not hesitate if you believe there is pertinent information that you must know.

- Remember there will be additional time to make any clarifications or salary negotiations after you are offered the job.

Employer Testing

Employer testing is very common today as part of the job interview process. An employer can tell a lot about your technical knowledge and communication skills through a test, especially if handwritten answers are required. Written responses reveal a lot about an interviewee. Write neatly when filling out employment applications or taking tests. Poor penmanship can make a bad impression on a prospective employer. When completing your application form, you should do the following:

- Be sure you understand all written test directions. If you are unclear about the instructions, verbally confirm them before you begin the test.
- Read each question carefully.
- Write legibly and clearly. Printing helps if your handwriting is poor.
- Budget your time wisely and do not dwell on one question.

Information to Bring to an Interview

The common information required at an interview is Social Security number, driver's license number, and a copy of your résumé. On your résumé, make a complete and chronological list of your education and training. List all of your past employment in sequence, and do not leave blank dates. If you stopped your employment to go to school, note the dates. This ensures your potential employer does not think you are trying to leave out an employer who may not give you a good reference. List the reasons for any breaks in your employment history.

You may wish to include copies of training and award certificates, transcripts, and letters of reference with your résumé. Typically, these will be verified anyway if listed on your résumé. Including copies with your résumé may speed up the verification procedure.

Three References

It is customary to provide references for a job. The quality of your references can mean a great deal to the employer. Some good references are teachers, past employers, supervisors, and fellow employees. Friends, family, and your clergy are not considered good references. Get permission from people before using them as a reference. For each reference, provide name, address, telephone number, and occupation. Also, note if the person was a past supervisor.

Chapter Summary

- An information technology (IT) position requires continuous education; a recognized certification is a way of proving your expertise in a computer technology specialty.
- Resources for conducting a job search are the Occupational Outlook Handbook; parents, neighbors, teachers, and guidance counselors; classified ads in the newspaper; the Yellow Pages; city, county, and state employment services; and the Internet.
- Arrive early or on time for your interview; during the interviewing process, smile and show a sense of cooperation and enthusiasm; and if tested by the prospective employer, be sure you understand instructions for the examination.

Review Questions

Answer the following questions on a separate sheet of paper. Please do not write in this book.

1. Why is continuing education required for an employee in the IT industry?
2. What is an entrepreneur?
3. Name at least three job search resources.
4. What is an interviewer trying to determine based on your answers and body language?
5. What items should you take to a job interview?
6. What information must be provided in your list of references?
7. What type of career would you like to have? How much training and education will this career require?
8. What traits do you think are required of successful entrepreneurs?
9. What professional goals do you hope to accomplish in the next five years? The next ten years?

Suggested Laboratory Activities

1. Go to the Microsoft website and download a copy of the requirements for the MTA Certification.
2. Go to the Microsoft website and download a copy of test objectives for the Configuring Windows 8 exam and the Managing and Maintaining Windows 8 exam.
3. Go to the Microsoft website and download a copy of the requirements for any MCSA exam that you think might be interesting.
4. Go to the Novell website and download the requirements for Certified Linux Professional (CLP) Certification.
5. Do a search on what colleges will give degree credit for certifications. See how much credit can be obtained and under what conditions.
6. Locate the Cisco Networking Academy nearest you. How much does a course cost, and how long does it run?
7. Visit the BICSI website and see what certifications are available.

Appendix A
List of Acronyms

A

ac	alternating current
ACK	acknowledge
ACPI	Advanced Configuration and Power Interface
ADSL	asymmetrical digital subscriber line
AGP	Accelerated Graphics Port
AI	artificial intelligence
AIFF	Audio Interchange File Format
ALU	arithmetic logic unit
AM	amplitude modulation
AMD	Active Matrix Display, *also* Advanced Micro Devices
ANSI	American National Standards Institute
AOL	America Online
APC	American Power Conversion
API	application program interface
APM	Advanced Power Management
ARCnet	Attached Resource Computer network
ARP	Address Resolution Protocol
ARPANET	Advanced Research Project Agency Network
ASCII	American Standard Code for Information Interchange
ASP	application service provider
ASPI	Advanced SCSI Programming Interface
ASR	Automated System Recovery
ATA	AT Attachment
ATAPI	AT Attachment Packet Interface
ATM	Asynchronous Transfer Mode
AUI	Attachment Unit Interface
A/V	audio/video
AWG	American Wire Gauge

B

BASIC	Beginner's All-purpose Symbolic Instruction Code
BAT	batch file
BBS	bulletin board system
BCC	blind carbon copy
BCD	binary coded decimal
BCU	Bus Controller Unit, *also* BIOS Configuration Utility
BDC	backup domain controller
BEDO DRAM	Burst EDO Dynamic Random Access Memory
BFT	Binary File Transfer
BGP	Border Gateway Protocol
BIOS	basic input/output system
BIT	binary digit
BIU	Bus Interface Unit
BMP	bitmap
BNC	British Naval Connector, *or* Bayonet Nut Connector, *or* Bayonet-Neill Concelman
BOOTP	Bootstrap Protocol
bps	bits per second
Bps	bytes per second
BRI	Basic-Rate Interface
BSD	Berkeley Software Distribution UNIX

C

CA	Certificate Authority
CAD	computer-aided design, *or* computer-aided drafting

CAD/CAM	computer-aided design/computer-aided manufacturing	cpi	characters per inch
CAL	Client Access License, *also* Computer-Assisted Learning, *also* Computer-Aided Logistics	cps	characters per second, *also* cycles per second
		CPU	central processing unit
		CRC	cyclic redundancy check
CAM	computer-aided manufacturing	CRT	cathode ray tube
CAS	Column Address Select	CSMA/CA	Carrier Sense Multiple Access with Collision Avoidance
CAV	constant linear velocity		
CBT	computer-based training	CSMA/CD	Carrier Sense Multiple Access with Collision Detection
CCD	charge-coupled device		
CCITT	Comité Consultatif International Téléphonique et Télégraphique	CSU/DSU	Channel Service Unit/Data Service Unit
CD	carrier detect, *also* compact disc, *also* collision detect	CTS	clear to send

D

CDFS	CD-ROM File System	DAC	digital-to-analog converter
CD-R	Compact Disc Recordable	daemon	Disk and Execution Monitor
CD-ROM	Compact Disc Read Only Memory	DARPA	Defense Advanced Research Projects Agency
CD-RW	Compact Disc Rewriteable		
CD-WO	Compact Disc, Write-Once	DAT	digital audio tape
CD-WORM	Compact Disc, Write-Once Read-Many	dB	decibel
		dc	direct current
CGA	color/graphics adapter	DCC	Direct Cable Connection
CGM	Computer Graphics Metafile	DDL	Dynamic Data Link, *also* Document Description Language, *also* Data Definition Language
CHAP	Challenge Handshake Authentication Protocol		
CHS	Cylinder, Head, Sector	DDR	Double Data Rate, *also* Dynamic Desktop Router
CID	Certified ID, *also* Caller Identification		
CIDR	Classless Inter-Domain Routing	DDR-SDRAM	Double Data Rate Synchronous Dynamic Random Access Memory
CIFS	Common Internet File System		
CISC	complex instruction set computer	DEC	Digital Equipment Corporation
CLV	constant linear velocity	DEK	Data Encryption Key
CMOS	complementary metal oxide semiconductor	DHCP	Dynamic Host Configuration Protocol
CMTS	Cable Modem Termination System	DHTML	Dynamic HTML
CMYK	cyan, magenta, yellow, black	DIB	Dual Independent Bus
CNA	Certified Netware Administrator, *also* Cisco Networking Academies	DIMM	dual in-line memory module
		DIN	Deutsche Industrie Norm (connector)
COA	Certificate of Authority	DIP	dual in-line package
COBOL	common business oriented language	DLC	Data Link Control
codec	compressor/decompressor	DLL	Dynamic Link Library

DMA	direct memory access
DNS	Domain Name System, or Domain Name Service
DOCSIS	Data Over Cable Service Interface Specification
DoD ARPA	Department of Defense's Advanced Research Project Agency
DoS	denial of services
DOS	disk operating system
dpi	dots per inch
DRAM	dynamic random access memory
DRDRAM	Direct Rambus Dynamic Random Access Memory
DSIMM	dual single in-line memory module
DSL	digital subscriber line
DSR	data set ready
DSS	digital satellite system
DTE	Data Terminal Equipment
DTR	data terminal ready
DUN	Dial-Up Networking
DVB	Digital Video Broadcasting
DVD	Digital Versatile Disc, or Digital Video Disc
DVDR	Digital Video Disc Recordable
DVI	Digital Video Interactive
DVM	Data/Voice Multiplexer

E

EBCDIC	Extended Binary-Coded Decimal Interchange Code
ECC	error code correction
ECMA	European Computer Manufacturers Association
ECP	Enhanced Capabilities Port
EDO	Extended Data Output
EDO DRAM	Enhanced Data Output Dynamic Random Access Memory
EDSI	Enhanced Small Devices Interface
EEPROM	electrically erasable programmable read only memory
EFS	encrypted file system

EGA	enhanced graphics adapter
EHF	extreme high frequency
EIA	Electronics Industries Association
EIDE	Enhanced IDE
EIGRP	Enhanced Interior Gateway Routing Protocol
EISA	Extended Industry Standard Architecture
EMI	electromagnetic interference
EMM	Expanded Memory Manager
EMP	Electromagnetic Pulse
EMS	expanded memory standard
ENIAC	Electronic Numerical Integrator Analyzer and Calculator
EOF	end of file
EOT	end of transmission, or end of text, or end of table
EP	electrophotographic process
EPA	Environmental Protection Agency
EPP	Enhanced Parallel Port
EPROM	erasable programmable read only memory
EPS	Encapsulated PostScript
ERD	Emergency Repair Disk
ESC	escape
ESD	electrostatic discharge
ESDI	Enhanced Small Device Interface
ESDRAM	Enhanced Synchronous Dynamic Random Access Memory
ESMTP	Extended Simple Mail Transfer Protocol
ESP	Encapsulated Security Payload, also Enhanced Serial Port
ETSI	European Telecommunications Standards Institute
EXT	external

F

FAQ	frequently asked questions
FAT	file allocation table
FC	fiber channel

FCC	Federal Communications Commission
FCPGA	Flip Chip Pin Grid Array
FDD	floppy disk drive
FDDI	Fiber Distributed Data Interface
FDHD	floppy drive, high-density
FDI	flat display, *also* floppy drive, *also* floppy disk, *also* full duplex
FDM	Frequency Division Multiplexing
FF	form feed
FIFO	first in first out
FLOPS	floating-point operations per second
FM	frequency modulation
FORTRAN	formula translator
FPM	Fast Page Mode
FPU	floating-point unit
FRU	field replaceable unit
FSB	front side bus
FTP	File Transfer Protocol, *or* File Transport Protocol

G

Gb	gigabit
GB	gigabyte
GDI	Graphical Device Interface
GHz	gigahertz
GIF	graphics interchange format
GUI	graphical user interface

H

HCL	Hardware Compatibility List
HD	hard disk, *also* high density
HDD	hard disk drive
HDSL	High bit-rate Digital Subscriber Line
HDTV	High-Definition Television
HMA	high memory area
HP	Hewlett-Packard
HPFS	High Performance File System
HTML	Hypertext Markup Language

HTTP	Hypertext Transfer Protocol
Hz	Hertz

I

IANA	Internet Assigned Numbers Authority
IBM	International Business Machines
IC	integrated circuit
ICANN	Internet Corporation for Assigned Names and Numbers
ICF	Internet Connection Firewall
ICMP	Internet Control Message Protocol
ICS	Internet Connection Sharing
ID	Identification
IDE	Integrated Development Environment, *also* Integrated Drive Electronics, *or* Intelligent Drive Electronics
IDN	Integrated Digital Network
IDSL	ISDN Subscriber Line
IE	Internet Explorer
IEEE	Institute of Electrical and Electronics Engineers
IETF	Internet Engineering Task Force
IIS	Internet Information Server
IMAP	Internet Message Access Protocol
I/O	input/output
IP	Internet Protocol
IPX	Internet Packet Exchange
IR	infrared
IRC	Internet Relay Chat
IrDA	Infrared Data Association
IRQ	interrupt request line
ISA	Industry Standard Architecture
ISDN	integrated services digital network
ISO	International Organization for Standardization
ISP	Internet Service Provider
IT	Information Technology
ITSP	Internet Telephony Service Provider

ITU	International Telecommunications Union

J

JPEG	Joint Photographic Experts Group

K

kbps	kilobits per second
kBps	kilobytes per second
kHz	kilohertz

L

LAN	local area network
LBA	logical block addressing
LCD	liquid crystal display
LCN	Logical Cluster Number
LDAP	Lightweight Directory Access Protocol
LEC	local exchange carrier
LED	light emitting diode
Li-ion	lithium-ion
LLC	Logical Link Control
LPT	line printer terminal
LQ	letter quality
LSB	least significant bit
LSI	large-scale integration
LUN	logical unit number

M

MAC	media access code, *also* media access control
MAN	metropolitan area network
MAPI	Message Application Programming Interface
MAU	Media Attachment Unit, *also* Media Access Unit, *or* Multistation Access Unit
MB	megabytes, *also* motherboard
Mb	megabit
MBps	megabytes per second

Mbps	megabits per second
MBR	Master Boot Record
MCA	Micro Channel Architecture
MCGA	multicolor/graphics array, *or* multicolor/graphics adapter
MDRAM	Multibank Dynamic Random Access Memory
Me	Millennium Edition (Windows)
MFT	Master File Table
MHz	megahertz
MIDI	musical instrument digital interface
MIME	Multipurpose Internet Mail Extensions
MIPS	million instructions per second
MO	magneto-optical
MODEM	modulator-demodulator
MOV	metal oxide varistor
MPEG	Moving Picture Experts Group
MSB	most significant bit
MS-DOS	Microsoft Disk Operating System
MZR	multiple zone recording

N

NAK	negative acknowledge, *or* not acknowledged
NAP	Network Access Point
NAS	Network Access Server, *also* network attached storage
NAT	Network Address Translation
NBT	NetBIOS on TCP/IP
NDS	Netware Directory Services, *or* Novell Directory Services
NetBEUI	NetBIOS Enhanced User Interface
NetBIOS	Network Basic Input/Output System
NFS	Network File System
NIC	network interface card
NiCad	nickel-cadmium
NiCd	nickel-cadmium
NiMH	nickel-metal hydride
NOS	network operating system

NSP	Network Service Provider
NT	New Technology (Windows), *also* Network Terminator
NTFS	New Technology File System
NVRAM	Non-Volatile Random Access Memory

O

OC	Optical Carrier
OCR	optical character recognition
OCX	OLE Custom Control, *or* OLE Control Extension
OEM	original equipment manufacturer
OLE	Object Linking and Embedding
OOP	object-oriented programming
OOPL	object-oriented programming language
OS	operating system
OSI	Open Systems Interconnection
OSPF	Open Shortest Path First
OSR 2	OEM Service Release 2 (Windows 95)
OTDR	Optical Time Domain Reflectometer

P

P2P	peer-to-peer, *also* point-to-point
PAP	Password Authentication Protocol
PBX	private branch exchange
PC	personal computer, *also* printed circuit
PCI	Peripheral Component Interconnect
PCMCIA	Personal Computer Memory Card International Association
PDA	personal digital assistant
PDC	primary domain controller
PDF	Portable Document Format
PDL	Page Description Language
PDU	Protocol Data Unit, *or* Packet Data Unit

PEL	Picture Element
Perl	Practical Extraction and Report Language
PGA	pin grid array, *also* Professional Graphics Adapter
PGP	Pretty Good Privacy
PIC	Lotus Picture
PIF	Program Information File
PIN	personal identification number
PING	Packet Internet Groper
PIO	Programmed Input/Output, *or* Programmable Input/Output
pixel	Picture Element
PLC	powerline communications
PLD	Programmable Logical Device
PnP	Plug and Play
PoP	Point of Presence
POP	Post Office Protocol
POP3	Post Office Protocol version 3
POSIX	Portable Operating System Interface for UNIX
POST	power-on self-test
POTS	plain old telephone service
PPGA	Plastic Pin Grid Array
ppm	page(s) per minute
PPP	Point-to-Point Protocol
PPTP	Point-to-Point Tunneling Protocol
PRI	Primary Rate Interface
PROM	programmable read only memory
PS/2	Personal System 2
PSTN	Public Switched Telephone Network
PVC	permanent virtual circuit

Q

QIC	Quarter-Inch Cartridge
QoS	quality of service

R

RAID	Redundant Array of Independent Disks, *or* Redundant Array of Inexpensive Disks

RAM	random access memory	SLIP	Serial Line Internet Protocol
RAS	Remote Access Server, *also* Remote Access Service, *also* Row Address Selection	SMB	Server Message Block
		SMM	System Management Mode
		SMTP	Simple Mail Transfer Protocol
RD	receive data	SNA	Systems Network Architecture
RDRAM	Rambus Dynamic Random Access Memory	SNMP	Simple Network Management Protocol
RF	radio frequency	SOHO	small-office/home-office
RFC	Request for Comments	SOM	Start of Message, *also* System Object Model
RGB	red, green, blue		
RIMM	Rambus In-line Memory Modules	SONET	Synchronous Optical Network
RIP	raster image processor, *also* Routing Information Protocol	SPARC	Scalable Processor Architecture
		SPD	serial presence detect
RISC	reduced instruction set computer	SPX	Sequenced Packet Exchange
RJ-11/12/45	Registered Jacks	SQL	structured query language
RLE	run-length encoding	SRAM	static random access memory
ROM	read only memory	SSD	Solid State Disk, *or* Solid State Drive
RS (RS-232)	recommended standard	SSL	Secure Sockets Layer
RTF	rich text format	STP	shielded twisted pair, *also* Secure Transfer Protocol
RTS	request to send		
		SVC	switched virtual circuit
		SVG	Scalable Vector Graphics
S		SVGA	super video graphics array
SAM	Security Accounts Manager		
SANS	System Administration, Networking and Security Institute	**T**	
		TAPI	Telephony Application Programming Interface
SAP	Service Advertising Protocol		
SAP	Serial Attached SCSI	TB	terabytes
SCSI	Small Computer System Interface	TCO	Total Cost of Ownership
SDRAM	Synchronous Dynamic Random Access Memory	TCP	Transmission Control Protocol
		TCP/IP	Transmission Control Protocol/ Internet Protocol
SDSL	Symmetric Digital Subscriber Line		
SEC	Single Edge Contact	TDM	Time Division Multiplexing
SET	Secure Electronic Transaction	TDR	Time Domain Reflectometer
SGML	Standard Generalized Markup Language	TFT	thin film transistor
		TFT-LCD	thin film transistor liquid crystal display
SGRAM	Synchronous Graphic Random Access Memory		
		TFTP	Trivial File Transfer Protocol
SIMM	single in-line memory module	TI	Texas Instruments
SIP	single in-line package	TIFF	Tagged Image File Format
SLDRAM	Sync Link Dynamic Random Access Memory	TLD	top-level domain

TPI	tracks per inch
TSR	terminate and stay resident
TTF	TrueType Font
TTL	time to live, *also* transistor-transistor logic
TTY	teletypewriter
TWAIN	Technology without an Interesting Name, *or* Toolkit without an Interesting Name

U

UART	universal asynchronous receiver-transmitter
UCS	universal character set
UDF	Universal Disk Format
UDMA	Ultra Direct Memory Access
UDP	User Datagram Protocol
UHF	ultrahigh frequency
ULSI	ultra large scale integration
UMB	Upper Memory Block
UNC	Universal Naming Convention, *or* Uniform Naming Convention
UPI	universal peripheral interface
UPS	uninterruptible power supply
URI	Universal Resource Identifier
URL	Uniform Resource Locator
USB	Universal Serial Bus
UTP	Unshielded Twisted Pair
UWB	ultra-wideband

V

VAR	value-added reseller
VB	Visual Basic
VC	Virtual Circuit
VCN	Virtual Cluster Number
VDSL	very high data-rate digital subscriber line
VDT	video display terminal
VESA	Video Electronics Standards Association
VFAT	virtual file allocation table

VGA	video graphics array
VHF	very high frequency
VLAN	virtual local area network
VLB	Video Electronics Standards Association (VESA) local bus
VLSI	Very Large-Scale Integration
VMM	Virtual Memory Manager
VMS	Virtual Memory System
VoIP	Voice over Internet Protocol
VOM	volt-ohmmeter, *also* volt-ohm milliameter
VPN	virtual private network
VR	virtual reality
VRAM	video random access memory
VxD	virtual device driver

W

W3C	World Wide Web Consortium
WAN	wide area network
WATS	wide area telephone service
WINS	Windows Internet Naming Service
WLAN	wireless local area network
WMF	Windows Metafile Format
WORM	write once, read many
WRAM	Windows Random Access Memory
WUSB	Wireless USB
WWW	World Wide Web
WYSIWYG	what you see is what you get

X

XGA	extended graphics array
XML	Extensible Markup Language
XMS	extended memory system

Y

Y2K	the year 2000

Z

ZIF	zero insertion force

Appendix B

Binary Math

Binary Math

Binary math accurately represents digital circuitry. In digital electronics, a circuit is either *on* or *off* or a voltage condition is *high* or *low*. For example, a digital circuit may have two distinct conditions: 5 volts present or 0 volts present.

Binary math uses only 2 numbers, 1 and 0, to represent an infinite range of numbers. The binary number system accomplishes this in basically the same way the decimal number system does, by placing numbers into discrete digit positions. The decimal number system fills these digits with values 0 through 9. The first digit position is commonly referred to as the 1s. The maximum value that can be entered here is 9. The second digit position must therefore be the 10s. If the maximum value of 9 is entered in both the 10s position and the 1s position, the resulting number is 99. The third position must therefore be the 100s position, and so on. Notice in **Figure B-1** that each of the positions can be expressed as an exponent of the base 10.

Figure B-1.

Digit Positions	1s	10s	100s	1,000s	10,000s	100,000s
Exponent	10^0	10^1	10^2	10^3	10^4	10^5
Range	0–9	10–99	100–999	1000–9999	10,000–99,999	100,000–999,999

Goodheart-Willcox Publisher

Note   The Range row indicates the range of number for which the selected digit position would be the leftmost digit, not the range of number that could contain that digit position.

Look at the number 2753. It contains the following:

2-1000s	2000
7-100s	700
5-10s	50
3-1s	3
Total	2753

Add the values together for a total of 2753.

Binary numbers are expressed in similar fashion. However, instead of each digit position being 10 times greater than the position before it, the value of each position is double that of the position before it. See **Figure B-2.**

Figure B-2.

Digit Positions	1s	2s	4s	8s	16s	32s	64s	128s
Exponent	2^0	2^1	2^2	2^3	2^4	2^5	2^6	2^7
Range	0–1	2–3	4–7	8–15	16–31	32–63	64–127	128–255

Goodheart-Willcox Publisher

Look at the binary number 101011000001 for example. It contains the following:

1-2048s	2048
0-1024s	0
1-512s	512
0-256s	0
1-128s	128
1-64s	64
0-32s	0
0-16s	0
0-8s	0
0-4s	0
0-2s	0
1-1s	1
Total	2753

As you can see, 101011000001 is the binary equivalent of 2753, **Figure B-3.**

Figure B-3.

2048s	1024s	512s	256s	128s	64s	32s	16s	8s	4s	2s	1s
1	0	1	0	1	1	0	0	0	0	0	1

Goodheart-Willcox Publisher

To convert the binary number to a decimal number, simply insert the value assigned to the location when a binary number 1 is in the location and then add the decimal numbers together. See **Figure B-4.**

Figure B-4.

32s	16s	8s	4s	2s	1s
1	0	1	1	0	1
32	+	8 +	4	+	1 = 45

Goodheart-Willcox Publisher

When converting a decimal number to a binary number, you simply reverse the previous operation. For example, to convert the decimal number 178 to a binary number, you must divide it by a series of "powers of 2." The "powers of 2" are 1, 2, 4, 8, 16, 32, 64, 128, 256, 512, 1024, 2048, and so on.

To convert the decimal number 178 to binary, start by finding the largest "power of 2" that does not exceed 178. The largest "power of 2" value that does not exceed 178 is 128 (2^7). Place a 1 in the binary number position that represents 128. See **Figure B-5**.

Figure B-5.

Powers of 2	128	64	32	16	8	4	2	1
Binary Digit	1							

Goodheart-Willcox Publisher

Subtracting 128 from 178 leaves 50. Fifty is less than 64 (2^6), the next smaller "power of 2." Therefore, you must insert a 0 in the 64s position, as seen in **Figure B-6**.

Figure B-6.

Powers of 2	128	64	32	16	8	4	2	1
Binary Digit	1	0						

Goodheart-Willcox Publisher

Next, 50 is larger than 32 (2^5), so place a 1 in the 32s position. See **Figure B-7**.

Figure B-7.

Powers of 2	128	64	32	16	8	4	2	1
Binary Digit	1	0	1					

Goodheart-Willcox Publisher

Next, subtract 32 from 50 and the difference is 18. The 18 is larger than 16 (2^4), so place a 1 in the 16s position. See **Figure B-8**.

Figure B-8.

Powers of 2	128	64	32	16	8	4	2	1
Binary Digit	1	0	1	1				

Goodheart-Willcox Publisher

Subtracting 16 from 18 leaves 2. The 2 is smaller than the next two "powers of 2," 8 (2^3) and 4 (2^2). That means the next two positions in the binary number are both 0s. See **Figure B-9**.

Figure B-9.

Powers of 2	128	64	32	16	8	4	2	1
Binary Digit	1	0	1	1	0	0		

Goodheart-Willcox Publisher

The next "power of 2" is 2 (2^1), and the number remaining from the last step is also 2. Therefore, a 1 goes into the 2s position. See **Figure B-10**.

Figure B-10.

Powers of 2	128	64	32	16	8	4	2	1
Binary Digit	1	0	1	1	0	0	1	

Goodheart-Willcox Publisher

There are no decimal numbers remaining, so the 1s position should be filled with a 0. The binary equivalent of the decimal number 178 is 10110010, **Figure B-11**.

Figure B-11.

Powers of 2	128	64	32	16	8	4	2	1
Binary Digit	1	0	1	1	0	0	1	0

Goodheart-Willcox Publisher

Appendix C

Number Conversion Table

Decimal	Binary	Octal	Hexadecimal
0	000000	0	0
1	000001	1	1
2	000010	2	2
3	000011	3	3
4	000100	4	4
5	000101	5	5
6	000110	6	6
7	000111	7	7
8	001000	10	8
9	001001	11	9
10	001010	12	A
11	001011	13	B
12	001100	14	C
13	001101	15	D
14	001110	16	E
15	001111	17	F
16	010000	20	10
17	010001	21	11
18	010010	22	12
19	010011	23	13
20	010100	24	14
21	010101	25	15
22	010110	26	16
23	010111	27	17
24	011000	30	18
25	011001	31	19
26	011010	32	1A
27	011011	33	1B
28	011100	34	1C
29	011101	35	1D
30	011110	36	1E
31	011111	37	1F

(Continued)

Decimal	Binary	Octal	Hexadecimal
32	100000	40	20
33	100001	41	21
34	100010	42	22
35	100011	43	23
36	100100	44	24
37	100101	45	25
38	100110	46	26
39	100111	47	27
40	101000	50	28
41	101001	51	29
42	101010	52	2A
43	101011	53	2B
44	101100	54	2C
45	101101	55	2D
46	101110	56	2E
47	101111	57	2F
48	110000	60	30
49	110001	61	31
50	110010	62	32
51	110011	63	33
52	110100	64	34
53	110101	65	35
54	110110	66	36
55	110111	67	37
56	111000	70	38
57	111001	71	39
58	111010	72	3A
59	111011	73	3B
60	111100	74	3C
61	111101	75	3D
62	111110	76	3E
63	111111	77	3F

Appendix D

Table of Standard ASCII Characters

Code	Character	Description
0	NUL	Null
1	SOH	Start of header
2	STX	Start of text
3	ETX	End of text
4	EOT	End of transmission
5	ENQ	Enquiry
6	ACK	Acknowledgment
7	BEL	Bell
8	BS	Backspace
9	HT	Horizontal tab
10	LF	Line feed
11	VT	Vertical tab
12	FF	Form feed
13	CR	Carriage return
14	SO	Shift out
15	SI	Shift in
16	DLE	Data link escape
17	DC1	Device control 1
18	DC2	Device control 2
19	DC3	Device control 3
20	DC4	Device control 4
21	NAK	Negative acknowledgment
22	SYN	Synchronous idle
23	ETB	End of transmit block
24	CAN	Cancel
25	EM	End of medium
26	SUB	Substitute
27	ESC	Escape
28	FS	File separator
29	GS	Group separator
30	RS	Record separator
31	US	Unit separator
32	SP	Space
33	!	
34	"	
35	#	
36	$	
37	%	
38	&	
39	'	
40	(	
41	)	

Continued	
42	*
43	+
44	,
45	-
46	.
47	/
48	0
49	1
50	2
51	3
52	4
53	5
54	6
55	7
56	8
57	9
58	:
59	;
60	<
61	=
62	>
63	?
64	@
65	A
66	B
67	C
68	D
69	E
70	F
71	G
72	H
73	I
74	J
75	K
76	L
77	M
78	N
79	O
80	P
81	Q
82	R
83	S
84	T

Continued	
85	U
86	V
87	W
88	X
89	Y
90	Z
91	[
92	\
93	]
94	^
95	_
96	`
97	a
98	b
99	c
100	d
101	e
102	f
103	g
104	h
105	i
106	j
107	k
108	l
109	m
110	n
111	o
112	p
113	q
114	r
115	s
116	t
117	u
118	v
119	w
120	x
121	y
122	z
123	{
124		
125	}
126	~
127	DEL

Glossary

A

A+ Certification. Certification awarded on successful completion of the CompTIA A+ exams. (1)

Accelerated Graphics Port (AGP). Bus designed exclusively for the video card. It supports data transfer of 32 bits at 254.3 MBps, 508.6 MBps, 1.017 GBps, and 2.034 GBps. (3)

accelerometer. Electromechanical device that measures acceleration forces. (12)

Access Control List (ACL). Database used to match a user SID to the resource and then allow or deny access to it. (17)

access time. Amount of time that passes between the issue of the read command and when the first data bit is read from the CD. (10)

Active Directory. Feature in Windows that allows files and information to be easily shared across large enterprise networks. (17)

active hub. Has a source of power connected to it. When a signal is received by an active hub, it is regenerated. (16)

active-matrix display. LCD display in which each individual cell in the grid has its own individual transistor. (8)

active partition. Designated boot disk for the system. (9)

actuator arm. Device that moves the read/write head over the disk. (9)

adapter teaming. Process that allows two or more network adapters to share the network load and ensure network reliability. (16)

address bus. Bus system that connects the CPU with the main memory module, used to identify memory locations where data is to be stored or retrieved. (3)

Address Resolution Protocol (ARP). Protocol used to resolve IPv4 addresses to physical addresses. (18)

ad-hoc network. Wireless formed between two or more wireless devices such as a workstation and a notebook. (12)

Advanced Access Content System (AACS). Standard used for content distribution and digital rights management that uses a security system based on a set of encryption keys that must be used to play the media. (10)

Advanced Access Control System. Digital rights management system for media content distribution. (10)

Advanced Configuration and Power Interface (ACPI). Open industry power management standard for desktops, laptops, and servers; it allows the operating system to control the power management features. (5)

Advanced Video Codec High Definition (AVCHD). Proprietary specification developed jointly by Sony and Panasonic that allows high-definition video to be burned to a standard DVD disc, which can then be played in a Blu-ray Disc player at high-definition resolution. (10)

Advanced Video Coding (AVC). Video compression standard used for high-definition video; also referred to as *H.264/MPEG-4*. (8)

adware. Designed to support advertisements, such as popups, and may also gather information about the user, which it sends data back to the originating source to keep track of the user's Internet habits. (14)

airplane mode. Disables wireless services so that the device cannot send or receive telephone calls or text messages. (12)

alkaline battery. Common battery found in small devices such as TV remote controls and some palmtops. (12)

alternating current (ac). Electrical current that reverses direction cyclically. It has no negative or positive markings because it is in a state of constant change or alternating polarities. (5)

alternating-frame rendering. Method of sharing the video workload in which each card is responsible for rendering every other frame. (8)

American Standard Code for Information Interchange (ASCII). First attempt to standardize computer character codes among the varieties of hardware and software. (1)

ampere (A). Scale of measurement for the volume of electron flow in a circuit. (5)

analog electronics. Electronic system that uses and produces varying voltage levels. Analog electrical circuits can be represented with a dimmer switch. (1)

Android. Mobile operating system derived from the Linux open source operating system. (12)

answer file. Text-based document used in conjunction with the Sysprep tool to configure the unattended destination computer. (17)

anti-static wrist strap. A strap, typically worn around the wrist that connects the technician to ground and bleeds off any electrostatic charge. (1)

Anything as a Service (XaaS). Hybrid of Saas, PaaS, and IaaS services, designed to meet a variety of needs. (18)

app. Software that allows the user to access the larger software application on the cloud service. (2)

app store. Location that provides software applications for portable devices such as smartphones and tablets. (12)

Apple picking. Method of stealing a user's mobile device while they are using it. (12)

application software. Designed for a specific purpose, such as creating databases or spreadsheets, word processing; also referred to as end-user software. (2)

archive bit. File attribute that indicates if a file has been backed up. (15)

arithmetic logic unit (ALU). CPU component that performs mathematical functions on data stored in the register area. (4)

aspect ratio. Ratio of a display area's height and width. (8)

assembly language. Low-level language in which a CPU's instruction set is written. (4)

AT Attachment (ATA). Standard for disk drive interface that integrates the controller into the disk drive; also referred to as *IDE* or *EIDE*. (9)

AT Attachment Packet Interface (ATAPI). Interface used for standard IBM PC AT and compatible systems for accessing CD devices. (10)

authentication. Process of verifying the identity of the user. (14)

Automatic Medium Dependent Interface Crossover (Auto-MDIX). Standard first introduced by Hewlett-Packard. Auto-MDIX is an electronic chip technology incorporated into the IEEE 1,000 gigabit Ethernet standard for network devices such as switches and network adapters. (16)

Automatic Private IP Address (APIPA). IP address that is automatically issued to a computer when a DHCP address cannot issue an IP address. (18)

B

back door virus. Virus designed to go undetected and leave a back door into your system. A back door is a hole in the security system of a computer or network. (14)

backfeed. Type of ohmmeter reading in which the resistance is measured through the circuit components even though the circuit is open. (5)

backoff interval. Period of time two network stations wait before trying to retransmit data after data packets from the two stations collide. (16)

backplane. Circuit board with an abundance of slots along the length of the board. (3)

bandwidth. Range of frequencies that an electronic cable or component is designed to carry. (13)

bar code reader. Device that converts bar code images into data. (7)

basic disk. Traditional FAT16, FAT32, exFAT, and NTFS file storage system. (9)

battery. Component that supplies voltage to the CMOS chip. Without the battery, information stored in the CMOS chip would be lost every time the computer is shut off. (1)

baud rate. Rate of the analog frequency that a modem transmits. (13)

benchmark test. Performance test conducted to compare different hardware and software. (9)

binary number system. System in which all numbers are expressed as combinations of 0 and 1; also known as the *base 2 number system*. (1)

biometrics. Science of using the unique physical features of a person to confirm their identity for authentication purposes. (12)

bit. Single binary unit of one or zero. (1)

bitmap (BMP). Graphics standard for uncompressed encoding of images. (8)

blackout. Condition that occurs when there is no voltage present. (5)

blue screen error. Blue screen that appears with an error code and then freezes the system; also referred to as *fatal errors*, *stop errors*, and *stop error messages*. (15)

Bluetooth. Name of a standard developed for short-range radio links between portable computers, mobile phones, and other portable devices. (12)

Bluetooth standard. Standard that connects low-powered devices over a short distance using the assigned 2.4-GHz frequency. (7)

Blu-ray Disc (BD). High-definition video and data format developed jointly by the Blu-ray Disc Association. (10)

Blu-ray Disc Plus (BD+). Standard used with Blu-ray Disc digital rights management systems that performs the same type of protection as DVD region codes. (10)

Blu-ray Disc Recordable (BD-R). Single-layer Blu-Ray disc that can only be recorded to once. (10)

Blu-ray Disc Recordable Erasable (BD-RE). Single-layer Blu-Ray disc that allows a user to add and back up data, music, or video multiple times. (10)

boot sequence. Step-by-step process of bringing a computer to an operational state. (2)

bootstrap program. Short program that runs the POST; searches for the Master Boot Record (MBR), which is typically located on the first section of the hard drive; loads into memory some basic files; and then turns the boot operation over to the operating system. (2)

botnet. Collection of infected computers that are controlled by a source computer. (14)

bridge. Device used to connect two dissimilar networks. (12)

brouter. Combination router and bridge. (18)

brownout. Flow of electrical power when low voltage is present. (5)

browser hijacker. Program that changes the Internet Explorer browser configuration, such as by replacing the default home page and or browser. (14)

buffer. Area used to temporarily store data before transferring it to a device. (6)

buffering. Technique used to play a downloaded file without skips or quiet spots during playback. (8)

bug. Error in programming. (2)

bus. Collection of conductors working together for a specific purpose.(3)

bus topology. Network topology in which a single conductor connects to all the computers on the network. (16)

bus unit. Network of circuitry that connects all the other major components together, accepts data, and sends data through the input and output bus sections. (4)

byte. Unit equal to eight bits. (1)

C

cable crimper. Tool designed to crimp (squeeze) an RJ-45 connector onto the end of a twisted pair cable, thus making the electrical connections between each of the eight conductors and the connector. (16)

cable modem. Transceiver similar to a DSL modem and allows existing cable television coaxial cable to be used for Internet access. (13)

cable tester. Tool used to test newly-made and existing network cables. A cable tester allows a technician to trace the exact location of cable runs inside walls, ceilings, or under floors to identify unmarked cables. (16)

cable tracer. Allows a technician to trace the exact location of cable runs inside walls, ceilings, under floors, to identify unmarked cables. The cable tracer receives the signal. and produces a tone if it is in close proximity to the cable. (16)

cache. Small temporary memory area that is used to separate and store incoming data and instructions. (4)

call center. Large collection of support people located in a common facility equipped with telephones and computer network support. (20)

candela. Light measurement based on candle illumination. (8)

carpal tunnel syndrome. Inflammation of the tendons in the hands and wrist, caused by repeating the same movement over and over without proper rest or support. (7)

Carrier Sense Multiple Access with Collision Avoidance (CSMA/CA). Protocol used by wireless networks to control and ensure the delivery of data. (16)

Carrier Sense Multiple Access with Collision Detection (CSMA/CD). Protocol used by Ethernet networks to control and ensure the delivery of data. (16)

cathode ray tube (CRT). Picture tube in which a beam of electrons sweeps across the glass tube, exciting phosphorous dots in the screen. (8)

CD-ROM File System (CDFS). Another name used for ISO 9660. (10)

central processing unit (CPU). Brain of the computer; location where most of the computer's calculating takes place. (1)

chain of custody. Method of preserving the evidence, tracking the exchange of evidence, and ensuring the integrity of the evidence. (20)

charged-coupled device (CCD). Series of light-activated capacitors contained in a single chip. (7)

chipset. Part connecting the motherboard buses and ports that run at different speeds. The chipset also handles data manipulation that would otherwise need to be performed by the CPU. (3)

circuit switching. Type of switching communication that makes a permanent connection for the duration of a transmission in which data is transmitted in a steady stream. (18)

Class A network. One of three classifications of the IPv4 network, supporting up to 16 million hosts on each of 127 networks. (18)

Class B network. One of three classifications of the IPv4 network, supporting up to 65,000 hosts on each of 16,000 networks. (18)

Class C network. One of three classifications of the IPv4 network, supporting 254 hosts on each of 2,000,000 networks. (18)

clean room. Room where dust and foreign particles have been completely eliminated. (15)

client. Individual PC or workstation that accesses a server's resources and shared files. (16)

client/server network. Networking model in which the network is made up of computers that are either clients or servers. (16)

client-side virtualization. Software application used to create multiple operating system environments on the host machine. (18)

cloud computing. Accessing a shared pool of resources and specialized services over the Internet. (2)

cluster. Grouping composed of one or more sectors and the smallest unit that a file will be stored in. Also referred to as *allocation units*. (9)

CMYK. Standard combination of colors (cyan, magenta, yellow, and black) used by color inkjet printers. (11)

coaxial cable. Core conductor surrounded by an insulator. (16)

Code Division Multiple Access (CDMA). One of the electronic techniques used to encode digital information when using radio as a medium. (13)

codec. Any hardware, software, or combination of hardware and software that can compress and decompress data. (8)

cold boot. When the electrical power switch is used to turn on the computer; also called a *hard boot*. (2)

color/graphics adapter (CGA). Video standard that featured two resolutions: 320×200 in four colors and a higher resolution of 640×200 in two colors. (8)

color palette. Collection of possible different colors that can be displayed on a monitor. (8)

color thermal printer. Printer that applies color by heating a special ribbon that is coated with wax-like material. (11)

colored books. Set of books that outline disc system specifications. (10)

Column Address Select (CAS). Time it takes to access the exact column location in the memory matrix after RAS. (6)

command interpreter. Contains a set of programs activated by text entered at the command prompt; another name for command.com and cmd.exe. (2)

command line interface (CLI). Operating system interface that allows commands for the computer to be issued by typing in text at a command prompt. (2)

command prompt. Program that produces the command line. (2)

Common Internet File System (CIFS). Network file-sharing protocol developed for early Microsoft operating systems. (18)

community cloud. Shared infrastructure of users who share a common interest or concern. (18)

Compact Disc Read Only Memory (CD-ROM). Optical disc able to store very large amounts of data. (10)

Compact Disc-Recordable (CD-R). Optical storage media that uses photosensitive reflective dye to simulate the pits and lands of a standard CD. (10)

Compact Disc-ReWritable (CD-RW). Improvement over the CD-R technology, featuring special discs that can be erased and rerecorded. (10)

company app. Application that ensures and enforces security policies on a mobile device. (12)

compiler. Special program that translates the higher-level language into machine language based on the CPU's instruction set. (4)

complex instruction set computer (CISC). CPU with a complex instruction set. (4)

CompTIA. Not-for-profit, vendor-neutral organization that certifies the competency level of technicians through examinations written to test specific areas. (1)

CompTIA A+ Certification exam. Series of tests measuring the fundamentals of computer technology and skills related to more advanced topics in computer technology. (21)

computer. Assembly of electronic modules that interact with computer programs known as *software* to create, modify, transmit, store, and display data. (1)

configuration file. File containing information such as the amount of memory and the type of video adapter present in the system. (2)

constant angular velocity (CAV). Method of reading data from a CD where the drive maintains the same RPM regardless of the data location. (10)

constant linear velocity (CLV). Method of reading data from a CD where the speed of the CD drive adjusts so that points on the inside and outside of the disc are read at a constant linear velocity. (10)

continuity. Ability of a device or component to allow an unobstructed flow of electrical energy. (5)

contrast ratio. Numeric expression in the form of a ratio used to describe the amount of contrast between the darkest and lightest pixel in the image. (8)

control bus. Bus used to deliver command signals from the processor to devices such as hard drives and modems. (3)

control unit. CPU component that controls the overall operation of the CPU. (4)

cookie. Small text file used to send information about a user to a server. (14)

cooling fan. Fan supplying a constant stream of air across the computer components. (1)

cooperative multitasking. When one program dominates the operating system but will allow another program to run while it is idle. (2)

cross talk. Imposition of a signal on one pair of conductors by another pair of conductors that runs parallel to it. (16)

current. Measured in amperes is the amount of electron flow in a circuit. (5)

customer support. Delivery of customer assistance, customer training, and customer services. (20)

cylinder. Vertical collection of one set of tracks. (9)

D

data. Information, which can be presented in alpha/numeric form (ABC or 123), visual form (pictures), and audible form (music or voices). (1)

data bus. Bus used to move data between components. (3)

data miner. Programs used to gather information about a user's Web browsing habits for marketing purposes. (14)

Data Over Cable Service Interface Specification (DOCSIS). Standard for cable modems that allows any DOSIS cable modem to communicate with any other DOCSIS cable modem. (13)

data transfer rate. Measurement of how much data can be transferred from a CD to RAM in a set period of time. (10)

decode unit. CPU component that decodes instructions and data and transmits the data to other areas in an understandable format. (4)

dedicated circuit. Electrical power distribution system designed to serve only computer equipment. (5)

dedicated server. Server with special functions, such as file servers, print servers, database servers, Web page servers, and administrative servers. (16)

deflection yoke. Electromagnets used to deflect the electron beam in a CRT. (8)

defragment. Rearranging clusters on the disk so each file is stored in consecutive clusters. (9)

degaussing. Correction of the remnant magnetic field. (8)

demarcation point. Location where the telephone company system ends and the residence ownership begins. (13)

Demilitarized Zone (DMZ). Area of a network system intentionally created to be less secure than the main network system and is directly accessible from the Internet. (19)

demultiplexer. Device that reverses the flow of data and voice over a T-carrier line by rearranging packets back into their original structures and releasing them to lower data rate lines. (13)

denial-of-service (DOS) attack. When a network server or web server is flooded with requests to the point that it cannot fulfill the requests. (14)

deployment image. Exact copy of all the files contained on the hard disk drive of the reference computer. (17)

depot technician. One who performs repair work usually covered by warranty. (20)

device bay. Drive bay designed to accommodate the easy hot swap of devices such as hard drives, tape drives, and optical drives. (1)

dialer. Program that automatically disables a telephone modem that is dialing a number and automatically switches to another phone number. (14)

differential backup. Operation that saves files that have changed since the last full backup of all files. (15)

digital camera. Type of camera used to capture and store images as digital data instead of on photographic film. (7)

digital electronics. Electronic system best represented by a simple switch, where there can only be two conditions in the switch circuit—either on or off. (1)

digital rights management (DRM). Any technology that ensures copyright protection for digital media such as digital music and video. (10)

digital subscriber line (DSL). Provides high-speed Internet access over telephone lines. A DSL can provide a constant connection to the Internet and can send both voice and data over the same line. (13)

Digital Versatile Disc (DVD). Highest storage capacity of all laser-based CD storage types; also referred to as *digital video disc*. (10)

digital-to-analog converter (DAC). Chip used to convert the digital signal from the computer to an analog signal that is displayed on the computer's monitor. (8)

digitizer pad. Pointing device consisting of a tablet and a puck or pen-like stylus. (7)

direct current (dc). Electrical energy flows in one direction, from negative to positive. (5)

direct memory access (DMA). Combination of hardware and software that allows the hard drive to transfer all the data directly to memory without involving the CPU. (3)

directory. File used to group other files together in a hierarchical file structure. Directories are referred to as *folders* in many operating systems. (2)

disk signature. Characteristic identifying the disk type and properties, so the Microsoft operating system can utilize the disk. (9)

diskless workstation. Workstation that runs without a floppy drive or hard disk drive. (16)

docking station. Electronic cradle providing power for a laptop, allowing users to turn the laptop into a full-size PC. (12)

domain. Organized collection of all groups and users on the network. (17) Category of a specific topic area covered in the CompTIA exam. (21)

Domain Name Service (DNS). Service that translates domain names to IP addresses and assists computers in identifying and talking to each other. (18)

domain user account. Available user account that provides access to network domain resources and to resources on the workstation. (17)

dot matrix printer. Printer that uses a pattern of very small dots to create text and images. (11)

dot pitch. Distance measured in millimeters between two color dots on the screen. (8)

driver. Small software program that enables the operating system to properly communicate with a peripheral device. (1)

DSL modem. Transceiver that allows for high-speed Internet access over existing phone lines. (13)

dual-boot system. Computer with two operating systems installed. (2)

dual-channel mode. Arrangement that is present when the DIMMs are arranged as a pair and in a specific way according to the motherboard manual; also known as *interleaved mode*. (6)

Dual Independent Bus (DIB). Bus architecture introduced with the Pentium Pro and Pentium II. (4)

dual in-line memory module (DIMM). Memory module in which the edge connectors are located directly across the circuit board from each other and do not connect electrically. (6)

dual in-line package (DIP). Chip that has two rows of connections, one row per side of the chip. (6)

dumpster diving. Act of inspecting a user or company's garbage to locate sensitive information. (14)

dye-sublimation printer. Printer that produces near photo quality printed images by vaporizing inks, which then solidify on paper. (11)

dynamic addressing. Act of automatically assigning IP addresses. (18)

dynamic disk. Improved version of the NTFS file system. (9)

dynamic execution. Term coined by Intel to describe the enhanced superscalar and multiple branch prediction features associated with the Pentium II processor. (4)

Dynamic Host Configuration Protocol (DHCP). Protocol written to replace the manual setup of IP addresses on a network. (18)

dynamic RAM (DRAM). Type of integrated circuit that uses capacitors to assist in storing data in the transistors. (6)

E

EFI System Partition (ESP). Special area of the hard disk drive intended for use solely by the firmware, typically containing files and data required to boot the computer system. The acronym EFI stands for Extensible Firmware Interface. (9)

electrically erasable programmable read-only memory (EEPROM). Read-only memory that can be erased electrically and written to more than once. (6)

electromagnetic interference (EMI). Interference or damage to components caused by magnets and magnetic fields. (1)

electron gun. Component that produces the electron beam, which sweeps across the inside of a monitor. (8)

electrophotographic process (EP). Photographic process using a combination of static electricity, light, dry chemical compound, pressure, and heat. (11)

electrostatic discharge (ESD). Release of energy (electrical current), created when an object with an electrostatic charge makes contact with a conductor. (1)

emoticon. Cartoon face character made from keyboard symbols, used to express emotions in e-mails, letters, and text messaging. (20)

eMTA modem. Transceiver that combines the functionality of a DOCSIS cable modem and a phone adapter in one device. The acronym eMTA stands for Embedded Multimedia Terminal Adapter. (13)

emulator. Software application acting as an interface between the user and a software application. (18)

encrypted file system (EFS). NTFS native encryption system that uses a file encryption key (FEK) to encrypt and decrypt the file contents. (9)

encryption. Method of encoding data that must be converted back to meaningful words by using an encryption key. The encryption key is a mathematical formula for substituting values in strings of data. (12)

encryption key. Mathematical formula for substituting values in strings of data. (12)

enhanced graphics adapter (EGA). Video standard used to improve the resolutions and color capabilities of the CGA standard. (8)

Enhanced Integrated Drive Electronics (EIDE). Term introduced by Western Digital Corporation to describe hard drives that originally used an ATA standard known as *ATA-2*, *Fast ATA*, or *Fast ATA-2*. (9)

erasable programmable read only memory (EPROM). Read-only memory that can be erased with an ultraviolet light and written to more than once. (6)

error code correction (ECC). Alternative form of data-integrity checking. (6)

Ethernet network. Network that communicates by broadcasting information to all the computers on the network. (16)

even parity checking. Data integrity checking method in which every time the number of bits counted is even, an extra bit of data is transmitted as a one to indicate even. (6)

examination objective. Target goal derived from industry surveys used to determine the actual job requirements of a PC service technician. (21)

executable file. Complete software program that runs when the file name is entered at the command prompt. These files have an .exe or .com file extension. (2)

expansion card. Board that can be easily installed in a computer to enhance or expand its capabilities. An expansion card allows the computer to be custom-designed to meet the needs of different consumers. (1)

expansion card slot. Receptacle for an expansion card, which allows the card to connect to the motherboard's circuitry. (1) Connector that allows devices to be quickly and easily plugged into the bus system. (3)

ExpressCard. Card used to add memory or expand a portable PC, designed to connect internally to either the USB 2.0 bus or the PCIe bus. (12)

extended file allocation table (exFAT). File system that is a proprietary Microsoft design for portable devices such as USB flash drives and flash memory cards. (9)

extended graphics array (XGA). Video standard that supports a resolution of 640×480 with 65,536 colors, or 1024×768 with 256 colors. (8)

external command. Individual, executable file found in addition to the internal command. (2)

external SATA. Port that provides a data connection to an external SATA device but does not provide power to the device. (1)

F

fail-over. Used by Microsoft to describe the process that occurs when one system fails and another system takes over. (16)

fake parity. When the parity bit is always set to one regardless of the true number of ones contained in the byte. (6)

FAT16. File system in which file storage information is recorded with 16 bits of data. (9)

FAT32. File system in which file storage information is recorded with 32 bits of data. (9)

fault tolerance. System's ability to recover after some sort of disaster. (17)

fiber-optic cable. Cable containing a glass or plastic center used to carry light. (16)

field. Complete sweep of the entire screen area. (8)

file. Program or a collection of data that forms a single unit. (2)

file extension. Second part of a file name, typically three additional characters long, indicating the function of the file. (2)

file system. Method of organizing files on a storage device. It is used by the operating system to keep track of all files on the disk. (2)

file table. Component of a file system used to organize files on a storage device. (2)

File Transfer Protocol (FTP). Protocol used for transmitting files across the Internet. (18)

firewall. Hardware device or software application that protects the computer from unauthorized access or malware delivered through a network or Internet connection. (14)

firmware. Hardware-specific software required to boot the computer and support communication between the operating system and hardware devices. Firmware interprets commands of higher-level software programs. (1)

flash BIOS. Electrically erasable programmable read-only memory (EEPROM) module, which can be erased electrically and then reprogrammed. (3)

flash memory. Solid-state, reusable data storage device that can retain data even when the electrical power is disconnected. (6)

flash ROM. ROM that can be erased in blocks using a high voltage. (6)

flex mode. Hybrid DIMM arrangement. (6)

floating point unit (FPU). Set of circuits incorporated into the processor that is used for mathematic computation. (4)

floppy disk. Soft magnetic disk used for storing small to moderate amounts of information. (9)

floppy disk drive. Component that reads and writes to floppy disks. (9)

floppy drive connector. Two-pin connector that delivers a +5 volt signal from the power supply. A variation of this connector has four wires and delivers both +12-volt and +5-volt signals; also called a *mini connector.* (5)

font. Design for a set of symbols, usually text and number characters. A font describes characteristics associated with a symbol such as the typeface, size, pitch, and spacing between symbols. (11)

form factor. Physical shape or outline of a motherboard and the location of the mounting holes; sometimes called the *footprint.* (3)

four-pin peripheral power connector. Hardware used to connect to ATA hard drives, CD-ROM drives, and DVD drives. These devices typically use the +12-volt level from the connector; also called a *Molex connector.* (5)

front side bus (FSB). Another term for *local bus.* (4)

fully qualified domain name (FQDN). Combination of both the computer name and the domain name. (19)

fuse. Cylinder shape of glass or ceramic with a metal cap on each end. Inside the cylinder is the fuse link. (5)

G

game pad. Any device used as an input for a game application. (7)

gas-plasma displays. Flat-panel displays that operate on the principle of electroluminescence. (8)

gateway. Networking device that translates information between two networks that use different protocols to communicate. (18)

geotracking. When a device is tracked by another device. (12)

global positioning system (GPS). Satellite-based navigation system developed by the Department of Defense (DoD). (12)

Global System for Mobile Communications (GSM). Wireless digital communication system for transmitting mobile voice and data. (13)

graphical user interface (GUI). Operating system interface that allows the user to perform functions by selecting on-screen icons rather than by issuing text-based commands. (2)

grayware. Collection of malware that is not regarded as very dangerous, but rather more of a nuisance. Examples of Grayware are popups, adware, joke programs, spyware, and data mining software. (14)

group. Collection of users organized together by similarities in their job tasks. (17)

GUID Partition Table (GPT). Area of the hard disk containing information about the disk partition and the type of storage media used (floppy disk or hard drive). (9)

gyroscope. Device that measures the vertical and horizontal orientation. (12)

H

hard disk drive (HDD) password. Hardware password used to prevent unauthorized access to the data stored on the hard drive; also known as the *drive lock password* or *hard disk drive lock password.* (14)

hard drive. Location where computer programs and data are stored; also called the *internal drive* or *hard disk drive.* (1)

hard reset. Returns the device to its original condition and removes all user data, passwords, and apps. (12)

heap. How Windows refers to the entire memory. (6)

heat spreader. Aluminum sheath capable of dissipating the heat generated by the high-speed data transfer rate. (6)

help desk. Central point of contact that provides technical support to clients. (20)

hexadecimal number system. System in which all numbers are expressed in combinations of 16 alphanumeric characters (0–F); also known as the *base 16 system.* (1)

High-bandwidth Digital Content Protection (HDCP). System that encrypts the data sent by a high-definition content player such as Blu-ray or HD-DVD to other devices such as a television or computer monitor via a physical connection. (10)

high-level format. Process used to prepare the disk for file storage. (9)

High Sierra format. Standard for compact discs, created so CDs could be read on any CD device. (10)

hive. Major grouping of the Windows Registry Editor; contains registry keys. (15)

hoax. False message spread about a real or unreal virus. (14)

Home Phoneline Networking Alliance (HomePNA) technology. Technology that allows existing home telephone lines to be used for the network media. (19)

home theater PC (HTPC). Customized computer used to enhance the television viewing experience, having all the capabilities of a typical PC plus additional software/hardware to support multimedia recording and playback. (8)

HomeGroup. Group of PCs sharing libraries and printers. (17)

HomePNA adapter. Networking device that allows every telephone jack connected together physically in a building to be part of the network. (19)

hot docking. Feature that allows users to dock or undock their laptop computer without the need to change hardware configurations. (12)

hot swap. Plug in or unplug a device while the PC is running. (1)

HP network re-discovery port monitor. Wireless port used to support connections to a wireless printer. (11)

hub. Device used to provide a quick and easy method of connecting network equipment together by cables. (16)

Human Interface Device (HID) standard. Classification of USB devices; a set of standards written for hardware device drivers to ensure compatibility between hardware devices and computers. (7)

hybrid cloud. Combination of two or more of the other cloud infrastructures. (18)

hybrid topology. Mixture of star, bus, and ring topologies. (16)

Hypertext Markup Language (HTML). Programming language used to create webpages. (18)

Hypertext Transfer Protocol (HTTP). Standard protocol used to transport webpage content across the Internet. (18)

hypervisor. Technical term used to identify the software that creates the virtual machine on the client device; also referred to as a *virtual machine monitor.* (18)

I

IEEE-1394. Bus system that provides a high rate of data transfer (speeds of 400 Mbps). A single IEEE-1394 port can serve up to 63 external devices in daisy-chain fashion. (3)

I/O bus. Bus that connects the processor to the expansion slots; also called an *expansion bus.* (3)

I/O port address. Memory address expressed in hexadecimal notation, which is used to identify a computer device such as a video card. (3)

incremental backup. Operation that backs up select files that have changed since the last backup of files. The archive bit is reset. (15)

Infrastructure as a Service (IaaS). Cloud service model providing storage and basic networking functions used by the consumer. (18)

infrastructure network. Wireless network that contains a wireless access point. (12)

inkjet printer. Printer with specially designed cartridges that spray a fine mist of ink as they move horizontally in front of a sheet of paper. (11)

input device. Equipment used to communicate with the PC system and provide the PC with data. (7)

instruction. Command given to the processor, or CPU. (4)

instruction set. Set of basic commands that control the processor. (4)

insulation displacement connector (IDC). Slotted post found on patch panels and punch down blocks. (16)

integrated circuit (IC). Collection of transistors, resistors, and other electronic components reduced to an unbelievable small size. (1)

Integrated Drive Electronics (IDE). Early standard for a disk drive interface that integrated the controller into the disk drive; a term commonly used when referring to the AT attachment. (9)

Integrated Memory Controller (IMC). Term used to describe when the memory controller is part of the processor. (4)

integrated services digital network (ISDN). Standard that allows a completely digital connection from one PC to another. (13)

interleave factor. Term used to describe how the sectors are laid out on a disk surface to optimize a hard drive's data access rate. (9)

internal bus. A bus that is part of the integrated circuit inside the CPU unit. (3)

internal command. Set of programs activated by text entered at the command prompt. These programs are wholly contained within the command processor program (command.com or cmd.exe). (2)

International Mobile Station Equipment Identity (IMEI). Identifies the mobile device and the user. (12)

Internet Connection Firewall (ICF). Software configured to keep unauthorized users from accessing the network. (19)

Internet Control Message Protocol version 6 (ICMPv6). Protocol and service for exchanging messages between network neighboring nodes on the same link. (18)

Internet Corporation for Assigned Names and Numbers (ICANN). Nonprofit organization that monitors the use of domain names, IP addresses, and related protocol. (18)

Internet Gateway Device Discovery and Control (IGDDC). Network connection sharing technology designed to discover and control network gateway devices such as routers. (19)

Internet Message Access Protocol (IMAP). E-mail protocol used to access e-mail from a server. (18)

Internet service provider (ISP). Provides a connection to the Internet, and many other services, such as e-mail, tools, and space to set up your own website, search engines, and local information provided by most ISPs. (13)

inverter. Electronic device used to convert the low voltage (12–18 Vdc) from the portable battery to a much higher voltage required by the CCFL. (8)

iOS. Proprietary mobile operating system iOS used for Apple devices, such as Apple iPhone, iPad, iPod touch, and other Apple products. (12)

IP address. Numeric identifier regulated and assigned through the Internet Corporation for Assigned Names and Numbers (ICANN). (18)

IPSec. Collection of protocols that encrypt and authenticate each Internet Control Message Protocol (ICMP) packet that uses an IP address over the Internet. (18)

ISO 9660. File system standard for CD-ROMs, which is an update on the High Sierra format. (10)

ISO image. Image that is the exact copy of data, made by copying all sectors containing data and ignoring the file system used. (10)

J

jailbreaking. Describes the process of overcoming the operating system's user limitations. (12)

K

kernel. Core of any operating system. (2)

kernel mode. Automatic mode of operation that oversees the system resources and processor actions. (15)

Kernel-based Virtual Machine (KVM) client. Machine having the virtualization software installed directly on the machine hardware rather than inside a host machine operating system; also referred to as a *bare metal device*. (18)

Keyboard-Video-Mouse (KVM). Switch is used to share a mouse, keyboard, and monitor with two or more computers or servers. (7)

keylogger. Malware that after being installed on a computer keeps track of all keys pressed by the user. It records the keystrokes in a file, which can later be retrieved in order to learn the user logon name, password, and other confidential information. (14)

L

L1 cache. Cache contained within the processor that is designed to run at the processor's speed. (4)

L2 cache. Cache mounted outside of the processor. (Note: The Pentium III incorporates the L2 cache in the processor.) (4)

land. Flat area between the pits in a compact disc. (10)

LED monitor. Portable LCD screen that uses an LED backlight. (8)

LED printer. Printer that uses an array of light-emitting diodes (LEDs) rather than a laser to write the image to the drum. (11)

library. Virtual collection of folders and files from different locations displayed as a single virtual folder. (17)

light pen. Input device that interacts with the light beam that creates the image on the monitor. (7)

liquid crystal display (LCD). Type of monitor using polarized light, which passes through liquid crystal to create an image on screen. (8)

lithium-ion (Li-ion) battery. Rechargeable battery found in most new portable computers. (12)

lithium-ion polymer (Li-poly) battery. Latest version of the lithium-ion class of battery which uses a polymer or polymer gel as the electrolyte. (12)

live support. Support in which a customer or client talks directly to support personnel for technical assistance, rather than use an FAQ list or web page. (20)

load balancing. Process that occurs when a computer has multiple network adapters installed and then balances or divides the exchange of packets between the multiple network adapters. (16)

local area network (LAN). Small network of computers contained in a relatively small area, such as an office building. (16)

local bus. Bus system that connects directly to the CPU and provides communications to high-speed devices mounted closely to the CPU; also called a *system bus*. (3)

local printer. Printer that connects directly to a PC. (11)

local printer connection. Phrase used to describe when a printer is connected directly to a computer. (11)

local user account. Available user account configured on the workstation to control access to specific resources on that specific workstation. (17)

logic bomb. Destructive program slipped into an application, which waits dormant until some event takes place, allowing the virus to spread to other computers before releasing its payload. (14)

logical drive. Separate storage area on a single drive that simulates a separate drive; also referred to as a *partition.* (9)

logical unit number (LUN). Identifier used with SCSI extenders to distinguish between (up to) eight devices on the same SCSI ID number. (9)

Long Term Evolution (LTE). Wireless digital communication system that is best for streaming music, videos, and high definition. (13)

loopback plug. Tool used to test an Ethernet network card. (16)

low-level format. Process that determines the type of encoding to be done on the disk platter and the sequence in which the read/write heads will access stored data. (9)

M

macro virus. Virus created using a macro programming language. It is attached to documents that use the language. (14)

magneto-optical (MO) drive. Disk drive that combines magnetic and optical principles to store and retrieve data. (10)

malicious software. Programs written for the express purpose of modifying a computer's configuration or causing damage to the computer system, also called *malware.* There are many different categories of malicious software, such as virus, worm, root kit, and more. (14)

man trap. Physical configuration that allows only one person access at a time. (14)

Master Boot Record (MBR). Area of the hard disk that contains information about the physical characteristics of the drive, the disk partitions, and the boot procedure; also referred to as the *boot sector.* (9)

MBR virus. Extremely destructive virus that attacks the master boot record (MBR) of a hard disk, resulting in hard disk failure. (14)

Measured Boot. Windows 8 security feature used to verify the successful launch of the operating system and store the information in the TPM. (14)

media access code (MAC) address. Hexadecimal number programmed into an adapter card's chip. (16)

memory address range. Assigned section of memory used as a temporary storage area for data before it is transferred. (3)

memory bus. Bus that connects the processor directly to the memory (3)

mesh topology. Network system in which each node connects directly to every other node on the network. (16)

Messaging Application Programming Interface (MAPI). Microsoft's proprietary e-mail protocol, very similar to IMAP. (18)

metal oxide varistor (MOV). Gate in a surge suppressor that becomes conductive at a given voltage, causing current to bypass the equipment plugged into the suppressor. (5)

metropolitan area network (MAN). Group of two or more interconnected LANs operating under a single management. (16)

MicroDIMM. More compact version of the standard SO-DIMM package. (6)

Microsoft Dynamic Link Library (DLL). Executable file that can be called and run by Microsoft software applications or by third-party software programs. (15)

Microsoft Reserved Partition (MSR). Partition on a data storage device, required for GUID partition tables; also referred to as *System Reserved partition.* (9)

MMX processor. Processor with an additional 57 commands that enhance its abilities to support multimedia technology. (4)

mobile broadband. Wireless Internet connection based on mobile phone technology. (13)

mobile hotspot. Portable wireless router that allows multiple devices to share a common Internet connection. (13)

modem. Electronic device used to convert serial data from a computer to an audio signal for transmission over telephone lines and vice versa. (13)

monochrome. Monitor type that displays only a single color, usually amber or green. (8)

motherboard. Circuit board covered by a maze of conductors which provide electrical current to the computer components and expansion slots. (1)

Moving Picture Experts Group (MPEG). Organization made up of professionals from all areas of the motion picture industry, with the goal to develop a standard format for recording motion picture video and sound. (8)

multicolor/graphics array (MCGA). Video standard supporting CGA and also providing up to 64 shades of gray. (8)

multi-factor authentication. Combination of two or more authentication techniques. (14)

multimedia. Format that includes interaction with audio and video. (8)

multiple-boot system. Computer with more than two operating systems installed. (2)

multiple branch prediction. Technique used to predict what data element will be needed next, rather than waiting for the next command to be issued. (4)

Multiple Input Multiple Output (MIMO). Device that uses multiple radio channels to transmit and receive data to increase the overall data rate. (13) Wireless technology that uses two or more streams of data transmission to increase the data throughput and range of the wireless network. (16)

multiple zone recording (MZR). Method of sectoring tracks so there are twice as many sectors in the outermost tracks as there are in the innermost tracks. (9)

multiplexer. Special electronic device that controls the flow of data and voice over a T-carrier line. (13)

Multipurpose Internet Mail Extensions (MIME). Specification for formatting non-text-based files for transmission over the Internet. (18)

multitasking. Ability of an operating system to support two or more programs running at the same time. (2)

multithreading. When data and parts of a program can be shared between two or more CPUs or between the two cores of a single CPU. (2)

multi-touch. Action of touching any surface-sensing device, such as a tablet touch screen or touch pad, with two or more fingers. (12)

musical instrument digital interface (MIDI). File standard developed for music synthesizers. (8)

N

nanosecond (ns). Unit of time equal to one billionth of a second. (6)

native resolution. Resolution that matches the pixel design of the display. (8)

network. Two or more computers connected together for the purpose of sharing data and resources. (16)

network administration. Use of network software packages to manage network system operations. (17)

network administrator. One person (or more) who has the highest security rating on the network and is responsible for delegating authority all the way down to the user level. (17)

network-attached storage (NAS). Form of data storage that provides a means of centralized file sharing with little administrative overhead. (19)

network interface card (NIC). Hardware used to connect media to individual network devices, such as workstations, file servers, and printers; also called a *network adapter card* and *Ethernet card.* (16)

network media. Means by which an electronic signal is transmitted. (16)

network operating system (NOS). Operating system that provides communications between computers, printers, and other intelligent hardware on the network. (16)

network printer. Printer connected via a wired or wireless network connection. (11)

network printer connection. Phrase used to describe when a printer is connected by other means than a direct connection to a computer; also referred to as shared printer connection. (11)

New Technology File System (NTFS). File system found in Windows NT and Windows 2000. NTFS features improve security and storage capacity and are compatible with FAT16. (9)

nickel-cadmium (NiCd) battery. Rechargeable battery used in early portable computers. Has a problem with memory effect. (12)

nickel-metal hydride (NiMH) battery. Second generation of a rechargeable battery used for portable computers. Has no problem with memory effect and holds a charge longer than the NiCad battery. (12)

node. Device connected to a client/server network. (16)

north bridge. Part once used to connect high-speed devices to the CPU, such as RAM and PCI slots. (3)

numerical aperture (NA). Numerical expression for the way the light is gathered and focused into a single point. (10)

O

octet. Eight-bit series of numbers. (18)

odd parity checking. Data integrity checking method in which every time the number of bits counted is odd, an extra bit of data is transmitted as a one to indicate odd. (6)

ohm. Unit of resistance, which is expressed with the letter R or the symbol omega (Ω). (5)

Open Systems Interconnection (OSI) model. Seven-layer reference model used to describe how hardware and software should work together to form a network communication system. (16)

operating system (OS). Software that provides a computer user with a file system structure and with a means of communicating with the computer hardware. (2)

optical character recognition (OCR). Type of software able to distinguish between the various letters, numbers, and symbols in a scanned image. (7)

optical mouse. Computer pointing device that traces movement by transmitting a light beam to a surface. (7)

organic LED display (OLED). New technology used to create the thinnest display, made from carbon-based materials rather than crystalline structures used for traditional electronic components. (8)

overclocking. Applying higher frequencies to a processor than the design specification. (4)

P

packet. Small unit of data into which larger amounts are divided for passage through a network. (16)

Packet Internet Groper (PING). Utility often used to verify network connections to websites. (18)

packet sniffer. Utility that captures packets on a network and displays their entire contents. (19)

packet switching. Type of switching communication that divides data into packets, which can take a variety of routes to get to their destination. (18)

packet writing. Records data in small blocks similar to the way hard drives store data. (10)

page file. Virtual memory located on the hard drive; also referred to as a *swap file.* (6)

paper jam. When a printer pulls one or more sheets through its mechanism and the paper becomes wedged inside. (11)

paper train. Route the paper follows through the printer. (11)

parallel ATA (PATA). Interface standard for the connection of storage devices. (9)

parallel transfer. Occurs when more than one bit of data is transferred side by side. Data is sent eight bits at a time. (1)

parity. Counting of either odd or even bits of the bytes transmitted. (6)

passcode lock. Set of numbers used as a password. (12)

passive hub. Connection point in the star topology. (16)

passive-matrix display. LCD display in which a grid of semitransparent conductors is run to each of the crystals that make up the individual pixels. (8)

password virus. Virus that steals passwords. (14)

pathname. String of characters used to identify a file's location in the directory structure. (2)

PCMCIA card. Card designed by the Personal Computer Memory Card International Association (PCMCIA) to add memory or expand a portable PC. The PCMCIA card is often referred to as a *PCM* or *PC card.* (12)

peer-to-peer network. Network administration model in which all the PCs connected together are considered equal. (16)

peripheral. Optional equipment used to display data or to input data. (1)

Peripheral Components Interface (PCI). Bus system featuring a 32-bit data bus that provides a high-speed bus structure needed for faster CPUs. (3)

persistence. Continuation of the glow after the electron beam ceases to strike the phosphor areas. (8)

personal area network (PAN). Short-range network, wired or wireless, that connects a user's devices such as a PC, cell phone, tablet, camera, and printer. (16)

pharming. Deceptive practice based on poisoning a Domain Name Service (DNS) server with an incorrect IP address for a Web site. (14)

phishing. E-mail used to impersonate a legitimate company or institution, thus fooling the user into believing the e-mail is from a trusted source. (14)

photocell. Electronic component that changes light energy into electrical energy. (10)

pit. Hole etched into a compact disc in order to record data. (10)

pitch. Unit of measure for the width of a font. (11)

pixel. Smallest unit of color in a screen display. (8)

pixel pitch. Distance between two same color pixels on the display area. (8)

Platform as a Service (PaaS). Cloud service model that supports programming software. (18)

plenum. Space above a ceiling or raised floor and is designed to carry return air in a closed air conditioning system. (16)

Plug and Play (PnP). Automatic assignment of system resources such as DMA channels, interrupts, memory, and port assignments. (3)

point. Unit of measure for the height of a font. Each point is equal to 1/72 of an inch. (11)

polarized light. Light consisting of waves that have the same. (8)

polymorphic virus. Type of virus that changes as it evolves to go undetected by antivirus programs. (14)

port forwarding. Router configuration set to forward packets to a destination computer/server by allowing specific ports to remain open to the destination. (19)

port number. Number in the range of 0 to 65,535; all software applications that use a network system use assigned port numbers to identify the software application or service. (14)

port replicator. External computer device that provides additional ports to be used by a computer system. (12)

port triggering. Router configuration that monitors outbound traffic by port number. (19)

Post Office Protocol 3 (POP3). E-mail protocol used to download e-mails (incoming) from an e-mail server. (18)

power. Amount of electrical energy provided or used by equipment. (5)

power bus. Bus system used to send electrical power to low-consumption devices such as speakers, lights, and switches. (3)

power eSATA (eSATAp). Port that provides an external SATA device with a data connection and electrical power; also called *eSATAp*. (1)

power good signal. Signal sent from the power supply to the motherboard that verifies the power supply is working properly. (5)

power-on password. Type of BIOS/UEFI password used to help prevent booting from external devices, such as flash drives or external hard drives; also known as the *power-on-password*. (14)

power-on self-test (POST). Simple diagnostic program that is initiated when electrical power is applied to the computer system. (2)

Power over Ethernet (PoE). Means to supply small amounts of electrical power to network devices such as a camera, IP phone, wireless access point, speakers, and phone or PDA charger. (16)

power supply. Source that converts the 120-volt ac power from the wall outlet to dc voltage levels used by the various computer components. (1)

powerline communications (PLC). Technology that enables existing power lines to be used as network media. (19)

preemptive multitasking. Multitasking with multiple programs to share control of the operating system; sometimes referred to as *time slicing*. (2)

primary partition. Partition used to contain the operating system, boot, and data files. (9)

principle of least privilege (POLP). Security principle that states a user should only have sufficient privileges to complete their work task. (14)

print queue. List of print jobs waiting to be completed and their status. (11)

print spooler. Software program that temporarily stores the data in RAM or an area on the hard drive. (11)

printer. Electromechanical device that converts computer data into text or graphic images printed to paper or other presentation media. (11)

printer driver. Component that converts specific file types to electronic signals that control how the image or document is printed on the paper. (11)

privacy filter. Device that attaches to a display and limits or reduces the viewing angle, thus reducing the risk of unauthorized viewing of the display unit. (14)

private cloud. Infrastructure model typically designed for exclusive use by an organization, such as a private corporation, government organization, or an educational organization like a university. (18)

processor affinity. Ability to select the number of CPU cores to apply to a software application. (4)

processor throttling. Controlling processor frequency to conserve battery life and produce less heat. (4)

professionalism. Businesslike characteristic reflected in a person and work environment. (20)

programmable read-only memory (PROM). Read-only memory that can be written to only once. (6)

proprietary recovery partition. Optional partition created by the system's Original Equipment Manufacturer (OEM); also known as the *Original Equipment Manufacturers (OEM) partition.* (9)

protected mode. Operating mode that supports multitasking and allows access to memory beyond the first 1 MB. (6)

protective MBR. Used to protect the GPT when legacy software tools are used to explore or repair the MBR. (9)

protocol. Set of rules used to govern communication between two devices. (7) Set of rules much like the rules that are used by two modes (13).

protocol suite. Combination of individual protocols, each designed for specific purposes. (16)

proxy server. Computer server that hides all the PCs in the LAN from direct connection with PCs outside of the LAN. (18); Computer server that functions as an intermediary between the Internet and a network client computer (19).

public cloud. Infrastructure open to the general public. (18)

public folders. Organizational feature in Windows that allows users to share files on a computer or network. (17)

punch down tool. Used for inserting twisted pair conductors into an insulation displacement connector (IDC); also used for inserting wires into RJ-45 keystone modules. (16)

Q

quad-channel mode. DIMM arrangement that supports four identical memory modules into the designated quad-channel slots. (6)

query. Locating and extracting data from a database system. (16)

R

radio-frequency identification (RFID). Electronic system that uses radio waves to identify objects or people. (14)

radio frequency interference (RFI). Interference produced by electronic devices that use radio waves. (1)

RAID. System of several hard drive units arranged in such a way as to ensure recovery after a system disaster or to ensure data integrity during normal operation. (17)

random access memory (RAM). Volatile memory system into which programs are loaded. When the computer's power is shut off, all data stored in RAM is lost. (1) Memory type that can store information, be erased, and have new information written to it. (6)

raster. Sweep of the electron beam. (8)

read-only memory (ROM). Memory that stores information permanently. (6)

read/write head. Mechanism that records information to and reads information from a magnetic medium. (9)

real mode. Operating mode in which only the first 1 MB of a system's RAM can be accessed. (6)

reduced instruction set computer (RISC). Type of CPU architecture that is designed with a fewer number of transistors and commands. (4)

refresh rate. Rate at which the electron beam sweeps across the screen. (8)

register. Small pocket of memory used to temporarily store data that is being processed by the CPU. (4)

register unit. CPU component containing many separate, smaller storage units known as registers. (4)

registered memory. Memory module that incorporates driver and synchronizing electronics as part of the unit. (6)

registrar. Private sector company to which users apply for an IP address or domain name. (18)

registry. Database that stores configuration information. (2)

registry keys. Folder containing additional registry values. (15)

remote wipe. Application that allows the user to wipe all information, data, and settings when the device is stolen. (12)

repeater. Piece of equipment that regenerates a weak digital signal. (18)

Resilient File System (ReFS). Microsoft file system with the capability to more likely recover after a major catastrophe such as a power outage or system failure. (9)

resistance. Opposition to the flow of electrical energy. (5)

resolution. Amount of detail a monitor is capable of displaying. (8)

response time. Amount of time it takes a TFT pixel to display after a signal is sent to the transistor controlling that pixel. (8)

ring topology. Network topology in which a single cable runs continuously from computer to computer. (16)

rollover cable. Special cable in which the pin order is completely reversed on the opposite end of the cable. (16)

root directory. Top of the directory structure. A root directory is analogous to a file cabinet drawer in a conventional, paper filing system. A root directory is also referred to as the *root*. (2)

rooting. When the user is able to take complete control of the device without limitations; applies to Android devices. (12)

rootkit. Collection of software programs an intruder installs on a computer, allowing the intruder to take total control at a level equal to the system administrator. (14)

router. Network device used to connect to the Internet and share the Internet connection with other devices in the home or office. (13); Hardware that supports communication between different types of networks, for example a home network and the Internet. (16)

Row Address Selection (RAS). Time it takes to start a memory read or to write the row location in the memory matrix; the first step of a memory access operation. (6)

run-length encoding (RLE). Graphics compression format that reduces image file size by recording strings of identical pixels. (8)

S

safe mode. Mode that boots the computer without some drivers and programs to allow for troubleshooting. (6)

sampling. Measuring an analog signal at regular intervals. (8)

sanitation. Removal of data from a storage media. (14)

Scalable Link Interface (SLI). Proprietary video card system owned by the NVIDIA Corporation. (8)

scanner. Tool used to read text into a computer or to create a digital version of an image. (7)

SCSI ID number. Unique number assigned to a device on a SCSI chain and used to identify that device. (9)

sectors. Subdivisions of tracks, usually about 512 bytes in size. (9)

Secure Shell (SSH). Security protocol providing secure access to a remote computer; also known as *Secure Socket Shell*. (18)

Secure Sockets Layer (SSL). Security protocol developed by Netscape Navigator to make HTTP-based Internet business transactions secure. (18)

Security Accounts Manager (SAM). Registry file used to maintain the user account database on a computer. (17)

Security Identifier (SID). Identification code used to determine what share and security permissions have been assigned to the user. (17)

security key. Encrypts the information one computer sends to another computer across the network. (12)

Security Set Identifier (SSID). Broadcasted name of the wireless access point. (12)

segment. Section of cable between two network devices; a portion of a network that shares a common collision or token passing domain. (16)

sequence number. Numeric assignment attached to each packet of data being transmitted, ensuring that the data will be reassembled in the exact order it was transmitted. (16)

Serial ATA (SATA). Developed to overcome the limitations of the ATA drive. (9)

Serial Attached SCSI (SAS). Latest development for SCSI technology. (9)

serial presence detect (SPD). Technology that identifies the type of RAM installed on a computer. (6)

serial transfer. Occurs when data is sent through a port one bit at a time in successive order. (1)

server. Powerful computer used to manage network resources and provide services such as security and file sharing. (16)

Server Message Block (SMB). Network file-sharing protocol that supports file sharing for client/server applications. (18)

service. Software application that performs specific network functions such as assigning network addresses or supporting remote access to a computer desktop. (14)

shadow mask. Metal mesh with triangular holes that a CRT's electron beam passes through, creating a crisper image. (8)

share. Any object shared across the network, such as a file, hard drive, DVD drive, printer, or scanner. (17)

shoulder surfing. Unauthorized viewing of a display to gain information. (14)

Simple File Sharing. Feature enabled by default used to designate the Shared Documents folder as a shared resource; first introduced by Windows XP. (17)

Simple Mail Transfer Protocol (SMTP). E-mail protocol used to upload and transfer e-mail messages (outgoing) between e-mail servers. (18)

Simple Network Management Protocol (SNMP). Type of protocol that collects information about network devices and configures network devices, such as servers, printers, switches, and routers. (18)

simultaneous threading. When two or more threads are executed at the same time. (4)

single-channel mode. Arrangement present when a single DIMM is installed, or multiple DIMMS of different memory capacity are installed in the motherboard memory slots; also referred to as *asymmetric mode.* (6)

single in-line memory module (SIMM). Memory module containing a row of DIP memory chips mounted on a circuit board. (6)

single in-line package (SIP). Memory chip having a single row of connections that run along the length of a chip. (6)

single port forwarding. Router configuration in which a single designated IP address is identified instead of all IP addresses in the local area network. (19)

Small Computer System Interface (SCSI). Uses an adapter board and connects up to seven devices on one flat ribbon cable. (9)

small-office/home-office (SOHO) network. Simple peer-to-peer LAN used to share resources and data in a home- or small-office environment. (19)

small outline DIMM (SO-DIMM). Small outline package of regular DIMM modules, used especially for laptop applications where space is compact. (6)

small outline RIMM (SO-RIMM). Small outline package of regular RIMM modules, used especially for laptop applications where space is compact. (6)

smart card. Credit card-like device with a chip embedded in the plastic, which allows the card to be used for a variety of purposes. (12)

social engineering. Act of manipulating people to get then to divulge confidential information about the computer system. (14)

Software as a Service (SaaS). Cloud service model that provides software applications to a user either through a thin client software application or through a web browser. (18)

software driver. Small package of programs that allow proper communication between the computer and the peripheral device. (2)

software patch. Fix for operating systems and application software that have already been released. (2)

solid ink printer. Type of printer that uses sold ink cartridges similar to wax. (11)

solid-state disc caching. Process that occurs when the SSD is used as a temporary storage location for frequently accessed files or programs. (9)

solid-state disk (SSD). Storage system designed with no moving parts and that consists entirely of DRAM chips. (6)

Solid State Drive (SSD). Storage device that uses Flash memory chips. (9)

south bridge. Part previously used to connect slower devices such as keyboard, mouse, printer, hard drive, and USB ports. (3)

spam. Unsolicited junk e-mail or junk electronic newsletters. (14)

spatial multiplexing (SM). Two of more streams of data transmitted in the same frequency channel. (16)

split-frame rendering. Method of sharing the video workload in which each card is responsible for an equal part of the frame image. (8)

spooling. Technique that stores in memory data to be printed so that printing operations can be completed in the background while other tasks are performed by the PC. (11)

spyware. Designed to track a user's habits, such as their Web browsing habits. (14)

standby power connection. Provides power to reactivate or wake up a system in standby, or sleep mode; also called *soft power.* (5)

star topology. Network topology in which a cable runs from each computer to a single point, forming a star. (16)

startup problem. Problem that causes the computer to lock up during the boot process. (15)

static IP addressing. Process that occurs when IP addresses are assigned manually. (18)

static RAM (SRAM). Integrated circuit technology based on digital flip-flop components. (6)

stealth virus. Type of virus, which hides from normal detection by incorporating itself into part of a known, and usually required, program for the computer. (14)

stylus. Type of pen used with the digitizer as a virtual pencil, paintbrush, or ink pen. (7)

subdirectory. Groupings of files; a file that subdivides the contents of a directory. A subdirectory is analogous to a folder within a folder in a conventional, paper filing system. Subdirectories are referred to as *subfolders* in many operating systems. (2)

subdomain. Division of a group of networks that function in a similar manner to folders in a file system, offering another way to organize a website. (18)

subnet mask. Number used to determine what subnet a particular IP address refers to. (18)

subscriber identity module (SIM). Integrated circuit used to securely authenticate a user's identity for a mobile device; also referred to as a *subscriber identification module*. (12)

super VGA (SVGA). Video standard supporting 16 million colors and various resolutions up to 1600 × 1200. (8)

superscalar execution. Processing multiple instructions simultaneously. (4)

surge. Flow of electrical power that occurs when a higher voltage than desired is present in the electrical system. (5)

switch. Hub that filters data packets and forwards them between network segments. (18)

switching hub. Enhanced active hub used to determine whether a signal should remain in the isolated section of the network or be passed through the hub to other parts of the network. (16)

synchronization. Act of matching data between two devices. (12)

synchronous. When data is transferred based on the same timing as the computer's clock signal. (7)

system image. Exact replicate of a hard drive partition including all personal and operating system files. (15)

System Management Mode (SMM). Standby mode developed for laptop computers to save electrical energy when using a battery. (4)

T

T-carrier lines. Lines designed to carry voice and data at a much higher rate than traditional phone lines. (13)

tailgating. When an unauthorized person closely follows an authorized person into a secure area. (14)

teamwork. Two or more people working toward a common goal. (20)

telephone jack. Location where the telephone line connects into the cabling; a standard connection used to attach devices such as modems and telephones to the wiring system. (13)

telnet. Protocol that allows a user to log on to a remote computer and download or upload files. (18)

tethering. Connecting a mobile device to another device. (13)

thin client. System supported by a cloud-based software application.(2); Computer that has minimal hardware resources. (16)

thin film transistor liquid crystal display (TFT-LCD). Display that consists of a matrix of thin film transistors, in which each transistor controls a single pixel. (8)

thread. Part of a software program that can be executed independently of the entire program. (4)

Tile. Shortcut to a Windows 8 program application. Tiles are similar to icons used on earlier Windows operating system desktops. (2)

time to live (TTL). Length of time the data in a packet is valid. (18)

tone generator. Tool used to test newly-made and existing network cables. A tone generator attaches to one end of a cable and transmits an analog or digital signal through the cable. (16)

topology. Physical arrangement of hardware and cabling in a network system. (16)

touch screen display. Computer display modified to accommodate input information by touch. (7)

TouchFLO. Action of touching any surface-sensing device, moving a finger across the display surface; another term used in similar fashion as multi-touch. (12)

trackball. Mouse with a ball embedded on top used to position the curser on the screen display. (7)

track. Concentric circle of data storage area on a disk. (9)

triple-channel mode. DIMM arrangement using three channels to support memory. (6)

Trojan horse. Class of virus that appears as a gift, such as a free download of a game or utility program, an e-mail attachment or some other item. (14)

Trusted Boot. Windows 8 security feature that checks the integrity of the operating system during the boot process and only allows digitally-signed software to boot and run on the computer. (14)

Trusted Platform Module (TPM). Integrated chip incorporated into the motherboard with the ability to create and store cryptographic keys. (14)

twisted pair cable. Most common choice for network wiring, consisting of four pairs of conductors twisted around each other. (16)

U

Ultra-Wideband (UWB). Short distance (10 meter) radio communication standard developed by the WiMedia Alliance. (7)

unattended installation. Automated installation of a new operating system or upgrade of an existing operating system. (17)

Uniform Resource Locator (URL). Global address for a website on the Internet. (18)

uninterruptible power supply (UPS). Power supply that ensures a constant supply of quality electrical power to the computer system. (5)

universal asynchronous receiver-transmitter (UART). Main chip in a modem that changes parallel data to serial data and vice versa. (13)

Universal Disk Format (UDF). File system structure accepted for CD-RW, magneto-optical disc, and DVD technology. (10)

Universal Mobile Telecommunications System (UMTS). 3G standard developed by the 3rd Generation Partnership Project (3GPP); a component of the International Telecommunication Union (ITU) set of communication standards. (13)

Universal Naming Convention (UNC). Path format that identifies a server and its share and uses backslashes to separate the server name from the share name. (19)

Universal Serial Bus (USB). Bus system designed to replace the function of expansion slots with a data transfer rate as high as 480 Mbps. The USB is accessed by plugging a USB device into the bus at a port opening in the case. Additional devices (up to 127) can be connected to the bus in a daisy-chain configuration. (3)

USB modem. Tiny mobile broadband device that plugs into any laptop with a USB port. (13)

USB standard. Developed by the USB Implementations Forum to describe how different classifications of devices should communicate with a PC. (7)

user. Individual who may use the network system resources. (17)

user mode. Actual user interface mode for the NT-based operation system. It is very restrictive and many areas are not accessible by the user or user program. (15)

V

vector font. Character design draws the outline of the letter rather than storing a separate bitmap pattern for each font; also referred to as an *outline font.* (11)

vector graphics. Graphics based on a series of mathematical formulas that can be converted into geometric shapes representing the image to be displayed. (8)

video graphics array (VGA). Minimum standard for video adapters; displays at a resolution of 640×480 with 16 colors or 320×200 with 256 colors. (8)

viewing angle. Measurement of the angle at which a person can adequately see an image on a display without it looking excessively distorted. (8)

virtual file allocation table (VFAT). Method of programming the FAT16 file system to allow long file capabilities similar to FAT32. (9)

Virtual Hard Disk (VHD). File that behaves exactly like a physical hard disk. (9)

virtual machine. Type of computer that runs two operating systems at the same time; also referred to as a *virtual PC.* (2)

virtual memory. Memory that supplements physical memory known as RAM. (6)

virtual private network (VPN). Security configuration that ensures data sent across the Internet is not intercepted, read, or modified. (19)

virtual smart card. Card simulation created by a combination of software and electronic integrated circuit. (14)

virtualization. When software applications are provided through cloud services. (2)

virus signature. Combination of characteristics that defines a particular virus, including such things as its length, file name(s) used, mode of infection or replication, and more. (14)

voltage. Amount of electrical pressure present in a circuit or power source. (5)

volt-amperes (VA). Alternative scale for measuring electrical power. (5)

volts (V). Scale used in measuring electrical pressure (electromotive force). (5)

volume mount points. System objects that allow a volume or additional hard drive to be attached to a directory structure. Volume mount points can be used to integrate a dissimilar file system into a logical file system. (9)

Volume Table of Contents (VTOC). Data structure that tells the CD drive how the data is laid out on the disc. (10)

W

Wake-on-LAN (WOL). Network adapter feature that allows the adapter to wake the computer from sleep or hibernation when network activity is detected. (16)

warm boot. Step used to restart a computer that is already running; also called a *soft boot*; using the reset button or key combination [Ctrl], [Alt], and [Delete] to restart a computer that is already running. (2)

watts (W). Scale used in measuring electrical power. (5)

Web Services for Devices (WSD). Printer port monitor service developed by Microsoft and first introduced in Windows Vista. (11)

webmail. Typically a free e-mail service, such as Gmail, Outlook.com, or Yahoo! Mail, based on using a web browser to access e-mail; also referred to as *HTML e-mail*. (18)

wide area network (WAN). Large number of computers, spread over a large geographic area and under control of a centrally located administrator. (16)

Wi-Fi. Any IEEE 802.11 wireless device that conforms to the Wi-Fi Alliance standard. (7)

Wi-Fi Protected Setup (WPS). Standard developed by the Wi-Fi Alliance and intended to make it easy to configure secure access to a wireless router. (16)

WiMAX. Wireless technology similar to Wi-Fi but has a much greater range, and the radio broadcast direction can be controlled. (13)

Windows Automated Installation Kit (WAIK). Collection of tools supporting the Windows deployment process. (17)

Windows CE. Mobile operating system designed as a compact Windows operating system to be used on devices that have limited hardware. (12)

Windows Internet Naming Service (WINS). Software service that resolves the computer name to the equivalent IP address on the network. (18)

Windows RT. Mobile operating system designed to run on the ARM processor; a lightweight version of Windows 8. (12)

wireless access point. Device used to support communications between wireless devices and a hard-wired network system. (12)

wireless range extender. Hardware used to extend the range of the wireless network. Another name for a wireless range extender is wireless repeater. (16)

wireless router. Combination of wireless access point, switch, and router. (16)

wireless topology. Network system that uses no cabling system between the computers; uses either infrared light or radio transmission to communicate between the network devices. (16)

Wireless USB (WUSB). Specification for USB wireless devices that uses the radio frequencies between 3.1 GHz to 10.6 GHz. (7)

word. Total amount of bytes a computer can process at one time. (1)

worm. Destructive program used to contaminate files on the infected computer and spread itself to other computers without prompting from the user. (14)

Z

zero insertion force (ZIF) socket. Processor socket equipped with a lever to assist in the installation of the CPU. (4)

Index